DATE DUE

			PRINTED IN U.S.A.

Literature Criticism from 1400 to 1800

Guide to Gale Literary Criticism Series

When you need to review criticism of literary works, these are the Gale series to use:

If the author's death date is:

You should turn to:

After Dec. 31, 1959
(or author is still living)

Contemporary Literary Criticism

for example: Jorge Luis Borges, Anthony Burgess,
William Faulkner, Mary Gordon,
Ernest Hemingway, Iris Murdoch

1900 through 1959

Twentieth-Century Literary Criticism

for example: Willa Cather, F. Scott Fitzgerald,
Henry James, Mark Twain, Virginia Woolf

1800 through 1899

Nineteenth-Century Literature Criticism

for example: Fedor Dostoevski, Nathaniel Hawthorne,
George Sand, William Wordsworth

1400 through 1799

Literature Criticism From 1400 to 1800
(excluding Shakespeare)

for example: Anne Bradstreet, Daniel Defoe,
Alexander Pope, Francois Rabelais,
Jonathan Swift, Phillis Wheatley

Shakespearean Criticism

Shakespeare's plays and poetry

Antiquity through 1399

Classical and Medieval Literature Criticism

for example: Dante, Homer, Plato, Sophocles, Vergil,
the Beowulf Poet

Gale also publishes related criticism series:

Children's Literature Review

This series covers authors of all eras who have written for the preschool through high school audience.

Short Story Criticism

This series covers the major short fiction writers of all nationalities and periods of literary history.

Poetry Criticism

This series covers poets of all nationalities and periods of literary history.

ISSN 0740-2880

Volume 15

Literature Criticism from 1400 to 1800

Excerpts from Criticism of the Works
of Fifteenth-, Sixteenth-, Seventeenth-, and
Eighteenth-Century Novelists, Poets, Playwrights,
Philosophers, and Other Creative Writers,
from the First Published Critical Appraisals
to Current Evaluations

James P. Draper
James E. Person, Jr.
Editors

 Gale Research Inc. • *DETROIT* • *LONDON*

STAFF

es P. Draper, James E. Person, Jr., *Editors*

. Daniel, Allyson J. Wylie, *Assistant Editors*

Jeanne A. Gough, *Permissions and Production Manager*

Linda M. Pugliese, *Production Supervisor*
Maureen A. Puhl, Jennifer VanSickle, *Editorial Assistants*
Donna Craft, Paul Lewon, Lorna Mabunda, Camille Robinson, *Editorial Assistants*

Victoria B. Cariappa, *Research Manager*
H. Nelson Fields, Judy L. Gale, Maureen Richards, *Editorial Associates*
Paula Cutcher, Alan Hedblad, Robin Lupa, Mary Beth McElmeel, *Editorial Assistants*

Sandra C. Davis, *Text Permissions Supervisor*
Josephine M. Keene, Denise Singleton, Kimberly F. Smilay, *Permissions Associates*
Maria L. Franklin, Michele M. Lonoconus
Shalice Shah, Rebecca A. Stanko, *Permissions Assistants*

Patricia A. Seefelt, *Permissions Supervisor (Pictures)*
Margaret A. Chamberlain, *Permissions Associate*
Pamela A. Hayes, Keith Reed, *Permissions Assistants*

Mary Beth Trimper, *Production Manager*
Mary Winterhalter, *External Production Assistant*

Arthur Chartow, *Art Director*
C. J. Jonik, *Keyliner*

The paper used in this publication meets the minimum requirements of American National Standard for Information Sciences—Permanence Paper for Printed Library Materials, ANSI Z39.48-1984. ∞™

Copyright © 1991
Gale Research Inc.
835 Penobscot Bldg.
Detroit, MI 48226-4094

Library of Congress Catalog Card Number 84-643570
ISBN 0-8103-6114-0
ISSN 0740-2880

Printed in the United States of America

Published simultaneously in the United Kingdom
by Gale Research International
(An affiliated company of Gale Research Inc.)

Contents

Preface   vii

Acknowledgments   xi

Preface

Literature Criticism from 1400 to 1800 (LC) presents criticism of world authors of the fifteenth through eighteenth centuries. The literature of this period reflects a turbulent time of radical change that saw the rise of drama equal in stature to that of classical Greece, the birth of the novel and personal essay forms, the emergence of newspapers and periodicals, and major achievements in poetry and philosophy. Much of modern literature reflects the influence of these centuries. Thus the literature treated in *LC* provides insight into the universal nature of human experience, as well as into the life and thought of the past.

Scope of the Series

LC is designed to serve as an introduction to authors of the fifteenth through eighteenth centuries and to the most significant interpretations of these authors' works. The great poets, dramatists, novelists, essayists, and philosophers of this period are considered classics in every secondary school and college or university curriculum. Because criticism of this literature spans nearly six hundred years, an overwhelming amount of critical material confronts the student. *LC* therefore organizes and reprints the most noteworthy published criticism of authors of these centuries. Readers should note that there is a separate Gale reference series devoted to Shakespearean studies. For though belonging properly to the period covered in *LC,* William Shakespeare has inspired such a tremendous and ever-growing corpus of secondary material that the editors have deemed it best to give his works extensive coverage in a separate series, *Shakespearean Criticism.*

Each author entry in *LC* attempts to present a historical survey of critical response to the author's works. Early criticism is offered to indicate initial responses, later selections document any rise or decline in literary reputations, and retrospective analyses provide students with modern views. The size of each author entry is intended to reflect the author's critical reception in English or foreign criticism in translation. Articles and books that have not been translated into English are therefore excluded. Every attempt has been made to identify and include the seminal essays on each author's work and to include recent commentary providing modern perspectives.

The need for *LC* among students and teachers of literature was suggested by the proven usefulness of Gale's *Contemporary Literary Criticism (CLC), Twentieth-Century Literary Criticism (TCLC),* and *Nineteenth-Century Literature Criticism (NCLC),* which excerpt criticism of works by nineteenth- and twentieth-century authors. Because of the different time periods covered, there is no duplication of authors or critical material in any of these literary criticism series. An author may appear more than once in the series because of the great quantity of critical material available and because of the aesthetic demands of the series's *thematic organization.*

Thematic Approach

Beginning with Volume 12, roughly half the authors in each volume of *LC* are organized in a thematic scheme. Such themes include literary movements, literary reaction to political and historical events, significant eras in literary history, and the literature of cultures often overlooked by English-speaking readers. The present volume, for example, focuses upon the cultural significance of the Age of Johnson. Future volumes of *LC* will devote substantial space to authors of Northern Humanism, the English Metaphysical poets, and the Spanish Golden Age, among many others. The rest of each volume will be devoted to criticism of the works of authors not aligned with the selected thematic authors and chosen from a variety of nationalities.

Organization of the Book

Each entry consists of the following elements: author or thematic heading, introduction, list of principal works (in author entries only), annotated works of criticism (each followed by a bibliographical citation), and a bibliography of further reading. Also, most author entries contain author portraits and other illustrations.

- The **author heading** consists of the author's full name, followed by birth and death dates. If an author wrote consistently under a pseudonym, the pseudonym is used in the author heading, with the real name given in parentheses on the first line of the biographical and critical introduction. Also located here are any name variations under which an author wrote, including transliterated forms for authors whose native languages use nonroman alphabets. Uncertain birth or death dates are indicated by question marks. The **thematic heading** simply states the subject of the entry.

- The **biographical and critical introduction** contains background information designed to introduce the reader to an author and to critical discussion of his or her work. Parenthetical material following many of the introductions provides references to biographical and critical reference series published by Gale in which additional material about the author may be found. The **thematic introduction** briefly defines the subject of the entry and provides social and historical background important to understanding the criticism.

- Most *LC* author entries include **portraits** of the author. Many entries also contain illustrations of materials pertinent to an author's career, including author holographs, title pages, letters, or representations of important people, places, and events in an author's life.

- The **list of principal works** is chronological by date of first book publication and identifies the genre of each work. In the case of foreign authors whose works have been translated into English, the title and date of the first English-language edition are given in brackets beneath the foreign-language listing. Unless otherwise indicated, dramas are dated by first performance, not first publication.

- **Criticism** is arranged chronologically in each author entry to provide a useful perspective on changes in critical evaluation over the years. For the purpose of easy identification, the critic's name and the composition or publication date of the critical work are given at the beginning of each piece of criticism. Unsigned criticism is preceded by the title of the source in which it appeared. All titles by the author featured in the critical entry are printed in boldface type. Publication information (such as publisher names and book prices) and parenthetical numerical references (such as footnotes or page and line references to specific editions of works) have been deleted at the editors' discretion to provide smoother reading of the text.

- Critical essays are prefaced by **annotations** as an additional aid to students using *LC.* These explanatory notes may provide several types of useful information, including: the reputation of a critic, the importance of a work of criticism, the commentator's individual approach to literary criticism, the intent of the criticism, and the growth of critical controversy or changes in critical trends regarding an author's work. In some cases, these notes cross-reference the work of critics within the entry who agree or disagree with each other.

- A complete **bibliographical citation** of the original essay or book follows each piece of criticism.

- An annotated bibliography of **further reading** appears at the end of each entry and suggests resources for additional study of authors and themes. It also includes essays for which the editors could not obtain reprint rights.

Cumulative Indexes

Each volume of *LC* includes a cumulative **author index** listing all the authors that have appeared in *Contemporary Literary Criticism, Twentieth-Century Literary Criticism, Nineteenth-Century Literature Criticism, Literature Criticism from 1400 to 1800,* and *Classical and Medieval Literature Criticism,* along with cross-references to the Gale series *Short Story Criticism, Poetry Criticism, Children's Literature Review, Authors in the News, Contemporary Authors, Contemporary Authors Autobiography Series, Contemporary Authors Bibliographical Series, Dictionary of Literary Biography, Concise Dictionary of Literary Biography, Something about the Author, Something about the Author Autobiography Series,* and *Yesterday's Authors of Books for Children.* Readers will welcome this cumulative author index as a useful tool for locating an author within the various series. The index, which includes authors' birth and death dates, is particularly valuable for those authors who are identified with a certain period but whose death dates cause them to be placed in another, or for those authors whose careers span two periods. For example, F. Scott Fitzgerald is found in *TCLC,* yet a writer often associated with him, Ernest Hemingway, is found in *CLC.*

Beginning with Volume 12, *LC* includes a cumulative **topic index** that lists all literary themes and topics treated in *LC, NCLC* Topics volumes, *TCLC* Topics volumes, and the *CLC* Yearbook. Each volume of *LC* also includes a cumulative **nationality index** in which authors' names are arranged alphabetically under their respective nationalities and followed by the numbers of the volumes in which they appear.

Each volume of *LC* also includes a cumulative **title index,** an alphabetical listing of the literary works discussed in the series since its inception. Each title listing includes the corresponding volume and page numbers where criticism may be located. Foreign-language titles that have been translated are followed by the titles of the translations—for example, *El ingenioso hidalgo Don Quixote de la Mancha (Don Quixote)*. Page numbers following these translated titles refer to all pages on which any form of the titles, either foreign-language or translated, appear. Titles of novels, dramas, nonfiction books, and poetry, short story, or essay collections are printed in italics, while individual poems, short stories, and essays are printed in roman type within quotation marks.

A Note to the Reader

When writing papers, students who quote directly from any volume in the Literary Criticism Series may use the following general forms to footnote reprinted criticism. The first example pertains to material drawn from periodicals, the second to material reprinted from books.

T. S. Eliot, "John Donne," *The Nation and the Athenaeum,* 33 (9 June 1923), 321-32; excerpted and reprinted in *Literature Criticism from 1400 to 1800,* Vol. 10, ed. James E. Person, Jr. (Detroit: Gale Research, 1989), pp. 28-9.

Clara G. Stillman, *Samuel Butler: A Mid-Victorian Modern* (Viking Press, 1932); excerpted and reprinted in *Twentieth-Century Literary Criticism,* Vol. 33, ed. Paula Kepos (Detroit: Gale Research, 1989), pp. 43-5.

Suggestions Are Welcome

In response to various suggestions, several features have been added to *LC* since the series began, including a nationality index, a Literary Criticism Series topic index, thematic entries, a descriptive table of contents, and more extensive illustrations.

Readers who wish to suggest new features, themes, or authors to appear in future volumes, or who have other suggestions, are cordially invited to write to the editors.

Acknowledgments

The editors wish to thank the copyright holders of the excerpted criticism included in this volume, the permissions managers of many book and magazine publishing companies for assisting us in securing reprint rights, and Anthony Bogucki for assistance with copyright research. We are also grateful to the staffs of the Detroit Public Library, Wayne State University Purdy/Kresge Library Complex, and the University of Michigan Libraries for making their resources available to us. Following is a list of the copyright holders who have granted us permission to reprint material in this volume of *LC*. Every effort has been made to trace copyright, but if omissions have been made, please let us know.

COPYRIGHTED EXCERPTS IN *LC*, VOLUME 15, WERE REPRINTED FROM THE FOLLOWING PERIODICALS:

Bulletin of Hispanic Studies, v. LII, October, 1975. © copyright 1975 Liverpool University Press. Reprinted by permission of the publisher.—*College Literature,* v. XVIII, 1990. Copyright © 1990 by West Chester University. Reprinted by permission of the publisher.—*Eighteenth-Century Life,* n.s. v. VIII, May, 1983. © 1983 University Center for International Studies, University of Pittsburgh. Reprinted by permission of the publisher.—*English Studies,* Netherlands, v. 44, June, 1963. © 1963 by Swets & Zeitlinger B.V. Reprinted by permission of the publisher.—*English Studies in Africa,* v. 28, 1985 for "Johnson's Dictionary and Attempts to 'Fix the Language' " by Geoffrey Hughes. Reprinted by permission of the publisher and the author.—*Essays in Literature,* v. XI, Spring, 1984. Copyright 1984 by Western Illinois University. Reprinted by permission of the publisher.—*Hispania,* v. 60, December 1977 for "Andrenio's Perception of Reality and the Structure of 'El Criticón' " by David H. Darst. © 1977 The American Association of Teachers of Spanish and Portuguese, Inc. Reprinted by permission of the publisher and the author.—*Hispanic Review,* v. 39, January, 1971 for "Gracián and the Moral Grotesque" by Paul Ilie. Reprinted by permission of the author.—*The Hudson Review,* v. XXIII, Summer, 1970. Copyright © 1970 by The Hudson Review, Inc. Reprinted by permission of the publisher. *The Journal of Aesthetics and Art Criticism,* v. XXI, Fall, 1962. Copyright © 1962 by The American Society for Aesthetics. Reprinted by permission of the publisher.—*The Journal of Medieval and Renaissance Studies,* v. 3, Spring, 1973. Copyright © 1973 by Duke University Press. Reprinted by permission of the publisher.—*Modern Age,* v. 25, Summer, 1981. Copyright © 1981 by the Intercollegiate Studies Institute, Inc. Reprinted by permission of the publisher.—*National Review,* New York, January 11, 1985. © 1985 by *National Review,* Inc., 150 East 35th Street, New York, NY 10016. Reprinted by permission.—*The New York Times Book Review,* November 16, 1952. Copyright 1952 by The New York Times Company. Reprinted by permission of the publisher.—*Philological Quarterly,* v. XLI, January, 1962 for "The 'Miss Lucy' Plays of Fielding and Garrick" by Charles B. Woods; v. 51, January, 1972 for "The Testimony of Literature, Spain (1618-1658)" by Juan Marichal; v. 54, Winter, 1975 for "A Century of 'Cymbeline'; or Garrick's Magic Touch" by George Winchester Stone, Jr. Copyright 1962, 1972, 1975 by The University of Iowa. All reprinted by permission of the publisher and the respective authors.—*Princeton Alumni Weekly,* v. 87, October 15, 1986 for "The Boundless Chaos of Living Speech" by Alvin B. Kernan. Reprinted by permission of the author.—*Renascence,* v. XXXVII, Winter, 1985. © copyright, 1985, Marquette University Press. Reprinted by permission of the publisher.—*Restoration and 18th Century Theatre Research,* v. XIV, May, 1975. Reprinted by permission of the publisher.—*The Review of English Studies,* v. XL, May, 1989. Reprinted by permission of Oxford University Press.—*Studies in Eighteenth-Century Culture,* v. 16, 1986. Copyright © 1986 American Society for Eighteenth-Century Studies. All rights reserved. Reprinted by permission of The University of Wisconsin Press.—*The Tablet,* v. 238, November 24, 1984. © 1984 The Tablet Publishing Company Ltd. 48 Great Peter Street, London SW1P 2HB. Reprinted by permission of the publisher.—*THOUGHT,* v. LIII, June, 1978. Copyright © 1978 by Fordham University Press. Reprinted by permission of Fordham University Press, New York.

COPYRIGHTED EXCERPTS IN *LC*, VOLUME 15, WERE REPRINTED FROM THE FOLLOWING BOOKS:

Bate, W. Jackson. From "Johnson and Satire in Manqué," in *Eighteenth-Century Studies in Honor of Donald F. Hyde.* Edited by W. H. Bond. Grolier Club, 1970. Copyright © 1970 by The Grolier Club. Reprinted by permission of the author.—Bayne-Powell, Rosamond. From *Eighteenth-Century London Life.* John Murray, 1937. Renewed 1966 by Robert Lane Bayne-Powell. Reprinted by permission of the publisher.—Berger, Jr., Harry. From *Second World and Green World: Studies in Renaissance Fiction-Making.* University of California Press, 1988. © 1988 by The Regents of the University of California. All rights reserved. Reprinted by permission of the publisher.—Blake, William. From *The Complete Writings of William Blake.* Edited by Geoffrey Keynes. Oxford University

PHOTOGRAPHS AND ILLUSTRATIONS APPEARING IN *LC,* VOLUME 15, WERE RECEIVED FROM THE FOLLOWING SOURCES:

The Granger Collection, New York: **p. 425.**

Age of Johnson

"The Age of Johnson" is the term most often used to describe the second half of the eighteenth century in England: roughly the period from 1750 to 1798, when Samuel Johnson—poet, lexicographer, essayist, novelist, journalist, and critic—dominated the English literary scene. It evolved out of the so-called "Augustan Age," which flourished during the reign of Queen Anne and typically extolled a strict, "neoclassical" sense of order, concentration, and economy in literature and in the fine arts, as well as logic, accuracy, "correctness," "good taste," and decorum. (Johnson, who began his writing career toward the end of that period, represents the culmination of Augustan stylistics.) However, as the century drew to a close, neoclassical standards were gradually synthesized to accomodate and reflect the changing tastes of an emerging generation. The latter half of the English eighteenth century, responding to German romantic thought and French Enlightenment thinking, witnessed a developing interest in human freedom, a widening scope of intellectual concerns and human sympathies, a developing appreciation of external nature and country life, and an evolving cult of the primitive. Influential political and religious events include the American and French Revolutions and the rise of Methodism. This period is widely considered the seedbed from which English Romanticism blossomed. Many commentators often label it the "age of sensibility" to emphasize the emergence of these new attitudes and an increasing reliance upon emotionalism and feelings as guides to truth and literary expression. Northrop Frye has defined the era as one of transition from "a reptilian Classicism, all cold and dry reason, to a mammalian Romanticism, all warm and wet feeling."

Eighteenth-century London thrived as the largest and wealthiest city in Europe. As such, it exerted considerable cultural and intellectual influence in both English and Continental affairs. Its predominance in English literary and artistic matters fostered an international reputation as a cosmopolitan center that attracted artists and intellectuals from throughout the world. Voltaire, Jean-Jacques Rousseau, Wolfgang Amadeus Mozart, Joseph Haydn, George Frideric Handel, Canaletto, and Louis François Roubillac were but a few writers and artists who streamed into London, compelled to visit the great capital at least once in their lifetimes. Contemporaries claimed that much of London's appeal lay in its striking diversity, its contrasts and contradictions, its extremes. In but a single day one could easily encounter vice, bribery, street crime, bad air, fires, huddled masses of humanity, unscrupulous lawyers, crumbling buildings, and lost faith, but London's amenities were equally accessible: felicitous taverns, the Strand's shops and theaters, dazzling city lights, commercial vigor and economic resilience, ceaseless hustle and bustle, the latest food and fashions, the Thames and its ships, green parks and spectacular shows, prolific newspapers and personalities. Johnson once quipped that "when a man is tired of London, he is tired of life; for there is in London all that life can afford."

The intellectual tone of mid-eighteenth-century England is generally characterized by two principal tendencies: reason and passion. These inclinations were manifest in literary and plastic arts, as evidenced by their pursuit of order, symmetry, and decorum on the one hand, and the cultivation of feelings, sensibility, and glorification of personal relationships on the other. Critics usually discuss the implications of reason and sentiment in terms of neoclassicism and romanticism. In literature the neoclassical penchant inspired satire, wit, argument, and plain prose; the cult of sensibility found expression in the psychological novel and in poetry of the sublime. Neoclassicists conceived nature in terms of order, regularity, and universality—standards that the romantics eventually rejected, favoring instead natural irregularity, or "wildness," and the freedom of individual expression. While Donald Greene has cautioned that "the great writers of the eighteenth century . . . were entirely unaware that they were "neoclassicists"; they did not use the term . . . nor is there any evidence that they thought of themselves as [such]," most critics agree that the literary achievements of eighteenth-century England reveal an unprecedented vitality and energy evinced by the moral intensity and imaginative variety that infuse the writings of Johnson, Laurence Sterne, and Oliver Goldsmith, among others.

Although many neoclassical ideals and mannerisms eventually were abandoned and replaced by romantic ideology, the movement permanently influenced English prose style. Neoclassicism simplified and refined English prose and revived the classical graces of order, polished form, unified structure, conciseness, and restraint. Nineteenth-century English critic Matthew Arnold fittingly dubbed the eighteenth century "our age of prose and reason." The age saw important developments in several literary genres, including the essay, imaginative fiction, literary criticism, prose satire and parody, historical writing, the letter and epistle, and the novel. Commonly characterized by clarity and a sense of contact with the reader—conditions considered essential to argument in print—prose writing challenged poetry as the most prestigious medium. Critics concur that the most rapid and diverse prose development occurred within the novel which established itself as a major literary form partly by the rational realism demonstrated in the works of Henry Fielding, Daniel Defoe, and Tobias Smollett and partly by the psychological probing evident in the novels of Sterne and Samuel Richardson. Commenting on the content of typical eighteenth-century novels, Leslie Stephen noted that "as the essayists were never tired of discussing the social phenomena of the time, from the most trifling to the most serious, the novelists were never tired of portraying the same phenomena, coloured by some favourite moral or sentiment." Several writers also introduced new elements to the novel during this period, thereby fostering additional technical improvements. Most early novelists followed a chronological sequence of events and generally claimed historical accuracy, but writers began to challenge these conventions as the genre matured. Sterne radically altered conventional chronology in his *Tristram Shandy* (1759-67), presenting life as a flux of events unrelated except in the mind of the person experiencing them, and Fielding consistently asserted the author's right to shape the spirit of the story and manipulate the narrative in the interests of artistic truth. After 1750, many novels tended to assume a sentimental attitude similar to Henry Mackenzie's *Man of Feeling* (1771), while others sought to depict Gothic horror as did Horace Walpole in *The Castle of Otranto* (1764). These innovations continued to flourish well into the nineteenth century.

Two other developments of the period include widespread growth of the periodical and significant advances in the social impact of printing technology. According to Rosamond Bayne-Powell, the power of the eighteenth-century press "for good or evil was enormous. The printed word among semi-literate people was looked upon with the greatest possible awe and respect." The extent to which printing technology affected social and institutional life in eighteenth-century England may be demonstrated by the proliferation of many previously unknown print products: posters, labels, newspapers and magazines, handbills, billheadings, theater bills, tickets, and pre-printed legal, sacred, and instructional forms such as marriage certificates, receipts, and indentures. Alvin Kernan suggested that the "simple usefulness [of the printed word] acquired an aura of authority . . . [which] grew into the authenticity that is probably the absolute mark of print culture, a generally accepted view that what is printed is true." The unprecedented spread of popular journalism in the eighteenth century offered readers, in the words of William Cowper, "a map of busy life, its fluctuations and its vast concerns." Although some publications existed merely as political propaganda, many periodicals aimed to please and instruct the public; Joseph Addison's *Spectator,* Sir Richard Steele's *Tatler,* and Johnson's *Rambler* are considered prime examples. Indicative of the contemporary attitude toward periodical literature, Johnson wrote that the "papers of the day, the *Ephemerae* of learning, have uses more adequate to the purposes of common life than more pompous and durable volumes." However, much of the material that appeared in the periodicals was provided by struggling hacks who lived in London's Grub Street. Since the eighteenth century the term "Grub Street" has connoted the personal attributes that characterize the group of writers who lived there and is sometimes used as a synonym for "literary trash," though it more accurately refers to earnest, would-be writers who struggled to establish themselves without any form of patronage—surviving in a near-hand-to-mouth existence. Despite the contemptuous criticism of Alexander Pope and others, it must be remembered that Johnson himself—who labored for years as a Grub-Street hack—once remarked that "no man but a blockhead ever wrote, except for money."

Nearly unlimited accessibility to and the prodigious quantity of printed books, periodicals, and pamphlets stimulated great discussions and debates among learned men and women as well as the general public. These discussions often took place at coffeehouses and dining clubs, and in the homes of literary men and women. In 1764 Johnson concurred with Sir Joshua Reynolds's suggestion for the foundation of what is perhaps the most famous London dining club of all time. Among the charter members, besides Johnson and Reynolds, were Goldsmith, Edmund Burke, Topham Beauclerk, and Bennet Langton; eventually many other famous men were admitted, including ballad collector Percy Smith, actor David Garrick, historian Edward Gibbon, economist Adam Smith, and Johnson's biographer, James Boswell. Simply called "The Club," but later known as The Literary Club, its members met weekly for supper or, when Parliament was in session, fortnightly dinners. Enjoying his reputation as a sort of literary dictator at these sessions, Johnson frequently dominated the conversation. Reynolds observed that the Club was primarily formed to give Johnson a forum to express himself.

The formidable influence and considerable renown of The Club spawned many lesser literary associations, most notably the Bluestocking Ladies, demonstrating that women, too, could be eighteenth-century litterateurs. The term "bluestockings" applies to women of pronounced intellectual interests who held London assemblies or "conversations"—the English equivalent of the French salon—to which were invited the leading literary and intellectual figures of the day, usually men. While there was no formal membership, the Bluestocking Ladies included Elizabeth Montagu, Hannah More, Fanny Burney, Hester Chapone, and Elizabeth Vesey. The origins of the group's name remain dubious, as Charles Pigott explained in 1794: "How they came to distinguish themselves by the appellation of bluestockings, it would be hard to decide, as the term conveys rather a light and lascivious idea; gradually leading the fancy upwards to the garter, and so on, to perhaps an improper and alarming height. We must therefore imagine, that the name originated in some happy and sudden flash of wit, which fortunately found a resemblance between things seemingly so unlike, as genius and coloured stockings."

The Age of Johnson was a vibrant era in the history of English literature, and most critics acknowledge that it was also a markedly transitional age. The neoclassicism that dominated the first half of the eighteenth century gradually yielded to the growing impulses of romanticism during the second half of the century. Commentary on the period vacillates between strictly neoclassical perspectives and "pre-romantic" viewpoints, but often echoes the closing chapter-title of Johnson's prose narrative *Rasselas* (1759): "A conclusion, in which nothing is concluded." However, most scholars point out that the wide spectrum of literary possibilities encompassed by the Age of Johnson fostered a vitality and energy rarely seen in English letters. Dorothy George, in *England in Transition* (1962), remarked that "we can regard the eighteenth-century as an age of corruption, oligarchy, privilege, materialism, or we can regard it as an age of common sense, good humor, reasonableness, and toleration—one view does not exclude the other."

JOHNSON'S LONDON

G. M. Trevelyan

[Trevelyan was an English historian and the grand-nephew of Thomas Babington Macaulay. Perhaps best-known for his History of England *(1926) and* British History in the Nineteenth Century *(1922), he was also recognized as an authority on Italian history. In the following essay, he sketches the social and cultural climate of eighteenth-century England.]*

It is often the custom to think of the eighteenth century, prior to the French Revolution, as a period of effete politeness and intelligence, of cultured and artificial decadence, of scepticism, atrophy, and want of enterprise—like the figure in Max Beerbohm's famous cartoons of the three centuries. The first reaction of many minds to the words 'eighteenth century' is a vision of beaux in coloured silk garments, drinking coffee out of small cups, while engaging in elegant philosophic small talk with ladies with towering powdered head-dresses and patched cheeks.

With regard to the continent of Europe, there is a certain amount of symbolical truth in this popular impression, but, for Britain, a more illuminating picture of the eighteenth century would be supplied by a vision of something more robust—Clive planted four-square across the breach of Arcot; Wolfe and his men scrambling up the precipitous forest track towards Quebec; Captain Cook's sails sweeping into Botany Bay; Wesley's lean face and long white hair, as he preaches to mass meetings of miners and throws powerful men into fits of hysteria; James Watt working in the instrument maker's shop, with thoughts in him that shall have their consequences in the history of mankind.

England, indeed, had also its Lord Chesterfields and its Beau Nashes, but they occupied a relatively small part of the scene. The eighteenth-century English, on the average, were an earnest, virile, original, unconventional, and energetic race. They practised self-help and individualism before the Victorians, but without bothering to write books about those virtues. That a man must help himself, seemed to them too natural to remark upon. If he did not, who else was to help him? Unless, indeed, he were cousin to a lord, or had a vote in a rotten borough, in which case the lord would provide. If they were to meet us, our eighteenth-century forefathers would, I shrewdly suspect, regard us as the decadents, with our grandmother, the State, running about after us all day long. If a man could not find honest employment, they expected him to be man enough to go to the Colonies or take to the Highway, in which latter case the State would sooner or later do its one useful office by him at Tyburn Gallows—and the admiring public would turn him into a ballad hero. Dr. Johnson's English were a sturdy crew.

With regard to the continent of Europe, the popular impression that the eighteenth century was effete and conventional has at least a certain relation to truth. The France that staggered on from the defeat of the ambitions of the Grand Monarch at Blenheim in 1704, to the final gulf of bankruptcy and revolution in 1789—that phoenix fire of an appalling rebirth—eighteenth-century France was in some senses effete. So, too, was Germany, with the exception of Frederick the Great's little Prussia; Germany, bled white by the Thirty Years War, was no longer the Germany of Luther, Albert Dürer, and the great merchant cities. Italy, too, the Italy of Piranesi's prints, was peaceful and stagnant—a land of hard-working, ragged, submissive peasants, of idle beggars, and of cultured dilettante nobles and clergy with few interests in life beyond the innocent occupation of reading to each other insipid compositions in verse, and disquisitions, learned and sentimental, on the monuments of antiquity—a land strangely different from the fierce and passionate Italy of the Middle Ages, of the later Risorgimento, or of modern Fascism.

A lethargic peace, not unfavourable to thought and culture as distinct from action, did in fact brood over much of eighteenth-century Europe. Until 1789 Europe, outside the small dominions of Frederick the Great, was energetic and creative only in thought, hardly at all in deed. It made no great industrial, social, or political change inside its own borders. And, except for the unsuccessful attempt of the French to drive us from India, continental Europe in that epoch made no great outward push at colonization in America, Africa, and the East, as the French, Spaniards, and Dutch had done in previous centuries, and as all European countries were destined to do in the nineteenth century.

But when we turn to the Britain of the period we have a different story to tell. This was the time when our fathers conquered Canada and half India, rediscovered and began to settle Australia, and traded on an ever-increasing scale all over the inhabited globe; reorganized British agriculture on modern methods; began the Industrial Revolution in our island, thence in later times to spread over the whole world; and if the thirteen American colonies were at the same time lost to the British Empire, it was the result less of decadence in Great Britain than of young and mutinous energies in English America.

And on this side of the Atlantic, Great Britain, over and above her efforts in the material sphere of war, industry, and commerce, could show no less wonderful achievements in the sphere of intellect and of culture. England produced not only the classical perfection of Johnson's conversations and Gray's and Goldsmith's writings, but the intellectual originality of men like Adam Smith, Bentham, and Blake, breaking up new soil of the mind and of the spirit. The historical genius of Gibbon was the perfect fruit borne by the widespread antiquarian learning common in the leisured class of the period, whence modern historical study emerged.

Indeed, Johnson's England was full of creative intellectual power both in the sciences and in the arts. In the country at large, the physical science of the Newtonian school—originated at the universities in the former age—was being applied by men of business to the processes of industry. It was in the later eighteenth century that Englishmen, taught by White of Selborne and Bewick of Tyneside, first learnt that peculiar interest in the bird life and natural history of their own land that has ever since distinguished them. It was the first great age of native English painting, with Reynolds and Gainsborough. The novel was being evolved by Defoe, Fielding, Richardson, Smollett, and Miss Burney, to be the principal instrument of literature in coming ages.

A mid-eighteenth-century view of London and the Thames. According to Richard Schwartz, London was "the center of government, of trade, of entertainment, of communications, of finance, of intellectual life, and of fashion."

Whether or not I am right in supposing that the England of the eighteenth century had an energy of spirit that was lacking elsewhere in the Europe of that day, it is at least certain that this view was then generally held upon the Continent. After the Marlborough wars with which the century opened, and, still more after the great victories of Chatham in two hemispheres in the Seven Years War, foreigners were always asking each other what was the secret of English success, and the answer they found was that the secret lay in our free institutions. In the days of Charles I and II our Parliament had been regarded abroad as a source of confusion and weakness to England. But the course of William III's and Marlborough's wars had changed that view completely. For the British Parliament had defeated the all-worshipped despotism of Louis XIV in a long-drawn contest, in which England had proved supreme alike in land warfare, in sea warfare, in diplomacy, and in financial strength. This unexpected event gave a prestige to our institutions which coloured European thought from the time of Marlborough right down to the French Revolution. The prosperity of England under Walpole, the constant increase of her trade and maritime power, her victories under Chatham in Canada and India, all confirmed the same impression. Even our great catastrophe—the loss of the American Colonies—was read in France as another demonstration of the power that freedom gives. It was not only our Parliament that was admired, but freedom of speech, press, person, and religious toleration. The England of the Revolution settlement stood for all these things, and in their strength it had triumphed over the despotic and intolerant institutions of France. Frenchmen were as eager as we ourselves to draw the lesson. They observed that whereas their own decline

might be dated from the renewed persecution of the Huguenots by the revocation of the Edict of Nantes, England had never looked back since she had given peace to her own religious discords by the Act of Toleration of 1689.

The criticisms passed by Montesquieu, Voltaire, and the Encyclopaedists on French and continental institutions in Church and State, would have received little attention if Louis XIV had triumphed at Blenheim, and if his descendants had dominated Europe, Canada, and India.

In our own day, men are somewhat confused in trying to draw general conclusions from contemporary events. The fall of the autocratic principle in Russia, Germany, and Austria, on the one hand, is countered by the fall of parliamentary government in Italy and its failure to fill the gap left in Russia by the disappearance of the Czardom. These signal failures, almost at the same moment, of despotic and of free government, render it difficult for men in our day to draw conclusions of universal applicability. We are, moreover, better aware than the Encyclopaedists of the diversities of men and things; but in the eyes of the eighteenth-century philosophers, human beings were thought of in the abstract. National differences were little understood. One panacea, it was held, would suit the whole human race, or at least all white men; and that panacea must clearly be parliamentary government and personal freedom, for it had been tried in England and had succeeded there. It had not yet been tried anywhere else— unless, indeed, in Holland, where also freedom had made a great nation out of a little clan.

Voltaire, in his *Lettres sur les Anglais,* told his countrymen:

> The English nation is the only one on earth which has managed to regulate the power of its kings while resisting them; where the lords are great without insolence and without vassals, and where the people takes part in the government without confusion. In England it is common to think (*communément on pense*); and literature has more honour than with us French. This advantage is a necessary outcome of their form of government.

Nothing is more touching and admirable than the personal relations of the French and English educated classes during this century of reason and good manners, in spite of the fact that two-fifths of its hundred years was spent in war between France and Britain. We breathe a harsher air in the international contests and alliances of our own era. Chatham was the admired man in the country on which he had heaped the disasters of the Seven Years War. To be a fellow countryman of Chatham, of Hume, of 'le grand Newton', opened every salon in Paris to the travelling Englishman. Gibbon was almost as much at home in the society of Paris as in that of London.

In those days, the English gentleman, once or oftener in his life, made the Grand Tour of France and Italy (hardly ever of Germany, and practically never of the English Colonies in America, which was one reason why we lost them). On the Grand Tour the English gentleman was received into the society of French salons and Italian petty Courts, mingling there with the foreign nobles and with the artists and men of letters whom they patronized. English tourists were not in those days isolated in cosmopolitan hotels from all contact with the life of the peoples in whose lands they travelled. This was partly because the travellers were in those days fewer and their Grand Tours more protracted. The Continent was visited not once in twelve months, but once in a lifetime, and then for a year or more on end. Moreover, there was a social freemasonry between the upper classes of all continental Europe that no longer exists. The noblesse of France and Italy and the gentry of England felt a mutual obligation and camaraderie that has no place in our busy world, where society is more mixed and classes are less distinguishable from one another in dress, education, and manners. At the present day, indeed, there seems, in theory at least, to be a greater camaraderie between the working classes of different countries. Cosmopolitanism was then upper class, it is now lower class. In the eighteenth century the English working man—then called the jolly yeoman or the industrious 'prentice—was intensely British, boasted himself a free-born Briton, and had no use for the frog-eating, priest-ridden Frenchman of his imagination. The average Englishman had not made the Grand Tour, and had no information about foreigners such as is being constantly poured in upon us to-day through newspapers, cinemas, books, pamphlets, and photographs. What the common English thought of the French you can see in Hogarth's uncomplimentary picture, entitled 'Calais Gate', in the National Gallery. This contempt for, and ignorance of, foreigners was extended not only to the Irish, but even to the Scots—who only became understood and admired in England in the age of Walter Scott, partly through the powerful influence of his pen.

Nor must it be supposed that even the gentry who had made the Grand Tour had been cosmopolitanized to a serious extent. Their portraits were painted not by foreign hands but by Gainsborough and Reynolds; their library shelves were weighted with luxurious editions of English history, poetry, and novels; their literary oracle was Dr. Johnson, the most abnormally English creature God ever made. The life that the English gentry lived was as different as possible from that of their continental friends. The nobles of France and Italy thought little of existence away from the Court of their master, the King or reigning Duke. But the English gentry, when they came to town, came first and foremost to their own Parliament, only secondarily to the King's Court—a place of dull ceremony, no longer the true heart of the land's activities as it had been under the Plantagenets and the Tudors. But the bulk of their lives the English gentlemen spent neither at Court nor yet in the purlieus of Parliament, nor in London at all; but in the country, among their neighbours of all classes whom they led, entertained, bullied, and at election time courted and bribed. It was to their country houses that they brought back the art treasures they had collected on the Grand Tour—treasures in our day being scattered oversea by the auctioneer's hammer. They lived among their neighbours, hunting foxes, shooting partridges, inclosing and draining land, improving breeds of sheep and cattle, governing the countryside as Justices of the Peace. Their whole manner of life and way of thought was English, and though every English gentleman was recognized as belonging to the same social level as the continental nobleman, he was also recognized as belonging to a separate and unique island species of the genus European gentleman.

There was therefore in eighteenth-century England, prior to the changes gradually made manifest by the Industrial Revolution, a national solidarity and unity of idea which bound Englishmen of all classes together and separated them from foreigners. Power, as we think looking back, was unduly concentrated in the hands of one class, the country gentry, but their monopoly was not popularly regarded as a grievance. The novelist Fielding is one of the very few contemporary critics of squirarchical power in the mid-eighteenth century. Classes were distinct in England—less distinct and rigid, indeed, than on the Continent at that time, but much more distinct and rigid than they are to-day. Wealth was very unevenly distributed. But there was little or no social discontent, and the national idea made every one proud of being a free-born Englishman.

> To glory we call you as freemen not slaves,
> For who are so free as the sons of the waves?

That song is the authentic popular voice of the England of Chatham. And therefore, when the French Revolution raised new issues between classes, and Tom Paine attacked the upper class monopoly of power, the first response of Englishmen to it was a decided rally to the English idea of national solidarity as distinct from the new French idea of equality and class war. But the Industrial Revolution was by that time busily at work sapping the old order in society; and therefore, early in the next century, at the time of Peterloo, we find an amount of conscious discontent and the arraying of class against class, from which the age of Johnson had been immune.

It is, indeed, arguable that a little more social discontent in the time of Walpole and Chatham might have prevented the Industrial Revolution, when it came, from developing on lines chosen with so little regard to the masses. In that case we might have avoided some at least of the dangerous class cleavages of the nineteenth and twentieth centuries. But that, like all the might-have-beens of history, is the merest speculation. Things were what they were, and the consequences will be what they will be.

If Johnson's England differed from Voltaire's France in her parliamentary constitution, in the greater amount of freedom secured to the individual citizen in speech, press, and person, and in the superior energies of the individual at home and overseas—England nevertheless shares with the rest of Europe one marked characteristic of the eighteenth century civilization, the lethargy of all established and chartered corporations. In England it was a great age for the energies of the private person—the adventurer, the merchant, the author—acting freely in a free community. But the chartered institutions were antiquated and corrupt. The universities, the endowed schools, the municipalities, the electoral bodies, had lost their old vigour and had not yet acquired the modern energies that gave them a fresh life in the following century. It was characteristic of the time that the established Church, just because it was established, was unable to accommodate itself to the new life brought to its service by Wesley; that the vast increase of British industry took place no longer, as in the Middle Ages, under cover of municipal protection, but for the most part outside the old municipal boundaries; that thought and learning were at a low ebb in the Oxford known to Gibbon and the Cambridge known to Wordsworth, although in every corner of the land private scholars were devoting their lives to antiquarian and classical lore.

It would appear that the chartered institutions and corporations—Church, universities, municipal bodies—were too secure; they had no fear of reform, and therefore they settled comfortably down to sleep. The undisturbed security of the chartered corporations is characteristic of the eighteenth century. But if privilege was immune from attack in England, it was partly because of the toleration which the privileged orders extended to those outside their own limits. The town municipalities and guilds no longer, as in the Middle Ages, pretended to control and direct all the industry and trade of the land. If the rotten municipalities of the eighteenth century had attempted to prevent the cloth and cotton manufacturers from spreading outside their jurisdiction, there would have been a sharp crisis, ending in a reform of the municipalities long before 1835. If the Church, after 1689, had continued to persecute Dissenters, the Wesleyans must have striven, like the Puritans before them, to annex or to overthrow the Church instead of leaving it on one side.

But the security of all chartered corporations from attack was based not merely on their tolerant practice towards outsiders, but also on the unreforming spirit of the age. The religious and political storms of the seventeenth century had spent their fury; the social and political storms of the modern era had not yet begun to blow. The intervening century of reason and toleration had the merits and defects of an era when existing institutions are taken for granted. It was therefore much sneered at in the retrospect by the more earnest and restless nineteenth century. We in the twentieth century are perhaps more nearly tempted to give a sigh of helpless envy in contemplating so fair and

peaceful a field for individual thought and energy as was presented by the age of Johnson, Wedgwood, and Reynolds.

'Let sleeping dogs lie' was Walpole's motto. 'Rejoice in our matchless constitution' was the lesson Blackstone taught to his contemporaries. According to the optimistic political philosophy of Blackstone and Burke, our British freedom was held to be based on the security of chartered corporations, and on the impotence of the central government to interfere with those rights and privileges. James II had attacked the chartered privileges of Parliament, Municipalities, Church, Universities, and the rights of freehold property. The attempt had cost him his throne, and the consequence was that for a hundred years after the Revolution no one ventured to attack chartered rights again, or even seriously to criticize their abuse. A habit of mind was formed which thought that 'whatever is is right', provided it can show a charter. The formidable Conservatism with which the eighteenth century ended, the anti-Jacobin Conservatism of the later Burke, Pitt, and Eldon, was based on a retrospective enthusiasm for the Revolution that had dethroned James II. That memorable event, so far from being merely a Whig shibboleth, was pleaded by the anti-Jacobin Tories a hundred years later as the palladium of our Constitution, henceforth unalterable. They held up the Conservative Revolution of 1689 as the touchstone which should render immune for all time all those institutions which James had illegally attacked, which the Radicals of a later age were proposing to alter in another direction and for a different purpose.

But long before the days of anti-Jacobins, in the mid-eighteenth century period of Walpole and Chatham, the holders of property and privilege, particularly of corporate rights, had felt so secure from criticism and reform that many abuses had grown up in Boroughs, Church, Universities, Civil Service, Army, and Parliament.

Before the Industrial Revolution, the mass of the people of all classes, though they worked for longer hours than now (eleven to thirteen hours normal) and for less pay, had the great advantage of living in the country instead of in the city; and even the dwellers in the moderate-sized cities of that time were not far removed from rural influence and tradition. The Tudor, Stuart, and early Hanoverian period, culminating in the eighteenth century, was the great period of English village life. In the Middle Ages the village had indeed been the normal scene of English life, but the medieval village was poverty-stricken and often famine- and plague-stricken; its inhabitants, even when not actually serfs, were nearly all of them engaged in a struggle with nature under harsh and difficult conditions. The medieval villagers were engaged in agriculture or in the simpler crafts immediately subsidiary to agriculture; the finer crafts, industry, and commerce of the Middle Ages had been centred in the walled cities for the most part. But, from the time of the rise of English cloth manufacture, many industries and crafts moved into the countryside, increasingly in Tudor and Stuart times. Workshops were more and more set up in the villages, which had become safe enough and civilized enough to be the scene of the most elaborate manufactures and, in particular, of the great weaving industry. The move back to the cities came with the Industrial Revolution, when industry from the end of the eighteenth century until our own day migrated back to urban areas, carrying with it far the greater part of the population.

But in the fortunate eighteenth century, many villages were centres of industry as well as of agriculture. The typical Englishman was a villager, but a villager accustomed to meet men of various crafts and occupations and classes—by no means, therefore, a mere rustic boor, ignorant of all save the plough handle. Moreover, some people are inclined to forget that ploughing and agricultural operations generally are an extremely skilled trade. But the village was alive with the activities of all sorts and conditions of men.

This, according to my fancy at least, was a more wholesome state of society than the village of the medieval serf on the one hand, or the present-day city and urban district, where dwell the millions divorced from nature and only very partially redeemed by education.

But the old system of village life and handicraft that culminated and began to decline in the eighteenth century, excellent as it was in many respects, could only maintain some 7 millions alive in this island, and then at a much lower standard of material comfort than that enjoyed by 42 millions in our own day. Indeed, it may be doubted whether English prosperity, such as it was in the time of Chatham, could have gone on much beyond the middle of the eighteenth century if it had not been for the great inventions and the Industrial Revolution. Already there was a fuel famine, due to the using up of the forests—a fuel famine that was killing our old timber-fed iron industry, and was rendering warmth and cooked food unattainable in the cottages of the poor in many districts. No fuel in the cottage meant a bread and cheese diet. The canals that brought coal to all parts of the island were the first great step towards the new era.

In the east and midlands the typical village was, as it is to-day, a large collection of houses round the parish church. But in the west and north the church stood with only a few houses near it, and the parish consisted of a number of scattered hamlets or scattered farms, looking to the parish church as their centre so far as they had any definite unity at all. The land of scattered hamlets in the west, and of scattered farmsteads in the north, generally meant inclosed fields round every farm. But in the east midlands, round the large centralized villages, the uninclosed open fields were still the prevailing method of cultivation until the great inclosures of the reign of George III.

There was great diversity of agricultural method, of tenure, and of social type in the various parts of England. Even in the same district one village differed from another in its social groupings and economic arrangements, much more than in the nineteenth century, when the village scene became more nearly monopolized by the tenant farmer and his employee, the landless agricultural labourer. But in the eighteenth century there was a great variety of craftsmen and manufacturers in or near the village, some supplying the needs of the village, others supplying the world market. There were large and small squires, large and small freehold yeomen, besides tenant farmers large and small. There were hired labourers who had no land, there were hired labourers who had also a little land or a garden of their own, there were men camped on or round the common, some making a respectable and hardy struggle with poverty, others little distinguishable from gipsies, thieves, or professional poachers. Amateur poaching, as a by-occupation, was one of the chief incidents of village life—an endless subject of talk and dispute, of tragedy and comedy. In most cottages and farmhouses the women and children engaged their spare time in spinning or minor handicrafts. And then there were the parish paupers, a terrible problem. Over this multiform and vigorous society, part agricultural, part industrial, the power of the squire loomed large, beneficent or tyrannical as the case might be—Sir Roger de Coverley or Squire Western—but always patriarchal.

There was no elective local government—no county councils or rural district councils, or even parish councils. Administration as well as justice, therefore, lay in the hands of the Justice of the Peace, who was usually a local squire, occasionally a parson. When the squire was also, like Coke of Norfolk, a successful agricultural improver and the maker of the well-being of the whole countryside, he commanded the affection as well as the obedience of his neighbours.

But apart from the power and influence of the squire, the village that lay in the shadow of the Hall had a life of its own, far more varied, independent, and energetic than the life of the village of serfs in the shadow of the medieval castle or manor-house. It was because of this greater freedom, variety, and energy that the English village of Stuart and early Hanoverian times proved capable of founding English-speaking America and beginning the Industrial Revolution. And in so doing it put a term to its own existence. (pp. 1-13)

G. M. Trevelyan, "The Age of Johnson," in Johnson's England: An Account of the Life & Manners of His Age, Vol. I, *edited by A. S. Turberville, Oxford at the Clarendon Press, 1933, pp. 1-13.*

Charles Churchill

[Churchill was a controversial English poet who is best known for his satirical attacks on the leading personalities of his day including Lord Bute, John Home, Tobias Smollett, and William Hogarth. In the following excerpt from his poem "The Times," published in 1764, he assails the preponderance of vice in eighteenth-century London.]

THE Time hath been, a Boyish, Blushing Time,
When Modesty was scarcely held a crime,
When the most Wicked had some touch of grace,
And trembled to meet Virtue face to face,
When Those, who, in the cause of Sin grown grey,
Had serv'd her without grudging day by day,
Were yet so weak an awkward shame to feel,
And strove that glorious service to conceal,
We, better bred, and than our Sires more wise,
Such paultry narrowness of soul despise,
To Virtue ev'ry mean pretence disclaim,
Lay bare our crimes, and glory in our shame.

Time was, e'er Temperance had fled the realm;
E're Luxury sat guttling at the helm
From meal to meal, without one moment's space
Reserv'd for business, or allow'd for grace;
E're Vanity had so far conquer'd Sense

To make us all wild rivals in expence,
To make one Fool strive to outvye another,
And ev'ry coxcomb dress against his brother;
E're banish'd Industry had left our shores,
And Labour was by Pride kick'd out of doors;
E're Idleness prevail'd sole Queen in Courts,
Or only yielded to a rage for sports;
E're each weak mind was with externals caught,
And Dissipation held the place of Thought;
E're gambling Lords in Vice so far were gone
To cog the die, and bid the Sun look on;
E're a great Nation, not less just than free,
Was made a beggar by Œconomy;
E're rugged Honesty was out of vogue,
E're Fashion stamp'd her sanction on the rogue;
Time was, that Men had conscience, that they made
Scruples to owe, what never could be paid.

Was One then found, however high his name,
So far above his fellows damn'd to shame,
Who dar'd abuse, and falsify his trust,
Who, being great, yet dar'd to be unjust,
Shunn'd like a plague, or but at distance view'd,
He walk'd the crouded streets in Solitude,
Nor could his rank, and station in the land
Bribe one mean knave to take him by the hand.
Such rigid maxims (O, might such revive
To keep expiring Honesty alive)
Made rogues, all other hopes of fame denied,
Not just thro' principle, be just thro' pride.

Our Times, more polish'd, wear a diff'rent face;
Debts are an Honour; Payment a disgrace.
Men of weak minds, high-plac'd on Folly's list,
May gravely tell us Trade cannot subsist,
Nor all those Thousands who're in Trade employ'd,
If faith 'twixt Man and Man is once destroy'd.
Why—be it so—We in that point accord,
But what is Trade, and Tradesmen to a Lord.

FABER, from day to day, from year to year,
Hath had the cries of tradesmen in his ear,
Of tradesmen by his Villainy betray'd,
And, vainly seeking Justice, bankrupts made.
What is't to FABER? Lordly as before,
He sits at ease, and lives to ruin more.
Fix'd at his door, as motionless as stone,
Begging, but only begging for their own,
Unheard they stand, or only heard by Those,
Those slaves in Livery, who mock their woes.
What is't to FABER? he continues great,
Lives on in grandeur, and runs out in state.
The helpless Widow, wrung with deep despair,
In bitterness of soul, pours forth her pray'r,
Hugging her starving babes, with streaming eyes,
And calls down vengeance, vengeance from the skies.
What is't to FABER? he stands safe and clear
Heav'n can commence no legal action here,
And on his breast a mighty plate he wears,
A plate more firm than triple brass, which bears
The name of PRIVILEGE, 'gainst vulgar awe;
He feels no Conscience, and he fears no Law.

Nor think, acquainted with small knaves alone,
Who have not shame outliv'd, and grace outgrown,
The great World hidden from thy reptile view,
That on such Men, to whom Contempt is due,
Contempt shall fall, and their vile Author's name
Recorded stand thro' all the land of shame.
No—to his porch, like Persians to the Sun,
Behold contending crowds of Courtiers run;
See, to his aid what noble troops advance,
All sworn to keep his crimes in Countenance.

Nor wonder at it—They partake the charge,
As small their Conscience, and their debts as large.

Propp'd by such Clients, and without controul
From all that's honest in the human soul,
In Grandeur mean, with insolence unjust,
Whilst none but knaves can praise, and Fools will trust,
Caress'd and Courted, FABER seems to stand
A mighty Pillar in a guilty land.
And (a sad truth to which succeeding times
Will scarce give credit, when 'tis told in rimes)
Did not strict Honour with a jealous eye
Watch round the Throne, did not true Piety,
(Who, link'd with Honour for the noblest ends,
Ranks none but honest Men amongst her friends)
Forbid us to be crush'd with such a weight,
He might in time be Minister of State.

But why enlarge I on such petty crimes?
They might have shock'd the faith of former times,
But now are held as Nothing—We begin,
Where our Sires ended, and improve in Sin,
Rack our invention, and leave nothing new
In vice, and folly for our sons to do.

Nor deem this censure hard; there's not a place
Most consecrate to purposes of grace,
Which VICE hath not polluted; none so high,
But with bold pinion She hath dar'd to fly,
And build there for her pleasure; none so low,
But She hath crept into it, made it know,
And feel her pow'r; in Courts, in Camps She reigns,
O'er sober Citizens, and simple Swains,
E'en in our temples She hath fix'd her throne,
And 'bove God's holy altars plac'd her own.

More to increase the horrour of our State,
To make her Empire lasting as 'tis great,
To make us in full-grown Perfection feel
Curses which neither Art, nor Time can heal,
All Shame discarded, all remains of pride,
MEANNESS sits crown'd, and triumphs by her side.
MEANNESS, who glcans out of the human mind
Those few good seeds which VICE had left behind,
Those seeds which might in time to Virtue tend,
And leaves the Soul without a pow'r to mend;
MEANNESS, at sight of whom, with brave disdain
The breast of Manhood swells, but swells in vain,
Before whom Honour makes a forc'd retreat,
And Freedom is compell'd to quit her seat;
MEANNESS which, like that mark by bloody CAIN
Borne in his forehead for a brother slain,
God, in his great and all-subduing rage,
Ordains the standing mark of this vile age.

The venal Heroe trucks his fame for gold,
The Patriot's virtue for a place is sold,
The Statesman bargains for his Country's shame,
And for preferment Priests their God disclaim.
Worn out with lust, her day of letch'ry o'er,
The Mother trains the daughter which She bore
In her own paths; The Father aids the plan,
And, when the Innocent is ripe for Man,
Sells her to some old Letcher for a wife,
And makes her an Adulteress for life,
Or in the papers bids his name appear,
And advertises for a L[IGONIER];
Husband and Wife (whom Av'rice must applaud)
Agree to save the charge of Pimp and Bawd;
Those parts they play themselves, a frugal pair,
And share the infamy, the gain to share,
Well-pleas'd to find, when They the profits tell,
That they have play'd the whore and rogue so well.

Nor are these things (which might imply a spark
Of Shame still left) transacted in the dark.
No—to the Public they are open laid,
And carried on like any other trade.
Scorning to mince damnation, and too proud
To work the works of darkness in a cloud,
In fullest vigour Vice maintains her sway:
Free are her Marts, and open at noon-day.
MEANNESS, now wed to IMPUDENCE, no more
In darkness skulks, and trembles as of yore
When the Light breaks upon her coward eye;
Boldly She stalks on earth, and to the sky
Lifts her proud head, nor fears lest time abate,
And turn her Husband's love to canker'd hate,
Since Fate, to make them more sincerely one,
Hath crown'd their loves with MOUNTAGUE their son.
A Son, so like his Dam, so like his Sire,
With all the Mother's craft, the Father's fire,
An Image so express in ev'ry part,
So like in all bad qualities of heart,
That, had They fifty children, He alone
Would stand as Heir Apparent to the throne.

With our own Island vices not content,
We rob our neighbours on the Continent,
Dance Europe round, and visit ev'ry court
To ape their follies, and their crimes import.
To diff'rent lands for diff'rent sins we roam,
And, richly freighted, bring our cargoe home,
Nobly industrious to make vice appear
In her full State, and perfect only here.

(pp. 391-95)

Be Grace shut out, be Mercy deaf, let God
With tenfold terrours arm that dreadful nod
Which speaks them lost, and sentenc'd to despair;
Distending wide her jaws, let Hell prepare
For Those who thus offend amongst Mankind,
A fire more fierce, and tortures more refin'd;
On Earth, which groans beneath their monstrous weight,
On Earth, alas! They meet a diff'rent fate,
And whilst the Laws, false grace, false mercy shewn,
Are taught to wear a softness not their own,
Men, whom the Beasts would spurn, should they appear
Amongst the honest herd, find refuge here.

No longer by vain fear, or shame controul'd,
From long, too long Security grown bold,
Mocking rebuke, they brave it in our streets,
And LUMLEY e'en at noon his mistress meets.
So public in their crimes, so daring grown,
They almost take a pride to have them known,
And each unnat'ral Villain scarce endures
To make a secret of his vile amours.
Go where We will, at ev'ry time and place,
SODOM confronts, and stares us in the face;
They ply in public at our very doors
And take the bread from much more honest Whores.
Those who are mean high Paramours secure,
And the rich guilty screen the guilty poor;
The Sin too proud to feel from Reason awe,
And Those, who practise it, too great for Law.

Woman, the pride and happiness of Man,
Without whose soft endearments Nature's plan
Had been a blank, and Life not worth a thought;
Woman, by all the Loves and Graces taught,
With softest arts, and sure, tho' hidden skill
To humanize, and mould us to her will;
Woman, with more than common grace form'd *here*,
With the persuasive language of a tear
To melt the rugged temper of our Isle,
Or win us to her purpose with a smile;

A coffeehouse of the Age of Johnson.

Woman, by fate the quickest spur decreed,
The fairest, best reward of ev'ry deed
Which bears the stamp of honour, at whose name
Our ancient Heroes caught a quicker flame,
And dar'd beyond belief, whilst o'er the plain,
Spurning the carcases of Princes slain,
Confusion proudly strode, whilst Horrour blew
The fatal trump, and Death stalk'd full in view;
Woman is out of date, a thing thrown by
As having lost its use; No more the Eye
With *female* beauty caught, in wild amaze,
Gazes entranc'd, and could for ever gaze;
No more the Heart, that seat where Love resides,
Each Breath drawn quick and short, in fuller tides
Life posting thro' the veins, each pulse on fire,
And the whole body tingling with desire,
Pants for those charms, which Virtue might engage
To break his vow, and thaw the frost of age,
Bidding each trembling nerve, each muscle strain,
And giving pleasure which is almost pain.
Women are kept for nothing but the breed;
For pleasure we must have a GANYMEDE,
A fine, fresh HYLAS, a delicious boy,
To serve our purposes of beastly joy.

Fairest of Nymphs, where ev'ry Nymph is fair,
Whom Nature form'd with more than common care,
With more than common care whom Art improv'd,
And Both declar'd most worthy to be lov'd,

[AYNAM] neglected wanders, whilst a croud
Pursue, and consecrate the steps [of STROUD.]
She, hapless maid, born in a wretched hour,
Wastes life's gay prime in vain, like some fair flow'r,
Sweet in its scent, and lively in its hue,
Which withers on the stalk from whence it grew,
And dies uncropp'd, whilst He, admir'd, carest,
Belov'd, and ev'ry where a welcome guest,
With Brutes of rank and fortune plays the Whore,
For their unnat'ral lust a Common Sew'r.

Dine with APICIUS—at his sumptuous board
Find all the world of dainties can afford—
And yet (so much distemper'd Spirits pall
The sickly appetite) amidst them all
APICIUS finds no joy, but, whilst he carves
For ev'ry guest, the Landlord sits and starves.

The forest Haunch, fine, fat, in flavour high,
Kept to a moment, smokes before his eye,
But smokes in vain; his heedless eye runs o'er
And loathes what He had deified before;
The Turtle, of a great and glorious size,
Worth its own weight in gold, a mighty prize
For which a Man of Taste all risques would run,
Itself a feast, and ev'ry dish in one,
The Turtle in luxurious pomp comes in,
Kept, kill'd, cut up, prepar'd, and drest by QUIN;
In vain it comes, in vain lies full in view;
As QUIN hath drest it, he may eat it too,
APICIUS cannot—When the glass goes round,
Quick-circling, and the roofs with mirth resound,
Sober he sits, and silent—all alone
Tho' in a croud, and to himself scarce known,
On grief he feeds, nor friends can cure, nor wine
Suspend his cares, and make him cease to pine.

Why mourns APICIUS thus? why runs his eye,
Heedless, o'er delicates, which from the sky
Might call down Jove? Where now his gen'rous wish
That, to invent a new and better dish,
The World might burn, and all mankind expire,
So he might roast a Phœnix at the fire.
Why swims that eye in tears, which, thro' a race
Of sixty years, ne'er shew'd one sign of grace?
Why feels that heart, which never felt before?
Why doth that pamper'd glutton eat no more,
Who only liv'd to eat, his Stomach pall'd,
And drown'd in floods of sorrow? hath Fate call'd
His Father from the grave to second life?
Hath CLODIUS on his hands return'd his Wife,
Or hath the Law, by strictest justice taught,
Compell'd him to restore the dow'r She brought?
Hath some bold Creditor against his will
Brought in, and forc'd him to discharge a bill,
Where Eating had no share? Hath some vain Wench
Run out his wealth, and forc'd him to retrench?
Hath any rival Glutton got the start,
And beat him in his own luxurious art,
Bought cates for which APICIUS could not pay,
Or drest old dainties in a newer way?
Hath his Cook, worthy to be slain with rods,
Spoil'd a dish, fit to entertain the Gods,
Or hath some Varlet, cross'd by cruel fate,
Thrown down the price of Empires in a plate?

None, none of these—his Servants all are try'd,
So sure, they walk on ice, and never slide;
His Cook, an acquisition made in France,
Might put a CHLOE out of countenance,
Nor, tho' old HOLLES still maintains his stand,
Hath He one rival glutton in the land;
Women are all the objects of his hate,

His debts are all unpaid, and yet his state
In full security and triumph held,
Unless for once a Knave should be expell'd;
His Wife is still a Whore, and in his pow'r,
The Woman gone, he still retains the dow'r;
Sound in the grave (thanks to his filial care
Which mix'd the draught, and kindly sent him there,)
His Father sleeps, and, till the last trump shake
The corners of the earth, shall not awake.

Whence flows this Sorrow then? behind his chair
Did'st Thou not see, deck'd with a Solitaire
Which on his bare breast glitt'ring play'd, and grac'd
With nicest ornaments, a Stripling plac'd,
A Smooth, Smug Stripling in life's fairest prime?
Did'st Thou not mind too, how from time to time,
The monstrous Letcher, tempted to despise
All other dainties, thither turn'd his eyes?
How He seem'd inly to reproach us all,
Who strove his fix'd attention to recall,
And how He wish'd, e'en at the Time of grace,
Like Janus, to have had a double face?
His cause of grief behold in that fair Boy;
APICIUS dotes, and CORYDON is coy.

Vain and unthinking Stripling! When the glass
Meets thy too curious eye, and, as You pass,
Flatt'ring, presents in smiles thy image there,
Why dost Thou bless the Gods, who made Thee fair?
Blame their large bounties, and with reason blame;
Curse, curse thy beauty, for It leads to shame.
When thy hot Lord, to work Thee to his end,
Bids show'rs of gold into thy breast descend,
Suspect his gifts, nor the vile giver trust;
They're baits for Virtue, and smell strong of lust.
On those gay, gaudy trappings, which adorn
The temple of thy body, look with scorn,
View them with horrour, they pollution mean
And deepest ruin; Thou hast often seen,
From 'mongst the herd, the fairest and the best
Carefully singled out, and richly drest,
With grandeur mock'd, for sacrifice decreed,
Only in greater pomp at last to bleed.
Be warn'd in time, the threat'ned danger shun,
To stay a moment is to be undone.
What tho', temptation proof, thy Virtue shine,
Nor bribes can move, nor arts can undermine,
All other methods failing, one resource
Is still behind, and Thou must yield to force.
Paint to thyself the horrors of a rape,
Most strongly paint, and, while Thou can'st escape,
Mind not his promises—They're made in sport—
Made to be broke—Was He not bred at Court?
Trust not his Honour; He's a Man of birth;
Attend not to his oaths—They're made on earth,
Not regist'red in Heav'n—He mocks at grace,
And in his Creed God never found a place—
Look not for Conscience—for He knows her not,
So long a Stranger, she is quite forgot—
Nor think thyself in Law secure and firm—
Thy Master is a Lord, and Thou a Worm,
A poor mean Reptile, never meant to think,
Who, being well supplied with meat and drink,
And suffer'd just to crawl from place to place,
Must serve his lusts, and think he does Thee grace.

Fly then, whilst yet 'tis in thy pow'r to fly,
But whither can'st Thou go? on Whom rely
For wish'd protection? Virtue's sure to meet
An armed host of foes, in ev'ry street.
What boots It, of APICIUS fearful grown,
Headlong to fly into the arms of STONE,
Or why take refuge in the house of pray'r,

If sure to meet with an APICIUS there?
Trust not Old Age, which will thy faith betray;
Saint SOCRATES is still a Goat, tho' grey;
Trust not green Youth; FLORIO will scarce go down,
And, at eighteen, hath surfeited the Town;
Trust not to Rakes—alas! 'tis all pretence—
They take up Raking only as a fence
'Gainst Common fame—place H[ERVEY] in thy view;
He keeps one Whore, as BARROWBY kept two;
Trust not to Marriage—T——took a Wife,
Who chaste as Dian might have pass'd her life,
Had She not, far more prudent in her aim,
(To propagate the honours of his name,
And save expiring titles) taken care
Without his knowledge to provide an heir;
Trust not to Marriage, in Mankind unread;
S[ACKVILLE]'s a married man, and S[TROUD] new wed.

Would'st Thou be safe? Society forswear,
Fly to the desart, and seek shelter there,
Herd with the Brutes—they follow Nature's plan—
There's not one Brute so dangerous as Man
In Afric's wilds—'mongst them that refuge find,
Which Lust denies thee here among Mankind;
Renounce thy name, thy nature, and no more
Pique thy vain pride on Manhood, on all four
Walk, as You see those honest creatures do,
And quite forget that once You walk'd on Two.

But, if the thoughts of Solitude alarm,
And Social life hath one remaining charm,
If still Thou art to jeopardy decreed
Amongst the monsters of AUGUSTA's breed,
Lay by thy sex, thy safety to procure;
Put off the Man, from Men to live secure;
Go forth a woman to the public view,
And with their garb assume their manners too.
Had the *light-footed* GREEK of Chiron's school
Been wise enough to keep this single rule,
The Maudlin Heroe, like a puling boy
Robb'd of his play-thing, on the plains of Troy
Had never blubber'd at Patroclus' tomb,
And plac'd his Minion in his Mistress' room.
Be not in this than Catamites more nice,
Do that for Virtue, which they do for vice.
Thus shalt Thou pass untainted life's gay bloom,
Thus stand uncourted in the drawing room,
At midnight thus, untempted, walk the street,
And run no danger but of being beat.

Where is the Mother, whose officious zeal
Discreetly judging what her Daughters feel
By what She felt herself in days of yore,
Against that Letcher Man makes fast the door,
Who not permits, e'en for the sake of pray'r,
A Priest, uncastrated, to enter there,
Nor (could her wishes, and her care prevail)
Would suffer in the house a fly that's male?
Let Her discharge her cares, throw wide her doors,
Her daughters cannot, if They would, be Whores,
Nor can a Man be found, as Times now go,
Who thinks it worth his while to make them so.

Tho' They, more fresh, more lively than the Morn,
And brighter than the noon-day Sun, adorn
The works of Nature, tho' the Mother's grace
Revives, improv'd, in ev'ry daughter's face,
Undisciplin'd in dull discretion's rules,
Untaught, and Undebauch'd by Boarding Schools,
Free and unguarded, let Them range the Town,
Go forth at random, and run pleasure down
Start where She will, discard all taint of fear,
Nor think of danger, when no danger's near.

Watch not their steps—They're safe without thy care,
Unless, like Jennets, they conceive by air,
And ev'ry one of them may die a Nun,
Unless They breed, like Carrion, in the Sun.
Men, dead to pleasure, as they're dead to grace,
Against the law of Nature set their face,
The grand, primæval law, and seem combin'd
To stop the propagation of Mankind;
Vile Pathicks read the Marriage Act with pride,
And fancy that the Law is on their side.

Broke down, and Strength a stranger to his bed,
Old L[IGONIER], tho' yet alive, is dead;
T[YRAWLEY] lives no more, or lives not to our Isle;
No longer blest with a CZ[ARINA]'s smile
T[YRAWLEY] is at P[ETERSBURGH] disgrac'd,
And M[OUNTAGUE], grown grey, perforce grows chaste;
Nor, to the credit of our modest race,
Rises one Stallion to supply their place.
A Maidenhead, which, twenty years ago,
In mid December, the rank Fly would blow
Tho' closely kept, *now,* when the Dog-Star's heat
Enflames the marrow, in the very street
May lie untouch'd, left for the worms, by Those
Who daintily pass by, and hold their nose.
Poor, Plain Concupiscence is in disgrace,
And Simple Letch'ry dares not shew her face
Least She be sent to Bridewell; Bankrupts made,
To save their fortunes, Bawds leave off that trade,
Which first had left off them; to *Well-close Square*
Fine, fresh, young Strumpets (for DODD preaches there)
Throng for subsistence; Pimps no longer thrive,
And Pensions only keep L[IGONIER] alive.

Where is the Mother, who thinks all her pain,
And all her jeopardy of travail, gain,
When a Man Child is born, thinks ev'ry pray'r
Paid to the full, and answer'd in an heir?
Shortsighted Woman! Little doth she know
What streams of sorrow from that source may flow,
Little suspect, whilst She surveys her Boy,
Her young NARCISSUS, with an eye of joy
Too full for Continence, that Fate could give
Her darling as a curse, that She may live,
E're sixteen Winters their short course have run,
In agonies of soul, to curse that Son.

Pray then, for daughters, Ye wise Mothers, pray;
They shall reward your love, nor make ye grey
Before your time with sorrow; They shall give
Ages of peace and comfort, whilst Ye live
Make life most truly worth your care, and save,
In spite of death, your mem'ries from the grave.

That Sense, with more than manly vigour fraught,
That Fortitude of Soul, that stretch of Thought,
That Genius, great beyond the narrow bound
Of Earth's low walk, that Judgment perfect found,
When wanted most, that Purity of Taste,
Which Critics mention by the name of chaste,
Adorn'd with Elegance, that easy flow
Of ready Wit, which never made a foe,
That Face, that Form, that Dignity, that Ease,
Those pow'rs of pleasing with that will to please,
By which LEPEL, when in her youthful days,
E'en from the currish POPE extorted praise,
We see, transmitted, in her Daughter shine,
And view a new LEPEL in CAROLINE.

Is a son born into this world of woe?
In never-ceasing streams let sorrow flow,
Be from that hour the house with sables hung,
Let lamentations dwell upon thy tongue,

E'en from the moment that he first began
To wail and whine, let him not see a man.
Lock, Lock him up, far from the public eye,
Give him no opportunity to buy,
Or to be bought; B——, tho' rich, was sold,
And gave his body up to shame for gold.

Let It be bruited all about the Town,
That He is coarse, indelicate, and brown,
An Antidote to Lust, his Face deep scar'd
With the Small Pox, his Body maim'd and marr'd,
Eat up with the Kings-evil, and his blood,
Tainted throughout, a thick and putrid flood,
Where dwells Corruption, making him all o'er,
From head to foot, a rank and running sore.
Should'st Thou report him as by Nature made,
He is undone, and by thy praise betray'd;
Give him out fair, Letchers in number more,
More brutal and more fierce, than throng'd the door
Of LOT in SODOM, shall to thine repair,
And force a passage, tho' a God is there.

Let Him not have one Servant that is male;
Where Lords are baffled, Servants oft prevail.
Some vices They propose, to all agree;
H——was guilty, but was M——free?

Give him no Tutor—throw him to a punk,
Rather than trust his morals to a Monk—
Monks we all know—We, who have liv'd at home,
From fair report, and Travellers, who roam,
More feelingly—nor trust him to the gown,
'Tis oft a covering in this vile town
For base designs; Ourselves have liv'd to see
More than one Parson in the Pillory.
Should He have Brothers, (Image to thy view
A Scene, which, tho' not public made, is true)
Let not one Brother be to t'other known,
Nor let his Father sit with him alone.

Be all his Servants, Female, Young, and Fair,
And if the Pride of Nature spur thy heir
To deeds of Venery, if, hot and wild,
He chance to get some score of maids with child,
Chide, but forgive him; Whoredom is a crime,
Which, more at this, than any other time,
Calls for indulgence, and, 'mongst such a race,
To have a bastard is some sign of grace.

Born in such times, should I sit tamely down,
Suppress my rage, and saunter thro' the town
As One who knew not, or who shar'd these crimes?
Should I at lesser evils point my rimes,
And let this Giant Sin, in the full eye
Of Observation, pass unwounded by?
Tho' our meek Wives, passive Obedience taught,
Patiently bear those wrongs, for which They ought,
With the brave spirit of their dams possess'd,
To plant a dagger in each husband's breast,
To cut off male increase from this fair Isle,
And turn our Thames into another Nile;
Tho', on his Sunday, the smug PULPITEER,
Loud 'gainst all other crimes, is silent here,
And thinks himself absolv'd, in the pretence
Of Decency, which meant for the defence
Of real Virtue, and to raise her price,
Becomes an agent for the cause of vice;
Tho' the Law sleeps, and, thro' the care They take
To drug her well, may never more awake;
Born in such times, nor with that patience curst
Which Saints may boast of, I must speak, or burst.

But if, too eager in my bold career,
Haply I wound the nice, and chaster ear,

If, all unguarded, all too rude, I speak,
And call up blushes in the maiden's cheek,
Forgive, Ye Fair—my real motives view,
And to forgiveness add your praises too.
For You I write—nor wish a better plan—
The Cause of Woman is most worthy Man—
For You I still will write, nor hold my hand,
Whilst there's one slave of SODOM in the land.

Let them fly far, and skulk from place to place,
Not daring to meet Manhood face to face,
Their steps I'll track, nor yield them one retreat
Where They may hide their heads, or rest their feet,
Till God in wrath shall let his vengeance fall,
And make a great example of them all,
Bidding in one grand pile this Town expire,
Her Tow'rs in dust, her Thames a lake of fire,
Or They (most worth our wish) convinc'd, tho' late,
Of their past crimes, and dangerous estate,
Pardon of Women with Repentance buy,
And learn to honour them, as much as I.

(pp. 398-409)

Charles Churchill, "The Times," in his The
Poetical Works of Charles Churchill, *edited
by Douglas Grant, Oxford at the Clarendon
Press, 1956, pp. 389-409.*

Richard B. Schwartz

[*A widely respected Johnsonian scholar, Schwartz is the
author of* Samuel Johnson and the New Science *(1971)
and* Samuel Johnson and the Problem of Evil *(1975).
In the following essay, he identifies several aspects of typical behavior in eighteenth-century London.*]

In Johnson's time, as in our own, observers drew a distinction between what one might find in the capital and what
one might find in the provinces. Then as now, however,
human nature did not change at the borders of the city.
Curiosities and perversities could be found virtually wherever they were sought. Yet the concentration of population within the city called attention to the actions, attitudes, and manners of the city's inhabitants. It is important for us to distinguish between those aspects of behavior
which might appear in the city and those which one could
find everywhere. The actions of the London mob, for example, might be duplicated elsewhere, but seldom with the
force of numbers which the capital made possible. An interest in investments and finance would be found wherever
there were people of means, but such interest would be
concentrated in the city. The city might offer examples of
extreme forms of behavior but one must hesitate before
drawing causal lines between extremism and an urban address, particularly considering the fact that the wealthy
often lived in the city for only a portion of the year, retiring to the countryside with the change of season or at the
end of a parliamentary session.

My intention here is to discuss several aspects of London
behavior which caught the attention of foreign visitors,
but with the caveat that "London" behavior could be
found in other places as well. What the foreigner found,
however, would certainly be a part of the daily life of the
capital, and while its importance could be exaggerated, the
fact that Londoners were inured to certain types of behavior is instructive in itself.

The London crowd was brash and abusive; the ridicule of passersby was one of its favorite pastimes. We misjudge the average eighteenth-century Londoner if we think of him as passive and subservient, knowing and enjoying his place within a hierarchic society. On the contrary, he was independent and assertive, although subject to political influences of a quite varied nature. Anecdotes abound concerning the Londoner and his exercise of individual liberty. For example, if the wealthy refused to move their coaches, the crowd would not hesitate to use the coaches as thoroughfares and walk right through them. Those who indulged in fashionable behavior were subject to the commentaries of the unappointed critic; there are several accounts, for example, of theatre-goers whose dress or hairstyles were so ridiculed by their fellows that they were forced to leave the premises.

Grosley noted that people in the street (day laborers, for example) were very rude to Frenchmen. In some cases the crowd moved from open insults to violent challenges. One Englishman wearing French clothes was told that if he ever again entered the neighborhood in Parisian dress he would be thrown into the Thames. Grosley's experience was that this sort of behavior was confined to the mob: "The politeness, the civility, and the officiousness of people of good breeding, whom we met in the streets, as well as the obliging readiness of the citizens and shopkeepers, even of the inferior sort, sufficiently indemnify and console us for the insolence of the mob; as I have often experienced." Moritz thought that anti-Semitism was stronger in England than in Germany. Saussure traced certain forms of British behavior to another prejudice, one involving pride: "I do not think there is a people more prejudiced in its own favour than the British people, and they allow this to appear in their talk and manners. They look on foreigners in general with contempt, and think nothing is as well done elsewhere as in their own country." Saussure also complains of rude and violent behavior on the part of the mob, particularly upon certain occasions, such as the Lord Mayor's Day:

> The populace on that day is particularly insolent and rowdy, turning into lawless freedom the great liberty it enjoys. At these times it is almost dangerous for an honest man, and more particularly for a foreigner, if at all well dressed, to walk in the streets, for he runs a great risk of being insulted by the vulgar populace, which is the most cursed brood in existence. He is sure of not only being jeered at and being bespattered with mud, but as likely as not dead dogs and cats will be thrown at him, for the mob makes a provision beforehand of these playthings, so that they may amuse themselves with them on the great day.

The hatred of foreigners was not confined to the London mob. In some cases in the provinces there was also a general antipathy toward strangers, including native Englishmen, some of whom were subjected to abuse by the suspicious. The villagers of Market Bosworth set their dogs on one man passing through for the simple reason that he was a stranger.

While the mob might be swayed by political demagogues of different ideological persuasions, its penchant for political fervor was not unique. As a people, the citizens of the eighteenth century were fiercely political, particularly those close to the center of political power in London. Ar-

chenholz comments on this phenomenon: "In general nothing is more difficult than to make an Englishman speak; he answers to every thing by *yes* or *no;* address him, however, on some political subject and he is suddenly animated; he opens his mouth and becomes eloquent; for this seems to be connected from his infancy with his very existence." Addison's obsessively political upholsterer (*Tatler* 155) reappeared frequently in the period in slightly different literary form, but in every guise he was representative of the influence of politics on the individual Englishman. Such behavior was not confined to the world of literature. At a lord mayor's procession early in the century one foreign traveler saw three naked men running through the streets of London, vowing they would never wear coat or shirt until James II was restored to his throne. Politicization extended to nearly every area of life. For example, with the Methuen Treaty (1703) it was agreed that Portugal would allow the importation of English cloth. In return, England would lower the duty payable on Portuguese wine. The drinking of port became a favorite Whig activity, in part because it was prejudicial to French trade. The Jacobites, of course, turned to claret or burgundy.

Political activities, though sometimes silly, were not usually harmful. We have spoken already of numerous forms of violence and brutality in eighteenth-century life. The point is worth restating. The dangers of English life in the eighteenth century were everywhere. For example, Lord Holland's Eton fagmaster had forced him to toast bread in his bare hands, with the result that his fingers were permanently deformed. While the newspapers recorded acts of criminal violence (for example, the case of Elizabeth Brownrigg, who was hanged in 1767 for torturing her apprentices to death, reported in detail in the *Annual Register*), much was simply taken for granted.

The theatre was a dangerous place. Moritz wrote of his experience at the Haymarket: "Every moment a rotten orange came whizzing past me or past my neighbour; one hit my hat, but I dared not turn round for fear one hit me in the face." Theatregoers came armed with rotten fruit and vegetables. They would probably not spend the 6d. for a theatre orange when one or two of them could be purchased outside for a halfpence. Poor Moritz was also a victim of vanity: "Behind me in the pit sat a young fop who continually put his foot on my bench in order to show off the flashy stone buckles on his shoes; if I didn't make way for his precious buckles he put his foot on my coat-tails."

A visitor to the House of Commons expecting decorous behavior and genteel debate was more likely to find constant milling about. Some would enter the room in spurs and sit cracking nuts or eating oranges while others attempted to speak. Gross and rough behavior were often the rule and not the exception. London, as Johnson noted, was not for the squeamish or the weak, and those who survived its challenges were likely to survive nearly anywhere else.

Some were not equal to its pressures and turned to suicide. Saussure reports that the property and land of suicides were confiscated and the suicides themselves buried at road crossings. He was shocked by the acceptance of the practice as well as the frequency of its occurrence: "I was much surprised at the light-hearted way in which men of this country commit suicide. I could not understand this mania, which astonished me as greatly as it does other foreigners." In some cases stakes were driven through the suicides' hearts, presumably to prevent the individual's ghost from rising. This was foregone if it could be proven that the person was insane.

Grosley attributed English melancholy to fog, humidity, and the smoke from coal fires, whose particles would "insinuate themselves into the blood of those who are always inhaling them, render it dull and heavy, and carry with them new principles of melancholy." His next comment is interesting: "Education, religion, public diversions, and the works of authors in vogue, seem to have no other end in view, but to feed and propagate this distemper." Archenholz thought that most suicides resulted from Deism, but the English climate and the London atmosphere were more often cited as causes. The weather's oppressiveness is more commonly discussed than its extremes. There were exceptional occurrences, such as the earthquake of 1750, which left gaping holes in London streets and toppled chimneys. There were also extremes, such as the severe winter of 1784, in which the ground was covered with two feet of snow and evergreen trees froze and split. This was, however, far from normal: the snow which Kalm experienced was seldom on the ground for more than two or three days. The coal smoke, on the other hand, was nearly always present, as was the damp.

We think of the eighteenth century as enlightened, even though there is good reason (as Professor Pocock and others have argued) to avoid the use of the term "enlightenment" when speaking of English intellectual history. Yet, if we speak of social history, particularly among the uneducated, we realize the extent to which superstition remained a common part of experience. Many, for example, believed that a dead man's hands could cure warts if the hands were rubbed against them. The touch of men who had been hanged was sought for its effect in curing goiter and swollen glands. In the mid-seventies a woman in Leicestershire was thrown into a pond to see if she was a witch, the notion being that witches rejected baptism and hence the water would reject them. Suspected witches were bound foot to hand (actually thumb to toe) in crisscross fashion before being tossed into the water. Usually a rope was tied to them to retrieve them if they demonstrated their innocence by sinking.

Suspected witches were sometimes weighed against the Bible; those found to be heavier were exonerated. In the seventeenth century it was not uncommon to encounter professional prickers, or witch finders. It was believed that a certain mark on the body indicated servitude to Satan. Satan, unfortunately, could be expected to hide the mark, and the mark would be insensitive. Thus, the suspected person was stripped and shaved of head and body hair; then any suspicious spots or marks were pricked with pins or sharp instruments. If no pain was apparent and no blood flowed when the pin was removed, it was assumed that the individual under examination was guilty. Although such practices were extremely rare in the eighteenth century, the last English witchcraft law was not repealed until 1736, and isolated examples of superstition and cruelty (such as the killing of a woman in Hertfordshire in 1751, reported in gory detail in the *Gentleman's Magazine*) still occurred.

While witches might not routinely be sought in the eighteenth century, the number of curious individuals a Londoner might encounter was potentially enormous. The Englishman has always prized his individuality and did so as much or more in the eighteenth century as in any other time. The eccentrics one meets in the pages of Fielding, Smollett, and Sterne had their counterparts in real life; Boswell remarks on the great "variety of characters" Johnson had encountered. One sometimes has the impression that bizarre behavior was the rule and not the exception. Of course, it *was* exceptional, but it was in no way uncommon. One understates the case by saying that the period contained many colorful personalities, for the list of such persons is enormous, ranging from George Psalmanazar, whose phoney "Formosan" language was taught to would-be missionaries, to John Woodward, who would disrupt proceedings at Royal Society meetings by grimacing at those he disliked. "Characters" were everywhere and their continual emergence markedly contributed to the texture of daily life. The rich were particularly prone to acts of bravado, too. When the eccentric fourth Earl Ferrers was hanged (with a silken rope—a peer's privilege) for shooting his servant, he went to the gallows in his silver-braided wedding suit, noting that the day of his wedding and the day of his execution were the two worst in his life. Serving the rich could be a dangerous occupation in these days of sometimes strange opulence. Lord North, for example, was presented with a tiger as a gift from a sea captain; the tiger proceeded to bite a hand off of each of his two feeders.

Extremes of other sorts were often encountered and noted. An enormous farmer named Spooner, who weighed 40 stone and 9 pounds and was 4'3" across the shoulders was once stabbed at Atherstone market, but the knife did not penetrate all of the layers of fat on his body. In the 1770s a woman died at the age of 128; she had taken her third husband at the comparatively youthful age of 92.

Criminals and prostitutes were particularly known for great skill or brazen behavior. Jonathan Wild is said to have picked the parson's pocket before his execution, and . . . Mary Young, the pickpocket, . . . equipped herself with artificial arms so that she could sit demurely in church while busily picking pockets. Kitty Fisher, the prostitute capable of commanding a fee of 100 guineas a night, is said to have boldly eaten a £1,000 banknote in a sandwich.

The period was one of great hoaxes. [Witness] . . . George Psalmanazar's "Formosan" language. There was also the "ghost" in Cock Lane, which Johnson investigated (the ghost was reputed to be that of Lanny Lynes, which accused Lanny's lover, William Kent, of poisoning her) and the more bizarre case of Mary Toft, the woman who, it was claimed, gave birth to rabbits. Her case was investigated by George I's own physician, Nathanael St. André, who arrived on the scene just in time to "deliver" the trunk of a rabbit, an action which shattered his reputation. St. André described Mary Toft's rabbit as "praeternatural."

The list of eccentricities and eccentrics is seemingly endless, from the Tahitian Omai, imported as a "noble savage" and lionized by London society, to Graham with his celestial bed and de Loutherbourg with his eidophusikon. Johnson's immersion in this world furnished an endless source of material for his curiosity and his fascination with human psychology and human behavior. It is a pity that he did not write more concerning the city, and we are, as has often been pointed out, deeply in Boswell's debt for the preservation of anecdotes, descriptions, and observations which would otherwise have passed into oblivion. Johnson's famous poem *London* is well worth considering in this connection. I have not discussed it up until now because its descriptive value is affected by its satiric intent, which leads Johnson to exaggerate certain of the city's ills in order to comment on politicians and political practices.

The poem has been criticized by scholarly commentators and not always for the right reasons. What is often overlooked is the fact that the poem has two narrators, only the second of which indulges in a lengthy jeremiad against the capital. The first speaker (the one who corresponds to the Juvenal figure in the poem Johnson is imitating) acknowledges the evils of the city:

> Tho grief and fondness in my breast rebel,
> When injur'd Thales bids the town farewell,
> Yet still my calmer thoughts his choice commend,
> I praise the hermit, but regret the friend,
> Resolved at length, from vice and London far,
> To breathe in distant fields a purer air,
> And, fix'd on Cambria's solitary shore,
> Give to St. David one true Briton more.
>
> For who would leave, unbrib'd, Hibernia's land,
> Or change the rocks of Scotland for the Strand?
> There none are swept by sudden fate away,
> But all whom hunger spares, with age decay:
> Here malice, rapine, accident, conspire,
> And now a rabble rages, now a fire;
> Their ambush here relentless ruffians lay,
> And here the fell attorney prowls for prey;
> Here falling houses thunder on your head,
> And here a female atheist talks you dead.

It is sometimes argued that Thales represents Johnson's friend the poet Richard Savage, though the dates will not permit such an interpretation. (It may be, however, that Savage—a notorious poseur and posturer—imitated Thales.) Regardless of Thales' identity, the Juvenalian parallel would suggest that the first speaker corresponds to the poet himself—Johnson—and that speaker remains in London at the poem's conclusion. From all that we know of Johnson's experience and attitudes, this is as it should be, for though he seldom distorted either the city's good features or its bad, he remained a lover of the city with all of its contrasts, contradictions, and extremes. Boswell can sometimes stress the favorable aspects of Johnson's life in the city; Johnson's *London* stresses the negative. The truth lies in between.

The charges quoted in the segment from Johnson's *London* are not exaggerated. One would easily find vice in Johnson's London, and bad air and bribery would be omnipresent. Danger, disruption, street crime, fire, and the mob would not be difficult to find either. There were predatory attorneys, lost faith, and falling buildings also, but the counterbalancing features should be remembered: the felicity which Johnson found in London taverns; the Strand's shops and the city's theatres; the city's lights, its commercial vigor, and economic resilience; the city's activity and power, its food and its fashions, its river and its ships; its parks and shows, its papers and its personalities. Most of all there is its history and the network of associations one encounters in every section and at every corner. Travelers then and now sometimes complain of the city,

but the occasions for complaint are dwarfed by the city's attractions. One sometimes hears the expression "only in London" as a pained *cri de coeur,* but most often one hears it as an expression of joy. (pp. 167-78)

> *Richard B. Schwartz, in his* Daily Life in Johnson's London, *The University of Wisconsin Press, 1983, 196 p.*

AESTHETICS OF NEOCLASSICISM

Edmund Burke

[*Burke was an Irish-born English statesman, philosopher, and critic. Widely recognized as the founder of modern Anglo-American conservatism, he ranks among the most important and influential English statesmen and political writers of the eighteenth century. In addition to his distinction as a political thinker, Burke wrote a pioneering work in the field of aesthetics,* A Philosophical Inquiry into the Origin of Our Ideas of the Sublime and the Beautiful *(1759). In the following excerpt from that work, he seeks to determine the basic guiding principles of individual taste in matters concerning aesthetic quality.*]

On a superficial view, we may seem to differ very widely from each other in our reasonings, and no less in our pleasures: but notwithstanding this difference, which I think to be rather apparent than real, it is probable that the standard both of reason and Taste is the same in all human creatures. For if there were not some principles of judgment as well as of sentiment common to all mankind, no hold could possibly be taken either on their reason or their passions, sufficient to maintain the ordinary correspondence of life. It appears indeed to be generally acknowledged, that with regard to truth and falsehood there is something fixed. We find people in their disputes continually appealing to certain tests and standards which are allowed on all sides, and are supposed to be established in our common nature. But there is not the same obvious concurrence in any uniform or settled principles which relate to Taste. It is even commonly supposed that this delicate and aerial faculty, which seems too volatile to endure even the chains of a definition, cannot be properly tried by any test, nor regulated by any standard. There is so continual a call for the exercise of the reasoning faculty, and it is so much strengthened by perpetual contention, that certain maxims of right reason seem to be tacitly settled amongst the most ignorant. The learned have improved on this rude science, and reduced those maxims into a system. If Taste has not been so happily cultivated, it was not that the subject was barren, but that the labourers were few or negligent; for to say the truth, there are not the same interesting motives to impel us to fix the one, which urge us to ascertain the other. And after all, if men differ in their opinion concerning such matters, their difference is not attended with the same important consequences, else I make no doubt but that the logic of Taste, if I may be allowed the expression, might very possibly be as well digested, and we might come to discuss matters of this nature with as much certainty, as those which seem more immediately within the province of mere reason. And indeed it is very necessary at the entrance into such an enquiry, as our present, to make this point as clear as possible; for if Taste has no fixed principles, if the imagination is not affected according to some invariable and certain laws, our labour is like to be employed to very little purpose; as it must be judged an useless, if not an absurd undertaking, to lay down rules for caprice, and to set up for a legislator of whims and fancies.

The term Taste, like all other figurative terms, is not extremely accurate: the thing which we understand by it, is far from a simple and determinate idea in the minds of most men, and it is therefore liable to uncertainty and confusion. I have no great opinion of a definition, the celebrated remedy for the cure of this disorder. For when we define, we seem in danger of circumscribing nature within the bounds of our own notions, which we often take up by hazard, or embrace on trust, or form out of a limited and partial consideration of the object before us, instead of extending our ideas to take in all that nature comprehends, according to her manner of combining. We are limited in our enquiry by the strict laws to which we have submitted at our setting out.

A definition may be very exact, and yet go but a very little way towards informing us of the nature of the thing defined; but let the virtue of a definition be what it will, in the order of things, it seems rather to follow than to precede our enquiry, of which it ought to be considered as the result. It must be acknowledged that the methods of disquisition and teaching may be sometimes different, and on very good reason undoubtedly; but for my part, I am convinced that the method of teaching which approaches most nearly to the method of investigation, is incomparably the best; since not content with serving up a few barren and lifeless truths, it leads to the stock on which they grew; it tends to set the reader himself in the track of invention, and to direct him into those paths in which the author has made his own discoveries, if he should be so happy as to have made any that are valuable.

But to cut off all pretence for cavilling, I mean by the word Taste no more than that faculty, or those faculties of the mind which are affected with, or which form a judgment of the works of imagination and the elegant arts. This is, I think, the most general idea of that word, and what is the least connected with any particular theory. And my point in this enquiry is to find whether there are any principles, on which the imagination is affected, so common to all, so grounded and certain, as to supply the means of reasoning satisfactorily about them. And such principles of Taste, I fancy there are; however paradoxical it may seem to those, who on a superficial view imagine, that

A meeting of The Club at Sir Joshua Reynolds's house, engraved by William Walker after a painting by James Doyle. Seated, left to right, are James Boswell, Samuel Johnson, Reynolds, David Garrick, Edmund Burke, Pasquale Paoli, Charles Burney, Thomas Warton, and Oliver Goldsmith.

there is so great a diversity of Tastes both in kind and degree, that nothing can be more indeterminate.

All the natural powers in man, which I know, that are conversant about external objects, are the Senses; the Imagination; and the Judgment. And first with regard to the senses. We do and we must suppose, that as the conformation of their organs are nearly, or altogether the same in all men, so the manner of perceiving external objects is in all men the same, or with little difference. We are satisfied that what appears to be light to one eye, appears light to another; that what seems sweet to one palate, is sweet to another; that what is dark and bitter to this man, is likewise dark and bitter to that; and we conclude in the same manner of great and little, hard and soft, hot and cold, rough and smooth; and indeed of all the natural qualities and affections of bodies. If we suffer ourselves to imagine, that their senses present to different men different images of things, this sceptical proceeding will make every sort of reasoning on every subject vain and frivolous, even that sceptical reasoning itself, which had persuaded us to entertain a doubt concerning the agreement of our perceptions. But as there will be very little doubt that bodies present similar images to the whole species, it must necessarily be allowed, that the pleasures and the pains which every object excites in one man, it must raise in all mankind, whilst it operates naturally, simply, and by its proper powers only; for if we deny this, we must imagine, that the same cause operating in the same manner, and on subjects of the same kind, will produce different effects, which would be highly absurd. Let us first consider this point in the sense of Taste, and the rather as the faculty in question has taken its name from that sense. All men are agreed to call vinegar sour, honey sweet, and aloes bitter; and as they are all agreed in finding these qualities in those objects, they do not in the least differ concerning their effects with regard to pleasure and pain. They all concur in calling sweetness pleasant, and sourness and bitterness unpleasant. Here there is no diversity in their sentiments; and that there is not appears fully from the consent of all men in the metaphors which are taken from the sense of Taste. A sour temper, bitter expressions, bitter curses, a bitter fate, are terms well and strongly understood by all. And we are altogether as well understood when we say, a sweet disposition, a sweet person, a sweet condition, and the like. It is confessed, that custom, and some other causes, have made many deviations from the natural pleasures or pains which belong to these several Tastes; but then the power of distinguishing between the natural and the acquired relish remains to the very last. A man frequently comes to prefer the Taste of tobacco to that of sugar, and the flavour of vinegar to that of milk; but this makes no confusion in Tastes, whilst he is sensible that the tobacco and vinegar are not sweet, and whilst he knows that habit alone has reconciled his palate to these alien pleasures. Even with such a person we may speak, and with sufficient precision, concerning Tastes. But should any man be found who declares, that to him tobacco has a Taste like sugar, and that he cannot distinguish between milk and vinegar; or that tobacco and vinegar are sweet, milk bitter, and sugar sour, we immediately conclude that the organs of this man are out of order, and that his palate is utterly vitiated. We are as far from conferring with such a person upon Tastes, as from reasoning concerning the relations of quantity with one who should deny that all the parts together were equal to the whole. We do not call a man of this kind wrong in his notions, but absolutely mad. Exceptions of this sort in either way, do not at all impeach our general rule, nor make us conclude that men have various principles concerning the relations of quantity, or the Taste of things. So that when it is said, Taste cannot be disputed, it can only mean, that no one can strictly answer what pleasure or pain some particular man may find from the Taste of some particular thing. This indeed cannot be disputed; but we may dispute, and with sufficient clearness too, concerning the things which are naturally pleasing or disagreeable to the sense. But when we talk of any peculiar or acquired relish, then we must know the habits, the prejudices, or the distempers of this particular man, and we must draw our conclusion from those.

This agreement of mankind is not confined to the Taste solely. The principle of pleasure derived from sight is the same in all. Light is more pleasing than darkness. Summer, when the earth is clad in green, when the heavens are serene and bright, is more agreeable than winter, when every thing makes a different appearance. I never remember that any thing beautiful, whether a man, a beast, a bird, or a plant, was ever shewn, though it were to an hundred people, that they did not all immediately agree that it was beautiful, though some might have thought that it fell short of their expectation, or that other things were still finer. I believe no man thinks a goose to be more beautiful than a swan, or imagines that what they call a Friezland hen excels a peacock. It must be observed too, that the pleasures of the sight are not near so complicated, and confused, and altered by unnatural habits and associations, as the pleasures of the Taste are; because the pleasures of the sight more commonly acquiesce in themselves; and are not so often altered by considerations which are independent of the sight itself. But things do not spontaneously present themselves to the palate as they do to the sight; they are generally applied to it, either as food or as medicine; and from the qualities which they possess for nutritive or medicinal purposes, they often form the palate by degrees, and by force of these associations. Thus opium is pleasing to Turks, on account of the agreeable delirium it produces. Tobacco is the delight of Dutchmen, as it diffuses a torpor and pleasing stupefaction. Fermented spirits please our common people, because they banish care, and all consideration of future or present evils. All of these would lie absolutely neglected if their properties had originally gone no further than the Taste; but all these, together with tea and coffee, and some other things, have past from the apothecary's shop to our tables, and were taken for health long before they were thought of for pleasure. The effect of the drug has made us use it frequently; and frequent use, combined with the agreeable effect, has made the Taste itself at last agreeable. But this does not in the least perplex our reasoning; because we distinguish to the last the acquired from the natural relish. In describing the Taste of an unknown fruit, you would scarcely say, that it had a sweet and pleasant flavour like tobacco, opium, or garlic, although you spoke to those who were in the constant use of these drugs, and had great pleasure in them. There is in all men a sufficient remembrance of the original natural causes of pleasure, to enable them to bring all things offered to their senses to that standard, and to regulate their feelings and opinions by it. Suppose one who had so vitiated his palate as to take more pleasure in the Taste of opium than in that of butter or honey, to be presented with a bolus of squills; there is hardly any doubt but that he would prefer the butter or honey to this nauseous morsel, or to any other bitter drug to which he had not been accustomed; which proves that his palate was naturally like that of other men in all things, that it is still like the palate of other men in many things, and only vitiated in some particular points. For in judging of any new thing, even of a Taste similar to that which he has been formed by habit to like, he finds his palate affected in the natural manner, and on the common principles. Thus the pleasure of all the senses, of the sight, and even of the Taste, that most ambiguous of the senses, is the same in all, high and low, learned and unlearned.

Besides the ideas, with their annexed pains and pleasures, which are presented by the sense; the mind of man possesses a sort of creative power of its own; either in representing at pleasure the images of things in the order and manner in which they were received by the senses, or in combining those images in a new manner, and according to a different order. This power is called Imagination; and to this belongs whatever is called wit, fancy, invention, and the like. But it must be observed, that this power of the imagination is incapable of producing any thing absolutely new; it can only vary the disposition of those ideas which it has received from the senses. Now the imagination is the most extensive province of pleasure and pain, as it is the region of our fears and our hopes, and of all our passions that are connected with them; and whatever is calculated to affect the imagination with these commanding ideas, by force of any original natural impression, must have the same power pretty equally over all men. For since the imagination is only the representative of the senses, it can only be pleased or displeased with the images from the same principle on which the sense is pleased or displeased with the realities; and consequently there must be just as close an agreement in the imaginations as in the senses of men. A little attention will convince us that this must of necessity be the case.

But in the imagination, besides the pain or pleasure arising from the properties of the natural object, a pleasure is perceived from the resemblance, which the imitation has to the original; the imagination, I conceive, can have no pleasure but what results from one or other of these causes. And these causes operate pretty uniformly upon all men, because they operate by principles in nature, and which are not derived from any particular habits or advantages. Mr. Locke very justly and finely observes of wit, that it is chiefly conversant in tracing resemblances; he remarks at the same time, that the business of judgment is rather in finding differences. It may perhaps appear, on this supposition, that there is no material distinction between the wit and the judgment, as they both seem to result from different operations of the same faculty of *comparing*. But in reality, whether they are or are not dependent on the same power of the mind, they differ so very materially in many respects, that a perfect union of wit and judgment is one of the rarest things in the world. When two distinct objects are unlike to each other, it is only what we expect; things are in their common way; and therefore they make no impression on the imagination: but when two distinct objects have a resemblance, we are struck, we attend to them, and we are pleased. The mind of man has naturally a far greater alacrity and satisfaction in tracing resemblances than in searching for differences; because by making resemblances we produce *new images,* we unite, we create, we

enlarge our stock; but in making distinctions we offer no food at all to the imagination; the task itself is more severe and irksome, and what pleasure we derive from it is something of a negative and indirect nature. A piece of news is told me in the morning; this, merely as a piece of news, as a fact added to my stock, gives me some pleasure. In the evening I find there was nothing in it. What do I gain by this, but the dissatisfaction to find that I had been imposed upon? Hence it is, that men are much more naturally inclined to belief than to incredulity. And it is upon this principle, that the most ignorant and barbarous nations have frequently excelled in similitudes, comparisons, metaphors, and allegories, who have been weak and backward in distinguishing and sorting their ideas. And it is for a reason of this kind that Homer and the oriental writers, though very fond of similitudes, and though they often strike out such as are truly admirable, they seldom take care to have them exact; that is, they are taken with the general resemblance, they paint it strongly, and they take no notice of the difference which may be found between the things compared.

Now as the pleasure of resemblance is that which principally flatters the imagination, all men are nearly equal in this point, as far as their knowledge of the things represented or compared extends. The principle of this knowledge is very much accidental, as it depends upon experience and observation, and not on the strength or weakness of any natural faculty; and it is from this difference in knowledge that what we commonly, though with no great exactness, call a difference in Taste proceeds. A man to whom sculpture is new, sees a barber's block, or some ordinary piece of statuary; he is immediately struck and pleased, because he sees something like an human figure; and entirely taken up with this likeness, he does not at all attend to its defects. No person, I believe, at the first time of seeing a piece of imitation ever did. Some time after, we suppose that this novice lights upon a more artificial work of the same nature; he now begins to look with contempt on what he admired at first; not that he admired it even then for its unlikeness to a man, but for that general though inaccurate resemblance which it bore to the human figure. What he admired at different times in these so different figures, is strictly the same; and though his knowledge is improved, his Taste is not altered. Hitherto his mistake was from a want of knowledge in art, and this arose from his inexperience; but he may be still deficient from a want of knowledge in nature. For it is possible that the man in question may stop here, and that the masterpiece of a great hand may please him no more than the middling performance of a vulgar artist; and this not for want of better or higher relish, but because all men do not observe with sufficient accuracy on the human figure to enable them to judge properly of an imitation of it. And that the critical Taste does not depend upon a superior principle in men, but upon superior knowledge, may appear from several instances. The story of the ancient painter and the shoemaker is very well known. The shoemaker set the painter right with regard to some mistakes he had made in the shoe of one of his figures, and which the painter, who had not made such accurate observations on shoes, and was content with a general resemblance, had never observed. But this was no impeachment to the Taste of the painter, it only shewed some want of knowledge in the art of making shoes. Let us imagine, that an anatomist had come into the painter's working room. His piece is in general well done, the figure in question in a good attitude, and the parts well adjusted to their various movements; yet the anatomist, critical in his art, may observe the swell of some muscle not quite just in the peculiar action of the figure. Here the anatomist observes what the painter had not observed, and he passes by what the shoemaker had remarked. But a want of the last critical knowledge in anatomy no more reflected on the natural good Taste of the painter, or of any common observer of his piece, than the want of an exact knowledge in the formation of a shoe. A fine piece of a decollated head of St. John the Baptist was shewn to a Turkish emperor; he praised many things, but he observed one defect; he observed that the skin did not shrink from the wounded part of the neck. The sultan on this occasion, though his observation was very just, discovered no more natural Taste than the painter who executed this piece, or than a thousand European connoisseurs who probably never would have made the same observation. His Turkish majesty had indeed been well acquainted with that terrible spectacle, which the others could only have represented in their imagination. On the subject of their dislike there is a difference between all these people, arising from the different kinds and degrees of their knowledge; but there is something in common to the painter, the shoemaker, the anatomist, and the Turkish emperor, the pleasure arising from a natural object, so far as each perceives it justly imitated; the satisfaction in seeing an agreeable figure; the sympathy proceeding from a striking and affecting incident. So far as Taste is natural, it is nearly common to all.

In poetry, and other pieces of imagination, the same parity may be observed. It is true, that one man is charmed with Don Bellianis, and reads Virgil coldly; whilst another is transported with the Eneid, and leaves Don Bellianis to children. These two men seem to have a Taste very different from each other; but in fact they differ very little. In both these pieces, which inspire such opposite sentiments, a tale exciting admiration is told; both are full of action, both are passionate, in both are voyages, battles, triumphs, and continual changes of fortune. The admirer of Don Bellianis perhaps does not understand the refined language of the Eneid, who if it was degraded into the style of the Pilgrim's Progress, might feel it in all its energy, on the same principle which made him an admirer of Don Bellianis.

In his favourite author he is not shocked with the continual breaches of probability, the confusion of times, the offences against manners, the trampling upon geography; for he knows nothing of geography and chronology, and he has never examined the grounds of probability. He perhaps reads of a shipwreck on the coast of Bohemia; wholly taken up with so interesting an event, and only solicitous for the fate of his hero, he is not in the least troubled at this extravagant blunder. For why should he be shocked at a shipwreck on the coast of Bohemia, who does not know but that Bohemia may be an island in the Atlantic ocean? and after all, what reflection is this on the natural good Taste of the person here supposed?

So far then as Taste belongs to the imagination, its principle is the same in all men; there is no difference in the manner of their being affected, nor in the causes of the affection; but in the *degree* there is a difference, which arises from two causes principally; either from a greater degree of natural sensibility, or from a closer and longer attention to the object. To illustrate this by the procedure of the senses in which the same difference is found, let us suppose a very smooth marble table to be set before two men; they both perceive it to be smooth, and they are both pleased with it, because of this quality. So far they agree. But suppose another, and after that another table, the latter still smoother than the former, to be set before them. It is now very probable that these men, who are so agreed upon what is smooth, and in the pleasure from thence, will disagree when they come to settle which table has the advantage in point of polish. Here is indeed the great difference between Tastes, when men come to compare the excess or diminution of things which are judged by degree and not by measure. Nor is it easy, when such a difference arises, to settle the point, if the excess or diminution be not glaring. If we differ in opinion about two quantities, we can have recourse to a common measure, which may decide the question with the utmost exactness; and this I take it is what gives mathematical knowledge a greater certainty than any other. But in things whose excess is not judged by greater or smaller, as smoothness and roughness, hardness and softness, darkness and light, the shades of colours, all these are very easily distinguished when the difference is any way considerable, but not when it is minute, for want of some common measures which perhaps may never come to be discovered. In these nice cases, supposing the acuteness of the sense equal, the greater attention and habit in such things will have the advantage. In the question about the tables, the marble polisher will unquestionably determine the most accurately. But notwithstanding this want of a common measure for settling many disputes relative to the senses and their representative the imagination, we find that the principles are the same in all, and that there is no disagreement until we come to examine into the preeminence or difference of things, which brings us within the province of the judgment.

So long as we are conversant with the sensible qualities of things, hardly any more than the imagination seems concerned; little more also than the imagination seems concerned when the passions are represented, because by the force of natural sympathy they are felt in all men without any recourse to reasoning, and their justness recognized in every breast. Love, grief, fear, anger, joy, all these passions have in their turns affected every mind; and they do not affect it in an arbitrary or casual manner, but upon certain, natural and uniform principles. But as many of the works of imagination are not confined to the representation of sensible objects, nor to efforts upon the passions, but extend themselves to the manners, the characters, the actions, and designs of men, their relations, their virtues and vices, they come within the province of the judgment, which is improved by attention and by the habit of reasoning. All these make a very considerable part of what are considered as the objects of Taste; and Horace sends us to the schools of philosophy and the world for our instruction in them. Whatever certainty is to be acquired in morality and the science of life; just the same degree of certainty have we in what relates to them in works of imitation. Indeed it is for the most part in our skill in manners, and in the observances of time and place, and of decency in general, which is only to be learned in those schools to which Horace recommends us, that what is called Taste by way of distinction, consists; and which is in reality no other than a more refined judgment. On the whole it appears to me, that what is called Taste, in its most general acceptation, is not a simple idea, but is partly made up of a perception of the primary pleasures of sense, of the secondary pleasures of the imagination, and of the conclusions of the reasoning faculty, concerning the various relations of these, and concerning the human passions, manners and actions. All this is requisite to form Taste, and the ground-work of all these is the same in the human mind; for as the senses are the great originals of all our ideas, and consequently of all our pleasures, if they are not uncertain and arbitrary, the whole ground-work of Taste is common to all, and therefore there is a sufficient foundation for a conclusive reasoning on these matters.

Whilst we consider Taste, merely according to its nature and species, we shall find its principles entirely uniform; but the degree in which these principles prevail in the several individuals of mankind, is altogether as different as the principles themselves are similar. For sensibility and judgment, which are the qualities that compose what we commonly call a *Taste,* vary exceedingly in various people. From a defect in the former of these qualities, arises a want of Taste; a weakness in the latter, constitutes a wrong or a bad one. There are some men formed with feelings so blunt, with tempers so cold and phlegmatic, that they can hardly be said to be awake during the whole course of their lives. Upon such persons, the most striking objects make but a faint and obscure impression. There are others so continually in the agitation of gross and merely sensual pleasures, or so occupied in the low drudgery of avarice, or so heated in the chace of honours and distinction, that their minds, which had been used continually to the storms of these violent and tempestuous passions, can hardly be put in motion by the delicate and refined play of the imagination. These men, though from a different cause, become as stupid and insensible as the former; but whenever either of these happen to be struck with any natural elegance or greatness, or with these qualities in any work of art, they are moved upon the same principle.

The cause of a wrong Taste is a defect of judgment. And this may arise from a natural weakness of understanding (in whatever the strength of that faculty may consist) or, which is much more commonly the case, it may arise from a want of proper and well-directed exercise, which alone can make it strong and ready. Besides that ignorance, inattention, prejudice, rashness, levity, obstinacy, in short, all those passions, and all those vices which pervert the judgment in other matters, prejudice it no less in this its more refined and elegant province. These causes produce different opinions upon every thing which is an object of the understanding, without inducing us to suppose, that there are no settled principles of reason. And indeed on the whole one may observe, that there is rather less difference upon matters of Taste among mankind, than upon most of those which depend upon the naked reason; and that men are far better agreed on the excellence of a description in Virgil, than on the truth or falsehood of a theory of Aristotle.

A rectitude of judgment in the arts which may be called a good Taste, does in a great measure depend upon sensibility; because if the mind has no bent to the pleasures of the imagination, it will never apply itself sufficiently to works of that species to acquire a competent knowledge in them. But, though a degree of sensibility is requisite to form a good judgment, yet a good judgment does not necessarily arise from a quick sensibility of pleasure; it frequently happens that a very poor judge, merely by force of a greater complexional sensibility, is more affected by a very poor piece, than the best judge by the most perfect; for as every thing new, extraordinary, grand, or passionate is well calculated to affect such a person, and that the faults do not affect him, his pleasure is more pure and unmixed; and as it is merely a pleasure of the imagination, it is much higher than any which is derived from a rectitude of the judgment; the judgment is for the greater part employed in throwing stumbling blocks in the way of the imagination, in dissipating the scenes of its enchantment, and in tying us down to the disagreeable yoke of our reason: for almost the only pleasure that men have in judging better than others, consists in a sort of conscious pride and superiority, which arises from thinking rightly; but then, this is an indirect pleasure, a pleasure which does not immediately result from the object which is under contemplation. In the morning of our days, when the senses are unworn and tender, when the whole man is awake in every part, and the gloss of novelty fresh upon all the objects that surround us, how lively at that time are our sensations, but how false and inaccurate the judgments we form of things? I despair of ever receiving the same degree of pleasure from the most excellent performances of genius which I felt at that age, from pieces which my present judgment regards as trifling and contemptible. Every trivial cause of pleasure is apt to affect the man of too sanguine a complexion: his appetite is too keen to suffer his Taste to be delicate; and he is in all respects what Ovid says of himself in love,

> Molle meum levibus cor est violabile telis,
> Et semper causa est, cur ego semper amem.

One of this character can never be a refined judge; never what the comic poet calls *elegans formarum, spectator.* The excellence and force of a composition must always be imperfectly estimated from its effect on the minds of any, except we know the temper and character of those minds. The most powerful effects of poetry and music have been displayed, and perhaps are still displayed, where these arts are but in a very low and imperfect state. The rude hearer is affected by the principles which operate in these arts even in their rudest condition; and he is not skilful enough to perceive the defects. But as the arts advance towards their perfection, the science of criticism advances with equal pace, and the pleasure of judges is frequently interrupted by the faults which are discovered in the most finished compositions.

Before I leave this subject I cannot help taking notice of an opinion which many persons entertain, as if the Taste were a separate faculty of the mind, and distinct from the judgment and imagination; a species of instinct by which we are struck naturally, and at the first glance, without any previous reasoning with the excellencies, or the defects of a composition. So far as the imagination and the passions are concerned, I believe it true, that the reason is little consulted; but where disposition, where decorum, where congruity are concerned, in short wherever the best Taste differs from the worst, I am convinced that the understanding operates and nothing else; and its operation is in reality far from being always sudden, or when it is sudden, it is often far from being right. Men of the best

Taste by consideration, come frequently to change these early and precipitate judgments which the mind from its aversion to neutrality and doubt loves to form on the spot. It is known that the Taste (whatever it is) is improved exactly as we improve our judgment, by extending our knowledge, by a steady attention to our object, and by frequent exercise. They who have not taken these methods, if their Taste decides quickly, it is always uncertainly; and their quickness is owing to their presumption and rashness, and not to any sudden irradiation that in a moment dispels all darkness from their minds. But they who have cultivated that species of knowledge which makes the object of Taste, by degrees and habitually attain not only a soundness, but a readiness of judgment, as men do by the same methods on all other occasions. At first they are obliged to spell, but at last they read with ease and with celerity: but this celerity of its operation is no proof, that the Taste is a distinct faculty. Nobody I believe has attended the course of a discussion, which turned upon matters within the sphere of mere naked reason, but must have observed the extreme readiness with which the whole process of the argument is carried on, the grounds discovered, the objections raised and answered, and the conclusions drawn from premises, with a quickness altogether as great as the Taste can be supposed to work with; and yet where nothing but plain reason either is or can be suspected to operate. To multiply principles for every different appearance, is useless, and unphilosophical too in a high degree. (pp. 11-27)

> *Edmund Burke, "Introduction on Taste," in his* A Philosophical Enquiry into the Origin of Our Ideas of the Sublime and Beautiful, *edited by James T. Boulton, University of Notre Dame Press, 1968, pp. 11-27.*

Emerson R. Marks

[*Marks is an American educator and author of several works on literary aesthetics and criticism. In the following essay, he exposes the antinomy of style in neoclassical poetics which "consists in the fact that the very features of expression which give fine verse its special power and allure may also constitute the vices and defects that mark poetic mediocrity and even downright trash."*]

From one literary period to another ideals of poetic language have tended to oscillate, in very rough fashion, between the poles of simplicity and ornateness. They involve vocabulary, tropical usages, syntax, and sometimes degrees of metrical regularity. The period of English poetry spanning the careers of Dryden and Dr. Johnson, despite its own initial reaction against the baroque involutedness of metaphysical verse, is generally regarded as favoring the pole of ornateness. "Poetry requires ornament," wrote Dryden, whom Johnson a century later praised for having supplied the "elegances of flowers of speech" which properly set it apart from prose. One of the triad of fatal poetical blemishes mentioned in *Rambler* 122 is "impropriety of ornament."

The concept of poetry as elegant discourse was of course neither an eighteenth-century discovery nor exclusively English, but an age-old commonplace. Four centuries earlier Dante had ascribed the beauty of his *Canzoni* to their ornamented words, though he was careful to assign prima-

Oliver Goldsmith, by Sir Joshua Reynolds.

ry value to their moral teaching ("la bontà è nella sentenza, e la *bellezza* nell' ornamento delle parole"). In his *Eléments de litérature* (1787) Johnson's French contemporary Jean Francois Marmontel could put it with dogmatic finality: "Le style de l'orateur et celui du poète a besoin d'être orné."

Romantic poetics opens with a violent swing to the opposite pole in Wordsworth's prefaces to *Lyrical Ballads*, in which the term *poetic diction*, honorific since its currency was initiated by John Dennis in 1696, suddenly labels a poetic vice. Thereafter critics tend increasingly to admit stylistic elaboration only when what is being said defies literal directness, and they have scant patience with the notion of a select poetic vocabulary. The older view was embodied in the traditional vestiary metaphor, the poet's thoughts "dressed" in attractive verbal garb. The organicist aesthetic orientation of the nineteenth century, hostile to so bald a severance of form and content, abandoned this metaphor. Words, Wordsworth observed, thinking primarily of poetry, are not the raiment but the incarnation of thoughts. Elegance, the central term of approval in the lexicon of European neoclassical literary theory, gradually acquired the faintly pejorative overtones it still retains. (The conceptual alteration in question here pertains to theory, not necessarily to the poets' actual practice.)

What I've just summarily characterized is a familiar topic exhaustively explored by literary historians. A related issue, which for lack of a less unwieldy phrase I will call *the antinomy of poetic style,* though it too has a history coterminus with that of poetics itself, has received nothing like the scrutiny it deserves. It consists in the fact that the very features of expression which give fine verse its special power and allure may also constitute the vices and defects that mark poetic mediocrity and even downright trash. A problem of both composition and theory in every age, it takes on special cogency during the eighteenth century, when the pendulum of theory was in the decorative sector of its arc.

This mysterious phenomenon receives attention in the earliest Western critical texts. In Longinus and Quintilian eighteenth-century writers found especially influential warnings against the betrayal of their inspiration to the attractions of a stylistic siren decked out in every charm of the maidenly muse. In "that high flying liberty of conceit proper to the Poet" their respected predecessor Sir Philip Sidney had apparently sensed no inherent destructive potential but only "some divine force," though in one place even he blames imitative poets for dressing up Matron Eloquence like a prostitute. In Quintilian's *Institutes of Oratory,* however, there are repeated condemnations of fancy phrase-making, deliberate striving after gilded verbiage, even though a whole section of that work is devoted to the many devices of stylistic heightening that orators and poets alike must master. For "where ornament is concerned," he observes, "vice and virtue are never far apart," and the anomaly becomes more piquant but no nearer solution when he adds that utter barbarisms in prose can actually be attractive in verse, a peculiarity sporadically noted in discussions of verse and prose from Aristotle's *Rhetoric* to modern structuralism. That the attributes of a vicious style often bear a resemblance of near identity to those of effective composition had been a staple of classical literary discussion well before Quintilian's time. For the three levels of good style first laid down in the *Rhetorica ad Herennium,* there are, says its author, faulty styles very closely related to them (*finitima et propinqua vitia*). What he calls the swollen style is easily mistaken for the grand, the loose for the middle, the meager for the simple. Similarly, for each of the four kinds of style roughly delineated in the Greek treatise *Peri hermeneias* (*On Style*) by one Demetrius, the author identifies corresponding "perversions": for the stately, the frigid; for the plain, the arid; for the forceful, the disagreeable. "In the same way," in Rhys Roberts' version, "there is a defective style perilously near to the elegant," namely the affected. Like others, Demetrius sees an analogy to the propinquity of his opposed styles in the similar relation of the moral virtues and vices. Courage, he notes, is next neighbor to rashness.

The paradox is most forcibly stressed in the Greek rhetorical treatise that became a near-sacred text for many of Johnson's contemporaries, Longinus' *On the Sublime.* "For our virtues and vices spring from much the same sources. And so while beauty of style, sublime expression, yes, and agreeable phrasing all contribute to successful composition, yet these very graces are the source and groundwork no less of failure than of success." The author therefore assumes it to be a part of his instructional duty to suggest how aspiring writers can "avoid the faults that go so closely with the elevated style." Beyond the admonition sounded at the outset, that sublimity, the great quality he is analyzing, bears a fatal likeness to its aesthetic opposite, tumidity, he detects the duplicity even in the individual figural devices that account for much of its appeal. Periphrasis is "a risky business"; hyperbole, overdone, "produces the opposite effect to that intended," and so on.

Ancient authorities, however, could supply no objective rationale to account for this disturbing trick of literary language. Instead, they offered psychological explanations of how authors fell victim to it and how readers could detect it. For the latter this meant having good taste, a criterion which in this application as in every other bears the curse of circularity. The generally assigned cause of the fault was a poet's overconscious art, his substitution of deliberate striving for the unsought promptings of genuine inspiration. The idea of self-defeating creative effort is so strongly emphasized by Longinus that we may conclude, in parody of his famous aphorism, that tumidity echoes the straining of a puny soul. Horace, in the *Ars poetica,* refines on this motif of compositional psychology. Most of us poets, he confesses, fall into obscurity by striving for concision, become flaccid by aiming at smoothness, and produce bombast by reaching for grandeur. Our well-intended efforts to avoid certain faults lead ironically not to their opposed beauties but to the vices kindred to those beauties, if we haven't properly learned our trade (*si caret arte*).

According to the author of the *Rhetorica ad Herennium,* Horace, and Demetrius, the plain style is as prone to this risk as the ornate. The eighteenth century, too, knew something of both cases. Pope tried to distinguish genuine simplicity from its fraudulent mimic, which he dubbed rusticity (he was speaking of pastorals), and everyone remembers his neat sample of it, adopted from Dryden's *Essay of Dramatic Poesy:* "And ten low Words oft creep in one dull line." But neoclassical theory held the main difference between verse and prose to consist in the cultivation of lexical and figurative embellishment in the one and its relative avoidance in the other. It is therefore not surprising that Johnson and David Hume—to instance only the more eminent—saw in the age's preponderant relish for poetry of excessive dictional refinement and imagistic elaboration the risk of "affectation" (Johnson), portending a "degeneracy of taste" (Hume). It is essential to keep in mind that neither of these men can even remotely be considered a harbinger of any Wordsworthian poetics of plain talk. On the contrary, both fully subscribed to the doctrine of their time that elegant turns of phrase and choice words, advisable in many kinds of prose, were virtual requirements in verse. "If his language be not elegant," Hume wrote, no author can please his readers. As for the much touted simplicity, he admits it can have no appeal if not "accompanied with great elegance and propriety." Yet precisely therein, he argues, lies the menace. So too Johnson. Writers on topics "probable and persuasory," a category inclusive a fortiori of poets, must be able "to recommend them by the superaddition of elegance and imagery, to display the colors of varied diction, and pour forth the music of modulated periods." He regards those writers as neither useless nor contemptible whose main effort is not to say anything new but to enhance familiar ideas "by fairer decorations." Yet within a few years of saying so he felt impelled to alert the public to the danger (Hume used the same word) inherent in this very process.

It would seem that in no other kind of human endeavor is it so true that there can be too much of a good thing as in the art of literature, and that the criticism of no other period is so pervaded by a troubled awareness of this fact as that produced in the eighteenth century. A kind of stylistic *nihil nimis,* locating excellence in a mean between extremes, is a constantly recurring theme. The mediating description of what makes for an effective ode set forth in Edward Young's "On Lyric Poetry" typically pairs its several qualities with their defective excesses. "To sum up the whole: Ode should be peculiar, but not strained; moral, but not flat; natural, but not obvious; delicate, but not affected; noble, but not ambitious; full, but not obscure; fiery, but not mad; thick, but not loaded in its numbers." The recommended moderation was not confined to the lyric. In every genre, as Henry Pemberton wrote, precisely because artful expression is necessary, "care must be taken to avoid excess."

No theory providing a set of terms for isolating and possibly resolving this aesthetic puzzle, from which the poets and readers of this rule-conscious literary era might have distilled appropriate rules, was ever devised. The futility of any attempt to do so is implied by the many endorsements, repeated to the century's end, of Longinus' recourse to the ineffable standard of an intuition nourished by experience. In the seventh of his *Discourses on Art,* Joshua Reynolds had no hesitation in prescribing the "ornaments" of meter and metaphor as indispensable to poetry. Yet "how far figurative or metaphorical language may proceed, and when it begins to be affectation"—did Reynolds have his friend the Rambler's admonitions in mind?—can be determined only by taste, which, to compound the problem, he regards as itself a cultural variable.

To name everyone who warned against meretricious verbal embellishment during the ages of Pope and Johnson would come near a roll call of major eighteenth-century critics. It was almost inevitably included in the many academic compendia of poetic rules and principles, like the Latin lectures delivered at Oxford by Joseph Trapp in 1711. Trapp found Ovid frequently guilty of inappropriate or excessive ornamentation, Homer himself occasionally so, the impeccable Virgil (*qui nil molitur inepte*) never. The views of the Trapps and the Pembertons tell us much. But with an aesthetic issue of such subtlety as this there is more profit in the witness of those who encountered it in their own creative practice, especially poets of the first rank who happen also to be critically articulate. We can be sure that Pope's inspired and agonized labors at an English Homer, including his study of the earlier translations he hoped to supersede, contributed to his discovery that the "sublime style is more easily counterfeited than the natural; something that passes for it, or sounds like it, is common in all false writers." But how distinguish the counterfeit from the real? Though Pope knows it is vital to do so, no more than anyone else can he find a touchstone. He repeats the familiar principle of propriety: avoid grand expressions with low or simple subjects. In both his Preface to the *Iliad* and his Postscript to the *Odyssey,* however, his language confesses that the problem is too complex and elusive to yield to any such critical rule of thumb. When "to be plain and when poetical and figurative" he calls "a great Secret" and "the great point of judgment." Had he himself discovered the secret? All he tells us is that poets can learn it from Homer, whose epics, Pope constantly reminds his readers, furnished Longinus with the finest examples of the true sublime.

Johnson's complaints that the studied elegance of modern poets too often crossed the line of mere ostentation are matched by Joseph Warton's denunciations of their "false refinement." More arresting is James Beattie's excoriation of the "finical style" of poets who concoct verses out of such periphrastic stereotypes as "syren song," "oaten reed" and the like. Its appearance in the very work in which he analyzes in detail, and advocates, the various devices of verbal elaboration essential to poetry bespeaks again their antinomial nature. Like the classical rhetoricians, he urges special care in the use of hyperbole, so efficacious in elevating discourse, because "employed injudiciously" it brings about the exactly opposite effect. In this figure above all, the sublime and the ludicrous reveal their common source. Of course the double-edged potency of literary language can be intentionally exploited, given the requisite talent, to produce delightful comic parody. Its repulsive twin is the kind of unintentional parody to which these eighteenth-century writers were calling attention.

What, in abstract terms, distinguishes injudicious rhetorical usage from its admired counterpart, or eloquent simplicity from the pedestrian, remained even more obscure to neoclassical inquirers than it has become since, and the mystery is still far from clarification. Hume judged it to be hard if not impossible "to explain by words where the just medium lies between the excesses of simplicity and refinement, or to give any rule by which we can know precisely the bounds between the fault and the beauty." The violation of the rule of propriety they came to see as at best but one type of the error, not its universal condition. Besides, that rule itself, derived from the classical doctrine of high, middle, and low styles first enunciated in the *Ad Herennium,* was already being challenged.

One aspect of that challenge has direct bearing on the antinomy of poetic expression. It was noticed that even if a trivial theme forbade ornate treatment, the corollary that serious subjects could never admit unadorned poetic style was patently untrue. It was recognized that a small but significant amount of excellent verse on weighty topics was actually devoid, or nearly devoid, of the usual embellishments. Beattie's citation of the moving lines spoken by King Lear on regaining consciousness and sanity is perhaps the most compelling instance in neoclassical discussion.

> Pray do not mock me:
> I am a very foolish fond old man,
> Fourscore and upward, not an hour more nor less;
> And, to deal plainly,
> I fear I am not in my perfect mind.
> Methinks I should know you and know this man,
> Yet I am doubtful; for I am mainly ignorant
> What place this is, and all the skill I have
> Remembers not these garments . . .

This sparse style was referred to as "easy poetry," a label singularly inept since, as Johnson observed in *Idler* 77, it is the hardest to write. The quality of ease, he notes, inheres mainly in the diction, which must be free of all artifice. The modern poets' "ambition of ornament and luxuriousness of imagery," he feels, has discouraged a proper appreciation of a style which, "tho' it excludes pomp, will admit greatness." By no means confined to "minute subjects," it is as well adapted to tragic declamation as to the pithy epigrammatic wit of a stanza by Cowley. Many lines of the soliloquy delivered by the hero in the last act of Addison's *Cato* Johnson finds to be "at once easy and sublime."

Johnson's illustration of the style which is diametrically opposite to easy poetry is no other than the four opening lines of Pope's *Iliad:*

> Achilles' *wrath,* to Greece the direful *spring*
> Of woes unnumber'd, *heav'nly* Goddess, sing,
> The [That] wrath which hurl'd to Pluto's *gloomy reign*
> The souls of *mighty* chiefs untimely slain.

When we recall that some twenty years later, in his final maturity, Johnson was to rate Pope's *Iliad* as "certainly the noblest version of poetry" ever written, a "poetical wonder," the severity of the censure he pronounces on these lines is somewhat startling. "In the first couplet," he declares, "the language is distorted by inversions, clogged with superfluities, and clouded by a harsh Metaphor; and in the second there are two words used in an uncommon sense, and two epithets inserted only to lengthen the line; all these practices may in a long work easily be pardoned, but they always produce some degree of obscurity and ruggedness."

Some of Johnson's disapprobation here may conceivably be ascribed to special pleading induced by his immediate purpose—to win appreciation for simplicity—some, but I think not much. It seems more likely that he shared the curious vacillation of his coevals on the subject of poetic figuration, in one breath prescribing it as necessary, in another conceding, even insisting, that the greatest emotional force can be embodied in the plainest words. In his popular *Lectures on Rhetoric and Belles Lettres* (1783) Hugh Blair taught that "Figures form *the constant Language of poetry*" (my italics). To see why, he suggested, we have only to compare the trite expression "the sun rises" with the magnificence of James Thomson's version of the same thought:

> But yonder comes the powerful king of day,
> Rejoicing in the east. . . .

Blair has apparently forgotten that only four pages earlier he had solemnly declared that often the most moving passages of verse, Virgil's for example, are "expressed in the simplest language." His shifts of ground are of a piece with Johnson's unfavorable references to the excessive verbiage of the very translation he elsewhere extolled. The censorious tone of his curt anatomy of Pope's lines precludes the explanation that he meant only to suggest that the translator's style, though admittedly admirable, was less suited to Homer's august matter than the "easy" style would have been. And surely—one cannot help remarking by the way—one item in his indictment, that the first couplet is "clogged with superfluities," comes awkwardly from the man whose finest poem opens, as Coleridge's gleefully malicious paraphrase of it lays bare, with triple-decked repetition:

> Let Observation, with extended View
> Survey Mankind from China to Peru.

The clashing ideals of poetic diction reflected in the speculations of neoclassical critics may well owe something to an imperfect accommodation of the reigning theory to the experience of readers. Although they may have comprised only a discriminating minority at the time, many lovers of poetry delighted both in the elegance of gorgeous verbal array and the "naked elegance"—to use Johnson's oxymoron-skirting phrase—of easy poetry. The orthodox doctrine had always recognized the appropriateness of even the most literal directness in certain kinds of prose, but poetry, as Dryden had said, demanded ornament. If admissible at all in verse, undecorated expression was confined to the humbler genres and subjects. To use it with tragic or epic material was, as Demetrius taught, to fall into its corresponding vice, aridity. Post-Romantic theory, having either totally abandoned this hierarchical stylistic, or else greatly relaxed it, presented no such impasse to a reader's actual experience of poetic beauty being attainable throughout the entire spectrum of verbal complexity. As a result critics have long been able to avoid the inconsistencies that troubled the earlier poetics. But these speculations would require for their full validation a range of evidence too digressive for my present concern.

To put the problem in a way more relevant here, the existence of easy poetry would seem to authorize a far more sweeping challenge to the decorative theory of poetic discourse than that entailed by the antinomy. The one protests only that the much prized devices of specialized diction, deviant syntax, and figurative expression (not to mention meter) by which poets beautify their speech may equally make it repellent. But the fact that great verse can apparently dispense entirely with these formalities supports the logical inference of the radical Wordsworthian conclusion: use only the language of common speech or of prose. Unfortunately, *experience,* to which Johnson argued all theory must finally yield, makes this position as untenable as the one it would replace. Eighteenth-century readers, critics, and poets, like those in ages before and since, could point to a vast body of poetry whose enduring appeal was obviously, perhaps even demonstrably, referable to its highly elaborate linguistic structure. For this too is a fact, whether the elaboration is appreciated as attractive "clothing" of paraphrasable ideas or as itself an "incarnation" of ideas expressible in no other way, as modern theory generally holds.

So the quandary of the stylistic antinomy persists. Luckily, my aim is not to propose a solution but only to take note of its main manifestations during a century much given to literary theorizing. One of the most interesting is an aspect of neoclassical Longinianism which lent powerful support to the antidecorative thrust of easy poetry. Although the *Peri hypsous* had been published in 1554 and appeared in an English translation by John Hall as early as 1652, its appreciable influence on English critical thought begins only with the French translation by Nicolas Boileau in 1674. The brief explicative preface by which he introduced the work to his readers may well have done more to bring the problematic nature of poetic style to the bemused awareness of Britons than Longinus' own remarks about the antinomy. Boileau well knew the bias toward ornate writing among the French *literati* of the time, who he feared might simply laugh at Longinus' laudatory citation of passages "qui bien que très sublimes, ne laissent pas d'être simples et naturels." And so he sets himself to explaining to an audience prone to equate fine writing with fancy phrasing "ce que Longin entend par Sublime." He does this by sharply separating "le Sublime" from "le style sublime." Whereas the sublime style depends on verbal pomp ("de grands mots"), the sublime itself, by which readers and hearers are irresistibly transported, consists in a single thought, image, or turn of phrase ("seule pensée . . . seule figure . . . seule tour de paroles"). The antinomy lying at the heart of the issue thus surfaces in Boileau's manipulation of his author's central term, because his two uses of it are not merely distinguished as to designation but set in mutually exclusive opposition. To enforce his point he rewords, in the "style sublime," the celebrated example of sublimity which Longinus cites from Genesis. "Le souverain Arbitre de la nature d'une seule parole forma la lumière," Boileau maintains, totally lacks the majesty of the stark scriptural form: *Dieu dit: Que la lumière se fasse, et la lumière se fit.*

Any careful student of the Greek treatise will see that Boileau's reading replaces its total thesis with a reductive extrapolation from one portion of it. Nonetheless, his is the interpretation predominant in the eighteenth-century concept of the sublime in England, which placed almost exclusive stress on Longinus' two innate sources of elevated discourse, noble thought and vehement feeling. The various figures of speech and thought which make up the three acquired sources were disregarded or even rejected outright. The sublime, Hugh Blair affirmed, cannot be attained "by hunting after tropes, and figures, and rhetorical assistances." The theoretical confusion certainly not caused, but much aggravated, by Boileau's preface was considerable. One senses a kind of tendentious irrelevancy in Beattie's imitation of Boileau's ploy. With proper acknowledgment of his French source, Beattie holds up for a comparison in Milton's disfavor that poet's elaboration of Jehovah's terse decree in *Paradise Lost* (VII, lines 243 ff.):

> "Let there be light," said God, and forthwith light
> Ethereal, first of things, quintessence pure
> Sprung from the deep, and from her native east
> To journey through the airy gloom began,
> Sphered in a radiant cloud, for yet the sun
> Was not. . . ."

Perhaps the most revealing evidence of the French critic's impact on the ambivalent evaluation of the poet's medium that prevailed during the ensuing century is provided by John Husbands, one of several who exalted the Hebrew poetry of the Old Testament. Husbands rejoices to find the scriptural style perfectly answerable to the traditional requirements, according to which, he writes, the *essence* of poetry inheres in lively discourse "adorn'd with Figures, varying according to the Greatness, Nature, and Quality of the Subject." Since their subject was nothing less than the mighty works of God, the Hebrew writers were especially favored by having lived in precivilized times. One article of the cultural primitivism of the Enlightenment held that pristine conditions of life fostered highly rhythmic and metaphorical expression. "No wonder therefore," Husbands reasons,

> that their Diction is something more flourish'd and ornamental, more vigorous and elevated, more proper to paint and set Things before our Eyes, than plain and ordinary Recital. . . .
>
> The Scripture abounds with a vast Variety of . . . beautiful Expressions, which breathe the true Spirit of Poetry. The Dawning of the Day the Hebrew expresses by *the Eyelids of the Morning.* Corners of the Earth are *Wings of the Earth.*

Yet with no attempt at reconciling the discrepancy, or even apparently noticing it, within a few pages Husbands grounds the superiority of the sacred writings over all other literature on the two "Beauties" of *simplicity* and *sublimity,* as being appropriate to momentous themes, which eschew "all Dress, and adventitious Ornament." Predictably, he then invokes Boileau's observations on the passage from Genesis adduced by Longinus (himself repeatedly named). From the same book of the Bible Husbands chooses his own samples of the plain sublime. In one he finds the "whole passion of Love" concisely and movingly conveyed: "And Jacob served seven years for Rachel, and they seemed unto him but a few Days, for the Love he had unto her." The beauty of such a passage, Husbands points out, "does not consist in a Flourish of Words, or Pomp of Diction, not in the *ambitiosa ornamenta* of Rhetorick." This after having just founded the essence and true spirit of poetry precisely in such verbal decoration.

The tone and language of the proponents of this strand of the eighteenth-century sublime suggest that it may represent a kind of unconscious evasion of the antinomial stylistic trap. Since legitimate embellishment is so prone to betrayal by its fraudulent double, and since the plain style is found to be consistent with the greatest expressive power, why not dispense with embellishment altogether? Yet this question, as noted, is readily answered out of common experience. Besides, the aesthetic ravishment examined by Longinus himself was also effected by passages in a style as remote as possible from plainness, by the periodic sentences of sustained involution in oratory or the enjambed verse paragraphs breathlessly piling image on image in epic or dramatic poetry. In fact to cap the contradiction, among the English Longinians themselves the favorite modern example of poetic sublimity was *Paradise Lost.* And in this judgment they were supported by many who were immune to the more outré symptoms of the Longinian fever, like Johnson, who named sublimity as the "characteristick quality" of Milton's epic.

The linguistic perversity that led Longinus to assign poetic vices and virtues to "much the same sources" is perhaps only the lexical form of a broader aesthetic ambivalence. Or is there, in literary art, beneath the aesthetic a moral incentive at work, a deep-seated suspicion that the smoke of verbal overplus conceals the flames of deception or insincerity? Jane Austen makes a sense of this very impulse an ingredient in the finely tuned sensibility of the heroine of *Persuasion.* At one point Anne Elliot checks her skepticism toward her snobbish family's boasts of social triumph. "She heard it all under embellishment. All that sounded extravagant or irrational in the progress of reconciliation might have no origin but in the language of the relators." However it may be, deep within the most discriminating readers' love of poetry there does seem to lurk an "antipoetic" motive. (It is not, typically, philistines who are repelled by manneristic flourish.) For this reason, the ambiguities that mark neoclassical theory of poetic discourse retain more than historical interest. True, its two chief strategies for dealing with the antinomy, the bans on excessive and inappropriate ornamentation, too often fail the test of poetry itself. Yet ambiguities and strategies alike are symptomatic of a perennial condition of our intercourse with the verbal arts. One of Samuel Johnson's several complaints about blank verse was that it could "hardly sustain itself without bold figures and striking images." For most readers today his generalization, even where it holds, will not seem a valid objection.

Yet it may contain its germ of truth. For some readers at any time, I suspect, the distaste of a more cynical moralist, Shakespeare's Jaques, touches a sympathetic chord even as they smile at the irony of its context: "Nay, then, God be wi' you, an you talk in blank verse." (pp. 215-32)

> *Emerson R. Marks, "The Antinomy of Style in Augustan Poetics," in* Johnson and His Age, *edited by James Engell, Cambridge, Mass.: Harvard University Press, 1984, pp. 215-32.*

Northrop Frye

[A Canadian critic and editor, Frye is the author of the highly influential and controversial Anatomy of Criticism *(1957), in which he argued that literary criticism can be scientific in its method and results, maintaining that judgments are not inherent in the critical process. Believing that literature is wholly structured by myth and symbol, Frye viewed the critic's task as the explication of a work's archetypal characteristics. In the following essay, originally published in 1956, he attempts to define the "age of sensibility" in terms of the eighteenth century's literary perspectives, characterizing its essential view of literature as "process" rather than as "product."]*

The period of English literature which covers roughly the second half of the eighteenth century is one which has always suffered from not having a clear historical or functional label applied to it. I call it here the age of sensibility, which is not intended to be anything but a label. This period has the 'Augustan' age on one side of it and the 'Romantic' movement on the other, and it is usually approached transitionally, as a period of reaction against Pope and anticipation of Wordsworth. The chaos that results from treating this period, or any other, in terms of reaction has been well described by Professor Crane in a recent article in the Toronto Quarterly ['On Writing the History of English Criticism, 1650-1800,' July 1953]. What we do is to set up, as the logical expression of Augustanism, some impossibly pedantic view of following rules and repressing feelings, which nobody could ever have held, and then treat any symptom of freedom or emotion as a departure from this. Our students are thus graduated with a vague notion that the age of sensibility was the time when poetry moved from a reptilian Classicism, all cold and dry reason, to a mammalian Romanticism, all warm and wet feeling.

As for the term 'pre-romantic,' that, as a term for the age itself, has the peculiar demerit of committing us to anachronism before we start, and imposing a false teleology on everything we study. Not only did the 'pre-romantics' not know that the Romantic movement was going to succeed them, but there has probably never been a case on record of a poet's having regarded a later poet's work as the fulfilment of his own. However, I do not care about terminology, only about appreciation for an extraordinarily interesting period of English literature, and the first stage in renewing that appreciation seems to me the gaining of a clear sense of what it is in itself.

Some languages use verb-tenses to express, not time, but the difference between completed and continuous action. And in the history of literature we become aware, not only of periods, but of a recurrent opposition of two views of literature. These two views are the Aristotelian and the Longinian, the aesthetic and the psychological, the view of literature as product and the view of literature as process. In our day we have acquired a good deal of respect for literature as process, notably in prose fiction. The stream of consciousness gets careful treatment in our criticism, and when we compare Arnold Bennett and Virginia Woolf on the subject of Mrs. Brown we generally take the side of Virginia Woolf. So it seems that our age ought to feel a close kinship with the prose fiction of the age of sensibility, when the sense of literature as process was brought to a peculiarly exquisite perfection by Sterne, and in lesser degree by Richardson and Boswell.

All the great story-tellers, including the Augustan ones, have a strong sense of literature as a finished product. The suspense is thrown forward until it reaches the end, and is based on our confidence that the author knows what is coming next. A story-teller does not break his illusion by talking to the reader as Fielding does, because we know from the start that we are listening to Fielding telling a story—that is, Johnson's arguments about illusion in drama apply equally well to prose fiction of Fielding's kind. But when we turn to *Tristram Shandy* we not only read the book but watch the author at work writing it: at any moment the house of Walter Shandy may vanish and be replaced by the author's study. This does break the illusion, or would if there were any illusion to break, but here we are not being led into a story, but into the process of writing a story: we wonder, not what is coming next, but what the author will think of next.

Sterne is, of course, an unusually pure example of a process-writer, but even in Richardson we find many of the same characteristics. Johnson's well-known remark that if you read Richardson for the story you would hang yourself indicates that Richardson is not interested in a plot with a quick-march rhythm. Richardson does not throw the suspense forward, but keeps the emotion at a continuous present. Readers of *Pamela* have become so fascinated by watching the sheets of Pamela's manuscript spawning and secreting all over her master's house, even into the recesses of her clothes, as she fends off assault with one hand and writes about it with the other, that they sometimes overlook the reason for an apparently clumsy device. The reason is, of course, to give the impression of literature as process, as created on the spot out of the events it describes. And in the very beginning of *Boswell in London* we can see the boy of twenty-one already practising the art of writing as a continuous process from experience. When he writes of his adventure with Louisa he may be writing several days after the event, but he does not use his later knowledge.

In poetry the sense of literature as a finished product normally expresses itself in some kind of regularly recurring metre, the general pattern of which is established as soon as possible. In listening to Pope's couplets we have a sense of continually fulfilled expectation which is the opposite of obviousness: a sense that eighteenth-century music also often gives us. Such a technique demands a clear statement of what sound-patterns we may expect. We hear at once the full ring of the rhyming couplet, and all other sound-patterns are kept to a minimum. In such a line as:

> And strains from hard-bound brains eight lines a year,

the extra assonance is a deliberate discord, expressing the difficulties of constipated genius. Similarly with the alliteration in:

> Great Cibber's brazen, brainless brothers stand,

and the fact that these are deliberate discords used for parody indicates that they are normally not present. Johnson's disapproval of such devices in serious contexts is written all over the *Lives of the Poets.*

When we turn from Pope to the age of sensibility, we get something of the same kind of shock that we get when we turn from Tennyson or Matthew Arnold to Hopkins. Our ears are assaulted by unpredictable assonances, alliterations, inter-rhymings and echolalia:

> Mie love ys dedde,
> Gon to hys death-bedde . . .

> With brede ethereal wove,
> O'erhang his wavy bed . . .

> The couthy cracks begin whan supper's o'er,
> The cheering bicker gars them glibly gash.
> But a pebble of the brook
> Warbled out these metres meet . . .

In many of the best-known poems of the period, in Smart's *Song to David,* in Chatterton's elegies, in Burns's songs and Blake's lyrics, even in some of the Wesley hymns, we find a delight in refrain for refrain's sake. Sometimes, naturally, we can see the appropriate literary influences helping to shape the form, such as the incremental repetition of the ballad, or Old Norse alliteration in *The Fatal Sisters.* And whatever may be thought of the poetic value of the Ossianic poems, most estimates of that value parrot Wordsworth, and Wordsworth's criticisms of Ossian's imagery are quite beside the point. The vague generalized imagery of Ossian, like the mysterious resonant names and the fixed epithets, are part of a deliberate and well unified scheme. *Fingal* and *Temora* are long poems for the same reason that *Clarissa* is a long novel: not because there is a complicated story to be told, as in *Tom Jones* or an epic of Southey, but because the emotion is being maintained at a continuous present by various devices of repetition.

The reason for these intensified sound-patterns, is, once again, an interest in the poetic process as distinct from the product. In the composing of poetry, where rhyme is as important as reason, there is a primary stage in which words are linked by sound rather than sense. From the point of view of sense this stage is merely free or uncontrolled association, and in the way it operates it is very like the dream. Again like the dream, it has to meet a censor-principle, and shape itself into intelligible patterns. Where the emphasis is on the communicated product, the qualities of consciousness take the lead: a regular metre, clarity of syntax, epigram and wit, repetition of sense in antithesis and balance rather than of sound. Swift speaks with admiration of Pope's ability to get more 'sense' into one couplet than he can into six: concentration of sense for him is clearly a major criterion of poetry. Where the emphasis is on the original process, the qualities of subconscious association take the lead, and the poetry becomes hypnotically repetitive, oracular, incantatory, dreamlike and in the original sense of the word charming. The response to it includes a subconscious factor, the surrendering to a spell. In Ossian, who carries this tendency further than anyone

else, the aim is not concentration of sense but diffusion of sense, hence Johnson's remark that anybody could write like Ossian if he would abandon his mind to it. Literature as product may take a lyrical form, as it does in the sublime ode about which Professor Maclean has written so well, but it is also the conception of literature that makes the longer continuous poem possible. Literature as process, being based on an irregular and unpredictable coincidence of sound-patterns, tends to seek the brief or even the fragmentary utterance, in other words to centre itself on the lyric, which accounts for the feeling of a sudden emergence of a lyrical impulse in the age of sensibility.

The 'pre-romantic' approach to this period sees it as developing a conception of the creative imagination, which became the basis of Romanticism. This is true, but the Romantics tended to see the poem as the *product* of the creative imagination, thus reverting in at least one respect to the Augustan attitude. For the Augustan, art is posterior to nature because nature is the art of God; for the Romantic, art is prior to nature because God is an artist; one deals in physical and the other in biological analogies, as Professor Abrams' *Mirror and the Lamp* has shown. But for the Romantic poet the poem is still an artefact: in Coleridge's terms, a secondary or productive imagination has been imposed on a primary imaginative process. So, different as it is from Augustan poetry, Romantic poetry is like it in being a conservative rhetoric, and in being founded on relatively regular metrical schemes. Poe's rejection of the continuous poem does not express anything very central in Romanticism itself, as nearly every major Romantic poet composed poems of considerable, sometimes immense, length. Poe's theory is closer to the practice of the age of sensibility before him and the *symbolistes* after him.

In the age of sensibility most of the long poems, of course, simply carry on with standard continuous metres, or exploit the greater degree of intensified recurrent sound afforded by stanzaic forms, notably the Spenserian. But sometimes the peculiar problems of making associative poetry continuous were faced in a more experimental way, experiments largely ignored by the Romantics. Oracular poetry in a long form often tends to become a series of utterances, irregular in rhythm but strongly marked off one from the other. We notice in Whitman, for instance, that the end of every line has a strong pause—for when the rhythm is variable there is no point in a run-on line. Sometimes this oracular rhythm takes on at least a typographical resemblance to prose, as it does in Rimbaud's *Saison en Enfer,* or, more frequently, to a discontinuous blend of prose and verse in which the sentence, the paragraph and the line are much the same unit. The chief literary influence for this rhythm has always been the translated Bible, which took on a new impetus in the age of sensibility; and if we study carefully the rhythm of Ossian, of Smart's *Jubilate Agno* and of the Blake Prophecies, we can see three very different but equally logical developments of this semi-Biblical rhythm.

Where there is a strong sense of literature as aesthetic product, there is also a sense of its detachment from the spectator. Aristotle's theory of catharsis describes how this works for tragedy: pity and fear are detached from the beholder by being directed towards objects. Where there is a sense of literature as process, pity and fear become states of mind without objects, moods which are common to the work of art and the reader, and which bind them together psychologically instead of separating them aesthetically.

Fear without an object, as a condition of mind prior to being afraid of anything, is called *Angst* or anxiety, a somewhat narrow term for what may be almost anything between pleasure and pain. In the general area of pleasure comes the eighteenth-century conception of the sublime, where qualities of austerity, gloom, grandeur, melancholy or even menace are a source of romantic or penseroso feelings. The appeal of Ossian to his time on this basis needs no comment. From here we move through the graveyard poets, the Gothic-horror novelists and the writers of tragic ballads to such *fleurs du mal* as Cowper's *Castaway* and Blake's Golden Chapel poem in the Rosetti MS.

Pity without an object has never to my knowledge been given a name, but it expresses itself as an imaginative animism, or treating everything in nature as though it had human feelings or qualities. At one end of its range is the apocalyptic exultation of all nature bursting into human life that we have in Smart's *Song to David* and the ninth Night of *The Four Zoas*. Next comes an imaginative sympathy with the kind of folklore that peoples the countryside with elemental spirits, such as we have in Collins, Fergusson, Burns and the Wartons. Next we have the curiously intense awareness of the animal world which (except for some poems of D. H. Lawrence) is unrivalled in this period, and is expressed in some of its best realized writing: in Burns's *To a Mouse*, in Cowper's exquisite snail poem, in Smart's superb lines on his cat Geoffrey, in the famous starling and ass episodes in Sterne, in the opening of Blake's *Auguries of Innocence*. Finally comes the sense of sympathy with man himself, the sense that no one can afford to be indifferent to the fate of anyone else, which underlies the protests against slavery and misery in Cowper, in Crabbe and in Blake's *Songs of Experience*.

This concentration on the primitive process of writing is projected in two directions, into nature and into history. The appropriate natural setting for much of the poetry of sensibility is nature at one of the two poles of process, creation and decay. The poet is attracted by the ruinous and the mephitic, or by the primeval and 'unspoiled'—a picturesque subtly but perceptibly different from the Romantic picturesque. The projection into history assumes that the psychological progress of the poet from lyrical through epic to dramatic presentations, discussed by Stephen at the end of Joyce's *Portrait*, must be the historical progress of literature as well. Even as late as the preface to Victor Hugo's *Cromwell* this assumption persists. The Ossian and Rowley poems are not simple hoaxes: they are pseudepigrapha, like the Book of Enoch, and like it they take what is psychologically primitive, the oracular process of composition, and project it as something historically primitive.

The poetry of process is oracular, and the medium of the oracle is often in an ecstatic or trance-like state: autonomous voices seem to speak through him, and as he is concerned to utter rather than to address, he is turned away from his listener, so to speak, in a state of rapt self-communion. The free association of words, in which sound is prior to sense, is often a literary way of representing insanity. In Rimbaud's terrifyingly accurate phrase, poetry of the associative or oracular type requires a 'dé-règlement de tous les sens.' Hence the qualities that make a man an oracular poet are often the qualities that work against, and sometimes destroy, his social personality. Far more than the time of Rimbaud and Verlaine is this period of literature a period of the *poète maudit*. The list of poets over whom the shadows of mental breakdown fell is far too long to be coincidence. The much publicized death of Chatterton is certainly one of the personal tragedies of the age, but an easier one to take than the kind of agony which is expressed with an almost definitive poignancy by Smart in *Jubilate Agno:*

> For in my nature I quested for beauty, but God, God, hath sent me to sea for pearls.

It is characteristic of the age of sensibility that this personal or biographical aspect of it should be so closely connected with its central technical feature. The basis of poetic language is the metaphor, and the metaphor, in its radical form, is a statement of identity: 'this is that.' In all our ordinary experience the metaphor is non-literal: nobody but a savage or a lunatic can take metaphor literally. For Classical or Augustan critics the metaphor is a condensed simile: its real or common-sense basis is likeness, not identity, and when it obliterates the sense of likeness it becomes barbaric. In Johnson's strictures on the music and water metaphor of Gray's *Bard* we can see what intellectual abysses, for him, would open up if metaphors ever passed beyond the stage of resemblance. For the Romantic critic, the identification in the metaphor is ideal: two images are identified within the mind of the creating poet.

But where metaphor is conceived as part of an oracular and half-ecstatic process, there is a direct identification in which the poet himself is involved. To use another phrase of Rimbaud's, the poet feels not 'je pense,' but 'on me pense.' In the age of sensibility some of the identifications involving the poet seem manic, like Blake's with Druidic bards or Smart's with Hebrew prophets, or depressive, like Cowper's with a scapegoat figure, a stricken deer or castaway, or merely bizarre, like Macpherson's with Ossian or Chatterton's with Rowley. But it is in this psychological self-identification that the central 'primitive' quality of this age really emerges. In Collins's *Ode on the Poetical Character*, in Smart's *Jubilate Agno*, and in Blake's *Four Zoas*, it attains its greatest intensity and completeness.

In these three poems, especially the last two, God, the poet's soul and nature are brought into a white-hot fusion of identity, an imaginative fiery furnace in which the reader may, if he chooses, make a fourth. All three poems are of the greatest complexity, yet the emotion on which they are founded is of a simplicity and directness that English literature has rarely attained again. With the 1800 edition of *Lyrical Ballads*, secondary imagination and recollection in tranquillity took over English poetry and dominated it until the end of the nineteenth century. The primitivism of Blake and Smart revived in France with Rimbaud and Gérard de Nerval, but even this development had become conservative by the time its influence reached England, and only in a few poems of Dylan Thomas, and those perhaps not his best, does the older tradition revive. But contemporary poetry is still deeply concerned with the problems and techniques of the age of sensibility, and while the latter's resemblance to our time is not a merit in it, it is a logical enough reason for re-examining it with fresh eyes. (pp. 311-18)

Northrop Frye, "Towards Defining an Age of Sensibility," in Eighteenth-Century English Literature: Modern Essays in Criticism, *edited by James L. Clifford, Oxford University Press, Inc., 1959, pp. 311-18.*

William Edinger

[In the following excerpt, Edinger surveys representative issues and attitudes of eighteenth-century poetic style.]

[In] opposing objects to ideas, and preferring the former, most seventeenth-century critics express their standard of poetic verisimilitude in a language which reflects the persistence of Aristotelian or realist assumptions about knowledge. These critics, however diverse their announced philosophical leanings, stressed the objective dimension of mimesis over the subjective: they were more interested in the writer's fidelity to objects or "things" than in his fidelity to his perception of objects or things. They were not unaware of the latter but tended to take it for granted that the two would or ought to coincide: poetry told the truth when the poet's concept of the thing and the thing in itself were the same—when, in effect, the poet knew its essence.

To think, says Bouhours, "is to Form in ones self the Picture of any Object spiritual or sensible. Now Images and Pictures are true no further then [sic] they resemble: so a Thought is true when it represents things faithfully: and it is false, when it makes them appear otherwise than they are in themselves." Here Bouhours is trying to explain what he means by truth in poetry and the belles lettres generally; elsewhere in the same work similar terms serve to define the "natural" and the "simple" in thought and style. By a "natural" thought, says Eudoxus, Bouhours's spokesman in the dialogue, I mean "something which is not far fetch'd, which follows from the nature of the Subject; I mean a kind of simple Beauty, plain without Art, such as the Ancients describe true Eloquence; one would say, that a Natural Thought should come into any body's Mind, and that it was in our Head before we read it; it seems easier to be found and costs nothing where e'er we meet it; *they come less in some manner out of the Mind of him that thinks than of the things that was spoke of*" (emphasis mine). This is Pope's standard of "what oft was thought":

> Something, whose Truth convinc'd at Sight we find,
> That gives us back the Image of our Mind.

True wit gives us back the image of our minds because it deals in universals, in what everyone knows latently if not self-consciously; and in the critical period terminating with Pope the concept or mental category is readily identified with its existential referent, so that the subject-object distinction remains relatively unimportant.

What is new in the stylistic criticism of the eighteenth century springs from a different set of assumptions. According to Boswell, Johnson praised Bouhours for showing "all beauty to depend on truth." But the premises which led to innovation in eighteenth-century thinking about style are best described as esthetic; and that, we may remember, is a term whose historical function has been to separate beauty from truth, "taste" from knowledge, and to group together all those responses to literature and the fine arts which can be discussed as imaginative, sympathetic, emotional, or something other than cognitive. In chapter 2 we had occasion to consider some of the theoretical disjunctions which stemmed from this separation of the esthetic and the cognitive in eighteenth-century criticism—the separation of sympathy from judgment, for example, and also the pragmatic or quasi-Ramist theory of verbal ornament which Addison derived from his sharp distinction between the pleasures of the imagination and those of the understanding. Now, however, we must turn our attention to other theoretical developments which, though arising in part from the principles of Addison's estheticism, and from Lockean psychology as presented by Addison, led eventually to a view of the nature and function of poetic language quite contrary to Addison's own.

In Addison's *Spectator* essays, then, the pleasures of the imagination are treated as independent of cognition. As we read through the papers on imagination we discover that Addison's approach to the subject is conditioned by certain Lockean principles which we have also had occasion to mention earlier. Do words (poetic or otherwise) give us knowledge of things? We know, said Locke, our own ideas of things, not things themselves; we know not real essences but nominal essences, aggregates of sense impressions which may vary considerably from perceiver to perceiver. Do words communicate ideas from writer to reader? Not, said Locke, unless they are qualified by extensive definition. Their ordinary function is not to transmit ideas but to excite them, so that, as James Harris correctly inferred from Locke's principles, there is no "real" Eve in *Paradise Lost,* but rather there is Milton's Eve, your Eve, and my Eve, depending upon the ideas each of us summons to give meaning to Milton's words. This view of knowledge and language informs the most important premise of Addison's esthetics, namely, that the pleasure afforded by mimetic works is to be traced not to that delight which accompanies all acts of cognition (where Aristotle had traced it), but to "that *action of the mind,* which compares the ideas arising from the original objects, with the ideas we receive from the statue, picture, description, or sound that represents them" (emphasis mine). In itself the difference between Addison and Aristotle may seem slight, but its historical consequences for theory and taste were enormous. Addison's "action of the mind" becomes in Joseph Priestley, for example, a "moderate exertion of the faculties"—a far more comprehensive expression. Priestley's comprehensiveness, however, was allowed for by Addison himself: we recall the value Addison attached to verbal suggestiveness, and the Proustian observation in *Spectator* 417 that "any single circumstance of what we have formerly seen, often raises up a whole scene of imagery, and awakens numberless ideas that before slept in the imagination; such a particular smell or colour is able to fill the mind, on a sudden, with the picture of the fields or gardens where we first met with it, and to bring up into view all the variety of images that once attended it."

The logic which links Locke and Addison with Archibald Alison, writing at the end of the century, is thus simple and direct. What Addison called the pleasure of imagination, says Alison, is in reality the "emotion of beauty," which arises from "the union of the pleasure of SIMPLE EMOTION, with that which is annexed, by the constitution of the human mind, to the Exercise of IMAGINATION." The emotion of beauty (also called the "emotion of taste") is the "peculiar pleasure" which results when "THE IMAGINATION IS EMPLOYED IN THE PROSECUTION OF A REGULAR TRAIN OF IDEAS OF EMOTION." From this it follows that poetical descriptions are beautiful in proportion to their power to stimulate associations charged with emotion. What we mean when we call a description "picturesque," Alison explains, is that we feel its power to "suggest an additional train of conceptions, besides what the scene or description itself would have suggested. . . . They are, in general, such circumstances, as coincide, *but are not necessarily connected,* with the character of the scene or description, and which at first affecting the mind with an emotion of surprise, produce afterwards an increased or additional train of imagery."

In Alison we find a theory of poetry as revery or mood, and what may fairly be called critical solipsism. After quoting a passage from Milton, Alison comments:

> In these [lines] and a thousand other instances that might be produced, I believe every man of sensibility will be conscious of a variety of great or pleasing images passing with rapidity in his imagination, beyond what the scene or description immediately before him can of themselves excite. They seem often, indeed, to have but a very distant relation to the object that at first excited them; and the object itself, appears only to serve as a hint, to awaken the imagination, and to lead it through every analogous idea that has place in the memory. It is then, indeed, *in this powerless state of reverie, when we are carried on by our conceptions, not guiding them,* that the deepest emotions of beauty or sublimity are felt, that our hearts swell with feelings which language is too weak to express, and that, in the depth of silence and astonishment, we pay to the charm that enthralls us, the most flattering mark of our applause.

Poet and reader are as hopelessly cut off from one another as the characters in *Tristam Shandy,* each bound by the arbitrary and mechanical workings of his own mind.

Midway between the moderate subjectivism of Addison and the extreme subjectivism of Alison lies Burke's analysis of poetic language in the *Enquiry,* perhaps the subtlest development of Lockean premises achieved by an eighteenth-century British critic. Accepting the Lockean equation between idea and image, Burke attacks the notion of *ut pictura poesis* by denying that *words* are the images of things. We do not, he argues, ordinarily visualize words of the class which he calls "simple abstract" (e.g., terms for simple qualities, such as red, blue, round, square, etc.) when we hear or read them, nor does their meaning depend in any way upon our visualizing them, nor do they gain in force when we visualize them. The same is true for words of the class called "aggregate words" (e.g., Locke's terms for "substances": man, horse, castle, etc.). As for the third class of "compounded abstract" words (e.g., virtue, honor, persuasion, docility: Locke's "mixed modes"), these cannot be visualized, since they stand primarily for aggregates of what Locke called "notions" as opposed to "ideas" (images); moreover, as "Mr. Locke has somewhere observed with his usual sagacity," words of this class are usually taught "before the particular modes of action to which they belong are presented to the mind," so that they acquire a power to affect us before we attach specific notions to them, and in fact continue to affect us even when we do not call up any part of the meaning

which we might legitimately attach to them. And to some words and phrases it is nearly impossible to assign any specific meaning at all: when we read in Milton the phrases "universe of Death" or "angel of the Lord" we summon neither images nor specific sets of "notions"; yet the phrases are affecting and, in context, sublime.

In the second place, Burke argues that even when poetic descriptions are meant to be visualized, their force depends much less than is commonly thought upon their excellence *as descriptions.* We do not sufficiently distinguish, Burke remarks, "between a clear expression, and a strong expression. . . . The former regards the understanding; the latter belongs to the passions. The one describes a thing as it is; the other describes it as it is felt." What critics have not noticed is that "we yield to sympathy, what we refuse to description. The truth is, all verbal description, merely as naked description, though never so exact, conveys so poor and insufficient an idea of the thing described, that it could scarcely have the smallest effect, if the speaker did not call in to his aid those modes of speech that mark a strong and lively feeling in himself. Then, by the contagion of our passions, we catch a fire already kindled in another, which probably might never have been struck out by the object described." In the third place, an accurate and detailed knowledge of any object, precisely represented (as far as that is possible) in words, is in the nature of the case relatively unaffecting. We not only yield to sympathy what we refuse to description; we refuse to description what we yield to ignorance. "It is our ignorance of things," says Burke, "that causes all our admiration, and chiefly excites our passions. Knowledge and acquaintance make the most striking causes affect but little."

These arguments support Burke's conclusion . . . that the business of rhetoric and poetry "is to affect rather by sympathy than imitation; to display rather the effect of things on the mind of the speaker, or of others, than to present a clear idea of the things themselves." In the *Enquiry* Burke will not allow that this mode of "display" constitutes an imitation; taking the latter term in the narrowest sense possible, he restricts it to the drama only. But for many other critics Burke's "display" came to be included in the notion of imitation, so that all animated writing could be seen as implicitly dramatic—imitative not primarily of things in themselves, but of the writer's perceptual process and of the particular consciousness engendered by his perceptions.

The assumption that what is sublime or pathetic in writing proceeds from the representation of subjective states of consciousness led to a theory of verbal ornament very different from the pragmatic view characteristic of seventeenth-century criticism. The newer view was a mimetic one, and found its classical authority in Longinus, a critic whose subjectivism complements that of the post-Lockean critics and estheticians at every point. Aristotle's theory of metaphor, we recall, is cognitive and ontological in emphasis. Metaphors, he says, are agreeable when they enable us "to get hold of new ideas easily": "when the poet calls old age 'a withered stalk', he conveys a new idea, a new fact, to us by means of the general notion of 'lost bloom', which is common to both things." For Aristotle metaphor involves the discovery of objective similarities— similarities founded on the real properties of things. In Cicero and Quintilian the pragmatic or rhetorical emphasis is primary: metaphors are a source of novelty, variety, liveliness; they illustrate or clarify. Longinus too is concerned with effect, and for him too the immediate justification of metaphor is rhetorical: metaphors dazzle, move, or please. But Longinus differs from the other classical authorities in tracing the power of metaphor to the sympathetic appeal of apparently spontaneous utterance. Metaphors and the other tropes are, he says, best used to "counterfeit" or imitate "spontaneous emotion," and the "right moment" for metaphor is "when emotion sweeps on like a flood and inevitably carries the multitude of metaphors along it." For art, as Longinus insists, "is only perfect when it looks like nature," that is, when it creates the illusion of unselfconscious "artless" speech. Otherwise the use of tropes will seem manipulative, for there is "an inevitable suspicion attaching to the unconscionable use of figures. It gives a suggestion of treachery, craft, fallacy." In this context, it should be noted, the word "nature" acquires a relatively precise significance, meaning, ultimately, consciousness and the normal expression of consciousness.

Despite the growth in Longinus's popularity after Boileau's translation of *Peri Hupsous* in 1674, the Longinian view of ornament made little headway in England before the eighteenth century. Dryden and even the otherwise Longinian John Dennis are among the critics who, thinking Ramistically of ornament as something added to plain speech, or as an alternative to normal expression, continued to uphold the common view that tropical language is out of place in the poetic representation of spontaneous expression (as in dramatic dialogue, for example), on the grounds that the use of tropes "showes remoteness of thought, or labour in the Writer." In Trapp and Addison, however, and later in Husbands and Manwaring, the Longinian approach to metaphor begins to legitimize the use of tropes in emotive utterance, appearing often in connection with the growing critical interest in "Hebrew poetry," whose figurative extravagance is now seen as the "natural" and appropriate expression of Oriental sensibility. This development reaches a kind of climax in the publication of Bishop Lowth's *Lectures on the Sacred Poetry of the Hebrews* (in Latin, 1753), after which time the mimetic doctrine of ornament occurs in such writers as Kames, Blair, Beattie, Gerard, Gibbon, Adam Smith, and, at least by implication, Johnson.

M. H. Abrams has traced the role of Longinian assumptions in the evolution of expressive theories of poetry. For Longinus himself the orator or poet was a mimetic artist, counterfeiting, not expressing, passion. But if poetry can be identified with figurative style, and if, as Longinus had suggested, the language of passion is naturally figurative, then it follows that passionate speech is inherently poetical. "Civil society," wrote Richard Hurd in 1749, "*tames us to humanity,* as Cicero expresses it," and "brings us down to one dead level" in speech as well as in manners. But when the violent passions arise, "we return again to the free and ferocious state of Nature. And what is the expression of that state? It is (as we understand by experience) a free and fiery expression, all made up of bold metaphors and daring figures of Speech." Hurd concludes that "Poetry, *pure Poetry,* is the proper language of Passion, whether we chuse to consider it as ennobling, or debasing the human character." Such assumptions received support from the contemporary pioneers of historical linguistics,

who stressed the radically metaphoric character of all language. The figures, Blair wrote about 1760, "are commonly considered as artificial modes of speech devised by orators and poets after the world had advanced to a refined state. The contrary of this is the truth. Men have never used so many figures of style as in those rude ages, when, besides the power of a warm imagination to suggest lively images, the want of proper and precise terms for the ideas they would express obliged them to have recourse to circumlocution, metaphor, comparison, and all those substituted forms of expression which give a poetical air to language." In 1772 the great linguist Sir William Jones explicitly rejected the notion of poetry as imitation, remarking that cultures such as the Moslem, with a theological ban on imitation in any form and a consequent lack of dramatic literature, nevertheless value and cultivate poetry of other kinds. Poetry, Jones believed, is the expression of feeling, and ought to be "sincere": "Petrarch was, certainly, too deeply affected with real grief, and the Persian poet [unidentified] was too sincere a lover, to imitate the passions of others."

Such a climate of opinion was conducive to the spread of the Longinian and Fénelonian doctrines of negative capability. Horace's dictum, *si vis me flere, dolendum est / Primum ipsi tibi* ("if you would have me weep, you yourself must first be moved"), a commonplace of seventeenth-century criticism, was now taken with a new literalness. Blair believed that "there is no possibility of speaking properly the language of any passion, without feeling it," and that it is not to a want of art but rather to "the absence or deadness of real emotion, that we must ascribe the want of success in so many Tragic Writers, when they attempt being pathetic." The dramatist who would write "natural" dialogue, Kames explains, must "assume the precise character and passion of the personage represented," adding that this is the "only difficulty; for the writer, who, annihilating himself, can thus become another person, need be in no pain about the sentiments that belong to the assumed character: these will flow without the least study, or even preoccupation; and will frequently be as delightfully new to himself as to his reader."

So conceived, imitation is indistinguishable from expression, and Art is swallowed up in Nature: the "natural" style is seen not as the product of skill, but as the direct manifestation of "genius." Wordsworth's 1802 preface to the *Lyrical Ballads* aptly illustrates the ambiguities in which the notion of art had involved itself, under the pressure of Longinian attitudes, by the end of the century. . . . Poetry here aspires to a standard of literal truthfulness with which not even the strictest Baconian devotée of fact could quarrel.

Although what I have called the mimetic theory of verbal ornament shades off into an expressivist literalism when pushed to an extreme, we shall continue to call it mimetic, partly on the ground that the term legitimately preserves our sense of the poet as a conscious artist (as the term "expressive" does not), and partly in order to reveal the inherent advantages of considering figurative language in mimetic rather than in pragmatic terms. The advantages are implicit in the fact that the mimetic theory of ornament obviates most of the problems which arise when poetry and rhetoric are conceived as alternatives to dialectic. To the Ramist or Platonic supposition that dialectic is the expression of thought itself, unadulterated by suasory considerations, the mimetic theorist replies that dialectic is the expression merely of one mode of thinking, and that there are other modes, and consequently other styles of expression organic to them. Figurative style is not to be conceived as an alternative to dialectic, or as dialectic-plus-ornament, but as the proper and indeed inescapable expression of a way of thinking which is neither better nor worse but simply other than abstract and logical.

This point of view, which makes us think of Coleridge, is in fact as old as the Port-Royal Logic. We have seen Arnauld reject the "Artificial and Rhetorical style compos'd of false Imaginations, Hyperboles, and forc'd Figures," whose vogue he associates with the Ramist approach to ornament, in favor of a "less Pompous, and more Barren" style adapted to exact reasoning. This sounds Cartesian. But the Port-Royal Logic contains not merely a mimetic theory of rhetoric, but a detailed analysis of the function of figurative language based on the subjectivist conception of mimesis which we have associated with Longinus and the literary theory of the later eighteenth century. The chief aim of the orator, declares Arnauld, is "to conceive things strongly and clearly in the Mind, and being conceiv'd to express 'em in such a manner, that they may imprint in the Breasts of the Hearers a clear and lively Image of the things express'd, *which not only represents the things barely as they are, but also the Motions and Affections with which they are conceiv'd*" (my emphasis). The figures of thought (and by implication the tropes as well) exist to portray the "Motion and Gesture of him that speaks." It is significant that Arnauld's most extensive discussion of figurative language occurs in a chapter of the *Logic* devoted to kinds of definition, for Arnauld is concerned with the ways in which ornament embodies meaning, and thus enters into the conceptual process of the speaker.

Arnauld notes that many words have the potential for two distinct kinds of meaning and may thus be defined in two ways. Philosophic definition gives the technical meaning of a term as it is used in scientific discourse, lexical definition the meaning as determined by common usage. The orator is usually concerned with the second kind, since he normally treats moral subjects in the context of ordinary experience rather than philosophically. The grammarians, Arnauld remarks, who are responsible for lexical definition, seldom give a complete account of the ordinary meanings of words because they neglect what today would be called their connotations. Arnauld's terms for the distinction between denotation and connotation are "principal" and "accessory" ideas, and he goes on to illustrate this distinction by explaining that the statement, *You lie,* is not equivalent to the statement, *You know the contrary of what you affirm,* because the former includes, in addition to the "principal" idea, the "accessory" ideas of scorn and contempt. The "accessory" aspect of meaning, Arnauld continues, is what chiefly determines the difference between a plain and a figured style, and he explains why one is often more "lovely" than the other:

> Which proceeds from hence, that figur'd expressions, besides the principal thing, signifie the Motion and Gesture of him that speaks, and imprint both the one and the other *Idea* in the mind, whereas simple expressions set forth only the naked Truth: For example, if this half verse of *Virgil,*

> *Usque adeone mori miserum est?*

> were express'd simply and without a Figure,

> *Non est neque adeo mori miserum.*

> Without doubt the sentence would not have had that force; and the reason is, because the first Expression signifies more then [*sic*] the second; for it does not only express the Thought, that it is not so miserable a thing as Men think to die; but it represents also the *Idea* of a Man, as it were provoking death, and undauntedly looking it in the face, which, without question is a great and lively Accession to the signification of the words.

The first expression signifies more than the second. Pragmatic theories of rhetoric obscure the relationship between the twin issues of right rhetoric, truth and persuasiveness, by treating them in separate frames of reference. Truth is abstract, a matter of logic and of the commonplace tradition; ornament, on the other hand, is said to please or move on account of its novelty, variety, or vividness. Arnauld reunites the issues of truth and persuasiveness in arguing that, if the ornamented expression is more pleasing or moving than its plain "equivalent," this is because it is more significant, and significant not only of the speaker's "feeling" or "emotion"—as though "emotion" were ever really separable from "thought"—but of a complex attitude or awareness on his part. This is the full meaning, then, for rhetorical theory, of Arnauld's maxim that "there is nothing lovely but what is true." The essential function of verbal ornament is not to persuade but to disclose—artistically to "imitate"—a complex act of apprehension. Conception and expression, invention and style, are here seen as aspects of one another, and figurative language as an instrument of thought. Implicit in this mimetic view of eloquence is a denial that moral truth is to be identified with logic or purely conceptual thinking; Arnauld's theory of ornament complements Pascal's *esprit de finesse* and Burke's conception of moral knowledge as a complicated and semi-intuitive "wisdom of the heart."

We have seen that subjectivist critical theory in eighteenth-century England tended to be esthetic in emphasis, in the sense that literary effects such as the beautiful, the pathetic, and the sublime were often treated without regard to questions of truth. The example of Arnauld shows clearly that this separation of pleasure from truth is not naturally incident to a subjectivist approach to mimesis. And after Arnauld, Fénelon shows the same thing more clearly still. [Elsewhere] we stressed the objectivist character of Fénelon's rhetorical thought, with its emphasis on "portraiture," or the concrete and dramatic rendering of the experience of people other than the speaker himself. But the *Dialogues on Eloquence* contain a subjective counterpart to "portraiture" in the theory of what Fénelon calls "movements," which refer to the depiction, in language or physical gesture, of the speaker's emotional response to his subject. In reply to the question, "What movement can there be in words?" Speaker A, Fénelon's principal spokesman, quotes from the *De Oratore* an asyndetic passage from a speech attributed to Gracchus ("Wretched: Where shall I go? What sanctuary remains to me? The Capitol?" etc.). Put these "broken sentences which so well mark nature in the transports of grief " into connected, declarative prose, says Speaker A, and they will lose their mimetic vivacity. For "the manner of saying things makes visible the manner in which one feels them, and it is this which strikes the listeners the more." In Fénelon the aims of "portraiture" and "movements," taken together, define the function of figurative language, which is, accordingly, to assist in registering the speaker's total (i.e., "objective") concrete reality. This distinction between objective and subjective mimesis reappears in Fénelon's *Letter to the French Academy,* where, after setting forth his ideal of poetic self-effacement in the interests of dramatic objectivity, Fénelon remarks that "the ancients did not think it enough to copy nature exactly: their pictures were moving, as well as true." When the poet speaks about himself, for example, let it be with the "tender simplicity" of a Catullus: "Odi, et amo: quare id faciam fortasse requiris. / Nescio, sed fieri sentio, et excrucior." "How much," asks Fénelon, "are the elaborate witty conceits of Ovid and Martial inferior to these negligent words; where the distracted heart alone speaks in a kind of despair?" Fénelon's point of view here is that of Johnson or Wordsworth: the "natural" expression of subjective experience has the objective truth of dramatic probability. Conversely, the conceited style falsifies the process of subjective apprehension as well as the nature of what the speaker apprehends.

English critics were late to grasp the advantages of the mimetic theory of ornament developed by Arnauld and Fénelon. In 1762, however, exactly a century after the appearance of *L'Art de Penser,* Adam Smith explicitly rejected the pragmatic view of ornament in favor of an Arnauldian approach to the nature of persuasive speaking. The ancients, said Smith, finding that what they called tropes and figures of speech were frequently met with in the most striking and beautiful passages of poetry and prose, unwisely concluded that the figures gave the passages their beauty. "But the case is far otherwise. When the sentiment of the speaker is expressed in a neat, clear, plain, and clever manner, and the passion or affection he is possessed of and intends, *by sympathy,* to communicate to his hearer, is plainly and cleverly hit off, then and then only the expression has all the force and beauty that language can give it." The figures of speech contribute to the beauty of expression "only so far as they happen to be the just and natural forms of expression . . . sentiment." "When they are more proper than the common forms of speaking, then they are to be used; but not otherwise." The ornaments, in short, are not ornaments when correctly used, but expressions as proper as the so-called proper ones from which they are distinguished in traditional rhetoric. They are proper because the "passion or affection" which they express is as vital a part of what is being communicated as the thought ("sentiment") of the speaker.

By regarding conception and style as inseparable, then, the mimetic theory of ornament overcame that "undoubtedly absurd and unprofitable and reprehensible severance between the tongue and the brain" which Cicero had so long ago complained of and freed rhetoric and poetry (considered as modes of discourse) from the awkward position of being in potential competition with dialectic. The influence of the theory upon critical practice was gradual, and did not manifest itself completely until the end of the eighteenth century. During the period between Lowth and Wordsworth, critics interested in describing the structure of "natural" styles in prose and poetry gave almost all of their attention to syntax. Discussions of "natural" style in

poetry emphasized the drama, Shakespeare being the universal favorite as a model of natural dialogue. The issues continued to be those raised by Dryden and the other seventeenth-century critics of declamation and conceit, and Shakespeare's "nature" was typically opposed to the connected "artificial" rhetoric of Dryden, Rowe, Corneille, and sometimes Racine.

Critics like Kames and Gerard elaborate the differences between these two general kinds of style with a new minuteness born of their fascination with the descriptive possibilities of associationism. For a mimetic style simply registers the motions of the mind, and the mind moves according to the laws of association, as *Hamlet* is often called upon to demonstrate:

> to die; to sleep;—
> To sleep? Perchance to dream! Ay, there's the rub . . .

But the laws of association are not to be taken as abstract principles which make unnecessary the poet's imaginative participation in his characters' feelings. Dramatic poetry fails, says Gerard, when the poet,

> having conceived some of the objects strictly connected with a passion, considers that object only in general and abstractly as a present perception; he therefore allows himself to run into such a train of thought as that object present to the mind would dictate if it were unconnected with any passion; he goes on coolly imagining such ideas as it suggests by means of any of the principles of association; and he makes the person possessed by the passion to express all these ideas. He feels not the passion, he has not the force of genius or sensibility of heart sufficient for conceiving how it would affect a person who felt it, or for entering into the sentiments which it would produce in him. The sentiments which he makes him utter might all be very proper in a description, a discourse, or a meditation occasioned by the view of such an object; but they are not natural to a person in whom that object produces a suitable passion. In order to conceive sentiments natural to him, the poet ought to have confined himself to the consideration of the object in this one point of view, as strictly connected with a passion and suggested by it; he ought to indulge only such a train of thought as it would lead to in these circumstances, or such a train as the passion with which it is presently connected would introduce into the mind of a person under the power of that passion.

The bad dramatic poet considers his object "only in general and abstractly": it is again the problem of conceptual over determination, the failure of negative capability, but described in a new and, in its way, very precise vocabulary. The effect of the new criticism is a sharpening of emphasis, a clarification of the demand for a perceptive and perceptual style in poetry.

We are apt to feel now that if spontaneity is the hallmark of "natural" style, that style should be spontaneous in diction as well as in syntax, and we are puzzled to find critics of the later eighteenth century paying so little attention to the problem of coterie language. There are, to be sure, signs of dissatisfaction with contemporary poetic diction, and the increasing taste for naturalistic and "minute" description bespeaks a demand for a more perceptive language than descriptive writing in the tradition of Pope normally affords. Nevertheless, Wordsworth's two prefaces to the *Lyrical Ballads* (1800, 1802), taken together, constitute the first thorough-going Longinian criticism of poetic diction in English [see excerpt below]. Here at last the principle of verisimilitude is separated from the classical and neoclassical doctrine of the three levels of style, and the latter doctrine—the main theoretical support of eighteenth-century "poetic diction" in Wordsworth's sense of the term—is repudiated, along with the pragmatic view of ornament with which Wordsworth rightly associates it. Thus to condemn "poetic diction" it is enough simply to identify it as such; it is not the "natural" language of imagination or feeling, but a specialized vocabulary of "phrases and figures of speech which from father to son have long been regarded as the common inheritance of poets." Its uses have been rhetorical rather than mimetic: "to elevate the style, and raise it above prose"; to minister to a cultural expectation that metrical writing will employ a "particular language"; to impress (as Wordsworth shrewdly says) "a notion of the peculiarity and exaltation of the Poet's character, and [to flatter] the Reader's self-love by bringing him nearer to a sympathy with that character." But these purposes conflict with mimetic truth. The genuine ornaments of poetry—"the emanations of reality and truth"—are to be sought in the nature of the subject, which, if "judiciously chosen," will "naturally, and upon fit occasion, lead him to passions the language of which, if selected truly and judiciously, must necessarily be dignified and variegated, and alive with metaphors and figures. I forbear to speak of an incongruity which would shock the intelligent Reader, should the Poet interweave any foreign splendour of his own with that which the passion naturally suggests."

But as Wordsworth's critical thinking matured he came to approach the problem of poetic diction from a somewhat different point of view. For lack of verisimilitude is neither the only nor the primary fault of eighteenth-century poetic diction. The principal difficulty with the eighteenth-century stock phrase—or "kenning," as Professor Tillotson significantly calls it—especially when it purports to imitate feeling or describe physical objects, lies precisely in its difference from the real kenning as found in *Beowulf* or Homer. The real kenning is a form of public language; in its unchanging conventionality it is an emblem of continuity and community of feeling, and therefore of the ritual or ceremonial function of the so-called primary epic. The modern reader does not wish it away, nor does he merely savor its quaintness; instead, because the experiences and concerns which epics celebrate—courage, death, national destiny—are universal, he participates in the community which the epic defines, if only self-consciously and temporarily, by a partially willed act of imagination; thus the kenning keeps for him some measure of its emblematic power. The neoclassical kenning is a form of public language too, inviting the reader to rehearse feelings and attitudes preestablished by and definitive of a community. But in this case the community is composed of certain poets and their readers; it is a coterie. A reader contemporary with it may wish to include himself in it or not. If he does, he will no doubt be moved by the conventionalities of its style in somewhat the same way as the participant in the larger community of the epic. But here we are dealing, not with universals, but with fashions in language and feeling; and fashions in both change, and the mannerisms which give the feelings currency become

dated. For the reader who survives the coterie, its kennings must lose their power (if they do not, indeed, become objects of disgust), for they are emblems now of the unworthy, of a community which found its identity in feelings now discarded or outgrown.

Such a reader will then perceive the essential difference between the two kinds of kenning, namely, that the valid kenning appears to be the product of a culture, while the literary kenning too obviously originates with a particular writer. Homer and the *Beowulf* poet are effaced and anonymous; it is not their voices we hear but the voices of their communities. But the eighteenth-century kenning is simply a characteristic and rather intrusive ornament imitated or plagiarized from Milton or Spenser or Pope or Virgil or someone else. The reader who has outgrown its community (as Wordsworth and Coleridge did in their twenties) reads these poets and their imitators as individuals, and in the context of individualism the kenning is merely a piece of stock diction asking for a stock response. It is neither public language nor private (in the sense of individual), for it registers merely an absence, a failure in experience or perception. It is a formula in the common and modern pejorative sense of the word, an abstract or empty universal, imitated and imitable, which is to say capable of repeated and mechanical use as a substitute for genuine intuition.

Wordsworth came increasingly to regard the mannerisms of eighteenth-century verse in this light as he became increasingly aware of the dependence of style upon perception. In the prefaces of 1800 and 1802, as we have seen, he stresses the Longinian principle of verisimilitude: eighteenth-century diction is faulty because it is not "a selection of language really used by men." Yet even here a concern for perceptual accuracy is evident; Wordsworth has "at all times endeavoured to look steadily at [his] subject," and hopes that there is in the *Lyrical Ballads* "little falsehood of description." His later criticisms of eighteenth-century diction stress its imperceptiveness. "The poetry of the period intervening between the publication of the Paradise Lost and the Seasons," he writes in a supplement to the preface of 1815, "does not contain a single new image of external nature; and scarcely presents a familiar one from which it can be inferred that the eye of the Poet had been steadily fixed upon his object." So too the period diction and predictable syntax of Pope's epitaphs, which Wordsworth examines in his *Essay on Epitaphs* (1810), convict Pope of writing out of habits which replaced an intuitive, sympathetic understanding of his subject. That the epitaph by its nature admits little more than the restatement of commonplaces is no objection in Pope's favor, for the poet's task is to rescue the commonplace from mere abstraction by experiencing it in language peculiarly his own: "it is required that these truths should be instinctively ejaculated or should rise irresistibly from the circumstances; in a word that they should be uttered in such connection as shall make it felt that they are not adopted, not spoken by rote, but *perceived* in their whole compass with the freshness and clearness of an original intuition." Where Pope's style is mechanical, language is all too obviously the "dress" of thought, and Wordsworth rejects the favorite neoclassical metaphor in rejecting the style: words "are not what the garb is to the body but what the body is to the soul, themselves a constituent part and power or function in the thought." "If words be not . . .

an incarnation of the thought, but only a clothing of it, then surely will they prove an ill gift; such a one as those possessed vestments, read of in the stories of superstitious times, which had power to consume and to alienate from his right mind the victim who put them on."

In the *Biographia Literaria* Coleridge criticizes Wordsworth's principle of verisimilitude in poetic diction by remarking that "were there excluded from Mr. Wordsworth's poetic compositions all, that a literal adherence to the theory of his preface *would* exclude, two-thirds at least of the marked beauties of his poetry must be erased." No one but a poet would have called a singing bird "busy," or have translated a beautiful May-day into "Both earth and sky keep jubilee"; the most perceptive diction is, in context, extraordinary, not commonplace, the expression of extraordinary powers of observation or imagination. (pp. 110-30)

After 1815 Wordsworth and Coleridge both bring poetic diction to the test of a perceptual standard, but the standard is informed by a theory of perception markedly different from any common in the eighteenth century. Their ideal poet is not, for example—or not merely—an accurate observer of nature in the Baconian sense, because he is not a recorder of normal appearances. Such observation is, in the Romantic view, passive and mechanical, whereas the observer who is moved by what he sees transfigures it. Their view that in its most valuable form perception is a creative activity of the mind carries Wordsworth and Coleridge equally far beyond the subjectivism of Burke's *Sublime,* with its implied antithesis between "distinct ideas" or accurate perceptions ("little," familiar, unim-

pressive) and "sublime" impressions which (when they are not produced by words alone unaccompanied by ideas of any kind) arise from acts of incomplete apprehension or simply misapprehension. For, although there is a place for the Burkean sublime in Wordsworth if not noticeably in Coleridge, both writers insist that the imaginative transformation of natural objects is not a misperception or distortion but a superior realization of what is there. The imaginative recreation of nature is to them inconceivable without that discriminating and captivated attention to the objects of vision or memory which is the source of the poet's precision of language.

Wordsworth insisted throughout his life that poetic descriptions ought to betray the marks of fresh and exact observation. Coleridge admired in Wordsworth

> the perfect truth of nature in his images and descriptions, as taken immediately from nature, and proving a long and genial intimacy with the very spirit which gives the physiognomic expression to all the works of nature. Like a green field reflected in a calm and perfectly transparent lake, the image is distinguished from the reality only by its greater softness and lustre. Like the moisture or the polish on a pebble, genius neither distorts nor false-colours its objects; but on the contrary brings out many a vein and many a tint, which escapes the eye of common observation, thus raising to the rank of gems what had been often kicked away by the hurrying foot of the traveller on the dusty high road of custom.

Thus the imaginative modification of natural appearances which Wordsworth and Coleridge have in mind is not an imposition of form from without but the disclosure of an immanent beauty which escapes ordinary observation. "Remember," says Coleridge in his essay "On Poesy or Art" (1818), "that there is a difference between form as proceeding, and shape as superinduced;—the latter is either the death or the imprisonment of the thing;—the former is its self-witnessing and self-effected sphere of agency." The artist who proceeds from a fixed concept, a "given form, which is supposed to answer to the notion of beauty," produces "emptiness" and "unreality"—*mere* abstractions, . . . outlines drawn according to a recipe." In contrast to this, the kind of imagination which Coleridge celebrates in Wordsworth is able to work directly upon perceptual materials, as an energy of focused response, contemplating "the ANCIENT of days and all his works with feelings as fresh, as if all had then sprang forth at the first creative fiat."

To describe the effect which this produces in Wordsworth's poetry, Coleridge employs the same radical formula that Johnson had used to describe true wit: natural and new. It is "the prime merit of genius and its most unequivocal mode of manifestation, so to represent familiar objects as to awaken in the minds of others a kindred feeling concerning them and that freshness of sensation which is the constant accompaniment of mental, no less than of bodily, convalescence." Thus Wordsworth is able "to give the charm of novelty to things of every day," not by an art which declares its abstracted separateness from the visual experience on which it draws, but simply "by awakening the mind's attention from the lethargy of custom, and directing it to the loveliness and the wonders of the world before us; an inexhaustible treasure, but for which, in con-

Historian Edward Gibbon, by Sir Joshua Reynolds.

sequence of the film of familiarity and selfish solicitude we have eyes, yet see not, ears that hear not, and hearts that neither feel nor understand."

The effect here attributed to Wordsworth's poetry is the effect which distinguishes the landscapes of his great contemporaries, Constable and Turner, from the many conventionally idealized landscapes of the eighteenth century. With the latter, studied form keeps the viewer within the boundaries of the work of art; natural objects are not only idealized but formulated—"drawn according to a recipe." With the former, and in Constable especially, the representation returns the observer to his own experience, giving him the sense that he knows intimately what he is beholding and that the painter has, as it were, merely revived his awareness of his own powers of observation. This effect has been celebrated in our time by Wallace Stevens, whose "necessary angel" represents (at least in part) the power to produce it. Responding to the claim that "poetry has to do with matter that is foreign and alien," Stevens replies, "On the contrary, its function, the need which it meets and which has to be met in some way in every age that is not to become decadent or barbarous, is precisely this contact with reality as it impinges upon us from outside, the sense that we can touch and feel a solid reality which does not dissolve itself into the conceptions of our own minds." In a broader context which includes the imitation of "the scenes of life" as well as "the prospects of nature," the effect described by Coleridge and by Stevens is the highest effect of poetry for Johnson too. (pp. 130-33)

William Edinger, in his Samuel Johnson and Poetic Style, *The University of Chicago Press, 1977, 272 p.*

"AGE OF PROSE AND REASON"

Matthew Arnold

[A poet and commentator on the social and moral life in Victorian England, Arnold is considered one of the most important English critics of the nineteenth century—though he is essentially regarded as an apologist for literary criticism. In all critical activities he advocated the doctrine of "disinterestedness" which stressed flexibility, curiosity, and a non-utilitarian approach to culture and art. He believed that the critic should judge a work of art according to its own qualities, unbiased by the influence of history and the limitations of subjective experience. In the following excerpt from a work originally published in 1880, Arnold characterizes eighteenth-century English literature as the "age of prose and reason."]

For my present purpose I need not dwell on our Elizabethan poetry, or on the continuation and close of this poetry in Milton. We all of us profess to be agreed in the estimate of this poetry; we all of us recognise it as great poetry, our greatest, and Shakespeare and Milton as our poetical classics. The real estimate, here, has universal currency. With the next age of our poetry divergency and diffi-

culty begin. An historic estimate of that poetry has established itself; and the question is, whether it will be found to coincide with the real estimate.

The age of Dryden, together with our whole eighteenth century which followed it, sincerely believed itself to have produced poetical classics of its own, and even to have made advance, in poetry, beyond all its predecessors. Dryden regards as not seriously disputable the opinion 'that the sweetness of English verse was never understood or practised by our fathers.' Cowley could see nothing at all in Chaucer's poetry. Dryden heartily admired it, and, as we have seen, praised its matter admirably; but of its exquisite manner and movement all he can find to say is that 'there is the rude sweetness of a Scotch tune in it, which is natural and pleasing, though not perfect.' Addison, wishing to praise Chaucer's numbers, compares them with Dryden's own. And all through the eighteenth century, and down even into our own times, the stereotyped phrase of approbation for good verse found in our early poetry has been, that it even approached the verse of Dryden, Addison, Pope, and Johnson.

Are Dryden and Pope poetical classics? Is the historic estimate, which represents them as such, and which has been so long established that it cannot easily give way, the real estimate? Wordsworth and Coleridge, as is well known, denied it; but the authority of Wordsworth and Coleridge does not weigh much with the young generation, and there are many signs to show that the eighteenth century and its judgments are coming into favour again. Are the favourite poets of the eighteenth century classics?

It is impossible within my present limits to discuss the question fully. And what man of letters would not shrink from seeming to dispose dictatorially of the claims of two men who are, at any rate, such masters in letters as Dryden and Pope; two men of such admirable talent, both of them, and one of them, Dryden, a man, on all sides, of such energetic and genial power? And yet, if we are to gain the full benefit from poetry, we must have the real estimate of it. I cast about for some mode of arriving, in the present case, at such an estimate without offence. And perhaps the best way is to begin, as it is easy to begin, with cordial praise.

When we find Chapman, the Elizabethan translator of Homer, expressing himself in his preface thus: 'Though truth in her very nakedness sits in so deep a pit, that from Gades to Aurora and Ganges few eyes can sound her, I hope yet those few here will so discover and confirm that, the date being out of her darkness in this morning of our poet, he shall now gird his temples with the sun,'—we pronounce that such a prose is intolerable. When we find Milton writing: 'And long it was not after, when I was confirmed in this opinion, that he, who would not be frustrate of his hope to write well hereafter in laudable things, ought himself to be a true poem,'—we pronounce that such a prose has its own grandeur, but that it is obsolete and inconvenient. But when we find Dryden telling us: 'What Virgil wrote in the vigour of his age, in plenty and at ease, I have undertaken to translate in my declining years; struggling with wants, oppressed with sickness, curbed in my genius, liable to be misconstrued in all I write,'—then we exclaim that here at last we have the true English prose, a prose such as we would all gladly use if we only knew how. Yet Dryden was Milton's contemporary.

But after the Restoration the time had come when our nation felt the imperious need of a fit prose. So, too, the time had likewise come when our nation felt the imperious need of freeing itself from the absorbing preoccupation which religion in the Puritan age had exercised. It was impossible that this freedom should be brought about without some negative excess, without some neglect and impairment of the religious life of the soul; and the spiritual history of the eighteenth century shows us that the freedom was not achieved without them. Still, the freedom was achieved; the preoccupation, an undoubtedly baneful and retarding one if it had continued, was got rid of. And as with religion amongst us at that period, so it was also with letters. A fit prose was a necessity; but it was impossible that a fit prose should establish itself amongst us without some touch of frost to the imaginative life of the soul. The needful qualities for a fit prose are regularity, uniformity, precision, balance. The men of letters, whose destiny it may be to bring their nation to the attainment of a fit prose, must of necessity, whether they work in prose or in verse, give a predominating, an almost exclusive attention to the qualities of regularity, uniformity, precision, balance. But an almost exclusive attention to these qualities involves some repression and silencing of poetry.

We are to regard Dryden as the puissant and glorious founder, Pope as the splendid high priest, of our age of prose and reason, of our excellent and indispensable eighteenth century. For the purposes of their mission and destiny their poetry, like their prose, is admirable. Do you ask me whether Dryden's verse, take it almost where you will, is not good?

> A milk-white Hind, immortal and unchanged,
> Fed on the lawns and in the forest ranged.

I answer: Admirable for the purposes of the inaugurator of an age of prose and reason. Do you ask me whether Pope's verse, take it almost where you will, is not good?

> To Hounslow Heath I point, and Banstead Down;
> Thence comes your mutton, and these chicks my own.

I answer: Admirable for the purposes of the high priest of an age of prose and reason. But do you ask me whether such verse proceeds from men with an adequate poetic criticism of life, from men whose criticism of life has a high seriousness, or even, without that high seriousness, has poetic largeness, freedom, insight, benignity? Do you ask me whether the application of ideas to life in the verse of these men, often a powerful application, no doubt, is a powerful *poetic* application? Do you ask me whether the poetry of these men has either the matter or the inseparable manner of such an adequate poetic criticism; whether it has the accent of

> Absent thee from felicity awhile . . .

or of

> And what is else not to be overcome . . .

or of

> O martyr souded in virginitee!

I answer: It has not and cannot have them; it is the poetry

of the builders of an age of prose and reason. Though they may write in verse, though they may in a certain sense be masters of the art of versification, Dryden and Pope are not classics of our poetry, they are classics of our prose. (pp. 34-42)

Matthew Arnold, "The Study of Poetry," in his Essays in Criticism, second series, *The Macmillan Company, 1924, pp. 1-55.*

Sir Leslie Stephen

[*Considered by some as the most important critic of the Victorian age after Matthew Arnold, Stephen has been praised for his intellectual vigor and moral insight and judgment. Other critics, however, argue that his work was deficient in aesthetic and formal analysis and that he failed to reconcile his moral and historical philosophies. In the following excerpt from a work first published in 1876, he reviews the principal genres that define eighteenth-century English literature: the essay, literary criticism, prose satire, the novel, and the prose works of the moralists.*]

There is [a] . . . wide province of literature in which writers of the eighteenth century did work original in character and of permanent value. If the seventeenth century is the great age of dramatists and theologians, the eighteenth century was the age in which the critic, the essayist, the satirist, the novelist, and the moralist first appeared, or reached the highest mark. Criticism, though still in its infancy, first became an independent art with Addison. Addison and his various colleagues set the first example of that kind of social essay which is still popular. Satire had been practised in the preceding century, and in the hands of Dryden had become a formidable political weapon; but the social satire of which Pope was, and remains, the chief master, began with the century, and may be said to have expired with it, in spite of the efforts of Byron and Gifford. De Foe, Richardson, Fielding, and Smollett developed the modern novel out of very crude rudiments; and two of the greatest men of the century, Swift and Johnson, may be best described as practical moralists in a vein peculiar to the time. . . . The rise of a class of comparatively educated and polished persons, large enough to form a public, and not so large as to degenerate into a mob, distinct from the old feudal nobility, and regarding the life of the nobles with a certain contempt as rustic and brutal, more refined again than that class of hangers-on to the Court, of merchants and shopkeepers stamped with the peculiarities of their business, which generated the drama of the Restoration, and, on another side, beginning to despise the pedants of colleges and cathedrals as useless and antiquated encumbrances, accounts for many of the most obvious phenomena of the time. After the long struggle of the end of the preceding century, the society called 'the Town' in the language of the essayists, definitely emerges, and is inclined to identify itself with the nation. Poets, novelists, essayists, and satirists consult its tastes, and consider Temple Bar as the centre of the universe. What are the characteristics in its intellectual relations of the literature which emerges?

Three tendencies, strongly marked in all this crowd of writers, may be noticed as sufficiently indicative of the contemporary modes of thought. The first is a speculative, the second an ethical, and the third an aesthetic tendency. They are intimately connected. . . . The first half of the century was a period of vehement discussion; the deists and their antagonists fought over questions of the deepest importance with an energy proportional to the interests at stake. But there is a tendency, strongly marked on both sides, which determines the limits of the controversy. Neither party wishes really to push matters to an extremity. The deists attack priestcraft with fierce hostility; but they do not wish to destroy theology. The priest once deprived of his exaggerated pretensions may be allowed to remain as a useful member of society, and the natural religion which is desired is to be but a modified and emasculated version of the old creed. The orthodox, on the other hand, have no inclination to attack the vital principles of their opponents. They admit the duty of free thought; they claim to be thoroughgoing rationalists, and they only desire to embody the teaching of reason in the old formula. Both sides tacitly evade certain crucial questions. Even Butler refrains from searching into the fundamental difficulty; and Hume alone dares to suggest the logical answer. This kind of intellectual indolence is revealed in the sphere of direct controversy by a general superficiality and readiness to put up with flimsy theories; and it is naturally connected with the cardinal fact that, in attacking the religious theory of the time, the deists were not animated, like their French successors, by any decided discontent with the social order. They were not seriously persecuted, and did not wish to inflict serious injury. To keep the clergy well under the heel of parliamentary authority would describe the ultimate limit of their political aspirations, as in a philosophical sense they wished generally to preserve theology, whilst getting rid of the supernatural. In literature the same tendency is marked by a stronger feeling. The strongest intellects of the day perceived, or felt instinctively, that the tendency of the deist speculations was to *undermine the whole social order,* and to undermine it in the interests of a flimsy creed. To any man with a strong sense of the *practical needs of the time,* the deists appeared to be superficial theorists who were gratifying their vanity *at the expense of the most important institutions.* They were insisting upon asking questions *which had better not be asked,* and to which they were prepared with no satisfactory answer. To stir the very foundations of society, a man must be prompted either by a passionate love of speculation, or by a distinct prospect of some fruitful result, or by a conviction of the absolute necessity of social reconstruction. Neither of the last two elements was present; and the pure love of enquiry is at all times the rarest of endowments. *The hidden fear of dangerous consequences, which kept the deists to half-truths, led men of strong, but not really speculative, intellects to object to speculation altogether.*

This sentiment is curiously expressed in the ablest writing of the time, down to the very end of the century, when it takes a rather different colouring. Why can't you let things alone? is the unanimous cry of the intellectual leaders. The old theology is effete; but a creed which is effete (an unlucky but a plausible doctrine!) is harmless. The deists are almost uniformly mentioned with a mixture of contempt and dislike. Addison dislikes them as much as he can dislike any one. Swift dislikes them, also, as much as he can dislike any one; and the phrase in his case represents, perhaps, the greatest intensity of aversion of which the human soul is capable. With the whole body of essayists,

from Steele downwards, a deist is a futile coxcomb, to be ridiculed like the 'virtuoso' and the fine gentleman. The novelists are equally clear. De Foe makes Robinson Crusoe preach sermons fit for a dissenting pulpit. Richardson has so great a contempt for infidels that he will not contemplate the possibility that even a Lovelace should disbelieve in a future state of rewards and punishments. Fielding, laughing over his beer and pipe at Richardson's namby-pamby sentiment, still has as hearty a contempt for a deist as for a methodist. Johnson turns the roughest side of his contempt to any one suspected of scepticism, and calls Adam Smith a 'son of a bitch.' When Burke endeavours to blast the deists with his fiery rhetoric at the end of the century, it is only that the wrath which had been smouldering whilst the Deism was comparatively masked bursts into flame as soon as the concealment vanishes. The common sense of the country was entirely on the side of Revelation as against Deism, and the ablest writers were but the mouthpiece of the common sense. The result, however, of this sentiment was not to give an actively orthodox tone to the writing of the time; for theology was for the most part almost as deistical as the deists.

A hatred for enthusiasm was as strongly impressed upon the whole character of contemporary thought as a hatred of scepticism. And thus the literary expression of the feeling is rather a dislike to all speculation than a dislike to a particular school of speculatists. The whole subject was dangerous, and should be avoided by reasonable men. A good common-sense religion should be taken for granted, and no questions asked. If the philosophy of the time was unfitted for poetry, it was, for the same reason, unfitted to stimulate the emotions, and therefore for practical life. With Shakespeare, or Sir Thomas Browne, or Jeremy Taylor, or Milton, man is contemplated in his relations to the universe; he is in presence of eternity and infinity; life is a brief dream; we are ephemeral actors in a vast drama; heaven and hell are behind the veil of phenomena; at every step our friends vanish into the vast abyss of ever-present mystery. To all such thoughts the writers of the eighteenth century seemed to close their eyes as absolutely as possible. They do not, like Sir Thomas Browne, delight to lose themselves in an Oh! Altitudo! or to snatch a solemn joy from the giddiness which follows a steady gaze into the infinite. The greatest men amongst them, a Swift or a Johnson, have indeed a sense—perhaps a really stronger sense than Browne or Taylor—of the pettiness of our lives and the narrow limits of our knowledge. No great man could ever be without it. But the awe of the infinite and the unseen does not induce them to brood over the mysterious, and find utterance for bewildered musings on the inscrutable enigma.

It is felt only in a certain habitual sadness which clouds their whole tone of thought. They turn their backs upon the infinite and abandon the effort at a solution. Their eyes are fixed upon the world around them, and they regard as foolish and presumptuous any one who dares to contemplate the great darkness. The expression of this sentiment in literature is a marked disposition to turn aside from pure speculation, combined with a deep interest in social and moral laws. The absence of any deeper speculative ground makes the immediate practical questions of life all the more interesting. We know not what we are, nor whither we are going, nor whence we come; but we can, by the help of common sense, discover a sufficient share of moral maxims for our guidance in life, and we can analyse human passions, and discover what are the moving forces of society, without going back to first principles. Knowledge of human nature, as it actually presented itself in the shifting scene before them, and a vivid appreciation of the importance of the moral law, are the staple of the best literature of the time. As ethical speculation was prominent in the philosophy, the enforcement of ethical principles is the task of those who were inclined to despise philosophy. When a creed is dying, the importance of preserving the moral law naturally becomes a pressing consideration with all strong natures. (pp. 366-71)

The moralising tendency thus directly expressed by poets and preachers, both lay and professional, may be traced through many other forms. The essayists preach a series of sermons, varying indefinitely in grace and power, upon every conceivable text, from the shortness of life to the extravagant size of feminine petticoats. The same material, treated in verse, and mixed with more or less poetical feeling, supplies the satires of Swift, Pope, Johnson, Young, Churchill, Mason, Cowper, and their innumerable imitators and rivals. The novelists have a similar didactic tendency. De Foe preaches incessantly; Richardson is ostentatiously and supereminently a moralist; Fielding, though his morality is of a rather different type, moralises as persistently as any contemporary preacher, and a good deal more forcibly. The theatre which had excited the indignation of Collier was partly occupied by the moralists, and sentimental comedies took the place of the cynical dramas of the Restoration. The morality, whether inculcated by direct precepts, or pompous allegory, or fictitious narrative, is much of the same stamp. Everywhere it expresses the remarks upon human life and conduct made by shrewd and sensible men, living in a society defaced by much coarseness and corruption, and stirred by no very strong passions or deep speculations; but yet comfortable, growing in wealth and mechanical knowledge, and profoundly impressed with the importance of the domestic virtues. (pp. 376-77)

The aesthetic tendency of the time is precisely in harmony with this moral sentiment. I have endeavoured to show how the poetry, in which the deepest thoughts of human beings should be reflected, had become merely argumentative, and had then died of inanition. A new form of art was developed which expressed more easily and fully the prevalent emotions of the time. The English novel, as the word is now understood, begins with De Foe. Though, like all other products of mind or body, it was developed out of previously existing material, and is related to the great family of stories with which men have amused themselves in all ages, it is, perhaps, as nearly an original creation as anything can be. The legends of saints which amused the Middle Ages, or the chivalrous romances which were popular throughout the seventeenth century, had become too unreal to amuse living human beings. De Foe made the discovery that a history might be equally interesting if the recorded events had never happened; and Richardson that a series of letters did not require real correspondents. Fielding, though his first novel was a parody of Richardson, was, no doubt, influenced, like Smollett, by the example of Le Sage, and, therefore, indirectly by the Spanish stories from which Le Sage drew his inspiration.

But, whatever the origin, the instinct gratified by the nov-

els, and the conditions of the time, sufficiently determined the form. The world of legend and of ideal grandeur had grown dim. A new social form was developing itself. What could men do more natural than talk about themselves? And thus, since the days of De Foe, we have derived unceasing amusement from looking into the mirrors which reflect, with more or less fidelity, the incidents and manners of our daily life. As the essayists were never tired of discussing the social phenomena of the time, from the most trifling to the most serious, the novelists were never tired of portraying the same phenomena, coloured by some favourite moral or sentiment. From Sir Roger de Coverley and Robinson Crusoe down to the appearance of a new type in Waverley, we have a vast family of fictitious characters, who are the most faithful reflection of the originals. Indeed, as the novel is substantially the embodiment of the remarks made by the ablest observers upon their contemporaries, we may in some sense admit Fielding's claim to be a writer of history more faithful than the elaborate fictions generally known under that name. No enchanted light of old romance colours or distorts his fictions; we do not feel that his characters are puppets in the hands of an irresistible destiny, or constituent atoms of a vast organism slowly developing under the action of gigantic forces; there is no tender regret for past forms of society or passionate aspirations for the future. But for insight into the motives of his contemporaries; for a power of seeing things as they are; for sympathy with homely virtues; and contempt for shams and hypocrites, Fielding is as superior to some later writers of equal imaginative force as they are superior to him in width of sympathy and delicacy of perception. His art is thus the most faithful representative of his age; he gives its coarseness and its brutalities, and sometimes with too little consciousness of their evils, though no one ever satirised more powerfully the worst abuses of the time. But he also represents the strong healthy common sense and stubborn honesty of the sound English nature, with a certain massive power of grouping and colouring which is peculiar to himself.

In Fielding and his beloved Hogarth we have the 'prosai-comi-epos'—I use Fielding's phrase—of the middle class of the time. Richardson, though a greater artist, is far inferior in sheer intellectual vigour; and Smollett is comparatively but a caricaturist. Fielding announced that his object is to give a faithful picture of human nature. Human nature includes many faculties which had an imperfect play under the conditions of the time; there were dark sides to it, of which, with all his insight, he had but little experience; and heroic impulses, which he was too much inclined to treat as follies. But the more solid constituents of that queer compound, as they presented themselves under the conditions of the time, were never more clearly revealed to any observer. A complete criticism of the English artistic literature of the eighteenth century would place Fielding at the centre, and measure the completeness of other representatives pretty much as they recede from an approach to his work. Others, as Addison and Goldsmith, may show finer qualities of workmanship and more delicate sentiment; but Fielding, more than any one, gives the essential—the very form and pressure of the time. (pp. 378-80)

Sir Leslie Stephen, "Characteristics: General Literature," in his History of English

Thought in the Eighteenth Century, Vol. II, *third edition, John Murray, 1927, pp. 366-80.*

C. E. Vaughan

[*Vaughan was a turn-of-the-century English educator and literary critic and editor. In the following excerpt from a work originally published in* The Cambridge History of English Literature *(1913), he focuses upon significant developments in the evolution of the novel, particularly the "novel of sensibility," during the mid-eighteenth century, highlighting the works of Laurence Sterne, Henry Mackenzie, Henry Brooke, and Fanny Burney.*]

The subject of this [essay] is, virtually, the history of the English novel from 1760 to 1780, a crucial period in the earlier stages of its growth. And the chief questions to be asked are: what are the new elements which these years added to the novel? how far has each of them proved of lasting value? and what is the specific genius of the two or three writers who stand out above the rest?

The answer to the first of these questions may be given, in summary form, at once. In the hands of Sterne and a group of writers who, though it may be without sufficient reason, are commonly treated as disciples of Sterne, sentiment began to count for more than had hitherto been held allowable. As a natural consequence, the individuality of these writers impressed itself more and more unreservedly upon a theme which, in the days of Defoe and even Richardson, had been treated mainly from without. Sterne, it need hardly be said, is undisputed master in this way of writing; and here, so far, at least, as his own century is concerned, he stands absolutely alone. Others, such as Brooke and Mackenzie, may use the novel as a pulpit for preaching their own creed or advancing their own schemes of reform. But their relation to Sterne, on this head, is, manifestly, of the slightest, and the effect produced is utterly different. A little more of personality, a great deal more of emotion and sentiment, may come into their work than any novelist before Sterne would have thought possible. But that is all. That is the one link which binds them to him, the one tangible mark which he left upon the novel of his generation.

Sterne is the sole novelist of first-rate importance in the period under review; for even Fanny Burney, inventive and sparkling though she is, can hardly lay claim to that description. And, thanks to his very originality, he stands aloof from the main stream of contemporary fiction. Apart from him, the writers of the time fall, roughly, into three groups: the novelists of 'sentiment and reflection,' who, though far enough from Sterne, are yet nearer to him than any of the others; the novelists of home life, who, in the main, and with marked innovations of their own, follow the chief lines laid down by Richardson in the preceding generation; and, finally, the novelists of a more distinctly romantic bent, Horace Walpole and Clara Reeve, who drew their theme from the medieval past, and supported the interest by an appeal to the sense of mystery and terror—Horace Walpole, no doubt, the more defiantly of the two and, perhaps, with less seriousness than has sometimes been imputed to him. It should be added that the romantic writers are of far less importance for their own sake than for that of the writers who followed during

the next fifty years, and of whom, in some measure, they may be regarded as precursors. (pp. 46-7)

Few writers have thrown down so many challenges as Sterne; and, if to win disciples be the test of success, few have paid so heavily for their hardihood. He revolutionised the whole scope and purpose of the novel; but, in his own country, at any rate, years passed before advantage was taken of the liberty he asserted. He opened new and fruitful fields of humour; and one of the greatest of his successors has denied him the name of humourist. He created a style more subtle and flexible than any had found before him; and all that Goldsmith could see in it was a tissue of tricks and affectations. But, if the men of letters hesitated, the public had no doubt. The success of *Tristram Shandy* swept everything before it. And here, as is often the case, the popular verdict has worn better than the craftsman's or the critic's.

Sterne was nothing if not an innovator. And in no innovation was he more daring than in that which widened the scope and loosened the structure of the novel. This was the first of his services to his brethren of the craft. It is, perhaps, the only one which has left a deep mark upon the subsequent history of a form which, when he wrote, was still in the early stages of its growth.

When *Tristram Shandy* began to appear (1760), there was real danger that the English novel would remain little more than a mirror of contemporary life: a reproduction, often photographically accurate, of the social conditions of the time. Defoe, Fielding, Smollett, each in his own way and according to the measure of his genius, had yielded to the impulse; Richardson alone, by striking into tragedy, had partially escaped. Sterne defiantly throws himself athwart the tradition of the elders. He delivers one blow after another at the fashion they had set. Tale of manners, picaresque adventure, types of contemporary humanity, plot itself, all go by the board. His very title is a resounding challenge to all accepted notions of what the novelist should attempt. And even the title falls very far short of what the novel actually provides. The *Life and Opinions* of the hero is the subject we are bidden to expect. The opinions, the character, the caprices of his father, his uncle, his uncle's servant—above all, of the author himself—is what we actually find. In other words, the novel has ceased to be a mirror of life and manners. It has ceased to be what Johnson, himself a heretic against his own theory, thought it must naturally be, 'a smooth tale, mostly of love.' It has become a channel for the outpouring of the author's own personality and idiosyncrasy; a stage from which, under the thinnest of disguises or with no disguise at all, he lays bare the workings of his heart, his intellect, his most fleeting imaginations, before any audience he can gather round him. If we compare *Tristram* with *Tom Jones,* with *Roderick Random,* with *Moll Flanders*—if we compare it even with *Pamela* or *Clarissa*—we shall see that the wheel has come full circle. Every known landmark has been torn up. And, in asserting his own liberty, Sterne, little as he may have cared about it, has won unbounded liberty for all novelists who might follow. Whatever innovations the future might have in store, it was hardly possible that they should go beyond the freedom triumphantly vindicated by Sterne. For whatever purposes future writers might wish to use the novel, it was hardly conceivable that they would not be covered by the principle which he had victoriously, though, it may be, unconsciously, laid down. The purpose for which Sterne used the novel was to give free utterance to his own way of looking at life, his own moral and intellectual individuality. So much granted, it was impossible to quarrel with those who used it for a more limited purpose; for embodying in a narrative form the passions stirred by any burning problem of the day; for giving utterance to their own views on any specific question, political, social or religious. The perils of such a task might be great. They could hardly, however, be greater, they would almost certainly be less great, than those which Sterne had already faced and conquered. And, with the success of *Tristram* before him, no critic could maintain that, given sufficient genius, the venture was impossible. The challenge of Sterne was wide enough to include all the other challenges that have followed. *The Fool of Quality, Nature and Art, Oliver Twist, Wilhelm Meister, Les Misérables*—all are covered by the unformulated formula of *Tristram*.

Not, of course, that the whole credit of the widening process should be given to Sterne. *Rasselas* in England, if *Rasselas* is, indeed, to be counted as a novel, much more *Candide* in France, had already pointed the way in the same direction. Both appeared in the year 1759, before the publication of the first volume of *Tristram*. Neither of them, however, attempts more than a fragment of the task which Sterne attempted and performed. In neither case does the author stake his whole personality upon the throw; he lets his mind work, or play, round a single question, or group of questions, and that is all. It was an easier venture, a smaller venture and one far less rich in promise, than that which, a few weeks later, launched the Shandy family upon their voyage round the world.

It is, then, as liberator that Sterne comes before us in the first instance. And it is as liberator that he has left his chief, perhaps his only enduring, mark upon the subsequent history of the novel. His other great qualities are almost purely personal to himself. His very originality has caused him to count for less, as a moulding influence, than many a writer not to be compared with him in genius.

And, first, his humour. The elements which go to make up this are strangely various and, for the most part, as strangely baffling and elusive. His handling of character is humorous to the very core. It is so with the figures that merely flit across the stage: Susannah and the scullion, Obadiah and Dr Slop, Eugenius and Yorick. It is so a hundred times more with those constantly before the footlights: above all, the undying trio, Walter Shandy, my uncle Toby and corporal Trim. (pp. 47-50)

It is just here, however, that Goethe found not only the most characteristic, but, also, the most helpful, quality of Sterne's genius—that from which there is most to be learned for the practical conduct of our lives. The very detachment from all that is commonly reckoned to belong to the serious interests of life, the readiness to escape from that for which other men are striving and fighting, to withdraw into the citadel of our bare, naked self and let the world go its way, to count all for nought, so long as our own ideal is kept intact, had, for him, a moral worth, a 'liberating' value, which it was hard to overrate. That it was the whole truth, Goethe was the last man to suppose. *Wilhelm Meister* is there to protest against so impossible a charge. But, as a half-truth, and one which the world

seems for ever bent on denying, he held, and he was right in holding, that it was beyond price. He recognised, and he was right in recognising, that, of all men who ever wrote, Sterne was the most firmly possessed of it himself, and the most able, by the magic of his art, to awaken the sense of it in others. 'Shandyism,' he says, in the words of Sterne himself, 'is the incapacity for fixing the mind on a serious object for two minutes together.' And Sterne himself he defines as 'a free spirit,' 'a model in nothing, in everything an awakener and suggester.'

So much as to Sterne's humour in the creation of character. This, however, is anything but the only channel through which his humour finds an outlet. He is rich in the humour of situation; rich, also, in that which gathers round certain instincts of man's nature. On the former, there is no need to enlarge: the less so, as it is often inseparably interwoven with the humour of character, which has already been sufficiently discussed. If we consider such scenes as that of Trim's kitchen discourse on mortality, or the collapse of Mr Shandy the elder upon his bed, or, above all, the curse of Ernulphus and all that leads up to it, we shall see at once the infinite art with which Sterne arranges his limelights and the astounding effects which he makes them produce. To say, as Goldsmith came near to saying, that Sterne's humour depends upon a judicious use of dashes and stars, upon the insertion of marbled sheets and other mechanical or pert devices, is not even a parody of the truth. As a criticism, it is incredibly beside the mark; only less so than Thackeray's—'The man is not a great humourist; he is a great jester.' (pp. 52-3)

The sentimentalism of Sterne goes much deeper and, in its more extreme forms, is, perhaps, less capable of defence. Here, again, no doubt, we are mainly, though, in this case, not solely, concerned with the actual effect stamped by the artist's hand upon our imagination. We have little—and, in that little, we have nothing *directly*—to do with the havoc which sentiment, as he nursed it, may have wrought with his personal conduct and his practical outlook on life. The truth is that sentiment so highly wrought—still more, sentiment so deliberately cultivated and laid out with such a manifest eye to effect—can hardly fail to rouse the suspicion of the reader. When the limelights are manipulated with design so palpable as in the death of Le Fevre or the story of the dead ass, the author goes far to defeat his own purpose. The spontaneity which is the first charm of sentiment is immediately seen to be wanting, and the effect of the whole effort is largely destroyed. More than that. We instinctively feel that, with the author himself, as a man, all can hardly be well. We are driven to cast doubts on his sincerity; and, when we look to his life, we more than half expect our doubts to be confirmed. Such suspicions inevitably react upon the imaginative pleasure which the picture itself would otherwise have given. There is an air of unreality, if not of imposture, about the whole business which, with the best will in the world, it is impossible wholly to put by.

Yet, the same command of effect, which, in matters of sentiment, is apt to prove perilous, is, elsewhere, brought into play with the happiest results. Give him a situation, a thought which appeals strongly either to his imagination or to his humanitarian instincts—for Sterne also, in his own curious way, is among the prophets—and no man knows so well how to lead up to it; how to make the most of it; how, by cunning arrangement of light and shade and drapery, to show it off to the best possible advantage. As stage-manager, as master of effective setting, he is without equal, we may almost say without rival, among novelists. And there are moments when such mastery is pure gain. Take the curse of Ernulphus, take Trim's reading of the sermon on conscience, take his oration upon death; and this will hardly be denied. There are, no doubt, other moments—those of sentimentality or indecency—when, from the nature of the theme, approval is not likely to be so unreserved. Yet, even here, we cannot but admire the cunning of the craftsman, deliberate yet light-handed, deeply calculated yet full of sparkle, nimbleness and humour.

From Sterne to his alleged disciples the descent is abrupt. Two only of these call for notice in this sketch: Mackenzie and Brooke.

Henry Mackenzie (1745—1831) passed a long and peaceful life at Edinburgh, where he held the post of attorney for the Crown, and subsequently of comptroller of the taxes, for Scotland. After the publication of *The Man of Feeling* (1771, the year of Scott's birth) he was recognised as the literary leader of Edinburgh society, and he may be said to have held that post by courtesy until his death, a year before that of Scott. In addition to his three novels, he wrote a successful play (*The Prince of Tunis,* 1773) and edited two successive periodicals, *The Mirror* (1779—80) and *The Lounger* (1785—7). He was also chairman of the committee which reported on Macpherson's *Ossian* (1805).

He is, of course, best known by his earliest work, *The Man of Feeling* (1771). At the time, this won for him a name which still survives as a tradition, but which is hardly justified by the intrinsic merits of the book, either in conception or in execution. It is, in fact, mainly remarkable as a record of the influences which, at this period, were battling for the mastery of the novel.

The form of it, which, at first sight, might be taken for picaresque, is, in reality, a reversion to a yet more primitive type of structure: that familiar to us from the Coverly papers. And it may be noted that *The Life of John Buncle, Esq.,* by Thomas Amory, the first part of which appeared some fifteen years earlier (1756), shows, with much better justification for itself, something of the same peculiarity. Mackenzie, however, does not, like Amory, write what professes to be an autobiography. He has not, therefore, the excuse of recording what give themselves out for 'actual facts.' On the contrary, he sets about to write a novel with a full-fledged hero to its credit. . . . It is manifest that the episodes are chosen, not in the least for the sake of the excitement they may offer, but solely to make call upon the virtuous, if ill-regulated, 'feelings,' and, still more, upon the tears, of the hero. And, neither in the spirit of the story, nor in its incidents, is there the smallest trace of humour. These things alone are enough to show that *The Man of Feeling* owes little or nothing to Fielding or Smollett; but that in form, if in nothing else, it casts back to Addison and the essayists. Some of the elements which, in the interval, the picaresque writers had employed for their own ends, may, doubtless, be fairly recognised as present. But they are bent to uses alien, indeed hostile, to those for which they were originally devised. They are no longer there for their own sake, or for the humour which

they offer. The sole purpose they serve is to furnish the stage on which the 'sentimental education' of the hero—and, through him, of the reader—is carried out.

It is in working the mine of sentiment that Mackenzie comes as near as he ever comes to Sterne. His methods and aims are utterly different. With him, as with the great humourist, the raw material is sentiment. But how raw the material remains in Mackenzie's hands! What a wide difference between his clumsy insistence and the light, airy touch of Sterne! Define Mackenzie as sentimentalist or sentimental moralist, and you have told almost the whole truth about him. Describe Sterne by the same terms, and almost everything remains unsaid. A slenderer thread of affiliation could not easily be conceived.

The debt of Mackenzie to Rousseau is, undeniably, more substantial. It is, however, a debt purely of sentiment, of the humanitarian feelings which Rousseau did more than any man to spread abroad through Europe. From the nature of the case, these feelings could not fail to make their way sooner, or later, into the novel. They had done so already in Sterne, and, by anticipation, even in Richardson; nor can it have been an accident that, in the preface to *The Man of Feeling,* Mackenzie should have placed himself behind the shield of Richardson and Rousseau; though he certainly goes far to destroy the force of the appeal by tacking on the name of Marmontel. For, in spite of their title, the *Contes Moraux* of that writer belong to a wholly different order. (pp. 54-7)

With Brooke, we return once more, in however loose a sense, to what may be called the sphere of influence of Sterne; and, like Mackenzie, he, too, has sat at the feet of Rousseau. To many readers, perhaps to most, the spirit of Brooke will seem much healthier, as his outlook is undoubtedly much wider, than that of Mackenzie. He writes in a far breezier spirit; and, as the picaresque model is more unreservedly adopted, there is far more variety in his incidents and his settings. The extreme looseness of structure which inevitably results from this is, no doubt, something of a drawback; but it is amply redeemed by the vivacity of the characters, and by the vividness of the ever-changing scenes through which they are led. It is redeemed, also, by the unfailing zest with which the author throws himself into the varying fortunes of his hero—whose pugnacity is hardly less conspicuous than his overflowing benevolence—and of the motley crew among whom his lot is cast. Moreover, full of 'feeling' as the book is, it is of the kind which leads as often to laughter as to tears. After a course of Mackenzie, we cannot but be grateful for this relief.

Henry Brooke (1703?—83) was born in Ireland and educated at Trinity college, Dublin; he lived in Dublin for the greater part of his life. In addition to his work in the novel, drama and poetry, he took some part in the political controversies of his time; issuing a warning against the Jacobite tendencies of the Irish catholics in the panic of 1745 (*The Farmer's Letters*), and subsequently pleading for a mitigation of the penal laws (1761). He was deeply affected by the religious movements of his day, that of the methodists as well as that of the mystics; a fact which did much to popularise his most important work, *The Fool of Quality.*

For our purposes, two things in particular deserve notice

in the work of Brooke. In the first place, *The Fool of Quality* (1766) is more deeply stamped with the seal of Rousseau—the Rousseau of the second *Discourse* and of *Émile*—than is any other book of the period. The contempt which Rousseau felt for the conventions of society, his 'inextinguishable hatred of oppression' in high places, his faith in the virtues of the poor and simple, his burning desire to see human life ordered upon a more natural basis—all this is vividly reflected upon every page of *The Fool of Quality*. It is reflected in the various discourses, whether between the personages of the story or between the author and an imaginary friend (of the candid sort), which are quaintly scattered throughout the book: discourses on education, heroism, debtors' prisons, woman's rights, matter and spirit, the legislation of Lycurgus, the social contract, the constitution of England—on everything that happened to captivate the quick wit of the author. Clearly, Brooke had grasped far more of what Rousseau came to teach the world, and had felt it far more intensely, than Mackenzie. Before we can find anything approaching to this keenness of feeling, this revolt against the wrongs of the social system, we have to go forward to the years immediately succeeding the outbreak of the French revolution; in particular to the years from 1790 to 1797—the years of Paine and Godwin, of Coleridge's 'penny trumpet of sedition'; or, in the field of the novel, the years of *Caleb Williams,* of *Nature and Art,* of *Hermsprong, or Man as he is not.* There, no doubt, the cry of revolt was raised more defiantly. For, there, speculation was reinforced by practical example; and the ideas of Rousseau were flashed back, magnified a hundredfold by the deeds of the national assembly, the convention and the reign of terror. And this contrast between the first and the second harvest of Rousseau's influence is not the least interesting thing in the story of the eighteenth century novel.

The second point which calls for remark is connected with the mystical side of Brooke's character, of which notice has been taken in an earlier chapter. Through the mystics, it will be remembered, Brooke was brought into touch with John Wesley and the methodists. It is, in fact, the methodistical, rather than the mystical, strain which comes to the surface in *The Fool of Quality*—though, in the discourse on matter and spirit, mentioned above, the author boldly declares, 'I know not that there is any such thing in nature as matter.' Such defiances, however, are rare, and, in general, the appeal of Brooke is of a less esoteric kind. He dwells much on conversion; and, as revised by Wesley, the book was long a favourite with methodists. The importance of this is to remind us of the bond which unites the literary with the religious revival of the eighteenth century. It is, of course, only in a small number of writers—Collins, Smart, Cowper, for instance—that the two strands are visibly interwoven. But it is probable that the emotional appeal of the religious revival was an awakening force to many writers, whether poets or novelists, who, in the outward ordering of their lives, were indifferent, or even hostile, to the 'enthusiasm' either of the methodist or of the evangelical. And it is certain that, from the general change of temper of which the religious revival was at once the cause and the symptom, both poet and novelist found the hearts of men more ready to receive their creations than would have been possible at any earlier period of the century. The same thing holds good as to the corresponding movement in the literature of Germany and, to a less degree, as to that in the literature of France.

If the pietists had not prepared the ground, Goethe, who himself owed not a little to intercourse with the 'beautiful soul'—the Moravian sister—would have found it much harder to win a hearing for his youthful poems and for *Werther*. If, in his earlier writings, Rousseau had not roughly challenged the speculative creed of 'the enlightenment,' *La Nouvelle Héloïse* and the Rêveries would probably have been written in a very different spirit; conceivably they might never have been written at all. (pp. 58-60)

From the novel of sentiment to that of terror, or of the far past, is a startling transition. And the harvest in this field is so poor that our account of it may be brief.

The fountainhead of both streams of romance is to be found in *The Castle of Otranto,* which was struck off at feverheat by Walpole in the summer of 1764 and published at the end of the year, or the beginning of the next. The execution is weak in the extreme. The 'history' is one vast anachronism, and the portents are absurd. Yet, in spite of these glaring defects, of which it is hard to suppose that the author was not in some degree aware, an entirely new turn is here given to the novel, and elements are brought into it which, at a later time and in hands more skilful, were to change it out of all knowledge. The book, as Walpole himself tells us, was written in conscious reaction against the domesticities and the sentiment of Richardson. It was a deliberate attempt to divert fiction from the channel along which it had hitherto flowed; to transport it from the sphere of close observation to that of free invention; to substitute for the interest of the present that of the past, the world of experience by that of the mysterious and the supernatural. The performance is bungling; but the design is in a high degree original and fruitful. It was, in fact, so original that, as sometimes happens in such cases, Walpole himself took fright at his own boldness. He is at the pains to explain that, all appearances to the contrary, his heart is still half with the novel of every-day life. 'It was not so much my intention to recall the glories of ancient romance as to blend the wonderful of old stories with the natural of modern novels.' And he appeals, in proof of his sincerity, to Matilda's avowal of her passion for Theodore. We are not bound to take him at his word. He may, with more kindness, be regarded as a wholehearted rebel, who led the forlorn hope in a cause which, years after, had its day of triumph. It is that which makes *The Castle of Otranto* a marked book—even more marked perhaps for its ultimate bearing on foreign literature than on our own.

Clara Reeve, to whom we now pass, led an entirely uneventful life (1729—1807), marked only by the publication of various tales, of which *The Old English Baron* has alone survived, and by her friendship with Mrs Brigden, Richardson's daughter, who revised that work in its earlier shape, *The Champion of Virtue.*

If there is some doubt about the intentions of Walpole, about those of Clara Reeve, his successor and disciple, there is none whatever. *The Old English Baron* (1777)—it had been published earlier in the same year as *The Champion of Virtue, a Gothic Tale*—is undeniably what *The Castle of Otranto* professes to be, 'an attempt to unite the merits and graces of the ancient Romance and of the modern Novel.' There is 'a sufficient degree of the marvellous,' in the shape of a ghost, 'to excite attention; enough of the manners of real life,' or what passes for such, 'to give an air of probability; and enough of the pathetic'—in the form of a love-story, with an interesting peasant, who turns out to be son and heir of the ghost (a murdered baron), for hero—'to engage the heart in its behalf.' It is quite true that the ingredients of *Otranto,* including the irresistible young peasant, were much the same. But they were differently mixed. In Walpole's book, the chief appeal was to 'terror' and to the romantic past. In *The Old English Baron,* these have sunk into little more than trimmings. The main stress on the part of the author lies upon a tale of righteous vengeance and of love. About the use of the marvellous, she is manifestly nervous. She reduces it, therefore, to the presence of an ordinary ghost, who contents himself with groaning beneath the floor, by way of instituting proceedings against his murderer. Even the medieval is a source of some alarm. And, considering what she makes of it, we can hardly be surprised. Walpole, absurd as novelist of the crusades—his scene is laid with delightful vagueness during the century and a half which covered them—at least contrives to give some faint flavour of the later middle ages to his characters and their setting. Clara Reeve can boast of no such success. A trial by combat, her supreme effort in this direction, is conducted with all the flourishes of forensic etiquette. The manners of the eighteenth century are transplanted straight into the fifteenth. The scene may be labelled 'A Feudal Castle'; in reality, it is the cedar parlour of Miss Byron and Sir Charles. The Gothic element and the element of terror being thus disposed of, nothing is left but that which 'engages the heart on its behalf': the eternal theme of 'virtue rewarded,' of injured innocence triumphant over treachery and crime. In the compromise which the authoress strove to effect, the 'modern Novel' carries off all the honours; the 'ancient Romance' is represented by little beyond garnish and appurtenance.

How far can it be said that the works comprised in the above group did anything to prepare the way for the historical and romantic novel, as it was subsequently shaped by Scott? The answer is: only in the vaguest and most rudimentary sense. The novel of terror—if by that we understand the terror which springs from the marvellous and supernatural—has never taken kindly to English soil. And it is manifest that Scott fought shy of the marvellous as an element of prose fiction. In appealing to terror, accordingly, neither Walpole nor Clara Reeve did much more than enter a claim that the borders of the novel might without treason be enlarged; that the novel was not bound down by the charter of its being to the presentation of current life in its most obvious aspects—of buying and selling, of marrying and giving in marriage. That, if judged by the permanent results, was all; but it was enough. The appeal to history told in the same direction; but it was far more fruitful of results. Walpole, it is true, did not make much of it; Clara Reeve still less. But they pointed the way which, with a thousand modifications suggested by his genius, Scott was triumphantly to follow. And the very defects of *The Old English Baron* may have aided him in the discovery, so often missed by his successors, that, in the historical novel, the history is of far less importance than the human interest and the romance. The earlier and greater *Waverleys,* in fact, can be called historical only by a stretch. It was not until Scott had worked for years upon the near past—a past which still made itself felt as a living force upon the present—that he plunged into the middle ages. Moreover, in spite of its stirring adventure, *Ivanhoe*

has always counted for less with the English reader than with those of Germany and France. (pp. 60-3)

With the novels of Fanny Burney we pass into another world. They stand far nearer to the novel as we know it than anything which had yet appeared. The picaresque scaffolding, the obtrusive moral, the deliberate sentiment—much more the marvellous and the medievalism—of the writers who had immediately gone before her are thrown to the winds. She sets herself to tell a plain story—enlivened, doubtless, with strange adventures, with characters still stranger—and that is all.

Yet in this very simplicity is contained a new and, as time has proved, a very fruitful conception of what the novel might achieve. Starting from the general plan laid down by Richardson, she limits, she adds, she modifies, until the result is something entirely different. The tragic element is the first to go. This, with other modifications, leaves her with a story of home life for the ground-work of her picture. And the introduction of a whole gallery of oddities, dogging the steps of the heroine at every turn, gives variety, zest and sparkle to what otherwise would have been a humdrum, and, perhaps, a slightly sentimental, tale. The novel of home life, it is not too much to say, is the creation of Fanny Burney. There is a great deal else, and a great deal more brilliant, in her creations. But it is this that makes them a landmark in the history of fiction. (pp. 63-4)

The first is a talent, not easily to be matched among English novelists, for telling a story; an unaffected delight in telling it, which wakens a like pleasure in the reader. The second is an amazing power—a power in which she is surpassed by Dickens only—of giving flesh and blood to caricature. 'My little charactermonger' was Johnson's pet name for her; and, in the sense just hinted at, she earned it ten times over. With infectious zest, she adds touch after touch of absurdity to her portrait, until the reader is fairly swept off his feet by the drollery of the figure she has conjured up. This particular talent is, no doubt, most conspicuous in her earliest two works, *Evelina* (1778) and *Cecilia* (1782). But it flashes out often enough in *Camilla* (1796) and, on occasion, even in *The Wanderer* (1814). In all this gallery of 'humourists' the most laughable is Mr Briggs, the ill-bred but not unkindly skinflint of *Cecilia.* But he is hard run by the Branghtons, still harder perhaps by Mr Smith, the 'gentleman *manqué,*' as Mrs Thrale called him, of *Evelina;* while Sir Hugh Tyrold and Dr Orkborne, the Admiral, Sir Jasper Herrington and Mr Tedman keep up the succession not quite unworthily, in the two later novels. But even to mention instances is to do injustice. For, after all, the most surprising thing is their unlimited abundance; the way in which they start up from every corner, from each rung of the social ladder, at the bidding of the author. For vulgarity, in particular, she has the eye of a lynx. Right and left, high or low, she unmasks it with unflagging delight, tearing off the countless disguises under which it lurks and holding it up, naked but not ashamed, to the laughter, and, sometimes, though not often, to the contempt of the reader. By the side of these lively beings, the figures of Smollett seem little better than stuffed birds in a museum. (pp. 64-5)

To the end Miss Burney remains what she was at the beginning: a keen observer, a great 'character-monger,' a supreme story-teller, the first writer to see that the ordinary embarrassments of a girl's life would bear to be taken for the main theme of a novel. 'To her we owe not only *Evelina, Cecilia* and *Camilla,* but also *Mansfield Park* and *The Absentee.*' When Macaulay ended his estimate of Miss Burney with these words, he said better than he knew. He was thinking of her as the first of a long line of woman novelists. He forgot that the innovation applied not only to her sex, but to her theme. (p. 66)

> *C. E. Vaughan, "Sterne and the Novel of His Times," in* The Cambridge History of English Literature: The Age of Johnson, Vol. X, *edited by Sir A. W. Ward and A. R. Waller, Cambridge at the University Press, 1964, pp. 46-66.*

CLUBMEN AND BLUESTOCKINGS

James Boswell

[*A Scottish diarist, biographer, and man of letters, Boswell is one of the most colorful and widely read figures in eighteenth-century English literature. He is esteemed for his inimitable conversational style and pictorial documentation of life in such works as* Journal of a Tour to the Hebrides *(1785) and* London Journal *(unpublished until 1950). Labelled the greatest of English biographers and best known for his* Life of Samuel Johnson *(1791), Boswell firmly established biography as a leading literary form through a conscious, pioneering attempt to recreate his subject by combining life history with anecdote, observation, dialogue, theme, and plot. In the following excerpt from the* Life, *he briefly recounts the founding of The Literary Club.*]

Soon after [Johnson's] return to London [in 1764], which was in February, was founded that CLUB which existed long without a name, but at Mr. Garrick's funeral became distinguished by the title of THE LITERARY CLUB. Sir Joshua Reynolds had the merit of being the first proposer of it, to which Johnson acceded; and the original members were, Sir Joshua Reynolds, Dr. Johnson, Mr. Edmund Burke, Dr. Nugent, Mr. Beauclerk, Mr. Langton, Dr. Goldsmith, Mr. Chamier, and Sir John Hawkins. They met at the Turk's Head, in Gerrard-street, Soho, one evening in every week, at seven, and generally continued their conversation till a pretty late hour. This club has been gradually increased to its present number, thirty-five. After about ten years, instead of supping weekly, it was resolved to dine together once a fortnight during the meeting of Parliament. Their original tavern having been converted into a private house, they moved first to Prince's in Sackville-street, then to Le Telier's in Dover-street, and now meet at Parsloe's, St. James's-street. Between the time of its formation, and the time at which this work is passing through the press, (June 1792,) the following persons, now dead, were members of it: Mr. Dunning, (afterwards Lord Ashburton,) Mr. Samuel Dyer, Mr. Garrick, Dr. Shipley Bishop of St. Asaph, Mr. Vesey, Mr. Thomas Warton, and Dr Adam Smith. The present members are, Mr. Burke, Mr. Langton, Lord Charlemont, Sir Robert Chambers, Dr. Percy Bishop of Dromore, Dr. Barnard Bishop of Killaloe, Dr. Marlay Bishop of Clonfert, Mr. Fox, Dr. George Fordyce, Sir William Scott, Sir Joseph Banks, Sir Charles Bunbury, Mr. Windham of Norfolk, Mr. Sheridan, Mr. Gibbon, Sir William Jones, Mr. Colman, Mr. Steevens, Dr. Burney, Dr. Joseph Warton, Mr. Malone, Lord Ossory, Lord Spencer, Lord Lucan, Lord Palmerston, Lord Eliot, Lord Macartney, Mr. Richard Burke, junior, Sir William Hamilton, Dr. Warren, Mr. Courtenay, Dr. Hinchliffe Bishop of Peterborough, the Duke of Leeds, Dr. Douglas Bishop of Salisbury, and the writer of this account.

Sir John Hawkins represents himself as a *"seceder"* from this society, and assigns as the reason of his *"withdrawing"* himself from it, that its late hours were inconsistent with his domestick arrangements. In this he is not accurate; for the fact was, that he one evening attacked Mr. Burke, in so rude a manner, that all the company testified their displeasure; and at their next meeting his reception was such, that he never came again.

He is equally inaccurate with respect to Mr. Garrick, of whom he says, "he trusted that the least intimation of a desire to come among us, would procure him a ready admission; but in this he was mistaken. Johnson consulted me upon it; and when I could find no objection to receiving him, exclaimed,—'He will disturb us by his buffoonery;'—and afterwards so managed matters, that he was never formally proposed, and, by consequence, never admitted."

In justice both to Mr. Garrick and Dr. Johnson, I think it necessary to rectify this mis-statement. The truth is, that not very long after the institution of our club, Sir Joshua Reynolds was speaking of it to Garrick. "I like it much, (said he,) I think I shall be of you." When Sir Joshua mentioned this to Dr. Johnson, he was much displeased with the actor's conceit. "*He'll be of us,* (said Johnson) how does he know we will *permit* him? the first Duke in England has no right to hold such language." However, when Garrick was regularly proposed some time afterwards, Johnson, though he had taken a momentary offence at his arrogance, warmly and kindly supported him, and he was accordingly elected, was a most agreeable member, and continued to attend our meetings to the time of his death.

Mrs. Piozzi has also given a similar misrepresentation of Johnson's treatment of Garrick in this particular, as if he had used these contemptuous expressions: if Garrick *does* apply, I'll black-ball him.—Surely, one ought to sit in a society like ours,

> Unelbow'd by a gamester, pimp, or player.

I am happy to be enabled by such unquestionable authority as that of Sir Joshua Reynolds, as well as from my own knowledge, to vindicate at once the heart of Johnson and the social merit of Garrick. (pp. 297-99)

> *James Boswell, in his* The Life of Samuel Johnson, *1811. Reprint by Everyman's Library, 1978, pp. 297-302.*

Charles Pigott

[*An ardent champion of the French Revolution, Pigott*

was an English author. Among his works is a reply to Edmund Burke's Reflections on the Revolution in France *(1790). In the following essay, he comments on the attributes of several members of the Bluestocking Club and includes his estimation of how it came to be known as such.*]

The Society of *blue stocking Fockies,* concerning which, it is incumbent on us to offer a few words, originated in a laudable resolution amongst certain *fine* ladies to establish an Aristocracy in the republic of letters.—"Oh! it was horrid that *low people, people of no fashion* should obtain public consideration by literary merit;" and therefore they aspired to a degree of monopoly, to become the arbiters of *all* works issuing from the press. Vanity, or rather a consciousness of the *just* deference due to their *rank* and *fortune,* encouraged them to hope that they should soon be able to pluck from plebeian brows the laurel and the bays.—In consequence of this powerful combination against the general efforts of genius and talents, great interest was made to be admitted members of so *august* and *enlightened* an association, by every species of *Lady Authors,* and their numerous train of humble dependents, from the accomplished Lady C-v-n, down to Mrs. Hannah M-re. A *good woman,* Mrs. Mont-gue (famous for her wealth, and annual dinner to the wretched chimney sweeper apprentices, as also for having *written a book,* in answer to Voltaire's criticisms on Shakespeare, unequal contest, a pigmy against a giant,) was a principal *ringleader* of this new *academy.* The meetings were to be held at her grand hotel in Portman Square, and it was there *wisely* decided, that her opinion, on all occasions, should be final and conclusive; nor is this respectful distinction to be wondered at, when we consider, that she had composed a work, which *some* persons had read, and which a *few* had praised.—The victory to be sure, was rather *partial,* because it evidently appeared from the lady's book, that Voltaire did not understand English, and that she herself was wholly ignorant of the French. Besides, she seemed so *unique,* so *liberal* in her annual banquet to the poor little *sweeps,* that all her decrees passed unanimously in the society. We, however, who examine the benevolencies of those who style themselves the Great, with an impartial eye, cannot discover any transcendant charity in a *public, ostentatious* expenditure of a few pounds *once a year,* out of an immense property, which bestows on the *Lady's dear self* every indulgence, and luxury *all the year round.* What a profanation of terms to call this charity; to bestow plenty one day, that famine may be more cruelly felt the next. These children of sorrow are trained to the hardest of all servitude, and yet perhaps, in every respect, they fare worse, if possible, than persons in any other condition of life. To behold these little victims of an arbitrary, unnatural Brute, regale themselves to-day, without procuring them the same consolation, or even a morsel of bread for to-morrow, must excite pain, rather than pleasure, in a truly *sensible,* compassionate heart.—They have an *equal* right from the God of all, and an *additional* right from their severe labour, to the comforts of society, and it is only the hardened deprivation, and cruelty of political institutions, that rob them of these comforts. Let us hear no more then, of Mrs. Mont-gue's public chimney sweeper *festival,* a substraction of five pounds, from an income of £8000 a year. It is provoking when one hears such language, an insult to reason, an outrage on humanity, and when we are told of a Lord, a Duke, or an *Esquire,* with

ten, twenty, forty thousand per annum, wasting more than half their estates on their hounds and their horses, their equipage, and their palaces; while on the other side, we are triumphantly told that these *grand seigneurs* bestow a few pecks of coals, and a few pounds of beef at *christmas,* on naked shivering villagers, the feeling heart recoils from the panegyric, and disdains the *virtue* of such *frozen charity.* But let us return to a more *agreeable* subject; the *dear ladies* under our more immediate consideration. How they came to *distinguish* themselves by the appellation of *blue stockings,* it would be hard to decide, as the term conveys rather a light and *lascivious* idea; gradually leading the fancy upwards to the garter, and so on, to perhaps an improper and alarming height. Now it is very well known, that the *fair* members of this *Lyceum,* are in general, chaste even to a fault; most of them preferring to let their charms be withered by time, than submit them to the *rude mercy* of that *odious monster man;* we must therefore imagine, that the name originated in some happy and sudden flash of wit, which fortunately found out a resemblance between things seemingly so unlike, as *genius* and *coloured stockings.*

Were we to enumerate all the members of this society, we should afford but little entertainment to our readers, for very few of them are known to the public by any literary excellence; yet we cannot pass over in silence, Mrs. Bull-r, a lady so extremely learned, as always to have a *Greek* book in her pocket; to the admiration of the ignorant, and wonder of the wife. Miss Hannah M-re deserves also to be celebrated for her religious zeal, and aristocratic ardour, a *downright* Bishop H-rsl-y in petticoats, and who is not only a *poetess;* but likewise a *patroness,* her *original* tragedy, being a proof of the one, and Anne Yearsley, *the muse of milk,* an evidence of the other. In truth, *Miss* Hannah had long been in search of a *genius* in low life, to whom, by affording protection, she might raise her own reputation, in a display of superior taste and discernment. Her first *genius* however, whom she found starving under a hay-stack, did not answer the purpose, so she was immediately restored to her original station; but with Anne Yearsly, she succeeded to her most sanguine hopes, as all who have read that *milkmaid's* poetical *sonnets* will testify. Our *amiable* patroness has a more powerful claim to the popularity she enjoys, as author of a pamphlet against the *murderous Atheists* of France, (for she is herself a most devout Orthodox christian, and attends her young ladies to church twice every Sunday) a book earnestly recommended and profusely circulated by that impartial critic, Mr. REEVES, and the profits arising from the sale of which, she most liberally applied to relief of the French refugee *papists;* but she has still additional claims on public gratitude; her charity knows no bounds, equally extended to all; Foreigners and Natives. The loyal Hannah is now at the head of a *patriotic* association, consisting intirely of *ladies,* for the express purpose, of providing our *brave* militia soldiers with shoes, which we must allow, is not only a noble, but also, a most *political* exertion on her part, as such examples of fervent loyalty, cannot fail prodigiously to increase her number of scholars; though the charity itself rather implies a kind of *oblique* censure on government, which out of the eleven millions already voted in the present year 1794, cannot spare wherewithall to keep the poor fellows feet properly *shoed.* Let her, however, go on in her career, and she may probably soon, like her renowned prototype Reeves, (who gets from the c-wn, paid by John Bull, £3000. a year for the *work* he performs), be at the head of a petticoat gang, united against Levellers and Republicans, for the preservation of grievances; and ultimately gain an appointment, suitable to her talents, equal to her *deserts.* May an *honourable pension* crown her *glorious labours.*

The remaining members of this eccentric society, are a Mrs. O-de, a lady of *little note,* but of *some fortune,* of a most *oily* address, and truly loyal conduct.—Lady L-can, . . . two delicate virgins of the name of B-rry, a variety of *old maids, Miss* Edward J-n-gh-m, and the Right Honourable *Lady* Horace W-lp-le, *Countess* of Orf-rd, the *sympathising guardian* of the immortal Chatterton, who in a fit of despair, put an end to his existence, in a wretched garret in Shoreditch, to avoid the horrors of being starved to death! Blush grandeur, shudder ye TI-TLED BOOKWORMS, ye effected patrons of genius, at recollection of his name. With these ladies, we conclude our characters; God help them all, and turn their hearts from *literature* to Charity. Amen. (pp. 188-96)

> Charles Pigott, *"The Blue Stocking Jockies"* and *"Case of Real Distress,"* in his The Female Jockey Club; or, A Sketch of the Manners of the Age, *fourth edition, D. I. Eaton, 1794, pp. 188-91, 191-96.*

Chauncey Brewster Tinker

[*Tinker was an American educator and literary critic and editor. His edition of the* Letters of James Boswell *(1924) established him as a leading authority on Boswell and Johnson. In the following excerpt, he describes the various types and distinguishing features of eighteenth-century literary salons in London, including profiles of prominent hostesses.*]

CONVERSATION PARTIES AND LITERARY ASSEMBLIES

Not the least pleasant of the social gatherings for conversation was the levee, or reception held on rising from bed. The custom was of course adopted by people of fashion in imitation of the popular court function, and it always retained something of the courtly atmosphere, its popularity in fine society being due to the sense of importance which it lent to the host or hostess. Madame de Tencin, for example, thus held court from eight o'clock in the morning, queening it over everybody, 'from the lowest tools to the highest.' Mascarille, it will be remembered, boasts that he never rises from bed without the company of half a dozen *beaux esprits.* Yet despite its imitation of the court, there must have been about this kind of reception a certain intimacy and ease that were lacking in the more formal assemblies held later in the day.

In England the levee had been known for perhaps a hundred years; but it first becomes of importance to the student of literature about the middle of the century. A good general impression of it may be obtained from the fourth plate of Hogarth's *Marriage à la Mode,* published in 1745. The hostess, half dressed, is seated at her toilet-table, under the ministrations of her hair-dresser, and is engaged in conversation with her lover, who is reclining on a sofa near by. In the background is seen the bed, one curtain of which is still drawn. A negro butler is passing chocolate to the guests who are ranged in front of the bed, while an

Italian tenor is regaling them with solos to the accompaniment of a flute. This latter point is significant in the satire, for it is evident that the hostess is incapable of conducting a true conversazione, and has therefore had recourse to providing her guests with other entertainment, while she pursues her amorous intrigue.

A later and even more familiar representation of the levee is found at the opening of the *School for Scandal,* where Lady Sneerwell is 'discovered' at her toilet. When this scene is correctly represented on the stage the lady's guests are shown as drinking chocolate at her levee, and there characteristically displaying their conversational gifts.

That the levee was at its best essentially a literary function is shown by the encouragement it received from Samuel Johnson. The account of his morning receptions is preserved for us by Dr. Maxwell, whose description must be quoted in full:

> About twelve o'clock I commonly visited him, and frequently found him in bed, or declaiming over his tea, which he drank very plentifully. He generally had a levee of morning visitors, chiefly men of letters; Hawkesworth, Goldsmith, Murphy, Langton, Steevens, Beauclerk, etc., etc., and sometimes learned ladies, particularly I remember a French lady of wit and fashion doing him the honour of a visit. He seemed to be considered as a kind of public oracle, whom everybody thought they had a right to visit and consult; and doubtless they were well rewarded.

When Johnson visited Boswell in Edinburgh after the tour of the Hebrides 'he had, from ten o'clock to one or two, a constant levee of various persons, of different characters and descriptions;' so that poor Mrs. Boswell was obliged to 'devote the greater part of the morning to the endless task of pouring out tea.'

This custom, thus sanctioned by fashion and by literary authority, was adopted by all who pretended to wit. In 1760, Goldsmith sneers at the philosophical beau who 'receives company in his study, in all the pensive formality of slippers, night-gown, and easy-chair.' Flavia, in the same author's *Double Transformation,* after marrying an Oxford Fellow, aspires to the reputation of a *femme savante:*

> Proud to be seen she kept a bevy
> Of powdered coxcombs at her levee.

By 1779 the function had become so popular that its name was frequently extended to any formal entertainment where conversation was the principal attraction, even when it was held in the evening.

The levee merged easily into the formal breakfast. This function might occur at any hour from eight o'clock in the morning to three in the afternoon. It was in 1750 that Madame du Bocage recorded her impressions of Mrs. Montagu's breakfasts, generalizing upon the custom of the nation in these words:

> In the morning breakfasts which enchant as much by the exquisite viands as by the richness of the plate in which they are served up, agreeably bring together both the people of the country and strangers [*i.e.,* both natives and foreigners].

The diaries and letters of Beattie, Mrs. Delany, Miss Burney, and Miss More are strewn with references to this fashionable meal. In the spring of 1774, Walpole professes himself frightened at the inundation of them coming on. A favourite diversion at these matutinal parties, as at entertainments later in the day, was the declamation of Thomas Sheridan (who would repeat Gray's *Elegy,* Dryden's *Ode,* and 'everything that everybody could say by heart'), the French readings of Tessier, the tragic recitations of Tighe (who expected his auditors to swoon from emotion), and, occasionally, bits of recitation or acting by Garrick. Sheridan gave so many of these literary breakfasts that Mrs. Boscawen suspected that he received money for them. At times such functions were more or less public, and were held in the Haymarket, at Vauxhall, or at Bath, in the Assembly Rooms.

The receptions of the later afternoon and evening are of a less definite character. Beattie describes a gathering at Mrs. Montagu's as 'an assembly or conversation or rout.' The entertainment was of wide scope, as in Italian and French drawing-rooms, and might include dancing, card-playing, and literary readings, as well as conversation. In this work we are concerned only with the literary aspect of these parties; the origin and the more serious results of the London salon are discussed elsewhere, so that the rest of this chapter may be devoted to a consideration of the means adopted for shining in conversation at these parties, and the attempt to connect such assemblies directly with the production of poetry.

It is surely a misfortune that contemporary descriptions of the conversazione should be generally satirical in tone;

Fanny Burney, one of the Bluestocking Ladies, painted by Edward Francis Burney. Johnson admired her novel Evelina *(1778) and considered Burney herself "a real wonder."*

but it is natural enough, for conversation, unsupported by other entertainment, tends, in large groups, to pedantry on the one hand, and to frivolousness on the other. English literature produced no Molière to satirize the salons; but the conversazione did give both character and title to one great comedy, the *School for Scandal.* Although this play is not, like the *Critique de l'École des Femmes,* an adequate criticism of the literary drawing-room, it does nevertheless preserve prominent aspects of it, and we shall have occasion to refer to it repeatedly in illustrating the nature of the conversazione. Another criticism of this entertainment is found in a book now totally forgotten, entitled, *Modern Manners, or the Country Cousins, in a series of Poetical Epistles.* This is the work of the Rev. Samuel Hoole, son of the translator of Tasso and Ariosto, and appeared in the year 1782. The poems describe the visit of a north-English family to London, somewhat after the manner of Smollett in *Humphry Clinker,* and of Anstey in the *New Bath Guide.* The tenth epistle is an account of Lady Chattony's conversazione. At that assembly old Mr. Ralph Rusty is served with lukewarm coffee and tea and a minute bit of cake, which made him long for more. The company splits up into groups, each with their backs turned on the rest. The first party which he joins is (naturally) talking scandal. . . . His second visit is to a group engaged in musical gossip. . . . He escapes from their gushing ecstasies only to fall on a political discussion. . . . Mr. Rusty's unhappy evening was concluded by listening to the tales of a young lord just returned from his travels, a buck who wishes to fight a duel with him because he laughs at incredible stories. (pp. 102-11)

We may notice, in the first place, that Lady Chattony has followed the best traditions of the salon in reducing her refreshments to a minimum, depending for the success of her reception entirely upon the conversation of her guests. The talk, again, is not confined to a large circle; but is broken up, after Mrs. Vesey's manner, into a series of small groups. We have the usual references to gossip, scandal, and chatter about clothes, politics, and the opera, with occasional approaches to Sheridan's method of satire, but with none of his cleverness.

It is inevitable that any satire on the conversazione should dwell on the tendency to scandal and gossip. So inevitable is their presence in the salons that it seems hardly necessary to point it out; but it is essential to be at the true explanation of their prevalence, which no satire is likely to point out. Scandal, and its sister, Gossip, are the short cuts to cleverness, and cleverness is the one indispensable thing to the frequenters of salons. This is abundantly evident in the *School for Scandal.* It is wit for which Lady Sneerwell's guests are striving, and they will mar a character that they may make a *mot.* 'There is no possibility,' says Lady Sneerwell, 'of being witty without a little ill-nature; the malice of a good thing is the barb that makes it stick,' and Lady Teazle is in practical agreement with her; 'I vow I bear no malice against the people I abuse; when I say an ill-natured thing 'tis out of pure good humour.'

Sheridan was not the only dramatist to satirize the salons and their scandalous talk. His comedy was imitated by Thomas Holcroft in *Seduction,* a play whose popularity on the stage was equalled by its popularity in print. (pp. 111-12)

Other aspirants to conversational fame adopted the . . .

habit of talking sentiments. Here again the *School for Scandal* reveals the trick of the salons, for Joseph Surface has won himself a place in the group by virtue of his philosophical and ethical maxims. Sheridan's brilliant satire of a reigning fad in literature and society was anticipated by Goldsmith in *She Stoops to Conquer,* in which, when Kate Hardcastle wishes to speak like a fine lady, she at once begins to talk sentiments. This habit of lending a semblance of depth to one's conversation by the introduction of philosophical aphorisms is no doubt as old as the salon itself. At its best, there is nothing contemptible in the sentiment, as the long and brilliant history of the maxim in French literature may prove. The reputation of Mme. de Sablé's salon was largely made by the maxim or *pensée,* and all the later salons afford examples of its vitality. Madame Geoffrin was famous for it. 'Madame Geoffrin,' wrote Mme. Necker, 'a mis toute sa raison en maximes,' and the same writer praises the work of English authors for their successful production of this type, finding these authors otherwise deficient in moral principles. The maxim, ethical sentiment, or philosophical truth sententiously expressed, did indeed attain substantial existence in the essays of Samuel Johnson, who fancied that mankind might come in time to 'write all aphoristically;' but in English conversation it never found a thoroughly congenial soil. 'Sentiments' were popular, but, like much that was popular, they were hollow too. The Dowager Countess Gower writes to Mrs. Delany that the bluestockings are at Sunning Wells, where they 'sport sentiments from morn till noon, from noon to dewy eve.' The pages of the *Wit's Magazine* teemed with collections of them: 'Flattery, like a cameleon, assumes the colours of the object it is nearest to.' The record of bluestocking maxims and sentiments preserved in letters and diaries is amazing, but not because of its brilliance. Mrs. Montagu wrote the following to Miss Burney, in reference to the character of Mr. Vesey, 'A frippery character, like a gaudy flower, may please while it is in bloom; but it is the virtuous only that, like the aromatics, preserve their sweet and reviving odour when withered.' This is exactly in the style of Julia, the once-fashionable heroine of *The Rivals,* who, in respect of her conversation, might be own sister to Joseph Surface: 'When hearts deserving of happiness would unite their fortunes, Virtue would crown them with an unfading garland of modest hurtless flowers; but ill-judging Passion will force the gaudier Rose into the wreath, whose thorn offends them when its leaves are dropped.'

Closely akin to the neatly-turned sentiment is the epigram and this, in all its forms, the salon, following Continental models, sought to stimulate. One thinks immediately of the poetical epigrams of Sir Benjamin Backbite, his impromptu verses on Lady Frizzle's feather catching fire, his rebuses, the charade which he made at Mrs. Drowsie's conversazione, and, above all, of that sprightly extempore conceit on Lady Betty Curricle's ponies:

> Sure never were seen two such beautiful ponies;
> Other horses are Clowns—and these macaronies;
> Nay, to give 'em this title I'm sure isn't wrong,
> Their legs are so slim and their tails are so long.

There was no more certain way of achieving a reputation for wit than by the impromptu composition of these little verses. No lover of Goldsmith will fail to remember Garrick's epigram on the poet who 'wrote like an angel and talked like poor Poll.' Less hackneyed is the couplet which

Dr. Young produced at the 'World,' a club of gentlemen who were amusing themselves after dinner by scratching verses, with their diamonds, upon the wine-glasses. Having no jewel of his own, Young, when his turn came round, was obliged to borrow Chesterfield's, and then wrote:

> Accept a miracle: instead of wit,
> See two dull lines with Stanhope's pencil writ.

It is difficult to find a volume of eighteenth century verse that does not bear witness to the popularity of the epigram. Every miscellany teems with them. No collected edition of poems was complete without a handful of them. They are recorded in every diary and commonplace-book, and were exchanged by friends in the course of familiar correspondence. High and low, the peer of wit and the pretender to it, vied with one another in the production of them. All alike seem to have reached a dead level of mediocrity. The charade which Johnson made in honour of his friend Dr. Barnard is no better and no worse than scores of impromptu verses quoted in Walpole's *Letters* or the *Asylum for Fugitive Pieces.*

Much of this, no doubt, seems trivial. But wherever the spirit of the salon appears, evidence of its presence is seen in the production and general esteem of such trifles: rebuses, anagrams, madrigals, enigmas, charades, and *bouts rimés.* The explanation of it all goes back, perhaps, to the Italian Renaissance, when, as Burckhardt has shown, an epigram could lay the foundation of a scholar's celebrity:

> It was held the greatest of all triumphs when an epigram was mistaken for a genuine copy from some old marble or when it was so good that all Italy learned it by heart, as happened in the case of some of Bembo's.

The popularity of epigrams in fine English society is amusingly illustrated by the entertainments provided by a certain Mrs. (afterwards Lady) Miller at her villa near Bath. The character and the results of her attempt to stimulate the production of literature are typical, and, as they have left a considerable record in print, it may be profitable to consider them somewhat at length. She introduced what she was pleased to term the 'little Gallic institution' of *bouts rimés.* Lists of riming words were distributed among her guests, who composed verses suggested by them, employing them in their given order. The resulting effusions were then placed in a vase decorated with laurel branches and pink ribbons, erected upon a 'modern altar.' 'It is at present,' writes this ingenious lady, 'the receptacle of all the contending poetical morsels which every other Thursday (formerly Friday) are drawn out of it indiscriminately, and read aloud by the gentlemen present, each in his turn. Their particular merits are afterwards discussed by them, and prizes assigned to three out of the whole that appear to be the most deserving. Their authors are then, and not before, called for, who seldom fail to be *announced* either by themselves, or, if absent, by their friends. Then the prize poems are read aloud a second time to the company, each by its author, if present, if not, by other Gentlemen, and wreaths of Myrtle presented publicly by the Institutress to each successful writer.'

When these verses were published they roused, if not the general esteem which the Institutress plainly expected for them, the interest of Miss Burney, the curiosity of Boswell, and the mirth of Walpole. (pp. 113-18)

Mrs. Miller's Institution appears, however, to have been an unqualified social success. The first edition of the verses was exhausted in ten days, and a second was published in the following year. Three similar volumes appeared at intervals, and the series was terminated only by the death of the Institutress. The publications received the compliment of an anonymous attack entitled *Sappho,* in which Mrs. Miller was satirically hailed as 'Mistress of the tuneful nine'; but a more deadly assault took the form of a solemn congratulatory *Epistle to Mrs. Miller,* in which that lady is said to

> Shine unmatched in old or modern time,
> A friend of Genius, Pleasure, Taste and Rhime,
> Which daily thrive beneath thy fostering hand
> And pour the tide of learning o'er the land.

An examination of the volume published in 1775 hardly seems to bear out these statements. The following production of the hostess herself it is difficult to describe with accuracy, for the word verse hardly seems appropriate to it:

> From Castor and Pollux, those twins of renown,
> Arose the great dance taught at Lacedæmon;
> Then a son of Achilles, with a barbarous name,
> Taught his soldiers to dance, those Cretans of fame.
> Wise philosopher Socrates also would know,
> From Aspasia the fair how to well point a toe.
> Pompous nuptials and feasts—e'en the grave Funerals
> Was danc'd at by princes, priests, people and all.

It is only fair to say that the verses in the volume do frequently rise from this level to that of mediocrity. The following specimen of *bouts rimés* may serve to indicate the type and contents of the volume:

> Hard to my muse it is, I must   confess,
> In six fixed rhymes aught witty to   express;
> Why did I mix with Wits? who must   detest
> And crush my follies which their sense   molest.
> Thus the poor mole, who rises into   light
> Dies when he meets the sun's refulgent   might.

There are other things to be said in amelioration of the harsh judgments one is inclined to pass upon Mrs. Miller. The later volumes are certainly less bad than the first. The praise of Mrs. Miller, which had formed the staple of the first volume, is somewhat mitigated in the others, and the names of the contributors occasionally emerge into the borderland of fame. Potter, William Hayley, Anna Seward, and Christopher Anstey are worthy of respect, and a poem by Garrick, though worthless, lends a certain distinction to the second volume. Anstey's poem, *An Election Ball,* which enjoyed something of the popularity of his *New Bath Guide,* was written upon a subject given out by Mrs. Miller, 'The ancient and modern Dress and Manners of the English Nation compared'; and the *Poetical Address* which prefaced it is addressed to Mr. Miller. In the former 'Clio' and the Tusculan 'vause' are celebrated, and in the latter the 'myrtle sprigs' and 'vocal swans of Bath.' These poems are still readable.

To Mrs. Miller must certainly be allowed the merit of having gathered about herself a group of persons who would have made the reputation of any London drawing-room. Her own inability to produce anything that should have more than the external appearance of verse does not seem to have repelled those of higher ability and finer taste. For such a woman it was in the nature of an achievement that

her Institution lasted six years; and the four volumes of so-called poetical contributions to it retain a certain melancholy interest as showing the result of a deliberate attempt by the world of fashion to stimulate the production of poetry. (pp. 119-22)

THE LONDON SALON

The London salon corresponds well enough, in its external aspects, with its Parisian prototype. . . . Differences in result there undoubtedly were, but the two were alike in aim. The London salon, like the Parisian, for example, depended for its influence partly on the beauty and interest of its material surroundings. Mrs. Montagu fascinated her guests with Chinese rooms, Athenian rooms, feather rooms, rooms decorated by Angelica Kauffmann, and other gorgeous apartments in her house in Hill Street and in her palace in Portman Square. Mrs. Vesey, less ambitious and more intimate, entertained her friends in a 'blue-room' or 'green-room,' and often in her little dressing-room which Mrs. Carter called 'the unostentatious receptacle of liberal society'—unostentatious, no doubt, but bizarre and successfully bizarre like everything that Mrs. Vesey touched.

Like the French hostesses, these women kept up in their assemblies a tone that was at once aristocratic and literary; they made conversation the chief entertainment of the drawing-room, and the patronage of letters their most elegant aim. Each of them attached to herself—perhaps it would be more proper to say, attached herself to—some writer, who frequently repaid her friendship with tributes in verse. These writers were, in general, women; and the friendships of the London salon are usually, though not always, feminine. They offer, therefore, as we shall see later, a notable contrast to literary friendships in Parisian salons.

Various English women—Mrs. Cholmondeley, Mrs. Crewe, Lady Lucan, Lady Hervey, Mrs. Greville, Mrs. Catherine Macaulay—had studied the Parisian salon at first hand; but none of them were so familiar with it, none so intimately acquainted with various Parisian hostesses, as Mrs. Montagu. As early as 1750 Madame du Bocage visited her in London and took breakfast at her house in Hill Street. The two ladies paid elaborate court to each other. Montagu presented du Bocage with compliments and an edition of Milton, and du Bocage (who was a professed poet) replied with compliments and a string of riming couplets, setting forth the merits of Montagu.

Again, when Madame Necker was in England, many years later, Mrs. Montagu saw much of her. The French lady, like every one, was pleased with her amiability, and, again like every one, amused at the stiffness of her conversation. When, in 1775, Mrs. Montagu went to Paris, her associations with the Neckers became fairly intimate. She was presented to 'all the *beaux esprits,*' and was even taken to see Madame Geoffrin, whose glory now was waning. On the sixth of July 1776, she met Madame du Deffand at dinner, and found her gay and lively. Madame du Deffand's comments on the bluestocking, in her letters to Walpole, are singularly indulgent, until corrected by Walpole. She is polite, thinks Madame du Deffand, but not over pedantic, and 'ennuyeuse, sans doute, mais bonne femme.' Mrs. Montagu hired a house at Chaillot, where she gave suppers for Madame du Deffand and the rest.

That she flattered them all, after the most approved Parisian fashion, no one who has read her letter to Madame du Deffand can doubt. It is one of the most skilful pieces of compliment which she ever devised, and was sent with a gift of two beautiful scent-boxes. (pp. 134-37)

In spite of the success of her Parisian visit, it may be questioned whether Mrs. Montagu was wholly satisfied with the spirit of the salons she visited. She had gone to Paris with the avowed intention of searching, among the provincial nobility, for 'some who are more in the *ton* of Louis XIV's court' than the ladies of Versailles. It was, as one might have suspected, the Rambouillet tradition that attracted her, rather than the later salon with its freer thought and freer manners, and its constant change of favourites. She should have gone to Paris at least as early as the days of Madame de Lambert.

But it is certain that Mrs. Montagu never succeeded in attaining to the ease of the Parisian salon. Friends feared that she would come back more artificial than ever. Mrs. Boscawen wished that she might get by heart Mrs. Chapone's chapter on Simplicity. But there was no such thing as simplicity in Mrs. Montagu's nature: all her instincts were for the elaborate, her methods in all things complicated, her manner grand, not easy. Her assemblies became even larger and more overpowering; the number of 'the Great' grew constantly larger.

Her salon was inevitably the reflection of her own character. She could be, as Mrs. Thrale witnessed, 'brilliant in diamonds, solid in judgment, critical in talk'; she could be, as Johnson freely admitted, 'par pluribus . . . variety in one.' But there was a certain stiffness in her character that inevitably communicated itself to her assemblies. Mrs. Chapone, who had every reason to love her, wrote to Pepys that he would always find in her good nature, 'though not accompanied with remarkable softness.' Fanny Burney was from the first rather overwhelmed by her grand manner, and Mrs. Delany found at one of her assemblies 'a formal, formidable circle,' where she had only 'a *whisper* with Mrs. Boscawen, another with Lady Bute, and a *wink* from the Duchess of Portland—*poor diet* for one who loves a plentiful meal of social friendship.' Six years later she was so dazzled by the brilliancy of one of Mrs. Montagu's assemblies that she fled incontinently.

Lady Louisa Stuart, who evidently did not like Mrs. Montagu, calls attention to another defect. 'There was a deplorable lack . . . of that art of kneading the mass well together, which I have known possessed by women far her inferiors. As her company came in, a heterogeneous medley, so they went out, each individual feeling himself single, isolated, and (to borrow a French phrase) embarrassed with his own person; which might be partly owing to the awkward position of the furniture, the malarrangement of tables and chairs. Everything in that house, as if under a spell, was sure to form itself into a circle or semicircle.' But all this is as nothing compared with the testimony of Lord Lyttelton. Mrs. Montagu was destined to receive the unkindest thrust from her own familiar friend. At some time in the decade of the sixties, Lord Lyttelton wrote an elaborate letter to a friend in criticism of the modern wits, whom he proclaimed 'not worth a beadsman's rosary.' The following passage can refer only to Mrs. Montagu:

No one can take more pains than Mrs. M—— to be surrounded with men of wit; she bribes, she pensions, she flatters, gives excellent dinners, is herself a very sensible woman, and of very pleasing manners; not young, indeed, but that is out of the question;—and, in spite of all these encouragements, which, one would think, might make wits spring out of the ground, the conversations of her house are too often critical and pedantic,—something between the dullness and the pertness of learning. They are perfectly chaste, and generally instructive; but a cool and quiet observer would sometimes laugh to see how difficult a matter it is for *la belle Présidente* to give colour and life to her literary circles.

There was, moreover, evidently much of the *femme savante* about Mrs. Montagu. Walpole described her in his most merciless manner as a 'piece of learned nonsense'; she and her friends, he continues, 'vie with one another till they are as unintelligible as the good folks at Babel.' This of course is not fair. When was Walpole ever fair? But it certainly may be taken as evidence that Mrs. Montagu did not hesitate to make a display of her knowledge. She had mastered the art, no doubt, of wearing her learning gracefully, but never that of gracefully dispensing with it. It cumbers her correspondence. With Garrick she must discuss Plautus, Terence, and Molière, with Elizabeth Carter the *Ethics* of Aristotle, with Beattie the Greek dramatists, Ossian, Homer, and the 'wilder Oriental poets.' But the reader has throughout the feeling that the writer is making the best of resources that are somewhat limited and undisciplined. Her knowledge of the classics was at best amateurish.

But this deficiency—if such it be—was not fatal. The learning of a professional scholar is by no means essential in the mistress of a salon. It may, indeed, as I have already shown, prove a serious obstacle to her success; for the means by which she diffuses her influence are of a totally different sort. With more essential things, high social rank, a large fortune, with, interest in the course of literature, and a faith in her own power to influence it for good, Mrs. Montagu was richly endowed. Without her there would have been no London salons; for all existed in more or less conscious imitation of hers. She alone succeeded in becoming a patron of letters. To say that she did not equal the great Frenchwomen in this art is merely to say that she was not a genius. She had the power of attracting people of real importance to her drawing-room, and even those who ridiculed her social methods were obliged to admit that they produced an effect. That effect it is difficult to estimate with precision; for it is by no means identical with that which she produced by her own writings or even by her patronage of writers. She has the honour of having assisted in spreading the esteem in which literature and men of letters were held at the close of the century, as opposed to the anomaly of their position fifty years earlier. Her achievement is not the less real because it cannot be exactly calculated.

A far more lovable figure than Mrs. Montagu is her friendly rival, Elizabeth Vesey. Though the daughter of a bishop, the wife of a Member of Parliament, and mistress of as popular a drawing-room as could be found in London, she was as free from vanity as from pretensions to literary gifts. She never dreamed of shining as a critical essayist; she scribbled no verses. She was a withered old lady with the heart of a child, who amused everybody by her enthusiasm and her naïve manners, which were always a bit slipshod. She was so notoriously informal that her guests forgot their elegant reserve, and became, like her, good-humoured and lively. She moves about her crowded assemblies like a fairy crone, her parchment skin seamed and shrivelled with age, her ear-trumpet dangling from her neck, while she distributes her promiscuous company, pats her guests on the arm, breaks up their cliques, and squares the social circle. She touched every one into good spirits with what Elizabeth Carter called the wave of her fairy wand. Everybody adored her, men and women alike. To Martin Sherlock she was 'good Mrs. Vesey—indeed she is *all* goodness'; and Horace Walpole bursts into momentary enthusiasm, 'What English heart ever excelled hers?'

If she found favour in the eyes of all London, it was not by any charms of person, for at the time of her great fame, she had long since lost every trace of beauty. In 1779, when Miss Burney first met her, she was a very pattern of old age, with 'the most wrinkled, sallow, time-beaten face' ever seen. But her vivid imagination never deserted her, and to the sophisticated people by whom she was surrounded she seemed a sort of ethereal meddler in human affairs. Her friends called her the Sylph. Mrs. Carter could detect nothing mortal in her save a love of London, and felt about her a suspicion of 'coral groves and submarine palaces.' If she was ordered to take fresh-water baths, she must, like a child, make a game of it all, play at being primitive, and rear in imagination an 'American hut' on the banks of the Liffey. She flitted eagerly about England and Ireland, anxious to know everybody and see everything. Mrs. Carter found her like Bartholomew Cokes, who wanted every plaything in the Fair. Indeed, the world must have seemed to Mrs. Vesey a vast toyshop with endless opportunities for play, for she could amuse herself by planning a *fête champêtre,* or by inventing a new teapot, lacking, to be sure, both spout and handle, but of 'a beautiful Etruscan form.' Her guests never knew what to expect, for she might present them with an atheist philosopher hot from the salons of Paris or set them to cutting out Indian figures and flowers, to paste on her dressing-room windows in imitation of painted glass. Dowagers marvel at her, and lament that oddities are become the fashion.

Her parties were informal to the point of becoming promiscuous. Her first aim was to get together every one of importance, literary, political, social, and ecclesiastical, to keep them broken up into small groups, and to insist on uniting those of different tastes and mood. She got Walpole side by side with Fanny Burney (whom he liked at once), and again side by side with Sir William Jones (whom he did not). She tried to present Dr. Johnson to the Abbé Raynal, and drew from the Great Moralist an immortal refusal. She was apparently even ambitious to marry Elizabeth Carter to Thomas Gray. Yet withal she had the rare gift of self-obliteration. She gave herself no airs. She was by nature absent-minded, and she affected to be more *distraite* than she actually was. When excitedly denouncing second marriages she could quite overlook (or *seem* to overlook) the fact that she herself had been married twice. 'Bless me, my dear! I had quite forgotten it.' Such wit was but ill-understood in salons which had never before witnessed the spectacle of a bluestocking laughing at herself. There is an Irish whimsicality about her re-

marks. When ill, she could declare that her only happy moment in fourteen days was in a fainting fit, or again that she was in dread of losing seven or eight of her senses. 'It's a very disagreeable thing, I think,' said she to Mr. Cambridge, 'when one has just made an acquaintance with anybody, and likes them, to have them die,' a sentiment that set Fanny Burney to 'grinning irresistibly,' and filliping the macaroon crumbs from her muff to hide her embarrassment. Mrs. Vesey somehow contrived to make even her deafness a source of amusement. When Lady Spencer brought her some silver ears to use instead of trumpets, she promptly tried them on before her guests, and greeted George Cambridge with one of them still clinging to her ear, but as she was moving away from him spilled it unaware. Surely this bluestocking is a very human sort.

Those who smiled at her naïveté forgot that it was a quality very near to wisdom. Her conversation, and perhaps her letters, revealed that instinctive knowledge of the human heart which is the peculiar possession of extreme innocence. 'Few people,' she said to Mrs. Carter, who quotes her words with approval—the *imprimatur* of common sense—'give themselves time to be friends'; and as if she only half understood the century into which she had been born, inquired 'why the head is always so suspicious of the heart.' The wise Carter, whose knowledge was so much more sophisticated, can but honour her for having the simplicity of a little child, though she would like to whip her for having its imprudence. But it was this very simplicity of soul that enabled the good creature to 'accommodate herself so fully to the awkward customs and manners of mere actually existing men and women.' Mrs. Carter finds it 'very surprising,' as does the student, and as did Montagu and all the dowagers, no doubt; but Miss Burney, with her keen observation, saw at once that her skill in selecting guests and her 'address in rendering them easy with one another' was an art that implied 'no mean understanding.' She had sufficient skill to persuade Horace Walpole, who professed to hate her 'Babels,' to come and join the Cophthi, and not to snub them one and all; she had the skill to keep always on good terms with Mrs. Montagu; she could attract the whole Literary Club on alternate Tuesdays, and filled her drawing-room with the most difficult people in England to manage. Yet her methods were always of the simplest, her collations modest though delicate, and her house, though interesting because of its oddity, was hardly an attraction apart from its mistress.

With all the new emotions of sentimentalism and romanticism, Mrs. Vesey was in full sympathy, and she must have done something to popularize these movements among the *beaux esprits* of London. She adored the *Sentimental Journey.* She and Mrs. Carter write each other of the solemn awe of storms at sea, of 'sublime and terrible' Welsh 'prospects,' of dim-lit Gothic cloisters, and the sad note of the owl at set of sun. She loved the poetry of Gray, and even tempted the shy poet into her drawing-room. She was obliged to pass much of her time in Ireland, and on her journeys there and back improved the opportunity of studying the wild scenery of Wales. She writes to Mrs. Carter of her journey through Anglesey and over Penmuenmaur. The story thrilled Mrs. Carter, for she wrote of it to Mrs. Montagu:

In the midst of her passage through these wild regions, she and Mrs. Hancock [Vesey's sister-in-law] were overtaken by a tempest which greatly heightened the sublime and terrible of the scene; and you may guess what a description such an adventure would furnish to an imagination like hers.

Mrs. Vesey, moreover, appears to have been alone among the blues in aspiring to the easier standards of French manners and to the new 'freedom of thought,' though she never really abandoned herself to them. She was one of the ladies who lent diversity to the amatory career of Laurence Sterne; but the flirtation, though feverish enough for a time, either escaped the notice of Mrs. Vesey's precise friends or was, by general consent, hushed up; for it expired at last quite harmlessly and left only a handful of letters as proof of its former vitality. Yorick and this earlier 'Eliza' met, it would appear, in 1762, when Sterne was at the height of his fame, and enjoying the pleasures of metropolitan life for a season. He heard Mrs. Vesey sing; walked twenty paces beside her; felt the 'harmonic vibrations' of a heart truly sentimental, and had no sooner left her than he opened an amatory correspondence with her. He would give one of his cassocks to explain the magic of her personality: 'I believe in my conscience, dear lady, if truth was known, *that you have no inside at all.* That you are graceful, elegant, and desirable, etc., etc.—every common beholder who can stare at you, as a Dutch boor does to the Queen of Sheba,—can easily find out—but that you are sensible, gentle, and tender and from one end to the other of you full of the sweetest tones and modulations require a deeper research.—You are a system of harmonic vibrations—the softest and best attuned of all instruments.—Lord! I would give away my other cassock to touch you.' Tristram Shandy protests that his head is turned.

We may follow them to Ranelagh, where they saunter lackadaisically, indifferent to the crowd and the fireworks, Mrs. Vesey uttering 'gentle, amiable, elegant sentiments in a tone of voice that was originally intended for a Cherub.' But the exposure was apparently too much for the tender frame of Yorick. In listening to Mrs. Vesey's voice, he lost his own, and now 'colds, coughs, and catarrhs' have so tied up his tongue that he can no longer whisper loud enough to explain Vesey's effect upon his heart. How often thereafter he was able to becassock himself and sit in the warm blue drawing-room listening to the music, we do not know. The romance did not last long, certainly; and we hear nothing more of it after the autumn of 1767, when Mrs. Vesey invited Sterne to visit her in Ireland, an invitation which his illness compelled him to decline.

Like the French ladies described by Sterne in the *Sentimental Journey,* Mrs. Vesey turned, at a certain age, to agnosticism. Mrs. Montagu had defied Voltaire, but Mrs. Vesey courted the Abbé Raynal. He responded with great vivacity and was often in her drawing-room during the year 1777. Mrs. Boscawen asserts that she once heard him talk for eight hours "successfully' and without interruption: 'One must have *heard and seen it to believe it;*' and Mrs. Chapone asserts that he talked steadily *from one at noon till one* in the morning. This particular conversation, however, did not occur at Mrs. Vesey's. She would never have permitted any one thus to turn conversation into a lecture.

Mrs. Vesey's interest in French agnosticism caused her friends grave concern. Twice Mrs. Carter denounced Voltaire when Mrs. Vesey demanded a pronouncement on his works, and at last wrote that she would as soon think of playing with toads and vipers, as of reading such blasphemy and impiety. She argued for the validity of revealed religion, but without great effect, for Mrs. Vesey continued to play with fire. She produced strange romantic thrills in herself by reading the Abbé Raynal during a violent thunderstorm. Byron, surely, could have understood this, but it was beyond the blues. ''Tis a dangerous amusement to a mind like yours, indeed to any mind,' wrote Mrs. Carter. But dangerous or not, it illustrates the curiosity of Mrs. Vesey's mind, and might furnish a historian of the Romantic Movement with an apt anecdote.

Because of the unpretentiousness of her character, Mrs. Vesey has always been ranked far below Mrs. Montagu, but it may be doubted whether the estimate is quite fair. There were many who found her assemblies more agreeable than Mrs. Montagu's more pretentious parties, especially after that lady's removal to Portman Square. Unlike Mrs. Montagu, she made no attempt to produce literature herself (and for this posterity should be grateful); but she appears to have had an instinctive appreciation, not surpassed by the other, of the true function of the salon. For it was the office of the bluestockings neither to reform the whole of London society by giving it a literary tone, nor to bring into existence a new school of authors dominated by their ideals; but rather to keep in motion, by means of social intercourse, the currents of thought, literary and philosophical. A true *conversazione* can create and vitalize a train of ideas, and Mrs. Vesey, with her broad and genial interests, was able to assemble the best representatives of the new ideas, and bring them into contact with society. This, if there be any, is the true office of the bluestocking, an office which Mrs. Vesey discharged with skill and with charm.

About Mrs. Montagu and Mrs. Vesey there revolved other luminaries. Certain of them—Elizabeth Carter, Hester Chapone, Hannah More, and Fanny Burney—though they presided over no salon, achieved an independent reputation as authors, and will therefore be considered in later chapters. Others of them—as Miss Monckton (still remembered for Reynolds's sentimental portrait of her), Lady Lucan, Lady Herries, Mrs. Greville, the admirable Mrs. Cholmondeley (niece of Walpole and friend of Miss Burney), and the sensible Mrs. Walsingham—have left, in general, little more than a name (and an adjective) to posterity. Others, who are more often encountered, demand a brief consideration.

There is, for example, the gracious figure of Mrs. Boscawen, wife of the Admiral, and one of the best-loved women in London. Boswell's compliment to her will be familiar to students of the *Life of Johnson:* 'If it be not presumptuous in me to praise her, I would say that her manners are the most agreeable and her conversation the best of any lady with whom I ever had the happiness to be acquainted.' Miss More described her parties in the words of Madame de Sévigné as 'all daffodil, all rose, all jonquil,' and dwelt on her power to make each of her guests feel that he had been the immediate object of her attention.

Her reputation was thus always rather social than literary. Her letters, indeed, were highly regarded by her friends, and were sometimes preferred to Mrs. Montagu's—a preference by no means audacious. The repeated comparison with Madame de Sévigné is certainly less happy. Mrs. Boscawen's letters, as preserved in Mrs. Delany's *Autobiography* and the *Memoirs of Hannah More,* have the affectionate intimacy but not the kindling wit and sprightliness which distinguish familiar correspondence at its best. It is sufficient to say of these letters that they have successfully preserved Mrs. Boscawen's pleasant personality.

Mrs. Boscawen emulated Mrs. Montagu as a patron of rising young authors by entering into warm personal relations with Hannah More. They first became intimate when, on the twelfth night of *Percy,* Mrs. Boscawen sent the successful dramatist a wreath of myrtle, laurel, and bay. This stimulated the young lady to an exhibition of that flattery for which she was already famous. In an *Ode to the Hon. Mrs. Boscawen,* Apollo himself is made to rebuke Hannah for wearing these floral honours, asserting that it is for Mrs. Boscawen that

> the faithful *myrtle blooms,*
> For her the sage's bay.
> And even thou shalt claim a name
> And challenge some renown;
> Boscawen's friendship is thy fame,
> Her praise thy LAUREL CROWN.

But the two ladies had only begun their career of compliment. Somewhat later Miss More sent to her patron a bottle of 'otto of roses,' having learned that that lady's organs 'partake the refinement that graces her mind.' This is not the first instance we have encountered of the use of incense in the bluestocking ritual.

Sir Joshua Reynolds's rendering of David Garrick as Kitely in Ben Jonson's drama Every Man in His Humour.

Mrs. Boscawen sometimes varied her flowery wreaths of praise with gifts and practical suggestions. When she learns that Miss More has been reading Homer and Tasso, she at once becomes ambitious for an English epic from the pen of a woman. 'Some spark,' she thinks, from these older geniuses, 'will communicate to that train of poetic fire, *qui vous appartient,* and the explosion will ascend in many a brilliant star.' The honourable lady demands and obtains an *Ode on the Marquess of Worcester's Birthday,* into which the author had the sense to weave a compliment to Mrs. Boscawen and to 'Glanvilla,' her estate. Meanwhile the patron is weeping her eyes red over *Percy,* circulating copies of Miss More's *Essays,* eliciting praises from friends and *beaux esprits*—all duly forwarded—and rebuking, very gently, the rising authoress for not proclaiming more loudly the greatness of the sex: 'where shall we find a champion if you (armed at all points) desert us?'

Miss More's chief tribute to Mrs. Boscawen, however, was her poem, *Sensibility,* published in 1782, in the form of an epistle to that lady. In rapturous verse Sensibility is hailed as the parent of charity, charm, and many other bluestocking virtues; but, above all, 'tis this that 'gives Boscawen half her power to please.' (pp. 137-56)

It is only necessary to add that it is to Mrs. Boscawen that we owe the painting of Opie's delightful portrait of Miss More. It does more to perpetuate the charm of the bluestocking ladies than all their congratulatory epistles—in prose or verse.

Mrs. Ord has by modern writers frequently been associated with Mrs. Montagu and Mrs. Vesey as originating the bluestocking *conversazioni.* Just why Mrs. Ord should have been chosen to complete the triad of ladies it is difficult to say. She is not mentioned in Miss More's *Bas Bleu,* in Dr. Burney's verses, or in Boswell's *Life of Johnson.* Her name occurs but once, and quite casually, in Walpole's *Letters;* and Johnson writes but once of having been present at her assembly. Even those who describe her parties speak rather of her guests than of herself, and praise her good nature without mentioning her conversation. Her talk was, it appears, considered heavy, so that Miss Burney herself was obliged to admit that it lacked both mirth and instruction, and that she loved Mrs. Ord for her friendliness but not for her brilliancy.

Nevertheless Mrs. Ord was one who early made the experiment of banishing cards and dancing from her evening parties and substituting undisturbed conversation as the staple of her entertainment. Like Mrs. Vesey she abhorred formality, and made her guests draw their chairs about a large table in the middle of the room, remarking—and it is one of the few remarks of hers that has been preserved—that a table was the 'best friend to sociable conversation.' Here, apparently, she succeeded in getting the unity without the hard formality of the dreaded circle.

She had, moreover, a skill in the choice of her guests which usually saved her from the charge of assembling crowds indiscriminately. Pepys and Dr. Burney unite in praising her ability to mix her ingredients, and for this the latter pronounces her an excellent cook. Miss More liked her assemblies because there she could have Sir Joshua and Mr. Cambridge all to herself or discuss the relative merits of Pope and Dryden, sitting apart with Mrs. Montagu and Horace Walpole.

Perhaps Mrs. Ord wished to take the place of Mrs. Thrale as the social patron of Fanny Burney. She it was who conducted Fanny to her royal prison at Windsor, who helped to keep her in touch with her old friends, who showered gifts upon her and carried her to oratorios, and who, when the young woman was worn out by her servitude, put the map of England into the hands of 'her child,' and bade her choose the journey she would take. This trip, which was through southwest England, lasted many weeks, and it was mid-September before the two finally drove out of Bath towards London in Mrs. Ord's coach-and-four. Nor did the services of this 'excellent and maternal' creature stop with this, for the very next year she carried Miss Burney to the 'salubrious hills of Norbury,' and there administered what the Diarist, in a flight of rhetoric worthy of her latest years, called 'the balsamic medicine of social tenderness.' But nothing came of this patronage in the way of literature, so that Mrs. Ord's kindness, though challenging our admiration, adds little to the movement we are tracing.

Another woman closely associated with Miss Burney, and one who profoundly influenced her life, was that venerable relic of the former age, Mary Granville Delany, whom Burke called 'not only the woman of fashion of the present age, but . . . the highest bred woman in the world.' 'Swift's Mrs. Delany,' they loved to call her, for she had known the great Dean in his latter days. Of the relationship, such as it was, she never tired of talking, and in this she was wise, for it was her chief claim to distinction in literary circles. The woman who could display a sheaf of private letters from Swift and to whom the *Spectator* was 'almost too modern to speak of ' was of course worshipped by every bluestocking in London; but she was never quite a blue herself. She did not wish to be. Miss More, it is true, claims her as one of the circle in her poem *Sensibility:*

> DELANY too is ours; serenely bright,
> Wisdom's strong ray, and virtue's milder light:
> And she who blessed the friend and graced the lays
> Of poignant Swift, still gilds my social days;
> Long, long protract thy light, O star benign!
> Whose setting beams with milder lustre shine.

But Mrs. Delany seldom allowed her lustre to shine upon the salon, and was anything but mild in her opinion of Mrs. Montagu's assemblies. She was more interested in the Royal Family than in the progress of literature, and despite her early associations, preferred the society of rank to that of genius. She was graciously pleased when Garrick received her friend the Duchess of Portland and herself '*very respectfully,*' and showed himself 'sensible of the honour' done him. She was vexed that Mason's tepid tragedy, *Elfrida,* should be 'prostituted' by a public performance, and 'the charms of virgins represented by the abandoned nymphs of Drury Lane.' 'Such a poem,' she continues, 'would have been represented in days of yore by the youthful part of the Royal family or those of the first rank. Indeed, in *these* our days (*save our own Royal Family*), it would be difficult to find representatives suited to such virtuous and refined characters.' Such a person, who was for ever protesting that she was in love with the King, the Queen, and the whole Royal Family, was in no position to mediate properly between authors and 'the Great.' Her one conception of serving them was to render them up, a living sacrifice, to the Royal Family, as Miss Burney (who was dazzled by the friend of Swift and the

friend of the Queen) discovered to her cost. When Miss Burney hesitated to enter upon her service as Dresser to Queen Charlotte—a post which her intimacy with Mrs. Delany had brought her—it was Mrs. Delany who was 'much mortified' that so flattering a proposal could cause a moment's hesitation.

Mrs. Delany is a significant figure in the history of the salon by virtue of the fascination which she exercised through her quondam connection with a great man; but of genuine interest in the salon she had little, and of influence upon the course of literature none at all.

Alone among the literary ladies of the age, Mrs. Thrale has retained the fascination which she exercised in her own time. The fame of the other bluestockings has gone from less to less; but hers has remained constant, if indeed it has not increased. This is of significance, for it shows either that she was more modern than her sisters or more universal. She might consistently have aspired to the title, 'Queen of the Bluestockings,' but she did not even care whether she was reckoned one of them, contenting herself with outwitting them at every point. It was she, for example, who captured the two authors most coveted by the mistresses of the salons, Johnson and Miss Burney, and 'planted' them in her house. Her friendship with the former, though it cannot be shown to have altered the course of his works, gave birth to an admirable series of familiar letters, which Hannah More found 'true letters of friendship which are meant to show kindness rather than wit.' But more important than such published results was the fame which Johnson lent to Mrs. Thrale by his residence at her home. The nearest approach to the true salon that we find in the eighteenth century in England is the dining-room at Streatham; the spectacle of Johnson there reading aloud from the proof-sheets of the *Lives of the Poets* is in exact accord with the best French traditions of the salon.

In many other respects Mrs. Thrale showed that she was capable of fulfilling the more important functions of a literary hostess. It was she who attempted to direct the genius of Fanny Burney towards the theatre, prevailing upon her to write a comedy. It is true that the resulting play, *The Witlings,* was not thought by Dr. Burney a fit successor to *Evelina,* and was accordingly destroyed; but in the absence of any proof to the contrary and in view of the influence which Mrs. Thrale could bring to bear in the theatrical world through Murphy and others, it is difficult to see why her advice to the young writer was not sound. Sheridan, than whom there was no better judge, gave similar counsel.

Finally, when, after her marriage and departure from England, as Mrs. Piozzi, she printed her *Anecdotes of the Late Samuel Johnson,* the value of what she had to tell and her vivacity in telling it enabled her to triumph over a slipshod style and an inaccurate method, and to establish, once for all, her reputation in the literary world, a reputation which the bluestockings were foolish enough to think she had lost for ever.

There is no need here to discuss the anomalies of Mrs. Thrale's character. They have been dwelt on unnecessarily and fruitlessly. She had no illusions about her friends, and least of all about her own importance. She looked out on the world in which she moved, shrewdly and, on the whole, sanely. She knew how to make people happy and how to put the Great at their ease. 'Mrs. Thrale,' says Mr. Seccombe, 'moved among them serene, lively, "a pretty woman still," an exorciser of melancholy, the cheeriest of hostesses, quite unconscious of erudition, gaily spontaneous, the queen of Streatham. Her wayward naturalness made her seem a rose among hot-house flowers. Her innate brightness enabled her, as has been said, to romp with learning and to play blind man's buff with the sages.' In the somewhat stifling atmosphere of salons such a personality is of the very highest worth. (pp. 157-65)

Chauncey Brewster Tinker, "Conversation Parties and Literary Assemblies" and "The London Salon," in his The Salon and English Letters: Chapters on the Interrelations of Literature and Society in the Age of Johnson, *The Macmillan Company, 1915, pp. 102-22, 134-65.*

PRINTING TECHNOLOGY

Alvin Kernan

[*Kernan is an American educator and author of several studies on Renaissance satire and modern theater. He also is the general editor of the Yale edition of Ben Jonson's collected works. In the following excerpt, he discusses the underlying "print logic" that dramatically transformed English culture during the eighteenth century and provides a general overview of the printing industry of Johnson's London.*]

We do not as yet have a detailed history of print in eighteenth-century England, but there are a great many specialized studies of different aspects of the printing and publishing trades, and in a survey of this material, Terry Belanger concludes that all the evidence points toward a transformation during the century from an oral-scribal society to a print society: "England in the 1790s was a well-developed print society; in the 1690s, especially once we leave London, we find relatively little evidence of one." The point requires some emphasis, for the standard historical view has assumed that England became and remained a print society after about 1500. There is, of course, no question that the national life was deeply affected in the 200 years between 1500 and 1700 by printed books, such as, by way of obvious example, vernacular bibles or the propaganda pamphlets of the civil war, but the weight of evidence increasingly suggests that it was not until about 1700 that printing began to affect the structure of social life at every level. Belanger lists many print products that became common for the first time in the eighteenth century, and in their very ordinariness they suggest how extensively print during this period expanded into and affected social and institutional life: posters, theater bills, newspapers and magazines, handbills, bill-headings, labels, tickets, "printed forms meant to be completed by hand . . . marriage certificates, printed indentures or receipts." In time, simple usefulness acquired an aura of authority as, for example, permanent records began to be printed, accu-

rate information conveyed in newspapers, and the society's privileged texts—legal, sacred, instructional—stabilized and stored in print. Gradually this kind of authority grew into the authenticity that is probably the absolute mark of print culture, a generally accepted view that what is printed is true, or at least truer than any other type of record.

In this general transformation to a print culture, letters and the entire world of writing, which were directly and continuously involved with printing, inevitably underwent radical, even revolutionary, changes. To mention only some of the most familiar print-related changes in letters at this time, the novel became the major literary form, and prose challenged poetry as the most prestigious medium; the author's copyright was legalized and censorship was nearly abolished; enormous numbers of literary works, both new and old, were printed and made available to readers; large public and private libraries became common; criticism became a standard literary genre; patronage nearly disappeared as authors began to be able to live by selling their writing; literacy increased and a new public audience of readers appeared; literary histories were written for the first time. Changes of this magnitude were cumulatively as revolutionary in the world of letters as the events of 1688 and 1789, with which they were socially coordinate, were in the political world, and like the related political changes, the literary changes were not random but followed a particular logic.

The "logic" of a technology, an idea, or an institution is its tendency consistently to shape whatever it affects in a limited number of definite forms or directions. Peter Berger, in *The Sacred Canopy,* describes, for example, the logic of tools such as the plow, and of language, and the way that their logics press on and impress both social activity and human consciousness:

> Once produced, the tool has a being of its own that cannot be readily changed by those who employ it. Indeed, the tool (say, an agricultural implement) may even enforce the logic of its being upon its users, sometimes in a way that may not be particularly agreeable to them. For instance, a plow, though obviously a human product, is an external object not only in the sense that its users may fall over it and hurt themselves as a result, just as they may by falling over a rock or a stump or any other natural object. More interestingly, the plow may compel its users to arrange their agricultural activity, and perhaps also other aspects of their lives, in a way that conforms to *its* own logic and that may have been neither intended nor foreseen by those who originally devised it. The same objectivity, however, characterizes the non-material elements of culture as well. Man invents a language and then finds that both his speaking and his thinking are dominated by its grammar. Man produces values and discovers that he feels guilt when he contravenes them. Man concocts institutions, which come to confront him as powerfully controlling and even menacing constellations of the external world.

Marshall McLuhan in *The Gutenberg Galaxy* traces the logic of print to the basic fact of the technology itself, "the mechanical spirit of movable types in precise lines." In a print culture, he argues, where what is printed is intensely true and the printed text is ultimately composed of the pieces of type in the printer's cases, texts and truth are therefore structured by the principal characteristics of type, which he lists as abstraction, uniformity, repeatability, visuality, and quantification. The printed book, with its potential infinity of abstract words, its standardized spellings, punctuation, and grammatical rules, its regular lines, numbered pages, and orderly format is the visible world of print logic or of the "spirit of movable types." Through the book, by the process McLuhan calls "the interiorization of technology," type extends its reality into the consciousness of readers: "Gutenberg typography filled the world the human voice closed down. People began to read silently and passively as consumers." And as they did so, print logic began to shape mental structures, imparting a sense of the world as a set of abstract ideas rather than immediate facts, a fixed point of view organizing all subject matter into an equivalent of perspective in painting, and the visual homogenization of experience. It also encouraged individualism, even solipsism, by the silent privacy in which the printed book is read: "The unconscious is a direct creation of print technology, the ever-mounting slag-heap of rejected awareness." And inevitably, McLuhan relentlessly goes on, as print logic changed mental structures, the social world was also changed by the increasing numbers of people whose minds were programmed by print logic. Rationalism, idealistic philosophy, consumerism, individualism, capitalism, and nationalism—"by print a people *sees* itself for the first time"—are all, in McLuhan's view, the inevitable consequences of movable type, the workings out in psychological and social life of print logic.

"It is quite easy," McLuhan states flatly, "to test the universal effects of print on Western thought after the sixteenth century, simply by examining the most extraordinary developments in any art or science whatever." In his applications of this hypothesis to modern western consciousness and society, McLuhan also applies it to letters and argues that some of the principal features of romantic and modern literature are closely related to the type which has been its primary medium for the last two hundred years or so. Print, he shows, for example, fixed the literary text, by giving it an objective and unchanging reality in its own right. In earlier oral cultures there could be no such thing as an exact text, since the particular form something took at any given moment always depended, as Parry and Lord in their studies of oral poetry have demonstrated, on performance. Even in a manuscript culture a work was seldom or never reproduced *exactly* the same way twice running, and so remained always a process, never becoming a completed, static object. But in a print culture, type makes it possible for the work to exist as a fixed object, infinitely and accurately reproducible, controlling, even "being" as it were, its own form independent of perception or accidents. Print thus makes poems into literary works of art and encourages thereby "a new hypnotic superstition of the book as independent of and uncontaminated by human agency." Printed books like the Bible, *Paradise Lost,* or Johnson's *Dictionary* have acquired enormous validity and transcendental authority in their own right. Even as print made the works of literature, so it also, McLuhan argues, made authors. In the words of E. P. Goldschmidt, "the Middle Ages for various reasons and from various causes did not possess the concept of 'authorship' in exactly the same significance as we have it now," but the factual, solid external existence of the printed book in numerous copies "told" the writer he was an author,

identified him as such on the title page, and offered him permanent existence in eternal fame.

Many of the formal properties considered central to romantic and modern literature are also, according to McLuhan, aesthetic expressions of print logic. The crucial literary concepts of a central plot and a single structure are extensions of the movement of type in precise lines, which generates "the notion of moving steadily along on single planes of narrative awareness . . . totally alien to the nature of language and consciousness." Even those ideal fictional worlds created by the imagination that are the fundamental assumption of romantic literature derive from "the power of print to install the reader in a subjective universe of limitless freedom and spontaneity." McLuhan's point is not that these leading ideas of romantic and modern literature, such as ideal text, author, and imagination, were unheard of in preprint cultures, but rather that when print became the dominant literary medium, it intensified these and other print-related values, while diminishing those manuscript qualities, such as rarity, with which it was not co-ordinate.

In her summary book, *The Printing Press as an Agent of Change,* Elizabeth Eisenstein has, in effect, tested McLuhan's brilliant insights—for they are little more or less than that—by looking at the historical effects of print on European culture of the Renaissance and Reformation. As a historian, Eisenstein is less concerned with nonobjective states of mind than McLuhan, and much more concerned with such solid details as, for example, print runs, costs and prices, the proportion of new books printed to old books reprinted, the accumulation of books on various subjects, and the growth of libraries. Her historical work tends to bear McLuhan out, however, and Eisenstein's leading "features of print culture" are very close to some of his basic principles of movable type. Eisenstein's subheadings in her second chapter provide a good scheme of her findings about the primary social effects of print logic: dissemination, standardization, reorganization, data collection, preservation, and amplification and reinforcement. Very briefly, these leading characteristics of print manifested themselves socially as: (1) the spread of knowledge as a result of the large number of printed books; (2) standardized printed texts which replaced the indeterminacy of oral performance and manuscript drift, and continued to replace imperfect printed copies with more accurate editions; (3) a rational organization of knowledge fostered by the inherent *esprit de système* of work in the printing house and its product, the printed book: "regularly numbered pages, punctuation marks, section breaks, running heads, indices"; and (4) "typographical fixity," the ability of printed books to give to the words and ideas they print a substantial and durable form, and to amplify this objectified verbal reality by the distribution of numerous identical copies of the same organization of words on the page.

In a print culture, McLuhan and Eisenstein, as well as other historians of print and writing, particularly Walter Ong and Eric Havelock, have shown us that everything that is affected by print—and almost everything eventually is—will reveal in some way and to some degree, depending on always complex circumstances, its leading characteristics, the impress of its logic. The basic elements of print logic as they have been variously defined interconnect and overlap, but writings on the subject like those of McLuhan and Eisenstein regularly emphasize three leading characteristics that for convenience can in our present discussion be called multiplicity, systematization, and fixity. The way in which these print qualities manifest themselves in the world can be illustrated most immediately and obviously with print's most characteristic product, the book: multiplicity—the printing press makes many different books and many copies of the same book; systematization—a book is systematically produced and internally ordered, and its existence forces the systematic structuring of knowledge; fixity—the book is objectively, durably, there, always the same or moving toward a "true" form.

These primary tendencies of print logic—multiplicity, systematization, and fixity—can provide a focus for the broad effects of print on letters in eighteenth-century England as we look . . . at the interlinking chain that extended from the print shop, to the publishers—or booksellers, as they were then known—to the marketplace and the Grub Street writers. To concentrate on the "logic" of the historical process is, of course, to simplify for the sake of clarity, and something of the actual complexity of what happened is suggested by the fact that although multiplicity and systematization are both openly and immediately at work in the Grub Street world of writing, the full effects of fixity appear only over a longer period of time and in more indirect ways. In fact, one of print's first effects on its products, whether books or authors, was, because of its tendency toward large numbers, to make them into common and therefore ephemeral commodities or even consumables. It was only cumulatively and gradually that the effects of fixity appeared. That is to say, there is at least some tension, if not downright contradiction, between two of the primary energies of print logic, multiplicity and fixity—what we might call the "remainder-house" and the "library" effects—which . . . has never entirely been resolved.

The old-style hand-press print shop, and the ways a bookseller-publisher conducted his business, are too well known to require detailed recounting, but a quick description of the print shop of William Strahan, Johnson's chief printer, and the bookselling business of his major publisher, Robert Dodsley, will reveal something of the complex and multifold ways print logic expressed itself in life, work, thought, and society.

At the center of the print shop of William Strahan, a young Scot who came to London to earn his fortune after learning the printing trade in Edinburgh, stood several of the old wooden hand-pulled presses, costing 15 guineas each, which had changed little since Gutenberg's time. In the 1750s, Strahan's printing house was located at 10 Little New Street, off Shoe Lane, in premises for which he paid a rent of £200 a year. Basic working materials for his presses were paper, which cost 12 to 20 shillings a ream of crown sheets, sized 15 by 20 inches, or 12 by 16 inches; a supply of good quality printer's ink; a number of cases of type, which cost 7s, 6d. a pair; and an assortment of relatively inexpensive ordering and locking devices (systematization and fixity at the mechanical level) such as composing sticks, galley trays, chases, and quoins. Strahan's account books still exist, and his biographer, J. A. Cochrane, has used them to study carefully the economics of Strahan's printing business. He estimates that in the 1750s

a capital investment of a few hundred pounds would set up a basic print shop.

The organization of labor in Strahan's shop, as in printing houses for the preceding three centuries, was an extension of print's logic of systematization to human activity. Strahan, who ran a large and active shop, remained the master printer and supervised operations; however, he hired a manager, whom he paid 30 shillings a week, and increased his income further by allowing him several apprentices. The shop was worked by these few apprentices and a number of journeymen whose weekly wage could rise as high as 1 guinea, good pay for that time. These journeymen were specialized, but the main divisions of labor were few. The compositor who set the type was paid on a piece-work basis, 8 shillings for an octavo sheet of 16 pages, or sometimes, after 1744, 4 pence per thousand letters. The proofreader or corrector got 2 pence for every shilling paid the compositor. The two men who worked the press itself, one to ink and one to pull, were together paid 1s. 2d. for every 250 perfected sheets, that is, printed on both sides. Their average rate of work has been computed by Cochrane at four impressions per minute, or about 250 perfected sheets in two hours, and average pay for a long workweek was therefore, Cochrane says, 15 to 17 shillings. In a large shop such as Strahan's, there were also other less skilled workers who hung the printed sheets up for drying, and later, stacked, folded, and bundled them in proper order, before sending them to the bookseller or the binder, binding ordinarily being done outside the printing shop.

In 1759 Strahan employed over 50 men in his shop and therefore when he operated continuously had a payroll of £40 to £50 a week. In computing his charges to his customers, Strahan used the standard method of adding one half of his wage costs to the actual wages paid for a job to cover material, overhead, and profit. For example, if his wage costs for 1,000 sheets of octavo came to 14 shillings he would add 7 shillings and bill 21 shillings total. Paper was the most expensive item in the entire process, and it was usually supplied by the bookseller, author, or whoever ordered the printing; but if Strahan supplied the paper, he would add its cost to his charges.

Strahan eventually became rich enough to take a seat as an M. P. and keep a coach—which was unusual enough for a printer to be remarked on favorably by Johnson, who sometimes had the use of it—and he did so not only by organizing his shop efficiently and keeping an eye on the pennies, but by adapting successfully to other economic realities of his situation. He eventually ran the largest print shop in London, with nine presses, and his combined fixed costs were high enough to make it very expensive for him to let his machinery stand idle or operate at less than full capacity. He did not pay his workers when there was no work for them, since he paid by the piece, but there was a strong incentive for him to keep his workforce adequately employed, and his capital investment, rent, and the money tied up in work completed but not yet paid for exerted a constant pressure on him, and in turn on those, including writers, who worked for him, to provide a steady flow of work to and through the presses. A little story Johnson told Boswell illustrates well how closely and carefully Strahan calculated these matters. While working on his *Dictionary*, which was printed in sections by Strahan, Johnson neglected to return at once some proof pages which had been sent him for correction. Strahan's boy was at the door immediately, and Strahan later explained patiently but forcefully to Johnson that his type—which cost money and was always short in the printing house—was tied up and his entire operations disrupted, until such time as the corrected proof was returned, corrections made in the set type, and the presses at work again. In view of this exemplary story of print, there is more than a little irony in the recent discovery that a number of authorial changes marked on *Dictionary* proofs that still exist were not made in the type.

Perhaps the proofs came too late, or perhaps it seemed too expensive to make changes which seemed unnecessary and delaying to a printer who always sought in all ways he could find, large and small, a steady flow of work for his presses. He was the friend and helper, sometimes the banker, of a number of authors who wrote books he printed; he sought and got various government printing contracts; he functioned as a publisher and bought copyrights—which was where the big money was—of books he would then print; and he entered into "congers" (joint venture groups) such as the combination that shared the financial risk for Johnson's *Dictionary*. All this effort to provide work for his presses made sense only if there were a ready market for the printed products, and though sales and distribution were primarily the realm of bookseller and wholesaler, Strahan inevitably became involved in this end of business as well, dealing directly with authors and books that were likely to sell, and serving as an agent and wholesaler to booksellers, particularly in North America.

Logical organization (system) and continuous, high-volume production (multiplicity) are the most prominent characteristics of Strahan's printing operation. Even at this handicraft stage, printing, if done efficiently, was capable of producing large numbers of printed products, and profits could be increased greatly by taking full advantage of this production potential and finding ready markets for the printed products. More presses, more printed materials, and more customers equaled more profits, and since the number of books produced had such important effects for letters, it will be worthwhile to try to summarize what we know about the bibliographic flood produced by Strahan and other printers in eighteenth-century England.

It is clear from the entry in *The Journal of The House of Commons* for 17 April 1695 that Parliament allowed the Licensing Act, the statute that legalized official censorship and limited the number of presses, to lapse in that year not because it infringed on the liberties of Englishmen but because it conferred a monopoly on the crown and a very limited number of booksellers to print, sell, import, and bind books and pamphlets. The main arguments for allowing the Act to lapse were commercial, not constitutional: the Act, it was argued, operated as a restraint on trade, as all forms of censorship do, by retarding the progress of imported books through customs, permitting only 20 printing houses in all England, and limiting the number of presses in each shop, usually to no more than two. After the lapse of the Licensing Act, the number of printers grew steadily, and by 1724 there were 75 printers in London, plus at least 28 more in the provinces. By 1785 there were 124 printers in London alone, and many more presses, since as many as nine were now concentrated in one

shop. By 1713, two thirds of the paper used in printing, which earlier had mostly been imported, was being produced in England, and with the opening of Caslon's type foundry in 1720, well-designed, high-quality English type became increasingly available. Counts of the number of printers and booksellers are notoriously imprecise and usually disagree with one another, but in his survey of the London book trade, Ian Maxted offers figures as hard as we are likely to get. His tables show that in 1668 there were 198 men employed in all the printing trades, working 65 presses—considerably more than the 40 the law strictly allowed—while in 1818 there were approximately 625 active presses worked by 3,365 masters, journeymen, and apprentices, a huge increase (multiplicity) over the 150-year period. The number of book-seller-publishers doubled during a somewhat shorter period, going from 151 in 1735 to 308 in 1802, though the number dropped in intervening years, to 72 in 1763, before rising again to 111 by 1772.

We lack, and probably will continue to lack, precise information about the number of books the printers produced in the eighteenth century. A number of recent scholarly projects have, however, given us more accurate estimations than we once seemed likely to have. (pp. 48-60)

The long-range trend . . . was a large increase in the number of presses, booksellers, and book titles printed in England and in London during the eighteenth century. The numbers, therefore, while telling us something extremely interesting about the ups and downs of the book publishing business during that time, provide in the end statistical support for, and additional explanation of, Belanger's thesis that it was during this time that Britain, along with the rest of western Europe, became a print culture; and they also show in specific terms how print's logical tendencies toward system and numbers were objectified in the social world. (p. 62)

The urgency and ingenuity of such poetic lives as those of Savage, Smart, Goldsmith, Chatterton, and Macpherson tell us not only that the eighteenth century was a literary watershed when the poetic role was no longer fixed, but also that there was an enormous concern about the form the poetic role should take. Print may have determined that henceforth all writers would be some kind of, to put it most crudely, Grub Street hack, but this life of *labor* rather than *work* was obviously unacceptable to the most intense writers of the day; and though they had to accept print realities to some degree, they also expended large amounts of energy and undertook great risks that threatened reputation, sanity, and even life to carve for themselves an acceptable poetic mask, a mask that was for them a realization of being itself. The extreme intensity and imagination these poets expended to make an acceptable, a liveable, poetic role for themselves, however mad the actions may now seem, serve to suggest, startlingly, the degree to which human feelings and existential values are involved in a radical change in the social arrangements of letters. That involvement is, of course, noticeably there in the activities of printers who buy coaches with their profits and booksellers who make an art of book design, but it is the hack writers violently determined to be something more than laborers for the book factory who make it obvious that the social construction of a new print-based system of letters was not a technologically determined process. Technology in the form of print plays a critical, perhaps even a primary, part in literary change in eighteenth-century England, but the new print-based literary system that was ultimately constructed was an interaction of print logic and human needs. (pp. 86-7)

Alvin Kernan, "Printing, Bookselling, Readers, and Writers in Eighteenth-Century London," in his Printing Technology, Letters & Samuel Johnson, *Princeton University Press, 1987, pp. 48-90.*

Allen T. Hazen

[*Hazen was an American educator and essayist. He regularly contributed articles on eighteenth-century literary and bibliographical topics to scholarly journals and was general editor of the Yale edition of* Samuel Johnson's Works *(1958-66). In the following essay, he traces the evolution of moveable type in the printing industry during the eighteenth century, focusing on the progression of type-styles encountered throughout Johnson's canon.*]

Printers are perhaps as conservative and unchanging as any craftsmen, and the printing of 1700 does not look radically unlike that of 1600; but during Johnson's later life new styles were steadily blossoming forth. Had Johnson's eyes been better, I think he might have blasted away at this typographic contraband somewhat as he did at neologism in language and at strange themes in poetry. For more than most men he liked the style familiarized to him in his youth, and he might have been expected to side vigorously with the many stand-patters who attacked Baskerville's slender types in 1757. It is pleasant to remember, however, that instead of decrying Baskerville, Johnson presented a copy of Baskerville's Virgil in 1769 to Trinity College, Oxford, in recompense for reading privileges extended to him there. His generosity was certainly not stirred by the importance of the text, since Baskerville's text has no independent value whatsoever; and he must therefore have presented the book because of its typographic excellence. But for the most part typographic change was unregarded by Johnson, and I shall refer to books not as printing specimens inspired by Johnson or treasured by him but as specimens of the changes taking place within the span of Johnson's life.

It is instructive to look at the *Miscellany* of John Husbands in 1731, in which Johnson first appeared in print, and to compare that with such sober later printing as the *Lives of the Poets.* The title page of Husbands, with its large type, might easily be mistaken for something printed in 1700, such as a tract by Defoe. The text of the volume, too, is in the older style, with its heavy types that belong artistically in a folio instead of in the cramped Oxford octavo. Old-fashioned, also, are the capitals for all nouns and the italics for all proper names, a style that was to give way within a generation (at least among progressive London printers) to the new style of capital letters for proper names only. Husbands' *Miscellany* is also printed in an older type, just when the more adaptable Caslon is superseding all other types.

Father Lobo's *Voyage to Abyssinia,* printed in Birmingham but published in London in 1735, is somewhat old-fashioned provincial printing and not otherwise notable.

The break from the older style is not precise in books writ-

ten by Johnson. Dodsley published *London* in 1738 in a format much like the Pope folios of the same time or a little earlier. But by 1749 the *Vanity of Human Wishes* is essentially a modern (i.e., mid-eighteenth century) book: the title page looks like those of the next twenty years, the type is Caslon, and the poem is printed in quarto, the size that replaced the earlier poetical folio. Quarto was to remain until 1800 the normal size for a small poetical pamphlet, and while the general trend to smaller sizes is easily understood, I am always a little startled at the suddenness with which folios dropped out after 1740. Up to 1740 the folio is normal; after 1740 it grows uncommon, and after 1750 it is scarcely used again for short poems.

The *Rambler* in 1750 is perhaps not a fair test, because Johnson and John Payne planned it to look like the *Spectator;* but the handsome *Rambler* in its pot folio looks in fact more like the printing of 1750 than of 1712. The folio keeps the older style of italics for all proper names and initial capitals for all nouns, but the pretty little reprint of 1752 in duodecimo adopts the new style which uses only initial capitals with roman letters for proper names and reduces nouns to lower case. The miscellaneous prose published by Johnson between 1740 and 1750 is of comparatively little typographic interest, although we may like to compare the title page of the *Drury-Lane Prologue,* printed by Cave in 1747, with the handsome Caslon title page of the *Plan of a Dictionary,* also printed in 1747. Cave clung to his old types, either from conservatism or inertia, and his long-time associate Johnson seems to have been well enough satisfied with the *Drury-Lane Prologue.*

Of the great *Dictionary* I scarcely know what to say. Finally published in 1755, it comes just at the middle of Johnson's literary career, a quarter century after Husbands' *Miscellany* and a quarter century before the *Lives of the Poets.* I do not know that its typographic excellence has ever been singled out for praise, and yet the pages of text filled with definitions and illustrations serve the reader well. There seems to me something almost Johnsonian in the sturdy independent way the folio columns present themselves, doing their duty without ostentation; and Strahan's title page with its solid refusal to be clever seems (perhaps by familiarity) to be well fitted to the text it describes.

The next major landmark in Johnson's publishing career, the edition of Shakespeare in 1765, is perhaps disappointing typographically. I have a sentimental fondness for that edition, and yet I confess that it always seems a dull piece of printing. The title pages are flat, the type of Johnson's famous Preface is too widely spaced for the type page, the paper is too thin, and the crowded pages of text and notes seem unsuccessful. Perhaps the octavo format is more to blame than the type or layout: the lines run over very frequently, especially in the notes, to produce a scattered look, Johnson's irregular annotation runs over to another page often enough to confuse us when we read, and a long note is often found to be a mere quotation from Warburton that pushes Johnson's comment far away from the passage he is annotating. Possibly only the majestic quartos that Pope used could have fused Johnson's notes and Shakespeare's text into an attractive page. The *Journey to the Western Islands,* written and printed somewhat hurriedly in 1775, makes a better impression on the reader than does the Shakespeare, probably because the pages are less crowded. It is good sturdy work, satisfactory but not glamorous.

Johnson's last major work, the *Lives of the Poets,* is perhaps not a fair test because the publication was even more than usually a booksellers' venture. It would have been possible for Johnson to advise about format and typography on any other book, but the *Poets* had been planned specifically as a competitive reply to Bell's Edinburgh-printed collection, and Johnson was engaged only to write some "little prefaces," one to be prefixed to each poet. That Johnson's liking for his task led him to write major critical essays does not affect the presumption that the format was determined in advance. But if the format of the *Poets* shows nothing of Johnson's typographic tastes, the little volumes are not unpleasing in themselves: the small format, pot octavo, is unusual and seems somewhat wasteful, but the well-spaced type makes judicious use of the small page and the careful presswork does honor to the fine letter paper that was used. The volumes are attractive if not revolutionary, and Johnson had every right to be pleased when he saw his little prefaces in print. The separate reprint of the *Lives* in 1781, four volumes in medium octavo, was planned more for compact utility than beauty, and it adds nothing to our estimate of Johnson's typographic enthusiasm.

Now if such a survey of the typography of Johnson's books shows chiefly that he paid no attention whatever to the type but merely allowed the stylistic changes of the time to be reflected in his books, one might fairly ask what Johnson's significance is in the matter. The correct answer seems to me to be that Johnson's very imperviousness to typography makes his books a better guide to what was happening between 1730 and 1780. Despite his indifference, his own books illustrate perfectly the change in average commercial printing from the older style (heavy angular continental types, crowded titles, and steady use of italics) to the newer style (the rounder Caslon that is now denominated Old Style, titles with homogeneous type, and italics severely restricted), a change that came just at that time with no assistance from Johnson.

Besides the general change in printing style during his life, Johnson lived through an era of important experimentation. In 1757, after long experimenting with type design, ink, and presswork, and with hot-pressed paper, Baskerville published his edition of Virgil. Two hundred years later, when the various eighteenth-century Old Style type faces have tended to fuse in our consciousness, we may find it hard to comprehend what caused all the excitement. Although the slender and pointed Baskerville letters are very different from the rounded Caslon, perhaps only a book designer would even think of saying today that one type is better (or worse) than the other. But in 1757 feelings ran high; men complained that the narrow Baskerville letters hurt their eyes and that the black ink and shiny paper reflected the glare. Benjamin Franklin proved by a pleasant trick that such people were merely unhappy because of the change from familiar to strange, and that they could not in fact differentiate the two types. I was amused by a similar experience a few years ago when a friend who aspired to some modicum of typographical understanding complained that Horace Walpole was ill-advised to use that horrid Baskerville type, and I could scarcely convince him that Walpole's type was actually not a horrid Basker-

ville but a dependable Caslon; his dislike of Walpole was genuine enough, but his disapproval of Walpole's choice of types was merely uninformed prejudice.

Baskerville's new type began to influence all type design: Moore and Fry in Bristol and Wilson in Glasgow soon began to offer types that were modified from Caslon in the direction of Baskerville. By the end of the century even the Caslon firm was offering a new font that was as close to Baskerville as it was to the earlier Caslon.

Boswell records that Johnson disapproved of Robert and Andrew Foulis when he met them in Glasgow, but Johnson was enough of a book collector to ask Boswell two years later to send him two books printed by the Foulis brothers. It would be pleasant if we could say that Johnson had requested a copy of the Foulis edition of Gray's *Poems.* The Foulis books were not directly influenced by Baskerville, but they established their own tradition of well-designed book production and careful presswork, to become notable as "trade" publishers who were fine printers.

Perhaps the most important of all fine printers during Johnson's lifetime was Bodoni of Parma, whose handsome editions of the classics began to appear shortly before Johnson died. Had Johnson been able to make his projected Italian journey, I think he would have thought Bodoni worth meeting; but he was unable to go, and I do not know that he was ever aware of Bodoni's work.

Meanwhile, a different manifestation of printing enthusiasm, the private press, was appearing in 1757 at Strawberry Hill. Both Baskerville and the Foulis brothers were commercial printers, important ones if not always entirely prudent. But although Walpole's first venture, Gray's *Odes,* can be called commercial since the edition was printed for Dodsley, Walpole's press was always a private one, presided over by one man—and a boy—and not run for profit. We know that Johnson read Gray's *Odes,* very probably in the Strawberry Hill edition, but we can suspect that his disapproval of the poetry was great enough to blind his eyes to the merits of the printing. There was little enough in Walpole, as a man or as an author, to appeal to Johnson; the rather foppish young man who in 1745 sat in Parliament out of a sense of duty but who preferred to dabble in society verse or to play whist with titled ladies would have seemed a useless dilettante to Johnson, who had learned by years of literary drudgery for Cave that worth rises with painful slowness when weighted down by poverty. Walpole's most important literary friends, besides, were Gray and Mason, almost the only literary men of the middle of the century to remain entirely outside of Johnson's orbit. And then when Walpole established his press he elected to print as his first offering Gray's two obscure odes. One would like to see Johnson's copy of this first Strawberry Hill book, perhaps underscored heavily and angrily at the line, "Give ample room and verge enough," underscored with what dark mutterings as he read. All in all, it is little to be wondered at that Johnson should have failed to praise the typography. Later books printed by Walpole were not written by Gray, at any rate, but one would not expect Johnson to be attracted by Vertue's collections dealing with the lives of the old painters, or by the *Mémoires du Comte de Grammont.* One volume, the handsomest product of the Strawberry Hill Press, might have been expected in Johnson's library.

This was the fine Lucan in quarto, with notes by Grotius and by Dr. Bentley. Such a book might well have seemed important to Johnson the classicist, whether or not he approved of Bentley as an editor of Milton. Two other editions of Lucan were in Johnson's library when he died, but not the Strawberry Hill edition. Perhaps it was too expensive, perhaps he had lost it; but I fear the simple truth was that he did not care about it.

An oddly attractive fact in bibliographical history is that Johnson's own publications, so unimpressive in format and typography, should now be the most eagerly collected of books from his century. Johnson was so regardless of printing style that he permitted and expected the printer to alter and regularize his own eccentric spelling, unlike Boswell who implored the printer to preserve his special orthography. Johnson was so regardless of the physical condition of his books that Garrick is said to have been unwilling to let him borrow any of his rare Shakespearean quartos. Perhaps it was not inappropriate, therefore, that Johnson's own writings were published in the normal range of formats during his lifetime, without ostentation or eccentric prettiness, as sturdy as his own notes on Shakespeare or his "Life of Dryden," and that they shared in the development of commercial printing during his lifetime, even if they lacked the special graces of the private press or of the new type designs. (pp. 403-09)

Allen T. Hazen, "New Styles in Typography," in The Age of Johnson: Essays Presented to Chauncey Brewster Tinker, *Yale University Press, 1949, pp. 403-09.*

PERIODICALS: "A MAP OF BUSY LIFE"

Samuel Johnson

[*One of the outstanding figures in English literature, Johnson was a prolific essayist, poet, lexicographer, and critic. Esteemed for their common-sensical approach and pleasant didacticism, Johnson's writings are distinguished by a direct and pungent prose style. In the following essay first published in* The Rambler *in 1751, he expounds on the value of journalists to modern society.*]

It is allowed that vocations and employments of least dignity are of the most apparent use; that the meanest artisan or manufacturer contributes more to the accommodation of life than the profound scholar and argumentative theorist; and that the public would suffer less present inconvenience from the banishment of philosophers than from the extinction of any common trade.

Some have been so forcibly struck with this observation that they have, in the first warmth of their discovery, thought it reasonable to alter the common distribution of dignity, and ventured to condemn mankind of universal ingratitude. For justice exacts that those by whom we are most benefited should be most honoured. And what labour can be more useful than that which procures to families and communities those necessaries which supply the wants of nature, or those conveniences by which ease, security, and elegance are conferred?

This is one of the innumerable theories which the first attempt to reduce them into practice certainly destroys. If we estimate dignity by immediate usefulness, agriculture is undoubtedly the first and noblest science; yet we see the plow driven, the clod broken, the manure spread, the seeds scattered, and the harvest reaped by men whom those that feed upon their industry will never be persuaded to admit into the same rank with heroes, or with sages; and who, after all the confessions which truth may extort in favour of their occupation, must be content to fill up the lowest class of the commonwealth, to form the base of the pyramid of subordination, and lie buried in obscurity themselves, while they support all that is splendid, conspicuous, or exalted.

It will be found, upon a closer inspection, that this part of the conduct of mankind is by no means contrary to reason or equity. Remuneratory honours are proportioned at once to the usefulness and difficulty of performances, and are properly adjusted by comparison of the mental and corporeal abilities which they appear to employ. That work, however necessary, which is carried on only by muscular strength and manual dexterity, is not of equal esteem, in the consideration of rational beings, with the tasks that exercise the intellectual powers, and require the active vigour of imagination, or the gradual and laborious investigations of reason.

The merit of all manual occupations seems to terminate in the inventor; and surely the first ages cannot be charged with ingratitude; since those who civilized barbarians, and taught them how to secure themselves from cold and hunger were numbered amongst their deities. But these arts once discovered by philosophy, and facilitated by experience, are afterwards practised with very little assistance from the faculties of the soul; nor is any thing necessary to the regular discharge of these inferior duties beyond that rude observation which the most sluggish intellect may practise, and that industry which the stimulations of necessity naturally enforce.

Yet, though the refusal of statues and panegyrics to those who employ only their hands and feet in the service of mankind may be easily justified, I am far from intending to incite the petulance of pride to justify the superciliousness of grandeur, or to intercept any part of that tenderness and benevolence which by the privilege of their common nature one man may claim from another.

That it would be neither wise nor equitable to discourage the husbandman, the labourer, the miner, or the smith, is generally granted; but there is another race of beings equally obscure and equally indigent, who because their usefulness is less obvious to vulgar apprehensions, live unrewarded and die unpitied, and who have been long exposed to insult without a defender, and to censure without an apologist.

The authors of London were formerly computed by Swift at several thousands, and there is not any reason for suspecting that their number has decreased. Of these only a very few can be said to produce, or endeavour to produce new ideas, to extend any principle of science, or gratify the imagination with any uncommon train of images or contexture of events; the rest, however laborious, however arrogant, can only be considered as the drudges of the pen, the manufacturers of literature, who have set up for authors, either with or without a regular initiation, and like other artificers, have no other care than to deliver their tale of wares at the stated time.

It has been formerly imagined that he who intends the entertainment or instruction of others must feel in himself some peculiar impulse of genius; that he must watch the happy minute in which his natural fire is excited, in which his mind is elevated with nobler sentiments, enlightened with clearer views, and invigorated with stronger comprehension; that he must carefully select his thoughts and polish his expressions; and animate his efforts with the hope of raising a monument of learning which neither time nor envy shall be able to destroy.

But the authors whom I am now endeavouring to recommend have been too long hackneyed in the ways of men to indulge the chimerical ambition of immortality; they have seldom any claim to the trade of writing but that they have tried some other without success; they perceive no particular summons to composition except the sound of the clock; they have no other rule than the law or the fashion for admitting their thoughts or rejecting them; and about the opinion of posterity they have little solicitude, for their productions are seldom intended to remain in the world longer than a week.

That such authors are not to be rewarded with praise is evident, since nothing can be admired when it ceases to exist; but surely though they cannot aspire to honour, they may be exempted from ignominy, and adopted into that order of men which deserves our kindness though not our reverence. These papers of the day, the *Ephemerae* of learning, have uses more adequate to the purposes of common life than more pompous and durable volumes. If it is necessary for every man to be more acquainted with his contemporaries than with past generations, and to rather know the events which may immediately affect his fortune or quiet than the revolutions of ancient kingdoms, in which he has neither possessions nor expectations; if it be pleasing to hear of the preferment and dismission of statesmen, the birth of heirs, and the marriage of beauties, the humble author of journals and gazettes must be considered as a liberal dispenser of beneficial knowledge.

Even the abridger, compiler and translator, though their labours cannot be ranked with those of the diurnal historiographer, yet must not be rashly doomed to annihilation. Every size of readers requires a genius of correspondent capacity; some delight in abstracts and epitomes because they want room in their memory for long details, and content themselves with effects, without enquiry after causes; some minds are overpowered by splendor of sentiment, as some eyes are offended by a glaring light; such will gladly contemplate an author in an humble imitation, as we look without pain upon the sun in the water.

As every writer has his use, every writer ought to have his patrons; and since no man, however high he may now stand, can be certain that he shall not be soon thrown down from his elevation by criticism or caprice, the common interest of learning requires that her sons should cease from intestine hostilities, and instead of sacrificing each other to malice and contempt, endeavour to avert

persecution from the meanest of their fraternity. (pp. 229-32)

Samuel Johnson, "Periodical Essays: Journalists," in his Samuel Johnson, *edited by* Donald Greene, *Oxford University Press, Oxford, 1984, pp. 229-32.*

Samuel Johnson

[*In the following essay, originally published in 1758, Johnson clarifies the essential objective of the responsible journalist.*]

It is an unpleasing consideration that virtue cannot be inferred from knowledge; that many can teach others those duties which they never practise themselves; yet, though there may be speculative knowledge without actual performance, there can be no performance without knowledge; and the present state of many of our papers is such that it may be doubted not only whether the compilers know their duty, but whether they have endeavoured or wished to know it.

A journalist is an historian, not indeed of the highest class, nor of the number of those whose works bestow immortality upon others or themselves; yet, like other historians, he distributes for a time reputation or infamy, regulates the opinion of the week, raises hopes and terrors, inflames or allays the violence of the people. He ought therefore to consider himself as subject at least to the first law of history, the obligation to tell truth. The journalist, indeed, however honest, will frequently deceive, because he will frequently be deceived himself. He is obliged to transmit the earliest intelligence before he knows how far it may be credited; he relates transactions yet fluctuating in uncertainty; he delivers reports of which he knows not the authors. It cannot be expected that he should know more than he is told, or that he should not sometimes be hurried down the current of a popular clamour. All that he can do is to consider attentively, and determine impartially, to admit no falsehoods by design, and to retract those which he shall have adopted by mistake.

This is not much to be required, and yet this is more than the writers of news seem to exact from themselves. It must surely sometimes raise indignation to observe with what serenity of confidence they relate on one day what they know not to be true, because they hope that it will please, and with what shameless tranquility they contradict it on the next day, when they find that it will please no longer. How readily they receive any report that will disgrace our enemies, and how eagerly they accumulate praises upon a name which caprice or accident has made a favourite. They know, by experience, however destitute of reason, that what is desired will be credited without nice examination; they do not therefore always limit their narratives by possibility, but slaughter armies without battles, and conquer countries without invasions.

There are other violations of truth admitted only to gratify idle curiosity which yet are mischievous in their consequences, and hateful in their contrivance. Accounts are sometimes published of robberies and murders which never were committed, men's minds are terrified with fictitious dangers, the public indignation is raised, and the government of our country depreciated and contemned.

These scribblers who give false alarms ought to be taught by some public animadversion that to relate crimes is to teach them, and that as most men are content to follow the herd, and to be like their neighbours, nothing contributes more to the frequency of wickedness than the representation of it as already frequent.

There is another practice of which the injuriousness is more apparent, and which, if the law could succour the poor, is now punishable by law. The advertisement of apprentices who have left their masters, and who are often driven away by cruelty or hunger; the minute descriptions of men whom the law has not considered as criminal, and the insinuations often published in such a manner that, though obscure to the public, they are well understood where they can do most mischief; and many other practices by which particular interests are injured are to be diligently avoided by an honest journalist, whose business is only to tell transactions of general importance, or uncontested notoriety, or by advertisements to promote private convenience without disturbance of private quiet.

Thus far the journalist is obliged to deviate from the common methods of his competitors by the laws of unvariable morality. Other improvements may be expected from him as conducive to delight or information. It is common to find passages in papers of intelligence which cannot be understood. Obscure places are sometimes mentioned without any information from geography or history. Sums of money are reckoned by coins or denominations of which the value is not known in this country. Terms of war and navigation are inserted which are utterly unintelligible to all who are not engaged in military or naval business. A journalist, above most other men, ought to be acquainted with the lower orders of mankind, that he may be able to judge what will be plain and what will be obscure; what will require a comment, and what will be apprehended without explanation. He is to consider himself not as writing to students or statesmen alone, but to women, shopkeepers, and artisans, who have little time to bestow upon mental attainments, but desire, upon easy terms, to know how the world goes; who rises, and who falls; who triumphs, and who is defeated.

If the writer of this journal shall be able to execute his own plan; if he shall carefully enquire after truth, and diligently impart it; if he shall resolutely refuse to admit into his paper whatever is injurious to private reputation; if he shall relate transactions with greater clearness than others, and sell more instruction at a cheaper rate, he hopes that his labours will not be overlooked. This he promises to endeavour; and, if his promise shall obtain the favour of an early attention, he desires that favour to be continued only as it is deserved. (pp. 544-46)

> *Samuel Johnson, "Later Prose: Of the Duty of a Journalist," in his* Samuel Johnson, *edited by Donald Greene, Oxford University Press, Oxford, 1984, pp. 544-46.*

Rosamond Bayne-Powell

[*Bayne-Powell was an English dramatist and author whose works primarily concern eighteenth-century English social history. In the following excerpt, she surveys the periodicals of eighteenth-century London and interprets their social influence.*]

"A leaf of political instructions is served up every morning with tea," said Goldsmith, and by his time the daily paper was a feature of London life.

The first English newspaper to be published every day was the *Daily Courant,* which appeared in 1702, and was soon followed by the *Post Boy.*

The age of Anne was prolific in newspapers. The Treasury with an eye to future taxation computed that in 1711 "there are published weekly about 44,000 newspapers viz. *Daily Courant, London Post, English Post, London Gazette, Postman, Postboy, Flying Post, Review,* and *Observator.*"

The *Review* was Defoe's paper and when it came to an end in 1713 he published a monthly journal with the title of *Mercurius Politicus,* thus reviving the name of the old paper which Milton had edited.

The *Tatler* and the *Spectator* were founded in 1709 and 1711, and enjoyed only too short a life.

The influence of these papers can hardly be exaggerated, and after more than two centuries they are still fresh and delightful. In an age when literature was frequently evil

Eighteenth-century English caricature of an author—"the picture of want and misery."

and base the *Tatler* and the *Spectator* stood for what was pure in thought and in style. They championed the poor, the downtrodden, the debtor, the ill-used child. They claimed a wider and fuller education for women, they denounced abuses and cruelties. They cared nothing for the sneering wits of the coffee houses, for reactionaries and bigots.

Steele tells us that he served the cause of women "to the last drop of ink," and he was equally the champion of the oppressed. The newspaper tax of 1711 killed the *Spectator,* though other worthless journals contrived to exist.

In 1710 Dr. King, the Jacobite Principal of St. Mary's Hall, Oxford, founded the *Examiner* and secured Swift as a contributor. Swift has been called "the father of the leading article," but he did not write for more than a few months. He gave it up when he obtained the Deanery of St. Patrick. The *Examiner* had, however, other brilliant contributors. Prior, Atterbury, Arbuthnot and Bolingbroke wrote for it. A number of other political journals followed, such as the *Craftsman,* the *Whig Examiner* and the *Medley.*

In spite of the Stamp Act newspapers became more numerous. The *Gentleman's Magazine* stated in 1731 that "no less than 200 half-sheets per month are thrown from the press only in London."

In 1733 the London journals included the *Daily Courant,* the *Craftsman, Fog's Journal, Mist's Journal,* the *London Journal,* the *Free Briton,* the *Grub Street Journal,* the *Weekly Register,* the *Universal Spectator,* the *Auditor,* the *Weekly Miscellany,* the *London Crier, Read's Journal,* the *London Evening Post, Œdipus or the Postman Remounted,* the *St. James' Post,* and the *London Daily Post,* later to be known as the *London Advertiser.*

Forty years later there were fifty-three newspapers circulating in London alone.

In 1750 Dr. Johnson began to edit the first number of the *Rambler,* a 2*d.* paper which came out twice a week.

It was an attempt to revive the non-political journal which deals with life and literature, but the venture was not a great success. The charm and gaiety of Steele and Addison were entirely lacking. Johnson wrote the whole of the ponderous thing himself, with only four contributions from outside, one of them being from Richardson. It lasted for about two years, and was then followed by such comparatively frivolous periodicals as the *Adventurer,* the *World* and the *Connoisseur.*

Johnson had contributed to the *Adventurer* but he disapproved of the other two papers, and in 1758 he began to edit the *Idler.* It hardly justifies its name, though it is less dull and boring than its predecessor. Wharton, Langton and Sir Joshua Reynolds contributed to it and it lasted for one hundred and three numbers.

In 1762 with Churchill's aid John Wilkes began to publish the *North Briton.* It contained the most bitter attacks on the Ministry and particularly upon Lord Bute. In the following year, having received an advance copy of the King's Speech from Pitt and Temple, Wilkes published his famous no. 45, which contained a most bitter and slashing attack upon the policy of the King's Ministers.

George III chose to consider this as a personal attack and took immediate proceedings against him. Wilkes pointed in vain to the opening words of his article.

"The King's Speech," he had said, "has always been considered, by the legislature and by the public at large, as the speech of the Minister."

He was arrested upon a general warrant, which means a warrant which did not give the name of the person to be arrested, and thrown into the Tower. A month later, however, he was released on a decision of Lord Chief Justice Pratt that his arrest was a breach of privilege. The matter came up again when the House of Commons declared no. 45 of the *North Briton* to be "a seditious libel" and in 1768 when Wilkes had returned from the Continent and was standing for Middlesex, he was sentenced to a year's imprisonment and a fine of £500 for his *Essay on Women* and no. 45 of the *North Briton.*

Wilkes was a man of infamous character; but he vindicated the liberty of the press and was to do it good service again in later years.

It is impossible to enumerate the countless weekly and bi-weekly papers which were produced in London during the century.

The *Observer,* still happily with us, was founded in 1791, and the official *London Gazette* has been published on Tuesdays and Fridays since 1666.

Lloyds List was first issued as a weekly paper in 1726. Its editor who had published a journal known as *Lloyds News* in the preceding century was a member of the famous house of Lloyds.

Perhaps the oldest English periodical was the *Bill of Mortality* published every week by the company of Parish Clerks. It had been established in the reign of Charles I and continued until the Registration Act of 1837 abolished the Bills of Mortality. It was sold at the Parish Clerk's Hall in London to parish clerks only, at the price of 16*d.* a quire with diseases on the back side, or 8*d.* without diseases. The clerks retailed it in their several parishes at 1*d.* each or 4*s.* for a yearly subscription. It is surprising that there should have been any demand, for even with the diseases on the back it must have been dull reading.

The oldest of the daily London newspapers which are still with us, the *Morning Post,* was established in 1772. It had then the sub-title of the *Daily Advertising Pamphlet,* and was indeed little more than a sheet of advertisements, dealing largely with State lotteries, and having eight pages measuring 12 inches by 8. After 1795 under the able editorship of Peter and Daniel Stuart it became a brilliant and popular newspaper.

The Times started its great career in 1785 with the name of the *Daily Universal Register,* but its title was changed three years later to the present one. Then, as now, it was published in Printing House Square under the auspices of the Walter family, and even in those early days it stood out for freedom of expression, and independence of thought.

John Walter, the first, had several clashes with a reactionary government, and even suffered fine and imprisonment in the service of his great paper. His chief offence lay in daring to suggest that the sons of George III had incurred the royal displeasure by conduct ill-befitting princes of the blood.

The *Morning Chronicle,* which lived for over ninety years, was founded by William Woodfall in 1769, and the *Morning Herald* in 1781. Henry Woodfall and his son published for many years a paper which was known as the *Public Advertiser,* the *General Advertiser,* the *London Daily Post,* and finally in 1798 the *Public Ledger.*

The *Letters* of Junius were published in this paper when it appeared as the *Public Advertiser.* They made an enormous difference to the sales, which were nearly doubled.

The mystery of the authorship was well preserved, and this, as much as the Letters themselves, conduced to the popularity of the paper.

There was certainly some kind of parliamentary reporting as early as the seventeenth century. News of what was going on was embodied in the papers, but the actual transcribing of words used in the House was first adopted by the *Gentleman's Magazine* in 1736. The publisher Edward Cave and a few friends took surreptitious notes, and reproduced them in his journal. This was held to be a breach of privilege and Cave was threatened with the rigour of the law. The reports, however, being popular with readers, Cave resolved to continue them. He published his parliamentary news with the heading of "Debates in the Senate of Lilliput" and disguised the names of the speakers under some absurd pseudonym, such as Wingul Pubrub for William Pulteney.

From 1740 to 1743 Dr. Johnson wrote the parliamentary news for this journal. He was careful, he said, not to "let the Whig dogs get the best of it." He still wrote about the senate of Lilliput and disguised the speakers' names under some sort of anagram.

Sometimes the notes brought to him from the House were so meagre that he "had nothing more communicated to him than the names of the several speakers, and the part which they had taken in the debate." The payment for contributions was never high. Thomas Holcroft received 5*s.* a column for what he supplied to the *Whitehall Evening Post.*

The reporter needed to be a man with a prodigious memory. There were those who could memorise a whole speech and going home could write it down verbatim. Others scribbled notes in secret in some corner of the House, and if they were detected would slip a half-guinea into the hand of the usher, who was generally quite willing to receive it. The salary of the reporter was usually about £1 a week, though there were men who commanded the princely sum of 30*s.*

As time went on the papers began to issue parliamentary reports more fully and accurately, and ministers would often supply copies of their speeches to the press. There were, however, those who still feared that garbled accounts of what went on in Parliament might do great harm outside, and there were others who dreaded the appearance of their own speeches in cold print.

In 1771 the printers of the *Morning Chronicle* and the *London Evening Post* were summoned to the House to be reprimanded by the Speaker as they knelt at the Bar.

A certain printer named Miller, who was a liveryman of the City, refused to come and a Serjeant-at-Arms was sent to arrest him. A fight ensued at the man's residence, and the Serjeant, instead of haling his man back to the House of Commons, found himself dragged off by a zealous constable to the neighbouring Guildhall. The Lord Mayor who was sitting with John Wilkes and another Alderman called Oliver, was outraged at this violation of ancient City charters. Miller was set free and the Serjeant-at-Arms was allowed bail on a charge of assault. The House of Commons was indignant and sent the Lord Mayor and Alderman Oliver, who both refused to make any sort of submission, as prisoners, to the Tower. Of John Wilkes they had already had such unpleasant experience that they did not dare proceed against him.

The Lord Mayor and Alderman became the heroes of the City. The mob cheered them to the echo, the Court of Common Council sent them the heartiest congratulations and the richest viands for their prison table. Writs of Habeas Corpus were demanded; but the Judges decided in favour of the Commons, and the Lord Mayor and Alderman Oliver remained in the Tower till the close of the parliamentary session. Then they came forth to the shouts, the bonfires and illuminations of an adoring City. They had put up a great fight for the privileges of the City, and incidentally for the freedom of the press, and after this time the right of reporting parliamentary speeches was never questioned.

The newspaper tax was a heavy clog upon circulation. The original duty in 1712 was a halfpenny on papers of half a sheet or less, and a penny on larger journals. In 1756 an additional halfpenny was added, and the tax was gradually raised to 1½*d.* and 2*d.*

A number of papers chiefly devoted to pornography and slander managed to evade the tax, and circulated furtively through the town.

The more reputable journals had a hard struggle to sell at the penny or twopence which was what most readers could afford. *The Times* cost as much as 4½*d.* or 6*d.* and there were few who could afford it. It could be read at the better clubs and coffee houses. Some of the inns took it in together with other papers, and charged a penny or two for their perusal.

There was a system which lasted for many years whereby a paper could be hired for an hour or two for a very small sum. The newsman went round to his customers and left *The Times* or whatever it might be, and called for it in an hour's or two hours' time. It cost more per hour to have a paper at breakfast-time than late in the evening, and many were the disputes and arguments about the time which had elapsed since it had been left or the lateness of its arrival.

The newsman blew his horn as he went along, to warn his paper reading clients that they must fold up the scanty sheets of print, and have them ready when he knocked upon the door.

When the evening papers came out, and there were several of these at the end of the century, the newsman sallied out again. The Royal Exchange had its own particular newsmen who must be served first and who rushed off immediately with the latest intelligence. Then when the London papers were distributed, the country papers had to be taken in bundles to the various inns and coach offices and despatched.

At Christmas the newsman came round with a copy of verses which he presented to his patrons, who in return gave him some small gratuity.

Cowper thus describes the contents of a newspaper:

> What is in it but a map of busy life,
> Its fluctuations and its vast concerns?
> Houses in ashes and the fall of stocks
> Births, deaths and marriages, the grand debate.
> The popular harangue, the tart reply
> The logic and the wisdom and the wit
> And the loud laugh.
> Cat'racts of declamation, thunder here,
> There forests of no meaning spread the page
> In which all comprehension wanders lost,
> While fields of pleasantry amuse us here
> With merry descants on a nation's woes.
> The rest appears a wilderness of strange
> But gay confusion; roses for the cheeks
> And lilies for the brow of faded age;
> Teeth for the toothless, ringlets for the bald.
> Heaven, earth and ocean plundered for their sweets.
> Nectarean essences, Olympian dews,
> Sermons and city feasts, and fav'rite airs
> Ætherial journeys, submarine exploits,
> And Katerfelto with his hair on end!

It seems, indeed, that the newspapers of the eighteenth century bore a strong resemblance to those of the present day. If we examined them, however, we should notice some great differences. Not only were they small in size and generally more expensive, but the most respectable allowed themselves a latitude which the lowest rag of the modern press would hardly contemplate. The highest in the land was subject to their attacks.

Georgiana, Duchess of Devonshire, young, beautiful and very unhappy, became the target for the abuse of newspaper writers and lampoonists, nor did they spare her husband. The Duke's amours were set out at length and in detail in the *Town and Country Magazine.* This periodical lived upon its scandals, which, unhappily for the victims, were generally founded upon fact.

Some papers levied a kind of blackmail.

When Cagliostro first came to England he was approached by a reporter who promised to write him up if he would hand over a sum of money. The Count indignantly refused, and the reporter went away to launch an attack upon him in his paper.

It seems strange that such libellous attacks should have been tolerated. Occasionally, it is true, some editor was thrashed by an indignant victim but usually newspaper calumnies were received with a shrug of the shoulders as something too degraded to be noticed. They also made very pleasant and exhilarating reading for the victim's friends.

Lord Ligonier certainly wished to prosecute a newspaper for having stated that he was eighty years of age.

"His lawyer," Walpole says, "told him it was impossible—a tradesman indeed might prosecute as such a report might affect his credit."

"Well, then," said the old man, "I may prosecute too, for I can prove I was going to marry a great fortune, who thought I was but seventy-four, the newspapers have said I am eighty and she will not have me."

The great art of newspaper advertisement was then in its infancy, but some advertisements make curious reading. Steele gives us a delightful account of this form of literature:

> To consider this subject," he says, "in its most ridiculous lights advertisements are of great use to the vulgar. First of all they are instruments of ambition. A man that is by no means big enough for the *Gazette,* may easily creep into the advertisements; by which means we often see an apothecary in the same paper of news with a plenipotentiary or a running footman with an ambassador.
>
> An advertisement from Piccadilly goes down to posterity with an article from Madrid, and John Bartlett of Goodman's Fields is celebrated in the same paper with the Emperor of Germany. . . .
>
> A second use which this sort of writing hath been turned to of late years has been the management of controversy, insomuch that above half the advertisements one meets with nowadays are purely polemical. The inventors of strops for razors have written against one another this way for several years, and that with great bitterness; as the whole argument pro and con in the case of the morning gown is still carried on after the same manner. I need not mention the several proprietors of Dr. Anderson's pills, nor take notice of the many satirical works of this nature so frequently published by Dr. Clark who has had the confidence to advertise upon that learned Knight, my very worthy friend Sir William Read. But I shall not interpose in their quarrel.
>
> Sir William can give him his own in advertisements that in the judgment of the impartial are as well penned as the doctor's.
>
> The third and last use of these writings is to inform the world where they may be furnished with almost everything that is necessary for life. If a man has pains in the head, cholicks in his bowels, or spots on his cloaths, he may here meet with proper cures and remedies. If a man would recover a wife or a horse that is stolen or strayed, if he wants new sermons, electuaries, asses' milk or anything else either for his body or his mind this is the place to look for them in public.

Steele dismisses this subject with a public admonition to Michael Parrot, that "he do not presume any more to mention a certain worm he knows of, which by the way has grown seven foot in my memory, for if I am not much mistaken, it is the same that was but nine foot long about six months ago."

Besides purely comic advertisements there are others which read curiously in these days.

"The pleasant villa at Fulham with orchards and fishponds" is now a pleasant dream, nor does anyone expect to rent a commodious residence in a fashionable London square for as little as £50 a year.

Dr. Johnson remembered "a washball that had a quality truly wonderful. It gave an exquisite edge to a razor." . . .

"The trade of advertising," he continues, "is now so near perfection that it is not easy to propose any improvement."

Newspaper advertisements may have been of great assistance to British trade, but they were of even more use in preserving the independence of the British press.

In Paris the Bureau d'Adresse exhibited all sorts of advertisements, and the newspaper editor was forced to eke out a precarious living by subsidies from factions or the Court.

In England a similar sort of institution known as the Register Office, carried on feebly for many years, and finally perished. Advertisers preferred the press, and the income which they brought to the various newspapers enabled some of them, at least, to preserve their integrity.

We have been considering newspapers and magazines as if they were one and the same thing, and indeed the difference between the two classes of periodicals was often very slight.

The *Tatler,* the *Spectator* and the *Idler* were called newspapers; in these days they would be known as magazines. The *Town and Country Magazine,* on the other hand, bears a very horrid resemblance to some of our more personal and scurrilous newspapers.

The *Gentleman's Magazine* was started in 1731 by Edward Cave, "Silvanus Urban," with the avowed object of collecting "essays on various subjects for entertainment, from the daily and weekly newspapers then circulating in England." Original contributions were also admitted. It was an excellent periodical and can still be read with pleasure. One of its best features were the obiturary notices which it published and which are still consulted.

Johnson wrote criticisms and essays for the *Literary Magazine* or *Universal Review,* which professed to contain, if not everything, at least a very great deal. In this periodical he defended Admiral Byng against the popular clamour, which led to his execution.

He also rose up as the champion of tea drinking against Jonas Hanway, who imputed every evil to that harmless practice.

The *Monthly Review* which was founded by Griffiths, the bookseller, in 1749, was the first periodical to devote itself exclusively to the criticism of new books. In religion and politics it was Low Church and Whig, and the High Church Tories set up a rival, the *Critical Review,* under the editorship of Smollett. Griffiths was furious and declared that his review was not written "by physicians without practice, authors without learning, or writers without judgment."

Smollett, though he might have no practice, was never lacking in repartee. He rejoined that his review on the other hand was not written "by a parcel of obscure hirelings under the restraint of a bookseller and his wife, who presume to revise, alter and amend the articles."

In 1749 the first magazine was founded for women. It was called *The Ladies' Magazine,* and came out once a fortnight. Many of its pages were filled with questions on English history, such as the following.

Q. Pray describe the persons of the English.

A. They are for the most part handsome, grey eyed, fair complexioned, have light hair and are well shaped. Their women are very beautiful and have greater privileges than those of other countries.

This magazine lasted for five years, and was followed in 1769 by another periodical which bore the same name, with the sub-title of *An Amusing Companion for the Fair Sex.* It contained articles on dress and needlework, with some literary criticism, and bore a strong resemblance to the women's magazines of the present day.

It even encouraged its readers to ask its advice and answered such questions as—"Are cats inhabited by evil spirits?" "Ought a woman to continue to live with a wicked husband?"

The influence of the press to-day is very great, though perhaps not so great as some newspaper men imagine; but in the eighteenth century its power for good and evil was enormous. The printed word among semi-literate people was looked upon with the greatest possible awe and respect. If some papers had a demoralising effect, others undoubtedly stood for honesty and decency, and their influence upon the moral progress of the century was very great. (pp. 357-68)

> *Rosamond Bayne-Powell, "Newspapers and Magazines," in her* Eighteenth-Century London Life, *John Murray, 1937, pp. 357-68.*

C. W. Previté-Orton

[*Previté-Orton was an English historian, essayist, and author. His works generally focused on classical and medieval topics. In the following excerpt from an essay originally published in* The Cambridge History of English Literature *(1913), he emphasizes the political nature of many eighteenth-century English periodicals, both newspapers and pamphlets.*]

The death of Henry Pelham in 1754 destroyed the equilibrium of English politics. 'Now,' said king George II, regretting, possibly, the minister more than the man, 'Now, I shall have no peace.' And he was right, for the leading whigs entered on an angry struggle for supreme power which only ended when, in 1757, the domination of the elder Pitt was, virtually, established. Round the duke of Newcastle, formidable by his phalanx of obedient votes, Pitt, the man of genius and of the public confidence, and the shrewd, but far from high-minded, Henry Fox arose a dense dust of controversy.

It was not merely the conflict of personal ambitions that was in question. Great public issues were rapidly raised and discussed, if, as rapidly, let fall again. The sober middle class were weary of the prevailing corruption which handed over the country's government to glaring incompetence. Tories, abandoning their vain hopes of a revolution, were eager to loose England from the Hanoverian tether which involved her in the intricacies of German politics, and to have done with the long feud with France. And both parties were anxious to see power held by men more representative than were the members of the existing narrow whig oligarchy, who, on their side, still believed in their hereditary mission to rule. Material for honest discussion there was in plenty.

At first, it seemed as if this kind of discussion would hold the field. In August 1755, *The Monitor* was founded by a London merchant, Richard Beckford, and was edited, and part written, by John Entick, of dictionary fame. Like its predecessors in political journalism, it consisted of a weekly essay on current events and topics: it was all leading article. The maintenance of whig principles and the uprooting of corruption formed its policy: good information, good sense and a kind of heavy violence of style were its characteristics. Soon, it was supplemented by a series of tory pamphlets, under the title *The Letters to the People of England,* written by John Shebbeare, a physician of some literary celebrity. They were not his first production; he had for some time been eminent in 'misanthropy and literature'; but they were distinguished beyond his other efforts by bringing him to the pillory. His politics, not the scurrility that tinged them, were in fault. He was a virulent tory, and in his *Sixth Letter* held up the reigning dynasty to public scorn. His highest praise is that he still remains readable. Logical, rhetorical, laboriously plain and, occasionally, cogent, his short paragraphs pretty generally hit the nail—often, no doubt, a visionary nail—on the head. Later, he was to enjoy court favour and be a capable pamphleteer on the side of George III; but his time of notoriety was gone.

Soon, however, the personal conflict asserted itself. In November 1756, Arthur Murphy, the dramatist, started *The Test,* with a view to capturing public favour for Henry Fox. But his amiable prosing and feeble giggle were soon over-crowed by the Pittite *Con-Test,* a far more able, and, also, more scurrilous, print, in some of the better essays of which we detect the pith and point of Shebbeare.

Save the honest *Monitor,* these Grub-street railers vanished with the whig feud which called forth their exertions, and the splendid success of the great commoner's ministry almost succeeded in silencing criticism. It required a new ferment of public opinion, a new conflict of principles and a renewed struggle for the possession of power to reawaken the fires of controversy, which, this time, were not to be quenched. George III's accession and his personal policy gave the signal. The new king was determined to choose his own ministers and break up the band of ruling whigs. The now loyal tories were to share in the government, and the system of king William's time was to be revived. The first literary sign of the change was a rally of pamphleteers for the defence and propagation of the royal views. In 1761, Lord Bath—the William Pulteney who, in the last reign, had led the opposition to Walpole and helped to set on foot *The Craftsman*—published his *Seasonable Hints from an Honest Man,* which contained an able exposition of the whig system and its vices, and outlined the new programme. Others followed, professional writers for the most part, such as the veteran Shebbeare and the elder Philip Francis—in his *Letter from the Cocoa-Tree to the Country Gentlemen,* which was not devoid of skill—and Owen Ruffhead, formerly editor of *The Con-Test.* But, in spite of the real ability displayed by these writers, their frequent ignorance of the true course of events and the lack of good faith habitual to them prevented them from attaining to any real excellence.

Meanwhile, events were moving rapidly. George III had

been able to oust Pitt and Newcastle from power and to promote his Scottish favourite, Lord Bute, to the office of prime minister. Bute had seen, from the first, that something beyond sporadic pamphlets was needed for converting public opinion to the new *régime,* discredited as it was by the dismissal of Pitt. For this, an imitation of *The Monitor* was the only means, a steady drumming of the same views and sentiments into the popular ear. It was all the more necessary, at the moment of Bute's accession to power, to set up a rival weekly journal, since *The Monitor* (in this representing the public) was a bitter opponent of the Scottish minister. Bute, however, cannot be called happy in his choice of means. Eminent literary talent was required, but not any sort of literary talent, and Tobias Smollett, famous as a novelist, was only to earn humiliation as a political controversialist. In vain his sheet, *The Briton,* discharged a weekly broadside of ferocious epithets on the opposition and its journalistic defenders. His persuasive powers were small, and he was fairly distanced in argumentative skill, raillery and vituperation. Arthur Murphy, writer of the dead *Test,* was soon summoned to Smollett's aid with a new paper, *The Auditor;* but, although more bitter than of old, he was not less feeble. The public judgment was only too clear. Neither of the ministerial papers would sell. Of course, Bute's unpopularity was partly at fault; but the scanty merit of the two champions was unable to surmount the weakness of their case.

The publication of *The Briton* provoked the appearance of the only one of these fugitive periodicals which has any reputation, *The North Briton,* edited by John Wilkes. That demagogue, on whom the mob-ruling mantle of Sacheverell descended, was sprung from a middle class family, typical of a respectability alien to the manners of its celebrated scion. . . . After producing a successful pamphlet concerning the breach with Spain, he proceeded to send contributions to *The Monitor,* in which he developed with much ingenuity the history of contemporary foreign favourites, and left his readers to point the obvious moral. Then, on the appearance of *The Briton,* he, in June 1762, started his rival print, *The North Briton.* Week by week, the new periodical continued its attacks on the government. It showed itself bold, to start with, in printing the ministers' names in full, without the usual subterfuges of dashes and stars; and it grew bolder as it went on, and as the odium into which Bute had fallen became more obvious. Nothing, however, gave a handle to the authorities by which, even under the existing law of libel, the writers could be brought to book, although *The Monitor* was subjected to lengthy legal proceedings. At last, Wilkes overstepped the line in No. 45, which bitterly impugned the truthfulness of the speech from the throne regarding the peace of Paris. The long government persecution of the libeller, which followed the publication of No. 45, and which finally resulted in the abolition of the tyrannic system of general warrants, also snuffed out *The North Briton.* The paper was subsequently revived; but it proved only the ghost of its former self. Wilkes, on the other hand, had yet to play the part of a full-fledged demagogue in his contest with king and parliament concerning the Middlesex election of 1768. Triumphant at last, he ended his life in 1797 as chamberlain of London and a *persona grata* with George III. In all his vicissitudes, he had kept in touch with public opinion.

It is not easy to describe the blackguard charm of Wilkes.

Notoriously self-interested and dissolute, ugly and squinting, he enjoyed a popularity by no means confined to the mob. Much may be ascribed to the singular grace of his manners. Even Johnson fell a victim to these. But he, also, possessed some very obvious virtues. He was brave, good-humoured and adroit. He had a sort of selfish kindliness. He was, moreover, manifestly on the right side: few people had any love for general warrants or for the infringement of the liberty of election. And he turned all these advantages to account.

His paper, *The North Briton,* may be regarded as the best example of its kind, the brief periodical pamphlet. It represents the type at which *The Briton* and the rest aimed, but which they could not reach. Like its congeners, it consisted of a weekly political essay. It was directed entirely to the object of overthrowing Bute and of reinstating the old group of whig families in alliance with Pitt. We notice at once in its polemic the scantiness of serious argument. Satire, raillery, scandal and depreciation in every form are there; but a real tangible indictment does not readily emerge from its effusions. In part, this peculiarity was due to the difficulty under which an opposition writer then lay in securing information and in publishing what information he possessed. When the preliminaries of peace or the jobbery of Bute's loan issues gave Wilkes his opportunity, he could be cogent enough. But a more powerful reason lay in the main object of the paper. Bute was safe so long as he was not too unpopular: he had the king's favour and a purchased majority in parliament. Therefore, he had to be rendered of no value to king and parliaiment. He was to be written down and to become the bugbear of the ordinary voter, while his supporters in the press were to be exposed to derision and thus deprived of influence. Wilkes and his allies in *The North Briton* were well equipped for this task. They were interesting and vivacious from the first, making the most of the suspicions excited by Bute. As the heat of battle grew and their case became stronger, the violence and abusiveness of their expressions increased till it reached the scale of their rivals. Still, even so, they continued to display an apt brutality wanting in the latter. In the earlier numbers, too, *The Briton* and *The Auditor* fell easy victims to the malicious wit of Wilkes. Perhaps the best instance of his fun is the letter which he wrote under a pseudonym to the unsuspecting *Auditor,* descanting on the value of Floridan peat, a mythical product, for mitigating the severity of the climate in the West Indies. An exposure followed in *The North Briton;* and poor Murphy could only refer to his tormentor afterwards as 'Colonel Cataline.'

But the scheme of *The North Briton* gave an easy opportunity for ironic satire. The editor was supposed to be a Scot exulting over the fortune of his countryman, and very ingenuous in repeating the complaints of the ousted English. There was nothing exquisite in this horseplay; but it was not badly done, and it had the advantage of appealing to strong national prejudice. The antipathy to the Scots, which was to disappear with startling suddenness during the American war of independence, had not yet undergone any sensible diminution. At root, perhaps, it was the dislike of an old-established firm for able interlopers. Scots were beginning to take a leading share in the common government, and their nationality was always unmistakable. Accordingly, old legends of their national character and a purseproud contempt for their national poverty lived ob-

stinately on; and *The North Briton* worked the vein exhaustively.

In the composition of his journal and in his whole campaign against the minister, Wilkes had for his coadjutor a more eminent man, who, unlike himself, is to be conceived of, not as a pleasant adventurer, but as a principal literary figure of the time, the poet and satirist Charles Churchill. The two men were fast friends, although their lives had flowed in very different streams until they became acquainted in 1761. (pp. 388-93)

Churchill so overtops his rivals in political verse that they scarcely seem worth mentioning. Mason, his frequent butt as a writer of pastorals—'Let them with Mason bleat and bray and coo'—shrouded himself in political satire under the name Malcolm Macgregor. Falconer, a naval officer, attacked Pitt from the court point of view. But both of these, and even Chatterton in his *Consuliad,* merely illustrate their inferiority to Churchill.

Prose was far more effective than verse in the political controversies which followed Bute's resignation. The weekly essay, in its old form, died out gradually; but the flood of pamphlets continued. They were in a more serious vein than formerly. Measures rather than men were in dispute, not so much because the public taste had changed, as because the more prominent politicians, with the exception of Pitt, presented few points of interest. The ability of many of these numerous pamphlets is undeniable. Some leading statesmen had a share in them. We find such men as George Grenville, an ex-prime minister, and Charles Townshend, leader of the House of Commons, defending or attacking current policy in this fashion. Others were

Johnson's biographer, James Boswell, by Sir Joshua Reynolds.

written by authors of literary eminence. Edmund Burke published a celebrated tract in defence of the first Rockingham ministry; Horace Walpole was stirred to address the public concerning the dismissal of general Conway in 1764; latest of all, Johnson took part as a champion of the government during the agitation about the Middlesex election, and in opposition to the accusations of Junius. Perhaps, however, the more effective among these pamphlets were due to political understrappers. Charles Lloyd, Grenville's secretary, wrote a series in support of his patron's policy, including a clever reply to Burke. Thomas Whateley, secretary to the treasury, defended the same minister's finance. These and their fellows worked with more or less knowledge of the ground, and, if their special pleading be conspicuous, they also dispensed much sound information.

Two pamphlets, which appeared in 1764, and dealt with the constitutional questions raised by the prosecution of Wilkes, stand well above their fellows in ability and influence. The first appeared, originally, as *A Letter to The Public Advertiser,* and was signed 'Candor.' It was an attack on Lord Mansfield for his charge to the jury in the Wilkes case and on the practice of general warrants. With a mocking irony, now pleasant, now scathing, the author works up his case, suiting the pretended moderation of his language to the real moderation of his reasoning. The same writer, we cannot doubt, under the new pseudonym 'The Father of Candor,' put a practical conclusion to the legal controversy in his *Letter concerning Libels, Warrants, etc.,* published in the same year. This masterly pamphlet attracted general admiration, and its cool and lucid reasoning, varied by an occasional ironic humour, did not meet with any reply. Walpole called it 'the only tract that ever made me understand law.' The author remains undiscovered. The publisher, Almon, who must have known the secret, declared that 'a learned and respectable Master in Chancery' had a hand in it. Candor's handwriting has been pronounced that of Sir Philip Francis; but, clearly, in view of Almon's evidence, he can only have been part author; and the placid, suave humour of the pamphlets reads most unlike him, and, we may add, most unlike Junius.

Candor's first letter had originally appeared in *The Public Advertiser,* and there formed one of a whole class of political compositions, which, in the next few years, were to take the foremost place in controversy. Their existence was due to the shrewd enterprise of the printer Henry Sampson Woodfall, who had edited *The Public Advertiser* since 1758. In addition to trustworthy news of events at home and abroad, Woodfall opened his columns to correspondence, the greater part of which was political. He was scrupulously impartial in his choice from his letter-bag. Merit and immunity from the law of libel were the only conditions exacted. Soon, he had several journals, such as *The Gazetteer,* competing with his for correspondents; but *The Public Advertiser's* larger circulation, and the inclusion in it of letters from all sides in politics, enabled it easily to distance the rival prints in the quality and quantity of these volunteer contributions. George III himself was a regular subscriber; it gave him useful clues to public opinion. The political letters are of all kinds—denunciatory, humorous, defensive, solemn, matter-of-fact, rhetorical and ribald. Their authors, too, were most varied, and are now exceedingly hard to identify. Every

now and then a statesman who had been attacked would vindicate himself under a pseudonym; more frequently, some hanger-on would write on his behalf, with many professions of being an impartial onlooker. There were independent contributors; and small groups of minor politicians would carry on a continuous correspondence for years. But neither single authors nor groups can be easily traced through their compositions. As is natural, their style seldom helps us to identify them. They wrote the current controversial prose, and, after 1770, their prose is tinged with a Junian dye. The pseudonyms throw little light on the matter. There was no monopoly in any one of them, and the same author would vary his pseudonyms as much as possible, chiefly with intent to avoid discovery and the decrease of credit which his communications might undergo if he were known, but, also, to provide sham opponents as a foil to his arguments and to create an illusion of wide public support for his views.

A good instance of the letter-writers was James Scott, a preacher of repute. In 1766, he contributed a series of letters to *The Public Advertiser,* signed 'Anti-Sejanus.' They were written in the interests of Lord Sandwich, and assailed, with much vehemence, the supposed secret intrigues of Bute. Scott used many other pseudonyms, and wrote so well that his later letters, which show Junius's influence in their style, were republished separately. From a private letter written by him to Woodfall, we learn that he, too, was a member of a group who worked together. Another writer we can identify was John Horne, later known as John Horne Tooke and as the author of *The Diversions of Purley*. He began to send in correspondence to the newspapers about 1764; but his celebrity only began when he became an enthusiastic partisan of Wilkes in 1768. Under the pseudonym 'Another Freeholder of Surrey,' he made a damaging attack on George Onslow, and, on being challenged, allowed the publication of his name. The legal prosecution which followed the acknowledgment of his identity, in the end, came to nothing, and Horne was able to continue his career as Wilkes's chief lieutenant. But the cool unscrupulousness with which Wilkes used the agitation as a mere instrument for paying off his own debts and gratifying his own ambitions disgusted even so warm a supporter as Horne. A quarrel broke out between them in 1771 concerning the disposal of the funds raised to pay Wilkes's debts by the society, The Supporters of the Bill of Rights, to which both belonged. Letter after letter from the two former friends appeared in *The Public Advertiser*. Horne, who, perhaps, had the better case, allowed himself to be drawn off into long petty recriminations on Wilkes's private life. Indiscreet expressions of his own were brought up against him, and the popularity of Wilkes, in any case, made the attempt to undermine him impossible. Yet 'parson Horne' had his triumph, too. The redoubtable Junius entered the controversy on Wilkes's side; Horne retorted vigorously, and proved the most successful critic of the greater libeller's productions. In truth, Junius's letters owed much of their success to his victims' inability to rebut his insinuations by giving the real facts in transactions which were necessarily secret. Horne's record was clear; he had no dignity to lose; he could pin Junius down by a demand for proof. Yet, even allowing for these advantages, his skill in dissecting his adversary's statements and his courage in defying the most formidable libeller of the day are much to his credit as a pamphleteer. Before long, Junius was glad to beat a retreat.

It was in the autumn of 1768 that the political letters of the unknown writer who, later, took the pseudonym of Junius, gained the public ear. But we know from his own statement that, for two years before that date, he had been busy in furtive, assassinating polemic; and it is possible that a careful search of newspaper files would result in the discovery of some of his earlier performances of 1766 and 1767. The time when he appears to have begun letter-writing tallies well with the objects pursued by him during the period of his known writings. He was an old-fashioned whig, and a warm, almost an impassioned, adherent of the former prime minister, George Grenville. Thus, the accession to power, in July 1766, of the elder Pitt, now Lord Chatham, with his satellite, the duke of Grafton, after a breach with Lord Temple, Grenville's brother, and their adherents, most likely, gave the impulse to Junius's activity. It was not, however, till October 1768 that he became clearly distinguishable from other writers in *The Public Advertiser.* By that time, Chatham's nervous prostration had rendered him incapable of transacting business, and the duke of Grafton was acting as prime minister in an administration which had become mainly tory. For some reason or other, Junius nursed a vindictive and unassuageable hatred against the duke, which it seems difficult to attribute only to the rancour of a partisan. The weakness of the loosely constructed ministry, too, would tempt their adversary to complete their rout by a storm of journalistic shot and shell. So, Junius, sometimes under his most constant and, perhaps, original signature 'C.', sometimes under other disguises, continued to add to the fury and cruel dexterity of his attacks. 'The Grand Council' ridiculed the ministers' Irish policy and their methods of business. A legal job which was attempted at the duke of Portland's expense furnished another opportunity. Nor was Junius content with these public efforts to discredit his foes. In January 1768, he sent Chatham an unsigned letter, full of flatteries for the sick man and of suggestions of disloyalty on the part of his colleagues. For the time being, however, Chatham continued to lend his name to the distracted ministry, which staggered on from one mistake to another. Those on which Junius, under his various *aliases,* seized for animadversion were small matters; but they were damaging, and his full knowledge of them, secret as they sometimes were, gave weight to his arguments. His ability seemed to rise with the occasion: the 'prentice hand which may have penned 'Poplicola's' attacks on Chatham in 1767 had become a master of cutting irony and merciless insinuation, when, as 'Lucius,' he, in 1768, flayed Lord Hillsborough. The time was ripe for his appearance as something better than a skirmisher under fleeting pseudonyms, and the series of the letters of Junius proper began in January 1769. They never, however, lost the stamp of their origin. To the last, Junius is a light-armed auxiliary, first of the Grenville connection, then, on George Grenville's death in 1770, of the opponents of the king's tory-minded ministry under Lord North. He darts from one point of vantage to another. Now one, now another, minister is his victim, either when guilty or when unable to defend himself efficiently. Ringing invective, a deadly catalogue of innuendoes, barbed epigrams closing a scornful period, a mastery of verbal fencing and, here and there, a fund of political good sense, all were used by the libeller, and contributed to make him the terror of his

victims. The choice and the succession of the subjects of his letters were by no means haphazard. His first letter was an indictment of the more prominent members of the administration. It created a diversion which made the letter-writer's fortune, for Sir William Draper, conqueror of Manilla, rushed into print to defend an old friend, Lord Granby. Thoroughly trounced, ridiculed, humiliated and slandered, he drew general attention to his adversary, who then proceeded to the execution of his main design. In six letters, under his customary signature or the obvious alternative Philo-Junius, he assailed the duke of Grafton's career as man and minister. Meanwhile, the agitation provoked by Wilkes's repeated expulsion from the commons, and his repeated election for Middlesex, was growing furious; and, in July 1769, Junius, following the lead of George Grenville, took up the demagogue's cause. For two months, in some of his most skilful compositions, he urged the constituency's right to elect Wilkes. Then, as the theme wore out, he chose a new victim. Grafton's administration depended on his alliance with the duke of Bedford, one of the most unpopular men in England. Junius turned on his foe's ally with a malignity only second to that which he displayed against Grafton himself. A triumphant tone begins to characterise the letters, for it was obvious that the Grafton ministry was tottering to its fall; and Junius decided on a bolder step. His information was of the best, and he was convinced that the king had no intention of changing his ministerial policy, even if Grafton resigned. The king, then, must be terrorised into submitting to a new consolidated whig administration. The 'capital and, I hope, final piece,' as it was called by Junius, who was conscious of his own influence with the public though he much overrated it, was an address to the king which contained a fierce indictment of George III's public action since his accession. It was an attempt to raise popular excitement to a pitch which would compel George to yield. But the libeller placed too much trust in his power over the ruling oligarchy and gave too little credit to the dauntless courage and resolution of the king. Lord North took up the vacant post of prime minister; and his talent and winning personality, assisted by the all-prevailing corruption and by the very violence of the opposition in which Junius took part, carried the day. It was the House of Commons which kept Lord North in power, and to its conquest the angry opposition turned. Junius now appears as one of the foremost controversialists on Wilkes's election, and as champion of the nascent radical party forming under Wilkes's leadership in the city of London. Other matters, also, were subjects of his letters, such as the dispute with Spain concerning the Falkland islands, and the judicial decisions of Lord Mansfield; but they are all subordinate to his main end. Ever and anon, too, he returns, now with little public justification, to the wreaking of his inexplicable hatred on the duke of Grafton, 'the pillow upon which I am determined to rest all my resentments.' But the game was up. Clearly, neither king nor commons could be coerced by an outside agitation, which, after all, was of no great extent. The quarrel of Wilkes and Horne wrecked the opposition in the city. Junius saw his scale kick the beam, and it was only the too true report conveyed by Garrick to the court, in November 1771, that he would write no more, which induced him to pen his final attack on Lord Mansfield, with which the collected letters close.

Junius vanishes with the publication of the collected edition of his letters. It was far from complete. Not only are the letters previous to 1769 omitted, but many of inferior quality or of transient interest, written during the continuance of the great series, usually under other pseudonyms, are absent. And, more remarkable still, there are certain letters of 1772, after the Junian series had closed, which he very anxiously desired not to be known as his, and which passed unidentified for years. Under fresh pseudonyms, such as 'Veteran,' he poured forth furious abuse on Lord Barrington, secretary at war. The cause, in itself, was strangely slight. It was only the appointment of a new deputy secretary, formerly a broker, Anthony Chamier, and the resignations of the preceding deputy, Christopher D'Oyly, and of the first clerk, Philip Francis. But, trifling as the occasion might be, it was sufficient to make the cold and haughty Junius mouth with rage.

Junius follows the habit of his fellow-correspondents in dealing very little with strictly political subjects. Personal recrimination is the chief aim of his letters, and it would hardly be fair to contrast them with those of a different class of authors, such as Burke, or even with the product of the acute legal mind of Candor. Yet, when he treats of political principles he does so with shrewdness and insight. He understood the plain-going whig doctrine he preached, and expounded it, on occasion, with matchless clearness. What could be better as a statement than the sentences in the dedication of the collected letters which point out that the liberty of the press is the guarantee of political freedom and emphasise the responsibility of parliament? And the same strong common sense marks an apophthegm like that on the duke of Grafton—

> Injuries may be atoned for and forgiven; but insults admit of no compensation. They degrade the mind in its own esteem, and force it to recover its level by revenge.

Yet these sentences betray in their sinister close the cast of Junius's mind. There is an evil taint in his strength, which could not find satisfaction in impartial reasoning on political questions. This partisanship merges at once into personal hatred, and his rancour against his chief victim, Grafton, can hardly be accounted for on merely political grounds. His object is to wound and ruin, not only to overthrow. Scandal, true or false, is the weapon of his choice. 'The great boar of the forest,' as Burke called him, loved the poison in which he dipped his tusks, and took a cruel pleasure in the torture he inflicted. Secure in his anonymity, no insult or counter-thrust could reach him. With frigid glee, he retorts upon accusations, which, of necessity, were vague and wide, by plausible insinuations against his opponents. 'To him that knows his company,' said Dr Johnson, 'it is not hard to be sarcastic in a mask.' And Junius, thus gripped with the obvious realities of his position, found no reply to this sarcasm.

But, however much he owed to his concealment and to his remarkable knowledge of the vulnerable points of his quarry (and, be it added, to the cunning with which he selected for his attack men who could not produce their defence), Junius holds a high position on his own literary merits. He was the most perfect wielder of slanderous polemic that had ever arisen in English political controversy. Not lack of rivals, but eminent ability, made him supreme in that ignoble competition. In invective which is uninformed by any generosity of feeling he stands unequalled.

His sentences, brief, pithy and pungent, exhibit a delicate equilibrium in their structure. Short as they are, their rhythm goes to form the march of a period, and the cat-like grace of their evolution ends in the sudden, maiming wit of a malign epigram. Direct invective, lucid irony, dry sarcasm mingle with one another in the smooth-ranked phrases. . . . . Junius possessed to perfection the art of climax.

The anonymity which he marvellously preserved enabled Junius to maintain that affectation of superiority which distinguished him. Never before were mere scandals and libellous diatribes presented with such an air of haughty integrity and stern contempt for the baseness of jacks-in-office. We have to make an effort in order to remember that this lofty gentleman, above the temptation of 'a common bribe,' is really engaged in the baser methods of controversy, and cuts a poor figure beside Johnson and Burke. But, from his impersonal vantage ground, he could deliver his judgments with more authority and more freely display the deliberate artifice of his style. Its general construction will appear from the passage on Grafton which has been quoted above. But he also uses a more shrouded form of innuendo than he there employs. He was very ingenious in composing a sentence, or even a whole period, of double meaning, and in making his real intent peculiarly clear withal. Perfect lucidity, indeed, is one of his chief literary qualities. In his most artificial rhetoric, his meaning is obvious to any reader. His wit, too, is of high quality, in spite of his laboured antitheses. It has outlived the obsolete fashion of its dress. It far transcends any trick of words; as often as not, it depends on a heartless sense of comedy. 'I should,' he wrote to the unhappy Sir William Draper, 'justly be suspected of acting upon motives of more than common enmity to Lord Granby, if I continued to give you fresh materials or occasion for writing in his defence.' He needs, we feel, defence himself. The best apology, perhaps, that can be offered for him is that he was carrying on an evil tradition and has to be condemned chiefly because of his excellence in a common mode.

Something, too, of his celebrity is due to the mystery he successfully maintained. The wildest guesses as to his identity were made in his own day and after. It was thought at first that only Burke could write so well, and most of the eminent contemporaries of Junius have, at one time or another, been charged with the authorship of the letters. Fresh light was cast on the problem by the publication, in 1812, of his private letters to Woodfall, with specimens of his handwriting, and subsequent research has at least laid down some of the conditions which must be satisfied if his identity is to be proved. Among them, we may take it that a coincidence of the real life of the author with the hints regarding himself thrown out in the letters is not to be expected. It was part of Junius's plan to avoid giving any real clue, and he was anxious to be thought personally important. But there are more certain data to go upon. The very marked handwriting of Junius is well known, although, to all seeming, it is a feigned hand. The dates of the letters show when the author must have been in London. His special knowledge is of importance. He had an inner acquaintance with the offices of secretary at war and secretary of state, and he was very well informed on much of the doings of contemporary statesmen and on the court. His politics show him to have been an adherent of George Grenville, who was anxious to draw Lord Chatham into alliance with the thoroughgoing whigs, and turn out the king's chosen ministers. The latter he hated to a man; but he had a singular antipathy to Grafton and Barrington. His power of hating is characteristic. We must find a man proud and malignant, yet possessed of considerable public spirit and of a desire for an honest, patriotic administration. Finally, we require a proof of ability, in 1770, to write the letters with their merits and defects. Later writings, even when tinged with the admired Junian style, are but poor evidence. Nor is the inferior quality of a man's later productions an absolute bar to his claims. He may have passed his prime. (pp. 398-408)

[The] letters of Junius seem to be brought home to a small group which included Calcraft, Francis and, perhaps, Lord Temple. They passed through Francis's hands, and he is their most likely author. He evidently wished to be thought so; but, if he was, the malignant talent they displayed could only develop in secrecy, or, perhaps, his prime was short. He remains in his real character a pretender only, in his assumed, a shade: *stat nominis umbra.*

In Junius, we have the culmination of a series of political writings; but his merits and defects do not exhaust theirs. Abuse and slander and political hatred are continually to be found in all. These blameworthy features should not obscure the quantity of solid facts and serious argument put forward for the public information, in many able and honest pamphlets and letters. It is easier for posterity than it was for the writers to judge of their fairness and accuracy; not so easy, perhaps, to perceive that, with their open discussion and criticism, they were the chief safeguards of the responsibility of government to public opinion. (p. 410)

C. W. Previté-Orton, "Political Literature (1755-1775)," in The Cambridge History of English Literature: The Age of Johnson, Vol. X, edited by Sir A. W. Ward and A. R. Waller, Cambridge at the University Press, 1964, pp. 388-410.

TRANSITION

William Wordsworth

[*A vital poet and critic of the English Romantic movement, Wordsworth outlined his poetic credo in his "Preface" to the 1800 edition of* Lyrical Ballads, *a collection of poetry by Samuel Taylor Coleridge and himself. Considered revolutionary at the time, the "Preface" challenged contemporary assumptions about poetry, maintaining that neither the language nor the content of poetry should be stylized or elaborate. In the following excerpt from the 1800 edition of that work, Wordsworth elucidates his belief that the aim of poetry is to provide pleasure while illuminating fundamental truths of human nature.*]

Several of my Friends are anxious for the success of these Poems from a belief, that if the views, with which they were composed, were indeed realized, a class of Poetry would be produced, well adapted to interest mankind permanently, and not unimportant in the multiplicity and in the quality of its moral relations: and on this account they have advised me to prefix a systematic defence of the theory, upon which the poems were written. But I was unwilling to undertake the task, because I knew that on this occasion the Reader would look coldly upon my arguments, since I might be suspected of having been principally influenced by the selfish and foolish hope of *reasoning* him into an approbation of these particular Poems: and I was still more unwilling to undertake the task, because adequately to display my opinions and fully to enforce my arguments would require a space wholly disproportionate to the nature of a preface. For to treat the subject with the clearness and coherence, of which I believe it susceptible, it would be necessary to give a full account of the present state of the public taste in this country, and to determine how far this taste is healthy or depraved; which again could not be determined, without pointing out, in what manner language and the human mind act and react on each other, and without retracing the revolutions not of literature alone but likewise of society itself. I have therefore altogether declined to enter regularly upon this defence; yet I am sensible, that there would be some impropriety in abruptly obtruding upon the Public, without a few words of introduction, Poems so materially different from those, upon which general approbation is at present bestowed.

It is supposed, that by the act of writing in verse an Author makes a formal engagement that he will gratify certain known habits of association, that he not only thus apprizes the Reader that certain classes of ideas and expressions will be found in his book, but that others will be carefully excluded. This exponent or symbol held forth by metrical language must in different æras of literature have excited very different expectations: for example, in the age of Catullus, Terence and Lucretius, and that of Statius or Claudian, and in our own country, in the age of Shakespeare and Beaumont and Fletcher, and that of Donne and Cowley, or Dryden, or Pope. I will not take upon me to determine the exact import of the promise which by the act of writing in verse an Author in the present day makes to his Reader; but I am certain it will appear to many persons that I have not fulfilled the terms of an engagement thus voluntarily contracted. I hope therefore the Reader will not censure me, if I attempt to state what I have proposed to myself to perform, and also, (as far as the limits of a preface will permit) to explain some of the chief reasons which have determined me in the choice of my purpose: that at least he may be spared any unpleasant feeling of disappointment, and that I myself may be protected from the most dishonorable accusation which can be brought against an Author, namely, that of an indolence which prevents him from endeavouring to ascertain what is his duty, or, when his duty is ascertained prevents him from performing it.

The principal object then which I proposed to myself in these Poems was to make the incidents of common life interesting by tracing in them, truly though not ostentatiously, the primary laws of our nature: chiefly as far as regards the manner in which we associate ideas in a state of excitement. Low and rustic life was generally chosen because in that situation the essential passions of the heart find a better soil in which they can attain their maturity, are less under restraint, and speak a plainer and more emphatic language; because in that situation our elementary feelings exist in a state of greater simplicity and consequently may be more accurately contemplated and more forcibly communicated; because the manners of rural life germinate from those elementary feelings; and from the necessary character of rural occupations are more easily comprehended; and are more durable; and lastly, because in that situation the passions of men are incorporated with the beautiful and permanent forms of nature. The language too of these men is adopted (purified indeed from what appear to be its real defects, from all lasting and rational causes of dislike or disgust) because such men hourly communicate with the best objects from which the best part of language is originally derived; and because, from their rank in society and the sameness and narrow circle of their intercourse, being less under the action of social vanity they convey their feelings and notions in simple and unelaborated expressions. Accordingly such a language arising out of repeated experience and regular feelings is a more permanent and a far more philosophical language than that which is frequently substituted for it by Poets, who think that they are conferring honour upon themselves and their art in proportion as they separate themselves from the sympathies of men, and indulge in arbitrary and capricious habits of expression in order to furnish food for fickle tastes and tickle appetites of their own creation.

I cannot be insensible of the present outcry against the triviality and meanness both of thought and language, which some of my contemporaries have occasionally introduced into their metrical compositions; and I acknowledge that this defect where it exists, is more dishonorable to the Writer's own character than false refinement or arbitrary innovation, though I should contend at the same time that it is far less pernicious in the sum of its consequences. From such verses the Poems in these volumes will be found distinguished at least by one mark of difference, that each of them has a worthy *purpose*. Not that I mean to say, that I always began to write with a distinct purpose formally conceived; but I believe that my habits of meditation have so formed my feelings, as that my descriptions of such objects as strongly excite those feelings, will be found to carry along with them a *purpose*. If in this opinion I am mistaken I can have little right to the name of a Poet. For all good poetry is the spontaneous overflow of powerful feelings; but though this be true, Poems to which any value can be attached, were never produced on any variety of subjects but by a man who being possessed of more than usual organic sensibility had also thought long and deeply. For our continued influxes of feeling are modified and directed by our thoughts, which are indeed the representatives of all our past feelings; and as by contemplating the relation of these general representatives to each other, we discover what is really important to men, so by the repetition and continuance of this act feelings connected with important subjects will be nourished, till at length, if we be originally possessed of much organic sensibility, such habits of mind will be produced that by obeying blindly and mechanically the impulses of those habits we shall describe objects and utter sentiments of such a nature and in such connection with each other, that the understanding of the being to whom we address ourselves, if he be in a healthful state of association, must nec-

essarily be in some degree enlightened, his taste exalted, and his affections ameliorated. (pp. 236-41)

[A] multitude of causes unknown to former times are now acting with a combined force to blunt the discriminating powers of the mind, and unfitting it for all voluntary exertion to reduce it to a state of almost savage torpor. The most effective of these causes are the great national events which are daily taking place, and the encreasing accumulation of men in cities, where the uniformity of their occupations produces a craving for extraordinary incident which the rapid communication of intelligence hourly gratifies. To this tendency of life and manners the literature and theatrical exhibitions of the country have conformed themselves. The invaluable works of our elder writers, I had almost said the works of Shakespear and Milton, are driven into neglect by frantic novels, sickly and stupid German Tragedies, and deluges of idle and extravagant stories in verse.—When I think upon this degrading thirst after outrageous stimulation I am almost ashamed to have spoken of the feeble effort with which I have endeavoured to counteract it; and reflecting upon the magnitude of the general evil, I should be oppressed with no dishonorable melancholy, had I not a deep impression of certain inherent and indestructible qualities of the human mind, and likewise of certain powers in the great and permanent objects that act upon it which are equally inherent and indestructible; and did I not further add to this impression a belief that the time is approaching when the evil will be systematically opposed by men of greater powers and with far more distinguished success.

Having dwelt thus long on the subjects and aim of these Poems, I shall request the Reader's permission to apprize him of a few circumstances relating to their *style,* in order, among other reasons, that I may not be censured for not having performed what I never attempted. Except in a very few instances the Reader will find no personifications of abstract ideas in these volumes, not that I mean to censure such personifications: they may be well fitted for certain sorts of composition, but in these Poems I propose to myself to imitate, and, as far as possible, to adopt the very language of men, and I do not find that such personifications make any regular or natural part of that language. I wish to keep my Reader in the company of flesh and blood, persuaded that by so doing I shall interest him. Not but that I believe that others who pursue a different track may interest him likewise: I do not interfere with their claim, I only wish to prefer a different claim of my own. There will also be found in these volumes little of what is usually called poetic diction; I have taken as much pains to avoid it as others ordinarily take to produce it; this I have done for the reason already alleged, to bring my language near to the language of men, and further, because the pleasure which I have proposed to myself to impart is of a kind very different from that which is supposed by many persons to be the proper object of poetry. I do not know how without being culpably particular I can give my Reader a more exact notion of the style in which I wished these poems to be written than by informing him that I have at all times endeavoured to look steadily at my subject, consequently I hope it will be found that there is in these Poems little falsehood of description, and that my ideas are expressed in language fitted to their respective importance. Something I must have gained by this practice, as it is friendly to one property of all good poetry, namely good sense; but it has necessarily cut me off from a large portion of phrases and figures of speech which from father to son have long been regarded as the common inheritance of Poets. I have also thought it expedient to restrict myself still further, having abstained from the use of many expressions, in themselves proper and beautiful, but which have been foolishly repeated by bad Poets till such feelings of disgust are connected with them as it is scarcely possible by any art of association to overpower.

If in a Poem there should be found a series of lines, or even a single line, in which the language, though naturally arranged and according to the strict laws of metre, does not differ from that of prose, there is a numerous class of critics who, when they stumble upon these prosaisms as they call them, imagine that they have made a notable discovery, and exult over the Poet as over a man ignorant of his own profession. Now these men would establish a canon of criticism which the Reader will conclude he must utterly reject if he wishes to be pleased with these volumes. And it would be a most easy task to prove to him that not only the language of a large portion of every good poem, even of the most elevated character, must necessarily, except with reference to the metre, in no respect differ from that of good prose, but likewise that some of the most interesting parts of the best poems will be found to be strictly the language of prose when prose is well written. The truth of this assertion might be demonstrated by innumerable passages from almost all the poetical writings, even of Milton himself. (pp. 242-46)

Is there then, it will be asked, no essential difference between the language of prose and metrical composition? I answer that there neither is nor can be any essential difference. We are fond of tracing the resemblance between Poetry and Painting, and, accordingly, we call them Sisters: but where shall we find bonds of connection sufficiently strict to typify the affinity betwixt metrical and prose composition? They both speak by and to the same organs; the bodies in which both of them are clothed may be said to be of the same substance, their affections are kindred and almost identical, not necessarily differing even in degree; Poetry sheds no tears "such as Angels weep," but natural and human tears; she can boast of no celestial Ichor that distinguishes her vital juices from those of prose; the same human blood circulates through the veins of them both.

If it be affirmed that rhyme and metrical arrangement of themselves constitute a distinction which overturns what I have been saying on the strict affinity of metrical language with that of prose, and paves the way for other distinctions which the mind voluntarily admits, I answer that the distinction of rhyme and metre is regular and uniform, and not, like that which is produced by what is usually called poetic diction, arbitrary and subject to infinite caprices upon which no calculation whatever can be made. In the one case the Reader is utterly at the mercy of the Poet respecting what imagery or diction he may choose to connect with the passion, whereas in the other the metre obeys certain laws, to which the Poet and Reader both willingly submit because they are certain, and because no interference is made by them with the passion but such as the concurring testimony of ages has shewn to heighten and improve the pleasure which co-exists with it.

It will now be proper to answer an obvious question, namely, why, professing these opinions have I written in verse? To this in the first place I reply, because, however I may have restricted myself, there is still left open to me what confessedly constitutes the most valuable object of all writing whether in prose or verse, the great and universal passions of men, the most general and interesting of their occupations, and the entire world of nature, from which I am at liberty to supply myself with endless combinations of forms and imagery. Now, granting for a moment that whatever is interesting in these objects may be as vividly described in prose, why am I to be condemned if to such description I have endeavoured to superadd the charm which by the consent of all nations is acknowledged to exist in metrical language? To this it will be answered, that a very small part of the pleasure given by Poetry depends upon the metre, and that it is injudicious to write in metre unless it be accompanied with the other artificial distinctions of style with which metre is usually accompanied, and that by such deviation more will be lost from the shock which will be thereby given to the Reader's associations than will be counterbalanced by any pleasure which he can derive from the general power of numbers. In answer to those who thus contend for the necessity of accompanying metre with certain appropriate colours of style in order to the accomplishment of its appropriate end, and who also, in my opinion, greatly under-rate the power of metre in itself, it might perhaps be almost sufficient to observe that poems are extant, written upon more humble subjects, and in a more naked and simple style than what I have aimed at, which poems have continued to give pleasure from generation to generation. Now, if nakedness and simplicity be a defect, the fact here mentioned affords a strong presumption that poems somewhat less naked and simple are capable of affording pleasure at the present day; and all that I am now attempting is to justify myself for having written under the impression of this belief. (pp. 247-57)

Having thus adverted to a few of the reasons why I have written in verse, and why I have chosen subjects from common life, and endeavoured to bring my language near to the real language of men, if I have been too minute in pleading my own cause, I have at the same time been treating a subject of general interest; and it is for this reason that I request the Reader's permission to add a few words with reference solely to these particular poems, and to some defects which will probably be found in them. I am sensible that my associations must have sometimes been particular instead of general, and that, consequently, giving to things a false importance, sometimes from diseased impulses I may have written upon unworthy subjects; but I am less apprehensive on this account, than that my language may frequently have suffered from those arbitrary connections of feelings and ideas with particular words, from which no man can altogether protect himself. Hence I have no doubt that in some instances feelings even of the ludicrous may be given to my Readers by expressions which appeared to me tender and pathetic. Such faulty expressions, were I convinced they were faulty at present, and that they must necessarily continue to be so, I would willingly take all reasonable pains to correct. But it is dangerous to make these alterations on the simple authority of a few individuals, or even of certain classes of men; for where the understanding of an Author is not convinced, or his feelings altered, this cannot be done without great injury to himself: for his own feelings are his stay and support, and if he sets them aside in one instance, he may be induced to repeat this act till his mind loses all confidence in itself and becomes utterly debilitated. To this it may be added, that the Reader ought never to forget that he is himself exposed to the same errors as the Poet, and perhaps in a much greater degree: for there can be no presumption in saying that it is not probable he will be so well acquainted with the various stages of meaning through which words have passed, or with the fickleness or stability of the relations of particular ideas to each other; and above all, since he is so much less interested in the subject, he may decide lightly and carelessly.

Long as I have detained my Reader, I hope he will permit me to caution him against a mode of false criticism which has been applied to Poetry in which the language closely resembles that of life and nature. Such verses have been triumphed over in parodies of which Dr. Johnson's Stanza is a fair specimen.

> I put my hat upon my head,
> And walk'd into the Strand,
> And there I met another man
> Whose hat was in his hand.

Immediately under these lines I will place one of the most justly admired stanzas of the "*Babes* in the Wood."

> These pretty Babes with hand in hand
> Went wandering up and down;
> But never more they saw the Man
> Approaching from the Town.

In both of these stanzas the words, and the order of the words, in no respect differ from the most unimpassioned conversation. There are words in both, for example, "the Strand," and "the Town," connected with none but the most familiar ideas; yet the one stanza we admit as admirable, and the other as a fair example of the superlatively contemptible. Whence arises this difference? Not from the metre, not from the language, not from the order of the words; but the *matter* expressed in Dr. Johnson's stanza is contemptible. The proper method of treating trivial and simple verses to which Dr. Johnson's stanza would be a fair parallelism is not to say this is a bad kind of poetry, or this is not poetry, but this wants sense; it is neither interesting in itself, nor can *lead* to any thing interesting; the images neither originate in that sane state of feeling which arises out of thought, nor can excite thought or feeling in the Reader. This is the only sensible manner of dealing with such verses: Why trouble yourself about the species till you have previously decided upon the genus? Why take pains to prove that an Ape is not a Newton when it is self-evident that he is not a man.

I have one request to make of my Reader, which is, that in judging these Poems he would decide by his own feelings genuinely, and not by reflection upon what will probably be the judgment of others. How common is it to hear a person say, "I myself do not object to this style of composition or this or that expression, but to such and such classes of people it will appear mean or ludicrous." This mode of criticism so destructive of all sound unadulterated judgment is almost universal: I have therefore to request that the Reader would abide independently by his own feelings, and that if he finds himself affected he would not suffer such conjectures to interfere with his pleasure. (pp. 261-64)

William Wordsworth, "Preface: 1800 Version (with 1802 Varients)," in Lyrical Ballads *by Wordsworth and Coleridge, edited by R. L. Brett and A. R. Jones, Methuen and Co. Ltd., 1963, pp. 235-66.*

Robert Shackleton

[*Shackleton was an English editor and essayist. In the following excerpt, he contrasts "enlightened" eighteenth-century Continental attitudes with contemporary English sentiments, basing his observations upon recorded incidents related to Johnson's visit to France in 1775.*]

A hasty answer to the problem of Johnson's relation to the Enlightenment could well be that his attitude was one of simple opposition. No outlook is more hostile to the aims of the Enlightenment than 'that fixed contempt' attributed to him by Macaulay 'for all those modes of life and those studies which tend to emancipate the mind from the prejudices of a particular age or a particular nation'. Johnson's own pronouncements, such as his celebrated declaration that it was difficult to settle the proportion of iniquity between Voltaire and Rousseau, often tend to confirm this view, as does his ostentatious refusal, related by Mrs. Piozzi, to meet Raynal visiting London at the height of his fame.

But if it is an error to regard Johnson's opinions as consistent and unambiguous, it would be still more wrong to think of the Enlightenment as a single-minded, tangible movement, or indeed, during the greater part of Johnson's life, as a movement at all. The picture of a cohesive band of allies, extending from Hume and Gibbon to Beccaria and the Verri brothers, and including Voltaire, Rousseau, Diderot, D'Alembert, D'Holbach, and a score of others, unitedly hostile to religion and monarchy, is wholly unhistorical. It is more accurate and profitable to see the Enlightenment as a series of impermanent and changing social groupings, whose members profess ideas which are far from forming a consistent corpus, which indeed are often contradictory, but which have some common features and develop out of a common origin. It consists of shifting alignments according to the controversies of the day. And since the Enlightenment is elusive and ill-defined, it is prudent in seeking to assess Johnson's attitude to it to begin cautiously and empirically; and since, however defined, it was to a large extent a French phenomenon, it is useful to consider some of the implications of Johnson's visit to France in 1775.

By this time some of the old struggles of the *philosophes* had subsided. The *Encyclopédie,* save for its less controversial supplement, had been completed ten years before. Voltaire was busy attacking the atheism of D'Holbach. Helvétius was dead, Rousseau was inactive. The Jesuits, expelled from France already in 1764, had been dissolved nine years later by Ganganelli's Bull *Dominus ac Redemptor.*

Mrs. Thrale, whose journal gives the fullest account of the journey, was Johnson's companion; but Baretti joined them at Dover and was the organizer of the tour. No great sympathy for new ideas was to be expected from this Piedmontese man of letters who, with his inimitable talent for inventing words, had in his *Frusta letteraria* castigated

Rousseau, Voltaire, Helvétius, Montesquieu, and D'Argens as *scompaginatori della mente umana* ('unsewers of the pages of the human mind') and referred to the *philosophes* as *filosofantelli*. Not for nothing did Voltaire describe him as the Zoilus of Italy. Another guide, Mrs. Strickland, *née* Towneley, was a member of an English Catholic family whose members in previous generations had, like other English Catholics, had an important role as intermediaries between France and England at a time when Ramsay and Bolingbroke were forging links between the two countries and when the nascent Enlightenment was still dallying with Jansenism.

Thus guided, Johnson passed eight weeks in France. He stayed for more than a single night only at Rouen, associated of old with advanced ideas and with cosmopolitan interests, and at Paris where Louis XVI was beginning his reign. The catalogue of persons met by Johnson during his journey is indicative of his sympathies and attitudes. He saw not a single leading figure of the Enlightenment, and no one who could lay undisputed claim to the title *philosophe*. He met some figures of the other camp, notably Fréron, the virulent enemy of Voltaire and editor of the *Année littéraire*. The illustrious Daubenton, natural historian, friend of Buffon, and contributor to the *Encyclopédie*, was his escort when he visited the Jardin des Plantes. Two sons of the famous clockmaker Julien Le Roy, themselves famous in different walks of life, paid their respects to his party. Three persons, however, can be singled out as particularly illustrating the background before which he moved: two ecclesiastics and a lady of fashion. (pp. 76-8)

Roffet, Hooke, and Madame Du Boccage represent aspects of the Enlightenment different from those ordinarily associated with it. Open-minded, tolerant, undoctrinaire, not seeing the incompatibility between religion and the new ideas, or looking back to, and taking their inspiration from, a time when that incompatibility had not yet been established, they are examples of a type which throws some light on Johnson's own position in relation to the Enlightenment.

Of Johnson's position it can first be said that whenever called on to pronounce on a current controversial issue, in relation to which opinions were clearly aligned into the contrasting camps of the *philosophes* and the *anti-philosophes*, or the 'enlightened' and the 'traditional', he was on the conservative side—and more rapidly and decisively if using the spoken and not the written word.

This is seen when he expresses himself on the subject of freedom of thought and expression. 'Suppose you and I,' he asks Boswell, 'and two hundred more were restrained from printing our thoughts: what then? What proportion would that restraint upon us bear to the private happiness of the nation?' Asked by Boswell in 1773 'if it was not strange that government should permit so many infidel writings to pass without censure', he replies, 'Sir, it is mighty foolish.' In the *Life of Milton* he discusses the relative merits of prior censorship and subsequent punishment, and concludes:

> It seems not more reasonable to leave the right of printing unrestrained, because writers may be afterwards censured, than it would be to sleep with doors unbolted, because by our laws we can hang a thief.

At a dinner on 7 May 1773 the theme of toleration was again discussed and Johnson, before being drawn by the chance of conversation to the extreme view that 'the only method by which religious truth can be established is by martyrdom' laid down a principle which throws light on the nature of his opposition to toleration:

> No member of a society has a right to *teach* any doctrine contrary to what that society holds to be true. The magistrate . . . may be wrong in what he thinks: but, while he thinks himself right, he may, and ought to enforce what he thinks.

This assertion of *cuius regio eius religio* and denial of toleration on *raison d'État* grounds shows that Johnson's dissent from the principle of toleration was not simply a traditionalist dissent. He is not arguing that since truth is in fact known and has been established, toleration can only generate error; he is arguing that established opinions must be enforced because they are established and not because they are true. This position, which Birkbeck Hill rightly likens to the 'profession de foi purement civile' of Rousseau's *Du contrat social,* is comparable to that strain of Hobbesian philosophy which runs through the Enlightenment and which marks Rousseau in spite of his many differences from Hobbes.

Johnson's attitude to Hobbes has in recent years been much discussed, and a distinguished American scholar has gone so far as to make this claim:

> The hard fact is that Johnson's conception of the state as a purely secular and rational institution is at least as atheistic as Hobbes's; indeed Johnson outdoes Hobbes in the rejection of metaphysics by discarding or ignoring the notion of a contract, to which Hobbes adheres. But in their emphasis on power as the central fact of government, to which all rights are subordinate, Johnson and Hobbes are very close.

The resemblance between their views is still more underlined by Johnson's insistence on the idea of sovereignty in *Taxation no Tyranny:* 'All government is ultimately and essentially absolute. . . . In sovereignty there are no gradations.' Dr. R. Voitle is less inclined to see Johnson as a disciple of Hobbes, and makes a careful comparison between his ideas and those of Cumberland. Johnson for him is much less an adherent of a Machiavelli-like belief in the autonomy of politics than is Hobbes, believing man to be essentially a social animal, subject already in the state of nature to a moral law. Voitle gives a graphic illustration of this view in a conversation between Johnson and Boswell about an unpunished murderer, and could have supported further the more general claim that for Johnson moral law stands higher than positive law by Cali's speech in the first act of *Irene:*

> Such are the woes when arbitrary power,
> And lawless passion, hold the sword of justice.
> If there be any land, as fame reports,
> Where common laws restrain the prince and subject,
> . . . Sure, not unconscious of the mighty blessing,
> Her grateful sons shine bright with every virtue.

But in either case, whether Greene stressing Hobbes or Voitle stressing Cumberland is right (and most will regard Voitle's case as conclusively argued) what is significant is that Johnson is discussing a problem which is central to the Enlightenment. The philosophy of Hobbes was a major preoccupation of the Enlightenment, and that fact is more important in relation to the Enlightenment than the nature of the specific attitudes adopted towards Hobbes and his ideas. Montesquieu was an avowed opponent of Hobbes and his work shows signs of the influence of Cumberland. Rousseau is Hobbesian in detail rather than in substance. Voltaire (in this at one with Rousseau) believes in sovereignty, while Montesquieu rejects it. That in which they and others are characteristic of their age and of the Enlightenment is their interest in, or even fascination with, the ideas of Hobbes. And Johnson is not different from them in this. In either case, moreover, it remains true that Johnson's position in political theory is one of moving from natural law (without ever renouncing it utterly) to utilitarianism, and no position is more characteristic of the Enlightenment than this.

If there is one doctrine which, more than any other, is essential to the Enlightenment, it is the belief, taken largely from Locke, that all ideas come from the senses. *An Essay concerning Humane Understanding* appeared in 1690, a French abridgement having already been published in the *Bibliothèque universelle* two years before. Translated *in extenso* by Pierre Coste in 1700, it did not, nevertheless, become well known in France until 1734 when Voltaire's *Lettres philosophiques* presented its ideas in greatly simplified and readily comprehensible guise. Thereafter, few indeed were the French *philosophes* who did not loudly assert that experience was the source of all knowledge, citing Locke as their mentor. Descartes, though his methodology of doubt was still often accepted, was disparaged as the discredited and superseded exponent of innate ideas. Johnson in this respect is at one with Voltaire, Diderot, and Helvétius. The belief in innate ideas is unfounded, though it can be explained; but 'judgement and ratiocination . . . draw their decisions only from experience'. This acceptance of Lockean sensationalism was from 1734 onwards the criterion of the true *philosophe* and Johnson was at one with the representatives of the early Enlightenment. Not only did he embrace the main doctrine, that ideas come from the senses ('every mind . . . is necessitated . . . to receive its informations and execute its purposes, by intervention of the body') but the concomitant notions are also accepted by him. One of these is the denial of a natural affection linking parents and children. Voltaire in his play *Mahomet* had put into the mouth of the Prophet the sentiments:

> On n'a point de parents alors qu'on les ignore.
> Les cris du sang, sa force, et ses impressions,
> Des cœurs toujours trompé sont les illusions.

Diderot, in the dedication to *Le Père de famille,* insists that the love of children for their parents is not a natural affection but is based on the recognition of benefits received. Johnson's views, as reported by Mrs. Thrale, are similar: 'Johnson always maintained that no such Attachment [as filial piety] naturally subsisted and used to chide me for *fancying* that I loved my Mother. . . . He denied parental Feeling entirely.' One of the eighteenth century's most discussed problems was that of the thinking soul. Locke, in some memorable pages of the *Essay concerning Humane Understanding,* had attacked Descartes's contention that the soul's essence and nature lay solely in thought. This controversy re-echoes through the eighteenth century. Voltaire in the *Lettres philosophiques,* D'Argens in *La Philosophie du bon sens,* the Abbé Yvon

in the article *Ame* of the *Encyclopédie,* had all made their pronouncements. They all took the side of Locke in denying that the soul continually thought; and Johnson, in a most interesting paper published in 1758, takes the same side, though for reasons different from Locke's:

> If it be impossible to think without materials, there must necessarily be minds that do not always think; and whence shall we furnish materials for the meditation of the glutton between his meals, of the sportsman in a rainy month, of the annuitant between the days of quarterly payment, of the politician when the mails are detained by contrary winds.

And if Johnson's argument here is in part facetious, it is still in the tradition of Locke who wrote: 'It is doubted whether I thought at all last night or no.'

Johnson's discipleship of Locke was doubtless achieved independently of Voltaire and those other *philosophes* who held him in the same esteem and who similarly adhered to the doctrines of sensationalism. He was brought closer to them by his admiration for Bayle. He respected him as a 'journalist' and made frequent use of the *Dictionnaire historique et critique,* which he possessed in the second edition. He describes it as 'a very useful work for those to consult who love the biographical part of literature, which is what I love most' and when someone spoke to him of a confutation of Bayle, he retorted: 'A confutation of Bayle, Sir! What part of Bayle do you mean? The greatest part of his writings is not confutable: it is historical and critical.' Bayle, according to one's standpoint, can be regarded either as one of the Enlightenment's greatest precursors or as one of its earliest figures. In either case his enormous role in eighteenth-century thought is incontestable, and Johnson's regard for him, when French opponents of the Enlightenment viewed him with detestation, is both surprising and significant. He cites from time to time the works (notably the éloge of Newton) of Fontenelle, who was Bayle's contemporary, though surviving until 1757, and Boswell gives a vivid picture of Johnson swinging on a low gate as he reads Trublet's memoirs on Fontenelle. Some of the obituary eulogies pronounced by Fontenelle in the Paris Academy of Sciences were translated into English by Johnson, either for the *Gentleman's Magazine,* like the lives of Boerhaave and Morin, or for James's *Medicinal Dictionary,* like the life of Tournefort.

A variety of special aspects of Johnson's affinities with the early Enlightenment could profitably be studied. He was at all times prone to argue in favour of luxury as a beneficial force in the economic life of a State, being at one in this with Mandeville and with Voltaire's poem *Le Mondain.* If he translates into English Crousaz's *Commentaire sur la traduction en vers . . . de l'Essai de M. Pope sur l'homme,* a critique of Pope by a prominent foe of the Enlightenment, at least he scatters throughout the work footnotes in defence of Pope; and in any case one of the aims of Crousaz had been to exculpate Pope from the charge of Leibnizianism and Johnson was as firm an opponent of Leibniz ('a paltry fellow') as Voltaire showed himself to be in *Candide.* The question of *Candide* and *Rasselas* and their respective situations in relation to eighteenth-century thought is too large to be studied here, but is full of significance. One of the most curious problems is that presented by the presence in Johnson's library of the works of Feijóo, both in the original Spanish and in English translation. This Spanish monk was the greatest figure in the early Enlightenment in Spain. An opponent of scholasticism, an advocate of the philosophy of experience, an admirer of Bacon, an enemy of all superstition, Feijóo is one of the eighteenth century's most remarkable figures. His range of interest was remarkable and an examination of his relation to Johnson would be a desirable piece of research.

Johnson's proposed translation of Fra Paolo Sarpi's *Istoria del Concilio tridentino* should not be overlooked, although the work was not completed. The role of this work in the development of the Enlightenment in Italy was second to none. In England too, as well as in France, its repercussions were considerable. The French translation by Le Courayer enjoyed great repute, and Le Courayer himself, favoured by Caroline of Anspach, represents a tradition which was both ecumenical and anticurialist. The appeal of Sarpi to the anti-ultramontanism of the Jansenists was natural, and Johnson, in interesting himself sympathetically in Sarpi, was coming close to one important aspect of the eighteenth-century Enlightenment, an aspect which was stronger in the middle of the century in Italy than in France, but which was not absent from France and of which the Abbé Roffet of Rouen would seem to have been a modest representative. The brief life of Sarpi which Johnson published in the *Gentleman's Magazine* in 1738 is intrinsically insignificant, since it is no more than a rough abridgement of Le Courayer's memoir published two years earlier, but that Johnson chose the subject is important. And although in 1775 he expressed a different view in the heat of conversation with Roffet, it does not, as Greene has pointed out, appear to have been with disapproval that he quoted a vigorous sentence from a letter written by Sarpi: 'There is nothing more essential than to ruin the reputation of the Jesuits; by the ruin of the Jesuits, Rome will be ruined; and if Rome is ruined, religion will reform of itself.'

Of all the different manifestations of the spirit of the Enlightenment none is more generally accepted as typical than the *Encyclopédie* of Diderot and D'Alembert, and nothing did more than the opposition to the *Encyclopédie*, crystallizing in its two suspensions, in 1752 and 1757, to force the *philosophes* into an organized movement with a common aim and with common enemies. Johnson's attitude to the *Encyclopédie* is important and conclusive.

In the first place he possessed the work, or at least he possessed, without doubt in the first edition, volumes I to VII, which suggests that when it fell into clandestinity he allowed his subscription to lapse. In the second place, as has been shown by Dr. Powell, he did in fact, doubtless unwittingly, contribute to it, for the article *Anglois*, contained in the supplement published by Robinet, is largely taken from Johnson's history of the English language prefaced to his *Dictionary*. In the third place, an enterprise of Diderot, immediately antecedent to the preparation of the *Encyclopédie*, was the translation into French of Robert James's *Medicinal Dictionary*, of which Johnson was in modest part author. Diderot's colleagues as translators were Toussaint and Eidous, themselves about to be collaborators in the *Encyclopédie*, while his publishers were the same *libraires associés* who were to bring out the *Encyclopédie*. At least one biographical article in James's work,

the life of Tournefort mentioned above, having been itself translated from the French of Fontenelle and probably by Johnson, was in turn retranslated into French by Diderot or one of his collaborators.

Apart from its initial aim of being simply a translation into French of Ephraim Chambers's *Cyclopaedia* (which Johnson possessed in the edition of 1741 and to the first edition of which his father had been a subscriber), the underlying purpose of the *Encyclopédie* was two-fold and the two parts are indicated by the two parts of the title. It was designed to spread knowledge while showing the interconnexions of its different branches, and it aspired, as a *Dictionnaire raisonné des sciences, des arts et des métiers,* to put on paper the existing state of knowledge. This second aim was closely allied, in the minds of Diderot and his collaborators, to the belief that manual arts and crafts were highly important aspects of the national life, to be regarded with respect and not with the scorn which past philosophers had sometimes shown. If there was one intellectual influence which more than any other inspired the Encyclopedists it was that of Bacon.

The initial privilege for the publication of the *Encyclopédie* was granted on 26 March 1745; on 8 March 1759 the Conseil d'État revoked the privilege, and the work, of which seven volumes had appeared in the years 1751-7, continued its existence and preparation in semi-clandestinity. Johnson's 'Short Scheme' for compiling a new dictionary of the English language was written in April 1746 and the *Dictionary* appeared in 1755. The lexicographical activity of Johnson came then within the period of production of the *Encyclopédie,* and Johnson's writings at this time show ideas often expressed across the Channel. In the preface to *The Preceptor* he produced an analytical survey of the different divisions of knowledge, in which the respective places of geometry, geography, astronomy, chronology, and history, and other branches of learning, were classified and arranged; while three years later in the *Rambler* he wrote of the 'mechanic arts' with an interest and enthusiasm not unworthy of Diderot. The second *Prospectus* of the *Encyclopédie* appeared at the end of 1750.

And in the *Discours préliminaire,* published at the end of June 1751 in the first volume, D'Alembert gives credit to Diderot for having acquired first-hand knowledge by personal visits to workshops. Johnson's article in the *Rambler* of 9 July 1751 speaks in admiration of the intricacies of mechanical arts, and explains how

> we enter the shops of artificers, observe the various tools by which each operation is facilitated, and trace the progress of a manufacture through the different hands that, in succession to each other, contribute to its perfection.

Citing Locke in support of his general theme, he goes on to assert that 'the most lofty fabrics of science are formed by the continued accumulation of single propositions' and in the same connexion mentions Bacon who, as 'l'immortel chancelier d'Angleterre', was praised to the skies by D'Alembert. Johnson two years later speaks of Bacon as having 'attained to degrees of knowledge scarcely ever reached by any other man. In 1777 he told Boswell that his interest in Bacon arose from his reading for the *Dictionary.*

The *Dictionary* appeared in 1755. The list of works of reference which had been Johnson's working tools shows how close some of his activities had been to those of the compilers of the *Encyclopédie.* The *Cyclopaedia* of Chambers, the *Lexicon technicum* of Harris, Savary's *Universal Dictionary of Trade and Commerce,* specific dictionaries of individual trades, these had been his constant companions. And when in the Preface he sums up his hopes for the work, 'I shall not think my employment useless or ignoble, if by my assistance foreign nations and distant ages gain access to the propagators of knowledge and understand the teachers of truth', he is expressing sentiments which ten years later Diderot echoed in the foreword to volume VIII of the *Encyclopédie,* where he expressed the hope that, in the eyes of posterity, he and his colleagues would not have lived wholly in vain.

Not long after the publication of the *Dictionary* Johnson wrote a preface for Rolt's *New Dictionary of Trade and Commerce,* which contains general reflections on dictionary-making, with particular reference to the utility of arts and trade, while in 1759 he puts on paper some thoughts on the functions of the three faculties of the mind, memory, reason, and imagination, which are reminiscent of the system of classification of human knowledge, based on these three faculties, which D'Alembert, following Bacon's example, had effected in the *Discours préliminaire* to the *Encyclopédie.*

The tasks of Johnson and of Diderot, in collecting information, classifying it, expressing it in readily comprehensible form, the one for the *Dictionary,* the other for the *Encyclopédie,* were similar. Diderot's enterprise was vaster, but Johnson worked single-handed; both encountered severe discouragement, indifference, and hostility; both were inspired by the same views about the spread of knowledge, about the significance of arts and crafts, both had a sense of working for future generations.

The situation of Johnson in relation to the Enlightenment is then by no means simple. He believed in the spread of knowledge. He accepted the empiricism of Locke. He leaned to utilitarianism in politics. His natural bent of mind was sceptical. In all these respects he was at one with Voltaire and with Diderot. Voitle has maintained that 'if Johnson let himself go, he might well turn into a deist.' And indeed, on one occasion, in conversation with Boswell, he let himself go to the point of declaring: 'The Christian revelation is not proved by the miracles alone, but as connected with prophecies, and with the doctrines in confirmation of which the miracles were wrought.' This sentiment, astonishing in the mouth of Johnson, was very close to one of the condemned propositions in the thesis of the Abbé de Prades, who had become notorious for his heterodox thesis presented to the Sorbonne, of which the Abbé Hooke, mentioned above as having been met by Johnson in Paris, had been examiner and whose doctrines he was deemed to have made his own. D'Argenson and Barbier, the two principal memorialists of the age, had reported the scandal provoked by Prades's having claimed that the miracles were efficacious as proofs of Christianity only if considered in conjunction with the prophecies. The Church had condemned, with unanimous voice, this thesis and the proposition in question as being false, temerarious, scandalous, evil-sounding, offensive to pious ears, blasphemous, and heretical, and the author had to take refuge abroad and to retire to the not very onerous position of

chaplain to Frederick the Great. This was the greatest crisis, so far, which the *philosophes* encountered, and Johnson is found to echo these dangerous sentiments.

This is one of the most paradoxical situations in a career by no means exempt from paradox. 'To be prejudiced,' Johnson wrote, 'is always to be weak'; and Montesquieu had written: 'Je me croirais le plus heureux des mortels, si je pouvais faire que les hommes pussent se guérir de leurs préjués.' But Johnson went on to write: 'There are prejudices so near to laudable, that they have often been praised, and are always pardoned.' He enjoyed prejudices and would not 'let himself go'. In the eighteenth century he would have been most at home with the learned *abbés* of its first three decades, men of inquiring minds, devoted to learning, disciples of Locke, hostile to ultramontanism. Such men (though not all having all these characteristics) were Buffier and Desmolets in France, Feijóo in Spain, Le Courayer in England, Passionei at Rome. Such a man, in many respects, was Benedict XIV himself. Johnson carried into the second half of the century the outlook, the ideas, and the sympathies of the earliest representatives of the Enlightenment. But to have aligned himself, in the public view or in the light of his own conscience, with the *philosophes* of 1770, atheists and materialists as they were, would for him have been unthinkable. (pp. 81-92)

> *Robert Shackleton, "Johnson and the Enlightenment," in* Johnson, Boswell and Their Circle *by Robert Shackleton and others, Oxford at the Clarendon Press, 1965, pp. 76-92.*

Donald Greene

[*Greene is a Canadian scholar of eighteenth-century English literature, particularly that of Johnson. His works include* Samuel Johnson: A Survey and Bibliography of Critical Studies *(1970), and an edition of Johnson's* Political Writings *(1977). In the following excerpt, he examines the historical implications of eighteenth-century English literary and aesthetic theory.*]

For many decades questions of eighteenth-century English artistic and literary taste and sensibility have usually been discussed in terms of two potent concepts, "neoclassicism" and "romanticism." A rough, but not too inaccurate, outline of the history of the English aesthetic from 1550 to 1850, as given in the great majority of literary histories from about 1870 onward, runs as follows: Three great movements can easily be discerned in the literary and artistic activity of the time, movements of, successively, action, reaction, then action again. The English Renaissance, dated approximately 1550-1650 and centering on the reign of Elizabeth I, is characterized by boldness, adventurousness, and exuberant individualism, culminating in the great "irregular" drama and poetry of Shakespeare and the extravagant conceits of Donne. In 1660, however, as a result of the traumatic experience of the Civil War, men's minds recoiled, in literature as well as in politics, from such qualities, and sought order, decorum, regularity, and stability instead. The means by which these ends were achieved were two: first, an increased emphasis on the importance of the classical (chiefly Latin) writers, Horace, Virgil, and Juvenal in particular, as providing literary models, critical principles, and norms of social conduct for modern man; and, second, the reliance of

The eighteenth-century conflict between the established order and the new rationalist-revolutionary is caricatured in "Smelling out a Rat." Here, the conscience of Dr. Richard Price, outspoken defender of the French Revolution, is troubled by the spirit of prescription, monarchy, and Christianity, bearing the distinctive nose and eyeglasses of Edmund Burke (author of Reflections on the Revolution in France *(1790).*

artists and writers on rigid rules, such as the dramatic unities, for the composition of their works and a corresponding distrust of the imagination. The fact that Charles II and his court spent many years of exile at the French court before returning to England is credited with having assisted this process, influential French writers and critics of the time (Corneille, Racine, Boileu) having been infected with the neoclassical virus even earlier and more strongly. Then in 1798 (though there had been foreshadowings in the shape of "pre-Romantics" such as Thomson, Gray, and the Wartons), *enfin Wordsworth vint,* along with Coleridge and Blake, to free the imagination from the shackles of these dead rules and models (and English literature lived happily ever after). To document the currency of such a picture from late nineteenth-and early twentieth-century textbooks of the history of English literature and criticism would be superlatively easy. One quotation will suffice here to illustrate it, the title of a lecture series given in the United States in 1884 by Edmund Gosse, *From Shakespeare to Pope: A History of the Decline of Romantic Poetry.*

Childish as this sketch appears when presented thus baldly, and drastically as details of it have later been modified—it is encouraging to note that the concept of "pre-

Romanticism," once accepted so unquestioningly, has been virtually abandoned by reputable modern literary historians—its essential elements still hold a powerful sway over the minds of students. Yet it is salutary to observe how comparatively recently this pattern was imposed on the historical data. The great writers of the eighteenth century, Dryden, Pope, Johnson (Swift has always been treated as an exception, sometimes even being termed a "Romantic" out of his time) were entirely unaware that they were "neoclassicists"; they did not use the term or any equivalent, nor is there any evidence that they thought of themselves as playing the role Arnold and others cast them in. Henry Hallam, in the earliest substantial literary history of the modern era, published between 1837 and 1839, manages to make a thorough and perceptive survey of the literature of Europe, including England, between 1400 and 1700 without displaying any awareness of a shift from "Renaissance exuberance" to "neoclassical restraint." The history of the genesis and propagation of the concept of a "neoclassical age" needs thorough investigation. It seems safe to say, however, that it was mainly an invention of the obscure academics and journalists who, from around 1840 to 1870, wrote the pioneering textbooks of the new school subject of English literature, which was just being introduced into the curriculum of English and

American colleges in the middle and late nineteenth century, and who felt a compulsion to provide a set of historical facts about the subject on which students could be examined. In short, the credentials of the concept are not so imposing that modern students need be frightened away from asking themselves whether, in spite of its wide currency, there is any compelling historical reason for accepting the hypothesis as valid.

This is not the place to enter into a detailed analysis of the question; but the student might usefully consider an alternative hypothesis that seems to fit the historical data at least as well as the "neoclassical" one—namely, that the eighteenth century, in England at least, far from representing a resurgence of reliance on previously abandoned classical rules and models, is, rather, the mid-point in a steady decline in reverence for the authority of the classical Latin and Greek writers, a decline which has been continuous from an apogee in the early Renaissance to the present, when the numbers of writers and critics who have any extensive first-hand acquaintance with the classics or regard them as in any way authoritative is small indeed. It is not surprising that Hallam failed to notice the occurrence of any "neo-classical" resurgence after 1660. He had recorded in detail that period in the early sixteenth century when "the real excellence of the ancients in literature as well as art gave rise to an enthusiastic and exclusive admiration of antiquity," the time when the test of a true intellectual was the ability to write "pure" Latin, "conformable to the standard of what is sometimes called the Augustan age, that is, of the period from Cicero to Augustus," and, by comparison, the time of Dryden, Defoe, Bunyan, and Swift must have seemed a far cry indeed from such "exclusive admiration." He was aware of the great indebtedness to classical literature of earlier writers like Marlowe, Spenser, Ben Jonson, Donne, Milton, and Shakespeare himself—the fact is that allusions to the classics occur more frequently in Shakespeare's plays than in those of Dryden or in Pope's verse epistles or Johnson's essays. It is true that Dryden, Pope, and Johnson were writing for an audience who they assumed had the basic grounding in Latin literature that was the hallmark of every educated Englishman from the Renaissance down to the beginning of the twentieth century. It is also true that they enjoyed and admired Horace and Juvenal, and used them for their own purposes. But that the domination of Horace and Juvenal over the minds of eighteenth-century writers was greater than that of Seneca and Ovid over sixteenth-century writers, or that Dryden and Pope succumbed to their spell more than Shelley, say, to that of Aeschylus, or Tennyson to that of Virgil, or that either Dryden or Pope recommended the classical writers as guides for the moderns more strenuously than T. S. Eliot and Ezra Pound were later to do, would be difficult to prove. It was Pope who wrote, with sturdy independence, "Of One Who Would Not Be Buried in Westminster Abbey" (himself):

> Heroes and kings, your distance keep,
> In peace let one poor poet sleep,
> Who never flattered folks like you.
> Let Horace blush, and Virgil too.

It was Ezra Pound who wrote "Homage to Sextus Propertius."

Any study of eighteenth-century literary and aesthetic theory in England must begin by deciding for itself whether or not it will accept *a priori* the postulate that an aggressive neoclassicism (or its more fashionable modern synonym, "Augustanism") was the dominant intellectual pattern of the age. If any such study does, it will face many difficult problems when considering the work of the leading critics of the century, on which it will often have to render the verdict of "inconsistent" or "ambivalent," of wavering aimlessly between desire to adhere to the dominant theory and desire to rebel against it. Such a verdict has often been passed on both the century's greatest literary critic, Samuel Johnson, and its greatest art critic, Joshua Reynolds. The net result is to discredit their criticism, and indeed the whole body of criticism of the eighteenth century, as the work of men who fundamentally could not make up their minds, who lacked the courage of their critical convictions. If, on the other hand, they are seen as men who, though inheriting a residual legacy of authoritarianism and apriorism in critical matters from the Renaissance (which had in turn inherited it from the Middle Ages), nevertheless moved steadily and consistently in the opposite direction, and contributed greatly to the erosion of that legacy, such charges will fail. There will be no more need to be apologetic about these critics than there is about, say, another famous contemporary, Henry Cavendish, who, though reared in the medieval and Renaissance belief in the theory of phlogiston (a product, in the end, of Aristotelian physics) and never bringing himself to the point of formally renouncing this theory, nevertheless, by his "modern" experimentation with hydrogen and nitrogen, made immensely valuable contributions to the development of modern chemistry.

The fancied necessity of finding evidence in the writings of Johnson, Reynolds, and others to support the view that, at least part of the time, they were militant "neoclassicists," has frequently led to serious misreadings of their writings. Both Johnson and Reynolds were fond of using the term "general" as one of critical approbation. Their modern expositors very often equate this with "abstract" and accuse them of preaching "abstractionism," though in fact Johnson never seems to have used "abstract" or "abstraction" as critical terms or said anything in favor of such a quality in imaginative writing. It is obvious, if one examines his texts without the presupposition that Johnson was a "neoclassicist," that by "general," as a term of approbation, he by no means meant "abstract." He illustrates his praise of Shakespeare's adherence to "general nature" by the example of King Claudius in *Hamlet,* and he makes it abundantly clear that it is not because Shakespeare's portrait of Claudius is an "abstract" representation of kingship that he admires it. On the contrary, he vigorously defends Shakespeare against the complaints of Voltaire and others that Claudius, in getting drunk, is much too *concrete,* too particularized, too little like the stereotype of a king. A little serious study of such passages soon convinces us that Johnson's position is precisely that of Ezra Pound when he praises Joyce's *Ulysses* and Eliot's *Prufrock:*

> James Joyce has written the best novel of the decade, and perhaps the best criticism of it has come from a Belgian who said, "All this is as true of my country as of Ireland." Eliot has a like ubiquity of application. Art does not avoid universals, it strikes at them all the harder in that it strikes though particularities. . . . [Eliot's] men in shirt-sleeves

and his society ladies are not a local manifestation: they are the stuff of our modern world, and true of more countries than one.

When Johnson praises "generality," he undoubtedly means "ubiquity of application" or "susceptibility of wide response," as no doubt Reynolds also does. And in the notorious passage in *Rasselas* where Imlac proclaims that the business of the poet is not to number the streaks of the tulips but "to exhibit . . . such prominent and striking features as recall the original to every mind," Johnson is surely saying no more than what Keats was later to say—that poetry should not surprise by "singularity; it should strike the reader as a wording of his own highest thoughts, and appear almost as a remembrance."

Indeed, the more one reads Johnson's remarks about how poetry should be written, the more strikingly his taste in poetry appears to resemble Wordsworth's. He detests archaic and contrived diction, the facile use of outworn mythology, unnatural inversion of normal English sentence order. Poetry, he thinks, should be communication among contemporary men in respect to contemporary issues and states of feeling, and its vehicle should be contemporary language. Gray's "images are magnified by affection; the language is laboured into harshness. . . . His art and his struggle are too visible, and there is too little appearance of ease and nature"; Collins' "diction was often harsh, unskillfully laboured and unjudiciously selected. He affected the obsolete when it was not worthy of revival; and he puts his words out of the common order, seeming to think, with some later candidates for fame, that not to write prose is certainly to write poetry." Johnson's objection to *Lycidas* is well summed up in Wordsworthian language—Milton's poem is patently *not* the spontaneous overflow of powerful feelings; and Johnson's own illustration of how an elegy should be written, "On the Death of Dr. Robert Levet," is a considerably Wordsworthian poem—even in its occasional descent into bathos, "His frame was firm, his powers were bright, / Though now his eightieth year was nigh."

The critique of *Lycidas* is indeed an important crux in the assessment of Johnson's criticism, and to some degree of eighteenth-century criticism in general. After a century and a half of denigration, some students have begun to examine Johnson's critique seriously and to understand that, far from its being an expression of old-fashioned reactionism, it is a revolutionary document. One student has gone so far as to term it "the end of Renaissance criticism":

> Johnson was in several ways a "new man," a man of our sensibility rather than a man of the Renaissance. . . . Johnson . . . just as we today, was not very interested in the "kinds" of literature as such, and demanded that poetry accord with "nature," the accordance to be tested by "my surveys of life." He wanted genuine passion in literature, and responded with passion to literature. He expected, as we expect, a funeral elegy to express the grief of the writer, not his adeptness at handling literary conventions; and at the end of his life, when he had lived much and suffered much, and forgotten nothing of the suffering, he found this desire for passion and above all for emotional truth in literature precisely in conflict with the Renaissance traditions which his education had affirmed. . . . Modern criticism begins with Johnson.

Johnson's strictures on *Lycidas* are clarified by his two earlier *Rambler* essays on the pastoral *genre*. For him, the emotional effect of a pastoral poem comes from what we would call its realism—he defines it simply as "a poem in which any action or passion is represented by its effects upon a country life." The pastoral poetry of Theocritus and Virgil pleases him because it springs from their actual experience, in childhood and youth, of rural life in northern Italy and Sicily, and their nostalgic recollection of it after they have become city dwellers. Later pastoral, like that of Spenser, Milton, and Pope, has failed because its writers have merely used a contrived rural setting as extrinsic ornament for declamation on current controversial political and religious questions, or an obituary of some recently deceased worthy, or simply to show off their own technical virtuosity; their shepherds are not countrymen whom they themselves have known, as Theocritus and Virgil did, but patently factitious stereotypes. Modern academic criticism rejects such an approach to the pastoral, and insists that we, as readers, accept it as an essentially artificial *genre* and train ourselves to sense the complex ironies implicit in the discrepancy between reality and illusion that it presents. But Johnson's ideal of the pastoral, though we may find it unacceptable, cannot be called reactionary or old-fashioned or, least of all, neoclassical. On the contrary, the ideal of presenting serious and universal human emotion in a realistic setting of "the simple life" is very modern. Crabbe, with Johnson's approval and assistance, would later attempt this; likewise Hardy, Frost, and many other late nineteenth- and early twentieth-century poets and novelists. It is a curious reflection that the work which Johnson's ideal of the pastoral most closely adumbrates is probably *Michael: A Pastoral Poem* (though he would also have approved of *The Death of the Hired Man*), and there are close resemblances between what is desiderated in *Ramblers* 36 and 37 and what is desiderated in the Preface to *Lyrical Ballads*.

The point of this long preamble is primarily to suggest that, much as eighteenth-century critical and aesthetic theory has been studied by later scholars, the usefulness of such study has too often been diminished by the attempt to fit the reading of the century's critical texts into a preconceived framework of intellectual history. The modern student should certainly at least try to approach the writings of eighteenth-century critics and aestheticians without such preconceptions, and only later, after he has familiarized himself with what these writers have actually been saying, consider whether or not there is any need to postulate such entities as "neoclassicism" and "Augustanism" to explain it. This, at least, would have been the method recommended, as it was followed by a great many of those writers themselves, products of a staunchly empiricist age. It is paradoxical, to say the least, that it has been by the exercise of a highly aprioristic procedure that the criticism of that age has been stigmatized as aprioristic.

That the century reveled in exploring the questions of what is artistically effective and why is apparent when one notes the 225 titles of books on general literary and aesthetic theory published between 1664 and 1800 which are listed in the *Cambridge Bibliography of English Literature,* followed by several hundred additional titles of works of criticism of particular genres and particular writers. "Dryden," said Johnson, "may be properly considered the father of English criticism," and certainly the contrast between the spotty and erratic history of English literary criticism before Dryden and the mighty proliferation of critics and theorists after him is striking. It would be wrong to try to explain this fact, as was once customary, by postulating an opposition between the creative imagination and the critical spirit, and asserting that the quantity of criticism produced by the eighteenth century is further proof that it was a cool, judicious age of reason, which bridled and restrained the soaring imagination—after all, as Eliot and others have pointed out, some of the greatest English critics have also been some of the greatest English poets. The phenomenon, on the contrary, is further proof of the century's exuberant curiosity, now ranging through scarcely explored territory, the complex operation of the human mind and emotions. Much of its critical effort was directed toward expanding taste, toward developing the reader's ability to respond to a wider range of literature—the difficult poetry of the politically unpopular Milton (Dryden and Addison), that of Chaucer (Dryden), the folk ballads (Addison and Percy—whom Johnson helped in preparing the *Reliques* for the press), Hebrew poetry (Lowth), Norse literature (Gray and others), the medieval romances, and Renaissance narrative poetry deriving from them, such as that of Spenser, Ariosto, and Tasso (Hurd), Middle English literature (Thomas Warton), above all Shakespeare, the modern editing of whose works begins with Rowe in 1709. As for cautious reliance on classical authority, Dryden himself may be said to have promulgated the century's declaration of critical independence in his splendid assertion, " 'Tis not enough that Aristotle has said so, for Aristotle drew his models of tragedy from Sophocles and Euripides; and *if he had seen ours, might have changed his mind.*"

In the short space of the present volume, there is no room to attempt even a summary of the century's vast production of "Essays on Criticism," "Essays on Taste," "Essays on Design," "Essays toward Fixing the True Standards of Wit," "Dissertations on Genius," "Observations on Style," and the like. Of course it may well be asked how useful it is to the student of the imaginative literature of the time to familiarize himself with all these—to what extent they will sharpen his understanding and appreciation of the literature itself. Much of this critical and aesthetic theorizing was written by men who were not greatly skilled, if at all, in any of the arts: Lord Kames, for instance, was a judge of the Scottish courts of justice, Alexander Gerard and Hugh Blair Presbyterian divines, Archibald Alison a Scottish Episcopalian divine (one wonders why theorizing about the nature of beauty should have so appealed to Scottish clergymen, of all people). And even when such theorizing is undertaken by a practitioner of the arts, it is an old truism that, as Coleridge observed of Wordsworth, his theory may give by no means an accurate report of his practice. An outstanding eighteenth-century illustration of this is Hogarth, who was very proud of the theory evolved in his *Analysis of Beauty* that an S-shaped curve of certain proportions ("the line of beauty") is the essential component of all artistically excellent design. But it has been pointed out that such a curve is preeminently characteristic of the rococo, which Hogarth detested, and it would be a hopeless task to try to locate the excellencies of Hogarth's own art in his use of the "line of beauty."

Aesthetics is, of course, a branch of philosophy or psy-

chology, and the most fruitful contributions to a satisfactory theory of aesthetics were made by philosophers, or rather psychologists in the guise of philosophers, as most of the great eighteenth-century British philosophers were. If Dryden was the father of English criticism, Locke was certainly the father of eighteenth-century English aesthetic theory. Locke's great service was to reject the old Greek theory that the human mind works with inherent "logic," and to propound instead the theory of "associationism"—that we think and feel what we do largely as a result of the fortuitous associations provided by our past experience of the things we see, hear, touch, taste, and smell. A child sees a cane and trembles, not because of any logical reasoning about the nature of canes, but because in the past it has been applied vigorously to his bottom; conversely, when he sees a bon bon, he smiles. Berkeley, especially in his *New Theory of Vision,* and David Hartley, in his *Observations on Man,* push this Pavlovianism even farther; and David Hume comes to the conclusion that all "reasoning" is simply habit, the product of "conditioning" by experience. As for aesthetics, Hume declares, "Beauty is no quality in things themselves: it exists merely in the mind which contemplates them; and each mind perceives a different beauty." The simple existential act of liking or disliking comes first; afterward we try to work out a rationale to explain our doing so. That there was a nexus between such empiricist aesthetics and the practical criticism of the time is evident when we consider such a passage as Johnson's "general observation" on *Julius Caesar* (and Johnson professed no admiration of Hume): "Of this tragedy," he begins, "many particular passages deserve regard, and the contention and reconcilement of Brutus and Cassius is universally celebrated." "But," adds Johnson coolly, "*I have never been strongly agitated in perusing it,* and think it somewhat cold and unaffecting," and this is enough to damn the work as far as Johnson is concerned.

Aesthetic theorists of the eighteenth century tend to be divided into two main classes, those who in the main concur with Locke and Hume and seek to find the causes of our liking or disliking something in the history of human experience, and those who, on the contrary, adhere to pre-Lockian psychology and postulate an "innate sense" in man which intuitively turns toward what is, in the nature of things, inherently and absolutely beautiful. The second group is not large, but a few influential eighteenth-century writers, notably Shaftesbury and, less dogmatically and more intelligently, Francis Hutcheson, stick to their Platonic guns and insist on the innate aesthetic sense which automatically responds to the true, the beautiful, and the good. The vast majority of English theorists and critics of the period fall, however, into the first category. There is Addison, whose *Spectator* essays on the imagination take an essentially psychological approach. There is Johnson, who shrewdly points out, among many other things, that the "unities" of time and place in the drama have no psychological justification, since the imagination of the spectator can quite as easily transfer him from Rome to Alexandria in the middle of a play as it transferred him from a hard theater seat in London to Rome at the beginning of it, and (in *Rambler* 60) that the source of the pleasure one gets from reading fiction or biography is what we should now call empathy. There is Burke, who finds that we are moved by "the sublime" (objects characterized by vastness, obscurity, a sense of power, and the like) when we have an "idea" of pain and danger without actually experiencing them, by contrast with our reaction to "the beautiful," whose characteristics are smallness, smoothness, delicacy, and so on. There is Lord Kames, who, though he begins by assuring us that taste is innate, nevertheless goes to great lengths to explain in associationist terms *why* some things are beautiful and others not (when you erect a "ruin" in your garden, be sure to construct it in Gothic rather than Greek style, because a Gothic ruin brings associations of time triumphing over strength, a melancholy but not unpleasing thought, whereas a Greek ruin represents the triumph of barbarity over taste, a gloomy and discouraging reflection). There are Hugh Blair (a stream running safely between banks is beautiful; a waterfall is sublime) and Archibald Alison, who is perhaps the most thoroughgoing associationist of them all—anything, he thinks, can be made affecting by association; there was, he tells us, a mathematician whose blood ran cold and whose hair stood on end when he read Newton's *Optics;* "The call of a goat among rocks," he says, "is strikingly beautiful, as expressing wildness and independence; in a farmyard, not so."

As interesting as all this may be to the student of the intellectual history of the time, it may be questioned whether much of it is actually relevant to the art of the Restoration and eighteenth century and the delight and instruction which that art is capable of affording to the modern listener, viewer, and reader. The truly great critics of the age, Dryden, Johnson and Reynolds, are also, as often happens, great executants of the arts they discuss; and Dryden and Johnson are much more critics than "metacritics"—they are concerned primarily with the concrete work before them, and very little with weaving grandiose generalizations about how the beautiful is to be defined. Reynolds, to be sure, in the fifteen presidential *Discourses* he delivered to the Royal Academy, tends to generalize more: it is a tendency inherent in the *genre* of the "presidential address," whether delivered to a gathering of artists, businessmen, university graduands, or even philological scholars.

Reynolds' *Discourses* have had an unenthusiastic reception for some time, largely, perhaps, because of Blake's witty aphorisms jotted in the margins of his copy of them. Yet the more one reads Reynolds, the more one is impressed by the seriousness and insight and the maturity and the *rightness* of so much of what he has to say. It becomes clear, for instance, as one studies the *Discourses* thoughtfully, that Reynolds is no more guilty than his friend Johnson of the most damning error that is charged against them both, that of advocating "generality," in the sense of "abstractness," in art: they are as well aware as Blake and Ezra Pound that the material of art is particularities, whatever the effect on the audience may be. And after so much elaborate theorizing in a vacuum, which lesser critics of the eighteenth century (as in other centuries) were so fond of indulging in, it is reassuring to be told by Reynolds, in his thirteenth *Discourse,*

> All theories which attempt to direct or control the Art, upon any principles falsely called rational, which we form to ourselves upon supposition of what ought in reason to be the end or means of Art, independent of the known first effect produced by the objects on the imagination, must be false and delusive.

It is clear that the greatest critics of eighteenth-century England were no more under the spell of "reason" than were its greatest philosophers and greatest poets. (pp. 159-71)

> *Donald Greene, "The Arts: A Note on Literary and Aesthetic Criticism and Theory," in his* The Age of Exuberance: Backgrounds to Eighteenth-Century English Literature, *Random House, 1970, pp. 159-71.*

FURTHER READING

Aldis, H. G. "Book Production and Distribution, 1625-1800." In *The Cambridge History of English Literature, Vol. XI: The Period of the French Revolution,* edited by Sir A. W. Ward and A. R. Waller, pp. 311-42. Cambridge: Cambridge University Press, 1964.

Traces the growth and development of the English press from the seventeenth century through the eighteenth century, highlighting significant perspectives and manifestations.

Aldis, Mrs. H. G. "The Bluestockings." In *The Cambridge History of English Literature, Vol. XI: The Period of the French Revolution,* edited by Sir A. W. Ward and A. R. Waller, pp. 343-65. Cambridge: Cambridge University Press, 1964.

Describes the social atmosphere of the leading English salons during the eighteenth-century.

Boas, Frederick S. *An Introduction to Eighteenth-Century Drama, 1700-1780.* 1953. Reprint. Westport, Conn.: Greenwood Press, 1978, 365 p.

Surveys the dramatic, political, and social significance of the principal English plays of the eighteenth century.

Brown, John. *An Estimate of the Manners and Principles of the Times.* 2 vols. 3d ed. London: L. Davis and C. Reymers, 1757.

A survey of moral and social issues in eighteenth-century English life, written by a clergyman and closely imitating Lord Shaftesbury's earlier study [see below].

Chapman, R. W. "Authors and Booksellers." In *Johnson's London: An Account of the Life and Manners of His Age,* Vol. II, edited by A. S. Turberville, pp. 310-30. Oxford: Clarendon Press, 1933.

Identifies major features of the publishing industry in eighteenth-century London.

Damrosch, Leo. "Introduction: Texts and Their Realities." In his *Fictions of Reality in the Age of Hume and Johnson,* pp. 3-15. Madison: University of Wisconsin Press, 1989.

Argues that eighteenth-century English authors of both imaginative writing and nonfiction "regarded reality as stable *and also* as relative."

Dickinson, H. T., ed. *Politics and Literature in the Eighteenth Century.* Totowa, N. J.: Rowman & Littlefield, 1974, 234 p.

Attempts to provide contemporary evidence of prevailing political opinions, reprinting eighteenth-century English political and imaginative literature as evidence.

George M. Dorothy. *London Life in the XVIIIth Century.* New York: Alfred A. Knopf, 1925, 457 p.

Portrays the conditions of lower-class life and work in eighteenth-century London.

Hipple, Walter John, Jr. *The Beautiful, The Sublime, & The Picturesque in Eighteenth-Century British Aesthetic Theory.* Carbondale, Ill.: Southern Illinois University Press, 1957, 390 p.

Reviews eighteenth-century aesthetic theory, analyzing the writings of prominent aestheticians.

Hogarth, William. *The Analysis of Beauty,* edited by Joseph Burke. Oxford: Clarendon Press, 1955, 247 p.

Explicates various aspects of eighteenth-century aesthetics.

Hudson, Nicholas. *Samuel Johnson and Eighteenth-Century Thought.* Oxford: Clarendon Press, 1988, 272 p.

Examines eighteenth-century philosophical and religious thought.

Krieger, Murray. "The Arts and the Idea of Progress." In *Progress and Its Discontents,* edited by Gabriel A. Almond, Marvin Chodorow, and Roy Harvey Pearce, pp. 449-65. Berkeley and Los Angeles: University of California Press, 1977.

Attempts to rectify historical discrepancies between the idea of progress and its relation to the liberal arts.

Miller, Henry K. "Some Relationships Between Humor and Religion in Eighteenth-Century Britain." *Thalia: Studies in Literary Humor* VI, No. 1: 48-59.

Assesses the historical relationships between humor and religious discourse during the Age of Johnson.

Namier, L. B. *The Structure of Politics at the Ascension of George III.* 2 vols. London: Macmillan and Co., 1929.

Surveys the political climate of England from 1760 onward, providing flow charts, maps, graphs, and appendices of parliamentary and royal financial accounts.

Pittock, Joan. "Taste and Augustanism." In her *The Ascendancy of Taste: The Achievement of Joseph and Thomas Wharton,* pp. 1-30. London: Routledge and Kegan Paul, 1973.

Considers the evolution of neoclassical critical techniques in eighteenth-century England.

Redford, Bruce. Introduction to *The Converse of the Pen: Acts of Intimacy in the Eighteenth-Century Familiar Letter,* by Bruce Redford, pp. 1-15. Chicago: University of Chicago Press, 1986.

Analyzes the characteristics of eighteenth-century "epistolary performance."

Rousseau, G. S. "Nerves, Spirits, and Fibres: Towards Defining the Origins of Sensibility." In *Studies in the Eighteenth Century: Papers Presented at the Third David Nichol Smith Memorial Seminar,* edited by R. F. Brissenden and J. C. Eade, pp. 137-58. Toronto: University of Toronto Press, 1976.

Interprets the scientific implications of the "age of sensi-

bility," refuting the common assertion that the social sciences were born in the eighteenth century.

Saintsbury, George. "The Prosody of the Eighteenth Century." In *The Cambridge History of English Literature, Vol. XI: The Period of the French Revolution,* edited by Sir A. W. Ward and A. R. Waller, pp. 245-56. Cambridge: Cambridge University Press, 1964.

Surveys the theoretical applications of eighteenth-century poetics.

Scholtz, Gregory F. "Anglicanism in the Age of Johnson: The Doctrine of Conditional Salvation." *Eighteenth-Century Studies* 22, No. 2 (Winter 1988-89): 182-207.

Refutes the notion that the eighteenth-century English Church embraced a "system of morality built on appeals to self-interest."

Shaftesbury, Anthony Ashley Cooper, 3rd Earl of. *Characteristics of Men, Manners, Opinions, Times, etc.* Edited by John M. Robertson. 2 vols. 1900. Reprint. Gloucester, Mass.: Peter Smith, 1963.

A collection of moral treatises originally published in 1711, which includes "A Letter Concerning Enthusiasm," "An Essay on the Freedom of Wit and Humor," and "An Inquiry Concerning Virtue or Merit." This work was generally considered a "dangerously influential" book throughout the eighteenth century.

Smith, D. Nichol. "The Newspaper." In *Johnson's England: An Account of the Life & Manners of His Age,* Vol. II, edited by A. S. Turberville, pp. 331-67. Oxford: Clarendon Press, 1933.

Discusses the features and habits of eighteenth-century English journalism.

Tillotson, Geoffrey. "Eighteenth-Century Poetic Diction." In *Eighteenth-Century English Literature: Modern Essays in Criticism,* edited by James L. Clifford, pp. 212-32. New York: Oxford University Press, 1959.

Centers on English poetic styles unique to the eighteenth century, indicating similarities with poetry of the following century.

Wheatley, H. B. "Letter Writers." In *The Cambridge History of English Literature, Vol. X: The Age of Johnson,* edited by Sir A. W. Ward and A. R. Waller, pp. 242-70. Cambridge: Cambridge University Press, 1964.

Considers the careers of several prominent eighteenth-century epistlers, including Horace Walpole, Fanny Burney, Elizabeth Montagu, and the Earl of Chesterfield.

Winton, Calhoun. "The Tragic Muse in Enlightened England." In *Greene Centennial Studies: Essays Presented to Donald Greene in the Centennial Year of the University of Southern California,* edited by Paul J. Korshin and Robert R. Allen, pp. 125-42. Charlottesville: University Press of Virginia, 1984.

Focuses on the principal themes of eighteenth-century dramatic tragedy, contrasting contemporary and twentieth-century tastes and interpretations.

David Garrick

1717-1779

English actor, dramatist, and poet.

While Garrick was recognized in his time as a brilliant and successful author, his reputation as a theater manager and actor has long overshadowed his literary achievements. As an author he is regarded primarily as a dramatist, though he published over 400 poems. He wrote and produced farces, satires, musicals, and adaptations of Shakespearean and non-Shakespearean works. Several of these works were performed well into the nineteenth century, and at least one, *The Clandestine Marriage,* is still often staged. In addition, his redactions of Shakespeare's plays earned him high praise from his contemporaries as well as from later literary scholars and historians. As Elizabeth P. Stein wrote in her *David Garrick, Dramatist,* "After Sheridan and Goldsmith . . . the third important dramatist of the period is David Garrick."

Born in Hereford in 1717, Garrick spent most of his childhood in Lichfield, where he was educated at the local grammar school. He spent a short amount of time in Lisbon learning the wine trade from an uncle, but scholars disagree about exactly when this took place, dating his residence abroad anywhere from 1726 to 1732. In 1735 Garrick and his younger brother, George, enrolled in the recently opened Edial Hall School run by Samuel Johnson. When the school closed, Garrick and Johnson set out together for London to pursue their fortunes. Garrick himself arranged to study privately with John Colson in Rochester before beginning legal studies at the Inns of Court, but his father's death and Colson's appointment to a chair at Cambridge cut short his studies. Having inherited a legacy from his uncle, who had also recently died, Garrick and his brother Peter decided to enter the wine trade, with David settling in London and Peter in Lichfield.

It was during this time in London that Garrick became involved in theater work. Having been introduced by Johnson to Edward Cave, editor of the *Gentleman's Magazine,* he took part in amateur theatricals at Cave's residence in St. John's Gate, Clerkenwell. He also began contributing verses and drama reviews to the *Gentleman's Magazine.* His first play, *Lethe; or, Esop in the Shades,* was performed in April 1740 at Drury Lane. In 1741 Garrick acted in Ipswich in Henry Giffard's production of Thomas Southerne's *Oroonoko*; he appeared under the pseudonym of Lyddall, the maiden name of Giffard's wife, because he had not yet revealed to his family his intentions to pursue a career in the theater. Garrick made his London debut the same year at Goodman's Fields Theatre. He played Richard III and was billed as "a gentleman, who never appeared on any stage." Alexander Pope was present at one of these performances and commented, "That young man never had his equal, and never will have a rival." Following his warm reception in this role, Garrick wrote to Peter: "My mind (as you must know) has been always inclined to the stage, nay so strongly so that all my illness and lowness of spirits was owing to my want of resolution to tell you my thoughts when here. Finding at last both my incli-

nation and interest required some new way of life, I have chosen the most agreeable to myself, and though I know you will be much displeased at me, yet I hope when you shall find that I may have the genius of an actor without the vices, you will think less severe of me and not be ashamed to own me for a brother." This letter ends with Garrick informing his brother that his farce *The Lying Valet* was to open at Drury Lane; it opened, in fact, at Goodman's Fields on November 30. Garrick, who had entered the world of drama with the warmest of receptions, now continued acting in other productions, appearing at Drury Lane and at Dublin's Smock Alley Theatre. The year 1747 saw further advancement in Garrick's career. His immensely popular farce *Miss in Her Teens; or, The Medley of Lovers* was presented at Covent Garden in January, and less than three months later Garrick and James Lacy became co-patentees of the Drury Lane, beginning a phase in Garrick's life that would last for nearly thirty years.

Theater business did not claim all of Garrick's attention at this time, however. Soon after the young Viennese dancer Eva Maria Violetti made her London debut in 1746, Garrick met the beautiful artist and immediately fell in love with her. He proposed marriage, but, perhaps owing to the unsavory reputation generally associated with the acting profession at the time, Violetti's English patrons, the Earl and Countess of Burlington, did not initially approve of the match. The earl and countess finally capitulated, however, and in June 1749 Garrick and Violetti were married. The marriage was an extremely happy one, marred only by the fact that they were unable to have children.

Garrick now began to expand his literary endeavors. In November 1748 he opened his production of Shakespeare's *Romeo and Juliet.* He altered the tragedy to delete any mention of Rosaline, Romeo's original love-interest, in order to eliminate the possibility that viewers would respond negatively to a young hero who could switch affections so quickly. He also retained Thomas Otway's own interpolated ending, in which Juliet is revived just before Romeo dies, to give the young lovers another scene together. This production was highly successful and encouraged Garrick to try further adaptations of both Shakespearean and non-Shakespearean dramatic works. Among these were Ben Jonson's *Every Man in His Humour* (1751), Voltaire's *Zaire* (1754), and Shakespeare's *King Lear* (1756) and *Hamlet* (1772).

Garrick also continued to write and produce original plays. Among the most memorable are *Lilliput,* a satiric drama produced in 1756 and based upon "The Voyage to Lilliput" in Jonathan Swift's *Gulliver's Travels* (1726), and *The Male Coquette; or, Seventeen Hundred Fifty-Seven,* a farce that opened the following year. Additionally, Garrick continued to manage Drury Lane, thereby exposing himself to tensions of a different sort from those to which he, the acclaimed actor, was accustomed. One event in particular stands out for the outcry it prompted. It was an established custom in the theaters of the day that after the main dramatic piece of the evening ended, patrons would be admitted to the afterpiece for half price. In January 1763, however, Garrick's playbills announced that "nothing under full price will be taken." This action incited a group of young men, known as "The Town," to rebel and insist upon the reinstatement of the old system. The group severely vandalized Drury Lane, and Garrick was forced to concede to their demands. The stress of such occurrences caused Garrick to fear for his health. In September of the same year, he and Eva Maria embarked on a European tour and did not return to England until April 1765.

Before leaving England, however, Garrick worked with George Colman the elder on a new comedy. Each man had his own sections to write, and the two efforts were later combined into one dramatic piece. Exactly how this labor was divided has been a point of contention for literary scholars and historians ever since, with one camp claiming that Garrick wrote most of the play, and the other giving Colman credit for a greater portion of the creation. In any event, *The Clandestine Marriage* was a phenomenal success and was touted as "the best comedy of the century." Literary critics point to the tightness of plot construction throughout and the relevance of each individual scene as two of the main reasons for the play's popularity. The action is fast-paced, the dialogue is witty and sharp, and there is no superfluous action or dialogue to confuse the audience. As a result, *The Clandestine Marriage* has long retained its appeal and is often revived today.

In 1769, prompted by his long-standing admiration for Shakespeare, Garrick devised a scheme for producing an elaborate festival, the "Shakespeare Jubilee." It was scheduled for September in Shakespeare's birthplace, Stratford-upon-Avon, and was meant to include feasts, balls, poetry readings, horse races, a parade, and fireworks. All went well until the designated week, when it rained incessantly in Stratford and the surrounding region. Most of the ceremonies and activities were rained out—indeed, nobles from throughout England found themselves and their carriages marooned in the sloppy quagmires that formed in the roads in and out of Stratford—and Garrick was forced to admit that the Jubilee festival was a disaster. In order to recoup some of Drury Lane's losses, he wrote a play entitled *The Jubilee.* This work incorporated the planned parade of Shakespearean characters, the "Ode upon Dedicating a Building and Erecting a Statue, to Shakespeare, at Stratford upon Avon," and witty dialogue that addressed many of the charges leveled against the festival, most notably by Samuel Foote. The play was a success with London audiences, and Lacy commented upon his partner: "Davy is an able projector, sir. This was a devilish lucky piece."

In 1773 Garrick was made a member of The Club, the select intellectual circle led by Samuel Johnson. As James Boswell recorded, Johnson maintained a personal liking for Garrick, calling him "the first man in the world for sprightly conversation"—this in spite of the fact that he considered the acting profession somewhat raffish and Garrick himself something of a pampered darling of the upper class, spoiled by attention. Still, Johnson would allow nobody to speak slightingly of "Davy"—except himself. And Garrick, after his admission into The Club, proved a vital and productive member; upon his death Johnson paid tribute to him by declaring that his place would not be filled for one year.

For some time Garrick had considered retirement, and by the mid 1770s, he sensed that the time was finally right. He gave his final stage performance on 10 June 1776, an event led up to by his performance of all his best-known and favorite roles at least once in the preceding month. At the end of his performance, Garrick made a short speech thanking the audience for their patronage and kindness over the years, saying, "This is to me a very awful moment: it is no less than parting for ever with those from whom I have received the greatest kindness, and upon the spot where that kindness and your favours were enjoyed." Although Garrick had retired from the stage, he still held half of the Drury Lane patent. He sold this to Richard Brinsley Sheridan in December 1776 and spent the rest of his life entertaining and visiting friends. During a visit to the countryside in December 1778, he was stricken with gout and shingles and decided to return to London. He went into a coma on 18 January 1779, and died two days later. He was buried with great ceremony in Westminster Abbey.

Garrick's dramatic works were generally well received by the eighteenth-century theater-going public. This is due in part to Garrick's having written plays and parts to suit particular actors or actresses; as a result, even below-average dramas came to life. His farces, satires, and comedies, based as they were on the author's private observations of London life, made members of society laugh at their own foibles. As Phyllis T. Dircks has written: "All of Garrick's plays are vitalized by his distinctive dramatic traits: fast-paced dramatic action, effective timing, careful craftsmanship, the use of topical material specifically directed to an English playhouse audience, and urbanity and wit in upholding the values of a civilized society." Among the most successful of these were *Lethe; or, Esop in the Shades* (1740), *The Lying Valet* (1742), *Miss in Her Teens* (1747), *Lilliput* (1757), *The Male Coquette; or, Seventeen Hundred Fifty-Seven* (1757), *The Guardian* (1759), *The Clandestine Marriage* (1767), *The Irish Widow* (1772), and *Bon Ton; or, High Life Above Stairs* (1775).

Commentators have long praised Garrick for his efforts to restore original readings to the adulterated and bowdlerized versions of Shakespeare's works that were commonly performed during the eighteenth century. Many of these early adaptations substituted "the bland verbiage of the Restoration" for the rich, powerful writing of Shakespeare himself, and Garrick recognized the value of the original text. Yet Garrick did not restore these plays to their initial form; he possessed a keen sense of what the public would most willingly pay to see, and he bowed to popular demands in many instances. In some cases, his adaptations of Shakespearean works were abysmal failures, but most of them enjoyed revivals well into the nineteenth century. Some scholars consider Garrick's Shakespearean adaptations to be travesties of the originals, while others claim that Garrick nevertheless did much to further the cause of text restoration, thereby promoting awareness of and respect for the works of Shakespeare.

Currently best remembered as an actor and theater manager, Garrick was recognized in his day as an accomplished dramatist. He wrote prolifically, composing many original poems, farces, satires, afterpieces, and musicals. He also made enduring efforts to restore original readings to Shakespearean texts. Thus it may be readily understood why Johnson commented that his friend's death "eclipsed the gaiety of nations, and impoverished the publick stock of harmless pleasure."

(See also *Dictionary of Literary Biography,* Vol. 84.)

PRINCIPAL WORKS

Lethe; or, Esop in the Shades   (drama)   1740
The Lying Valet   (drama)   1741
Macbeth [adaptor; from the drama *The Tragedy of Macbeth* by William Shakespeare]   (drama)   1744
Othello [adaptor; from the drama *The Tragedy of Othello, the Moor of Venice* by William Shakespeare]   (drama)   1745
Miss in Her Teens; or, The Medley of Lovers: a Farce in Two Acts, as it is Perform'd at the Theatre-Royal in Covent-Garden   (drama)   1747
Romeo and Juliet [adaptor; from the drama *The Tragedy of Romeo and Juliet* by William Shakespeare]   (drama)   1748
Every Man in His Humour [adaptor; from the drama *Every Man in His Humour* by Ben Jonson]   (drama)   1751
Katharine and Petruchio [adaptor; from the drama *The Taming of the Shrew* by William Shakespeare]   (drama)   1754
The Fairies [adaptor; from the drama *A Midsummer*

Night's Dream by William Shakespeare]   (drama)   1755
Florizel and Perdita [adaptor; from the drama *The Winter's Tale* by William Shakespeare]   (drama)   1756
King Lear [adaptor; from the drama *The Tragedy of King Lear* by William Shakespeare]   (drama)   1756
Lilliput [adaptor; from the satire *Travels into Several Remote Nations of the World, in Four Parts; by Lemuel Gulliver, First a Surgeon, and then a Captain of Several Ships* by Jonathan Swift]   (drama)   1756
The Tempest [adaptor; from the drama *The Tempest* by William Shakespeare]   (drama)   1756
The Male-Coquette; or, Seventeen Hundred Fifty-Seven   (drama)   1757
The Guardian   (drama)   1759
High Life below Stairs   (drama)   1759
*Harlequin's Invasion   (pantomime)   1759
Cymbeline [adaptor; from the drama *Cymbeline* by William Shakespeare]   1761
The Farmer's Return from London   (drama)   1762
The Clandestine Marriage [with George Colman the elder]   (drama)   1766
The Country Girl [adaptor; from the drama *The Country Wife* by William Wycherley]   (drama)   1766
Neck or Nothing   (drama)   1766
Cymon   (drama)   1767
A Peep Behind the Curtain; or, The New Rehearsal   (drama)   1767
The Dramatic Works of David Garrick, Esq.; Now First Collected in Three Volumes   (drama)   1768
†The Jubilee   (drama)   1769
Hamlet [adaptor; from the drama *The Tragedy of Hamlet, Prince of Denmark* by William Shakespeare]   (drama)   1772
The Irish Widow   (drama)   1772
A Christmas Tale   (drama)   1773
The Meeting of the Company; or, Baye's Art of Acting   (drama)   1774
Bon-Ton; or, High Life Above Stairs, a Farce in Two Acts   (drama)   1775
The Theatrical Candidates: A Musical Prelude   (drama)   1775
The Poetical Works of David Garrick, Esq.   (poetry)   1785
Letters of David Garrick   (letters)   1963
The Plays of David Garrick: A Complete Collection of the Social Satires, French Adaptations, Pantomimes, Christmas and Musical Plays, Preludes, Interludes, and Burlesques, to Which Are Added the Alterations and Adaptations of the Plays of Shakespeare and Other Dramatists from the Sixteenth to the Eighteenth Centuries. 7 vols.   (drama)   1980-82

*Includes the poem "Heart of Oak."

†Includes "An Ode upon dedicating a Building, and erecting a Statue, to Shakespeare, at Stratford upon Avon."

Oliver Goldsmith   (essay date 1759)

[*In the following excerpt attributed to Goldsmith, the critic unfavorably reviews* High Life below Stairs.]

Just as I had expected, before I saw this farce [*High Life Below Stairs*], I found it, formed on too narrow a plan to afford a pleasing variety. The sameness of the humour in every scene could not at last fail of being disagreeable. The poor, affecting the manners of the rich, might be carried on thro' one character or two at the most, with great propriety; but to have almost every personage on the scene almost of the same character, and reflecting the follies of each other, was unartful in the poet to the last degree.

The scene was also almost a continuation of the same absurdity; and my Lord Duke and Sir Harry (two footmen who assume these characters) have nothing else to *do* but to talk like their masters, and are only introduced to speak, and to shew themselves. Thus, as there is a sameness of character, there is a barrenness of incident, which, by a very small share of address, the poet might have easily avoided.

From a conformity to critic rules, which, perhaps, on the whole, have done more harm than good, our author has sacrificed all the vivacity of the dialogue to nature; and though he makes his characters talk like servants, they are seldom absurd enough, or lively enough, to make us merry. Though he is always natural, he happens seldom to be humorous.

The satire was well intended, if we regard it as being masters ourselves; but, probably, a philosopher would rejoice in that liberty which Englishmen give their domestics; and, for my own part, I cannot avoid being pleased at the happiness of those poor creatures, who, in some measure, contribute to mine. The Athenians, the politest and best-natured people upon earth, were the kindest to their slaves; and if a person may judge, who has seen the world, our English servants are the best treated, because the generality of our English gentlemen, are the politest under the sun.

But not to lift my feeble voice among the pack of critics, who, probably, have no other occupation but that of cutting up every thing new. I must own, there are one or two scenes that are fine satire, and sufficiently humorous; particularly the first interview between the two footmen, which, at once, ridicules the manners of the great, and the absurdity of their imitators. (pp. 154-56)

> *Oliver Goldsmith, in an originally unsigned essay titled "A Word or Two on the Late Farce, Called 'High Life Below Stairs',"* in The Bee, *No. V, November, 3, 1759, pp. 154-57.*

The Monthly Review　(essay date 1769)

[*In the following excerpt from an unsigned review in* The Monthly Review, *the critic praises the artistry and imagery of* "An Ode upon Dedicating a Building, and Erecting a Statue, to Shakespeare, at Stratford upon Avon."]

This ode ["**An Ode Upon Dedicating a Building, and Erecting a Statue to Shakespeare, at Stratford upon Avon**"], though not intended as a mere vehicle for music, should not be brought to the test of severe criticism, as a literary performance intended for the dispassionate leisure of the closet.

The Author wrote part of it for his own elocution, and part for music; for those parts which, in compositions of the like kind, have been condemned to be neither sung nor said, in what is called *Recitative,* he spoke; which, as may easily be imagined, produced a very great effect.

He is known to be peculiarly happy in catching and improving hints from local and temporary circumstances, and, perhaps, the ode before us is the greatest example of this rare felicity that he ever gave; so that, taking it for all in all, it may be the best that could possibly have been produced upon the occasion.

One instance of the Author's skill appears in the beginning of this performance. Shakespeare is not named till the 30th verse, yet every preceding line contributes to his being there named with advantage.

'To what Genius,' says he, 'shall Gratitude erect the temple and the statue? does not the heart confess its lord! It is he who trod the flowery margin of the Avon, while Nature directed his path, and sportive Fancy, in wanton circles, flew round him: but before our joy breaks out in the fascinating strains of music, let Silence, for a moment, hold us in awful suspence; then let Rapture sweep the strings, and Fame, with all her tongues, pronounce SHAKESPEARE! SHAKESPEARE! SHAKESPEARE!'

The repetition of the name, so long deferred, and the immediate joining in of other voices and music, produced the effect he intended, and gratified his utmost hope.

In the prologue which Mr. Garrick spoke when he first became a patentee, and which was written by his celebrated friend Mr. Samuel Johnson, are these verses:

> Each scene of many-colour'd life he drew,
> *Exhausted worlds and then imagin'd new,*
> *Existence saw him scorn her bounded reign,*
> And panting Time toil'd after him in vain.

This thought is happily adopted in the ode, and is in some measure made new by contrasting Shakespeare with Alexander:

> Tho' Philip's fam'd unconquer'd son,
> Had ev'ry blood-stain'd laurel won;
> He sigh'd—that his creative word,
> (Like that which rules the skies,)
> Could not bid other nations rise,
> To glut his yet unfated sword:
>
> But when our Shakespeare's matchless pen,
> Like Alexander's sword, had done with men;
> He heav'd no sigh, he made no moan,
> Not limited to human kind,
> He fir'd his wonder-teeming mind,
> Rais'd other worlds, and beings of his own!

The Author then wishes for one spark of Shakespeare's 'muse of fire,' that he might tell

> How fitting on his magic throne,
> Unaided and alone,
> In dreadful state,
> The subject passions round him wait;
> Who tho' unchain'd, and raging there,
> He checks, inflames, or turns their mad career;
> With that superior skill,
> Which winds the fiery steed at will,
> He gives the awful word—
> And they, all *foaming,* trembling, own him for their lord.

With these, his slaves, he can *controul,*
Or *charm* the soul;
So realiz'd are all his *golden dreams,*
Of *terror, pity, love,* and *grief,*
Tho' conscious that the vision only seems,
The *woe-struck* mind finds no *relief.*

In these lines there is great ardour of imagination; and the Author was not at leisure to consider that he attributed to all the passions what could be proper or true only with respect to some; or that the passions which should have been exhibited on this occasion, are those which the Poet *excites,* rather than those he *represents.* Raging, is a fit word to signify the excess of jealousy, hatred, or indignation; but not of pity, or sorrow, or love: as these passions cannot with propriety be said to *rage,* much less can they with propriety be said to *foam.* The passions which Shakespeare *commands* are principally terror and pity, and these should not have been confounded, by an indiscriminate imputation of the same attributes. This ardour has also betrayed him into the impropriety of giving the epithet of *golden* to the dreams of *Terror* as well as to those of *Love,* and representing the mind as *woe-struck* by a golden dream of *love,* as well as by a golden dream of grief. Perhaps, however, the epithet *golden* might be used to express the excellence of Shakespeare's fictions, and not their species. It may also be remarked, that there is no proper opposition between the words *controul* and *charm.* To *charm* is to *controul* by power more than natural; it is also to *delight,* but, taken in that sense, the mind that is *charmed* is *controuled* by the power of the charmer; and the soul that is *delighted* in this verse, is *woe-struck* in the next but three.

The following air is very poetical, especially the thought in the fourth verse, which is repeated in the last:

Though crimes from death and torture fly,
The swifter muse,
Their flight pursues,
Guilty mortals more than die!
They live indeed, but live to fee!
The scourge and wheel,
On the torture of the mind they lie;
Should harrass'd nature sink to rest,
The poet wakes the scorpion in the breast,
Guilty mortals more than die!

In the next stanza, Shakespeare is represented as a *magician,* fired by *charms,* and *spells,* and *incantations*; but there is some incongruity in this image; a magician is not the *subject* of charms and spells, and incantations, but the *agent* that employs them.

The Author then, by a natural and pleasing transition, exhibits the comic powers of Shakespeare; and, in this instance, he has almost rivalled the humour of the great master he celebrates.

His representation of the birth of Falstaff from the brain of Shakespeare, his calling him first a Mountain, as a contrast to the Mouse which a Mountain was said to bring forth, and then a World, and his illustration, by observing that Falstaff and the World are both of them *round* and *wicked,* would do honour to any imagination.

While Fancy, Wit, and Humour spread
Their wings, and hover round his head,
Impregnating his mind,
Which teeming soon, as soon brought forth,

Not a tiny spurious birth,
But out a mountain came,
A mountain of delight!
Laughter roar'd out to see the sight,
And Falstaff was his name!
With sword and shield he, puffing, strides;
The joyous revel-rout
Receive him with a shout,
And modest Nature holds her sides:
No single pow'r the deed had done,
But great and small,
Wit, Fancy, Humour, Whim, and jest,
The huge, misshapen heap impress'd;
And lo—SIR JOHN!
A compound of 'em all,
A comic world in ONE.

A I R.

A world where all pleasures abound,
So fruitful the earth,
So quick to bring forth,
And the world too is wicked and round.

As the well-teeming earth,
With rivers and show'rs,
Will smiling bring forth
Her fruits and her flow'rs;
So Falstaff will never decline;
Still fruitful and gay,
He moistens his clay,
And his rain and his rivers are wine;
Of the world he has all, but its care;
No load, but of flesh, will he bear;
He laughs off his pack,
Takes a cup of old sack,
And away with all sorrow and care.

Upon this occasion it may be observed, that the advantage of speaking his own composition, much more than counterbalanced any superiority in correctness or beauty that might have been found in the composition of another.

A man always has images and conceptions antecedent to terms; the exhibiting these images and conceptions forcibly and precisely, in another mind, is what he labours to effect, not by the terms only, but by that pronunciation and manner which faithful Nature always suggests, when the images and sentiments are first conceived, and which Garrick preserves till the repetition: but a man who speaks the composition of another, very often substitutes no image under the terms; perhaps seldom, perhaps never, the very same, with all its circumstances, which the term was intended to convey; he therefore can be prompted to no aid of the term, as expressive of that image, by tone, gesture, or aspect. Every man has a peculiar manner, always natural and expressive, of conveying, jointly, by word, aspect, and gesture, such ideas as he is able to conceive; but no man can have acquired a peculiar manner of expressing ideas which he is not able to conceive: when therefore he is to express such ideas, he must become a mere creature of imitation, and adopt the manner peculiar to some other, or attempt a fantastic and imaginary excellence, by the rules that have been absurdly given for producing what no rules can produce. (pp. 234-37)

"Shakespeare's Jubilee," in The Monthly Review, *London, Vol. XLI, September, 1769, pp. 234-38.*

Joseph Knight   (essay date 1894)

[*Knight was a longtime drama critic for the* Athenaeum *and editor of* Notes and Queries. *He was the author of* Life of Dante Gabriel Rossetti *(1887),* Theatrical Notes *(1893), and* David Garrick *(1894). In the following excerpt from his biography of Garrick, Knight offers a short, mixed appraisal of Garrick's skill as a dramatist and poet, having stated elsewhere in his book that "It is as an actor that Garrick appeals to us, and not as a dramatist."*]

In the most famous theatrical picture ever painted Sir Joshua shows us Garrick between tragedy and comedy. In his case alone among actors previous to the present century it is impossible to say whether he was greater in tragedy or comedy, whether Lear, Archer, or Abel Drugger was the most absolute masterpiece. He seems himself to have leant to light comedy, to the Archers and Rangers of previous playwrights. . . . Frank mirth is aimed at in the few pieces constituting his existing dramatic baggage. The alterations of Shakespeare and other great dramatists impudently classed as his works are serious and lachrymose from whatever point they are regarded. Many of his *pièces d'occasion,* moreover, he has had the grace to leave unprinted. What are entitled to be called his dramatic works, though principally adaptations such as **Miss in her Teens, Bon Ton,** the **Guardian,** and the **Irish Widow,** are thoroughly humorous and genuinely diverting. (p. 312)

A few of Garrick's plays have, as has been said, ingenuity of construction and vivacity. On the whole, like that of Christian in the *Pilgrim's Progress,* his march towards immortality will be the speedier and the more comfortable when the burden of his general dramas falls from him. His occasional verses are sometimes happy. What Johnson said of his talk is almost true of his verses—"Garrick's conversation is gay and grotesque. It is a dish of all sorts, but all good things. There is no solid meat in it: there is a want of sentiment in it." (pp. 335-36)

> *Joseph Knight, in his* David Garrick, *Kegan Paul, Trench, Trübner & Co., Ltd., 1894, 346 p.*

Frederick W. Kilbourne   (essay date 1906)

[*In the following excerpt, Kilbourne outlines Garrick's adaptation of* Hamlet, *concluding that the play was hurt by the alterations.*]

Garrick in 1772 was so foolish as to make an alteration of *Hamlet,* thereby demonstrating that his professed reverence for Shakespeare was rather hypocritical and that a good actor may be a very poor playwright. Garrick's revision, which he did not venture to print, although he at first intended to do so, seems to have been undertaken chiefly to free the play from features criticised by Voltaire, who in the preface to his *Semiramis* had called *Hamlet* "a coarse and barbarous piece," and had gone on to point out some of the gross absurdities, with which, in his opinion, the play abounded. According to Davies, Garrick divided the acts differently, but made no great changes in the action or dialogue until toward the end of the play. The plotting scenes between the King and Laertes to destroy Hamlet were entirely changed and Laertes was rendered more estimable. Hamlet, having escaped from Rosencrantz and

Guildenstern, returned with a firm resolve to avenge his father's death. The gravediggers and Osric were rejected absolutely; the fate of Ophelia was not mentioned; her funeral was omitted; and the Queen, instead of being poisoned on the stage, was led from her seat and reported to be in an insane condition, due to her sense of guilt. When Hamlet attacked the King, the latter drew his sword, defended himself, and was killed in the rencounter. Laertes and Hamlet then died of mutual wounds.

The account given by Boaden in his *Life of J. P. Kemble,* adds a little to this, and differs from it in some respects, especially as to the conclusion. Among the additional particulars, we are told that Garrick cut out the voyage to England and the execution of Rosencrantz and Guildenstern (he must mean the references to Hamlet's artifice to get them killed and to the report of their deserved fate); that all the wisdom of the Prince is omitted; that Hamlet bursts in upon the King and his court and is reproached by Laertes for being the cause of his father's and his sister's deaths; that, when they are both at the height of their anger, the King interposes and is stabbed by Hamlet. The remainder of the play is said to have been as follows: "The Queen rushes out, imploring the attendants to save her from her son. Laertes, seeing treason and murder before him, attacks Hamlet to revenge his father, his sister, and his King. He wounds Hamlet mortally, and Horatio is on the point of making Laertes accompany him to the shades, when the Prince commands him to desist, assuring him that it was the hand of Heaven, which administered by Laertes 'That precious balm for all his wounds.' " We then learn that the miserable mother had dropped in a trance before she could reach her chamber door, and Hamlet implores for her "an hour of penitence ere madness end her." He then joins the hands of Laertes and Horatio, and commands them to unite their virtues (as a coalition of ministers) to "calm the troubled land." The old couplet as to the bodies concludes the play.

Whichever of these two accounts is right, one thing at least is self-evident, Garrick has sadly mangled Shakespeare's play. We can detect the application of some of the dramatic principles so dear to the classicists. The violation of the unities is made somewhat less pronounced through the omission of young Fortinbras or at least his return; the gravediggers disappear because their jocularity was regarded as incongruous with the tragic affairs amongst which it is placed; the character of Laertes is elevated to make him such a model of virtue as a true hero should be; and Osric is removed perhaps for the same reason as the gravediggers, or perhaps because it was regarded as against all rules to introduce a new character near the end of a play. Garrick, in his anxiety to get rid of the gravediggers, forgot to give poor Ophelia a Christian or any other burial, thus showing his failure to have a thorough command of all the action of the play, as well as thereby depriving us of many of the fine lines and passages of the original. (pp. 153-55)

We are pleased to learn that the theatre-goers of the day, who were beginning to tire of the continual presentation of Shakespeare in adulterated form, were not very favorably disposed towards this version, not even the acting of Garrick being able to make them take kindly to it. It was not often played, and after the revival of the original in 1780 was no more heard of. The day of Shakespeare alteration was nearing its end and few serious original attempts to correct the great Elizabethan were made after this date. Even if he were lacking in art as the playwrights and critics declared, the people began to prefer Shakespeare with all his imperfections on his head rather than with amendments.

Tate Wilkinson, manager of the theatres at Hull and York, who published in 1790 his memoirs, which are full of entertaining and valuable information as to the London and Dublin theatres, applied to Victor for a copy of Garrick's "Hamlet" as acted at Drury Lane. Victor in his reply said: "It is not in my power to send you the corrections lately made in 'Hamlet'; no such favor can be granted to anyone. I presume the play will never be printed with the alterations, as they are far from being universally liked; nay, they are greatly disliked by the million, who love Shakespeare with all his glorious absurdities and will not suffer a bold intruder to cut him up." (p. 156)

> Frederick W. Kilbourne, "Julius Caesar— Macbeth—Hamlet—King Lear—Othello," in his Alterations and Adaptations of Shakespeare, The Poet Lore Company, 1906, pp. 142-72.

Frank A. Hedgcock   (essay date 1911)

[In the following excerpt from a work first published in French in 1911, Hedgcock focuses on Garrick's dramatic and poetic writings, charging him with lack of originality.]

Was the eighteenth century right in thus exalting the comedian [Garrick] to a place beside the poet [Shakespeare]; and must we really see in him "the man who resuscitated Shakespeare in his entirety"?

If the latter phrase means that Garrick, by the intensity of his acting, gave to Shakespeare's plays all the penetrative force of which they are susceptible, and that he showed how much passion and genius they contained, then the answer may well be in his favour; but if, by "resuscitating Shakespeare in his entirety," is meant, placing his works on the stage as he wrote them, then Garrick is far indeed from deserving such praise.

And first of all, it is an error to believe that, at the moment of Garrick's début, Shakespeare's works were buried in oblivion. "The tendency of public taste [in favour of the Heroic drama] had not prevented the actors from constantly having the name of Shakespeare on their playbills. At the time of Garrick's appearance Shakespeare's plays were, at any rate, acted quite as much in London as they are now, and the great, generally-known characters, such as Hamlet, Richard III., King Lear, Shylock, Othello, Falstaff, etc., belonged to the permanent répertoire of every distinguished actor." All the principal players, from Betterton to Quin, had seen in his tragedies the best vehicle for their talents. As to the comedies, they had been neglected for a time in favour of the school of Farquhar, Wycherley, and Congreve; but from about 1730 managers had once more begun to stage them and the public to appreciate them. Garrick, then, inaugurated no movement in favour of Shakespeare; rather did he profit by that already commenced.

One must assuredly accord him praise for continuing that movement and for restoring to the stage pieces that had not been played for years. Antony and Cleopatra, as well as The Two Gentlemen of Verona, was revived in a good arrangement, made by means of cuts only. Timon of Athens, which had not seen the footlights since the Restoration, was given at Drury Lane in 1771, but in a version which still contained no few verses foreign to the original. Macbeth, considered since 1660 as a melodrama of which the first two acts were capable of pleasing by their animation, but the last three were dull and void of interest, became once more a tragedy of the highest class; our actor-manager suppressed the additions due to Dryden and D'Avenant, but he retained verses introduced from Middleton, and, with his own hand, added to his own part a speech in articulo mortis.

This revival was discretion itself compared with his "improvement" of The Taming of the Shrew and A Midsummer Night's Dream. It is true that these pieces had not been seen for many years; but can one say that they were seen beneath the disguise with which Garrick loaded them? In his hands the first became **Katharine and Petruchio,** and figures under that title in the actor's **Dramatic Works.** The under-plot is entirely removed; we find Bianca already married to Hortensio, and thus the amusing scenes between the different suitors for her hand disappear. With them vanishes Petruchio's reason for demanding Kate in marriage. Thus simplified and reduced to classic unity, the play falls into three parts: Petruchio's courtship of the shrew; the marriage, the hurried departure of the couple, and their arrival at the bridegroom's home; the scenes (much abridged) in which Kate is brought to reason, and the tableau which shows us the scold reduced to meekness. With characteristic clumsiness Garrick takes from Katharine a portion of her final speech on the duties of the model wife, and, by transferring it to the victorious husband, destroys all its veiled comic tone. Shakespeare's joyous farce finishes on a grave note suitable for a homily on the whole duty of woman.

As to the Midsummer Night's Dream, it was coolly turned into an opera, for the use of the reigning tenor and of two Italian singers, by the addition of twenty-eight songs or choruses, the words of which were borrowed from other pieces of Shakespeare's, from Milton, Waller, Dryden, or written by Garrick himself. Needless to say that such vulgarly comic characters as the Athenian artisans found no place amid the trills and recitatives; with them disappeared "the most lamentable comedy and most cruel death of Pyramus and Thisby." The love-passages between Demetrius and Helena, Lysander and Hermia, are also removed. Titania becomes amorous, for no reason whatever—but then, this is an opera—with a clown whom she finds sleeping in the forest. In a word, all the dreamy fancy and all the rich playfulness of the charming pastoral are suppressed; and in that lies the importance to the literary historian of Garrick's alterations of Shakespeare: they mark French influence at its high tide, just before the turn. The French mind, positive, realist, and intellectual, has never shown much sympathy for the visionary creations, so unlike anything in heaven or on earth, of our romantic imaginative poets. Now Garrick's was a French mind, formed in what may be called a French century.

But in the place of what he destroyed he set original productions from his own pen—songs, terrible in their triviality, their nudity unadorned save by strings of commonplaces. Thus:

> With mean disguise let others nature hide,
> And mimick virtue with the paint of art;
> I scorn the cheat of reason's foolish pride,
> And boast the graceful weakness of my heart.
> The more I think, the more I feel my pain,
> And learn the more each heavenly charm to prize;
> While fools, too light for passion, safe remain,
> And dull sensation keeps the stupid wise.

Or,

> Joy alone shall employ us,
> No griefs shall annoy us,
> No sighs the sad heart shall betray;
> Let the vaulted roof ring,
> Let the full chorus sing,
> Blest Theseus and Hippolit-a.

Dare we set in comparison with such verses some of the original lines discarded by Garrick? Let us risk, at least, a short and well-worn passage:

> I know a bank where the wild thyme blows,
> Where ox-lips and the nodding violet grows,
> Quite over-canopied with luscious woodbine,
> With sweet musk-roses and with eglantine:
> There sleeps Titania sometime of the night,
> Lull'd in these flowers with dances and delight;
> And there the snake throws her enamell'd skin,
> Weed wide enough to wrap a fairy in:
> And with the juice of this I'll streak her eyes,
> And make her full of hateful fantasies."

If music was necessary, is that unworthy of music?

For this production Garrick composed a Prologue, one of his weakest, in which he asked pardon for daring to put an English opera on the stage:

> An Op'ra too! play'd by an English Band!
> Wrote in a Language which you understand!
> I dare not say *who* wrote it—I could tell ye,
> To soften matters, Signor Shakespearelli.

And he adds, with becoming modesty:

> This awkward Drama (I confess the offence)
> Is guilty, too, of Poetry and Sense.

Except for the remains of Shakespeare's poetry, the piece cannot fairly be declared guilty on the first count; and, as for the second, the play has been so cut about that little sense remains. But then, as Garrick remarks: "Even the best poetry would appear tedious when only supported by Recitative."

The truth is that Garrick was not capable of appreciating Shakespeare as a poet; fanciful pieces like the *Dream* or *The Tempest* were to him formless and barbaric compositions. As to the latter play, our self-styled admirer of Shakespeare, once enthroned at Drury Lane, revived the ridiculous pantomime into which Dryden and D'Avenant had turned it; and that, although Shakespeare's *Tempest,* almost in its pristine beauty, had been acted at the same theatre two years earlier. One can imagine with what raciness Peg Woffington must have played the part of Hippolyte, the man who has never seen a woman—a character added to balance that of the innocent Miranda—and how

she must have fired off her share of the broad jokes which pass between Miranda, Dorinda, Ferdinand, and Hippolyte on the subject of marriage and children!

After this first attempt Garrick allowed *The Tempest* to slumber until 1756; then he turned it into another opera in the style of *The Fairies,* which the same composer, Smith, fitted with music and in which the same tenor, Beard, played the principal part.

A like heaviness of touch and the same absence of all poetic feeling characterize his remodelling of *Romeo and Juliet.* "The chief design of the alteration in the following play," declares Garrick in his "Advertisement," "was to clear the original as much as possible from the jingle and quibble which were always the objections to reviving it. The sudden change of Romeo's love from Rosaline to Juliet was thought by many, at the first revival of the play, to be a blemish in his character; an alteration in that particular has been made, more in compliance to that opinion than from a conviction that Shakespeare, the best judge of human nature, was faulty. Bandello, the Italian novelist, from whom Shakespeare has borrowed the subject of this play, has made Juliet to wake in the tomb before Romeo dies: this circumstance Shakespeare has omitted, not, perhaps, from judgment, but from reading the story in the French or English translation, both which have injudiciously left out this addition to the catastrophe."

Consequently Garrick, following the example of Otway, who had already demolished *Romeo and Juliet* to construct *Caius Marius* with the débris, takes upon himself the task of correcting the author whom he was wont to call, "The god of my idolatry."

The changes introduced are of two sorts: the first have reference to the structure of the piece, the others to detail and poetic form. All allusion to Rosaline having been suppressed, Garrick is obliged to make cuts in the first two acts and to change the order of certain scenes. A grave alteration, in more than one sense, is that by which he awakens Juliet in the tomb before Romeo is yet dead, thus introducing a sensational scene, with plenty of contortions and groans for himself, followed by a funeral procession and a dirge, to verses of his own composition, worthy, perhaps, of a place in some opera libretto, but hardly equal to the society in which they find themselves. Thus the actor reinforces the value of his own part, the manager makes his "show" more splendid and more attractive, and the shade of Shakespeare is, doubtless, enchanted at seeing his omissions repaired.

The changes in poetical form bear especially on two points: the romantic spirit and somewhat euphuistic fancy of this work of Shakespeare's youth are carefully eliminated. All "quibble" is removed; for example, the second scene of Act I., where Romeo and Benvolio indulge in a duel of wit, and several of Mercutio's dazzling verses, not forgetting the objectionable pun: "Ask for me to-morrow, and you will find me a *grave* man." All expressions that might seem excessive are suppressed or toned down; thus in—

> These violent delights have violent ends,
> And in their triumph die; like fire and powder,
> That, as they *kiss* consume;

Garrick and his wife, Eva Maria Violetti, as painted by William Hogarth.

Garrick decides that "kiss" is passing strange, and alters it to "meet." Juliet's cry—

> Prodigious birth of love it is to me
> That I must love a loathèd enemy,

is omitted entirely.

Thanks to this fondness for curtailing, pruning, and attenuating, some ridiculous errors slip into the text; thus, for Tybalt's fine antithesis:

> Romeo, the *love* I bear thee can afford
> No better term than this—thou art a villain,

Garrick substitutes, "the *hate* I bear thee"; which is, of course, more readily intelligible to the pit. (pp. 60-70)

Secondly, all the rhymed portions of the play are reduced to prose, so that no inharmonious "jingle" may remain; in other words, Garrick dared to *unpoetize* some of the finest passages, so as to produce a form of speech more closely assimilated to everyday conversation. (p. 70)

In preparing the *Winter's Tale* for the stage, Garrick saw an occasion for correcting other defects in his favourite author. There is, alas! an interval of sixteen years between the third and the fourth act of this play. Garrick found a simple remedy for this lengthy violation of the unity of time: he suppressed the first three acts entirely, and had the events they contain recounted by one of the characters in the opening scene of the piece. There were, then, in the

original *Winter's Tale,* two parts: in the first, we follow the growth of jealousy in Leontes' heart, we see the passion suddenly burst forth and turn the just king, tender husband, and faithful friend into a suspicious and cruel tyrant. This exposition, with its condensed and solid action, its rapid happenings and touching scenes, must count among Shakespeare's best work; compared with it, the conclusion, brought about by the well-worn trick of a recognition and by the unexpected change of a statue into a woman, is feeble, and is hardly saved from disaster by some pretty scenes of country life, and by the amusing, but supernumerary, character of Autolycus. Between these two halves, Garrick did not hesitate one moment; with what one is obliged to call his habitual bad taste in such matters, he chose the inferior portion, because it did not infringe the classical rules of unity. In order to make a piece of ordinary length out of the two acts he preserved, he added songs and verses of his own; yet he has the impudence to say in his Prologue, in which Shakespeare's genius is compared to good wine:

> In this night's various and enchanted cup
> Some little Perry's mixt for filling up.
> The five long acts from which our three are taken
> Stretched out to sixteen years, lay by, forsaken.
> Lest, then, this precious liquor run to waste,
> 'Tis now confin'd and bottled for your taste.
> 'Tis my chief wish, my joy, my only plan
> To lose no drop of that immortal man!

A little more of Shakespeare's champagne and a little less of Garrick's gooseberry juice would have made a better mixture!

It is of these arrangements of Garrick's that Theo. Cibber said in 1756: "Were Shakespeare's Ghost to rise, wou'd he not frown indignation on this pilfering Pedlar in poetry, who thus shamefully mangles, mutilates, and emasculates his Plays? The *Midsummer Night's Dream* has been minc'd and fricasseed into an indigested and unconnected thing, call'd **The Fairies**: the *Winter's Tale* mammoc'd into a Droll; *The Taming of the Shrew* made a Farce of; and *The Tempest* contorted into an Opera. Oh! what an agreeable Lullaby might it have prov'd to our Beaus and Belles to have heard Caliban, Sycorax, and one of the Devils trilling of Trios! And how prettily might the North-Wind (like the tyrant Barbarossa) be introduc'd with soft Musick! . . . Rouse, Britons, rouse, for shame! and vindicate the Cause of Sense, thus sacrificed to Mummery! Think you see *Shakespeare's Injur'd Shade* . . . sighing over . . . your Non-resistance to this Profanation of his Memory. He grieves to see your tame submission to this merciless *Procrustes* of the stage, who, wantonly as cruelly, massacres his dear remains. . . . Yet this sly Prince would insinuate, all this ill-usage of the Bard is owing, forsooth, to his love of him!"

We do not imagine for one moment that Cibber's criticism is inspired by pure admiration for the great dramatist and by enlightened respect for his works; but it would be idle to deny that his protests are well founded.

Of all Garrick's nefarious attempts on Shakespeare's pieces, the most celebrated is his travesty of *Hamlet.* "I had sworn I would not leave the stage till I had rescued that noble play from all the rubbish of the fifth act. I have brought it out without the Grave-diggers' trick and the Fencing-match." It is evident that the strictures of his

French friends had not failed to produce their effect, and that Garrick had not read in vain the writings of that Voltaire whom, like a good Englishman, he detested. So he attempted to clear his favourite poet of all barbarity and vulgarity; and, at the same time, he relieved the *dreamy inaction of Hamlet by plenty of exclamations and business.* It was, doubtless, the very moderate success that attended his well-meant efforts which prevented Garrick from publishing his arrangement. (pp. 74-7)

Resuming, then, this question of Garrick's attitude towards Shakespeare's plays, we may say that his enthusiasm, undoubtedly sincere, for the dramatist was corrupted by two influences: first, by the taste of an age which mingled many reserves with its admiration for the great Elizabethan—the eighteenth century, nourished on the criticism of Boileau, Rapin, le père Le Bossu, and of their English disciples, Rymer, Dennis, Gildon and others, did not appreciate Shakespeare's luxurious fancy, deplored his ignorance of rules, and regretted his many "deviations from the art of good writing"; and, secondly, by the exigencies of the actor-manager, who was anxious to increase the effect of his own parts at the poet's expense, and to present a spectacle capable of pleasing the general public. To this latter influence are chiefly due the adaptations of *Romeo and Juliet* and of *Macbeth,* as well as the preservation of Cibber's and of Tate's monstrosities. The two influences combined produced the opera of **The Fairies** and that of **The Tempest.** The first drove Garrick to regularize *A Winter's Tale* and *The Shrew* and to expurgate *Hamlet.* It is here that the actor's panegyrists, by pleading the taste of the day, can find for his sacrilegious doings the best excuse; but even here, it should be added, Garrick was a reactionary. (pp. 79-80)

When one reads **The Poetical Works of David Garrick, Esq.,** one sees at once why he would have been well advised in not meddling with Shakespeare's plays. It would be incredible that he could ever have imagined his poetical powers sufficient to allow him to correct the great writer's defects and to match his majestic verse, did we not remember that rhymers even feebler than he had dared undertake the same task. What is particularly lacking in Garrick is originality, both in conception and in execution, in the whole scheme of a poem and in its details. When he tries his hand at a satire, he imitates Pope and Churchill, but remains far behind his models. When he wishes to write a fable in verse he takes La Fontaine's magic pen; but, ignorant of the spell that made dumb things speak and lacking the *bonhomme's* delicate fancy, he produces a laborious compilation, void of grace. In his most ambitious attempt, the **"Ode"** to Shakespeare, he borrows his form from Dryden; but he does not succeed in discovering one new or personal thought, and the images which he employs are either commonplaces or quotations, avowed and unavowed. It is certain that in this piece, written for so important an occasion—the apotheosis of Shakespeare and himself—he has given the fullest measure of his talent; and the result is a perfect cento, a collection of tags, odd-ends, and copybook lines, brought together from every quarter; true actor's poetry, owing its inspiration to memory alone. We do not, of course, reproach him with the use of phrases quoted between inverted commas, such as: "The god of our idolatry" (*Romeo and Juliet,* Act II. sc. ii.); "On the torture of the mind they lie" (*Macbeth,* Act III. sc. ii.), etc.; but at every moment epithets and metaphors shame-

lessly stolen are to be met with. We note at random: "Fame . . . with all her trumpet tongues" (cf. "His virtues . . . trumpet-tongued," *Mac.,* Act I. sc. vii.); "The penitential tear" (cf. "Penitential groans," *Gent. of Verona,* Act III. sc. iv.); "Marble-hearted monster" (cf. "Marble-hearted fiend," *Lear,* Act I. sc. iv.); "Nature's glory, Fancy's child, Never sure did witching tongue, Warble forth such woodnotes wild" (cf. "Or sweetest Shakespeare, Fancy's child, Warble his native wood-notes wild," *L'Allegro*); "And modest Nature holds her sides" (cf. "And laughter holding both her sides," *ibid.*); "Leading the nymph Euphrosyne, goddess of joy and liberty" (cf. commencement of *L'Allegro*); "Songs of triumph to him raise" (cf. "See, the conquering hero comes," in Handel's oratorio *Saul,* libretto by Morell), etc. Even those expressions which cannot be assigned to any particular author are old and worn and belong to all the hack writers; for example: magic art—full tide of harmony—our humble strains—demons of the deep—spirits of the air—buskin'd warriors—tuneful numbers—etc., etc.

When Garrick writes society verses and occasional lines he is more at ease. He possessed the knack necessary for turning a neat compliment to a lady, the wit required for aiming a dart at some rival or critic. In throwing off these trifles he had no need of poetry, and in this subordinate class there is nothing better than his verses—

"To the Countess of Burlington"

(Written in a Prayer-book she gave him)

> This sacred book hath Dorothea given
> To show a straying sheep the way to heav'n;
> With forms of righteousness she well may part
> Who bears the spirit in her upright heart.

Or those on Johnson's Dictionary, completed in 1755:

> Talk of war to a Briton, he'll boldly advance
> That one English soldier will beat ten of France; . . .
> First Shakespeare and Milton, like gods in the fight,
> Have put their whole Drama and Epic to flight;
> In Satires, Epistles, and Odes would they cope,
> Their numbers retreat before Dryden and Pope;
> And Johnson, well arm'd, like a hero of yore,
> Has beat forty French, and will beat forty more.

In the same style were the Prologues and Epilogues of which he rhymed more than a hundred, turning them off at the rate of one in a couple of hours. These little monologues often represented a whole scene in epitome, and were, no doubt, sprightly and effective when spoken and *played* by a good actor; to-day, when we *read* them, after the lapse of a century and a half, much of their brilliancy has departed and they remind one of the faded tinsel of some theatre wardrobe. Here is Peg Woffington complaining of a new regulation which forbids beaux to penetrate behind the scenes:

> No beaux behind the scenes! 'tis innovation
> Under the specious name of reformation!
> Public complaint, forsooth, is made a puff;
> Sense, order, decency, and such like stuff.
> But arguments like these are mere pretence;
> The beaux, 'tis known, ne'er gave the least offence,
> Are men of chastest conduct and amazing sense.
> Each actress now a locked-up nun must be,
> And priestly managers must keep the key. . . .

Or let us listen for a moment to Mrs. Pritchard, in her rôle of Queen Bess, indulging in patriotic sentiment:

> If any here are Britons but in name,
> Dead to their country's happiness and fame,
> Let 'em depart this moment; let 'em fly
> My awful presence and my searching eye.
> No more your Queen, but upright judge I come
> To try your deeds abroad, your lives at home. . . .
> Since that most glorious time that here I reigned,
> An age and half! what have you lost or gain'd?
> Your wit, whate'er your poets sing or swear,
> Since Shakespeare's time is somewhat worse for wear.
> Your laws are good; your lawyers good, of course;
> The streams are surely clear, when clear the source.
> In greater stores these blessings now are sent ye;
> Where I had one attorney you have twenty . . .

Lastly, let us hear Garrick, *propriâ personâ,* reciting for the command night which brought him back to the stage, November 14th, 1765, a prologue which ended thus:

> The Chelsea pensioner, who, rich in scars,
> Fights o'er in prattle all his former wars,
> Tho' past the service, may the young ones teach
> To march—present—to fire—and mount the breach.
> Should the drum beat to arms, at first he'll grieve
> For wooden leg, lost eye, and armless sleeve;
> Then cocks his hat, looks fierce, and swells his chest:
> "'Tis for my king, and, zounds! I'll do my best."

To these sketches of his old pupil's Johnson accorded no small praise when he said: "Dryden has written prologues superior to any that David Garrick has written, but David Garrick has written more good prologues than Dryden has done. It is wonderful that he has been able to write such a variety of them." But that was the limit of his poetic talent. (pp. 82-8)

His comedies had much the same qualities as his prologues—plenty of "go" and a number of brightly, if roughly, sketched characters; but they were lacking in originality, and were usually borrowed from French pieces. We will give a rapid outline of **Lethe,** his first attempt, produced in 1740, revived in 1756, and constantly touched up and altered by the author.

Pluto, at Proserpine's request, has granted a boon to mortals: all those who wish to forget some of life's ills may come and drink of the waters of Lethe, provided that Æsop, stationed as examiner on the near bank, consider the reasons they give for their desire sufficient. Thus a whole series of characters defiles before the audience: a poet who would forget the ill success of his latest play; a miser who would forget that he must one day die and leave his money; etc. The most amusing sketches are old Lord Chalkstone and Mrs. Riot; the former (founded on Lord Foppington in Cibber's *Careless Husband* and developed later into the Lord Ogleby of **The Clandestine Marriage**) is an old roué, eaten up by the gout, but perfectly contented with life, thanks to wine, women, and his flatterer, Mr. Bowman; the second a would-be fine lady, to whom Sheridan's Mrs. Malaprop perhaps owed a hint. There is also a Frenchman, who is in England "pour polir la nation," and who states thus his qualifications for the task: "I speak de French, *j'ai bonne adresse,* I *danse un minuet,* I sing de littel chansons, and I have—a tolerable assurance; *en fin,* Sir, my merit consists in one vord—I am foreignere; and, *entre nous,* vile de Englis be so great a fool to love de foreignere better dan demselves, de foreignere vold be

more great a fool did they not leave deir own countrie, vere dey have noting at all, and come to Inglande, vere dey want for noting at all, *perdie. Cela n'est il pas vrai, Monsieur Æsop?"* Æsop advises him to return to France, but the visitor replies that he prefers to be *le Marquis de Pouville* (horrible name!) in England rather than to remain plain *Jean Frisseron le coiffeur* in France.

This little sketch is light, but sparkling; the dialogue is good and the characters vigorously drawn. From it one may judge of the meaning of the word *comedy* for Garrick—a series of situations in which amusing and ridiculous types of humanity can be brought together to expose their peculiarities before the eyes of the audience. As for the plot, that was always as slight as might be, and he preferred to take it ready-made from the works of some predecessor. Here, as in the poems, composing power is lacking, and it is worthy of note that, in the only one of his pieces which is important from its structure, he had the assistance of his friend George Colman. (pp. 89-90)

The Lying Valet—a development of the second act of Motteux's curious medley, *The Novelty; or, Every Act a Play,* with reminiscences of a French comedy by Hauteroche—turns on the endeavours of Sharp, valet to Gayless, an indebted beau, to prevent Melissa, his affianced bride, from discovering the true state of the master's fortunes. The situations are amusing, if somewhat forced. Sharp, a close relation of the *valet fourbe* that Molière and Beaumarchais have rendered immortal, is a lively rogue. Garrick, when young, must have been very vivacious in the part.

A Miss in her Teens, or A Medley of Lovers, provides a somewhat insufficient frame for the portraits of Fribble, an effeminate dandy, and Flash, a cowardly bully, two suitors with whom Miss Biddy has amused herself during her lover's absence at the wars. In his adaptation Garrick has certainly not weakened the French piece on which he has founded his own. Fribble and Flash are better drawn than the original Dorante and Lisimon; but they owe a good deal to Maiden, in *Tunbridge Walks,* and to Captain Brazen, in Farquhar's *Recruiting Officer.* But, indeed, bullies and dandies are favourite characters in all the comedies of the day.

The Male Coquet, acted at first in 1757 as **The Modern Fine Gentleman,** again runs on old lines. Daffodil is a male flirt who loves to have the reputation of a gallant, but who never lets his passion pass beyond the platonic stage. Several married women whose affections he has trifled with decoy him to a rendezvous in Hyde Park, and expose him to the laughter of their friends. Daffodil is an amusing character, but he reminds one of Congreve's Vain-love and Tattle.

In the same way, when in **Neck or Nothing** we see Martin Belford's servant disguise himself as a gentleman in order to marry a woman of fortune, we are reminded of a part of *The Way of the World.* **A Peep behind the Curtain** is likewise, as its sub-title *The New Rehearsal* confesses, only another version of the Duke of Buckingham's famous farce. **The Guardian,** in which we see the middle-aged Mr. Heartly slowly brought to understand that his ward, Miss Harriett, prefers him to the very foolish young suitor he had proposed for her, is a really excellent little comedy; but it is a very close adaptation of Fagan's *La Pupille,* of which Voltaire used to declare that it was the best short piece in the French language.

These pieces, then, betray little talent on Garrick's part beyond that of knowing how to choose in his predecessors' works incidents or characters capable of development in different surroundings, and of giving them new life by the addition of smart, up-to-date dialogue; that *is* talent, of course, but not of a very high class. In France his value as an author was never overrated. Although Madame Riccoboni, a fervent worshipper, might tell him, "I have re-read all your charming pieces; you have embellished many of our subjects," yet even she had to admit that they had not the charm of novelty. Grimm, in spite of his admiration for the actor, says plainly: "Garrick is the author of several pieces, but they are said to be mediocre"; and later Meister, when he directed the *Correspondance littéraire,* declared, after having read the French translation of Garrick's dramatic works, that he knows not whether to attribute its want of interest to unskilfulness on the translator's part or the feebleness of the pieces themselves. (pp. 91-3)

> *Frank A. Hedgcock, in his* A Cosmopolitan Actor: David Garrick and His French Friends, *Duffield and Company, 1912, 442 p.*

R. W. Babcock   (essay date 1930)

[*In the excerpt below, Babcock discusses the ground-swell of public opposition to alterations of Shakespeare's works during the 18th century, focusing upon Garrick's role in and opinions of this matter.*]

Opinion favorable to alterations of Shakespeare proceeded, with some opposition, to about 1775 and after that generally disintegrated. The chief alterer from 1750 to 1775 was Garrick, and the chief proponent of these adaptations was F. Gentleman, who was quite agreeable to Garrick's manipulations as well as those of all others. The plays most generally changed were *Richard III, Timon of Athens, King Lear, Romeo and Juliet, Cymbeline,* and *Hamlet.* It will be best to take up the current in favor of alterations first.

The *British Magazine* in 1767 praised Cibber's adaptation of *Richard III:* "The late laureat has . . . made up a compleat tragedy of Richard the Third, which may vie with the best pieces of our great dramatic poet." Similarly, the *Monthly Review* in 1768 approved Dance's alteration of *Timon of Athens* and in 1771, Cumberland's. Francis Gentleman in 1770 applauded Tate's *Lear* (rejecting Colman's) and offered some suggestions himself for further alteration; he also accepted Cibber's *Richard III* and Garrick's *Romeo and Juliet* and *Cymbeline.* Two years later the *Macaroni and Theatrical Magazine* approved Garrick's adaptation of *Hamlet:*

> To clear this piece of these charges (which were in part not ill-founded) has been the task of the present revisor [Garrick]: how far he has succeeded, the applauses of a crowded and judicious audience have already testified.

Bell's *Edition* of Shakespeare, 1774, followed the theatres in expunging "obscure, indelicate" passages, and finally, Mrs. Griffith in 1775 may be cited as a feminine representative of this waning point of view: Tate's *Lear* is better

because "our feelings are often a surer guide than our reason." This date practically concludes the critics' approval of the mangling of Shakespeare in this century.

On the other side is an interesting development, from several points of view. Individual plays are rescued from alterations and restored to Shakespeare; prompter's changes are rejected; Garrick is flayed, and there is also an appeal to retain Shakespeare's original language. (pp. 447-48)

[In 1776] the *Universal Magazine* explained, defensively and humorously, Garrick's alteration of *Hamlet:* The gravediggers complain to Garrick about being left out of the play. Garrick answers: ". . . the age does not like to be reminded of mortality: 'tis . . . very disgustful to a well-bred company"; whereupon Shakespeare is allowed to appear in spirit and in imitation of the famous "Angels and ministers of grace defend us" scene, addresses Garrick:

> Freely correct my Page;
> I wrote to please a rude unpolish'd age;
> Thou, happy man, art fated to display
> Thy dazzling talents in a brighter day;
> Let me partake this night's applause with thee,
> And thou shalt share immortal fame with me.

But the most vigorous and comprehensive objectors to alterations of Shakespeare appeared in 1784 and 1791, in Tom Davies and the Edinburgh *Bee.* Davies successively, with some disgust, rejected Cibber's *King Lear,* Davenant's *Macbeth,* Garrick in general and his *Macbeth* in particular, Buckinghamshire's *Julius Caesar,* Tate's *Lear,* Colman's *Lear,* and Garrick's *Hamlet.* This wholesale overthrow of the alterers turned the tide in favor of Shakespeare, for *The Bee* in 1791 continued the devastation: "Shakespeare said just enough in one significant line [in *Measure for Measure*], which is only spun out, in the five finical modern ones"; "with what a disgraceful motely [*sic*] of nonsense and absurdity has this modern poet [Aaron Hill] confounded the beauties of Shakespeare in this play"; "Florizel and Perdita, or the Sheep-Shearing . . . Shakespeare is here mangled as usual"; and the final, slashing blow: "Benedict was . . . grossly injured by Garrick's alterations . . . it is impossible both to alter and amend him [Shakespeare]." This last sweeping statement the *Monthly Mirror* fully corroborated in 1797 by attacking Garrick again:

> Shakspere has always suffered from unskilful alterations, as is plainly proved from many vain attempts which are buried in oblivion; and I question whether *Romeo and Juliet* has gained much by the amendments of Mr. Garrick.

Such a rejection of Garrick's adaptations as that just suggested was by no means new. Horace Walpole in 1769 remarked on Garrick's "insufferable nonsense about Shakespeare." Johnson the same year laughed at Garrick "as a shadow" of Shakespeare, with the addendum that "Many of Shakspeare's plays are the worse for being acted, *Macbeth,* for instance." In 1785 he attacked Garrick even more vigorously: "He has not made Shakspeare better known," and (to Garrick directly): "I doubt much if you ever examined one of his [Shakespeare's] plays from the first scene to the last." Garrick himself in 1776 was rather dubious about his procedure: "I have ventured to produce *Hamlet* with alterations. It was the most impudent thing

I ever did in all my life; but I had sworn I would not leave the stage till I rescued that noble play from all the rubbish of the fifth Act." And finally his biographer, Arthur Murphy, in 1801 corroborated Garrick's doubt, for he says that Garrick, after altering *Hamlet,* "saw his error" because "he never published his alterations." (pp. 449-50)

R. W. Babcock, "The Attack of the Late Eighteenth Century upon Alterations of Shakespeare's Plays," in Modern Language Notes, Vol. XLV, No. 7, November, 1930, pp. 446-51.

Elizabeth P. Stein   (essay date 1938)

[*In the excerpt below, Stein surveys and evaluates several of Garrick's original dramatic works, including* The Clandestine Marriage. (*In an unexcerpted portion, Stein concludes that "after Sheridan and Goldsmith, . . . the third important dramatist of the period is David Garrick.")*]

The Farmer's Return from London, an exceedingly clever and swiftly-moving little interlude, gave the dramatist through his Farmer, a really superb character sketch, an opportunity to satirize the Cock Lane Ghost affair, which kept London agog for quite a while; the inattentiveness of the *beau monde* at the theatre; the critics in the pit; and the noisiness of the spectators in the upper gallery. In this highly diverting playlet is also found one of Garrick's many thrusts at sentimental comedy, a form with which he was entirely out of sympathy and to which he was never reconciled. *The Farmer's Return from London* is important also for Garrick's sympathetically realistic portrayal of the characters of the farmhouse kitchen. In his ridicule of the prevailing follies of the day here as well as in his other plays, Garrick is decidedly in the spirit of the classical tradition of comedy; but in his sympathetic delineation of humble folk like the Farmer and his family in *The Farmer's Return from London,* he is directly in line with the humanitarian phase of the romantic movement.

The Jubilee is a series of scenes built around the pageant of Shakespearean characters which the heavy rainfall at Stratford-upon-Avon prevented Garrick from exhibiting, as he had originally planned, in the streets of the town during the Jubilee festivities (September, 1769). The playlet is significant for its kindly ridicule of the Stratfordians' reception of the Jubilee visitors, for its rollicking good humor, its breath of the out-of-doors, its bustling tavern scene, very much in the spirit of Shakespeare and of Farquhar—another dramatist whom Garrick loved from his boyhood days—and, finally, for its use of the transparency before De Loutherbourg. The employment of this scenic device here as well as in *Harlequin's Invasion* ten years previous, and the fact that Garrick ordered Shakespeare's birthplace and five windows of the Town Hall at Stratford-upon-Avon enveloped, as part of the Jubilee program, in transparencies, prove conclusively that De Loutherbourg was not, as has been generally and erroneously believed, the first to make use of the transparency.

Although in form and spirit the admirable little one-act play, *The Meeting of the Company; or, Bayes's Art of Acting,* follows in the footsteps of the classic example of the burlesque-rehearsal drama of Buckingham, Garrick's is the better organized of the two. In it he satirizes the idiosyncrasies of the players in general; the ridiculously grandiose manner and the inflated style of the tragedians of the period in particular; and the bad behavior of the spectators at the theatre. In introducing upon the stage some members of his company in their own names, and in permitting them to engage in back-stage gossip and, principally, in a discussion of the manner of acting tragedy and comedy, Garrick shows a similarity to Molière in *L'Impromptu de Versailles* (1663). There is, however, this difference. Garrick's is a play of lively action; Molière's is a brilliant discussion. It is this rapidity and bustle of action that distinguishes Garrick also from his contemporaries and, with the exception of Farquhar, to whom in this respect he bears a close resemblance, sets him apart, likewise, from the comic dramatists of the Restoration. More closely still he resembles in his achieving of a briskly-moving play his Elizabethan master, Shakespeare. Even those plays which Garrick adapted from the French take on the vigor and robustness of the English temper. In its hearty good fun, kindly ridicule, skilful characterization, and swiftly-moving action, *The Meeting of the Company* is typical of Garrick's work at its best.

As for the sprightly little piece, *The Theatrical Candidates* (1775), its significance lies in the fact that here again Garrick re-states his position with regard to pantomime and sentimental comedy. His attitude toward the first *genre* does not differ in this playlet from the one he manifests in *Harlequin's Invasion.* As regards sentimental comedy, Garrick holds that comedy and tragedy, except in Shakespeare's plays, must not trespass on each other's territory. But Garrick's concession to Shakespeare in so far as his tragedies were concerned, was not very great, for those that held the boards during the Restoration and the eighteenth century, were given without their comic scenes. In fact, Garrick himself, in the tragedies of Shakespeare which he presented at his theatre, never restored the comic portions that the preceding age had expunged. Besides, three years prior to the presentation of *The Theatrical Candidates,* Garrick, in conformity with the tenets of "regular" tragedy, had altered *Hamlet* (1772) to exclude the low comedy scenes of the gravediggers, so that the exception he makes for Shakespeare seems to be in favor only of the tragic elements in his comedies. Save for this ineffectual surrender to Shakespeare's method, comedy and tragedy, according to Garrick, must hold to their separate provinces.

His is, therefore, decidedly the classical attitude, and from it he rarely swerves. Except for the sentimental elements in *The Lying Valet* (1741), and except, too, for Lord Ogleby's intermediary efforts in behalf of the clandestinely married pair, and for Sir John Melvil's apology to Fanny Sterling for his blunder in courting her, Garrick does not permit any sentiment to enter into his plays and particularly not into his criticism of the human follies that he parades before us. For the pathos and the sympathy of sentimental comedy, Garrick substitutes humor and kindly ridicule and thus steers in the course of genuine comedy. It is true that the moral *pronunciamentos* uttered from time to time by the commentator, a character which finds its way from Jonson's and also from Molière's comedies into a number of Garrick's, might give the impression that the eighteenth-century dramatist is dealing in sentiments. But this is not the case. Like Jonson's and like Molière's, Garrick's, too, is the comedy of manners, that combines with it comedy of morals, a form which not only ridicules human frailties, as the other does, but also insists upon the correction of these. But following in the footsteps of his masters, he does not permit the expository moral declarations to become obtrusive; they do not dominate. The function of comedy with Garrick, as his plays prove, is not to preach but to evoke laughter, and this he accomplishes through ridicule of the idiosyncrasies and follies of his characters. Garrick remembers always that he is first and foremost a dramatist; the play is his chief concern. "*Action, Action, Action*" is his *desideratum,* and to secure this, he permits no obstacle to impede the rapidity of movement which is so characteristic of his best comedies.

The commentator, the moral element in Garrick's comedies, serves the same purpose that he does in Jonson's and in Molière's, that of presenting not the sentimental but the common sense aspect of the problem at hand. Censure rather than compassion is the method Garrick adopts; and in his censure he has learned from his masters, Jonson, Molière, and the comic dramatists of the Restoration, to detach himself from the object of his ridicule. Still, the bludgeon that Jonson and Molière occasionally use and to which Wycherley practically always resorts, is not at all present in Garrick's satire. His is rather the light, bantering, good-humored, Horatian type, although in several episodes of *Lethe* (1740), in *Lilliput* (1756), in *The Male-Coquette* (1757), in moments in *The Irish Widow* (1772), and in *Bon Ton* (1775), Garrick strikes a more serious note, not serious enough, however, to take these plays out of the realm of pure comedy. The problem in these plays is of a more weighty nature than in the others—*Miss in Her Teens* (1747), for instance. But despite the seriousness that sometimes manifests itself in his work, Garrick is never cruel; his pen is never dipped in gall. His desire is to paint the foibles and fopperies of the age in such a manner as to make them appear absurd and unattractive. To accomplish this, Garrick, throughout his plays, assumes the part of a keenly observant spectator who stands aloof from his fellow-men; notes their absurdities and weaknesses; permits these fools to file before us; points out their faults; and asks us to use society's weapon—derisive laughter—for those who dare to digress from her accepted standards. "Folly and Vice should never be spared," says Æsop in *Lethe.* To cure folly by ridicule becomes Garrick's purpose in a number of plays already considered, as well as in all of the ten two-act afterpieces and in the one full-length comedy, *The Clandestine Marriage*. . . . (pp. 254-58)

Two of these *petite-pièces,* *The Lying Valet* (1741) and *Neck or Nothing* (1766), both adaptations of French plays, are not written in the comedy of manners vein in which the others of the group under consideration are. In fact, *Neck or Nothing* with its plots and counterplots, disguises, and bustle of action, savors something of the comedy of intrigue. Since justice in Garrick's plays is always effected, vice is not permitted to go unpunished, and *Neck or Nothing* ends on a moral note as does also *The Lying Valet,* the second endeavor in Garrick's career as a dramatist. The latter afterpiece with its sentimental hero and its sentimental heroine together with its final wind-up in a scene of reclamation of the reckless squanderer and a general reconciliation of all concerned, is Garrick's only out and out concession to the sentimental muse. The idea of the remorseful hero came ready to his hand from his

source material, Motteux's *All Without Money* (1697); but Garrick, by causing Gayless to suffer intensively all through the play, as Needmore in the original does not, motivates the reformation of his hero, as is not the case in Motteux's play. Gayless's promise in the end to walk the straight and narrow path has, therefore, a more genuine ring than has Needmore's. Here, then, is the only instance in which Garrick, in pointing out folly—extravagance in this case—takes the kindly and forgiving attitude toward human frailties instead of the critical one that he adopts in *Lethe,* which precedes *The Lying Valet,* and in his other plays.

Except for Gayless, not one of the erring characters in any of Garrick's plays reforms or holds out any promise to do so. To list but a few instances: the incompatible pairs, Mr. and Mrs. Riot (*Lethe*) and Lord and Lady Flimnap (*Lilliput*) go their different ways philandering as before. Lord Minikin, who married a fortune, does not repent his flirtation with his wife's cousin, Tittup; nor does this lady feel any qualms over her coquetting with his lordship. The other half of this ill-mated pair, Lady Minikin, who married a title, does not express any regrets for philandering with Tittup's *fiancé,* Colonel Tivy; and this gentleman, when he discovers that the delightful Tittup is offered to him without the stipulated dowry, withdraws his promise of marriage to her and goes off in quest of another fortune. Daffodil, the Male-Coquette, slinks away without any promise whatsoever of reformation; and as for the fashionable ladies of his coterie who sought his love, Sophia states the case correctly when she points out to Tukely the futility of his efforts to persuade them to see Daffodil's duplicity:

> Why will you give yourself this unnecessary Trouble, Mr. *Tukely,* to convince these Ladies, who had rather still be deluded, and will hate your Friendship for breaking the Charm?

These ladies, it is true, are very much annoyed at discovering Daffodil's hypocrisy, but Garrick does not wring from them a promise that they will mend their ways. On the contrary, he recognizes the power of habit and knows the instantaneous redemption of persons addicted to vices of one sort or another to be false. He laughs at Orpheus's "qualm of conscience" (*Peep Behind the Curtain,* II, i) that causes him on a sudden to forsake his mistress and to venture into Hades to seek his wife. Such unexpected and hence unmotivated change of heart points to an optimism which sees merely the favorable aspects of life and in its self-deception ignores the existence of evil. Garrick's, however, is the healthy, common sense optimism that detects the presence of folly and vice, points them out, and has the courage to attempt to combat them out of existence. It is true that in Harriet (*The Guardian*) and in Fanny (*The Clandestine Marriage*) we have what at first appear to be heroines of the sentimental type; but upon closer examination we discover that they are delineated not sympathetically but critically. By endowing these girls with an excess of sensibility, Garrick causes them to depart from the norm and so to become ridiculous. Character exploitation for comic effects is his method here. (pp. 258-60)

Since Garrick was so decidedly opposed to sentimental comedy, one is led to suspect that he was attracted to his source material for *The Lying Valet* not for its regenerated rake, nor for its love interest—for this in Garrick's plays never becomes a passion but merely a pivot upon which the plot turns—but rather for the opportunities which the superb part of Sharp, the lying valet, gave him as an actor. It is upon this character, therefore, that Garrick the dramatist concentrated and lavished his efforts. That he was successful both in the creation and in the interpretation of this rôle can be gathered not only from his own enthusiastic account of the first performance of the piece, but from the fact, too, that he was obliged to play it throughout his acting career. Sharp, the lying valet, follows in the footsteps of the knavish and intriguing master's man of the Molièresque comedy. The scheming valet, in fact, a pair of valets, find their way both into *Miss in Her Teens* and *Neck or Nothing.*

Another borrowing that Garrick brought over from the comedies of Molière and his followers into his own is the pert lady's maid, the *soubrette,* who plays a part in the love affairs of her mistress just as the valet does in those of his master. Sometimes, as is the case in *Neck or Nothing,* the valet's efforts are in his own behalf and against his master. But usually, as in *Miss in Her Teens,* valet and maid unite to bring about a happy culmination of the love affair of master and mistress. Except for the one instance of *Neck or Nothing* in which two arrant knaves, one personating his master and the other aiding him in the scheme, attempt to extort from a wealthy citizen the dowry he was to have given with his daughter, Garrick, after *Miss in Her Teens,* leaves the resourceful valet type of servant and seeks the models for his domestics in Restoration comedy and in life about him. His servants become less contriving but more humorous and more human. They either try to reason their masters out of their folly as do Ruffle in *The Male-Coquette* and Thomas in *The Irish Widow;* or else, convinced of the futility of curing their masters of their weaknesses, these valets, Lord Chalkstone's Bowman and Lord Ogleby's Canton, cajole them into showing these follies off. Brush and the Sterling Chambermaid recall the servant pair in Cibber's *Love's Last Shift,* and Davy, Sir Trotley's otherwise proficient and obedient servant in *Bon Ton,* acquires, during his one day's sojourn in London, all the vices and the impertinence of the domestic gentry of the city, Garrick's delightful hit at the servant class of London.

Still another character familiar to the plays of Molière, although he appears also in Jonson, is the amorous old fool who courts a young girl very much against her will, and who, in the end, is either forced of his own accord to relinquish her to her lover, or else, through some trick, is cheated out of marriage with her. It is in comic aspects of wooing such as these rather than in serious love plots that Garrick is successful.

An important character that Garrick again took from Jonson's comedies is the commentator, who in Molière is known as the *raisonneur.* He serves as the dramatist's spokesman. He is sufficiently detached from the erring characters to see their faults, to expose these, and to present the common sense view of the problem under consideration. That is the office of Æsop in *Lethe,* Bolgolam in *Lilliput,* Sir William and Tukely in *The Male-Coquette,* Sir John Trotley in *Bon Ton,* Bates in *The Irish Widow,* and of various of the maids in the plays.

From Molière comes the false pretender to good taste and

The playbill from Garrick's London debut at Goodman's Fields Theatre.

great learning. Lady Fuz's professed passion for Shakespeare; her domination over the weak-willed Sir Toby, her husband, whom she forces into enacting with her scenes from *Romeo and Juliet*; her close watch over her daughter and her attempt to inveigle her into playing Juliet to the Romeo of the obese Sir Toby, when, in fact, the romantic Fanny would rather marry the man she loves than espouse the cause of Shakespeare; her enraptured attention to Glib's nonsensical burletta as it is being rehearsed before her—these suggest Molière's *Les Femmes savantes* (1672). Of course, Buckingham's burlesque inspired the rehearsal portion of the play. The songs of the burletta of *Orpheus,* in their extravagant humor, their delightful satire, and their lilting quality, anticipate the lyrics of William S. Gilbert. Both *A Peep Behind the Curtain* and *The Meeting of the Company* are superb burlesques on matters theatrical and serve as worthy forerunners of the better known play by Sheridan, *The Critic* (1777).

The *parvenu* aping the ways of his betters is a figure eternal in literature as it is in life. The classic example in drama is, of course, M. Jourdain in *Le Bourgeois gentilhomme* (1669) of Molière. But the "cit" with his newly acquired wealth, striving for place and prestige in the social world, was too obvious a figure in eighteenth century England for Garrick to have found it necessary to go to Molière for inspiration. Sterling in *The Clandestine Marriage* is not the fantastically foolish and vainly credulous M. Jourdain. "Sotte vanité," M. Jourdain's ruling idiosyncrasy, is not

Sterling's folly. On the contrary, Sterling is shrewd and not very easily imposed upon. He has more facets to his character than has M. Jourdain, chief of which is his inordinate desire for enormous wealth which he hopes will bring him power and recognition:

> Mind now, how I'll entertain his Lordship and Sir John—We'll shew your fellows at the other end of the town how we live in the city—They shall eat gold—and drink gold—and lie in gold—Here Cook! butler! (*calling*) What signifies your birth and education, and titles? Money, money, that's the stuff that makes the great man in this country.

Money with Sterling, as with all successful self-made business men, is the everlasting measure by which achievement is gauged. But plebeian and materialistic as this is, Sterling has a capacity for shrewd observation of which M. Jourdain seems incapable. Of the two *parvenus,* Sterling is more realistically presented. Like M. Jourdain, his folly consists in his attempt to buy his way into a class of society to which he does not belong and which he is determined to ape. But whereas M. Jourdain's manoeuvres are fantastic and grotesque, Sterling's are realistic and highly amusing.

The greater portion of Sterling's portrait, particularly that which presents him as the *bourgeois gentilhomme,* belongs to Garrick. This portrayal together with the one of Sterling's counterpart in petticoats, the vulgar Mrs. Heidelberg, a character which is entirely Garrick's and which, moreover, heralds the more famous Mrs. Malaprop, are two of the best examples of comic character delineation in the eighteenth century drama.

Restoration comedy also provided a fertile field from which Garrick gleaned much of his material. Not only was this material good theatre, but with fashionable society in the eighteenth century hardly unchanged from what it was in Restoration days, Garrick found little difficulty in making situations and characters from the comedies of this period prove useful in his ridicule of the follies and vices of the *beau monde* of his own time. In **The Male-Coquette** he shows us "fashionable virtue coquetting with fashionable vice." In Daffodil we discover the vain, cruel, passionless rake of the Horner type, trifling with the affections of a number of women, who, like those of Horner's coterie, are content to carry on an intrigue, provided their reputations remain unimpaired. Just such an individual is also Lady Flimnap. Moreover, she assumes much the same attitude towards marriage and husbands as do the fashionable ladies in Restoration comedy:

> It is below a Woman of Quality to have either Affection or Oeconomy; the first is vulgar and the last is mechanic.

So Lady Flimnap expresses herself in **Lilliput.** The *ennui* of the marital state is thus set forth by this same lady.

> I say, my Lord, had I been happy enough to have been born—bred—and married in *England,* I might then have been as fond as I am now sick of Matrimony . . .

In her attitude towards her lord and master, Lady Flimnap again is the fashionable lady of the time: "I do despise my Husband, heartily despise him." This same genteel incompatibility between husband and wife is exemplified also in Lady Minikin:

> I may with truth aver, that no woman of quality ever had, can have, or will have, so consummate a contempt for her Lord, as I have for my most honourable and puissant Earl of Minikin . . .

in Lord Minikin who hopes that his lady has "no intentions . . . of being fond of him;" in Mrs. Riot who informs Æsop that "One's Husband . . . is almost next to Nothing"; and in Lord Chalkstone who married for convenience and his wife for position.

With the attitude of the *élite* of the eighteenth century equally as cynical towards marriage as that of the same class in Restoration society, jealousy, as in the earlier age, came to be looked upon as a vulgar passion, and, hence, it was not to be indulged in by fashionable ladies and gentlemen. With their complete disregard of the marriage vows and with jealousy playing no part in their emotional composition, the husbands and wives of the *beau monde* were free to carry on their individual intrigues much as they desired.

It is this pursuit of lawless gallantry and disregard of the sanctity of the marriage vow that Garrick satirizes in a number of his plays. He recognizes the importance of normal marriages to the entire social structure, and anything inimical to such marriages or to normal family life in general, he does not permit to go unchallenged. He is particularly earnest in his censure of the arranged marriage, whether it be one of convenience or one which forces a young girl to accept a suitor who is altogether repugnant to her. Moreover, he grasps every opportunity to point out that disparity of ages, of outlook upon life, or of station in society, is fatal to a happy union. In Garrick's plays marriages without inclination either fail or do not materialize.

As for the young men and young girls in his comedies, except for those he holds up to ridicule for some one foolish idiosyncrasy or another, they are wholesome and likable and eager to be married. The young women, however, are more individualized than the men. These latter, for the most part, are the handsome conventional lovers, who in the end always win the heroines.

Tittup (**Bon Ton**), however, is the typical heroine of the comedy of manners who cherishes her independence too much for her to wish to relinquish it. With her, as with her Restoration sisters, love is not a passion but a pastime. Like Daffodil and also like Lord Minikin, the rake who pursues her, but to whom she, like the heroines of Restoration comedy, never acknowledges her love, Tittup enjoys the chase for its own sake. When, however, Colonel Tivy, the rake who expects to marry her for her fortune, demands to know her mind, she, in a miniature proviso scene, bargains with him for her freedom after marriage. But Tittup belongs to the upper stratum of society. The girls of the *bourgeoisie,* as depicted by Garrick, are the future mothers of England's sturdy citizenry. They are not interested in the fashionable philanderings of the fine lady of the time, but, on the contrary, they are eager for marriage and, moreover, with the men of their own choosing. They look forward to an honorable position in the home where they do not expect to dominate, but rather to live in faithful companionship with their husbands.

Not only immorality but the callousness and cruelty of the Restoration era, which likewise manifested themselves in the life of the fashionable world of the eighteenth century, also come into the range of Garrick's shafts of satire. He attacks a society which allows a Lord Chalkstone to "back" his mother's life against the lives of five other women, among them the "Mad-Woman at Tunbridge, at Five Hundred each *per Annum*"; and when his mother outlived them all but the insane one, his lordship "hedg'd off a dam'd Jointure" for himself. Again Garrick criticizes the brutality of the age in the episode of the mishap to Daffodil's cousin, Dizzy. Immediately upon the latter's fall down the stairs of the fashionable gentlemen's club, Lord Rackett agrees, upon one condition only, to lay a wager of fifty pounds that Dizzy "don't live till Morning." The condition demands that all assistance to him be barred; "not a physician or a surgeon sent for, or," Lord Rackett threatens, "I am off" (II, ii). Daffodil is determined that no help shall be given his cousin; but Dizzy recovers despite all wagers against his life. Incidentally, here as well as in the Chalkstone episode, we get Garrick's ridicule of the fashionable practice of wagering. Nor is Garrick less severe in his censure of Lord Minikin's friend, Colonel Tivy, "a man of wit, and a fine gentleman," who will be happy, indeed, when Sir Tan Tivy, his brother, breaks his neck, for then the Colonel will come into an estate of six thousand pounds a year. In his criticism of this cruelty of man toward man, Garrick makes another move in the direction of the humanitarian aspect of romanticism. (pp. 260-66)

Although Garrick appropriated many characters and situations from the comedies of the Restoration, the moral tone that he injected into his plays is his own. There is no attempt on his part, as there is with the comic writers of the earlier period, to make vice attractive; nor does he permit wrong-doing, as these other dramatists usually do, to go undetected and unpunished. On the contrary, whereas Dorimant is permitted, after his many transgressions and philanderings, to expect the hand of the charming Harriet in marriage, Daffodil's *amours* are exposed, and the rake, jeered at by the very ladies who had hoped to win his love, sneaks away in confusion and defeat. The doting fop, Whittle, is tricked into surrendering fortune and lady to his nephew; and the rake, Lord Minikin, is not only deprived of the coquette, Tittup, but is made to face his lawyers and creditors in order to learn that his "dissipation of fortune and morals," as Sir John Trotley points out, "must be followed by years of parsimony and repentance."

As for Garrick's indebtedness to the Elizabethan dramatists, we discover that he chose to borrow from Shakespeare and from Jonson. Besides the Whittle-Nephew-Widow plot of *The Irish Widow,* which recalls the one of Morose-Dauphine-Epicœne in Jonson's *The Silent Woman* (1609), Garrick also owes to this dramatist several characters, particularly the commentator, and the cowardly blustering soldier who appears in *Miss in Her Teens* and also in *Harlequin's Invasion.* But Flash of the first play differs from Gasconade of the other in that he is not a rascal as is Gasconade, who for fame and fortune decapitates the meek, sleeping Tailor Snip, but merely a lily-livered braggart with a bold front, who deserts his comrades-in-arms at the first smell of powder, and once home, seeks to impress with his regimentals the lady whose heart he wishes to win. When, however, he finds her beset by a number of suitors, Flash attempts to bully them into surrendering the field completely to him. Gasconade savors something more of Falstaff than of Bobadil, who served rather as the pattern for Flash.

The various expressions from Shakespeare's plays that Garrick wove into the dialogue of his own; the healthy broad humor of his low comedy scenes; the very existence of such scenes in Garrick's pieces; the duel between the two timorous combatants, Flash and Fribble in *Miss in Her Teens,* a situation strongly reminiscent of the similar one in *Twelfth Night*; Daffodil's Falstaff-like description of his encounter with a "dozen fellows," and Sophia's query, "In Buckram, my Lord," words which betray the fact that at this moment Garrick's thoughts wandered to the Gadshill episode in I *Henry IV*: these show Shakespeare's influence on Garrick to have been a decided one. As in Shakespeare, there are in Garrick's plays no surprises or unexpected turns. One is prepared, although the characters are not, for what is to ensue. Hence it is that one can sit back with a feeling of superiority and laugh at the blunders of the characters who, in the course of the action, become more and more enmeshed in the intricacies of the web which they unsuspectingly weave about themselves. Not surprise but expectation is what we find in Garrick's plays, a trick that he learned from a careful study of the technique of the master Elizabethan dramatist. The *dénouement* with Garrick is always a natural outcome of the steps in the action of his play.

From our examination of his comedies, we learn that in choice of material as well as in method of presentation, Garrick is eclectic. With the pressure of theatre business heavy upon his hands; with long and arduous rehearsals to direct and a variety of difficult parts to learn and to play almost every night; with a vast correspondence to carry on; and with numerous manuscript plays presented to him by aspiring dramatists to read—Garrick found it more convenient to adapt his plays than to create them. Even in his original work there are echoes of borrowings. Like Shakespeare, the god of his idolatry, and like Molière, Garrick took his material wherever he found it, absorbed and assimilated it, imbued it with his geniality, delightful and kindly humor, flashes of his wit, his vivacity, and the charm of his personality, which make his borrowings peculiarly his own. He modeled his plays upon those he knew best and admired most, the successful dramas in the repertory of his theatre and others in the magnificent dramatic collection in his library. His wide and varied selection of material shows an extensive and thorough acquaintance with the drama of France, of Italy, and of England from Elizabeth's day through that of his own. Moreover, it is not unlikely that those of Jonson's characters which trace their lineage back to Latin comedy and find their way also into Garrick's plays, the eighteenth century dramatist knew in the original, for his library boasted of the complete works of Plautus and Terence, and more than this, one of Garrick's early teachers was Samuel Johnson.

Garrick tried his hand at many forms of the drama, and, with the exception of his serious plays, he was highly successful with them all. He had an uncanny sense for detecting situations which would make good theatre; and with the skill of a master craftsman, he welded these together into extremely diverting and effective acting plays. The texts of these are replete with stage directions, indicating rapid and continuous movement. The five acts of *The Clandestine Marriage* permitted a normal unfolding of plot and the presentation of characters on a full-length canvas; but the two-act miniature comedy, the medium in which Garrick chose for the most part to work, demanded a more concentrated treatment both in plot development and in character delineation. Of necessity, therefore, Garrick introduces his principal characters fairly early, sets them a-talking, and through a rapid give and take dialogue which, together with the "business" indicated in the text, insures for the play from the very start a briskly moving action, gives an insight into the natures of his characters, and presents the expository material necessary to set the play going.

The characters in Garrick's comedies are the result of his keen observation of life about him. Although they bear descriptive names, indicating the ruling idiosyncrasy which the dramatist wished to ridicule, yet they do not belong to the humour type of character. Garrick's people are not generalizations tending to the abstract, but are decidedly particularized individuals with more facets than one. They are not, like the humour character, governed mechanically by merely one dominant trait, but, in addition to this dominant idiosyncrasy, they possess also some inconsistencies which make them more diversified and flexible and, hence, more human. The follies that Garrick's characters manifest are, therefore, eradicable, which is not usually the case with humours. In the delineation of his characters Garrick adopts rather the lighter method of Restoration comedy than the one of the comedy of humours. Like his own acting, Garrick's plays are studies in characters, miniature presentments, it is true, but of extraordinarily fine detail. His ability as a painter of full-length portraits manifests itself in the superb characterizations in *The Clandestine Marriage.*

Garrick was keenly interested in people, and into his plays he introduced many kinds from almost every station in eighteenth-century life. Detesting sham and affection, he mirrors with fidelity the shallow ambitions of the *bourgeoisie* and the pettiness, the brutality, the philanderings, and the foppish frivolities of the socially important. From the fashionable fool in high life, who forgets that rank carries with it important obligations to his fellow-beings; through the rank and file of the middle class, from which emerges the *parvenu,* whose over-reaching strivings to improve his social status lead him to ape the manners and mode of life of his betters; down to the rogue who depends for his existence upon the agility of his wits, Garrick's is a procession not only of excellently delineated characters, presented with a technical skill that makes them pulsate with life, but also of many capital acting parts.

In pointing out the follies and weaknesses current in the society of his day, Garrick's satire is always deftly aimed and within bounds. Except for Canton's reference in *The Clandestine Marriage* (II, i) to the *Sejanus* and *Anti-Sejanus* disputes in the daily papers, neither politics nor religion plays any part in Garrick's comedies. Moreover, the maliciously bitter and personal sting which makes the scurrilous farces of Fielding and Foote decidedly topical and, hence, less universal in appeal, is absent in Garrick's satire. He strikes at the thing rather than at the individual. By choosing to ridicule the universal human foibles and

follies, Garrick not only makes his plays the abstracts and brief chronicles of his own age, but gives them a permanent quality which Fielding's and Foote's, by reason of the nature of their satire and choice of topics, lack. Foote's pieces, as Professor Thorndike pointed out, "are too hasty and too extravagant to have much value apart from his own impersonations. They left behind them a tradition that was confined mainly to farce." Garrick does not employ the grotesquely extravagant cartoonist method of Foote, nor the maliciously personal attacks of Fielding, nor the slap-stick processes frequently used by writers of farces to evoke laughter. He gains his effects rather through a study of character and sometimes, as in the case of Harriet in *The Guardian,* Fanny Sterling, and Fribble, through an intensification of the idiosyncrasy he wished to ridicule. But his satire is always kindly. Sometimes his satire strikes a more serious note than usual, but for the most part, Garrick's plays are bubbling over with hearty good fun and rollicking humor. We laugh readily with Garrick as he parades his procession of fools before us. In this, then, lies another of Garrick's claims to recognition as an important dramatist of the eighteenth century. Not only are his plays valuable for their manifold allusions to the conditions of the contemporary stage and contemporary society; for their masterfully constructed plots and skilful character delineations; but principally for the fact that, despite the prevailing sentimental vogue, they kept the comic spirit in drama alive during the eighteenth century. (pp. 268-72)

> *Elizabeth P. Stein, in her* David Garrick: Dramatist, *The Modern Language Association of America, 1938, 315 p.*

George Winchester Stone, Jr.   (essay date 1948)

[*An American educator, literary critic, and essayist, Stone has written extensively on the 18th-century theater. In the following excerpt he analyzes Garrick's adaptation of* King Lear, *praising him for restoring Shakespearean text to Nahum Tate's popular version of the tragedy.*]

Since [Garrick] chose to be regarded as Shakespeare's priest from 1741 through 1779, and since accumulated evidence from letters, journals, prologues, epilogues, and recorded conversation indicates his genuine interest in performing as much and as pure Shakespeare as he could, many a later critic has condemned him for not restoring *King Lear* entire.

Cross, the prompter, noted in his Diary for the night of 28 October 1756:—"*KING LEAR*—with restorations from Shakespeare." The box receipts, which had averaged £140 nightly for the preceding fortnight, shot up to £200 for the occasion.

Examination of Garrick's entire connection with the versions of Shakespeare and Tate reveals more than the prompter's statement, and demonstrates the dilemma of an eighteenth-century mind caught between an ideal liking for Shakespeare and a canny understanding of box-office appeal.

Garrick started with Tate, but ended with a play much closer to Shakespeare. Thoroughly apprised of the mainsprings of tragic appeal as Pity and Fear, he alternately dissolved his audience in tears and froze them with horror (if we can credit the hyperbole of mid-century comment). But pity won, for Garrick saw in *King Lear* a Shakespearean play which could surpass competition from all writers of pathetic tragedy and could command the emotional pleasure of tears more successfully than sentimental comedy. Tapping the strong vogue for the pathetic and sentimental, Garrick skillfully met public desire for these dramatic types in his production of *King Lear,* and without much sacrificing the sacredness of Shakespeare's text. Study of his text and his performance in the title role reveals the extent of his skill. (p. 91)

In . . . early performances Garrick was using Tate's script. Yet soon the interpretation he gave to the character was based on Shakespeare's rather than Tate's text. Curious testimony to this fact is found in Samuel Foote's *Examen of the New Comedy call'd the Suspicious Husband,* to which he added a "Word of Advice to Mr. Garrick." Three fourths of Foote's letter vindicates Garrick's Lear from the criticism of an anonymous pamphlet entitled a *Treatise on the Passions.* Foote finds the pamphleteer ignorant of Shakespeare's text, hence unable to realize that Garrick's actions though accompanied by Tate's wording were instigated by the authentic Shakespearean play. . . . (p. 92)

Foote advised Garrick to change costume in the fourth act; to abolish use of a handkerchief at the end of the curse; to curb the spirit of his rage at Regan and Cornwall; and to abandon the fainting called for by Tate's lines in the concluding act when Lear discovers Kent and Caius to be identical. He urged profounder irony in the speech to Regan beginning, "Dear daughter I confess that I am old." He concluded with a question that stemmed from Addison's comment, "Why will you do so great an injury to Shakespeare as to perform Tate's execrable alteration of him? Read and consider the two plays seriously, and then make the public and the memory of the author some amends by giving us Lear in the original, fool and all."

We can never know how soon Garrick acted upon this advice. We do know that toward the end of 1753 and during the spring and summer of 1754 a flurry of criticism concerning *King Lear* appeared in *The Adventurer* and in *Gray's Inn Journal.* Professor Nichol Smith sees in Warton's essays in the *Adventurer* a definite turning from neoclassicism towards romanticism. Be that as it may, Warton tells explicitly of Garrick's influence upon his own appreciation of *King Lear*:

> I should be guilty of insensibility and injustice, if I did not take this occasion to acknowledge that I have been more moved and delighted by hearing this single line—
>
> O me, my heart! my rising heart—but down.
>
> spoken by the only actor of the age who understands and relishes these little touches of nature, and therefore the only one qualified to personate this most difficult character of Lear, than by the most pompous declaimer of the most pompous speeches in *Cato* or *Tamerlane.*

In the history of stage texts the most illuminating point in Warton's praise is the fact that the single line which so impressed him is Shakespeare's, but is nowhere to be found in Tate. By gradual infiltration Garrick was restor-

ing to the stage Shakespeare's wording as well as Shakespeare's character emphasis. In these two subtle ways he was aligning himself with Addison and Foote, and was satisfying his own ideals concerning Shakespeare's text. (pp. 93-4)

The first printed text of Garrick's revised version seems to be that published by Bell in 1773, "regulated from the prompt books with permission of the managers." The Bell editors used as bases for their texts sometimes old prompt copies, sometimes the latest ones. The texts of *King Lear,* identical in Bell's 1773 and 1774 printings may well represent accurate transcriptions of Garrick's 1756 play. But Garrick apparently did not leave his 1756 revision without further restorations from Shakespeare. A duodecimo printed for C. Bathurst in 1786, after Garrick's death, bears the title *KING LEAR, Altered from Shakespeare by David Garrick, Esq., Marked with the Variations in the Manager's Book at the Theatre Royal in Drury Lane.* This edition differs from the Bell text by including more lines from Shakespeare and excluding more lines from Tate. The cast listed places Garrick and Miss Younge in the leading roles. Miss Younge played Cordelia to his Lear during the last years of his performing.

Collation of three texts, Tate 1681, Bell 1774 and Garrick 1786 shows the extent to which Garrick deserves praise for restoring Shakespeare and banishing Tate.

The *Lear Variorum* runs to 3,201 lines. Tate cut the play by one third. The Bell edition, though cutting sweepingly from Tate, restored sufficient from Shakespeare's text to expand the Tate count by 255 lines. The Garrick version cut eighteen Tate lines remaining in Bell, and restored fifty additional Shakespearean lines. As a result Garrick's version, whether viewed from the 1774 or 1786 text, is far from Tate's in title, scene and act division, in language, character emphasis, and in pointed moral. In overall structure, however, some similarity still exists, for Garrick retained the happy ending, a shortened version of the love between Egar and Cordelia, Cordelia's confidante Arante, and omitted the Fool.

In retaining these structural features, he continued, as a manager, to sacrifice to the altar of poetic justice, to bow to the shrine of neo-classical dramatic theory which allowed no comic element to enter the province of tragedy, and to cater to public taste for tears and pathos. Yet what a refreshing play his is compared with Tate's! The triumph of Shakespeare in scene after scene in all his plays often lies in sheer weight of wording. When Tate altered Shakespeare's phraseology, time and again he took the lustre from the jewels he was restringing. In the restoration of Shakespeare's wording Garrick was able to pay best honor to the God of his idolatry, though as manager he left offerings at other shrines.

Witness the effect. Edmund's soliloquy upon bastardy opens Tate's play, and this villain speaks with the tongue of the "fuddling" laureate:

> Thou Nature art my Goddess, to thy law
> My services are bound; why am I then
> Depriv'd of a son's right, because I came not
> In the dull road that custom has prescribed?
> Why bastard, wherefore base, when I can boast
> A mind as gen'rous, and a shape as true
> As honest madam's issue? Why are we

Held base, who in the lusty stealth of nature
Take fiercer qualities than what compound
The scanted births of the stale marriage bed;
Well then, legitimate Edgar, to thy right
Of law I will oppose a Bastard's cunning.
Our father's love is to the bastard Edmund
As to legitimate Edgar; with success
I've practis'd on both their easie natures;
Here comes the old man chaf'd with th' information
Which last I forg'd against my brother Edgar,
A tale so plausible, so boldly utter'd
And heighten'd by such lucky accidents
That now the slightest circumstance confirms him
And base born Edmund spite of law inherits.

Upon the heels of this Lear divides the kingdom and Tate gives first inkling of Edgar's love for Cordelia.

Garrick restored Shakespeare's opening scene in which Kent and Gloucester discuss the probable division of the kingdom. In 1774 Garrick still retained Tate's lines of love making between Edgar and Cordelia. They are marked for excision, however, in the 1786 text. When in Garrick's versions at the opening of the second scene Edmund soliloquizes, he does so in Shakespeare's rich idiom:

Thou Nature art my Goddess, to thy law
My services are bound. Wherefore should I
Stand in the plague of custom, and permit
The curiosity of Nations to deprive me
For that I am some twelve or fourteen moonshines
Lag of a brother? Why bastard? Wherefore base?
When my dimensions are as well compact
My mind as generous, and my shape as true
As honest madam's issue? Why brand they us
With base? with baseness? bastardy? base, base?
Who in the lusty stealth of nature take
More composition and fierce quality
Than doth, within a dull, stale, tired bed,
Go to the creating a whole tribe of fops
Got 'tween sleep and wake? Well then,
Legitimate Edgar, I must have your land:
Our father's love is to the bastard Edmund
As to the legitimate. Fine word 'legitimate'
Well my legitimate, if this letter speed,
And my invention thrive, Edmund the base
Shall top the legitimate:—I grow, I prosper;
Now Gods stand up for bastards!

The restoration is complete and exact, giving the actor of Edmund's part more of a characterization than did the meagre lines of Tate. Edmund was again presented, after seventy years, not merely as a treacherous, scheming villain, but as a man possessing certain intellectual curiosity, who saw not only the injustices of custom towards natural sons, but observed also the tyranny of words which in themselves create attitudes and shape prejudices. He played with the words 'bastard' 'base' and 'legitimate' repeating them until they lost all significance. Garrick understood the difference between the charged effect of Shakespeare's speech which made for drama, and the briefed utterance of Tate which produced merely the introduction to a story.

When Tate's Lear asks an expression of love from Goneril she replies:

Sir, I do love you more than words can utter
Beyond what can be valu'd rich or rare,
Nor liberty, nor sight, health, fame or beauty
Are half so dear; my life for you were vile;

As much as child can love the best of fathers.

In the 1774 text Garrick had restored some Shakespearean lines:

I do love you, Sir,
Dearer than eyesight, space and liberty,
Beyond what can be valued rich or rare
No less than life with grace, health, beauty, honor,
As much as child ere loved or father found,
A love that makes breath poor, and speech unable,
Beyond all manner of so much I love you.

In the 1786 text appears the exact and complete restoration:

Sir, I do love you more than words can wield the matter
Dearer than eyesight, space, etc. . . .

Similar care is to be noted in the restoration of Lear's ensuing words:

Tate's Lear:

Of all these bounds, ev'n from this line to this
With shady forests and wide skirted meads
We make thee Lady, to thine and Albany's issue
Be this perpetual—what says our second daughter?

Garrick's Lear (1774, 1786) and Shakespeare's:

Of all these bounds ev'n from this line to this,
With shadowy forests and with champains rich'd
With plenteous rivers, and wide skirted meads
We make thee Lady—to thine and Albany's issue
Be this perpetual, what says our second daughter?
Our dearest Regan, wife of Cornwall, speak.

Such careful restorations even in places of no great dramatic significance and in words, which travelling swiftly across the footlights mean little in the sum total of impression, show the respect which Garrick held for Shakespeare's text. His faithfulness to text extended to cut passages as well as to expanded ones. Shakespeare's Kent belabors Lear's treatment of Cordelia in an earnest speech of eleven lines, which Tate cut to three. Garrick left the speech at three lines but made sure the wording was Shakespeare's.

A final example, from the heath scene, points the difference between Tate and Garrick as text-makers. Lears from Betterton to Garrick attuned themselves to the brewing storm in Tate's phraseology:

Blow winds and burst your cheeks, rage louder yet,
Fantastic light'ning singe, singe my white head:
Spout cataracts, and hurricanoes fall,
'Till you have drown'd the towns and palaces
Of proud ingrateful man.

But Garrick restored the pounding words of Shakespeare:

Blow winds and crack your cheeks! Rage! Blow!
Ye cataracts and hurricanoes, spout
'Till you have drench'd the steeples, drown'd the cocks!
You sulphurous and thought executing fires,
Vaunt courriers of oak-cleaving thunderbolts,
Singe my white head! and thou all-shaking thunder
Strike flat the thick rotundity o' the world!
Crack Nature's mold, all germens spill at once
That make ingrateful man.

Garrick's play, however, is not all pure Shakespeare. It is cut to suit acting purposes of the day. It retains Arante, the female companion which Tate provided for Cordelia. Her appearance is brief and she fades out completely during the storm scene. Only once is a Shakespearean character which remains, changed. Shakespeare's Regan, cruelest of the sisters, reaches the climax of her cruelty in her command to the servants who have gouged out Gloucester's eyes:

> Go, thrust him out at th' gates, and let
> Him smell his way to Dover . . .

Garrick retained the Tate version at this point, wherein Regan taunts Gloucester, "if those eyes fail thee call for spectacles," leaving it to the dying Cornwall to say:

> Turn out the eyeless villain; let him smell
> His way to Cambray . . .

Garrick eliminated entirely Tate's scene at the beginning of the fourth act where Regan and Edmund are "amorously seated in a grotto listening to music." Though Garrick retained the happy ending he cut the moral curtain speech which Tate devised for Edgar:

> Our drooping country now erects her head,
> Peace spreads his balmy wings, and plenty blooms.
> Divine Cordelia all the gods can witness
> How much thy love to empire I prefer!
> Thy bright example shall convince the world
> (Whatever storms of Fortune are decreed)
> That Truth and Virtue shall at last succeed.

Differences between the Tate version and the 1774 text are too numerous for further listing. Their quality has been accurately suggested by the foregoing examples. Differences between the 1774 and the 1786 texts are marked not in outline but in the further restorations of Shakespeare which appear in the latter. Just when Garrick made these restorations we have no way of telling. What we do know is that from 1747 until the close of his stage career he was giving the play more and more of a Shakespearean flavor.

It may be argued that Garrick could afford to restore Shakespeare's wording in an age which had known so much Shakespeare editing, and had seen as much Shakespearean criticism as had the mid-part of the eighteenth century, whereas Tate in 1681 was forced to rewrite lines for the sake of clarity. The pleading of such a case in justification of Tate is sound, but should in no way belittle the efforts and real accomplishments of Garrick. (pp. 96-101)

> *George Winchester Stone, Jr., "Garrick's Production of 'King Lear': A Study in the Temper of the Eighteenth-Century Mind," in* Studies in Philology, *Vol. XLV, No. 1, January, 1948, pp. 89-103.*

Fredrick L. Bergmann   (essay date 1952)

[*Bergmann is an American educator who has written extensively on Garrick's career as an author. In the following excerpt from his authoritative study of* The Clandestine Marriage, *he discusses both the influence of 18th-century acting traditions and Garrick's intent in the creation of the play.*]

I have referred to **The Clandestine Marriage** as a fusion of farce, sentimental comedy, and comedy of manners. In this fusion the manners element predominates. If we ask why this highly successful play was built on such a combination of types, we shall see a remarkable instance of the influence of the actor and the manager in moulding public taste while yet catering to the public's fancy in dramatic fare. For it is evident that Garrick was not in sympathy with the vogue of sentimental comedy, even though, as a clever manager of Drury Lane, he continued to produce sentimental comedies before full houses at great financial profit and to the delight of the playgoers. But Garrick himself was a man who liked laughter better than weeping. His definition of comedy is found in a letter to Mrs. Benjamin Victor regarding a play he had just read: "I said indeed that the Comedy wanted interest, but not of ye *Passions*—I meant a Comic interest, resulting from ye varing [sic] humours of the Characters thrown into spirited action & brought into interesting Situations, naturally arising from a well constructed fable or Plot—this, with a good Moral, deduc'd from ye whole, is all I wish or look for in a *Comedy.*" Comedy, for Garrick, is to be at once mirth-provoking and corrective. Writing to Colman in 1761 about a Colman play, Garrick said, "I have read yr last & think it a fine Plan a little too hastily finish'd—there is Strength, & good Sense, but I would more laugh & pleasantry—." Miss Elizabeth P. Stein, who has made a valuable contribution to the study of Garrick as a non-sentimental writer, summarizes the actor's view of comedy as "to paint the vices and foibles that flesh is heir to and to hold them up to ridicule with the hope that the audience will laugh at them and thus correct them." Such comedy calls forth mirth, not tears. Garrick's alarm at the vogue of sentimentalism is indicated in a letter to the Reverend Charles Jenner, in which he asks his friend to write a comedy "calculated more to make an Audience Laugh than Cry" and reveals his fear that unless writers make a stand for genuine comedy "the Stage in a few years, will be (as Hamlet says) like Niobe all tears." So Garrick, though he often shielded himself behind Dr. Johnson's famous dictum, "The drama's laws the drama's patrons give," reacted against the taste of the playgoers, protesting that Hugh Kelly's immensely popular sentimental comedy, *False Delicacy,* is a sermon, not a play, and that the public would soon expect Drury Lane to wear a steeple. And even though he rejected *She Stoops to Conquer* for presentation at his house, his prologue hailed the change in taste it demanded. Likewise in the prologue of his own alteration of Tomkis' *Albumazar* he indicated his delight in the new taste for laughter rather than for sentimental melancholy.

Yet the fact remained that Drury Lane had profited not a little from the presentation of sentimental comedies; and so Garrick, in adding his name to Colman's in a joint dramatic piece, intended to insure the success of the comedy by keeping it sentimental enough to please the public and yet satirical enough to make it a comedy of manners. The sentimental element enters into the characterization of Fanny, the virtuous daughter who has a tendency to tears and fainting in moments of stress, and Lovewell, who displays some of the symptoms of a "man of feeling." It also enters into the change of heart of Lord Ogleby, who has a kind of fifth-act repentance which enables the play to end on a happy note. But on the other hand, Fanny is a girl of spirit who has been—and intends to remain—disobedient to her father; and Lovewell does not neglect to consider the financial value of witholding the announcement of his clandestine marriage to Fanny. Furthermore,

Lord Ogleby is a true descendent of the old fops of Restoration comedy. The coarseness is now gone, but in him the satire and spirit of the comedy of manners remain.

All this is important in a consideration of the influence of the actor on the drama of the day. Garrick the manager owed a considerable share of his fortune and the reputation of his theater to the popular appeal of sentimental comedy. And yet in his own writings he is not sentimental. His afterpieces—of which *Lethe,* a kind of forerunner of the play we are considering, is the first and one of the best—exploit the satirical vein. And of fourteen older non-Shakespearean plays which he revised for presentation at Drury Lane, more than half are clearly satirical, humorous works from the pens of Jacobean and Restoration dramatists. It seems that Garrick carefully played up to that element in the public which appreciated the kind of satirical comedy which had once ruled the boards—albeit without the coarseness—and was attempting to wean the audiences away from plays which were "like Niobe all tears." The process of weaning was continued in *The Clandestine Marriage,* for, as George Nettleton has said, it is genuine comedy, and with plays like it and *The Jealous Wife,* which Garrick helped Colman to write, "it is idle to maintain that [Goldsmith] was the first to turn comedy back from tears to laughter." (pp. 151-54)

The picture we get, then, is one of Garrick the manager, whom aspiring dramatists were still showering with one sentimental comedy after another, many of which made box-office history, joining with his friend Colman to write the kind of play which Garrick felt should be the standard for comic writing. And in this venture the two made a remarkable success, partly because some touches of sentimentalism were included, but more especially because Garrick in his own writing and acting had prepared his public to relish another kind of drama as well. The influence of the actor on the drama of his day begins to emerge.

Although the problem of who wrote exactly what parts of the play has had more consideration over the years than the play itself, there is no need to trace here the history of the quarrel. Briefly, in ascribing parts of the writing to the two authors the Colmanites gained ground increasingly up to 1935, when E. R. Page in his *George Colman the Elder* gave Garrick credit merely for polishing the play and resolving the plot. A telling rebuttal came two years later from Miss Stein, whose ingenious chapter in her *David Garrick, Dramatist* sets out not only to prove Page and a long line of Colmanite predecessors wrong, but also to reverse the claim that Colman was the writer and Garrick the polisher. Miss Stein credits Garrick with the main action, the entire Ogleby plot with all its associated characters, especially Canton and Brush, for all the Heidelberg scenes—in fact, for almost the entire play. And so the matter has stood, with no conclusive answer as to the ascription of specific parts.

The MS. drafts for the play in the Folger Library cast new light on this problem of authorship and demonstrate the controlling influence of the actor. Four hands are evident in the 120 sheets of the MS.: Colman's briefly, Garrick's preponderately, that of an amanuensis who was probably William Hopkins, the Drury Lane prompter, briefly, and that of another amanuensis in an early version of Act V. The MS. indicates that Garrick actually wrote at least half of the play; how much more he may have written we can-

not know for certain, for the MS. does not cover the whole play. Although a detailed study of the MS. and its provenance does not lie within the scope of this paper, a brief summary regarding the authorship of the play as revealed therein is in order. The MS. indicates that, in addition to a careful preliminary synopsis, Garrick's portion of *The Clandestine Marriage* includes the following:

> Act II: The opening scene of Brush and the chambermaid, and Lord Ogleby's levee scene.
> Act III: The scene between Mrs. Heidelberg and Miss Sterling regarding Fanny's supposed plot to thwart Miss Sterling's marriage; a scene (later omitted) in which they attempt to trap Lovewell into revealing his regard for Fanny; and the scene in which Lovewell and Fanny decide to ask Lord Ogleby for aid, which was later transposed to Act IV.
> Act IV: The famous garden scene, including the repartee of Ogleby and Canton, the Swiss sycophant; Fanny's interview with Ogleby in which the old lord images that she is in love with him; Lovewell's subsequent interview with Ogleby; and finally Sir John's admission to his uncle of love for Fanny.
> Act V: Entire.

This would leave for Colman or as undecided all of Act I; Sir John's interview with Lovewell in which he seeks aid in proposing marriage to Fanny, their interruption by Sterling's party on tour of the garden, and Sir John's actual proposal in Act II; the lawyer scene which opens Act III and Sir John's interviews with Sterling and Mrs. Heidelberg later in the same act; and two episodes in Act IV, one concerning Mrs. Heidelberg's threat to cut the Sterling family out of her will, and the other Miss Sterling's appeal to Lord Ogleby. Other than Act I, then, the chief parts of the play not in Garrick's MS. are the majority of the Sir John Melvil scenes and the satire on lawyers. This would indicate that the most important parts of the play are by Garrick, including the Ogleby material, much of the clandestine marriage plot, and the masterful fifth act, the best writing in the entire comedy.

One additional point regarding authorship requires some clarification. Whereas there has been general agreement (as Colman himself agreed in his letter of 4 December 1765 to Garrick) that Garrick wrote the Ogleby material in Act II and all of Act V, some question has remained as to the authorship of the excellent satiric portrait of the old fop in Act IV—the scene in which Ogleby mistakenly assumes that Fanny is madly in love with him. This is the only important Ogleby scene in which there has been a question of authorship. Without departing from the subject of this paper so far as to give detailed consideration of the problem, I believe it may be said with reasonable certainty that the scene in question is Garrick's. First of all, the scene is in Garrick's hand in the Folger MS., and it is no mere copy of a previously written scene. It is beyond a reasonable doubt an original writing, replete with reworking and polishing. Second, there is in the MS. a sheet headed "G—takes—," a notation in Garrick's hand following a jointly written synopsis which will be mentioned hereafter. This sheet indicates that Garrick was to write, in addition to the levee of Act II and certain other scenes, this very garden episode, which he described as

Fanny's discovering Scene to my Lord

E. I. Portbury's engraving from William Hogarth's famous portrait of Garrick as Richard III.

his mistake in his own Favor & Consequences.
previous to this a Short Scene with Canton.

Here is strong evidence that Garrick had taken the scene in question as his own. Colman's case depends mainly on his letter of 4 December, in which he says that "in the conduct as well as dialogue of the fourth act, I think your favourite, Lord Ogleby, has some obligations to me," a claim which Garrick surely refutes in his reply of 5 December, in which he refers to Ogleby as "my portion of the play." Colman was, of course, smarting under Garrick's refusal to play the part, and his claim to "some obligation" in Ogleby is in the nature of a taunt, as Garrick himself says. However this may be, the MS. factors involved—Garrick's taking on the writing of the scene, and the original nature of his MS. version—indicate that Garrick wrote this satiric portrait and give support to Miss Stein's argument, in *David Garrick, Dramatist,* that internal evidence likewise proves his authorship.

With Garrick's share of the play more definitely established, we may ask how the actor went about writing a play. Looking at the play in the Folger MS. as an example of the impact of the actor on the writing of drama, I find several points that are emphasized. At the outset, the choice of subject is realistic and contemporary so that all the parts may be done in mid-century costume and all the acting may be as "natural" as walking into a coffee house in the Strand. Here Garrick puts his worship of naturalness on the stage in his own dramatic vehicle. Even more important is Garrick's conception of the play in terms of actual contemporary stage personalities rather than in terms of stock characters of literary tradition. This is evident in three synopses of the play, one by Colman and two by Garrick, which have been preserved. Colman's, which was published by his son as "Addenda" to his edition of the Colman letters in 1820, names the characters (all but one of which were later changed) and most of the chief players. A second synopsis, purportedly by Garrick and available through excerpts printed by John Forster in the second edition of his *Life and Times of Oliver Goldsmith* (1854), uses no character names at all but only the names of the intended players—for example, the opening scene is sketched as follows: "Enter Bride and O'Brien (who are secretly married), complaining how unhappy she is, and how disagreeably situated she is on account of their concealing their marriage. . . . The audience must learn that Mrs. Clive, the aunt, has two nieces, co-heiresses, and one of them is to be married to O'Brien, the son of Garrick and nephew of Yates." The third synopsis, which is a part of the Folger MS., includes a summary of Act I by Colman and the remainder by Garrick. Although both Garrick and Colman were careful to use character names in this synopsis, which is apparently the latest written of the three, yet they begin with the cast of characters and players, which indicates that the first consideration of the dramatists was to write parts for the best actors and actresses available at Drury Lane. It is obvious in all three synopses that the part of Lord Ogleby was written for Garrick and designed to exploit his prime qualities as the leading actor of the day, and that Mrs. Clive was to be Mrs. Heidelberg, Miss Pope to act the part of Miss Sterling, and Miss Bride that of Fanny. The care with which the comedy was adapted to the actors is best seen in Garrick's portion of the Folger synopsis, and the garden scene in Act IV furnishes a good example. Here Ogleby is mirth-provoking and riotous comedy, the kind the actor made famous in his creation of the simple-minded Abel Drugger, the coxcomb Bayes, Lord Chalkstone the dandy, and drunken Sir John Brute. In fact, it may almost be said that Ogleby expresses the total of Garrick's comic talents. Fortunately for the early performances of the play, the part also fitted the genius of Thomas King, who took the role after Garrick refused it on the grounds of ill health. King, who had studied well under Garrick, made the most of his talent for dry, epigrammatic humor in creating the part. (pp. 154-58)

Another indication of the impact of the actor on play writing may be seen in the fact that Garrick betrays continual interest in the stage effects which certain actions will produce. This interest may best be seen in the synopses. Colman, in his summary of the play, concerns himself only casually with stage effects: his interest in this line is nothing like that of Garrick the actor. In outlining such a scene as Ogleby's levee, Garrick uses considerable detail, envisioning the parade of actors as they cross the stage to pay their respects to his lordship. He is also careful about emptying the stage at the right moment. And he arranges to have some characters on the stage but outside the action, as in the garden scene of Act IV, so that they may quickly and naturally be brought into the action when they are needed. Thus Canton is "walking in the garden" while the interview between Ogleby and Fanny is taking place, so that he may be readily at hand for the "fine dialogue . . . of flattery and vanity," as Garrick calls it, which is to follow. Another good example of Garrick's eye to the staging of the play is found in the last act, where he carefully plans the setting of the gallery outside the various bedchambers with "a lamp (sconce) in the middle of the stage; the stage branches drawn up." Later he has Mrs. Heidelberg and Miss Sterling draw down the sconce and put it out so that, concealed in the half-light, they may watch the unraveling of the plot. In no play before this time do we have actual evidence of such carefully detailed preliminary work as the three synopses of *The Clandestine Marriage* indicate. The more interesting fact, however, is that in the synopses of Garrick the actor the details of staging are far more explicit than they are in the outline sketched by Colman the playwright.

A further point which emerges is that the actor carefully maintained in his character portrayal the pattern of successful characterization as he knew it from previous stage experience. For example, he thinks of Canton as "another species of the *Bowman* kind," a statement which not only identifies the Swiss with Garrick's own Bowman in the farce *Lethe,* but also indicates the identity of Ogleby with

Lord Chalkstone in the same play. There can be no doubt that Chalkstone in Garrick's first play is a forerunner of Ogleby, nor can we doubt that the success of the early farce played a large part in the framing of the character of the gouty old Lord in *The Clandestine Marriage.* Worthy of note also is Garrick's care to preserve sharp contrasts in character which his audience could grasp and enjoy immediately. Thus he sees Sterling as "a fine contrast to my lord with his vulgar notions of grandeur" and notes with relish the contrast between Lovewell's astonishment and behavior and Sir John's blandness when the latter informs the clandestine husband of his desire to marry Fanny.

Notable also in a consideration of the actor as playwright is his preservation of a rational concept of unity of plot, as is indicated, for example, when he insists that Ogleby and Sterling, in the levee scene, touch on "some little matter of the family marriage business" so that "the main stream of the play may flow through every scene of it, which is not always thought necessary or comply'd with by our modern dramaticks." His careful attention to the unity of the whole is likewise seen in his concern about what the audience would think as to the passage of time during the action of the play. He suggests that the acts take up the intermediate time between the meals, each meal being supposed to take place during the music between the acts.

Also evident is Garrick's ability to sharpen the focus on characterization immediately. Of the portions of the play we now know to have been written by Garrick this is perhaps best seen at the beginning of Act II, where the dialogue between Brush and Sterling's chambermaid is a carefully calculated introduction to Lord Ogleby, who has not yet appeared on the stage. The comments of the two servants are skillfully planned so that the audience will have planted in their minds certain high points to note with particular interest when Ogleby finally appears. This is good play construction, traditional, of course, with actor-playwrights. One of the major interests of the entire first act lies in keying the audience for the arrival of the old lord, but he does not appear. Now, just before his first entrance, the anticipation is sharpened and the attention of the audience is focused, not upon the clandestine marriage plot nor upon the marriage-of-convenience sub-plot, but upon the chief comic character alone. In the concentrated art of the drama this is skillful economy. The achievement is that of a man of the theatre, not a dilettant writer of plays.

A final point to be noted in the Folger MS. is Garrick's method of composition. His tendency was to write hastily—a copious flow of composition—and to revise with care. One notices an inclination to long speeches in the earliest drafts, followed by careful reworking which breaks up the long speeches so that speed of pace improves, so that more humor is engendered, so that the entire company is occupied and no one actor walks off with the whole dialogue—in short, so that acting results. A good example may be found at the opening of Act II. Here time and again Brush is made, in the revisions, to interrupt the chambermaid's speeches, which originally were too long; and also his remarks are amplified to point up character and to insert humor. Thus when the chambermaid fears that Ogleby will break in upon them, Brush in the first version merely explains that the gouty old lord is too sore from the evening's walk which Sterling forced him upon; but in the revision Garrick enlarged the reply to bring in the satire on Ogleby's physical condition ("What with qualms, Age, Rhumatism, and a few surfeits in his Youth," Brush says, "he must have a great deal of brushing, oyling, screwing & winding up to set him a going for ye Day") and to identify Canton's sycophantic type and his activity in the household. Other revisions smooth the unfolding of the plot and intensify characterization. In regard to the former, the most extensive revision in the MS. occurs near the end of the last act. It took four different writings by Garrick to acquit Sir John of involvement with Fanny and to bring Lovewell out of her bedroom at just the right moment, a part of the sentimental element which was finally hit upon to resolve the plot.

In summary, then, it may be said that the MS. reveals half a dozen valid examples of the actor's method of composing drama. Garrick tailored the play to fit the capabilities of a company of actors whose strength and weaknesses he knew intimately. He betrayed continual interest in stage effects. He preserved in his characterization certain surefire techniques which his previous experience in writing and acting had proved. He sharpened characterization and economized on exposition by planting in the minds of the audience certain high points regarding main characters before their appearance on the stage. And he wrote at first hurriedly and then revised with great care in order to get the most out of his entire company of players.

Reading the Garrick MS. with an eye to both the minute and the extensive revisions made in the course of its composition gives a picture of a careful writer at work, a playwright who kept in mind not only the capabilities of his actors and the inclinations of his audience, but also his own ideal of true comedy. Nor is this all. If we consider the MS. as a play rather than as a problem in authorship, we shall find few better examples of a player bringing his own personality, taste, and dramatic ideas to bear on writing for the stage. The result is a brilliant comedy, typical of the best in the creative drama of the late eighteenth century. (pp. 159-62)

> *Fredrick L. Bergmann, "David Garrick and 'The Clandestine Marriage'," in* PMLA, *Vol. LXVII, No. 2, March, 1952, pp. 148-62.*

Charles B. Woods (essay date 1962)

[*In the excerpt below, Woods hypothesizes that similarities between Garrick's* Lethe *and* Miss in Her Teens: or, The Medley of Lovers *and Henry Fielding's* The Virgin Unmask'd *indicate the strong possibility of the two authors' secret collaboration on* Miss Lucy in Town, *a play historically ascribed to Fielding alone.*]

The first certain evidence of Garrick's intentions with respect to the professional theatre was the production of his afterpiece **Lethe, or Esop in the Shades** at Drury Lane on April 15, 1740. This play has a curious history which has never been fully described. Garrick tinkered with it throughout his career; it exists in a number of versions, both in print and in manuscript; some of the versions were extremely popular on the stage. Garrick even read a version at Court when, after his retirement as manager of

Drury Lane, he was summoned by George III to appear before the Royal Family in 1777. The point I wish to stress about **Lethe,** however, is that its earliest versions contain episodes which form a sequel to *The Virgin Unmask'd.* Manifestly, Garrick's first effort as professional dramatist, as well as his acting at St. John's Gate, indicates his familiarity with Fielding's plays.

Lethe is an attack on social follies set in a Lucianic underworld; it follows a fashion of the day that was popular for both dramatic and non-dramatic satire (Fielding had used the form for plays and periodical essays). The plot resembles that of *The Virgin Unmask'd* in being a frame for a procession of comic characters. Pluto has given mortals the privilege of drinking from the river Lethe "as a Sovereign Remedy against their Care." After Mercury has conducted them to the Styx and Charon has ferried them over to Elysium, Æsop is to "distribute the Waters." Naturally we have a parade of mortals before Æsop, and in the first version of the play, which has never been printed and exists only in a Larpent MS., they include an attorney, a beau, a drunken man, his extravagant wife, and our old friends Miss Lucy and Mr. Thomas, who, although they have been married only a month, want to "drink some Leithe [*sic*] to forget one another & to be unmarried again"— at least that is how Miss Lucy explains their presence. As in Fielding's play, the erstwhile footman is more sensible than his bride. "Several young Ladies of my Acquaintance" have advised Lucy, she says, that "I should be a fine, compleat Lady if I would procure a Seperate Maintainance" [*sic*]. But Thomas hopes that Æsop's wisdom will "alter her Intentions, & save us both from Ruin." Lucy has little inclination to reform, however, and for the edification of Æsop, who wants to know what she calls "a fine Lady," she sings what is obviously meant to be the most memorable musical number of the whole show—an eight-stanza song. " 'Tis call'd," she says, "the Life of a Belle in Imitation of the Life of a Beau." The first and last stanzas will suggest its spirit:

> What lives are so happy as those of the Fair,
> Who scarcely a Moment from pleasure can spare,
> But leave their Husbands Reflection & Care,
> Such, such is the Life of a Belle. . . .
>
> Plays, Balls, & Ridotto's each Night she attends;
> And sometimes Quadrille with a few Female Friends;
> And something in Secret—but here my Song ends.
> Such, such &c—

Now Mrs. Clive created Garrick's Miss Lucy, just as she had created Fielding's, and for two seasons in Fielding's *The Miser* the same actress had been singing with great success an interpolated song called "The Life of a Beau." This song had originally appeared in 1738 in James Miller's *The Coffee House,* a disastrous failure produced but once; Mrs. Clive, apparently feeling that the song was too good to lose, introduced it into her favorite part of Lappet in *The Miser;* thus a song associated with a Fielding play furnished a hint to Garrick.

The first performance of **Lethe** was the only one at Drury Lane until 1749, when it was revived under Garrack's management in a thoroughly reworked version that no longer presented characters named Mr. Thomas and Miss Lucy (some of their old lines were assigned to a new couple, Mr. and Mrs. Tattoo). But **Lethe** with Miss Lucy and her husband had a most successful run at another theatre,

Goodman's Fields, where it was performed more than thirty times between April 1741 (a year after its Drury Lane production) and May 1742. Newspaper advertisements for the first Goodman's Fields performance on April 7, 1741, ended with these words: "and the Part of Miss Lucy by Miss Hippisley. In which Character will be introduc'd a Song, call'd "The Life of a Belle," that Scene being a Sequel to the *Virgin Unmask'd*. This scene was advertised more than once during the Goodman's Fields run, suggesting that the connection with *The Virgin Unmask'd* was considered an especially attractive feature. (pp. 296-98)

On May 6, 1742, a new sequel to *The Virgin Unmask'd* appeared at Drury Lane. It was another afterpiece with songs, called *Miss Lucy in Town;* and this time the whole play, instead of episodes as in **Lethe,** was concerned with the heroine's adventures after marriage. Fielding, who had not written for the stage since the Licensing Act, acknowledged that he was part author, but asserted that his share had been a very small one. So far as I know, his collaborator was never revealed and no candidates have been proposed. I should like to suggest that David Garrick was the co-author. If the major responsibility for *Miss Lucy in Town* was Garrick's, it was his second attempt at portraying Miss Lucy and his third play; his second play, **The Lying Valet,** had appeared at Goodman's Field's in 1741 a few weeks after his debut as Richard III. It is interesting to note that Garrick's fourth play, by this method of counting, entitled **Miss in Her Teens: or, The Medley of Lovers** is strikingly reminiscent of *The Virgin Unmask'd* in that its most famous scene presents a sixteen-year old country miss with a fortune of £15,000 standing between two quarreling suitors who have drawn their swords but are really not eager to fight.

Miss Lucy in Town is a rather risqué farce for its period. The authors seem to have taken a hint from Vanbrugh and Cibber's *The Provok'd Husband,* possibly the most popular comedy of the century, which has an amusing "low" plot depicting the mishaps of a country family in London. Through sheer ignorance of city ways these yokels take lodgings in a house of ill fame. In the new afterpiece, Miss Lucy and her husband make exactly the same blunder when they come to London from the country after six weeks of marriage. But the situation is handled with much less delicacy than in the predominantly sentimental *Provok'd Husband;* indeed the humors of a bawdy house are exploited with Restoration frankness. We have the bawd, Mrs. Haycock—a notorious prostitute in real life was named Mrs. Haywood—haggling with her customers as she tries to get the best price for Lucy, who is blithely unaware of what is being planned for her. (Mr. Thomas is conveniently out of the way because as soon as possible he has rushed out to find a tailor so that he may "appear like a Gentleman.") The procession of Mrs. Haycock's customers permits a slashing satiric attack on titled aristocrats, Jewish stock-brokers, and English and Italian singers. The Italian opera received a terrific ribbing, we learn from one of Horace Walpole's letters, when Mrs. Clive (who created Miss Lucy for the third time) sang a duet with Beard (who played Signor Cantileno) and both ridiculed well-known opera performers.

> Our operas are almost over; there were but three and forty people last night in the pit and boxes. There is a little simple farce at Drury Lane, called

> *Miss Lucy in Town,* in which Mrs Clive mimics the Muscovita admirably, and Beard Amorevoli intolerably. But all the run is now after Garrick, a wine merchant who is turned player at Goodman's Fields.

Fortunately Mr. Thomas gets back from the tailor's before his wife has succumbed to her most dangerous suitor, Lord Bawble, who has been recognized by Cantileno as one of the directors of the opera. Lucy is eager to desert Thomas for the noble lord, but the former footman maintains his rights against the privileges of rank. The last speech in the play is assigned to Lucy's father, Goodwill, who seems to have little excuse for being present except to echo the ending of *The Virgin Unmask'd*. "Henceforth," says Goodwill, "I will know no Degree, no Difference between Men, but what the Standards of Honour and Virtue create—The Noblest Birth without those is but Splendid Infamy; and a Footman with these qualities, is a Man of Honour."

Does the text of *Miss Lucy* tend to support the theory that Garrick was part author? I believe that it does, although the evidence falls short of proof. Near the opening of the play Miss Lucy learns from Tawdry, one of Mrs. Haycock's employees, about the life led by the modern fine lady. Some of this dialogue sounds like a prose version of the song in **Lethe.** To Lucy's question " . . . are there no Sights for a fine Lady to see," Tawdry replies: "O yes, Madam, there are Ridotto's, Masquerades, Court, Plays, and a thousand others. So many that a fine Lady has never Time to be at home but when she is asleep." The same routine had been outlined in "The Life of a Belle"; the second stanza tells of the fine Lady sleeping "All morning when other are up & Employ'd," and the third describes her breakfasting at noon and hurriedly slipping on a gown so that she may take the chair at her door and set out on her round of pleasures. After the heroine of *Miss Lucy* has been told what kind of life she may expect in town, she also has a song, which begins:

> If flaunting & ranting
> If noise & Gallanting
> Be all in fine Ladies requir'd
> I'll warrant I'll be
> As fine a Lady
> As ever in Town was admir'd

If the success of **Lethe** at Goodman's Fields in 1741 and 1742 had made audiences want to hear Miss Lucy talk and sing about the life of a fine lady, the authors of *Miss Lucy in Town* decided to exploit this precedent set by Garrick, who in **Lethe** had built upon some hints in *The Virgin Unmask'd* that for Lucy the *summum bonum* was a coach and six. The presence of the "fine lady" material, of course, does not *prove* that Garrick had a hand in *Miss Lucy in Town,* but Fielding was sensitive about taking suggestions from contemporary playwrights without acknowledgment.

The same consideration applies to another similarity between *Miss Lucy in Town* and the Goodman's Fields version of **Lethe.** The ending of the GF version (as given in the 1745 edition) differs from that of the original Drury Lane production: two new characters, a Frenchman and Teague, are accosted by Lucy after she has run on stage exclaiming, "I have given my Husband the Slip, and I wish I could find one to run away with—." She offers herself as wife to each of the new characters, is rejected by both, and then, seeing her husband approaching, says: "Here comes one, I must have—Where have you been, dear Bud?" This new turn to her character, a naive disloyalty to her husband reminding one of Margery Pinchwife's, is developed by the authors of *Miss Lucy in Town* to such an extent that it becomes the foundation of the plot: the last Miss Lucy is more than willing to exchange Thomas for Lord Bawble; she says she hates her husband and even has the impudence to deny that she is married to him. In fact she is reconciled to him only after she is convinced that she cannot have another mate. It may be doubted whether Fielding, without Garrick's approval, would have collaborated in such an extension of the traits that first appear in *Lethe.* At least it is safe to assert that the characterization of Miss Lucy is consistent in the two plays which depict her in the married state. Of course Garrick might have gone to Fielding for suggestions about Miss Lucy and Thomas when *Lethe* was written; if he did, it would have been natural for the two dramatists to collaborate on another play concerned with those characters.

Because of its deeper satiric bite and more coherent plot, *Miss Lucy in Town* is a better play to read than either of its predecessors. It seems to have been cordially received in the theatre. Although it was brought on very late in the season, it had at least seven performances in May. It is interesting that Garrick acted four times at Drury Lane during the same month, giving his first performances at a patent theatre. Fairly early in the next season, on 27 October 1742, *Miss Lucy in Town* was revived and ran well for a dozen performances until the first of December. Then the afterpiece apparently disappeared from the repertory in its original form. (pp. 299-303)

> Charles B. Woods, "The 'Miss Lucy' Plays of Fielding and Garrick," in Philological Quarterly, *Vol. XLI, No. 1, January, 1962, pp. 294-310.*

John Hainsworth   (essay date 1973)

[*In the excerpt below, Hainsworth surveys Garrick's poetry, highly praising the comic verses, prologues, and epilogues.*]

David Garrick will be known as an actor for as long as the English theatre continues to exist. As a theatre manager he is remembered for the innovations, notably in stage lighting and scenic design, that were introduced at Drury Lane during his management. As a playwright he survives still—if only because of *The Clandestine Marriage* written in collaboration with George Colman the elder. His brilliance as a letter-writer is evident in the magnificent three-volume edition of his letters brought out by D. M. Little and G. M. Kahrl in 1963. And, of course, he is known as an associate of Dr Johnson and a member of the famous Club. But David Garrick as a poet? This aspect of his achievement has been almost lost sight of. Yet verse-writing was an activity that he persisted in throughout his busy and successful adult life. 'It seems', says his friend and biographer Arthur Murphy, 'that his close connection with Dr. Johnson at Litchfield [*sic*], gave him an early turn for versification . . . If we except the pleasures he enjoyed in conversation with his friends, poetical composition was his chief recreation from the fatigue of his profession.'

There has been no new edition of these poems since Kearsley published *The Poetical Works of David Garrick, Esq.* in 1785. Professor Mary E. Knapp, it is true, brought out a check-list of his poems in 1955, and lists, in all, 479 items, some of them unknown to Kearsley. But the only other significant recognition of him as a poet that I know of, has come from David Nichol Smith, who includes two items by Garrick in *The Oxford Book of Eighteenth Century Verse.* One of his choices is the song Garrick wrote for his patriotic pantomime *Harlequin's Invasion,* usually known by the first line of its chorus, 'Heart of Oak', and so traditional that its authorship has been widely forgotten. Nichol Smith's other choice is two stanzas of the poem Garrick wrote **"To Mr. Gray, on the Publication of his Odes"**:

> Repine not, Gray, that our weak dazzled eyes
> Thy daring heights and brightness shun;
> How few can track the eagle to the skies,
> Or like him gaze upon the sun!
>
> The gentle reader loves the gentle Muse,
>   That little dares, and little means,
> Who humbly sips her learning from *Reviews,*
>   Or flutters in the *Magazines.*

These lines owe their effectiveness to the imagery, and especially to the eagle imagery of the first stanza and the way the final verb 'flutters' is played off against it. But what Garrick actually says about Gray through this imagery is extremely vague and general. This vagueness and generality are failings typical of Garrick whenever he ventures outside the field of light verse. From his **"Ode on the death of Mr. Pelham,"** for instance, no impression emerges of an individual person or even of a recognisable type. The qualities which Garrick perceives in the deceased prime minister are merely ideals:

> No selfish views t' oppress mankind,
> No mad ambition fir'd thy mind,
> To purchase fame with blood;
> Thy bosom glow'd with purer heat:
> Convinc'd that to be truly great,
> Is only to be *good.*

There is nothing beyond uninspired commonplace to be found, either, in the **"Ode on Shakespeare"** that Garrick wrote to be delivered by himself at the great Stratford Jubilee, where he would clearly have wished to be at his best; or in the various epitaphs that he wrote for his friends. One is even tempted to take seriously the remark of Samuel Foote that he was afraid of dying before Garrick, in case Garrick should write his epitaph.

Garrick was more in his element with the comic epitaph. His famous quip on Goldsmith was delivered extempore at a meeting of the Club:

> Here lies Nolly Goldsmith, for shortness call'd Noll,
> Who wrote like an angel, but talk'd like poor Poll.

Garrick also claimed extemporaneousness for his couplet on Dr John Hill, the well-known purveyor of patent medicines, who had reviled the Drury Lane management after his farce *The Rout* had been badly received:

> For physic and farces,
> His equal there scarce is;
> His farces are physic,
> His physic a farce is.

Such verse as this is merely an extension of conversational wit, and so strongly suggestive of its social origin that one is tempted to speculate on who was present in the company that first heard it. Garrick also has a slightly longer piece relating to this affair of John Hill and his farce. This is a step further in the direction of literature and shows Garrick's muse *fluttering* 'in the Magazines'. It makes use of the fact that, at the first performance of *The Rout,* the playwright's name had been withheld, and he had been designated merely as 'A Person of Honour':

> Says a friend to the Doctor, 'Pray give it about
> That this farce is not yours, or you'll miss of the pelf;
> What had come of your *Nerves,* or your *P[o]x* or your
>   *Gout,*
> Had these embrios crawl'd forth as begot by yourself?
> Let your Muse, as your pamphlets, come forth (I advise
>   ye)
> Like a goddess of old, with a cloud cast upon her.'
> 'You're right,' quoth the Doctor, 'and more to disguise
>   me,
> I'll give myself out for a *Person of Honour.*

This is still more witticism than wit, however, and writing it in verse serves only to make it sound a little more clever. It is instructive to set these lines beside Charles Churchill's account of Hill in "The Rosciad." Churchill's superiority is that his lines are more than just witticism: they make a statement more complex than Garrick's and they use the peculiar resources of poetry to achieve their complexity. (pp. 359-61)

It is not, of course, fair to show up the deficiencies of Garrick's verse by comparing lines he wrote for a magazine with an extract from a consciously literary work like "The Rosciad." A fairer comparison would be between "The Rosciad" extract and lines from Garrick's poem **"The Fribbleriad."** This is a more ambitious literary project, a contribution to that mock-heroic genre to which "The Rosciad" also belongs—a genre so popular at this time that Christopher Smart had even written a "Hilliad" about Dr Hill. A 'fribler' [sic] had been defined by Richard Steele in *Spectator* No. 288 as 'one who professes rapture and admiration for the woman to whom he addresses, and dreads nothing so much as her consent'. There is a character called Fribble in Garrick's play *Miss in her teens.* According to Garrick's friend Arthur Murphy, he represents a phenomenon of the times, 'the pretty gentlemen, who chose to unsex themselves, and make a display of delicacy that exceeded female softness'. In the course of acting the role of Fribble, Garrick was said to mimic eleven fashionable gentlemen of the time. The poem **"The Fribbleriad,"** however, was not published till 1761, fourteen years after the first performance of the play. It was a rejoinder to attacks on Garrick's abilities as an actor made in print by a certain Thaddeus Fitzpatrick. In his poem, Garrick comically takes it for granted that these attacks were a belated act of vengeance, prompted by 'fribbles' who had recognised themselves in the play. The poem describes a 'Panfribblerium'—a meeting of fribbles at Hampstead to discuss the form of their revenge on Garrick. At one stage the Chairman, Fizgig, who represents Fitzpatrick, calls on Sir Diddle, a character who has already appeared in *Miss in her teens,* to address the meeting:

> Sir DIDDLE then he thus address'd—
> ''Tis yours to speak, be mute the rest.'
> When thus the knight—'Can I dissemble?

> 'Conceal my rage, while thus I tremble?
> 'O FIZGIG! 'tis that Garrick's name,
> 'Now stops my voice, and shakes my frame—
> 'His pangs would please—his death—oh lud!
> 'Blood, Mr. FIZGIG, blood, blood, blood!'
> The thought, too mighty for his mind,
> O'ercame his powers; he star'd; grew blind;
> Cold sweat his faded cheek o'erspread,
> Like dew upon the lily's head;
> He squeak'd and sigh'd—no more could say
> But blood—bloo—blo—and died away.
> Thus when in war a hero swoons,
> With loss of blood, or fear of wounds,
> They bear him off—and thus they bore
> Sir DIDDLE to the garden-door.

The obvious criticism of such verse is that the tetrameters limit metrical flexibility and make for an effect of doggerel. This is not entirely a fair criticism, as it is largely this effect of doggerel that deflates the heroics into mock-heroics and makes the epic similes sound comic. The device is a simple one, but then the end in view is also simple. Garrick's aim is merely to ridicule his fribbles. The more complex and serious kind of statement that Churchill has achieved is not attempted.

One has to go to Garrick's prologues and epilogues to find a complexity in any way approaching Churchill's. It is on these theatrical pieces that Garrick's claim to be remembered as a poet must mainly rest. And yet, of course, the complexity there achieved is not of the same kind as that to be found in a literary work like "The Rosciad." For the prologues and epilogues are not literature but drama. (pp. 362-64)

The imagery and wit of Garrick, in his prologues and epilogues, were singled out for special praise in his own day. Thus, in a prologue delivered at the Haymarket theatre in 1775, the speaker excuses his own lack of these things on the grounds that they are in short supply: Garrick is making so much use of them elsewhere:

> In Prologue Writing, modern Bards agree,
> The only Art, is Wit and Simile;
> But *for* that Art, we ever must complain,
> While ROSCIUS uses it at Drury-Lane.

Both wit and imagery are very effectively used in Garrick's Epilogue to the Rev. John Brown's tragedy of *Athelstan,* and used in a way that is peculiarly appropriate to the theatre. Mrs Cibber, who has just been playing the tragic heroine, tells of the different ways in which different sections of the audience react to tragedy:

> As men with different eyes a beauty see,
> So judge they of that stately dame—Queen Tragedy.
> The Greek-read critic, as his mistress holds her,
> And having little love, for trifles scolds her:
> Excuses want of spirit, beauty, grace,
> But ne'er forgives her failing, time and place.
> How do our sex of taste and judgment vary?
> Miss 'Bell adores, what's loath'd by lady Mary:
> The first in tenderness a very dove,
> Melts, like the feather'd snow, at Juliet's love:
> Then, sighing, turns to Romeo by her side,
> 'Can you believe that men for love have dy'd?'

This is a passage which well repays an analysis of its dramatic merits. The 'Queen Tragedy', referred to at the beginning, is no mere allegorical figure whom the audience have to imagine. Mrs Cibber is clearly intended, by a significant change in her deportment, to take the role upon herself, her past achievements in this theatre, and not just her performance this evening, making her a strong candidate for the throne in question. 'The Greek-read critic' is at first titillated with the idea of having Mrs Cibber as his mistress, and then wittily abused as one so lacking in true feeling that he would care more about whether she arrived at the right time, in the right place, than about her personal qualities. The imagery associated with Miss Bell is satisfyingly rich on a purely literary level:

> The first in tenderness a very dove,
> Melts, like the feather'd snow, at Juliet's love.

Dove, it is true, is a conventional enough image for tenderness, but the conventionality is redeemed by what follows. The richness can be demonstrated if one asks what the connection is between the two images *dove* and *snow.* They are associated because both are white, because snow-flakes are like feathers (compare Hopkins: 'Flake-doves sent floating forth at a farm-yard scare!'), and because the dove represents tenderness, which, like snow, turns to water (*melts*). The imagery is not just literary, however; it involves a dramatic relationship. Juliet, in whom the tears originate, is not just a random representative of tragedy, but one of the roles in which Mrs Cibber herself most excelled. And Miss Bell, to whom the imagery relates, is supposed to be someone in the audience Mrs Cibber is addressing—some members of the audience, that is, are recognising themselves in the portrait—recognising themselves, though, with a certain amount of comic detachment, because the imagery contains also an element of poetic exaggeration, of which both speaker and audience are aware. Comedy gains the upper hand at the end of the passage quoted, in the stock joke about the shallowness of men's love. There is more here than just a joke, however, for the suggestion that Romeo and Juliet may be located in the audience as well as on stage, carries the serious implication that the stage world and the real world are essentially one—or, at least, that the one mirrors the other.

This is to labour over a passage that would make its impact in the theatre without any need of analysis. The point of analysing it is to show that it can only achieve its full impact in the theatre. (pp. 365-66)

Yet, dramatic as Garrick's prologues and epilogues are, they are not dramatic in quite the same way that a play is dramatic. For a play involves a sustained fiction; the actor is consistently pretending to be someone else; the audience are all the time being asked to assume the reality of the fictitious world they see before them on the stage. There always is an element of fiction in a prologue or epilogue, even when the speaker addresses the audience in his own person. For he is pretending to speak his thoughts extempore, whereas, in fact, they have been carefully prepared and versified; and they are not his own thoughts, either, unless author and speaker happen to be the same person. Yet the fiction is never as complete as in a play, for even when the speaker of an epilogue acts the role he has just been playing, as in 'Sir Anthony Branville's Address to the Ladies', he is now in a different and more personal relationship with the audience, addressing them directly from the apron, and sometimes with the curtain dropped behind him. (p. 367)

In the skill with which he tailors prologues and epilogues to their speakers, Garrick is without rival. This is hardly surprising, since his success as a manager depended on his being able to gauge with accuracy the abilities of actors and actresses. An interesting illustration of the pains Garrick would take in this matter is the epilogue he wrote for the occasion of Mrs Pritchard's retirement from the stage. To try to ensure *her* satisfaction, in the copy of the epilogue he sent her, he marked lines she could omit if she wished, and offered variant readings. Knowing that Mrs Pritchard would be deeply moved by the occasion, he makes her say:

> I now appear myself, distress'd, dismay'd,
> More than in all the characters I've play'd.

And the epilogue is so worded that any tears she sheds will help rather than hinder the effect aimed at. 'She spoke her farewell epilogue,' says Thomas Davies, 'with many sobs and tears, which were increased by the generous feelings of a numerous and splendid audience.' (pp. 372-73)

His intimate and many-sided knowledge of his theatre provided Garrick with a much firmer foundation for his poetry than any literary tradition could do—which is, no doubt, the main reason why these theatrical pieces are, generally, superior to anything else he wrote. This is the basis, too, for his eminence, if not preeminence, amongst writers in this genre. Dr Johnson even compared him favourably with Dryden. 'Dryden has written prologues superiour to any that David Garrick has written; but David Garrick has written more good prologues than Dryden has done'. With the first part of this statement there can be no quarrelling. For sheer dramatic effectiveness, nothing in Garrick can quite equal, for instance, Dryden's Epilogue to *An Evening's Love.* Here the way the actress mimics the audience's behaviour and makes fun of their critical attitudes allows her to show off her abilities, and, at the same time, involves the audience, in a delightfully provocative way, in her performance. She also makes them laugh at French manners, but wittily justifies the author's borrowing of a French plot. If she is a good deal more bawdy than Garrick could permit, the bawdiness is made to seem not adventitious, but a genuine and amusing revelation of the speaker's character. Dryden shows in this epilogue that he can excel Garrick even in those dramatic qualities where Garrick is strongest. The first part of Dr Johnson's verdict is unassailable, therefore. It is doubtful, however, if the second part of it—that 'David Garrick has written more good prologues than Dryden has done'—is soundly based in arithmetical calculations. But whatever Garrick's status relative to Dryden, or indeed, to anyone else, there are reasons enough why a modern reader might find a study of his prologues and epilogues worthwhile. Many of them still make lively and enjoyable reading— that is one reason. But for anyone interested in the history of the theatre they have a special importance. In them, in quite a unique way, the dead facts of history are brought to life again. As Garrick himself has pointed out in his Prologue to **The Clandestine Marriage,** the art of the actor lacks the durability of other arts:

> The painter dead, yet still he charms the eye;
> While England lives, his fame can never die:
> But he, who *struts his hour upon the stage,*
> Can scarce extend his fame for half an age;
> Nor pen nor pencil can the Actor save,
> The art, and artist, share one common grave.

A note in rhyme sent with some tickets from Garrick to the architect Sandby.

Prologues and epilogues—and especially those of Garrick—to some extent ameliorate this situation. In them, so carefully tailored, as they often are, to the aptitudes of a particular speaker, there is captured something, at least, of the art and stage personality of the dead performer. Also accessible through them is the audience to which they were originally addressed—and to which they were also tailored. And this not just because of the vivid portraits of that audience which they occasionally provide, but in a more existential way, too. For the imaginative reading and re-reading of these verses provides the nearest possible approximation to actually becoming oneself a part of that eighteenth-century audience. They bring to life for the reader a theatrical community, and this not in any merely external way, but by enabling him to feel for himself the tensions within it, by giving him a personal and unique experience of its intimate life. (pp. 374-76)

> *John Hainsworth, "David Garrick, Poet of the Theatre: A Critical Survey," in* Studies in the Eighteenth Century, Vol. II, *edited by R. F. Brissenden, Australian National University Press, 1973, pp. 359-76.*

George Winchester Stone, Jr.   (essay date 1975)

[*In the following excerpt, Stone examines Garrick's alteration of Shakespeare's* Cymbeline.]

The apparent formlessness of Shakespeare's play [*Cymbeline*] did, indeed, baffle and disturb most of Garrick's contemporaries who used the critical standards of Aristotle as measurement, and as usual none was more sure of his judgment on this point than Dr. Johnson:

> It has many just sentiments, some natural dialogue, and some pleasing scenes, but they are obtained at the expense of incongruity. To remark the folly of the fiction, and absurdity of the conduct, the confusion of the names, and manners of different times, and the impossibility of the events in any system of life, were to waste criticism upon unresisting imbecility, upon faults too evident for detection, and too gross for aggravation.

Garrick, doubtless with flashing eye and evident zest, took up the challenge, and many who wrote were of the opinion that in doing so he rendered his age signal service in altering the play and producing it. Benjamin Victor wrote of the Garrick version: "*Cymbeline* is a tragedy written by Shakespeare; with some little alterations, by which the stage is enriched with another excellent play." Arthur Murphy, after quoting the Dr. Johnson blast, remarks:

> In the play before us, all is confusion, a wild chance of heterogeneous matter. The poet may be said to have placed in view a monster fifty furlongs in length. And yet Garrick thought fit to revive the play, because he knew that amidst all its imperfections, a number of detached beauties would occur to surprise and charm the imagination.

Subsequent critics have agreed, but a discordant note appears in the note by Horace Walpole, who saw one of the early Garrick performances. We have a fragmentary impression of his reaction in an extant piece of a letter to George Montagu (8 December 1761) in which he notes that he crowded into the packed pit, was uncomfortable, saw no one he knew. The play appeared to him "as long as if everybody in it went to Italy in every act and came back again. With a few pretty passages and a scene or two it is so absurd and tiresome that I am persuaded Garrick . . . " And we will never know the conclusion of the sentence.

Garrick's version was printed first in 1762, and his advertisement tells rather completely the nature of his alteration:

> The admirers of Shakespeare must not take it ill that there are some scenes, and consequently many fine passages, omitted in this edition of *Cymbeline*. It was impossible to retain more of the play and bring it within the compass of a night's entertainment. The chief alterations are in the division of the acts, in the shortening of many parts of the original, and transposing some scenes.

Examination of the text reveals Garrick's consistent practice in fitting Shakespeare for the eighteenth-century stage, namely in letting the sheer weight of Shakespeare's wording come across the footlights, without trying to substitute his own poetic values, as so often did the seventeenth-century and early eighteenth-century alterers, from Tate to Hawkins.

He makes a slight reduction of characters, for as his play opens the First Gentleman's lines are given to Pisanio. A few words are changed here, and two sentences are added to fit them to the new speaker. The first Act is reduced from the five scenes of the original to two. The first of these includes Shakespeare's scenes i, iii, and v, embracing all the action which in the Act takes place in Britain. The second scene is Shakespeare's iv, wherein Posthumus arrives at Rome, meets Iachimo, and makes the fatal wager. This scene is retained word for word, with the omission of but three and a half lines. Shakespeare's third scene, however, which presents Cloten in converse with two Lords after the fight with Posthumus, is omitted altogether. A speech of commiseration on Imogen, given by a second Lord in Shakespeare's Act II, is transposed and given to Pisanio in Act I. Garrick's rearrangement is of distinct advantage to the producer, as it calls for only one shift of scenery, yet retains all the important expository material necessary for the development of the plot and the introduction of the characters. Cloten's part alone is shorn, and we meet him in Act I only by the comments of others.

The second Act begins with Shakespeare's Act I, scene vi, that is with Iachimo's visit to Imogen. It then proceeds in sequence through the first three scenes of Shakespeare's Act II, and here we see Cloten making a fool of himself before two Lords, Iachimo gathering evidence from Imogen's bedroom, and Cloten's awakening the heroine with his aubade, "Hark, hark the Lark at Heaven's Gate Sings . . . " The Act closes with Imogen's conversation with him and her realization of the loss of her bracelet. The entrance of Cymbeline and his queen in Shakespeare's third scene is moved forward to Garrick's first one. The new element in this act comes in the third scene, and proved to grant lasting pleasure to theatre-goers. Cloten after the dawn song says to his attendants:

> Come now to our dancing, and if she is unmovable

to this she is an unmovable princess, and not worth my notice.

Then follows a dance, after which Cloten knocks upon her chamber door. The dance was highly advertised:

> In Act II will be introduc'd a masque by Mr. Vincent, Signor Giorgi, Signor Lochery, Signora Giorgi, & c., with Singing by Mrs. Vincent.

Little cutting took place in this Act.

Garrick's Act III begins with Shakespeare's Act II, scene iv, in which the location changes to Rome, and in which Iachimo boasts the success of his expedition to Imogen's chamber. The action proceeds in order through Shakespeare's III, iii. We see Posthumus' cynical reaction to Iachimo's story, we learn of Cymbeline's refusal to pay tribute to Augustus, we learn of Pisanio's orders to kill Imogen, and we meet with Bellarius, Guiderius and Arviragus. A portion of Shakespeare's fifth scene follows in which the certainty of war with Rome is made known, and Imogen's absence is discovered. The Act ends with Shakespeare's fourth scene as Imogen and Pisanio approach Milford Haven. One hundred and forty-nine lines are excised from the Act, over half of them from the scene of purely political import relative to Britain's tribute to Rome. Two and a half lines are added to Posthumus' speech to Philario in scene i, not indicated in Shakespeare. They speak with pride about the British sovereign, and doubtless are praise for, or advice to, the newly crowned George III:

> . . . and more than that
> They [the Britons] have a King whose love and justice
> To them may ask and have their treasures, and their blood.

Garrick's Act IV begins with Shakespeare's Act III, scene v, line 70, in which Cloten professes his love and disdain for Imogen, decides to pursue her to Milford Haven, to rape her, and to "foot her home again." Shakespeare's sixth scene follows in which Imogen meets her mountaineer brothers. The seventh scene between senators and tribunes at Rome is omitted. Shakespeare's fourth act then proceeds in order through the killing of Cloten, and the burial of Fidele (Imogen) with him under a blanket of flowers. The dirge is much shortened and changed:

> BEL. Let us lay the bodies each by each
> And straw 'em o'er with flowers, and on the morrow
> Shall the earth receive 'em.
>
> ARV. Sweet Fidele,
> Fear no more th' heat o' th' sun,
> Nor the furious Winter's blast
> Thou thy worldly task hast done,
> And the dream of life is past.
>
> GUID. Monarchs, sages, peasants must
> Follow thee and come to dust.
> [Exeunt with the Body.]

The scene here shifts to Shakespeare's third scene, a room in Cymbeline's palace, in which we learn of the Queen's illness, of the approach of Roman troops, and of the lack of communication from Posthumus. After this brief interlude we are returned to finish Shakespeare's second scene. The Act ends with Imogen's awakening, her mistaking the dead Cloten for Posthumus, and her joining the Roman troops under Lucius.

Garrick's Act V begins with Shakespeare's IV, iv, wherein the three mountaineers decide to fight for Britain. Shakespeare's V, i, immediately follows disclosing Posthumus as he changes from "Italian weeds" to British peasant's garb, in order to join the British troops. He conquers Iachimo in the next scene, and sets him free. The latter submits with a twinge of conscience, that was thoroughly acceptable to the eighteenth century, but hardly consistent with the Italian's character:

> With Heav'n against me, what is sword or shield!
> My guilt, my guilt o'erpowers me and I yield.

Shakespeare's third scene follows, in which the Britons gain the field, but much more quickly than in the original. Pisanio and a Lord retail the necessary information to us in half the number of lines used in Shakespeare. Shakespeare's fourth scene, the long prison one, is completely excised, and his fifth scene follows, wherein Cymbeline learns of the death of his Queen and of her perfidy, and makes the series of discoveries which give him a new lease on life and bring the play to a close, with reconciliations all round.

Five hundred and twenty-four lines were cut from this act at first by Garrick, and, according to a note in his advertisement, forty-five more (those containing the information of the Queen's death) were eliminated on the stage after the first night. One can only agree with the eighteenth-century critics that the alteration makes an excellent acting text, presenting as it does a well-developed story, and injuring no important character in the excisions. A Gentleman, some Senators, Tribunes, and a Soothsayer vanish to be sure, and Cloten's opportunities for making a fool of himself are reduced, but the former are hardly missed, and sufficient chance is left the latter to display his character adequately. One gathers that Thomas King, and succeeding Clotens responded to the burden thus placed on the actor to come through effectively. The play was produced "with new scenes and habits" (scenery and costumes) and surely deserved its success, relying as it did on full use of the Shakespearean dialogue, without attempting to "improve" it. (pp. 315-18)

George Winchester Stone, Jr., "A Century of 'Cymbeline'; or Garrick's Magic Touch," in Philological Quarterly, *Vol. 54, No. 1, Winter, 1975, pp. 310-22.*

Don Rintz   (essay date 1975)

[*In the following excerpt, Rintz investigates the charge that Garrick plagiarized the tomb scene in his adaptation of* Romeo and Juliet *from Thomas Otway's* Caius Marius.]

David Garrick's most significant alteration of Shakespeare's *Romeo and Juliet* was the revision of the tomb scene. In the final act, Juliet awakens from her drugged sleep to find Romeo dying of the apothecary's poison. The lovers have a few brief moments together before Romeo dies and Juliet stabs herself.

The alteration was immediately popular. From its first performance in 1748 to the end of the eighteenth century, Garrick's adaptation of *Romeo and Juliet* was the most frequently produced of Shakespeare's plays. It was presented on London stages some 456 times—compared with 360 performances of *Hamlet*, 338 of *Richard III*, 288 of *Macbeth*, 197 of *King Lear*, and 191 performances of *Othello*. The popularity of Garrick's version continued well into the nineteenth century; and even as late as 1875, Sir Charles Wyndham used Garrick's tomb scene in his own production of *Romeo and Juliet*.

Garrick was very proud of his revision of the tomb scene and was elated by its popularity and critical acclaim. In the Advertisement for the first edition of his version, he explained that the public approbation of the scene had prompted him to be bold enough to publish it:

> The favourable Reception of the new Scene in the fifth Act has met with, induc'd the Writer to print it, and if he may be excus'd for daring to add to *Shakespeare*, he shall think himself well rewarded in having given *Romeo and Juliet* an Opportunity of shewing their great Merit.

Eighteenth century critics were especially delighted with the altering of the ending. Allowing Romeo and Juliet a short time together before their death was a poignant moment which some said was worthy of Shakespeare himself. Otway had first used this twist of the plot in *Caius Marius*. One writer thought that Shakespeare would have thanked Otway for this refinement of his play.

Garrick believed that Shakespeare not only would have approved of the change but might have adopted it himself had he read the version of the legend which told the story that way. (p. 31)

Garrick further believed that his rewriting of the final scene was responsible for its effectiveness on the stage. At least one critic was not willing to give him the credit for it. MacNamara Morgan—who was himself an adapter of Shakespeare—agreed that the revised ending was effective—"perhaps the finest Touch of Nature in any Tragedy ancient or modern." But Morgan was no friend of Garrick's, and he could not allow a paltry player the credit for so successful a piece of dramatic writing. He maintained that it was Otway who was responsible for this very moving addition to *Romeo and Juliet*:

> It is very strange, therefore, that it has not been inquired into, who the Author was, that made so happy an Alteration. I have heard it attributed to one of the Players; and it passes current that his Knowledge of the Stage enabled him to do it. But that we may not learn to set too small a Value on the tragic Genius, by imagining, that every little Smatterer can, with such Delicacy, touch the human Heart; know, none but that Genius, who comes next to Shakespeare's self, cou'd draw so fine a Stroke. It was Otway altered it. Compare the Tomb Scene in *Romeo and Juliet* with that in *Caius Marius*, which is but another Alteration of the same Play, and there you will find this noble Incident, and the very Words of the whole Scene, with very little Alteration.

The attack was vicious and completely in error. Anyone who took the time in the eighteenth century (or anyone who takes the time today) to compare Otway's and Garrick's scenes as Morgan suggested, would find that it was

Garrick who was responsible for the dramatic effectiveness of the scene. The rewriting—except for the borrowing of a few lines from Otway—is original with Garrick.

Garrick was incensed by Morgan's attack. He answered the charge of plagiarism in his introductory remarks to the edition of 1753:

> Mr. Otway in his *Caius Marius,* a Tragedy taken from *Romeo and Juliet,* has made use of this affecting Circumstance, but it is a matter of Wonder that so great a dramatic Genius did not work up a Scene from it of more Nature, Terror and Distress—Such a Scene was attempted at the Revival of this Play, and it is hop'd, that an Endeavour to supply the failure of so great a Master will not be deem'd arrogant, or the making use of two or three of his Introductory Lines, be accounted a Plagiarism.

He continued his remarks in an ironic tone, which one must admit, admirably succeeded in turning the tables on Morgan:

> The Persons who from their great Good-nature and Love of Justice have endeavour'd to take away from the present Editor the little Merit of this Scene by ascribing it to Otway, have unwittingly, from the Nature of the Accusation, paid him a Compliment which he believes they never intended him.

Garrick also carefully protected himself against the charge of plagiarism. In the first two editions of his adaptation he had, indeed, used a few more than two or three of Otway's introductory lines for his new scene.

The scene begins when Romeo drinks from the vial of poison. Shakespeare's lines are rearranged as a prelude to Juliet's awakening:

> [ROM.] No more—here's to my love—eyes, look your last;
> Arms, take your last embrace; and Lips, do you
> The doors of breath seal with a righteous kiss.—

There follow sixty-seven lines which comprise Garrick's revision. Several of them, at the beginning, come comletely from Otway or closely parallel lines from *Caius Marius.*

Garrick:

> [ROM.] Soft—soft—she breathes, and stirs!
> [Juliet *wakes.*
>
> JUL. Where am I? defend me, powers!
>
> ROM. She speaks, she lives; and we shall still be bless'd!

Otway:

> [MAR. JUN.] She breaths and stirs.—
> [Lavinia *wakes.*
> *Lavin. in the Tomb.* Where am I? bless me, Heav'n!
> 'Tis very cold: and yet here's something warm—
> *Mar. jun.* She lives, and we shall both be made immortall.

Lavinia's line, " 'Tis very cold: and yet here's something warm," is faintly echoed a few lines later in Garrick's scene when Juliet awakens a bit more saying, "Bless me!

how cold it is! who's there!" These may be the two or three introductory lines to which Garrick referred.

But there are a few more borrowings. Juliet, still not fully conscious, does not recognize Romeo. She mistakes him for her father, and as Romeo "brings her from the tomb" (according to the stage direction in Garrick's version), several more echoes of Otway are heard.

Garrick:

> JUL. Why do you force me so—I'll ne'er consent—
> My strength may fail me, but my will's unmov'd,—
> I'll not wed *Paris,—Romeo* is my husband—

Otway:

> [LAVIN.] What have they done with me? I'll not be used thus?
> I'll not wed *Sylla. Marius* is my Husband.

However, the most complete and direct borrowing from Otway is yet to come. In the first two editions of his version, when Juliet finally recognizes Romeo, Garrick provided Juliet with three very beautiful lines:

> Had'st thou not come, sure I had slept for ever;
> But there's a sovereign charm in thy embraces
> That can revive the dead.

They were written for Lavinia by Otway:

> Hadst thou not come, sure I had slept for ever.
> But there's a sovereign Charm in thy embraces
> That might do Wonders, and revive the Dead.

One can understand why Garrick lifted these lines of Lavinia's for his own Juliet; but he certainly must have feared that they would be used against him as evidence of plagiarism. The three lines were removed from his third edition which was printed after Morgan's attack. They do not appear in any of the subsequent editions of Garrick's version of *Romeo and Juliet* which I have examined. Thus did Garrick strengthen his assertion that he borrowed only a few introductory lines from Otway.

He had no need to be so defensive. Even in the first two editions borrowings from Otway number, at most, nine of the sixty-seven lines which comprise his new scene. He reduced that number to six in 1753.

Most critics gave Garrick the credit he deserved. Francis Gentleman wrote: "The whole dying scene does Mr. Garrick great credit as being worthy the matchless author he has furnished it to." Thomas Davies said that the scene had been written "with a spirit not unworthy of Shakespeare himself;" and Arthur Murphy was lyrical in his praise. In a comparison of Garrick's and Otway's final scenes, he wrote:

> Garrick, beyond all question, has shewn superior skill. He rouzes a variety of passions; we are transported with joy, surprise, and rapture, and, by a rapid change, we are suddenly overwhelmed with despair, and grief, and pity. Every word pierces to the heart, and the catastrophe as it now stands, is the most affecting in the whole compass of the drama.

Garrick's version of *Romeo and Juliet* presented a dramatically effective treatment of Juliet's awakening scene, and it was his "Knowledge of the Stage" which enabled him to do it. In the eighteenth century, the tomb scene was thought to be Garrick's finest contribution to Shakespeare's play. It has evoked praise from admirers of Shakespeare even to the present time. Garrick's lines may not be completely worthy of Shakespeare; but the impact of his scene is.

Shakespeare's own knowledge of the stage makes it seem probable that had he been familiar with the version of the legend which told the story that way, Shakespeare himself could not have resisted the chance to dramatize the star-crossed lovers' final meeting. But Shakespeare did not write the scene; and Otway wrote it without distinction; but Garrick wrote it passing well. (pp. 32-5)

> *Don Rintz, "Garrick's 'Protective Reaction' to a Charge of Plagiarism," in* Restoration and 18th Century Theatre Research, *Vol. XIV, No. 1, May, 1975, pp. 31-5, 50.*

George Winchester Stone, Jr. and George M. Kahrl (essay date 1979)

[*American educators and literary critics, Stone and Kahrl specialize in studies of eighteenth-century literature. In the following excerpt from their critical biography of Garrick, they examine common elements in Garrick's original dramatic works.*]

From Garrick's own plays, from his adaptations both in comedy and tragedy, and from his statements in correspondence with playwrights one sees developing a handful of common denominators which reveal his guiding principles in playwriting. His cardinal one (and doubtless the basis for the success of his plays and adaptations) derives from the inextricable combination in him of playwright *and* actor. Aesthetic effectiveness of drama for him (as distinct from the novel, say) flowered only when it was acted on stage before audiences. Excellent acting he thought could bring words to life, and present events to thrill in tragedy, amuse in comedy, or throw the house into an uproar with farce. He wanted, as he wrote to Baron Grimm, to leave actors something to do. Grimm, in turn, thought Garrick "perfected his great talents by a profound study of human nature, and by researches full of shrewdness and broadness of thought." Observation from mingling with London's crowd, was reinforced often by note taking of details at various ceremonies, where he gained copy bound to come out after passing through the alembic of his imagination into a piece for the stage. "Mr. Garrick was on Monday morning last in the Chapel to see the Installation, and at night at the opera house at the ball, in both which places he seemed very attentive to what was going forward, particularly in the former, as he took notes. So that from the indefatigible attention of that manager to lay before the public everything that is curious, we may expect to be presented . . . with a full and true account of the Installation of the Knights of the Bath." To alertness for copy, Garrick in writing also kept in mind the capacities of his fellow actors to carry off the unique qualities of the characters he sketched. Evidence comes occasionally from manuscripts submitted to the Lord Chamberlain for licensing, where at times actor's names appear instead of character names appearing in the later printed texts.

All studies of his plays have taken care to point out the sources from which he worked, often with elation over discovery of the seed plot in a continental piece, and accounting him heavily derivative. What he did with the materials at hand, however, was not only what counted, but what marks his creativity in refashioning, the distant and the old. His friend Thomas Warton reminds us of the sort of "malicious triumph one feels in detecting the latent and obscure source from whence an original author has drawn some celebrated descriptions; yet this," he continues, "soon gives way to the rapture that results from contemplating the Chymical energy of true genius which can produce so noble a transmutation."

All in all, however, Garrick showed major concern for an actively moving plot (clear enough for audiences to follow), for sparkling dialogue, for hints in the dialogue for potential characterization (which the actor's art could make effective), for a confluence of people and events at the close to bring about exciting curtain, for a healthy self-spoofing again and again (tucked away almost as a signature in his farces), for touches of contemporary relevance (topical and cheering), and for basic morality.

Ample evidence relating to the first four of his guidelines: plot, character, topical reference, and dialogue has appeared in the discussion of his several plays. A word more about curtain effectiveness in his merging of characters and events, about his self-spoofing signature, and about his principles of basic morality.

Garrick the player, the reader of many plays, the writer of many others, and the manager interested in exciting curtain scenes which would entice the return of audiences repeatedly, saw to it that his farces, entertainments, and adaptations showed a confluence of all threads of action, and a convergence of all parties for the final curtain. The convention was, to be sure, time honored. His French sources did this sort of thing brilliantly. But no characters of Garrick's casts left the theatre for lodgings or the tavern early. He constructed his plays so that everyone counted, and counted in a finale. They were not only there for the country dance and the bow at the close, but nearly always had a speaking part in the finish. Sharp, Kitty, Melissa, Gayless, Justice Guttle, Mrs Gadabout, Beau and Mrs Trippet, daughters and servants cry out in chorus at the end of *The Lying Valet,* "A dance!" "By all means," agrees the hungry Justice Guttle—"but after supper!" Fourteen characters make up the cast of *The Clandestine Marriage,* including a maid and a chambermaid. Twelve of them have speaking parts right up to the drop of the curtain, and so it goes with *May Day, Bon Ton, The Guardian* and Garrick's others. No use to labor the point, but Garrick the writer was Garrick the actor, *and* Garrick the manager all in one. If as manager he was forcing rehearsals (as indeed he did) and doing all he could to emphasize ensemble performance with full and interested participation by all hands throughout each piece (as indeed he did), he was writing to give opportunity for each actor to stay with the ensemble till the end.

A personal signature (runes for Cynewulf, a tail and bob rhyme for the Townly Dramatist, a self-portrait of the artist among the angels, Hitchcock's appearance somewhere in a crowd in all his motion pictures) has been traditional in all branches of art. Garrick's hidden signature in his own plays (so many of which were published anonymously) turns up in a line or comment which anticipates and disarms criticism of the author by tossing a shaft of silvery laughter at David Garrick the manager or the actor—small in stature. He had used the device in forms other than dramatic, as we know—as early as 1744 poking fun at himself in **"An Essay upon Acting,"** and again in 1765 in his fable of *The Sick Monkey*—but there "testing, just testing," as a microphone operator might say.

Examples: In Garrick's *Peep Behind the Curtain* (1767) lover Wilson devises a ruse to enter the theatre in order to snatch Miss Fuz from her stage-struck mother, who is watching a rehearsal.

> MARVIN: But how will you gain entrance to Drury Lane?

> WILSON: I was near being disappointed there, for unluckily the acting manager, *who scarce reached my third button,* cocked up his head in my face and said I was too small for a hero . . .

In *The Jubilee* one asks—"The Steward—have you seen him, Ralph?"

> RALPH: Yes I ha' seen him—not much to be seen tho'. . . . He's not so big as I, but a great deal plumper—he's old enough to be wiser too.

In *The Meeting of the Company* Bayes tells Weston that by use of his "equalizing" formula he shall be both hero and fine gentleman, "and you won't be the first 'little man' who has tried to be both."

Possibly this iteration was a defense of sorts, subconsciously marking an insecurity in the extrovert, but it appears generally in such professional and sophisticated form that one is inclined not to attribute a substratum of despair to it. The custom of "puffing" a play, a performance, or an actor was common. Garrick followed this practice, but occasionally used this device of what one might call the "anti-puff" with amusing effectiveness.

A final common denominator, which indeed says something about Garrick the man as well as the professional dramatist is a constant turn of phrase in his plays about moral action. He knew how to titillate, understood the pleasures of mild shock in the risqué and the ribald, from the wealth of Restoration plays handed down to him, but found a new theatrical value in supporting the change in moral practices of his time. His plays as a whole and in their several parts emphasize moral improvement in men and manners. Considerable initiative seems to be present in his treatment. Perhaps he was but following a similar trend in all the arts of the late eighteenth century, yet many commended him for walking arm in arm with a movement for uplifting the tone of the community. Some even felt he was breaking ground and taking the lead as a creative dramatist, as a producer, and as a person whose private life seemed exemplary.

Garrick corresponded with 41 clergymen during his professional years, including the archbishops of Canterbury and York, eight bishops and two deans. The Anglican clergy were deeply interested in the cultural movements of the period, and Garrick sensed the value of their approval of his writings. Staunch polemicists such as William Warburton credited Garrick with more than a modicum of leadership in the movement: "I honour you for your repeated endeavours in stemming the torrent of vice and folly. You do it in a station where most men, I suppose, would think you might fairly be dispensed with from bearing your part in the duty of a good citizen on such a necessary occasion; but it is for this very thing I chiefly honour you."

The situations Garrick sets up in his plots, and the dialogue by which he communicates them are racy, occasionally risqué, but not licentious or obscene. Generally so sprightly is his dialogue that what might become vapid and preachily insipid escapes such clogs. The movement to improve men and morals began long before Garrick appeared. General identification of aesthetics with moral behavior, stemming from the Greeks, was freshened by Addision in the *Spectator* papers (1711). Moralism in drama moved into the obvious utilitarian category in somewhat heavy-footed fashion with George Lillo, while Garrick was still a schoolboy in Lichfield. "The more extensively useful the moral of a tragedy," wrote Lillo, "the more excellent that piece must be of its kind." Garrick, probably by conviction, certainly by business instinct, and flattered by the comments of the clergy, bestrode this horse and rode it consistently.

In his **"Advertisements"** to editions to *The Country Girl* and *The Chances* Garrick spoke to the point, reflecting the social atmosphere within which he worked. Of *The Chances,* "Should the play in its present state be thought a more decent entertainment, it is all the merit claimed from these necessary though slight additions and alterations." The play as he adapted it looks back through the Duke of Buckingham's text to the original base in Fletcher's play. It clears the text of some "exceptionable passages" from Buckingham, omits lines directly referring to the Deity (perhaps as a bow to his clerical friends), and underscores the change in character wrought in Don John by tagging on some final lines: "My former vanities are past and gone / Now I change the wild wanton for the sober plan / And like my friend become a moral man."

For *The Country Girl* (his adaptation of Wycherley's *The Country Wife*) Garrick explained, "Though nearly half . . . is new written, the Alterer claims no merit but his endeavour to clear one of our most celebrated comedies from immorality and obscenity." By excising Horner, the Fidgets, and Squeamishes he unloaded most of what was perceived at the time as the super-charged immorality of Wycherley. Margery Pinchwife became Garrick's Peggy Thrift, whose guardian Jack Moody gives out that they are married to prevent assaults upon her virtue. Pace picks up in the streamlining of Wycherley's movement and the reduction of his cast of 14 to Garrick's of seven. Attitude changes as the old central "cuckold" theme shifts to a traditional triangle one. At the play's end Moody becomes an about-to-be husband, so instead of provoking a guffaw at Pinchwife's new-cut horns the conclusion brings off a romantic climax in which two young lovers are united at the expense of a jealous old man. Garrick rewrote the play (his fullest alteration of an older one) to bring out a new young actress Miss Ann Reynolds (Peggy), and to advance the fortunes of young Samuel Cautherly (Belville). It had a season's success, running 13 times, including a "Command," and a "Benefit" performance. Public reaction showed not only in the box office, but in the pages of *The Critical Review* (November, 1766), "It must . . . be allow'd that the writer of *The Country Girl* has considerably improved on his original in the concentration of the fable; not only converting the libidinous Horner into the modest Mr. Belville, but by dissolving the marriage between Margery Pinchwife, and representing his heroine as a simple spinster." Garrick in no sense pandered to public taste. From his position of power, and from good conscience he subtly molded it.

But Garrick's professional approach, even where morality and theological overtones were involved, always considered three elements—the probability of stage success for the *text* (either a fresh-created one, or an old one to revive), *capabilities* of his actors, and the pulse of probable *audience response*. On the very point under discussion—the moral impact of plays—comparison of *The Country Girl* (revived for particular circumstances prevailing in his company in 1766) with Garrick's adaptation a decade earlier of James Shirley's *The Gamester* is apposite. The blandness of the former, suiting the young performers of the main roles and agreeable to the audience, differs considerably from the dark ironies of the latter, in which Garrick himself played Wilding. He knew that he in his acting could control the results of performing the old "bed trick," and could handle the psychological revenge which his stage wife sets up for him (the cuckold theme not minimized but made imaginary). At the same time he could ridicule in the brittle "comedy of manners" style the contemporary 1757 scene in the tavern sequences of the Old Barnacle subplot. Barnacle wants his sheepish nephew to gain the reputation of a contemporary "blade" of gentlemanly distinction, hence pays to have him beaten in a brawl. "Blades" he believes "roar in brothels, break windows, swear dammes to pay their debts, and march like walking armaries, with poiniards, pistols, rapiers and batons, as though they would murder all the King's people, and blow down the streets." The play as Garrick adapted it, remains tough, a farcical piece of social satire. All comes clean in the end when Wilding reforms:

> The Syren's voice shall charm my ear no more,
> With joy I quit that treacherous or fatal shore
> Where a friend's ruin is by friends enjoyed,
> And every virtue is by turns destroyed!

Garrick had sought in his prologue to remind the audience that the piece came straight from the English, not the French, tradition, painting "English manners, Englishmen." But some hissing had occurred on the first night. Somewhat disturbed Garrick sent the play to Warburton for comment. Warburton seeing a tough morality in it approved the piece. He accounted for the hissing: "It was not the virtue of the audience which took offense at a supposed adultery; it was not their vice which was disappointed when they saw none committed; it was their vanity which was shocked, in finding themselves outwitted by the poet. They had sat long enough in their suspense to be secure in their sagacity, that Wilding had been really cuckolded; and to find themselves mistaken at the last, was enough to put them out of humour."

Garrick in these matters was professional but not a prude. He experimented both with his own texts and with his adaptations, thus testing the limits of public taste. His *Lilliput* received a bad review, . . . seeming to put into the mouths of children (who played the parts) "immoral sentiments and sophisticated frippery." That petite afterpiece

is more subtle than the critic for the *Theatrical Examiner* found it. Garrick tweaked lots of noses therein, and its run was well-accepted. Garrick likewise saw the "brawniness" of Wycherley, so revived *The Plain Dealer,* having asked Isaac Bickerstaff to trim it for the stage. Even with Bickerstaff's excisions of speeches and reduction of the obvious sensuality of the Olivia-Manly-Fidelia triangle, the strict moralists in London protested. But the public at the box office paid scant attention to the protesters.

"If the Wantons of Charles's days," wrote Garrick in his advertisement to *The Country Girl,* "is now so reclaimed as to become innocent without being insipid, the present editor will not think his time ill employed" in adding variety to the entertainment of the public. The heart of the matter, Garrick was then convinced, lay in the "absolute necessity for *reforming* many plays of our most eminent writers; for no kind of wit ought to be received as an excuse for immorality, nay it becomes still more dangerous in proportion as it is more witty. Without such reformation our English comedies must be reduced to a very small number and would pall by too frequent repetition or what is worse continue shameless in spite of public disapprobation." And such sentiments were just what the public wanted to hear and read.

Moral influence comes through so patently in flashes of Garrick dialogue, in prologue, epilogue, and advertisement, that one may wonder a bit whether a certain ambivalence might not be present in the seeming iterative overkill. Many a remark is capable of being benignly spoofed by a look, a wink, an intonation in the acting. But as Garrick was a man of his times, not of ours, no call appears to re-create him in the image of another age. Yet one recalls Sharp's line, "Oh the delights of impudence and a good understanding!" as basic to Garrick's own character. The temptation is great to grant Garrick, the professional Garrick, the possibility, which sophisticated men of all times have seized upon, of playing both sides of the street, occasionally, to please composite audiences. The thought has its appeal, but the evidences for moral action are indeed deeply embedded in his texts. Garrick the actor saw, as he wrote or adapted, the effective way of turning seeds and sketches into agreeable interpretations. (pp. 282-89)

> *George Winchester Stone, Jr. and George M. Kahrl, in their* David Garrick: A Critical Biography, *Southern Illinois University Press, 1979, 771 p.*

Helen R. Smith   (essay date 1979)

[*In the excerpt below, Smith provides a succinct overview of Garrick's best-known original dramatic works.*]

The author of some twenty-two new plays, in addition to adaptations and a great deal of light occasional verse, Garrick has no great claim to literary originality: he wrote to a required formula to serve an immediate need.

He did not usually invent the plots for his plays. As manager he accurately anticipated what new pieces were needed each season and what would suit his audiences. Most of his plays are afterpieces, the two-act light comedies which followed the full five-act mainpiece on each day's playbill. These lasted less well and a considerable number were needed each season. Garrick, helped no doubt by his

Engraved invitation to Garrick's funeral at Westminster Abbey.

Huguenot descent, read French fluently and turned to contemporary dramatists in Paris for suitable ideas for plots, although his characters are entirely English. His afterpieces, like *The Lying Valet, Miss in her Teens,* and the rather sentimental *The Guardian,* are lively comedies of situation and character, containing a fair amount of social satire, and were usually well received, whether or not Garrick played in them himself.

His best-known play, the five-act *The Clandestine Marriage,* is one of the few plays in the century to approach the standard of Goldsmith's and Sheridan's great comedies and it is still occasionally performed. As it was written in collaboration with George Colman, each author deserves some of the credit for the play's great success. Disputes about their respective contributions have been largely settled by an examination of the surviving manuscript in the Folger Shakespeare Library, which shows that Garrick wrote at least half the play, most materially the scenes involving the ridiculous Lord Ogleby, and generally tightened the construction [see excerpt dated 1952]. The old fop, brilliantly characterized by Thomas King in the original production, was the one part which at the end of his career Garrick wished he himself had played. It is generally assumed that this time Garrick invented the basic plot, and it was considered original and amusing enough to form the basis for Cimarosa's lively opera *Il matrimonio segreto* in 1792. Compared with Lord Ogleby, however,

the opera's oddly named Count Robinson is a disappointing figure.

Other plays of Garrick's were written merely as vehicles for the display of the scenery, costumes, singing, dancing and special effects expected of a Christmas entertainment. *Lilliput,* written for a company of children in 1756, *Cymon,* and *A Christmas Tale,* are examples of this type of work; the third proving the vehicle for one of the most magnificent achievements of the great theatrical painter, de Loutherbourg. It is difficult now to imagine that their vapid plots and thin verse were very entertaining; but the first two survived with alterations into the nineteenth century, and *Cymon* was remembered well enough to be considered worth burlesquing by J. R. Planché as late as 1850.

These plays contain a great deal of music, and although Garrick himself had no ear, he possessed a happy facility in writing rhythmical and melodious verses which he was prepared to pay the best contemporary composers, Arne, Boyce, and Dibdin to set, and which became popular songs. **"Heart of oak,"** inserted into his spectacular *Harlequin's Invasion* (which shows Shakespeare triumphing over Harlequin), is perhaps his most widely known work, although not many people today remember who wrote the words for William Boyce.

Garrick's greatest claim to literary excellence comes from his many theatrical prologues and epilogues. He wrote other topical verse, one piece of which, **"To Mr. Gray on his Odes,"** was actually printed in a limited edition on Horace Walpole's private press at Strawberry Hill; there are also longer satires, but he knew his audiences well, and his lively wit and facility in couplets were ideally suited to charming and cajoling them into the right mood. (pp. 43-8)

> *Helen R. Smith, in her* David Garrick, 1717-1779: A Brief Account, *The British Library, 1979, 80 p.*

Jeffrey Lawson Laurence Johnson   (essay date 1983)

[*In the excerpt below, Johnson examines Garrick's alteration of* Hamlet, *commending him for retaining the dramatic character of the tragedy.*]

From 1743, when he began to manage Drury Lane, until 1763, when he took his extended grand tour, Garrick had the precedent of previous playwrights to plead for his alterations of Shakespeare's plays. However, whereas Davenant, Dryden, and others added lines, Garrick cut them to provide space for explosively emotional visual additions of his own creation. Garrick trusted his unique acting style, combining elaborate pantomime with rapid stage movement, to add psychological depth to character. Although a dreadful playwright by the standards of any century, Aaron Hill, in *The Art of Acting* (1753), sums up the visual quality of Garrick's style:

> To act a passion well, the actor never must attempt its imitation, 'til his fancy has conceived so strong an image, or idea, of it, as to move the same impressive springs within his mind, which form that passion, when 'tis undesigned, and natural.

It was this type of psychological development Garrick felt was missing in most modern tragedy and in Thomas Sheridan's elocutionary style. What delighted him about Shakespeare's works was that in play after play, Shakespeare wrote speeches and soliloquies that show interesting and unique minds at work. Writing to Sir John Hussey Delaval, Garrick waxed enthusiastic on the performing of Shakespeare's soliloquies: "In the Speaking of Soliloquys, the great art is to give variety, & which can only be obtain'd by a strict regard to the pauses—the running the different parts of a monologue together, will necessarily give a monotony & take away yet spirit and Sense of ye Author." These moments of silence on stage gave Garrick time to create what he felt the most necessary part of an actor's art: the visual association of the ideas that produced the character's formal speeches. . . . So, on those occasions when Garrick found Shakespeare writing long speeches relating events that happened offstage, he had no qualms about cutting them. Probably because of its narrative quality, for example, Garrick cut Gertrude's eighteen-line speech on the death of Ophelia. After cutting such long narrative speeches, Garrick created a fast-moving plot centered on characters in a sequence of dramatic conflicts.

Because of its excessive length, *Hamlet* had been a problem from the opening of the theatres in 1660. All of the Restoration quartos consulted print the following statement or a variant of it:

> This Play being too long to be conveniently Acted, such places as might be least prejudicial to the Plot or Sense, are left out upon the Stage: but that we may no way wrong the incomparable Author, are here inserted according to the Original Copy with this mark

(pp. 15-16)

Garrick's alteration of *Hamlet* is no mere digested version, however. The playing script demonstrates his sensitivity to dramatic character and its expression in acting that reveals psychological complexity. He restores over six hundred lines in the first three acts of the play. Generally, these lines are reinstated to give characters time to react and to provide proper motivations for their reactions. In earlier versions, the Player's speech concerning Pyrrhus and Priam had been cut extensively: Garrick restores some twenty lines to the speech. Stone and Kahrl note that Garrick's restoration gives some point to Polonius' "This is too long." However, the whole simile on Illium, in both the Davenant and the Wilks-Hughs versions, does give a clear verbal cue to Polonius' expression of exasperated boredom. Significantly, most of the twenty lines Garrick reinstates center around Hecuba, stressing the Queen's reaction to the murder of Priam. These added lines present Hamlet with a shocking comparison between the actions of Hecuba and Gertrude. Also, they provide Garrick sufficient time to create a pantomime of enough emotional depth to give probability to the soliloquy, "O what a rogue and peasant slave am I." Like Garrick, Francis Gentleman realized that the Player's speeches on Pyrrhus and Priam

> are meant to realize the characters of the main action, are evidently proposed as a contrast of fiction to what it is necessary the audience should think is truth. At the beginning of the soliloquy which concludes the second act, Hamlet gives himself force and reality by alluding to the Player's fictitious feeling, compared with his own substantial cause for grief.

Actually, the "O what a rogue and peasant slave am I" soliloquy concludes Act III of the Garrick version and is meant to balance the "How all occasions do inform against me" soliloquy, which Garrick restored to Act V, and which was heard for the first time in production since the closing of the theatres. Both of these soliloquies feature, as Gentleman notes, "the breaks and pauses, such as occur in *Hamlet, Lear, Macbeth,* and other plays of Shakespeare. . . . They not only give variation to voice, but also agreeable transition to the features." The "O what a rogue and peasant slave" soliloquy, after winding through an emotional labyrinth, ends in Hamlet's resolution to create "The Mousetrap." "How all occasions do inform against me," set against a backdrop of military preparations, leads to the final deadly confrontation between Hamlet and Claudius.

Act IV of Garrick's *Hamlet* ends with the long scene between Hamlet and his mother. As indicated by the restorations that Garrick made to the Player's speech on Hecuba, Garrick felt Hamlet's love for his father and despair over his mother were the core motivations for most of the young prince's behavior. Garrick's emphasis on Hamlet's filial nature is clearly shown in Georg Christoph Lichtenberg's account of the excellent soliloquy: "O that this too, too solid flesh would melt." Garrick is completely overcome by tears of grief, felt with only too good cause, for a virtuous father and on account of light-minded mother, who not only wears no mourning, but feels no sorrow, at a time when all toadies should be wearing black; tears which flow all the more unrestrainedly, perhaps, since they are the sole relief of an upright heart in such a conflict of warring duties.

Indeed, Garrick felt the only confrontation between Hamlet, Gertrude, and the Ghost such a dramatic highlight that he included it in *The Jubilee,* his afterpiece celebrating the glory of Shakespeare:

> Hamlet in ye Closet Scene follow
> Queen ye Ghost in Horror.

Garrick's concern for Gertrude as a capital character and his desire to resolve the conflict between the prince and his mother lead him to introduce the following revised addition at the end of *Hamlet:*

> HAMLET: Where is the wretched Queen
> (Enter Messenger.)
>
> MESSENGER: Struck with the horror of the scene, she fled—
> But 'ere she reach'd her chamber door, she fell
> Intranc'd and motionless—unable to sustain
> The Load of Agony and Sorrow.
>
> HAMLET: O my Horatio—watch the wretched Queen;
> When from this trance she wakes—O may she
> breathe an hour of Penitence, 'ere Madness ends her.

Garrick's verse, though not in Shakespeare's manner, effectively satisfies eighteenth-century notions of poetic justice. Furthermore, it points up the actress who has just left the scene and reveals the ensemble nature of the plays that Garrick, as actor-manager, staged at Drury Lane.

Garrick's condensation of Acts IV and V would run for about thirty minutes on stage. In contrast, Acts IV and V of *Hamlet,* on PBS' *The Shakespeare Plays,* ran for nearly two hours. In *The Dramatic Censor,* Francis Gentleman complimented Shakespeare on the great number of his major parts: "Shakespeare, in all his pieces, seems to have had great regard to his capital characters." This is certainly proved true by the seven major figures in the last two acts of *Hamlet:* Hamlet, Claudius, Laertes, Gertrude, the Grave-Diggers, and Osric. Two hours' traffic on the stage may carry seven major figures, but thirty minutes will not support even half that number. Therefore, Garrick cut some characters and condensed the parts of others. In the case of Laertes, he was aided by general acting traditions, for the scene between Claudius and Laertes in which they plot the death of Hamlet had been greatly cut in all previous acting versions of *Hamlet* and was generally disliked by critics. Garrick's elimination of the Claudius-Laertes scene was the least controversial change in his promptbook of *Hamlet.*

Now Garrick had a decapitalized Laertes and had been able to cut about a half an hour of stage time, but he had a new problem caused by his own views on acting. Because of his own critical and popular successes as Richard III,

Lothario, and Jaffeir, Garrick was convinced that audiences believed what they heard only when it was reinforced with simple clear action on the stage. However, Garrick had shown the audience no crime sufficient to justify Laertes' death at the end of the play. Betterton and Wilks had played Hamlet, and both had killed Laertes without compunction. But Garrick, whose sense of theatrical justice was as intense as Johnson's sense of moral justice, could not kill a nice young man with a newly dead father and a slightly mad sister. So the fencing match was out, and Garrick wrote a weak restoration-of-the-kingdom speech:

> HAMLET: O I die Horatio—but one thing more,
> O take this hand from me—unite your Virtues—
> (joins Horatio's hand to Laertes')
> To calm this troubled Land—I can no more
> Nor have I more to ask but mercy Heav'n (dies.)
>
> (pp. 16-18)

In his 1765 acting edition, Garrick had made one brief cut at the beginning of the Osric scene; but disliking topical humor in tragedy as much as he adored it in comedy, he soon gave up this character, aptly called by Gentleman "a fantastical mushroom." So with the elimination of the fencing match, Garrick could safely swat Shakespeare's waterfly, a character whose humor seemed more at home in the court of James I than that of George III. With a cut-out Osric, a weak, but morally correct Laertes, and a Gertrude who had already had her capital scene at the end of Act IV, Garrick was left with Hamlet, Ophelia, Claudius, and the Grave-Diggers. Although Johnson had criticized Shakespeare's conclusions in general, and at the conclusion of his *Tom Thumb* Fielding had lampooned the general blood bath in *Hamlet,* everyone liked the Grave-Diggers. In the "Preface" to his edition of Shakespeare, Johnson neatly sums up this universal approbation: "And the grave-diggers themselves may be heard with applause." Francis Gentleman, who disliked every other incident in Act V, liked the Grave-Diggers; and even Lichtenberg, whose admiration of Garrick verged on idolatry, condemned Garrick's most radical cut: "The grave diggers' scene is omitted. They retain it at Covent Garden. Garrick should not have done this." (p. 19)

For once, Garrick's desire for rapidity of plot (fable) and clarity and consistency of character came into headlong conflict with two of Shakespeare's most static and best loved comic characters. Garrick's performing version of Act V (Acts IV & V in Shakespeare) consists of ten clear visual sequences. Eight of these sequences center on the conflict between Hamlet and Claudius, with many of Claudius' lines restored to make him a more formidable adversary for Hamlet. Sequences six and eight center on the mad Ophelia, giving variety to the action and bringing a halt to a quickness of plot development that could seem melodramatic to the audience. The beginning of Garrick's Act V follows Shakespeare's Act IV with great care. Gertrude informs Claudius of Hamlet's murder of Polonius, and Claudius realizes that Hamlet meant to murder him: "It had been so with us, had we been there." Finally, the king withdraws in a state of mental confusion over Polonius' death and Hamlet's behavior. This short sequence of verbal action and visual reaction, in which through the actor's use of mime and stage movement the audience sees a character's mind at work, in this case that of the evil Claudius, is an example of the visual quality of Shakespeare's art Garrick most admired and what he wished most clearly to point up to his audience.

In the second sequence, Hamlet enters, has a brief interchange with Rosencranz and Guildenstern, observes their behavior, and properly reasons that they are fools and the King's toadies. The third sequence is a confrontation between Claudius and Hamlet over the death of Polonius and Hamlet's mad actions before the King. After this sequence Hamlet exits, leaving the stage to Claudius, who finally evolves a plan of action against Hamlet that is suitable to the King's malevolent nature:

> And England, if my present Love thou hold'st at aught
> Let it be testify'd in Hamlet's death
> O do it England—for like a Hectic in my Blood he rages,
> And thou must cure me.

The first four sequences of Garrick's Act V center around Claudius, and Claudius' dilemma over Hamlet, which is finally resolved at the end of section four. Claudius' character is developed quickly, but according to the pattern established in Shakespeare's original. First Claudius hears what Hamlet has done; then observes Hamlet's behavior; and finally, based on what he has just seen, resolves to put Hamlet to death.

For the climax Garrick restored Hamlet's soliloquy, "How all occasions do inform against me," now heard for the first time on the eighteenth-century London stage. To provide a proper visual lead in for this crucial speech, he allots a twenty-four line scene between Hamlet and Rosencranz and Guildenstern, allowing them time to describe the offstage army and Hamlet time to realize that this military fanfare informs against him. The longest individual speech in Act V, "How all occasions do inform against me," abounds in the pauses that Garrick so loved because they gave him many chances "to shift situations so often, that the eye can hardly have time to find out and dwell upon the defect [of his shortness of figure]." The speech shows a mind emotionally ranging, as it "thinks too precisely on the event," from calm deliberation ("What is a man / If his chief good and Market of his Time / Be but to sleep and feed") to sarcasm ("Rightly to be great / Is not to stir without great argument; / But greatly to find quarrel in a Straw, / When honor's at stake"). In the first twenty-six lines, the actor presumably used a variety of hand gestures: counting reasons, picking straws, dividing thoughts, and breaking egg-shells. Finally, the soliloquy shifts to self-recognition: "How stand I then that have a Father kill'd, / A Mother Stain'd." As Shakespeare wrote it, this is where Hamlet's soliloquy ends its emotional development: the original final line is, "My thoughts be bloody, or be nothing worth." This statement moves Hamlet back into a generalized mood of introspection. In Shakespeare's original this is dramatically acceptable because it has another act to run, wherein Hamlet will be exposed to the deceased Ophelia, a chop-fallen skull, the poisoned Queen, and a falling sparrow. But Garrick's Hamlet has only ten minutes of stage time left, so he must come to some resolve. In imitation of the Shakespearean pattern of resolution that concluded "O what a rogue and peasant slave am I," Garrick wrote Hamlet the following exit lines: "The Hour is come—I'll fly my Keepers—sweep to my revenge." Although not as quotable as "The play's the thing / Wherein I'll catch the conscience of the King," Garrick's lines stress to the audience that Hamlet's next

appearance will be sudden, bloody, and very theatrical. Also, they allow the actor to sweep grandly off the stage. Finally, they are a splendid example of "those probable Strokes of Art wch Ye first Poets make use of to reconcile strange Events to ye minds of an audience," which Garrick told Lord Bute were sadly lacking in Home's *Douglas.*

After this emotional peak and clear foreshadowing of the end of the play, the dramatic tension built up in the audience is relaxed in sequences six through eight, dealing with Ophelia and Laertes. Although he could have compressed Ophelia's mad scenes into one long frenzied section, as Ambroise Thomas did in his opera *Hamlet* (1868), Garrick gives Ophelia sequences six and eight in which to develop and refine her musical madness. In sequence six he allows Ophelia seventeen lines of introduction; and in sequence eight, Ophelia's last appearance in the play, Garrick adds special stage directions to prepare the audience for her reentry. He also gives Laertes, who had entered in sequence seven, six lines of reaction to her plight, thus reengaging the audience's sympathy for the rejected maid and allowing Mrs. Smith, the actress playing Ophelia, to move down center stage for her last scene. By centering the audience's attention on Ophelia and concentrating her action in the last act, Garrick has given his mad maiden an importance second only to that of Hamlet himself. If Lichtenberg's reaction to Ophelia is in any way typical, then Mrs. Smith owed much to her director, David Garrick: "She was played by Mrs. Smith, a young woman and good singer, who is admirably suited to the part. . . . The songs, which she sang charmingly, were fraught with such plaintive and tender melancholy that I fancied that I could still hear them far into the night when I was alone."

As mentioned earlier, Garrick, like Betterton, Wilks, and Davenant, had not capitalized Laertes' character. In Garrick's *Hamlet,* however, Polonius' son is no mere puppet to hold the sword Hamlet runs onto at the play's conclusion. Garrick restores eleven lines of introduction for Laertes that had never been performed in the eighteenth century, knowing that in the roar of offstage shouting, none of Laertes' speech would be clearly heard; the only thing the audience would understand clearly would be that the young man was coming on stage. Once Laertes is on stage, his character follows a consistent pattern carefully designed by Garrick. After hearing of his father's death, Laertes is won over by the king and decides to refer this matter to arbitration. In Shakespeare, these speeches occur after Laertes has seen his mad sister. Since the plotting scene is cut, Garrick thought this too cold a response to a father dead and a sister maddened, so he moved it to a point earlier in the action when Laertes was still at the listening stage of his character development. Throughout Ophelia's final mad scene, all of Laertes' lines indicate how much moved the brother is by his sister's plight.

After Ophelia's exit, Laertes has seen enough to be motivated for revenge, and the play suddenly leaps forward to its rapid conclusion. Sequences nine and ten begin Hamlet's sweep to his revenge, as the prince appears without warning during Laertes' rumination on what he has seen of Ophelia's suffering. Because of the visual power of Ophelia's madness, Laertes is ready for vengeance, and sequence nine ends with a very brief version of the scene in Shakespeare's *Hamlet* where Laertes and Hamlet bicker over the grave of Ophelia. Of course, in Garrick's version

Ophelia's grave is undug, and both men are fighting over a woman who is still very much alive, even if she is a bit balmy.

Sequence ten, the last thirty-six lines of Act V, is almost completely the work of David Garrick, and his autograph manuscript of the conclusion, in the Folger Library, indicates that he actually prepared two endings for his *Hamlet*. . . . In this first ending, after Hamlet kills the King, Gertrude screams "Hamlet, Hamlet," and swoons. In his death speech, Hamlet's "watch the wretched Queen" refers to her visibly recumbent body. The great advantage to Garrick's first ending is that it eliminates the Messenger, a pop-up figure worthy of a Tom Stoppard take-off. But there are a number of disadvantages to having Gertrude swoon. From a performer's point of view, a good actress could have so over-developed her swoon that it would have been as fatal to the ending of *Hamlet* as Laertes' sword is to the prince. Also, in an age of sensibility, some members of the audience fresh from a reading of Mackenzie's *Man of Feeling* (1771), at the time a best seller, might have felt the Queen had actually died of a broken heart.

Over the Queen's swoon speech Garrick wrote an "x"; and the "x" addition, consisting of one page 4½" by 6½", is pasted in front of Garrick's first ending. Combined with Garrick's first ending, this is the version printed by Stone in his 1931 article and recently reprinted by Stone and Kahrl in their biography of Garrick (1979); however, the fact that it is a merged version seems to have escaped critical attention until now. In the "x" version, Garrick's liberal use of "etc" shows that this was written after the fold-out version, and is, at the very least, Garrick's third ending to *Hamlet,* and his final thought on the matter. The Messenger, possibly a member of the court who has followed Gertrude off stage, appears and makes his awkward but short speech. As for the fate of Gertrude and the division of the kingdom, these lines satisfy Garrick's sense of dramatic unity, but because he had no Shakespearean model to go by, they do sound rather lame. The other lines I take to be mere verbal cues for the actors to do something visual. Given the emphasis that Garrick put on the relationship of Hamlet and Gertrude, I presume that in his rush to help his raving mother Hamlet literally runs into Laertes' drawn sword. This visual pattern would satisfy Garrick's sense of theatrical justice, for Laertes cannot kill Hamlet unless he is to die himself. Also, this would add a rather poignant irony that would be novel to an audience that had seen Hamlet over and over again. Thus, the recognition-and-surprise theme that Stone and Kahrl see as basic to Garrick's revivals of older plays would be evident at the conclusion of *Hamlet*. At all events, when the visual hurly-burly is done, instead of the bloody carnage mocked by Fielding and deplored by Gentleman the audience is presented with the dead King and dying Hamlet. The conflict that Garrick saw as basic to *Hamlet* has been resolved, and thanks to Garrick's design of verbal action leading to clear visual reaction the audience sees and feels this final resolution.

Considering the extreme rush of the end of Act V, it is small wonder Garrick felt Osric and the Grave-Diggers would break the audience's concentration, causing them to fail to perceive the character motivations he had worked so hard to clarify. Indeed, action and reaction are

the controlling principles of Garrick's Act V. Claudius observes Hamlet, Claudius decides what to do, Hamlet hears of Fortinbras' army, he comes to an immediate decision on what to do about the King. Garrick's ending is a carefully controlled turmoil meant to provoke an emotional frenzy in the audience. Whereas Betterton and Quin had relied on vocal beauty to enrich poetic speeches, Garrick felt that merit in an actor consisted in displaying visible motivations for accompanying verbal statements. Garrick's condensation of Acts IV and V shows his careful attention to the character consistency in Claudius, Ophelia, and Hamlet, which had previously been obscured in post-Restoration stage presentations. (pp. 19-23)

> *Jeffrey Lawson Laurence Johnson, "Sweeping up Shakespeare's 'Rubbish': Garrick's Condensation of Acts IV & V of 'Hamlet',"* in Eighteenth-Century Life, *n.s. Vol. VIII, No. 3, May, 1983, pp. 14-25.*

Linda R. Payne   (essay date 1986)

[*In the following excerpt, Payne examines the literary style of Garrick's song lyrics and their purpose within his adaptations of* A Midsummer Night's Dream, Anthony and Cleopatra, The Winter's Tale, *and* Romeo and Juliet.]

Although his theatrical reputation is what endures, in his own time Garrick was also known for his song lyrics, not only in the theater, but in the street, pub, and coffee house as well. For the theater alone, he composed lyrics to more than 106 songs for plays (his own or others), including ten primarily musical Garrick adaptations or original plays. Many of the lyrics were topical; they were often light, bantering, or satirical, and included love songs, drinking songs, pastorals, dirges, and epithalamia. He collaborated with the important English composers of his day, among them William Boyce, Thomas and Michael Arne, and John Christopher Smith, Jr. We might guess that Garrick put so much creative energy into the musical side of production not only because he wished to please his spectacle-hungry audience, but also because he considered music an intrinsic part of the dramatic effect he sought to achieve. This view is confirmed by a letter he wrote to his close friend, the music historian Dr. Charles Burney, referring to music as "that nice feeling of ye passions (without which everything in ye dramatic way will cease to entertain)."

Given his own general practise as well as the demand of public taste for music and dance, it is not surprising that Garrick provided additional music for those Shakespeare plays that he adapted. He based his contributions to the periodic examination with all-sung English opera on *A Midsummer Night's Dream* (*The Fairies,* 1755) and *The Tempest* (1756). In his landmark history, Burney could recollect "no English operas in which the dialogue was carried on in recitative, that were crowned with full success, except the *Fairies,* set by Mr. Smith in 1756, and *Artaxerxes,* by Dr. Arne in 1763."

Although Garrick followed the eighteenth-century tradition of interpolating new incidental songs into plays written by other playwrights, his additions were generally less wanton than the almost ludicrously unrelated bits of spectacle interrupting the course of many period plays. Biographers Stone and Kahrl say of his songs that "the intellectual content of many is slight, but one must bear in mind that the song quality depends on a context of music, play, and theatrical setting." A closer look at Garrick's incidental songs for the Shakespeare adaptations will illustrate his approaches to supplementing the play text, as well as the relationship between the success of the song and the success of Garrick's characterization and fidelity to Shakespeare.

The second edition (1758) of Garrick's adaptation of *Antony and Cleopatra* included a page of verse, headed with the note, "The Song at p. 39, being thought too short, an addition was made to it while the play was in rehearsal, and it is as follows." The song that follows has two stanzas of six lines each, an expansion of Shakespeare's one-stanza, six-line "Come, thou monarch of the vine." This provides the only example of Garrick's words mixed with Shakespeare's within the same song. Shakespeare's lines are these:

> Come, thou monarch of the vine,
> Plumpy Bacchus with pine eyne!
> In thy vats our cares be drowned,
> With thy grapes our hairs be crowned.
> Cup us, 'till the world go round,
> Cup us, 'till the world go round!

Garrick did not merely append additional lines to the poem, but instead arranged his new and expanded version to exploit Shakespeare's rhyme and motif in the best way possible:

> Come, thou monarch of the vine,
> plumpy *Bacchus*, with pink eyne;
> thine it is to cheer the soul,
> made, by thy enlarging bowl,
> free from wisdom's fond control,
> free from wisdom's fond control.
>
> Monarch, come; and with thee bring
> tipsy dance, and revelling.
> In thy vats our cares be drowned;
> with thy grapes our hairs be crowned;
> cup us 'till the world go round.
> cup us 'till the world go round.

Garrick's couplets in trochaic tetrameter follow Shakespeare's quite faithfully both in rhythm and diction. The main stylistic difference is found in the syntax: Shakespeare's couplets are all closed, while Garrick includes an open couplet in each verse to lead into the repeated refrain line. By preserving the rhythm, Garrick not only retained the flavor of the original, but also made it possible to use any extant musical setting by merely repeating the stanza. In 1750, Thomas Chilcot had written such a setting, which Garrick would have known about and had access to.

Despite their brevity, Garrick's six new lines demonstrate his goal of highlighting the work of Shakespeare rather than competing with it. This song is sung by Enobarbus during the scene aboard the ship, when Antony is reunited with Caesar and Lepidus. The scene is designed to underscore Antony's decay, and Garrick's lines 4-6 more blatantly state the case, foreshadowing Caesar's "Strong Enobarbe / Is weaker than the wine." The same lines heighten the justification for Caesar's disgust.

Similarly, for his 1756 adaptation of *The Winter's Tale,* Garrick wrote a song which was not only published with the play but printed with its music in *The London Magazine* (February 1756) and *Universal Magazine* (March 1756). In Garrick's alteration of the play, which had not been successfully produced in the century, the characterization of Perdita became perhaps the most essential element in the success of the three-act *Florizel and Perdita* as a "Dramatic Pastoral."

In order to shorten the play and maintain the unities (which the sixteen-year span of *The Winter's Tale* violates perhaps more outrageously than any other of Shakespeare's plays), Garrick cut much of the second half of the drama, knit the rest together with narrative exposition, and set it all in Bohemia. The sheepshearing event, therefore, becomes the key to the main action. (The Hermione plot is somewhat tacked onto the end, so as not to lose the dramatic potential of the episode of the statue's quickening.) The shortened format and lighter tone made the play suitable fare not only for a mainpiece but for an afterpiece as well, and even rival John Rich used it that way at Covent Garden.

As he often did, Garrick provided in the prologue to the play a rationale or apology for his strategies of adaptation. The entire prologue is an extended analogy featuring the dramatist as innkeeper (at the sign of "Shakespeare's Head"), with images of food and drink and many puns employed. Garrick claims to have altered the play in order to preserve it:

> Lest then this precious liquor run to waste,
> 'Tis now confined and bottled for your taste.
> 'Tis my chief wish, my joy, my only plan,
> To lose no drop of that immortal man!

This alteration received much criticism from the later bardolaters in the vein of Frank Hedgecock's quip in 1912, "A little more of Shakespeare's champagne and a little less of Garrick's gooseberry juice would have made a better mixture." However, Garrick's biographer and rival playwright Arthur Murphy provides us with the prevailing contemporary view, pronouncing Shakespeare's "business" to be so "complicated and heterogeneous," that the "strictest attention cannot find a clue to guide us through the maze." He judged that "Garrick saw that the public would be little obliged to him for a revival of the entire play, and therefore with great judgment, extracted from the chaos before him a clear and regular fable."

The sheepshearing had already been the focus of a brief musical afterpiece at Covent Garden, and Garrick wanted to make the lasting impression. To introduce the song, he added a line for the old shepherd: "Come, come, daughter, leave for a while these private dalliances and love-whisperings, clear up your pipes, and call, as custom is, our neighbors to your shearing." Perdita dutifully obeys. The following lyrics were then inserted into Garrick's published version of the play:

> Come, come, my good shepherds, our flock we must shear;
> In your holy-day suits, with your lasses appear.
> The happiest of folk are the guiltless and free,
> And who are so guiltless, so happy as we?
>
> We harbor no passions by luxury taught;
> We practice no arts with hypocrisy fraught;
> What we think in our hearts you may read in our eyes;

For, knowing no falsehood, we need no disguise.

By mode and caprice are the city dames led,
But we as the children of nature are bred;
By her hand alone we are painted and dressed;
For the roses will bloom when there's peace in the breast.

That giant, Ambition, we never can dread;
Our roofs are too low for so lofty a head;
Content and sweet cheerfulness open our door,
They smile with the simple and feed with the poor.

When love has possessed us, that love we reveal;
Like the flocks that we feed are the passions we feel;
So, harmless and simple, we sport and we play,
And leave to fine folks to deceive and betray.

Perdita's song reveals all the typical illogic of the pastoral form. The city is associated with "passions by luxury taught," with hypocrisy, "mode and caprice," and ambition. Country folk, on the other hand, are "guiltless and free" (the published song sheets read "guileless and free"), happy, content and sweet, and the companions of cheerfulness. Yet the central lovers turn out, of course, to be nobility disguised (Florizel) and undiscovered (Perdita). They leave the Edenic existence they have praised to live at court, where Perdita is to "put on / This novel garment of gentility, / And yield a patched behavior." Polixenes's line immediately following the song points up the paradox well: "This is the prettiest low-born lass that ever / Ran on the green-sord; nothing she does or seems / But smacks of something greater than herself, / Too noble for this place."

Garrick employs closed couplets in this song, grouping them this time in four-line stanzas. He writes in iambic tetrameter, which matches the meter of Shakespeare's "Lawn as white as driven snow," "Jog on, jog on," and "Get you hence," although Shakespeare had used a more interesting 4/3/4/3 stanza for "Will you buy any tape" and "But shall I go mourn for that, My dear." Shakespeare also varies his rhyme scheme between aabb couplets and an abab pattern. Garrick's syntax is sometimes a bit contorted, with unnaturally inverted word order. (pp. 165-70)

The sweetness and sentimental mood of the sheepshearing song, so suitable for the guileless Perdita, was of course familiar to the midcentury audience accustomed to "sentimental comedy." The strength of that sentiment no doubt enabled the song to stand alone as a "hit" apart from the comedy. It is obvious that the song is longer by far than any of Shakespeare's, and its twenty lines make it considerably longer than the lengthened version of **"Come, thou monarch."** The length also suggests that it was intended both to support dramatic characterization or motivation and to entertain independently. Dr. Johnson's cynicism about this song only highlights Garrick's sentiment and humanity. When Mrs. Thrale praised Garrick as a master of light, lively verse, she singled out the line, "I'd [*sic*] smile with the simple, and feed with the poor"; to which Johnson replied, "Nay, my dear Lady, this will never do. Poor David! Smile with the simple! What folly is that! And who would feed with the poor that can help it? No, no; let me smile with the wise and feed with the rich."

Yet many of those contemporary critics who disliked the adaptation spoke well of the song, as did actor and Garrick biographer Thomas Davies: "The sheep-shearing was

Another artistic rendition of Garrick as Richard III.

preserved, with a very pleasing song on the subject, which Mrs. Cibber, in the part of Perdita, sung with that sweet simplicity which became the character." What would have mattered most to Garrick, however, was that, according to Arthur Murphy, the line "The roses will bloom when there's peace in the breast" was "heard for a long time in every street in the metropolis."

The funeral dirge Garrick wrote for Juliet for his 1750 production of *Romeo and Juliet* may not have been sung in the streets, but it was continually sung in the theater into the next century. (p. 171)

Garrick's processional scene was still being performed by Kemble's company in Paris, and probably inspired a corresponding movement in Berlioz's *Romeo and Juliet*. It had apparently been dropped by 1878 when Fanny Kemble expressed pleasure at its demise. Yet she noted that even during her career the procession had been performed (c. 1830), although her description of the music seems to indicate that the dirge may have been supplanted by traditional funeral music more in keeping with that period. (p. 174)

In this case Garrick's song did not have to share the stage with Shakespeare's songs. The processional dirge is pompous and majestic, with the weighty lyrics contributing to the overall effect of the occasion. The new lyrics were appended to the end of the second printing by Tonson and Draper:

CHORUS

Rise, rise!
Heart-breaking sighs
The woe-fraught bosom swell;
For sighs alone,
And dismal moan,
Should echo *Juliet's* knell.

—AIR

She's gone—the sweetest flow'r of May,
That blooming blest our sight;
Those eyes which shone like breaking day,
Are set in endless night!

She's gone, she's gone, nor leaves behind
So fair a form, so pure a mind;
How could'st thou, Death, at once destroy,
The *Lover's* hope, the *Parent's* joy?

Thou spotless soul, look down below,
Our unfeign'd sorrow see;
O give us strength to bear our woe,
To bear the loss of Thee!

The strongly accented dimeter of three lines in the chorus, with which the procession begins and ends, lends the proper rhythmic quality to "*Juliet's* knell." The rhyme of the words "swell" and "knell" also accentuate the bell's tolling. The first and third verses have an even hymn stanza, 4/3/4/3, matched by an abab rhyme scheme. Garrick achieves variety, and also adds to the solemnity of the second, gravest verse, by rhyming it aabb in a weightier tetrameter quatrain.

Even in this formulaic setting, we again see character detailed through Garrick's lyrics. Juliet is "the sweetest flow'r of May," of fair form, pure mind, and spotless soul. In describing her eyes "which shone like breaking day" and are "set in endless night," Garrick picks up Shakespeare's dawn imagery. That first stanza, containing both the flower and dawn images, is also more lyrical than the others because of its alliteration as the flower "blooming blest our sight." The final verse is given added grandeur by its long vowel sounds. (pp. 175-76)

Still, we might wonder why someone interested in promoting "pure Shakespeare" would have made an opera out of *A Midsummer Night's Dream* or *The Tempest,* or why he would have felt compelled to write a funeral dirge for Juliet or a sheepshearing song for Perdita. Part, but not all of the answer lies in Garrick's intimate connection with the audience for whom he wrote and his uncanny ability to sense their pleasure. Yet, putting generations of theater fashion and of artistic and scholarly concern aside, Garrick was first an actor; therefore, for him the heart of drama was the human heart—and surely part of his love affair with Shakespeare was inspired by a sense of human as well as artistic kinship.

His devout study of characterization enabled him as an adaptor to retain the full intensity of Shakespeare's characters even in the shorter acting versions of the eighteenth century. A chief purpose of his songs, beyond adding the color and fun his audience craved, was to heighten characterization; through the interplay of music and lyric he could accomplish this economically and forcefully. Song

can reveal human emotion and touch human emotion, the essential chord Garrick strove to strike.

Prior to Fiske's work and the Stone-Kahrl biography, Garrick's musical contributions were generally too little noticed and too little valued. While there is little evidence about Garrick's interest in music away from the theater, he was certainly vitally concerned with the role of music in producing dramatic effects. In some respects, his music for the Shakespeare adaptations may give the best indication of what he felt that role should be, because we know the seriousness of his purpose in those adaptations went beyond mere entertainment. He approached the writing of lyrics as a playwright, striving for characterization and dramatic effect, more than as a poet fulfilling convention. These songs, all written within the period 1750-1763, both add to our picture of Garrick's developing writing skills and provide a new perspective from which to appreciate his treatment of "the God of his Idolatry." (pp. 177-80)

> *Linda R. Payne, "Garrick's Incidental Lyrics: Supplementing, Not Supplanting Shakespeare," in* Studies in Eighteenth-Century Culture, *Vol. 16, 1986, pp. 165-81.*

FURTHER READING

Babcock, Robert Witbeck. *The Genesis of Shakespeare Idolatry, 1766-1799: A Study in English Criticism of the Late Eighteenth Century.* Chapel Hill: University of North Carolina Press, 1931, 307 p.
> Scattered references to Garrick. Explores the burgeoning critical and popular interest in Shakespeare and his works during the late eighteenth century.

Barton, Margaret. *Garrick.* London: Faber & Faber, 1948, 324 p.
> General biography of the actor and playwright.

Beatty, Joseph M., Jr. "Garrick, Colman, and *The Clandestine Marriage.*" *Modern Language Notes* XXXVI, No. 3 (March 1921): 129-41.
> Argues that Colman was responsible for a majority of the plot of *The Clandestine Marriage,* while Garrick's main contribution was Act V.

Bergmann, Fred L. "Garrick's *Zara.*" *PMLA* LXXIV, No. 3 (June 1959): 225-32.
> Examines Garrick's treatment of text in his adaptation of Aaron Hill's *Zara,* which brought the play closer to its original source, Voltaire's *Zaire.*

Burnim, Kalman A. *David Garrick, Director.* Pittsburgh: University of Pittsburgh Press, 1961, 234 p.
> Discusses Garrick's direction of several plays, focusing on staging, props, and other managerial duties.

Copeland, Nancy. "The Source of Garrick's *Romeo and Juliet* Text." *English Language Notes* XXIV, No. 4 (June 1987): 27-33.
> Examines Garrick's adaptation of the tragedy, concluding that he based his version on Alexander Pope's text.

Cutts, John P. "Garrick's Use of Milton in His Version of *A Midsummer Night's Dream*." *Neuphilologische Mitteilungen* LXXX (1979): 78-80.

Concise discussion of Garrick's use of passages from John Milton's "L'Allegro" as bases for song lyrics in his operatic rendition of *A Midsummer Night's Dream*.

Dircks, Phyllis T. *David Garrick*. Boston: Twayne Publishers, 1985, 152 p.

Discusses Garrick's dramatic works, subdividing them into the categories of farces and satires, musical plays, adaptations of Shakespearean plays, adaptations of other works, and occasional poetry.

Fitzgerald, Percy. *The Life of David Garrick; From Original Family Papers, and Numerous Published and Unpublished Sources*. 2 vols. London: Tinsley Brothers, 1868.

Lengthy early biography, not completely accurate in matters of fact.

Gentleman, Francis. *The Dramatic Censor; or, Critical Companion*. 2 vols. 1770. Reprint. New York: AMS Press, 1975.

Contains scattered references to Garrick, with special commentary reserved for his adaptations of *Cymbeline* and *Romeo and Juliet*, and his collaboration with George Colman, the elder, on *The Clandestine Marriage*.

Gottesman, Lillian. "Garrick's 'Lilliput'." *Restoration and 18th Century Theatre Research* XI, No. 2 (November 1972): 34-7.

Outlines the plot of Garrick's play based on Jonathan Swift's satire *Gulliver's Travels*, highlighting some differences between the story lines of each.

Kendall, Alan. *David Garrick: A Biography*. London: Harrap, 1985, 215 p.

Useful recent biography containing extended discussions of several important events pertaining to Garrick's life and career.

Knapp, Mary E. *A Checklist of Verse by David Garrick*. Charlottesville: University of Virginia Press, 1955, 69 p.

List of poetry written by Garrick, divided into the categories of occasional verse, prologues and epilogues, theatrical skits, and songs. Also contains an index of first lines and indicates the source of each poem.

MacMillan, Dougald. "David Garrick as Critic." *Studies in Philology* XXXI, No. 1 (January 1934): 69-83.

Considers scattered pieces of literary criticism by Garrick, concluding that the dramatist based his critical opinions upon no established criteria.

Murphy, Arthur. *The Life of David Garrick, Esq.* 2 vols. London: J. Wright, 1801.

Early biography focusing on Garrick's life as an actor.

Pedicord, Harry William. "Shakespeare, Tate, and Garrick: New Light on Alterations of *King Lear*." *Theatre Notebook* XXXVI, No. 1 (1982): 14-21.

Brief comparison of Garrick's adaptation of *King Lear* to that of Nahum Tate's alteration and Shakespeare's original.

Reynolds, Sir Joshua. "Reynolds on Garrick." In his *Portraits*, edited by Frederick W. Hilles, pp. 97-99. New York: McGraw-Hill Book Co., 1952.

A scathing character sketch, discovered in this century among a cache of James Boswell's private papers. Reynolds depicts Garrick as a self-obsessed fame-seeker who "died without a real friend, though no man had a greater number of what the world calls friends."

Stone, George Winchester, Jr. "Garrick's Long Lost Alteration of *Hamlet*." *PMLA* XLIX, No. 3 (September 1934): 890-921.

Compares Garrick's textual cuts in *Hamlet* to previous adaptations, defending the dramatist against critical claims that his version of the tragedy is a "mutilation."

——. "Garrick's Handling of *Macbeth*." *Studies in Philology* XXXVIII, No. 4 (October 1941): 609-28.

Presents an overview of Garrick's emendation of Shakespeare's *Macbeth* from the Theobold text.

Baltasar Gracián y Morales

1601-1658

(Also wrote under pseudonyms Lorenzo Gracián, Lorenço Gracián, and García de Marlones) Spanish philosopher and moralist.

Gracián is recognized as one of the most important figures of Spain's Siglo de Oro, or Golden Age. An innovative author whose compact and complex writing style challenges even the most careful reader, Gracián sought to transform the Europe of his day by providing guides to successful moral living. By continually emphasizing the importance of prudence and self-knowledge, his works challenge his readers to work toward and achieve personal excellence. As Virginia Ramos Foster, a leading Gracián scholar, wrote, Gracián "examined life, its chronic frailties as well as its joys, literature, politics, and, above all, man himself as the chief 'actor' of life. We are made aware of a world that is depressing and often absurd, where disorder is more common than normalcy. Nevertheless, the glimpses of hope shine through this pessimistic despair. Man and society can be transformed and redeemed through human efforts and achievements."

Born in 1601 at Belmonte near Calatayud, Baltasar Jeronimo Gracián y Morales was the son of Francisco Gracián, a lawyer, and Angela Morales. Little is known of his early childhood except that he lived most of it in Toledo with his uncle, Antonio Gracián, who was the chaplain of the Chapel of San Pedro de los Reyes. It was here that Gracián studied humanities and philosophy, leaving Toledo in 1616 to study at the Jesuit school in Zaragoza. The time spent under instruction in Zaragoza had a tremendous influence upon the young man. Deciding to dedicate his life to the Jesuit order, Gracián entered the novitiate of the Jesuits in Tarragona in 1619, taking his first set of perpetual vows in 1621. For the next two years, Gracián studied philosophy at the College of Calatayud, following that with four years of theology in Zaragoza. Ordained as a priest in 1627, Gracián was a professor of grammar at the Jesuit school in Calatayud until 1630. From 1631 until 1636, he taught at Lérida and Gandía, taking his final vows in 1635. After his term at Gandía, Gracián went to Huesca, where he met the renowned Spanish humanist Vincencio Juan de Lastanosa. This man proved a most generous and supportive patron of Gracián and his literary efforts.

The Spanish political situation was one of great turmoil during most of Gracián's life. A significant event was the 1640 peasant uprising in Cataluña, a rich region comprised of the Spanish provinces of Barcelona, Gerona, Lérida, and Tarragona. Known for their separatist tendencies, the Catalans formed their own republic, placing themselves under the protection of the French monarchy. This upheaval strongly influenced the writings of Spanish authors for years to come, Gracián included. When Philip IV came to the throne in 1621, Gracián was appalled by what he saw as the monarch's disregard for personal moderation and Christian morality. As the Spanish court in Madrid became increasingly decadent and untrustworthy,

the young Jesuit set out to rectify the situation in the manner he felt best: through teaching and writing.

Gracián held several service and teaching posts until 1658. He had been publishing his works ever since the release of *El héroe* (*The Hero*) in 1637, usually without the permission of his supervisors and under a pseudonym—practices that were criticized but generally tolerated. Following the publication of *El criticón* (*The Critick*), however, Gracián was reported to the Jesuit General in Rome for refusing to obey commands to quit writing. The superior of the Jesuits, who found the pessimistic and cynical tone of *The Critick* offensive, ordered the removal of the author from his teaching post and put him on a rigid diet of bread and water. Gracián asked to leave the order, but permission was denied and he was exiled to Tarazona. He died on 6 December 1658.

Gracián's first publications were treatises on the expected deportment of the well-bred, well-behaved, exemplary gentleman. The first of these, *The Hero,* outlines a plan for self-conduct in the manner of Baldassare Castiglione's *The Courtier* and Machiavelli's *Prince. The Hero* was published in 1637 without the permission of Gracián's supervisors. To protect himself from censure, Gracián released the work under the pseudonym Lorenzo Gracián, Infanzon. His identity was later determined, and Gracián was reprimanded for insolence. His superiors granted permission for a second edition in 1639, but Gracián retained the use of a pen name nonetheless. Commentators consider this work especially important for what it reveals about Gracián's works in general, containing as it does precepts that were to reappear throughout his later publications. As Foster stated "What Gracián shows us in his first treatise is an affirmation of heroism, based on virtue and pragmatic rules that set forth ideals that perhaps lie far beyond his reach and ours." This was followed in 1640 by a second unauthorized treatise, *El político don Fernando el Católico,* which applied the ideals set forth in *The Hero* to a specific historical figure, Ferdinand the Catholic. In 1646, with the permission of his Jesuit superiors, Gracián published *El discreto* (*The Compleat Gentleman*) under the name Lorenzo Gracián. This treatise, which develops another set of guidelines for the prototypical ideal man, evidences a markedly pessimistic quality that is less noticeable in earlier works but that saw further development in later publications. In 1647, again under the pseudonym Lorenzo Gracián, the Jesuit published *El oráculo manual y arte de prudencia* (*The Oracle*), a collection of 300 maxims for moral living and personal success that treats the themes of self-knowledge, prudent living, and Gracián's idea of *desengaño*—"disappointment." This work is recognized as an influence upon such authors as François de La Rochefoucauld and Voltaire. The negative tone of *The Compleat Gentleman* is even more apparent in this work; as one critic noted, "[As *The Oracle*] teaches one how to get ahead in the world it pessimistically implies the ultimate vanity of all worldly success." The prevalence of conceits in *The Oracle* is also considered significant. Foster noted that Gracián scholar Romera Navarro judged this work to be "the most *conceptista* ["euphuistic"] work in all of Spanish literature."

The Oracle was succeeded by *Agudeza y arte de ingenio* in 1648. This is the definitive version of an earlier work, *Arte de ingenio,* published in 1642. Concerned with the use of conceits and wit in literature, especially poetry, *Agudeza* was at the time unique in several ways. First, as Foster pointed out, "This interest in conceptual relationships [conceit and wit] emphasized the rare, the unique, and the surprising by means of analogical extremes or opposites and likenesses; it was a 'clever wit' that was held to effect such unexpected analogies. And wit came to be the source not only of intellectual pleasure but also of a moral instruction." Similarly, Leland Chambers commented that Gracián's method "brings together lyric poetry, epic poetry, oratory (in the form of sermons), prose fiction, history, biography, drama, the emblem, the parable, fable, the apologue, allegory, several varieties of wordplay, witty remarks and retorts, the epistle, moral philosophy, gestures, deeds and even conversation to prove that the mind and imagination, given the opportunity and a properly founded set of circumstances, can move them all into life by means of wit."

The Critick was Gracián's last major work and is his only work of fiction. Published in three parts under the pseudonyms Garcia de Marlones and Lorenzo Gracián, it is an ambitious allegory satirizing European life and vanities. Experience and prudence, two qualities deemed necessary in Gracián's earlier works, are once again emphasized and shown to be essential components of a successful, moral life. Categorized by some scholars as an allegorical novel reminiscent of John Bunyan's *Pilgrim's Progress* and Edmund Spenser's *Faerie Queene, The Critick* follows Critilo (rational man) and Andrenio (passionate man) through their life-journeys. Foster concisely summarized twentieth-century views of *The Critick:* "The novel is an interesting piece of literature, rich in imagery, vocabulary, moral philosophy, classical mythology, imaginative visions, complicated allegorical conceits, and abstract ideas. Its art is thoroughly complicated. . . . It is a splendid example of the baroque *Gesamtkunstwerk. . . . The Master Critic* is nothing more nor less than an allegory of life, both as a general human circumstance and as a seventeenth-century European reality. On the one hand, it is an encomium of the individualism of man and, on the other, a severe censure of man's behavior and of Gracián's own times."

An innovative stylist and literary theorist, Gracián is recognized as a leading figure in the history of Spanish literature. In an effort to counteract what he saw as the increasing corruptness and decadence of his contemporaries, especially as displayed at the Spanish court in Madrid, he wrote works meant to guide readers to lives of personal perfection and morality. . . . While the study of Gracián's works has frustrated many scholars because of the author's typically intricate literary style, many critics recommend the effort, for "[what] the modern reader will find in Gracián . . . is a writer who demonstrates the creative and intellectual ferment of the baroque, an age which he both described in his allegorical novel and an aesthetics, which he codified and promoted in his critical treatise."

PRINCIPAL WORKS

El héroe   (prose)   1637
  [*The Hero,* 1726]
El político don Fernando el Católico   (prose)   1640
El discreto   (prose)   1646
  [*The Compleat Gentleman,* 1710]
El oráculo manual y arte de prudencia   (prose)   1647
  [*The Art of Prudence,* 1702; also published as *The Art of Worldly Wisdom,* 1892; also published as *The Oracle,* 1953]
*Agudeza y arte de ingenio en que se explican todos los modos y diferencias de conceptos   (prose)   1648
El criticón. 3 vols.   (prose)   1651-57
  [*The Critick,* 1681]
El comulgatorio   (prose)   1655
Obras completas   (prose)   1944, 1960, 1967, 1969

*Revised edition of *El arte de ingenio, tratado de la agudeza* (1642?).

Joseph Jacobs   (essay date 1892)

[*In the following excerpt from the introduction to his translation of the* Oráculo manual *Jacobs examines the literary tone and style of Gracián's maxims.*]

[That the **Oráculo Manual** of Balthasar Gracian] is the best book of maxims is a foregone conclusion, because there is none other. Schopenhauer, who translated the book, observes that there is nothing like it in German, and there is certainly none approaching it in English, and if France or Italy can produce its superior, it is strange that its fame has remained so confined to its native country.

Not that there are not books teaching the art of self-advancement in almost all languages. The success of Dr. Smiles's volume on Self-Help is a sufficient instance of this. Curiously enough, Dr. Smiles's book has had its greatest success in Italy, where it has given rise to quite a *letteratura selfelpista,* as the Italians themselves call it. Or rather not curiously, for if you wish to find the most unromantic set of ideals nowadays you must go search among the Romance nations.

Gracian does not, however, compete with Dr. Smiles. He does not deal with *Brodweisheit;* he assumes that the vulgar question of bread and butter has been settled in favour of his reader. He may be worldly, but he is thinking of the great world. He writes for men with a position and how to make the most of it. Nor is the aim he puts before such persons an entirely selfish one. "The sole advantage of power is that you can do more good" is the only rational defence of ambition, and Gracian employs it (Max. CCLXXXVI).

Indeed the tone of the book is exceptionally high. It is impossible to accuse a man of any meanness who is the author of such maxims as—

> "One cannot praise a man too much who speaks well of them who speak ill of him" (CLXII).

> "Friends are a second existence" (CXI).

> "When to change the conversation? When they talk scandal" (CCL).

> "In great crises there is no better companion than a bold heart" (CLXVII).

> "The secret of long life: lead a good life" (XC).
>
> (pp. XXXI-XXVII)

The characteristic of the book is this combination or rather contrast of high tone and shrewdness. Gracian is both wisely worldly and worldly wise. After all, there does not seem to be any inherent impossibility in the combination. There does not seem any radical necessity why a good man should be a fool. One always has a certain grudge against Thackeray for making his Colonel Newcome so silly at times, though perhaps the irony, the pathos, the tragedy of the book required it. As a matter of fact the holiest of men have been some of the shrewdest, for their friends at least, if not for themselves.

The explanation of the combination in Gracian is simple enough. He was a Jesuit, and the Jesuits have just that combination of high tone and worldly wisdom as their *raison d'être.* And in the case of the **Oráculo** the mixture was easily effected by Gracian or his friend Lastanosa. For Gracian had written at least two series of works in which this contrast was represented by separate books. Two of these describing the qualities of the Hero and the Prudent Man (**El Heroe** and **El Discreto**) were published and are represented in the **Oráculo.** Two others dealing with the

Gallant and the Cautious Man (**El Galante** and **El Varon Atento**) are referred to by Lastanosa in the preface to **El Discreto,** and are also doubtless represented in the book before us. One may guess that the section on Highmindedness (CXXVIII) or on Nobility of Feeling (CXXXI) comes from **El Galante,** while "Better mad with the rest of the world than wise alone" (CXXXIII) smacks of **El Varon Atento.** At times we get the two tones curiously intermingled: "Choose an heroic ideal" (LXXV) seems at first sight a noble sentiment, but Gracian goes on to qualify it by adding, "but rather to emulate than to imitate."

The modernness of the tone is the thing that will strike most readers apart from these contrasts. Here and there one may be struck by an archaic note. "Never compete" would scarcely be the advice of a worldly teacher nowadays. But on the whole there is a tone of modern society about the maxims which one would scarcely find in contemporary English works like Peacham's, or even in contemporary French authors like Charron. The reason is that modern society is permeated by influences which Gracian himself represented. The higher education of Europe for the last two and a half centuries has been in the hands of Jesuits or in schools formed on the *Ratio Studiorum.* And Society in the stricter sense traces from the Hôtel Rambouillet, where one-half the influence was Spanish. Gracian thus directly represents the tone of the two Societies which have set the tone of our society of today, and it is no wonder therefore if he is modern.

Even in his style there is something of a modern epigrammatic ring. At times there is the euphuistic quaintness, *e.g.* "One must pass through the circumference of time before arriving at the centre of opportunity." But as a rule the terseness and point of the maxim approximate to the modern epigram. "El escusarse antes de ocasion es culparse" might be both the source and the model of *Qui s'excuse s'accuse.* The terseness is indeed excessive and carried to Tacitean extremes. "A poco saber camino real," "Ultima felicidad el filosofar," "Harto presto, si bien." Gracian jerks out four or five words where a popular preacher would preach a sermon. Yet I cannot agree with the writers who call him obscure. He is one of the writers that make you think before you grasp his meaning, but the meaning is there, and put plainly enough, only tersely and very often indirectly, after the manner of proverbs. There is indeed no doubt that he and his predecessors were influenced by the form of the Spanish proverb in drawing up aphorisms and maxims. I say predecessors, for aphorismic literature at any rate was no novelty in Spain. Among the long list of books on aphorisms possessed by the late Sir William Stirling-Maxwell, and still at Keir, there are fully a dozen Spanish ones who precede Gracian (Hernando Diaz, Lopez de Corelas, and Melchior de Santa Cruz are the most important, though the latter is more full of anecdotage). Among them is a book of *Aforismos* by Antonio Perez, whose *Relaciones* has been the chief means of blackening Philip II.'s character. The former are undoubtedly of the same style as Gracian, and probably influenced him, though, as they are aphorisms and not maxims, I have not been able to quote parallels in the Notes. Thus "Una obra vale millares de graçias" . . . has the same proverbial ring. It is curious to see Lytton's "The pen is mightier than the sword" anticipated by Perez' "La pluma corta mas que espadas afiladas," or Voltaire's "Speech was given us to conceal our thoughts" in Perez' "Las palabras, vestido de los conçeptos". This last example has all Gracian's terseness, while Perez' "Amigos deste Siglo, rostros humanos, coraçones de fieras" has both terseness and cynicism. Certainly the only other work in Spanish or any other literature preceding Gracian on anything like the same lines is this book of *Aforismos* by Antonio Perez.

It is somewhat of a question, to my mind, how far Gracian was the author of the final form of the maxims as we have them in the **Oráculo**. Those taken from *El Heroe* and *El Discreto* differ from their originals with great advantage. They are terser, more to the point and less euphuistic. Now the Address to the Reader has all these qualities, and we may assume was written by its signatory, Don Vincencio de Lastanosa. It is just possible that we owe to him the extreme terseness and point of the majority of the maxims of the **Oráculo Manual.** It must not, however, be assumed that they are all as pointed and epigrammatic as those I have quoted. Gracian seems advisedly to have imbedded his jewels in a duller setting. At times he views with the leaders of the great sect of the Platitudinarians, and he can be as banal as he is brilliant. Even as it is, his very brilliancy wearies, and after fifty maxims or so one longs for a more fruity wisdom, a more digressive discussion of life like those learned, wise, and witty essays of Mr. Stevenson, which may some day take higher rank as literature than even his novels.

Perhaps, after all, the weariness to which I refer may be due to the cautious tone of the book. To succeed one must be prudent; that is the great moral of the book, and if so, does it seem worth while to succeed? If life is to be denuded of the aleatory element, is it worth living? Well, Gracian meets you when in that temper too. It is indeed remarkable how frequently he refers to luck; how you are to trust your luck, weigh your luck, follow your luck, know your unlucky days, and so forth. Is all this a confession that after all life is too complex a game for any rules to be of much use? Granted, but there is one thing certain about life, and that is put by Goethe in the lines which I, following Schopenhauer, have placed at the head of my translation. One must be either hammer or anvil in this world, and too great an excess of idealism only means that the unideal people shall rule the world. To guard against both extremes we have the paradoxical advice I have heard attributed to Mr. Ruskin, "Fit yourself for the best society, and then—never enter it."

Whether any ideal person will learn to rule the world by studying Gracian's or any one else's maxims is somewhat more doubtful, for reasons I have given above in discussing proverbs. The man who can act on maxims can act without them, and so does not need them. And there is the same amount of contradiction in maxims as in proverbs. Thus, to quote an example from the book before us, from Max. CXXXII it would seem best to keep back an intended gift: "long expected is highest prized"; whereas from Max. CCXXXVI we learn that "the promptness of the gift obliges the more strongly." Which maxim are we to act upon? That depends on circumstances, and the judgment that can decide on the circumstances can do without the maxims. I cannot therefore promise success in the world to whosoever may read this book; otherwise I should perhaps not have published it.

But whether Gracian's maxims are true or useful scarcely affects their value. To the student of literature as such, the flimsiest sentiment or the merest paradox aptly put is worth the sublimest truth ill expressed. And there can be little doubt that Gracian puts his points well and vigorously. I cannot hope to have reproduced adequately all the vigour and force of his style, the subtlety of his distinctions, or the shrewdness of his mother-wit. But enough, I hope, has emerged during the process of translation to convince the reader that Gracian's **Oráculo Manual** has much wisdom in small compass and well put. (pp. XXXVIII-XIV)

Joseph Jacobs, from an introduction to The Art of Worldly Wisdom, *by Balthasar Gracian, translated by Joseph Jacobs, 1892. Reprint by The Macmillan Company, 1944, pp. XVII-XLV.*

E. Sarmiento　(essay date 1933)

[*Sarmiento is an English educator who has written widely on Spanish literature. In the excerpt below, he examines* El Criticón *in detail, focusing on the moral theories of Gracián as well as his literary style and technique.*]

[*El Criticón*], the longest of any of [Gracian's] books, seems also to have been the longest time in writing, since six years elapsed between the appearance of the first and third parts. It can likewise claim to be the work of greatest value that the author wrote. This value is twofold. Primarily, it is an allegory of life, and its chief theme is conduct: but it is equally important and interesting from another point of view: as a work of art of a certain type. As moral teaching, or doctrine of conduct, this book links up with other of its author's works, the smaller treatises, **El Heroe, El Discreto,** and the **Oráculo Manual.** As a work of art, it bears a relation to the author's study of the peculiar art and aesthetic he was exponent of in the **Agudeza y Arte de Ingenio.**

El Criticón (the book of *crisis,* crises, or perhaps better, critiques), consists as we have seen of three parts, each of the first two containing thirteen *crisis,* and the last, twelve. A crisis, a genre peculiar to this book, (so Barclay's—Barcalayo as Gracián calls him—*Satiricon*) is a moral study of some aspect of life. The three collections of crises cover a threefold division of the life of man: *la primavera de la niñez y el estio de la juventud* is the first, the second is *el otoño de la varonil edad,* and the last is *el invierno de la vejez.*

In the first crisis, shipwrecked Critilo (the prudent and discreet man of judgment) comes upon Andrenio (the natural man), who had been cast in infancy upon the island of St. Helena. With these two characters, anticipating perhaps both Crusoe and the Noble Savage, we start this curious novel of which the plot is entirely concerned with the interior mental life, and of which the incidents are without exception, symbolical statements with an attempt at suggesting a conventional verisimilitude. Each of the remaining thirty-six crises begins abruptly with a moral fable, or an apologue, told always as an incident that took place at the beginning of creation. It usually turns out that this fable that we have been reading is being spoken by some character in the novel, perhaps not before introduced, to Critilo and Andrenio; or else that it is the thoughts of Critilo himself,—never of course of Andrenio. The substance of the crisis then follows, the symbolic event, or the vision of life that is shown to Critilo and Andrenio, or some other method of presenting the critique. This invariably closes by leaving the two protagonists in some uncertain situation, and we are always invited to follow them into the next crisis, both a crisis and a criticism.

After the meeting of Critilo with Andrenio who is much younger than Critilo, being still in the "spring of childhood" while Critilo is "swanlike in his whiteness and more so in his song," Critilo enquires of Andrenio his story, teaches him to speak, tells him his own history, warns him against mankind and the world which they are about to enter (for they have sighted a vessel), and on their entry into it, assumes the lead in this first of their adventures together. They proceed to Spain, and there in place of the peninsular topography that we expect, they start on a symbolical journey through life and through Europe. Critilo always slow in undertaking and reserved in judgment, Andrenio carried away by his uncontrolled emotions and instincts. Finally they reach Madrid, deceitful court, where Andrenio is seduced by a woman, Falsirena. Critilo had told Andrenio that he was in search of his betrothed whose family had carried her off from India before their child had been born, and here in this half-real, half-symbolical Madrid, they seek news of her. Andrenio is also intent on discovering his parentage. It is eventually discovered of course that Andrenio is the son of Felisinda, Critilo's lost mistress, and son, therefore to Critilo. After their adventures in Madrid, they set out for Rome in the second part. "In the Autumn of full Manhood," and at the summit of a mountain, they meet Salastano in a library and museum. This represents Gracián's friend and patron, Lastanosa, and his palace at Huesca. They continue through France, where they discuss the French, meet the nymph of art and letters, and discuss literary affairs. They journey through the wilderness of hypocrisy, which deals with false religion and kindred dangerous topics, and after other experiences, come to *la casa de los locos*. In the third part, "the winter of old age," they near Rome, under the protection of the balanced judge of affairs, *el Acertador,* and the revealer of allegories, *el Descifrador*. In Rome they are present at the proceedings of a learned academy, and then watch the wheel of time, which carries events round in an eternal repetition. They finally proceed to the island of immortality which is the life of fame only to be reached by deeds of worth in life.

The reader in following this account of the book will at once think of possible sources and comparisons for the various situations in which Gracián places his heroes. Fundamentally the idea is comparable to two of Cervantes' novels: first to the *Quijote,* and secondly to his less well-known *Persiles y Segismunda*. In matter and in intention the *Criticón* is comparable to the former, in manner to the latter, and affords an unequalled opportunity for setting the pre-Góngora *culterano* and the later *conceptista* together. There is no intention of suggesting any closer relationship between these two books: but a discussion of them as admitting of comparison is likely to prove fruitful in understanding the movements both aesthetic and moral of which Gracián is an outstanding representative. The difference between Cervantes' curious but beautiful work, and Gracián's work is that the latter is far more concentrated, the "interest" of a journey far less important to Gracián than to Cervantes' *novela septentrional,* and with

regard to object, Cervantes can hardly be said to have one, beyond that of producing strange combinations of sounds, of images, of persons, of being in fact a *culterano* work of art, whereas Gracián's object is to produce a moral guide full of thought, condensed. This is of course typical of the two schools of art: one aimed at producing beauty whether in words, rhythms or images, without too great a preoccupation for justifying it, the other aimed at the production of a beauty in the operations of thought, in relationships seen and expressed.

Amongst Gracián's creditors are those he himself mentions, first as we have seen: Barclay with whose *Satyricon* the *Criticón* has one point in common, the insistence on national characteristics, an anticipation of the modern taste for race-psychology. Boccalini, too (*el Boquelino*), whose *Ragguagli* Gracián mentions, and to which the crises may be compared individually in form, has some share in the formation of the *Criticón.* Nor must one forget *un filósofo, mi libro le llamaba el sabio indocto* which seems unmistakably to be a reference to the story of Hayy Ibn Yaqzan.

But all these questions of influence and sources do not constitute, any more than similar questions with respect to the influence of the *Criticón* upon *Robinson Crusoe, Gulliver's Travels,* or the *Pilgrim's Progress,* the real interest of the book, which is that of the moral ideas it contains, and the beauty with which they are expressed.

The impression left by this complex work, both emotional and aesthetic, is profound and difficult of analysis. In its mere content, the moral questions that the book treats and the solutions that it gives to the problems raised are a study sufficiently difficult. But when those moral problems are presented not directly, but in a form itself of artistic value, the two strands become increasingly hard to disentangle. The more so that it is the art that is difficult, unemotional, deliberate, and the moral attitude that wells up spontaneously from the author's mind, and makes its appeal not by ordered logic and metaphysic, but by a deep appeal to the eternal pessimism in human nature, presenting a stoical indifference to such trumperies as personal immortality, holding out the development of character as in itself desirable, to be crowned with an immortality of influence and fame, faintly suggesting philosophic immortality, or more nearly a Butlerian life after death.

As art, the appeal of the *Criticón* is intellectual, as philosophy its appeal is to deep-seated emotions. Its account of humanity is that its life is a tale that is told, its fundamental inspiration seems in fact drawn from Ecclesiastes, and its theory of conduct based on the contemporary feeling for *el hombre de bien, l'homme de bien,* the courtier, a conception which Gracián found in the making, and to the development of which in the second half of the XVIIth century, his works contributed greatly, both in France and in Germany. The art of the *Criticón* is mental, a thing of patterned ideas and balanced words, with short broken rhythms that make an irresistible assault upon the reader. A most important quality of the general view of life presented in this book is its complete independence of religion and of the faith that undoubtedly Gracián held. What constitutes this work's appeal is its undeniable truth, its sense of inevitable melancholy, a just vision of both truth and art, free from fervour, and an amazing imagery expressed with consummate technique of writing.

The Theories of Gracián

By theories is here not meant an ordered exposition of any moral scheme, but the body of notions which though not explicitly, yet quite clearly inform the whole of Gracián's work.

Briefly the moral position of Gracián is this. Creation is beautiful with a strange and difficult beauty, man is inherently bad and prone to work evil. The only remedy for this defect of mankind is Art, or *artificio,* to wrench him back into line with the rest of the work of the Great Architect. The mainspring of this course of action is the Will; its method is to restore by *artificio* the lost harmony of the world, and shape by force the wayward inclinations of human nature.

The artistic achievement can only be: self-reliance, spiritual independence and solitude, and the reward an eternity of fame, obtained not so much by way of reward as by way of the natural outcome of this rightly-directed activity: for there is in Gracián no dwelling on reward and punishment.

Although plainly there is no startling novelty for us in these propositions, the intervening two and a half centuries of philosophy and art having made us more than familiar with all these ideas, yet for Gracián's own time, there is a certain daring in thus presenting a theory of conduct completely devoid of religious doctrine, and based only on the very essentials of what may be called the religious attitude as distinct from the rationalist attitude. For of course, the stress laid on the will is the pure essence of the *Spiritual Exercises* of St. Ignatius; the fundamental assumption that man is bad is equally necessary to Christianity and to Gracián's undoctrinal pessimism, and was especially emphasized in the Catholicism of the Counter-Reform which had to repair the damage done to religion by humanism; the doctrinal attitude was as much emphasized by the heresies of the period which the Counter-Reform had likewise to combat. Yet these dogmas, or rather their content, is presented by Gracián quite empty of dogmatic force; although man is seen to be inherently bad in contrast to nature, there is no suggestion of sin and the Fall, only of stupidity, *necedad.* The whole controversy of Grace that was raging during the years that the *Criticón* was writing, is ignored by Gracián, while Calderón was still producing plays and *autos* full of these urgent matters. It may even be more correct to say that Gracián presents us in the *Criticón* with the philosophical attitude in which the religious sentiment of his day was lodged, rather than with the religious attitude itself.

It is useless and unjustifiable to conclude from this that Gracián was secretly an unbeliever, or even that he was lukewarm. We can only suppose Gracián to have been a man of amazing broadness of mind and richness of intellect. He was capable of supplying an ethical theory and a moral goal without having recourse to the entirely non-human and supernatural means and motives of religion, showing therein what is perhaps the obverse of the mystical strain in the Spanish character: a capacity to live the philosophic, the spiritual life, bare even of religion. This is strictly in accordance moreover with the teaching of the Church which nobly insists on the natural capacity of man for acquiring some idea of God. Obviously the value of supernatural religion is precisely that it is supernatural: Gra-

cián in stressing natural ethics, like the Mohammedan theologians, only grants the fuller dignity to Revelation. Clearly the mind that justly appreciates this is fruitful ground for the sowing of the seed.

These few fundamental conceptions are the basis for the journey through life which is the thread uniting the various incidents of the *Criticón:* on this journey in which all things are vanity, and all man's instincts to be resisted, the chief things necessary are prudence and foreknowledge to avoid falling into the pits dug along the way by the weaknesses inherent in human nature: superficiality, appearance, lack of substance, and short-circuiting vice. The good for Gracián is the Christian standard of morality, or more accurately, the bad for him, is its accepted standard of sin, with an additional evil, common to Gracián and to the Preacher, foolishness; there is one more evil peculiar to Gracián's outlook: that of not being anything at all, *huero, no ser hombre.* The more fundamental standard that for Gracián justifies these ideas is that of the goal he holds out to all who make the journey through life: the isle of immortality, the fame of posterity, the idea which is the seed of a Spinozistic immortality, and which held such attraction for Renan.

Gracián in this connection repudiates the fame of an evildoer as no true immortality, in much the same way as Plato in some dialogues denies the existence of Ideas of evil. It is worthy of note that Gracián does not succumb to the temptation of making Hell an eternity of ill-fame. This supports the contention that Gracián retained his faith, for otherwise we might have expected him inevitably to have "rationalized" this doctrine: his "island of immortality" is not a substitute for Heaven, he "believed in" both.

We might hazard an alternative presentation of Gracián's theory of conduct by attempting to subsume it under a purely aesthetic scheme. This method has its dangers, for since all the teaching of the *Criticón* is implied and not explicit, any account that ventures out of the broadest generalities, or does not merely systematize Gracián's own words, is of necessity purely personal. On the other hand, the aesthetic attitude seems so natural to Gracián, that it would appear to be possible to understand him as taking conduct also as an artistic activity. If this be so, then his doctrine could be set out in this way:

1) Man is corrupt in a Universe of beauty and order.
2) Salvation is in the exercise of the will, to make of life harmony and order by:—
    a) discovery of the beauty that exists in Nature, i.e., knowledge and
      the pursuit of truth;
    b) expressing this, i.e. art;
    c) expressing it in life and action as well as in the material of art, i.e. conduct;
3) The effect of this activity will be the achievement of the command, frequently repeated throughout the *Criticón: see persona, ser hombre;* and admission to the isle of immortality.

The expression of harmony and beauty in life through conduct is not any conception of "sweetness" such as we are accustomed to in modern suggestions of this kind. It is an idea quite devoid of any sentiment. It is neither the effort to alter reality as exemplified by such fashions in manners as that of the *précieuses* in France, nor that of the English "decadents" of the 1890's. But neither has it anything to do with an "acceptance" of life, of reality, such as all the "back-to-nature" movements seek to express, best expounded by the most famous of naturists: Rousseau. It is an attitude of superiority to reality without ignoring it, and an effort to utilise reality in the construction of a formal vision of it which is beauty. It involves the exercise of the qualities of judgment, balance, self-reliance, expressed by Gracián's highest term of commendation: *ser hombre,* together with a spiritual solitude and an inevitable sense of illuminating disillusion. It is an attitude far more easily related to that of the mystics in their philosophical aspect, than to any other, a judgment which is not by any means incompatible with Gracián's exclusion of religion.

The qualities of judgment and prudence are the marks of Gracián's ideal character that so far have attracted most attention, both in France and Germany in the XVII century as well as in the movement towards Gracián represented by M. André Rouveyre in France today. These are qualities however which are not brought out so much in the **Criticón** as in the smaller treatises, especially the **Oráculo manual.**

Some Aspects of the Technique of the **Criticón**

In considering the **Criticón** as a work of art, we are confronted with the question of originality. We have already touched on the question of sources, and it is quite clear from the most summary review of all the works mentioned by Gracián himself, and those which Criticism may suggest, that they can have had little influence on Gracián himself, and but little on the **Criticón,** none certainly on the form of it. Apart from the impossibility of originality in any cultured mind (a fact which Gracián himself pointed out: *todo está ya en su punto . . .*), it quickly reveals itself a quality not worth having, except in that measure possible for all and so resolved into qualities like sincerity and understanding.

The **Criticón** is original because out of all the varied components of the material, knowledge, theory, experience, and imagination, there is evolved an organic and whole expression, comparable to a classical picture where all is dominated by a notion of order, of relationship. Its value is as such, not in its expression of a past age, or any other extrinsic thing. The fundamental point in considering the **Criticón** as art is this one of order. Gracián chooses the philosophic foundation of his time to give expression to this root idea. Secondly he chooses largely and definitely man as the instrument through which to convey this idea of order. The third thing to consider is that Gracián in company with the thought of the Counter-Reform, accepts a duality which if not technically dualism, is close to it, and artistically indistinguishable from it; it is the foundation of the insistence on balance in Gracián's idea of art. This is a balance far removed from that of classical architecture, which is a balance of repose; the balance of the art of Gracián, present in the **Criticón,** preached in the **Agudeza de Ingenio,** is like the balance of Baroque architecture, a balance of tension. The symmetry is of opposition, not of complement. Finally, besides its essential function of imparting form, the life of a work of art resides also in another quality: power. The **Criticón** not only is the work of a mind rich in informing genius, but is efficient

in the performing of its function far beyond the requisite of power. Its beauty and originality, its singleness and individuality are presented with an intensity proper to the greatest art. A consideration of the points of technique which have produced this intensity is not without interest.

One of the most striking things about the writing of the **Criticón** is the rhythm. The gentle flow of these half-dozen words: *Asi como el de la indagadora natural filosofia, levantando mil testimonios a la naturaleza. . . .* This moderate unit of rhythm is the most frequent one in the book, so much so, that the general impression is one of several small divisions to a chapter (*crisi*), rather than one or two ample movements. In the same way, the incident is treated as a quick succession of images, not a prolonged and single action. *Confesaron todos la enterisima verdad y convirtieron sus incredulidades en aplausos.* In the same way again, and in obedience to the same underlying demand for brevity, the steps in any incident are invariably conveyed with terse, concentrated phrases. . . . This terseness is introduced even in conversation. . . . It will be noticed that here as everywhere, the rhythm *Asi como de la indagadora natural filosofia* with its complement *levantando mil testimonios a la Naturaleza,* appears, as it is constantly appearing, sometimes interrupted, sometimes lengthened, always at the base of the sentence. This rhythm has a certain resemblance to that of the versicles and responses that occur in the liturgy, and especially in the Roman Office; it is nevertheless far more regular than these are, at least in their recited form (as distinct from their plain-chant setting). Let us go back to the first of our quotations: there is a definite break at *filosofia,* corresponding to the "versicle," followed by the "response" *levantando mil testimonios a la naturaleza,* practically a repetition of the first half. There are four syllables less in the second arm of this particular example, but the number of well-defined stresses is constant, four. The number of syllables is not, within limits, of importance to this rhythm, for the second half or arm may contain less than the first, and yet retain the identity of the first by its stresses. Besides this well-separated "versicle-and-response" division, there is another fairly constant characteristic, the nature of the stress-order within the first half of the unit. We have in the examples chosen: *indagadora natural filosofia,* a heaping-up of syllables in the adjective preceding the final stress; or more clearly, with a *palabra esdrújula* (proparoxy-tone): *enterisima verdad,* an effect that is extremely common in the **Criticón.** Any close examination of prose rhythm is attended by the great difficulty that so much more license is admissible in prose than in verse without the loss of the general pattern; our type rhythm sometimes appears considerably lengthened so far as number of syllables goes, yet unmistakably retaining its character, as in the long phrases quoted above, *El que no tiene amigos . . .* Later on we find a much shortened form: *Saludóles muy a lo cielo para ganar más tierra.* The break at *cielo* is not to be mistaken, and the stresses number only three, but the effect is maintained in two ways; first there is an emphasis in meaning on the two important words in each section, *cielo* and *tierra;* and secondly, in the second arm, the three stresses follow one another without intervening unstressed syllables: *(ga) nar más tie (rra).* The first device has the effect of giving more than normal value to one stress in each of the arms of the phrase, the second by bringing the stresses in succession, forces the reader to dwell on each with more pressure than he would otherwise have done, making up for the shortness in respect of number of syllables, and so far from losing the rhythm, by these compensations bringing it clearly out, conforming with the type rhythm that has already been established in the mind's ear. Despite the freedom, or because of it, the dominant rhythmic impression to be obtained from the *Criticón* is surprisingly uniform for a prose work, and the variations themselves become established effects.

But if the rhythm of *Asi como el de la indagadora natural filosofia* is the basic rhythm throughout the book, this does not preclude the introduction of other types. . . . There is a series of deeper emotional passages on page 311 of Cejador's edition, Volume II, too long for quotation, beginning: *Sobre esta tan llana verdad venia echando el contrapunto de un singular desengaño el cortesano discreto . . .* continued to *el grave peso de sus muchos yerros* on page 313, where the rhythm is subtly manipulated in a new manner. The last pun in the context is not so much flippant, as curiously and emotionally charged with the overtone of *peso de hierro*. The first phrase with its reference to musical counterpoint is noteworthy in view of the passages that follow, they are three times interrupted with an interval of short rhythms, and finally lead up to the long passage of protracted rhythms: *Dime no caminas . . .* These variations are comparatively few however over the whole work, and the standard remains that of *indagadora natural filosofia*.

It is this rhythm too, with its demand upon the rapid conveying of impression and incident, and breaking-up of the phrase in consequence, and ultimately its influence even upon the vocabulary, that is at the root of most of the other linguistic devices in the book. This demand for quick or rather concentrated phrase and expressive vocabulary results in a remarkable manipulation of tense, and the utilisation of all the resources of the Spanish verb, both in meaning and in form, for the sake of obtaining a conformity to rhythm here, or there a reflection. So too with inversion, the omission of the article, and other devices in the maintaining of rhythm appear also indissolubly linked to the psychological processes of which the rhythms are the expression, and which likewise, they stimulate.

Contrast in the presentation of images is encouraged by having them placed one in each arm of the type rhythm: returning to the quotations already employed: *filosofia, naturaleza; cayere, levantar; verdad, aplausos;* these are pairs of words and of ideas that by placing in key position in the two arms of the rhythmic phrase, increase their mutual opposition.

The vivid imagery and *imagisation* thus rendered essential for effective contrast and balance, comparable to the balancing of statuary and decorative motifs on a Baroque façade is exemplified here: *un retorcido caracol que hurtó a un fauno, y alentándole de vanidad. . . .* Everywhere there is juxtaposition of contrasts, even the abrupt juxtaposition of contrasts, and the unity of assault on the reader is always one form or other of the type-rhythm we have noted. Hence the succinctly-evoked images and *imagisations* of thought or incident, a close psychological study of some of these images should reveal much of interest. The wonderful vitality of certain of the symbols seems to be almost pathologically maintained, the less pleasant aspects of life seem to excite as much pleasure as disgust in the author; but most interesting of all are some which

seem to exercise an irresistible fascination over Gracián. The swan, *cisne canoro,* is constantly appearing, perhaps most memorably in this passage: *Oianse en los estanqués cantar los cisnes en todo tiempo.* This swan-obsession is shared with Góngora, and seems part of the poetic convention of the period, a fact which gives it more importance of course, since it is in the conventions of a literature and artistic style that we can grasp its most intimate significance. Another image constantly utilised is that of Narcissus; the stars haunt Gracián's mind, and the moon, especially *los cuernos de la luna: Tan alto las alas que tal vez temi quedar enganchado en alguna de las puntas de la luna, o estrellado en el cielo.* Here too we have a pun far less humorous in effect and intention than it is purely poetical.

Also due to the rhythmic demands is the frequent clipping of the phrase to enable it to fit better within the scheme: *exageró sentimientos; en vez de brazos batia alas,* continuing without a connecting verb: *tan volantes que . . . ; tanto gusto como deseo,* and similar smaller units of contrast, especially those on the basis: *no tal y tal, si tal otro;* which are comparable to the key constructions that Don Dámaso Alonso has studied in Góngora. In the use of the verb, two tenses lend themselves to concentrated expression, and to clipping when necessary: the preterite used in preference to the imperfect or the present perfect (containing too a more marked tonic stress), and the *-ra* form of the past subjunctive, with its additional meanings of a past anterior and of a conditional anterior. The preterite especially is utilised by Gracián, and undoubtedly is intended to avoid the unpleasant effect of a too repetitive imperfect, moreover by avoiding the too-recent present perfect, aids the *imagisation* of incident, contributing to the rhythm and the contrasts, by removing events to the luminousness of the remotely past, despite the knowledge that in fact the preterite in question is referring to events which have only just occurred, or continue to exist. . . . Then there is this use of the terseness of the Spanish verb—in which we must be struck with the frequency with which Gracián omits its subject pronoun—applied to other tenses: *bajemos a comer, no diga el otro simple lector. . . .* The use of the enclitic forms, especially such combinations as produce proparoxytones, or even words with their tonic accent still further removed from the end, *viéronla, mirándoselas, ahogándose,* often serves to emphasize the speed in the first arm of a rhythm: *Viéronla a veces de repente. . . .*

Parallel with this economy in words is a concentration of emotion and of occurrence; in this sentence there is a situation which could be expanded almost indefinitely, certainly out of all proportion with the length of the sentence itself: *Asi lo confesó uno a la que le decia: Yo soy aquélla, respondiéndole: Ya no soy aquél.* (pp. 235-49)

The power of the *Criticón* is not however, solely due to the carefully constructed rhythms which close examination reveals as determining practically all its resources. There would still seem to be two things not absolutely dependent on the rhythmic construction and other elements which in their turn are determined by it. There are in the first place, the actual ideas presented by the author, as distinct from the images through which they are presented (for these as we have seen do derive their quality in a large measure from the rhythmic exigencies of the prose), and in the second place is the smallest stylistic unit of all: the word. Although vocabulary is not independent of the rhythm to the same extent as the ideas contained in the book (for after all, there would be no book at all without the ideas the author sets forth in it!),—we have seen already how for example the verb and smaller grammatical constructions are very largely so determined, yet there is a great freedom for the further enhancing or loss of power in the quality of the vocabulary so far as it is free.

We have already said that the fundamental notion Gracián wishes to convey is the aesthetic view of life best expressed by the word *order*. The activity that Gracián seems to suppose is the specifically human is to perceive and express order. This inevitably constitutes a moral scheme, and the ideas selected to convey this fundamental notion of order are necessarily moral ideas. It is of value to consider them here in their capacity of artistic contribution to the work of art, rather than their significance as a guide to conduct. In considering the larger elements of style, we saw that everything with an admirable unity depended on the rhythm which Gracián had consistently used throughout his book, and that that rhythm, rather than conceived on the grand scale of fluency, was short, clearly divisible into two shorter waves, and ended in an abrupt descending movement: the rhythm of pessimistic thought rather than of melancholy feeling. This shortness, this breaking-up into compact elements appears throughout Gracián's work. The *Criticón* as a whole is itself divided up into short self-contained sections; and all his other works (short in themselves), likewise divide up into brief sections of at most three (octavo) pages. (The *Agudeza* is an exception.) Gracián with his intense admiration for brevity (*lo bueno si breve dos veces bueno, y lo malo menos mal*), would almost seem to have modelled his literary work upon the art of the medallist in which he and Lastanosa were such loving connoisseurs. Similarly with his ideas. The images that express them were compact we saw, the ideas themselves are single, detached, clear, "unmetaphysical" (referring, we may suppose, to the contemporary movement towards complexity in philosophy, he says, *El engaño anda metafísico*), not systematized into any vast synthesis. So in his practical recommendations, the three hundred maxims of the *Oráculo* are precisely maxims; unconnected in form, they have only the psychological unity that belongs to work sprung from a single personality. The main ideas which continually filter through, or rather break through like dry sand-dust from the pages of the *Criticón* are a bare half-dozen; considerable work is required to erect them into any kind of connected system: yet they are unmistakably and insistently present in every episode of the book. God has created a work of beauty; man is from the beginning corrupt, and when not corrupt a born fool; there are pitfalls at every step in the journey of the man determined to live "righteously," i.e., according to reason and in view of beauty; woman is rarely the great lady whose price is above rubies, too often she is *buscada cuando hermosa, y cuando fea, ella busca;* above all, the dominant note of the whole: *hacerse hombre, ser persona*, make oneself a soul, be something attain depth, a continual insistence on interior strength, and complete independence of the crowd, *el vulgo*. These few, simple, clear, and monotone ideas are all the music that those rhythms play, all the vision those harsh images make, the only stay for the journey that all must go: the ideas of Gracián are not by any means comfort for the afflicted, but meat for the strong.

It is this very simplicity, strength, and harshness that enables even the vocabulary to acquire and give again a contribution to the power of this work of art, apart from the forced offering that is levied through the medium of verb and syntax in the service of the rhythm.

Perhaps nowhere outside the *Criticón* is such a wealth of effective, heavily-charged phrase. Were the ideas not so simple, so few, and so direct, mere groups of two or three words could never acquire such significance as they do here. (pp. 250-52)

The last point to be considered in this preliminary examination of the technique of Gracián's style is the aspect of the *Criticón* as a novel. Let it be conceded at once that this term can only by much stretching be applied to the *Criticón.* On the other hand the author evidently considered it as some species of novel, with a thin thread of plot running through it; a distinctly novelistic flavour in the first few crises where the two main characters first come in contact, and the method of joining each crisi on to the next with an invitation to see what happens next, all suggest that Gracián supposed himself to be writing some kind of novel. We have mentioned Cervantes' *Persiles y Segismunda,* and only hinted at the *Quijote,* recalling that both it and the *Criticón* are novels of two complementary characters who set out on a symbolical journey. But there is a passage where Gracián follows a convention dear to Cervantes. I refer to the making the characters speak of themselves as characters in a book. In volume II of the Cejador edition, page 309, we find this: *Esto bastará por ahora, les dijo el cortesano no diga el otro simple lector: ¿De qué pasan estos hombres que nunca se introducen comiendo ni cenando, sino filosofando?* There is in fact here a double reference to Cervantes. First there is in the text itself a hint of that *universal poético* in opposition to the *verdad histórico* as Américo Castro defines the situation, which is of the very essence of the *Quijote,* and secondly there is this conception of making characters behave as conscious beings aware of their existence as characters in the mind of their creator and in the pages of his book.

The reverse process is resorted to on another occasion, where the author cynically has recourse to abstractions to place his characters in a desired situation. . . . So Gracián with all his psychological acumen refuses to waste it in achieving "verisimilitude," and treats his characters as marionnettes, giving us rather the full value of his command over the image and language than a novel in the legitimate sense. (pp. 253-54)

E. Sarmiento, "A Preliminary Survey of Gracián's 'Criticón'," in Philological Quarterly, *Vol. XII, No. 3, July, 1933, pp. 235-54.*

Dorothy M. McGhee (essay date 1937)

[*McGhee is an American educator who specializes in the study of Romance languages and literatures. In the following excerpt, she discusses the possible influence of Gracián's El Criticón on Voltaire's Candide.*]

Perusal of some Voltairian conte material not long ago elicited two cursory observations which have since seemed to be confirmed by more detailed reading. They concern the evident interest which the seventeenth-century Spanish moralist, Gracián, appears to have evoked in Voltaire.

The observations, as first made, were these: that in a list of Voltaire's library, works of Gracián stand out prominently, in both Spanish and French; that *El Criticón,* a moralistic tale of a traveling *naif* and his realist-tutor, presents not only an interesting link in the adventure genre, but seemingly a hint of the Candide-Martin relationship of the *conte philosophique.* The suggestion of a connection, conscious or not, between *El Criticón* and *Candide* was, on first observation, based upon superficial comparison. The present brief inquiry will attempt to confirm the point that a reasonably close connection does exist—one which receives attention neither in editions of the contes nor in other critical works on the period.

Naturally, when indicating so-called "connections" with anything Voltairian, we must use prudently the words *source* and *influence.* M. Morize, speaking of "les 'sources' de *Candide,*" significantly puts the word *sources* in quotation marks. Voltaire, as we know, adapted and amalgamated much of what he read. Therefore, in endeavoring to clarify the present connection, we shall say that this interesting Gracián *naif,* among the number preceding Voltaire, probably had more place in the contes, and particularly in *Candide,* than has hitherto been observed.

The present conclusions are based upon three major points as evidence: (1) that the Voltairian library contains a noticeable amount of Gracián; (2) that Voltaire mentions the seventeenth-century author with evident admiration; and (3) that distinct comparisons of *El Criticón* and *Candide,* each with its traveling, world-chastened pupil and his practical companion, bring the two works into very close parallel.

First, as to library items, brief but significant. An unpublished manuscript catalogue of Voltaire's private library, now in Leningrad, loaned by Professor George R. Havens, lists the Gracián works thus: 1 vol. *Las Obras de gracián* (sic), fol. 46 vo.; 1 *Héros* de gratian (1637), fol. 12 vo.; 3 *Criticón* de gratian, fol. 12 vol.; 1 *Maximes* de gratian, fol. 12 vo. In number, this list assumes a place with those foreign works and authors most read by Voltaire: for example, Cervantes, Lope de Vega, or, in his own century, let us say Addison, Bolingbroke, or Swift. Also, when speaking of book items, we recall the point stressed by Desnoiresterres, that Voltaire's library was limited and practical, that it showed the person and was meant for use.

Gracián should have been, to Voltaire, a kindred spirit, if we may judge from their ideas and spiritual sympathy. It will be recalled that in one respect the Spain and France of these two centuries were comparable; much of the satiric pungency of Spain was evident in the seventeenth, of France, in the eighteenth. Gracián, like Voltaire, had defied church tradition; had held out constantly against absolutism and for tolerance. He had seen the first two sections of his *Criticón* condemned, and had boldly written the third with an even more forceful hand. He might have been a *philosophe,* had he lived in France a century later. The pen of each was a tireless force against war, Gracián with a less caustic expression, true, but certainly with as bitter a hatred. *El Criticón* and *Candide* present some similarities in this respect, as we shall note. The attitude of each *conteur* toward his work seems significantly close— "conducting the reader through workshops of judgment," as Gracián expresses it. Each was analyzing a universal Soul of Man: Gracián, subtly, calmly and at length; Vol-

taire, sharply, sardonically, in sallies. The laugh of each was fearless and practical.

Voltaire, in common with his century and particularly with the *philosophes,* evidenced a frequent scorn for Spain. Such scorn, however, was directed largely against fanaticism and a resultant lack of what Voltaire called "la saine philosophie." He had had much occasion to speak seriously and with admiration, of its seventeenth-century literary figures—of Cervantes, Lope and Quevedo, and we know his predilection for the picaresque genre, enriched by Spanish authors.

Voltairian mention of Gracián is, like the library citation, brief but significant. . . . Voltaire's coupling the names of Lope and Gracián [in a 1767 letter to the Marqués de Miranda] is a significant intimation that Gracián enjoys his high esteem.

In placing *El Criticón* and Candide side by side for comparison, it will be granted, first of all, that certain contrasts appear: (1) in the length of the two works (three volumes, as compared with slightly over one hundred pages); (2) in the manner of expressing themes—moral allegory as against the *conte philosophique;* and (3) in tone, austerity as against sardonic brittleness. There are also certain general similarities: (1) each work is a journey of a *naif* (Andrenio, Candide) accompanied by a realistic companion (tutor Critilo, observer Martin), all with closely allied characteristics; (2) each forms a part of a series—the *Criticón,* of a long moralistic group, *Candide,* of the contes, which might all be termed one great journey of the ingenuous hero; (3) both authors insist upon the conflicting duality of Man, though that point is in formula, and (4) both authors, at full maturity in these works, produced climaxes of contained rage.

With regard to the journey itself, *some* points are simply in the adventure formula:

> 1. Madrid and Paris both become Babylons of confusion, injustice and evil.

> 2. There are typical buffetings of Fate, interpolations, multiple variations of Destiny.

> 3. The hero, constantly warned, just as constantly falls into abysses. *But,* apart from formula, the peregrinations end, for both heroes, in a disillusionment which is *avowed* and turned to profit.

Characteristics of the *naif* and his companion are particularly close:

> 1. We find Andrenio termed the *inexperto* and Critilo the *sabio,* to couple with Candide the *naïf* and Martin the *philosophe.*

> 2. Andrenio allegorically accepts bonds of flowers, and Critilo, those of books—Candide the bond of hyperidealism, and Martin, of rigid objectivity.

> 3. Docility is stressed as a characteristic in both heroes.

Another striking point is that one passage in the *Criticón,* using the very word *cándidos* seems to fit rather nearly the Voltairian hero. It concerns a miraculous fountain, which can transform attitudes. . . . (pp. 778-82)

Andrenio and Candide, nearing the conclusion of their journeys, still present comparisons:

> 1. Both have traveled, read and conversed with wisdom, but refused counsel.

> 2. Critilo, like Martin, has supplied the objections, in the form of *pero* (compare Voltaire's usual turning of *mais* into the unexpected "et").

> 3. In common with the *naïf*, neither of the two has grown wiser with experience, *but* each comes to understanding at the point of *complete* disillusionment. That stage is again marked by similarity in the two tales. Gracián has Andrenio express it: "contento, no; pero desengañado, sí." Voltaire's Candide mentally makes the same comment as he decides to limit himself to the present, "exercer ses talents,"—"cultiver notre jardin."

Though it is to be expected that subjects will be found in common among satirists, the following are notably akin in the two authors:

> 1. The theme of the search for happiness, so constant in the contes and so recurrent in Gracián—"Leave chimeric schemes and develop the present," say both in substance.

> 2. The advisability, for happiness' sake, of "oneness" of sight or hearing (witness the one *good* eye of *Le Crocheteur Borgne*—the stress upon *willingness* to hear, in Gracián).

> 3. Among institutions, insistence upon the futility of War. Voltaire must have had infinite sympathy with such passages as *El Criticón,* II, 60-67, in which War is backed by two devils, self-aggrandizement and misunderstanding.

> 4. The power of money to determine friendship, a subject that looms large in both authors.

Another point of correspondence draws our interest in this same connection. Like Voltaire's Babouc and Candide, Andrenio begins by uttering, optimistically, "Oh qué bueno va el mundo," then sees, bit by bit, his ideals brought to earth. Demagogues rule; merit is ostracized. But, in Gracián as in Voltaire, the world is passable, neither all good nor all evil. We think of Babouc's statue, and its significant moulding of the two elements in one mass.

Content has been the exclusive argument in making these comparisons. Stylistically, likenesses might appear in any other two satirists—devices, plays on words, paragraphs in word-pattern formation, series of aphorisms. But *El Criticón,* with its particular construction, protagonists, and mode of presentation, seems sufficiently close to *Candide* to have evoked some memory, whether conscious or not, in the later Voltairian conte. In such a rôle, *El Criticón* should, then, be included among the important *probable* readings that went to make up these composite *contes philosophiques* of Voltaire. (pp. 782-84)

> *Dorothy M. McGhee, "Voltaire's 'Candide' and Gracián's 'El Criticón'," in* PMLA, *Vol. LII, September, 1937, pp. 778-84.*

Gerald Brenan (essay date 1951)

[*Brenan was a British travel writer and literary historian who lived most of his life in Spain. In the following excerpt from his history of Spanish literature, he gives a concise analysis of Gracián's literary style, especially in regard to* El Criticón.]

Spanish literature down to the twentieth century has been sparing of those discursive books that deal in a general way with human life and thought, such as for example Montaigne's or Bacon's *Essays* or La Bruyère's *Caractères*. The principal exception to this are the works of Baltasar Gracián. (p. 271)

Gracián's principal works comprise several short treatises: *The Hero,* 1637; *The Politician,* 1640; *The Man of Discretion,* 1646; *The Manual Oracle and Art of Prudence,* 1647; *Agudeza y arte de ingenio,* 1640 (a book of literary criticism); and a long allegorical novel, *El Criticón,* 1651-7. The titles of the first three books explain themselves: they are treatises on the ideal qualities that should be possessed by heroes, politicians and courtiers. They aim at doing for that age what Baldassare Castiglione's great book *The Courtier* had done for the Italian Renaissance. As one would expect, they are deeply tinged with the Jesuit ideology. The great quality of the hero is prudence, by which is meant knowing how to adapt means to ends. He must be aware of his own limitations and be free from illusions. Moreover, he must be a man of general culture, refined in his manners, keen in his perceptions, a perfect master of himself and well able to conceal his thoughts and feelings. He must love subtlety and ingenuity and prefer new styles to old. This last is a point to be noticed. The sixteenth century, though it had shown more originality and creative power than the seventeenth, had suffered from a great dread of novelty. The word 'new' had come to have for most Spaniards the meaning of 'bad'. The fact that no sooner was Philip II dead than this fear of the new gave way to a deliberate search for it was due partly to the general law of reaction, partly to the fact that the court was now the centre of fashion, but still more perhaps to the influence of the Jesuits, who were trying to impose on the medieval Catholic world a more polished and up-to-date conception of society and of religion.

Gracián was a strong opponent of Machiavelli. Refuting the ethics of *The Prince* had become one of the duties of every writer on politics, yet one cannot help noticing that a good deal of diluted Machiavellianism creeps into his precepts. This is understandable when one remembers that the success of the Jesuits was due more than anything else to their assimilation of the political theories of the Italian Renaissance and its preoccupation with the idea of power. Hence the *Spiritual Exercises,* their great system of education, their new casuistry, their monopoly of the office of confessor to kings and ministers. But, being realists, they were necessarily also men of common sense and so Gracián's criticisms of the cult of illusions and unrealizable ends are very much more to the point than Quevedo's. What one misses, in comparing his views to those of Castiglione, is the note of simplicity and generosity. The Baroque age, one cannot say it too often, was a tight, contracted age, turned in on itself and lacking self-confidence and faith in the future.

Gracián is a notable stylist. He writes in a dry, clipped, epigrammatic idiom in which every phrase has been carefully polished and refined. He expresses himself in understatements which keep back a certain part of his meaning:

his conceits are few, but well chosen: every word is premeditated. Nothing more unlike the grand diction of Quevedo or the copious arabesque of Vélez de Guevara can be imagined, yet he is a more affected writer than they are, for his language smells of the study and is little touched by the rhythms of ordinary speech. Now a stilted or distorted idiom is justified when it produces effects of vividness or emotion that cannot be obtained in any other way: when, that is, it takes a step nearer to poetry. But Gracián's tone is never raised above that of ordinary conversation: the effect he aims at is *agudeza* or subtlety. I confess therefore that I would regard it as a bad style, especially as I find it tedious to read, if it were not that so many good judges admire it extremely.

Gracián's principal work, composed towards the end of his life, is *El Criticón.* This is a long, closely written allegorical novel in which he sets out his philosophy of life. It begins with the shipwreck of Critilo, who stands for rational and civilized man, and his meeting on an otherwise uninhabited island with a savage called Andrenio, who represents the man of untamed passions and instincts. They become friends and, by reasoning upon the order and beauty of Nature, convince themselves of the existence of God. It is curious that Gracián should thus be repeating the theme of the famous philosophic romance by Ibn Tufail, a Spanish Muslim philosopher who was born at Guadix early in the twelfth century. But it was a coincidence, for Ibn Tufail's work was not then known in the West.

The part of the book describing the life of the two men on the desert island occupies only four chapters. The rest is a description of their adventures when they leave the island and visit the world. The picture we get is a very pessimistic one. 'O life, you should never have begun, but once begun you ought never to end', exclaims Critilo as he battles with the waves, and these words may be said to form the text on which the book is written. Critilo and Andrenio suffer innumerable deceptions and misfortunes, yet the pessimism is not complete, for we see them rise out of their difficulties and by a continual struggle for self-perfection acquire a share in the only kind of immortality that human society offers—that of the great heroes, poets and artists.

The book is packed with acute observations on human nature, with anecdotes, epigrams and critical judgments. It is clearly the work of a man of unusual culture, intelligence and originality and it offers us a sympathetic and civilized approach to life, similar to that which we may suppose to have been held by Góngora. Dragged out of the limbo of forgotten tomes by Schopenhauer's extravagant praise and, it must be said, partly misunderstood by him, it is today one of the best known (though perhaps least read) of Spanish classics. (pp. 271-74)

> Gerald Brenan, "Quevedo and Gracián," in his The Literature of the Spanish People: From Roman Times to the Present Day, *Cambridge at the University Press, 1951, pp. 258-74.*

L. B. Walton   (essay date 1953)

[*In the following excerpt, Walton provides a brief over-*view of Gracián's works, paying special attention to the Oráculo manual. *He maintains that this particular work is an "anthology of the apothegms, maxims, epigrams, and general obiter dicta to be found scattered throughout the other works of the author." Walton also surveys the literary style of several of Gracián's treatises.*]

In order to explain the significance of the *Oráculo manual* something must first be said concerning the works of which it is an epitome or anthology. Excluding *El Comulgatorio* (1655), which is no more than a guide to devotions, these works are five in number, *El Héroe* (1637), *El Político Fernando* (1640), *El Discreto* (1646), *Agudeza y arte de ingenio* (1648) (revised ed. of *El Arte de ingenio, tratado de la Agudeza*) [1642?], and *El Criticón* (1651-7).

In *El Héroe* Gracián gives us a kind of *catalogue raisonné* of the qualities, 'primores' he calls them, which should characterize the ideal leader and man of action.

The 'hero' of Gracián, be it noted, is no semi-mystical figure with the light of battle in his eyes, bearing a book and a sword. Nor is he a superman, nor a humanitarian philanthropist, nor yet an altruist. He is, first and foremost, an astute man of sound judgment, great-hearted, quick in action, and courageous. His most outstanding quality will be 'despejo,' a Spanish word which defies adequate English translation but which might be rendered, approximately, by 'ready wit combined with charm.' Some of the 'heroic' qualities enumerated by Gracián are of especial interest as revealing the author's own character and temperament. Moving, as he did, in a social circle superior to that in which he was born; dependent for success in his literary career upon the favours of the great, among whom, perhaps, he was never completely at his ease; an object of envy to his less cultured fellow priests, the quality most essential to him personally was discretion. He early came to realize that, as La Rochefoucauld was to put it later, 'il n'y a rien d'aussi difficile que le commerce des hommes.' Seeing around him everywhere the disastrous consequences of human stupidity, he was almost fanatical in his detestation of fools. Warmth is not a characteristic of Gracián as a writer. It is, nevertheless, undoubtedly there when he is portraying an ass. We gather that he would have agreed up to a point with the proverbial division of mankind into 'knaves and fools' and there can also be little doubt that, in spite of his priestly office, he preferred the company of the former to that of the latter.

The hero, says Gracián, must be continually on his guard against fools and the shallow judgments of the mob. He should not reveal all his good qualities at once but should keep some distinction up his sleeve as a surprise. The multitude never respects a man whom it thinks it has completely fathomed. The hero must, above all, know how to hold his tongue and if he has been guilty of some foolish blunder he must know how to cover it up.

He should avoid the company of poor or unfortunate persons and should deliberately parade some weakness in order to appease the envious. Also, says Gracián, we must not forget that sheer luck plays a large part in the careers of the great. The fault *is* sometimes in our stars that we are underlings and the tide in the affairs of men *is* frequently missed owing to sheer ill fortune. *Pace* the moralists, our own experience surely bears out this view of Gracián's. Most men whom fortune has favoured will, if they are honest, admit that the secret of their success is about twenty per cent hard work, five per cent ability, and seventy-five per cent sheer luck. (pp. 9-10)

These awkward facts of experience, ignored by Samuel Smiles and the majority of Puritan moralists, did not escape the keen and observant eye of the Jesuit priest. We must, however, bear in mind that, as a priest, the Spanish writer would probably equate 'fate' or 'luck' with the 'inscrutable designs' of Providence. Events have for the religious-minded an esoteric significance even when their outward aspect is purely fortuitous. The significant point is that, for Gracián, success in life is not necessarily the reward of piety and thrift. Also, from the Catholic point of view, wealth and power do not carry, as they do in our modern commercial civilizations, any necessary implication of superiority, or title to respect. In the age of Gracián, wealth was, in itself, no general social passport, even from the purely mundane angle.

El Héroe is the child of a mind well stocked from the classics and Italian writers on political philosophy. Gracián may also owe something to the *Honnête Homme* (1630) of Nicolas Faret. It is interesting to note that he explicitly condemns Machiavelli in the **Criticón,** I. 7, as a 'falso político' although in the **Héroe** he may have intended to show that worldly success is not incompatible with Christian ethics. If so, he can scarcely be regarded as having attained his object.

El Político Don Fernando el Católico appeared at Zaragoza in 1640 and was dedicated to the Viceroy of Aragon, the Duque de Nocera. Its object was to depict a model ruler in the person of King Fernando I, 'the Catholic,' and to expound his political theories. Fernando, says Gracián, founded an empire, a task for which destiny alone can supply the necessary qualities. The two essential virtues in a monarch are courage and prudence. He must also be astute and able to conceal his true motives, especially when he is preparing for war. He must surround himself with trustworthy and able ministers. Gracián calls attention to the disunity of the Spain of his own day and contrasts it with the unity achieved by Fernando I (Queen Isabella is not mentioned, possibly because she was a woman!) and the comparative stability of France. There is nothing original in the **Político,** which is, indeed, inferior to the Italian political treatises of the time and to Quevedo's political writings. Gracián's notion that distinctive ages of history produce distinctive types of ruler is interesting, if facile and unconvincing. In one era, he says, the monarch will be a statesman, in another a warrior, in another a voluptuary, and so on.

The **Político** simply sets down the facts concerning Fernando's policy, accompanied, invariably, by eulogistic comment. There is no attempt to evolve a philosophy of history, no attempt at character analysis. Gracián, was, however, like so many authors, an exceedingly poor judge of his own works. He thought very highly of *El Político* and in his **Criticón** ranks it with famous political treatises such as Machiavelli's *Il Principe.*

El Discreto (1646) is addressed to the ordinary man of the world. It is very difficult to find an appropriate English rendering of the title, which has also puzzled Gracián's French translators; Amelot de la Houssaie renders 'Discreto' by 'Discret,' while Fr. Courbeville paraphrases with 'L'Homme universel.' Gracián aimed at portraying what came to be regarded later as the distinguishing qualities of the eighteenth-century French 'honnête homme,' or of the English 'gentleman.'

As we have seen, prudence was a virtue much admired by Gracián and perhaps one need go no further than 'the man of discretion' in order to find his essential idea of the personality which he wishes to depict.

The qualities of the 'discreto' he calls 'realces' and each of the twenty-five chapters of the work deals with one of these. There is no fixed plan of composition. We find dialogues, letters, allegories, essays, all brought in to illustrate the virtues in question.

Some of the essays, which have as sub-title 'discurso académico,' may have been read at meetings of Lastanosa's *salon.*

The first chapter is important as throwing some light upon Gracián's use of the words 'genio' and 'ingenio.' One of the greatest difficulties which the translator has in dealing with Gracián is to be found in the variety of senses in which he uses certain quite common Spanish words. In *El Héroe,* 'ingenio' is used to indicate the intellectual faculties as opposed to 'agudeza,' 'finesse,' 'wit.' In *El Discreto* it also means 'aptitude for acquiring knowledge,' while 'genio' is used in the sense of 'innate tastes' and 'character.' Vagueness in the use of words is characteristic of Gracián. Nevertheless, generally speaking, one may say that 'genio' and 'ingenio' were employed during his age as in the sense of the French 'génie' and 'esprit,' respectively.

A certain assurance of manner is a mark of the 'discreto,' an assurance which, in fools, takes the form of insolence and arrogance, common also, says Gracián, among the wealthy. He must be 'galante' (another troublesome world for the translator), and the Conde de Aranda is quoted as a model of 'gallantry.' He must be consistent and of equable disposition, urbane and tolerant. Lastanosa is given as a model of urbanity. He must be 'quick in the uptake' and must divine, up to a point, unspoken thoughts. The idea that a man of the world should be something of a mind-reader is characteristic of Gracián and he returns to it in the **Criticón.** He must have a sense of humour, but know when to stop joking. He must have discrimination and must not be too easy-going. He must know when he has gone far enough in a negotiation and be able to get out at the right moment; he must be able to display his merits without vulgar ostentation. He must not give way to moods, nor be aggressive in conversation. 'He must,' says Gracián, employing a metaphor from the bullring, 'watch from behind the barrier of his wisdom the antics of the bulls of folly.'

Gracián's reputation as a cultivator of 'conceptismo' and 'culteranismo,' those often perverse forms of literary style so popular in Spain during the seventeenth century, is mainly due to his *Agudeza y arte de ingenio* of which more will be said later. Here we need only comment on the curious fact that, while the **Oráculo manual,** so highly praised by Schopenhauer, has been neglected by the majority of Gracián's critics, the **Agudeza** was for long generally regarded as his only title to fame, or, perhaps we should say, infamy.

El Criticón is Gracián's most ambitious work and embodies a lifetime of reading and experience. It might well be described as a secular *Pilgrim's Progress* and one episode, the visit to the Fair of the World, recalls a similar incident in Bunyan's masterpiece. It is, indeed, true that both books are allegorical romances. There, however, the similarity ends. The two works differ from one another profoundly, as do the temperaments of their respective authors. Gracián is the aloof, objective observer of human folly and wickedness, while Bunyan is the burning enthusiast, proclaiming his 'message' on every page. Gracián approaches his theme in the spirit of a pagan philosopher and develops it as a cultured man of the world. It was less dangerous for him to attack social evils through the mouths of his characters than to indulge in direct criticism. *El Criticón,* nevertheless, was a major cause of his ultimate downfall and disgrace. It is, indeed, an extraordinarily courageous book coming, as it did, from the pen of a Jesuit priest who did not hesitate to criticize, although but implicitly, his own Order. It is also an indisputably great book which, if it had been written in a less obscure and tortured style, might well have received as much attention as the world's other great allegorical and satirical romances. More will be said later concerning the translations of Gracián's works. It is, however, interesting to note here that Part I of the *Criticón* appeared in an English version by Paul Rycaut as early as 1681 and it has been suggested that Defoe may have derived the conception of Robinson Crusoe from this rendering.

The *Oráculo manual y arte de prudencia* (1647) is, as we have observed, a kind of compendium or anthology of the apothegms, maxims, epigrams, and general *obiter dicta* to be found scattered throughout the other works of the author.

It is the book by which Gracián is best known outside Spain and it has been translated into no less than eight modern European languages. To what extent may one regard it as the product of Gracián's unaided genius? The three hundred Maxims of which it consists are original in their mode of expression rather than in their content. As M. Coster rightly observes: 'On n'invente pas en morale.' Gracián has drawn upon the common stock of Western European thought as exemplified, more especially, in the works of the Roman moralists, such as Seneca and the younger Pliny. There are indications that he was also acquainted with the works of Francis Bacon and he owes something to his own countrymen, Francisco Gómez de Quevedo and Antonio Pérez. Borrowings of this kind were universal at the time, and if Gracián is to be charged with plagiarism he should, with justice, be accompanied in the dock by many figures greater than he. He is certainly as original as La Rochefoucauld who, directly or indirectly, probably laid him under contribution. With this observation one may, perhaps, put aside a somewhat unprofitable topic and turn to matters of greater interest.

What kind of work is the *Oráculo?* It is, as the author describes it, a 'handbook' and its object is severely practical. The literature of the period abounded in guides to heaven above; the *Oráculo* is strictly concerned with man's fortunes on the earth beneath. It may seem strange that such a book as this, an odd compound of shrewdness, cynicism, and moralizing, should be the work of a minister of religion. Gracián, however, was a very special kind of minister, a Jesuit priest, with no inconsiderable experience of men and things both directly, in the palaces of the aristocracy and on the battlefield, and indirectly, in the confessional.

Whatever faults Roman Catholic priests may have, they are rarely, if ever, what the Americans describe, in picturesque simile, as 'yellow-mouthed.' The hearing of confessions over a long period must surely tend to eradicate any starry-eyed notions concerning human behaviour. It might be stretching the point rather far to say that the *Oráculo* could only have been written by a Catholic priest. It is, nevertheless, the kind of book which one might well expect from a cleric of Gracián's temperament, culture, and experience. As a priest, he was accustomed to advising penitents on spiritual matters. In the *Oráculo* he addresses his readers in his character of courtier and man of the world. He says to them, in effect: 'If you want to get on in life do what this book tells you, although I do not say that getting on in life should be your chief object, or even that it is a laudable object.' The approach of Samuel Smiles is very different. Gracián is nearer to Lord Chesterfield. His cynicism, however, goes deeper than that of the Englishman because the Spanish priest believed that 'getting on' in life was fundamentally unimportant. There is no cynicism more profound than that of the unworldly.

Apart from the deliberate opening gambit in which Gracián tells us that everything on earth has already been done as well as it possibly can be done, 'especially the job of being a great man,' the *Oráculo* is a book without a plan. The Maxims follow one another indiscriminately and there is no underlying conception to link them together. The same idea is frequently expressed in different forms. The quintessence of the advice which Gracián offers his readers might be summed up as follows: Know yourself, your weakness as well as your strength; know also how to conceal shortcomings and make a discreet display of your merits. Others, however, are at the same game, so *they* must be known as well. Penetrate behind their masks; be something of a clairvoyant, see through them and divine their thoughts. Do not exaggerate, and remember, also, that truth itself can sometimes be used in order to deceive. A wise man will have to deal, mainly, with fools because they are in the majority. He can, however, always get the better of them. Combine the subtlety of the serpent with the candour of the dove. Think with the few and speak with the many. Neither hate nor love on a permanent basis and remember that a friend turned enemy is the most dangerous of all foes, and that even the best friend may change. One must, of course, have friends because they increase one's power, but do not trust them too far. One really good friend, and no more, is the ideal, but do not even venture to put all your eggs into that basket. Avoid poor and unlucky folk like the plague and cultivate those who can be of use to you. Learn how to foster goodwill in others. It is better that others should suffer than oneself.

The *Oráculo* produces an impression of almost complete secularity. Its atmosphere is almost entirely of this world and its pessimism and cynicism were, later, to find an echo in the thought of La Rochefoucauld, Schopenhauer, and, possibly, Nietzsche. Was Gracián, then, a hypocrite and a double-dealer? Some of his critics have thought as much. Their judgment in this respect is almost certainly erroneous and arises either from lack of knowledge or from failure to appreciate the significance of Gracián's works. The Roman Catholic Church taught, and still teaches, that there are two orders of being, the natural and the supernatural; also that natural man, while not entirely corrupt, has but little to commend him. The Jesuits, while they believed in free will, regarded man's volition as enfeebled and perverted by original sin. While man is not altogether devoid of a certain natural benevolence, as distinct from supernatural charity, it would, from the Catholic point of view, be an occasion for surprise if people normally behaved well 'off their own bat,' so to speak. This, one feels, is the true explanation of Gracián's disarming observation at the end of the *Oráculo* to the effect that the best advice of all is: 'Be a saint.'

THE STYLE OF GRACIAN

Preciosity, Marinism, Gongorism, Euphuism, call it what you will, is not, as some critics would have us believe, a stylistic phenomenon which has its origins solely in the soil of Spain. It seems to flourish most luxuriantly at the point in its history when a civilization has reached its cultural zenith and is beginning to follow a downward spiral. When everything that can be said has been said upon a theme, for example, such as sexual love, the only task left to the erotic poet is to say the same things in a different way. When all possible topics for moral exhortation have been exhausted, the preacher must keep the interest of his congregation alive by varying his technique, a fact of which ministers of religion in later days have been as conscious as were the Catholic clergy in the age of Gracián. (pp. 10-18)

In Spain, 'preciosity' took two forms. There was, on the one hand, 'culteranismo,' the art of playing with words, and, on the other, 'conceptismo,' the art of playing with ideas. Marini in Italy, and Luis de Góngora in Spain, were outstanding exponents of the first technique, while Quevedo distinguished himself in the second, and Gracián in both. Quite apart from the influence of pulpit oratory and the general stylistic tendencies of his age, Gracián was temperamentally inclined towards highly sophisticated art forms. Anything which the mob, 'los necios,' the fools, could easily understand would naturally appear to him as of little, if any, value. Like Marini, he regarded obscurity as the essence of all great art. Where style is concerned, 'good' and 'difficult' were to him synonymous. Environmental influences in the form of Lastanosa's *salons* fostered cultural esotericism, and the wonder is not that Gracián became a 'cultista' and a 'conceptista' but that he was not more extreme in his practice of the stylistic techniques then so highly in favour. The maxims of the *Oráculo* are, it is true, difficult to interpret, and they are intentionally so. They are not meant to be swallowed at one gulp but to be rolled meditatively around the intellectual palate, as one might savour a fine old brandy with the physical organ. They presuppose a certain acquaintance with the classics and the contemporary literature of Italy and Spain. Some of them require a gloss for their proper elucidation. But surely similar things could also be affirmed of, say, the poetry of Mr. T. S. Eliot, who is now ungrudgingly awarded the approbation of the orthodox.

It is true that the *Criticón* abounds in obscure allusions to contemporary personalities and events, but so do the works of many non-Spanish writers who are hailed as geniuses. If Luis de Góngora, a far more obscure and diffi-

cult writer than Gracián, is accepted to-day as the genius which he undoubtedly was, why should some critics jib at the complexities of Gracián?

It is possible to find fault with the *Agudeza y arte de ingenio* on other and more serious grounds. While it is, professedly, a treatise on style, it has no clear plan and is replete with inconsistencies. With his head full of the writings of his greatly admired Alonso de Ledesma and the sermons of Paravicino, Gracián set out to produce a book of literary precepts for the guidance of would-be practitioners in the aforementioned styles. He does not even succeed in producing a satisfactory definition of either 'culteranismo' or 'conceptismo.' His theories concerning poetic diction, the use of neologisms and archaisms, are ill presented and confused. He praises the worst extravagancies of Ledesma, and exalts the second-rate Luis Carillo y Sotomayor to the highest heaven of poesy. For Gracián he is the prince of Spanish 'cultistas.' Luis de Góngora, the greatest poet of that age, meets with slightly better treatment than his predecessor, Herrera. He is, says Gracián, a 'swan in his conceits' but the most famous of all Góngora's 'cultista' poems, *Las Soledades* and *El Polifemo,* are dismissed with the briefest of mention. Quevedo is praised for his 'incessant puns' and Lope de Vega is somewhat unjustifiably ranked as an outstanding 'conceptista.'

It has been suggested that the *Agudeza* was a piece of plagiarism and, whether this be the case or not, the work, which has often been regarded as the sole criterion of Gracián's merits as a writer, is not comparable in worth with either the *Oráculo* or the *Criticón.*

Gracián's stylistic peculiarities may be summarized, very briefly, as follows. The 'agudeza' is no new phenomenon in literature. The ancients knew it, although they had no theories about it. It is a 'beautiful concordance, an harmonious correlation between intelligible extremes expressed by an act of the intelligence.' 'What beauty is to the eyes and harmony to the ears, the "concepto" is to the understanding.' Another definition of the 'concepto' is 'an act of the understanding which expresses the correspondence which is to be found between objects.' Gracián goes on to distinguish two species of 'agudeza,' the second of which he subdivides into three varieties. Much has been written upon the precise nature of this treatise. Croce regards it as dealing with both 'conceptismo' and 'culteranismo' while Menéndez y Pelayo says that it is exclusively 'conceptista.' We shall not attempt to expound these arguments here but merely call attention to the fact that Gracián makes a clear distinction (one of the few such in the book) between 'natural' and 'mannered' style ('estilo natural' and 'estilo artificioso') and observes that the 'natural' variety is like bread, in that one never wearies of it. He also states quite clearly that two things are necessary to constitute a perfect style, the material element, which consists of the actual words employed, and the formal element, representing the ideas which the words express. Some, he says, are satisfied with the 'soul' of the 'agudeza' alone. This is not enough. It is difficult to interpret this observation as other than a statement of the author's belief that both 'conceptismo' and 'culteranismo' must be present to produce a perfect style. He emphasizes his point when he avers that if attention is paid merely to the words, their collocation and their material 'pulidez,' the result will be a 'bastardo cultismo.' The older writers, he goes on to say, concentrated entirely on the 'concepto' while his contemporaries laid the main emphasis upon 'cultismo.' Of the two, Gracián maintains that the former were on more correct lines.

Gracián belongs, in fact, to both schools and his style is characterized by the following outstanding features: (1) careful avoidance of the simple and obvious idea or word; (2) forced antitheses of ideas and/or words; (3) comparisons and parallelisms; (4) plays on words; (5) inversion (subject placed after the verb); (6) constant use of metaphors, many of them forced and obscure; (7) use of words in a different sense from the normal one; (8) use of neologisms; (9) Latinisms (e.g. suppression of the article); (10) use of ellipsis; (11) use of odd epithets.

In spite of these mannerisms, most of his works have a superficial and deceptive appearance of simplicity, owing to the brevity of the sentences as compared with the long, meandering clauses so common in Spanish literature of the 'Golden Centuries.' Everywhere, except in the **Criticón,** we sense an effort towards extreme concision. A maxim of the **Oráculo** is rather like one of those Chinese boxes which were fashionable playthings in the Edwardian era. It appears to be a complete object in itself but on opening it another box is revealed, and on opening that, another, and so on until one reaches the core, a miniature so small that it can scarcely be handled. The miniature box might be compared to the ultimate idea of a Maxim of the **Oráculo.** It has taken a great deal of time and much intellectual effort to discover it and when it is at last found it is sometimes a mere platitude dressed up to look like an epigram. But the process of discovering it in the original Spanish is entertaining and a valuable piece of intellectual gymnastics. (pp. 18-22)

> *L. B. Walton, in an introduction to* The Oracle: A Manual of the Art of Discretion, *by Balthasar Gracián, translated by L. B. Walton, J. M. Dent & Sons Ltd., 1953, pp. 1-48.*

L. B. Walton   (essay date 1959)

[*In the excerpt below, Walton investigates the similarities between Gracián's* El Criticón *and John Bunyan's* Pilgrim's Progress, *determining that "the analogies, though sometimes striking, are no more than coincidental."*]

While Bunyan and Gracián were both masters of the allegorical novel they were, as individuals, poles apart. There are, however, one or two interesting biographical parallels. The idea of the *Pilgrim's Progress* came to Bunyan in gaol, where he was twice confined for his opposition to the policy of the Establishment. Gracián, as we know, came under ecclesiastical censure and discipline when he persisted in writing the Third Part of *El Criticón.* Bunyan was at one time a soldier and served in the New Model Army (1644). Gracián was for a time an army chaplain and witnessed much bloodshed (1646).

While some of the analogies between the *Pilgrim's Progress* and *El Criticón* are striking, there are also fundamental differences in tone between the allegories. Bunyan was austere and limited in his outlook, a typical Puritan. His knowledge of literature was confined to Holy Writ, interpreted according to the tenets of a Calvinistic Evangelicalism. Roman Catholicism was repugnant to him, as to all exponents of his creed. When Christian meets with Pope and Pagan in the Valley of the Shadow of Death, Bunyan writes: "Pagan has been dead for many a long day and, as for the other, though he may yet be alive, he is by reason of age . . . grown so crazy and stiff in his joints that he can now do little more than sit in his Cave's mouth, grinning at Pilgrims as they go by and biting his nails because he cannot come at them."

Apart from his knowledge of Biblical lore, Bunyan was a near ignoramus. His work is, however, rich in mystical insight, and reveals the author as a "God-intoxicated" man. But he is no psychologist. His characters are little more than allegorical figure-heads. Gracián's work, on the contrary, is rich in subtle psychological insight. Bunyan was of poor and humble parentage, a tinker by trade. Gracián came of good bourgeois stock on his father's side and was welcomed in urbane and aristocratic circles. His work shows him to have been a man of wide scholarship. He owes much, both stylistically and ideologically, to his knowledge of the ancient classics, and is deeply indebted to classical mythology, moral philosophy, and the work of various Italian humanists and political philosophers. The intellectual climate in which he worked was utterly different from that of the humble Bunyan. The Puritans set great store by austerity and respectability, condemning the theatre, dancing, and other secular amusements as wiles of the Devil. Theologically, they were much concerned with the doctrines of Justification by Faith, Predestination and Election. Eternal Damnation was regarded as the only alternative to Heavenly Bliss. Bunyan, a layman, wrote several religious works or tracts on religious topics. Gracián wrote only one book, *El Comulgatorio* (1655) of a specifically religious character. Some critics have regarded it as a sop to the clerical Cerberus, for, unlike any of Gracián's other works, it is purely devotional and might have done something to refute the charges of frivolity and secularism brought against him. Here, however, we are in the dangerous realm of speculation.

There are certainly some striking resemblances between the *Pilgrim's Progress* and *El Criticón.* Both works contain episodes in which the world is presented to us as a Fair, as an Enigma requiring interpretation and, by Bunyan, as a Dream. While Gracián does not introduce us to it in *El Criticón,* the conception of the world as a dream or fantasmagoria was, nevertheless, part of the climate of opinion in his day. It is unnecessary to remind Hispanists of Calderón's *La vida es sueño.* The idea of death as an awakening to eternal reality, as "the moment of truth", is also a commonplace of Catholic theology. This dream symbolism was not a special feature of Puritan thought. While Bunyan tells us that his vision of the pilgrimage came to him *in* a dream, he takes a step further when he describes life in this world *as* a dream, and a dream requiring interpretation. This he does in the dogged rhyme he uses (he was a very bad poet) in his apology for his book, to explain its meaning and purpose.

> This book is writ in such a Dialect
> As may the Minds of listless Men affect
> It seems a Novelty, and yet contains
> Nothing but sound and honest Gospel-strains
> Wouldst thou then read Riddles and their Explanation.
> Wouldst thou be in a Dream and yet not sleep?

À propos of Bunyan's "honest Gospel-strains", Gracián seems to have been more at home in the witty and urbane atmosphere of aristocratic salons than in the society of theologians and clerics. The latter found him a difficult person to handle and there can be little doubt that his social contacts were the object of disapproval tinged with envy. If his secular activities were unpleasing to Catholic priests, austere Puritans would have regarded them as actually sinful. As we know, the tone of *El Criticón* is almost entirely secular and pagan. Apart from the resemblances which we are about to discuss, one outstanding ideological similarity between the *Pilgrim's Progress* and *El Criticón* deserves emphasis. For both writers, the world is dominated by the lie in the soul and, for both writers, this is its besetting and major fault. Both Bunyan and Gracián continually harp upon the falsity of the world, in which seekers after truth are condemned out of hand. In *El Criticón* Gracián's views concerning the majority of his fellow creatures appear to be misanthropic. The consoling hope of eventual bliss through Divine Redemption is not mentioned. For Bunyan, however, eternal happiness in Heaven awaits the justified sinner and this belief does something to mitigate the pessimism of his world picture. Gracián's Heaven, La Isla de la Inmortalidad, on the contrary, is not the traditional Christian one. It is populated by the wise rather than by the godly.

There are also considerable differences between the *Pilgrim's Progress* and *El Criticón*. Gracián mingles actual historical characters with purely symbolic and mythical figures. Here we are concerned only with the allegorical and symbolic elements in the two works. It should also be noted that in both books important episodes and symbolic figures are not confined merely to the pictures which the respective authors give of the world as a Fair. The Interpreter is introduced at an early stage in Bunyan's story, the scene of which is partly set in the approaches to Vanity Fair. El Descifrador, whose function is similar to that of Bunyan's Interpreter, does not appear until Part III of *El Criticón*. Discounting Christian's wife, Christiana, and his children, whose pilgrimage, on similar lines, is recorded in Part II of the *Pilgrim's Progress,* Bunyan's book has two protagonists rolled into one, for we are told that, prior to his conversion, Christian was known as Graceless. Gracián's work has two distinct heroes, if one can describe Andrenio as such, for the author appears to regard him as an object of patronage and, indeed, at times, almost as a stooge. Critilo, Andrenio's sagacious and worldly mentor, is obviously the author's ideal. Critilo, be it noted, has little to say, explicitly, about God or the Devil. He has, however, much to observe concerning the follies, vices and general stupidity of mankind. In comparing the *Pilgrim's Progress* with *El Criticón* a distinction should be made between the aforementioned figures of the Interpreter and El Descifrador. Bunyan's characters are, as a rule, straightforwardly symbolic. Evangelist, Help, Mr. Worldly Wiseman, Mr. Legality, Formalist, Hypocrisy, Mistrust, Timorous, Piety, Prudence, Charity, and Christian himself, are obvious examples. Of whom is the Interpreter symbolical? An Apostle, a Prophet perhaps? He takes Christian into his house and interprets the significance of various persons and objects in answer to direct questions from Christian: "What means this?" He first shows Christian a picture symbolizing Christ. He then takes him into a parlour full of dust and calls upon a man to sweep it. Then he requests a damsel to sprinkle the room with water. In answer to Christian's question, the Interpreter replies: "This Parlour is the heart of man that was never sanctified by the sweet Grace of the Gospel. The dust is his original sin. . . . He that began to sweep at first is the Law; but she that brought water and did sprinkle it is the Gospel." Christian is then taken into a room where there are two children, Passion and Patience, and the Interpreter points out that Passion wanted the good things of this world, Patience being content to wait until the next one. Then follow the allegories of the room with the Fire, the Man in Armour, the Man in an Iron Cage, the Man on a Cloud, all on the same simple and obvious religious lines.

Notwithstanding his somewhat similar role, Gracián's El Descifrador is a very different kind of person from the Interpreter. He is not concerned with theology, but rather with the hidden motives underlying human behaviour. . . . While, as we have observed, Bunyan's Interpreter confines himself to explaining the meaning of a simple religious allegory, Gracián's El Descifrador appears to revel in subtlety for its own sake.

Bunyan's Vanity Fair is far less rich in incident than Gracián's La Feria de Todo el Mundo. Nevertheless, his description of the Fair has something in common with Gracián's account of the Feria. It is situated, says Bunyan, in the Town of Vanity, through which the Devil and his minions have arranged that all Pilgrims to the Celestial City must pass. (It is) "a Fair wherein should be sold all sorts of Vanity." It lasts all the year long. "Therefore at this Fair are all such Merchandises sold, as Houses, Lands, Trades, Places, Honors, Preferments, Titles, Countries, Kingdoms, Lusts, Pleasures, and Delights of all sorts, as Whores, Bawds, Wives, Husbands, Children, Masters, Servants, Lives, Blood, Bodies, Souls, Silver, Gold, Pearls, Precious Stones, and what not? And moreover, at this Fair there are at all times to be seen Jugglings, Cheats, Games, Plays, Fools, Apes, Knaves and Rogues, and that of every kind. . . . And as in Fairs of less moment, there are the several rows and Streets under their proper names (*viz.* Countries and Kingdoms) where the Wares of this Fair are soonest to be found. Here is the Britain Row, the French Row, the Italian Row, the Spanish Row, the German Row, where several sorts of Vanities are to be sold." It will be observed that the general description of the Fair tallies to some extent with that which Gracián gives us of his Feria. Bunyan, however, unlike Gracián, enters into little detail. One would like to have heard more, for example, of the Cheats and Jugglings.

Comparatively little happens during Christian's visit to the Fair. On being asked what the Pilgrims will buy, they reply, "We buy the Truth." The response of the vendors is to beat them, smear them with dirt, and put them into a cage. They are examined, re-examined, and eventually charged with being guilty of the hubbub in the Fair. They are put in irons and led in chains up and down the streets. Eventually they are brought to trial, with Lord Hategood on the bench. False witness is given against Faithful by Envy, Superstition and Pickthank. Faithful attempts to defend himself on religious grounds. His pleas, however, are unavailing and he is eventually beaten and put to a painful death. Meanwhile, Christian resumes his pilgrimage with a new companion, Hopeful. So end the chief incidents in the episode of the Fair. There is no extensive detail, no subtlety of any kind. The religious allegories are of the simplest and the theological disquisitions of the pilgrims often seem tedious to a layman. (pp. 28-33)

There are some interesting similarities between Bunyan's scripturally inspired picture of the Valley of the Shadow of Death and the Valle de las Fieras described by Gracián. Bunyan's Valley is "as dark as pitch and infested by Hobgoblins, Satyrs and Dragons of the Pit. There is a continual howling and yelling. It is overhung by clouds of confusion and Death spreads his wings over it." In the middle of the Valley Christian passes the Mouth of Hell and is beset by fiends. The place is full of snares, traps, gins and pitfalls. It is "every whit dreadful, being utterly without order."

In Gracián's Valle, "todo era confusión y fiereza, espectáculo verdaderamente fatal y lastimero." It is infested with "ejércitos de fieras, leones, tigres, osos, lobos, serpientes y dragones." Here it must be noted that Gracián's Valle describes a natural, not a spiritual hell. There are no diabolical figures, as in Bunyan's Valley. Both writers are, however, fascinated by monstrosities, and Bunyan's description of the fiend, Apollyon, would, doubtless, have pleased Gracián. "He was hideous to behold, he was clothed with scales like a fish, had wings like a dragon, feet like a bear . . . and his mouth was as the mouth of a lion." (p. 34)

Apart from his own inventions, Gracián describes various monsters of classical mythology, satyrs, centaurs, serpent men and so forth. . . . Among Gracián's own monstrous creations, the gigantinano and the sombra de hombre are ingenious and original. It is to be noted that, where symbolism exists, it is on the natural or mythological, not, as in Bunyan, on the religious plane.

The writer of this article would venture to claim that some curious and interesting analogies between the *Pilgrim's Progress* and *El Criticón* have here been revealed, notwithstanding the fundamental differences between the tone and style of the two works. These analogies would appear to be entirely fortuitous. (pp. 34-5)

As to any possible influence on the *Pilgrim's Progress*, it must be noted that the last edition of Part I of this work appeared in 1688. . . . Rycaut's rendering of Part I of *El Criticón* was published in 1681. As all the other editions of Part I of the *Pilgrim's Progress* pre-date Rycaut's translation, and as there are few novelties in the 1688 edition of Bunyan's work, chronology does not appear to be of importance in this case. Part II of the *Pilgrim's Progress*, which was published in 1684, contains little that is fundamentally new. (p. 35)

The *Pilgrim's Progress* has but one source of inspiration—Holy Writ. Gracián's *El Criticón* has many sources. Of the two works the *Pilgrim's Progress*, for all its relative simplicity, is, perhaps, more original in spirit and feeling.

Dr. Antonio Rodríguez Pastor has indicated a possible analogy between the Critilo—Andrenio and Robinson Crusoe—Man Friday antitheses. The first part of *Robinson Crusoe* appeared in 1719. Unlike Bunyan, Defoe (1659-1731), who became a prolific writer in his later years, was acquainted with a wide range of literature and might well have seen Rycaut's rendering of Part I of *El Criticón*. No virtual impossibility is involved, such as we meet with in the case of the *Pilgrim's Progress*. Defoe lived,

moreover, at a time when there was a growing interest in Spanish literature. One of his predecessors in the journalistic world of his day was Roger L'Estrange, translator of Quevedo's *Los Sueños*. But so far as the *Pilgrim's Progress* and *El Criticón* are concerned, the analogies, though sometimes striking, are no more than coincidental. They may thus serve as a warning to "source hunters" in other fields. (pp. 35-6)

> *L. B. Walton, "Two Allegorical Journeys: 'Pilgrim's Progress' and 'El Criticón',"* in Bulletin of Hispanic Studies, *Vol. XXXVI, 1959, pp. 28-36.*

Herman Iventosch   (essay date 1961)

[*Iventosch is an American educator who has published several works on Spanish literature. In the excerpt below, he provides in-depth interpretations of the allegorical names in* El Criticón.]

The study of invented literary names has lagged far behind that of toponyms and historical family names, and yet imaginative literature has produced an uncommon number of names which not only achieved extensive common use (especially in the Renaissance) but from time immemorial have formed an important element of literary invention. I am concerned here with the particular case of moral-allegorical names in the foremost didactic work of the Spanish Baroque. They are of interest both because they illustrate a continuing historical phenomenon and because in the day of "mannered" literary techniques they came to be key ingredients in one writer's didacto-literary system.

As Romera-Navarro has pointed out, the allegorical element is of utmost importance in the **Criticón.** The grand scheme in the work is the voyage of man (Critilo and Andrenio) through life, a voyage complicated by innumerable encounters with personified virtues and vices, as well as with occasional historical personages, that are met on the way. The principals of this allegory and many of the minor actors are typified by invented names: 'honor' is *Honoria,* 'hypocrisy' *Hipocrinda,* etc. The practice of thus highlighting the essential nature of a character, or in this case of personifying man's principal virtues and vices, has been designated as the "only rhetorical device" which can be traced uninterruptedly to Homer, and Gracián included it as a prime stylistic device in his **Agudeza y arte de ingenio** (1642, 1648).

In the **Agudeza** it is demonstrated that this stylistic device will seek not only the absolute creation of names but will, perhaps with preference and more often, adapt names hoary with antiquity, and with or without alteration, will find their "correspondence and correlation" which will make them adaptable to allegorical use. Gracián then implies that a higher *agudeza* will be achieved if the name is changed, that is, if by an alteration of the name (*Roma* reversed, *Amor,* the 'love' of the church), its potential *correspondencia* is more thoroughly plumbed. Hereby, an infinitude of new meanings may be revealed, and the practice will produce in the **Criticón** *Andrenio,* which probably combines *Andrés* and *Andronio,* even as it derives from Greek *anēr,* gen. *andrós* 'man'; *Sofisbella,* which fuses Greek *sophía* 'wisdom' with a popular seventeenth-century form of *Isabel, Isbella; Vegecia* 'Old-age,' which probably hearkens back to the likes of the Roman writer *Vegetius* (Sp. *Vegecio*), etc. Even the absolute inventions usually reveal some onomastic element: *Hipocrinda* 'hypocrisy' with the common name-suffix *-inda,* as *Lucinda;* or *Falimundo* 'falseness of the world' or 'world of the false,' but with *mundo* reflecting also the likes of *Rosamunda* and *Segismundo,* the stem, in Gracián, being Latinized in manneristic fashion back to the infinitive *fallere* rather than the participle *falsus,* the usual source of the Spanish derivatives. The idea of the mystery and hidden meanings of language undoubtedly goes back not only to Homer and Plato but also to the concept of the sacredness of language and the word, and the Jesuit Gracián does not hesitate to attribute to *Dios* his own private interpretation of the exalted term.

Like *Crisi,* the chapter title name in the **Criticón,** the name *Critilo* is also derived from the Greek verb *krino,* 'judge.' Rescuing Andrenio from shipwreck, Critilo is his mentor, his guide, and much more—as we shall see—in the pilgrimage through life. He is, in brief, as his name conveys, the rational part of man, the part which by the divine gift of reason, may see the truth; who not only has the oft-mentioned Gracianesque qualities of practical conduct, but also possesses the vision necessary to avail himself of virtue in the pilgrimage toward salvation; he is the elite, thus, not ony of the world, but also the "elite" part of man. The name *Cratilo* (Plato's *Cratylus*) probably provided a general onomastic mold for Gracián, as with a slight *trastrocar* it yields a new allusion. Its alteration on the basis of *krino, kritos,* gives the *correspondencia* to 'reason' and 'judgment' which the author requires.

The name *Andrenio* likewise suggests its Greek origin (*anēr, andrós*). Its form, as noted, probably emerges from both *Andrés* and *Andronio* (*Andronicus*), and in Gracián's scheme is symbolic of 'raw, untutored man.' He is Critilo's "otro yo," and almost any page will reveal variations on the "Andrenio," or the raw, unprincipled, carnal, ingenuous, etc., element in all men: Andrenio can be the simple one in search of wisdom; he can be the head which is kicked about like a football, . . . or, as is illustrated when they approach Virtelia's palace, he can be the spontaneous and unreflective man who will not face the hardships of virtue. . . . The name now reveals a greater dramatic and intellectual message. Gracián has created the name *Andrenio* 'man' because "man" has a particular significance in his semantics. "Man," the raw material, is distinguished regularly by the Jesuit from *persona,* or "man" under control of reason. In the **Criticón** Andrenio is called "hombre o bestia. . . ." *Andrenio,* thus, translates Spanish *hombre* with its exact etymological meaning from rare Latin *homo* 'gross man' (see any good Latin lexicon). As Jansen points out, *hombre* may sometimes include an additional attribute, "hombres substanciales y de fondo", or "hombres de veras", in which instance it becomes equivalent to *sabio, persona,* and the rest. But *hombre* alone cannot convey a "real human being" (*wirklicher Mensch*), and is generally equivalent to just "man"—the flesh, the instincts (see *Falsirena*)—or "animal," as noted above. The effect of the name *Andrenio,* then, is to abstract all the qualities which Gracián associates with simple "man," and to portray them onomastically in the individual who depicts them. We have seen only a fraction of the characteristics which Andrenio exhibits. His name is a dramatic summation of them all.

Critilo, meanwhile, is Ariel forever struggling against him, never with entire success. The name *Critilo*—'judge,' 'rational man'—synthesizes the various Gracianesque notions of *sabio, héroe, persona,* and the rest, while the act of combining him and *Andrenio,* his "otro yo," probably reflects orthodox Christian polarized man as Critilo pursues his task of education of his baser self (*Andrenio*). In any instance, the pair highlight Gracián's dualistic concept of man. *Critilo* "higher man" is equipped with the Stoical qualities (Gracián carries on the immemorial task of attempting to reconcile pagan and Christian thought) of prudence, moderation, and impassivity, as Gracián, like Mateo Alemán, arms Christian man with extraordinary powers of 'judgment' to enable him to cope with the universal deceit around him (Baroque *desengaño*).

Artemia. The exterior resemblance of this name to *arte* makes it possible under the canon of "agudeza nominal" for her to personify the 'arts' or 'reason.' It should be noted that the form is one of two (with *Honoria*) that corresponds to "agudeza nominal" without a *trastrocar;* or should we say, that the *trastrocar* is entirely mental, the traditional form of the name being maintained intact. But a bold *correspondencia* is effected by supposing the name to be compounded from *arte,* especially since it had already acquired a traditional literary usage, with perhaps no allusive content except occasionally to 'virginity' (from *Artemis*). Artemia, reminiscent of the long tradition of the Liberal Arts, will achieve miracles, as did they: she converts the "villano zafio" to "cortesano galante"; the *vizcaíno* to "eloquente secretario" (the language of Biscayans was parodied in Spain, as is well known, from Lope de Rueda, through Cervantes, to modern times); and she makes a "César de un escribano," "hombres graves" from "hombres muy livianos." This queen is a worker of prodigious deeds; and to climax her feats, she produces "un hombre que discurría" from a wooden rod. . . . The ideal of the Liberal Arts . . . in both Antiquity and the Middle Age as the glory of man's mind and as bequeathed by God lived in Gracián as he used this name. *Artemia* means quite simply, then, 'reason,' and although she is once called *Saber,* the broad symbolism of 'wisdom' is reserved for *Sofisbella. Artemia,* thus, synthesizes a prime motif in Gracián: she symbolizes the absolutely miraculous power of reason; she creates a man who not only *discurría* but thereupon also *valía.* She is seen to be, of all the queens, perhaps the "queen of queens," since she represents in essence the same glorification of 'reason' and 'judgment' that is typified by Critilo.

Falimundo. The derivation of this name has already been analyzed. He is *engaño* 'deception,' and is vaguely conceived of as a monarch with a "Babilonia, que no corte" where Andrenio is held captive. As might be expected, there is only one defense against this evil potentate—logically Artemia 'reason,' who assures Critilo, playing again upon the *arte* in her name, that " . . . no nos ha de faltar *ardid* contra el engaño."

The treatment of these various allegorical names now permits us to make a generalization on them and Falimundo, a generalization which has been suggested in reference to Andrenio and which will apply generally to the other principal allegorical figures. It has been mentioned that sometimes specifically, sometimes only vaguely—as here, with Falimundo—the allegorical personages are kings, queens, and the like. It follows that rulers have courts, and that courts have courtiers and their other sundry retainers around them. Gracián has given the invented names to the monarchs of successive courts, the *primor* of the "agudeza nominal" being reserved for the chief figures who, in their position of eminence, have sway over many followers. The followers, accordingly, portray the various components of the major vice (or virtue) which is abstracted and synthesized by the fantastic ruler-appellation. We have mentioned how *Andrenio* may synthesize all qualities which Gracián associates with "man." *Deceit,* too, is a broad concept, and at the "juegos bacanales" at the "Babilonia, que no corte" of Falimundo, the whole throng attend. . . . The "agudeza nominal," a thing of wit and beauty, is consciously given to the main virtues and vices, to the 'crises' of man's life, while the infinite components of these virtues and vices—here courtiers—maintain everywhere their direct names—*la Lujuria, la Codicia, la Justicia*—as personified qualities, or the unpersonified ones shown above for Falimundo. This process, we think, is of striking originality in Gracián. *Artemia* could have been simply *el Saber,* and was briefly so called, as we have seen. But *Artemia,* by virtue of historical reminiscence and sex (*Artemis*), is a queen, and can rule over many subjects, the components of the 'arts.' Falimundo might have been *el Engaño,* but the onomastic ending in *-mundo,* as well as its geographic connotation, . . . and the opportunity to Latinize the stem, proves both more *agudo,* more regal, hence more synthetic, since he can be endowed with a court—and thus more efficient intellectually and more dramatic novelistically than the direct name. In the allegorical voyage the high points and stops along the road are signalized by the *primor* of an "agudeza nominal."

Falsirena. Unlike *Falimundo, Falsirena* points to the traditional Spanish derivation from the participle *falsus* (Spanish *falso*) which form is dictated by the initial *s* of *sirena,* the key concept of the personage who will represent 'woman,' "False" and a "Siren." The heavy medieval reflection would be overbearing did not Gracián qualify it by saying his Siren represents "la mala muger." The functions of the Sirens in Homer are of course commonplaces of Western literature and, as such, make available to Gracián a wealth of images with which to express his Christian sensuality, his "mundo, demonio, carne." The Sirens appear, first, with their sisters, the "furias, parcas, . . . arpías. . . . Falsirena's palace coalesces with Circe's pigsty, where Andrenio is discovered on the ground with other victims. In short, a series of traditional antique pictures is evoked by the name *Falsirena* to personify Gracián's Christian distrust of the flesh; and we are again reminded of the reconciliation, or attempted reconciliation, which had been going on since the early Middle Ages, of the Antique and Christian imagination. Most of these allegorical personages—principals, as noted, on the pilgrimage—do not appear again once they have been seen (except *Felisinda* 'happiness,' who will draw the pilgrims on throughout the novel); but Falsirena, long after her principal action, almost at the end of the voyage, is recalled as having been a necessary test on the road to virtue " . . . el escarmiento en la casa de Falsirena."

Felisinda. There are numerous names fashioned on *felix, -icis.* The meaning of the root, 'joyous,' defines her mission

in the **Criticón** as both doctrinal 'happiness' and as the amorous object of Critilo and Andrenio. Like Falimundo, Falsirena, and others, she exhibits a compound name, *Felis-inda,* which combines both 'joyous' and the common onomastic suffix *-inda,* as in *Lucinda.* But the *correspondencias* are more ample in "agudeza nominal." It is probably hardly accidental that "happiness" emerges from and is constantly recalled by the reader as having been associated with remote India, nor that this allegorical personification of happiness should have a name terminating with *-inda,* which is not only suffix but directly relevant to 'India.' *Felisinda* might thus have a message of 'happiness in India,' or 'happiness remote and inaccessible,' since this is precisely the quality she personifies, the unattainability of happiness on earth to Christian man. . . . The name *Felisinda* thus compliments in onomastic terms the doctrinal material cited above, even though, like Artemia, her name might occur as an ordinary feminine denomination. . . . A semi-amorous and novelistic slant is given to the sermon by this love-quest after *Felisinda,* but its connection with the doctrinal matter is obvious. At the court of Hipocrinda, where of course the "lovers" seek Felisinda out, they must leave emptyhanded, since certainly "la verdadera felicidad" is not to be found there, but only at the implied end of the pilgrimage, death, and the contemplation of the divine.

Hipocrinda, Virtelia: These two queens are treated together since they are closely associated in the text.

Hipocrinda represents 'hypocrisy,' and will be best explained here in her function as "queen vice," . . . the queen in whose court pullulate *la Simonía, la Usura, el Festejo,* specific "hypocrisies," and especially the "falso hermitaño y verdadero embustero," commonplace for religious hypocrisy. The function of queen for a prime vice has been efficacious up to this point, but as we reach "hypocrisy" Gracián finds it expedient to consider her also as the Mother Superior of a convent, since the first hypocrisy to our Jesuit is the religious one. Thus the abstraction of *Hipocrinda* "rules" over an additional series of specific hypocrites: the false hermit, a false priest, a gluttonous priest, false alcalde, and finally, a *professo,* who "más . . . huele a ladrón que a monge," all these being concretions of the major vice typified by Hipocrinda. In the religious and moral sphere, however, the aim of hypocrisy is the cloak of *virtue,* and our "falso hermitaño" will accordingly stand athwart the path and urge the pilgrims away from one who is designated "alma de la alma, vida de la vida . . . realce de todas las prendas, corona de las perfecciones, y perfección de todo el ser," Queen Virtelia.

The regal personification, as well as the suggestion of the devoted search, . . . is maintained in her. *Virtelia* 'virtue,' however, is perhaps the queen most pregnant with allegorical possibilities: the path to her palace is an ascent, symbolical of the vices and also of the trials to be endured in achieving virtue. . . . Such a goal is reminiscent of either the Christian pilgrim through life, or the knight errant. Virtelia must have a guide to her palace, as Hipocrinda did to hers; and this guide is, logically, *Lucindo,* a name—like Artemia—of a traditional form, given here with a new *correspondencia,* "light," or "varón de luces," who, as a counterpart for wisdom, will 'light,' the way to virtue. Moreover, Virtelia has the most peopled court of all the characters: *la Sabiduría, la Paciencia, la Justicia, la Equidad, la*

Castidad, la Honestidad, la Sagacidad, "gran ministra de Virtelia," all these are "virtue," and all are courtiers to Queen Virtelia. Finally, Virtelia is a "queen judge." Reminiscent of Solomon or Portia, she sits on a throne of justice (*la Justicia* is a handmaiden of hers, as noted) and answers pleas for boons: e.g., she gives courage to the soldier; skill to the priest in praying, to the farmer in planting, etc. The *agudeza Virtelia* stands as a beacon mark on man's pilgrimage through life, while all attendant "virtues" throng around her to explain what virtue is to the *vulgus.*

Honoria. As the reader knows, an *Honorius* was a Roman emperor of the West (A.D. 395—423) and an *Honoria* the licentious daughter of Valentinian who refused marriage with Attila the Hun. Many others doubtless exist, and the name is of such common stuff, both in ancient and modern times, that the measure of innovation in Gracián is small. The fact of her regal personification is supplemented by the attendant appearance of the celebrated and feared Momus, whose presence here will take us again into the ancient world as well as into the well-known seventeenth century conception of honor. For Honoria is represented as dwelling in a palace of glass, so that we are here reminded of the "honor play" and of Lope and Calderón. The Roman deity was styled *Honos* or *Honor,* but Gracián creates a feminine deity with deliberate effect. As a woman, she will serve several functions impossible to an allegorizing *Honor.* On the one hand, since it is Gracián's intention to disclose that there is *no* honor left in the world, Momus will step forward and say that, since Honoria is a woman, it is doubtful that she really represents what her name designates. . . . An additional classical reference will now be to regard Honoria as the mother of an "honorable" son, Pedro Pablo Zapata, the former governor of Aragón, whose exile signifies the departure of all "honor" from life. Many deities might be suggested as models of this mother and son, but Aphrodite and Eros, the son gaining his qualities from his mother, is the likely inspiration for Honoria and Zapata. The conclusion here is that the only "Honoria" possible is attainable in books and libraries, in the typical Stoic notion that the only personal integrity possible is in wisdom and in freedom from human passion. That *Honoria,* like Felisinda, eludes man's search, is a seeming reference to a contemporary earthly state, the seventeenth century in Spain, and not, as in *Felisinda,* a description of the divine plan.

Sofisbella. Gracián again seeks out the Greek lexicon to fashion the name of the queen who will personify 'wisdom.' The whole name combines the Greek *soph-* with a special form of *Isabel,* Gracián, like many writers of his time, transforming the Spanish *-bel* to the Italian *-bella,* to produce the Spanish sense of 'beautiful,' thus 'wisdom beautiful.' Each queen discussed so far has represented a maximum vice or virtue in the Christian's pilgrimage on earth; Sofisbella does the same. . . . What with *Critilo,* the 'critic,' and *Artemia,* the 'arts,' *Sofisbella,* 'glorious wisdom,' is a sort of culmination of the others. We now have reached, in a sense, the highest plane of earthly attainment, with only *Vegecia,* 'old-age,' ahead of us, and even she, of course, will offer—as her greatest boon—wisdom. . . . It is, then, crucial that Sofisbella, like Felisinda and Honoria, be beyond man's reach in this bitterest of all worlds; she dwells only, finally, in that sacred precinct, the library. . . . The absence of Sofisbella climaxes the bitter scene. . . . (pp. 215-27)

Vegecia. The important fact regarding *Vegecia* is not so much that her name suggests the Roman writer *Vegetius* (Spanish *Vegecio*), although this is generally a necessary attribute of the invented name, but that she is thereupon coupled with *Janus,* the Roman deity of the two doors. Through these doors will pass the two possibilities of man—those typified by *Andrenio* and *Critilo*—one through the door of *horrores,* or just the decrepitude of old age, and the other, *Critilo,* through the door of *honores,* or the wisdom accessible to some in old age. The name *Vegecia,* unproductive of any allusion beyond the exterior resemblance to *vejez,* in addition to the reminiscence of *Vegetius,* must perforce be combined with *Janus,* so that Gracián, when necessary, can conceive of a variation on his *agudeza nominal,* namely, the creation of a sort of *Vegecia-Jano,* the original *agudeza* expanded with an additional antique name to fulfill the allegorical picture which the author seeks. Queen Vegecia, the *honores* part of her, commands a large retinue, the qualities of whom she keynotes and synthesizes, in the Graciánesque technique we have described: *La Cordura, la Autoridad, el reposo* (the uncapitalized names are no different in allegorical function than those capitalized), *el assiento, la madurez, la prudencia, la gravedad, la entereza.*

Wherever convenient, Gracián turns also to name conceits for his minor characters. We have already mentioned *Lucindo* as the "varón de luces," symbol of wisdom and guide to Virtelia. There is also an *Egenio* (Latin *egenus* 'deserving, needing'), whose name is qualified by Gracián: " . . . este era su nombre, ya definición". He is thus named because he has a sixth sense, considering that "necessity" " . . . es ingeniosa, inventiva . . . ", or as English has it, the "mother of invention" comprises a sense additional to the usual five. *Volusia* (from the Roman jurist *Volusius,* in preference to the popular *Volupia* or *voluptas*) 'sensuality' compliments the functions of Falsirena.

The majority of the minor inventions are dedicated, however, to a favorite antipathy of the severe Jesuit: to the *Buena Miel,* as he styles the individual lacking in self-assertion and independence. There are a variety of these characters: a *Pachorra* 'phlegm, indolence,' whose very lethargy prevents the exercise of self-assertion; *Don Fulano de Macapán* 'Sir Candy' or 'Sir Creampuff'; *Buenas Entrañas, Canónigo Blandura, Dexado,* "y bien dexado de todos"; similarly, *Juan de Buen Alma, Boncampaño, Buen Hombre, Hombre de su Palabra.* . . . The very number of these names verifies the Jesuit's particularly violent scorn for the soft and the passive, and these personal traits can doubtless be grouped with those that Gracián feels impede the exercise of judgment and criterion.

Various other evils are also onomastically portrayed: a *Buñuelo de Viento* is a windy preacher; treacherous and false qualities are represented by *Raposo* and *Tracillas,* and a *Duque de Bernardina. Marrajo* 'uncouth' is considered by Romera-Navarro to refer again to Salinas, and an *Infanta doña Toda* is reduced by Gracián to *doña Nada* in a mockery of the pretension of lineage.

Clearly, the *primores* of the "agudeza nominal" are reserved in general for very special figures, the few unimportant ones above to the contrary notwithstanding. This is a process which we have already commented on and which we will summarize now.

Since it is clear that the invented names are given to the principal allegorical personages, let us see, briefly, the system we may extract from them. *Critilo* and *Andrenio* are of course *Man;* and *Man,* not a eulogy of reason or a critique of the world's evil, is the subject of the *Criticón.* More than Man, indeed, the conduct of Christian man is the subject of the novel. The *Criticón,* then, in all senses of the word, is a grave sermon, albeit with a special emphasis on worldly and profane activity; a definition of what man's nature is, *Critilo* and *Andrenio,* and what his actions should be in this most evil of all worlds.

But man must dwell briefly on earth. This fact is symbolized by the presence of *Falimundo,* who is emblematic not just of the 'falseness of the world,' or the 'world of the false,' but *of* the world. The world is of course "false" to the believing Christian. *Falimundo* will personify, with *Falsirena,* the emptiness of corporeal existence. *Falsirena* has a somewhat complex function, but her basic nature is a shallow disguise for "life itself." Gracián, to be sure, embellishes his sermon with varied tales of temptation and lust, as we have seen, in the pictures drawn from the remote Sirens and Circe. But the end product is a *Falsirena,* partly, to be sure, in the Medieval sense, signifying the female corruption of man, but more important, a *Falsirena* who is corporeal existence itself, "mundo, demonio, carne," in Gracián's own words.

If, then, the names noted depict man and his state in the world, there stands the "flower" of Queens, *Virtelia,* opposed to them. Up to this point we have, in a sense, treated what we may call the negative aspects of man's passage on earth. Is there no positive element to man's life? There is only one, says Gracián, virtue. Virtue, as we have said, is a complex concept, so that the components thereof—including even such daring concepts as the famous "santa astucia"—as if a homiletic explanation from the pulpit, teem through her court. *Virtelia* 'virtue' is a real and attainable end for man, but instead he seeks *Felisinda* 'joy' (Critilo, too), in his weak flesh, but of course in vain. As noted, she spans the novel, giving it movement forward until *Vegecia* 'old age' is reached. *Vegecia* is crucial since she symbolizes man's last and best chance for wisdom, after "la loca juventud" has passed. The place of reason and wisdom has been amply discussed here. *Artemia* and *Sofisbella* are at once a doubling of the emphasis on this imperative demand and a distinct reflection of the medieval preoccupation with *scientia* and *sapientia,* and again attest the Jesuit's respect for the stoic's stand, even while neither queen is to be found on earth.

Honoria and *Hipocrinda* remain for our consideration. The absence of the first, with the bitter acknowledgment of the second, allows an intense sense of contemporary satire to enter this otherwise profoundly doctrinal work: *Honoria,* for her reflection of the Spanish preoccupation with *pundonor; Hipocrinda,* because she reflects the contemporary obsession with universal hypocrisy, the leitmotif of *Guzmán de Alfarache,* and a favorite subject for satire in Gracián's day.

A very clear conclusion to our discussion may now be stated. Gracián has availed himself of the *primor* of the "agudeza nominal" to symbolize man and his main concerns on earth. His invented names have highlighted the main aspects of the moral message and have offered us an onomastic passage through the nature of man and his moral life itself.

Thus the didactic nature of the *Criticón* is clear. The preacher's art is to give life to his sermon. The invented names we have discussed make the allegorical personifications more outright personal, and thus are more easily absorbed by the reader; they are more vividly representative of the qualities personified (cf. *la Hipocresía* for 'hypocrisy,' as the contemporary writer of the *auto* would have said, in contrast to Gracián's *Hipocrinda*); and are more likely to be remembered in the course of the novel. In the *Criticón* the author seeks by literary means to reach his congregation with the maximum impress possible. In Gracián, thus, as perhaps nowhere else, the intellectual exercise of conceptism attains a fine synthesis of aesthetic ideal and moral purpose. The demonstration that the whole of man and his moral 'crises' can be signalized by a series of invented allegorical names reveals the originality of Gracián's technique and the efficacy with which he practiced his own doctrine of "Agudeza nominal." (pp. 228-33)

> *Herman Iventosch, "Moral-Allegorical Names in Gracián's 'Criticón'," in* Names, *Vol. IX, 1961, pp. 215-33.*

Otis H. Green   (essay date 1966)

[*Green is an American literary historian who specializes in Spanish literature. In the excerpt below from an essay originally published in his* Spain and the Western Tradition *(1966), he examines the role of* desengaño *("awakening to the nature of reality") in* El Criticón.]

Independent of and quite separate from the awareness of national decline . . . ; independent, also, of the widespread idea of a cyclical movement of history and a growing-old both of the world and of the human race; independent of—or at least not caused by—Counter-Reformational pressures imposed from above to cause a return to a hell-fire conception of humanity; and finally no less independent of causative effects produced by the racism that darkened many aspects of the life of Spain, there grew up in our period a literature of considerable bulk on the subject of disillusionment.

This was no new phenomenon, but a differentiating tone of intensity was perceived even by contemporaries. Fray Francisco Palanco, in his approbation of Quevedo's treatise *On the Constancy and Patience of Saintly Job* (1641), declared that those meditations have a greater Christian utility

> than other works of the author; for although he always has appeared as *desengañado* [that is to say, undeceived by the beguilements of life] even when his writings were festive and jocose in nature, in his earlier poems and essays the disillusionment was a sort of play-acting, a holiday jousting in which the lances were thrown for pleasure, not in anger. Here, on the contrary, there is no play, no jesting. The lances are thrown in all seriousness, and their steel points are so sharp that they penetrate to the in most recesses of any thoughtful heart. The author does not flatter; he strikes.

This *desengaño* is related to the sort of awakening to the nature of reality that the Prodigal Son must have experienced: "I will arise and go to my father." This waking to true awareness is called *caer en la cuenta:* to have the scales fall from one's eyes, to see things as they are. Such a state of mind is desirable. Disillusionment comes to be viewed, even to be venerated, as a sort of wisdom—the wisdom of the Stoic *sapiens,* or wise man of antiquity, who was fully aware of what constituted the *summum bonum,* the supreme good, and was utterly unenticed by everything else; a wisdom perhaps not unlike what the French mean today by their phrase *n'être pas dupe,* to be nobody's fool. (pp. 141-42)

Covarrubias, in his *Tesoro de la lengua castellana,* recognizes the positive values that the word *desengaño* may connote. Under the key word *Desengañar* he he defines the noun *desengaño* as "the clear and straightforward manner whereby we undeceive another; or the truth itself which undeceives us." In harmony with the second of these meanings, Fray Luis de León, in the dedication of his edition of the works of Santa Teresa, tells how the human soul becomes *desengañada de lo que la false imaginación le ofrecía*—freed from the enticements of the false images of things, conjured up by the imagination—and Quevedo in his treatise *The Cradle and the Grave* (1633) applies the same figure of speech to the last breath of every person: *desengaña al hombre de sí mismo*—it corrects all false ideas of the self. (p. 142)

Caer en la cuenta—to come to oneself—was the phrase most used in connection with the type of *desengaño* we are considering [in relation to Gracián and *El Criticón*]. It signified a passing from ignorance to knowledge, an awakening from the falsity of one's dream. Baltasar Gracián—no pessimist—in the allegory of this awakening which he entitled *El Criticón,* places the blame for life's confusion where it belongs: on man, not on the Creator. "Numerous and great are the monstrosities which appear each day in the dangerous pilgrimage which is our life," he causes Critilo to lament at the beginning of *Crisi* V of Part III, and continues:

> The most monstrous of all is the placing of Deceit at the world's front gate and Disillusionment at the exit—a disastrous handicap sufficient to ruin our life entirely, since . . . to make a misstep at the beginning of life causes one to lurch headlong with greater speed each day and end up in utter perdition. Who made such an arrangement, who ordained it? Now I am more convinced than ever that all is upside down in this world. Disillusionment should stand at the world's entrance and should place himself immediately at the shoulder of the neophyte, to free him from the dangers that lie in wait for him. But since the newcomer—by an opposite and contrary arrangement—makes his first encounter with Deceit (who at the beginning presents everything to him in perverted and reversed order), he heads for the left-hand road, and strides on to destruction.

Critilo looks about in vain for his Decipherer, but the latter has disappeared in the universal confusion of smoke and ignorance. By rare good fortune, however, a bystander who has overheard the lament comes forward and says: "You have every reason to complain of the senselessness of the world, but you should not ask who ordained it, but who has upset it; not who disposed it as it is, but who has put everything into reverse. For you must know that the

Supreme Artificer planned things very differently at the beginning, since He stationed Disillusionment on the threshold of the world, and cast Deceit into outer darkness."

To Critilo's repeated question, who did bring this about?, the stranger replies: "Who? Men themselves."

The allegory has its key. The author refers, under the name of *Disillusionment,* to the Tree of the Knowledge of Good and Evil; under the name of *Deceit,* to Lucifer, the leader of the rebellious angels and universal adversary of mankind (see Gen. 2:17; 3:3 and 7). The stranger explains to Critilo that, had it not been for man's initial willful sin, every new entrant into the world would have been warned by the Tree of the Knowledge of Good and Evil: "Remember that you were not born for the world but for heaven; the enticements of the worldly vices will bring you only death, as the rigors of virtue will give you life; trust not in your youth: its substance is mere glass."

In *Crisi* VIII of Part III, Critilo and Andrenio arrive at the Cave of Nothingness. On learning its name, Andrenio asks, "What do you mean, Cave of Nothingness, when into it plunge the great current of the century, the torrent of the world, populous cities, great courts, entire kingdoms?" The Honest One replies that, in spite of appearances, there is absolutely nothing in that cave. "But what do they do who plunge into it?" Andrenio asks, and is told: "What they alway did." "What do they end up as?" he asks again, and is answered: "They become their own achievement: they were nothing, they did nothing, they end up as nothing." At that moment someone rushes forward and, explaining that he has found no profession so attractive as doing nothing, slips inside the cave. Another man, a gentleman followed by a retinue of servitors, comes with the same purpose and, disregarding the pleas of the Honest One, follows his predecessor into Nothingness, never to be heard from again. Men of valor disappear to become men of no value; flowering geniuses, to wither and decay.

In *Crisi* VII of Part II Andrenio asks the Hermit: "What is the purpose of all the statues that you have here?" "Oh," replies the Hermit, "they are idols of the imagination, phantoms of appearance; they are all empty, but we make believe they are full of substance and solidity. A man crawls into the statue of a wise man, imitates his voice and words, and all obey him."

But not everything is farce in this world of farces. In *Crisi* X the pilgrims ask the Queen of Equity how they may arrive at the dwelling of her ladyship Happiness. By way of answer the Queen calls four of her handmaidens (the cardinal virtues), points to the first of them, and says: "This one, who is Justice, will tell you where and how to look; this second one, Prudence, will reveal her to you; with the third, who is Fortitude, you shall reach her; and with the fourth, whose name is Temperance, you will make her yours." At this point there is a harmonious blast of trumpets as a fragrant zephyr begins to stir. The pull of the stars becomes actually perceptible, and the wind, growing stronger, lifts them toward heaven. "He who wishes to know where they stopped must seek them farther on."

"He . . . must seek them farther on"—here is another indication, among so many that seem to have been overlooked in the writings of Gracián, that his "essays"—in the sense of *experiments* in the manner of Montaigne—have to do with this world only, though the beyond is ever present in the author's mind as the haven where life's little bark comes to rest, where—to revert to abstract language—confusion gives way to meaning.

Caer en la cuenta—to awaken to awareness—is really an extension of the task laid upon the individual not only by Socrates but by the whole tradition of Christian theology. Gracián's innocent savage Andrenio—Everyman—starts his journey toward comprehension from exactly this point of departure: "the first time that I recognized myself and was able to form a conception of my person." On this basis he forms his ideas of the world and of his fellow men. *Thou* is but an extension of *I:* "in you I perceive myself portrayed more vividly than in the silent crystal of a fountain." Thus for Gracián—more Augustinian than Cartesian—*existence* is the primary datum: I live, therefore I am. "In a confused and disoriented way," writes José Antonio Maravall, "Gracián is the first writer to consider life as a radical and inexorable reality upon which other realities depend."

The awakening to awareness of Gracián's Andrenio, his *caer en la cuenta,* is portrayed in a vivid allegory in *Crisi* VIII of Part I. In the "Court of Confusion" Andrenio had suffered a general obfuscation of the senses and of the mind, had become separated from his mentor Critilo, and was lost. The latter, searching for him, appealed to Artemia, later revealed as none other than Wisdom or Knowledge, a worker of marvels and prodigies who was by many considered a sorceress; unlike Circe, however, she did not convert men into beasts but used her magic to transform bestial men into men of reason. Critilo tells her that his alter ego must surely be at the court of the King Who Is Famous Without Being Named. Artemia comprehends at once: surely Andrenio is at the Babylonlike court of her great enemy, King Falseworld. She calls one of her chief ministers, the Prudent One, and entrusts the quest to him. It is a wise choice. El Prudente has difficulties. All he has to go by is a description, and Andrenio, after residing in the city of King Falimundo, is so changed that not even his mentor Critilo would recognize him. His eyes are dull, half closed, and almost blind, since the ministers of Falimundo take great care to obfuscate every man's vision; he could not even hear well in that court and Center of Lies. Even so, the Prudent One finds him one day, "losing many days in seeing how other men lost their property and even their conscience." It happens that there is a great ball game going on, and the huge balls have a strange appearance. "They seem to be human heads," Andrenio remarks to the man who has come to seek him. The fact is, they are indeed human heads—heads more full of wind than of understanding, full of tow or cotton stuffing, full of trickery and of lies. One party of players throws them upward toward their felicity, the other band casts them down amid suffering and calamities; and this goes on until the ball bursts and lands in the stinking mud of a grave.

"Who are you, who see so much?" asks the neophyte. "Who are you who are so blind?" asks the Prudent One. The conversation thus begun, Andrenio is assured that he will never have access to King Falseworld, whose very existence depends on his not being recognized. That is the reason that visitors to his court are all but blinded. Since the king cannot be seen face to face and in direct light, An-

drenio is led up onto a high hill. "It seems to me that I see much better than before," says the younger man, and the older one rejoices, since in seeing and in knowing lies the young man's salvation. Straining his eyes "to see if he could perceive any reality," Andrenio is thwarted by the window blinds of the palace. He is told to turn his back, since the things of this world must be seen in reverse in order to be seen straight. Then the Prudent One brings out a mirror: "Look well, and try to satisfy your desire." Andrenio looks, trembles, utters a cry. "What is the matter? What do you see?" "What do you expect me to see? A monster, the most horrible sight of my life! Get him out of my sight!"

"Keep your promise," the Prudent Ones replies. "Note well that face of a fox, that torso of a serpent, that camel's spine, those lower parts of a siren, those leper's hands . . . He even speaks in falsetto." To Andrenio's cries of horror the old man replies: "Enough; this is what I desired." The cause of so much horror is the famous king, unknown to all, who holds the world in his grasp because he lacks one thing only—the truth. This is the great hunter who with a universal net ensnares mankind, the judge to whom all appeal in order to condemn themselves. This is none other than King Deceit.

Andrenio would fain seek the safety of distance, but the old man is still not satisfied: Andrenio must know those surrounding the king. A sea monster more frightful than Ariosto's woman-devouring Orc and more false than Rojas' Celestina is the king's mother. Her name is Falsehood (*Mentira*), and her attendants are Yes and No; others in her train are Ignorance, Malice, Human Folly, Perdition, Confusion, Scorn, Intrigue.

As they leave that Babel the old man asks: "Are you content, Andrenio?" "No, not content," is the reply, "but enlightened" (*desengañado*). They move out into the daylight, and Andrenio seems actually half happy (full happiness being impossible). Asked what is lacking, he tells the old man of his lost companion and mentor, Critilo, who had departed for Queen Artemia's court. "Be comforted," says el Prudente, "for we too shall go there. He who freed you from Deceit, where else could he take you but to the presence of Knowledge, by which I mean to the court of the discreet Queen you mention."

In all of this we have the exposition of an optimistic doctrine. Andrenio goes forth from his encounter with Falimundo not only *desengañado* but also relatively content, which is all any man can aspire to. He is on his way to the court of Queen Artemia, who is none other than Knowledge. His guides to happiness are the four cardinal virtues. Andrenio is, thus, a sort of primeval Adam on the human level. (There is no Fall in Gracián's anthropology, purposely limited to the secular sphere.) From within his imperfection (ever with him), Andrenio exercises the power of relative self-perfection; achievement of his self-realization is what Critilo, his mentor, represents. Critilo, or Human Reason, is not perfection; but in Gracián's thought he is the possibility of—the gift of striving toward—perfection. When Andrenio has his relapses, Critilo needs the help of a transcendent ethic, of someone outside himself who will help him "ransom his 'other I,' who has fallen captive, one knows not how, nor into whose power." The world for Andrenio is thus a balcony from which to see, a platform on which to live. From it he contemplates reality, receiving the testimony not only of things but of their Creator, of men, and of himself.

A similar optimism lies at the heart of Gracián's other great concept, that of the Superior Man. In this sense he is a precursor of Carlyle's *Heroes and Hero Worship.* The very existence of these culture heroes implies an anthropological optimism. Man, says Gracián, "is not born ready-made." His self-realization incorporates new elements into his own being. Critilo is the symbol of the myth of Prometheus, complementary to the myth of Adam. Gracián in all these matters moves within the inherited orbit of Aristotelianism; to him, "becoming a person" consists in achieving full rational development. This every man does by making choices: "where there is no choice there is no perfection." The human personality is, therefore, an artistic artifact.

The process of maturation can occur only in society: the great individual rises above the common and general human condition. Precisely because this condition is general, Gracián pays scant attention to lineage, to nobility: all anyone needs is to be a man. Self-transformation from an ordinary into an extraordinary creature is a general human trait. Gracián's individuals are merely that—individuals—and yet the life adventure of each is similar to that of every other. What one individual can offer, in opposition to other individuals, is eminence—the exaltation of this quality or that. Gracián's *Discreto,* his Intelligent Man or *Sapiens,* obtains a universal knowledge, so that moral philosophy makes him prudent; natural philosophy makes him wise; history makes him well-informed; poetry awakens his creative powers; rhetoric renders him eloquent; classical studies give him discretion; cosmography imparts to him an acquaintance with the world; and the reading of the Holy Scripture makes him devout. Thus in every branch of learning—human and divine—he achieves perfection.

Engaño (the only escape from which is blessed *desengaño*) is a strictly human deceit. At the beginning of *Crisi* IV of Part III of *El Criticón,* a pilgrim surveys the starry heavens and declares that the best book in the world is the world itself—an extended parchment, with stars for letters. "The words of that heavenly scroll are easy to understand, even though the astrologers call them enigmas. The difficulty—the real difficulty—is in learning to read what lies below, from the rooftops downward, because, since all is in cipher and human hearts are sealed and inscrutable, the best of readers is constantly at fault. And if you have not studied well and memorized the code to the cipher, you will be simply lost, unable to read a word or recognize a letter, not even a pen-stroke or a tilde." God, in other words, does not deceive; the universe was created in holy wisdom and love. It is human hearts that are "sealed." (pp. 145-52)

> Otis H. Green, "Desengaño," in his The Literary Mind of Medieval & Renaissance Spain, The University Press of Kentucky, 1970, pp. 141-70.

Paul Ilie　(essay date 1971)

[*Ilie is an American educator who has written extensive-*

ly on Spanish literature. In the following excerpt, he analyzes the use and effect of the grotesque in El Criticón.]

It has long been evident to scholars that the presence of distortion and monstrosity in *El Criticón* makes these elements prime factors for consideration when dealing with the work's esthetic and philosophical disposition. (p. 30)

However, it was not until Gerhart Schröder published *Baltasar Graciáns "Criticón"* that any serious attention was given to the details of Gracián's grotesque. This study not only provided much needed information about the literary background of the "allegorical grotesque," but it also established the validity of such categories as the "Bildgroteske" and the "Sprachgroteske." Schröder's orientation is ethical and philosophical, with emphasis on the roles of contradiction, antithesis, disillusion, and the implications of the thesis that Gracián's grotesque becomes "die Bildstruktur, die Ausdruck des 'Verkehrten,' d.h. des dem Geist Entgegengesetzten ist." With this sort of approach articulated at last, it is now possible for critics to look more carefully at the nature and workings of the grotesque in *El Criticón* from the standpoint of esthetic analysis and exegetical meaning.

At the very least, it is demonstrable that many of the aforementioned antagonistic forces make up a counterpoint of dissonances, a fairly coherent subesthetic of grotesque motifs and effects. Much can also be done along two other lines of thought: evaluating Schröder's survey of the origin and typological development of the more bizarre images used by Gracián, and, perhaps more useful at this point, locating the position of these images in the evolution of grotesque literature in Spain. It is this second area which I intend to explore here, conscious of the vast preparation brought to this field by scholars of the Spanish Renaissance and Baroque, a preparation which might caution them against some of the generalizations which I will make later on. Nevertheless, there is a need for the type of approach that is undertaken from another perspective. While Gracián's work is the product of a complex tradition before him, his esthetic does not end there. It also represents one phase in the creation of forms and concepts that, over the centuries, has come to be known as the grotesque mode. And conversely, the history of esthetic ideas in Spain does not begin with the twentieth century, and it is necessary, in order to speak intelligently about the Valle-Incláns and the Solanas, to understand earlier literary periods: first the Romantic grotesque, then the epochs of Goya and Torres Villarroel, then the Baroque of Gracián and Quevedo, and so on in a receding process that has been the traditional direction of scholarly investigation. (pp. 30-1)

The grotesque in *El Criticón* does not stand out as an independent phenomenon against a background of undistorted elements. Neither does it appear in easily isolated passages that can be separated from the general prose fabric, as in the case of the grotesque portraits in Torres' *Visiones y visitas.* Nor is it, finally, a part of the self-contained episodes that frequently occur in Romantic works, where scenes of fantasy and supernaturalism alternate with other moods and episodes. In *El Criticón,* the grotesque is a function of context. Its deformations have a functional role requiring an explanation set in terms of the work's basic themes, which themselves do not suffer any deformation. These themes include, above all, Gracián's ideas about Nature, a concept which must be posited explicitly by the work if its grotesque violations of the natural order are to be understood. There is also the problem of what role is cast for artistic forms—especially architecture—and, finally, what patterns are imposed upon the conventions of allegorical symbolism.

This kind of thematic approach must, of course, deal with both form and idea. Philosophically speaking, Gracián makes use of a "moral grotesque," a technique of distortion that upholds the moralistic idealism of the Golden Age while rejecting many of the esthetic ideals of that Age. Gracián prepares a metaphysical groundwork that slopes away from theology toward the ethics of Nature and society. But at the same time, his formal expression depends upon allegories that break away from classical restraint and proliferate their animal motifs until the entire structure becomes swollen and deformed. This revision of allegorical convention is one aspect of Gracián's grotesque, and others, like the use of metamorphosis and carnivalesque grotesquerie, have new implications that will all be discussed in Part Two.

First, however, we must be clear as to what notions of natural order and cosmic harmony were posited by Gracián and held as a contrasting background for the grotesque reliefs of his more fantastic scenes. His representation of reality is more than simply abstract and unreal, for he makes very concrete statements about the structure of social reality and the inherent traits of Nature. Gracián's representation is often antinatural, so to speak, conceived in opposition to the natural workings of the universe. The narrative situation itself comes about because Critilo is "un náufrago, monstruo de la naturaleza y de la suerte," a phrase which suggests the violation of an underlying principle, the belief in the existence of predictable laws and equilibrium both in Nature and in the course of human events. Even Fortune's wheel is a circle, although the direction of its spin is beyond human divination. Gracián also refers to "la sabia naturaleza," to "el concierto, la firmeza y la variedad desta gran máquina criada," and to the fact that Nature and Fortune are two counterbalancing forces.

Everything, then, indicates that the concept of Nature involves a structural order that is harmonious but free to produce variants, and that due to the peculiar tension arising from Nature's role in the universal concert of discords, such variants can sometimes become monstrous. This structure within Nature is further detailed by Gracián in two similar areas. The first of these points to generic order, a hierarchy in which "los inferiores sirven a los superiores" in three categories: "la sensible sobre la vejetante" and a "tercer grado de vivientes mucho más perfectos." These groups refer to plant, animal, and human life, and when the grotesque emerges it is from the disruption of the hierarchy, with results conveyed by such words as "monstrimuger" and "serpihombre." Thus, deformation becomes synonymous with deviant variation, with whatever deviates from the fixed order of life. Then, too, there is a second aspect to Gracián's idea of Nature. This concerns the structural support for the vital order just described, a framework that provides the means whereby life can take on a physical dimension. Such an arrangement is classical in structure, with emphasis on symmetry, proportion, stability, and beauty. In a long passage describing these physical properties of Nature, the key phrase is "prolixa ana-

tomía de su artificiosa composición." That is, Nature's beauty is conceived of both analytically, in terms of its structural composition, and universally, as a total phenomenon that responds to the laws of growth and harmony. Once again, the breakdown of this arrangement has grotesque consequences, but even without them, the wondrous and gigantic vision described in the passage ("tan agradable laberinto de prodigios") pushes the frontiers of reality to their farthest limit.

In all of this, it goes without saying that the natural world is the work of a Divine Creator. But whatever the relationship between God and Nature may be, it is also clear that the conditions leading up to the grotesque stem from the deterioration of an "armonía tan plausible de to do el universo, compuesta de una tan estraña contrariedad que, según es grande, no parece avía de poder mantenerse el mundo un solo día." Just as the notion of a prodigious universe makes it possible for immensity to overflow into gigantism and monstrosity, so too does the tension of contrasts make it easier for exaggerated and distorted elements to rush forward in the event of a temporary disruption. Although this seldom happens in *El Criticón's* realm of natural phenomena, there are cases, as in one violent storm, where Nature seems to be on the verge of a cataclysm. Thus, Critilo's observation that "todo este Universo se compone de contrarios y se concierta de desconciertos" can be interpreted in either direction, toward concord or toward discord. Gracián did, therefore, as an artist, become aware that individual elements are in themselves disproportionate, even though they find their just equilibrium in the larger concert of harmonies.

These ideas are not very new from the standpoint of intellectual history. But their esthetic implications are far from being commonplace, at least as far as literary practice is concerned. They have little to do with Aristotelian poetics or, for that matter, with the theories of Plato, Horace, or the Renaissance theorists. It is true that evidence exists to show that among the latter several thinkers were aware of the artistic potential of discord. However, there is no study indicating that the literary practice of using discords on the grotesque scale devised by Gracián had been realized before *El Criticón.* In terms of actual esthetic procedure, therefore, Gracián's notion of a harmony of disharmonies offers a new alternative to the literary depiction of reality, whether the latter be idealistic or realistic, allegorical or picaresque. It opens the way to the use of conflict, violence, and, ultimately, destruction, all of which increase the probability of distortion in the presence of any of these elements.

This potential for distortion is stressed less in the world of natural phenomenon than in the moral realm. . . . Although the transition is vague, a bridge exists between natural order and moral order, and once it is crossed we are led directly to the Christian landscape of ethics and aphorisms that is so typical of the itinerary followed by Critilo and Andrenio. And the grotesque enters each time a perversion of Christian morality is depicted in terms of the violation of the norms that I have been describing thus far. Here, then, is the link to the moral aspect of the grotesque in *El Criticón.* Having defined the norms of reality as consisting of order, structure, and the conflict of opposites, Gracián projects them into the ethical realm. What happens in the natural world has its counterpart in the world of value judgments.

This is not to say that evil and vice are not portrayed by other techniques as well. Nor are these norms the only ones that guide Gracián's philosophy in this work. As I suggested at the beginning, the grotesque is a function of the narrative as a whole, and it is only one esthetic mode in the author's total allegory. But, granted all of this, there can be no doubt that his grotesquerie goes beyond the animal symbolism and bestial representations of the Dantesque tradition. Gracián consciously links moral aberration to a corresponding deformation of the natural and human orders. In a sweeping transvaluation, "todo anda al rebés, y todo trocado de alto abaxo . . . las bestias hazen del hombre y los hombres hazen la bestia. . . ." What methods are actually used in this animalization will be discussed in another context; at this point it is enough to note that the origin of the moral grotesque is the transformation just described, influenced as it is by the intention to deform Nature and human life.

There is one final aspect to be considered with regard to the norms of symmetry, order, and beauty in the natural realm. This is the problem of their deterioration. An analogy with architecture is developed in this connection, a fact which should not surprise us given Gracián's concept of a "structure" in Nature. Architectural parallels are also appropriate for conventional reasons as well, since they evoke the work of Roman and Italian antecedents like Vitruvius, Raphael, and Luca Signorelli. Then too, there is the etymological link between *grotta* and *grottesco,* a link which brings Nature and architecture closer together under the two auspices of esthetic experience and philosophical discourse. A good example is the description of "la cueva de la nada," a scene where abstract elements are combined with natural ones in an architectonic manner. . . . This passage is, first of all, in the mainstream of the early grotesque tradition because of its setting. Moreover, the adjective *bruta* is reminiscent of the linguistic identification of *brutesco* and *grutesco* in the seventeenth century. Beyond this, what makes the cave so horrible and ugly is its physical isolation from the grandeur of Nature, and its moral kinship with the vileness of materialism. Neither cause by itself is particularly conducive to the grotesque, but together with the deliberate exclusion of architectural beauty, their result at least in Gracián's mind is a grotto of horrors antithetical to everything shapely and noble in the universe.

On the other hand, *El Criticón* shifts away from Renaissance grotesque associations with arabesque design and other bizarre architectural decorations. Although this type of ornamentalism was called *grottesco* because styles similar to it were discovered after certain late fifteenth century excavations, its fantastic scrollwork had little to do with the ominous mood that subsequently grew out of the grotto-like scenes of later periods. The word *grottesco,* and the grotesque adornments associated with architecture, traditionally evoked an air of whim, caprice, and, above all, relative calm. Thus, the wild *gruta* motif so prominent in Part One of *El Criticón* represents a violence and upheaval far removed from the architectural tranquility of the Renaissance. This fact is consistent with Gracián's dialectic of Nature's opposites, and, in addition, it brings new implications to the entire idea of natural and

artificial distortion. For example, one mountain-grotto setting becomes a study in space and sound, without reference to Renaissance grotesque motifs: ". . . conmovióse todo él [el monte], temblando aquellas firmes paredes, bramava el furioso viento vomitando en tempestades por la boca de la gruta, començaron a desgajarse con horrible fragor aquellos duros peñascos y a caer con tan espantoso estruendo que parecía quererse venir a la nada toda aquella gran máquina de peñas." What is grotesque in this scene is not so much the deformation of a particular architectural design, but the imminent breakdown of a universal concept: Gracián's law of balanced opposites. The landscape is rent asunder, and the laws of harmony are opposed by forces of disintegration within Nature. Thus, the episode depicts more than just a menacing storm. It is the author's way of conveying grotesque horror by depicting an elementary stage of naturistic evil in the world.

This naturistic or "natural" evil, arising without human cause in a realm beyond human control, constitutes the physical base of the world's moral evil, which is the author's real subject. With it, Gracián can represent any perversion of Christian morality against the background of a horrible or threatening Nature. The importance of this technique should not be underestimated, for by identifying it in this way, we can understand how the monstrous storms and supernatural backdrops of the Romantic period came to be different from those of the Baroque, especially in their detachment from the ethical concerns of the Christian world. In Gracián, we have the primitive prototypes of the violent landscapes and Gothic terror of Romanticism. (pp. 31-8)

What we have, then, is the kind of grotesque that developed in Europe from Dante to the Baroque, in which horrible forms function not autonomously but as part of a larger Christian cosmology, and where deformation usually serves an ulterior didactic purpose. This is the tradition inherited by Gracián and modified by him through the *concordia discors topos* discussed in Part One. Inherent in this grotesque, and absent in its subsequent Romantic forms, is the shifting of a convulsive order from the physical plane to the moral one. Also, the wilder aspects of Nature grow uncontrolled, forming an appropriate background for the human vices depicted by the narrative. On the other hand, the means used to describe these upheavals is the conventional technique of animal symbolism. But in contrast to the Dantesque tradition, Gracián's allegory turns into grotesquerie because of the inordinate presence of corporal as well as moral correspondences between animals and men. Thus, we find strained physical parallels mixed with excessive conceits, all built upon a moral foundation whose lesson is made graphic by a familiar, yet fantastic, realism:

> Tenían otros cabeças de camellos, gente de cargo y de carga; muchos, de bueyes en lo pesado, que no en lo seguro; no pocos de lobos, siempre en la fábula del pueblo; pero los más, de estólidos jumentos, mui a lo simple malicioso . . . Todos eran hombres a remiendos, y assí, quál tenfa garra de león y quál de osso e[1] pie; hablava uno por boca de ganso, y otro murmurava con ozico de puerco; éste tenía pies de cabra, y aquél orejas de Midas; algunos tenían ojos de lechuza y los más de topo; risa de perro. . . .

This lack of economy in animal representations certainly helps to make the entire scene bizarre. But *El Criticón* is a work with various kinds of bestial presences, ranging from classical monsters to straightforward animal allegories (I, 151-152, 190, 229; II, 195-196; III, 80). Thus, the piling up of bestialized men and humanized beasts in this particular case tends to broaden the traditional category of animalizations while it also distorts the normal configuration of the work's allegorical form. From an esthetic standpoint, this nominalistic catalog of physical correspondences is less conventional than the "Tiersymbolik" emphasized by Schröder, just as the purely imagistic qualities of style are more dramatic than the conventions of a "Psychologie der Körperdefekte." (pp. 38-9)

The idea . . . of Nature's values being reversed harks back to what what we have just seen: moral perversion taking the external guise of a physical transvaluation. There is also the suggestion that the element of *capricho*—whim, fantasy, chimera, grotesque humor—had entered Gracián's awareness, although the extent to which he approached Bosch's methods is an uncertain matter. We cannot know whether he intended to emulate the painter or not, but the fact that he was conscious of the *capricho* as an esthetic possibility, drawing an analogy between it and his own work, should be sufficient even for cautious critics. We should also remember that Bosch's paintings can also be interpreted in allegorical terms, which is to say that their deformations, like those of *El Criticón,* conform to definite iconographical patterns. Similarly, both Gracián and Bosch reflect the grotesque in its early stages, as it had developed from the Middle Ages to the Baroque. Therefore, the notion of *capricho* enters as a new factor in the deformation of medieval allegorical motifs, gaining significance both as a technique and as an attitude in the light of what was to come in the decades after Goya.

Beyond the interrelationship between moral transvaluation, physical inversion, and Gracián's ironic self-awareness, there is one further point. That is the concept of monstrosity. The theory and practice of monstrous creation is not new in Gracián, although no one has studied his debt to the esthetic forms popularized by such models as *La Divina Commedia,* the chivalric novels, emblem literature, and other compendia of monsters and fiends. But what makes Gracián interesting in this respect is that he marks the high point in one particular stage of grotesque development: Baroque moralism. This means that along with the Christian lesson to be learned from the presence of these monstrosities, there is also a good deal of attention paid to their physical anatomies. . . . What should be evident at once is that Gracián's moral grotesque breaks the form of the conventional animal allegory. The author is clearly on the verge of a formal exercise here, juxtaposing animalistic parts at will without concern for an immediate one-to-one relationship between those parts and their possible symbolic meaning. His ultimate purpose, true, remains as ethical as Schröder's exposition shows it to be, and the total picture of distortion conveys the feeling of moral revulsion which is so central to Gracián's didactic position. But in its details—not all quoted above—the picture is irrational. It lacks the logic of an inner vocabulary of images that might be translated into a comprehensive moral symbolism. In fact, the details are gratuitous from a didactic point of view, and their justification lies mainly in the design of their Baroque surface. In this stylistic excess, then, we have the significance of the moral grotesque: it goes beyond normal allegory by piling up an ornate superstructure of motifs that have intrinsic formal value without enriching the essence of the moral structure beneath it. And this, needless to say, is a Baroque phenomenon. (pp. 39-41)

The moralistic force, however, is always in the background, and can be described by such statements as: " . . . siendo el hombre persona de razón, lo primero que executa es hazerla a ella esclava del apetito bestial. Deste principio se originan todas las demás monstruosidades, todo va al rebés en conseqüencia de aquel desorden capital. . . ." And yet what is truly the novel element in *El Criticón* is not this medieval account of moral failure, but the Baroque amalgamation of endless forms into an overgrown mass of impossible identity. . . . On the other hand, there is an important element in common with classical tradition, and this is the area of metamorphosis. Here, Gracián makes it clear that the physiological changes he is attempting to describe go beyond the conventions of antiquity. As we read in one episode, "—Aquí—dixo Andrenio—alguna Circe habita que assí transforma las gentes. ¿Qué tienen que ver con éstas todas las metamorfosis que celebra Ovidio?" The answer, supplied by the thoughtful reader, is that esthetically they have little to do with each other, for many reasons.

One reason is that Ovid did not seek to draw a strong moral lesson, while Gracián does. Another is that the changes in form suffered by the figures of mythology were often the logical consequences of the events and personalities involved, whereas Gracián's figures are irrational. But the most important differences are esthetic in character. There is no purity of form in Gracián's grotesque figures: at best they are hybrids and more often they are mongrel, or else they sprawl unrecognizably, with their individual parts identifiable but their general appearance remaining beyond recognition. The concept of metamorphosis, therefore, is realistic for Ovid and just the opposite for Gracián. Of course, both writers created comparable fantasies in that their myths and fictions do not represent situations in reality. But only in Ovid do the transformed shapes correspond to plausible forms—and sometimes even whole entities—in reality. The monstrous mutations in *El Criticón,* on the other hand, are not intended to have formal verisimilitude. Their overall structures may have symbolic meaning, but they are grotesque insofar as they fail to conform to the proportions of real or imaginary animals.

Be this as it may, what places Gracián's metamorphosis in a more modern context in comparison to Ovid's is its dehumanization of existence. As we know, twentieth century portraits of dehumanized man range from the loss of self and the acquisition of masks or mannequin shapes, to the physiological transformation of human figures into lesser forms of organic existence. The scale on which this occurs in Gracián is obviously much more reduced, but once again it is the quality rather than the extent which is significant. What is essential in any grotesque dehumanization is the replacement of human factors by nonhuman ones. In a contemporary framework, this involves the substitution of mineral and vegetal states for higher forms of life. In *El Criticón,* the vocabulary alluding to these conditions is similar, and the philosophy which is implied has an unmistakable ring of modernity. (pp. 42-4)

It is in this symbolic representation of the lack of human

substance that Gracián's grotesque draws closest to the modern age. In particular, there are two areas where this is true: the use of puppets and pastiche figurines to ridicule human dignity, and the use of masks to disguise personality or the lack of it. Men with wax torsoes stuffed with cloth or cotton are the seventeenth century counterparts of contemporary figures symbolizing the demise of the hero. And the masked carnival at which they sport is the scene of psychological evasion as well as moral deceit. Thus, part of *El Criticón* makes a fairly modern statement about personality and values by means of images that are still being used by cultivators of the grotesque mode.

For example, during the "juegos bacanales" celebrated with disguises, people and animals alike change their identities by assuming the appearance of their opposites. Thus, the serpent dresses as a dove, and the usurer as an almsgiver. The result is a didactic description that covers the esthetic framework with so heavy a tapestry of dissembling that the original carnival form is overshadowed. At the same time, Gracián attempts to relate the incident to his reader's experience by alluding to the Spanish practice of masquerading ("Andavan las máscaras más validas que en la misma Barcelona"). In this way, he provides an instance of Baroque carnivalesque behavior, another subject which in subsequent literary periods becomes a favorite motif for Romantics and surrealists. The difference, however, is that Gracián's norms are "de todos modos, no sólo de diablura, pero de santidad y de virtud." His deformation is achieved not only through what we now consider to be the conventional carnival mask, but also through nondeformed, realistic masks. That is, his carnival can be created without deformation. Whereas traditional celebrations—Bacchanalia, witches' Sabbaths, pre-Lenten carnivals—produce only distorted faces, Gracián's scene produces undistorted types as well. This is because reality in one case is assumed to be normal, and hence victimized by perverse disguises, whereas in the other case reality is already perverse. Therefore, in the latter, it would be inappropriate to conceal one deformation by masking it with another. Thus, the most eligible carnival masks for whores, adulterers, and rapacious beasts are those that represent austere penitents, faithful friends, and domestic animals. Since the figures are already morally misshapen, their participation in the general grotesquerie can only become possible through the guise of normal, undistorted shapes.

This throws us back again to the fact that we are dealing with a grotesque mode based on moral precepts. But what of the problem of personality and human substance? Here, Gracián's condemnation of immorality extends to a grotesque representation of people psychologically corrupted by vice. Physically dehumanized because they have forfeited human dignity, and mentally stunted by Gracián's refusal to invest them with human personality, they parade before the reader like marionettes of a later age. . . . The diminution of man's social and moral status is a conventional theme in *El Criticón,* but the reduction of his vital movements to a mechanical analogy is far from being commonplace in the Golden Age. If Gracián's outlook causes him to regard human beings as the "semilla de títeres," his own sensibility itself bears the seed of a new flowering of the grotesque in later periods. References to sawdust and hinges instead of to blood and muscle cause the description to turn upon a formally grotesque axis

rather than a philosophical one. Thus, the animation of characters, rather than their analysis, makes the most impressive statement about life in a post-heroic age. On the other hand, despite his anticipation of Romantic motifs, Gracián's grotesque remains a Baroque phenomenon for several reasons. Its technique runs away with itself, impatiently jumping from figure to figure instead of elaborating an episode built around one grotesque subject. This lack of economy, plus the cumulative effect of many self-sufficient metaphors, creates a typically Baroque edifice of image upon image that exhausts the reader with its ponderous size.

Fundamentally, however, the grotesque in *El Criticón* is subordinated, while the concept of man as marionette is developed with prosaic ethical directness. But it is significant that the puppet image was not abandoned by Gracián, since the relationship between mannequins and the fall from heroism has, from his time to our own, come to be axiomatic. . . . I would suggest, however, that perhaps for the first time a Baroque writer has found a fairly original image through which he might express his vision of the fall from heroism. All of the famous conceits of the early Baroque—Quevedo's crumbling walls, Lope's shipwrecked beach, Cervantes' wooden horse—have a traditional basis for their inventiveness, and in any case, would later be exchanged for new metaphors in subsequent generations. In contrast, Gracián's marionettes reflect a different sensibility, and one whose ramifications would be exploited by Europeans everywhere after the eighteenth century. This is not to make false comparisons about the quality of images in the early and late Spanish Baroque. Nor should we forget the place that puppets had on the non-grotesque popular stage. But the point is that a deep-seated preoccupation with decadence in the mid-seventeenth century found an unusual, if not unique, metaphor for its expression. What is more, this metaphor is grotesque, detached from classical tradition, and conceived at the early dawn of a new sensibility rather than in the twilight of an old one. In other words, just as we found changes in the concept of metamorphosis from Ovid to Gracián, so now we find an image that opens up new possibilities for the future of grotesque esthetics. In the last two quotations, we witness a deliberate attempt to reduce the human dimension to a stilted, mechanical framework. This may be in keeping with the general bent of seventeenth century moralism, and even with Gracián's own philosophy. But its formal expression does not reflect the techniques of literary convention. As we have seen, traditional allegories are like realistic statues: both groups rely on representationalism rather than deformation. The episodes discussed in this article have been no less moralistic, but they are unmistakably deformed renditions of men and events. And here again we are faced with the central issue. At certain moments, the balanced harmonies of Renaissance philosophy and art, and of Counter-Reformational cosmology, are upset by the distorted forms of Gracián's moral grotesque. (pp. 44-8)

Paul Ilie, "Gracián and the Moral Grotesque," in Hispanic Review, *Vol. 39, No. 1, January, 1971, pp. 30-48.*

Juan Marichal (essay date 1972)

[*Marichal is a Spanish-born American educator and literary scholar. In the excerpt below, he contends that* El Criticón *reflects the social and political turmoil of the baroque age.*]

The eleven years between the Treaty of Westphalia (1648) and the so-called Peace of the Pyrenees (1659) are a political and social turning-point in the history of Latin Europe. The centralized power of the monarchies asserts itself, weakening the nobility and giving an increasing importance to the royal bureaucracies, to the *noblesse de robe.* Those changes are not entirely equivalent to what the Duc de Saint-Simon called "l'anéantissement de la noblesse." Nor are they completely either what the same bitter pen described as the beginning of "un long règne de vile bourgeoisie": but those eleven years do mark without any doubt the victory of the bureaucrats over the aristocrats, of the lawyers over the landed oligarchy. My purpose here is to discuss the writings of Gracián—and specifically his *Criticón, The Critic*—in the light of those changes in the social and political structure of the Baroque monarchies of Latin Europe; or rather, to hear Gracián's explicit and implicit testimony on the nature of those changes.

Gracián's book was published in three successive stages, 1651, 1653, 1657, corresponding to three periods of a European journey. It is, of course, a book of essays—I continue to be shocked by those scholars who persist in calling it an "allegorical novel"—it is indeed a long "essay on the times." Gracián saw himself primarily as a spectator of his European century—if I am allowed an anachronistic license I would say that Gracián was actually the first Orteguian Spanish "spectator" before Ortega. His field of vision and thought was the totality of Europe. And in many ways he was the last Spaniard—until Ortega precisely—to be a normal European, without the self-consciousness of so many latter-day *Europeizantes.* (p. 245)

[Gracián] wrote the first part of *The Critic* in Huesca between 1646 and 1651, as a very eminent historian the Jesuit Father Battlori has shown. Gracián was then the inhabitant, so to speak, of the library of his close friend Lastanosa, one of the best private libraries of Spain and probably of Europe. . . . Within that excellent library—and Lastanosa's house was also a museum, and he even had a small zoo in his very special gardens—from the library Gracián looked across the Pyrenees into the rest of Europe and from that library he also observed the Spanish monarchy. Gracián's location is new in the Spanish intellectual history of that century: it actually represents a change of perspective that is, in itself, an essential aspect of his testimony. Merleau-Ponty, the late French philosopher, established what I believe is a useful distinction: "Il y a un centre de l'histoire qui est l'action politique et une périphérie qui est la culture." If we contrast Gracián with his Baroque predecessor Quevedo, that distinction is quite applicable because Quevedo, forty years before, in the 1610's, was placed in the very center of power while Gracián was to be in that periphery of history which is culture. And in a very strict sense in his case: Huesca is in the geographical periphery of Spain, and Gracián was in the library of Lastanosa instead of being like Quevedo in the corridors of the Madrid center of power, the Royal Palace. This displacement of the main intellectual spectator of his times

shows already what has happened in that Europe of the Baroque. Let me indicate immediately that Gracián did not consider that he was a sort of exile; nor can he be compared to those writers who in the Renaissance write in praise of the village against the court. Gracián does not make a single allusion to rural happiness, to the so-called purity of country life: for Gracián life was culture and culture was not necessarily found in the village. But it was not found in the court either. Here is the novelty of Gracián, and the novelty of Lastanosa, his patron. Court and Culture are self-excluding, as also are Politics and Morality. A contemporary of Gracián, a distinguished Spanish diplomat, wrote the following in his book *El embajador:*

> There are two ways of being a good man, one is the absolute way, and it can not be achieved if one is a member of the government unless the King or the Republic would be perfect. The other way is the relative one, this meaning that one will love what is just (*amará las cosas absolutamente justas*) but in practice one will follow the orders of the King and the laws of the land.

We have here the well-known theory of the tacitists of the Baroque Age of Latin Europe. But Gracián, at least in *The Critic,* did believe that it was necessary for the person to achieve as much moral goodness as possible and this, of course, was tantamount to withdrawal from the center of power. The aim of culture was the making of the Person, and only away from Power could this aim be reached.

This was a radical change in the orientation of the intellectual in Spanish life, because since the middle of the fifteenth century men of letters had tended to be in the center of power—as royal secretaries, for instance. Quevedo, of a family precisely of royal bureaucrats, had attacked those writers who opposed political action. But Gracián had no doubts: *un hombre de bien,* a man of integrity, had to be removed from the center of power. That is, for Gracián there are two kinds of men, two possibilities of life for men: to be *ordinary* and to be *persons.* And his essays are a theory of the *person,* a description of the road to personal perfection. This road does not go through the court, through the capital of the Monarchy. I should indicate that "Court" became, in Spanish, equivalent to "Capital," to Madrid. That court is seen by Gracián embodied, so to say, in the Madrid theaters, and these are what he calls *acorralada necedad,* that is "the stupidity of the corral," having in mind that theaters were called "corrales" because of their original location in back patios of houses or palaces. Gracián has, thus, utmost disdain for an author applauded in such "corrals," Lope de Vega: he was, Gracián said of Lope, full of "viento popular." (And, of course, this negative characterization of Lope's art is perhaps the best formula of his art for us today: "llenóse de viento popular"). The Court, the Capital, the Theater, are dominated by what Ortega would have called the Masses; and I should put in here another parenthesis and point out again the similarity of some aspects of Gracián, and Ortega. Those masses of the Capital are noisy and noise is, for Gracián, the very negation of the possibility of expansion for the person:

> Acertaron a pasar por una plaza, la de mayor concurrencia, donde hallaron un numeroso pueblo, dividido en enjambres de susurro, aguardando algunos de sus espectáculos vulgares. (They went

through a square, full of people, spread in swarms
of murmur, waiting for their vulgar spectacles.)

The intensity of Gracián's disdain for the masses is seen
in that coupling of *enjambres* and *susurro*: he wants, of
course, to show men in groups in that square as swarms
of bees. Any man who wants to be himself, who wants to
be a person, must get away from the noise of those
swarms. This includes also the Princes of the Monarchy;
they also ran the same danger and they were not protected
by the level of their social highness:

> aunque sea un príncipe, en no sabiendo las cosas,
> quererse meter en hablar de ellas, a dar su voto en
> lo que no sabe, ni entiende, al punto se declara
> hombre vulgar y plebeyo, porque el vulgo no es otra
> cosa que una sinagoga de ignorantes presumidos.
> (The Prince if he talks when he does not know be-
> comes also a vulgar man, because vulgarity is the
> assembly of pretentious, ignorant men.)

Let us put aside the anti-Semitic note in the text just quoted. Gracián warns in that text that the Prince must be
aware that the Court is a constant danger, intellectually
speaking, because men are constantly talking about what
they do not know. This, of course, is related to Gracián's
cautions regarding words and verbal expression: his sense
of stylistic economy.

But above all the Court, Madrid, is the center of falsehood
and individual servility. "Los áulicos siempre están con-
templando el rostro del Príncipe y brujuleándole los afec-
tos" ("The courtiers are always observing the Prince's face
as if it were the North star"). That Gracián was expressing
himself sincerely is seen in his letters to Lastanosa, from
Madrid, in the spring of 1640: "Me volvería con mucho
gusto al estudio de Vuestra Merced, to do es embeleco,
mentiras, gente soberbia y vana . . . " ("I would return
with pleasure to your library. All here is lies, people full
of pride and vanity . . . ") But what is perhaps quite a
shock for readers of our day is Gracián's view of the University, and in particular of the University of Salamanca,
the oldest in Spain. Since a man who wants to be a person
should have culture it would be assumed that Gracián sees
the University as the proper place for such a man, for such
a process of becoming a person. Not in the least! The University, and Salamanca specifically, is described as "plaza
de armas contra las haciendas." That is, the University of
Salamanca had been primarily a School of Law, whose
graduates would become royal officials. The motto of the
University since the 13th century had been, "the King for
the University, the University for the King." In short, the
University was seen by Gracián as the human source of
what was to be called, later on, in France, *use armature
d'avocats.* The early French Republic was considered to
have such a skeleton of lawyers, but in fact all the post-
Renaissance monarchies were built upon such an *armature.* And those lawyers were seen by the nobility as their
real enemies, since they were both the mind and the hand
of the centralist Monarchy. Historians of Spain have not
seen this important fact of social conflict: and of course I
cannot blame them for not having seen it, because the
Spanish monarchy of the Baroque Age did not show insti-
tutionally this conflict as in France. There was nothing
like the French highly organized *noblesse de robe* in Spain,
and the aristocracy had expressed itself only through some
writers, writers such as Quevedo, who were its mouth-
pieces, in a literal sense. It is true that Gracián did not like

Quevedo. He thought Quevedo wanted to please vulgar
tastes. He refers to Quevedo as being similar to tobacco
leaves: they are pleasant to smell but they go up in smoke.
Quevedo was also the opposite pole of Gracián, being such
a verbal torrent, a writer who excelled in abundance instead of the excellence in conciseness characteristic of
Gracián. But there is a clear connection between the two
regarding their identification with an aristocracy—with
an oligarchy—which sees its power slowly but surely eroded by the men of black gowns, by the Salamanca graduates. (pp. 247-50)

There is no doubt that Gracián saw the social mobility
taking place in the Spain of the 1650's as the victory of the
"many." And it is understandable that some anti-
democratic writers of the last century have used Gracián
for their criticism of the Europe of the masses. Of course,
I cannot agree with the late Aubrey Bell when in his book
on Gracián he writes: "It was not to be expected that Gracián, who made superiority his motto, should be attracted
by democracy and he handles it severely in *The Critic.*"
I frankly do not see where Gracián deals with democracy
in his essays. It is true that he contrasts the lives of the few
chosen persons with all the others, and he called them
"todo lo demás es número" ("and the rest is numbers").
It is true also that he claims that masses of men do not understand nuances and that they are not therefore good
judges in matters of artistic and literary taste. That is why
Gracián never admired Cervantes, because the author of
Don Quijote had had popular success. And Gracián complained bitterly about what he called the intellectual preponderance of barbers: "si el barbero del lugar no quiere,
nada valdrá el sermón más docto" ("if the village barber
does not approve of it, the best sermon will be considered
as worthless"). All these views have nothing to do with a
criticism of democracy. On the other hand, Gracián was
writing to praise the values and the historical function of
the aristocracy, of the aristocracies. And that was the
principal reason for his extraordinary impact on the Europe of the Baroque Age.

In 1650 a young Englishman who had just graduated from
Cambridge University arrived in Madrid to learn Spanish
and to try to arrange for payment of a debt that the Spanish monarchy had with his father. Weeks and months
passed and, not wanting to waste his time, he registered
at the University of Alcalá to study Spanish. There he was
well received and liked: his knowledge of Latin and interest in poetry made many friends for him. And some of
these were reading then the first part of *El Criticón,* just
published in 1651, with the pen-name Lorenzo Gracián.
Paul Ricaut, who was later to be known as Sir Paul Ricaut, and who became an illustrious member of the Royal
Society (he was to be also an important Arabist) left Spain
without his monies but with the beginning of a translation
of that first part of *El Criticón* which he published in 1681
in London, after having been in several countries of the
Near East as an English diplomatic representative. Let me
add in parenthesis that Ricaut was the first to point out
the connection between Gracián and the Arabic treatise
of Abentofail, *The Self-taught Philosopher.* This little episode has, also, a special historical significance by showing
the contrast between the impecunious condition of the
Spanish monarchy and the exportable resources of its culture. Spain was obviously going downhill, politically
speaking, but Gracián was to be read as probably no other

Spanish writer—until Ortega again—has been read beyond the Pyrenees. And one of the reasons for his impact was precisely that *The Critic* (and other works) were giving to the embattled aristocracies of Latin Europe some sort of consolation. I think that the late Fernand Baldensperger, in his article, "L'arrière-plan espagnol des *Maximes* de La Rochefoucault," has pointed out how all the *Frondeurs* were psychologically strengthened by the *morale de seigneurs* coming out of Spain. I do not know if I should agree with Baldensperger when he says that Gracián was a sort of typical Spanish intellectual: "un de ces intellectuels d'outremonts qui appliquent leur savoir à renforcer et guider l'autorité." It is true that the three Spaniards who have been widely read, and who have had considerable influence, outside of Spain in their own times, have been Gracián, Juan Donoso Cortés, and José Ortega y Gasset. And of the three of them, at least two are obvious defenders of authority and of the identification of culture and aristocracy. But Baldensperger is mistaken when he sees Gracián as the official exponent, so to speak, of the Spanish monarchy. His influence comes precisely from the fact that he also expresses in Spain "un désenchantement d'aristocrates à demi résignés." And if Gracián was able to "articuler fièrement" the views of that aristocracy it was partially because the Spanish nobility also felt itself being displaced by "un long règne de vile bourgeoisie" in spite of all other appearances. The structure of the Spanish state was not then "moins bourgeois" than in France: I would even say that it was a little more so. I should mention here that when Gracián selects two names to exemplify his idea of the person that he calls *hombre substancial,* he puts together the Duke of Osuna and the Prince of Condé. Two men of the same temper, and one of them had died in defeat and in prison: he was the Spaniard, not the Frenchman.

In conclusion we could say that Gracián's explicit and implicit testimony opens a new view on the social tensions within the Spanish Monarchy of the Baroque Age. And this shows again that literature is always a mirror of the times. On the other hand, it is not the only one, and we must always use it only as a way of seeing a historical period from within itself. . . . The historian of literature and the historian of society have nothing to lose by joining their efforts to achieve the aim of historical reconstruction: to make of distant men credible characters in the fiction of centuries and nations that we call history. (pp. 251-54)

> *Juan Marichal, "The Testimony of Literature, Spain (1618-1658)," in* Philological Quarterly, *Vol. 51, January, 1972, pp. 245-54.*

J. B. Hall   (essay date 1975)

[In the excerpt below, Hall examines Gracián's theory of history as a cyclical process.]

Impermanence, mutability, and the constant changes brought about by the passing of time, are themes common enough in the writings of Gracián and of other moralists of the seventeenth century. However, surprisingly little attention seems to have been paid to Gracián's ideas concerning the actual nature of the temporal or historical process, an omission which it is hoped at least partially to remedy in the present study.

Gracián's final and most extensive statement on the process of history is to be found in the tenth chapter of the third part of his *Criticón* (1657). It is introduced by an account of an ancient belief that each person's life is like a circle: a man's first ten years are, according to this theory, influenced by the uncertain Moon, and thus a time of emotional instability and excessive sentimentality, 'ya llorando, ya riendo, sin saber de qué se enoja, sin saber con qué se aplaca'. Then, until he reaches twenty, he undergoes the influence of Mercury, acquiring 'docilidades, con que se va adelantando ya muchacho, al paso que en la edad, en la perfección'. Venus rules him from twenty to thirty, and the Sun from thirty to forty; next comes Mars, and from fifty to sixty he is governed by Jupiter, 'influyendo soberanías'. From sixty to seventy he is influenced by melancholy Saturn, 'con humor y horror de viejo', and then at seventy a second childhood begins. . . . Gracián, though not accepting this theory *in toto,* at least recognizes it as true insofar as a man's declining years often do reflect his infancy, and he was clearly drawn by its satisfying neatness; he calls it an 'ingenioso jeroglífico de la rueda de la humana vida', and we should note that the *Criticón* itself might be said to have a circular structure, in that Critilo's escape from spiritual death or oblivion, as he and Andrenio finally arrive at the Island of Immortality, recalls his escape from physical death at the opening of the story when he struggled out of the sea to reach the island paradise of St Helena.

After his disquisition on the ages of man, Gracián returns to the adventures of Critilo and Andrenio who are now in Rome and have been led by the Cortesano to the highest of the city's hills, from where the entire world may be surveyed. Taking the wondrous telescope offered by their guide, Andrenio looks at a number of European countries, starting with Spain. . . . History, it would seem, is repeating itself, and the affairs of nations come full circle in the course of time, tracing a pattern to which the life of man, the microcosm, also conforms. Since the process never stops there is no permanent or lasting change, and as the pattern is circular nothing in the world is ever really new. . . . These words of the Cortesano are further stressed by the enormous Rueda del Tiempo which Critilo and Andrenio see next. (pp. 371-72)

It is clear from the above that Gracián is advancing here that view of history as a cyclic process which was still widely held in his time, though fated (together with the theory of decline, which looked back to a lost Golden Age) to be replaced by the concept of history as constant progress and improvement. The cyclic theory offers its adherents ample scope for an optimistic interpretation of history: its regular pattern provides evidence of divine order, of God's grand design, while the notion that there is nothing really new in the world can be an additional source of reassurance, eliminating the possibility of any totally unfamiliar development in human affairs, and enabling the more perceptive to assure themselves of success by a judicious reading of the signs of the times. A further implication of the theory is that good fortune and bad are justly and evenly distributed in this life. Views such as these are, as we shall see, commonly proposed in Gracián's earlier works, but here in the final part of the *Criticón* he inclines towards a pessimistic reading of time's cyclic pattern; he stresses the impermanence of existence, the fact that no human institution or achievement, however noble or worthy, is free from overthrow or decay. The 'Alforjas del Tiempo' provide the Cortesano with a series of depressing examples on the eternal instability of life, in which power and authority are constantly being torn away from those who wield them, so that Africa, formerly 'madre de prodigiosos ingenios, de un Augustino, Tertuliano, y Apuleyo', is now 'un barbarismo, engendradora de alarbes', while Greece, once so brilliant, has become 'un solecismo en poder de los bárbaros traces', and Italy, 'que mandaba a todas las demás naciones', is now reduced to impotence and subjection. In his description of the Rueda del Tiempo, Gracián continues to concentrate on the negative aspect of the changes wrought by time, repeatedly stressing the decline of the worthy and the triumph of the base, the collapse of noble lineages, and the elevation of the low-born. (pp. 372-73)

Gracián concedes of course that the cyclic theory of history recognizes the existence of periods of happiness and prosperity, but as Andrenio pertinently observes, this is of scant comfort for anyone obliged to live in a time of misery. . . . Nor does the cyclic pattern as presented here seem even to ensure an ultimate balance between good fortune and bad, since according to the Cortesano the world must endure four rulers like Nero, five like Caligula and eight like Heliogabalus for a single Augustus; for one like Cyrus, then like Sardanapalus. . . . Admittedly, some hope for Europe is glimpsed a little later, as the Cortesano sees in Mariana of Austria the qualities displayed by Blanche of Castile (the thirteenth-century Queen Regent of France). . . . Alexander himself seems to have returned in the figure of Pope Alexander VII. . . . The pessimism, then, is not absolute, but the episode of the Rueda del Tiempo remains for the most part very depressing, with its emphasis upon decay and loss and the impossibility of permanent change for the better, all mankind's achievements being doomed to eventual destruction as time rolls on remorselessly. Even the suggestion, made hopefully by Andrenio, that the regular pattern of history might at least enable men to profit from past experience and ward off future disasters, is firmly rejected by the Cortesano. . . . (pp. 373-74)

In his earlier writings, however, including the first and second parts of the *Criticón,* Gracián had drawn much more positive and optimistic conclusions from time's cyclic pattern. In the third chapter of part one (1651), Critilo describes nature's unending process of self-renewal. . . . The emphasis here is not on the inevitability of decline but rather on life's constantly triumphing over death in the world around us. . . . Later, in the sixth chapter of part two (1653), Critilo and Andrenio visit Fortuna, at whose bidding Time revolves his Wheel. Fortuna, to their surprise, is not blind but rather possesses the keenest of sight, and she denies that she is in any way unjust or cruel, asserting that on the contrary she distributes good fortune and bad impartially, her fairness being symbolized by her garment, 'la mitad de luto y la otra mitad de gala,' while she is attended by Equidad who carries a pair of scales. Fortuna is not the goddess of pagan antiquity whom Machiavelli had revived; the changes which she brings about in human affairs are never random, for they are the result of God's providence. . . . In a long speech she justifies the constant changes which Time brings about at her command, pointing out that it would be unfair for the powerful to keep their power for ever. . . . As Time's Wheel

turns the humble are exalted and the mighty fall, but this is a source of consolation to the oppressed and a warning to tyrants, a reminder that power and authority are uncertain things. . . . (pp. 374-75)

A similarly favourable interpretation of the cyclic theory of history is usual in Gracián's other works prior to the *Criticón.* In the *Héroe,* for instance (1637), the cyclic pattern of human affairs is shown as offering the discerning man who reads the signs of the times an opportunity of avoiding misfortune and gaining prosperity. . . . In the *Político* (1646), Gracián notes that the success enjoyed by any monarch depends largely upon the kind of era through which his country is passing during his reign, whether a period of growth ('juventud') or of decline ('vejez'). . . . Clearly Gracián has in mind here the regular alternations produced by the Wheel of Time, and the implication would seem to be that a nation's adversities resulting from 'vejez' are ultimately balanced by the good fortune enjoyed during 'juventud'. The point is made more directly in the *Discreto* (also 1646), where nature's eternal variability and the constant ebb and flow of human affairs are viewed optimistically as being indicative of universal harmony. . . . One is reminded here of Gracián's statement in chapter three of the first part of the *Criticón* that 'todo este universo se compone de contrarios y se concierta de desconciertos', and he makes the point again in the following chapter of the *Discreto,* in which he compares each man's life with its ups and downs to 'una representación trágica y cómica' in which good fortune and bad are fairly balanced, 'viniéndose a igualar las dichas con las desdichas.' Elsewhere in the *Discreto,* Gracián turns aside from the pattern of each individual's life to consider again the cyclic pattern of history in general; the world, he maintains, is characterized by the regular repetition of what has gone before. . . . Originality and novelty are now impossible. . . . Man can do nothing really new, being able only to choose between various courses of action already performed countless times before, yet this is not a cause for disillusionment and despair, but rather an encouraging reminder of our possession of the noble gift of free-will, a right use of which enables the man of sense to stand out from the ordinary mass of humanity. . . . Later, in the dialogue between the author and Canon Manuel Salinas y Linaza, the mutability of the world is shown in the fact that all men reach by their efforts a peak or 'punto de perfección' in their careers and then inevitably begin to decline. However, we do not dwell long on what the Canon calls 'la infelicidad de nuestra inconstancia', for the impermanency of life is seen as providing a stimulus for man to exploit to the full those times of good fortune which he experiences and to make the most of his personal talents before they fade with age. The emphasis again is on opportunity. . . .(pp. 375-76)

Gracián's view of history prior to the final part of his *Criticón* is overwhelmingly optimistic; it would seem reasonable to suppose that his eventual inclination towards a mostly negative and depressing interpretation of the cyclic process of historical change was due largely to the intense personal bitterness and frustration which marked his final years. His outlook on life could hardly fail to be influenced by the well-known difficulties with his superiors arising out of his publication of the *Criticón* without their permission, and culminating in his punishment, exile to Graus and vain attempts to move from the Company of Jesus to some other order. As Batllori has shown, official reports on Gracián during this period reveal the increased melancholy of a man of habitually rather gloomy temperament, . . . and in addition to his personal problems Gracián seems to have been greatly concerned over the present state of Spain and the progress of the wars in Flanders and Italy, topics which crop up in his correspondence during his last years.

Gracián's changed view of the historical process in the third part of the *Criticón* needs of course to be interpreted carefully. Although he now comes to deny that good fortune and bad are balanced in this life, or that it is possible to avoid disaster by observing the regular pattern of history, and stresses the impermanence of man's achievements, Gracián's pessimism is not total; he sees, for instance, the possibility of better things in Mariana of Austria, Christina of Sweden, and Pope Alexander VII, and his pessimism in any case is limited to the material world. Mutability and death can be seen in different ways, in the light of time or in the light of eternity, and we need to bear in mind that Gracián's now bleaker and more negative interpretation of history is balanced by his awareness of the existence of another world, free from the ravages of the passing of time. Although he may not mention the Christian hierarchy of values very often, he certainly advocates them, and he reveals in fact what Romera-Navarro calls 'el pesimismo y el optimismo del cristiano', which is orthodox *desengaño,* the Christian's recognition of the transience and imperfection of material things, and their worthlessness compared with the things of God. . . . Everything on earth is shortlived and subject to decay and decline with the exception of virtue, which alone is immune to the mutability of the world . . . so that even though a man's achievements come eventually to nothing as the Wheel of Time rolls on, the memory of his virtues at least is preserved among other men after his death, and these virtues assure him of true immortality in Heaven. The pessimism with which Gracián comes to view the temporal or historical process should not, then, be exaggerated or seen as a giving way to total despair, but nonetheless it remains very striking. (pp. 376-78)

> *J. B. Hall, "The Wheel of Time: Gracián's Changing View of History," in* Bulletin of Hispanic Studies, *Vol. LII, No. 4, October, 1975, pp. 371-78.*

Virginia Ramos Foster   (essay date 1975)

[*In the following excerpt from her monograph on Gracián, Foster analyzes the allegorical form and themes of* El Criticón.]

Man's allegorical journey as expressed in Western literature recalls numerous titles: Homer's *Odyssey,* Virgil's *Aeneid,* Dante's *Divine Comedy,* Bunyan's *Pilgrim's Progress,* and Spenser's *Faerie Queen,* among others. In the literature of seventeenth-century Spain, Quevedo's *Sueños* (Dreams) and Gracián's *Criticón (The Master Critic)* represent the culminating works of this particular fictional mode. (p. 68)

Although all literature can be called allegorical in the sense that it is metaphoric of human experience, it is valuable to stress allegory as a particular, or a more narrowly

defined, modality of premodern literature. To seek out differences between a work like the famous *Lazarillo de Tormes* and *The Master Critic* is instructive. The former is quasi-naturalistic in that throughout the stages of the journey of life, there are abstract values but there is also, to be sure, the narrative attempt to give the impression of day-to-day life. *The Master Critic,* however, is quite abstract and nonnaturalistic in its narrative elaboration. For example, it uses the common allegorical procedure of personification (the embodiment of abstract concepts, usually virtues and vices, in the forms of persons whose only function is to *personify* those qualities—by extension, animals and monsters may also be used). Also, in the movement from incident to incident, no intrinsic anecdotal justification is given, nor is there more than a purely abstract correspondence with day-to-day experience. (Of course, this does not mean that the work does not deal with profound human experience but only that the latter is identified and presented in nonnaturalistic terms.) In *The Master Critic* all of these elements—nonnaturalistic development, use of stereotyped personifications, as well as widely recognizable mythological figures—are part of the identification of the work as allegory in the specialized sense.

The Master Critic is not only Gracián's longest and most mature work (it was written over a period of six years and published in three different parts in 1651, 1653, and 1657), but it is also his only work of fiction. The novel is an interesting piece of literature, rich in imagery, vocabulary, moral philosophy, classical mythology, imaginative visions, complicated allegorical conceits, and abstract ideas. Its art is thoroughly complicated; its length is awesome. Indeed, Gracián can hardly be said to have followed his own famous dictum of brevity. In short, his work is a summa of social criticism, a compendium of almost all the literary and moral thought to be found in his previous writings. It is a splendid example of the baroque *Gesamtkunstwerk.* Published in defiance of his superiors and a source of antagonism and ill-will between the author and his order, *The Master Critic* is nothing more nor less than an allegory of life, both as a general human circumstance and as a seventeenth-century European reality. On the one hand, it is an encomium of the individualism of man and, on the other, a severe censure of man's behavior and of Gracián's own times.

Unfortunately, although the book has become a Spanish classic, it no longer enjoys the wide reading public it once had. In the nineteenth century, Schopenhauer, who shared the pessimism of Gracián, declared that *The Master Critic* is one of the best books in the world. As an alternate opinion from the twentieth century, the Argentine poet Jorge Luis Borges totally repudiates Gracián as a man and as an artist:

> Labyrinth, quibbles, emblems,
> Such bleak laborious minutiae
> Were all this Jesuit knew of poetry,
> Which he had reduced to stratagems.
>
> No music in his soul; but this inane
> Herbarium of metaphors and punning
> And a veneration of cunning
> And contempt for the human and superhuman.
>
> Homer's ancient voice he never heard,
> Or the voice—silver and moonlight—of Virgil;
> Nor saw Oedipus the accursed in exile

Nor Christ who is dying on a piece of board.

The stars, the radiant eastern stars
That is the vast aurora slowly fade,
Of these he blasphemously said
Chickens of the celestial acres.

As ignorant of divine love he was
As of that other burning in the bone;
The Pale One surprised him one afternoon
As he was reading El Marino's stanzas.

His later destiny is not given;
The dust that yesterday was his frame
Loosened to the changes of the tainted grave,
The soul of Gracián rose up to heaven.

What did he feel then contemplating plainly
The Archetypes and the Splendors?
Perhaps he cried and told himself: Vainly
I sought nourishment in shadows and errors.

What happened when the relentless
Sun of God, The Truth, put forth its fire?
Maybe the light of God left him blind there
In the center of the endless heavens.

I know another ending. Doped on his themes
Infinitesimal; Gracián never noticed heaven
And turns over in his memory as ever
Labyrinths, quibbles and emblems
(Translated by Irving Feldman)

General Characteristics

The plan of the novel, although not original in its broad outlines, is unique and significant in terms of theme, structure and philosophy. It is a philosophic-didactic compendium consisting of thirty-eight rambling chapters which recount the travels, adventures, and misadventures of Critilo, the archetype of intellect and reason, and Andrenio, the archetype of instinct and passion. Together the two characters can be said to constitute in a complementary sense the totality of man's nature. Throughout the novel, both are spokesmen on a variety of subjects. The two protagonists, like Dante, and many another "lost traveler," are led by a series of guides who are both mythological and allegorical figures in their journey through life in order to find Felisinda, who personifies happiness, and in order to become *personas* (i.e., truly persons). In their wanderings, which are very much reminiscent of the more naturalistic picaresque mode in Renaissance and baroque fiction, they go from the Island of Santa Elena to Madrid, Castilla, Aragón, the Pyrenees, France, Picardy, Germany, the Alps, Italy, and Rome, finally ending up on the Island of Immortality. Together they experience all kinds of difficulties and perils. But in spite of their misfortunes and disillusionments, they manage to attain self-perfection. And although the tone of *The Master Critic* is strongly pessimistic and misanthropic, Gracián does present an exit for man: an immortality based on artistic, political, social, and cultural achievements.

Obviously Gracián had read widely and had absorbed the many literary influences of his day. For example, Menéndez y Pelayo has been able to discover an oriental influence in *The Master Critic;* José Montesinos regards the novel as a picaresque creation; Romera Navarro emphasizes the Byzantine elements of the work. What a balance sheet of the historical investigations on the novel shows is that it is an amalgam of Oriental, classical, and Western literary traditions, with Oriental apologues, descriptive narration, moral and philosophic digressions, allegorical conceits, picaresque wanderings, circumstantial exempla, social criticism, and satire. Although it is generally believed that Gracián's knowledge of Greek is secondhand, he is, however, able to make many allusions to Greek writers with whose work he is familiar: Homer, Aesop, Heliodorus, Lucian, Aristotle, Plato, Sophocles, Euripides, Aristophanes, and Plutarch.

Likewise, the influence of Latin writers on *The Master Critic* is overwhelming. From Cicero and Seneca Gracián has taken the sententious maxims and literary modes of moral intent. He does not surpass them in profundity of thought, but he does excel them in conciseness of style and conceptual rapidity. Horace, Ovid, and Virgil are the poets who have left their mark on Gracián, while he also shares an attitude of bitter satire with Martial, Persius, and Juvenal. The humor and fresh spirit of the New Comedy of Plautus and Terence are also evident throught the novel. And the philosophy of historians like Pliny, Tacitus, Caesar, and Suetonius permeates Gracián's thinking. Romera Navarro is one literary historian who has emphasized the unusual importance of the Roman world in *The Master Critic.*

Throughout his writings, Gracián's theory of conduct for the ideal man centers on prudence and reason. This theory is sustained in *The Master Critic,* where man himself has become the vehicle through the allegorical framework for conveying the Jesuit's ideas. In order to capture the spirit of the work, it is essential to place it within the frame of reference of the baroque and the Counter-Reformation in Spain, a time when the organization of knowledge was based on complex dualities, counterpoints, ambivalences, and opposites.

In *The Master Critic* symmetry, totality, and harmony function not as complementary terms but rather as opposites. This constant tension is developed through the interplay of the two protagonists, who discover life in opposite ways, see reality in different perspectives, and think antithetically. Together, however, they form a total human personality, and together theirs is the quest for identification, happiness, and fulfillment. The following list of characteristics associated with each demonstrates the dialectical nature of the two characters; the complexity of the novel rests on the allegorical depiction of their antithetical yet complementary nature:

Critilo	*Andrenio*
Intellectual	Emotive
Mature	Immature, inexperienced
Independent, self-reliant	Dependent, unreliable
Stoic	Epicurean
Teacher	Pupil
Father	Son
Perspicacious	Gullible
Introvert	Extrovert
Spiritual	Corporal
Quiet	Noisy

Antonio Prieto has discussed this duality as the structural justification of the work:

The meeting of shipwrecked Critilo with Andrenio

on the Island of Santa Elena will be the meeting of human duality, in which reason and prudence blend with nature and imprudent generosity to form the human totality, the main actor of the narrative. It is a synthesis of two halves whose analysis and separation Gracián uses to show that mixture of opposites which dualizes the narrative subject and which ends in a synthesis with Gracián's incorporation of the individual in his composition as a person. The subject is dualized in this fashion in an allegorical play of synthesis-analysis-synthesis, which in the Baroque mode of contrasts is going to point out the composition of opposites which govern existence in their travels across the "stage" of the world. In his development, the narrative subject will be portrayed by a narrative form rich in opposites and tied to the technique of counterpoint which will resort expressively to the frequent use of antithesis, oxymoron, and homonymy. It is a perfect gauging of the narrative subject to the word, which under conceptism, structures **The Master Critic** in a tight correspondence of all its elements.

Narrative Organization

The first-time reader of **The Master Critic,** which is a highly imaginative as well as an extravagantly diffuse work, is astounded by Gracián's busy world, populated with hosts of both real and imaginary characters, many of the latter grotesque. This narrative world is further enriched by the accumulation of allegories, ideas, events, commentaries, and elaborate and sustained puns. In the introductory remarks to his reader, Gracián announces the moral purpose of his all-encompassing, baroque *Gesamtkunstwerk:* . . .

> I have attempted to join the dryness of philosophy with the entertainment of invention, the piquant of satire with the sweetness of the epic. . . . Beginning with fair Nature, I move on to elegant Art, and I end up with useful Morality.

From the outset, the author establishes the static, moral backdrop of the novel. (pp. 68-74)

Themes

An examination of **The Master Critic** from a thematic point of view immediately opens up the work for the reader in terms of Gracián's moral goal. In addition to an intricate plot supported by a vast erudition, one finds that the novel contains a multitude of recurring ideas and commentaries voiced by the characters, primarily by the sagacious Critilo, who is the archetypal educator and civilizer of not only Andrenio but of all humanity. We can see how the name of the protagonist bears a direct relationship to the title, **The Master Critic:** Critilo is the critic, the observer, the decipherer, and the interpreter of life—he is, in short, Gracián's literary alter ego in a world of constant discovering, seeing, and telling.

In keeping with baroque and Counter-Reformation thought, the novel probes the nature of the world. For Gracián, the world is a complex system of deceits, an enigma, a labyrinth of lies and ambiguities. What prevails is man's constant battle against *parecer* ("appearance; what seems to be") and *ser* ("what is"). Critilo, like many of the subsidiary guides, counselors, sages, and personifications of wisdom that appear throughout the novel, stresses the importance of *ver* ("seeing"), man's strongest weapon against an otherwise deceptive world. Man is imprisoned within a façade of false appearances and what is needed is an inner eye (as St. Ignatius of Loyola also insisted), a keen perceptivity in order to *see* beyond superficial realities. Gracián believes that the real heroes of life do not accept apparent truths but rather pursue profound significant ones. Ver along with *saber* ("knowing") are the principal keys for a worthwhile existence.

Besides the eternal battle between illusion and reality—and it must be remembered that Critilo is repeatedly obliged to explain what Andrenio *really* sees and experiences as they venture through life—man must set as his goal to *ser persona,* to become a person, through rational, prudent activity. In a sense, Gracián liberates human life from a dependence on the supernatural; his consciousness does not primarily focus on God but rather on man, his intellect and reason. It is precisely this concept of *ser* ("being") that is so highly prized by Gracián. After all, **The Master Critic** is man's quest for ser, both in this life and after death, and it is a quest described wholly within a secular, nontheological context.

Clearly, the themes of **The Master Critic** are not faithful to the restrictive prevailing Catholic beliefs, for Gracián's moral precepts do not deal with the religious issues of grace and original sin attributable to his more orthodox contemporaries. That is, the Jesuit deviated from the traditional norm of theocentricity espoused by great literati like Dante, Bunyan, Cervantes, and Calderón, to name a few, whose views of the world are ultimately God-centered. For his day, Gracián is a free and daring soul who set his novel within a pagan, secular world. Critilo speaks infrequently about God and the devil, but he turns to contemplate at length the human condition, its follies, vices, and stupidities. Since **The Master Critic** is not a theocentric work of literature, its author elaborates not on theology but on human behavior, and the major concerns of the composition rest on the latter. Look, for instance, at the allegories which stress secular subjects, such as honor, fortune, valor, all of which constitute substantial principles for this life. Likewise, the events of the characters' journey emphasize man, not religion, while the symbolism in the work follows the same orientation based on nature and myth. Nonetheless, Gracián remains a participant in Counter-Reformation Spain and a proponent of Aristotelian-Thomistic philosophy. Consequently he continues to believe that reason is man's superior faculty and with it he is able to solve his problems and difficulties.

The theme of nature plays an integral role in Gracián's world of fiction, both from a physical point of view in that the protagonists must deal with nature physically and psychologically—they must overcome her many adversities—and from an aesthetic point of view. In the opening chapters, the discussions concerning nature foreshadow somewhat the primitivism of Rousseau, principally in terms of the rustic joys of nature and the innocence of the noble savage as symbolized by Andrenio. The beauty and harmony of nature and the universe are incomparable in their supreme perfection. Nature is viewed as a capricious phenomenon filled with harmonious discords. God is not only the Prime Mover but the consummate artist who has created the world with his own agudeza and ingenio. Moreover, God's art provides man with a supreme means of attaining knowledge: . . .

Only the infinite knowledge of the Supreme Maker could find the way, the order, and the harmony of such a beautiful and perennial variety.

He cannot be seen, but he is known and, like a sovereign prince who is secluded in his inaccessible incomprehensibility, he speaks to us through his creatures. This is how a philosopher so aptly defined this universe, an immense mirror of God. My book, the unlettered wiseman called it, where in ciphers of creatures he studied the divine perfections.

Critilo and his pupil view the cosmos of nature, in typical baroque fashion, as a magnificent theater filled with awesome wonders like celestial time, the starry heavens, the seas, day, and other mysteries. But what brings discord and disorder to this otherwise utopian setting of nature is man, far worse even than the beasts. *The Master Critic* abounds in misanthropic attitudes toward man, who with his prime sin of foolishness perverts, corrupts, and transgresses against nature and the universe. Critilo repeatedly tells Andrenio that life is a constant battle against evil and, in fact, warns him against man whose morality and corporality are bestial: . . .

for if men are not beasts it is because the more beastly for the former have often learned from the cruelty of the latter. We have never been in greater danger than we are now among these latter. . . .

Believe me when I say that there is no wolf, no lion, no tiger, no basilisk that can touch man; he exceeds them all in his ferocity.

However, man is nonetheless capable of understanding truth and beauty through artistic and abstract expression. Thus man, who possesses a complex duplicity, figures simultaneously as both the destroyer of harmony and nature and as the Maker who through Will can direct his intellectual and artistic energies to restoring to nature its beauty and balance.

As is well known, *The Master Critic* has the distinction of being unrelentingly pessimistic in affirming that life is a constant death, man is bad, and society is irremediably corrupt. Basically it is man himself who is the theme of *The Master Critic,* man who is defined and redefined within the network of infinite situations and possibilities open to human conduct and behavior. In his departure from scholastic ideas, Gracián believes that man does not fall by birth from Christian grace. Rather, he willfully and stupidly chooses evil in order to satisfy his natural propensity for baser needs and desires. It is significant that during their travels, Critilo and his guides reject all that is physical and carnal as highly repugnant. Man, however, can be redeemed, not by divine redemption, but by human achievement. The highest moral good in Gracián's work is *ser hombre, ser persona,* "to be a man, to be a person." The novel does not shape a traditional, didactic vision of heaven or hell as a reward or punishment for man. Rather man's reward, the culmination of human happiness, lies in fame, in an immortality and an eternal life through posterity, whereas damnation consists of an existence in eternal oblivion. Critilo's and Andrenio's final destination strikes a secular and intellectual note. They end up on the Island of Immortality because the two have fulfilled their destiny as *personas,* having subjugated all of their passions through reason and the use of the Golden Mean, the prin-

ciple of moderation so esteemed by pre-Christian and Christian moralists alike.

Contemporary Commonplaces

The preceding details can only serve to provide a comprehensive trajectory of the thematic framework of the narrative. In addition, every page of *The Master Critic* offers the reader a didactic medley of ideas and advice. Some of the most significant motifs include the following *topoi,* "commonplaces."

Misogyny. Like Quevedo, Gracián maligns women, who are the frequent targets of his hostility and criticism. Critilo is the major spokesman of Gracián's misogyny, for he has suffered severe trauma because of Felisinda, who, besides representing the embodiment of happiness, is the *belle dame sans merci.* Critilo repeatedly warns Andrenio about feminine treachery. He is clearly antimarriage (wives imprison men) and often blames the shocking condition of the world on woman, the Pandora of all evils. And although, like Felisinda, several women figures, both real and fictitious, are portrayed as aesthetically or intellectually pleasing, many are physically and spiritually repulsive, grotesquely presented as fact and ugly hags, liars, hypocrites, and monsters.

Journey of Life. This topic provides the narrative structure of the work which represents Everyman's peregrination through life in search of *desengaño* ("undeluded truth"). The protagonists follow a linear progression as they engage in activities corresponding to the chronological stages of age.

Theatrum mundi. For Critilo and Andrenio the whole celestial and terrestrial world is a stage where men, as the principal actors, reach awareness, knowledge, and possible self-perfection. The world as a theater, filled with conflict and deceit, also emerges as a place of marvels and intellectual pleasures. The novel also views life as a play with a natural beginning, middle and end.

Complaint on Death. Gracián's eschatological concerns climax in the Cave of Death, where Death appears as a leveler—"all men must die"—of humanity. Death, from her horrible throne of cadavers, somewhat pathetically complains of her experiences with mortals who neither understand nor accept her.

Criticism of Clergy and Monastic Life. In the allegorical episode on the Wasteland of Hipocrinda, Gracián boldly denounces the fraud and hypocrisy of the religious life. Hipocrinda's house (she is the personification of Hypocrisy) actually emerges as a convent whose members lead an epicurean life of carnality and vice under the guise of holiness and virtue. By means of fiction, Gracián covertly satirizes and censures the spiritual licentiousness of the times.

Ubi sunt. Many characters reiterate a disillusionment with the affairs of the world, especially those related to Spain. Consequently there is a yearning for the glories, triumphs, and successful men of times past and a longing for such deeds and magnificence of spirit to return once again to Spain and elsewhere: . . .

for this is not the century of man—that is, of those of other times. What? Did you expect to find now a don Alonso the Magnanimous in Italy, a Great Captain in Spain, a Henry IV in France . . . ?

There are no longer heroes such as these in the world, nor any recollection of them. . . .

Will another Alexander the Great come into the world, a Trajano and the great Theodosius? That would be a great thing!

Fortune even laments the scarcity of wise people—there are not even two wise persons in one kingdom while *necios,* "fools," are infinite in number.

Continuity. Especially in The Wheel of Time adventure the characters gain insights into the meaning of time as an omnipresent feature of reality. Through the magic of the Courier, they become aware of a fixed cosmic hierarchy, and the circular nature of time; likewise they see that history repeats itself among a web of ambiguities and that there is a pattern of eternal return. Time is interpreted as continuity with an alternation of highs and lows in temporal events. Closely paralleling this concept throughout **The Master Critic** lies the system of correspondences in the universe: between the animal world and the human world, nature and life, fable and reality, past, present and future times, the microcosm of man and the macrocosm of God, harmony and strife.

Vulgo. Gracián, an elitist, censures the masses as mindless, ignorant, and insensitive creatures who have no destiny to fulfill in this life or in the next. Critilo shuns them for their capriciousness, mediocrity, and lack of imagination (for example, they replace Truth with Lie), and Gracián unmercifully satirizes their absurdity frequently in the work. Approximately three-quarters of humanity belongs to the mob of monsters who march across the pages of **The Master Critic** like the characters of a painting by Hieronymus Bosch. The *vulgo* is defined in these terms by El Sabio: . . .

the masses are nothing but a synagogue of pretentious ignoramuses who, the less they understand of things, the more they speak of them.

Contempt of the World. Incisive invectives against the world and its deceits fill **The Master Critic:** Critilo explains that the world is essentially man's prison, where he is subjected to physical pain and sickness, spiritual unrest, and sorrow, with death as the final punishment and loss. Man is born crying, lives in a theater of tragedies, and dies miserably. Gracián revolts against the senses, carnal love, selfishness, and ambition, because they all highlight this virtually existential condition.

Scorn for the Court. Gracián regards the city as the den of iniquity—the wise and the godly have left for the natural life, while the beasts have come to the cities to become courtiers. . . .

Without a doubt the few men that were left have retired to the mountains . . . in order not to see what is happening in the world, and the beasts have come down to the cities and have become courtiers.

Life in the court is portrayed as a microcosm of all the evils that exist in the world at large: extravagant, vain women and idle, stupid men who pursue a life of pleasure as parasites of society. Grand women are, in reality, adulterous, while great lords are cowards who pervert honor. (One will recall that the court presented major problems for seventeenth-century Spanish society.)

Boy and Old Man. The wise and older Critilo helps Andrenio to acquire maturity and an understanding of life: theirs is a parent-child relationship both figuratively and literally. At the start, Andrenio has practically no knowledge of life, but an active participation in life, with its attendant sensations and experiences, have enriched him and made him a person.

Letter Writing. The epistolary style is considered to be the greatest science. For example, Luis Vives's book *De conscribendis epistolis,* the *Arte de escribir cartas,* (Art of Letter Writing) is cited as the magnum opus in the quarrel between the arts and science. During this quarrel it is also decided that men with great imagination choose natural philosophy (Plato) while men of prudent judgment are interested by ethics (Seneca).

Landscapes. Atmospheric scenery is often drawn throughout the novel: there are many descriptions centering on the sea, violent landscapes, sinister storms, flowers, greenery, steep hills, mountain grottoes, caves, forests, the sea, meadows, the figurative Alps of Old Age, and the Island of Immortality. In **The Master Critic** Gracián associates geography with age, which he sees as a steady progression upward: youth is spent in the lower, flowery regions (springtime), middle age along the steep, less verdant hills (autumn), and finally, old age high up in the region of the Alps (winter).

Book of Nature, Book of the World. Countless are the times that the commonplace of the book as a symbol of the universe is used. Gracián accords the Book of Nature—that is, the experiences of life—the superior ranking. In the same vein, however, great writings and books nourish man's spirit and intellect. The Palace of Sofisbella, of wisdom personified, as well as Salastano's Museum (in real life the house and library of Gracián's friend and patron Lastanosa), are kingdoms of knowledge for mankind.

The World Upside Down. Corruption and decadence beset Spain in a topsy-turvy world full of chaos and values in reverse. Man has perverted natural laws like honor and virtue. Lies replace truth, vanity and a youthful appearance are treasured values, women rule the world and men, wars predominate, and passions enslave humanity, for which lying, cheating, and malice are the standard norms of life. Materialism is rampant and laziness and idleness are the great ethics. (pp. 81-9)

National Psychology and Praise of Countries. Romera Navarro has pointed out Gracián's concern for the personalities of the nations that he satirizes: Germans are famous as gluttons and drunkards, Spaniards are proud, the French greedy, and the Portuguese boastful. The English are fickle and Protestant, the Italians are liars, and the Turks are barbarians. At the same time Gracián praises several countries, he simultaneously criticizes them. Spain, of course, is the most important nation in Europe, and she is both hated and envied. Italy is praised for her genius and her contributions to art, literature, philosophy, and political writings. Rome is the center of culture, history, religion and beautiful buildings. Lisbon is characterized as a good place with wealth, abundance, and a peculiar bent for the fantastic. France is "the flower of the kingdoms," blessed with holy kings and brave and wise men, while Brazil is a paradise of sugar.

Locus Amoenus. The topic of a beautiful, restful, and harmonious nature, a refuge *from* mankind, abounds in *The Master Critic,* especially in Crisis I and II of Part One.

Deus Artifex. God is the Maker of man as well as creator of a perfectly ordered universe, which is a perfect work of art: . . .

> This is the prodigious effect of the infinite wisdom of the Creator, whereby He organized all things in accordance with their weight, number, and measure: for, if one observes carefully [one sees that] every created thing has its center with respect to place, its duration in time, and its special end in action and existence. For this reason you will see that they are subordinated each to each in accordance with the degree of their perfection. The elements, which are lowest in the scale of nature, join to form mixed bodies; and among the latter, the lesser ones serve the greater. Those herbs and plants which are at the bottom of the scale of life (since their life is merely vegetative), moving and growing till they attain the point of their perfection with the passage of time beyond which point they cannot advance, nonetheless serve as nutriment for sentient beings, which are in the second rank of life, enjoying sentient life in addition to life which is merely vegetative; and these [sentient beings] are the animals of the earth, the fishes of the sea and the fowls of the air: these crop grass, live in trees whose fruit they eat, in whose branches they nest, among whose trunks they hide to defend themselves, with whose leaves they cover themselves, and beneath whose shade they take shelter from the sun. But all of them, trees and animals, live in the service of another and third rank of living beings, much more perfect and greatly superior, which, over and above growth and sense, can reason, ponder, and understand; and this is man, who at the end of the creative process is ordained and given existence for and toward God, to recognize Him, love Him, and serve Him.

Arms and Letters. Gracián upholds the cerebral life of the Muses: music, literature, history, philosophy, political and spiritual writings. However, *The Master Critic* praises the life of the warrior who has fought (physically and/or figuratively) with the noble ends of honor and fame. Since heroism is a prime virtue for Gracián, the novel is indeed a catalogue of heroes both historical and fictional: Alexander the Great, Vasco de Gama, Isabel and Ferdinand, James the Conqueror, The Cid, and so forth.

Fortune. This topic, which is a constant in all of Gracián's writings, is ambivalently portrayed as a capricious and powerful arbiter of life as well as a mediatress of justice and the divine world. She has favored Spain with "rivers of silver, mountains of gold, gulfs of pearls." The work speaks against her fickle nature and suggests that men neither blindly follow her nor humbly submit to her but rather face up to her with reason and good judgment.

Solitude. The Master Critic reflects upon this topic in both negative and positive ways. Critilo never restrains Andrenio's desire to be with the mad *vulgo.* On the one hand, solitude increases man's shortcomings, but on the other, solitude enables man to cultivate an interior life so that he can live wisely in a world of mediocrity and ordinary people. (pp. 89-92)

> *Virginia Ramos Foster, in her* Baltasar Gracián, *Twayne Publishers, 1975, 171 p.*

David H. Darst   (essay date 1977)

[*Darst is an American educator who has written widely on Spanish literature. In the following excerpt, he outlines the plot of* El Criticón *and traces the moral development of Andrenio throughout his journey.*]

The major themes that comprise the subject matter of Baltasar Gracián's philosophical novel *El Criticón* are well known. The author depicts the civilized world as *al revés* and *al contrario* from the way it should be (these terms appear no less than one hundred and seventy-three times in the novel). He reiterates that the depraved human condition is the cause for it, and he urges the individual to be alert and wary in order to penetrate society's guileful meanness. Gracián likewise teaches that one must consciously strive for an *aurea mediocritas* by seeking the middle path between vice and excessive virtue; for only then will one become what the author terms a *persona.* These themes recur in every country through which Critilo and Andrenio travel (Spain, France, Germany, and Italy), and they form a major part of the ethical philosophy Gracián espouses for the successive ages of adolescence, youth, manhood, and senescence. This continual reiteration of themes tends to deemphasize the structural distinction among the three Parts, however, and has generated a proclivity among students to consider *El Criticón* uniform in composition, consisting of little more than a monotonous discourse on the same Neo-Stoic doctrine couched in a multitude of different allegories.

The consideration of the novel's vast panoply of incidents, places, and characters as apparently static in presentation invariably includes the two allegorical travelers. E. Correa Calderón expresses a commonly accepted critical judgment about Andrenio and Critilo when he describes them as "flat" characters who remain unchanged in their philosophical and psychological constitution. . . . Miguel Romera-Navarro holds the same view. . . . A more recent critic, Margarita Levisi, also considers the pilgrims a pair of opposites, although she intuits that the two form as well an organic unity representing Man. . . . (p. 907)

It is indeed true that Gracián has to some extent intentionally polarized the inherent characteristics of his two heroes in the first lines of the novel by referring to Critilo as "lo juizioso" and to Andrenio as "lo humano." This supposed constancy of relationships between the two men is quite superficial, however. As I plan to demonstrate in this [discussion], Andrenio's perception of reality changes decidedly in each Part of the novel as he progresses from youth through manhood to old age, and the changes he undergoes are intimately related to the particular themes and structure of each Part.

The most notable transformation in Andrenio's character is in Parts One and Two, and for a very logical reason. The definitive form of *El Criticón* comprises three distinct Parts: "Primera parte en la primavera de la niñez y en el estío de la juventud," "Segunda parte en el otoño de la varonil edad," and "Tercera parte en el invierno de la vejez." They were published in 1651, 1653, and 1657, respectively. This three-part format was not the original one envisioned by Gracián, however. As Miguel Romera-Navarro explains in a note to the *Prólogo* to the first Part the Jesuit's initial intention was to compose solely a two-part work. . . . Thus Gracián intended to write only a diaeretic work in which the first section would examine adolescence and youth while the following one would depict manhood and old age. It should come as no surprise, then, that Parts One and Two present a formal consonance and a growth in Andrenio's perception of reality that manifest dualities rather than some tripartite vision of the world, as would be expected if Gracián had intended from the beginning to compose *El Criticón* in three stages. (pp. 907-08)

Obviously, if Andrenio (and to a lesser extent Critilo) is to mature at all as he passes to another age in life, he must undergo an expansion in his awareness of the outer world which parallels the physical growth from youth to manhood. A close scrutiny of Andrenio's actions and the nature of the events presented by Gracián in Parts One and Two will demonstrate that there is a remarkably clear difference in the intentions of the two Parts.

Gracián based his pattern for organizing Andrenio's experience on the Aristotelian idea that the human being possesses three distinct souls, known as the vegetative, the sensitive, and the rational souls. Man is born with the vegetative soul, which rules his life during childhood. . . . Youth is "la vida sensitive," where the senses reign supreme. Solely in manhood, "la vida racional," does a person have the opportunity to gain full utilization from his three higher faculties.

In Gracián's novel, the first three chapters describe the vegetative stage of man's life. They are therefore dedicated exclusively to a disquisition on the natural world in all its beauty, variety, and abundance, and God's provident plan for it. This configuration includes a discussion of the *Concierto de el universo,* as the marginal note in Crisi i relates; an extensive description of the sun, moon, and the stars (Crisi ii); and an entire Crisi dedicated to "La hermosa naturaleza" (the title of Crisi iii). The next three chapters are transitional ones. As their titles indicate—"El despeñadero de la vida," "Entrada del mundo," and "Estado del siglo"—they are primarily intended to educate Andrenio before his passage into the first responsible phase of life, the "vida sensitiva," into which the two travelers enter at the beginning of Crisi vii. . . . (pp. 908-09)

Despite the fact that the first three chapters treat natural philosophy and the initial vegetative state of man, they present the major themes of Part One; themes, moreover, that are not prevalent in Part Two. In the author's introductory statements to Crisi ii, which form a kind of *judicium* before the *experimentum* that follows, Gracián departs from the topic of the order and the concert of nature to decry the deadly sins of *codicia, sobervia, desvanecimiento,* and *gula.* At the beginning of Crisi iv, he repeats the motif, this time pondering the vicious conditions of the *syrado, codicioso, confiado, perezoso, desvanecido, hipócrita, sobervio, jugador, glotón* and *bebedor.* These "pasiones," as the Jesuit terms them, are the enemies against which Andrenio and Critilo will struggle throughout Part One, for they are mentioned specifically in every one of the chapters. In Crisi v, where the allegorical journey through life begins at the trifurcation of the road into two extreme paths and a middle way, the two travelers watch the highways of vice and excessive virtue taken by *vanos, vengativos, glotones, lascivos, avaros,* 'otros que todo el día andavan alrededor moliédose y moliendo, sin passar adelante ni llegar jamás al centro" (*envidiosos*), and

"otros: todo se les iba en començar a caminar" (*perezosos*). In Crisi vi, they encounter vain men, misers, and a general group of "esclavos de sus apetitos, siervos de sus deleites;" and in Crisi vii a register at the beginning of the chapter includes *gula, lascivia, codicia, sobervia,* and *ira.* The final chapter presents a résumé of all the passions that have assaulted Critilo and Andrenio throughout their journey: *sobervia, codicia, engaño, ira, gula, inconstancia, simplicidad, infidelidad, barbaridad, astucia, atrocidad, injusticia, delicias, cobardía, temeridad, pereza,* and *luxuria.* There is thus in Part One a constant repetition of all the sensual vices to which man is subject, with particular emphasis on the sins to which a youth is most susceptible.

Another theme predominates in Part One that is related intimately with the passions, for it describes what men become when they let their appetites seize control of their actions. Immediately following the introductory section in Crisi iv, Critilo forewarns Andrenio what to expect from civilized society. . . . Critilo then compares man to the lion, the tiger, the elephant, the bull, the bear, the dog, and the wolf. To emphasize the analogy, he repeats the motif, describing men as lions, bulls, serpents, dragons, basilisks, bears, dogs, and elephants. The theme recurs at the "Entrada del mundo" (Crisi v), where the unwary children led by Evil Inclination are set upon and devoured by "exércitos de fieras, leones, tigres, osos, lobos, serpientes y dragones," representing, of course, the diverse sensual passions to which adolescents are subject. In the next chapter, when Andrenio and Critilo enter the Plaza Mayor, they expect to encounter men, but instead "avía leones, tigres, leopardos, lobos, toros, panteras, muchas vulpejas, ni faltavan sierpes, dragones y basiliscos." Quirón explains to them, moreover, that the lions are the powerful, the tigers are the assassins, the wolf is a greedy man, the vixen is a courtesan, and the serpent is a prostitute. In Crisi vii, tigers are equated with the cruel, lions with the proud, bears with the dishonest, and crows with thieves. The plethora of comparisons of men with animals gives the first Part the appearance of a veritable bestiary. Gracián repeats the central idea of the Part in a variety of ways, and his moral lesson is always the same: vice "convierte los hombres en bestias." When man allows his sensitive nature to gain control of his faculties, he becomes a lion in his pride, an old dog in his greed, a turtle in his laziness.

From Critilo's lengthy speeches on the vices and the bestiality of man in Crisis v, vi, and vii, which cover the transitional period between early childhood and youth, Andrenio has received a broad indoctrination on how to traverse the next phase in life's pilgrimage without falling victim to the passions; but it is of little benefit. In accordance with an age ruled by the senses, Crisis vii through xii present Andrenio stumbling and falling into sin at every opportunity. His first experience as a youth is indicative of what happens to him throughout Part One. It takes place in the City of Deceit (Crisi vii), where the streets are named Hypocrisy, Ostentation, and Artifice; and where in the Plaza Mayor the populace presents a comedy which is the greatest delusion of all, for it is the tragedy of life. When Critilo desires to leave so as to continue the straight path, Andrenio, "cchizado de la vanidad," makes ridiculous excuses to remain; and Critilo ponders the remedy that will rescue his friend.

In the next Crisi, Critilo leaves Andrenio in the clutches

of vanity and continues to the palace of Artemia. . . . The Prudente Anciano, whom Artemia sends to free Andrenio from his captivity, finds the youth completely changed in physiognomy and blinded by sin. The Wise Man carries his charge from the city and makes him view it in a mirror, because "las cosas del mundo todas se han de mirar al rebés para verlas al derecho." Andrenio is immediately enlightened, and they travel to the palace of Artemia, where the youth, in accordance with the sensitive life through which he is passing, discourses at length on the moral anatomy of man.

Andrenio's next experience as a youth takes place on the way to Court when he and Critilo fall into the hands of bandits who bind the pilgrims' hands with flowers and books, characterizing thereby the respective obsessions of delight and wisdom. Critilo immediately escapes and returns to Artemia to request that the Sabio who had earlier rescued Andrenio return to free the youth again. Andrenio obtains freedom on his own, however, by making a rope out of the very flowers that bound him; and he again declares that he has experienced the *desengaño* necessary to avoid falling into error. Nevertheless, when the two travelers arrive at Court, Andrenio falls under the spell of "Los encantos de Falsirena" (Crisi xii) and has to be rescued by Critilo and an allegorical character called Egenio: "Salieron todos a la luz de dar en la cuenta, desconocidos de los otros, pero conocidos de si." After such a strong indoctrination, Andrenio avoids the pitfalls in the last Crisi, "La feria de todo el mundo," which functions as a summary by treating all the various vices to which man is subject; and he and Critilo advance toward Aragon and manhood.

In sum, at every opportunity in Part One Andrenio fell victim to his beastly passions, vanity and lust in particular; and Critilo, the Prudente Anciano, and Egenio had to come to the youth's aid to extract him from the pits and mires into which he descended. Yet the experiences endowed Andrenio with an invaluable measure of perceptive knowledge about the reality of the visible world. . . . In keeping with the dominance of the sensitive soul, Gracián is telling his readers, the major objectives for a young man are control of the appetites and, of most significance, the acquisition of the ability to SEE the world as it really is. If a youth can accomplish these ends, he will avoid many of the pitfalls in the journey through manhood.

The thematic images in the first sections of Part Two are markedly different from those in the earlier Part, for Gracián concentrates on the presentation of opposite values. As youth was "la vida sensitiva," so manhood is "la vida racional." While a young man naturally desires to seek pleasure and delight, a man of middle age attempts naturally to live by the dictates of his intellect. . . . In short, man strives to achieve a modus vivendi characterized by moral virtue rather than by vice and passion. Gracián therefore formulates a thematic structure for Part Two that illustrates how Andrenio and Critilo advance in the accruement of exemplary moral values.

The first allegorical figure the two travelers encounter in Part Two, for example, is Argos, a strange figure with eyes covering his body. . . . After Andrenio and Critilo pass through the Custom's House of Life (Crisi i), where they admire the way almost everyone acquires ethical rectitude in manhood, Argos gives them a special preparation for their journey:

> Después, Argos con un extraordinario licor alambicado de ojos de águilas y de linzes, de coraçones grandes y de celebros, les dió un baño tan eficaz, que a más de fortalecer mucho, haziéndolos más impenetrables por la cordura que un Roldán por el encanto, al mismo punto se les fueron abriendo muchos y varios ojos por todo el cuerpo, de cabeça a pies; que avían estado ciegos con las legañas de la niñez y con las inadvertidas passiones de la mocedad; y todos ellos tan perspicazes y tan despiertos, que ya nada se les passava por alto; todo lo advertían y lo notavan.

With such a powerful ointment, neither the father nor the son will succumb to the passions, nor will they be mistaken as to the identity of others, as occurred in the first Part; rather both of them will recognize immediately in virtually every instance the vices and deceits to which most of their fellow travelers are subjected.

In 'La carcel de oro" (Crisi iii), for instance, the two pilgrims are not deceived into believing that such a place is worthy of entrance, although at the end of the Crisi both are caught in a fine gold net. After this episode, Andrenio leaves Critilo at "El museo del discreto" (Crisi iv) and journeys to the "Plaça del populacho y corral del vulgo" (Crisi v) to see the "sabios de fortuna"; but he immediately comprehends that the wisdom expressed there is false knowledge. In contrast to his actions in Part One, Andrenio is horrified at the sight of so many "hombres a remiendos," and flees from the plaza of his own free will, "tan arrepentido como desengañado." When a false hermit guides the two travelers to feigned virtue, Andrenio again sees clearly through the disguises and roles of the inhabitants; and upon arriving at the "Anfiteatro de monstruosidades" (Crisi ix), Andrenio is the first to explain: "O casa engañosa, por fuera toda maravillas, y por dentro monstruosidades!" Finally, in Crisi xiii the pair comes upon a strange figure whom Critilo presumes is Ostracismo, but whom Andrenio properly recognizes: "A mi me pareció en aquel mirar de mal ojo, en el torcer de boca, en el hazer gestillos, en el modillo de hablar y en el enfadillo, que era la Embidia."

Andrenio's ability to perceive reality so well in Part Two has been facilitated, according to Gracián, by the fact that middle age is naturally free of error because it represents the highest physical level of man. (pp. 909-12)

Moreover, the allegorical countries to which Andrenio and Critilo travel are signs of virtues rather than vices: "Descubrían países nunca andados, regiones nunca vistas, como la del Valor y del Saber, las dos grandes provincias de la Virtud y la Honra, los países del Tener y del Poder, con el dilatado reino de la Fortuna y del Mando." This particular itinerary is repeated at the end of Part Two when the pilgrims reach the Alps to enter old age. The Man of Extremes lists for them the virtues that they have acquired in manhood: "El honroso saber, el acomodado tener, la dulce amistad, el importante valor, la ventura deseada, la virtud hermosa, la honra autorizada, y desta vez el mando verdadero."

These two indexes are accurate résumés of the eight different locales visited by Andrenio and Critilo. In the first part of Crisi iii they meet Gerión, an allegorical representation of *amistad*. They then observe "La carcel de oro," the extreme of the virtue *tener*. In Crisi iv they visit "El museo del discreto," which represents the acquirement of *saber;* and in Crisi v they see the contrary of *saber* in the vulgarity of the people at "La plaça del populacho." The "Hiermo de Hipocrinda" in Crisi vii is the antithesis of the *valor* that is delineated in the "Armería del valor" of Crisi viii. Crisi ix, "El anfiteatro de monstruosidades," depicts the extremes of the mean *virtud,* which is allegorized by the figure of Virtelia in Crisi x. Crisi xi presents *honor* in the form of Honoria, and Crisi xii examines the last virtue of the journey, which is *mando.* The final Crisi, "La jaula de todos," functions in the same way as "La feria de todo el mundo" did in Part One; it sums up the action and leads to the next age of mankind. Throughout Part Two, then, there is a very strict coordination of events to present the moral virtues in the order described by Gracián at the beginning and at the end of the Part; and, in most cases, Gracián continues the presentation of the topsy-turvy world so characteristic in his prose works by dramatizing the opposite of the virtues his travelers are acquiring.

Crisi ii, "Los prodigios de Salastino," comes before the pilgrims begin their allegorical journey through manhood, but it serves a double purpose in Gracián's plan. . . . The whole Crisi is an encomium of Lastanosa in particular and of famous men in general; for to Gracián the most effective answer to his vision of vicious men as beasts in Part One is a full representation of virtuous men as heroes in Part Two. For this reason, throughout the second Part he mentions virtually every famous man of the epoch, as well as noted warriors, politicians, rulers, and thinkers of ancient times. In fact, there is a minimum of three hundred different references to noted persons in Part Two, with the largest concentrations in Crisi ii, iv, and viii. Parts One and Three combined do not have nearly the number of heroes as does this Part. The praise of famous men was also intended to be the culminating moment of *El Criticón;* for Gracián originally planned for his two pilgrims to end their journey and to experience the pleasures of old age at the palace of the Spanish ambassador to Germany, don Francisco de Moura.

It is clear, then, that from the beginning of *El Criticón* the Jesuit envisioned a bipartite work which would show man's development from domination by the senses in adolescence and youth to rational self-awareness in manhood and senescence. However, as Gracián began writing the final Crisi of Part Two, he must have realized that he could not possibly append old age to it because the last years of the people he saw around him marked a decided *descent* from virtue into vice; so he decided to dedicate an additional Part to old age in order to express that movement. Furthermore, the Jesuit had continually preached that manhood was the mean between the two extremes of the delights of youth and the aggravations of senility. It was therefore aesthetically impossible to attach an extreme to the mean presented in Part Two. Since this paradox evidently did not occur to Gracián until the last Crisi of Part Two, he was faced with the structural problem of adding a third section to what was supposed to have been a unified dual representation of man's journey through life. To resolve the difficulty, he simply incorporated into Part Three the same thematic material that he had delineated in both earlier Parts, presenting Andrenio as the embodiment of an old man subject to the passions and Critilo

as one who lives according to the dictates of virtue. Thus the Jesuit describes within a single framework two contrary sides of old age: *horrores* and *honores*.

This conjunctive method differs completely from the manner in which Gracián displayed his protagonists in the first two Parts. In this Part, the maturation of Andrenio's perceptive ability ceases to concern Gracián, because he manipulates his two travelers in a wholly different way. To conform to his earlier system, the Jesuit would have had to show both Critilo and Andrenio meritorous of honor and fame, as throughout Parts One and Two he has presented them struggling and triumphing together. In order to demonstrate the evil side of old age, however, he arrests Andrenio's growth in awareness and uses him to illustrate the worst characteristics of senescence, while Critilo becomes the personification of one who enjoys the honors bestowed on those who lead a virtuous life. This polarization of attitudes categorically separates Andrenio spiritually and physically from Critilo, and prohibits the development of either character, for they now serve merely as types who personify two contrary conditions of old age.

Gracián introduces the dual theme of honors and horrors in the first section of Crisi i, when the two pilgrims meet a man who walks toward one direction but has his head turned in the other. He is Janus and, as he says, he represents the two sides of old age. This gentleman takes them to the palace of Vejecia, which has two entrances. One is a "puerta de los horrores," through which Andrenio passes; and the other is a "puerta de los honores," through which Critilo enters. Thus, for the next four pages the reader follows Andrenio to behold the pains suffered by old people; and then he views Critilo, who examines the honors that come to those who live prudently. (pp. 912-14)

Thus the two personages remain throughout Part Three. Andrenio, who has regressed in perception to a state equivalent to that of the vegetative and sensitive souls of Part One, falls into the pit of vice (Crisi ii), joins the hysterical mass of people who flee the truth (Crisi iii), is deluded by deceivers and falsifiers (Crisi iv), becomes lost in "El palacio sin puertas" (Crisi v), takes the extreme path of simplicity (Crisi vi), wants to rest before climbing the mountain to the Palace of Vanity (Crisi vii), and stumbles in the darkness of "La cueva de la nada" (Crisi viii). Critilo, on the other hand, has no problems in coping with any of these impediments, for he has progressed logically from the rational life to a state of Nestorine wisdom.

When the two leave the Cave of Nothingness, they proceed to Rome, where the final four segments take place. These Crisis form a certain unified whole, because they treat the metaphysical problems of Happiness, Time, Death, and Immortality, respectively. Although Andrenio and Critilo still view the world from antithetical perspectives, as when the former sees Death as ugly, sad, poor, and despicable, and the latter as beautiful, happy, rich, and agreeable, neither of the two participates actively in any of the proceedings. They are mere observers to the allegories that explain the Jesuit's philosophy of these four concerns. They both listen attentively when their guide presents the final and most important advice of the work. . . . When they arrive at the Isle of Immortality, they are both admitted because of the meritorious journey that they undertook in life.

Such is the thematic and structural framework of the three Parts of *El Criticón.* Gracián allegorizes in all three sections the general notions that the world is topsy-turvy, that man is the cause for it, that to see society in a proper perspective one must be constantly alert, and that the most efficacious manner to remain aware of dangerous pitfalls is to tread the mean between vice and excessive virtue. He formulates a binary pattern for the first two Parts, and coordinates Andrenio's perceptive ability to the respective moral considerations in each section, for Andrenio lacked control over the appetites in Part One, but was able to proceed through Part Two in a virtuous way because of the expertise he had acquired. The third Part fuses the themes of virtue and vice; Andrenio experiences the horrors of senescence while Critilo reaps the honors that may come to the elderly. This polarity of the characters' situations eliminates the possibility for Andrenio to enhance his perceptive awareness during the last stage of his epic journey. Consequently, Andrenio's perception of reality is strictly determined by the thematic structure that Gracián creates for Part Three, as it was likewise coordinated to the sensitive life of Part One and the rational life of Part Two. Structure, in other words, comes before character, and therefore dictates what kind of character there should be in each Part. The novel, in sum, exhibits a brilliantly organized pattern of events; and it outlines intelligibly the path man should follow and the dangers that will beset him in the hazardous pilgrimage through life. (pp. 914-15)

> *David H. Darst, "Andrenio's Perception of Reality and the Structure of 'El Criticón'," in* Hispania, *Vol. 60, No. 4, December, 1977, pp. 907-15.*

FURTHER READING

Abbott, Don. "La Retórica y el Renacimiento: An Overview of Spanish Theory." In his *Renaissance Eloquence: Studies in the Theory and Practice of Renaissance Rhetoric,* pp. 95-104.

Berkeley and Los Angeles: University of California Press, 1983.

> Discusses Gracián's part in restructuring rhetoric during the late Renaissance, considering especially the impact of the *Agudeza y arte de ingenio.*

Duff, M. E. Grant. "Balthasar Gracian." *The Fortnightly Review* CXXIII (1 March 1877): 328-42.

> Translations of several of the maxims in the *Oráculo manual.*

Grady, Hugh H. "Rhetoric, Wit, and Art in Gracián's *Agudeza.*" *Modern Language Quarterly* 41, No. 1 (March 1980): 21-37.

> Informative study of Gracián's use of conceit, simile, and metaphor in the *Agudeza.*

Hafter, Monroe Z. "Gracián's Reputation in Eighteenth-Century Spain." In *Homenaje a Rodríguez-Moñino: Estudios de Erudición que le Ofrecen sus Amigos o Discípulos Hispanistas Norteamericanos,* Vol. 1, pp. 233-40. Madrid: Editorial Castalia, 1966.

> Discusses Gracián's possible influence upon Spanish authors of the eighteenth century.

Roscoe, Thomas. "Lyric Poetry of Spain at the Close of the Sixteenth and Commencement of the Seventeenth Century." In *Historical View of the Literature of the South of Europe,* Vol. II, edited by J. C. L. Simonde de Sismondi, translated by Thomas Roscoe, pp. 341-67. London: Henry G. Bohn, 1846.

> Concise critique of Gracián's works, describing them as "at times unintelligible" and "tedious."

Sarmiento, E. "Gracián's *Agudeza y Arte de Ingenio.*" *Modern Language Review* XXVII (1932): 280-92, 420-29.

> Insightful, critically recognized analysis of the *Agudeza.*

Trask, Willard R. "Mannerism: Baltasar Gracián." In *European Literature and the Latin Middle Ages,* edited by Ernst Robert Curtius, translated by Willard R. Trask, pp. 293-301. New York: Pantheon Books, 1953.

> Salutes Gracián's *Agudeza y arte de ingenio* as a "summa of agudeza" and "a national achievement."

Samuel Johnson

1709-1784

English essayist, lexicographer, critic, poet, and dramatist.

Perhaps the best known and most often-quoted English writer after Shakespeare, Johnson ranks as the major literary figure of the second half of the eighteenth century. Yet the large and varied canon of his writings has often been overshadowed by his personality. Thus he is remembered as the witty conversationalist who dominated the literary scene of London—the man immortalized by James Boswell in *The Life of Samuel Johnson, LL.D.* (1791). Johnson, known in his day as the Great Cham of Literature, displayed a vigorous reasoning intelligence, a keen understanding of human frailty, and a deep Christian morality. These traits are especially evident in works as diverse as the poem "The Vanity of Human Wishes" and the prose narrative *The History of Rasselas, Prince of Abissinia*, as well as in his *Dictionary of the English Language* and his *Prefaces, Biographical and Critical, to the Works of the English Poets*, a work better known as *The Lives of the Poets*. Wrote nineteenth-century English critic William Hazlitt: "[Johnson] left behind him few wiser or better men." Today he may be considered the quintessential embodiment of English letters.

Born in Lichfield in 1709 to Sarah Ford and Michael Johnson, a bookseller, Johnson suffered from scrofula, which seriously affected his eyesight and disfigured his face. This necessitated a visit to Queen Anne in 1712 to receive the "royal touch," then thought to be a cure for the disease. He was educated at Lichfield Grammar School and later at Pembroke College, Oxford, but a shortage of money forced him to leave the latter institution without a degree in 1729, after a residence of only 13 months. After his father's death in 1731 Johnson lived in Birmingham, where he translated the French version of *A Voyage to Abyssinia*, by Father Jerome Lobo, which he published anonymously in 1735. The same year he married Elizabeth Porter, a widow twenty years his senior— "dear Tetty" he called her. He established a boarding school at Edial, near Lichfield, but admitted failure two years later and closed the school. Then, in company with David Garrick, one of his former pupils, he went to London to make a career as a man of letters; "Tetty" joined him shortly thereafter. Once in London, he performed editorial work for Edward Cave's *Gentleman's Magazine*, to which he submitted essays, poems, reviews, and a series of brief biographies. His most notable contributions appeared between 1740 and 1743 and were entitled "Debates in Magna Lilliputia." These essays eloquently—perhaps too eloquently—recreate parliamentary proceedings. As a result, they were widely accepted as authentic speeches of the great politicians of the day. In 1738 Johnson anonymously published his immediately successful *London: A Poem, In Imitation of the Third Satire of Juvenal*, which contains protests against political corruption, the dangers of the London streets, and the miseries of the unknown and impecunious author. One of Johnson's closest friends

during this period of poverty and hackwork was Richard Savage, a failed writer whom Johnson joined in nocturnal odysseys through Grub Street. His *Account of the Life of Mr. Richard Savage*, published anonymously in 1744, was the first of his prose works to captivate the public. Today, it is admired for its lively depiction of Grub Street life and is considered a milestone in the art of biography. Johnson next turned to Shakespearean work, publishing his *Miscellaneous Observations on the Tragedy of Macbeth* in 1745. *Miscellaneous Observations* also contains a preliminary proposal for a new edition of Shakespeare's plays, but Johnson laid that project aside after it was suggested that he compile a dictionary of the English language. In 1747 he published his *Plan of a Dictionary of the English Language*, dedicating the work to Lord Chesterfield—who, in fact, cared little about the project. In the meantime, Garrick had achieved considerable success as an actor and by 1747 had become manager of Drury Lane Theater. Johnson wrote a prologue for the first performances managed by Garrick. Garrick, in turn, produced Johnson's tragedy *Irene* in 1749, thirteen years after it had been written; it ran for nine days and was never revived again. Subsequently Johnson published his second Juvenalian imitation, "The Vanity of Human Wishes," in which the personal vicissitudes of scholars, philosophers, and legislators from the modern and ancient worlds are used to illustrate the pitfalls of political ambition, the uselessness of military conquest, and the anguish that accompanies literary production.

Beginning in 1750, Johnson published a semiweekly periodical, the *Rambler,* each issue of which comprised a single anonymous essay on contemporary literary and social conditions. Fervently believing that it is the writer's duty to make the world a better place, to "redeem the time," Johnson crafted these essays in various forms: allegories, sketches of archetypal humans, literary criticism, and lay sermons. A few days after the last number of the *Rambler* appeared in 1752, Johnson's "dear Tetty" died. During the next few years he confined his literary efforts to work on the *Dictionary* and irregularly contributed to another weekly periodical, published by John Hawkesworth, *The Adventurer.* In 1755 Johnson and his amanuenses finally finished the 40,000-word *Dictionary* which surpassed earlier dictionaries of its kind, primarily in precision of definition. Johnson's lexicographical work is particularly esteemed for the literary illustrations that distinguish subtle nuances of meaning for particular words. Johnson, however, was acutely conscious of its imperfections: refutable orthography, uncertain etymology, and the fact that, as he said, some words were budding and some were falling away. Nonetheless, the *Dictionary* firmly established Johnson's literary reputation and led to his receiving an honorary M.A. degree from Oxford University. Lord Chesterfield, striving to make amends for his previous lack of regard, hailed Johnson as the supreme dictator of the English language—only to provoke what is perhaps the most famous of Johnson's letters: a scornful rebuke of Chesterfield's self-serving praise and a defense of his own initiative and industry without the assistance of a patron. Soon thereafter, Johnson once again focused his attention on Shakespeare, formally issuing his *Proposals for Printing the Dramatick Works of William Shakespeare* in 1756. Despite the commercial success of the *Dictionary,* which nevertheless failed to relieve his money problems, Johnson continued to write essays, reviews, and political articles for various periodicals. One of his most notable works from this period is his review of Soame Jenyns's *Free Inquiry into the Nature and Origin of Evil,* in which, with supreme irony, Johnson demolished the author's conjecture of a substrata of incorrigibly depraved beings who deceive and torment others for their own pleasure. From 1758 to 1760 Johnson contributed a regular weekly essay to the *Universal Chronicle.* These essays, appearing under the heading "The Idler," exhibit the moralist and social reformist perspectives of the *Rambler* pieces, but also treat the lighter side of the human condition through comical character sketches. In 1759, informing his printer that he had "a thing he was preparing for the press" to defray the expense of his mother's impending funeral, Johnson wrote *The History of Rasselas, Prince of Abissinia* in the evenings of one week. Essentially an essay on "the choice of life," *Rasselas* tells the tale of an innocent young man's quest for the secret of happiness. With his sister and Imlac, a poet-philosopher, Rasselas contemplates fundamental problems of life and art, but the conclusion—"a conclusion, in which nothing is concluded"—resolves little. This work also contains Johnson's celebrated definition of the "business of the poet". According to Imlac, the poet inspects "not the individual, but the species . . . he does not number the streaks of the tulip;" and the poet writes "as

the interpreter of nature, and the legislator of mankind . . . presiding over the thoughts and manners of future generations." Some critics view *Rasselas* as Johnson's spiritual autobiography.

In 1762 George III conferred upon Johnson a pension of £300 a year, thereby relieving him the drudgery of hackwork. The next year his accidental meeting with Boswell in Thomas Davies's bookshop in Covent Garden inaugurated one of the most famous literary companionships in history. Boswell's diary entry recording the event noted that Johnson's "conversation is as great as his writing." In 1764 Johnson gladly concurred with Joshua Reynolds's proposal for the founding of what still ranks as the most famous London dining club of all time. Simply called "The Club," it was later known as The Literary Club. Among the original members, besides Johnson and Reynolds, were Edmund Burke, Topham Beauclerk, Bennet Langton, and Oliver Goldsmith; eventually Boswell, Edward Gibbon, Charles James Fox, and several others were admitted to membership. It was at meetings of the Club that Johnson uttered many of his renowned epigrams and opinions. Indeed, Reynolds once admitted that the Club was formed primarily to give Johnson a forum to express himself verbally and in company. One of the most comforting friendships of Johnson's life began in 1765 when he was introduced to Henry Thrale, owner of a Southwark brewery, and his wife, Hester Lynch Salusbury, a famous hostess and, later, the self-styled "provider and conductress of Dr. Johnson." Treated as one of the family, Johnson spent weeks and months at the Thrales's country house at Streatham as well as at their London house in Southwark. The same year Johnson's *Plays of William Shakespeare* appeared in eight volumes—eleven years after being adumbrated. A lifelong student of Shakespeare, Johnson corrected textual corruptions, elucidated obscurities of language, and examined Shakespeare's textual sources. For his Shakespearean work Johnson received the degree of LL.D. from Trinity College, Dublin, and a similar honor ten years later from Oxford. Although he continued writing prologues and dedications for friends, Johnson no longer devoted his work exclusively to problems of literature and ethics. Instead he expounded his essentially pragmatic political philosophy in a series of pamphlets on the power politics of English and French colonialism, most notably in *The False Alarm, The Patriot,* and *Taxation No Tyranny.* The last-named polemic, perhaps his best known outburst against colonial American claims, was written in reply to the resolutions passed by the American Continental Congress of 1774. Enjoying unprecedented leisure in the mid-1770s, Johnson extensively toured Great Britain and visited the Continent. Having traveled to Scotland and the Hebrides with Boswell in 1773, Johnson published his impressions two years later in *A Journey to the Western Islands of Scotland,* which describes the customs, religion, education, commerce, and agriculture of eighteenth-century Highland society. Johnson also traveled with the Thrales to North Wales in 1774 and to France in 1775.

In 1777 Johnson agreed to write biographical prefaces for an "elegant and accurate" edition of the works of English poets, ranging from the time of John Milton onwards; instead, his prefaces were separately issued as *The Lives of the English Poets.* Completed in 1781, this ten-volume work contains fifty-two essays and a wealth of biographical material. Critics have charged, however, that in some cases the criticism is ill advised, even unfair, particularly in the cases of the Metaphysical poets, Milton's "Lycidas," and Thomas Gray's "Odes." Johnson's criticism in the *Lives* generally reflects such neoclassical tendencies as "good taste," polish, "common sense," and reason. Johnson himself said that he best loved the biographical part of literature—a fact especially apparent in the *Lives*—and claimed that he came nearest to actual enjoyment of writing while composing the *Lives.* However, his personal prejudices about any given poet's life influenced his critical assessment of the poet's works—he made no attempt to separate the poetry from the poet. Between the death of Henry Thrale in 1781 and Hester Thrale's subsequent remarriage in 1784, Johnson slowly realized that the ease and intimacy of the Streatham days were coming to an end. (The widow's remarriage, in particular, deeply distressed him.) In 1783 Johnson had a paralytic stroke that left him seriously debilitated until the spring of the following year. After visiting his native Lichfield for the last time in the summer of 1784, he returned to London in November, and though his physical condition had considerably worsened, his mind remained alert. Johnson died on 13 December 1784 and was buried in Westminster Abbey. Within a year his *Prayers and Meditations* was published. This highly personal volume publicly revealed his oftenrepeated, but seldom-kept, resolutions and private repentance—a testimony to the sincerity of one man's humility and ceaseless heart-searching.

Johnson's reputation as a man of letters rests as much on his life and personality as it does on his writings. This is evidenced by the scope, depth, and sheer bulk of the corpus of Johnsonian criticism, much of which is pure character analysis. Boswell's account of his life, particularly from the time of their meeting onwards, was perhaps most responsible for "Johnsonizing" England, and it fostered an image of Johnson as a gifted and original writer and masterful conversationalist. Nonetheless, Johnson was revered by his contemporaries as a skilled poet, brilliant lexicographer, and sensitive moralist. Critics hailed him as the "new" Alexander Pope upon publication of "The Vanity of Human Wishes," and the *Dictionary,* initially well received, remained a standard until the appearance of the *Oxford English Dictionary* well over a century later. Equally, *Rasselas* supplemented the popular moral themes of Johnson's earlier *Rambler* and "Idler" essays while satisfying eighteenth-century readers' tastes for what Pope termed "impressive truth in fashion drest."

Critics continued to admire most of Johnson's works in the decade following his death, but in time commentators began to fault Johnson for what they considered his highly Latinate, formal, and overly balanced prose style as well as for his wordiness and narrow critical method. Some critics singled out *Lives of the Poets,* chastising Johnson for his harsh appraisal of Milton and his prejudicial assessments of other works and authors, notably Gray and his "Odes." Horace Walpole, presaging this posthumous estimation of Johnson's works, wrote in 1779: "[It] may be usefull to caution young Authors against partiality to his Style & manner, both of which are uncommonly vicious & unworthy of Imitation by any Man who aims at excellence in writing of his own Language." By the early nineteenth century Johnson's folk image—the man of Boswell's *Life*—had come to dominate critical thinking, leav-

ing little room for studies of the works themselves. William Hazlitt evidenced this approach when he wrote in 1818: "His good deeds were as many as his good sayings . . . all these, and innumerable others, endear him to the reader, and must be remembered to his lasting honour." Indeed, this sort of assessment was typical until the last years of the nineteenth century. When critics did focus on Johnson's works, they generally turned to his *Dictionary* and *Lives of the Poets.* Leslie Stephen favorably remarked that the *Dictionary* "was a surprising achievement, and made an epoch in the study of language," while Thomas Babington Macaulay mirrored the views of his contemporaries when he appraised *Lives of the Poets:* "They are the judgments of a mind trammelled by prejudice and deficient in sensibility, but vigorous and acute." Similarly, the *Rambler* essays were dismissed as didactic lay sermons, and other prose works were labeled "unreadable." Thus, by the turn of the century, interest in Johnson's literary works was at a low point, but the man himself continued to loom large in readers' minds.

The bicentenary of Johnson's birth in 1907 sparked a major revaluation of the Johnson canon. Throughout the twentieth century, critical emphasis shifted from the amusing idiosyncrasies and the pointed commentaries of the man to his ethical and moral standards, his appraisals of the human condition, and the compass, strength, and method of his reasoning. Some scholars noted that Johnson's writings on morals closely anticipated the theories, if not the language, of Austrian neurologist Sigmund Freud, while others ranked Johnson just below Pope and John Dryden as masters of heroic-couplet verse. Even *Lives of the Poets,* the most favorably received of Johnson's works, was reconsidered. No longer perceiving Johnson as a strictly neoclassical critic, scholars contended that he employed an empirical approach in his criticism; thus some critics have cited Johnson as the father of New Criticism. Recently, commentators have turned to Johnson's Shakespearean work, countering a common nineteenth-century claim that, in the words of Heinrich Heine, "Garrick got a better hold of Shakespeare's thought than Dr. Johnson." Likewise, Johnson's political tracts, long viewed as abusive expressions of his conservative prejudice against the rights of the people, are seen today as an extension of his lifelong concern with political morality and order.

Today, after a long eclipse, Johnson is once again preeminent in the history of English letters, and mention of his name commands an almost god-like reverence in the English-speaking world. According to Malcolm Muggeridge: "Dr. Johnson will go on being remembered, not so much for his achievements as a writer as for the mysterious quality of greatness that he exudes."

(See also *Dictionary of Literary Biography,* Vols. 39, 95.)

PRINCIPAL WORKS

A Voyage to Abyssinia. By Father Jerome Lobo, A Portuguese Jesuit [translator] (travel essay) 1735
London: A Poem, In Imitation of the Third Satire of Juvenal (poetry) 1738
"Debates in the Senate of Magna Lilliputia" (essays) 1740-43; published in periodical *The Gentleman's*

Magazine; also published as *Debates in Parliament by Samuel Johnson, LL.D.,* 2 vols., 1787

An Account of the Life of Mr. Richard Savage, Son of the Earl Rivers (biography) 1744

Miscellaneous Observations on the Tragedy of Macbeth (criticism) 1745

The Plan of a Dictionary of the English Language; Addressed to the Right Honourable Philip Dormer, Earl of Chesterfield (essay) 1747

"Prologue and Epilogue, spoken at the opening of the Theatre in Drury-lane 1747" (poetry) 1747; published in periodical *The Gentleman's Magazine*

Irene: A Tragedy (drama) 1749

The Vanity of Human Wishes (poetry) 1749

*The Adventurer. 2 vols. [with Richard Bathurst, John Hawkesworth, Joseph Warton, and others] (essays) 1753-54

†*The Rambler.* 2 vols. (essays) 1753

A Dictionary of the English Language: in which The Words are deduced from their Originals, and Illustrated in their Different Significations by Examples from the best Writers. 2 vols. (dictionary) 1755

Proposals for Printing the Dramatick Works of William Shakespeare (essay) 1756

"A Free Inquiry into the Nature and Origin of Evil by Soame Jenyns" (criticism) 1757; published in periodical *The Literary Magazine, or Universal Review*

The Prince of Abissinia. 2 vols. (prose narrative) 1759; also published as *The History of Rasselas, Prince of Abissinia,* 1787

‡*The Idler.* 2 vols. (essays) 1761

The Plays of William Shakespeare, in Eight Volumes, with the Corrections and Illustrations of Various Commentators; To which are added Notes by Sam. Johnson. 8 vols. [editor] (dramas) 1765

The False Alarm (essay) 1770

The Patriot (essay) 1774

A Journey to the Western Islands of Scotland (travel essay) 1775

Taxation no Tyranny; an Answer to the Resolutions and Address of the American Congress (essay) 1775

Prefaces, Biographical and Critical, to the Works of the English Poets. 10 vols. (criticism) 1779-81; also published as *The Lives of the English Poets, and a criticism of their works,* 3 vols., 1781

"On the Death of Dr. Robert Levet" (poetry) 1783; published in periodical *The Gentleman's Magazine*

The Poetical Works of Samuel Johnson, LL.D. (poetry) 1785

Prayers and Meditations, composed by Samuel Johnson, LL.D. (meditations) 1785

The Works of Samuel Johnson, LL.D. 11 vols. (criticism, drama, essays, poetry, prose narrative, and travel essays) 1787

Letters to and from the late Samuel Johnson, LL.D. 2 vols. (letters) 1788

A Sermon, written by the late Samuel Johnson, LL.D. for the Funeral of his Wife (sermon) 1788

The Celebrated Letter from Samuel Johnson, LL.D. to Philip Dormer Stanhope, Earl of Chesterfield; now first published, with notes, by James Boswell, Esq. (letter) 1790

An Account of the Life of Dr. Samuel Johnson, from his birth to his eleventh year, written by himself (autobiography) 1805

A Diary of a Journey into North Wales, in the year 1774; By Samuel Johnson, LL.D. (diary) 1816

The Yale Edition of the Works of Samuel Johnson. 14 vols. (criticism, diaries, drama, essays, letters, meditations, poetry, prose narrative, travel essays, and sermons) 1958-78

*Originally published as individual numbers from 7 November 1752 to 9 March 1754.

†Originally published as individual numbers from 20 March 1750 to 14 March 1752. Johnson did not write Nos. 10, 15, 30, 44, 97, 100, and 107.

‡Originally published in 104 numbers of *The Universal Chronicle, or Weekly Gazette.* Johnson did not write Nos. 9, 15, 33, 42, 54, 67, 76, 79, 82, 93, 96, and 98.

Samuel Johnson   (essay date 1755)

[*In the following excerpt from the preface to his* Dictionary, *Johnson describes his intent and method of compilation, acknowledging merits and shortcomings alike.*]

It is the fate of those who toil at the lower employments of life to be rather driven by the fear of evil than attracted by the prospect of good; to be exposed to censure, without hope of praise; to be disgraced by miscarriage, or punished for neglect, where success would have been without applause, and diligence without reward.

Among these unhappy mortals is the writer of dictionaries; whom mankind have considered, not as the pupil, but the slave of science, the pioneer of literature, doomed only to remove rubbish and clear obstructions from the paths through which Learning and Genius press forward to conquest and glory, without bestowing a smile on the humble drudge that facilitates their progress. Every other author may aspire to praise; the lexicographer can only hope to escape reproach, and even this negative recompense has been yet granted to very few.

I have, notwithstanding this discouragement, attempted a dictionary of the English language, which, while it was employed in the cultivation of every species of literature, has itself been hitherto neglected; suffered to spread, under the direction of chance, into wild exuberance, resigned to the tyranny of time and fashion, and exposed to the corruptions of ignorance, and caprices of innovation.

When I took the first survey of my undertaking, I found our speech copious without order, and energetic without rules: wherever I turned my view, there was perplexity to be disentangled, and confusion to be regulated; choice was to be made out of boundless variety, without any established principle of selection; adulterations were to be detected, without a settled test of purity, and modes of expression to be rejected or received, without the suffrages of any writers of classical reputation or acknowledged authority.

Having therefore no assistance but from general grammar, I applied myself to the perusal of our writers; and noting whatever might be of use to ascertain or illustrate any word or phrase, accumulated in time the materials of a dictionary, which, by degrees, I reduced to method, establishing to myself, in the progress of the work, such rules as experience and analogy suggested to me; experience, which practice and observation were continually increasing; and analogy, which, though in some words obscure, was evident in others.

In adjusting the ORTHOGRAPHY, which has been to this time unsettled and fortuitous, I found it necessary to distinguish those irregularities that are inherent in our tongue, and perhaps coeval with it, from others which the ignorance or negligence of later writers has produced. Every language has its anomalies, which, though inconvenient, and in themselves once unnecessary, must be tolerated among the imperfections of human things, and which require only to be registered, that they may not be increased, and ascertained, that they may not be confounded: but every language has likewise its improprieties and absurdities, which it is the duty of the lexicographer to correct or proscribe. (pp. 307-08)

In settling the orthography, I have not wholly neglected the pronunciation, which I have directed by printing an accent upon the acute or elevated syllable. It will sometimes be found that the accent is placed by the author quoted on a different syllable from that marked in the alphabetical series; it is then to be understood that custom has varied, or that the author has, in my opinion, pronounced wrong. Short directions are sometimes given where the sound of letters is irregular; and if they are sometimes omitted, defect in such minute observations will be more easily excused than superfluity.

In the investigation both of the orthography and signification of words, their ETYMOLOGY was necessarily to be considered, and they were therefore to be divided into primitives and derivatives. A primitive word is that which can be traced no further to any English root; thus *circumspect, circumvent, circumstance, delude, concave,* and *complicate,* though compounds in the Latin, are to us primitives. Derivatives are all those that can be referred to any word in English of greater simplicity.

The derivatives I have referred to their primitives, with an accuracy sometimes needless; for who does not see that *remoteness* comes from *remote, lovely* from *love, concavity* from *concave,* and *demonstrative* from *demonstrate?* But this grammatical exuberance the scheme of my work did not allow me to repress. It is of great importance, in examining the general fabric of a language, to trace one word from another by noting the usual modes of derivation and inflection; and uniformity must be preserved in systematical works, though sometimes at the expense of particular propriety.

Among other derivatives, I have been careful to insert and elucidate the anomalous plurals of nouns and preterites of verbs, which in the Teutonic dialects are very frequent, and, though familiar to those who have always used them, interrupt and embarrass the learners of our language.

The two languages from which our primitives have been derived are the Roman and Teutonic: under the Roman I comprehend the French and provincial tongues; and under the Teutonic range the Saxon, German, and all their kindred dialects. Most of our polysyllables are Roman, and our words of one syllable are very often Teutonic. (pp. 310-11)

The words which are represented as thus related by descent or cognation do not always agree in sense; for it is incident to words, as to their authors, to degenerate from their ancestors, and to change their manners when they change their country. It is sufficient, in etymological inquiries, if the senses of kindred words be found such as may easily pass into each other, or such as may both be referred to one general idea.

The etymology, so far as it is yet known, was easily found in the volumes where it is particularly and professedly delivered; and, by proper attention to the rules of derivation, the orthography was soon adjusted. But to COLLECT the WORDS of our language was a task of greater difficulty: the deficiency of dictionaries was immediately apparent; and when they were exhausted, what was yet wanting must be sought by fortuitous and unguided excursions into books, and gleaned as industry should find, or chance should offer it, in the boundless chaos of a living speech. My search, however, has been either skilful or lucky; for I have much augmented the vocabulary. (p. 312)

The words, thus selected and disposed, are grammatically considered; they are referred to the different parts of speech; traced, when they are irregularly inflected, through their various terminations; and illustrated by observations, not indeed of great or striking importance, separately considered, but necessary to the elucidation of our language, and hitherto neglected or forgotten by English grammarians.

That part of my work on which I expect malignity most frequently to fasten is the EXPLANATION, in which I cannot hope to satisfy those who are perhaps not inclined to be pleased, since I have not always been able to satisfy myself. To interpret a language by itself is very difficult; many words cannot be explained by synonyms because the idea signified by them has not more than one appellation; nor by paraphrase, because simple ideas cannot be described. When the nature of things is unknown, or the notion unsettled and indefinite, and various in various minds, the words by which such notions are conveyed, or such things denoted, will be ambiguous and perplexed. And such is the fate of hapless lexicography that not only darkness, but light, impedes and distresses it; things may be not only too little, but too much known, to be happily illustrated. To explain requires the use of terms less abstruse than that which is to be explained, and such terms cannot always be found; for as nothing can be proved but by supposing something intuitively known, and evident without proof, so nothing can be defined but by the use of words too plain to admit a definition. (p. 315)

The solution of all difficulties, and the supply of all defects, must be sought in the examples subjoined to the various senses of each word, and ranged according to the time of their authors.

When first I collected these authorities, I was desirous that every quotation should be useful to some other end than the illustration of a word; I therefore extracted from philosophers principles of science; from historians remarkable facts; from chemists complete processes; from divines striking exhortations; and from poets beautiful descriptions. Such is design, while it is yet at a distance from execution. When the time called upon me to range this accumulation of elegance and wisdom into an alphabetical series, I soon discovered that the bulk of my volumes would fright away the student, and was forced to depart from my scheme of including all that was pleasing or useful in English literature, and reduce my transcripts very often to clusters of words in which scarcely any meaning is retained: thus to the weariness of copying, I was condemned to add the vexation of expunging. Some passages I have yet spared which may relieve the labour of verbal searches, and intersperse with verdure and flowers the dusty deserts of barren philology.

The examples, thus mutilated, are no longer to be considered as conveying the sentiments or doctrine of their authors; the word for the sake of which they are inserted, with all its appendant clauses, has been carefully preserved; but it may sometimes happen, by hasty detruncation, that the general tendency of the sentence may be changed: the divine may desert his tenets, or the philosopher his system.

Some of the examples have been taken from writers who were never mentioned as masters of elegance, or models of style; but words must be sought where they are used; and in what pages eminent for purity can terms of manufacture or agriculture be found? Many quotations serve no other purpose than that of proving the bare existence of words, and are therefore selected with less scrupulousness than those which are to teach their structures and relations.

My purpose was to admit no testimony of living authors, that I might not be misled by partiality, and that none of my contemporaries might have reason to complain; nor have I departed from this resolution but when some performance of uncommon excellence excited my veneration, when my memory supplied me from late books with an example that was wanting, or when my heart, in the tenderness of friendship, solicited admission for a favourite name.

So far have I been from any care to grace my pages with modern decorations that I have studiously endeavoured to collect examples and authorities from the writers before the Restoration, whose works I regard as *the wells of English undefiled,* as the pure sources of genuine diction. Our language, for almost a century, has, by the concurrence of many causes, been gradually departing from its original Teutonic character, and deviating towards a Gallic structure and phraseology, from which it ought to be our endeavour to recall it, by making our ancient volumes the ground-work of style, admitting among the additions of later times only such as may supply real deficiencies, such as are readily adopted by the genius of our tongue, and incorporate easily with our native idioms.

But as every language has a time of rudeness antecedent to perfection, as well as of false refinement and declension, I have been cautious lest my zeal for antiquity might drive me into times too remote, and crowd my book with words now no longer understood. I have fixed Sidney's work for the boundary beyond which I make few excursions. From the authors which rose in the time of Elizabeth, a speech might be formed adequate to all the purposes of use and elegance. If the language of theology were extracted from Hooker and the translation of the Bible; the terms of natural knowledge from Bacon; the phrases of policy, war, and navigation from Raleigh; the dialect of poetry and fiction

from Spenser and Sidney; and the diction of common life from Shakespeare, few ideas would be lost to mankind for want of English words in which they might be expressed.

It is not sufficient that a word is found, unless it be so combined as that its meaning is apparently determined by the tract and tenor of the sentence; such passages I have therefore chosen, and when it happened that any author gave a definition of a term, or such an explanation as is equivalent to a definition, I have placed his authority as a supplement to my own, without regard to the chronological order that is otherwise observed. (pp. 318-20)

Thus have I laboured, by settling the orthography, displaying the analogy, regulating the structures, and ascertaining the signification of English words, to perform all the parts of a faithful lexicographer: but I have not always executed my own scheme, or satisfied my own expectations. The work, whatever proofs of diligence and attention it may exhibit, is yet capable of many improvements: the orthography which I recommend is still controvertible, the etymology which I adopt is uncertain, and, perhaps, frequently erroneous; the explanations are sometimes too much contracted, and sometimes too much diffused, the significations are distinguished rather with subtlety than skill, and the attention is harrassed with unnecessary minuteness.

The examples are too often injudiciously truncated, and perhaps sometimes, I hope very rarely, alleged in a mistaken sense; for in making this collection I trusted more to memory than, in a state of disquiet and embarrassment, memory can contain, and purposed to supply at the review what was left incomplete in the first transcription.

Many terms appropriated to particular occupations, though necessary and significant, are undoubtedly omitted; and of the words most studiously considered and exemplified, many senses have escaped observation.

Yet these failures, however frequent, may admit extenuation and apology. To have attempted much is always laudable, even when the enterprise is above the strength that undertakes it. To rest below his own aim is incident to every one whose fancy is active, and whose views are comprehensive; nor is any man satisfied with himself because he has done much, but because he can conceive little. When first I engaged in this work, I resolved to leave neither words nor things unexamined, and pleased myself with a prospect of the hours which I should revel away in feasts of literature, the obscure recesses of northern learning which I should enter and ransack, the treasures with which I expected every search into those neglected mines to reward my labour, and the triumph with which I should display my acquisitions to mankind. When I had thus inquired into the original of words, I resolved to show likewise my attention to things; to pierce deep into every science, to inquire the nature of every substance of which I inserted the name, to limit every idea by a definition strictly logical, and exhibit every production of art or nature in an accurate description, that my book might be in place of all other dictionaries whether appellative or technical. But these were the dreams of a poet doomed at last to wake a lexicographer. (pp. 321-22)

Of the event of this work, for which, having laboured it with so much application, I cannot but have some degree of parental fondness, it is natural to form conjectures.

Those who have been persuaded to think well of my design will require that it should fix our language, and put a stop to those alterations which time and chance have hitherto been suffered to make in it without opposition. With this consequence I will confess that I flattered myself for a while; but now begin to fear that I have indulged expectation which neither reason nor experience can justify. When we see men grow old and die at a certain time one after another, from century to century, we laugh at the elixir that promises to prolong life to a thousand years; and with equal justice may the lexicographer be derided who being able to produce no example of a nation that has preserved their words and phrases from mutability shall imagine that his dictionary can embalm his language, and secure it from corruption and decay, that it is in his power to change sublunary nature, or clear the world at once from folly, vanity, and affectation. (p. 324)

If the changes we fear be thus irresistible, what remains but to acquiesce with silence, as in the other insurmountable distresses of humanity? It remains that we retard what we cannot repel, that we palliate what we cannot cure. Life may be lengthened by care, though death cannot be ultimately defeated: tongues, like governments, have a natural tendency to degeneration; we have long preserved our constitution, let us make some struggles for our language.

In hope of giving longevity to that which its own nature forbids to be immortal, I have devoted this book, the labour of years, to the honour of my country, that we may no longer yield the palm of philology without a contest to the nations of the continent. The chief glory of every people arises from its authors: whether I shall add any thing by my own writings to the reputation of English literature must be left to time: much of my life has been lost under the pressure of disease; much has been trifled away; and much has always been spent in provision for the day that was passing over me; but I shall not think my employment useless or ignoble, if by my assistance foreign nations, and distant ages, gain access to the propagators of knowledge, and understand the teachers of truth; if my labours afford light to the repositories of science, and add celebrity to Bacon, to Hooker, to Milton, and to Boyle.

When I am animated by this wish, I look with pleasure on my book, however defective, and deliver it to the world with the spirit of a man that has endeavoured well. That it will immediately become popular I have not promised to myself: a few wild blunders, and risible absurdities, from which no work of such multiplicity was ever free, may for a time furnish folly with laughter, and harden ignorance in contempt; but useful diligence will at last prevail, and there never can be wanting some who distinguish desert; who will consider that no dictionary of a living tongue ever can be perfect, since while it is hastening to publication, some words are budding, and some falling away; that a whole life cannot be spent upon syntax and etymology, and that even a whole life would not be sufficient; that he whose design includes whatever language can express must often speak of what he does not understand; that a writer will sometimes be hurried by eagerness to the end, and sometimes faint with weariness under a task which Scaliger compares to the labours of the anvil and the mine; that what is obvious is not always known, and what is known is not always present; that sudden fits

of inadvertency will surprise vigilance, slight avocations will seduce attention, and casual eclipses of the mind will darken learning; and that the writer shall often in vain trace his memory at the moment of need for that which yesterday he knew with intuitive readiness, and which will come uncalled into his thoughts tomorrow.

In this work, when it shall be found that much is omitted, let it not be forgotten that much likewise is performed; and though no book was ever spared out of tenderness to the author, and the world is little solicitous to know whence proceeded the faults of that which it condemns; yet it may gratify curiosity to inform it that the *English Dictionary* was written with little assistance of the learned, and without any patronage of the great; not in the soft obscurities of retirement, or under the shelter of academic bowers, but amidst inconvenience and distraction, in sickness and in sorrow: and it may repress the triumph of malignant criticism to observe that if our language is not here fully displayed, I have only failed in an attempt which no human powers have hitherto completed. If the lexicons of ancient tongues, now immutably fixed, and comprised in a few volumes, be yet, after the toil of successive ages, inadequate and delusive; if the aggregated knowledge and cooperating diligence of the Italian academicians did not secure them from the censure of Beni; if the embodied critics of France, when fifty years had been spent upon their work, were obliged to change its economy, and give their second edition another form, I may surely be contented without the praise of perfection, which, if I could obtain, in this gloom of solitude, what would it avail me? I have protracted my work till most of those whom I wished to please have sunk into the grave, and success and miscarriage are empty sounds: I therefore dismiss it with frigid tranquillity, having little to fear or hope from censure or from praise. (pp. 326-28)

> *Samuel Johnson, "A Dictionary of the English Language: Preface," in* Samuel Johnson, *edited by Donald Greene, Oxford University Press, 1984, pp. 307-28.*

William Kenrick   (essay date 1765)

[*Kenrick was an English journalist, dramatist, and critic who was noted for the savagery of his attacks upon Johnson and his circle. Having succeeded Oliver Goldsmith as a reviewer for the* Monthly Review *in 1759, he was dismissed from that position in 1765 after publishing the review excerpted below as well as his* Review of Doctor Johnson's New Edition of Shakespeare: in which the Ignorance, or Inattention, of that Editor is exposed, and the Poet defended from the Persecution of his Commentators *(1765). In the following excerpt from an originally unsigned review of* The Plays of William Shakespeare, *Kenrick expresses "apprehension" toward Johnson's treatment of Shakespeare in his preface and supporting commentary, maintaining that "there are many evident marks of the want of ingenuity or industry in the Commentator."*]

It is a circumstance very injurious to the productions even of the best writers, that the public prepossession is up in their favour before they make their appearance; especially if such prepossession hath been kept any considerable time in a state of expectation and suspense: delay being in itself a kind of disappointment, which prepares the mind for a still greater mortification, and even disposes us to conceive ourselves disappointed if we are not gratified with something superior to what we had at first a right to expect. A number of apologies are ready, and various are the pleas admitted, in justification of a precipitated performance. Errour and inadvertence are imputed, as natural effects, to haste; and even ignorance itself finds a convenient shelter under the pretence of rapidity of composition. A very different fate attends on those works, whose publication, having been long promised and frequently deferred, is supposed to be delayed only to render them by so much the more valuable when they appear, as their appearance may have been procrastinated.

Under this disadvantage lies the present edition of Shakespeare; a poet, who least requires, and most deserves, a comment, of all the writers his age produced. We cannot help thinking it, therefore, a misfortune almost as singular as his merit, that, among so many ingenious scholiasts that have employed themselves in elucidating his writings, hardly one of them hath been found in any degree worthy of him. They all seem to have mistaken the route, in which only they could do honour to themselves, or be useful to the reader. Engaged in the piddling task of adjusting quibbles, and restoring conundrums, they have neglected the illustration of characters, sentiments and situations. Instead of aspiring to trim the ruffled bays that have a little obscured his brow, they have been laboriously and servilely employed in brushing the dirt from his shoes. Instead of strewing flowers, and planting fresh laurels, on his tomb, they have been irreverently trampling down the turf, that had otherwise covered his dust with perpetual verdure. From the present Editor, it is true, we hoped better things. But what shall we say? when he himself confesses, that, as to 'the poetical beauties or defects of his author, he hath not been very diligent to observe them: having given up this part of his design to chance and caprice.' This is surely a strange concession to be made by the author of the proposals for printing this work by subscription! We were by them given to understand, that the Editor would proceed in a manner very different from his predecessors; and were encouraged to hope that Shakespeare would no longer be commented on, like a barren or obsolete writer; whose works were of no other use than to employ the sagacity of antiquarians and philologers. But perhaps our Editor found the task, of commenting on Shakespeare as a *poet,* much more difficult than he had conceived it to be. It might sound as harsh in the ear of the public, to tax a writer whom it hath so much honoured by its approbation, with want of capacity for writing such a commentary, as it doubtless would, in the ears of Dr. Johnson, to hear himself charged with want of application to it, when he acknowledges the great encouragement he has had the honour of receiving for that purpose. We should be very tender, be the occasion what it would, of laying any writer of acknowledged merit under the necessity of pleading guilty either to the charge of ignorance or indolence. But we cannot help subscribing to the opinion of a very ingenious critic, when he affirms, that 'every writer is justly chargeable with want of knowledge when he betrays it on the subject he is treating of, let him be ever so capable of treating other subjects, or however justly founded may be his reputation for learning in general.' It hath been observed, in some remarks already published on this occasion, that our Editor's notes, few and exception-

able as they are, lay claim to our admiration, if we reflect on the extreme indolence of the Writer; who is naturally an *idler.* How far such a plea may be satisfactory to the purchasers of this edition, we know not; but we have too high an opinion of the Editor's character, to think he will more readily acquiesce under the imputation of ingratitude than under that of incapacity. At the same time, however, we cannot but express our apprehensions, that every judicious reader, who may accompany us through a fair and impartial review of his preface and commentary, will think, with us, that there are many evident marks of the want of ingenuity or industry in the Commentator.

We find little in the first five pages of our Editor's preface, but trite and common-place reflections, on our veneration for antiquity, and on the general talents of Shakespeare; delivered in that pompous style which is so peculiar to himself, and is so much admired by some kind of readers. In some places, however, he is less verbose; and then he is generally sensible, instructive and entertaining. (pp. 285-87)

Dr. Johnson prefers Shakespeare's comic scenes to his tragic: in the latter, he says, 'there is always something wanting, while the former often surpasses expectation or desire. His tragedy seems to be skill, and his comedy instinct.' As this is a general assertion, unsupported by any particular examples, we cannot very easily controvert it; but we are apt to suspect it is founded in a great degree on the preference which the Editor himself may possibly be disposed to give to comedy in general. Different auditors, as he observes, have different habitudes; so that, were we to put this assertion to the proof by particular applications, we should possibly find *quot homines tot sententiœ.*

After having enumerated the various excellencies of this great poet, our Editor proceeds to mention his faults; faults, says he, *'sufficient to obscure and overwhelm any other merit.'* The first defect he charges him with, is, indeed, a very capital one; from which we should be glad, and shall endeavour, to exculpate him. (pp. 290-91)

Shakespeare is here charged with 'sacrificing virtue to convenience,' for no other reason than that he seemed more careful to please than instruct, and to write without any moral purpose. But if it be admitted, as our Editor actually admits, that a system of social duty may be selected from his writings, and that his precepts and axioms were virtuous; we may justly ask, whether they are less so for dropping casually from him? Must a writer be charged with making a sacrifice of virtue, because he does not professedly inculcate it? Is every writer *ex professo* a parson or a moral philosopher? It is doubtless always the *moralist*'s duty, to strive at least, to make the world better; but we should think it no inconsiderable merit in a *comic-poet,* to be able to divert and amuse the world without making it worse; especially if he should occasionally drop such virtuous precepts and axioms, as would serve to form a system of social duty. We are, for these reasons, so far from thinking that the barbarity of his age cannot extenuate the fault here censured, that we think he stands in need of no other excuse than our Editor hath on another occasion made for him, viz. his ignorance of poetical composition. He did not know that the rules of criticism required the drama to have a particular moral; nor did he conceive himself bound, as a *poet,* to write like a *philosopher.* He carries his persons, therefore, indifferently through right and wrong, for the same reason as he makes them laugh and cry in the same piece; and is justifiable on the same principles; it is a strict imitation of nature; and Shakespeare is the Poet of Nature. Were our Poet now living, and possessed of Dr. Johnson's critical knowledge, we presume he would make no more nor greater sacrifices of *virtue* to *convenience* than his Editors may have done. (pp. 291-92)

The next fault our immortal Poet is charged with, is the want of connection and consistence in his plots; from which charge, with all the aggravating circumstances enumerated by the learned Editor, we shall not undertake to defend him, any more than from the charge, of paying no regard to distinction of time or place. It is certain he makes no scruple of giving, to one age or nation, the customs, institutions, and opinions of another, not only at the expense of likelihood, but even of possibility. But surely our Editor will admit that the barbarity of his age may extenuate this fault; since, by his own confession, Shakespeare was not the only violater of chronology in his time: Sidney, his contemporary, who wanted not the advantages of learning, having, in his *Arcadia,* confounded the pastoral with the feudal times, the days of innocence, quiet and security, with those of turbulence, violence, and adventure.

Shakespeare is said to be seldom very successful in his comic scenes, when he engages his characters in raillery or repartee, or as Dr. Johnson more quaintly expresses it, 'reciprocations of smartness and contests of sarcasm.' Their jests, we are told, are commonly gross and their pleasantry licentious: nor will, it seems, the barbarity of his age excuse our Poet with regard to this defect, any more than the former. (p. 292)

As to the quirks and quibbles of Shakespeare's clowns, which sometimes infect the graver parts of his writings, we cannot be of Dr. Johnson's opinion. He affirms that 'A quibble is to Shakespeare, what luminous vapours are to the traveller; he follows it at all adventures, it is sure to lead him out of his way, and sure to engulf him in the mire. It has some malignant power over his mind, and its fascinations are irresistible. Whatever be the dignity or profundity of his disquisition, whether he be enlarging knowledge or exalting affection, whether he be amusing attention with incidents, or enchaining it in suspence, let but a quibble spring up before him, and he leaves his work unfinished. A quibble is the golden apple for which he will always turn aside from his career, or stoop from his elevation. A quibble, poor and barren as it is, gave him such delight, that he was content to purchase it, by the sacrifice of reason, propriety and truth. A quibble was to him the fatal *Cleopatra* for which he lost the world, and was content to lose it.'

Quaintly as all this is expressed, and boldly as it is asserted, we cannot be persuaded that Shakespeare's native genius was not too sublime to be so much captivated with the charms of so contemptible an object. How poorly soever it might descend to trifle with an *ignis fatuus* by owl-light, we cannot think an eagle, soaring in the direct beams of the meridian sun, could be allured, to look down with pleasure on the feeble glimmerings of a rush-light. It is not impossible, indeed, that the necessity of accommodating himself in this particular so frequently to the humour and taste of the times, had rendered a practice habitual to him,

which his own better taste and judgment could not fail to condemn. (pp. 292-93)

We shall leave our Readers to determine, whether what the present Editor hath above advanced, is sufficient to invalidate this plea; or whether they will take the Editor's word for Shakespeare, rather than Shakespeare's word for himself.

In speaking of our poet's faults in tragedy, the Editor says, 'his performance seems constantly to be worse as his labour is more. The effusions of passion which exigence forces out, are for the most part striking and energetic; but whenever he solicits his invention, or strains his faculties, the offspring of his throes is *tumour, meanness, tediousness, and obscurity.*' And again—'His declamations or set-speeches are commonly cold and weak, for his power was the power of nature; when he endeavoured, like other tragic writers, to catch opportunities of amplification, and instead of inquiring what the occasion demanded, to show how much his stores of knowledge could supply, he seldom escapes without the *pity* or *resentment* of his reader.' It is a pity our Editor does not refer us to the particular passages, that justify these general assertions. For, admitting the truth of them, yet if it be very seldom, as we will venture to say it is, that Shakespeare appears reduced to the necessity of straining his faculties; if he be hardly ever endeavouring, like other tragic poets, at amplification, or to make an impertinent display of his knowledge, what shall we say to the candour of that commentator, who lays hold of a few defects, *ubi plura nitent,* on which to found a general charge against his author? Were we disposed to be as harsh and severe on the learned Annotator, as the Annotator himself hath been on his GREAT, INIMITABLE Author, we might here appeal to the public, to decide which of them most demands our *pity* or merits our *resentment.*

He goes on.—'It is incident to Shakespeare to be now and then entangled with an unwieldy sentiment, which he cannot well express, and will not reject; he struggles with it a while, and if it continues stubborn, comprises it in such words as occur, and leaves it to be disintangled and evolved by those who have more leisure to bestow upon it.'

We know not whether this *incident* might not be called with more propriety a misfortune rather than a fault, and be imputed with greater justice to the then imperfect state of our language than to Shakespeare. But be this as it may; certain it is, that if our poet be sometimes entangled with his sentiments for want of words, our Editor is not seldom entangled with his, through a multiplicity of them; or, if he may understand his own meaning, it is not always the case with his reader, who, as he says of the poet, struggles with it for a while, and if it continues stubborn, leaves it comprised in the words that invelop it, to be disintangled and evolved by those who have more leisure to bestow upon it. It is possible that, in this, he may betray the want of patience, though we cannot admit that he betrays a want of judgment; being fully of opinion with our Editor, that where the language is intricate the thought is not always subtle, nor the image always great where the line is bulky. 'The equality of words to things,' as he justly observes, 'is very often neglected, and trivial sentiments and vulgar ideas disappoint the attention, to which they are recommended by sonorous epithets and swelling figures.'

Having thus endeavoured to prove the faults of Shakespeare 'sufficient to obscure and *overwhelm any other merit,*' our Editor attempts dexterously to change sides, and to stand up in his defence, against those who have accused him, of violating those laws, which have been instituted and established by the joint authority of poets and of critics; we mean, the unities of action, place and time.

'From the censure, which this irregularity may bring upon him,' says Dr. Johnson, 'I shall with due reverence to that learning which I must oppose, adventure to try how I can defend him.'

It happens, however, very unluckily for our Editor, that, in spite of that respect which he is so notoriously ready to pay to his opponents, he shews himself to be as indifferent a pleader *for* Shakespeare as he hath proved *against* him. Nay, we entertain some suspicion that the critical Reader will, on a due consideration of what is hereafter advanced, be apt to think Dr. Johnson too little acquainted with the nature and use of the drama, to engage successfully in a dispute of so much difficulty as that which relates to the breach or observation of the dramatic unities. (pp. 294-95)

It appears, on the whole, that the unities are essential to the drama, though not in that degree as hath been asserted by the critics; so that the result of Dr. Johnson's enquiries concerning them, is as erroneous as his supposition of the necessity on which they were founded. (p. 381)

Our Editor proceeds next to give an account of what he hath done, or attempted to do himself, and to apologize for what he hath not done, or confessedly found himself unable to do. We cannot help being somewhat apprehensive, however, that the readers of this part of Dr. Johnson's preface, will be apt to think he hath, in more places than one, betrayed a consciousness of the want of application in his pretended endeavours, as well as of the ill success attending them. There runs, indeed, through the whole of this preface, such a mixed and inconsistent vein of praise and censure respecting others; and of boasting and excuse regarding himself, that we think we discover it to be the production of a wavering pen, directed by a hand equally wearied and disgusted with a task, injudiciously undertaken, and as indolently pursued. (p. 387)

As to the work itself; the present Editor hath prefixed the several prefaces of Pope, Theobald, Hanmer and Warburton, as also the dedication and preface of Heminge and Condell, and Shakespeare's life by Mr. Rowe. Of Mr. Pope's notes the Editor hath retained the whole; in order, as he says, that no fragment of so great a writer may be lost. With Dr. Johnson's leave, however, as Mr. Pope's attempts on Shakespeare do so little honour to his memory, a future editor who affected to revere that memory ought to have suppressed them; at least those of them which were the most exceptional.—Of Theobald's notes, the *weak, ignorant, mean, faithless, petulant, ostentatious* Theobald, the present Editor hath generally retained those which he retained *himself* in his second edition; and these, we must acquaint our Readers, are not a few nor unimportant.—Of Sir Thomas Hanmer's notes, Dr. Johnson professes, and we find no reason to disbelieve him, that he hath inserted them all.—To Dr. Warburton he is still more obliged than to any of the preceeding commentators, at least in point of quantity.—To the author of the *Canons of Criticism* he is also equally obliged in point of quality;

but we know not to what cause we must impute it, that the Editor is so extremely sparing of confessing his obligations, from this quarter.

As to the Editor's own notes, it possibly will not be expected they should be so numerous, or so important, as those he had an opportunity of borrowing from his predecessors: the Reader will meet with some of them, however, here and there interspersed among the rest, and like the rest, *bona quædam, mala, mediocra.* If the Reader should complain that these are too few and insignificant, we can only impute their paucity and want of importance to a notion entertained by the Editor (the most unfortunate sure that ever entered into the head of a commentator!) that the Reader is more, and better pleased with what he finds out himself, than with what the most sagacious scholiast can point out to him. But this plea, if admitted, would of course be urged too far, and even supersede the task of any commentator at all. Indeed Dr. Johnson seems full as little solicitous about the success of his annotations, as he could possibly be about the composing them; it is to be wished, however, for the sake of his own reputation, that he had always treated the poet with the same candour as he *professes* to have observed toward his brother commentators. (pp. 388-89)

> *William Kenrick, in a review of "Johnson's 'Edition of Shakespeare's Plays'," in* The Monthly Review, *London, Vol. XXXIII, October-November, 1765, pp. 285-301, 374-89.*

Horace Walpole   (essay date 1779?)

[*An English author, politician, and publisher, Walpole is best known for his memoirs and voluminous correspondence, which provide revealing glimpses of life in England during the last half of the eighteenth century. In the following excerpt from a short study possibly written in 1779, he comments on Johnson's style and manner of writing, noting that both "are uncommonly vicious and unworthy of imitation."*]

Dr. Johnson's works have obtained so much reputation, and the execution of them, from partiality to his abilities, has been rated so far above their merit, that, without detracting from his capacity or his learning, it may be useful to caution young authors against admiration of his *style* and *manner;* both of which are uncommonly vicious, and unworthy of imitation by any man who aims at excellence in writing his own language.

A marked *manner,* when it runs through all the compositions of any master, is a defect in itself, and indicates a deviation from nature. The writer betrays his having been struck by some particular tint, and his having overlooked nature's variety. It is true that the greatest masters of composition are so far imperfect, as that they always leave some marks by which we may discover their *hand.* He approaches the nearest to universality, whose works make it difficult for our quickness or sagacity to observe certain characteristic touches which ascertain the specific author.

Dr. Johnson's works are as easily distinguished as those of the most affected writer; for exuberance is a fault as much as quaintness. There is meaning in almost every thing Johnson says; he is often profound, and a just reasoner—I mean, when prejudice, bigotry, and arrogance do not cloud or debase his logic. He is benevolent in the application of his morality; dogmatically uncharitable in the dispensation of his censures; and equally so, when he differs with his antagonist on general truths or partial doctrines.

The first criterion that stamps Johnson's works for his, is the loaded style. I will not call it verbose, because verbosity generally implies unmeaning verbiage; a censure he does not deserve. I have allowed and do allow, that most of his words have an adequate, and frequently an illustrating purport, the true use of epithets; but then his words are indiscriminately select, and too forceful for ordinary occasions. They form a hardness of diction and a muscular toughness that resist all ease and graceful movement. Every sentence is as high-coloured as any: no paragraph improves; the position is as robust as the demonstration; and the weakest part of the sentence (I mean, in the effect, not in the solution) is generally the conclusion: he illustrates till he fatigues, and continues to prove, after he has convinced. This fault is so usual with him, he is so apt to charge with three different set of phrases of the same calibre, that, if I did not condemn his laboured coinage of new words, I would call his threefold inundation of synonymous expressions, *triptology.*

He prefers learned words to the simple and common. He is never simple, elegant or light. He destroys more enemies with the weight of his shield than with the point of his spear, and had rather make three mortal wounds in the same part than one. This monotony, the grievous effect of pedantry and self-conceit, prevents him from being eloquent. He excites no passions but indignation: his writings send the reader away more satiated than pleased. If he attempts humour, he makes your reason smile, without making you gay; because the study that his learned mirth requires, destroys cheerfulness. It is the clumsy gambol of a lettered elephant. We wonder that so grave an animal should have strayed into the province of the ape; yet admire that practice should have given the bulky quadruped so much agility.

Upon the whole, Johnson's style appears to me so encumbered, so void of ear and harmony, that I know no modern writer whose works can be redde aloud with so little satisfaction. I question whether one should not read a page of equal length in any modern author, in a minute's time less than one of Johnson's, all proper pauses and accents being duly attended to in both.

His works are the antipodes of taste, and he a schoolmaster of truth, but never its parent; for his doctrines have no novelty, and are never inculcated with indulgence either to the froward child or to the dull one. He has set nothing in a new light, yet is as diffuse as if we had everything to learn. Modern writers have improved on the ancients only by conciseness. Dr. Johnson, like the chymists of Laputa, endeavours to carry back what has been digested, to its pristine and crude principles. He is a standing proof that the Muses leave works unfinished, if they are not embellished by the Graces. (pp. 361-62)

> *Horace Walpole, "General Criticism on Dr. Johnson's Writings," in his* The Works of Horatio Walpole, Earl of Orford, *Vol. IV, G. G. and J. Robinson, 1798, pp. 361-62.*

William Blake   (essay date 1784-85)

[*An English poet and artist, Blake is viewed as one of the most important literary figures of the nineteenth century. His works are esteemed for their dense thematic texture, their compressed and allusive style, and the impassioned, prophetic tone which characterizes many of them. Despite being virtually unknown and often dismissed as a lunatic in his own time, Blake is considered the most extreme of the English Romantic writers and ranks today as one of the greatest poets of his age. In the following excerpt from his* An Island in the Moon—*a work most likely written in 1784 or 1785—Blake reflects a prevalent critical estimation of Johnson's immediate posthumous reputation, associating Johnson with bawdy humor and rejecting any presumed preeminence of his philosophical importance.*]

> "I say, this evening we'll all get drunk—I say—dash! an Anthem,
> "an Anthem!" said Suction.
> > "Lo the Bat with Leathern wing,
> > Winking & blinking,
> > Winking & blinking,
> > Winking & blinking,
> > Like Doctor Johnson."
>
> *Quid.* " 'Oho', said Dr. Johnson
> To Scipio Africanus,
> 'If you don't own me a Philosopher,
> I'll kick your Roman Anus'."
>
> *Suction.* " 'Aha', To Dr. Johnson
> Said Scipio Africanus,
> 'Lift up my Roman Petticoat
> And kiss my Roman Anus'."

(p. 54)

> *William Blake, "An Island in the Moon," in his* The Complete Writings of William Blake, *edited by Geoffrey Keynes, Oxford University Press, London, 1966, pp. 44-63.*

James Boswell   (essay date 1791)

[*A Scottish diarist, biographer, and man of letters, Boswell is one of the most colorful and widely read figures in eighteenth-century English literature. He is esteemed for his inimitable conversational style and pictorial documentation of life in such works as* Journal of a Tour to the Hebrides *(1785) and* London Journal *(unpublished until 1950). Labelled the greatest of English biographers and best known for his* Life of Samuel Johnson *(1791), Boswell firmly established biography as a leading literary form through a conscious, pioneering attempt to recreate his subject by combining life history with anecdote, observation, dialogue, theme, and plot. In the following excerpt from the* Life, *he appraises "The Vanity of Human Wishes" and recounts the production of Johnson's tragedy* Irene.]

In January, 1749, [Dr. Johnson] published **"THE VANITY OF HUMAN WISHES, being the Tenth Satire of Juvenal imitated."** He, I believe, composed it the preceding year. Mrs. Johnson, for the sake of country air, had lodgings at Hampstead, to which he resorted occasionally, and there the greatest part, if not the whole, of this Imitation was written. The fervid rapidity with which it was produced, is scarcely credible. I have heard him say, that he composed seventy lines of it in one day, without putting one of them upon paper till they were finished. I remember when I once regretted to him that he had not given us more of Juvenal's Satires, he said, he probably should give more, for he had them all in his head; by which I understood, that he had the originals and correspondent allusions floating in his mind, which he could, when he pleased, embody and render permanent without much labour. Some of them, however, he observed were too gross for imitation.

The profits of a single poem, however excellent, appear to have been very small in the last reign, compared with what a publication of the same size has since been known to yield. I have mentioned upon Johnson's own authority, that for his **LONDON** he had only ten guineas; and now, after his fame was established, he got for his **"Vanity of Human Wishes"** but five guineas more, as is proved by an authentick document in my possession.

It will be observed, that he reserves to himself the right of printing one edition of this satire, which was his practice upon occasion of the sale of all his writings; it being his fixed intention to publish at some period, for his own profit, a complete collection of his works.

His **"Vanity of Human Wishes"** has less of common life, but more of a philosophick dignity than his **"London."** More readers, therefore, will be delighted with the pointed spirit of **"London,"** than with the profound reflection of **"The Vanity of Human Wishes."** Garrick, for instance, observed in his sprightly manner, with more vivacity than regard to just discrimination, as is usual with wits, "When Johnson lived much with the Herveys, and saw a good deal of what was passing in life, he wrote his **'London,'** which is lively and easy: when he became more retired, he gave us his **'Vanity of Human Wishes,'** which is as hard as Greek. Had he gone on to imitate another satire, it would have been as hard as Hebrew."

But **"The Vanity of Human Wishes"** is, in the opinion of the best judges, as high an effort of ethick poetry as any language can shew. The instances of variety of disappointment are chosen so judiciously, and painted so strongly, that, the moment they are read, they bring conviction to every thinking mind. That of the scholar must have depressed the too sanguine expectations of many an ambitious student. That of the warrior, Charles of Sweden, is, I think, as highly finished a picture as can possibly be conceived.

Were all the other excellencies of this poem submitted, it must ever have our grateful reverence from its noble conclusion; in which we are consoled with the assurance that happiness may be attained, if we "apply our hearts" to piety:

> Where then shall hope and fear their objects find?
> Shall dull suspense corrupt the stagnant mind?
> Must helpless man, in ignorance sedate,
> Roll darkling down the torrent of his fate?
> Shall no dislike alarm, no wishes rise,
> No cries attempt the mercy of the skies?
> Inquirer, cease; petitions yet remain,
> Which Heav'n may hear, nor deem Religion vain.
> Still raise for good the supplicating voice,
> But leave to Heaven the measure and the choice.
> Safe in His hand, whose eye discerns afar

> The secret ambush of a specious pray'r;
> Implore His aid, in His decisions rest,
> Secure, whate'er He gives, He gives the best:
> Yet when the sense of sacred presence fires,
> And strong devotion to the skies aspires,
> Pour forth thy fervours for a healthful mind,
> Obedient passions, and a will resign'd;
> For love, which scarce collective man can fill;
> For patience, sovereign o'er transmuted ill;
> For faith, which panting for a happier seat,
> Counts death kind Nature's signal for retreat.
> These goods for man the laws of Heaven ordain,
> These goods He grants, who grants the power to gain;
> With these celestial wisdom calms the mind,
> And makes the happiness she does not find.

Garrick being now vested with theatrical power by being manager of Drury-lane theatre, he kindly and generously made use of it to bring out Johnson's tragedy, which had been long kept back for want of encouragement. But in this benevolent purpose he met with no small difficulty from the temper of Johnson, which could not brook that a drama which he had formed with much study, and had been obliged to keep more than the nine years of Horace, should be revised and altered at the pleasure of an actor. Yet Garrick knew well, that without some alterations it would not be fit for the stage. A violent dispute having ensued between them, Garrick applied to the Reverend Dr. Taylor to interpose. Johnson was at first very obstinate. "Sir, (said he) the fellow wants me to make Mahomet run mad, that he may have an opportunity of tossing his hands and kicking his heels." He was, however, at last, with difficulty, prevailed on to comply with Garrick's wishes, so as to allow of some changes; but still there were not enough.

Dr. Adams was present the first night of the representation of **IRENE** and gave me the following account: "Before the curtain drew up, there were catcalls whistling, which alarmed Johnson's friends. The Prologue, which was written by himself in a manly strain, soothed the audience, and the play went off tolerably, till it came to the conclusion, when Mrs. Pritchard, the Heroine of the piece, was to be strangled upon the stage, and was to speak two lines with the bow-string round her neck. The audience cried out *'Murder! Murder!'* She several times attempted to speak; but in vain. At last she was obliged to go off the stage alive." This passage was afterwards struck out, and she was carried off to be put to death behind the scenes, as the play now has it. The Epilogue, as Johnson informed me, was written by Sir William Yonge. I know not how his play came to be thus graced by the pen of a person then so eminent in the political world.

Notwithstanding all the support of such performers as Garrick, Barry, Mrs. Cibber, Mrs. Pritchard, and every advantage of dress and decoration, the tragedy of *Irene* did not please the publick. Mr. Garrick's zeal carried it through for nine nights, so that the author had his three nights' profits; and from a receipt signed by him, now in the hands of Mr. James Dodsley, it appears that his friend, Mr. Robert Dodsley, gave him one hundred pounds for the copy, with his usual reservation of the right of one edition.

Irene considered as a poem, is entitled to the praise of superiour excellence. Analysed into parts, it will furnish a rich store of noble sentiments, fine imagery, and beautiful language; but it is deficient in pathos, in that delicate power of touching the human feelings, which is the principal end of the drama. Indeed Garrick has complained to me, that Johnson not only had not the faculty of producing the impressions of tragedy, but that he had not the sensibility to perceive them. His great friend Mr. Walmsley's prediction, that he would "turn out a fine tragedy writer," was, therefore, ill-founded. Johnson was wise enough to be convinced that he had not the talents necessary to write successfully for the stage, and never made another attempt in that species of composition.

When asked how he felt upon the ill success of his tragedy, he replied, "Like the Monument;" meaning that he continued firm and unmoved as that column. And let it be remembered, as an admonition to the *genus irritabile* of dramatick writers, that this great man, instead of peevishly complaining of the bad taste of the town, submitted to its decision without a murmur. He had, indeed, upon all occasions a great deference for the general opinion: "A man (said he) who writes a book, thinks himself wiser or wittier than the rest of mankind; he supposes that he can instruct or amuse them, and the publick to whom he appeals, must, after all, be the judges of his pretensions."

On occasion of this play being brought upon the stage, Johnson had a fancy that as a dramatick authour his dress should be more gay than what he ordinarily wore; he therefore appeared behind the scenes, and even in one of the side boxes, in a scarlet waistcoat, with rich gold lace, and a gold laced hat. He humourously observed to Mr. Langton, "that when in that dress he could not treat people with the same ease as when in his usual plain clothes." Dress indeed, we must allow, has more effect even upon strong minds than one should suppose, without having had the experience of it. His necessary attendance while his play was in rehearsal, and during its performance, brought him acquainted with many of the performers of both sexes, which produced a more favourable opinion of their profession than he had harshly expressed in his **"Life of Savage."** With some of them he kept up an acquaintance as long as he and they lived, and was ever ready to shew them acts of kindness. He for a considerable time used to frequent the *Green-Room,* and seemed to take delight in dissipating his gloom, by mixing in the sprightly chit-chat of the motley circle then to be found there. Mr. David Hume related to me from Mr. Garrick, that Johnson at last denied himself this amusement, from considerations of rigid virtue; saying, "I'll come no more behind your scenes, David; for the silk stockings and white bosoms of your actresses excite my amorous propensities." (pp. 111-17)

> *James Boswell, in his* The Life of Samuel Johnson, *1791. Reprint by J. M. Dent & Sons Ltd., 1976, 646 p.*

William Mudford   (essay date 1802)

[*In the following excerpt, Mudford underscores some of the distinctive qualities of Johnson's poetry, focusing on "London" and "The Vanity of Human Wishes."*]

[Some lines of Johnson's poetry] may justly contest even the superiority with Pope. But **"London"** presents less of these than the **"Vanity of Human Wishes."** Yet the former

is said to have obtained the approbation of a man (Pope) well qualified to judge; who declared that the author of such an excellent work could not be long concealed. This story is related, but is, I think, little deserving of credit. Pope, whose ear was accustomed to the nicest harmony, and who could easily discern the minutest deviation from propriety, can hardly be supposed to have overlooked the many weak lines and puerile tautologies which this presents; and if he saw them, it can as little be supposed that he would have conferred upon it such a disqualified commendation.

It is an invidious mode of criticism to detect and expose trifling errors in a work, which otherwise abounds in beauties; it displays a mean appetence to detraction; and a mind void of sensibility. Yet as much indiscriminate praise has been lavished on this poem of Johnson's, and has even been preferred by some to his **"Vanity of Human Wishes,"** and as its faults have been hitherto unnoticed, a few remarks may be offered without any disingenuous imputation. I am far from wishing to detract in the smallest degree from the great fame of Johnson, and I am besides aware, that no examination of his poetry can do it, however severe it may be. He has been read, and praised, and imitated, as a philosopher, a moralist, and an elegant prose writer; but none yet ever did, or ever can, confer upon him the appellation of poet. I therefore only propose to myself, in exposing a few trifling errors, to give confidence to unambitious modesty, and to instruct the blind admirers of this stupendous genius that even *he* is not infallible.

It is always deemed unlucky to stumble upon the threshold. In the third couplet however, Johnson has fallen into a manifest tautology.

> Resolved at length from vice and London *far*
> To breathe in *distant* fields a purer air.

This indeed was hardly to have been expected from the usual correctness of his language, which was in general scrupulous of the words adopted, even to a fault. Yet we have the same impropriety again, a few lines afterwards.

> With slavish tenets *taint* our *poisoned* youth.

It is impossible to taint a body already poisoned. If there be a weaker line in the namby pamby verses of Philips, or the dull page of Tate, I will confess my inability to discover it. It is indeed surprising, that the perspicuity of Johnson's mind, which could so readily detect the deviations of other poets, should have been incapable of correcting his own. But the fondness of a parent, rarely beholds the imperfections of his offspring.

The concluding line of this poem is remarkably weak, and the last part is indeed a mere languid iteration of the former.

These are a few of the faults of this imitation, and these are sufficient to answer my purpose. I now hasten to the more agreeable task of pointing out some of its most striking beauties, which I trust will be more agreeable to my reader. The description of London is spirited and just; for who can deny but that

> Here malice, rapine, accident, conspire,
> And now a rabble rages, now a fire;
> Their ambush here relentless ruffians lay,
> And here the fell attorney prowls for prey;

> Here falling houses thunder on your head,
> And here a female atheist talks you dead.

There is something colloquial and vulgar in the expression *talks you dead,* which is not suited to the dignity of poetry. In these lines also, he uses the initial resemblances, or alliterations, though he censures them in his life of Gray.

Johnson had the power of reasoning in verse, though he did not always reason with cogency, nor did he possess the vigour of Pope in condensing much meaning in a few words. That is a power granted but to few, and is not much the effect of study. But he is seldom more pleasing than in the following lines:

> But thou, should tempting villainy present
> All Marlborough hoarded or all Villiers spent,
> Turn from the glittering bribe thy scornful eye,
> Nor sell for gold what gold can never buy,
> The peaceful slumber, self approving day,
> Unsullied fame, and conscience ever gay.

After enumerating with indignation, the vices and snares of the metropolis, the poet takes occasion to break out into the following exclamation.

> Has heaven reserved in pity to the poor
> No pathless waste or undiscovered shore?
> No secret island in the boundless main?
> No peaceful desert yet unclaimed by Spain?
> Quick let us rise, the happy seats explore,
> And bear oppression's insolence no more.
> This mournful truth is every where confessed,
> *Slow rises worth by poverty depressed.*

These are perhaps the beauties of *Johnson's poem,* but they surely are not the *beauties of poetry.*

"The Vanity of Human Wishes" is by far more energetic, and more pleasing than **"London."**—Whether it be that the author had improved his taste or his judgment; whether he was seized with some sudden inspiration, or whether he was intent upon exposing what he had long beheld with pain and anxiety, I know not; but it certainly contains more masterly touches, more spirited delineations, more vigour of sentiment, and compression of language than his **"London."** This was indeed his favourite topic.

His **"Vanity of Human Wishes"** was published the year preceding the commencement of his *Rambler.* It may therefore be expected to contain some of those sombre pictures, and doleful declamations which that work presents. And this expectation will not be disappointed, for it does in fact abound in them, and they are, in consequence, the most pleasing parts of the poem. Some of these therefore, I shall transcribe, as exhibiting more happy efforts of Johnson's poetic powers.

I will not vouch for the truth of the following lines, but must affirm, that they afford a rich repast to the melancholy mind, and to those whom disappointment have taught the necessity of patience.

> On ev'ry stage the foes of peace attend,
> Hate dogs their flight, and insult mocks their end.
> Love ends with hope, the sinking Statesman's door
> Pours in the morning worshipper no more;
> For growing names the weekly scribbler lies,
> To growing wealth the dedicator flies,
> From every room descends the painted face
> That hung the bright palladium of the place;

> And smoked in kitchens or in auctions sold,
> To better features yields the frame of gold:
> For now no more we trace in ev'ry line
> Heroic worth, benevolence divine;
> The form distorted justifies the fall,
> And detestation rids the indignant wall.

There is much of keen satire and animated diction in this passage, and it would have been no disgrace to the pen of Pope or Dryden. It has indeed been the opinion of some, that had Johnson cultivated poetry, he would have equalled the former author in his versification, and in his language. Of this no one can be certain; and all conjectures are vain; but there exist no solid grounds for the inference. Those who regard poetry as mechanical, may perhaps believe it; but those who consider it as intuitive and not to be acquired, will reject it as idle. What Johnson could not attain at forty years of age, it is not likely he ever would attain afterwards. It is my opinion, that no labour or study, however assiduous, could possibly have ever rendered him equal to Pope, whose melody and genius yet remain unequalled.

I have been told that the author could never read the following description of the student's progress without tears. Why he should have been so powerfully affected by a description to which he was familiar, it is now in vain to enquire; it does not possess sufficient pathos to draw tears, I believe, from the eyes of any other reader.—But this story is, I think, little probable, for "wonders are willingly told and willingly believed." I shall, however, transcribe the passage, and then leave my reader to consult his own feelings and determine whether it be really so affecting as to make him weep.

> When first the college rolls receive his name,
> The young enthusiast quits his ease for fame;
> Resistless burns the fever of renown
> Caught from the strong contagion of the gown:
> O'er Bodley's dome his future labours spread,
> And Bacon's mansion, trembles o'er his head.
> Are these thy views? proceed, illustrious youth,
> And Virtue guard thee to the throne of truth.
> Yet should thy soul indulge the gen'rous heat,
> 'Till captive science yields her last retreat;
> Should reason guide thee with her brightest ray,
> And pour on misty doubt resistless day,
> Should no false kindness lure to loose delight,
> Nor praise relax, nor difficulty fright;
> Should tempting novelty thy cell refrain,
> And sloth effuse her opiate fumes in vain;
> Should beauty blunt on fops her fatal dart,
> Nor claim the triumph of a letter'd heart:
> Should no disease thy torpid veins invade,
> Nor Melancholy's phantoms haunt thy shade;
> Yet hope not life from grief or danger free,
> Nor think the doom of man revers'd for thee;
> Deign on the passing world to turn thine eyes,
> And pause awhile from learning to be wise;
> There mark what ills the scholar's life assail,
> Toil, envy, want, the patron, and the jail.
> See nations, slowly wise, and meanly just,
> To buried merit raise the tardy bust.
> If dreams yet flatter, once again attend,
> Hear Lydiat's life and Galileo's end,
> Nor deem, when learning her last prize bestows,
> The glittering eminence exempt from foes.
> See when the vulgar 'scapes despis'd or aw'd,
> Rebellion's vengeful talons seize on Laud.
> From meaner minds, tho' smaller fines content,

The plunder'd palace or sequester'd rent;
Mark'd out by dangerous parts he meets the shock,
And fatal learning leads him to the block.
Around his tomb let art and genius weep;
But hear his death, ye blockheads, hear and sleep.

To this description praise cannot be denied; for its general vigour and harmony render it a distinguished part of the poem before us. But the propriety of the expression, *lettered heart,* is, I think, doubtful.

In point of accuracy and spirit, the description of old age, beginning 1. 255, and ending 290, is entitled to high commendation. But it is not, upon the whole, equal to the former. This was, indeed, a subject he delighted to expatiate upon; and has, in the *Rambler,* described almost every possible misery attendant on that state of debility; and I know not whether those delineations have not more of true poetry in them than the present.

After considering the infelicities of old age, as incident to all men, he proceeds to shew that even the decline of *him* who is exempt from *scorn or crime;* whose life *melts with unperceived decay;* and whose *night congratulating conscience cheers,* is not exempt from some distress, either more or less, and proceeding from a different cause.

Yet e'en on this, her load misfortune flings,
To press the weary minutes' flagging wings;
New sorrow rises as the day returns,
A sister sickens or a daughter mourns.
Now kindred merit fills the sable bier,
Now lacerated friendship claims a tear.
Year chases year, decay pursues decay,
Still drops some joy from with'ring life away:
New forms arise, and different views engage,
Superfluous lags the veteran on the stage,
Till pitying nature signs the last release,
And bids afflicted worth retire to peace.

From these quotations it is, I think, manifest how far superior the present poem is to the **"London"** of Johnson. While the former contains nothing that is remarkable, this frequently presents striking lines and paragraphs, and is often laboured into dignity; the language is more pure, the ideas more vivid, and the versification more harmonious: yet Johnson's claim to poetry is very doubtful. He was too much given to reasoning and declamation ever to attain those heights of sublimity which astonish and delight. If he seldom offends by his harshness he as seldom exhilarates by his vivacity; and though he did not detract from our poetic dignity, he cannot be said to have added any thing to it. As his reflections were always melancholy, so his writings have the same cast: and as this is a disease which does not allow very vigorous or very frequent excursions to the intellect, his images are not much varied; and analogous ideas are generally excited by events the most dissimilar. It was not in his power to assume much variety, nor did he seek to improve this inability by labour; for he was, I believe, little ambitious of the title of poet; an indifference proceeding, perhaps, from a consciousness of natural disqualifications for the exercise of that exalted function. The soft graces he never could attain, though he sometimes exhibits strength and elegance. He was, indeed, soon aware that his abilities did not consist in poetry; for he began it late, and abandoned it early: and it is very probable that had he been exempt from want, he never would have produced the imitations of Juvenal. In short, his poetic character may be given in his own words: "He

is elegant but not great; he never labours after exquisite beauties; and he seldom falls into gross faults. His versification is smooth, but rarely vigorous; and his rhymes are remarkably exact." (pp. 68-80)

William Mudford, in his A Critical Enquiry into the Moral Writings of Dr. Samuel Johnson, *Cobbett and Morgan, Pall Mall, and R. Faulder, 1802, 144 p.*

William Hazlitt   (essay date 1819)

[*An English essayist, Hazlitt was one of the most important critics of the Romantic age. He was a deft stylist and a master of the prose essay. He utilized the critical techniques of evocation, metaphor, and personal reference—three innovations that greatly influenced the development of literary criticism in the nineteenth and twentieth centuries. In the following excerpt from his* Lectures on the English Comic Writers, *a work first published in 1819, he places Johnson's writings in the "middle rank between startling novelty and vapid common-place," but upholds Johnson's literary reputation in consideration of his conversational skills.*]

The dramatic and conversational turn which forms the distinguishing feature and greatest charm of the *Spectator* and *Tatler,* is quite lost in the **Rambler** by Dr. Johnson. There is no reflected light thrown on human life from an assumed character, nor any direct one from a display of the author's own. The *Tatler* and *Spectator* are, as it were, made up of notes and memorandums of the events and incidents of the day, with finished studies after nature, and characters fresh from the life, which the writer moralises upon, and turns to account as they come before him: the **Rambler** is a collection of moral Essays, or scholastic theses, written on set subjects, and of which the individual characters and incidents are merely artificial illustrations, brought in to give a pretended relief to the dryness of didactic discussion. The **Rambler** is a splendid and imposing common-place-book of general topics, and rhetorical declamation on the conduct and business of human life. In this sense, there is hardly a reflection that had been suggested on such subjects which is not to be found in this celebrated work, and there is, perhaps, hardly a reflection to be found in it which had not been already suggested and developed by some other author, or in the common course of conversation. The mass of intellectual wealth here heaped together is immense, but it is rather the result of gradual accumulation, the produce of the general intellect, labouring in the mine of knowledge and reflection, than dug out of the quarry, and dragged into the light by the industry and sagacity of a single mind. I am not here saying that Dr. Johnson was a man without originality, compared with the ordinary run of men's minds, but he was not a man of original thought or genius, in the sense in which Montaigne or Lord Bacon was. He opened no new vein of precious ore, nor did he light upon any single pebbles of uncommon size and unrivalled lustre. We seldom meet with any thing to 'give us pause;' he does not set us thinking for the first time. His reflections present themselves like reminiscences; do not disturb the ordinary march of our thoughts; arrest our attention by the stateliness of their appearance, and the costliness of their garb, but pass on and mingle with the throng of our impressions.

After closing the volumes of the **Rambler,** there is nothing that we remember as a new truth gained to the mind, nothing indelibly stamped upon the memory; nor is there any passage that we wish to turn to as embodying any known principle or observation, with such force and beauty that justice can only be done to the idea in the author's own words. Such, for instance, are many of the passages to be found in Burke, which shine by their own light, belong to no class, have neither equal nor counterpart, and of which we say that no one but the author could have written them! There is neither the same boldness of design, nor mastery of execution in Johnson. In the one, the spark of genius seems to have met with its congenial matter: the shaft is sped; the forked lightning dresses up the face of nature in ghastly smiles, and the loud thunder rolls far away from the ruin that is made. Dr. Johnson's style, on the contrary, resembles rather the rumbling of mimic thunder at one of our theatres; and the light he throws upon a subject is like the dazzling effect of phosphorus, or an *ignis fatuus* of words. There is a wide difference, however, between perfect originality and perfect common-place: neither ideas nor expressions are trite or vulgar because they are not quite new. They are valuable, and ought to be repeated, if they have not become quite common; and Johnson's style both of reasoning and imagery holds the middle rank between startling novelty and vapid common-place. Johnson has as much originality of thinking as Addison; but then he wants his familiarity of illustration, knowledge of character, and delightful humour.—What most distinguishes Dr. Johnson from other writers is the pomp and uniformity of his style. All his periods are cast in the same mould, are of the same size and shape, and consequently have little fitness to the variety of things he professes to treat of. His subjects are familiar, but the author is always upon stilts. He has neither ease nor simplicity, and his efforts at playfulness, in part, remind one of the lines in Milton:—

————The elephant
To make them sport wreath'd his proboscis lithe.

His Letters from Correspondents, in particular, are more pompous and unwieldy than what he writes in his own person. This want of relaxation and variety of manner has, I think, after the first effects of novelty and surprise were over, been prejudicial to the matter. It takes from the general power, not only to please, but to instruct. The monotony of style produces an apparent monotony of ideas. What is really striking and valuable, is lost in the vain ostentation and circumlocution of the expression; for when we find the same pains and pomp of diction bestowed upon the most trifling as upon the most important parts of a sentence or discourse, we grow tired of distinguishing between pretension and reality, and are disposed to confound the tinsel and bombast of the phraseology with want of weight in the thoughts. Thus, from the imposing and oracular nature of the style, people are tempted at first to imagine that our author's speculations are all wisdom and profundity: till having found out their mistake in some instances, they suppose that there is nothing but commonplace in them, concealed under verbiage and pedantry; and in both they are wrong. The fault of Dr. Johnson's style is, that it reduces all things to the same artificial and unmeaning level. It destroys all shades of difference, the association between words and things. It is a perpetual paradox and innovation. He condescends to the familiar till we are ashamed of our interest in it: he expands the little till it looks big. 'If he were to write a fable of little fishes,' as Goldsmith said of him, 'he would make them speak like great whales.' We can no more distinguish the most familiar objects in his descriptions of them, than we can a well-known face under a huge painted mask. The structure of his sentences, which was his own invention, and which has been generally imitated since his time, is a species of rhyming in prose, where one clause answers to another in measure and quantity, like the tagging of syllables at the end of a verse; the close of the period follows as mechanically as the oscillation of a pendulum, the sense is balanced with the sound; each sentence, revolving round its centre of gravity, is contained with itself like a couplet, and each paragraph forms itself into a stanza. Dr. Johnson is also a complete balance-master in the topics of morality. He never encourages hope, but he counteracts it by fear; he never elicits a truth, but he suggests some objection in answer to it. He seizes and alternately quits the clue of reason, lest it should involve him in the labyrinths of endless error: he wants confidence in himself and his fellows. He dares not trust himself with the immediate impressions of things, for fear of compromising his dignity; or follow them into their consequences, for fear of committing his prejudices. His timidity is the result, not of ignorance, but of morbid apprehension. 'He runs the great circle, and is still at home.' No advance is made by his writings in any sentiment, or mode of reasoning. Out of the pale of established authority and received dogmas, all is sceptical, loose, and desultory: he seems in imagination to strengthen the dominion of prejudice, as he weakens and dissipates that of reason; and round the rock of faith and power, on the edge of which he slumbers blindfold and uneasy, the waves and billows of uncertain and dangerous opinion roar and heave for evermore. His **Rasselas** is the most melancholy and debilitating moral speculation that ever was put forth. Doubtful of the faculties of his mind, as of his organs of vision, Johnson trusted only to his feelings and his fears. He cultivated a belief in witches as an out-guard to the evidences of religion; and abused Milton, and patronised Lauder, in spite of his aversion to his countrymen, as a step to secure the existing establishment in church and state. This was neither right feeling nor sound logic.

The most triumphant record of the talents and character of Johnson is to be found in Boswell's *Life* of him. The man was superior to the author. When he threw aside his pen, which he regarded as an incumbrance, he became not only learned and thoughtful, but acute, witty, humorous, natural, honest; hearty and determined, 'the king of good fellows and wale of old men.' There are as many smart repartees, profound remarks, and keen invectives to be found in Boswell's 'inventory of all he said,' as are recorded of any celebrated man. The life and dramatic play of his conversation forms a contrast to his written works. His natural powers and undisguised opinions were called out in convivial intercourse. In public, he practised with the foils on: in private, he unsheathed the sword of controversy, and it was 'the Ebro's temper.' The eagerness of opposition roused him from his natural sluggishness and acquired timidity; he returned blow for blow; and whether the trial were of argument or wit, none of his rivals could boast much of the encounter. Burke seems to have been the only person who had a chance with him: and it is the unpardonable sin of Boswell's work, that he has purposely omitted their combats of strength and skill. Goldsmith asked, 'Does he wind into a subject like a serpent, as Burke does?' And when exhausted with sickness, he himself said, 'If that fellow Burke were here now, he would kill me.' It is to be observed, that Johnson's colloquial style was as blunt, direct, and downright, as his style of studied composition was involved and circuitous. As when Topham Beauclerc and Langton knocked him up at his chambers, at three in the morning, and he came to the door with the poker in his hand, but seeing them, exclaimed, 'What, is it you, my lads? then I'll have a frisk with you!' and he afterwards reproaches Langton, who was a literary milksop, for leaving them to go to an engagement 'with some *un-idead* girls.' What words to come from the mouth of the great moralist and lexicographer! His good deeds were as many as his good sayings. His domestic habits, his tenderness to servants, and readiness to oblige his friends; the quantity of strong tea that he drank to keep down sad thoughts; his many labours reluctantly begun, and irresolutely laid aside; his honest acknowledgement of his own, and indulgence to the weaknesses of others; his throwing himself back in the post-chaise with Boswell, and saying, 'Now I think I am a good-humoured fellow,' though nobody thought him so, and yet he was; his quitting the society of Garrick and his actresses, and his reason for it; his dining with Wilkes, and his kindness to Goldsmith; his sitting with the young ladies on his knee at the Mitre, to give them good advice, in which situation, if not explained, he might be taken for Falstaff; and last and noblest, his carrying the unfortunate victim of disease and dissipation on his back up through Fleet Street, (an act which realises the parable of the good Samaritan)—all these, and innumerable others, endear him to the reader, and must be remembered to his lasting honour. He had faults, but they lie buried with him. He had his prejudices and his intolerant feelings; but he suffered enough in the conflict of his own mind with them. For if no man can be happy in the free exercise of his reason, no wise man can be happy without it. His were not time-serving, heartless, hypocritical prejudices; but deep, inwoven, not to be rooted out but with life and hope, which he found from old habit necessary to his own peace of mind, and thought so to the peace of mankind. I do not hate, but love him for them. They were between himself and his conscience; and should be left to that higher tribunal, 'where they in trembling hope repose, the bosom of his Father and his God.' In a word, he has left behind him few wiser or better men. (pp. 99-104)

> *William Hazlitt, "On the Periodical Essayists," in his* Essays and Belles Lettres: The English Comic Writers & Miscellaneous Essays, *edited by Ernest Rhys, J. M. Dent & Sons, Ltd., 1910, pp. 91-105.*

Sir Walter Scott (essay date 1821)

[*A Scottish author of historical romances, Scott was one of the leading proponets in the early nineteenth century of verisimilitude and historical accuracy in literature. Although he never truly formulated a guiding or central theory to his work, his criticism reflects a high regard for realism and the desire to assess an author's place in literary history. In the following excerpt from an essay first published in 1821, Scott favorably comments on Johnson's literary accomplishments, focusing on* Rasselas *and contrasting it with Voltaire's* Candide.]

Of all the men distinguished in this or any other age, Dr. JOHNSON has left upon posterity the strongest and most vivid impression, so far as person, manners, disposition, and conversation, are concerned. We do but name him, or open a book which he has written, and the sound and action recall to the imagination at once, his form, his merits, his peculiarities, nay, the very uncouthness of his gestures, and the deep impressive tone of his voice. We learn not only what he said, but form an idea how he said it; and have, at the same time, a shrewd guess of the secret motive why he did so, and whether he spoke in sport or in anger, in the desire of conviction, or for the love of debate. It was said of a noted wag, that his bon-mots did not give full satisfaction when published, because he could not print his face. But with respect to Dr. Johnson, this has been in some degree accomplished; and, although the greater part of the present generation never saw him, yet he is, in our mind's eye, a personification as lively as that of Siddons in *Lady Macbeth,* or Kemble in *Cardinal Wolsey.*

All this, as the world well knows, arises from Johnson having found in James Boswell such a biographer, as no man but himself ever had, or ever deserved to have. The performance, which chiefly resembles it in structure, is the life of the philosopher Demophon, in Lucian; but that slight sketch is far inferior in detail and in vivacity to Boswell's *Life of Johnson,* which, considering the eminent persons to whom it relates, the quantity of miscellaneous information and entertaining gossip which it brings together, may be termed, without exception, the best parlor-window book that ever was written. Accordingly, such has been the reputation which it has enjoyed, that it renders useless even the form of an abridgement, which is the less necessary in this work, as the great Lexicographer only stands connected with the department of fictitious narrative by the brief tale of **Rasselas.** (pp. 235-36)

When we consider the rank which Dr. Johnson held, not only in literature, but in society, we cannot help figuring him to ourselves as the benevolent giant of some fairy tale, whose kindnesses and courtesies are still mingled with a part of the rugged ferocity imputed to the fabulous sons of Anak; or rather, perhaps, like a Roman Dictator, fetched from his farm, whose wisdom and heroism still relished of his rustic occupation. And there were times when, with all Johnson's wisdom, and all his wit, this rudeness of disposition, and the sacrifices and submissions which he unsparingly exacted, were so great, that even his kind and devoted admirer, Mrs. Thrale, seems at length to have thought that the honor of being Johnson's hostess was almost counterbalanced by the tax which he exacted on her time and patience.

The cause of those deficiencies in temper and manners, was no ignorance of what was fit to be done in society, or how far each individual ought to suppress his own wishes in favor of those with whom he associates; for, theoretically, no man understood the rules of good-breeding better than Dr. Johnson, or could act more exactly in conformity with them, when the high rank of those with whom he was in company for the time required that he should put the necessary restraint upon himself. But during the greater part of his life, he had been in a great measure a stranger to the higher society, in which such restraint is necessary; and it may be fairly presumed, that the indulgence of a variety of little selfish peculiarities, which it is the object of

James Boswell, Oliver Goldsmith, and Johnson at the Mitre Tavern in London, engraved by R. B. Parkes after a painting by Eyre Crowe.

good-breeding to suppress, became thus familiar to him. The consciousness of his own mental superiority in most companies which he frequented, contributed to his dogmatism; and when he had attained his eminence as a dictator in literature, like other potentates, he was not averse to a display of his authority: resembling in this particular Swift, and one or two other men of genius, who have had the bad taste to imagine that their talents elevated them above observance of the common rules of society. It must be also remarked, that in Johnson's time, the literary society of London was much more confined than at present, and that he sat the Jupiter of a little circle, sometimes indeed nodding approbation, but always prompt, on the slightest contradiction, to launch the thunders of rebuke and sarcasm. He was, in a word, despotic, and despotism will occasionally lead the best dispositions into unbecoming abuse of power. It is not likely that any one will again enjoy, or have an opportunity of abusing, the singular degree of submission which was rendered to Johnson by all around him. The unreserved communications of friends, rather than the spleen of enemies, have occasioned his character being exposed in all its shadows, as well as its lights. But those, when summed and counted, amount only to a few narrow-minded prejudices concerning country and party, from which few ardent tempers remain entirely free, an over-zeal in politics, which is an ordinary

attribute of the British character, and some violences and solecisms in manners, which left his talents, morals, and benevolence, alike unimpeachable.

Of **Rasselas,** translated into so many languages, and so widely circulated through the literary world, the merits have been long justly appreciated. It was composed in solitude and sorrow; and the melancholy cast of feeling which it exhibits, sufficiently evinces the temper of the author's mind. The resemblance, in some respects, betwixt the tenor of the moral and that of *Candide,* is striking, and Johnson himself admitted, that if the authors could possibly have seen each other's manuscript, they could not have escaped the charge of plagiarism. But they resemble each other like a wholesome and a poisonous fruit. The object of the witty Frenchman is to induce a distrust of the wisdom of the great Governor of the Universe, by presuming to arraign him of incapacity before the creatures of his will. Johnson uses arguments drawn from the same premises, with the benevolent view of encouraging men to look to another and a better world, for the satisfaction of wishes, which in this seem only to be awakened in order to be disappointed. The one is a fiend—a merry devil, we grant—who scoffs at and derides human miseries; the other, a friendly though grave philosopher, who shows us the nothingness of earthly hopes, to teach us that our affections ought to be placed higher.

The work can scarce be termed a narrative, being in a great measure void of incident; it is rather a set of moral dialogues on the various vicissitudes of human life, its follies, its fears, its hopes, its wishes, and the disappointment in which all terminate. The style is in Johnson's best manner; enriched and rendered sonorous by the triads and quaternions which he so much loved, and balanced with an art which perhaps he derived from the learned Sir Thomas Brown. The reader may sometimes complain, with Boswell, that the unalleviated picture of human helplessness and misery, leaves sadness upon the mind after perusal. But the moral is to be found in the conclusion of the **"Vanity of Human Wishes,"** a poem which treats of the same melancholy subject, and closes with this sublime strain of morality:—

> Pour forth thy fervors for a healthful mind,
> Obedient passions, and a will resign'd;
> For Love, which scarce collective man can fill;
> For Patience, sovereign o'er transmuted ill;
> For Faith, that, panting for a happier seat,
> Counts death kind nature's signal of retreat:
> These goods for man the laws of Heaven ordain;
> These goods He grants, who grants the power to
> gain.
> With these celestial Wisdom calms the mind,
> And makes the happiness she cannot find.

(pp. 241-45)

Sir Walter Scott, "Samuel Johnson," in his The Lives of the Novelists, *A. Denham & Co., 1872, pp. 235-45.*

Thomas Babington Macaulay   (essay date 1856)

[*Macaulay was a distinguished historian, essayist, and politician of mid-nineteenth-century England who often contributed erudite, highly opinionated articles to the* Edinburgh Review *which were later collected in* Critical and Historical Essays *(1843). His most enduring work is his five-volume* History of England from the Accession of James II *(1849-61), which, despite criticism of its strong Whig bias, is revered for its consummate rhetorical and narrative prose. In the following excerpt from an essay originally published in the* Encyclopedia Britannica *in 1856, he describes the circumstances surrounding the composition Johnson's major works, including their critical and popular reception.*]

About a year after Johnson had begun to reside in London, he was fortunate enough to obtain regular employment from Cave, an enterprising and intelligent bookseller, who was proprietor and editor of the *Gentleman's Magazine.* That journal, just entering on the ninth year of its long existence, was the only periodical work in the kingdom which then had what would now be called a large circulation. It was, indeed, the chief source of parliamentary intelligence. It was not then safe, even during a recess, to publish an account of the proceedings of either House without some disguise. Cave, however, ventured to entertain his readers with what he called **"Reports of the Debates of the Senate of Lilliput."** France was Blefuscu; London was Mildendo: pounds were sprugs: the Duke of Newcastle was the Nardac secretary of State: Lord Hard-

wicke was the Hurgo Hickrad; and William Pulteney was Wingul Pulnub. To write the speeches, was, during several years, the business of Johnson. He was generally furnished with notes, meagre indeed, and inaccurate, of what had been said; but sometimes he had to find arguments and eloquence both for the ministry and for the opposition. He was himself a Tory, not from rational conviction—for his serious opinion was that one form of government was just as good or as bad as another—but from mere passion, such as inflamed the Capulets against the Montagues, or the Blues of the Roman circus against the Greens. . . . It is easy to guess in what manner debates on great party questions were likely to be reported by a man whose judgment was so much disordered by party spirit. A show of fairness was indeed necessary to the prosperity of the *Magazine.* But Johnson long afterwards owned that, though he had saved appearances, he had taken care that the Whig dogs should not have the best of it; and, in fact, every passage which has lived, every passage which bears the marks of his higher faculties, is put into the mouth of some member of the opposition.

A few weeks after Johnson had entered on these obscure labours, he published a work which at once placed him high among the writers of his age. It is probable that what he had suffered during his first year in London had often reminded him of some parts of that noble poem in which Juvenal had described the misery and degradation of a needy man of letters, lodged among the pigeons' nests in the tottering garrets which overhung the streets of Rome. Pope's admirable imitations of Horace's *Satires and Epistles* had recently appeared, were in every hand, and were by many readers thought superior to the originals. What Pope had done for Horace, Johnson aspired to do for Juvenal. The enterprise was bold, and yet judicious. For between Johnson and Juvenal there was much in common, much more certainly than between Pope and Horace.

Johnson's **"London"** appeared without his name in May 1738. He received only ten guineas for this stately and vigorous poem: but the sale was rapid, and the success complete. A second edition was required within a week. Those small critics who are always desirous to lower established reputations ran about proclaiming that the anonymous satirist was superior to Pope in Pope's own peculiar department of literature. It ought to be remembered, to the honour of Pope, that he joined heartily in the applause with which the appearance of a rival genius was welcomed. He made inquiries about the author of **"London."** Such a man, he said, could not long be concealed. The name was soon discovered; and Pope, with great kindness, exerted himself to obtain an academical degree and the mastership of a grammar school for the poor young poet. The attempt failed; and Johnson remained a bookseller's hack. (pp. 182-85)

[The] most remarkable of the persons with whom at this time Johnson consorted was Richard Savage, an earl's son, a shoemaker's apprentice, who had seen life in all its forms, who had feasted among blue ribands in Saint James's Square, and had lain with fifty pounds' weight of irons on his legs in the condemned ward of Newgate. This man had, after many vicissitudes of fortune, sunk at last into abject and hopeless poverty. His pen had failed him. His patrons had been taken away by death, or estranged by the riotous profusion with which he squandered their bounty, and the ungrateful insolence with which he rejected their advice. He now lived by begging. He dined on venison and champagne whenever he had been so fortunate as to borrow a guinea. If his questing had been unsuccessful, he appeased the rage of hunger with some scraps of broken meat, and lay down to rest under the Piazza of Covent Garden in warm weather, and, in cold weather, as near as he could get to the furnace of a glass house. Yet, in his misery, he was still an agreeable companion. He had an inexhaustible store of anecdotes about that gay and brilliant world from which he was now an outcast. He had observed the great men of both parties in hours of careless relaxation, had seen the leaders of opposition without the mask of patriotism, and had heard the prime minister roar with laughter and tell stories not over decent. During some months Savage lived in the closest familiarity with Johnson; and then the friends parted, not without tears. Johnson remained in London to drudge for Cave. Savage went to the West of England, lived there as he had lived everywhere, and, in 1743, died, penniless and heartbroken, in Bristol gaol.

Soon after his death, while the public curiosity was strongly excited about his extraordinary character, and his not less extraordinary adventures, a life of him appeared widely different from the catchpenny lives of eminent men which were then a staple article of manufacture in Grub Street. The style was indeed deficient in ease and variety; and the writer was evidently too partial to the Latin element of our language. But the little work, with all its faults, was a masterpiece. No finer specimen of literary biography existed in any language, living or dead; and a discerning critic might have confidently predicted that the author was destined to be the founder of a new school of English eloquence.

The **"Life of Savage"** was anonymous; but it was well known in literary circles that Johnson was the writer. During the three years which followed, he produced no important work; but he was not, and indeed could not be, idle. The fame of his abilities and learning continued to grow. Warburton pronounced him a man of parts and genius; and the praise of Warburton was then no light thing. Such was Johnson's reputation that, in 1747, several eminent booksellers combined to employ him in the arduous work of preparing a Dictionary of the English Language, in two folio volumes. The sum which they agreed to pay him was only fifteen hundred guineas; and out of this sum he had to pay several poor men of letters who assisted him in the humbler parts of his task. (pp. 186-87)

Johnson had flattered himself that he should have completed his *Dictionary* by the end of 1750; but it was not till 1755 that he at length gave his huge volumes to the world. During the seven years which he passed in the drudgery of penning definitions and marking quotations for transcription, he sought for relaxation in literary labour of a more agreeable kind. In 1749 he published the **"Vanity of Human Wishes,"** an excellent imitation of the Tenth Satire of Juvenal. It is in truth not easy to say whether the palm belongs to the ancient or to the modern poet. The couplets in which the fall of Wolsey is described, though lofty and sonorous, are feeble when compared with the wonderful lines which bring before us all Rome in tumult on the day of the fall of Sejanus, the laurels on the doorposts, the white bull stalking towards the Capitol, the

statues rolling down from their pedestals, the flatterers of the disgraced minister running to see him dragged with a hook through the streets, and to have a kick at his carcase before it is hurled into the Tiber. It must be owned too that in the concluding passage the Christian moralist has not made the most of his advantages, and has fallen decidedly short of the sublimity of his Pagan model. On the other hand, Juvenal's Hannibal must yield to Johnson's Charles; and Johnson's vigorous and pathetic enumeration of the miseries of a literary life must be allowed to be superior to Juvenal's lamentation over the fate of Demosthenes and Cicero.

For the copyright of the **"Vanity of Human Wishes"** Johnson received only fifteen guineas.

A few days after the publication of this poem, his tragedy [*Irene*], begun many years before, was brought on the stage. His pupil, David Garrick, had, in 1741, made his appearance on a humble stage in Goodman's Fields, had at once risen to the first place among actors, and was now, after several years of almost uninterrupted success, manager of Drury Lane Theatre. . . . Garrick now brought *Irene* out, with alterations sufficient to displease the author, yet not sufficient to make the piece pleasing to the audience. The public, however, listened with little emotion, but with much civility, to five acts of monotonous declamation. After nine representations the play was withdrawn. It is, indeed, altogether unsuited to the stage, and, even when perused in the closet, will be found hardly worthy of the author. He had not the slightest notion of what blank verse should be. A change in the last syllable of every other line would make the versification of the **"Vanity of Human Wishes"** closely resemble the versification of *Irene.* (pp. 188-90)

About a year after the representation of *Irene,* he began to publish a series of short essays on morals, manners, and literature. This species of composition had been brought into fashion by the success of the *Tatler,* and by the still more brilliant success of the *Spectator.* A crowd of small writers had vainly attempted to rival Addison. The *Lay Monastery,* the *Censor,* the *Freethinker,* the *Plain Dealer,* the *Champion,* and other works of the same kind, had had their short day. None of them had obtained a permanent place in our literature; and they are now to be found only in the libraries of the curious. At length Johnson undertook the adventure in which so many aspirants had failed. In the thirty-sixth year after the appearance of the last number of the *Spectator* appeared the first number of the *Rambler.* From March 1750 to March 1752, this paper continued to come out every Tuesday and Saturday.

From the first the *Rambler* was enthusiastically admired by a few eminent men. Richardson, when only five numbers had appeared, pronounced it equal, if not superior, to the *Spectator.* Young and Hartley expressed their approbation not less warmly. Bubb Dodington, among whose many faults indifference to the claims of genius and learning cannot be reckoned, solicited the acquaintance of the writer. In consequence probably of the good offices of Dodington, who was then the confidential adviser of Prince Frederic, two of his Royal Highness's gentlemen carried a gracious message to the printing office, and ordered seven copies for Leicester House. But these overtures seem to have been very coldly received. Johnson had had enough of the patronage of the great to last him all his life, and was not disposed to haunt any other door as he had haunted the door of Chesterfield.

By the public the *Rambler* was at first very coldly received. Though the price of a number was only twopence, the sale did not amount to five hundred. The profits were therefore very small. But as soon as the flying leaves were collected and reprinted they became popular. The author lived to see thirteen thousand copies spread over England alone. Separate editions were published for the Scotch and Irish markets. A large party pronounced the style perfect, so absolutely perfect that in some essays it would be impossible for the writer himself to alter a single word for the better. Another party, not less numerous, vehemently accused him of having corrupted the purity of the English tongue. The best critics admitted that his diction was too monotonous, too obviously artificial, and now and then turgid even to absurdity. But they did justice to the acuteness of his observations on morals and manners, to the constant precision and frequent brilliancy of his language, to the weighty and magnificent eloquence of many serious passages, and to the solemn yet pleasing humour of some of the lighter papers. On the question of precedence between Addison and Johnson, a question which, seventy years ago, was much disputed, posterity has pronounced a decision from which there is no appeal. Sir Roger, his chaplain and his butler, Will Wimble and Will Honeycomb, the Vision of Mirza, the Journal of the Retired Citizen, the Everlasting Club, the Dunmow Flitch, the Loves of Hilpah and Shalum, the Visit to the Exchange, and the Visit to the Abbey, are known to everybody. But many men and women, even of highly cultivated minds, are unacquainted with Squire Bluster and Mrs. Busy, Quisquilius and Venustulus, the Allegory of Wit and Learning, the Chronicle of the Revolutions of a Garret, and the sad fate of Aningait and Ajut.

The last *Rambler* was written in a sad and gloomy hour. Mrs. Johnson had been given over by the physicians. Three days later she died. She left her husband almost broken-hearted. . . . Yet it was necessary for him to set himself, as he expressed it, doggedly to work. After three more laborious years, the *Dictionary* was at length complete.

It had been generally supposed that this great work would be dedicated to the eloquent and accomplished nobleman to whom the prospectus had been addressed. He well knew the value of such a compliment; and therefore, when the day of publication drew near, he exerted himself to soothe, by a show of zealous and at the same time of delicate and judicious kindness, the pride which he had so cruelly wounded. Since the *Ramblers* had ceased to appear, the town had been entertained by a journal called *The World,* to which many men of high rank and fashion contributed. In two successive numbers of *The World* the *Dictionary* was, to use the modern phrase, puffed with wonderful skill. The writings of Johnson were warmly praised. It was proposed that he should be invested with the authority of a Dictator, nay, of a Pope, over our language, and that his decisions about the meaning and the spelling of words should be received as final. His two folios, it was said, would of course be bought by everybody who could afford to buy them. It was soon known that these papers were written by Chesterfield. But the just resentment of Johnson was not to be so appeased. In a letter written with

singular energy and dignity of thought and language, he repelled the tardy advances of his patron. The *Dictionary* came forth without a dedication. In the preface the author truly declared that he owed nothing to the great, and described the difficulties with which he had been left to struggle so forcibly and pathetically that the ablest and most malevolent of all the enemies of his fame, Horne Tooke, never could read that passage without tears.

The public, on this occasion, did Johnson full justice, and something more than justice. The best lexicographer may well be content if his productions are received by the world with cold esteem. But Johnson's *Dictionary* was hailed with an enthusiasm such as no similar work has ever excited. It was indeed the first dictionary which could be read with pleasure. The definitions show so much acuteness of thought and command of language, and the passages quoted from poets, divines and philosophers are so skilfully selected, that a leisure hour may always be very agreeably spent in turning over the pages. The faults of the book resolve themselves, for the most part, into one great fault. Johnson was a wretched etymologist. He knew little or nothing of any Teutonic language except English, which indeed, as he wrote it, was scarcely a Teutonic language; and thus he was absolutely at the mercy of Junius and Skinner. (pp. 190-95)

He proposed to bring out an edition of Shakespeare by subscription; and many subscribers sent in their names, and laid down their money; but he soon found the task so little to his taste that he turned to more attractive employments. He contributed many papers to a new monthly journal, which was called the *Literary Magazine.* Few of these papers have much interest; but among them was the very best thing that he ever wrote, a masterpiece both of reasoning and of satirical pleasantry, the review of Jenyns's *Inquiry into the Nature and Origin of Evil.*

In the spring of 1758 Johnson put forth the first of a series of essays, entitled *The Idler.* During two years these essays continued to appear weekly. They were eagerly read, widely circulated, and, indeed, impudently pirated, while they were still in the original form, and had a large sale when collected into volumes. *The Idler* may be described as a second part of the *Rambler,* somewhat livelier and somewhat weaker than the first part.

While Johnson was busied with his *Idlers,* his mother, who had accomplished her ninetieth year, died at Lichfield. It was long since he had seen her; but he had not failed to contribute largely, out of his small means, to her comfort. In order to defray the charges of her funeral, and to pay some debts which she had left, he wrote a little book in a single week, and sent off the sheets to the press without reading them over. A hundred pounds were paid him for the copyright; and the purchasers had great cause to be pleased with their bargain; for the book was *Rasselas.*

The success of *Rasselas* was great, though such ladies as Miss Lydia Languish must have been grievously disappointed when they found that the new volume from the circulating library was little more than a dissertation on the author's favourite theme, the **"Vanity of Human Wishes,"** that the Prince of Abyssinia was without a mistress, and the Princess without a lover; and that the story set the hero and the heroine down exactly where it had taken them up. The style was the subject of much eager controversy. The *Monthly Review* and the *Critical Review* took different sides. Many readers pronounced the writer a pompous pedant, who would never use a word of two syllables where it was possible to use a word of six, and who could not make a waiting woman relate her adventures without balancing every noun with another noun, and every epithet with another epithet. Another party, not less zealous, cited with delight numerous passages in which weighty meaning was expressed with accuracy and illustrated with splendour. And both the censure and the praise were merited.

About the plan of **Rasselas** little was said by the critics; and yet the faults of the plan might seem to invite severe criticism. Johnson has frequently blamed Shakespeare for neglecting the proprieties of time and place, and for ascribing to one age or nation the manners and opinions of another. Yet Shakespeare has not sinned in this way more grievously than Johnson. Rasselas and Imlac, Nekayah and Pekuah, are evidently meant to be Abyssinians of the eighteenth century: for the Europe which Imlac describes is the Europe of the eighteenth century; and the inmates of the Happy Valley talk familiarly of that law of gravitation which Newton discovered, and which was not fully received even at Cambridge till the eighteenth century. What a real company of Abyssinians would have been may be learned from Bruce's *Travels*. But Johnson, not content with turning filthy savages, ignorant of their letters, and gorged with raw steaks cut from living cows, into philosophers as eloquent and enlightened as himself or his friend Burke, and into ladies as highly accomplished as Mrs. Lennox or Mrs. Sheridan, transferred the whole domestic system of England to Egypt. Into a land of harems, a land of polygamy, a land where women are married without ever being seen, he introduced the flirtations and jealousies of our ball-rooms. In a land where there is boundless liberty of divorce, wedlock is described as the indissoluble compact. "A youth and maiden meeting by chance, or brought together by artifice, exchange glances, reciprocate civilities, go home, and dream of each other. Such," says Rasselas, "is the common process of marriage." Such it may have been, and may still be, in London, but assuredly not at Cairo. A writer who was guilty of such improprieties had little right to blame the poet who made Hector quote Aristotle, and represented Julio Romano as flourishing in the days of the oracle of Delphi. (pp. 195-98)

One laborious task indeed he had bound himself to perform. He had received large subscriptions for his promised edition of **Shakespeare;** he had lived on those subscriptions during some years; and he could not without disgrace omit to perform his part of the contract. His friends repeatedly exhorted him to make an effort; and he repeatedly resolved to do so. But, notwithstanding their exhortations and his resolutions, month followed month, year followed year, and nothing was done. He prayed fervently against his idleness; he determined, as often as he received the sacrament, that he would no longer doze away and trifle away his time; but the spell under which he lay resisted prayer and sacrament. His private notes at this time are made up of self-reproaches. "My indolence," he wrote on Easter eve in 1764, "has sunk into grosser sluggishness. A kind of strange oblivion has overspread me, so that I know not what has become of the last year." Easter 1765 came, and found him still in the same state, "My time," he

wrote, "has been unprofitably spent, and seems as a dream that has left nothing behind. My memory grows confused, and I know not how the days pass over me." Happily for his honour, the charm which held him captive was at length broken by no gentle or friendly hand. He had been weak enough to pay serious attention to a story about a ghost which haunted a house in Cock Lane, and had actually gone himself, with some of his friends, at one in the morning, to St. John's Church, Clerkenwell, in the hope of receiving a communication from the perturbed spirit. But the spirit, though adjured with all solemnity, remained obstinately silent; and it soon appeared that a naughty girl of eleven had been amusing herself by making fools of so many philosophers. Churchill, who, confident in his powers, drunk with popularity, and burning with party spirit, was looking for some man of established fame and Tory politics to insult, celebrated the Cock Lane Ghost in three cantos, nicknamed Johnson Pomposo, asked where the book was which had been so long promised and so liberally paid for, and directly accused the great moralist of cheating. This terrible word proved effectual; and in October 1765 appeared, after a delay of nine years, the new edition of **Shakespeare.**

This publication saved Johnson's character for honesty, but added nothing to the fame of his abilities and learning. The preface, though it contains some good passages, is not in his best manner. The most valuable notes are those in which he had an opportunity of showing how attentively he had during many years observed human life and human nature. The best specimen is the note on the character of Polonius. Nothing so good is to be found even in Wilhelm Meister's admirable examination of Hamlet. But here praise must end. It would be difficult to name a more slovenly, a more worthless, edition of any great classic. The reader may turn over play after play without finding one happy conjectural emendation, or one ingenious and satisfactory explanation of a passage which had baffled preceding commentators. Johnson had, in his **"Prospectus,"** told the world that he was peculiarly fitted for the task which he had undertaken, because he had, as a lexicographer, been under the necessity of taking a wider view of the English language than any of his predecessors. That his knowledge of our literature was extensive is indisputable. But, unfortunately, he had altogether neglected that very part of our literature with which it is especially desirable that an editor of Shakespeare should be conversant. It is dangerous to assert a negative. Yet little will be risked by the assertion, that in the two folio volumes of the English **Dictionary** there is not a single passage quoted from any dramatist of the Elizabethan age, except Shakespeare and Ben. Even from Ben the quotations are few. Johnson might easily, in a few months, have made himself well acquainted with every old play that was extant. But it never seems to have occurred to him that this was a necessary preparation for the work which he had undertaken. He would doubtless have admitted that it would be the height of absurdity in a man who was not familiar with the works of Æschylus and Euripides to publish an edition of Sophocles. Yet he ventured to publish an edition of Shakespeare, without having ever in his life, as far as can be discovered, read a single scene of Massinger, Ford, Decker, Webster, Marlow, Beaumont, or Fletcher. His detractors were noisy and scurrilous. Those who most loved and honoured him had little to say in praise of the manner in which he had discharged the duty of a commentator. He had, however, acquitted himself of a debt which had long lain heavy on his conscience; and he sank back into the repose from which the sting of satire had roused him. He long continued to live upon the fame which he had already won. (pp. 199-202)

He had early read an account of the Hebrides, and had been much interested by learning that there was so near him a land peopled by a race which was still as rude and simple as in the middle ages. A wish to become intimately acquainted with a state of society so utterly unlike all that he had ever seen frequently crossed his mind. But it is not probable that his curiosity would have overcome his habitual sluggishness, and his love of the smoke, the mud, and the cries of London, had not Boswell importuned him to attempt the adventure, and offered to be his squire. At length, in August 1773, Johnson crossed the Highland line, and plunged courageously into what was then considered, by most Englishmen, as a dreary and perilous wilderness. After wandering about two months through the Celtic region, sometimes in rude boats which did not protect him from the rain, and sometimes on small shaggy ponies which could hardly bear his weight, he returned to his old haunts with a mind full of new images and new theories. During the following year he employed himself in recording his adventures. About the beginning of 1775, his *Journey to the Hebrides* was published, and was, during some weeks, the chief subject of conversation in all circles in which any attention was paid to literature. The book is still read with pleasure. The narrative is entertaining; the speculations, whether sound or unsound, are always ingenious; and the style, though too stiff and pompous, is somewhat easier and more graceful than that of his early writings. His prejudice against the Scotch had at length become little more than matter of jest; and whatever remained of the old feeling had been effectually removed by the kind and respectful hospitality with which he had been received in every part of Scotland. It was, of course, not to be expected that an Oxonian Tory should praise the Presbyterian polity and ritual, or that an eye accustomed to the hedgerows and parks of England should not be struck by the bareness of Berwickshire and East Lothian. But even in censure Johnson's tone is not unfriendly. The most enlightened Scotchmen, with Lord Mansfield at their head, were well pleased. But some foolish and ignorant Scotchmen were moved to anger by a little unpalatable truth which was mingled with much eulogy, and assailed him whom they chose to consider as the enemy of their country with libels much more dishonourable to their country than anything that he had ever said or written. They published paragraphs in the newspapers, articles in the magazines, sixpenny pamphlets, five shilling books. One scribbler abused Johnson for being blear-eyed; another for being a pensioner; a third informed the world that one of the Doctor's uncles had been convicted of felony in Scotland, and had found that there was in that country one tree capable of supporting the weight of an Englishman. Macpherson, whose Fingal had been proved in the *Journey* to be an impudent forgery, threatened to take vengeance with a cane. The only effect of this threat was that Johnson reiterated the charge of forgery in the most contemptuous terms, and walked about, during some time, with a cudgel, which, if the impostor had not been too wise to encounter it, would assuredly have descended upon him, to borrow the sublime language of his own epic poem, "like a hammer on the red son of the furnace." (pp. 208-10)

Unhappily, a few months after the appearance of the *Journey to the Hebrides,* Johnson did what none of his envious assailants could have done, and to a certain extent succeeded in writing himself down. The disputes between England and her American colonies had reached a point at which no amicable adjustment was possible. Civil war was evidently impending; and the ministers seem to have thought that the eloquence of Johnson might with advantage be employed to inflame the nation against the opposition here, and against the rebels beyond the Atlantic. He had already written two or three tracts in defence of the foreign and domestic policy of the government; and those tracts, though hardly worthy of him, were much superior to the crowd of pamphlets which lay on the counters of Almon and Stockdale. But his *Taxation No Tyranny* was a pitiable failure. The very title was a silly phrase, which can have been recommended to his choice by nothing but a jingling alliteration which he ought to have despised. The arguments were such as boys use in debating societies. The pleasantry was as awkward as the gambols of a hippopotamus. Even Boswell was forced to own that, in this unfortunate piece, he could detect no trace of his master's powers. The general opinion was that the strong faculties which had produced the *Dictionary* and the *Rambler* were beginning to feel the effect of time and of disease, and that the old man would best consult his credit by writing no more.

But this was a great mistake. Johnson had failed, not because his mind was less vigorous than when he wrote *Rasselas* in the evenings of a week, but because he had foolishly chosen, or suffered others to choose for him, a subject such as he would at no time have been competent to treat. He was in no sense a statesman. He never willingly read or thought or talked about affairs of state. He loved biography, literary history, the history of manners; but political history was positively distasteful to him. The question at issue between the colonies and the mother country was a question about which he had really nothing to say. He failed, therefore, as the greatest men must fail when they attempt to do that for which they are unfit; as Burke would have failed if Burke had tried to write comedies like those of Sheridan; as Reynolds would have failed if Reynolds had tried to paint landscapes like those of Wilson. Happily, Johnson soon had an opportunity of proving most signally that his failure was not to be ascribed to intellectual decay.

On Easter Eve 1777, some persons, deputed by a meeting which consisted of forty of the first booksellers in London, called upon him. Though he had some scruples about doing business at that season, he received his visitors with much civility. They came to inform him that a new edition of the English poets, from Cowley downwards, was in contemplation, and to ask him to furnish short biographical prefaces. He readily undertook the task, a task for which he was pre-eminently qualified. His knowledge of the literary history of England since the Restoration was unrivalled. That knowledge he had derived partly from books, and partly from sources which had long been closed; from old Grub Street traditions; from the talk of forgotten poetasters and pamphleteers who had long been lying in parish vaults; from the recollections of such men as Gilbert

Walmesley, who had conversed with the wits of Button; Cibber, who had mutilated the plays of two generations of dramatists; Orrery, who had been admitted to the society of Swift; and Savage, who had rendered services of no very honourable kind to Pope. The biographer therefore sate down to his task with a mind full of matter. He had at first intended to give only a paragraph to every minor poet, and only four or five pages to the greatest name. But the flood of anecdote and criticism overflowed the narrow channel. The work, which was originally meant to consist only of a few sheets, swelled into ten volumes, small volumes, it is true, and not closely printed. The first four appeared in 1779, the remaining six in 1781.

The Lives of the Poets, are, on the whole, the best of Johnson's works. The narratives are as entertaining as any novel. The remarks on life and on human nature are eminently shrewd and profound. The criticisms are often excellent, and, even when grossly and provokingly unjust, well deserve to be studied. For, however erroneous they may be, they are never silly. They are the judgments of a mind trammelled by prejudice and deficient in sensibility, but vigorous and acute. They therefore generally contain a portion of valuable truth which deserves to be separated from the alloy; and, at the very worst, they mean something, a praise to which much of what is called criticism in our time has no pretensions.

"Savage's Life" Johnson reprinted nearly as it had appeared in 1744. Whoever, after reading that life, will turn to the other lives will be struck by the difference of style. Since Johnson had been at ease in his circumstances he had written little and had talked much. When, therefore, he, after the lapse of years, resumed his pen, the mannerism which he had contracted while he was in the constant habit of elaborate composition was less perceptible than formerly; and his diction frequently had a colloquial ease which it had formerly wanted. The improvement may be discerned by a skilful critic in the *Journey to the Hebrides,* and in the *Lives of the Poets* is so obvious that it cannot escape the notice of the most careless reader.

Among the lives the best are perhaps those of Cowley, Dryden, and Pope. The very worst is, beyond all doubt, that of Gray. (pp. 212-15)

Since his death the popularity of his works—the *Lives of the Poets,* and, perhaps, the "Vanity of Human Wishes," excepted—has greatly diminished. His *Dictionary* has been altered by editors till it can scarcely be called his. An allusion to his *Rambler* or his *Idler* is not readily apprehended in literary circles. The fame even of *Rasselas* has grown somewhat dim. But, though the celebrity of the writings may have declined, the celebrity of the writer, strange to say, is as great as ever. Boswell's book has done for him more than the best of his own books could do. The memory of other authors is kept alive by their works. But the memory of Johnson keeps many of his works alive. The old philosopher is still among us in the brown coat with the metal buttons and the shirt which ought to be at wash, blinking, puffing, rolling his head, drumming with his fingers, tearing his meat like a tiger, and swallowing his tea in oceans. No human being who has been more than seventy years in the grave is so well known to us. And it is but just to say that our intimate acquaintance with what he would himself have called the anfractuosities of his intellect and of his temper serves only to strengthen

our conviction that he was both a great and a good man. (pp. 219-20)

Thomas Babington Macaulay, "Samuel Johnson," in his Critical, Historical and Miscellaneous Essays, *Vol. VI,* Sheldon and Company, *1862, pp. 172-220.*

Leslie Stephen   (essay date 1874)

[*Considered by some as the most important critic of the Victorian age after Matthew Arnold, Stephen has been praised for his intellectual vigor and moral insight and judgment, while others argue that his work was deficient in aesthetic and formal analysis and that he failed to reconcile his moral and historical philosophies. In the following excerpt from an essay originally published in 1874 in the* Cornhill Magazine, *he alleges that Johnson's adherence to eighteenth-century literary conventions render much of his canon "unreadable."*]

In the lives of most eminent men we find much good feeling and honourable conduct; but it is an exception, even in the case of good men, when we find that a life has been shaped by other than the ordinary conventions, or that emotions have dared to overflow the well-worn channels of respectability. The love which we feel for Johnson is due to the fact that the pivots upon which his life turned are invariably noble motives, and not mere obedience to custom. More than one modern writer has expressed a fraternal affection for Addison, and it is justified by the kindly humour which breathes through his *Essays.* But what anecdote of that most decorous and successful person touches our hearts or has the heroic ring of Johnson's wrestlings with adverse fortune? Addison showed how a Christian could die—when his life has run smoothly through pleasant places, secretaryships of state, and marriages with countesses, and when nothing—except a few overdoses of port wine—has shaken his nerves or ruffled his temper. A far deeper emotion rises at the deathbed of the rugged old pilgrim, who has fought his way to peace in spite of troubles within and without, who has been jeered in Vanity Fair and has descended into the Valley of the Shadow of Death, and escaped with pain and difficulty from the clutches of Giant Despair. When the last feelings of such a man are tender, solemn, and simple, we feel ourselves in a higher presence than that of an amiable gentleman who simply died, as he lived, with consummate decorum.

On turning, however, from Johnson's life to his writings, from Boswell to the *Rambler,* it must be admitted that the shock is trying to our nerves. The *Rambler* has, indeed, high merits. The impression which it made upon his own generation proves the fact; for the reputation, however temporary, was not won by a concession to the fashions of the day, but to the influence of a strong judgment uttering itself through uncouth forms. The melancholy which colours its pages is the melancholy of a noble nature. The tone of thought reminds us of Bishop Butler, whose writings, defaced by a style even more tiresome, though less pompous than Johnson's, have owed their enduring reputation to a philosophical acuteness in which Johnson was certainly very deficient. Both of these great men, however, impress us by their deep sense of the evils under which humanity suffers, and their rejection of the superficial optimism of the day. Butler's sadness, undoubtedly, is that of a recluse, and Johnson's that of a man of the world; but the sentiment is fundamentally the same. It may be added, too, that here, as elsewhere, Johnson speaks with the sincerity of a man drawing upon his own experience. He announces himself as a scholar thrust out upon the world rather by necessity than choice; and a large proportion of the papers dwell upon the various sufferings of the literary class. Nobody could speak more feelingly of those sufferings, as no one had a closer personal acquaintance with them. But allowing to Johnson whatever credit is due to the man who performs one more variation on the old theme, *Vanitas vanitatum,* we must in candour admit that the **Rambler** has the one unpardonable fault: it is unreadable.

What an amazing turn it shows for commonplaces! That life is short, that marriages from mercenary motives produce unhappiness, that different men are virtuous in different degrees, that advice is generally ineffectual, that adversity has its uses, that fame is liable to suffer from detraction;—these and a host of other such maxims are of the kind upon which no genius and no depth of feeling can confer a momentary interest. Here and there, indeed, the pompous utterance invests them with an unlucky air of absurdity. 'Let no man from this time,' is the comment in one of his stories, 'suffer his felicity to depend on the death of his aunt.' Every actor, of course, uses the same dialect. A gay young gentleman tells us that he used to amuse his companions by giving them notice of his friends' oddities. 'Every man,' he says, 'has some habitual contortion of body, or established mode of expression, which never fails to excite mirth if it be pointed out to notice. By premonition of these particularities, I secured our pleasantry.' The feminine characters, Flirtillas, and Cleoras, and Euphelias, and Penthesileas, are, if possible, still more grotesque. Macaulay remarks that he wears the petticoat with as ill a grace as Falstaff himself. The reader, he thinks, will cry out with Sir Hugh, 'I like not when a 'oman has a great peard! I spy a great peard under her muffler.' Oddly enough Johnson gives the very same quotation; and goes on to warn his supposed correspondents that Phyllis must send no more letters from the Horse Guards; and that Belinda must 'resign her pretensions to female elegance till she has lived three weeks without hearing the politics of Button's Coffee House.' The Doctor was probably sensible enough of his own defects. And yet there is a still more wearisome set of articles. In emulation of the precedent set by Addison, Johnson indulges in the dreariest of allegories. Criticism, we are told, was the eldest daughter of Labour and Truth, but at last resigned in favour of Time, and left Prejudice and False Taste to reign in company with Fraud and Mischief. Then we have the genealogy of Wit and Learning, and of Satire, the Son of Wit and Malice, and an account of their various quarrels, and the decision of Jupiter. Neither are the histories of such semi-allegorical personages as Almamoulin, the son of Nouradin, or of Anningait and Ayut, the Greenland lovers, much more refreshing to modern readers. That Johnson possessed humour of no mean order, we know from Boswell; but no critic could have divined his power from the clumsy gambols in which he occasionally recreates himself. Perhaps his happiest effort is a dissertation upon the advantage of living in garrets; but the humour struggles and gasps dreadfully under the weight of words. 'There are,' he says, 'some who would continue blockheads' (the Alpine Club was not yet founded), 'even on the

summit of the Andes or the Peak of Teneriffe. But let not any man be considered as unimprovable till this potent remedy has been tried; for perhaps he was found to be great only in a garret, as the joiner of Aretæus was rational in no other place but his own shop.'

How could a man of real power write such unendurable stuff? Or how, indeed, could any man come to embody his thoughts in the style of which one other sentence will be a sufficient example? As it is afterwards nearly repeated, it may be supposed to have struck his fancy. The remarks of the philosophers who denounce temerity are, he says, 'too just to be disputed and too salutary to be rejected; but there is likewise some danger lest timorous prudence should be inculcated till courage and enterprise are wholly repressed and the mind congested in perpetual inactivity by the fatal influence of frigorifick wisdom.' Is there not some danger, we ask, that the mind will be benumbed into perpetual torpidity by the influence of this soporific sapience? It is still true, however, that this Johnsonese, so often burlesqued and ridiculed, was, as far as we can judge, a genuine product. Macaulay says that it is more offensive than the mannerism of Milton or Burke, because it is a mannerism adopted on principle and sustained by constant effort. Facts do not confirm the theory. Milton's prose style seems to be the result of a conscious effort to run English into classical moulds. Burke's mannerism does not appear in his early writings, and we can trace its development from the imitation of Bolingbroke to the last declamation against the Revolution. But Johnson seems to have written Johnsonese from his cradle. In his first original composition, the preface to Father Lobo's *Abyssinia,* the style is as distinctive as in the **Rambler.** The Parliamentary reports in the *Gentleman's Magazine* make Pitt and Fox express sentiments which are probably their own in language which is as unmistakably Johnson's. It is clear that his style, good or bad, was the same from his earliest efforts. It is only in his last book, the **Lives of the Poets,** that the mannerism, though equally marked, is so far subdued as to be tolerable. What he himself called his habit of using 'too big words and too many of them' was no affectation, but as much the result of his special idiosyncrasy as his queer gruntings and twitchings. Sir Joshua Reynolds indeed maintained, and we may believe so attentive an observer, that his strange physical contortions were the result of bad habit, not of actual disease. Johnson, he said, could sit as still as other people when his attention was called to it. And possibly, if he had tried, he might have avoided the fault of making 'little fishes talk like whales.' But how did the bad habits arise? According to Boswell, Johnson professed to have 'formed his style' partly upon Sir W. Temple, and on *Chambers's Proposal for his Dictionary.* The statement was obviously misinterpreted: but there is a glimmering of truth in the theory that the 'style was formed'—so far as those words have any meaning— on the 'giants of the seventeenth century,' and especially upon Sir Thomas Browne. Johnson's taste, in fact, had led him to the study of writers in many ways congenial to him. His favourite book, as we know, was Burton's *Anatomy of Melancholy.* The pedantry of the older school did not repel him; the weighty thought rightly attracted him; and the more complex structure of sentence was perhaps a pleasant contrast to an ear saturated with the Gallicised neatness of Addison and Pope. Unluckily, the secret of the old majestic cadence was hopelessly lost. Johnson, though spiritually akin to the giants, was the firmest ally and subject of the dwarfish dynasty which supplanted them. The very faculty of hearing seems to change in obedience to some mysterious law at different stages of intellectual development; and that which to one generation is delicious music is to another a mere droning of bagpipes or the grinding of monotonous barrel-organs. (pp. 7-13)

In one of the **Ramblers** we are informed that the accent in blank verse ought properly to rest upon every second syllable throughout the whole line. A little variety must, he admits, be allowed to avoid satiety; but all lines which do not go in the steady jog-trot of alternate beats as regularly as the piston of a steam engine, are more or less defective. This simple-minded system naturally makes wild work with the poetry of the 'mighty-mouthed inventor of harmonies.' Milton's harsh cadences are indeed excused on the odd ground that he who was 'vindicating the ways of God to man' might have been condemned for 'lavishing much of his attention upon syllables and sounds.' Moreover, the poor man did his best by introducing sounding proper names, even when they 'added little music to his poem:' an example of this feeble though well-meant expedient being the passage about the moon, which—

> The Tuscan artist views
> At evening, from the top of Fiesole
> Or in Valdarno, to descry new lands, &c.

This profanity passed at the time for orthodoxy. But the misfortune was, that Johnson, unhesitatingly subscribing to the rules of Queen Anne's critics, is always instinctively feeling after the grander effects of the old school. Nature prompts him to the stateliness of Milton, whilst art orders him to deal out long and short syllables alternately, and to make them up in parcels of ten, and then tie the parcels together in pairs by the help of a rhyme. The natural utterance of a man of strong perceptions, but of unwieldy intellect, of a melancholy temperament, and capable of very deep, but not vivacious emotions, would be in stately and elaborate phrases. His style was not more distinctly a work of art than the style of Browne or Milton, but, unluckily, it was a work of bad art. He had the misfortune, not so rare as it may sound, to be born in the wrong century; and is, therefore, a giant in fetters; the amplitude of stride is still there, but it is checked into mechanical regularity. A similar phenomenon is observable in other writers of the time. . . . The form, too, of the **Rambler** is unfortunate. Johnson has always Addison before his eyes; to whom it was formerly the fashion to compare him for the same excellent reason which has recently suggested comparisons between Dickens and Thackeray—namely, that their works were published in the same external shape. Unluckily, Johnson gave too much excuse for the comparison by really imitating Addison. He has to make allegories, and to give lively sketches of feminine peculiarities, and to ridicule social foibles of which he was, at most, a distant observer. The inevitable consequence is, that though here and there we catch a glimpse of the genuine man, we are, generally, too much provoked by the awkwardness of his costume to be capable of enjoying, or even reading him.

In many of his writings, however, Johnson manages, almost entirely, to throw off these impediments. In his deep capacity for sympathy and reverence, we recognise some of the elements that go to the making of a poet. He is always a man of intuitions rather than of discursive intellect; often keen of vision, though wanting in analytical power.

For poetry, indeed, as it is often understood now, or even as it was understood by Pope, he had little enough qualification. He had not the intellectual vivacity implied in the marvellously neat workmanship of Pope, and still less the delight in all natural and artistic beauty which we generally take to be essential to poetic excellence. His contempt for *Lycidas* is sufficiently significant upon that head. Still more characteristic is the incapacity to understand Spenser, which comes out incidentally in his remarks upon some of those imitations, which even in the middle of the eighteenth century showed that sensibility to the purest form of poetry was not by any means extinct amongst us. But there is a poetry, though we sometimes seem to forget it, which is the natural expression of deep moral sentiment; and of this Johnson has written enough to reveal very genuine power. The touching verses upon the death of Levett are almost as pathetic as Cowper; and fragments of the two imitations of Juvenal have struck deep enough to be not quite forgotten. We still quote the lines about pointing a moral and adorning a tale, which conclude a really noble passage. We are too often reminded of his melancholy musings over the

> Fears of the brave and follies of the wise,

and a few of the concluding lines of the **"Vanity of Human Wishes,"** in which he answers the question whether man must of necessity

> Roll darkling down the torrent of his fate,

in helplessness and ignorance, may have something of a familiar ring. We are to give thanks, he says,

> For love, which scarce collective man can fill;
> For patience, sovereign o'er transmuted ill;
> For faith, that, panting for a happier seat,
> Counts death kind nature's signal for retreat;
> These goods for man, the laws of heaven ordain,
> These goods He grants, who grants the power to gain,
> With these celestial wisdom calms the mind,
> And makes the happiness she does not find.

These lines, and many others which might be quoted, are noble in expression, as well as lofty and tender in feeling. Johnson, like Wordsworth, or even more deeply than Wordsworth, had felt all the 'heavy and the weary weight of all this unintelligible world;' and, though he stumbles a little in the narrow limits of his versification, he bears himself nobly, and manages to put his heart into his poetry. Coleridge's paraphrase of the well-known lines, 'Let observation with extensive observation, observe mankind from China to Peru,' would prevent us from saying that he had thrown off his verbiage. He has not the felicity of Goldsmith's 'Traveller,' though he wrote one of the best couplets in that admirable poem; but his ponderous lines show genuine vigour, and can be excluded from poetry only by the help of an arbitrary classification.

The fullest expression, however, of Johnson's feeling is undoubtedly to be found in **Rasselas.** The inevitable comparison with Voltaire's *Candide*, which, by an odd coincidence, appeared almost simultaneously, suggests some curious reflections. The resemblance between the moral of the two books is so strong that, as Johnson remarked, it would have been difficult not to suppose that one had given a hint to the other but for the chronological difficulty. The contrast, indeed, is as marked as the likeness. *Candide* is not adapted for family reading, whereas **Rasselas** might be a textbook for young ladies studying English in a convent. *Candide* is a marvel of clearness and vivacity; whereas to read *Rasselas* is about as exhilarating as to wade knee-deep through a sandy desert. Voltaire and Johnson, however, the great sceptic and the last of the true old Tories, coincide pretty well in their view of the world, and in the remedy which they suggest. The world is, they agree, full of misery, and the optimism which would deny the reality of the misery is childish. *Il faut cultiver notre jardin* is the last word of *Candide,* and Johnson's teaching, both here and elsewhere, may be summed up in the words 'Work, and don't whine.' It need not be considered here, nor, perhaps, is it quite plain, what speculative conclusions Voltaire meant to be drawn from his teaching. The peculiarity of Johnson is, that he is apparently indifferent to any such conclusion. A dogmatic assertion, that the world is on the whole a scene of misery, may be pressed into the service of different philosophies. Johnson asserted the opinion resolutely, both in writing and in conversation, but apparently never troubled himself with any inferences but such as have a directly practical tendency. He was no 'speculatist'—a word which now strikes us as having an American twang, but which was familiar to the lexicographer. His only excursion to the borders of such regions was in the very forcible review of Soane Jenyns, who had made a jaunty attempt to explain the origin of evil by the help of a few of Pope's epigrams. Johnson's sledgehammer smashes his flimsy platitudes to pieces with an energy too good for such a foe. For speculation, properly so called, there was no need. The review, like *Rasselas,* is simply a vigorous protest against the popular attempt to make things pleasant by a feeble dilution of the most watery kind of popular teaching. . . . He was too reverent and cared too little for abstract thought to share the scepticism of Voltaire. In this miserable world the one worthy object of ambition is to do one's duty, and the one consolation deserving the name is to be found in religion. That Johnson's religious opinions sometimes took the form of rather grotesque superstition may be true; and it is easy enough to ridicule some of its manifestations. He took the creed of his day without much examination of the evidence upon which its dogmas rested; but a writer must be thoughtless indeed who should be more inclined to laugh at his superficial oddities, than to admire the reverent spirit and the brave self-respect with which he struggled through a painful life. The protest of *Rasselas* against optimism is therefore widely different from the protest of Voltaire. The deep and genuine feeling of the Frenchman is concealed under smart assaults upon the dogmas of popular theology; the Englishman desires to impress upon us the futility of all human enjoyments, with a view to deepen the solemnity of our habitual tone of thought. It is true, indeed, that the evil is dwelt upon more forcibly than the remedy. The book is all the more impressive. We are almost appalled by the gloomy strength which sees so forcibly the misery of the world and rejects so unequivocally all the palliatives of sentiment and philosophy. The melancholy is intensified by the ponderous style, which suggests a man weary of a heavy burden. The air seems to be filled with what Johnson once called 'inspissated gloom.' *Rasselas,* one may say, has a narrow escape of being a great book, though it is ill calculated for the hasty readers of today. Indeed, the defects are serious enough. The class of writing to which it belongs demands a certain dramatic picturesqueness to point the moral effectively. Not only the long-winded sentences, but the slow evolution of thought and the deliberation with which he works out his pictures of misery, makes the general effect dull beside such books as *Candide* or *Gulliver's Travels.* A touch of epigrammatic exaggeration is very much needed; and yet anybody who has the courage to read it through will admit that Johnson is not an unworthy guide into those gloomy regions of imagination which we all visit sometimes, and which it is as well to visit in good company. (pp. 13-20)

Johnson's political pamphlets, besides the defects natural to a writer who was only a politician by accident, advocate the most retrograde doctrines. Nobody at the present day thinks that the Stamp Act was an admirable or justifiable measure; or would approve of telling the Americans that they ought to have been grateful for their long exemption instead of indignant at the imposition. 'We do not put a calf into the plough; we wait till he is an ox'—was not a judicious taunt. He was utterly wrong; and, if everybody who is utterly wrong in a political controversy deserves unmixed contempt, there is no more to be said for him. We might indeed argue that Johnson was in some ways entitled to the sympathy of enlightened people. His hatred of the Americans was complicated by his hatred of slaveowners. He anticipated Lincoln in proposing the emancipation of the negroes as a military measure. His uniform hatred for the slave trade scandalised poor Boswell, who held that its abolition would be equivalent to 'shutting the gates of mercy on mankind.' His language about the blundering tyranny of the English rule in Ireland would satisfy Mr. Froude, though he would hardly have loved a Home Ruler. He denounces the frequency of capital punishment and the harshness of imprisonment for debt, and he invokes a compassionate treatment of the outcasts of our streets as warmly as the more sentimental Goldsmith. His conservatism may be at times obtuse, but it is never of the cynical variety. He hates cruelty and injustice as righteously as he hates anarchy. Indeed, Johnson's contempt for mouthing agitators of the Wilkes and Junius variety is one which may be shared by most thinkers who would not accept his principles. There is a vigorous passage in the *False Alarm* which is scarcely unjust to the patriots of the day. He describes the mode in which petitions are generally got up. They are sent from town to town, and the people flock to see what is to be sent to the King. 'One man signs because he hates the Papists; another because he has vowed destruction to the turnpikes; one because it will vex the parson; another because he owes his landlord nothing; one because he is rich; another because he is poor; one to show that he is not afraid, and another to show that he can write.' The people, he thinks, are as well off as they are likely to be under any form of government; and grievances about general warrants or the rights of juries in libel cases are not really felt so long as they have enough to eat and drink and wear. The error, we may probably say, was less in the contempt for a very shallow agitation than in the want of perception that deeper causes of discontent were accumulating in the background. Wilkes in himself was a worthless demagogue; but Wilkes was the straw carried by the rising tide of revolutionary sentiment, to which Johnson was entirely blind. Yet whatever we may think of his political philosophy, the value of these solid sturdy prejudices is undeniable. To the fact that Johnson was the typical representative of a large class of Englishmen, we owe it that the Society of Rights did not develop into a Jacobin Club. The fine phrases on which Frenchmen became intoxicated never turned the heads of men impervious to abstract theories and incapable of dropping substances for shadows. There are evils in each temperament; but it is as well that some men should carry into politics that rooted contempt for whining which lay so deep in Johnson's nature. . . . His incapacity for speculation makes his pamphlets worthless beside Burke's philosophical discourses; but the treatment, if wrong and defective on the theoretical side, is never contemptible. Here, as elsewhere, he judges by his intuitive aversions. He rejects too hastily whatever seems insipid or ill-flavoured to his spiritual appetite. Like all the shrewd and sensible part of mankind, he condemns as mere moonshine what may be really the first faint dawn of a new daylight. But then his intuitions are noble, and his fundamental belief is the vital importance of order, of religion, and of morality, coupled with a profound conviction, surely not erroneous, that the chief sources of human suffering lie far deeper than any of the remedies proposed by constitution-mongers and fluent theorists. The literary version of these prejudices or principles is given most explicitly in the **Lives of the Poets**—the book which is now the most readable of Johnson's performances, and which most frequently recalls his conversational style. Indeed, it is a thoroughly admirable book, and but for one or two defects might enjoy a much more decided popularity. It is full of shrewd sense and righteous as well as keen estimates of men and things. The **"Life of Savage,"** written in earlier times, is the best existing portrait of that large class of authors who, in Johnson's phrase, 'hung loose upon society' in the days of the Georges. The **Lives** of Pope, Dryden, and others have scarcely been superseded, though much fuller information has since come to light; and they are all well worth reading. But the criticism, like the politics, is woefully out of date. Johnson's division between the shams and the realities deserves all respect in both cases, but in both cases he puts many things on the wrong side of the dividing line. His hearty contempt for sham pastorals and sham love-poetry will be probably shared by modern readers. 'Who will hear of sheep and goats and myrtle bowers and purling rivulets through five acts? Such scenes please barbarians in the dawn of literature, and children in the dawn of life, but will be for the most part thrown away as men grow wise and nations grow learned.' But elsewhere he blunders into terrible misapprehensions. Where he errs by simply repeating the accepted rules of the Pope school, he for once talks mere second-hand nonsense. But his independent judgments are interesting even when erroneous. His unlucky assault upon *Lycidas,* already noticed, is generally dismissed with a pitying shrug of the shoulders. 'Among the flocks and copses and flowers appear the heathen deities; Jove and Phœbus, Neptune and Æolus, with a long train of mythological imagery, such as a college easily supplies. Nothing can less display knowledge, or less exercise invention, than to tell how a shepherd has lost his companions, and must now feed his flocks alone; how one god asks another god what has become of Lycidas, and how neither god can tell. He who thus grieves can excite no sympathy; he who thus praises will confer no honour.' (pp. 22-6)

Lycidas repelled Johnson by incongruities, which, from his point of view, were certainly offensive. Most modern readers, I will venture to suggest, feel the same annoyances, though they have not the courage to avow them freely. If poetry is to be judged exclusively by the simplici-ty and force with which it expresses sincere emotion, *Lycidas* would hardly convince us of Milton's profound sorrow for the death of King, and must be condemned accordingly. To the purely pictorial or musical effects of a poem Johnson was nearly blind; but that need not suggest a doubt as to the sincerity of his love for the poetry which came within the range of his own sympathies. Every critic is in effect criticising himself as well as his author; and I confess that to my mind an obviously sincere record of impressions, however one-sided they may be, is infinitely refreshing, as revealing at least the honesty of the writer. . . . If Johnson's blunder in this case implied sheer stupidity, one can only say that honest stupidity is a much better thing than clever insincerity or fluent repetition of second-hand dogmas. But, in fact, this dislike of *Lycidas,* and a good many instances of critical incapacity might be added, is merely a misapplication of a very sound principle. The hatred of cant and humbug and affectation of all vanity is a most salutary ingredient even in poetical criticism. Johnson, with his natural ignorance of that historical method, the exaltation of which threatens to become a part of our contemporary cant, made the pardonable blunder of supposing that what would have been gross affectation in Gray must have been affectation in Milton. His ear had been too much corrupted by the contemporary school to enable him to recognise beauties which would even have shone through some conscious affectation. He had the rare courage—for, even then, Milton was one of the tabooed poets—to say what he thought as forcibly as he could say it; and he has suffered the natural punishment of plain speaking. It must, of course, be admitted that a book embodying such principles is doomed to become more or less obsolete, like his political pamphlets. And yet, as significant of the writer's own character, as containing many passages of sound judgment, expressed in forcible language, it is still, if not a great book, really impressive within the limits of its capacity. (pp. 27-8)

[We] frequently meet touches of the conversational Johnson in his controversial writing. *Taxation no Tyranny* is at moments almost as pithy as Swift, though the style is never so simple. The celebrated **"Letter to Chesterfield,"** and the letter in which he tells MacPherson that he will not be 'deterred from detecting what he thinks a cheat by the menaces of a ruffian,' are as good specimens of the smashing repartee as anything in Boswell's reports. Nor, indeed, does his pomposity sink to mere verbiage so often as might be supposed. It is by no means easy to translate his ponderous phrases into simple words without losing some of their meaning. The structure of the sentences is compact, though they are too elaborately balanced and stuffed with superfluous antitheses. The language might be simpler, but it is not a mere sham aggregation of words. His written style, however faulty in other respects, is neither slipshod nor ambiguous, and passes into his conversational style by imperceptible degrees. The radical identity is intelligible, though the superficial contrast is certainly curious. We may perhaps say that his century, unfavourable to him as a writer, gave just what he required for talking. . . . His greatest literary effort, the **Dictionary,** has of necessity become antiquated in use, and, in spite of the intellectual vigour indicated, can hardly be commended for popular reading. And thus but for the inimitable Boswell, it must be admitted that Johnson would probably have sunk very deeply into oblivion. A few good sayings would have been preserved by Mrs. Thrale and others, or have been handed down by tradition, and doubtless assigned in process of time to Sydney Smith and other conversational celebrities. A few couplets from the **"Vanity of Human Wishes"** would not yet have been submerged, and curious readers would have recognised the power of **Rasselas,** and been delighted with some shrewd touches in the **Lives of the Poets.** But with all desire to magnify critical insight, it must be admitted that that man would have shown singular penetration, and been regarded as an eccentric commentator, who had divined the humour and the fervour of mind which lay hid in the remains of the huge lexicographer. And yet when we have once recognised his power, we can see it everywhere indicated in his writings, though by an unfortunate fatality the style or the substance was always so deeply affected by the faults of the time, that the product is never thoroughly sound. His tenacious conservatism caused him to cling to decaying materials for the want of anything better, and he has suffered the natural penalty. He was a great force half wasted, so far as literature was concerned, because the fashionable costume of the day hampered the free exercises of his powers, and because the only creeds to which he could attach himself were in the phase of decline and inanition. A century earlier or later he might have succeeded in expressing himself through books as well as through his talk; but it is not given to us to choose the time of our birth, and some very awkward consequences follow. (pp. 30-2)

Leslie Stephen, "Dr. Johnson's Writings," in his Hours in a Library, Vol. II, *revised edition, G. P. Putnam's Sons, 1899, pp. 1-32.*

Matthew Arnold   (essay date 1878)

[*A poet and commentator on the social and moral life in Victorian England, Arnold is considered one of the most important English critics of the nineteenth century—although essentially regarded as an apologist for literary criticism. In all critical activities he advocated the doctrine of "disinterestedness" which stressed flexibility, curiosity, and a non-utilitarian approach to culture and art. He believed that the critic should judge a work of art according to its own qualities, unbiased by the influence of history and the limitations of subjective experience. In the following excerpt from an essay originally published in* Macmillan's Magazine *in 1878, Arnold defines the value of Johnson's* Lives of the Poets *as "admirably fitted to serve as . . . a fixed and thoroughly known centre of departure and return to the student of English literature."*]

If we could but take, I have said to myself, the most important of the lives in Johnson's [*Lives of the Poets*], and leave out all the rest, what a text-book we should have! The volumes at present are a work to stand in a library, "a work which no gentleman's library should be without." But we want to get from them a text-book, to be in the hands of every one who desires even so much as a general acquaintance with English literature;—and so much acquaintance as this who does not desire? The work as Johnson published it is not fitted to serve as such a textbook; it is too extensive, and contains the lives of many poets quite insignificant. Johnson supplied lives of all whom the booksellers proposed to include in their collection of Brit-

ish Poets; he did not choose the poets himself, although he added two or three to those chosen by the booksellers. Whatever Johnson did in the department of literary biography and criticism possesses interest and deserves our attention. But in his *Lives of the Poets* there are six of preeminent interest; the lives of six men who, while the rest in the collection are of inferior rank, stand out as names of the first class in English literature—Milton, Dryden, Swift, Addison, Pope, Gray. These six writers differ among themselves, of course, in power and importance, and every one can see, that, if we were following certain modes of literary classification, Milton would have to be placed on a solitary eminence far above any of them. But if, without seeking a close view of individual differences, we form a large and and liberal first class among English writers, all these six personages—Milton, Dryden, Swift, Addison, Pope, Gray—must, I think, be placed in it. Their lives cover a space of more than a century and a half, from 1608, the year of Milton's birth, down to 1771, the date of the death of Gray. Through this space of more than a century and a half the six lives conduct us. We follow the course of what Warburton well calls "the most agreeable subject in the world, which is literary history," and follow it in the lives of men of letters of the first class. And the writer of their lives is himself, too, a man of letters of the first class. Malone calls Johnson "the brightest ornament of the eighteenth century." He is justly to be called, at any rate, a man of letters of the first class, and the greatest power in English letters during the eighteenth century. And in these characteristic lives, not finished until 1781, and "which I wrote," as he himself tells us, "in my usual way, dilatorily and hastily, unwilling to work and working with vigour and haste," we have Johnson mellowed by years, Johnson in his ripeness and plenitude, treating the subject which he loved best and knew best. Much of it he could treat with the knowledge and sure tact of a contemporary; even from Milton and Dryden he was scarcely further separated than our generation is from Burns and Scott. Having all these recommendations, his *Lives of the Poets* do indeed truly stand for what Boswell calls them, "the work which of all Dr. Johnson's writings will perhaps be read most generally and with most pleasure." And in the lives of the six chief personages of the work, the lives of Milton, Dryden, Swift, Addison, Pope, and Gray, we have its very kernel and quintessence; we have the work relieved of whatever is less significant, retaining nothing which is not highly significant, brought within easy and convenient compass, and admirably fitted to serve as a *point de repère,* a fixed and thoroughly known centre of departure and return, to the student of English literature.

I know of no such first-rate piece of literature, for supplying in this way the wants of the literary student, existing at all in any other language; or existing in our own language, for any period except the period which Johnson's six lives cover. A student cannot read them without gaining from them, consciously or unconsciously, an insight into the history of English literature and life. He would find great benefit, let me add, from reading in connection with each biography something of the author with whom it deals; the first two books, say, of *Paradise Lost,* in connection with the life of Milton; *Absalom and Achitophel,* and the *Dedication to the Æneis,* in connection with the life of Dryden; in connection with Swift's life, the *Battle of the Books;* with Addison's, the *Coverley Papers;* with Pope's, the imitations of the *Satires* and *Epistles* of Horace. The *Elegy in a Country Churchyard* everybody knows, and will have it present to his mind when he reads the life of Gray. But of the other works which I have mentioned how little can this be said; to how many of us are Pope and Addison and Dryden and Swift, and even Milton himself, mere names, about whose date and history and supposed characteristics of style we may have learnt by rote something from a handbook, but of the real men and of the power of their works we know nothing! From Johnson's biographies the student will get a sense of what the real men were, and with this sense fresh in his mind he will find the occasion propitious for acquiring also, in the way pointed out, a sense of the power of their works. (pp. 189-95)

The [lives of these six poets] cover a period of literary and intellectual movement in which we are all profoundly interested. It is the passage of our nation to prose and reason; the passage to a type of thought and expression, modern, European, and which on the whole is ours at the present day, from a type antiquated, peculiar, and which is ours no longer. The period begins with a prose like this of Milton: "They who to states and governors of the commonwealth direct their speech, high court of parliament! or wanting such access in a private condition, write that which they foresee may advance the public good; I suppose them, if at the beginning of no mean endeavour, not a little altered and moved inwardly in their minds." It ends with a prose like this of Smollett: "My spirit began to accommodate itself to my beggarly fate, and I became so mean as to go down towards Wapping, with an intention to inquire for an old schoolfellow, who, I understood, had got the command of a small coasting vessel then in the river, and implore his assistance." These are extreme instances; but they give us no unfaithful notion of the change in our prose between the reigns of Charles I. and of George III. Johnson has recorded his own impression of the extent of the change and of its salutariness. Boswell gave him a book to read, written in 1702 by the English chaplain of a regiment stationed in Scotland. "It is sad stuff, sir," said Johnson, after reading it; "miserably written, as books in general then were. There is now an elegance of style universally diffused. No man now writes so ill as Martin's *Account of the Hebrides* is written. A man could not write so ill if he should try. Set a merchant's clerk now to write, and he'll do better." (pp. 200-02)

[The] century so well represented by Dryden, Addison, Pope, and Swift, and of which the literary history is so powerfully written by Johnson in his lives, is a century of prose—a century of which the great work in literature was the formation of English prose. Johnson was himself a labourer in this great and needful work, and was ruled by its influences. His blame of genuine poets like Milton and Gray, his over-praise of artificial poets like Pope, are to be taken as the utterances of a man who worked for an age of prose, who was ruled by its influences, and could not but be ruled by them. Of poetry he speaks as a man whose sense for that with which he is dealing is in some degree imperfect.

Yet even on poetry Johnson's utterances are valuable, because they are the utterances of a great and original man. That indeed he was; and to be conducted by such a man through an important century cannot but do us good, even though our guide may in some places be less competent than in others. Johnson was the man of an age of prose. Furthermore, he was a strong force of conservation and concentration, in an epoch which by its natural tendencies seemed moving towards expansion and freedom. But he was a great man, and great men are always instructive. The more we study him, the higher will be our esteem for the power of his mind, the width of his interests, the largeness of his knowledge, the freshness, fearlessness, and strength of his judgments. The higher, too, will be our esteem for his character. His well-known lines on Levett's death, beautiful and touching lines, are still more beautiful and touching because they recall a whole history of Johnson's goodness, tenderness, and charity. Human dignity, on the other hand, he maintained, we all know how well, through the whole long and arduous struggle of his life, from his servitor days at Oxford, down to the *Jam moriturus* of his closing hour. His faults and strangenesses are on the surface, and catch every eye. But on the whole we have in him a good and admirable type, worthy to be kept in our view for ever, of "the ancient and inbred integrity, piety, good-nature and good-humour of the English people." (pp. 216-18)

Matthew Arnold, "Johnson's 'Lives,'" in his Essays in Criticism, third series, *The Ball Publishing Co., 1910, pp. 183-219.*

Edmund Gosse   (essay date 1888)

[*Gosse was an English translator and critic of Scandinavian literature who was responsible for introducing Henrik Ibsen's "new drama" to English audiences. His other works include studies of John Donne, Thomas Gray, Sir Thomas Browne, and important early articles on French authors of the late nineteenth century. Largely viewed as a popularizer, much of his commentary lacks depth and is not considered in the first rank of modern critical thought, but his broad interests and knowledge of foreign literatures lend his works much more than a documentary value. In the following excerpt from a work originally published in 1888, Gosse provides a critical chronology of Johnson's writings.*]

All that [Bishop William] Warburton fancied himself to be, Dr. Samuel Johnson was. In the person of this ever-fascinating hero of the world of books we find the dictator of letters, the tyrant over the consciences of readers, that the militant bishop of Gloucester was too ready to conceive himself to be. Johnson holds a place in some respects unique in literature. Other writers, however sympathetic or entertaining their personal characters may have been, live mainly in their works; we read about them with delight, because we have studied what they wrote. But with Johnson it is not so. If we knew nothing about his career or character, if we had to judge him solely by the works he published, our interest in him would shrink to very moderate proportions. Swift and Pope, Berkeley and Gray, Burke and Fielding, have contributed more than Johnson to the mere edifice of English literature. But, with the exception of Swift, there is no one in the eighteenth century who can pretend to hold so high a place as a man of letters. The happy accident by which he secured the best of all biographers is commonly taken to account for this fact, but the character, the wit, the vigour, must have first existed to stimulate a Boswell and to entrance generation after generation. The fact is that Johnson's indolence and the painful weight of his physical temperament prevented his literary powers from being fully expressed in the usual way; but they were there, and they found a vehicle in speech at the dinner-table or from his tavern-throne. He talked superb literature freely for thirty years, and all England listened; he grew to be the centre of literary opinion, and he was so majestic in intellect, so honest in purpose, so kind and pure in heart, so full of humour and reasonable sweetness and yet so trenchant, and at need so grim, that he never sank to be the figure-head of a clique, nor ever lost the balance of sympathy with readers of every rank and age. His influence was so wide, and withal so wholesome, that literary life in this country has never been since his day what it was before it. He has made the more sordid parts of its weakness shameful, and he has raised a standard of personal conduct that every one admits. He was a gruff old bear, "Ursa Major," but it would surely be hard to find the man or woman, whose opinion is worth having, who does love almost more than revere the memory of Sam Johnson. (pp. 282-83)

[In] 1735 he performed a piece of hack-work for a Birmingham bookseller, *A Voyage to Abyssinia,* from a French abridgment of Father Lobo's Portuguese travels. The anonymous preface to this translation is Johnson's earliest original publication. This preface is written in a very characteristic style, though not, as has been carelessly stated, in his more pompous manner. (p. 283)

From this time, for twenty years, Johnson was more or less dependent for support on the labours of his pen, and the iron entered deeply into his soul. He suffered from a physical inability to prolong the effort of writing, and he absolutely required leisurely intervals of repose and meditation. Hence, even when employment was abundant, he often failed to take full advantage of it, and not less often the work he did gave dissatisfaction to his stupid taskmasters. As a schoolmaster he had already failed because he had "the character of being a very haughty, ill-natured gent, and had such a way of distorting his face" that it frightened the lads. (p. 284)

In May of [1738] S. J. published, in folio, an imitation of the Third Satire of Juvenal, under the title **"London,"** for which he received ten guineas. This poem, though to be somewhat eclipsed by a later success, enjoyed the favour of the town. It was a vigorous but certainly not an inspired study in heroic couplets in the manner of Pope, who was still before the public as a living force, one of whose satires appeared on the very same day as **"London."** The latter poem is not always marked by the author's later seriousness of purpose; Johnson affects in it to scorn and puff away the city which he had really learned to find already indispensable, and which he was presently to love with passion. After the thirty-fourth line the sentiments of **"London"** are placed in the mouth of "indignant Thales," in whom the person of Savage has been usually recognised; he is represented as seeking retirement in Wales. There is pathos in the nervous lines in which the poet expresses the misery of those who, poor and enlightened, are obliged to endure the insolence of blockheads. Johnson, here at least, speaks from the heart, and not less when he asks the question, "When can starving merit find a home?" The Orgilis passage is the best in the poem, which only extends to about two hundred and sixty lines.

Two trifling publications belong to the year 1739, *The Complete Vindication,* an ironical defence of the licensers for suppressing Brooke's tragedy of *Gustavus Vasa,* and a satire, ***Marmor Norfolciense,*** for which latter it was absurdly rumoured afterwards that Johnson suffered a state prosecution. For the next four years he was busy in writing out the reports of the parliamentary debates for *The Gentleman's Magazine,* under the transparent disguise of **"Debates in Magna Lilliputia."** . . . *The Account of the Life of Mr. Richard Savage* appeared in 1744; it is the longest and most elaborate of Johnson's essays in biography, and may still be read with great pleasure, in spite of various patent faults. It recounted, with all detail, a scandal, into the truth of which Johnson had not taken the pains to inquire; it was but careless in the statement of facts which lay easily within the writer's circle of experience; and it treated with extreme indulgence a character which, in a stranger, would have called down the moralist's sternest reproof. The critical passages now escape censure only because so few in the present day read the works examined. But the little book was undeniably lively; it contained several anecdotes admirably narrated, and its graver parts displayed the development of Johnson's studied magnificence of language. Good biography was still rare in England, and *The Account of Savage* attracted a great deal of notice. (pp. 284-86)

In 1745 he printed a pamphlet on ***Macbeth,*** and in 1747 the prospectus of a vast scheme which he had formed, that of an English Dictionary, on a scale hitherto unattempted. He dedicated his ***Plan of a Dictionary*** to Lord Chesterfield, who sent him ten pounds, and then took no further interest in the matter, to his own lasting misfortune. For eight years no more was heard of this projected work. In 1748 Johnson spent a short holiday at Hampstead, where he wrote his longest and best poem, **"The Vanity of Human Wishes,"** published in 1749. This is a study in heroic verse, like **"London,"** but it extends to another hundred lines, and is, moreover, a much finer and more accomplished production. It is an imitation of the Tenth Satire of Juvenal, and is written in a very grave and even melancholy vein, though without unseemly bitterness. It was not much liked when it appeared; Garrick declared it was "as hard as Greek." The public had become accustomed to a thinner and smarter kind of satire, to the lucid snip-snap of the immediate followers of Pope, and **"The Vanity of Human Wishes"** was voted obscure. It is certainly weighted with thought, and the closeness with which the Latin original is followed gives a certain tightness of phrase, the result of a meritorious concentration. But it is perhaps the most Roman poem in the language, the one which best reflects the moral grandeur of Latin feeling and reflection; and it has contributed more familiar quotations to the language than any other work of Johnson's. Such a passage as the following gives a very favourable notion of Johnson as a didactic poet:

On what foundation stands the warrior's pride,
How just his hopes, let Swedish Charles decide;
A frame of adamant, a soul of fire,
No dangers fright him and no labours tire;
O'er love, o'er fear, extends his wide domain,
Unconquer'd Lord of passion and of pain;
No joys to him pacific sceptres yield,
War sounds the trump, he rushes to the field;
Behold surrounding kings their power combine,
And one capitulate, and one resign;

Peace courts his hand, but spreads her charms in vain,
'Think nothing gained,' he cries, 'till nought remain;—
On Moscow's walls till Gothic standards fly,
And all be mine beneath the polar sky.'
The march begins in military state,
And nations on his eye suspended wait;
Stern Famine guards the solitary coast,
And Winter barricades the realms of Frost;
He comes, nor want nor cold his course delay,—
Hide, blushing glory, hide Pultowa's day.

A pleasing incident now broke into the monotony of Johnson's gray and laborious existence. His old pupil, David Garrick, had risen into success more rapidly than Johnson had, and was now manager of Drury Lane Theatre. When he was keeping school at Edial Hall, in 1736, Johnson had written a blank verse tragedy on a Turkish subject, but had vainly attempted, in later years, to get it acted. Garrick loyally determined that he would produce it, and after some obstinate struggles with the author, who could not be brought to yield willingly to any stage requirements, *Mahomet and Irene* was acted on the 6th February 1749. Johnson was present, and did not, on this occasion, "suspend the soft solicitudes of dress." He gained nearly £300 by the play, which, however, did not run for more than nine nights, and was never revived. Garrick had introduced the incident of Irene's being strangled on the stage, and to Johnson's mingled mortification and satisfaction, the audience hissed and called out "Murder! murder!" In future, on the stage, as in the printed play, the heroine was forced out by the mutes, crying for mercy, and was seen no more. The tragedy was presently published under the title of *Irene.* Johnson's solitary play labours under the disadvantage of being perfectly uninteresting. It was founded on a tragedy, by one Charles Goring, that had been acted at Drury Lane forty years before; there was no plot worth mentioning, no development of characters, no bustle or intrigue. The conduct of the speeches and the versification is closely modelled on that of the sentimental tragic poet Rowe, whose plays had been popular in Johnson's early youth; what Johnson said of Rowe's plays, long afterwards, might be repeated almost verbally as a criticism of *Irene.* The most amusing thing about the whole incident of this play is Johnson's odd remark to Garrick about the white stockings of the actresses.

Posterity is more ready to realise the Sage in the character of "a majestic teacher of moral and religious wisdom" than as one whose scarlet waistcoat fluttered the dovecotes of Drury Lane. Since the days of Addison and Steele, or since, to be more exact, the *Guardian* of 1713, there had been made many attempts to rival the great social newspapers of the reign of Anne. But none of these had been successful, and Johnson, finding himself now moderately famous, determined to issue a new periodical. It was difficult to find a name; but one night he sat down on his bed, and determined not to go to sleep till he had thought of a title. The *Rambler* occurred to him at last, and he sank to rest contented. On the 20th of March 1750 the first number of this little newspaper appeared, and it closed on the 14th of March 1752. The death of his wife, a few days after the latter date, has been given as the cause of Johnson's discontinuance of a periodical of which he was probably weary. He wrote the *Rambler* unaided, with the exception of five numbers—of these one was written by Richardson; two by Elizabeth Carter (1717-1806), the translator of Epictetus; one by Hester Mulso, better

known as Mrs. Chapone (1727-1801); and one by Catherine Talbot (1720-1770). These ladies deserve mention, not merely as dear and lifelong friends of Johnson, but as apt disciples of his moral manner. Johnson's authorship was at first kept secret, but his style was now familiar to careful readers, and was promptly recognised. The publisher complained that "the encouragement as to sale" was not in proportion "to the raptures expressed by the few that did read it." The *Rambler* is "too wordy," as the author confessed; he tried to be a little lighter in manner in the twenty-nine papers he contributed in 1752 and 1753 to Hawkesworth's *Adventurer,* and somewhat later we shall be called, in describing the *Idler,* to speak of him as a periodical writer at his best.

Meanwhile the mighty *Dictionary* had been slowly progressing, and in April 1755 it was published in two folio volumes. It hardly belongs to literature, except in connection with two short essays, in which Johnson shows himself at his best as a prose-writer, namely, the dignified and pathetic preface, which can scarcely be read to the close without emotion, and the astonishing letter, on the subject of a patron's duties, which he addressed to Chesterfield on the 7th of February 1755. In these two short compositions, in each of which the author is singularly moved, his English, though always stately and formal, is lifted out of the sesquipedalian affectation of magnificence which has amused the world so much, and which was beyond question a serious fault of Johnson's style. Here, and especially in the letter to Chesterfield, he is simple, terse, and thrilling, and, as the occasion was a private one, we may take it that in the extraordinary fire and pungency of the sentences we have something like a specimen of that marvellous power in conversation which made Johnson the wonder of his age. (pp. 286-89)

There is something of the same brightness and ease in the papers of the *Idler,* a series of essays published by Johnson from the 15th of April 1758 to the 5th of April 1760 in a newspaper called the *Universal Chronicle.* He took less trouble with his *Idlers* than with his *Ramblers,* and the result is more pleasing. Johnson as an essayist is most happy when he analyses a character, in the manner of La Bruyère, mingling criticism with narrative; the best example is the sketch of Dick Minim. He possessed shrewdness, judgment, singular knowledge of human nature, and plentiful wit; somehow all these qualities, though fused by his literary genius, did not quite produce a great essayist.

Perhaps it might be said that the best of Johnson's *Idlers* was the long apologue which appeared in book form while he was publishing his shorter weekly essays. The agreeable story of *The Prince of Abyssinia* (known from the seventh edition onwards by the name of its hero, *Rasselas*) was composed in the evenings of one week, to defray the expenses of his mother's funeral and to pay her debts. He received one hundred pounds as the first payment for this book, which appeared in April 1759, about three weeks after Voltaire's *Candide.* Johnson was interested in this latter fact, and said that "If they had not been published so closely one after the other . . . it would have been in vain to deny that the scheme of that which came latest was taken from the other." The resemblance, however, appears somewhat slight to a modern reader; Johnson has all the advantage in health and profundity, Voltaire in wit and intellectual daring. *Rasselas* is not a brilliant ro-

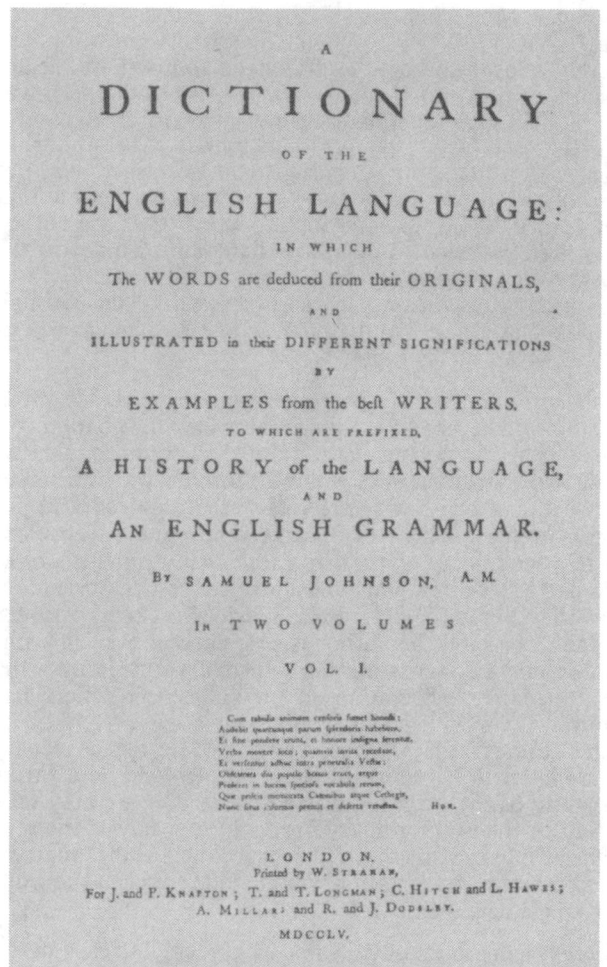

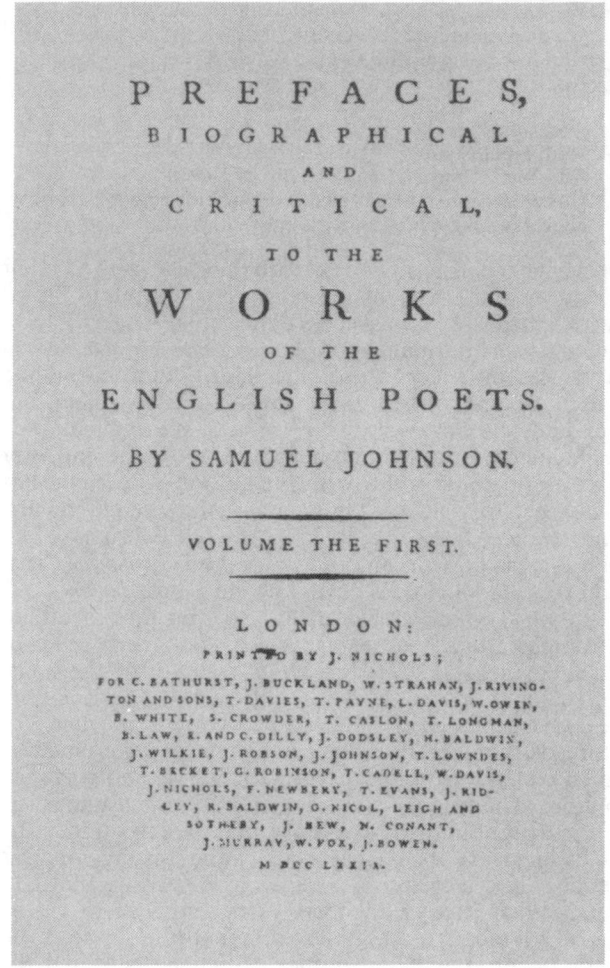

Title page of the first edition of Johnson's Dictionary *(1755) and* Prefaces, Biographical and Critical to the Works of the English Poets *(vol. 1, 1779).*

mance; the artless young person who flies to it as a story of African adventure will be sadly disappointed. It is a description in measured and elegant prose of how Rasselas became discontented in his Happy Valley, how he fled from it, in company with his sister Nekayah, under the guidance of an old man of infinite resource named Imlac, and how, after some mild and incredible incidents, they resolved to return to Abyssinia. The charm of the book is its humanity, the sweetness and wholesomeness of the long melancholy episodes, the wisdom of the moral reflections and disquisitions; nor is there wanting here and there the gentle sunshine of a sort of half-suppressed humour. *Rasselas* enjoyed an instant success, and was reprinted seven or eight times before Johnson died.

The toilsome part of Johnson's life closed with the publication of the ***Dictionary;*** and with his acceptance of a pension of £300 from the king a few years later he attained positive ease. . . . In 1764 the "Club" was created; among its original members were—besides Johnson—Reynolds, Burke, Goldsmith, and Hawkins. Garrick, C. J. Fox, and Boswell were soon added. To Johnson his semi-presidential chair at the Club was, as he said, "the throne of human felicity," and it was from this social palace that his edicts went forth to the world. He was no lon-

ger anxious to write. He loitered for nine years over a very perfunctory edition of Shakespeare, which finally appeared in 1765. For five years more he was silent, until in 1770 he contributed to the Wilkes controversy a tract, ***The False Alarm,*** on the Tory side. Having once plunged into the giddy waters of political pamphleteering, the old Tory veteran could not induce himself to withdraw. He published in 1771 ***Thoughts on the late Transactions respecting the Falkland Islands,*** which was geographical as well as polemical. In 1774 he attempted to stem the tide then flowing against the court party by a tract entitled ***The Patriot,*** and in 1775 he took the wrong side about America in ***Taxation no Tyranny.*** In 1776 these four treatises were issued in one volume, as ***Political Tracts,*** by S. J. It may be noticed that Johnson's full name appeared on no titlepage during his lifetime. Of the political pamphlets it may be said that they were forcible, but entirely without historical breadth or sympathy. (pp. 290-92)

Late in the year [1774] appeared his ***Journey to the Western Islands,*** which is not to be compared for interest with Boswell's later work on the same theme. It was, however, read with curiosity and respect, for Johnson's reputation was now in its full splendour. In 1775 Oxford made her old disciple an LL.D., and Johnson a few months later entered into controversy with the "foolish and impudent" James Macpherson, whose version of Ossian he regarded with contempt. Johnson properly mistrusted the literary honesty of Macpherson, and openly told him that his book was an imposture in a letter only less famous than the Chesterfield specimen.

Johnson's literary work now seemed to be wellnigh ended, but in 1777 he undertook a labour of biography and criticism, which was perhaps, had he considered his responsibilities, the most arduous he had ever thought of. This is the book usually reprinted as **Lives of the English Poets,** but published in 1779-1781 as **Prefaces, biographical and critical, of the most eminent of the English Poets.** The life of Savage, though too long for the system of the book, was worked in, and so were other lives that Johnson had already written. The poets themselves appeared in sixty-eight volumes, and Johnson's **Lives** in a special edition of four volumes. The selection was arbitrary, although there was no intention of throwing scorn on Chaucer and Spenser by opening the roll of fame with Cowley. This was done merely to suit the convenience of the publisher. The **Lives** are of very various interest and value. Some of the worst are those in which Johnson deals with great men, such as Milton and Gray; some of the best are those in which he allows himself to meditate around very little men, as in the case of Edmund Smith. . . . The book is full of wit and thought, but although a charming companion it is one of the worst of guides. Johnson was a competent critic only within a certain sharply-defined groove.

In 1782 the death of his old dependant, the "useful and companionable" Robert Levett, called forth what is certainly the most tender, and towards close the most admirable of Johnson's minor poems:

> His virtues walked their narrow round,
> Nor made a pause, nor left a void;
> And sure the Eternal Master found
> The single talent well employed.
>
> The busy day, the peaceful night,
> Unfelt, uncounted, glided by;
> His frame was firm, his powers were bright,
> Though now his eightieth year was nigh.
>
> Then with no fiery throbbing pain,
> No cold gradations of decay,
> Death broke at once the vital chain,
> And freed his soul the nearest way.

These stanzas might have been signed by Matthew Arnold, so modern are they in their workmanship. (pp. 292-94)

After Johnson's death every scrap of his manuscript that could be found was printed, his **Prayers and Meditations** in 1785, his **Sermons** in 1788-89, his **Diary in North Wales** in 1816; and in 1791 Boswell set the topstone to the edifice of Johnson's glory by his immortal biography. (pp. 294-95)

> *Edmund Gosse, "Johnson and the Philosophers," in his* A History of Eighteenth Century Literature (1660-1780), *The Macmillan Company, 1924, pp. 273-309.*

Lytton Strachey   (essay date 1906)

[*Strachey was a twentieth-century English literary critic and biographer whose inconoclastic reexaminations of historical figures revolutionized the course of modern biography. In his major biographies,* Eminent Victorians (1918), Queen Victoria (1921), *and* Elizabeth and Essex: A Tragic History (1928), *he disclosed previously overlooked complexities in his subjects' personalities. Scholars regard his literary criticism as incisive and interestingly written and, although he wrote on a wide variety of topics, his discussions of French literature are particularly insightful. In the following excerpt from an essay originally published in the* Independent Review *in 1906, he considers the overall "good quality" of Johnson's criticism in* The Lives of the Poets, *but notes that the individual critical portraits "are never right."*]

No one needs an excuse for re-opening the **Lives of the Poets;** the book is too delightful. It is not, of course, as delightful as Boswell; but who re-opens Boswell? Boswell is in another category; because, as every one knows, when he has once been opened he can never be shut. But, on its different level, the **Lives** will always hold a firm and comfortable place in our affections. After Boswell, it is the book which brings us nearer than any other to the mind of Dr. Johnson. That is its primary import. We do not go to it for information or for instruction, or that our tastes may be improved, or that our sympathies may be widened; we go to it to see what Dr. Johnson thought. Doubtless, during the process, we are informed and instructed and improved in various ways; but these benefits are incidental, like the invigoration which comes from a mountain walk. It is not for the sake of the exercise that we set out; but for the sake of the view. The view from the mountain which is Samuel Johnson is so familiar, and has been so constantly analysed and admired, that further description would be superfluous. It is sufficient for us to recognise that he is a mountain, and to pay all the reverence that is due. In one of Emerson's poems a mountain and a squirrel begin to discuss each other's merits; and the squirrel comes to the triumphant conclusion that he is very much the better of the two, since he can crack a nut, while the mountain can do no such thing. The parallel is close enough between this impudence and the attitude—implied, if not expressed—of too much modern criticism towards the sort of qualities—the easy, indolent power, the searching sense of actuality, the combined command of sanity and paradox, the immovable independence of thought—which went to the making of the **Lives of the Poets.** There is only, perhaps, one flaw in the analogy: that, in this particular instance, the mountain was able to crack nuts a great deal better than any squirrel that ever lived.

That the **Lives** continue to be read, admired, and edited, is in itself a high proof of the eminence of Johnson's intellect; because, as serious criticism, they can hardly appear to the modern reader to be very far removed from the futile. Johnson's æsthetic judgments are almost invariably subtle, or solid, or bold; they have always some good quality to recommend them—except one: they are never right. That is an unfortunate deficiency; but no one can doubt that Johnson has made up for it, and that his wit has saved all. He has managed to be wrong so cleverly, that nobody minds. When Gray, for instance, points the moral to his poem on Walpole's cat with a reminder to the fair that all that glisters is not gold, Johnson remarks that this is 'of no relation to the purpose; if *what glistered* had been *gold, the cat would not have gone into the water; and, if she had, would not less have been drowned.*' Could anything be more ingenious, or more neatly put, or more obviously true? But then, to use Johnson's own phrase, could anything be of less 'relation to the purpose'? It is his wit—and we are speaking, of course, of wit in its widest sense—that has sanctified Johnson's perversities and errors, that has embalmed them for ever, and that has put his book, with all its mass of antiquated doctrine, beyond the reach of time.

For it is not only in particular details that Johnson's criticism fails to convince us; his entire point of view is patently out of date. Our judgments differ from his, not only because our tastes are different, but because our whole method of judging has changed. Thus, to the historian of letters, the *Lives* have a special interest, for they afford a standing example of a great dead tradition—a tradition whose characteristics throw more than one curious light upon the literary feelings and ways which have become habitual to ourselves. Perhaps the most striking difference between the critical methods of the eighteenth century and those of the present day, is the difference in sympathy. The most cursory glance at Johnson's book is enough to show that he judged authors as if they were criminals in the dock, answerable for every infraction of the rules and regulations laid down by the laws of art, which it was his business to administer without fear or favour. Johnson never inquired what poets were trying to do; he merely aimed at discovering whether what they had done complied with the canons of poetry. Such a system of criticism was clearly unexceptionable, upon one condition—that the critic was quite certain what the canons of poetry were; but the moment that it became obvious that the only way of arriving at a conclusion upon the subject was by consulting the poets themselves, the whole situation completely changed. The judge had to bow to the prisoner's ruling. In other words, the critic discovered that his first duty was, not to criticise, but to understand the object of his criticism. That is the essential distinction between the school of Johnson and the school of Sainte-Beuve. No one can doubt the greater width and profundity of the modern method; but it is not without its drawbacks. An excessive sympathy with one's author brings its own set of errors: the critic is so happy to explain everything, to show how this was the product of the age, how that was the product of environment, and how the other was the inevitable result of inborn qualities and tastes—that he sometimes forgets to mention whether the work in question has any value. It is then that one cannot help regretting the Johnsonian black cap.

But other defects, besides lack of sympathy, mar the *Lives of the Poets.* One cannot help feeling that no matter how anxious Johnson might have been to enter into the spirit of some of the greatest of the masters with whom he was concerned, he never could have succeeded. Whatever critical method he might have adopted, he still would have been unable to appreciate certain literary qualities, which, to our minds at any rate, appear to be the most important of all. His opinion of *Lycidas* is well known: he found that poem 'easy, vulgar, and therefore disgusting.' Of the songs in *Comus* he remarks: 'they are harsh in their diction, and

not very musical in their numbers.' He could see nothing in the splendour and elevation of Gray, but 'glittering accumulations of ungraceful ornaments.' The passionate intensity of Donne escaped him altogether; he could only wonder how so ingenious a writer could be so absurd. Such preposterous judgments can only be accounted for by inherent deficiencies of taste; Johnson had no ear, and he had no imagination. These are, indeed, grievous disabilities in a critic. What could have induced such a man, the impatient reader is sometimes tempted to ask, to set himself up as a judge of poetry?

The answer to the question is to be found in the remarkable change which has come over our entire conception of poetry, since the time when Johnson wrote. It has often been stated that the essential characteristic of that great Romantic Movement which began at the end of the eighteenth century, was the re-introduction of Nature into the domain of poetry. Incidentally, it is curious to observe that nearly every literary revolution has been hailed by its supporters as a return to Nature. No less than the school of Coleridge and Wordsworth, the school of Denham, of Dryden, and of Pope, proclaimed itself as the champion of Nature; and there can be little doubt that Donne himself—the father of all the conceits and elaborations of the seventeenth century—wrote under the impulse of a Naturalistic reaction against the conventional classicism of the Renaissance. Precisely the same contradictions took place in France. Nature was the watchword of Malherbe and of Boileau; and it was equally the watchword of Victor Hugo. To judge by the successive proclamations of poets, the development of literature offers a singular paradox. The further it goes back, the more sophisticated it becomes; and it grows more and more natural as it grows distant from the State of Nature. However this may be, it is at least certain that the Romantic revival peculiarly deserves to be called Naturalistic, because it succeeded in bringing into vogue the operations of the external world—'the Vegetable Universe,' as Blake called it—as subject-matter for poetry. But it would have done very little, if it had done nothing more than this. Thomson, in the full meridian of the eighteenth century, wrote poems upon the subject of Nature; but it would be foolish to suppose that Wordsworth and Coleridge merely carried on a fashion which Thomson had begun. Nature, with them, was something more than a peg for descriptive and didactic verse; it was the manifestation of the vast and mysterious forces of the world. The publication of *The Ancient Mariner* is a landmark in the history of letters, not because of its descriptions of natural objects, but because it swept into the poet's vision a whole new universe of infinite and eternal things; it was the discovery of the Unknown. We are still under the spell of *The Ancient Mariner;* and poetry to us means, primarily, something which suggests, by means of words, mysteries and infinitudes. Thus, music and imagination seem to us the most essential qualities of poetry, because they are the most potent means by which such suggestions may be invoked. But the eighteenth century knew none of these things. To Lord Chesterfield and to Pope, to Prior and to Horace Walpole, there was nothing at all strange about the world; it was charming, it was disgusting, it was ridiculous, and it was just what one might have expected. In such a world, why should poetry, more than anything else, be mysterious? No! Let it be sensible; that was enough. (pp. 59-63)

Lytton Strachey, "The Lives of the Poets," in his Books & Characters: French & English, *Chatto and Windus, 1922, pp. 59-64.*

G. K. Chesterton   (essay date 1909)

[*Regarded as one of England's premier men of letters in the first half of the twentieth century, Chesterton is best known today as a colorful bon vivant, a witty essayist, and as the creator of the Father Brown mysteries and the fantasy* The Man Who Was Thursday *(1908). Much of his work reveals a childlike enjoyment of life and reflects his pronounced Anglican and, later, Roman Catholic beliefs. His essays are characterized by their humor, frequent use of paradox, and chatty, rambling style. In the following excerpt from an essay originally published in the* Daily Graphic *in 1909, he attributes Johnson's primary appeal to twentieth-century readers to the directness of his emotionalism.*]

It is possible that there are still people in England who do not adore Dr. Johnson. These persons must be removed, if possible, by persuasion. A short and plain attempt to persuade them must take precedence of subtler questions in every discussion of the great man. Now this old and superficial misunderstanding of Johnson (now nearly extinct) expresses itself in two main popular notions—that he was pedantic and that he was rude. He occasionally was rude; he never was pedantic. He was probably the most unpedantic man that ever lived; certainly you and I are much more pedantic than Dr. Johnson. For pedantry means the worship of dead words; and his words, whether long or short, were always alive. He played long words and short words against each other with impromptu but infallible art. I am far from books, and I quote from memory, but I think that a Scotchman, vexed at the ritual jeers of Johnson against his country, said: "Do you remember that God made Scotland?" Johnson replied promptly: "Sir, you are to remember that he made it for Scotchmen." Then, after a pause, he said in grave meditation: "Comparisons are odious; but God made hell." Now the vague popular opinion of Johnson would concentrate on long words like "comparisons" and "odious", and retain the impression that he was pedantic. It would be just as easy to concentrate on words like "hell" and give the impression that he was vulgar. The only true way of testing the matter is to look at the whole sentence and ask oneself if there is a single word, long or short, out of its place. Johnson was the reverse of pedantic, for he used long words only where they would be effective. Generally it came to this, that he spoke pompously when Boswell spoke flippantly and flippantly when Boswell spoke pompously—a very sound rule. When Boswell confronted him with the brute facts of a lonely tower and a baby, he answered, with distant dignity: "Sir, I should not much like my company." But when Boswell justified some morally backsliding bishop or vicar with that elaborate hash of sophistry and charity which is still used to excuse the rich, Johnson answered him with a few short words, so full of Christianity and common sense that I should not be allowed to print them.

The charge of rudeness is much more real; but about this also an impression still surviving requires a great deal of correction. Taken in conjunction with the charge of pedantry, it has created the image of a bullying schoolmaster, a superior person who thinks himself above good manners. Now Johnson was sometimes insolent, but he was never superior. He was not a despot, but exactly the reverse. It was his sense of the democracy of debate that made him loud and unscrupulous, like a mob. It was exactly because he thought the other men as clever as himself that he sought in desperate cases to bear them down by clamour. Everyone knows the brilliant description of him by one of his best friends: "If his pistol misses fire he knocks you down with the butt of it." But few realise that this is the act of a simple and heroic fellow fighting against a superior force. Johnson was a man of great animal impulsiveness and of irregular temper, but intellectually he was humble. He always went into every conflict with the idea that the other man was as good as he was, and that he might be defeated. His bellowings and bangings of the table were the expressions of a fundamental modesty. We can feel this element, I think, in everything he said, down to those last awful words upon his death-bed, when he spoke of Burke, the one man who had really excited and arrested him, "If I saw him now it would kill me." His fate in these respects has been strange. He has been called the pedant par excellence because he was the one thoroughly unpedantic person of a pedantic age. He has been called a conversational tyrant, because he was the one man of his mental rank who was ready to argue with his inferiors. On the one hand it is often said that he translated English into Johnsonese. But let it be remembered that he was the only man of his time who could translate Johnsonese back into English. Half a hundred critics in that age might have said of a play, "It does not possess sufficient vitality to preserve it from putrefaction", but only Johnson could have said also, "It has not wit enough to keep it sweet." There were numerous great men in the eighteenth century who kept a club or court of dependents, where they had things entirely their own way. I need not prove the point; the greatest satirist of that age has made the image immortal.

> Like Cato gave his little Senate laws,
> And sat attentive to his own applause.

But Johnson was the reverse of attentive to people who were applauding him. Johnson was furiously deaf to people who were contradicting him. So far from being a stately and condescending king like Atticus, Johnson was a kind of Irish member in his own Parliament. All these are but broken and incidental examples; everything about the man rang of reality and honour; he never thought he was right without being ready to give battle; he never thought he was wrong without being ready to ask pardon.

We have all heard enough to fill a book about Dr. Johnson's incivilities. I wish they would compile another book consisting of Dr. Johnson's apologies. There is no better test of a man's ultimate chivalry and integrity than how he behaves when he is wrong; and Johnson behaved very well. He understood (what so many faultlessly polite people do not understand) that a stiff apology is a second insult. He understood that the injured party does not want to be compensated because he has been wronged; he wants to be healed because he has been hurt. Boswell once complained to him in private, explaining that he did not mind asperities while they were alone, but did not like to be torn to pieces in company. He added some idle figure of speech, some simile so trivial that I cannot even remember what it was. "Sir," said Johnson, "that is one of the happiest similes I have ever heard." He did not waste time in formally withdrawing this word with reservations and that word with explanations. Finding that he had given pain, he went out of his way to give pleasure. If he had not known what would irritate Boswell, he knew at least what would soothe him. It is this gigantic realism in Johnson's kindness, the directness of his emotionalism, when he is emotional, that gives him his hold upon generations of living men. There is nothing elaborate about his ethics; he wants to know whether a man, as a fact, is happy or unhappy, is lying or telling the truth. He may seem to be hammering at the brain through long nights of noise and thunder, but he can walk into the heart without knocking. (pp. 118-21)

> G. K. Chesterton, "The Real Dr. Johnson," in his The Common Man, *Sheed and Ward*, 1950, pp. 118-21.

Irving Babbitt   (essay date 1927)

[*Babbitt was one of the founders of the New Humanism movement which arose during the twentieth century's second decade. The New Humanists were strict moralists who adhered to traditional conservative values in reaction to an age of scientific and artistic self-expression. In regard to literature, they believed that the aesthetic qualities of a work of art should be subordinate to its moral purpose. That Babbitt was more a theorist than a literary critic is evident in his several books that propound his concept of humanism which substituted faith in humanity for faith in God. In the following excerpt from an essay originally published in the* Southwest Review *in 1927, he places Johnson's conception of the imagination within a neoclassical framework.*]

As is well known, the imagination was under suspicion during the neo-classical period. This suspicion extended far beyond the bounds of literature in the narrower sense and was variously grounded. Philosophers like Descartes and Spinoza objected to the imagination because it was an obstacle to truth, a truth which, as they conceived it, was to be achieved by abstract reasoning. The imagination was also attacked, especially by Pascal, in the name of religion. According to Pascal, the imagination is a 'proud power,' a 'mistress of error,' which overwhelms the reason in which the philosophers put their trust. Man can hope to escape from the deceits of imagination only by a divine succor, the illumination of grace. The imagination is at times attacked on both rationalistic and religious grounds as, for example, by Malebranche in his *Recherche de la Vérité.*

The hostility of the literary critics of the period to the imagination has somewhat different grounds. Though, like the philosophers, they oppose 'reason' to imagination, by reason they mean not so much abstract reasoning as intuitive good sense. By intuitive good sense one may determine what is normal or 'probable' and so achieve centrality in one's point of view. Imagination, on the other hand, tends to pull one off center. For example, false wit is, according to La Bruyère, eccentric wit; and it is eccentric, because 'it has too much imagination in it.' Dr. Johnson echoes many predecessors when he declares the imagination 'a licentious and vagrant faculty, unsusceptible of limitations, and impatient of restraint.' This distrust of the imagination can be explained historically as a recoil not only from the school of conceits but also from the extravagance of the mediæval type of fiction, as it appears in the romances of chivalry. The neo-classicist was at times all the more hostile to this type of fiction in that he had personally experienced its perils. According to Bishop Percy, Johnson 'when a boy was immoderately fond of reading romances of chivalry and he retained his fondness for them through life . . . . Yet I have heard him attribute to these extravagant fictions that unsettled turn of mind which prevented his ever fixing in any profession.'

A movement looking to the rehabilitation of the imagination got under way in the eighteenth century and gained ground with surprising rapidity in view of the extent of the previous distrust. The important period in this movement is that which extends from the publication of Addison's papers on the imagination in *The Spectator* (1712) to Young's *Conjectures on Original Composition* (1759). It was at this time that the phrase 'creative imagination' or 'creative fancy' began to gain currency. If it could be shown that Dr. Johnson shared this new attitude towards the imagination there might be some justification for affirming with a recent writer that 'he was an important motive force behind that tidal wave of revolt which eventually was to engulf the outworn creed (of neo-classicism).' On the contrary, Johnson displays the full neo-classic suspicion of the imagination, combined at times with a type of suspicion that reminds one of Pascal. On the other hand, he has little or nothing of the distrust of the imagination, based on an overweening faith in abstract reason, that one finds in a Descartes or a Spinoza. As a preliminary to understanding his attitude, one needs to distinguish between two main meanings of the word 'imagination' in the period that preceded him. As used by the philosophers, the word refers to the various impressions of sense or else to a faculty that stores up these impressions. When Hobbes, for example, defines imagination as 'decaying sense,' he is still very close to the conception of fancy (*phantasia*) set forth by Aristotle in his *Psychology*. The literary critics, on the other hand, often use the word imagination in a sense that derives, not from Aristotle's *Psychology*, but from his *Poetics*. Aristotle, it will be remembered, does not employ the word 'fancy' or 'imagination' at all in the *Poetics*. What the neo-classic critic was later to call imagination he there describes as 'fable' or 'myth' or 'fiction.' The right relationship, according to Aristotle, between the truth that the poet can give us and fiction is of crucial importance for our whole subject. The poet, he tells us in a familiar passage of the *Poetics* (Chapter IX), is superior to the historian because the truth that he gives us is less implicated than that of the historian in the particular. Homer is the greatest of poets, he adds in Chapter XXIV, because he has the most of this general truth and his success in achieving it is due to the fact that he is the most accomplished of liars.

Critics during the neo-classic period, as well as more recently, seem to have found it singularly difficult to grasp this Aristotelian conception of representative fiction, of truth through illusion. From Robortelli, who published his commentary on the *Poetics* in 1548, to the present day, they have tended on various grounds to put their truth or reality in one compartment and their fiction or illusion in another. One may illustrate the neo-classic form of this tendency from Dr. Johnson. He never tires of telling us that poetry should aim not at the particular but at the general. He does not as a rule, however, associate his general truth with a right use of fiction or, if one prefers, with a certain quality of imagination. On the contrary, instead of dwelling on a possible coöperation between truth and fiction, he inclines to set the two in sharp opposition to one another. According to Hawkins, 'he could at any time be talked into a disapprobation of all fictitious relations, of which he would frequently say they took no hold of the mind.' He was especially unwilling to admit any relation between fiction and religious truth. Like Boileau he therefore rejects the Christian epic because it introduces fiction into a domain where truth alone is appropriate. 'The good and evil of Eternity,' he says, 'are too ponderous for the wings of wit.'

Though Boileau would have religious truth and fiction sharply segregated, he encouraged fiction in one of the main senses that the word had come to have in the neo-classic period—the use, namely, of the pagan myths. Johnson, though in general sympathy with Boileau, breaks with him sharply at this point. 'The rejection and contempt of fiction (i.e., fiction in the sense of the classical myths) is,' he says, 'rational and manly.' Granted that classical fiction had become intolerably trite in the hands of minor poets, one is inclined to ask whether Johnson felt sufficiently how profoundly poetical this fiction had once been, nay, how poetical it may still be, if employed imaginatively. We do not think of him as striving that he might

> Have sight of Proteus rising from the sea;
> Or hear old Triton blow his wreathéd horn.

Towards another main type of fiction Johnson was implacable—namely, the type that appears in the pastoral. He would have none of it even in a Milton. He sickened at the mere mention of lambs and shepherds' crooks and was especially angered, we are told, by any praise of the Golden Age. Here again one may grant all that Johnson says about the more factitious forms that the pastoral theme had assumed and at the same time ask whether he does justice to the poetry of which the pastoral is capable. No classicist can afford to follow Schiller in his *Essay on Simple and Sentimental Poetry,* and grant the first place to the idyllic imagination; at the same time he must recognize that man is never perhaps more spontaneously imaginative than when he yields to his Arcadian longings. 'Turn where you will in mythology and literature,' says Mr. P. E. More, 'and you will find this pastoral ideal haunting the imagination of men. . . . Were one to attempt to display its universality by illustration, one would need to abridge the libraries of the world into a few pages.'

The idyllic imagination was assuming a new importance in the time of Johnson as a result of its association by Rousseau and other primitivists with a state of nature to which men were actually invited to return. More or less innocent illusion was thus being converted into dangerous delusion. Dr. Johnson not only failed, as it seems to me, to do justice to the poetry of pastoral fiction; he also failed—though, in view of his condemnation of Rousseau, it is not possible to speak so confidently on this point—to perceive its full peril. The pastoral dream to which the princess succumbs in *Rasselas* is of the conventional rather than of the new primitivistic type.

Of the peril of fiction in general, of the ease with which illusion passes over into delusion, Johnson was only too acutely conscious. Chapter 43 of *Rasselas* on 'The Dangerous Prevalence of Imagination' not only gives the key to this work, but, taken in connection with *Rambler* 89 on **"The Luxury of Vain Imagination,"** points to one of Johnson's constant preoccupations. The neo-classic distrust of the imagination is, as I have already said, reinforced in him by that of the Christian. Traditionally, however, the Christian has been more inclined than was Johnson to invite a man to enter into himself. The man who enters into himself may achieve true meditation instead of becoming the puppet and plaything of vain conceits. It is this latter possibility that Johnson seems to take too exclusively into account. He himself rather dreaded being alone. He appears to have been happier when drinking tea with Mrs. Thrale. He associated with his solitary moments the fits of 'hypochondriac obnubilation' to which, as he tells us, he was subject. There is no evidence that he cultivated in a notable degree 'that inward eye which is the bliss of solitude' in the sense that a Christian saint would have given to the phrase 'inward eye.' In the sense that Wordsworth gave to the phrase Johnson did not of course cultivate the inward eye at all. 'Solitude,' he says, 'is a state dangerous to those who are too much accustomed to sink into themselves.' In his account of the 'recluse' who regales himself with 'airy gratifications,' who yields to 'an invisible riot of mind,' who is unable to distinguish between the 'labor of thought' and 'the sport of musing,' Johnson anticipates admirably much of our modern psychology. 'The dreamer,' he says, 'retires to his apartments, shuts out the cares and interruptions of mankind, and abandons himself to his own fancy; new worlds rise up before him, one image is followed by another, and a long succession of delights dances round him. He is at last called back to life by nature, or by custom, and enters peevish into society, because he cannot model it to his own will.'

This passage, written in 1751, runs curiously parallel to the passage in the *Confessions* in which Rousseau narrates how in 1756 at the Hermitage he made of his 'creative imagination' a means of escape into a 'land of chimeras' and how rudely he rebuffed visitors who interrupted him at the moment when he was on the point of setting out for *'le monde enchanté.'* In this particular use of the creative imagination Rousseau has had innumerable followers. The person who indulges in this quality of fiction is termed by the psycho-analyst in his own special jargon, the 'introvert' or victim of 'autistic' thinking. Johnson does not fall into the pseudo-scientific fallacies of psycho-analysis, especially in his dealing with the problem of the will. He does, however, remind one at least remotely of the psycho-analyst by the remedy he proposes for the maladjustment that grows out of the flight from the real into some world of fiction. He puts his emphasis on outer activity rather than on the inner activity by which Christian and Aristotelian alike would adjust themselves to a higher reality, an adjustment that Aristotle relates specifically in the *Poetics* to a right use of fiction or illusion.

One should add that though Johnson was in general very prone to see illusion passing over into delusion, he refused to admit any such passage precisely at the point where most neo-classic critics discovered it—namely, in the type of drama that conformed to the three unities. It is well known that the doctrine of the three unities arose in Italy during the sixteenth century and was imposed on the European drama in connection with the Quarrel of the Cid.

In the name of pseudo-probability, the illusion of a higher reality that true tragedy requires is converted by this doctrine into literal deception. Various attacks on the unities had been made in the eighteenth century before Johnson, one of the earliest being by a French writer, La Motte-Houdard, who is in his total tendency pseudo-classical. To those familiar with these previous attacks on the unities the attack in the **"Preface to Shakespeare"** (1765) will not seem especially original. There is no doubt, however, that Johnson's refutation of the idea of literal deception is masterly and definitive. Towards the end of this refutation he suggests that there may be other and better reasons for observing the unities than those based on a false verisimilitude. As a matter of fact, the unities have been revived in our own day, largely through the influence of Ibsen, because they have been found to make for concentration, a prime requirement of good dramatic technique. The larger question of verisimilitude in the Aristotelian sense still remains unsolved. A melodrama may observe the unities or approximate them and in other respects display excellent dramatic technique, and yet remain wildly improbable, because its action is not motivated with reference to normal human experience. It is not enough to make a plea as Farquhar already does in his attack on the unities in his *Discourse upon Comedy* (1702) for 'a free and unlimited flight of imagination.' The value of the imagination that is thus free to 'wander wild,' that is not in other words disciplined to any norm, is precisely the problem raised by the whole modern movement. Critics contemporary of Dr. Johnson complained that, though he had shown that we are not actually deluded at a play by the observance of the unities or by any other device, he did not do justice to the degree of illusion that a play may actually produce—for example, when he says that a 'play read affects the mind like a play acted.' What is certain is that he did not bring together adequately the idea of fiction or illusion and the idea of verisimilitude. As I have been pointing out, he tends, like most neo-classic critics, to set imagination and reason (or judgment), illusion and verisimilitude, in sharp opposition to one another. The contrast that he establishes in *Rasselas* is between a merely deceitful fancy and 'sober probability.' Unfortunately, there is truth in the assertion of observers so different as Pascal and Napoleon that imagination governs mankind. Anyone who wishes, therefore, to make a right appeal to men will not be satisfied with opposing cool reason or judgment to imagination but rather one quality of imagination to another. Johnson indeed has an occasional remark of admirable perspicacity regarding the mechanical opposition between judgment and imagination that runs through the neo-classic movement. 'It is ridiculous,' he says, 'to oppose judgment to imagination; for it does not appear that men have necessarily less of one as they have more of the other.' If he had developed adequately the hint he has thus thrown out, if he had done justice to the rôle of fiction or illusion in both life and art, if he had linked with a right use of the imagination, the 'grandeur of generality' that he is always opposing to what seems to him every deviation from normal human experience, the romantic rebels would have been left without any legitimate grievance. As it was, these rebels simply took over the neo-classic opposition between reason and imagination and turned it upside down. Instead of sacrificing imagination to reason, they were ready to sacrifice reason to what A. W. Schlegel calls the magic of genuine illusion. (pp. 80-93)

I have already suggested that the 'nature' of Wordsworth and other primitivists is in no small measure a projection of the idyllic imagination and in so far is not 'real' in any sense of that much-abused word. At all events, it is not yet clear that the type of imagination by which one is enabled, according to Wordsworth, to enter into communion with 'nature' is more important than the type that he dismisses so disdainfully, the type that M. Legouis describes as 'the gift of feigning, of arbitrarily combining the features of a legend or story.' One should add that this type of imagination cannot afford to be entirely arbitrary, if it is to meet the Aristotelian requirement of probability; it must in short be disciplined to normal human experience. In proportion as it is thus disciplined it gains in reality in the humanistic and not in the current naturalistic sense. Persons are still found sufficiently naïve to suppose that the word 'romantic' is specially hard to define as compared with other general terms like 'real,' 'ideal,' 'nature,' 'imagination.' As a matter of fact, a certain integrity has been maintained in the use of the word 'romantic' in spite of a bewildering multiplicity of specific applications. What was called romantic in the Middle Ages is still romantic, whereas, in the case of the word 'real' in particular, there have been since the mediæval period radical changes of meaning. An urgent task, if we wish to escape from our present confusion, is therefore to define above all the words real (or realism) and imagination, not only separately but in their relation to one another. If definition of the kind I have in mind is carried out with sufficient thoroughness, the way may be opened for the theory and possibly the practice of that art of representative fiction to which Johnson, in spite of his genuine humanistic wisdom, does not seem to me to have done entire justice, and to which even less justice has been done in the movements that have succeeded one another since his day. (pp. 94-6)

Irving Babbitt, "The Problem of the Imagination: Dr. Johnson," in his On Being Creative and Other Essays, *Houghton Mifflin Company, 1932, pp. 80-96.*

Alfred Noyes   (essay date 1930)

[*Noyes was an English poet and prose writer whose works temperamentally and stylistically reflect those of earlier eras, particularly the age of William Wordsworth and the age of Alfred, Lord Tennyson. Although a prolific writer popular with the reading public, especially for his poem "The Highwayman," Noyes was never recognized as an important poet by most critics. In the following excerpt, he distinguishes the originality of Johnson's thought from what he terms the "mere novelty" of other writers.*]

The modern man, having lost his roots, tends to forget that originality is a matter of origins, not of superficial effects. Origins are not of to-day, or yesterday. It was one of the most individual personalities of the eighteenth century—Doctor Johnson—who said that originality had nothing in common with mere novelty. There are hosts of running readers at the present day who, being unable to grasp the connection between the beginning and end of a sentence, would misinterpret that statement as a defence of the dullest conservatism, though of course it is exactly the opposite. It is a defence of the true originality. We may turn the sentence round and say "mere novelty has nothing to do with originality." The truth of that statement has been recognised in every age and in every nation, except when the age was corrupt and the nation dying. The death and dissolution of Athens are described in a single sentence in the Acts of the Apostles. "All the Athenians and strangers which were there spent their time in nothing else, but either to tell, or to hear, some new thing." Paul accused them, not of intelligence, but "superstition." The recognition of the true nature of originality is the master-key to the character of Johnson, and to all real greatness of the intellect and the spirit, which comes not to destroy, but to fulfil. It is no paradox to say that real originality is fundamentally incompatible with mere novelty; for everything that is creative is rooted in a common ground of reality and develops its future out of its past. Growth, growth, and yet again growth, is the law of the arts and of the intellect; but there is no growth without roots, and the roots run back through the ages.

Novelty can easily be achieved by the simple method of telling a lie. You may say that horses have five legs. It is new, but of no value. You may paint, or write, in a way that is equally false, equally new, and seems very effective to a certain kind of jaded mind, especially if the lie be concerned with things a little less obvious. But the artificial novelties that are stuck into the ground to startle and trick the hasty observer into a foolish momentary admiration will perish and leave no memory behind them. There is perhaps no single truth of which the full realisation would be more salutary at the present time. Johnson returns to it again and again. He opens his great preface to **Shakespeare** with it: "That praises are without reason lavished on the dead, and that the honours due only to excellence are paid to antiquity, is a complaint likely to be always continued by those who, being able to add nothing to truth, hope for eminence from the heresies of paradox." He makes of course due allowance for mere prejudice, and remarks that "while an author is yet living we estimate his powers by his worst performance, and when he is dead, we rate them by his best," but he returns to his text again and again. There is a hint perhaps, here, of his own vanity of human wishes. "Nothing can please many," he says, "and please long, but just representations of general nature. The irregular combinations of fanciful invention may delight awhile, by that novelty of which the common weariness of life sends us all in quest; but the pleasures of sudden wonder are soon exhausted and the mind can only repose on the stability of truth."

Again, in dealing with the metaphysical poets, in his **"Life of Cowley,"** he says: "Their thoughts are often new, but seldom natural. They are not obvious, but neither are they just; and the reader, *far from wondering that he missed them,* wonders more frequently by what perverseness of industry they were ever found."

Far from wondering that he missed them! This great man, through all the ponderous trappings of his age, by dint of sheer sincerity, was on the verge of a critical discovery here of the very first importance—a theory of art that Plato would have understood, before him; and Wordsworth after him; but very few others in the history of literature; a theory that fully accounts for the dilemma in which modern criticism finds itself.

On a subsequent page he says of the same metaphysical poets:

> As they were wholly employed on something unexpected and surprising, their courtship was void of fondness and their lamentation of sorrow. Their wish was only to say what they hoped had never been said before. Nor was the sublime more within their reach than the pathetic; for they never attempted that comprehension and expanse of thought which at once fills the whole mind, and of which the first effect is sudden astonishment and the second rational admiration. Those writers who lay on the watch for novelty could have little hope of greatness; for great things cannot have escaped former observation. Their attempts were always analytic. They could no more represent by their slender conceits and laboured particularities, the prospects of nature or the scenes of life, than he who dissects a sunbeam with a prism can exhibit the wide effulgence of a summer noon.

This, we may say, in flat contradiction of the stupid contempt of Macaulay, is great criticism. It is great in its grasp of first principles. When Johnson praised or blamed particular poems in detail the prejudices of his age made him an unreliable judge, especially of the technique of verse. But whenever he wrote of general principles, his own sincerity led him directly to the heart of the matter. Perhaps the most significant sentence of all for my present purpose is that in which he says of the same hunters for novelty, "it will be readily inferred that they were not successful in representing or moving the affections."

Johnson himself has moved the affection of all those who care for English literature. He has moved them through heavy disadvantages, with all the odds against him. Born in poverty, scarred with disease, uncouth in person and manner, the wielder of a literary style that even to his own contemporaries seemed occasionally to be making little fishes talk like whales, he nevertheless ruled the literary world of London for a third of a century as no man has ever ruled it before or since, and he has been loved almost as a personal friend by thousands of readers down to the present day.

Although Johnson was dogmatic almost to the point of arrogance, he was able to compel all kinds of persons, no matter what were their views, to like him. Boswell's *Life* has given us more opportunities of liking him, but it would be a mistake to attribute too much to the instrument on which the great personality of Johnson played his sonorous voluntaries. We have long ago ceased to believe that Boswell was the kind of inspired idiot depicted by Macaulay. Boswell had a singular talent for collecting and arranging his material; but, even for the sake of an antithesis, we must not regard him as in other respects a fool. Nor need we attribute inspiration to him. The simple straightforward talent was his own, but the material, and whatever inspiration was to be found in his work, was Johnson's. Take away from Boswell the prayers composed by Johnson, the letters written by Johnson, and, above all, the sentences spoken by Johnson, and there is not much left. But one faculty Boswell had that was essential to his task, a faculty that all lovers of Johnson must have—it accounts to a great extent for their love of him—the ineradicable delight of human nature in playing the game of "let's pretend." All through his life, although he was one of the sincerest men in the history of literature, Johnson asked his friends to come and play with him at the splendid game of "I'll be dictator, and you shall be my court." In boyhood, we are told, he frequently rode to school on the back of a school-fellow, who seemed to have taken his own ignominious part for granted; and one of the chief ingredients in the delicious dish provided by Boswell is just this spice of humour which enters into some of the gravest passages in the book. How far it unconsciously entered into Boswell's description of Johnson's interview with the King, or perhaps we should say the King's interview with Johnson, it is difficult to decide. In any case the modern reader is asked to play his part of "let's pretend" in a very delicious little comedy. Johnson, surrounded by an awe-struck crowd of friends after the great event, gravely informed them that, on the whole, he was very well pleased with his Majesty, both as to what his Majesty said, and as to his Majesty's manners, which he commended as really quite excellent. It was implied, too, that his Majesty probably felt the intellectual strain to a certain extent, and that this was probably the cause why his Majesty did not seek a further interview with his august subject. Again and again, too, there were occasions when the most amazing questions were asked of Doctor Johnson, not with a view to discovering his real opinion, but with a view to discovering what might be called the absolute truth on the most recondite subjects. Questions, for instance, like: "Will you inform me, sir, whether God created the onion before He created the potato." On which, Johnson, if he were in an amiable mood, would sometimes deliver judgment; but if he were a little tired of play, would say peremptorily: "That, sir, is a question which I am not bound to answer." Or there was that extraordinary letter which he wrote to Boswell on the eve of one of Boswell's journeys abroad, to something like this effect: "Pray, sir, take careful note, when you are in Holland, of the following matters, on which I require more information:

"(*a*) Whether in Holland there is much orange peel used for medicinal purposes;

"(*b*) What do they do with the pips;

"(*c*) Whether a Dutch duck is larger than an English duck;

"(*d*) How many Scotchmen there are in Antwerp."

A mysterious purpose was implied in many of these requests which one feels sure were never carried out; and, occasionally, when Dr. Johnson was in a mischievous mood, he delighted in shattering the very illusion he had created, as when—at the very height of his autocratic fame—he stood, in all his immense bulk, at the top of a gently sloping hill and remarked: "I have not rolled down a hill since I was at school, and I intend to do so now." Whereupon, despite the earnest solicitations of his attendant friends, the great man did, then and there, lie down and roll from the top to the bottom of that hill like a human avalanche.

In another way, there was the same feeling of "let's pretend" about his poetry, which is considerably underrated at the present day. There was of course a good deal of very direct humour in his verses, as in:

> If a man who turnips cries
> Cries not when his father dies,
> 'Tis a proof that he had rather

Have a turnip than his father;

or

> Hermit hoar, in solemn cell
> Wearing out life's evening grey,
> Strike thy bosom, sage, and tell
> What is bliss, and which the way.
>
> Thus I spoke and speaking, sighed,
> Scarce represt the starting tear,
> When the hoary sage replied:
> 'Come, my lad, and drink some beer.'

The burlesque solemnity of this strikes one as more genuine than the tragic tones of that modern Professor of Latin, in lyrics of a similar brevity and exactly the same rhythm, who seems to take the hangman's noose and malt as the best answer to life's riddle.

But there are subtler effects which have been deliberately reproduced by stylists like Stevenson. It is the same sort of "let's pretend" that we get in Stevenson, who always had something up his sleeve, although it was rather a larger something and a more portentous sleeve. Who for instance could be quite sure that the following lines were by Johnson and not by Stevenson? They were lines written to Miss—on her giving the author a gold and silver network purse of her own weaving:

> Though gold and silk their charms unite
> To make thy curious web delight,
> In vain the varied work would shine
> If wrought by any hand but thine:
> Thy hand that knows the subtler art,
> To weave those nets that catch the heart.

In other ways, too, he transcended his own age and "dipt into the future." There is a curious anticipation in *Rasselas* of Tennyson's prophetic vision of the airy navies grappling in the central blue.

> You, sir, whose curiosity is so extensive, will easily conceive with what pleasure a philosopher, furnished with wings, and hovering in the sky, would see the earth, and all its inhabitants, rolling beneath him. . . . How must it amuse the pendent spectator to see the moving scene of land and ocean, cities and deserts. . . . How easily shall we trace the Nile through all his passage; and examine the face of nature from one extremity of the earth to the other. . . . I have considered the structure of all volant animals, and find the folding continuity of the bat's wings most easily accommodated to the human form. Upon this model I shall begin my task. . . . If men were all virtuous I should with great alacrity teach them all to fly. But what would be the security of the good, if the bad could at pleasure invade them from the sky? *Against an army sailing through the clouds, neither walls, nor mountains, nor seas could afford any security. A flight of northern savages might hover in the wind, and light at once with irresistible violence upon the capital of a fruitful region that was rolling under them.*"

It is true that his philosopher came to grief; but this was the eighteenth century. In the same fable, in his own massive way, Johnson anticipates an imagination of a very different kind.

In the matter of literary "origins" there are few "discoveries" to be made nowadays among the more famous works;

yet one of the most curious "origins" of all is to be found, I believe, in ***Rasselas, Prince of Abyssinia.*** The wild romanticism of "Kubla Khan" seems, at first sight, to be remote indeed from the stately prose of Johnson's Eastern tale; but I should not be surprised to hear that Coleridge had been comparing it with Purchas's Pilgrims before he fell asleep and dreamed that broken and many-coloured dream. Johnson's description of the happy valley in which the palace of the prince was built, gives us a daylight picture of the very scene that Coleridge saw by glimpses of the moon. There are the "gardens bright with sinuous rills," and there the "sacred river" that escaped through "a dark cleft of the mountains, and fell with dreadful noise from precipice to precipice, till it was heard no more"; unless it echoes again through "the caverns, measureless to man" of "Kubla Khan." In the happy valley:

> The shadow of the dome of pleasure
> Floated midway on the waves,

and in the palace of Rasselas, too, which was raised about thirty paces above the surface of the water, "all the artificers of pleasure were called to gladden the festivity." If Purchas be the common origin of both there are still touches in the tale of the Prince of Abyssinia which seem to reappear in "Kubla Khan," and are not to be found in the "Pilgrims."

It will be remembered that the wildest and most musical passage in "Kubla Khan" was inspired by a dream within the dream, and that this was not of Xanadu.

> A damsel with a dulcimer
> In a vision once I saw.
> *It was an Abyssinian maid* . . .

It would be to consider too curiously to trace these suggestions beyond their own flying gleams of indirect light into the caverns of Kubla Khan; but it seems probable that, in the strange fashion of dreams, the colours of ***Rasselas*** had somehow got interwoven with the more obvious colours of Purchas in the poem of Coleridge.

The deepest note stressed in ***Rasselas*** is again the note of human affection, which was the origin of all Johnson's groping after a world of more permanent values than are to be found in the world around us.

His own extraordinary power over the affections of others, in turn, was due to the true originality and force of a character rooted in those permanent realities. He was and is loved, in a large measure, because he was the exact opposite of the false novelty hunters whom he criticised. His "conservatism" draws its strength from the unfailing springs of truth, and was therefore a part of his real originality. For, in many respects, it was opposed to the whole spirit of his age. Its veracity made short work of cant, in literature, as in life; it was the formal Johnson who, when Voltaire attacked Shakespeare, gave the complete answer to the formal theory of the ancient "unities." Voltaire whenever he is mentioned by Johnson seems to shrink to the dimensions of a dancing-master. In the essay on Milton, discussing the sources of "Paradise Lost," Johnson wrecks Voltaire in a single sentence. "Voltaire," he remarks, "tells a wild and unauthorised story of a farce seen by Milton in Italy which opened thus: 'Let the Rainbow be the Fiddle-stick of the Fiddle of Heaven.' " And there Johnson leaves it. Yet in his criticism of the defects both of Shakespeare and of Milton he is far shrewder, far truer and far more independent of authority than any later critic. Macaulay, when he poured contempt on Johnson's critical powers, was the conventionalist, Johnson the original thinker. Johnson's remark that Shakespeare "threw away the world for a quibble," not only goes to the heart of the chief fault of Shakespeare but suggests the greatness of that capacity which alone prevented that fault from becoming intolerable. There are whole speeches in Shakespeare which are nothing more or less than bad punning, and Johnson had the courage to say so.

No other critic of Shakespeare has so completely maintained his own intellectual balance, both for praise and for blame. Take for instance his comment on some of the most famous lines in "Hamlet":

> For who would bear the whips and scorns of time
> The oppressor's wrong, the proud man's contumely,
> The insolence of office and the spurns
> That patient merit of the unworthy takes?

In themselves of course they are great poetry. They are lines that, in every syllable, would strike home to the author of the **"Vanity of Human Wishes,"** and, perhaps for that very reason, he lays his finger on their dramatic weakness. "It may be remarked," he says, "that 'Hamlet' in his enumeration of miseries, forgets, whether properly or not, that he is a prince, and mentions many evils to which inferior stations only are exposed."

Again, in his comments on "Macbeth" there is an extraordinary breadth of view. He quotes the passage:

> Here lay Duncan
> His silver skin laced with his golden blood
> And his gash'd stabs looked like a breach in nature
> For ruin's wasteful entrance.

"Mr. Pope," he says, "has endeavoured to improve one of these lines by substituting gory blood for golden blood; but it may easily be admitted that he who could on such an occasion talk of 'lacing the silver skin,' would lace it with 'golden blood.' No amendment can be made to this line, of which every word is equally faulty, but by a general blot." Yet even here he is not dogmatic, and is prepared to state the other side. "It is not improbable," he adds, "that Shakespeare put these forced and unnatural metaphors into the mouth of Macbeth as a mark of artifice and dissimulation to show the difference between the studied language of hypocrisy and the natural outcries of sudden passion." That is of course the answer, and would be adopted at once by the conventional enthusiasm of the ordinary commentator. But Johnson bends his great brows over it like a thunder-cloud, gives us both aspects of the matter in two strong, terse paragraphs, and refuses to decide between them. Why? His mind was ranging, far and wide, over the poet's works. He knew that Shakespeare was one of the immortals, so he would not lightly decide against him, but he knew that Shakespeare was often guilty of a certain fault, on occasions when it could not glibly be turned into a merit. He simply could not be sure; and there, being a very great critic, and having cleared his mind of cant, he left it, for his readers to brood over, as they brood over Shakespeare himself. Others abide our question. It was Johnson, on this occasion, that smiled and was still.

But what an example to the hasty judgments of those critics of the present day who, having no standards of judgment, deliver their arbitrary blame and praise, mistaking the chatter of the hour for fame, and the novelty of the hour for greatness. It did not prevent him from writing:

> When learning's triumph o'er her barbarous foes
> First rear'd the stage, immortal Shakespeare rose;
> Each change of many-coloured life he drew,
> Exhausted worlds, and then imagined new;
> Existence saw him spurn her bounded reign
> And panting Time toiled after him in vain.

It is not what the later romantic poets would regard as the highest kind of poetry, yet that last line has been incorporated in the language. Neither that line nor its predecessor means quite what the critics who have quoted them suppose; but we must not expect too much. There is, of course, a rather subtle reference to Shakespeare's disregard of the classic "unities" of Time and Place. The passage is perhaps the truest single thing that any poet has ever said in verse about Shakespeare. When Swinburne, for instance, wanted to write about Shakespeare, he simply went into a religious ecstasy, and wrote lines like:

> All stars are angels, but the sun is God.

Swinburne thought he had no religion, and his own nature as a poet revenged itself by forcing him, when he attempted to write about Victor Hugo or Shakespeare, to write an unconsciously religious poem. Johnson, on the other hand, had a religion, and he saw terrestrial things in a just proportion.

It is equally to be remembered by those who think that Johnson was unable to appreciate the beauty and power of Shakespeare that, shortly before he died, he repeated to his own physician those lines which so poignantly express his own lifelong torment of the mind:

> Canst thou not minister to a mind diseased,
> Pluck from the memory a rooted sorrow,
> Raze out the written troubles of the brain,
> And with some sweet oblivious antidote
> Cleanse the stuff'd bosom of that perilous stuff
> Which weighs upon the heart?

It is one of the most grimly ironical characteristics of almost every generation that the crowd, following the latest fashions of the hour with perfect unanimity and complete conventionality, regards the lonely rebels, who refuse to follow, as representatives of the conventional mind. The ground shifts with each generation, and each forgets that what was glorious and lonely rebellion in a former day may be merely fashionable in the next. Voltaire was the spirit of the age of Johnson: and, in the age of Voltaire, this great, uncouth, pugnacious leader of English literature worshipped at St. Clement Dane's and knelt at his bedside, as humbly as a child, to say his prayers, remembering always in them poor "Tetty," as he called her, the wife who had been his best and only real friend in his younger days. This, in another man, might have meant little; but in Dr. Johnson, with his range of intellect, in the age of Voltaire, it meant that he was one of the loneliest figures in the world. Lonely, in spite of his love of children; lonely, in spite of the gaieties of Mrs. Thrale, lonely, in spite of the amazing collection of helpless and half-witted creatures with whom he filled his house. Loneliest of all, perhaps, in those hours when to escape his own brooding thoughts he talked to the friends who wondered whether his preoc-

cupation was due to his personal fear of death. Like all men of genius, he had to wrestle with a dark angel, and there was none to understand him.

It is the custom to-day to accept the shallow judgment of Macaulay on Johnson's own writings; yet, in some of the essays of the *Rambler* there are passages of prose infinitely finer than anything that Macaulay ever wrote, passages that give the clue to his own carelessness of fame, his indolence, and his brooding upon death. The style is of his own day; but it is only a narrowly time-bound critic who will accept (for instance) the involved periods of Henry James as excellent, and will dismiss the balanced and lucid prose of Johnson as worthless. It has a grave elegiac quality, the slow waves of it breaking in measured cadences, and through their very regularity somehow conveying the immeasurable sadness of the great Roman soul that breathed through them. Listen to this:

> When a friend is carried to his grave, we at once find excuses for every weakness, and palliations of every fault. We recollect a thousand endearments, which before glided off our minds without impression, a thousand favours unrepaid, a thousand duties unperformed, and wish, vainly wish, for his return, not so much that we may receive, as that we may bestow happiness, and recompense that kindness which before we never understood.

When he began to publish his *Rambler,* his wife had said to him, quietly: "I knew you could write, but I did not know you could write like this." It was probably the happiest moment of his life. The last number of the *Rambler* was dated with the day of her death. Mrs. Meynell, in the beautiful essay in which she defended Mrs. Johnson against the brutal ridicule of Macaulay, has said well that her real epitaph is not that which is inscribed on her tomb. It is hidden, as it was hidden in Johnson's heart, yet it beats, as that great heart beats, through every syllable of the masterpiece of English prose in which he declined the favour of Lord Chesterfield. Almost the saddest words in our tongue, I think, are those terrible phrases: "It comes too late. I am solitary and cannot impart it."

Their formal balance gives them the strength of a terrible restraint, a dreadful reserve which, if it were broken down, would show a great soul upon the rack, but a soul that, even upon the rack, is its own master. "It comes too late. I am solitary and cannot impart it." *Cannot impart it.* What does that mean? It might have pleased *her.* They would have talked about it, had a pleasant little gossiping time over their fourth dish of tea. "When the book comes out, we will do this and that and the other." But now—too late—

"I am solitary and cannot impart it."

But the realisation of his loss was no new thing to him. He had never lived merely in the present, and he was acquainted in youth with every grief that might befall him, though he did not know when or where. It was this "awareness" that gave to his writings a quality that has never been fully appreciated, an undertone of the music of eternity. Again and again, in the *Rambler* we hear that note.

Some of those classic essays, with their great measured cadence, have a place in English prose very like that of Gray's "Elegy" in English verse; and, if he did not altogether appreciate Gray, it is perhaps in part because he knew beforehand—only too well—what Gray had to tell him.

> Can storied urn or animated bust
> Back to its mansion call the fleeting breath?
> Can honour's voice provoke the silent dust,
> Or flattery soothe the dull, cold ear of death?

It is a continuation of his own **"Vanity of Human Wishes,"** and he had explored it all again and again in his prose. Compare for instance those verses, with this passage from the **Rambler,** taken almost at random:

> The influence of greatness, the glitter of wealth, the praises of admirers, and the attendance of supplicants, appeared vain and empty things when the last hour seemed to be approaching. . . . His friends expected to please him by accounts of the growth of his reputation; but they soon found how vainly they attempted by flattery to relieve the solicitude of approaching death. Riches, authority and praise lose all their influence when they are considered as riches which to-morrow shall be bestowed upon another, authority which shall this night expire for ever, and praise which, however merited, or however sincere, shall, after a few moments, be heard no more. Everything that terminated on this side of the grave was received with indifference. It had little more prevalence over his mind than a bubble that had now broken, a dream from which he was awake. His powers were engrossed by the consideration of another state.

It was not the personal fear of death that oppressed him—as some of his lighter-minded friends supposed. It was the awful presence of the eternities and, in part, his dread of severance from what seemed dearer than life, "the loss of those whom we have loved with tenderness." "Friendship between mortals," he wrote, "can be contracted on no other terms than that one must some time mourn for the other's death; and this grief will always yield to the survivor one consolation proportionate to his affliction; for the pain, whatever it be, that he himself feels, his friend has escaped."

He was never able to put these thoughts aside. They were true; they besieged him with their truth, their dreadful original truth; and sometimes, in spite of their truth, they were too much for him. This was why he distracted himself with his friends, and disliked to be alone. But even when he was with his friends he would sometimes be overheard murmuring a prayer to himself. His sympathy with Catholicism was partly due to his intense realisation of the naturalness of "praying for the dead." His sacraments were summed up in the idea of communion, with those he loved, and with God. He had greater affections than he ever displayed, and they were made all the more poignant by his preoccupation.

> The dusky strand of death inwoven here
> With dear love's tie, makes Love itself more dear.

Boswell writes, with innocent vanity, how Johnson travelled down to Dover to see him off on his European travels. But he misses the almost pathetic wistfulness of that great figure standing on the shore, and gazing after the ship. It probably never occurred to Boswell how greatly Johnson would miss him. Johnson writes to him, formally enough, asking for certain information that could be of no possible use to him; and Boswell is again flattered at the request, not seeing that the pathetically comic list of things about which Johnson required to be told conceals the simple affectionate desire of the arrogant old emperor of English literature to get a message from his little friend, a message of any sort.

Yet, in all this brooding over the inevitable end, there was an infinite courage. One remembers how, at the end of his life, when the surgeon was trying to relieve him of his dropsy by an incision, Johnson urged him to cut deeper. There was courage in his desire to live; courage, and the pathos of courage in his desire to see Rome before he died; courage, and the deep root of all true courage, in his contemplation of that other state, and that other City, eternal in the heavens, which illumined all his prayers. **"The Vanity of Human Wishes"** ends with a glimpse of the Abiding beyond the transient; and of that which enfolds all changes and can never change. Whole volumes of theology are compressed into one of its couplets:

> Safe in His power, whose eyes discern afar
> The secret ambush of a specious prayer.

The superficial contradiction between the prayer "Thy will be done," and the very act of praying is transcended in the depths of the Divine wisdom; and, in that noble conclusion of the poem, if it be read aloud in the right way, there is a slow, deep pulse as though the great heart of its author were throbbing through all the iron restrictions of the eighteenth century. It is customary almost to ignore Johnson as a poet; but, behind all the dignity and formality of those lines, there are tears hidden; pangs of mortal grief, and the passion of an immortal and unconquerable spirit, gazing through Life and Time and Death, into the depths of the Eternal.

> Still raise for good the supplicating voice,
> But leave to Heaven the measure and the choice.
> Safe in His power, whose eye discerns afar
> The secret ambush of a specious prayer;
> Implore His aid, in His decisions rest,
> Secure whate'er He gives He gives the best.
> Yet when the sense of sacred presence fires,
> And strong devotion to the skies aspires,
> Pour forth thy fervours for a healthful mind,
> Obedient passions, and a will resigned;
> For love, which scarce collective man can fill,
> For patience, sovereign o'er transmuted ill;
> For faith, which panting for a happier seat,
> Counts death kind Nature's signal for retreat.
> These goods for man the laws of Heaven ordain;
> These goods He grants, who grants the power to gain;
> With these celestial wisdom calms the mind,
> And makes the happiness she does not find.

The language and the manner are far removed from those of our day. Many poets have written couplets which may strike us as more "brilliant"; but I know of none in the language which, if read with the simple integrity of spirit that is their due, are so likely to fill the reader's eyes with unexpected tears. (pp. 323-29)

Alfred Noyes, "The Originality of Doctor Johnson," in The Bookman, *London, Vol. LXXVII, No. 462, March, 1930, pp. 323-29.*

T. S. Eliot   (lecture date 1944)

[Perhaps the most influential English poet and critic of the first half of the twentieth century, Eliot's works embody many of the qualities denoted by the term Modernism: experimentation, formal complexity, artistic and intellectual eclecticism, and a classicist's view of the artist working at an emotional distance from his or her creation. Upholding the values of traditionalism and discipline and espousing an overall conservative world view, he strongly affected critical thought in his lifetime, largely through his belief that poets must be conscious of the living tradition of literature in order to artistically and spiritually validate their work. In the following excerpt from the text of a lecture delivered in 1944, Eliot appraises Johnson's criticism in The Lives of the Poets, *focusing on the text's reflection of eighteenth-century poetic "sensibilities."]*

It is primarily with Johnson as a critic, as the author of **The Lives of the Poets,** that I am here concerned. But I shall have something to say of his poetry also; because I think that in studying the criticism of poetry, by a critic who is also a poet, we can only appreciate his criticism—its standards, its merits, and its limitations, in the light of the kind of poetry that he wrote himself. I consider Johnson one of the three greatest critics of poetry in English literature: the other two being Dryden and Coleridge. All of these men were poets, and with all of them, a study of their poetry is highly relevant to the study of their criticism, because each of them was interested in a particular kind of poetry.

If this relevance is less apparent in the case of Johnson, than with Dryden and Coleridge, it is for trivial reasons. A great deal of bibliography has accumulated about Johnson, yet relatively little has been written about his writings; his two long poems have been neglected; and as for **The Lives of the Poets,** few educated persons have read more than half a dozen of them, and of these half-dozen, what is remembered is chiefly the passages with which everyone disagrees. One reason for indifference to his criticism, is that he was not the initiator of any poetic movement: he was a secondary poet at the end of a movement which had been initiated by greater poets than he, and his poems represent a personal variation of a style which was well established. Dryden, and Coleridge in partnership with Wordsworth, represent for us something *new* in poetry in their time. What Dryden wrote about poetry is therefore more exciting than what Johnson wrote. In his critical essays, he was outlining laws of writing for two generations to come: Johnson's view is retrospective. Dryden, concerned with defending his own way of writing, proceeds from the general to the particular: he affirms principles, and criticizes particular poets only in illustration of his argument; Johnson, in the course of criticizing the work of particular poets—and of poets whose work was ended—is led to generalizations. Their historical situations were quite different. It is not, in the long run, relevant to our judgement of an author's greatness, whether he comes at the beginning of an age or at the end; but we are inclined to favour unduly the former. Of Johnson's influence there is nothing to say; and we are always impressed by a reputation for influence, as influence is a form of power. But when the tide of influence, which a writer may set in motion for a generation or two, has come to its full, and another force has drawn the waters in a different direction, and when several tides have risen and fallen, great writers remain of equal potentiality of influence in the future. It remains to be seen whether the literary influence of Johnson, as, in political thought, the influence of his friend of the other party, Edmund Burke, does not merely await a generation which has not yet been born to receive it.

An obvious obstacle to our enjoyment in reading **The Lives of the Poets** as a whole—and we must read it as a whole if we are to appreciate the magnitude of Johnson's achievement—is that we have not read the works of many of the poets included, and no inducement of pleasure or profit can be offered us to do so. Some of his minor eighteenth-century poets I have read in order to understand why Johnson approved of them; some I have only glanced at; and there are a number, of whom Johnson's commendation is so mild or his treatment so perfunctory, that I have not bothered even to look them up. Nobody wants to read the verses of Stepney or Walsh; I hardly think that any Ph.D. candidate would be encouraged by his advisers to devote his thesis to a study of the work of Christopher Pitt. Johnson's assertion that Yalden's poems 'deserve perusal' is no more convincing than a letter of introduction written for an importunate visitor whom the writer wants to get rid of. The student of the history of literary taste may be struck by Johnson's remark that 'perhaps no composition in our language has been oftener perused than Pomfret's *Choice*' and want to find out why. But the common reader will probably be more discontented by Johnson's omissions, than made curious by all his inclusions. Everyone knows that the collection represented the choice of a group of booksellers, or publishers, who presumably thought that the works of all these authors were saleable, and who certainly thought, with more evident reason, that prefaces by Dr. Johnson would go far to compensate for the want of copyright, in commending their edition to the public. We may be pretty sure that Johnson himself, though he did his best by everybody, would not have thought all of his authors worth including. Yet we know that Johnson had some liberty to add to the collection, for we are told that he suggested three of the poets, of one of whom, Sir Richard Blackmore, I shall have something more to say.

That the predecessors and contemporaries of Shakespeare, and the metaphysical poets before Cowley, were at that time unsaleable, would have been justification for the booksellers' vetoing any proposal by Johnson for their inclusion. But there is no evidence that Johnson wanted to include them; the evidence goes to show that his acquaintance with them was very limited, and that he was perfectly content to edit a library of poetry which began with Cowley and Milton. The very fine **"Preface to Shakespeare"** is a separate work, and shows no evidence of awareness of the need to estimate any poet in relation to his predecessors and contemporaries. Yet this very innocence of the historical and comparative methods which modern criticism takes for granted, contributes to the singular merit of this **"Preface"**; and the virtues of Shakespeare to which he calls attention, are mostly those in which Shakespeare was unique, which he did not share, even in degree, with the other dramatists.

This limitation of the area of English poetry is a positive

characteristic of importance. It would be a capital error to attribute the narrow range of Johnson's interests solely to ignorance, or solely to lack of appreciation, or even to both. To say that his ignorance was due to lack of understanding, would probably be truer than to say that his lack of understanding was due to ignorance: but it is not so simple as that. If we censure an eighteenth-century critic for not having a modern, historical and comprehensive appreciation, we must ourselves adopt towards him, the attitude the lack of which we reprehend; we must not be narrow in accusing him of narrowness, or prejudiced in accusing him of prejudice. Johnson had a positive point of view which is not ours; a point of view which needs a vigorous effort of imagination to understand; but if we can grasp it, we shall see his ignorance or his insensibility in a different light. Walter Raleigh says of Johnson that 'he had read immensely for the *Dictionary,* but the knowledge of English literature which he had thus acquired was not always serviceable for a different purpose. In some respects it was even a hindrance. Johnson's *Dictionary* was intended primarily to furnish a standard of polite usage, suitable for the classic ideals of the new age. He was therefore obliged to forego the use of the lesser Elizabethans, whose authority no one acknowledged, and whose freedom and extravagance were enemies to his purpose.'

To the poet and critic of the eighteenth century, the values of language and literature were more closely allied than they seem to the writers and to the reading public of today. Eccentricity or uncouthness was reprehensible: a poet was prized, not for his invention of an original form of speech, but by his contribution to a common language. It was observed by Johnson and by men of his time, that there had been progress in refinement and precision of language, as of refinement and decorum of manners; and both these attainments, being recent, were highly esteemed. Johnson is able to censure Dryden, for his bad manners and bad taste in controversy. Now it is generally observable of mankind, that in the elation of success in some course which we have set ourselves, we can be oblivious of many things which we have been obliged to resign in the accomplishment of it. We do not take kindly to the thought that, in order to gain one thing, we may have to give up something else of value. With these lost values the path of history is strewn and always will be: and perhaps a purblindness to such values is a necessary qualification, for anyone who aspires to be a political and social reformer. The improvement of language, which the eighteenth century had achieved, was a genuine improvement: of the inevitable losses only a later generation could become aware.

Johnson, certainly, saw the body of English poetry from a point of view which took for granted a progress, a refinement of language and versification along definite lines; and which implied a confidence in the rightness and permanence of the style which had been achieved—a confidence so much stronger than any we can place in the style, or styles, of our own age that we can hardly see it as anything but a blemish upon his critical ability. The emphasis upon, the care for, the common style and the common rules, which Johnson exhibits, and which make him sometimes appear to measure great genius by the standards suitable only to smaller minds, may lead to an exaggeration of the value of pedestrian poetry which conforms, over that of work of individual genius which is less law-abiding. Yet

the obtuseness which we are apt to attribute to Johnson is seldom apparent in his positive affirmations, but chiefly by silence; and this silence is evidence, not of individual insensibility, but of an attitude which is difficult for us to assume. From Johnson's point of view, the English language of the previous age was not sufficiently advanced, it was still 'in its infancy'; the language with which earlier poets worked was too rough, for those poets to be treated on the same footing with those of a more polished age. Their work, when they were not of the very highest rank, was a subject of study more suitable for the antiquary than for the cultivated reading public. The sensibility of any period in the past is always likely to appear to be more limited than our own; for we are naturally much more aware of our ancestors' lack of awareness to those things of which we are aware, than we are of any lack in ourselves, of awareness to what they perceived and we do not. We may ask then whether there is not a capital distinction to be drawn between a limited sensibility—remembering that the longer extent of *history* of which we have knowledge, makes all minds of the past seem to us limited—and a defective sensibility; and accordingly ask whether Johnson, within his proper limits, is not a sensitive as well as judicial critic; whether the virtues he commended in poetry do not always remain virtues, and whether the kinds of fault that he censured do not always remain faults and to be avoided.

Even if I have not yet succeeded in making my meaning very clear, I hope that I have done something to unsettle your minds, and to prepare for an investigation of the charge against Johnson of being insensitive to the music of verse. A modern reader remembers nothing more clearly, from a reading of *The Lives of the Poets,* than Johnson's remarks on the versification of Donne and of Milton's *Lycidas.* If we recall no other opinion of Johnson, we recall the following:

> The metaphysical poets were men of learning, and to show their learning was their whole endeavour: but unluckily resolving to show it in rhyme, instead of writing poetry they only wrote verses, and very often such verses as stood the trial of the finger better than of the ear; for the modulation was so imperfect that they were only found to be verses by counting the syllables.

Of the work of Cleveland, and some of the other minor metaphysicals, this judgment would be sound enough; but that Johnson included Donne in this censure, we can be sure from his observation that Ben Jonson resembled Donne 'more in the ruggedness of his lines than in the cast of his sentiments'. Nowadays we regard Donne as a very accomplished craftsman indeed, as a versifier of signal virtuosity, and what Johnson denotes as 'ruggedness' strikes our ear as a very subtle music. But the judgment on *Lycidas,* as well known as the judgment on the metaphysical poets, equally outrages our sensibility. Johnson declares that in this poem 'the diction is harsh, the rhymes uncertain, and the numbers unpleasing'. With some other of Johnson's remarks about *Lycidas* we may find it possible to agree. If we think that an elegy requires the justification of unfeigned and cordial regret, we may find the poem frigid. The conjunction of Christian and classical imagery is in accord with a baroque taste which did not please the eighteenth century: and I must admit for myself that I have never felt happy in the spectacle of Fr. Camus and St. Peter marching in the same procession, like a couple of professors strolling down King's Parade on their way to hear the university sermon. But surely it is the musical virtue of the verse which clothes the absurdities in grandeur, and makes all acceptable. So we ask, was Johnson insensible to the music of verse? Had he, had the whole of his generation, defective hearing?

There is perhaps no more stubborn cause of extreme differences of opinion, between respectable critics of poetry, than a difference of ear: and by 'ear' for poetry I mean an immediate apprehension of two things which can be considered in abstraction from each other, but which produce their effect in unity: rhythm and diction. They imply each other: for the diction—the vocabulary and construction—will determine the rhythm, and the rhythms which a poet finds congenial will determine his diction. It is the immediate favourable impression of rhythm and diction which disposes us to accept a poem, encourages us to give it further attention and to discover other reasons for liking it. This immediacy may be lacking, in the reading of the poetry of one generation by another. Not until a literature has arrived at maturity—not, perhaps, until it has passed the moment of maturity and advanced far into later age, can critics perceive that rhythm and diction do not simply improve, or deteriorate, from one generation to another, but that there is also pure change, such that something is always being lost, as well as something being gained. In the perfection of any style it can be observed, as in the maturing of an individual, that some potentialities have been brought to fruition only by the surrender of others; indeed, part of our pleasure in early literature, as of the delight which we take in children, is in our consciousness of many potentialities not all of which can be realized. In this respect, primitive literature can be richer than that which follows. A literature is different from a human life, in that it can return upon its own past, and develop some capacity which has been abandoned. We have seen in our own time, a renewed interest in Donne; and, after Donne, in earlier poets such as Skelton. A literature can also renew itself from the literature of another language. But the age in which Johnson lived, was not old enough to feel the need for such renewal: it had just arrived at its own maturity. Johnson could think of the literature of his age, as having attained the standard from which literature of the past could be judged. In a time like ours, in which novelty is often assumed to be the first requisite of poetry if it is to attract our attention, and in which the names of *pioneer* and *innovator* are among the titles most honoured, it is hard to apprehend this point of view. We easily see its absurdities, and marvel at the assurance with which Johnson could reprehend *Lycidas* for the absence of the merit which we find most conspicuous in it, and could dismiss Donne for the roughness of his diction. And when Johnson writes of Shakespeare, we are puzzled by Johnson's silence about the mastery of versification. Here there was no prejudice against a particular fashion of writing, as when he discusses the metaphysicals; no personal dislike of the man, as when he treats of Milton; but only the acutest observation, the highest esteem, the most just and generous praise: but he assigns to Shakespeare the very highest rank among poets, on every other ground than that of the beauty of rhythm and diction.

My point is that we should not consider this obtuseness, which to us is very strange, as a personal defect of Johnson which diminishes his stature as a critic. What is lacking

is an historical sense which was not yet due to appear. Here is something which Johnson can teach us: for if we have arrived at this historical sense ourselves, our only course is to develop it further; and one of the ways in which we can develop it in ourselves is through an understanding of a critic in whom it is not apparent. Johnson fails to understand rhythm and diction which to him were archaic, not through lack of sensibility but through specialization of sensibility. If the eighteenth century had admired the poetry of earlier times in the way in which we can admire it, the result would have been chaos: there would have been no eighteenth century as we know it. That age would not have had the conviction necessary for perfecting the kinds of poetry that it did perfect. The deafness of Johnson's ear to some kinds of melody was the necessary condition for his sharpness of sensibility to verbal beauty of another kind. Within his range, within his time, Johnson had as fine an ear as anybody. Again and again, when he calls attention to beauties or to blemishes in the work of the poets of whom he writes, we must acknowledge that he is right, and that he is pointing out something that we might not have noticed independently. It may prove that his criteria are permanently relevant.

There is another consideration, in the problem of the difference between the sensibilities of one century and another, which is worth mention. That is the problem of the emphasis on sound or on sense. The greatest poetry, I think we may agree, passes the most severe examination in both subjects. But there is a great deal of good poetry, which establishes itself by a one-sided excellence. The modern inclination is to put up with some degree of incoherence of sense, to be tolerant of poets who do not know themselves exactly what they are trying to say, so long as the verse sounds well and presents striking and unusual imagery. There is, in fact, a certain merit in melodious raving, which can be a genuine contribution to literature, when it responds effectually to that permanent appetite of humanity for an occasional feast of drums and cymbals. We all want to get drunk now and again, whether we do or not: though an exclusive addiction to some kinds of poetry has dangers analogous to those of a steady reliance upon alcohol. Besides the poetry of sound—and, from one point of view, occupying an intermediate position between the poetry of sound and the poetry of sense—there is poetry which represents an attempt to extend the confines of the human consciousness and to report of things unknown, to express the inexpressible. But with this poetry I am not here concerned. Between the two extremes of *incantation* and *meaning* we are I think to-day more easily seduced by the music of the exhilaratingly meaningless, than contented with intelligence and wisdom set forth in pedestrian measures. The age of Johnson, and Johnson himself, were more inclined to the latter choice. Johnson could accept much as poetry, which seems to us merely competent and correct; we, on the other hand, are too ready to accept as poetry what is neither competent nor correct. We forgive much to sound and to image, he forgave much to sense. And to exceed in one direction or the other is to risk mistaking the ephemeral for the permanent. Johnson sometimes made mistakes. I referred, a little earlier, to Sir Richard Blackmore.

Impressed by Johnson's assertion that Blackmore's *Creation* alone was a poem which 'would have transmitted him to posterity among the first favourites of the English

Muse', and his statement that it was by his own recommendation that Blackmore was included in the library which he introduced, I read the poem with some curiosity. I came to the conclusion that Johnson's praise of this poem shows a grievous lapse in two directions. In the first place, the poem almost at once violates some excellent rules which Johnson himself, in treating of a greater poet, had laid down for the use of triplet and alexandrine in the rhymed couplet form. Instead of reserving the triplet [three lines rhyming together and alexandrine as the third line] for the conclusion of a period, where this termination can be very effective, Blackmore introduces a triplet almost at the start; and presently offers us an alexandrine as the second line of a couplet. What is much worse, the versification is sometimes no better than that of a schoolboy's exercise. But Johnson, like all good churchmen and all good Tories, abominated Hobbes—a notable atheist and totalitarian. He must have been blinded to defects which he would have reproved in Dryden or Pope, by the satisfaction he got from the following lines alluding to that philosopher:

> At length Britannia's soil, immortal dame!
> Brought forth a sage of celebrated name,
> Who with contempt on blest Religion trod,
> Mocked all her precepts, and renounced her God.

To apply the kind of minute criticism in which Johnson excelled, we may remark that the first line is bad grammar, because *dame* is grammatically in apposition to *soil* instead of to *Britannia;* and we may censure the second line by remarking that Hobbes's name was not celebrated until a long time after his birth. We should expect also, that the personification of Religion, as a helpless female stamped upon by Hobbes, would be too inelegant for Johnson's taste. I think that this is the kind of lapse which can most severely be censured in a critic—the lapse from his own standards of taste. And secondly, my reading of the poem led me to suspect that even on grounds of content Johnson should have rejected it. For Johnson—and it is a very important thing about him—was one of the most orthodox churchmen, as well as one of the most devout Christians, of his day: and Blackmore seems to me to be expressing pure deism. I can only suppose that deism so permeated the atmosphere of the century that Johnson's nose failed to respond to its smell.

I want however to distinguish this species of error—the critic's failure to apply his own standards—from those apparent errors which spring from the principles of a particular mind at a particular time, and which no longer seem to us errors in the same sense, once we succeed in apprehending the point of view. Such will be found, and they will at first bewilder us, in Johnson's various remarks about writers of blank verse. For this kind of verse, he appears to give the highest place to Akenside, of whom he says, that 'in the general fabrication of his lines he is perhaps superior to any other writer of blank verse'. Even leaving out of account the blank verse of the great dramatic poets of a previous age—or the dramatic verse of Otway at his best—this seems at first an extravagant assertion.

Nowadays we use words so loosely that a writer's meaning may sometimes be concealed from us, simply because he has said exactly what he meant. To extract the meaning from Johnson's assertion about Akenside, we must first compare Akenside's versification with that of other blank

verse writers of his century; we have also to compare what Johnson has said about the others, and with what he said about Milton's verse. In his essay on Milton, you will remember that Johnson confirms the words of Addison who said of Milton *the language sunk under him.* Johnson goes on to say that Milton 'had formed his style by a perverse and pedantic principle' and that 'he was desirous to use English words with a foreign idiom'. But, having made this criticism, he goes on to utter the highest praise: Milton 'was master of his language to its full extent'. And in mentioning the weaknesses of 'heroic' blank verse; particularly the difficulty, in speaking it, of preserving the metrical identity of each line; and finally, after saying everything that can be said against blank verse, he makes the handsome admission: 'I cannot prevail upon myself to wish that Milton had been a rhymer; for I cannot wish his work to be other than it is; yet, like other heroes, he is to be admired rather than imitated.' The acknowledgment of Milton's greatness as a versifier is unequivocal. But there are laws, for the use of words and the construction of sentences, which Milton defies. The lawbreaker should not be praised for his lawlessness; and a second-rate poet may be more law-abiding than a poet of great genius. So, Akenside, 'in the general fabrication of his lines,' may be more correct than Milton; and if we value correctness, in that respect superior.

I do not think that the history of blank verse since Milton's time altogether gives him the lie. 'The music of the English heroic lines strikes the ear so faintly,' says Johnson, 'that it is easily lost.' That is true: the alternative danger is a monotonous thumping, which ceases to have any music at all. What Johnson failed to remark is, that Milton made blank verse a successful medium for the heroic poem, by that very eccentricity which Johnson reproves.

Johnson did, however, see the verse of Milton as an exception. He admits that there are purposes for which blank verse remains the proper medium; though he does not trouble to define and particularize those purposes. Of Young's *Night Thoughts* he says:

> This is one of the few poems in which blank verse could not be changed for rhyme but with disadvantage. The wild diffusion of the sentiments, and the digressive sallies of imagination would have been compressed and restrained by confinement to rhyme.

His approval of the use of blank verse by Thomson in his *Seasons* expresses a similar approval:

> His is one of the works in which blank verse is properly used. Thomson's wide expansion of general views, and his enumeration of circumstantial varieties, would have been obstructed and embarrassed by the frequent intersections of the sense, which are necessary effects of rhyme.

Let us return to Akenside, the author upon whose blank verse Johnson has bestowed such high commendation:

> In the general fabrication of his lines, he is perhaps superior to any other author of blank verse; his flow is smooth, and his pauses are musical; but the concatenation of his verse is too long continued, and the full close does not occur with sufficient frequency. The sense is carried on through a long intertexture of complicated clauses, and, as nothing is distinguished, nothing is remembered.

The exemption [Johnson continues, generalizing from his criticism of Akenside] which blank verse affords from the necessity of closing the sense with the couplet betrays luxuriant and active minds into such self-indulgence, that they pile image upon image, ornament upon ornament, and are not easily persuaded to close the sense at all. Blank verse will therefore, I fear, be too often found in description exuberant, in argument loquacious, and in narration tiresome.

To say that the concatenation of Akenside's verse is too long continued, and that the sense is carried on through a long intertexture of complicated clauses, is a censure which is fully justified by our examination of Akenside's lines; though it is only fair to remark that this concatenation, these complicated clauses, were exactly what Milton was able to manipulate with conspicuous and solitary success. But the general observations on the dangers of blank verse are such as later writers in this form would have done well to ponder. And Johnson could not foresee that later poets would also be able to exhibit in the rhymed couplet, through their desire to extend the resources of this form beyond the rigid limits imposed by the best eighteenth-century verse, the same exuberance, the same loquacity, and the same tiresomeness that Johnson lists as the vices of blank verse. We have only to look at William Morris for examples. (pp. 184-98)

I cannot help wondering how many blank verse poems of the nineteenth century will be perused by posterity with any greater excitement, than we now derive from those of Thomson, Young, or Cowper. There will remain *Hyperion, The Prelude* [which, however tedious in many places, has to be read entire], a few fine short pieces of Tennyson, some dramatic monologues of Browning. But in general, I think that the nineteenth-century poems which promise to remain permanently pleasurable, are poems in rhyme.

That Johnson regarded blank verse as more suitable for the theatre than rhyme, we may infer from his preference for *All for Love* among Dryden's heroic plays, and from his having chosen blank verse as the medium for his own tragedy *Irene.* That Johnson failed to understand the peculiarities of *dramatic* blank verse is evident from this play: for we find the blank verse to be that of a writer who thought and felt in terms of the rhymed couplet. I have already observed, that in all of Johnson's high and just praise of Shakespeare as a dramatic poet, he speaks as if Shakespeare had written in a language of which the sense had been preserved, but of which the sound meant nothing to us: for there is not a word about the music of Shakespeare's verse. Johnson holds that blank verse is more suitable to the stage, simply because it is nearer to prose: in other words, people conversing do occasionally produce an unconscious iambic pentameter, but almost never fall into rhyme. I do not think that this judgment is altogether valid. If Johnson failed, on the one hand, to appreciate the special music of dramatic blank verse, he was also deceived in thinking that blank verse is necessarily the more conversational form. I remarked long ago, that Dryden seems to me to approximate more closely to the tones of conversation in his rhymed plays than he does in *All for Love.* Johnson's *Irene* has all the virtues which verse by Johnson should be expected to have; and for Johnson, who did not ordinarily labour at his writing, it appears a very painstaking piece of work. His verse has none of the dra-

matic qualities; it is correct, but correctness in such isolation becomes itself a fault. The play would be more readable to-day, if he had written it in rhyme; the whole would be more easily declaimed, and the good things more easily remembered; it would lose none of its excellence of structure, thought, vocabulary and figures of speech. What would be mellifluous in rhyme, is merely monotonous without it.

I have been occupied so far, primarily with the task of trying to reduce some of the obstacles to the appreciation of Johnson as a critic. Before closing, there remain two incidental opinions of Johnson which I must face, because otherwise I should expose myself to the charge of evading them. The first is Johnson's opinion of choral drama, which was unfavorable; the second is his attitude towards religious or devotional verse, which was condescending. I must therefore direct the jury on these two points.

If *Paradise Regained* has been too much depreciated, *Samson Agonistes* has in requital been too much admired. It could only be by long prejudice, and the bigotry of learning, that Milton preferred the ancient tragedies, with their encumbrance of a chorus, to the exhibitions of the French and English stages, and it is only by a blind confidence in the reputation of Milton, that a drama can be praised in which the intermediate parts have neither cause nor consequence, neither hasten nor retard the catastrophe.

I may have occasion to remind you again, how emphatically Johnson was *modern* in his time: his preference of the French and English theatre to the Greek is only one example of this. I should wish to qualify his reproof of Milton, in the passage I have just quoted, by saying that I do not believe it was primarily long prejudice, or the bigotry of learning, which led Milton to write his play on the Greek model. I think that it was first of all a knowledge, conscious or unconscious, of what were his own gifts. He chose, in *Samson,* the one subject most suitable for him; and he took the Greek model because he was a poet, and not a dramatist, and in this form he could best exhibit his mastery and conceal his weaknesses. What is more odd, however, since Johnson holds up French as well as English drama for imitation, is that he makes no reference to the case, inconvenient for his thesis, of Racine's *Athalie.* Racine was a poet of the theatre, if there ever was one; in *Athalie* he employs the chorus; and *Athalie,* I think, is a very great play indeed. But, with this exception, Johnson was judging choral drama according to dramatic standards which I do not think that most of us apply to *Samson.* For many people, *Samson* is the most readable of Milton's major works: certainly, more readable than *Paradise Regained.* We can even enjoy *Samson,* as we can enjoy *Comus,* when it is performed. But I do not believe that anyone could enjoy them directly as drama: we need either to be pretty familiar with the text, or else have a very quick ear for the appreciation of verbal beauty. Otherwise, I do not think that the plot or the characterization of either piece would long hold our attention.

I am inclined to believe that on the whole Johnson, if he is allowed to criticize *Samson* as drama, is right. I do not believe that he appreciated the dramatic force of the Greek conventions in their own place and time. Indeed, I doubt whether it was possible for anyone to do so in the undeveloped state of archaeological knowledge in his time: certainly, our own understanding of the Greek plays as plays has been immensely extended by recent study and research. But the real question is whether the form of Greek drama can be naturalized for the modern world. And I suspect that the chief justification for Milton, as for some later poets, in imitating the Greek form of drama, is that the use of a chorus enables poets with no skill in the theatre, to make the most of their accomplishments, and thereby conceal some of their defects.

Johnson's opinions on religious verse are most fully stated in his **"Life of Waller."** It is there that he observes

> Let no pious ear be offended, if I advance, in opposition to many authorities, that poetical devotion cannot often please. . . .

> Contemplative piety, of the intercourse between God and the human soul, cannot be poetical. . . .

These and other words might have been transposed into his **"Life of Watts,"** and are confirmed there by the following:

> His devotional poetry is, like that of others, unsatisfactory. The paucity of its topics enforces perpetual repetition, and the sanctity of the matter rejects the ornaments of figurative diction.

As a criticism of Watts, this is just enough. To a generation which has learned to admire the religious sonnets of Donne, the lyrics of George Herbert, Crashaw and Vaughan, it seems narrowly perverse. I think that we have to take account, not only of the limitations of the literary taste of his time, but of its religious limitations also. The two support each other here: for as it did not occur to the mind of Johnson that there were poetic values, in earlier periods, which had vanished during the perfecting of those of his own, so I do not think that it could occur to him that there was a religious sensibility which had disappeared also. Johnson's strictures are applicable to *most* of the religious verse that has been written since, as well as to that of his own time. What vitiates his condemnation, is the absence of any discrimination between the religious poetry of public worship, and the religious poetry of personal experience. In the hymn, the anthem, the sequence, the intrusion of personal experience would be impertinent; and perhaps for this reason the poetry of public worship is at its best in the impersonal eloquence of the Latin language. It is true that some devotional religious verse appears to be equally valid in both contexts. Some of George Herbert's poems are found in hymnals: yet I always feel them to be less satisfactory as hymns than those of Watts; for I am always aware of the personality of Herbert, and never conscious of any personality of Watts. But most of the devotional poetry of the eighteenth century has the merit neither of the one kind nor of the other. The reasons why good poetry in this kind was not written, and the reasons why Johnson could not recognize its possibility, have to do with the limitations of religious sensibility in that century. I say limitations, rather than lack of sensibility, for no one can read Johnson's *Prayers and Meditations* or Law's *Serious Call* without acknowledging that this age also has its monuments of religious devotion. (pp. 199-204)

T. S. Eliot, "Johnson as Critic and Poet," in his On Poetry and Poets, Farrar, Straus, and Cudahy, 1957, pp. 184-222

Joseph Wood Krutch   (essay date 1944)

[*Krutch is widely regarded as one of America's most respected literary and drama critics. A conservative and idealistic thinker, he consistently advocated human dignity and the preeminence of literary art. Much of his literary criticism is characterized by the themes of two works: in* The Modern Temper *(1929) he argued that scientific thought denied human worth, rendering tragedy obsolete; and in* The Measure of Man *(1954) he attacked modern culture for depriving humanity of a sense of individual responsibility necessary for making important decisions in an increasingly complex era. In the following excerpt, he analyzes* Rasselas, *distinguishing Johnson's "ordinary pessimism" from his tragic sense of life.*]

Johnson's style has no doubt been called "laborious" more often than it has been called anything else, but the implications of the adjective are not to be taken to include slowness of composition, for Johnson was likely to dash off at top speed even those compositions which seem heavy and involved. "When," he once observed, "a man writes from his own mind, he writes very rapidly. The greatest part of a writer's time is spent in reading, in order to write: a man will turn over half a library to make one book." And it is Boswell who tells Bennet Langton's story about the time when Johnson, on a visit to Oxford in 1759, asked him one evening when the post went out and, on being told that it would leave in about half an hour, said merely: "Then we shall do very well." He instantly sat down, composed an *Idler* (about a thousand words), and when Langton asked to read it, replied: "Sir, you shall not do more than I have done myself." He then folded the paper and dispatched it to London, where it was due at the printer's next day.

It was not until many years later that Johnson made his often-quoted remark: "No man but a blockhead ever wrote, except for money," but it is against the background of the profession of letters as he saw it at this time that the statement must be interpreted, and it is not cynical in the way that it is often assumed to be. Johnson did not love money, which he never accumulated and which he gave freely away. He put upon it the value commonly put upon it by the poor, and this is a very different thing from the value put upon it by the rich. To write for money meant, in Johnson's case, merely to write from necessity, and his statement means no more than that he could not conceive how anything except necessity could drive a man to do what he found so painful to his constitutional indolence, so much less entertaining than reading or conversation. Like many, perhaps like most, good writers, he found the process of composition disagreeable in itself even though he composed rapidly, and he spoke for many when he said: "I allow that you may have pleasure from writing, after it is over, if you have written well; but you don't go willingly to it again."

The desire to excel and to win admiration Johnson certainly had, but that desire alone was not enough to overcome his inertia, and it is noticeable that all his major works were accomplished either because he wrote under the pressure of immediate necessity or because he had previously committed himself to something from which he could not honorably escape. Thus *Rasselas* (1759), his most important work between the publication of the *Dictionary* and the appearance of his edition of *Shakespeare,* was composed, quite literally, to "defray the expense of his mother's funeral, and pay some little debts which she had left." (pp. 168-69)

Many who have never read **Rasselas** are, nevertheless, aware of the fact that it tells the story of a prince who escaped from a happy valley in order to find out for himself what men were like and how they fared. In accordance with the peculiar custom of his country (which took this means of preserving highborn persons from the temptations of political intrigue) he had been imprisoned in a sort of earthly paradise provided with every luxury and inhabited by a cultivated group of his fellow countrymen who had voluntarily agreed to commit themselves for life to this luxurious confinement.

Unlike most of his fellow prisoners, Rasselas was not content. He had some need which survived the satisfaction of every definable want and he plotted with his philosopher-guide, Imlac, to escape. Joined by his sister and her maid, they finally practised a tunnel through one of the surrounding mountains, went forth into the world, saw the unhappiness of every human condition and, in the end, decided to return to their prison because they had learned what Imlac knew from the beginning—that "Human life is everywhere a state, in which much is to be endured, and little is to be enjoyed."

To Johnson's contemporaries the book was a dazzling specimen of that "true wit" which consists in achieving the perfect statement of something which "oft was thought but ne'er so well expressed." For that reason they admired it with an enthusiasm which the nineteenth cen-

tury, brought up to admire novelty, paradox, perversity and eccentricity, found it difficult to understand; and in so far as we inherit the taste of that century, we too are likely to approach **Rasselas** with prejudice. But it is actually more original, or at least more tinged with the color of Johnson's own personality, than seems to have been generally remarked—possibly because in the days when it was promptly accepted as a classic there was so much less tendency than there is now to assume that individual personality, the difference between one temperament and another, is the most interesting thing which writing can reveal. Actually, Johnson did something more than merely rephrase the commonplaces which have long served to demonstrate that all is vanity. He was not content merely to indicate how men's plans go astray and men's ambitions are frustrated. His pessimism, in other words, was not merely of that vulgar sort which is no more than a lament over the failure of worldly prosperity. It was, instead, the pessimism which is more properly called the tragic sense of life, and he would undoubtedly have approved the lines of that modern poet who proclaims:

> The troubles of our proud and angry dust
> Are from eternity, and shall not fail.

Since the two things, ordinary pessimism and the tragic sense of life, are easily confused, since, indeed, they are at least mingled if not confused in **Rasselas** itself, it might be worth while in analyzing the tale to build the analysis around some attempt to separate them. Let us, then, begin on the lowest level.

Told in outline as it was told above, the story would seem

The Thrales' country house in Surrey, Streatham Park, where Johnson spent much time in his later years.

to be no more than a device for introducing a survey of some of the various conditions of life, and its hero no more than a naïvely neutral observer. Some portion of it is, indeed, precisely that. A series of very short chapters disposes of various ways of life with almost perfunctory brevity, though often with wit. Shepherds, the travelers find, are too rude and too stupid to tell them whether or not the pastoral life is as peaceful as poets have maintained; a hermit they discover just as he is about to return to public life, a philosopher just at the moment when a personal calamity has robbed him of all his philosophy. A professional sage whose society they cultivate soon exhibits Johnson's own weakness by demonstrating that he prefers their foolish conversation to the solitary pleasure of his own wise thoughts, and when they ask him point-blank to advise them what way of life they should choose, he can only reply that he is not able to do so, since he himself has chosen wrongly. Indeed, the only person who will consent to advise them is an optimist who accepts the universe and who believes in living in accordance with nature, but who defines that process thus: "To live according to nature, is to act always with due regard to the fitness arising from the relations and qualities of causes and effects; to concur with the great and unchangeable scheme of universal felicity; to cooperate with the general disposition and tendency of the present system of things." But "The Prince soon found that this was one of the sages whom he should understand less, as he heard him longer. He, therefore, bowed, and was silent, and the philosopher, supposing him satisfied and the rest vanquished, rose up and departed, with the air of a man that had cooperated with the present system."

But by far the best chapter in the latter half of the book is one which deals with a visit to the Pyramids and includes, indeed, what is probably the finest single paragraph in the whole work. Moreover, this chapter is interesting, and one paragraph in it unforgettable, because it treats so powerfully a theme which the earlier sections had introduced but had allowed, for the most part, to remain suggested rather than systematically developed—the theme, that is to say, which has already been called the tragic rather than the merely pessimistic theme.

Rasselas, we here perceive, did not leave the valley merely in order to find out whether, in any vulgar sense, men prospered more outside it than he did within its confines. He knew that he had in the fullest measure that security and plenty and ease for which men commonly say they perform their labors and he was prepared not to be surprised that others led lives more troubled than his. Nor was it merely that he was consumed with vague curiosity. Actually he was seeking the answer to a tremendous question. "That I want nothing," said the prince, "or that I know not what I want, is the cause of my complaint," and it is the "know not what I want" that is really important. Sometimes Rasselas supposes that this sense of wanting something unspecifiable is merely the result of having had all possible desires satisfied. "I have already," he says, "enjoyed too much; give me something to desire." But Johnson is both too little an ascetic and too profoundly concerned with the ultimate nature of man to allow his hero to rest content with so simple an explanation of his infelicity. The difficulty is not merely that all desires are satisfied, but rather that man has some desire which nothing in his experience is capable of satisfying.

'What,' said he, 'makes the difference between man and all the rest of the animal creation? Every beast, that strays beside me, has the same corporal necessities with myself: he is hungry, and crops the grass, he is thirsty and drinks the stream, his thirst and hunger are appeased, he is satisfied and sleeps: he rises again and is hungry, he is again fed, and is at rest. I am hungry and thirsty, like him, but when thirst and hunger cease, I am not at rest; I am, like him, pained with want, but am not, like him, satisfied with fulness. The intermediate hours are tedious and gloomy; I long again to be hungry, that I may again quicken my attention. The birds peck the berries, or the corn, and fly away to the groves, where they sit, in seeming happiness, on the branches, and waste their lives in turning one unvaried series of sounds. I, likewise, can call the lutanist and the singer, but the sounds, that pleased me yesterday, weary me to-day, and will grow yet more wearisome to-morrow. I can discover within me no power of perception, which is not glutted with its proper pleasure, yet I do not feel myself delighted. Man surely has some latent sense, for which this place affords no gratification; or he has some desires, distinct from sense, which must be satisfied, before he can be happy.'

After this, he lifted up his head, and seeing the moon rising, walked towards the palace. As he passed through the fields, and saw the animals around him, 'Ye,' said he, 'are happy, and need not envy me, that walk thus among you, burdened with myself; nor do I, ye gentle beings, envy your felicity; for it is not the felicity of man. I have many distresses, from which ye are free; I fear pain, when I do not feel it; I sometimes shrink at evils recollected, and sometimes start at evils anticipated: surely the equity of providence has balanced peculiar sufferings with peculiar enjoyments.'

Perhaps the fact that Rasselas, when he indulges in these reflections, is dwelling in an earthly paradise tends to suggest that such thoughts are likely to occur only to a man so situated, but Johnson's own life was certainly not passed in any happy valley and yet a boredom of tragically grandiose implications was the evil always ready to assert itself even when other evils had been temporarily banished. Indeed, and as we shall see, both his theory of aesthetics and his general theory of human nature rest ultimately upon the desperate assumption that, since man never finds any really self-justifying activity, he must, if life is to be tolerable at all, fill it up with those temporary satisfactions which are gained by the gratification of the easily wearied senses and the parallel gratification of that less easily wearied but still far from limitless appetite for knowledge to which he generally gives no more exalted name than "curiosity."

But though almost the entire substance of another **Rasselas** could easily be compiled out of Johnson's recorded sayings and the identification between himself and his hero could be completely established, he nowhere else takes so definitely as he does in this tale the step which carries him from a rationalistic despair to the point where he asks the question which the Greeks had asked: "What activity is appropriate to man? In doing what does he fulfill his function and thus satisfy himself?"

Sometimes, as for instance when writing to Baretti, Johnson speaks of life as everywhere "supported with impatience and quitted with reluctance." Here his attitude seems almost Schopenhauerian, and suggests the conviction that life is endured only because the irrational will is stronger than the rational judgment. But though the passage from *Rasselas* just quoted seems at least to hint the possibility that the existence of a need must imply the existence somewhere of an answer to it, that hint has disappeared again in the later passage, which is not only the most eloquent Johnson ever wrote on this theme but perhaps, in all literature, the most magnificent tribute ever paid to the power of Boredom.

Rasselas and his companions have, in the course of their travels, just visited the Pyramids.

> 'We have now,' said Imlac, 'gratified our minds with an exact view of the greatest work of man, except the wall of China.
>
> 'Of the wall it is very easy to assign the motive. It secured a wealthy and timorous nation from the incursions of barbarians, whose unskilfulness in arts made it easier for them to supply their wants by rapine than by industry, and who, from time to time, poured in upon the habitations of peaceful commerce, as vultures descend upon domestic fowl. Their celerity and fierceness, made the wall necessary, and their ignorance made it efficacious.
>
> 'But, for the pyramids, no reason has ever been given adequate to the cost and labour of the work. The narrowness of the chambers proves that it could afford no retreat from enemies, and treasures might have been reposited, at far less expense, with equal security. It seems to have been erected only in compliance with that hunger of imagination, which preys incessantly upon life, and must be always appeased by some employment. Those who have already all that they can enjoy, must enlarge their desires. He that has built for use, till use is supplied, must begin to build for vanity, and extend his plan to the utmost power of human performance, that he may not be soon reduced to form another wish.
>
> 'I consider this mighty structure, as a monument of the insufficiency of human enjoyments. A king, whose power is unlimited, and whose treasures surmount all real and imaginary wants, is compelled to solace, by the erection of a pyramid, the satiety of dominion and tastelessness of pleasures, and to amuse the tediousness of declining life, by seeing thousands labouring without end, and one stone, for no purpose, laid upon another. Whoever thou art, that, not content with a moderate condition, imaginest happiness in royal magnificence, and dreamest that command or riches can feed the appetite of novelty, with perpetual gratifications, survey the pyramids, and confess thy folly!'

(pp. 175-80)

Voltaire's *Candide* was published the same year as *Rasselas* (probably some two months earlier). Johnson himself, says Boswell, remarked "that if they had not been published so closely one after the other that there was not time for imitation, it would have been in vain to deny that the scheme of that which came latest was taken from the other," and comparison became an inevitable topic for commentators. Johnson thought that "*Candide* . . . had more power in it than any thing that *Voltaire* had written"; Voltaire, acknowledging a copy of the first French

translation sent him by its maker, wrote less ambiguously: "Il m'a paru d'une philosophie aimable, et très-bien écrit." Boswell, who of course was always ready with the correct moral sentiments, remarks:

> Voltaire, I am afraid, meant only by wanton profaneness to obtain a sportive victory over religion, and to discredit the belief of a superintending Providence: Johnson meant, by shewing the unsatisfactory nature of things temporal, to direct the hopes of man to things eternal. Rasselas, as was observed to me by a very accomplished lady, may be considered as a more enlarged and more deeply philosophical discourse in prose, upon the interesting truth, which in his **"Vanity of Human Wishes"** he had so successfully enforced in verse.

Such was the line usually taken—as, for example, by one of Johnson's early nineteenth-century editors who did not hesitate to run the risk of exaggerating the effect of the printed word in order to make the contrast more vivid and who roundly announced that, while "the one demoralized a continent, and gave birth to lust, and rapine, and bloodshed; the other has blessed many a heart, and gladdened the vale of sorrow, with many a rill of pure and living water."

But such easy contrasts seem hardly worth drawing. That Voltaire is ribald and ferocious, Johnson melancholy and pietistic, is obvious enough. Yet the very fact that comparisons are drawn seems to suggest that those who make them may have some uneasy sense that, despite the obvious contrasts, there are apparent similarities which ought to be explained away. Indeed, the two lines of argument advanced by the two moralists coincide precisely at the point where Johnson, in a passage quoted above, pays ironical respect to the special system of optimism which is the principal object of Voltaire's attack. However antithetical the temperaments of the two men may have been, they find equally absurd the proposition that this is the best of all possible worlds in the simple sense that Pope had proclaimed when he wrote:

> All discord harmony not understood;
> All partial evil universal good.

Neither is prepared to accept either Spinoza or Leibnitz, or the popular vulgarization of the two.

But the contrast between them is not the simple contrast between the cynic and the Christian, each refusing for a different reason to agree that the world is good. To afford so simple an antithesis, Voltaire would have had to be more of a cynic, and Johnson, if not more of a Christian, at least a Christian of either a more mystical or a more sentimental sort, and hence readier than he was to find a really effective consolation in the reflection that this life is merely the prelude to another. Actually, Johnson was, in one respect, more of a cynic than Voltaire, because Voltaire believed in the possibility of reform while Johnson did not. And if it is not cynicism that prevents him from insisting upon the adequacy of the pietistic solution which he makes a show of offering, it is two things which would have driven a different temperament to cynicism—namely, what he himself called his "obstinate rationality" coupled with an appetite for living which he was too contemptuous of cant to pretend to deny.

Rasselas does not so much end as break off. His contemporaries supposed that Johnson intended to write a continuation, but it seems equally likely that once he had written enough to fill the two small volumes he had agreed to deliver, he stopped because he did not like to write and because, in this particular case, he did not know what more to say. "It was now the time of the inundation of the Nile . . . They deliberated awhile what was to be done, and resolved, when the inundation should cease, to return to Abissinia." Thus the tale concludes, and on the basis of the final sentence one would seem justified in saying that the moral is not that no career leads to happiness and that therefore happiness should not be sought for, but rather the almost Epicurean conclusion that since the ultimate source of human unhappiness "is from eternity," the most fortunate men are those who, like the inhabitants of the Valley, are at least relieved from all the secondary causes of distress and possess in the largest measure the palliatives of security and pleasure. Rasselas and Imlac do return to physical comfort and security.

Shortly before, the sister of Rasselas has been made to say: "To me the choice of life is become less important; I hope, hereafter, to think only on the choice of eternity," and thus Johnson pays to orthodoxy, as he always does, the tribute of formal profession. But these formal professions cannot mean to him what they would have meant had they been as simply and vividly believed in as some have believed them, and here they constitute only the formal rather than the effective moral. Interpreted in the light of his own life as he lived it, the conclusion of *Candide* ("Let us cultivate our garden") would be almost as appropriate to *Rasselas* and therein, perhaps, lies one of the resemblances between the two books which made champions of English respectability so anxious to labor the obvious differences between them.

Boswell, who passed much more easily and more completely than Johnson through the series of steps which lead from the acceptance of orthodoxy to the determination to cultivate pleasantly the garden of this temporary state, could write with enviable ease:

"But if we walk with hope in 'the mid-day sun' of revelation, our temper and disposition will be such, that the comforts and enjoyments in our way will be relished, while we patiently support the inconveniences and pains. After much speculation and various reasonings. I acknowledge myself convinced of the truth of Voltaire's conclusion, *'Après tout c'est un monde passable.'*"

Johnson himself once wrote Mrs. Thrale: *"Vivite laeti* is one of the great rules of health"; and though he might well have suspected of lightness anyone who found it so easy to supply *Rasselas* with Boswell's gloss, he had no theoretical disagreement with it and in his own more troubled way attempted to put its recommendations into practice. Again and again when he is faced with the necessity either of consoling others or of facing some sorrow of his own, the steps are the same. First, the consolations of religion. Then, to others or to himself, the advice: Seek the palliatives for those ills which are susceptible of no radical remedy. That the man as well as the child can be pleased with a rattle and tickled with a straw is indeed one of nature's most kindly laws. (pp. 181-84)

Joseph Wood Krutch, in his Samuel Johnson, *Henry Holt and Company, 1944, 599 p.*

Allen Tate (essay date 1949)

[*Tate's works are closely associated with two critical movements, Agrarianism and New Criticism. A conservative thinker and convert to Catholicism, Tate's most important criticism treats modern poetry, Southern traditions, and the legacy of the Civil War. Attacking the tradition of Western philosophy, which he felt had alienated persons from themselves, one another, and from nature by divorcing intellectual from natural functions in human life, Tate viewed literature as the principal form of knowledge and revelation which restores human beings to a proper relationship with nature and the spiritual realm. In the following excerpt from an essay originally published in 1949, he contrasts Johnson's use of figurative language in* The Lives of the Poets *with the Metaphysical poets' style, focusing on "apparent contradictions within Johnson's criticism."*]

Johnson came to *The Lives of the Poets* when a great age of English poetry was about ending; he had lived through the age, he had formed his sensibility, and disciplined his mind, in it; and it was a poetry to which the Metaphysical style had contributed little. If we refuse to see him as a part of a positive culture, in which personal prejudice can at times, in certain persons, receive the discipline of objectivity which transcends the disorder of unacknowledged opinion, we shall the more readily see in our disagreements with him a failure of understanding on his part.

These general remarks will serve to expose the bias of the narrow enquiry that follows. Whether it is a proper field of enquiry cannot be determined in a short essay. I shall not be concerned with Johnson's criticism as a whole, or with the permanent value of his particular judgments; I shall try to investigate a contrast, very broadly conceived, in the use of figurative language, with Johnson on one side and the Metaphysical style on the other. For this purpose I quote, to begin with, four lines from Denham's "Cooper's Hill" and a part of Johnson's commentary:

> O could I flow like thee, and make thy stream
> My great example, as it is my theme!
> Though deep, yet clear; though gentle, yet not dull;
> Strong without rage, without o'erflowing full.

> The lines in themselves [says Johnson] are not perfect; for most of the words, thus artfully opposed, are to be understood simply on one side of the comparison, and metaphorically on the other; and if there be any language which does not express intellectual operations by material images, into that language they cannot be translated.

Johnson adds that the passage has "beauty peculiar to itself, and must be numbered among those felicities which cannot be produced at will by wit and labor. . . ." (If he was right in saying that "almost every writer for a century has imitated" the lines, we might reasonably expect him to have turned upon them his best critical powers.) The imperfection of the metaphor, he seems to say, lies in its failure to work both ways; that is, the qualities that Denham would like to achieve in his style cannot be found literally in the river. The literal and the metaphorical cannot be reciprocally interchanged. I am a little puzzled that Johnson should see in this discrepancy a defect; for ordinarily it would be a defect from our point of view today, but not from his: the approach to identity of "vehicle" and "tenor" was not a feature of metaphor which the neoclassical critics thought possible or desirable. Johnson I think has an altogether different point in mind.

If we look again at the third part of the sentence, we shall be struck by the negatives in both the conditional and the independent clause. What is Johnson getting at when he says that it is the fault of the passage that the intellectual qualities which Denham desires cannot be "translated" into nonmaterial images? Remove the negatives and we get something like this: If there is a language which can express intellectual operations by material images, into that language the passage can be translated; but it cannot be translated into abstract language. And that is Johnson's real objection to the lines. The tenor of the figure, to be convincing, ought to have translatability into a high degree of abstraction; it ought to be detachable from the literal image of the flowing river. If we bring our own prejudices into play at this point, we should have to decide that Johnson's opinion of the lines is scarcely consistent with his calling them a "felicity" "which cannot be reproduced at will by wit and labor"; for, to parody Johnson himself, figurative language comes naturally if not elegantly to our lips; systematic abstraction is the result of labor. What Johnson seems to detect here is the doubtful application of the operations of the mind to the river; it is a one-way metaphor in which the tenor is compromised by the vehicle. I believe it is fair to say that Johnson liked his tenors straight, without any nonsense from the vehicles. His remark that the "particulars of resemblance are perspicaciously collected," seems incomprehensible.

Johnson would doubtless agree with us in finding little in common between Denham's lines and the fourth stanza of Donne's "A Nocturnall upon S. Lucie's Day." Let us look briefly at that stanza, as well as we can, with the eyes that Johnson turned upon Denham.

> But I am by her death, (which word wrongs her)
> Of the first nothing, the Elixer grown;
> Were I a man, that I were one,
> I needs must show; I should preferre,
> If I were any beast,
> Some ends, some means; Yea plants, yea stones detest,
> And love; All, all some properties invest;
> If I an ordinary nothing were,
> As shadow, a light, and body must be here.

I do not know how to paraphrase the tenor of these lines, because I run at once into Johnson's difficulties with Denham. There are probably no abstractions, more abstract than Donne's own language, into which the distinction between an "ordinary nothing" and the "Elixer" of the "first nothing" can be paraphrased. The tenor can be located only in its vehicle, the specific metaphorical structure of the passage. One of Johnson's counts against the Metaphysical poets was the failure to represent the "operations of intellect" (to say nothing of their wilful neglect of the "scenes of life" and the "prospects of nature"), a quality that Johnson found preeminently in Pope. Yet it must seem to us that Donne is more nearly an *intellectual* poet than Pope (if the designation have meaning at all), for many of Donne's poems are, at one level or another, semi-rational operations elaborately drawn out. (These misunderstandings seize upon one slippery term after another, which will never be fixed, though it is the perpetual task of criticism to misunderstand its "problems" in new terms at intervals of about fifty years.) Johnson knew Donne's

poetry thoroughly, much of it by heart, and he quotes him extensively; but his scattered comment is so brief that we cannot reconstruct a coherent view. We can only surmise that he would have found it "improper" and "vicious" for a man to imagine himself less than an "ordinary nothing." He tells us that "whatever is improper or vicious is produced by a voluntary deviation from nature in pursuit of something new and strange." (pp. 491-95)

Johnson's piety is well known; his views on Christianity were forthright, uncompromising, and beyond controversy; I do not intend to discuss them here. I will cite two brief paragraphs from the **"Life of Waller,"** concerning the relation of poetry and Christian worship:

> Contemplative piety, or the intercourse between God and the human soul, cannot be poetical. Man, admitted to implore the mercy of his Creator, and plead the merits of his Redeemer, is already in a higher state than poetry can confer.
>
> The essence of poetry is invention; such invention as, by producing something unexpected, surprises and delights. The topics of devotion are few, and being few are universally known; but, few as they are, they can be made no more; they receive no grace from novelty of sentiment, and very little from novelty of expression.

There is a certain common sense in these paragraphs, if we read them very freely: Poetry is not religion, or even a substitute for it. But what Johnson actually says is that religious contemplation is not a subject for poetry; and this is nonsense. The first paragraph evinces an ignorance of religious poetry, or an indifference to it, comparable to the incapacity of an American critic three generations later, whose critical style was influenced by Johnson: Edgar Allan Poe. Whether poetry can confer a state either higher or lower than that of contemplative piety becomes a meaningless question if we ask first whether it can *confer* any sort of state. Whether religious experience can be the subject of poetry is another question equally unreal. One does not ask whether a man has two arms and two legs, and expect to deduce the Laputan answer; for he obviously has both. Great devotional poetry obviously exists. (What was Johnson doing with St. John of the Cross, the poems of St. Thomas Aquinas, or even, for that matter, with the Psalms of David?) At the end of Johnson's second paragraph one finds another dubious distinction between sentiment and expression. The sentiment remains unknown without the expression, whether it be "novel" or common. (Johnson's rhetorical parallelism frequently leads him by the nose, into saying more, or something else, than he means.) Whether from novelty of sentiment or of expression it is difficult to see how the "topics" of devotion could receive "grace." No one has ever asserted that they did, unless it be the grace snatched beyond the reach of art. Is this "grace" of the "higher state than poetry" supernatural grace sacramentally conferred? No one has ever asserted that poetry could confer it. Some poems (and their apologists) have asserted that we can get along without it; but that is another problem.

No historical considerations have entered into my rough treatment of Johnson; I am reading him out of his time, in my own time, countering his explicit prejudice with prejudice, perhaps not sufficiently explored, of my own. It would be instructive but beside the point to show that

Johnson's strictures upon religious poetry are neoclassical criticism at a level of insight where as literary critic he could turn out the light, and revert to private feelings at a depth untouched by his "positive training." Johnson, like most critics whose philosophical powers are in themselves not impressive (and unlike Coleridge), is at his best when he is reading or comparing texts. If we continue to think of Johnson at his best as a critic with a positive training in the English neoclassical school, we shall understand more sympathetically his insistence that the end of poetry is delight leading to instruction; its means, invention. What he finds wrong with religious poetry is probably the same thing that he finds wrong with Denham. The devotional objects, being "universally known," provide a fixed "tenor" for which no new metaphorical vehicle or invention is adequate or necessary; for only the tenor is "true." Institutional religion is the immense paraphrase, no longer, if ever, seen as resting upon a metaphorical base, of the religious experience. The imaginative act of returning the paraphrase to the hazards of new experience (new vehicles) is an impiety, even a perversity which he reproves in the Metaphysical poets.

The foregoing digression into the quotations from the lives of Denham and Waller has seemed to me necessary in order to form as clear a notion as possible of Johnson's assumptions about metaphor. Nowhere in the **"Life of Cowley,"** which I shall now glance at, shall we find so close a scrutiny of language as his analysis of Denham's couplets, or a limitation upon the province of poetry so clearly defined in ultimate religious terms, as in the paragraphs on Waller. The **"Life of Cowley"** ends with a formidable string of quotations, none of which receives a thorough going over. His strictures upon Cowley and Donne take the form of generalizations from a considerable body of poetry, but like Aristotle on poetic diction he leaves the application to us. I conceive his criticism of the Metaphysicals to be grounded in certain philosophical assumptions of his time about the meaning of Reason and Nature: I have neither competence nor space to deal extensively with such questions. Doubtless the New Learning of the seventeenth century, which Mr. Wimsatt finds typically reflected in Johnson, and the philosophy of Locke, gave a rationalistic tinge to his conceptions of reason and nature, and buttressed his literary neoclassicism and thus his views on the province of poetry.

We must now make what we can of some crucial passages from the **"Life of Cowley"**:

> . . . they [the Metaphysical poets] neither copied nature nor life; neither painted the forms of matter nor represented the operations of intellect . . . they were not successful in representing or moving the affections.

> They had no regard to that uniformity of sentiment which enables us to conceive and to excite the pains and pleasures of other minds; they never enquired what on any occasion they should have said or done; but wrote rather as beholders than partakers of human nature. . . . Their wish was only to say what had never been said before.

The first of these excerpts contains Johnson's general objection, which could easily take us philosophically far afield. If we roughly equate "nature" with "forms of matter," and "life" with "operations of intellect," we get the solid objects of eighteenth century physics (inorganic: no internal change), and a rationalistic epistemology which orders the objects in fixed relations. I am not able to develop this inference further, but it may be sufficient for my purpose to guess that we have here, in the "operations of intellect" upon the "forms of matter," Locke's secondary qualities in a stable relation to the primary; so that the perception of qualities and discourse about them are a single act of mind. Likewise in Johnson's representation and moving of the affections there is both a perceptual and a cognitive limit beyond which the poet exceeds the known and fixed limits of emotion. Thus the Metaphysical poets failed to enquire into the limits of what can be said; they failed to respect, in ignoring the strict conventions of imitation, the neoclassical standard of generalized emotion, scene, and character; they lacked the uniformity of sentiment which Johnson's positive culture supported. Because they wrote outside the eighteenth century canon they wrote outside, rather than within, human nature.

At this point one should pause to distinguish certain historical differences between the situation of Donne and the old age of English Baroque, when in the 1770's it had passed into Rococo. What little I know about these differences is better known by the scholars in the two fields, though perhaps few scholars know both; I should not in any case wish to rely too much upon terms taken from architecture. And we must not assume that the Rococo artist ought to understand the origins of his style in the Baroque; there is no reason why Johnson should have understood Donne. The age of Johnson had achieved in verse a *period* style. Whatever may have been its remote origins in the age of Donne (it became something very different from its origins), it was a style that we could not write today, and was perhaps inconceivable to Donne and his contemporaries. With the exceptions of Milton (excluding "Lycidas") and Shakespeare, both of whom were so "great" that he could scarcely miss them, he lacked the critical terms and the philosophical temper for the estimation of poetry outside his period style. Perhaps a high development of period style always entails upon its critics a provincial complacency towards the styles of the past which have not directly contributed to it (one thinks of Pound and early Eliot on Milton, both men concerned about a language for a period); and we get almost inevitably a progressive view of poetry. One of the aims of Johnson's proposed, but never written, History of Criticism was to give "An Account of the Rise and Improvement of that Art." But there is no invidious inference to be drawn from his prospectus; there is no evidence that a bad poet after Dryden could win his praise.

Whether he preferred Cowley as a forerunner of his own period style, to Donne, or whether the committee of forty-three booksellers who underwrote the *Lives* did not consider Donne a poet of enough "reputation" to justify a new edition, is a scholar's question; yet it is not without an answer of the internal sort if we are willing to glance at Johnson's praise of Cowley's "Of Wit." Of this poem he says:

> The Ode on Wit is almost without a rival. It was about the time of Cowley that *wit*, which had been till then used for *intellection*, in contra-distinction to *will*, took the meaning, whatever it be, which it now bears. . . . Of all the passages in which poets have exemplified their own precepts, none will easi-

ly be found of greater excellence than that in which
Cowley condemns exuberance of wit.

He then quotes the fifth stanza, of which we may glance
at these lines:

> Several lights will not be seen,
> If there be nothing else between.
> Men doubt because they stand so thick i' the skie,
> If those be stars which paint the Galaxie.

If this does not exhibit the excess of conceit against which
it was written, then one has wasted one's life in the concern for poetry, (a possibility that must always be kept in
view); but short of facing such a crisis one must regretfully
impute to Johnson a lapse of judgment at a moment when
his prejudice is flattered. The passage flatters Johnson otherwise: lines three and four are a couplet that Dryden, in
a fit of absent-mindedness, might have written, and that,
but for the extra syllable in the fifth foot of the third line,
could have been written by Pope in a moment of fatigue.

I have disclaimed any ability to estimate Johnson's specific criticism of the Metaphysical poets; but I seem to have
been judging it, perhaps inevitably; exposition without incidental judgment is not possible. But I now return to the
more neutral enquiry into the contrasting uses of figurative language, of which Johnson stands for one extreme
and Donne for another. The instructive paragraph for this
purpose, in the **"Life of Cowley,"** has not had much attention from critics of either Johnson or Donne; I quote it entire:

> Nor was the sublime more within their reach than
> the pathetic; for they never attempted that compre-
> hension and expanse which at once fills the whole
> mind, and of which the first effect is sudden aston-
> ishment, and the second rational admiration. Sub-
> limity is produced by aggregation, littleness by dis-
> persion. Great thoughts are always general, and
> consist in positions not limited by exceptions, and
> in descriptions not descending to minuteness. It is
> with great propriety that subtility, which in its orig-
> inal import means exility of particles, is taken in its
> metaphorical meaning for nicety of distinction.
> Those writers who lay on the watch for novelty,
> could have little hope of greatness; for great things
> cannot have escaped former observation. *Their at-
> tempts were always analytic; they broke every image
> into fragments; and could no more represent, by
> their slender conceits and laboured particularities,
> the prospects of nature, or the scenes of life, than he
> who dissects a sunbeam with a prism can exhibit the
> wide effulgence of a summer noon.*

Up to the last sentence of this remarkable pronouncement,
about half of the ghost of Longinus is the presiding, if
somewhat equivocal authority. (Longinus did not *oppose*
the "sublime" to the "little.") Great things, even in Johnson's testimony, had escaped former observation before
Shakespeare, and Shakespeare left a few to Pope. But it is
good neoclassical doctrine: "But when t'examine every
part he came, / Nature and Homer were, he found, the
same." It is the doctrine of the Grandeur of Generality
given a critical formula in the phrases "positions not limited by exceptions" and "descriptions not descending to minuteness." If Mr. Leavis is right in saying that Johnson
had little dramatic sense (he could still have had it and
written **Irene**), it is a defect that seems general in that age,
when men assumed a static relation between the mind and

its object, between poet and subject. The universals that
have not escaped former observation are again the big tenors which must not be limited by too many exceptions in
the vehicles: invention is all very well if the poet doesn't
mean it too hard; if he does it will not win rational admiration for the "minute particulars" in which Blake saw the
life not only of poetry but of the spirit. We can scarcely
blame Johnson if in describing what poetry ought to be he
described the weak side of Pope's and his own.

But the remarkable last sentence of the paragraph might
well be set down as the main text of this commentary: I
hope I shall not give it an unfair reading. "Their attempts," says Johnson, "were always analytic; they broke
every image into fragments." He asks us to prejudge Cowley and his fellows before we are given to understand how
we should judge them: it is, generally speaking, bad to
break things. What are the "attempts" of the Metaphysicals? Their poems, or isolated figures? I assume that he
means this: they used metaphor in such a way as to produce analytic effects; they got inside the object and exhibited it as a collection, or dispersion, of "laboured particularities." I confess that I do not understand what I have
just written: I can think of no poem of the Metaphysical
school of which Johnson's words or my own gloss would
be a just description. One could play with an irresponsible
sorites, and take analytic to mean in the Kantian and, for
Johnson, anachronistic sense, a predicate containing nothing that is not already in the subject. Johnson would then
be censuring the Metaphysicals for having done what he
should have praised them for: for giving us "images" the
qualities of which were already known. His censure is for
the Kantian synthetic judgment; for the Metaphysical
flight beyond the predictable character of the object, or for
the internal exploration of new imaginative objects not
known in the neoclassical properties. Johnson I daresay
did not know that he was a neoclassicist; so he boggles at
the violation of what he deemed the eternal principles of
style discovered by the ancients and rediscovered by his
own forerunners for the improvement of English poetry.
By analytic I take it that he also meant the assertion of
marginal similarities as total, like the lovers-compasses
simile which virtually claims an identity on the thin
ground that lovers, like compasses, must lean towards
each other before they can become the two congruent lines
of the embrace. By analytic he means a fragmentation of
objects in pursuit of "occult resemblances."

The famous phrase brings us to the even more famous
"definition" of Metaphysical poetry, in which it occurs:

> But wit, abstracted from its effects upon the hearer,
> may be more rigorously and philosophically con-
> sidered as a kind of *discordia concors;* a combina-
> tion of dissimilar images, or discovery of occult re-
> semblances in things apparently unlike.

One is constantly impressed by Johnson's consistency of
point of view, over the long pull of his self-dedication to
letters. There is seldom either consistency or precision in
his particular judgments and definitions—a defect that
perhaps accounts negatively for his greatness as a critic:
the perpetual reformulation of his standards, with his eye
on the poetry, has done much to keep eighteenth-century
verse alive in our day. His theories (if his ideas ever reach
that level of logical abstraction) are perhaps too simple for
our taste and too improvised; but his reading is disciplined

and acute. There is no doubt that the definition of Metaphysical wit is an improvisation of terms, but it represents the result of long and sensitive meditation on a body of verse which he could not like but the importance of which he had to acknowledge. A brief scrutiny of this definition turns up the astonishing metaphor of sound, *discordia concors,* coming after the promise to give us not a psychological but an epistemological view of wit. We were to have got what wit is, not how it affects us. I don't want to quibble about this matter; I want to emphasize the essential accuracy of one of the great critical insights. It is a new insight based upon a long critical tradition going back to the *Poetics* (Chapter 22):

> It is a great thing indeed to make a proper use of these poetical forms, as also of compounds and strange words. But the greatest thing by far is to be a master of metaphor. It is the one thing that cannot be learned from others; and it is also a sign of genius, since a good metaphor implies an intuitive perception of the similarity in dissimilars.

It would have been helpful in the past twenty-three hundred years if Aristotle had told us what a good metaphor is, and settled the matter. How far should the perception of similarity go? The *Poetics* seems to be a fragment, and we shall not get Aristotle's wisdom (if he had it) for our folly. We have Johnson's, in the second sentence after the quotation above; and he writes what is possibly his best descriptive criticism of the Metaphysical style:

> The most heterogeneous ideas are yoked by violence together. . . .

By what kind of violence? A poetry of violence may have its own validity in its own time, and even for other times. Again we confront Johnson's point of view done up in an approximate generalization, which for all its heuristic accuracy begs the question which it conceals. The question is how much violence is allowable, and at what point does the yoking of dissimilars in similarity overreach itself and collapse under the strain? It would be critical folly to decide how much stretch Johnson would allow, a folly of which he was happily not guilty. The allowed stretch is the stretch of one's age (with one eye on other ages), the tensions within the religious and moral struggle that the poet must acknowledge in himself.

If we may reasonably get around this defeating relativism, what direction shall we take? One direction is towards the chasm; to the leap into the unhistorical and timeless generalization of the late Paul Valéry; but only skeptics who believe in unicorns had better travel that road. Another road leads to the Palace of Wisdom where there aren't any poets; and criticism may want in the end to get along without poetry. Between the chasm and the feather bed (Mr. Blackmur's version of the Palace of Wisdom), somewhere between the down and the up, lies the region that most critics inhabit without quite knowing where it is. That is not too desperate an ignorance, if one remembers that Poe was Valéry's unicorn (desperate skepticism indeed) and that autotelism is usually a bed of feathers that no longer sing. I am not confident that Johnson would like this mixture of feathers, a Palace, and a unicorn; and I am not sure that he would not be right.

Nor can I be sure that his failure to understand Donne as we think we understand him was a real failure. I have concealed the questions I have put to him, as he concealed his, by begging them. One would prefer to *note down,* as dispassionately as possible, his dogmatic rejection of all religious poetry which is not pietistic or devotional; his static psychology of perception; his fixed natural order; his fixed decorum in diction. It all adds up to a denial of validity to what in our age has been called a poetry of experience. A poetry of experience is incipiently a poetry of action; hence of drama, the sense of which Johnson seems to have lacked. The minute particulars of the wrestling with God, which we find in Donne and Crashaw, bring the religious experience into the dimension of immediate time. Johnson's implied division of poetry into the meditative and the descriptive (implied also in his own verse) fixes its limits, arresting the subject within the frame of pictorial space: *ut pictura poesis,* for his typical *period* verb for the poetic effect is that the poet *paints.* The breaking up of the image, of which he accuses the Metaphysical poets, is the discovery of a dynamic relation between the mind and its objects, in a poetry which does not recognize the traditional topic; the subject becomes the metaphorical structure, it is no longer the set theme. The ideas that result from the dynamic perception of objects (language itself is thus an object) are in constant disintegration; so inferentially are the objects themselves. The "object" which poetry like "The Extasie" or "The Canonization" suggests that we locate, is not an existence in space, but an essence created by the junction of the vehicle and the tenor of the leading metaphor. It is not *in* space; it moves with experience in time. (pp. 495-507)

> *Allen Tate, "Johnson on the Metaphysical Poets," in his* Essays of Four Decades, *The Swallow Press Inc., 1968, pp. 491-508.*

Ian Jack   (essay date 1952)

[*Jack is a Scottish educator and literary scholar who, in several full-length critical works, has examined English poetry from the Augustan era through the late nineteenth century. In the following excerpt, he identifies the Juvenalian features of "The Vanity of Human Wishes" which distinguish it as a "tragical satire . . . not only deeply pessimistic, but pessimistic in an almost medieval way."*]

As Edward Young pointed out, the term 'satire' is not 'unapplicable to graver compositions. Ethics, Heathen and Christian, and the Scriptures themselves, are, in a great measure, a satire on the weakness and iniquity of men.' **"The Vanity of Human Wishes,** 'a poem of the moral and didactic species', is in many ways more reminiscent of the Book of Job, of Prior's *Solomon* or Johnson's own ***Rasselas,*** than of *Hudibras* and *The Rape of the Lock, MacFlecknoe* and the *Epistle to Arbuthnot.* It is a discourse without a plot, a pessimistic survey of human life in which the poet enforces his lesson with a series of *exempla* in the manner of a preacher. Like its model it ends with the short didactic coda conventional in the classical *satura,* which was commonly made up of a major part which attacks vice, and a minor part in which virtue is recommended.

It is the prominence of the element of attack which makes **"The Vanity of Human Wishes,"** like its Juvenalian original, a satire in the English sense of the word. What distinguishes it from the *Essay on Man,* for example—a poem with which it has marked similarities—is that it takes its tone from its primary rhetorical function of 'diminishing' human life. While several of the finest passages in the *Essay on Man* have this function, Pope's main intention is to survey human life and make sense of it. Johnson does not aim at explanation: his concern, like Juvenal's, is to underline the insecurity of man's existence and the futility of selfish ambitions. This intention gives **"The Vanity of Human Wishes"** its characteristic accent.

In Juvenal Johnson found a perfect model. The affinity of Juvenal's Stoicism with certain aspects of Christianity was early recognized by the Church. The Tenth Satire, on which Johnson's poem is founded, was particularly popular. 'This Divine Satyr', as Dryden called it, is the first of the more reflective satires which contrast so strongly with those which go before that a German scholar was driven to the theory that there were two Juvenals. Throughout the Middle Ages it furnished preachers with topics and examples, and it continued to be used in this way in the seventeenth and eighteenth centuries. Dryden mentions that it was recommended, along with the satires of Persius, in a pastoral letter written by the Bishop of Salisbury, 'to the serious perusal and practice of the divines in his diocese, as the best commonplaces for their sermons, [and] as the store-houses and magazines of moral virtues, from whence they may draw out, as they have occasion, all manner of assistance for the accomplishment of a virtuous life'.

It was not only the similarity between Juvenal's ethical position and his own that appealed to Johnson, as to so many Christians before him. He was impressed also by Juvenal's magnificent rhetoric. Juvenal was a professional pleader for many years before he began to write satire, and his poems owe a considerable debt to the rhetorical theory of his time. In his work Johnson found at once a sombre reading of life which had much in common with his own and an object-lesson in the art of impressing what he had to say on the minds of his readers.

When Joseph Warton remarked that Johnson 'certainly would not have succeeded so well if he had ever attempted to imitate Horace', he had in mind not only the differences between the work of the two great Latin satirists which are most evident to the modern reader, but also the interpretations of their work made current by the editions and commentaries of the scholars of the Renaissance. As has been mentioned earlier, the editors of Horace and Juvenal did not scruple to deduce from the works of the satirist of their choice universal rules of satire. Juvenal's admirers held that Horace's satires were written in a style too low for the true dignity of satire, while Vossius and others insisted that '*Horatian* Satire is the only true one; and the Writings of *Juvenal* and *Persius* have no Pretence to that Title'. From this controversy was born the theory that there were two different species of satire, each legitimate and each governed by its own rules. 'The Comick Satirist', Dennis remarked, 'who owes no small Part of his Excellence to his Experience, that is, to the Knowledge of the Conversation and Manners of the Men of the World, [will] be in all likelihood more agreeable to the discerning Part of a Court, and a great Capital'; while 'the Tragick Satire, which like Tragedy fetches its Notions from Philosophy and from common Sense, [will] be in all probability more acceptable to Universities and Cloisters, and all those Recluse and Contemplative Men, who pass most of their Time in their Closets, all which Persons are suppos'd to have Philosophy from Study, and common Sense from Nature'. This difference of tone, which resulted in a difference of style, is the heart of the distinction. And as Horace's man-of-the-world manner, casual, urbane, insinuating, confidential, was a perfect model for Pope; so the declamatory grandeur of Juvenal, with its tone of a dignified public utterance, austere, exacting, sternly censorious, afforded Johnson the precedent and the example that he required. 'He could not rally', as Dryden said of Juvenal, 'but he could declaim; and as his provocations were great, he has revenged them tragically.'

The personal quality of the *Imitations of Horace* contrasts with the impersonality of **"The Vanity of Human Wishes."** In Pope's epistolary satires, as in Horace, autobiography is a prominent element: in Johnson's great poem, as in the Tenth Satire of Juvenal, it is completely lacking. While Pope chats wittily with his friends, rising only occasionally, and with the most carefully managed of transitions, to a more elevated tone, Johnson is in the pulpit throughout, addressing a congregation. Pope chooses for his examples living men and women, often the objects of strong personal animosity. Johnson, aiming at a detachment and grandeur rivalling that of History itself, confines himself to 'the most eminent vices among the greatest persons'. Disdaining Atticus, Sporus, and Atossa he writes of Wolsey, Charles of Sweden, Galileo, and 'Persia's tyrant'.

As the thoughts of Juvenal are 'much more elevated' than those of Horace, they are fittingly expressed in a style akin to that of tragedy. To gain a similar effect Johnson used much more 'numerous' verse than that of the *Imitations of Horace,* and a 'sublime and lofty' diction:

> The march begins in military state,
> And nations on his eye suspended wait;
> Stern Famine guards the solitary coast,
> And Winter barricades the realms of Frost;
> He comes, not want and cold his course delay;—
> Hide, blushing Glory, hide Pultowa's day:
> The vanquish'd hero leaves his broken bands,
> And shews his miseries in distant lands;
> Condemn'd a needy supplicant to wait,
> While ladies interpose, and slaves debate.
> But did not Chance at length her error mend?
> Did no subverted empire mark his end?
> Did rival monarchs give the fatal wound?
> Or hostile millions press him to the ground?
> His fall was destin'd to a barren strand,
> A petty fortress, and a dubious hand;
> He left the name, at which the world grew pale,
> To point a moral, or adorn a tale.

Dryden's remark that Juvenal's expressions are 'sonorous and more noble' than Horace's applies also to the comparison between **"The Vanity of Human Wishes"** and Pope's epistolary satires.

The abstract generality of idiom noticeable in some degree in all Johnson's writing is used with great skill to contribute to the elevation of the style of his 'tragical satire'. In many passages abstractions and personifications are the key-words:

> In full-blown *dignity,* see Wolsey stand,
> *Law* in his voice, and *fortune* in his hand:
> To him *the church, the realm,* their *pow'rs* consign,
> Thro' him the rays of regal *bounty* shine,
> Turn'd by his nod the stream of *honour* flows,

His smile alone *security* bestows:
Still to new heights his restless *wishes* tow'r,
Claim leads to *claim*, and *pow'r* advances *pow'r;*
Till *conquest* unresisted ceas'd to please,
And *rights* submitted, left him none to seize.

Such abstractions are very different from the type commonly associated with unsuccessful Augustan verse. They are the manifestation and embodiment of concentrated meaning and a weighty seriousness.

In the work of many poets there is some characteristic of style which becomes most evident when they are writing at the top of their bent. This unusual fondness for abstract personifications is Johnson's characteristic. Just as Donne's images tend to become more and more daring as his inspiration catches fire, so the better Johnson is writing the more prominent abstract personifications become. It is when he has gathered all his powers and is deploying his poetic rhetoric with supreme effect that he makes the fullest use of abstractions and personifications:

Are these thy views? proceed, illustrious youth,
And *virtue* guard thee to the throne of *Truth!*
Yet should thy soul indulge the gen'rous heat,
Till captive *Science* yields her last retreat;
Should *Reason* guide thee with her brightest ray,
And pour on misty *Doubt* resistless day;
Should no false *Kindness* lure to loose delight,
Nor *Praise* relax, nor *Difficulty* fright;
Should tempting *Novelty* thy cell refrain,
And *Sloth* effuse her opiate fumes in vain;
Should *Beauty* blunt on fops her fatal dart,
Nor claim the triumph of a letter'd heart;
Should no *Disease* thy torpid veins invade,
Nor *Melancholy's* phantoms haunt thy shade;
Yet hope not life from *grief* or *danger* free,
Nor think the *doom* of man revers'd for thee.

Critics have often fallen into the danger of condemning one species of personification by contrast with another. It is the task of the critic to be empirical, judging each example as he meets it, and making no attempt to lay down universal laws for poetry. To condemn Johnson's abstract sort of personification out of hand, contrasting it (for example) with Keats's use of the figure, is as futile as it would be to condemn the prose of De Quincey by comparing it with Swift's. Just as De Quincey and Swift were aiming at different effects, and used different means to attain them, so Johnson and a Romantic poet aim, in their use of personification, at different results. It is not surprising that they use different methods. To condemn Johnson for 'failing to bring his personifications to life' (by which is usually meant failing to bring them before the mind's eye) is uncritical. That was not the sort of effect that he wished to gain.

Elevation of style is not the only result of Johnson's use of an unusually abstract idiom. An effect of philosophic generality, and a remarkable conciseness, are equally noteworthy. Johnson belonged to an age which found generalizations about human life exciting, when many critics held, with Imlac, that the true poet 'must divest himself of the prejudices of his age or country; . . . must consider right and wrong in their abstracted and invariable state; . . . must disregard present laws and opinions, and rise to general and transcendental truths, which will always be the same'. The use of highly generalized figures in **"The Vanity of Human Wishes"** exemplifies one of the most direct ways in which the poet can give expression to his general observations. What Rymer called 'the greater force and emphasis [of] the *abstract*' was thus a rhetorical effect with a philosophical basis. Further, *Worth* and *Science* are not only dignified and philosophical ways of saying *those who deserve a reward* and *men of learning:* they are also remarkably concise. Similarly in the lines

Around his tomb let Art and Genius weep,
But hear his death, ye blockheads, hear and sleep,

Art and *Genius,* which contrast with the concrete and undignified *ye blockheads,* are more concise as well as more dignified than their concrete equivalents. Such effects led Joseph Warton to remark on the 'diction remarkably close and compact' of this poem.

Closely connected with his preference for abstraction is Johnson's use of what may be termed 'the generic article'. Instead of *learned men* he may say *Science:* equally he may say *the knowing.* He felt this to be a gain in elevation and in philosophical generality, though not in conciseness. This use of the generalized individual for the species is very common in **"The Vanity of Human Wishes."** Nothing is more characteristic than the frequency of such phrases as *the vassal. . . the lord; the hind; the needy traveller; the toiling statesman; th' insidious rival and the gaping heir; the glitt'ring eminence;* and *the plunder'd palace.*

Johnson uses the definite article in a number of other ways very similar to this 'generic' use. For example:

At once is lost the pride of aweful state,
The golden canopy, the glitt'ring plate,
The regal palace, the luxurious board,
The liv'ried army, and the menial lord.

There is no rhetorical device which gives Johnson greater help in the attainment of that 'grandeur of generality' to which he aspired:

The festal blazes, the triumphal show,
The ravish'd standard, and the captive foe,
The senate's thanks, the gazette's pompous tale,
With force resistless o'er the brave prevail.

What could be simpler? *The* + generalized adjective + generic noun. Yet the result is poetry of no mean order.

With the same object of impressing on the reader the abundance and irrefutability of the evidence Johnson makes telling use of schematic figures based on parallelism and repetition. These vary from the simple repetition in lines 25-26—

For gold his sword the hireling ruffian draws,
For gold the hireling judge distorts the laws

—through the more extended repetition of 'him' and 'his' in the passage about Wolsey to the skilful rhetoric of the closing lines:

For love, which scarce collective man can fill;
For patience sov'reign o'er transmuted ill;
For faith, that panting for a happier seat,
Counts death kind Nature's signal of retreat:
These goods for man the laws of heav'n ordain,
These goods he grants, who grants the pow'r to gain;
With these celestial wisdom calms the mind,
And makes the happiness she does not find.

Such passages suggest that excessive emphasis is often

placed on the part played by the couplet in the rhetoric of Augustan verse. In **"The Vanity of Human Wishes"** it is not the couplet but the verse-paragraph that is the basic unit of composition. Like Pope in the best parts of the *Essay on Man* Johnson here succeeded in weaving his end-stopped couplets into a larger unity. The irresistible march of the lines forms a fitting accompaniment to the massive accumulation of sombre statements about life and bears witness to his rhetorical skill.

Like the Idea of Tragedy and Comedy, the Idea of Horatian and Juvenalian Satire acted as an inspiration to poets; it provided masks, bearing, and gesture which enabled them to express their deepest feelings within the necessary cloak of stylization. It is fitting that the great age of verse satire in England should have drawn to a close with a poem in which the greatest man of letters of the century found in Juvenal as perfect a model as the greatest poet of the period had found in Horace.

Yet Johnson's debt to Juvenal should not blind us to the originality of his achievement. 'The general character of this translation', he remarked of the version of Juvenal by Dryden and his associates, 'will be given when it is said to preserve the wit, but to want the dignity of the original. The peculiarity of Juvenal is a mixture of gaiety and stateliness, of pointed sentences, and declamatory grandeur. His points have not been neglected; but his grandeur none of the band seemed to consider as necessary to be imitated, except Creech.' Johnson took for his model one of the most sombre of Juvenal's satires, and the quality which he was most concerned to reproduce was not the wit of his original but its grandeur. In spite of the wish that Democritus would revisit the world and improve it 'With chearful wisdom and instructive mirth', there is even less humour in Johnson's poem than in Juvenal's. In his hands the Juvenalian satire became a sermon of incomparable weight and authority.

It is hard to see how the old fallacy that the eighteenth century was an age of facile optimism could have survived a reading of Johnson's 'tragical satire', which is not only deeply pessimistic, but pessimistic in an almost medieval way. In tone it has a manifest affinity to the tradition of *contemptus mundi,* while the lesson it enforces is the lesson of Erasmus in *The Praise of Folly:*

> Were any one plac'd on that Tower, from whence *Jove* is fancied by the Poets to Survey the World, he would all around discern how many Grievances and Calamities our whole Life is on every Side encompassed with: How Unclean our Birth, how Troublesome our Tendance in the Cradle, how liable our Childhood is to a Thousand Misfortunes, how Toilsome and full of Drudgery our Riper Years, how Heavy and Uncomfortable our Old Age, and lastly, how Unwelcome the Unavoidableness of Death. Farther, in every Course of Life how many Wracks there may be of torturing Diseases, how many unhappy Accidents may casually occurr, how many unexpected Disasters may arise, and what strange Alterations may one Moment produce? Not to mention such Miseries as Men are mutually the Cause of, as Poverty, Imprisonment, Slander, Reproach, Revenge, Treachery, Malice, Cousenage, Deceit, and so many more, as to reckon them all would be as puzz'ling Arithmetick as the numbring of the Sands.

(pp. 135-45)

Ian Jack, " 'Tragical Satire': The Vanity of Human Wishes," in his Augustan Satire: Intention and Idiom in English Poetry, 1660-1750, *Oxford at the Clarendon Press, 1952, pp. 135-45.*

René Wellek   (essay date 1955)

[*Wellek employed a critical method, as demonstrated in* A History of Modern Criticism *(1955-65) and outlined in his* Theory of Literature *(1949), which describes, analyzes, and evaluates a work solely in terms of the problems it poses for itself and how the writer solves them. Wellek's critical methods are reflected in the work of the New Critics, though he was not a member of that group and rejected their more formalistic tendencies. In the following excerpt, he argues that Johnson embraced a "liberal" neoclassicist perspective in his literary criticism.*]

Samuel Johnson (1709-84) cannot be considered simply as a representative of English neoclassicism. He does, it is true, hold to many of its commonplaces and share most of its tastes. But he differs clearly from the neoclassical creed on some important issues. In him certain of its elements have overgrown all others and led to consequences which are destructive of its very essence. Dr. Johnson is, of course, no romanticist or even unconscious forerunner of romanticism: he is rather one of the first great critics who have almost ceased to understand the nature of art, and who, in central passages, treats art as life. He has lost faith in art as the classicists understood it and has not found the romantic faith. He paves the way for a view which makes art really superfluous, a mere vehicle for the communication of moral or psychological truth. Art is no longer judged as art but as a piece or slice of life. This new view comes out very clearly in Johnson's famous **"Preface"** to his edition of Shakespeare (1765).

> This therefore, is the praise of Shakespeare, that his drama is the mirror of life; that he who has mazed his imagination, in following the phantoms which other writers raise up before him, may here be cured of his delirious extasies, by reading human sentiments in human language, by scenes from which a hermit may estimate the transactions of the world, and a confessor predict the progress of the passions. . . . Shakespeare has no heroes; his scenes are occupied by men, who act and speak as the reader thinks he should himself have spoken or acted on the same occasion. . . . The dialogue of this author is often so evidently determined by the incident which produces it, and is pursued with so much ease and simplicity, that it seems scarcely to claim the merit of fiction, but to have been gleaned by diligent selection out of common conversation, and common occurrences.

This view, that literature is "a just representation of things really existing and actions really performed," that the "legitimate end of fiction is the conveyance of truth," that the novelists should be "just copiers of human manners," recurs again and again. There runs through Johnson a deep suspicion of all fiction and all art. According to Hawkins he "could at any time be talked into a disapprobation of all fictitious relations, of which he would frequently say they took no hold of the mind." "The rejection and contempt of fiction is rational and manly" is another of his sayings. We can see this preference for truth running through all Johnson's judgments. It comes out with ludicrous violence in a story, also told by Hawkins: "Talking with some persons about allegorical painting, he said: 'I had rather see the portrait of a dog I know, than all the allegorical painting, they can show me in the world.' " It comes out even more strikingly in his preference for domestic tragedy: "What is nearest touches us most. The passions rise higher at domestic than at imperial tragedies." *Timon of Athens* is a "domestic tragedy, and therefore strongly fastens on the attention of the reader." A pathetic and moving scene in *Henry VIII* (IV. ii), in which Catharine of Aragon hears of the death of Wolsey and speaks of her own last wishes, was to Johnson "above any other part of Shakespeare's tragedies, and perhaps above any scene of any other poet, tender and pathetic, without gods, or furies, or poisons, or precipices, without the help of romantic circumstances, without improbable sallies of poetical lamentation, and without any throes of tumultuous misery." (pp. 79-80)

The second great principle of Dr. Johnson's criticism after "reality" is, of course, "moral truth," morality. Didacticism has a venerable tradition in criticism, and I am not disposed to dispute its rights if they are properly limited. In Johnson they are not always properly limited. Instead, his didactic criterion often becomes a demand for mere moralizing, for a selection from nature which frequently runs counter to his own principle of reality. In *Rambler* No. 4 he discusses modern fiction and begins by saying: "It is justly considered as the greatest excellency of art, to imitate nature; but it is necessary to distinguish those parts of nature, which are most proper for imitation: greater care is still required in presenting life, which is so often discolored by passion, or deformed by wickedness." He draws the conclusion that "many characters ought never to be drawn." The purpose of novels is "to teach the means of avoiding the snares which are laid by Treachery for Innocence . . . to give the power of counteracting fraud, without the temptation to practice it; to initiate youth by mock encounters in the art of necessary defence, and to increase prudence without impairing virtue." Perfect heroes are not objectionable, and "vice, for vice is necessary to be shewn, should always disgust." Johnson also frequently required poetical justice. He sides with the general public in preferring a happy ending for *King Lear*. "I was many years ago so shocked by Cordelia's death, that I know not whether I ever endured to read again the last scenes of the play till I undertook to revise them as an editor." Johnson feels "some indignation" that Angelo in *Measure for Measure* is not punished. He even endorses Iago's warning to Othello ("She did deceive her father, marrying you"), solemnly moralizing on deceit and falsehood as "obstacles to happiness." He thought that "perhaps Shakespeare meant to punish Juliet's hypocrisy" when she asked to be left alone:

> For I have need of many orisons.

But Johnson's concept of poetic justice is not always so obtusely literal minded.

In the *Lives* there is a passage which admits that "since wickedness often prospers in real life, the poet is certainly at liberty to give it prosperity on the stage. For if poetry is an imitation of reality, how are its laws broken by exhibiting the world in its true form? The stage may sometimes gratify our wishes, but if it be truly the mirror of life, it ought to shew us sometimes what we are to expect." The demand for reality here triumphs over the demand for morality with the argument that reality is instructive and hence moral. But more frequently the moralist is dominant, to the exclusion and even detriment of the critic. Johnson preferred Richardson to Fielding for moral and political reasons; he condemned *Tom Jones* as a "vicious book" and Fielding as a "barren rascal." He despised Sterne for his impiety and obscenity. In spite of his admiration he had strong moral reservations against Swift; and of course Johnson is the most famous of those critics who, like Tolstoy and Shaw, complain of Shakespeare's lack of morality. (pp. 82-4)

Johnson has been widely admired for this type of pronouncement, for his sturdy common sense, for his attitude of "no nonsense." At the same time, therefore, he has been dismissed—especially on the Continent—as a "British superstition." It seems hard to deny that in Johnson we can observe a slipping of the grasp on the nature of art and an anticipation of standards of realism and moralism which will make art really as superfluous as it seemed to many Englishmen of the 19th century. It must have become so to Johnson, who in his later years felt that his conversation did as much good as his writings.

But it is impossible to dismiss him as a mere moralist or expounder of a realistic view which confounds art and life. For Johnson moralism and realism combine with a strong and emphatic exposition of many of the central neoclassical tenets, especially the basic rationalistic view of art, and with a trained and self-conscious taste which worked with remarkable sureness within the body of accessible literature. That Johnson is not a narrow authoritarian is obvious; he condemns the imitation of ancient authors. "No man ever yet became great by imitation," he says in *Rambler* No. 154, and repeats it in *Rasselas.* On the other hand Johnson recognizes the greatness of many ancients and the importance of the argument based on tradition and general agreement. "What mankind has long possessed they have often examined and compared; and if they persist to value the possession, it is because frequent comparisons have confirmed opinion in its favor." "What has been longest known has been most considered, and what is most considered is best understood."

Literature is thus not imitation of ancient writers, but representations of general nature, of "general manners or common life," as "reason and nature are uniform and inflexible" and "human nature is always the same." Realism, Dr. Johnson frequently recognizes, is thus not accurate copying nor is it merely selection by moral criteria; it is rather the depiction of the general, the universal, the typical. There is, I think, a certain undeniable contradiction between Johnson's many purely realist or moralist pronouncements and this abstractionism. There is a contradiction between his constant recommendations of the abstract, the generalized and universal, and his actual practical love of life, of its concrete particularity. The abstract neoclassicism clashes with the new realism; but the former, while deplorable in its desiccated abstractness, did something for Johnson: it gave him a hold on art, some view of the nature and function of art which would not simply identify it with a slice of life, selected and judged by moral standards.

He recognizes that realism is not enough. "If the world be promiscuously described, I cannot see of what use it can be to read the account: or why it may not be as safe to turn the eye immediately upon mankind as upon a mirror which shows all that presents itself without discrimination." His usual remedy is moral selection. But this moral selection is assumed to proceed to "general and transcendental truths." Thus Johnson arrives at his condemnation of the particular, the local and transient, a thesis which he formulated possibly more sharply than any other critic of high repute. In the tenth chapter of **Rasselas** is the famous passage: "The business of a poet is to examine, not the individual, but the species; to remark general properties and large appearances: he does not number the streaks of the tulip, or describe the different shades in the verdure of the forest." "Poetry," he says, discussing the pastoral, "cannot dwell upon the minuter distinctions, by which one species differs from another, without departing from that simplicity of grandeur which fills the imagination; nor dissect the latent qualities of things, without losing its general power of gratifying every mind by recalling its conceptions." This view appears quite frequently. Thus Shakespeare is praised as the "poet of nature," a term which is, to a modern reader, surprisingly explained by what follows:

> His characters are not modified by the customs of particular places . . . by the peculiarities of studies or professions . . . or by the accidents of transient fashions or temporary opinions; they are the genuine progeny of common humanity . . . His persons act and speak by the influence of those general passions and principles by which all minds are agitated, and the whole system of life is continued in motion. In the writings of other poets a character is too often an individual, in those of Shakespeare it is commonly a species.

The same view underlies the discussion of the metaphysical poets. Johnson objects to their failure to reach the sublime. "Sublimity is produced by aggregation, and littleness by dispersion. Great thoughts are always general, and consist in positions not limited by exceptions, and in descriptions not descending to minuteness." We find this criterion again and again: Butler's *Hudibras* cannot last, because it is full of allusions comprehensible only at a particular time; a poem by Casimir (Sarbieski) expresses a thought "more generally, and therefore more poetically" than a poem by Cowley; Edgar's speech in *King Lear* describing the cliff of Dover is censured for "its observations of particulars, its attention to distinct objects," choughs and crows, the samphire gatherer and the fishermen. Johnson feels that the "one great and dreadful image of irresistible destruction" is "dissipated and enfeebled" by these details. On the other hand, Gray's "Elegy" "abounds with images which find a mirror in every mind, and with sentiments to which every bosom returns an echo." (pp. 84-6)

Historically most important was Johnson's attack on the rules. He follows partly the usual line of recognizing that genius is above rules, that there "is always an appeal open from criticism to nature." But this would be little but giving up the question. More frequently and more consistently he recognizes that it is the aim of criticism "to establish principles: to improve opinion into knowledge," to discover "principles of judgment on unalterable and evident truth," to use rules as "instruments of mental vision." These basic principles must be distinguished from arbitrary local prescriptions: "The accidental prescriptions of authority, when time has procured them veneration, are often confounded with the laws of nature." Some laws of criticism are to be considered "fundamental and indispensable, others only as useful and convenient; some as dictated by reason and necessity, others as enacted by despotic antiquity; some as invincibly supported by their conformity to the order of nature and operations of the intellect; others as formed by accident, or instituted by example, and therefore always liable to dispute and alteration." This is, in itself, a fairly widespread idea accepted by Voltaire among others, but the dividing line between nature and custom drawn by Johnson involved a rejection of the rigid unities of time and place, and a defense of tragicomedy. In practice this was especially a defense of Shakespeare as a great English classic.

Johnson criticizes the unity of space with a recognition of the falsity of the usual neoclassical assumption of delusion. . . . The same argument holds good with respect to the unity of time. Johnson concedes that "probability requires that the time of action should approach somewhat nearly to that of exhibition. . . . But since it will frequently happen that some delusion must be admitted, I know not where the limits of imagination can be fixed." Especially the interval between acts can be imagined as long as the author thinks fit. Thus nothing is essential but the unity of action. In these arguments Johnson correctly grasps what modern aestheticians would call "aesthetic distance."

Tragicomedy is defended by Johnson with fundamentally realistic arguments. "The connexion of important with trivial incidents, since it is not only common but perpetual in the world, may surely be allowed upon the stage, which pretends only to be the mirror of life." Specifically Johnson defends Shakespeare's mixture of tragedy and comedy by going so far as to deny the distinctions of genres in him. "Shakespeare's plays are not in the rigorous and critical sense either tragedies or comedies, but compositions of a distinct kind; exhibiting the real state of sublunary nature, which partakes of good and evil, joy and sorrow, mingled with endless variety of proportion and innumerable modes of combinations; and expressing the course of the world, in which the loss of one is the gain of another." "When Shakespeare's plan is understood, most of the criticisms of Rymer and Voltaire vanish away. The play of *Hamlet* is opened, without impropriety, by two sentinels; Iago bellows at Brabantio's window, without injury to the scheme of the play, though in terms which a modern audience would not easily endure; the character of Polonius is seasonable and useful; and the grave-diggers themselves may be heard with applause." Johnson accepts Menenius, the clownish senator in *Coriolanus,* and defends the fact that King Claudius, a king, is represented as a drunkard in *Hamlet.* Shakespeare "always makes nature predominant over accident." (pp. 87-9)

While Johnson is thus liberal in the matter of decorum in characterization, he holds firmly to neoclassical views about decorum in language. His own theory and practice of style leans in the direction of the abstract, the grandiose, the ornamental. In *Adventurer* No. 115 he distinguishes a plain style, "clear, pure, nervous and expressive," which is used in the discussion of science and demonstration, but argues that if the "topics be probable and persuasory, the author must recommend them by the superaddition of elegance and imagery, to display the colors of varied diction, and pour forth the music of modulated periods." Elsewhere he says: "The pebble must be polished with care, which hopes to be valued as a diamond; and words ought surely to be labored, when they are intended to stand for things."

Yet in his criticisms of Shakespeare and other writers Johnson does not stand very strictly by the ideal of splendid diction. Shakespeare is praised especially for his comic dialogue, which seems to Johnson a "style which never becomes obsolete, a conversation above grossness, and below refinement where propriety resides." Many times Shakespeare is censured for his "disproportionate pomp of diction," his "tumor" and even bombast. Gray's odes excite Johnson's dislike, partly for the "cumbrous splendor" of their diction. We may be surprised, in view of a general similarity of Johnson's own style with that of Jeremy Taylor or Sir Thomas Browne, to see how severely he censured Browne's style as "rugged, pedantic, obscure, harsh, uncouth." Much of this can be explained by the traditional rhetorical theories of levels of style and by Johnson's own interest in the stabilization and purification of the English language. Johnson devoted years of his life to the *Dictionary,* which is not merely a descriptive thesaurus of the English language but a work which aims to prescribe good usage and to censure words. It includes words such as "abstrude," "adjugate," "advesperate," and "agriculation," but either excludes many other words as obsolete or colloquial or lists them with notes stating that they are "low," "improper," "corrupt," "barbarous," "unauthorized," or "lacking in etymology." ("Punch," for example, is of a lower order than the Arabic "sherbet.") We thus can hardly be surprised that Johnson did not like "low" diction in a tragic context and devoted a whole number of the *Rambler* (No. 168) to a discussion of Lady Macbeth's speech (I, v, 51ff.):

> Come, thick night!
> And pall thee in the dunnest smoke of hell,
> That my keen knife see not the wound it makes;
> Nor heav'n peep through the blanket of the dark,
> To cry: Hold, hold!

"Dun" is criticized as an epithet "now seldom heard but in the stable," and "knife" as the "name of an instrument used by butchers and cooks in the meanest employments." "Who does not, from the habit of connecting a knife with sordid offices, feel aversion rather than terror?" Johnson can hardly "check his risibility" when he thinks of the two unfortunate words "peep" and "blanket." There are elsewhere censures of "studied barbarity" in Spenser's *Shepheardes Calender* and of mean diction used by kings in *Henry V* or *Richard II.* But on the whole Johnson's views of diction are moderate and carefully graduated according to genre and context. (pp. 90-1)

His attitude toward versification is somewhat different. Even more than in the matter of diction, Johnson was convinced that his own time had achieved the pinnacle of perfection. English versification is a "science" which excludes "all casualty" and aspires to "constancy." Thus, once established, it cannot and should not be changed. After

Pope, "to attempt any further improvement of versification will be dangerous." A whole *Rambler* essay (No. 86) is devoted to the distinction between "pure" and "mixed" measure in English heroic pentameters. By "pure" Johnson means lines which fulfill the metrical patterns exactly. He admits only grudgingly the necessity of "mixed" measures, i.e. those which allow "substitution," especially in the first measure. The possibility of using more unaccented syllables than two in a measure is not even mentioned, and triplets and alexandrines, while admitted as necessary, are condemned. Dr. Johnson's ear must have been early attuned only to the heroic couplet, whose niceties and differences he was obviously very well able to perceive and to describe. But he had considerable difficulties even with blank verse, a meter sanctioned in his eyes by the precedents of Shakespeare and Milton. In discussing Milton's arguments against rhyme, he professes to see a strong difference between English and the classical languages which can do without rhyme. "The music of the English heroic line strikes the ear so faintly that it is easily lost, unless all the syllables of every line cooperate together; this cooperation can be only obtained by the preservation of every verse unmingled with another as a distinct system of sounds, and this distinctness is obtained and preserved by the artifice of rhyme." "Blank verse left merely to its numbers has little operation either on the ear or mind: it can hardly support itself without bold figures and striking images." Thus the sublime Milton is admitted: also Young's *Night Thoughts* and Akenside's *Pleasures of Imagination;* but most of the contemporary blank verse, especially in didactic or burlesque subjects, excites Johnson's disfavor. "But it is blank verse" suffices to condemn a poem by David Mallet.

Johnson was even more hostile to and apparently simply incapable of reading lyrical measures of greater complexity and diversity. He dislikes the "Pindaric madness" of Cowley, observing that the "great pleasure of verse arises from the known measure of the lines and uniform structure of the stanzas." Dryden's and Pope's "Odes for St. Cecilia's Day" are similarly said to "want the essential constituent of metrical compositions, the stated recurrence of settled numbers." Most famous, of course, are Johnson's strictures upon the minor poems of Milton: even the songs of *Comus* are "not very musical in their numbers," and *Lycidas* is written in "unpleasing numbers." Thus his highest praise goes out to Pope. If we can believe Boswell, Johnson said that "a thousand years may elapse before there shall appear another man with a power of versification equal to that of Pope."

Johnson is thus firmly rooted and even enclosed in the taste of his own age. He seems hardly touched by two of the new motifs of 18th-century criticism: aesthetics and cosmopolitanism.

There is hardly any discussion of beauty in Johnson's writings. The discussion which introduces No. 92 of the *Rambler* (1751) seems to come to relativistic conclusions. Beauty is "merely relative and comparative," and Johnson seems to grant that it is "little subject to the examinations of reason." But then he takes away this concession to skepticism by an appeal to the verdict of the ages, the common sense of humanity. The long continuance of the reputation of certain writings "proves that they are adequate to our faculties, and agreeable to nature." He announces the possibility of "reducing some regions of literature under the dominance of science" and enters into a discussion of the relation of sound and sense in verse. Beauty, in literature, seems to Johnson to be largely confined to beauty of language and versification, the sonority of sound, the regular recurrence of meter. Now and then, apparently under the influence of his friend Edmund Burke's *Inquiry into the Origin of Our Ideas of the Sublime and the Beautiful* (1756), Johnson distinguishes between the beautiful and the sublime, between attention to the vast and to the minute. Milton is characterized in terms of sublimity or "gigantic loftiness." "Sublimity is the general and prevailing quality of this poem [*Paradise Lost*]; sublimity variously modified, sometimes descriptive, sometimes argumentative." (pp. 92-3)

[Johnson] certainly shows little interest in speculations about genius and imagination. Not that he never uses these terms: he always recognizes the necessity of genius in a poet, i.e. the necessity of his having some innate gift of nature. In describing the genius of Pope, he enumerates the standard qualities: invention, imagination, judgment. He would say that "the highest praise of genius is original invention." Discussing Shakespeare, Johnson can praise invention as the "first and most valuable" power of the poet and understand it as "that which is able to produce a series of events," to "strike out the first hint of a new fable: hence to introduce a set of characters and to wind up the whole in a pleasing catastrophe." But "genius" has none of the romantic connotations. It is simply *ingenium*, "a mind of large general powers, accidentally determined to some particular direction." In a conversation Johnson went so far as to say that "had Sir Isaac Newton applied himself to poetry, he would have made a very fine epic poem. I could as easily apply to law as to tragic poetry." Boswell objected, "Yet, sir, you *did* apply to tragic poetry, not to law." Johnson answered, "Because, sir, I had not money to study law. Sir, the man who has vigor, may walk to the east, just as well as to the west, if he happens to turn his head that way." The implication that any man of parts could be a poet if he wills so, that there is no difference between the gifts for poetry, law, or mathematics, does not disturb Johnson, as he wanted the poet to be assimilated to man in general.

Thus Johnson cannot show any interest in the new theory of creative imagination. It is not, however, a sufficient demonstration of his distrust of imagination to point to Imlac's discourse in *Rasselas* (ch. 43) on the "Dangerous Prevalence of Imagination" or the 89th *Rambler* on **"Luxury of Vain Imagination."** Johnson there disapproves of day dreaming, escapism, and, as other passages in *Prayers and Meditations* show, simply of "sensual images and loose thoughts." "Imagination" is understood as the power of visualizing absent things, the common use of the 18th century. "Imagination selects ideas from the treasures of remembrance, and produces novelty only by varied combinations." In purely literary contexts Johnson accepts imagination as part of the poet's equipment. He would say about Pope: "He had Imagination, which strongly impresses on the writer's mind and enables him to convey to the reader the various forms of nature, incidents of life, and energies of passion, as in his *Eloisa, Windsor Forest,* and the *Ethic Epistles.*" The inclusion of the *Ethic Epistles,* which we could hardly call "imagina-

tive," is enough to show that "imagination" here is used merely as the power of representation. (pp. 95-6)

The same attitude comes out in Johnson's discussions of imagery, simile, metaphor, and symbolism. Johnson can be very amusingly literal-minded in criticizing metaphors, of which he requires perfect consistency and rational progression. He censures, for instance, the first stanza of Gray's "Progress of Poetry" for "confounding the images of 'spreading sound' and 'running water,' " or shows a surprising incomprehension of ordinary metaphorical expression when he comments on the conclusion of Gray's "Ode on a Cat": "If what glistered had been 'gold,' the cat would not have gone into the water; and, if she had, would not less have been drowned." In close succession two figures by Addison are ridiculed for mixed or "broken" metaphor, *catachresis*. Johnson is also opposed to figures drawn from art to illustrate nature. " 'Idalia's velvetgreen' has something of cant. An epithet or metaphor drawn from Nature ennobles Art; an epithet or metaphor drawn from Art degrades Nature." This is a common rhetorical theory which seems to be based on a theological view of the inferiority of man's work to God's, but which, applied rigorously, would make short work of much of the metaphorical wealth of poetry today and during the Renaissance. (pp. 97-8)

Johnson's incomprehension of the centrally metaphorical character of poetry illuminates and is in turn illuminated by his attitude toward religious poetry. In many contexts Johnson condemns religious poetry. In discussing Cowley's *Davideis* he shows that he thinks poetry and imagery as "amplification" (of sacred history) are "frivolous and vain: all addition to that which is already sufficient for the purposes of religion seems not only useless, but in some degree profane." Speaking of Waller's sacred poems, Johnson explains again that "poetical devotion cannot often please." He allows that doctrines of religion may be defended in a didactic poem and that the beauties of nature may be praised in a descriptive poem. The subject of the description "is not God, but the works of God." But "contemplative piety, or the intercourse between God and the human soul, cannot be poetical. Man admitted to implore the mercy of his Creator and plead the merits of his Redeemer is already in a higher state than poetry can confer." This can be interpreted as meaning that prayer is a higher state than poetic contemplation, and one apparently excludes the other. "The essence of poetry is invention; such invention as, by producing something unexpected, surprises and delights. The topics of devotion are few, and being few are universally known; but, few as they are, they can be made no more; they can receive no grace from novelty of sentiment, and very little from novelty of expression." ("Grace" here means adornment, ornament; "sentiment" the content, the subject matter; "expression" the rhetorical form.) "Omnipotence cannot be exalted; Infinity cannot be amplified; Perfection cannot be improved." Exactly the same ideas underlie the criticism of *Paradise Lost:* "The good and evil of Eternity are too ponderous for the wings of wit." *Paradise Lost* is vitiated by a constant confusion of spirit and matter, especially in the narration of the war in heaven. Isaac Watts's devotional poetry is also unsatisfactory. "The paucity of its topics enforces perpetual repetition, and the sanctity of the matter rejects the ornaments of figurative diction." It seems surprising to be told so, in view of the Bible's figurative diction so recently described by Bishop Lowth. But one must recognize that Johnson here joins in an old critical debate in which Boileau had taken the side Johnson accepted: the Christian marvelous was condemned. Johnson takes this side in the controversy for deep personal reasons: religion is for him completely divided from fiction, the gulf between God and man being almost as great as in Calvinistic doctrines. Though he was an Anglican he was incapable of sharing the older view of a Chain of Being, the gradual ascent from nature to God, the whole metaphorical view of the universe, its correspondences and relations among which poetry as well as religion weaves a web.

Johnson was also untouched by the new cosmopolitanism. He did, of course, read some French and Italian literature. But his critical writings contain only the most perfunctory references to modern foreign authors: occasional praise for La Bruyère's *Characters* or Cervantes are the high points. "Corneille," he said to Mrs. Piozzi, "is to Shakespeare as a clipped hedge is to a forest." Boileau's "Tenth Satire" is inferior to Pope's "Characters of Women," though "he surely is no mean writer to whom Boileau shall be found inferior." "As to original literature the French have a couple of tragic poets who go round the world, Racine and Corneille, and one comic poet, Molière." Fénelon's *Télémaque* is "pretty well." Voltaire has not stood his trial yet and nobody reads Bossuet. It will not surprise us that Rousseau excited his contempt. "I think him one of the worst of men; a rascal who ought to be hunted out of society. . . . I would sooner sign a sentence for his transportation, than that of any felon who has gone from the Old Bailey these many years. Yes, I should like to have him work in the plantations." But this is hardly literary criticism, and we must not forget that Johnson was needling Boswell, who made a pilgrimage to Switzerland to see Rousseau. There is nothing beyond the bare names in Johnson concerning Dante, Petrarch, or Boccaccio. Tasso's *Aminta* is condemned specifically as a pastoral, and *Orlando Furioso* is criticized for the enchanted wood to which we follow "Rinaldo with more curiosity than terror."

But Johnson was not only touched but deeply involved in the general awakening of the historical sense and specifically in the revived interest in early English literature and in literary antiquarianism and historiography. There is, of course, the evidence of his *Dictionary,* which shows that he had read in practically every earlier English writer, though it may be difficult in some cases to distinguish between real reading and mere sampling by him or an amanuensis. There is the Introduction to the *Dictionary,* which is a history of the English language, and in which, incidentally, Johnson has something to say about early English literature. He quotes specimens of Anglo-Saxon and Middle English from Hickes's *Thesaurus,* and remarks, with an unusual suspension of judgment, that "our ignorance of the laws of their metre and the quantities of their syllables excludes us from that pleasure which the old bards undoubtedly gave to their contemporaries." Johnson wanted to edit Chaucer. His edition was to contain "remarks on his language, and the change it had undergone from the earliest times to his age, and from his to the present, with notes explanatory of customs, etc. and references to Boccace, and other authors from whom he has borrowed, with an account of the liberties he has taken in telling the stories." Yet Johnson could not have appreciated

Chaucer highly. He says, of Dryden's retelling the "Nun's Priest's Tale," that the "Tale" seems "hardly worth revival," and he censures Dryden's praise of the "Knight's Tale" as "hyperbolical." Johnson smiled at some of the excesses of antiquarianism: in *Rambler* No. 177 he ridicules an antiquary proudly displaying "a copy of the *Children in the Wood,* which he firmly believed to be of the first edition." "Chevy Chase" is condemned for "chill and lifeless imbecility." Medieval mysteries are "wild dramas." But for linguistic reasons Johnson read some of the romances, dipped even into Lydgate, and, of course, prepared his great edition of Shakespeare, which, besides its critical preface and comments on the individual plays and passages, is also a work of textual criticism and historical elucidation. (pp. 99-102)

We get Johnson's nearest approach to a literary history of England in the *Lives of the Poets* (1779-81), which are of course primarily biography and straight criticism, but which contain an implicit scheme of the history of English poetry of the preceding century. The choice of lives was prescribed by the booksellers who ordered them, and thus from the outset Johnson was limited to the living tradition of poetry, from Cowley to Gray. He himself seems to have urged only the inclusion of minor poets such as Blackmore, Watts, Pomfret, and Yalden. Nothing came of a suggestion made by George III that Spenser should have been included. In the **"Life of Cowley"** Johnson starts with a discussion of the metaphysicals as background and foil to the tradition he is about to treat in full, and he stresses everywhere the anticipations and steps which led to its establishment. The reform begins with Waller and Denham, who "traced the new scheme of poetry." The actual founder of the new style was Dryden: "To him we owe the improvement, perhaps the completion of our metre, the refinement of our language, and much of the correctness of our sentiments." Before the time of Dryden "there was no poetical diction: no system of words at once refined from the grossness of domestic use and free from the harshness of terms appropriated to particular arts." Johnson always points out either relapses from or approximations to this ideal norm. Addison "debased rather than refined" the versification which he had learned from Dryden. And Pope, of course, is the summit of perfection.

This view of a progress of English poetry toward an ideal technical norm attained especially by Pope is curiously enough combined in Johnson with a constant recognition of the historical point of view and pleadings for some relativity of standards. He recognized that wit "has its changes and fashions, and at different times takes different forms." He explicitly states that "to judge rightly of an author we must transport ourselves to his time, and examine what were the wants of his contemporaries, and what were his means of supplying them." As early as the *Observations on Macbeth* (1745), Johnson had stated that "in order to make a true estimate of the abilities and merit of a writer, it is always necessary to examine the genius of his age and the opinions of his contemporaries." However, he uses the historical argument largely as an apology for shortcomings and mistakes in older literature. Thus Dryden's "Threnodia Augustalis" has the "irregularity of meter, to which the ears of that age however were accustomed"; Milton's verse was "harmonious, in proportion to the general state of our metre in Milton's age"; Waller's poem "On the Danger of the Prince on the Coast of Spain" may be "justly praised, without much allowance for the state of our poetry and language at that time."

Once, in Johnson's defense of Pope's translation of Homer, the historical argument is prominent and effective. "Time and place will always enforce regard. In estimating this translation consideration must be had of the nature of our language, the form of our meter, and, above all, of the change which two thousand years have made in the modes of life and the habits of thought" since Pope "wrote for his own age and his own nation." But the historical argument which seems to Johnson valid in case of an adaptation of a work of remote antiquity did not affect his central view of English literature as one continuous effort toward the establishment of a timeless norm, that of Pope and Dryden. Johnson certainly believed in progress (despite all personal pessimism as to the possibility of human happiness). He rejected the view that the world "was in its decay" and that "souls partake of the general degeneracy." "Every age," he thought, "improves in elegance. One refinement always makes way for another." But the new dispensation seems firmly established. Since Dryden, English poetry has had "no tendency to relapse to its former savageness." This faith or hope may help explain Johnson's acrimonious criticism of Gray's and Collins' attempts to revive what he considered an obsolete and essentially superseded diction and versification. It explains in part the harshness of his comments on Milton's early poems, which he knew were not only highly valued by his contemporaries but had also become the models of a new Miltonic school of which he disapproved as of any archaism. He did not and could not very well see that he himself stood almost at the end of a great tradition. The stirring of the new seemed to him only the odd, perverse, and, at the most, partially successful revival of old and worn-out things. His own critical work is certainly varied enough, unified without being monotonous, strongly rooted in the tradition but still far from merely dogmatic in its acceptance of it. Johnson, while holding firm to the main tenets of the tradition of neoclassical criticism, constantly reinterprets them in a spirit for which it is difficult to avoid a term he would have hated: liberal. (pp. 102-04)

> *René Wellek, "Dr. Johnson," in his* A History of Modern Criticism: 1750-1950, The Later Eighteenth Century, *Vol. 1, 1955. Reprint by Yale University Press, 1965, pp. 79-104.*

John Wain   (essay date 1959)

[*Perhaps one of the most prolific English authors of contemporary fiction and poetry, Wain is regarded as a significant, if minor, twentieth-century critic. Central to his critical stance is the belief that, in order to judge the quality of a piece of literature, the critic must make a moral as well as an imaginative judgement. In the following excerpt from an essay originally published in the* London Observer *in 1959, he attempts to explain the "reverence" that Johnson commands in the English-speaking world.*]

Dr. Johnson is one of those myth-figures, like King Alfred or Nelson, of whom virtually every English person has heard. Most people think of him as an intellectual version of John Bull (a character invented by Arbuthnot some years before Johnson was born, and very much of the peri-

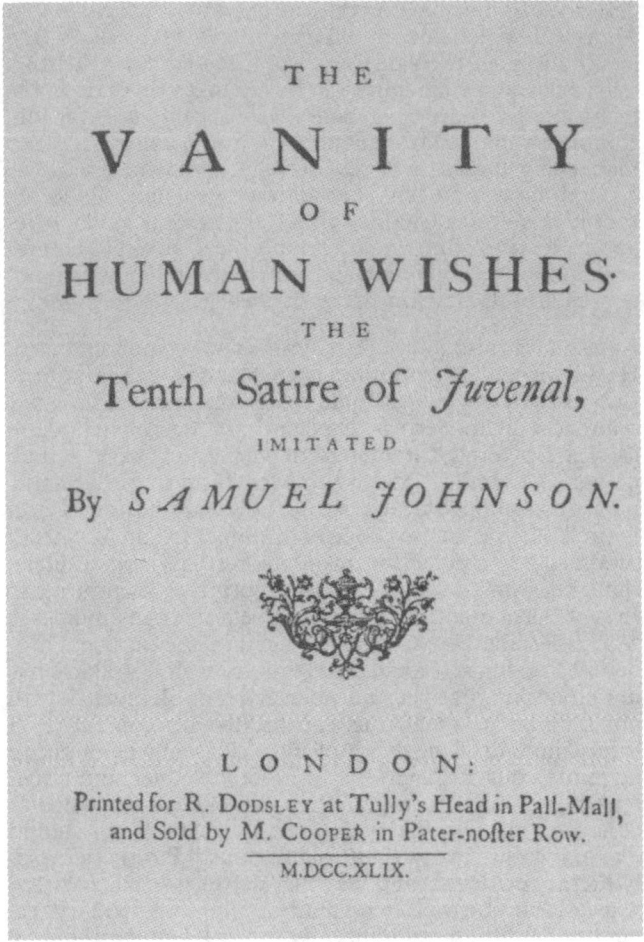

Title page of the first edition of The Vanity of Human Wishes *(1749), Johnson's second Juvenalian imitation.*

od). At school they read a few extracts from Boswell's *Life,* and get from it the impression that Johnson began every sentence with 'Sir' and contradicted every remark addressed to him. This is the sum of their knowledge.

For a myth-figure, this will do, being quite as substantial as Lady Hamilton or the burnt cakes, but it is as well to remind ourselves that behind the two-dimensional popular image stands a great and tragic character, full of paradox and enigma, calling out passionate loyalty and strong dislike not only during his lifetime but unbrokenly ever since. (pp. 171-72)

It used to be the fashion to decry Johnson's powers as a writer and claim that he was important solely as a character. In fact, by any objective standard he was one of the best writers of the eighteenth century; whether or not he was what people now understand by the word 'poet', he could write movingly and memorably in verse; if **"The Vanity of Human Wishes"** is not a poem, it is hard to know what else to call it. And Johnson's prose, grave, sonorous, heavily charged with meaning, gives the lie to the slander of 'Johnsonese', by which the Victorians meant an emptily inflated style. This prose is heavy because it is densely packed.

As a literary critic, Johnson was a conservative. His sensibility was formed during the first half of the eighteenth century, a period that was itself backward-looking and time-marking; and, though his working life stretched through the years that saw the rise of the novel, the renewed interest in mediaeval literature, balladry, and primitive art, and the shift from classic to romantic generally, he remained, like most critics, faithful to the taste of his early days. In the *Lives of the English Poets,* his most formidable repository of critical judgments, he is usually at his best in dealing with writers whose vogue passed away with his own youth.

The *Lives* may be Johnson's major critical work, but his most delightful critical writing occurs in the notes to his edition of Shakespeare. This took nine years to prepare and was published when Johnson was fifty-six, so that the notes show the working of his mind during the hard-pressed years when he laboured in the heat of the day, whereas the *Lives* are the fruit of his lionised old age.

These notes show the force and freshness of Johnson's intelligence better than anything except the very best pages of Boswell. The stage direction 'Exit Pistol' in *Henry V* may not seem to call for a footnote: but it moves Johnson to write, with loving sadness:

> The comick scenes of the history of Henry the fourth and fifth are now at an end, and all the comick personages are now dismissed. Falstaff and Mrs. Quickly are dead; Nym and Bardolph are hanged; Gadshill was lost immediately after the robbery; Poins and Peto have vanished since, one knows not how; and Pistol is now beaten into obscurity. I believe every reader regrets their departure.

Such a comment reveals Johnson's loving absorption in the play. At other times his remarks show a vigilant desire to make Shakespeare's work directly available to the reader's moral life, by pointing out the lessons to be learnt from seemingly trivial lines. In *Much Ado About Nothing,* Leonato, the father of the wronged girl Hero, is so stunned by the brutal scene of rejection at the altar that he acquiesces in the friar's counter-scheme with the numb, almost indifferent words

> Being that I flow in grief,
> The smallest twine may lead me.

Johnson is ready with the comment:

> Men overpowered with distress eagerly listen to the first offers of relief, close with every scheme, and believe every promise. He that has no longer any confidence in himself, is glad to repose his trust in any other that will undertake to guide him.

The impression is of reading Shakespeare in company with a man who is prepared at every turn to weigh the author against his own long and rugged experience of life.

As writer and critic, then, he is still interesting. Nevertheless, it is true that Johnson's chief hold over our minds is as a moral hero, a great personal example. With all his faults and foibles, he lived a brave and unselfish life. Starting with every handicap—bad sight, poor health, no money, and uncouth appearance and uncontrollable nervous habits—he fought his way up to recognition as one of the great men of his time. Once there, he made no effort to turn his reputation to worldly advantage in pursuit of

money or power; he gave away most of what he earned, keeping back only enough to supply his basic needs, and filled his house with a crowd of peevish old creatures who could not look after themselves.

All this was visible to the world. But the real heroism of Johnson's life lay in his unceasing struggle against the darkness within his own mind. Physically he never knew fear, but on another level he was haunted by neurotic guilt and the dread of eternal punishment. In the year of his death, a friend, trying to reason him into calmness, asked what precisely he understood by the term 'damned'. Johnson burst out passionately: 'Sent to Hell, Sir, and punished everlastingly!' When urged to rely on the merciful nature of God, he pointed out that, since Hell undoubtedly existed, it was part of the wisdom of God that some souls should be sent there, and why not his?

A man of strong passions and appetites will easily fall into temptations, and Johnson's *Prayers and Meditations* are full of piteous appeals for leniency from God and promises to amend ('O Lord, let me not sink into total depravity; look down upon me, and rescue me at last from the captivity of sin'). At times his reason threatened to give way; when he was living in Mrs. Thrale's house at Streatham, which he did intermittently for twenty years, he appears to have made her promise to lock him up, and even put him in irons, if he actually ran mad; among her effects, sold off at her death in 1823, was 'Johnson's padlock, committed to my care in 1768'.

Partly because he could never get the fear of Hell out of his mind, and partly because he had suffered and come through such desperate privations, Johnson was extremely hardhearted about trivial sufferings. In a world where many poor wretches were starving, and where the gates of Hell might at any moment yawn beneath one's feet, it seemed to him impious and wicked to complain about boredom, or a headache, or the spiteful remark of an acquaintance. He was also very suspicious of Utopians who claimed that with a little engineering human life could be made happy. To him, unhappiness was the permanent normal condition of human life, and this inclined him to political conservatism, since to throw over existing institutions in the belief that new ones would bring happiness seemed to him a self-indulgent folly. As he declared in *Rambler* No. 32:

> The cure for the greatest part of human miseries is not radical but palliative. Infelicity is involved in corporeal nature, and interwoven with our being; all attempts therefore to decline it wholly are useless and vain: the armies of pain send their arrows on every side, the choice is only between those which are more or less sharp, or tinged with poison of greater or less malignity; and the strongest armour which reason can supply will only blunt their points, but cannot repel them.

Johnson's whole way of life, as well as his intellectual position, can be deduced from that passage. Human suffering could be met, but only by putting on armour supplied by 'reason', and taking reasonable advantage of the 'palliative' cures, innocent diversions which enabled a man to forget his unhappiness. No one ever threw himself into blameless enjoyments with more zest than Johnson, who loved a good dinner and an evening's talk so well that he declared 'a good tavern or inn' the happiest invention of the human mind. Mrs. Thrale, who saw his domestic side, said that he 'always hated to be left out of any innocent merriment that was going forward. . . . I verily think, if he had had good eyes, and a form less inflexible, he would have made an excellent mimic.'

Conviviality, even 'buffoonery', were one side of Johnson; neurotic dread and melancholia were another; the strong, rapid play of a masterly intelligence was a third. But none of these quite explains the reverence in which he was held. As Johnson lay dying, Fanny Burney sat for hours in tears on the stairs leading up to his room, hoping that she might be called in to receive his blessing. No mere John Bull, intellectual or otherwise, inspires that kind of devotion. Johnson had a greatness of mind, a tragic and heroic stature, that we can feel across two hundred and fifty years. (pp. 173-76)

> *John Wain, "Samuel Johnson," in his* Essays on Literature and Ideas, *Macmillan and Co. Ltd., 1963, pp. 171-76.*

Dina Abdul-Hamid Al Aoun   (essay date 1959)

[*In the following excerpt, Al Aoun centers on the education and character of the Prince in* Rasselas.]

Dr. Johnson's *History of Rasselas, Prince of Abyssinia* is one of the few books of its kind which, written as it was, under the pressing exigencies of time and want, have commanded the interest and admiration of subsequent generations. . . . This would underline the fact that it is not merely a curious period-piece or an historical indicative document for the student of eighteenth century thought, and that it does not depend for fame on the particularity of its style but that it is a composition with the elements of deep and universally appealing philosophy sustained by a reticent but, nevertheless, eloquent personal note—elements which raise a work of art to the level of the classics.

The title of the book is explicatory of its nature like most pre-twentieth century writings before the fashion for obscurantist titles, and places it in a certain form and a certain tradition of literature. It is an eighteenth century novel in the prevalent and convenient setting of an Oriental background. As to the tradition it does not so much fall into the category as is reminiscent of the pupil and mentor theme which engaged the pens of some of the most eminent writers of Europe from the Middle Ages onwards, and which illustrates the preoccupation from Plato down into the eighteenth century with the education or rather the character of a prince.

This I have found to be a point of interest upon re-reading *Rasselas,* so much so, since the concept of a just ruler and his requirements of character and education has lost none of its interest or urgency with the vast developments and political ideas and forms of government.

By choosing to set his story in a distant land Johnson used an expedient literary convention dating back farther than More's completely imaginary *Utopia* and more common in the eighteenth century, when political and social satire prevailed more extensively, than in any other period of European literature, producing such masters of the art as Pope, Swift and Voltaire. At such a time writers were in greater need of projecting their ideas and criticisms into far away or imaginary countries, both to add an aura of romance to their tale (a trait growing more distinct towards the latter part of the century) and to escape the censure or penalty incurred by their attack on the established order of things. But Johnson's choice of a figure of high rank as the central figure of his tale, although it finds many echoes in classical and post-classical literature, deviates from the usual pattern and may here invite a few remarks and demand one or two points of comparison and contrast.

Dr. Johnson, in his choice of title and theme, has gathered the specific ingredients which would appeal to contemporary readers, for any work of art, however individual, is not only inevitably an echo of its time, but, in order to be great, has to be creative within the disciplined framework of its own period. The Oriental Tale, influenced by the many travel books composed earlier on, was a very fashionable literary form. Hence Johnson's introduction of the philosophical Abyssinians in a manner which could be reminiscent of Rousseau's Noble Savage, had it not been for his explicit refutation of the fallacy of inherent goodness and pastoral bliss in Chapter XIX and his conviction that learning is the prime requisite of a good man, and his very Augustan assertion of Reason as opposed to the Imagination, which for him is a sign of disequilibrium: "All power of fancy over reason is a degree of insanity", says Imlac.

It may be worth noting here that the Oriental theme had appeared in one of Johnson's *Rambler* essays (No. 190, January 11th. 1752) among others, but here specifically anticipating the philosophy of the pursuit of happiness subsequently leading to resignation and acceptance, a philosophy stated also in **"The Vanity of Human Wishes"** and elaborated in *Rasselas.* The essay ends with the majestic words of Abouzaid:

> I shall henceforth do good and avoid evil, without respect to the opinion of men and resolve to solicit only the approbation of that being whom alone we are sure to please by endeavouring to please him.

The importance accorded to the education of a prince has, we have seen, weighed on the minds of most great writers through the centuries, but we find an even more insistent and widespread preoccupation with the subject in the eighteenth century, both in England and on the continent of Europe. In England this has an immediate significance in the fact that not only is it the natural outcome of a generation proud of its scientific achievements, but it uncovers also the desire of the thinkers of the age to find and establish a parallel for the stability of society, by regarding the apex of the social pyramid to be represented by the person of the ruler. They also wished to divest themselves of the traditional Jacobite loyalties and convince themselves that, even in the domain of the foreign and, no doubt, unsympathetic Hanoverian rule 'whatever is, is right'.

Johnson writes (in spite of his possible loyalty to the House of Stuart, which is really a love for tradition and order and is, in this passage, transferred to the ruling representative of the House of Hanover):

> Why all this childish jealousy of the power of the crown? The crown has not power enough. . . . In

no government can a power be abused long. Mankind will not hear it. If a sovereign opposes his people to a great degree, they will rise and cut off his head. There is a remedy in human nature against tyranny, that will keep us safe under every form of government.

In this passage are the seeds of British democratic conviction, that peculiar blend of fierce individual independence and innate love of order, stability and balance. This is once more apparent in Hannah More's *Hints Towards Forming the Character of a Young Princess* (1805):

> The prince is an individual being placed on a pedestal of peculiar elevation; but he should learn that he is placed there as a minister of good to others. . . . This is not a period when any wise man would wish to diminish either the authority or the splendour of kings. . . . Nevertheless, these outrages which have lately been committed against the sancity of the throne furnish new and most powerful reasons for assiduously guarding princes by every respectful admonition, against any tendencies to exceed their just prerogatives and for checking any propensity to overstep, in the slightest degree, their well defined rights.

This is the distinct demarcation line between the idea of the ruler enjoying the Divine Right of Kings and the eighteenth century idea of the prince for whom the emphasis has been shifted from prerogatives to duties. Madame de Genlis in France showed a similar preoccupation and similar sentiments in her play for young people entitled *Vathek* (1782).

Yet Johnson's divergence from the traditional methods of presenting the subject of education, of transforming the mentor-pupil theme, is, to me, the chief point of interest in *Rasselas.* If we contrast it with Machiavelli's *Prince,* for example, we find that the latter book heads the tradition of manuals for princes, which developed into manuals for gentlemen during the eighteenth century. These manuals were transformed from repositories of wisdom and learning (wordly, as in Machiavelli or moralistic, as in Fénelon) into handbooks for 'correct gentlemanly behaviour'; we should also find that *Rasselas* is not simply an example of the development of ideas about government, between 1500 and 1700, but it also contains a subjective element which proves the danger of pigeon-holing writers and periods of literature, such as the common representation of Johnson as a type-figure of Augustan impersonality.

Johnson's *Rasselas,* however, maintains a link with its precursors in that it abounds with the prince's remarks on his conception of a just ruler and an ideal government. In Chapter VI he says: "Kings are accountable for injustice permitted as well as done. If I were Emperor not the meanest of my subjects should be oppressed with impunity". Imlac also says in Chapter XXX: "Those who have kingdoms to govern have understandings to cultivate". And the book ends with the prince's decision to go back and form a kingdom in which he hopes to exercise the wisdom he has learned during his travels, if not to enjoy the happiness, which, he has been convinced by Imlac and his own experience is only an illusion.

A point at which Johnson's acceptance of tradition coincides with his diversion away from it is the figure of Rasselas. Whatever Johnson may have thought about him at first, he is to us distinctly, if remotely, suggestive of the figure of the tragic hero and his preponderance in the classical and Shakespearean conception of tragedy. But more interesting is the subtle fusion of that regal concept with the robust English, democratic but mystical figure born of *Everyman* and the imagination of Bunyan. In *Rasselas* the prince becomes Everyman, and the symbolism (present even in mediaeval minds) of the ruler as a representative of the multitude is particularly accentuated.

Although the idea of educating a prince is important in *Rasselas* the core of the tale lies in the theme of the 'choice of life' and its relation to happiness, which raises questions in the mind of the reader that, like all important philosophical questions, remain unresolved. In this manner Johnson sets out to refute the prevalent mood of eighteenth century optimism inculcated by philosophers such as Berkeley, Leibniz, the complacently pious works of Soame Jenyns and the Machiavellian, aristocratic smugness of Lord Chesterfield. This he does in favour of the solid virtues of an enlightened 'bourgeoisie'. Rasselas is an allegorical representation of eighteenth century optimism contrasted with Johnson's own sense of Christian pessimism of which Imlac is the spokesman.

But Johnson, popular as he was in the capacity of moralist among his contemporaries, was not able to stem the tide of optimism, which does not so much end with the eighteenth century, (giving way to the sometimes fantastic gloom and prophecy of nineteenth century writers) as change from an optimism of acceptance to an optimism of progress, as Professor Willey has brilliantly shown in his *Eighteenth Century Background.*

Johnson, although he is a typically eighteenth century figure, nevertheless shows us many links with the age to come and its writers, especially in *Rasselas.* A very interesting point is the embryonic presence of Shelley's fiery theory about poets being the unacknowledged legislators of mankind, which we find in the concluding lines of Imlac's Dissertation upon Poetry (Chapter X) in almost the same words: "He must write as the interpreter of nature and the legislator of mankind; and consider himself as presiding over the thoughts and manners of future generations as being superior to time and place". The difference, perhaps, is that Shelley, with Romantic optimism, believed poets *to be* legislators of mankind, whereas Johnson, with his rare balance and innate pessimism, only imagined such a state of affairs in the ideal.

Another significant passage in *Rasselas,* because of its truth, is the speech of the old sage (Chapter XLV):

> Let the gay and the vigorous expect pleasure in their excursions; it is enough that age can obtain ease. To me the world has lost its novelty; I look round and see what I remember to have seen in happier days. I rest against a tree and consider, that in the same shade, I once disputed upon the annual overflow of the Nile with a friend who is now silent in the grave. I cast my eyes upwards, fix them on the changing moon, and think with pain on the vicissitudes of life.

In this and many other passages, which emerge from among the weighty, ponderous eighteenth century utterances of good sense and transcend the deliberate balance of phrases and sentiments, there emerges Johnson, the

Man of Feeling, not Johnson, the tyrant of the dinner table, but the Johnson of the **Prayers and Meditations,** lonely and introspective, very much akin to nineteenth century men of letters. There is a sense, therefore, in regarding this passage, rather than the final chapter, as the conclusion which Johnson would have had us carry away from his tale. (pp. 15-20)

> *Dina Abdul-Hamid Al Aoun, "Some Remarks on a Second Reading of 'Rasselas'," in* Bicentenary Essays on "Rasselas," *edited by Magdí Wahba, Cairo Studies in English, 1959, pp. 15-20.*

Jeffrey Hart   (essay date 1960)

[*Hart is an American educator, columnist, and author who has served as an editor of the* Burke Newsletter *and currently serves as a senior editor of the conservative biweekly* National Review. *Among his better known works are* The Political Writers of Eighteenth-Century England *(1964),* The American Dissent *(1966), and* From This Moment on: America in Nineteen Forty *(1987). In the following excerpt, he identifies three major themes in Johnson's* A Journey to the Western Islands.]

Boswell's account of the famous tour through Scotland has received far more attention than Johnson's. And what Boswell has to offer is more accessible to the reader. One can open Boswell's book almost anywhere and find an entertaining description or a memorable anecdote. Who will ever forget that encounter with the ancient Highland widow who fearfully expected to be raped by Johnson? And equally memorable is the conversation between Dr. Johnson and the Rev. Hector MacLean—'about seventy-seven years of age, a decent ecclesiastick, dressed in a full suit of black clothes, and a black wig'—a conversation in which the participants, because hard of hearing, spoke simultaneously, 'each continuing to maintain his own argument, without hearing exactly what the other said'. Boswell's account of the tour provides, *par excellence,* what one expects of a book by Boswell, and Johnson could not have competed with him on his own ground. To the reader looking for anecdotes, Johnson is disappointing. His book presents us with no memorable personalities, except of course his own. Indeed, Johnson deliberately muted his descriptions of people. Concerning a Mr. Nairne, who is given a genuine individuality by Boswell, Johnson merely reports that they were accompanied on the first day by 'another gentleman, who could stay with us only long enough to show us how much we lost at separation'. Such treatment is characteristic, for his subject, to distinguish it from Boswell's, is not 'personality'. Nor, because of its subject and method, can one *sample* Johnson's version. To appreciate its power, one must read it through. It is not a simple chronicle of the trip Johnson took with Boswell. Rather, it is a highly-wrought work of art, possessing a complex organisation. Its themes, and to Johnson they were themes of compelling importance, are interwoven, contrasted, counterpointed, and modulated; its greatness derives largely from its manner of organisation.

At a first glance Johnson's book seems to make a rather modest claim. It appears to describe merely a casually conceived trip around Scotland. Yet we cannot read far

without observing that Johnson is making use of a device familiar to eighteenth-century analysts of society. The observer learns the truth about social institutions and about the historical process by studying them in a strange locale. So accustomed has he been to his own society that he cannot really see it. When he arrives in a strange country, however, he achieves the necessary detachment, and is able to see its manners and institutions with an instructive, and often destructive, clarity. Montesquieu's *Lettres persanes* comes to mind as an example of this strategy, as does Goldsmith's *The Citizen of the World.* Swift, of course, used a variation of it in *Gulliver's Travels.* One could see the truth about society, these authors imply, only if one abandoned the conventional point of view and took a fresh look. And Johnson employed the same device in **A Journey to the Western Islands.**

The book has three large concerns, which constitute its three major themes. The first is the destruction of pre-Reformation Christian culture. Johnson gradually becomes aware how great a tragedy this destruction was; the reader's awareness of the tragedy grows with Johnson's, and gains intensity from the contrast between this grand theme, the darkest and most mournful of the three, and Johnson's patter of detailed observation concerning agricultural and industrial processes. The second major theme compares, by implication, this destruction, which occurred in the past, with an analogous destruction Johnson sees taking place in the present: the destruction of Highland culture. The third theme is the rise of middle-class, progressive culture, toward the values of which Johnson maintains an ambivalent attitude.

At St. Andrews, 'a city once archiepiscopal', in whose university philosophy had been taught by the Latinist Buchanan, Johnson surveys 'a city, which only history shews to have once flourished', and he gazes upon the remnants of 'ancient magnificence, of which even the ruins cannot long be visible, unless some care be taken to preserve them'. He examines the ruins of the cathedral, 'of which the foundations may still be traced'. Though it appears to have been 'a spacious and majestick building, not unsuitable to the primacy of the kingdom', it has all but disappeared, 'demolished, as is well known, in the tumult and violence of Knox's reformation'. Johnson castigates the fanaticism of the reformers. He tells us that Cardinal Beatoun 'was murdered by the ruffians of reformation, in the manner of which Knox has given what he himself calls a merry narrative'. In the mind of the reader, at this point, the question inevitably arises: What did Knox's reformation achieve, what results can justify all this destruction? Johnson answers that the destruction was purely wasteful, a making of nothing out of something: the former fanaticism, incapable of settling in a moderate course, has yielded to 'laxity of practice and indifference of opinion'. The crumbling cathedrals reflect, for Johnson, a crumbling of values.

The city of St. Andrews itself, Johnson points out, also has decayed. 'One of its streets is now lost; and in those that remain, there is the silence and solitude of inactive indigence and gloomy depopulation.' The university there is wasting away. One of its three colleges has been sold, and the college chapel is now a greenhouse. Johnson reflects reproachfully that this nation, in which 'the commerce is hourly extending, and the wealth increasing, denies any participation of its prosperity to its literary societies; and while its merchants and nobles are raising palaces, suffers its universities to moulder into dust'. At the very beginning, then, in his account of the visit to St. Andrews, Johnson introduces two of his major themes, and by associating images of past destruction and present decay, he sets up one of his theses: the potential barbarism of an entirely commercial society. He develops this thesis, and complicates it, as the narrative proceeds. As we shall see, he does not permit it to remain unqualified. Yet for the present, here at St. Andrews, as he walks amid the ruins of the ancient university city, he can reflect only upon the tragedy which has left this debris. He compares the destruction wrought by Knox and the reformers with the destruction of civilisation by Alaric and the 'Goths'. Thus, behind the destruction of Scottish culture looms the destruction of Rome; and beyond that, because of what Rome meant to the Augustan imagination, the possibility that, in the end, the idea of civilisation itself might be destroyed. Johnson sees the university, which the indifference of a commercial society has permitted to decay, as the victim of barbarism. His mind, he says, was filled 'with mournful images and ineffectual wishes'.

The theme of the destruction of pre-Reformation Christian culture, a theme of which the first grand chords are sounded here at St. Andrews, reverberates all through the book. Skeletons of dead churches stand out against the grey sky and against the gaunt landscape. The monastery at Aberothick, whose 'ruins afford ample testimony of its ancient magnificence', has crumbled, has been inundated by grass and weeds. And yet, despite its decay, Johnson feels that he 'should scarcely have regretted [his] journey, had it afforded nothing more than the sight of Aberothick'. A sentimental appreciation of ruins had become, by this time, quite fashionable, and connoisseurs even went so far as to construct artificial ruins on their estates. But clearly, in Johnson's account, we find no such indulgence, no sentimentality. He gives us only a bare statement. In context, however, and as the narrative proceeds, the bare statement acquires resonance, accumulates meanings. It is much more than antiquarianism that attracts Johnson to the past.

When Johnson reaches the city of Old Aberdeen, where stands King's College, the first president of which was Hector Boethius, he finds that it 'has the appearance of a town in decay'. In marked contrast, nearby New Aberdeen 'has all the bustle of prosperous trade, and all the shew of increasing opulence'. One senses, I think, considerable bitterness behind the description of New Aberdeen, with its bustle of trade and 'shew of increasing opulence'. And Johnson's observation, amid all this evidence of mutability, that prosperous New Aberdeen 'must be very lasting', surely possesses ironic overtones.

At Elgin, the ruins of another once magnificent cathedral again demonstrate to Johnson 'the waste of reformation'. He picks over the ruins and lovingly recounts details: how the choir and the chapter house may still be identified, but how 'the body of the church is a mass of fragments'. He tells us that after the Reformation the lead roofs of the cathedrals at Elgin and Aberdeen were to be sold for money to pay the army, even though their sale could have brought very little. 'I hope every reader will rejoice,' he

writes, 'that this cargo of sacrilege was lost at sea.' In the next paragraph he points the moral for England:

> Let us not, however, make too much haste to despise our neighbours. Our own cathedrals are mouldering by unregarded dilapidation. It seems to be part of the despicable philosophy of the time to despise monuments of sacred magnificence, and we are in danger of doing that deliberately, which the Scots did not do, but in the unsettled state of an imperfect constitution.

This passage, though perfectly adequate to make Johnson's point, represents a softening of what he had originally written. Before revision the passage read:

> Let us not, however, make too much haste to despise our neighbours. There is now, as I have heard, a body of men not less decent or virtuous than the Scottish council, longing to melt the lead of an English cathedral. What they shall melt, it were just that they should swallow.

Johnson's book, though describing only Scotland, is also about England, for he sees in Scotland social and cultural developments which, more slowly, and superficially more 'acceptably', are also taking place in England.

At Raasay, and in other islands, the theme recurs: 'throughout the few islands which we visited, we neither saw nor heard of any house of prayer, except in Skye, that was not in ruins'. Johnson fulminates against the 'malignant influence of Calvinism' which has 'blasted ceremony and decency together'. Mourning over the destruction of church buildings and the decay of religion, Johnson contrasts ironically the 'sleepy laziness' of the medieval men who built the churches to the 'fervid activity' of those who have permitted them to fall. At Col he sees two more ruined chapels: 'Two chapels were erected by their ancestors, of which I saw the skeletons, which now stand faithful witnesses of the triumph of Reformation.' The tone darkens. At Mull: 'We travelled many hours through a tract, bleak and barren, in which, however, there were the reliques of humanity; for we found a ruined chapel in our way.'

Was it only his own intense Christian commitment, we may ask, that led Johnson to make this theme so prominent, to give so much space to descriptions of church ruins? I think not. He omitted references to Christianity from *Rasselas.* He could have done so here, had he chosen. In most of his political writing, indeed, Christianity plays no part at all. But Johnson was, I think, particularly impressed in Scotland, because of the nature of the country, with the kind of triumph represented by culture, both secular and religious. Culture, Johnson seems to be saying, must be regarded as a triumph of the will and the imagination, a triumph especially heroic here in Scotland, because won over a harsh and bleak environment, the maleficence of which connotes the cruelty of the universe itself. It is this awareness that informs Johnson's sense of tragic loss. There are no trees in Scotland, he says again and again. Crops are grown with difficulty here. In Scotland, he says, one is not 'in the artificial solitude of parks and gardens' where one feels flatteringly self-sufficient. Rather, one is in a desert, and the 'phantoms which haunt a desert are want, misery, and danger; the evils of dereliction rush upon the thoughts; man is made unwillingly acquainted with his own weakness, and meditation shows him only how little he can sustain, and how little he can perform'. Though man is weak, Johnson sees, he once accomplished much here, and now little more remains than the ruins, the ruins and the finally triumphant environment.

All of the observations Johnson makes concerning ruined chapels and cathedrals prepare the reader for the climax of this theme: the visit to Inch Kenneth and then to Iona. Here the perception of tragic loss all but overwhelms the narrative. The theme separates itself from all lesser concerns, and concludes in passages of grand and sombre music. At Inch Kenneth Johnson finds

> a venerable chapel, which stands yet entire, except that the roof is gone. It is about sixty feet in length and thirty in breadth. On one side of the altar is a bas relief of the blessed Virgin, and by it lies a little bell; which, though cracked, and without a clapper, has remained there for ages, guarded only by the venerableness of the place. The ground round the chapel is covered with gravestones of Chiefs and ladies; and still continues to be a place of sepulture.

The silent bell, the silent Chiefs and ladies, prepare one for the Virgilian sadness Johnson felt at Iona, the visit to which called forth one of his greatest passages:

> We were now treading that illustrious island, which was once the luminary of the *Caledonian* regions, whence savage clans and roving barbarians derived the benefits of knowledge and the blessings of religion. To abstract the mind from all local emotion would be impossible, if it were endeavoured, and would be foolish, if it were possible. Whatever withdraws us from the power of our senses; whatever makes the past, the distant, or the future predominate over the present, advances us in the dignity of thinking beings. Far from me and my friends be such frigid philosophy as may conduct us indifferent and unmoved over any ground which has been dignified by wisdom, bravery, or virtue. That man is little to be envied, whose patriotism would not gain force upon the plain of *Marathon,* or whose piety would not grow warmer among the ruins of *Iona.*

Johnson wanders among the unroofed churches and ruined convents of the ancient religious community. 'The bottom of the church is so encumbered with mud and rubbish, that we could make no discoveries of curious inscriptions. . . . The chapel of the nunnery is now used by the inhabitants as a kind of general cow-house. . . . The graves are very numerous, and some of them undoubtedly contain the remains of men, who did not expect to be so soon forgotten.' Iona, he observes, is now populated by inhabitants who are 'remarkably gross'. This island, 'which was once the metropolis of learning and piety, has now no school for education, nor temple for worship, only two inhabitants that can speak *English,* and not one that can write or read'.

Thus we reach the climax of one theme of **A Journey to the Western Islands,** the destruction of pre-Reformation Christian culture. The second theme is the destruction of Highland culture, which proceeded rapidly after Culloden, and which entered its final stages at the time of Johnson's tour in 1773. Like the first theme, this one develops slowly, grandly, with gradual increments of power. At first Johnson sees mainly the disagreeable side of Highland culture, and condescends to its rudeness and vio-

lence. Indeed, he never comes to admire it unequivocally: Highlanders, he maintains, have little respect for fact. Their tales are overly tall. In the midst of this dying feudal culture, Johnson remains a partisan of the Enlightenment. But he does discover that there was much to admire in Highland culture by way of honour, courage, gaiety, and loyalty. He recalls how Highlanders were always fiercely independent, yet how all 'on the first approach of hostility came together at the call to battle, as at a summons to a festal show'. To lose this spirit, he says, 'is to lose what no small advantage will compensate'. Indeed, the very fact of Johnson's enduring sympathies with the attitudes of the Enlightenment makes his discovery of valuable qualities in Highland culture particularly impressive. He is forced, by the virtues he finds in Highland culture, to reflect critically upon the commercial culture which in Scotland, as in England, is sweeping all else before it.

> It may likewise deserve to be inquired, whether a great nation ought to be totally commercial? whether amidst the uncertainty of human affairs, too much attention to one mode of happiness may not endanger others? whether the pride of riches must not sometimes have recourse to the protection of courage?

Johnson gradually realises that the destruction of Highland culture is tragic, and he sees that the tragedy is being exacerbated by the fact that the destruction is going forward according to the dictates of a distant central authority which has no sense of responsibility to the inhabitants. Nothing is replacing the old culture. The land is being depopulated by emigration. He passes a devastating political judgment: 'To hinder insurrection, by driving away the people, and to govern peaceably, by having no subjects, is an expedient that argues no great profundity of politics.' Johnson's sense of loss is intensified by his perception that a community, once destroyed, is irrecoverable. Will the Highlanders be happy in America? They will not, he replies, be 'happy as a nation, for they are a nation no longer', He believes, as Burke did, that the continuity of institutions must be maintained. Reflecting on the planting of trees, he observes:

> But there is a frightful interval between the seed and the timber. He that calculates the growth of trees, has the unwelcome remembrance of the shortness of life driven hard upon him. He knows that he is doing what will never benefit himself; and when he rejoices to see the stem rise, is disposed to repine that another shall cut it down.

In its context, this passage acquires larger meanings. Self-interest, narrowly conceived, is not enough: there must be something which endures. Immediate profits are not an adequate criterion for well-being. A generation owes much to those which preceded it, and as much to those still to be born.

At Anoch Johnson hears for the first time of 'the general dissatisfaction, which is now driving the Highlanders into the other hemisphere'. Each successive mention of emigration is more ominous, both because we are gradually becoming aware of the extent of the exodus, and because, as we examine the intricate communal structure through Johnson's eyes, our sense of what is being lost is deepened. Though Johnson sees much poverty as he journeys through the Highlands, he also observes, admiringly, that 'everything in these countries has its history'.

In the course of his journey through the Highlands, his admiration grows. 'At Dunvegan,' he writes, 'I had tasted Lotus, and was in danger of forgetting that I was ever to depart . . .' The Laird of Muack he discovers to be a fine example of *noblesse oblige* who, 'having all his people under his immediate view, seems to be very attentive to their happiness. The devastation of the smallpox, when it visits places where it comes seldom, is well known. He has disarmed it of its terror at *Muack,* by innoculating eighty of his people'. Innovation, Johnson implies, should, if possible, go forward within the forms of the existing society. He finds the young Laird at Col particularly attractive:

> Wherever we roved, we were pleased to see the reverence with which his subjects regarded him. He did not endeavour to dazzle them by any magnificence of dress: his only distinction was a feather in his bonnet; but as soon as he appeared, they forsook their work and clustered about him: he took them by the hand, and they seemed mutually delighted. He has the proper disposition of a Chieftain, and seems desirous to continue the customs of his house. The bagpiper played regularly, when dinner was served, whose person and dress made a good appearance; and he brought no disgrace upon the family of *Rankin,* which has long supplied the Lairds of *Col* with hereditary musick.

This Laird, Johnson observes, is improving the land by means of the newer agricultural techniques. He has planted orchards, and has introduced cultivation of turnips, with which cattle may be fed during the hard winters. But the Highlands in general are not being permitted such peaceful evolution, which would preserve the continuities of local culture. Instead, they are being subjected to a ruinous repression: 'There was perhaps never any change of national manners so quick, so great, and so general, as that which has operated in the Highlands, by the last conquest, and the subsequent laws.' The Highland Chiefs, he observes, have been stripped of most of their influence, and as they 'gradually degenerate from patriarchal rulers to rapacious landlords, they will divest themselves of the little that remains'. The destruction of the old order, the abandonment of mutual obligations between ruler and ruled, far from 'liberating' the Highlanders, will expose them to the greed of 'rapacious landlords'. No fabric of custom and tradition will stand between the Highlanders and behaviour based upon the narrowest conception of self-interest. Edmund Burke, a few years later, was to see a similar peril in the convulsions of France.

The repressive laws, Johnson sees, have accelerated the transition from an agricultural and traditional society to one subject to the vicissitudes of commerce. The commercial society is fluid, socially mobile, Johnson says, for money 'confounds subordination, by overpowering the distinctions of rank and birth'. He finds in every quarter the dissolving effect of money on the old social order: 'and I saw with grief the chief of a very ancient clan, whose island was condemned by law to be sold for the satisfaction of his creditors'. At times, he finds himself torn between the values of two moral worlds: 'The commodiousness of money is indeed great; but there are some advantages which money cannot buy, and which therefore no wise man will by the love of money be tempted to forego.' This

process, in which money was rendering ineffectual the ties which bound the old society together, had been under way in England for more than a century. Those Tory writers who, like Johnson, admired many of the values of traditional society, expressed their grief over the change in such works as *The Dunciad* and *The Deserted Village.*

Many Highlanders responded to the destruction of their way of life by emigrating. At the beautiful island of Raasay Johnson finds a deceptive cheerfulness: 'nothing but civility, elegance, and plenty'. Before dinner there is dancing, and after dinner the ladies sing Erse songs. 'I inquired the subjects of the songs, and was told of one, that it was a love song, and of another, that it was a farewell composed by one of the islanders that was going, in the epidemical fury of emigration, to seek his fortune in *America.*' An atmosphere of melancholy, more portentous because not mentioned, pervades the remaining scenes at Raasay:

> Such a seat of hospitality, amidst the winds and waters, fills the imagination with a delightful contrariety of images. Without is the rough ocean and the rocky land, the beating billows and the howling storm: within is plenty and elegance, beauty and gaiety, the song and the dance. In Raasay, if I could have found an Ulysses, I had fancied a *Phoeacia.*

And yet, no sooner is this idyllic note struck, than, in the following paragraph, which describes Dunvegan, we come upon evidence that this culture is doomed: 'The port is made by an inlet of the sea, deep and narrow, where a ship lay waiting to dispeople *Sky,* by carrying the natives away to *America.*' Johnson finds that 'whole neighbourhoods formed parties for removal', and he pleads that 'some method to stop this epidemic desire of wandering' be sought. He suggests that the Highlanders' plaids and weapons be returned to them, and that subsidies be provided to protect them from the rapidly rising rents.

And yet, though Johnson saw, perhaps more clearly than anyone of his time, what had been lost in Scotland through the destruction of pre-Reformation Christian culture and through the disintegration of Highland culture, he was not oblivious to the advantages of the progress that had in fact occurred. New Aberdeen, lacking, indeed, tradition, and the richness that tradition provides, and populated largely by tradesmen, yet shows an orderliness which he does not find unattractive. 'The houses are large and lofty, and the streets spacious and clean.' Even out of evil, he perceives, some good may come: 'I was told at *Aberdeen* that the people learned from Cromwell's soldiers to make shoes and plant kail.' Johnson's many and curiously detailed observations concerning agricultural and industrial processes, because in a minor key, serve as a contrast to his great tragic themes. Yet they do more. In the midst of tragedy, Johnson tells us, life must go on. Just as *Hamlet* includes Fortinbras and Horatio, Johnson's book makes room within itself for the normal, the minimal. Though history is tragic, he makes us see, it may alternatively be perceived to consist not 'of illustrious actions, or elegant enjoyments':

> the greater part of our time passes in compliance with necessities, in the performance of daily duties, in the removal of small inconveniences, in the procurement of petty pleasures, and we are well or ill at ease, as the main stream of life glides on smooth-

ly, or is ruffled by small obstacles and frequent interruption.

Indeed, after all his description of the tragedy of history, in the full awareness of what has been lost, Johnson is able to admit that there is a good side to the new society that is evolving, a society with which he would never be on easy terms. Coming down out of the Highlands—in the narrative at this point one feels that one is entering another world—Johnson observes that at Glasgow there may be found thriving commerce and obvious prosperity, and he remarks, 'the greatness of many private houses'. His approval, to be sure, is not unqualified. The cathedral, though it escaped destruction, has never been completed, and the 'college has not had a sufficient share of the increasing magnificence of the place'. Because of the very clarity of his perceptions, Johnson's sympathies remain divided. One gathers, on the one hand, that the rising middle-class culture embodied much that repelled him. It provided neither the intense loyalties nor the motives for personal heroism which were part of feudal culture, and it lacked the spiritual heights and depths of the old Christian culture. The new middle-class produced, characteristically, as Yeats was to put it, a

> rational sort of mind
> That never looked out of the eye of a saint
> Or out of drunkard's eye.

Indeed, its commitment, at least at the start, to a narrow definition of self-interest, cut it off from the most generous impulses of the old culture. Such losses, Johnson saw, were tragic. He was far too intelligent to share the complacent progressivism of many of his lesser contemporaries, who, though they congratulated the past for producing them at last, were a bit grudging in their congratulations because the past, inexplicably, had taken so long about it. Like those other eighteenth-century writers who now speak to us with undiminished, and perhaps with increased, authority—Pope, Swift, Burke—Johnson quarrelled profoundly with the ascendant cultural forces of his time. Yet even so, Johnson chose to end his book, and by doing so criticise his own tragic vision, with a perfect example of the enlightened humanitarianism which is the kind of thing middle-class culture at its best can provide. At Edinburgh he visits a school for the deaf and dumb, 'who are taught to speak, to read, to write, and to practice arithmetick, by a gentleman, whose name is Braidwood'. At this school Johnson

> found some of the scholars waiting for their master, whom they are said to receive at his entrance with smiling countenances and sparkling eyes, delighted with the hope of new ideas.

Thus, in *A Journey to the Western Islands,* Johnson develops three major themes: the destruction of pre-Reformation Christian culture, the disintegration of Highland culture, and the rise of middle-class, progressive culture. By superimposing the present upon the past, by treating the themes simultaneously, he is able to generate some ironic analogies: of the 'enlightened' commercial classes to the 'Goths' who had destroyed Rome, for example, the same analogy Pope had made in *The Dunciad.* The lesser concerns of the book draw further meaning from the major themes. 'Ossian' infuriates him, in part, no doubt, because it represents a sentimental lie, an attempt to say that something is alive which has long been dead. In creating the various shades of meaning, Johnson's personality as narrator plays an important part: his scepticism, his Englishness, his sense of himself as a product of the Humanist tradition, his complicated commitment to the Enlightenment. The elements of his personality modify, and are modified by, the grand themes of his narrative, which develop slowly, rise out of a minute and often seemingly dispassionate cataloguing of detail: Johnson has in common with Defoe, from whom he differs so much in other ways, an impressive circumstantiality. And because these themes develop slowly, their cumulative effects, as at Iona, are the more powerful.

Johnson had seen so much in Scotland. He had seen, as it were, the entire pattern of European history since the Reformation. And even more than this. In his large vision of mutability he had seen one kind of truth about all of history. In his final sentence, with an irony worthy of Socrates, he tells us that his narrative represents 'the thoughts of one who has seen but little'. (pp. 44-58)

Jeffrey Hart, "Johnson's 'A Journey to the Western Islands': History as Art," in Essays in Criticism, *Vol. X, No. 1, January, 1960, pp. 44-59.*

Geoffrey Tillotson   (essay date 1961)

[*Tillotson was an English educator, author, and critic of eighteenth-century and nineteenth-century English literature and writers. Notable among his works are* Augustan Studies *(1961) and* Essays in Criticism and Research *1942. In the following excerpt, he extols Johnson's linguistic insights as stated in his* Dictionary *and related writings.*]

There are two pieces of extended writing connected with the **Dictionary.** The body of the **Dictionary** could not, in its very nature, be more than a series of short items, but as usual Johnson took the opportunity to deliver himself at large on the principles of the work he was concerned in doing. Eight years before the **Dictionary** was published, he brought out his **"Plan of an English Dictionary"**, and when the work was completed he affixed to it a **"Preface."** The **"Plan"** is enough to show that Johnson had been conscious of the nature of English words long before there had been any question of his making a dictionary. It shows a magnificent grasp of what lay ahead. When the time came for him to write his **"Preface"** he did not need to supersede the **"Plan"** at any important point. **"Plan"** and **"Preface"** together are two of the most remarkable writings we have about the matters they treat of.

The **"Plan"** and the **"Preface"** show that Johnson saw his work as concerned not so much with words as with language. That is one of the supreme merits of the **Dictionary.** It is possible for a dictionary-maker to do his work quite happily on a much lower plane. He is paid to take the words of the language, to arrange them in alphabetical order and to give us an account—some account—of their meaning. And this had been what dictionary-makers up to that time had felt to be all that was expected of them. But Johnson came to see that to isolate a word in dictionary fashion was to destroy something essential in its nature. He saw English words as things belonging to what he called 'a living tongue', and he saw that the advantage of belonging to a living tongue was that words were themselves alive in the sense that their meaning depended upon the various places they had occupied, or were occupying, among their fellows. He saw words as gregarious things, as things, as it were, that had faces which lit up only when in company. There are no more interesting passages in his **"Plan"** and **"Preface"** than those which deal with the subtleties that words owe to their successive contexts.

'Names,' he said, 'have often many ideas.' And again:

> When the construction of a word is explained, it is necessary to pursue it through its train of phraseology, through those forms where it is used in a manner peculiar to our language, or in senses not to be comprised in the general explanations.

And these are some of the phrases he uses: 'exuberance of signification', 'nice and subtle ramifications of meaning', and—a phrase now common which he seems to have invented—'shades of meaning'. He despaired of seizing these distinctions, but he saw that we could discern them by noting words in their place in the living language, especially when it is written or spoken by those who understand 'the genius of the tongue'—again the phrase is his and again he seems to have invented it. In the **"Plan"** of the *Dictionary* he gave the idea this modern turn:

> The signification of adjectives may be often ascertained [i.e., pinned down] by uniting them to substantives; as, *simple swain, simple sheep.* Sometimes the sense of a substantive may be elucidated by the epithets annexed to it in good authors; as, the *boundless ocean,* the *open lawns.*

Now it had been the dream of some of Johnson's contemporaries and some of his immediate predecessors, that English could become fixed in a changeless state. Johnson himself had begun with hoping that he might make that dream come true.

We can understand why in the eighteenth century there was a wish to see English fixed. The literary ideal of its great writers was the ideal of correctness. And that was an ideal partly, sometimes mainly, dependent on the means of expression, on language. Prose writers often had new thoughts and so needed to have them understood. Poets had old thoughts mainly, and so looked to expression to justify their expressing them once again. And yet they saw that English had proved itself a broken reed. It had been a language so given to change that the writings of one age had become progressively unintelligible to later ages. If it was still possible to discern that Chaucer was a great poet, that was because this greatness had proved too lively to be quite extinguished by its medium. And not only Chaucer. Atterbury, the friend of Pope, said that much of Shakespeare was unintelligible at that date. Did it not follow that the same doom was awaiting the would-be correct writings of Swift, Addison and Pope? Pope certainly thought so:

> And such as Chaucer is shall Dryden be.

This feeling about the transience of English was sharpened by the admiration these men felt for the comparative fixity of Latin—what survived of Latin literature made use of a language that, beside English, appeared beautifully stable. Pope himself purposed to help in a formal way the fixing of English. He had the idea of making a dictionary which should draw its words from the best English writers of the sixteenth and seventeenth centuries. And it was Pope's plan apparently that was passed on to Johnson, who speaks of Pope's solicitude 'for the success of this work'. Johnson came to see that nobody could fix a living language any more than King Canute could fix the sea. Even so he did something towards saving it from unnecessary change. Along with other great writers he worked, both as writer and lexicographer, in the spirit of that exhortation in his **"Preface:"** 'We have long preserved our constitution, let us make some struggles for our language.'

Because of the outcome of the struggles we can still read the writing of Swift and Pope—I mean skim along the surface, of course—almost as effortlessly as their first readers.

And so to my third point. Johnson complained, when speaking of those subtle verbs *get, take,* and so on, that in English we had too many of them. Modern linguists will resent that complaint. But Johnson himself knew it was an idle one. He saw his office as that of 'registering' not 'forming' the language. We can see how wise he was when we think of the vain endeavours that Robert Bridges, say, engaged himself in. Bridges assumed that language could be shaped according to the desires of those interested in shaping it. What a pity he did not read Johnson's Preface which proclaims that 'to enchain syllables and to lash the wind, are equally the undertakings of pride, unwilling to measure its desires by its strength'.

My final point brings me back to what I said about Johnson and truth. Everybody knows that when, half-way through his vast *Dictionary,* he arrived at the word 'lexicographer' he allowed himself the pleasure of intruding into his definition the phrase 'a harmless drudge', but he did so because he himself was as incapable of the mindlessness of drudgery as of the inanity of harmlessness. 'I am not yet so lost in lexicography,' he assures us in the **"Preface,"** 'as to forget that *words are the daughters of earth, and that things are the sons of heaven.* Language is only the instrument of science [i.e., knowledge], and words are but the signs of ideas.' He was not so lost as to forget to make of his *Dictionary* more than a dictionary. He made of it the occasion for a long series of inlets into great literature. For Johnson great literature embodied truth. He had a passion for 'true, evident and actual wisdom'. All his writings were means of honouring it. Even his *Dictionary* honours it. For when he chose to show words actively alive in his exhibits, he chose to show them so in exhibits worth reading on their own account. We of the twentieth century with our weakness for snippets can think of each dozen pages of his *Dictionary*—and there are about 3,000 pages—as offering us a tear-off calendar of great thoughts! As well as everything else, his *Dictionary* is an anthology of 'beauties'. Of course, they could only be brief beauties, but it is interesting to learn that their number had to be reduced on revision, and it is amusing to see the amplitude of some of those that were retained. So interesting are these examples as pieces of truth that the *Dictionary* comes near to defeating its own ends. It is a dictionary that can be read, and in practice we find ourselves reading it. In other words, it is made to serve the ends that are served by *The Rambler, Rasselas* and the *Lives of the Poets.* When Anna Seward said that all Johnson's writings were poetry—that is, writings that added delight to instruction—she made an exception of his orthographical works. But she need not have done so. (pp. 224-28)

Geoffrey Tillotson, "Johnson's Dictionary," in his Augustan Studies, *The Athlone Press, 1961, pp. 224-28.*

Frederick W. Hilles (essay date 1965)

[*Hilles was an American educator, author, and esteemed Johnsonian scholar whose works include* The Age of Johnson *(1949) and* New Light on Dr. Johnson *(1959). In the following excerpt, he finds that the theme, literary style, and structural pattern of Johnson's* Rasselas *presents a balanced view of the world.*]

Of the various adverse judgements passed upon **Rasselas** my favourite is the one written by Richardson's prosy friend Hester Mulso Chapone. It is my favourite because, though made up of a series of negatives, it is so positive. Johnson, she said: 'ought to be ashamed of publishing such an ill-contrived, unfinished, unnatural and uninstructive tale. . . . I think the one maxim one can deduce from the story is that human life is a scene of unmixed wretchedness.' This criticism I should characterize as ill-natured, unfair, unbalanced, and unintelligent, but it nicely sums up the objections to the book that have been made during the past two centuries. **Rasselas,** we are told, is structurally weak; it is artificial; it is hopelessly pessimistic.

When characterizing the book as ill-contrived and unfinished, Mrs. Chapone is only one of many readers who have regarded it as a series of moral essays loosely strung together on a plot-thread of the flimsiest. Admittedly it lacks the careful organization we find in *Tom Jones* (what book does not?), but analysis proves that **Rasselas** is in fact, like most books of its period, well-constructed. It is composed of three roughly equal parts, each closely related to the other two.

In the first part we are in the Happy Valley, a garden of Eden, an earthly paradise, described in words that recall ideal communities in epic and romance. We are introduced to a prince who lives in this idyllic spot, and we discover that he is anything but happy, is on the contrary unspeakably bored. Within the valley is security; outside, he is told, man preys upon man; 'discord is always raging'. His old teacher, attempting to convince his pupil that he should be happy, says: 'Sir, if you had seen the miseries of the world, you would know how to value your present state.' Like other teachers before and after him, he finds that what he has said has an effect directly opposite to what was intended. 'Now, said the prince, you have given me something to desire; I shall long to see the miseries of the world, since the sight of them is necessary to happiness.' Almost half of this first section is devoted to preparation for his travels in the form of discussions with the poet Imlac, whose experiences foreshadow what Rasselas will discover for himself.

The second part of the book begins when Imlac leads Rasselas, his sister Nekayah, and her companion Pekuah into the world of men. Settling in Grand Cairo, the young people compare various ways of living by conversing with men and women from all walks of life. Episode follows episode in a carefully balanced fashion. Urban life is con-

trasted to the rural. Within the city the epicurean offsets the stoic, the one lazily sinking beneath man's proper level, the other foolishly preaching what is beyond the powers of mere humans. In the country the travellers meet shepherd, landlord, and hermit, the first depicting debased human nature, man in an animal state, and the last an intelligent person attempting unsuccessfully to do what social beings cannot do, attempting to escape from all representatives of his species. The prince and his sister examine respectively the lives of the great and the humble and, comparing notes, find that every home is 'haunted by some fury that destroys its quiet'. They debate the advantages or disadvantages of youth and age, celibacy and matrimony, early and late marriages. This section of the tale—a period of exploration for the young people—ends with the comparison of past and present, which is made concrete by their visit to the Pyramids. This central section is a kind of keystone on which everything in the book depends. Throughout there are equal stresses between 'on the one hand' and 'on the other'. Man must not do this; man cannot do that. To use Pope's verbs, man must not creep; he cannot soar.

In the final section the observers become participants. Pekuah is abducted by the Arab chieftain, and as a result not she alone, but her royal companions as well, learn what suffering is. This episode occupies roughly half the section and almost the same amount of space is devoted to the travellers' personal involvement in the life of the mad astronomer. The sombre chapters on insanity, old age, and death lead to a conclusion, which like the ending of *Candide* has apparently meant different things to different readers. For the moment I shall merely say of it that the last sentence takes us back to the first one, neatly rounding off a skilfully organized little tale. The book, in short, is not loosely episodic. It has been carefully put together, moving us from light to dark, from youth to age, from vicarious living to disillusioning experience.

Rasselas, we have seen, has been criticized for being unnatural, artificial. There never have been, there never will be, such bloodless creatures, we are told, as the prince and his sister. The language they speak is language that no human being has ever been heard to use; the experiences they have are too neatly contrived. Criticism of this sort would rule out many of the literary masterpieces of the world. Criticism of this sort led Tolstoi to declare that *King Lear* was a silly play, that Shakespeare was a second-rate author. Johnson, an abstractionist, has reduced his characters to the essentials, has obliterated from them all 'accidentals'. His fictitious men and women are deliberately stylized, his language appropriately formal. Writing when Longinus was in the ascendant, writing immediately after his friend Burke had published his *Essay on the Sublime and Beautiful,* he chose to make use of the Grand Style. The tone is set in the opening sentences.

> Ye who listen with credulity to the whispers of fancy, and persue with eagerness the phantoms of hope; who expect that age will perform the promises of youth, and that the deficiencies of the present day will be supplied by the morrow; attend to the history of Rasselas prince of Abissinia.

The mood is hortatory, imperative. The language suggests the epic. Rasselas, we find, 'was the fourth son of the mighty emperour, in whose dominions the Father of waters begins his course; whose bounty pours down the streams of plenty, and scatters over half the world the harvests of Egypt'. The conception is vast, the ideas lofty, the pace stately. Words and phrases reach our minds through ear as well as eye. Period balances period, sound echoes sound, to produce a hypnotic effect. The style is what Johnson called 'persuasory'. Incantation, applied at the outset to a never-never land, charms the reader (*charms* in its original sense), draws him out of his everyday existence, so that by the time the story gets under way he can look upon this world with an uncommon objectivity. Shall we examine one of the two great works made by the hands of men? The Pyramid, Imlac states,

> seems to have been erected only in compliance with that hunger of imagination which preys incessantly upon life, and must be always appeased by some employment. . . . Whoever thou art, that, not content with a moderate condition, imaginest happiness in royal magnificence, and dreamest that command or riches can feed the appetite of novelty with perpetual gratifications, survey the pyramids, and confess thy folly!

Or, we may focus not on man's works, but on the workings of man's mind:

> He who has nothing external that can divert him, must find pleasure in his own thoughts, and must conceive himself what he is not; for who is pleased with what he is? He then expatiates in boundless futurity, and culls from all imaginable conditions that which for the present moment he should most desire. . . . In time some particular train of ideas fixes the attention, all other intellectual gratifications are rejected, the mind, in weariness or leisure, recurs constantly to the favourite conception, and feasts on the luscious falsehood whenever she is offended with the bitterness of truth. By degrees the reign of fancy is confirmed; she grows first imperious, and in time despotick. Then fictions begin to operate as realities, false opinions fasten upon the mind, and life passes in dreams of rapture or of anguish.

We do not read *Rasselas* for the story. We read it for a view of life that is presented majestically in long sweeping phrases. We read it, to adopt Johnsonian terminology, for the colours of varied diction, for the music of modulated periods. What Johnson achieves in this 'artificial' manner is the grandeur of generality. Diction, rhythms, character, and plot are all of a piece.

That the book is didactic is a truism. The question is whether a work of art may at the same time be instructive and aesthetically pleasing. Johnson of course would snort at the doubter. 'The only end of writing is to instruct.' 'He that thinks reasonably must think morally.' Johnson was living in an England that believed in progress, in an England that was rapidly growing in wealth and power. The riches of the Indies, west as well as east, were being diverted to her shores. The prevailing philosophy, even among those who were not well-to-do, was shallowly optimistic. In his essays and in his great poem Johnson had already attacked this attitude. Like Gulliver he might have bemoaned the fact that his voice had not been heard; in any event he repeated his attack in *Rasselas,* repeated it knowing that what he had to teach was of vital importance to Everyman.

Voltaire, if he was not speaking ironically, was out of step with the world when he characterized the philosophy underlying *Rasselas* as *aimable*. *Un*pleasant, *dis*agreeable, is the word one expects to hear. Certainly Johnson is not painting a rosy picture of the world. When writing his *Essay on Man,* Pope told a friend that his aim was 'to make mankind look upon this life with comfort and pleasure, and put morality in good humour'. *Rasselas* might be considered Johnson's *Essay on Man,* but it hardly makes this life seem comfortable or pleasant.

Speaking of *Rasselas* Professor Cazamian says: 'Le pessimisme est souffrant, non point ironique.' I confess that I do not understand this sentence. Irony, I should say, is all-pervasive. In the opening section in the Happy Valley our unhappy hero is not alone. 'Great Prince, said Imlac, . . . I know not one of all your attendants who does not lament the hour when he entered this retreat.' In the Happy Valley none is happy. The central section begins with Chapter XVI, 'They enter Cairo and find every man happy.' Characteristic of this section is the stoic who, we soon discover, is quite unstoical. And the final section begins with a situation that shrieks irony. Pekuah is kidnapped because she prefers what she thinks is safety to entering the pyramids. Or what of the final chapter, a conclusion in which nothing is concluded? The entire book has dealt with the vanity of human wishes, and repeatedly the characters are made to realize that those in great places are most insecure. Yet at the end Pekuah wishes (the verb is Johnson's) to go into a convent *where she will be prioress,* Nekayah desires (again the verb is Johnson's) to found a college *in which she will preside,* and Rasselas desires a little kingdom, 'but he could never fix the limits of his dominion, and was always adding to the number of his subjects'.

The book is filled with psychological insights developed through irony. The melancholy prince soliloquizes on man and is delighted with himself as he talks about 'the miseries of life', happy 'from consciousness of the delicacy with which he felt, and the eloquence with which he bewailed them'. A similar note is struck when Imlac tells of meeting the great Mogul: 'though I cannot now recollect any thing that he uttered above the power of a common man, he dismissed me astonished at his wisdom, and enamoured of his goodness.' This in turn is echoed by the philosopher of Cairo who, as he finished his discourse, 'looked round him with a placid air, and enjoyed the consciousness of his own beneficence'.

Non point ironique? Chapter IV shows our hero resolving to run away.

> He past four months in resolving to lose no more time in idle resolves, and was awakened to more vigorous exertion by hearing a maid, who had broken a porcelain cup, remark, that what cannot be repaired is not to be regretted. . . . He, for a few hours, regretted his regret, and from that time bent his whole mind upon the means of escaping from [not the Happy Valley but] the valley of happiness.

The ground tone, no doubt, is one of sorrow. The picture of humanity is not gay; the smile of the author is a sad smile. But is it really true that this is a pessimistic book? Supported by the definitions of pessimism in the *Oxford English Dictionary* I should ask whether the author here preaches 'the doctrine that this world is the worst possible'? Does his book, even faintly, suggest that 'everything naturally tends to evil'? Pessimism presents a view of life that is devoid of hope, the sort of view that James Thomson offers in *The City of Dreadful Night.* (pp. 111-17)

Admittedly the sentences usually extracted from *Rasselas* are not cheerful. 'The life of a solitary man will be certainly miserable.' 'Marriage has many pains, but celibacy has no pleasures.' 'Human life is every where a state in which much is to be endured, and little to be enjoyed.' But these negatives—and this, as far as I know, has not been pointed out—are regularly counterbalanced by positives. The book attempts to set for us, to use Imlac's words, the limits of sober probability, to discriminate between what man must not and what man can not do. It is a child of its time; it is the product of neo-classic thought, emphasizing the necessity of some sort of control over human behaviour. 'He does nothing who endeavours to do more than is allowed to humanity', we read, but also: 'Do not suffer life to stagnate', or, 'Few things are impossible to diligence and skill.' Above the ground tone of sorrow is a melodic line that is vigorous, energetic, vibrant. The characters in this sad book enjoy many moments of pleasure. Life is worth living to them so long as it is not allowed to stagnate, so long as they have something to desire, so long as they are mentally active. At the end of the book they are still day-dreaming, but it is made explicit that they *know* they are dreaming. They now know that ahead of them are disappointments, injustices, sorrows. Their eyes have been opened to realities, and they are now in a position to face those realities. The outlook on life here presented is not pessimistic but realistic. What Henry James said of Hawthorne is equally applicable to the author of *Rasselas:* 'He is no more a pessimist than an optimist. . . . To a considerable degree ironical . . . [he is] neither bitter nor cynical.'

A few months before he wrote *Rasselas* Johnson sent to his friend Bennet Langton a letter of condolence, which ended with words that throw light on the book he was about to write.

> Let us endeavour to see things as they are, and then enquire whether we ought to complain. Whether to see life as it is will give us much consolation I know not, but the consolation which is drawn from truth, if any there be, is solid and durable, that which may be derived from errour must be like its original fallacious and fugitive.

This, I repeat, is not pessimism, but realism. To get at the solid and the durable we must see life as it is.

Now to see life as it is is the message of Jonathan Swift; it is the message of Voltaire in *Candide.* Johnson is the product of the same age that produced Swift and Voltaire. All three seek to dispel illusions, but Johnson's manner of doing so differs sharply from the others. In *Candide,* in Gulliver's last voyage, our pretensions as human beings are stripped off in such a way as to leave us bleeding and sore. Johnson's approach to human fallibility is one of sympathy. He comes closest to Voltaire, perhaps, when he describes the unfortunate inventor in the Happy Valley. After labouring for a year on his flying machine, the 'artist' appeared one morning on a promontory, ready to test his handiwork. He 'waved his pinions a while to gather air, then leaped from his stand, and in an instant dropped into the lake. His wings, which were of no use in the air, sustained him in the water, and the prince drew him to land,

half dead with terrour and vexation.' As G. B. Hill pointed out long ago, 'Johnson is content with giving the artist a ducking. Voltaire would have crippled him for life at the very least; most likely would have killed him on the spot.' Voltaire tends to be destructive; Johnson constructive.

Assuming for the moment that Horace Walpole's famous aphorism is true ('This world is a comedy to those that think, a tragedy to those that feel'), *Rasselas* presents a view of the world that is somewhere between the extremes. It is, to state the obvious, a thoughtful book, but clearly one that is the result of deep feeling. Certain modern commentators stress—overstress, I should say—the comic elements in the book, just as the more orthodox critics have dwelt overmuch on the tragic sense of life that informs it. The literary style (words and sentences evenly balanced) and the structural pattern (aspects of life carefully compared and contrasted) support the balanced view of the world that the book offers. The whole produces a gyroscopic effect, creates a state of equilibrium. After closely inspecting the world, Rasselas and his friends are less likely to lose their balance. As they have acquired wisdom, they have achieved poise. (pp. 117-19)

Once, when praising Lord Kames's *Elements of Criticism,* Johnson added: 'I do not mean that he has taught us any thing; but he has told us old things in a new way.' In *Rasselas* Johnson tells us nothing that is new, but he tells us what is true, and tells it so effectively that people in all parts of the globe and from all walks of life have come under its spell. (p. 120)

[*Rasselas*'s] longevity, its triumph over space as well as time, its popularity with rich and poor, orientals and occidentals, today as well as yesterday, is directly related to its author's theory of literature. *Rasselas* depicts human nature in general. It is the story of Everyman, believer or non-believer, Christian or Jew, Mahometan or Buddhist. It does not attempt to justify the ways of God to man. It does not ask the question why. Why does evil exist? That is a question not to be asked—not to be asked, because the will of the Supreme Being, as Imlac puts it, is unsearchable. But there are other questions, such as: What are the chief causes of man's unhappiness? or What objectives are proper to man? These are questions to be asked. And these are questions that are put compellingly to every reader of *Rasselas.* (pp. 120-21)

> *Frederick W. Hilles, " 'Rasselas', An 'Unin-structive Tale'," in his* Johnson, Boswell and Their Circle, *Oxford at the Clarendon Press, 1965, pp. 111-21.*

W. K. Wimsatt   (essay date 1968)

[*Wimsatt was an American educator, critic, and essayist who contributed critical and historical articles and reviews to numerous journals. He also served as co-editor for* Literary Criticism: A Short History (*with Cleanth Brooks, 1957) and* Samuel Johnson on Shakespeare (*1960). In the following excerpt, he identifies chronological discrepancies in the narrative of* Rasselas *and highlights Johnson's adaptation of the major conventions of the "oriental tale."*]

Johnson most likely began to write *Rasselas* not long after Saturday, 13 January, 1759, when he seems first to have heard of his mother's serious illness. A week later, on Saturday, 20 January, he wrote to the publisher William Strahan that he would deliver the book to him on Monday night, and that the title would be "The Choice of Life/ or/ The History of. . . . Prince of Abisinnia". The several learned editors of **Rasselas** have, accordingly, not been inclined to take literally Johnson's later statement to Reynolds, as reported by Boswell, that he not only wrote **Rasselas** "in the evenings of one week", but "sent it to the press in portions as it was written". In portions, as it was corrected during days subsequent to Monday, 22 January, perhaps. It is not difficult to imagine revisions and afterthoughts even during the original week of rapid composition. One of the most obvious internal suggestions of such afterthought, or at least of a certain absent-mindedness during the course of writing, appears in the development of the character of the lady Pekuah. We hear of her first, momentarily, in the escape from the happy valley (chapter XV). "The princess was followed only by a single favourite, who did not know whither she was going . . . The princess and her maid turned their eyes toward every part, and, seeing nothing to bound their prospect, considered themselves as in danger of being lost in a dreary vacuity. They stopped and trembled". A second very brief allusion occurs in the next chapter (XVI), as they arrive at Cairo. "The princess . . . for some days, continued in her chamber, where she was served by her favourite as in the palace of the valley". Thereafter, for fourteen chapters (XVII-XXX), or during the whole first period at Cairo, including the trip to the cataract of the Nile to visit the hermit, we miss this personage altogether, until in chapter XXXI, at the great Pyramid, she reappears abruptly: " . . . the favourite of the princess, looking into the cavity, stepped back and trembled. 'Pekuah, said the princess, of what art thou afraid?' " In the first edition, this was the first introduction of the lady's name. For the second edition, Johnson went back and inserted this name after the word "favourite" in the sentence quoted above from chapter XVI. We remember that Pekuah, through her terror of the gloomy inside of the pyramid, remains outside and in chapter XXXIII is kidnapped by a band of Arab horsemen and becomes the central object of attention during six succeeding chapters (to XXXIX). She reappears thereafter, to the end of the story, in every family conversation (chapters XLIV, XLV, XLVII, XLIX); and in chapter XLVI, her interest in the stars, acquired while she was a prisoner of the Arab chief, is exploited when the ladies invade and civilize the mad astronomer. Once he had conferred a few colours upon this lady, Johnson found her a convenient enough addition to his *dramatis personae*. It is possible that, having in chapters XV and XVI, provided for her presence, he then forgot her, or even deliberately left her out of sight, for seventeen chapters. But it seems at least possible—to me it seems more likely—that he first conceived of the lady Pekuah as his travellers stood at the entrance of the Pyramid, and he bethought himself of Arab horsemen on the horizon and the opportunity to give his story an impetus towards action which at that juncture it badly needed. In that case, he went back (nothing could be simpler) and inserted the allusions to a "favourite" in chapters XV and XVI, and in the second edition the name Pekuah in chapter XVI.

As Geoffrey Tillotson has already observed, Johnson throughout **Rasselas** is preoccupied with the passage of time and pays close attention to the number of days, months, and years which measure out his story. At the age of twenty-six, for example, when he first becomes restless in his confinement, Rasselas lets twenty months slip away in day-dreaming, then awakes and estimates with chagrin that, since the active life of man, between infancy and senility, amounts to no more than forty years, he has just allowed a twenty-fourth part of his life to run to waste ($12 \times 40 = 480 \div 20 = 24$). In contrast to such numerical nicety, the following curious sequence occurs in chapters XIX, XX, and XXI. Rasselas and his friends hear of a hermit, famous for sanctity, who lives near the "lowest cataract of the Nile". They set out to visit him but stop during the "heat" of the [first] day at the tents of some shepherds, whose barbarous conversation proves disgusting to the princess (chapter XIX). Presumably they do not linger for the afternoon or spend the night with these shepherds. But: "On the *next day* [the italics are mine] they continued their journey", says the first sentence of chapter XX. Again they stop during the "heat" of the day, but this time at the "stately palace" of a very prosperous gentleman. He entreats them to stay. They do. And the "next day" he entreats them again. They "continued", in fact, "a few days longer, and then went forward to find the hermit". Then the next chapter (XXI) begins: "They came on the third day, by the direction of the peasants, to the hermit's cell". By the direction of the peasants? Some might argue that this means simply "*the* peasants" of that region. But this kind of slipshod phrasing is not like Johnson. It appears to me all but certain that "peasants" is one of Johnson's occasional quiet or pronominal "elegant variations". He means the "shepherds" with whom they stopped at midday during chapter XIX. After that, and "on the third day" after setting out, they came to the hermit's cell. It seems to me very likely that the episode of the prosperous country gentleman is something which occurred to Johnson at some time after he had written the sequence about the shepherds and the hermit (chapters XIX, XXI), and that, wishing to get it in, he wrote it in where he could, but without noticing a slight derangement of the details of the itinerary. The stop with the shepherds is a brief episode which does not sidetrack the journey to the hermit. Chapter XX, on the downfall of a prosperous country gentleman, is an extended intrusion into that journey. **Rasselas** is in a sense a travel story, but it is not on the whole a picaresque story.

The third example of narrative absent-mindedness which I wish to notice does, however, give us another exception to that rule. Chapter XL (immediately after the narrative of Pekuah's captivity with the Arab), begins: "They returned to Cairo . . . none of them went much abroad. The prince . . . one day declared to Imlac, that he intended to devote himself to science, and pass the rest of his days in literary solitude. 'Before you make your final choice, answered Imlac, you ought to examine its hazards . . . I have just left the observatory of one of the most learned astronomers in the world.' " For the space of five chapters (XL, XLI, XLII, XLIII, XLIV) Imlac continues a nonstop lecture upon the mad delusion by which the astronomer believes himself possessed of the power to control the seasons, bringing rain or sunshine to any part of the world as his conscience dictates. We discover that not only Rasselas but Nekayah and Pekuah are present during the whole conversation (chapters XLIII and XLIV). Then chapter XLV breaks into this sequence as follows: "The evening was now far past, and they rose to return home.

As they walked along the bank of the Nile, delighted with the beams of the moon quivering on the water, they saw at a small distance an old man." But this does not really make sense. If we look back through the involvements of Imlac's long discourse on the mad astronomer, to the beginning of chapter XL, we remember that they are already at home and have been during the whole episode. (Looking back yet farther, a long way back, to chapter XXV, one might recall that during the first period at Cairo the prince and princess "commonly met in the evening in a private summer-house on the bank of the Nile". But this summer-house either was on the grounds of the main house rented and magnificently furnished in chapter XVI, or it was not. If not, if it was away from home, nothing in chapters XL-XLIV intimates that they have now gone there.) The episode of the mad astronomer has not been concluded. After chapter XLV, "They discourse with an old man", the long and dramatically important chapter XLVI immediately resumes the story of the astronomer, telling how he is visited by the ladies, Nekayah and Pekuah, and under the softening influence of feminine conversation is gradually cured of his delirious fantasy. Chapter XLV, devoted to the old man, a characteristically and passionately Johnsonian projection of the bitterness of old age, is a stark intrusion into the sequence about the astronomer. In its absent-minded opening, it seems to me another of Johnson's afterthoughts, so important that it had to go somewhere. Where else would seem better when the other episodes were already in sequence?

I have been urging genetic inferences and have not meant to imply that the actual inconsistencies which I observe (with the possible exception of Pekuah's long absence from the stage) are in any sense aesthetic deficiencies. They do, however, appear to me as complements of and accents upon a much larger and more clearly observable character of the whole story—what I would describe as its highly episodic, and hence very lumpy or bumpy, structure. One recent critic of **Rasselas,** Professor Kolb, has said that it is arranged in two main parts, one in the happy valley, one after the escape. Another critic, Professor Hilles, has discerned three main parts: 1. in the valley, chapters I-XIV; 2. the escape and a period of relatively detached and orderly *observation* at and near Cairo, chapters XV-XXX; 3. beginning with the abduction of Pekuah and the grief of Nekayah, a period of greater personal *involvement* and, at the end, of more somber experience, chapters XXXIII-XLIX. In the chapters following the episode of Pekuah's abduction (if I may expand this theme a little), the mad astronomer is not merely observed, but converted from his delirium and received into the family; even the bitter old man comes home with them for a brief conversation. A climax of experience and reflection is reached in the ante-penultimate chapters, with the visit to the Catacombs, Imlac's argument for the immortality of the soul, and Nekayah's conclusion: "To me . . . the choice of life is become less important; I hope hereafter to think only on the choice of eternity".

Nevertheless, I believe that the forty-nine chapters of the tale fall even more readily into another and more piecemeal pattern—more readily because with more aesthetic immediacy, more clearly segmented colouring. Thus: 1. chapters I-VI, the *unrest* of Rasselas in the valley, climaxed by the attempt at flying; 2. chapters VII-XV, the *story* of Imlac (surely too long in proportion to the whole

book) and the implausible *escape* by tunnelling through the mountain; 3. chapters XVI-XXII, the first period at Cairo, *exploratory,* varicoloured, embracing the visit to the hermit; 4. chapters XXIII-XXIX, an extended *conversation,* on public and private life, on marriage and celibacy, between Rasselas and Nekayah; 5. chapters XXX-XXXIX, *adventures:* the Pyramids, abduction and recovery of Pekuah; 6. chapters XL-XLIX, return to Cairo and more *somber* experiences: the mad astronomer, the bitter old man, the Catacombs, the end. In each of these six segments, certain subdivisions can of course be seen. The first period in Cairo is notable for the rapid succession of separately sought-out episodes. The relentlessly continued conversation between the prince and his sister (chapters XXIII-XXIX) occupies the middle of the whole story as a prolonged central stasis or dead center. The sequence in which Pekuah is the focus of attention (chapters XXXI-XXXIX) is notable for the relative continuity of the adventure story. The visit to the Pyramids which begins this part, or ends the preceding, seems like a heavy punctuation mark (the accent of antiquity and the tomb), and this indeed is echoed in a second and similar punctuation, the visit to the Catacombs, which signals the end of the whole. The second period at Cairo, though it has fewer incidents than the first, is a sort of counterpart to the first, echoing its structure across the interval of the long conversation and the long adventure. Inside one episode in each Cairo period, a shorter and abruptly introduced intercalary episode, as we have seen, stands out like a special bump or knob in the grain of the story. The embittered and malignant old man looks out from his knot-hole or niche back across the chapters to the fearful and ruined country gentleman. But it is difficult to say just what is accomplished for the whole pattern by features of this sort. It is difficult, on the whole, to speak of the "structure" of **Rasselas** in a sense anything like that in which one speaks of the structure of a play by Shakespeare or of a novel by Fielding or Jane Austen. **Rasselas** has the kind of structure which satisfies, more or less, its modest requirements as a quasi-dramatic narrative—not the causal progression, the beginning, middle, and end of the Aristotelian "whole", but a structure of accumulation, something like that of a series of laboratory reports, or a series of chapters on animals sighted or taken, on a hunt across the veldt with gun or camera. "Eye Nature's walks, shoot Folly as it flies, And catch the Manners living as they rise." (pp. 111-17)

To put the matter conventionally and moderately, it is a paradox that a man who had Johnson's preference for both the homely and the abstract should undertake an oriental tale at all. Or better, it is a strangely fit incongruity that this tale, which both tries and refuses to be oriental, should contain as one of its most memorable exhibits a discourse on the art of poetry in which occurs the following sequence of assertions: 1. "I could never describe what I had not seen . . . I ranged mountains and deserts for images and resemblances, and pictured upon my mind every tree of the forest and flower of the valley". 2. "The business of a poet . . . is to examine, not the individual, but the species; to remark general properties and large appearances: he does not number the streaks of the tulip". 3. "He must be acquainted likewise with all the modes of life . . . and trace the changes of the human mind as they are modified by various institutions and accidental influences of climate and custom".

The local colour of *Rasselas,* the "oriental imagery" to the "charms" of which Boswell alludes, is not luxuriant. It is even very thin, and we may at moments wish it were thicker. It has a curiously deductive and even conjectural character—like the effort of a man who has read long ago a book of eastern travels for the purpose of translation, perhaps too has dipped into another book or two in the more recent past.

The most conspicuous colour consists simply in the proper names of places, persons, and offices. We are "oriented" at the outset (chapter I) by the names "Abissinia", "Egypt", and "Amhara". Soon we follow Imlac (chapters VIII-XII) from "Goiama", near the "fountain of the Nile", by way of "the shore of the red sea", to "Surat", and to "Agra, the capital of Indostan", city of the "great Mogul", and thence to "Persia", "Arabia", "Syria", "Palestine", "many regions of Asia", "Egypt", "Cairo", and "Suez"—the latter names pre-establishing for us the route which will be followed by the fugitives from the valley a few chapters hence. Later, the sequence of adventure chapters (XXX-XXXIX) gives us "old Egyptians", the "Pyramids" (over and over), a "troop of Arabs", "Turkish horsemen", the "Bassa" at Cairo, the "borders of Nubia", "the monastery of St. Anthony", "the deserts of Upper-Egypt", the "Arab's fortress" on an "island of the Nile . . . under the tropick".

"How easily shall we then trace the Nile through all his passage", says the aeronautical artist back in chapter VI. This is the first of altogether fifteen allusions by name to that great geographical feature and symbol. The escapees from the happy valley behold "the Nile, yet a narrow current, wandering beneath them". The hermit of chapter XXI lives "near the lowest cataract of the Nile". The "annual overflow" or "inundation" of the Nile is a leitmotif of chapters XLI-XLV, dealing with both the mad weather-maker and the sad old man. ("I rest against a tree, and consider, that in the same shade I once disputed upon the annual overflow of the Nile with a friend who is now silent in the grave.") In chapter XLIX, the Conclusion, a final "inundation of the Nile" confines the prince and his friends to reflection at home (as, long since, in the happy valley, Rasselas and Imlac had been brought together in "domestick amusements" forced upon them by an "inundation" from the lake). "No man", says the wise and aphoristic Nekayah, concluding an earlier chapter of conversation (XXIX), "can, at the same time, fill his cup from the source and from the mouth of the Nile". But Johnson has come close to doing just this.

Another vehicle of exoticism may be identified here and there in a certain courtly, ceremonious, and archaic flourish of words—what Professor Hilles has called "the Grand Style", an aspect of the sublime. This occurs a few times in the author's own voice, as in the opening of the first chapter: "Ye who listen with credulity to the whispers of fancy . . . attend". More often it is from the mouths of the characters—no doubt what the country gentleman of chapter XX detected as the "eloquence of Imlac . . . and the lofty courtesy of the princess". (It is Miltonic—like "Daughter of God and Man, immortal Eve".) As Rasselas saw the animals by moonlight, " 'Ye', said he, 'are happy . . . nor do I, ye gentle beings, envy your felicity'." (chapter II). " 'Dear princess', said Rasselas, 'you fall into the common error of exaggeratory declamation'." (chap-

ter XXVIII). " 'My dear Pekuah', said the princess . . . 'Remember that you are companion of the princess of Abissinia'." (chapter XXXI). "Whoever thou art, that . . . imaginest happiness in royal magnificence, and dreamest . . . perpetual gratifications, survey the pyramids, and confess thy folly!" (chapter XXXII). Here Imlac echoes the rhythm of the narrator in the first sentence of the book. "Illustrious lady", said even the Arab outlaw, "my fortune is better than I had presumed to hope". "Lady", said he, "you are to consider yourself as sovereign". (chapter XXXVIII, XXXIX). Probably the most full-blown instance in the book returns us, characteristically, to geography and to the mighty river. In chapter XXV, "The princess and her brother commonly met in the evening in a private summerhouse on the bank of the Nile . . . As they were sitting together, the princess cast her eyes upon the river that flowed before her". And:

> "Answer", said she, "great father of waters, thou that rollest thy floods through eighty nations, to the invocations of the daughter of thy native king. Tell me if thou waterest, through all thy course, a single habitation from which thou dost not hear the murmurs of complaint?"

Certain other details of local colour are much less distinctive. At the start (chapter I) we are treated to "mountains", "rivulets", a "lake", "fish of every species", water falling "from precipice to precipice", "the banks of the brooks . . . diversified with flowers", "beasts of prey", "flocks and herds", "beasts of chase frisking in the lawns". We hear also of a "palace" with "squares or courts", "arches of massy stone", "upper stories", "private galleries", "subterranean passages", "columns", and "unsuspected cavities" closed with "marble". Such terms, so frequent throughout the work, whenever the argument seems to call for some evocation of physical decor, work as local colour mainly or only in conjunction with the proper names of places and persons which we have seen. It seems scarcely extreme to say that these combinations make the kind of local colour a schoolboy might supply. When I was in the eighth grade, we studied geography (which that year was Africa), and we had to write an imaginary journey through Egypt. I can still remember, approximately, one sentence of my composition—because it struck me at the time as so neatly yet richly executed. "Turning a bend in the Nile, we came in sight of the giant Assouan Dam."

Certain other descriptive details are indeed more specially exotic. These, however, are scarce. I attempt the following approximately exhaustive list. In the "torrid zone" of chapter I, we find the "monkey" and the "elephant". At the start of Imlac's travels in chapter VIII, we have "camels" and "bales" of goods. In chapter IX and again in XII, we have a "caravan", and in chapter X the "mosque of Mecca". In chapter XVIII, at Cairo, a "spacious building", with "open doors", housing a "school of declamation, in which professors read lectures", seems, in spite of its vagueness, much like a part of the ancient Alexandrian world. The shepherds in chapter XIX live in "tents". At the estate of the prosperous country gentleman in chapter XX, "youths and virgins" are "dancing in the grove" near a "stately palace". In XXI, the hermit's "cell" is a "cavern" beneath "palm-trees". In XXX, as we begin to think of the Pyramids, we hear of "fragments of temples" and "choked aqueducts". In XXXII appear "galleries" and "vaults of marble"; in XXXIII, "dark labyrinths". The travel in the desert (chapters XXXI-XXXIX) gives us "tents" (nine times), "camels" (three), "ounces of gold" (three), "deserts" and "the desert", a "monastery", a "refectory", and a "prior"; in XXXVIII appear "carpets", "finer carpets", Pekuah's "upper vest" (with "embroidery"), "the lance", "the sword", "palaces", "temples", "granite", "porphyry"; in XXXIX, "the tropick", a "couch", "turrets", two special plums: "crocodiles" and "river-horses", "needlework", "silken flowers", and another plum: the "seraglio". In the final expedition, to the catacombs (XLVII-XLVIII), we have a "guard of horsemen", "sepulchral caves", a "labyrinth of subterraneous passages", "embalming" and "embalmed" bodies, "caverns".

A few ingenious manipulations of this slender exotic store, cunning jointures of it with the Johnsonian philosophic and plastic staple, stand out. In chapter I, just as I become mildly annoyed at "beasts of chase frisking in the lawns" and "the sprightly kid . . . bounding on the rocks", I am moderately diverted by "the subtle monkey frolicking in the trees, and the solemn elephant reposing in the shade". (No matter whether elephants would really be found in that mountain fastness.) By a somewhat different sort of conjunction, it seems to me, Johnson creates a moment of interesting local colour in chapter XXXIX, as Pekuah looks out on the "winding" river from her island prison: "The crocodiles and river-horses are common in this unpeopled region . . . For some time I expected to see mermaids and tritons, which, as Imlac has told me, the European travellers have stationed in the Nile". And here let us quote too that moment of pregnant phrasing from chapter XXX: "The most pompous monument of Egyptian greatness, and one of the most bulky works of manual industry . . . are the pyramids". And from chapter XXXVIII, the Arab's observation to the lady Pekuah that

> buildings are always best preserved in places little frequented, and difficult of access: for, when once a country declines from its primitive splendour, the more inhabitants are left, the quicker ruin will be made. Walls supply stones more easily than quarries, and palaces and temples will be demolished to make stables of granite, and cottages of porphyry.

By a slight extension of the idea of the exotic, perhaps we can bring in such learned words from the realm of *Mathematical Magick* as Johnson borrowed from his archaic dictionary source of that title, or from other "philosophic" sources, and worked into chapter VI, the story of an attempt at the art of flying: "the tardy conveyance of ships and chariots", "the swifter migration of wings", "the pendent spectator", "volant animals", "the folding continuity of the bat's wings". And with these we come close to yet a wider category of somewhat notable descriptive phrases—all those, I should say, which, without including any word in any way exotic or bizarre, yet by some special energy of compression are likely to strike our attention or force on us the feeling that the description has "texture". In chapter I, the lake is "frequented by every fowl whom nature has taught to dip the wing in water . . . every blast shook spices from the rocks, and every month dropped fruits upon the ground. All animals that bite the grass, or brouse the shrub . . . wandered in this extensive circuit". Such phrases as these may be looked on as Johnsonian substitutes for local colour.

A recent observer from the vantage point of Saudi-Arabia has expounded the extreme unrealism of the journey made by the princely party of fugitives, by ups and downs, through the nearly impassable tropical forests of the Abyssinian plateau, and then down the steep seven or eight thousand feet from the eastern escarpment to the narrow coastal plain and the port where they stayed several months. (This was probably Massawa, a typical Red Sea port, a "horrible place", lying under relentless sun, in saturation humidity.) No less dimly realized seem their "quick and prosperous" coastal voyage [of twenty or thirty days] in a primitive sailing dhow, their slow trip by camel caravan under the desert stars to Cairo, and finally what must have been the astonished arrival of this party of Coptic Christians amid the teeming contrasts of a vast Islamic city.

Johnson, we know, had long enjoyed some awareness of the Abyssinian locale, for as a young man he had written and published (1735) a translation from a French version of the seventeenth-century Portuguese Jesuit Father Jerome Lobo's *Voyage to Abyssinia*. Of recent years, the scholarship of sources has been urging Johnson's debt to other writers on Abyssinia. Lobo, it is clear, could not have been his only source, for Lobo said the prison of the princes was a rocky and "barren summit". But the paradise on the Abyssinian hill was a commonplace—"where Abassin kings their issue guard, Mount Amara—by some supposed True Paradise, under the Ethiop line". One of the reasons why Johnson was interested in Lobo's *Voyage* was that the Jesuit missionary and diplomat himself was more interested in human character and mores, the hardships and vicissitudes of the human adventure, than in exotic or fantastic colourations. Thus, Lobo reports of the crocodiles (which Pekuah saw from the Arab's island fortress): "Neither I nor any with whom I have convers'd about the *Crocodile*, have ever seen him Weep, and therefore I take the Liberty of ranking all that hath been told us of his Tears, amongst the Fables which are only proper to amuse Children". And Johnson, in a Preface to Lobo which Boswell by quoting has made the best-known part of the book:

> THE *Portugese* Traveller, contrary to the general Vein of his Countrymen, has amused his Reader with no Romantick Absurdities or Incredible Fictions . . . HE appears by his modest and unaffected Narration to have described Things as he saw them, to have copied Nature from the Life, and to have consulted his Senses not his Imagination; He meets with no *Basilisks* that destroy with their Eyes, his *Crocodiles* devour their Prey without Tears, and his *Cataracts* fall from the Rock without Deafening the Neighbouring Inhabitants.

Samuel Johnson—both Johnson the man and Johnson the translator of Lobo and the narrator of *Rasselas*—no doubt believes that even the local colours, the geography, the flora, the fauna, the architecture, and the costumes, of exotic places are far less exotic than is commonly reported. Beyond doubt, he believes that human living and human nature in Amhara or in Cairo are far less exotic than is commonly supposed, are indeed essentially the same as in London.

> THE Reader . . . will discover, what will always be discover'd by a diligent and impartial Enquirer, that wherever Human Nature is to be found, there

is a mixture of Vice and Virtue, a contest of Passion and Reason.

General human nature is of course Johnson's theme—vice and virtue, passion and reason. Why not then generalized local colour? The deliberate simplification, even complacent ignorance about the actual colours of life in the supposed locale of Johnson's story, is a kind of counterpart and symbol of the general human truth he would be getting at.

Various critical questions might be asked about *Rasselas,* but surely the main question must always be: What are we to make of the fact that the obvious element of morality is cast in the shape of an oriental tale? Or, what are we to make of the fact that the equally obvious oriental tale is invested with so much morality? The problem, or the task, of a writer who would tell a moral tale is, of course, to get the story and the morality together. He will have to do better than give us a close juxtaposition or rapid alternation of plot and sermon (programme and commercial plug), or a set of essays in a curiously wrought frame, a series of *Ramblers* inserted in a version of the *Arabian Nights.* "We do not read *Rasselas* for the story", says Professor Hilles. "We read it for a view of life that is presented majestically in long sweeping phrases." But he immediately adds: "Diction, rhythms, character and plot are all of a piece". So that he really has a warmer affection for the story (character and plot) than, for instance, Professor Kolb, who, while implying some distress at those critics who "have been content to praise the wisdom and ignore the narrative", at the same time (and on the same page) concludes "that the tale is not the principle which best explains . . . the book . . . the problem of happiness rather than the element of 'story' emerges . . . as the determinant by reference to which questions about the book's structure may be most adequately answered". The structure is "didactic". And this seems to imply somehow that we can call it a "narrative", but not a "tale" or a "story".

In the second section of this essay, I have already given up the "structure" of *Rasselas* so far as that idea pretends to any Aristotelian or organistic and dramatic implications. But then a story does not have to have *much* structure in order to be a story. It is a story if it has any characters and places at all, and if the characters do any talking at all and move about a little, from one place (or one state) to another. The story of *Rasselas* as such, a certain movement of certain persons in certain places—loosely constructed, vaguely characterized, largely undramatic or half-heartedly dramatic as it may be, unfictional fabric of a fiction that it is—has, nevertheless, some kind of imaginative bearing on the moral ideas. This is not an original thesis. "The eastern background", says Professor Kolb, "provides . . . the aura of strange and distant lands where human happiness is commonly thought to be complete and lasting; . . . reminding us of the superficial likenesses and essential differences between *Rasselas* and ordinary oriental tales with their happy-ever-after conclusions." "The judgement of human life", says Professor Leyburn, "would leave a very different impression if it were presented stripped of such aesthetic distance as the regions of the Nile provide." Oriental decor had been used in Augustan England for stories of adventure and fantasy (*Arabian Nights* and *Persian Tales*). It had well-established didactic uses too—as in *Spectator* and *Rambler* visions and apo-

logues. An oriental spokesman could be used to throw a strange and skeptical perspective on Western mores (Montesquieu's *Persian Letters,* Goldsmith's *Chinese Letters*—just after *Rasselas*). The peculiar twist of Johnson's *Rasselas* is that he uses a sort of nominally or minimally exotic tale for the purpose of displaying the most homely human materials and of asserting a workaday perspective upon them. The philosophy of *Rasselas* (Johnson's resistance to eighteenth-century "optimism") might readily enough become our theme now, but I am pushing, not the philosophy but the literary actualization of it, trying to improve the view that it is important for Johnson's antirationalist and conservative purpose that he *should* have a story, of sorts, and a foreign scene.

The Johnsonian substitutes for local colour, we have said, are abstractive, at moments "philosophic", and all but invisible. They may, for that very reason, have a broader spread than we have so far mentioned. It was Johnson himself who observed of Sir Thomas Browne that he "poured a multitude of exotick words", and Johnson's friends Boswell and Arthur Murphy who thought that Browne was a main source for Johnson's own "Anglo-Latin" peculiarities. "How he differed so widely from such elegant models [the Augustans] is a problem not to be solved, unless it be true that he took an early tincture from the writers of the last century, particularly Sir Thomas Browne." Twenty-five years ago I ventured the opinion that Browne "deserves the name 'exotick' which Johnson applies to him", but that this name would sit "curiously on Johnson himself". "Where Browne uses remote terms to make us think of remote things"—Pharaoh, mummy, golden calf, scorpion, and salamander—"Johnson 'familiarizes' ". That much is still true. But, on the other hand, I will now undertake to argue that Johnson's whole way of moral writing, what we may call the *Rambler* style, is a form of moderate exoticism which did not find its ideal setting until he wrote *Rasselas.* During the course of producing his 208 *Ramblers,* Johnson tried out a number of domestic settings of voices for the Rambler mood: the country housewife and her kitchen (no. 51), Mr. Frolick the Londoner in the country (no. 61), Quisquilius the curio-collector (nos. 82-83), Nugaculus the gossip (no. 103), Mrs. Busy (no. 138), Captator the legacy-hunter (nos. 197-198). But in all such instances, the more dramatic he makes the treatment, the more the peculiar Rambleresque pomp of phrasing thins out. This happens even in the exotic setting of the Greenland idyll of Anningait and Ajut (nos. 186-187). Perhaps it happens too with the several oriental tales, including that of the Emperor Seged of Ethiopia (nos. 204-205). Yet with the Emperor Seged, Johnson was verging on the discovery of a curiously heightened affinity between story and philosophic idiom. Perhaps the *Rambler* had been all along a series of oriental apologues without the plot and local colour?—the Rambler himself a kind of Abyssinian sage without the name and the overt ethnic colouration? It was a strange language, that language of the Rambler in his own persona. Who really talked that way? Not Dryden or Addison, or Lord Chesterfield. Not really Johnson himself, except perhaps in the moments of his conversation when he was being the consciously pompous self-parodist or when Mrs. Thrale and Burney had come into the library at Streathem to "make" him "speak" a *Rambler.*

The part of *Rasselas* which we remember best and carry

away with us for allusion and quotation—the portable part—is beyond question the aphoristic moralism, the lugubrious orotundity. "We do not read *Rasselas* for the story." "Human life is everywhere a state in which much is to be endured, and little to be enjoyed." Who says this? Imlac, Rasselas, Nekayah, the Stoic philosopher, the hermit, the Arab, the mad astronomer, the old man? Any one of these, at the right moment, might say it. Actually, of course, we remember it is Imlac, near the end of his narrative of his own life (chapter XI)—the same Imlac who later, seated in one of the "most spacious chambers" of the great Pyramid, discourses so eloquently, in a vein of inverse romantic vision: "It seems to have been erected only in compliance with that hunger of imagination which preys incessantly upon life, and must be always appeased by some employment . . . I consider this mighty structure as a monument of the insufficiency of human enjoyments" (chapter XXXII). The same Imlac, who when the prince looks on a fissure in the rocks as a "good omen" of escape from the valley, replies—almost like a wound-up automation, a speaking toy-philosopher: "If you are pleased with prognosticks of good, you will be terrified likewise with tokens of evil . . . Whatever facilitates our work is more than an omen, it is a cause of success . . . Many things difficult to design prove easy to performance".

"Marriage has many pains, but celibacy has no pleasures." Who says this? Any one of several characters might say it. Actually the speaker is the maiden princess Nekayah, in the course (chapter XXVI) of that lengthy and soon

quarrelsome conversation with her brother about such profound issues: public and private life, youth and age, celibacy or marriage. The same princess who a few pages later, in the accents of a proto-Screwtape, "reckons" for us "the various forms of connubial infelicity . . . the rude collisions of contrary desire . . . the obstinate contests of disagreeable virtues, where both are supported by consciousness of good intention . . ." (chapter XXVIII). The same princess whom we have already heard, seated in the summer-house by the bank of the Nile, utter her apostrophe to that mighty "father of waters" who rolls his "floods through eighty nations".

The courtly and ceremonious discourse which we have already noticed as a kind of local colour is only the most obvious instance of a lofty and reflective idiom which plausibly pervades nearly the whole of this oriental tale. (The notion of an oriental sage, philosopher, poet, emperor, prince, is an easy one for us to entertain. Who ever heard of an oriental buffoon or ninny?) The *Rambler* idiom, Johnson's own idiom, if we like, an expansion of homely human wisdom into the large perspective of Latinate philosophic diction, is projected across time and space, straight from London and Fleet Street, to cover appropriately, with a veil of the delicately exotic, scenes which we know, by a more than willing suspension of disbelief are enacted at places along the Nile from Amhara to Cairo.

The notion of *Rasselas* as a "comedy" (Johnson's "greatest comic work") has been urged by two recent writers. A third, Professor Hilles again, thinks that they "overstress" the "comic element". Probably they do overstress it. Professor Tracy sees a "comic" (perhaps, rather, a "satirical") reduction of man's fatuousness, shrewd laughter at the prince's chronic failure of common sense, demolition of the poet Imlac's "grandiloquent . . . rapture". Professor Whitley finds "pure comedy of ideas" in the episodes of the first period at Cairo, "comedy of emotion and behaviour", and "deflated oriental romance", in Pekuah's abduction, "dark comedy" in the later chapters about the mad astronomer and the catacombs. Probably we are on safer ground if we are content to say, with Professor Hilles, simply that the attitude prevailing in the story is not, as so often said, "pessimistic", not morose, not cynical, not even satirical; it is rather, gently "ironic" and "realistic". The "smile of the author is a sad smile". Yes—though one may need to insist that it *is* a smile. With Professor Hilles, we must differ from certain critics who have supposed that a "tragic sense of life . . . informs it". It appears to me next to impossible that anyone should be moved either to tears or to shudders at any part of *Rasselas.* "In a short time the second Bassa was deposed. The Sultan [at Constantinople], that had advanced him, was murdered by the Janisaries." But that was, if not a long time ago, yet very far in another country. (The chapter, XVIII, where the Stoic philosopher mourning the death of his daughter is put in a position of nearly laughable contrast to his declamation of the preceding day is perhaps the only part of the whole book that verges on the uncomfortable.) "In a year the wings were finished and, on a morning appointed, the maker appeared furnished for flight on a little promontory: he waved his pinions a while to gather air, then leaped from his stand, and in an instant dropped into the lake." There we have the characteristic motion of the story as action—the immediate and inevitable plunge, so inevitable and so confidently foreseen as to warrant not the smallest flourish or comment. " 'I . . . resolve to return into the world tomorrow'. . . He dug up a considerable treasure which he had hid among the rocks, and accompanied them to the city, on which, as he approached it, he gazed with rapture." (chapter XXI). At many moments the comic smile of the narrator is turned directly on one or another of his characters. " 'But surely, interposed the prince . . . Whenever I shall seek a wife, it shall be my first question, whether she be willing to be led by reason?' " (chapter XXIX). More often, however, or in general, the smile of this narrator envelops in a less direct way, in a more reticent parodic spirit, the whole of his own Abyssinian tale. He is very close to the endlessly meditative and controversial nature of each of his personae. What does the narrator think of his own "Tale" when he gives his chapters titles such as these: "The prince continues to grieve and muse", "A dissertation on the art of flying", "Imlac's history continued. A dissertation upon poetry", "Disquisition upon greatness", "Rasselas and Nekayah continue their conversation", "The dangerous prevalence of imagination", "The conclusion, in which nothing is concluded"?

In real life, Johnson sometimes indulged in a complacent self-consciousness and amusement at his own inflations. His moments of self-parody are celebrated. In his essays too, **Ramblers** and **Idlers,** a sort of shackled playfulness often parodies the solemn parade. A shadow of grimace accents some restrained contrast between gravity of diction and homeliness or meanness of sentiment. In **Rasselas,** the Johnsonian speaker has translated himself into a realm of sober fantasy where the grim smile, the sad smile, the wan smile, can be more or less constant. Probably it was some feeling like this about the tale that prompted Voltaire to say that its philosophy was *aimable.* Indeed there are profoundly reflective and even solemn moments—and they occur increasingly in the later chapters—at the Pyramids, in the conversation about the astronomer's madness, in the confrontation with the savagely embittered old man, and finally at the Catacombs, in the contemplation of death and immortality. But the last seems to me the only place where it may be impossible to find a smile. Here the initially dominant tone is metaphysical sobriety ("as thought is, such is the power that thinks; a power impassive and indiscerptible"), and this deepens at the end to theological solemnity ("The whole assembly stood a while silent and collected . . . 'To me', said the princess, 'the choice of life is become less important: I hope hereafter to think only on the choice of eternity' "). But this is an exceptional moment, not the ground tone of the book and not its conclusion. The conclusion, in which nothing is concluded, reverts to the basic plan.

It is not possible to smile sympathetically at nothingness without a degree of participation. Johnson's way of laughter is not the high-comedy way of the wit and his butts, but a quieter way of partly encumbered rehearsal and laboured formulation. Martin Price has deftly alluded to the "gently preposterous oriental setting" of Johnson's tale, "the self-mocking formality of its dialogue, the balance and antithesis of characters as well as dialogue, and the circularity of its total structure". All this is the *imagination* of Johnson's quasi-oriental and ceremonious notale—"the wine of absurdity", or absurdity mitigated only in its own rich self-contemplation. In our day, Albert Camus has explained absurdity in Kantian terms as "the

division between the mind that desires and the world that disappoints". Johnson's **Rasselas** has much in common with modern versions of the absurd—with a *Godot* or a *Watt.* One main difference, which may disguise the parallel for us, is that the modern versions of the descent take place at a level which is, to start with, subterranean, the very sub-cellar or zero level of modern man's three-century decline from the pinnacles of theology and metaphysics. Johnson's descendental exercise, with its saving theological clause in the Catacombs, takes place at a level still near the top of the metaphysical structure. It is of course all the richer for this. In the "endgame" played at the modern level, a nearly complete numbness and boredom is roused only as occasional stabs and jolts of obscenity reach a buried nerve. In the more spacious and better lighted areas available to Johnson, there was still eloquence—an eloquence profound and moving as it verges continually on a smiling absurdity. (pp. 117-30)

> *W. K. Wimsatt, "In Praise of Rasselas: Four Notes (Converging)," in* Imagined Worlds: Essays on Some English Novels and Novelists in Honour of John Butt, *edited by Maynard Mack and Ian Gregor, Methuen & Co., Ltd., 1968, pp. 111-36.*

Marvin Mudrick   (essay date 1970)

[*Mudrick is a controversial American essayist and literary critic. His most recent work, consisting chiefly of contributions to literary reviews, has been criticized by some commentators as lowbrow and unscholarly, while others have labeled it highly original and imaginative. According to one commentator, Webster Schott, "If Mudrick is tough and demanding he also succeeds in making the books he praises seem to require our reading." In the following excerpt, Mudrick contrasts the intentions of Johnson the writer and Johnson the man.*]

Johnson's reputation is deadly. . . . Of all the great literary figures, he is in his own work the least read from mere curiosity and the most effectively mutilated by his academic keepers, who smack their lips over the soundness of the bullying old eccentric of the moral essays, quarantine Boswell with labels like "libidinous puppy" (along alleys, on deserted bridges, in boudoirs, even burning penitently with the clap, the young Scotsman couldn't get enough of London whores and actresses), and never blink at the unbridled despondencies with which the Christian Doctor flattens any residual hopefulness in the utterly damnable human race:

> The depravity of mankind is so easily discoverable, that nothing but the desert or the cell can exclude it from notice. The knowledge of crimes intrudes uncalled and undesired. They whom their abstraction from common occurrences hinders from seeing iniquity, will quickly have their attention awakened by feeling it. Even he who ventures not into the world, may learn its corruption in his closet. For what are treatises of morality, but persuasives to the practice of duties, for which no arguments would be necessary, but that we are continually tempted to violate or neglect them? What are all the records of history, but narratives of successive villanies, of treasons and usurpations, massacres and wars?

Though a pale ray may now and then penetrate his megrims, it hardly alters the atmosphere of exanimate platitude:

> That familiarity produces neglect, has been long observed. The effect of all external objects, however great or splendid, ceases with their novelty: the courtier stands without emotion in the royal presence; the rustic tramples under his foot the beauties of the spring, with little attention to their colour or their fragrance; and the inhabitant of the coast darts his eye upon the immense diffusion of waters, without awe, wonder, or terror.

down, down to the lowest circle of bathos:

> That every day has its pains and sorrows is universally experienced, and almost universally confessed; but let us not attend only to mournful truths; if we look impartially about us we shall find that every day has likewise its pleasures and its joys.

If, really, we look impartially about us, nothing in "our present state" will serve. "Of riches," declares Johnson, "as of every thing else, the hope is more than the enjoyment" (one of the **Rambler**'s or **Idler**'s multitudinous generalizations on which "Speak for yourself" is the appropriate comment). Pleasure? there's nothing in it: "Such is . . . [its] emptiness . . . that we are always impatient of the present. Attainment is followed by neglect, and possession by disgust; and the malicious remark of the Greek epigrammatist on marriage may be applied to every other course of life, that its two days of happiness are the first and the last." Indeed he goes so far as to make a statement of such stunning ignorance that, even neglecting to remind Johnson of the fact of laughter, the libidinous puppy or one of those obliging actresses could have corrected it any night in the world:

> Pain is less subject than pleasure to caprices of expression. The torments of disease, and the grief for irremediable misfortunes, sometimes are such as no words can declare, and can only be signified by groans, or sobs, or inarticulate ejaculations. Man has from nature a mode of utterance peculiar to pain, but he has none peculiar to pleasure, because he never has pleasure but in such degrees as the ordinary use of language may equal or surpass.

Sometimes the fear of the world (as well as, in this instance, a recollection of Swift) contracts into a strong metaphor:

> It is well known, that, exposed to a microscope, the smoothest polish of the most solid bodies discovers cavities and prominences; and that the softest bloom of roseate virginity repels the eye with excrescences and discolorations. The perceptions as well as the senses may be improved to our own disquiet, and we may, by diligent cultivation of the powers of dislike, raise in time an artificial fastidiousness, which shall fill the imagination with phantoms of turpitude, shew us the naked skeleton of every delight, and present us only with the pains of pleasure, and the deformities of beauty.

And just once, unintentionally, the moralist's rhetoric of rejection knots itself up into an agonized indictment of a God whose only guarantee to mankind is posthumous:

> It is scarcely to be imagined, that Infinite Benevo-

> lence would create a being capable of enjoying so much more than is here to be enjoyed, and qualified by nature to prolong pain by remembrance and anticipate it by terror, if he was not designed for something nobler and better than a state, in which many of his faculties can serve only for his torment, in which he is to be importuned by desires that never can be satisfied, to feel many evils which he had no power to avoid, and to fear many which he shall never feel: there will surely come a time, when every capacity of happiness shall be filled, and none shall be wretched but by his own fault.

Boswell calls him "The Sage"; but impersonal judiciousness, sustained and moderate reflection, prudence and resource with their comfortable aphorisms (*à la* his remarkably different transatlantic contemporary, Benjamin Franklin), Christian or at least stoic submissiveness to the will of God and the nature of things—all the traits answerable to what the Enlightenment, of which Johnson was England's most illustrious representative, identified as wisdom—are in neither his character nor his writing. No renunciatory and expiatory metaphysic is large enough for him; he suffers pain and terror unrelieved by the consolations of philosophy; he is burdened, not as he thinks by the guilt and self-hatred whose pious names he borrows from the eighteenth-century remains of Christian dogma, but by the sense of unused capacity ("there will surely come a time, when every capacity of happiness shall be filled, and none shall be wretched but by his own fault"), the personal sense of waste and loss, the immoderateness of desire, the weight of his inapplicable talents and passions.

Johnson's preoccupation in the essays is not so much religious or moral as hydrostatic: his most personal imagery is less of sin and penance than of filling and killing time, of voids and the hope of repletion. "Such things . . . as other philosophers often attribute to various and contradictory causes," according to Mrs. Thrale, "appeared to him uniform enough; all was done to fill up the time . . . One man, for example, was profligate and wild, as we call it, followed the girls, or sat still at the gaming-table. 'Why, life must be filled up (says Johnson), and the man who is not capable of intellectual pleasures must content himself with such as his senses can afford.' " A favorite word of Johnson's is "vacuity": about riches (as elsewhere about every other human preoccupation), he remarks (in **The Idler** Number 73) that "we find them insufficient to fill up the vacuities of life." If Johnson were more religious or more moral, his essays would be considerably livelier. Nor is it his sesquipedalian propensities that damage them: the Johnsonian style is much less an unabridged-dictionary creature than used to be alleged: so preposterous a passage as this (from **The Rambler** Number 20)—" . . . when from the adscititious happiness all the deductions are made by fear and casualty, there will remain nothing equiponderant to the security of truth. . . ."—is hard to find. The prevailing defect of the style is its gross and very personal exaggeration of the eighteenth-century notion that style, at the height of the civilized elegance which the Augustans felicitated themselves on having achieved, is merely the more or less shapely vessel of thought. Since for Johnson the public moralist all serious thought is a reminder of entropy and the end of the world, he does everything he can to excogitate and adorn, the more mechanically and tautologically the better, a structure of statement that will disguise the anarchic desperation of the contents:

The general voice of mankind, civil and barbarous, confesses that the mind and body are at variance, and that neither can be made happy by its proper gratifications, but at the expence of the other; that a pampered body will darken the mind, and an enlightened mind will macerate the body. And none have failed to confer their esteem on those who prefer intellect to sense, who controul their lower by their higher faculties, and forget the wants and desires of animal life for rational disquisitions or pious contemplations.

The very idea of desire can't be risked; it is so perilous that Johnson surrounds it with tattered blankets of allegory and mythological metaphor:

Nothing is more fatal to happiness or virtue, than that confidence which flatters us with an opinion of our own strength, and by assuring us of the power of retreat precipitates us into hazard. Some may safely venture further than others into the regions of delight, lay themselves more open to the golden shafts of pleasure, and advance nearer to the residence of the Sirens; but he that is best armed with constancy and reason is yet vulnerable in one part or other, and to every man there is a point fixed, beyond which if he passes he will not easily return. It is certainly most wise, as it is most safe, to stop before he touches the utmost limit, since every step of advance will more and more entice him to go forward, till he shall at last enter the recesses of voluptuousness, and sloth and despondency close the passage behind him.

No epigram would have seemed more pernicious to Johnson than Blake's "The road of excess leads to the palace of wisdom." Johnson requires no advice to be excessive: he is all appetite, incapable of restraint except by absolute suppression. "Every thing about his character and manners," says Boswell, "was forcible and violent; there never was any moderation; many a day did he fast, many a year did he refrain from wine; but when he did eat, it was voraciously; when he did drink wine, it was copiously. . . ." Johnson is an unhappy ogre at the feast of life. His appetite appalls the other guests and soon enough himself; its inordinateness is the guarantee of its ultimate failure; excess as much as abstinence is a *memento mori:*

. . . as we advance forward into the crowds of life, innumerable delights sollicit our inclinations, and innumerable cares distract our attention; the time of youth is passed in noisy frolicks; manhood is led on from hope to hope, and from project to project; the dissoluteness of pleasure, the inebriation of success, the ardour of expectation, and the vehemence of competition, chain down the mind alike to the present scene, nor is it remembered how soon this mist of trifles must be scattered, and the bubbles that float upon the rivulet of life be lost for ever in the gulph of eternity. . . .

At the edge of eternity, within a month of his death, seventy-five years old, the victim of a paralytic stroke, suffering from asthma and dropsy, constipated, tormented by insomnia, barely able to walk, even then he cannot be moderate or simply yield: for recreation he drives out in a friend's coach ("I struggle hard for life," he writes to Dr. Burney. "I take physick, and take air; my friend's chariot is always ready. We have run this morning twenty-four miles, and could run forty-eight more. *But who can run the race with death?*"); "such was his intellectual ardour even

at this time," says Boswell, "that he said to one friend, 'Sir, I look upon every day to be lost, in which I do not make a new acquaintance'; and to another, when talking of his illness, 'I will be conquered; I will not capitulate' "; alone, he doses himself ferociously with a whole pharmacopoeia of emetics, cathartics, and narcotics, administers enemas to himself often several times daily, and in his "Sick Man's Journal" in Latin ("medical treatises should be in Latin") notes everything—dosages, food and drink, quantity of urine, quantity and quality of stool, amount of sleep, apparent changes in the state of his mind and body (together at least!).

"His figure was large and well formed," says Boswell, "and his countenance of the cast of an ancient statue; yet his appearance was rendered strange and somewhat uncouth, by convulsive cramps, by the scars of that distemper which it was once imagined the royal touch could cure, and by a slovenly mode of dress. He had the use only of one eye; yet so much does mind govern and even supply the deficiency of organs, that his visual perceptions, as far as they extended, were uncommonly quick and accurate. So morbid was his temperament, that he never knew the natural joy of a free and vigorous use of his limbs: when he walked, it was like the struggling gait of one in fetters; when he rode, he had no command or direction of his horse, but was carried as if in a balloon." Mrs. Thrale reports that he told her husband once "that he had never sought to please till past thirty years old, considering the matter as hopeless." "With all possible . . . delicacy" Boswell states that Johnson's "conduct, after he came to London, and had associated with Savage and others, was not so strictly virtuous, in one respect, as when he was a younger man. It was well known, that his amorous inclinations were uncommonly strong and impetuous." Boswell "never knew a man laugh more heartily." . . . (pp. 278-84)

He was immobilized and irrepressible. Boswell notes that Johnson "feared death, but he feared nothing else, not even what might occasion death. . . . One day, at Mr. Beauclerk's house in the country, when two large dogs were fighting, he went up to them, and beat them till they separated; and at another time, when told of the danger there was that a gun might burst if charged with many balls, he put in six or seven, and fired it off against a wall. Mr. Langton told me, that when they were swimming together near Oxford, he cautioned Dr. Johnson against a pool, which was reckoned particularly dangerous; upon which Johnson directly swam into it. He told me himself that one night he was attacked in the street by four men, to whom he would not yield, but kept them all at bay, till the watch came up, and carried both him and them to the roundhouse." Saying that Johnson "feared death, but . . . nothing else," Boswell momentarily forgets—what was well known among their circle of friends—that Johnson feared madness also: indeed there is evidence, in a letter by Johnson (in French!) to Mrs. Thrale and in some guarded remarks she confides to her diary, that her responsibility, when Johnson while residing in her home anticipated an onset, was to chain and manacle him in his locked room, enforce this "confinement and severity" (as she referred to it) with a whip, and keep the keys till he felt able to trust his faculties again. At every age he was a man of unaccommodatable passions: "How many Times," exclaims Mrs. Thrale in her diary, "has this great, this formidable Doctor Johnson kissed my hand, ay & my foot too upon his knees!'' When he wrote his reluctant farewell letter to her—he was seventy-four—he wrote like the broken-hearted lover he was as he thanked her for "that kindness which soothed twenty years of a life radically wretched."

If he had been Dickens or Dostoevsky, he would have written disorderly melodramatic triple-decker novels brimming with incidents from the common life that was as much his element as theirs. Instead he wrote poets' biographies as austere as lighthouses, eighteenth-century poems and occasionally superb eighteenth-century criticism, an epochal dictionary, a brilliantly annotated edition of Shakespeare (in which, without questioning Shakespeare's primacy, Johnson was the last and most astute English critic to suggest that the "licentiousness" of Shakespeare's diction didn't necessarily contribute to the unshackled expressiveness of the English language), moral essays and romances rather too categorical and funereal even for the taste of the time, and he spent his life in other people's drawing-rooms talking unstoppably into the night: " 'I lie down (said he) that my acquaintance may sleep; but I lie down to endure oppressive misery, and soon rise again to pass the night in anxiety and pain.' By this pathetic manner," comments Mrs. Thrale, "he used to shock me from quitting his company," which he made "exceedingly entertaining when he had once forced one, by his vehement lamentations and piercing reproofs, not to quit the room, but to sit quietly and make tea for him, as I often did in London till four o'clock in the morning."

The strangest fact of all about Johnson is that he is a character in other people's books. Our sense of his unprecedented magnitude depends on vivid and particular accounts by others, who—themselves figures bounded by their somewhat complacent century—could not have known how far his life was from being the exemplary eighteenth-century life they must have been convinced it would seem to an admiring posterity. If the vain and shrewd Mrs. Thrale hadn't pampered the famous old man and noted him down in the very pulsations of his nature—

> To recollect . . . and to repeat the sayings of Dr. Johnson, is almost all that can be done by the writers of his life; as his life, at least since my acquaintance with him, consisted in little else than talking, when he was not absolutely employed in some serious piece of work; and whatever work he did, seemed so much below his powers of performance, that he appeared the idlest of all human beings; ever musing till he was called out to converse, and conversing till the fatigue of his friends, or the promptitude of his own temper to take offence, consigned him back again to silent meditation.

—if (in a book immeasurably greater than the collected works of its subject) Boswell had not recorded him triumphantly talking away on every one of the world's questions in a thousand drawing-rooms, if all that remained of him was his writing, then we might make clever guesses at his personal virtues and shortcomings and even concede his idiosyncratic greatness but we would not begin to imagine how prodigious a phenomenon we had missed.

His marvelous powers of conversation are, in his formal writing, confined and often smothered by the self-mortifying compulsion to set down not personal casualty

but, as his contemporaries and his conscience saw it, universal truth. In the tiny fragment, written in his sixties, of a memoir of his childhood, he tantalizes us with intimations of what he might have written if he hadn't been the lifelong prisoner of himself. . . . "A story is a specimen of human manners," he said to Mrs. Thrale, "and derives its sole value from its truth." The glow of his memoir is in its relying solely on the truth, with which in this instance art or calculation seems to have nothing to do.

Truth is the first test of everything: "Johnson was known to be so rigidly attentive to it," says Boswell, "that even in his common conversation the slightest circumstance was mentioned with exact precision. The knowledge of his having such a principle and habit made his friends have a perfect reliance on the truth of every thing that he told, however it might have been doubted if told by many others. As an instance of this, I may mention an odd incident which he related as having happened to him one night in Fleet-street. 'A gentlewoman (said he) begged I would give her my arm to assist her in crossing the street, which I accordingly did; upon which she offered me a shilling, supposing me to be the watchman. I perceived that she was somewhat in liquor.' This, if told by most people, would have been thought an invention; when told by Johnson, it was believed by his friends as much as if they had seen what passed."

The important truth is the truth of human manners: to a friend commenting on the beauty of the landscape through which they were traveling, Johnson retorted that "a blade of grass is always a blade of grass, whether in one country or another: let us if we *do* talk, talk about something; men and women are my subjects of enquiry; let us see how these differ from those we have left behind." (pp. 284-88)

He was a great, good, kind, loving, companionable man. Once when Miss Helen Maria Williams, "an elegant and accomplished young lady," was in his company, "he asked her to sit down by him, which she did, and upon her inquiring how he was, he answered, 'I am very ill indeed, Madam. I am very ill even when you are near me; what should I be were you at a distance?' " Boswell

> . . . was surprised at his talking without reserve in the publick postcoach of the state of his affairs; "I have (said he,) about the world I think above a thousand pounds, which I intend shall afford Frank [his servant] an annuity of seventy pounds a year." Indeed his openness with people at a first interview was remarkable. He said once to Mr. Langton, "I think I am like Squire Richard in *The Journey to London,* 'I'm never strange in a strange place.' " He was truly *social.* He strongly censured what is much too common in England among persons of condition,—maintaining an absolute silence, when unknown to each other; as for instance, when occasionally brought together in a room before the master or mistress of the house has appeared. "Sir, that is being so uncivilised as not to understand the common rights of humanity."

He loved and needed his hosts of friends more continuously and more intensely than any of them could love and need him in return; he loved women often for themselves and always as the special consolation of men; he loved children and the young ("you have at least a chance for virtue till age has withered its very root"); he had himself been miserably poor for many years, and

. . . loved the poor [observes Mrs. Thrale] as I never yet saw any one else do, with an earnest desire to make them happy.—What signifies, says some one, giving halfpence to common beggars? they only lay it out in gin or tobacco. "And why should they be denied such sweeteners of their existence (says Johnson)? it is surely very savage to refuse them every possible avenue to pleasure, reckoned too coarse for our own acceptance. Life is a pill which none of us can bear to swallow without gilding; yet for the poor we delight in stripping it still barer, and are not ashamed to shew even visible displeasure, if ever the bitter taste is taken from their mouths." In consequence of these principles he nursed whole nests of people in his house, where the lame, the blind, the sick, and the sorrowful found a sure retreat from all the evils whence his little income could secure them . . .

The strongest essays by this Christian Tory, who thunderously supported rank and subordination, are devoted to attacking capital punishment, parental tyranny, vivisection, war and other conflicts about property, debtors' prisons; advocating the abolition of imprisonment for debt, he doesn't hesitate to hold the creditor more culpable (because impelled by meaner vices) than the debtor:

It is vain to continue an institution, which experience shews to be ineffectual. We have now imprisoned one generation of debtors after another, but we do not find that their numbers lessen. We have now learned, that rashness and imprudence will not be deterred from taking credit; let us try whether fraud and avarice may be more easily restrained from giving it.

Swift's *saeva indignatio* is more noticed, but Johnson's indignation has none of the misanthropy and self-congratulation of Swift's. Johnson's has always an unencumbered straightforwardness of motive, as when in the greatest book review ever written he assesses the silliness of the "philosopher" Soame Jenyns, who in his *Free Enquiry into the Nature and Origin of Evil* derived a system of benignant universal hierarchy from Pope's *Essay on Man* ("Whatever is, is right"). . . . (pp. 289-90)

The ogre who ate up Jenyns skin, bones, and all was not—though Jenyns must have thought he was—one of those superior beings who invent and savor human suffering. He was not even a mortal proud of his parts. His powers, though they repelled evil and affectation and illuminated the world for everyone who knew him, could not exorcise his fear of the vengeance of God:

I have now begun the sixtieth year of my life. How the last year has past I am unwilling to terrify myself with thinking. This day has been past in great perturbation. I was distracted at Church in an uncommon degree, and my distress has had very little intermission. . . .

Twelve years later, another birthday prayer commemorated "a life radically wretched":

I have forgotten or neglected my resolutions or purposes [which] I now humbly and timorously renew. Surely I shall not spend my whole life with my own total disapprobation. Perhaps God may grant me now to begin a wiser and a better life.

Almighty God, my Creator and Preserver, who hast permitted me to begin another year, look with

mercy upon my wretchedness and frailty. Rectify my thoughts, relieve my perplexities, strengthen my purposes, and reform my doings. Let encrease of years bring encrease of Faith, Hope, and Charity. . . .

It would never have occurred to him that he had in fact done enough, he could not help remembering how much had been promised and how much left undone in the terrifying range of his powers. (p. 292)

Marvin Mudrick, "The Ogre at the Feast of Life," in The Hudson Review, *Vol. XXIII, No. 2, Summer, 1970, pp. 278-92.*

W. Jackson Bate   (essay date 1970)

[*Bate is an American educator, critic, and literary historian. His works include* The Achievement of Samuel Johnson *(1955),* Coleridge *(1968), and* John Keats *(1963), for which he received the Pulitzer Prize in biography in 1964. In the following excerpt, he posits that much of Johnson's career is marked by a struggle with "satire and the deflection of it," creating a distinct literary type which Bate labels "satire manqué" or "satire foiled."*]

Considering the literary atmosphere in which Johnson grew up, it is surprising that he did not turn more than he did to satire—certainly the most brilliant mode of English writing from the 1680's to the 1740's and one that pervaded every form. Almost everyone was aware that in this one way, if in no other, modern English literature was excelling not only the English Elizabethan and seventeenth-century past (a matter very important to Augustan England) but probably the ancients as well, and possibly even neo-classic France. Satire in Greece, however inventively fertile for later literatures, had not been a major *genre*. Roman satire, though stronger than Greek, was no more so than English, and it was less varied. Even French satire could be forgivably regarded by the literary patriot as thinner—not in range of objects, perhaps, but in intensity and variety of emotion; nor was there the same earthiness of humor, the same gift for burlesque and farce, that can serve as supplements and extensions to wit.

To a gifted writer born in 1709, the attractions of satire were not only strong but, one would think, irresistible, if he possessed even a fraction of the psychological endowment of a Pope or Swift for writing it; and Johnson possessed far more than a fraction. It is hard, in fact, to think of a single qualification for satire that he did not have, and generally to a strong degree. Take first the range and readiness of his humor—itself an indication of his quickness to sense incongruity, disparity, pretense, as well as the psychological need to put things at arm's length. "No man loved laughing better," said Mrs. Thrale, "and his vein of humour was rich, and apparently inexhaustible." She quotes Arthur Murphy's remark that Johnson was "incomparable at buffoonery," adding that with "less inflexible features" he "would have made an admirable mimic." "In the talent of humour," said Sir John Hawkins, "there hardly ever was Johnson's equal, except perhaps among the old comedians." And Hawkins goes on to mention how much this would disconcert grave people like the scholar William Warburton. In such tributes we feel the union of surprise and reassurance common in reactions to other aspects of Johnson. The surprise, and with it the human reassurance, is that a man who could so easily subsume whatever the Warburtons of the world are able to contribute, if he could be brought to devote to it a fraction of his mind, and who added so much else, should at the same time be so free of the defensive solemnities and rigidities of the specialized. This was the Johnson who, despite his age, could suddenly climb a tree, roll down a hill, or, on the northern tour, put on a splendid imitation of the newly discovered animal in Australia, the kangaroo.

But Mrs. Thrale was also thinking of Johnson's readiness and aggressive militance of reply: "Promptitude of thought, indeed, and quickness of expression, were among the peculiar felicities of Johnson: his notions rose up like the dragon's teeth sowed by Cadmus already clothed, and in bright armour too, fit for immediate battle." The readiness and the aggressive strength at least match, possibly exceed what we find in the life of any satirist of whom we know personally anything at all. The same may be said of his personal temptations to make full expressive use of them—the irritabilities and impatience of temperament, the eagerness to confute, the large floating dissatisfactions, the physical suffering; all of which he strove so hard to control, though the struggle to do so naturally produced its own further tensions. Our point in mentioning them is only to remind ourselves that he was by no means lacking in *temperamental* incentives. Mrs. Thrale, taking 20 as a perfect score, gave Johnson 16 for humor. But for "good humour," that is, good nature, a quality in which Boswell excelled—she gave him 0. (She gave Boswell 19 for "good humour" but 3 for humor itself.) Struggling so hard to attain "good humour," maintaining at all times that it could be acquired, it was possible for Johnson to get very hot-tempered about it.

Then there is the power of *reductionism*—of quickly, through an exasperated brush of the fingers, sifting a thing down to the lowest common denominator. Reductionism is of course the essence of satire, and it is as habitual in Johnson as it is in the greatest of satirists, Jonathan Swift. If we go through the records of the conversations, at least a quarter of the memorable remarks—the replies or observations that have passed into legend—are severely, even drastically, reductive. Take one of a score that would occur at once to a Johnsonian. I select it precisely because it is unfair both to the subject and to Johnson. For the point is the way in which this habit of expression is so ready that it can arise immediately, as a stock response, before he has even had a chance to consider a matter. Goldsmith teases him for going so little to the theater any more. (Johnson had loved the theater when he was younger, but he was now neither hearing nor seeing very well.) The reply is: "Why Sir, our tastes greatly alter. The lad does not care for the child's rattle, and the old man does not care for the young man's whore." In this quick, impatient jostle, not just one thing is being reduced but the whole lot. The lad with his whore and the child with his rattle are not much luckier than the playgoer. This sort of thing happens again and again throughout the recorded conversations, though frequently supplemented (as is the case with the remark quoted above) with second thoughts.

This same temptation to reductionism is constantly stirring throughout the three series of the moral essays. Thus, in speaking of the specialization and isolation of scholars

and scientists: "He who is growing great and happy by *electrifying a bottle,* wonders how the world can be engaged by trifling prattle about war and peace." Here we have the satirical habit. Or the whole frantic zeal and scramble of writing, scholarship, criticism, and reviewing is suddenly brought to heel in that magnificent phrase, "the epidemical conspiracy for the destruction of paper." The reduction is often to the physical, and to the physical of the most elementary sort—even to mere space to be filled. Open the essays at random: Fame, the "desire of *filling* the minds of others": "he who *places* happiness in the *frequent repetition* of his name . . .": "filling the vacuities of his mind with the news of the day"; or Zephyretta, who, after marriage, had "in four and twenty hours spent her stock of repartee." Or there is the quasi-mechanical, as in the account of poor Tim Ranger (*Idler* 64), who after learning that laughter is necessary for success in society, struggled hard to acquire the art, suffering often from bad timing or deficiency in loudness and length, until "I attained at last such flexibility of muscles, that I was always a welcome auditor." Then there are the almost brutally concrete verbs. Speaking of the effect of custom and familiarity on feeling, and the tendency of men to grow less tender with age because of this (*Rambler* 78): He who when young melted at the loss of every friend begins, in age, to look with less concern "upon the grave into which his last friend was *thrown,* and into which himself is ready to *fall.* . . ." But more often (as in his style generally) we have the immediate clutch into condensed but restless and suggestive abstraction in which Johnson is unrivalled, as in his dismissal of the belief that one can write better at one season of the year than another—"imagination operating upon luxury." (The formula could prove infectious to his friends: e.g., Mrs. Thrale's own remark on another occasion, "arrogance acting upon stupidity.") Often the effect is close to a slap: the fortune-hunter's opportunity to "walk the Exchange with a face of importance"; "a frown of importance"; the travelers in *Adventurer* 84, thrown together in the stage-coach, whose first effort, in order to inspire each other with the proper veneration, was "employed in collecting importance into our faces"; or Lady Bustle "who has no crime but luxury, nor any virtue but chastity." Or think of that "unwillingness to be pleased" which always so infuriated him with its stock assumption that superiority is more effectively demonstrated by disapproval than by praise: "elegance refined into impatience"; the "cultivation of the powers of dislike"; "the stare of petulant incredulity"; "the stratagems of well-bred malignity."

These fidgety, tart phrases that bristle through the moral essays (or the conversations) are often joined by something darker that shows Johnson's kinship with Hobbes, Swift, and Mandeville: a deeply pessimistic conviction of the frightening and unsleeping strength of human egotism and vanity. Sometimes it is fairly innocent. There is that blustery group in the *Rambler* rushing out to the countryside, with the rest of the fashionable world, who, in missing the coach, lose the pleasure of "alarming villages with the tumult of our passage, and disguising our insignificancy with the dignity of hurry." There is the moral philosopher discoursing to his audience, and "swelling with the applause which he has gained by proving that applause is no value." But this sense of the power of egotism can lead to sharper attacks. One of many is *Rambler* 188, where the modest, good-natured man is pictured as loved only because he cannot be envied—"His only power of giving pleasure is not to interrupt it," and by keeping quiet and concealing his imbecility leads his companions to think that his silence comes "not from inability to speak but from eagerness to hear"—to hear *them*. (Here we recall Johnson's own struggle to attain "good humour," and how he once despondently admitted to Henry Thrale that he had never even "sought to please till past thirty years old, considering the matter as hopeless.") But again what we are mentioning is found mainly in phrases or individual sentences: critics, whose "acrimony is excited merely by the pain of seeing others pleased, and of hearing applauses which another enjoys"; "the treachery of the human heart" that can lead the critic to gratify his "own pride or malignity *under the appearance* of contending for elegance of propriety"; "Many need no other provocation to enmity than that they find themselves excelled"; "We are inclined to believe those we do not know, because they have never deceived us"; or most of *Rambler* 183 on envy. Mrs. Chapone, after talking with Johnson, "wondered to hear a man, who by his actions shews so much benevolence, maintain that the human heart is naturally malevolent, and that all the benevolence we see in the few who are good is acquired by reason and religion." In the *Tour to the Hebrides,* when Lady McLeod asked whether man's feelings were not by themselves directed to the good, she was shaken by Johnson's reply, "No Madam, no more than a wolf." In "a low voice" she replied: "This is worse than Swift."

Lastly there are those prolonged outbursts of laughter that puzzled Boswell, Garrick, Fanny Burney, and most others—but did not, I think, so much puzzle Mrs. Thrale—where Johnson's intellect pierces through the pretenses and self-delusions that fill up so much of life, and he sees their grotesque futility against the large backdrop of doom that everyone shares. Examples would be the scene in Fanny Burney's *Diary* where they are trying or pretending to persuade her to turn her talents now to the drama ("Streatham—a Farce"); or the episode in Boswell of Langton's will, in which Johnson's ridicule, as it uncoils, hurls out one stinging detail after another, ending in the final snort "I'd have his will turned into verse, like a ballad."

Yet Johnson was not a satirist, and in fact, said Mrs. Thrale, had "an aversion to general satire." We could put it more strongly and say that he had a hatred and fear of satire, which is what led him to be so antagonistic to Swift. To Johnson, Swift was a frightening example of what not to be, and all the more because of Johnson's own temptations. Against this background, Johnson's life-long struggle for good-humor (a "willingness to be pleased") and his efforts to check or suppress anger suddenly light up. They show that he did not dare to release the satiric impulse partly because it was so strong. But something else is involved—the charity and justice he is always bringing to "helpless man." He could not simply watch. He had to participate; and his own willing participation sets a bar to satire.

What happens, therefore, is that ridicule, anger, satiric protest, are always in the process of turning into something else. It is the *process* that is important. We have here what amounts to another *genre* or form of writing, the essence of which is not satire at all but which begins with

satiric elements and an alert satiric intelligence (indeed an imagination that often seems most fertile and concrete when stung by exasperation); and then the writer—still fully aware of the satiric potentialities, still taking them all into account—suddenly starts to walk backward and move toward something else. As a result much of the writing of the middle period of Johnson's career—that is from the late 1740's down through the *Rambler* (1750-52) and the *Adventurer* (1753-54) to the *Idler* (1758-60) and *Rasselas* (1759)—falls into a distinctive literary type, eminently characteristic of Johnson, that we might call "satire *manqué*" or "satire foiled." Take as a quick example, obvious because it is narrative and also relatively self-contained, Chapter 18 of *Rasselas*—the encounter with the Stoic philosopher. He talks with energy and brilliance of the government of the passions. He gives all the clichés. He mentions examples of heroes who endured, and tells how to use reason in expecting calamities. Rasselas is naturally enthusiastic. The satirical situation that is being built up is twofold. There is the philosopher himself, with his pretensions, and there is Rasselas, who is so naive as to take the philosopher at his word. The reader has every reason to expect that at least one of them, probably both, will be exposed. Then Rasselas wants to visit the man at home—wants really to get to know him. This disconcerts the philosopher, who "hesitates until Rasselas puts a purse of gold in his hand." At this point the frame for satire becomes more pronounced. The philosopher, for all his talk, is glad to have the gold; and at the same time we have Rasselas still believing in the philosopher's pretensions even after having, in effect, bribed him. This man, he says to Imlac, will henceforth be his "guide." But then, as the moment arrives for satiric exposure, the situation is changed. There is exposure indeed, but only of naked and "helpless man." When Rasselas goes expectantly to visit the sage, what has happened is that a real blow has fallen on him: the philosopher's only child is dead. Plunged in grief, the Stoic violates his own precepts, but does not for that reason become an object of laughter or censure. When Rasselas starts to quote back to him the earlier remarks about expecting death and calamity, the philosopher rightly replies: "You speak like one who has never felt" the loss of those dearest to us: "What comfort . . . can truth and reason afford me? of what effect are they now, but to tell me, that my daughter will not be restored?" Only superficially or theoretically is the incident an undercutting of the philosopher. He has a real distress. In so far as there is satire left at the end, and there is not much, it turns on satirists themselves, or at least on people who like Rasselas are so naive as to expect human nature to live up always to every principle we try to assert. And does it really satirize Rasselas? "Without hope there can be no endeavour." For a youth of Rasselas' age not to have expected more would have been a frightful indictment of him. For anyone of whatever age not to have assumed that a man's precepts could be evaluated apart from his practice—his own life—would also indicate some limitation or rigidity of mind.

Among the portraits in the periodical essays, one example may be cited: *Rambler* 73, a letter supposedly written by that stock figure in satire, the legacy hunter—an account quickly etched with a savage directness we might expect from Swift or Mandeville. As we read of this family sitting about and waiting for the death of three elderly, wealthy aunts, we also recall Johnson's affinity with Juvenal, the "angry" satirist. The story is both grotesque and ugly. But the anger and exasperation, before the short sketch is finished, are suffused by a sadness and a final charity that completely transform them. The aging nephew, who has waited so long and has kept consoling himself that "all are mortal," finds that he himself is altogether "mortal"—that he has, as his own life has been passing, become the helpless victim of time and habit. Having for so long been "corrupted with an inveterate disease of wishing," he is now "accustomed to give the future full power" over his mind—to be "unable to think on anything but wants" and, despite his years, to "start away from the scene before me to some expected enjoyment."

But the portraits are not the main example. Working there on so small a scale—often no more than a page or two—Johnson tends to put the character sharply and reductively, and only afterwards, usually in another essay, seeking to palliate or explain. It is in the directly expository moral essays, which are the finest part of the three periodical series, that we especially find this drama of thought and expression moving from the reductive to explanation and at times something close to apology. For almost every impatiently reductive phrase we cited earlier there is more than supplement. That remark "He who is growing great and happy by electrifying a bottle" comes from a man whose interest in science is equalled by few humanists of the past three centuries. The hunger and scramble for "reputation"—socially, intellectually, or in any other way—are repeatedly burlesqued, sometimes in the concrete example of a portrait but more often in a few sentences: the young who think that everyone who approaches them must be either an "admirer or a spy," when the cruel truth is that no one is even thinking of them; the lecturer (**Rambler** 159) who agonizes with the fear that renown or infamy is suspended on every syllable when, as a matter of fact, whatever he says will be only too quickly forgotten; the author in *Rambler* 146—one of the finest of the essays—who on the day of publication, with beating heart, walks out to the coffee-houses, like a monarch in disguise, expecting to overhear remarks about his book, prepared to bear with stoicism or good humor any censure, and then finding that no one is even aware of the book. And yet the excuse, or at least explanation, is quickly at hand: the need of everyone to conceal his own unimportance from himself, and the doomed wrestle of that need with the fact that the bulk of mankind—occupied, as Johnson reminds us, in shortening their way to some new possession or trying to ward off some expected calamity—have very little time to spare for the "reputation" of others, past or present; that names that had hoped to range over entire kingdoms shrink at last to items in a library catalogue, consulted or noticed by a few solitary students. So even with the evils that sprout from or through envy, including gossip and slander—the almost instinctive readiness of the human animal to try to pull others down, most strident in its *Schadenfreude* (and therefore most evil) when it can release itself through the guise of maintaining virtue or "standards." In minds not constantly "corrected," by reason or religious belief, or preferably by both, this becomes the source of most of the daily anxiety and misery of human life and also a direct expression of the "treachery of the human heart." And yet (as Johnson concludes **Rambler** 76): "It is generally not so much the desire of men sunk into depravity to deceive the world as themselves. . . . " We have, in effect, throughout the periodical essays, a dialogue between two parts of a divided self. . . . (pp. 145-53)

For what we have suggested by this phrase "satire *manqué*" **"The Vanity of Human Wishes,"** written back in 1748, is the prototype as it is for much else in the prose-writing that follows. Think of the astonishingly savage things one finds in that poem: the whole huge crowd of humanity (condemned to live so briefly and die so quickly) still occupied in making traps and snares for each other; the scramble for riches, and for power, of these short-lived beings, whom he pictures as groping over a misty, snare-laden heath next to a cliff; the "fawning" niece, "hot for a legacy" (these are strong words); the "growing statesman," fighting for power, undercutting others, besieged, as he rises, with "suppliants," while his predecessor is now downgraded, and

> the *sinking* statesman's door
> Pours in the morning worshipper no more.
> For *growing* names the weekly scribbler lies,
> For *growing* wealth, the dedicator flies.

And in one house after another the portrait of the sinking statesman is taken down from the wall, torn from its frame, and either hung in the kitchen or else sold in auctions, while "To better features yields the frame of gold."

And so things go on. But then something starts to happen to all these people, caught up in the huge, greedy scramble Johnson describes. They all begin to stumble and weaken. Disease, misfortune, old age begin to club or push them imperceptibly into weariness, defeat, staleness, illness and finally death. In short, Johnson starts to sympathize and to share. And this strange, powerful poem, this apparent satire which, as Sir Walter Scott said, could draw tears from people who would scorn sentimental poetry, softens its mockery by dissolving it within a wider understanding. We think of that remark Johnson could sometimes be overheard muttering to himself: "And then he died, poor man." The poem begins to turn, in other words, into a form of tragedy, though the tragedy is modified by the strong religious hope at the end. Haunting the poem, and even more the prose-writing of the next decade, is the movement of emotion and thought in William Law's *Serious Call*—that book Johnson had picked up as a college student, expecting to laugh at it, and then found an "overmatch" for him. One by one, William Law, following the pattern of *Ecclesiastes*, had touched on the ambitions and hungers of the human heart and imagination, showing how each new possession, each new step of achievement, quickly ceases to fill the heart, which can ultimately find stability and purpose only through religion. Of special interest both critically and psychologically, are the ways in which the creative use of a *genre* often leads (in fact almost always *can* lead) to at least its temporary extinction. If the essence of a living form is that it is being developed from one point to another, it is safe to assume that, whatever the direction, it will not remain at a middle point. This is one of the obvious truths that we are always forgetting in our formalistic haste to classify, define, or (to use Johnson's term) "circumscribe" a mode or expression.

Throughout the 1750's, when Johnson is in his forties, the periodical essays qualify—we might say that they also encapsulate—still further the satiric restiveness and exasperation on which we have touched; and the need to write essays so frequently for a deadline not only gave opportunities but helped to incite the reconsiderations to which Johnson was always inclined. This is one major difference between the **Idler** (1758-60) and the two earlier series. With **Rasselas** (1759) we have the culmination of what we have been noticing and also—as far as the major writing is concerned (as contrasted with the conversation)—its substantial though not its complete end. Forced to write the book on short notice, Johnson almost instinctively adopts a conventional satiric framework that would have surprised no one. The situation at the start would be completely familiar—an intelligent but inexperienced man about to view society and the modes of human life. Here, it would have seemed, was another satiric work in the vein of Gulliver or Montesquieu's *Persian Letters,* where the "naive stranger" confronts and questions the social order from the standpoint of uncorrupted common sense or reason. There is perhaps no clearer illustration of Johnson's deflection of satire than the simple fact that **Rasselas** does not take this familiar and expected course, the course on which it even seems at first to be heading. Instead, as the story progresses, it is rather as though Swift's Brobdingnagian King, or Goldsmith's visiting Chinaman, in *The Citizen of the World,* were forced to recognize that their rational expectations were not so much naive as callow.

In relation to literary precedent or tradition, then, **Rasselas** embodies the fading of satire into a more profound analysis of human experience, and a similar movement recurs in particular episodes, notably in that of the Stoic philosopher discussed above. If the method and intention of satire *per se* is correction by ridicule, we have virtually none in **Rasselas.** In this sense especially, **Rasselas** marks a further stage in Johnson's wrestle with satire and deflection of it, already apparent in **"The Vanity of Human Wishes"** a decade before.

But if satire could be described (as it hardly can) in another way—not as correction *by* or *through* ridicule, but as the *presentation of the ridiculous for the sake* of correcting it, **Rasselas** provides numerous examples. The "correction" occurs through paced and sympathetic analysis. In this sense, what we have been calling "satire *manqué*" could also be described as a carrying further of satire into meditative reflection. But an anomaly must be presented before it can be accounted for, and the presentation itself can often verge on comedy.

The mad astronomer, to take one example, becomes a completely sympathetic figure almost at once. Yet even in his case there are touches, as Johnson introduces him, that stir remembrances of the way that Swift would have treated him. For the astronomer could have been easily included in Swift's gallery of madness in the essay on the "Mechanical Operation of the Spirit." He is another of those unfortunate persons who, having given their brains an "unlucky-shake," as Swift puts it, suffer large delusions of self-importance. The astronomer's mania that he personally regulates the weather and the seasons seems hardly less grotesque than anything Swift invented: "What must have been the misery of half the globe, if I had limited the clouds to particular regions, or confined the sun to either side of the equator!" Among the first things we learn of the astronomer, as Imlac describes him, is that, having devoted "forty years in unwearied attention to the motions and appearances of the celestial bodies," he "admits a few

friends once a month, to hear his deductions and enjoy his discoveries." Whether we discern conscientious zeal or merely vanity, the image—"admits a few friends once a month"—is already satiric, and especially for a writer who is so quick to attack seclusion or withdrawal as a means either for virtue or for knowledge. But our point now is that Johnson immediately diverges into a more sympathetic treatment and ends in extended reflective analysis. The purpose of the episode, it turns out, is to explain how such delusions can fasten on the mind and how they can be cured. Ultimately Johnson has as much real interest in satire as William James.

Of course, the anomaly most exploited throughout is Rasselas himself. His function has already been indicated in the episode of the Stoic philosopher but in general it may be said that he unites two roles, the "naive stranger" and the "enthusiast." In both roles he can at times appear slightly ridiculous, and on such occasions he exists to be corrected. He is an enthusiast for learning ("The prince began to love learning, and one day declared to Imlac, that he intended to devote himself to science, and pass the rest of his days in literary solitude"), for happiness and goodness (he thinks they go together: "if I had the choice of life, I should be able to fill every day with pleasure . . . I would relieve every distress, and should enjoy the benedictions of gratitude"), and for justice ("Surely," said the prince, "my father must be negligent of his charge, if any man in his dominions dares take that which belongs to another"). And he asks the reasonable questions of the "naive stranger" in a similar tone: "Is there such depravity in man, as that he should injure another without benefits to himself?" The same vulnerable innocence appears more strongly in Nekayah's enthusiastic approach to the old man: "an evening walk must give to a man of learning like you, pleasure which ignorance and youth can hardly conceive. . . . Everything must supply you with contemplation and renew the consciousness of your own dignity."

A satirist would simply let the questions stand ("Is there such depravity in man, as that . . . "), but in Johnson there is always the explanatory reply, implicitly exposing the question as insufficiently reflecting while also phrasing it in such a way that its valuable (indeed necessary) innocence is strengthened even though it cannot remain sheltered. Yes, says Imlac, there is such depravity; and, without in the least justifying it, he goes on to explain why. Moreover, the emperor cannot eradicate injustice from his dominions, and "the time will come when you will acquit your father. . . . Subordination supposes power on one part, and subjection on the other; and if power be in the hands of men, it will sometimes be abused." Rasselas himself later remarks that "He that has much to do will do something wrong." So much has he learned in the meantime.

Examples of naiveté corrected could be further accumulated; they are indeed the basic gesture or posture of the plot. Perhaps the most curious is the episode before the visit to the Pyramids, where even humanistic moralism is made to sound naive in the mouth of Rasselas. Like a good Johnsonian, Rasselas is less than eager to visit the Pyramids, and he expresses himself with something of the burly reductionism with which Johnson so often silenced opponents in conversation: "My curiosity," says Rasselas, "does not very strongly lead me to survey piles of stone, or mounds of earth; my business is with man." Once again Imlac replies in patient analysis, in the finest and the most penetrating sentences of the book ("that hunger of imagination which preys incessantly upon life . . . "), and once again Rasselas is convinced. The episode stands as a further reminder that Johnson was just as strongly identified with the naive expectations of Rasselas as the mournful wisdom of Imlac. The process of correction, throughout the book, was self-correction.

Johnson's later work, from the **"Preface to Shakespeare"** down to the *Lives,* is as great as it is because it is the product of a mind—indeed the product of a *life*—that has actively subsumed some of the most powerful temptations to satire of any major intelligence in literary history, while at the same time it has moved beyond them. From here on, after the crucial middle period of his career, the thought (moral, critical, or both) and the style itself involve a dialectic, indeed a drama, in which the promptitude of a reductive and powerful exasperation (with a still more matured sharpness of phrase acquired from years of habit) is almost immediately found at wrestle with charity and generality of reflection, held in suspension, supplemented, and then placed beneath a larger proscenium. Never, in the history of literature, has a spokesman for the humanities, and for the ideals of the humanities, been more directly and personally involved in all that the humanities must work in and through (scientific, psychological, imaginative, moral), if they are to be as relevant to human life in general as they can and should be; and this also includes the struggle of the human heart, in such time as we have, with its own impatience before its own ideals—its frustrations, its rivalries, its angers, its occasional despairs. Never, from here on in his major writing, have we been able to feel with another writer that we are so close to having a friend in court: one who would more than take for granted all that we try to protest, whether in moments of anger, indignation, hope, or religious aspiration. To no one since the Renaissance can we so aptly apply that old Greek epigram about Plato: that, in whatever direction we go, we find him returning on his way back. (pp. 154-60)

> *W. Jackson Bate, "Johnson and Satire Man-qué," in* Eighteenth-Century Studies in Honor of Donald F. Hyde, *edited by W. H. Bond, The Grolier Club, 1970, pp. 145-60.*

Leopold Damrosch, Jr.   (essay date 1972)

[*Damrosch is a Filipino-born American educator whose studies concentrate upon Johnson and eighteenth-century literature. In the following excerpt, he investigates the relationship between the satiric elements and the overall tragic quality of "The Vanity of Human Wishes."*]

Among Johnson's noncritical works the two which have continued to enjoy the greatest esteem are **"The Vanity of Human Wishes"** and *Rasselas.* The first is a formal "imitation" of a classical satire and the second is rich in gently satirical effects, but both are often described as having an affinity with tragedy. In my view *Rasselas,* despite its inconclusive conclusion and its exposure of the perpetual frustration of human desires, succeeds in resolving tragic, comic, and satiric elements into a perspective of harmony

and detachment. And although to many readers it may seem darker than this, its tragic elements are finally too tenuous and ambiguous to repay extended treatment here.

The case is quite different with **"The Vanity of Human Wishes,"** in which Johnson achieves what Ian Jack (adapting a phrase of Dryden's) has called "tragical satire." The poem has been the subject of so many excellent critical discussions that a comprehensive analysis here would be neither necessary nor useful. My purpose is a more limited one: to investigate what is meant by the tragic quality which critics have consistently found in it, and to try to see what relation this quality may have to the satiric elements which it also contains.

"The Vanity of Human Wishes" is offered as an imitation of the tenth satire of Juvenal, in the specialized sense of "imitation" as it is defined in the *Dictionary:* "A method of translating looser than paraphrase, in which modern examples and illustrations are used for ancient, or domestick for foreign." The poet, then, will show his skill in adapting suitable modern instances to the argument of his model. Johnson does not imply any significant alteration of tone and implication: that would detract from the success of the imitation, "which pleases when the thoughts are unexpectedly applicable and the parallels lucky" (**"Life of Pope"**). The greatest difficulty of the imitator will be in preserving fidelity to the original:

> The man of learning may be sometimes surprised and delighted by an unexpected parallel; but the comparison requires knowledge of the original, which will likewise often detect strained applications. Between Roman images and English manners there will be an irreconcileable dissimilitude, and the work will be generally uncouth and party-coloured; neither original nor translated, neither ancient nor modern.

Juvenal's tenth satire had already been translated by Dryden, whose version was reasonably faithful to the literal sense of the original but seemed open to criticism for its prevailing tone. This poem, in particular, was considered sufficiently solemn to serve as a magazine of materials for preachers. Thus Johnson's opinion of Dryden's version, and his decision to enter into competition with it, were based on well-accepted assumptions.

> The general character of this translation will be given when it is said to preserve the wit, but to want the dignity of the original. The peculiarity of Juvenal is a mixture of gaiety and stateliness, of pointed sentences, and declamatory grandeur. . . . It is therefore perhaps possible to give a better representation of that great satirist, even in those parts which Dryden himself has translated, some passages excepted, which will never be excelled.
>
> (**"Life of Dryden"**)

Let us pause, then, to see what we can surmise about Johnson's conception of his task. He had to furnish modern instances in place of Roman ones, while preserving a fairly strict fidelity to their effect in the original; and he had to capture the tone of his model, which comprised two quite different aspects, wit and grandeur. To Juvenal he applies the term "that great satirist," and we are certainly not led to suppose that the poem, though declamatory and weighty, is anything other than a satire. He intended, we may suppose, to "imitate" that quality in Juvenal which has been called "a vehement and burning passion, like the 'saeva indignatio' of Swift."

Yet the difference between his poem and Juvenal's is so striking, particularly in this matter of tone, that it has led a series of modern critics to deny its satiric intention. The Roman poet mercilessly exposes the result of intemperate desire and belittles his subjects with cruel caricature. Johnson, on the contrary, shows a deep sympathy for the common fate of man, and quite early in the poem suggests a radical divergence from Juvenal's attitude. Democritus, according to the original, "laughs at all the Vulgar Cares and Fears; / At their vain Triumphs, and their vainer Tears" (Dryden's version). In the same passage in Johnson the emphasis is wholly different: "All aid the farce, and all thy mirth maintain, / Whose joys are causeless, or whose griefs are vain". There would seem to be an implied exception of genuine suffering, which is not "vain" and is therefore not included in the "farce." And later in the poem there are two passages of more or less autobiographical content, the descriptions of the scholar and of innocent old age, that illustrate the point.

The neoclassical writers who called Juvenal "tragical" were principally alluding to the technical matter of his elevated style, or in Dennis's words "the violent Emotions and vehement Style of Tragedy." But a number of modern critics have found tragedy, in its metaphysical sense, in **"The Vanity of Human Wishes,"** in consonance with Walter Scott's remark that its "deep and pathetic morality . . . has often extracted tears from those whose eyes wander dry over pages professedly sentimental." From various excellent discussions of this kind, that of Mary Lascelles may be chosen as exemplary. Her conclusion is that Juvenal employs a satiric irony to expose the distance between our pretensions and our powers, while Johnson regards the human condition with a deeper kind of tragic irony. Thus, "Johnson's response to the man who plays high and loses all is the Shakespearean—that is, the tragic—response"; and again, "The awe and pity with which Johnson contemplates the spectacle of human unfulfilment makes of **"The Vanity of Human Wishes"** a great tragic poem."

Miss Lascelles' position suggests the approach of what we may call the tragic school of interpreters, which has been to emphasize the portraits, especially those of Wolsey and Charles XII. In Juvenal the fall of Sejanus, for example, is full of circumstantial detail, which is intended to focus the reader's attention on the fickleness and hypocrisy of the people who first supported and then reviled him (as in Ben Jonson's *Sejanus*). Johnson presents his Wolsey with far greater dignity, and with only the briefest allusion to the hostility of the former sycophants (four lines, to Juvenal's twenty-five). The passage ends in a generalized allusion to Shakespeare's *Henry VIII*, with Wolsey seeking "the refuge of monastic rest" and reproaching the broken faith of kings. It is very much like the outline of a tragedy.

This kind of interpretation compels us to recognize that parts of the poem, at least, are either not satiric at all, or satiric in a very peculiar way. The point is best illustrated in the often-noticed disparity between Juvenal's Hannibal and Johnson's Charles XII of Sweden. Johnson was well aware of the antiheroic convention in Augustan satire, as for example in Prior's ballad on the taking of Namur or Swift's satirical elegy on Marlborough; in a way he draws

upon it in the terrible lines, "From Marlb'rough's eyes the streams of dotage flow, / And Swift expires a driv'ler and a show", with the deep irony of compelling Swift and the man he hated to share the closed unity of a couplet, just as they have had to share the fate of man. But he is often interested in effects of a very different kind. Dryden renders Juvenal's account of Hannibal fairly literally in lines like these:

> A Sign-Post Dawber wou'd disdain to paint
> The one Ey'd Heroe on his Elephant. . . .
> Go, climb the rugged *Alps,* Ambitious Fool,
> To please the Boys, and be a Theme at School.

The sarcasm is brutally unforgiving. For Johnson the subject aroused more solemn emotions.

> The death of great men is not always proportioned to the lustre of their lives. Hannibal, says Juvenal, did not perish by a javelin or a sword; the slaughters of Cannae were revenged by a ring. The death of Pope was imputed by some of his friends to a silver saucepan, in which it was his delight to heat potted lampreys.
>
> **("Life of Pope")**

Johnson perceives the ironies in the situation, but in Pope's case his reference is mild and humane, with its pleasant use of the phrase "it was his delight." And he transformed Juvenal's Hannibal into the great portrait of Charles XII of Sweden.

> His fall was destin'd to a barren strand,
> A petty fortress, and a dubious hand;
> He left the name, at which the world grew pale,
> To point a moral, or adorn a tale.

It is Johnson, not schoolboys, whose moral is pointed and whose tale is adorned.

Further analysis of the passage would demonstrate that Charles, though he exhibits definite limitations of vision and perhaps even of humanity, is heroic in the sense that figures in Augustan satire seldom are. He is an overreacher, he is deluded, but he is certainly not ignoble. But can we go further, and claim that he is genuinely tragic? Eliot remarked that "these thirty-two lines compose a paragraph which is, in itself, quite perfect in form: the rising curve of ambition, the sudden calamity, and the slow decline and degradation." The effect seems to be that of a miniature tragedy, and Johnson actually contemplated writing one on this subject.

Against such a view at least three objections can be raised. One is that the tragedy, if it exists at all, is only potentially present, since the story is not especially particularized. Johnson's characters are really emblematic figures, as indeed the transposition of Roman and modern examples would suggest; they are the agents or representatives of abstract forces that are larger than any individual, however great. Thus we see Wolsey, "Law in his voice, and fortune in his hand", and thus Charles XII, "Unconquer'd lord of pleasure and of pain". What we have is more like the prospectus for a tragedy than the tragedy itself, and Charles is present mainly in order to support a thesis. Moreover, the shapely form which Eliot describes suggests something quite different from the quality of most political tragedies, which might be characterized in the words of Bacon's essay "Of Great Place": "The standing is slippery; and the regress is either a downfall, or at least an eclipse." For

Johnson the rise and fall of great men seems a relatively slow and stately process, like the waxing and waning of the moon, or growth and decay. In tragedy it is perhaps more like mountain-climbing: immense skill expended in the face of ever-present danger, and the stroke of disaster coming like a sudden blow.

A related objection is that the simple *de casibus* exemplum, while it is fundamental to the idea of the tragic, is (considered simply in itself) an inadequate basis for tragedy as the artistic imitation of an action. Modern criticism would not care to accept as tragic all of the stories related by Chaucer's Monk, and in fact the type, depending on its treatment, need not be tragic at all. Humpty Dumpty is a *de casibus* figure. If the Charles XII passage is tragic, it must be so by virtue of its imaginative presentation, however brief (as I have argued in opposition to Joyce, or at any rate Stephen Dedalus, in Chapter 1).

Finally, an even more fundamental objection may be advanced: that a tragic interpretation of Charles XII is a wilful misreading of Johnson's intention, which is satiric. Howard D. Weinbrot, approaching the poem from a formal analysis of Augustan satire, inverts the values of the tragic school and regards it as an assault on human pride. Thus Charles is seen as "super-human but inhuman," held up as an example to avoid, not to admire or sympathize with. Such a view is a useful corrective to the notion that we have any clear—much less any intimate—understanding of Charles' feelings, but it does not really disprove the possibility of tragic emotion. Many tragic heroes are inhuman in their greatness, arrive at a fate which is both appropriate and effected by their own actions, and do not necessarily "learn" from their fall.

A fully satiric treatment of Charles is implied in a brief allusion in the *Essay on Man:*

> Heroes are much the same, the point's agreed,
> From Macedonia's madman to the Swede;
> The whole strange purpose of their lives, to find
> Or make, an enemy of all mankind!
> Not one looks backward, onward still he goes,
> Yet ne'er looks forward farther than his nose.

When Johnson quoted these lines from memory, Boswell objected to "Yet ne'er looks forward farther than his nose" as being low. Johnson replied, "Sir, it is intended to be low: it is satire. The expression is debased, to debase the character." And in *Adventurer* 99, where he defends "projectors" from the unthinking derision of the Augustan satirists, he describes Charles XII as one of those true projectors whose ambitions should be regarded with revulsion.

> I cannot conceive, why he that has burnt cities, and wasted nations, and filled the world with horror and desolation, should be more kindly regarded by mankind, than he that died in the rudiments of wickedness; why he that accomplished mischief should be glorious, and he that only endeavoured it should be criminal: I would wish Caesar and Catiline, Xerxes and Alexander, Charles and Peter, huddled together in obscurity or detestation.

For whatever reason, he did not choose, four years earlier, to present Charles in this light in **"The Vanity of Human Wishes."**

But considerations like these should not lead us to suppose that the poem is altogether remote from satire. One may imagine that Johnson knew he was ignoring much of Juvenal's sarcastic acerbity, and that he was transforming passages of vivid (not to say grotesque) particularity into something much more solemn and general. But it is quite another matter to believe that he intended the poem to be essentially unsatiric, or, what is more important, that it would actually convey that impression to us if we were not reading selectively. It is clear that the tragic school, from Scott to Miss Lascelles, have been responding to something that really exists in **"The Vanity of Human Wishes."** But in so doing they have not given full weight to another equally real aspect, which led Joseph Warton to write, "The imitations of Horace by Pope, and of Juvenal by Johnson, are preferable to their originals in the appositeness of their examples and in the poignancy of their ridicule." For this one-sidedness of emphasis the comparison with Juvenal is partly to blame. The difference between Johnson's version and its model is so apparent that critics have been inclined to regard it as one of kind rather than degree. And their approach, emphasizing as it does the great set-piece portraits, is likely to neglect other passages which have considerable poetic merit and are essential to the structure of the poem.

Here, however, we must ask what kind of structure **"The Vanity of Human Wishes"** may reasonably be said to have. Early in the poem Johnson follows Juvenal quite closely, and appears to recommend the example of jesting Democritus. Later he departs a good deal from his source and for much of the time, at least, evokes a mood which has been called tragic. What, then, should we make of Democritus? One critic concludes that he has been "unsuitably" retained; another takes the somewhat desperate course of declaring **"The Vanity"** a failure, which abruptly drops its mocking program and attempts a treatment quite unsuited to its subject. But another possibility all but forces itself upon us: that Johnson has attempted to do more than one thing in this poem, to join both the satiric and the tragic modes in a larger whole.

To take this approach need not imply an especially high claim for the "unity" of the poem, or an assertion that it embodies some kind of symbolic *concordia discors*. Indeed, I shall urge that the terms of the argument explicitly deny the possibility of reconciling its discordant elements, except by escaping them entirely in the way proposed by the ending of the poem. If I am right, then Johnson is making a virtue of his tendency, which Geoffrey Tillotson has noticed, to conduct an argument rather erratically through a series of quite independent paragraphs. Or, looking at it in another way, Johnson obeys the principle of organization by accretion which Ralph Cohen finds in the Augustan mode: the verse paragraphs are carefully shaped within themselves, but assembled in the larger structure with an additive rather than an organic effect. In either case, one cannot claim too subtle an interrelation of parts. **"The Vanity of Human Wishes,"** even more than Juvenal's tenth satire, is a very miscellaneous poem. One could easily fabricate reasons to explain why Johnson expands one passage or contracts another, but perhaps it is wisest to assume that he has a right to be simply idiosyncratic in these matters. To take a relatively trivial example, there is no obvious reason why he should substitute modern parallels for all but one of Juvenal's portraits, retaining Xerxes (though adding "the bold Bavarian" as well). I am tempted to believe simply that the passage had a special imaginative fascination for him. We know that he alluded to it later, on two quite different occasions, and that a couplet from it was his favorite in all of his poetry.

Let us return, at this point, to the lines, "From Marlb'rough's eyes the streams of dotage flow, / And Swift expires a driv'ler and a show." This couplet is the only direct reference to Juvenal's Swiftian disgust at the impotence of old age, which he mocks with a vehement obscenity that the Loeb translator feels obliged to omit and Dryden to render more witty and less explicit:

> The limber Nerve, in vain provok'd to rise,
> Inglorious from the Field of Battel flies:
> Poor Feeble Dotard, how cou'd he advance
> With his Blew-head-piece, and his broken Lance?

Dryden if anything softens Juvenal's revulsion in the lines,

> The Skull and Forehead one Bald Barren plain;
> And Gums unarm'd to Mumble Meat in vain:
> Besides th' Eternal Drivel, that supplies
> The dropping Beard, from Nostrils, Mouth, and
>   Eyes.

To compare these lines with Johnson's treatment of old age may easily lead us to call his version tragic, but we should not forget that the prevailing tone of the passage is satiric as much as sympathetic. The lines inspired by Johnson's aged mother, in which Nature at least "bids afflicted worth retire to peace," have frequently been mentioned as if they were the entirety of the section. But in fact they are an expansion of Juvenal's brief reference to the sorrows of age *even when* it is not contemptible; and they are preceded by lines which correspond perfectly to Warton's opinion of the poignancy of Johnson's ridicule. The dotard loses the pleasures of the senses, and "shuns to know, / That life protracted is protracted woe"—a sentence which is often quoted, and justly so, as a typically Johnsonian statement about the life of man. Thus far we may presume that Johnson intends a degree of sympathy; we all feel a kind of horror when we consider that "time hovers o'er, impatient to destroy, / And shuts up all the passages of joy." As he so often does, Johnson universalizes the condition by attributing it to a force, *Time,* to which we are all in bondage, and gives it point and immediacy by the brilliant stroke of personification: Time is *impatient* to destroy.

The old man, then, is tedious to himself, and with this we may easily sympathize. On the other hand, we must do justice to the epigrammatic skill with which Johnson depicts another aspect of his condition: he is tedious to others, and insofar as it is worth their while to humor him, he encourages moral debasement of a particularly despicable kind.

> But everlasting dictates croud his tongue,
> Perversely grave, or positively wrong.
> The still returning tale, and ling'ring jest,
> Perplex the fawning niece and pamper'd guest,
> While growing hopes scarce awe the gath'ring sneer,
> And scarce a legacy can bribe to hear;
> The watchful guests still hint the last offence,
> The daughter's petulance, the son's expence,
> Improve his heady rage with treach'rous skill,
> And mould his passions till they make his will.

From the loathsome old man—loathsome morally, not just physically—the emphasis shifts to the predatory heirs, whose skill in fawning is "perplexed" by the rambling confusion of his stories and jests. He has become so appalling that even a legacy is barely reward enough for their attentions. And at last, tyrannical though he is, he becomes the victim and they the agents, as they "hint," "improve," and "mould" his feelings, until—with a neat pun—"they make his will." Johnson has often been praised for the strength and vitality of his verbs, but his adjectives and participles as well show a peculiarly Augustan accuracy of implication. The tale is "still returning"—the listeners perceive with despair that, like fate, it looms once again into view; the jest is "ling'ring," as it stumbles laboriously through its familiar course. And the sycophants' role forbids them to deflect the tale and the jest; on the contrary, they are obliged to welcome them with every sign of delight.

Thus far, I have suggested that **"The Vanity of Human Wishes"** contains two predominant modes, those of satiric attack and tragic sympathy. Sometimes they alternate; sometimes they appear more intimately joined. But it is not necessary to claim that they are reconciled in any profound way, for, as I have intimated, Johnson denies the possibility of real reconciliation. The overtly religious conclusion to the poem does not emerge logically from it, but is supplied, as if from outside, as the only possible escape from its dilemmas. We have been given a series of impressions of human life, producing emotions which are varied and perhaps even contradictory. Just as in the final sentence of *Rasselas,* we are offered no means of finding stability amid the vicissitudes of life, but are advised instead to redirect our attention to "the choice of eternity."

The radical difference between Juvenal's ending and Johnson's has often been noticed. The Roman poet recommends the Stoic posture which Johnson so often criticized as inhuman, and far from endorsing the efficacy of prayer, instructs his reader to concede as little as possible to the gods.

> Yet, not to rob the Priests of pious Gain,
> That Altars be not wholly built in vain;
> Forgive the Gods the rest, and stand confin'd
> To Health of Body, and Content of Mind:
> A Soul, that can securely Death defie,
> And count it Nature's Priviledge, to Dye.

Mens sana in corpore sano: this is the answer to both of the themes of Juvenal's satire, the vanity of ambition (for power, wealth, and so on), and the final disillusionment with life itself. Johnson would probably agree with the former ("the wisest justice on the banks of Trent"), but his answer to the latter is the reverse of Juvenal's: only "celestial wisdom," acting for a benevolent God, can make "the happiness she does not find."

In this sense **"The Vanity of Human Wishes"** is not only didactic, but actually homiletic. If I were to guess at Johnson's conception of his relation to Juvenal, I would surmise that he wanted us to be struck by precisely this difference between the two poems. While admiring the aptness of his modern parallels and the weighty solemnity of his language, we will have noticed how much less mocking his version is, and how a tragic feeling keeps breaking in upon the satire, though never wholly displacing it. We know from Johnson's many discussions of Stoicism that he cannot have regarded Juvenal's answer as in any sense adequate, so that it deserves the criticism of the **Rambler:** "The folly of human wishes and persuits has always been a standing subject of mirth and declamation, and has been ridiculed and lamented from age to age; till perhaps the fruitless repetition of complaints and censures may be justly numbered among the subjects of censure and complaint." Mere censure, mere mirth and declamation, are "fruitless"; Johnson's method is to lead us through the stages of the Roman poet's argument, and then to show that religion reveals a conclusion of which Juvenal had not the slightest intimation. Thus I suggest that he intended his Christian ending as a kind of tour de force, answering the despair of the classical poet with the truth of revelation, and making the happiness he could not find.

The title which Johnson gave his imitation suggests this correction of classical by means of Biblical wisdom. We are meant to think of Ecclesiastes, to which he often alluded in his sermons and periodical writings.

> The numerous miseries of human life have extorted in all ages an universal complaint. The wisest of men [Solomon] terminated all his experiments in search of happiness, by the mournful confession, that "all is vanity"; and the antient patriarchs lamented, that "the days of their pilgrimage were few and evil."

To dwell upon the miseries of life would be useless, and indeed cruel, if it did not perform the essential service of distracting man from the illusory pleasures of this world and impelling him to fix his attention on eternity.

> Some have endeavoured to engage us in the contemplation of the evils of life for a very wise and good end. They have proposed, by laying before us the uncertainty of prosperity, the vanity of pleasure, and the inquietudes of power, the difficult attainment of most earthly blessings, and the short duration of them all, to divert our thoughts from the glittering follies and tempting delusions that surround us, to an inquiry after more certain and permanent felicity.
>
> (Sermon V)

In particular, this "inquiry" involves a redirection of two of man's most fundamental passions, those of hope and fear. In his sermon on the text, "I have seen all the works that are done under the sun; and behold, all is vanity and vexation of spirit," Johnson says that Solomon "had taken a survey of all the gradations of human life," just as **"The Vanity of Human Wishes"** begins with observation surveying mankind; and Solomon reached a similar conclusion, that "the history of mankind is little else than a narrative of designs which have failed, and hopes that have been disappointed." Before undertaking his "survey," Johnson asks,

> Then say how hope and fear, desire and hate,
> O'erspread with snares the clouded maze of fate,
> Where wav'ring man, betray'd by vent'rous pride,
> To tread the dreary paths without a guide,
> As treach'rous phantoms in the mist delude,
> Shuns fancied ills, or chases airy good.

If man is indeed "without a guide"—Johnson takes for granted the inadequacy of Juvenal's *mens sana* in this regard—then the catalogue of human folly and misery must compel us to raise the question again, in even more pessimistic terms.

> Where then shall Hope and Fear their objects find?

> Must dull Suspence corrupt the stagnant mind?
> Must helpless man, in ignorance sedate,
> Roll darkling down the torrent of his fate?

In the first published edition the final line read "Swim darkling down the current of his fate"; the revision forcibly enhances the idea of utter helplessness.

Hope and *Fear* are not the vague, indefinite terms that they have become today, but denote a view of the human condition that Johnson believes to be both psychologically and theologically true. First of all, these emotions are an inseparable part of life; as Imlac found, not even the Happy Valley could empower him to "bid farewell to hope and fear." But more importantly, empiricist psychology defines them as a sort of double mainspring of human life. "Every man is conscious," Johnson writes in a sermon, "that he neither performs, nor forbears any thing upon any other motive than the prospect, either of an immediate gratification, or a distant reward." The answer to the vanity of human wishes, then, is to redirect these basic drives in the right way. "To live religiously, is to walk, not by sight, but by faith; to act in confidence of things unseen, in hope of future recompense, and in fear of future punishment." Thus Aspasia's eloquence briefly impels Irene to recognize the emptiness of "The glitt'ring vanities of empty greatness, / The hopes and fears, the joys and pains of life." Aspasia seizes the hint, and urges her friend, "let nobler hopes and juster fears succeed." Only in heaven will hope and fear cease to be necessary.

In effect, **"The Vanity of Human Wishes"** counsels a Boethian withdrawal from the inevitable disappointments and sorrows of the temporal world. It warns against subservience to "delusive Fortune," and urges the lesson of the passage from Boethius which Johnson translated for the 1752 edition of the *Rambler* (repeating his use of the word "darkling"):

> O Thou whose pow'r o'er moving worlds presides,
> Whose voice created, and whose wisdom guides,
> On darkling man in pure effulgence shine,
> And chear the clouded mind with light divine.
> 'Tis thine alone to calm the pious breast
> With silent confidence and holy rest:
> From thee, great God, we spring, to thee we tend,
> Path, motive, guide, original, and end.

It is now time to draw back a little from the poem, and to ask whether it does in fact convey the impression which, if my argument is correct, Johnson intended that it should. Is Ian Jack right in seeing an "almost medieval" pessimism in the *contemptus mundi* tradition? Does the poem genuinely escape the tragic (and the satiric) by refusing to be bound by transitory hopes and fears, in the way that *Antony and Cleopatra*—to take an extrareligious example—seems to escape from the confines of tragedy?

> 'Tis paltry to be Caesar:
> Not being Fortune, he's but Fortune's knave,
> A minister of her will.

These are questions which every reader must answer for himself. For my own part, I am inclined to think that even in this poem the moralist never quite suppresses the man. As Gray wrote in the lines which Johnson singled out for particular admiration,

> For who to dumb Forgetfulness a prey,
> This pleasing anxious being e'er resign'd,

Left the warm precincts of the cheerful day,
Nor cast one longing ling'ring look behind?

And, retreating still further from the poem, it is possible
to distinguish between the meaning it is intended to enforce and the meaning we give it if we cannot share Johnson's religious premises. Like Pascal, he wins through to
his knowledge of a higher truth by exposing the sickening
inadequacy of any temporal truth; but for many readers
today this is a conclusion which may be imaginatively understood but not shared. In this case, the main body of the
poem may take on a different appearance, and become
something much closer to tragedy than Johnson designed
it to be. Nor is such an interpretation an anachronistic,
twentieth-century misreading. To illustrate my meaning
I cannot do better than to quote the following passage
from F. M. Cornford's brilliant study of Thucydides' *History* as a tragic drama:

> Elpis had not to the Greek the associations which
> Christianity has given to "Hope"; she is not a vir-
> tue, but a dangerous passion. The future is dark and
> uncertain, and although rational foresight (*gnóme*)
> can see a little way into the gloom, Fortune, or
> Fate, or Providence, is an incalculable factor which
> at any moment may reverse the purposes and defeat
> the designs of man. Elpis is the passion which de-
> ludes man to count on the future as if he could per-
> fectly control it; and thus she is a phase of infatuate
> pride, a temptress who besets prosperity.

Man in this sense is, we may say, condemned indeed to
"tread the dreary paths without a guide" (8), he is indeed
the helpless victim of delusive Fortune, but to know these
things is not to be able to escape them.

Such reflections as these may help to explain why the
"tragic" elements of **"The Vanity of Human Wishes"** have
so often been admired, and indeed interpreted as setting
the tone of the poem as a whole. But although it is idle to
ask that our aesthetic response be governed by the presumed intention of the writer, it may yet be true that Johnson intended the poem to have an effect that was neither
tragic nor satirical, moving beyond both into a larger and
more comprehensive vision. It should be emphasized that
no absolute statement of value is intended in a phrase like
"larger and more comprehensive vision." A work which
draws upon tragedy and satire at once may lack the intensity and penetration of either kind at its best, and may
seem more discursive than imaginative. May it not also
seem peculiarly Johnsonian? (pp. 139-59)

> *Leopold Damrosch, Jr., in his* Samuel Johnson
> and the Tragic Sense, *Princeton University
> Press, 1972, 267 p.*

Russell Kirk   (essay date 1981)

[*An American historian, political theorist, novelist, journalist, and lecturer, Kirk is one of America's most eminent conservative intellectuals, admired for the incisive-
ness of his ideas and criticism. One of Kirk's early books,*
The Conservative Mind *(1953), which provided a major
impetus to the conservative revival that has since developed, describes conservatism as a living body of ideas
"struggling toward ascendancy in the United States"
and traces its genesis to the thought of such predecessors
as Edmund Burke, John Adams, and Alexis de Tocque-*

*ville. In the following excerpt, he explicates Johnson's
conception and defense of the eighteenth-century social
and moral order, comparing Johnson's convictions with
those of Edmund Burke and Adam Smith.*]

What Matthew Arnold called "an epoch of concentration" impends over the English-speaking nations. The revolutionary impulses and the social enthusiasms that dominated our century since their great explosion in Russia are
now confronted by a countervailing physical and intellectual force. Fanatic ideology has been, in essence, rebellion
against the old moral order of our civilization. To resist
ideology, certain principles and usages of order have been
waked, quite as they stirred against French innovating
fury after 1790. We have entered upon a time of reconstruction and revaluation; we discern a resurrected conservatism in politics and philosophy and letters.

Britain during Arnold's "epoch of concentration" became, despite its disillusion, a society of high intellectual
achievement, the revolutionary energy latent in it diverted to reconstructive ends. That the epoch of concentration
displayed moral qualities so powerful, that it did not sink
into a mere leaden reaction, Arnold attributed to the influence of Edmund Burke. Indeed Burke succeeded in death,
beyond his own last expectations, at his labor of upholding
the order of civilization. "The communication of the
dead is tongued with fire beyond the language of the living." Let me add to the name of Edmund Burke the great
names of Samuel Johnson and Adam Smith; and permit
me to suggest to you, very succinctly, how these three men
of the latter half of the eighteenth century explained and
defended that social and moral order which endures to our
own present troubled decade.

Although the three great men knew one another, they
were not intimates; Smith and Johnson, indeed, were adversaries. Burke was a practical leader of party, Johnson
a poet and a critic, Smith a professor (nominally) of moral
philosophy. (Actually, he at once converted his Glasgow
appointment into a chair of finance and political economy.) Johnson was a Tory; Burke and Smith were Whigs.
Doubtless their ghosts would be astonished to find their
names joined amicably near the end of the twentieth century. Yet it may be said of them what T. S. Eliot wrote of
the partisans of the English Civil Wars: they "Accept the
constitution of silence / And are folded in a single party."
What party, nowadays? Why, we may call it the party of
order.

All three men were moralists; all were realists and shrewd
observers; all gave primacy to order in the commonwealth. I propose to touch briefly upon some of their several convictions, to compare the three, and to suggest their
relationships. (pp. 226-27)

"The first Whig was the Devil." A good many people
know little more of Samuel Johnson's politics than this
witticism, which does suggest, indeed, Johnson's emphasis
on ordination and subordination. But Johnson was a political thinker of importance, though no abstract metaphysician in politics.

It will not do to look at Johnson through the spectacles
of "the Whig interpretation of history" or on the basis of
silly commentaries in popular literature-textbooks which
result from ignorance of Johnson's doctrines and milieu.
The political Johnson was a reasonable, moderate, and

generous champion of order, quick to sustain just authority, but suspicious of unchecked power. If one analyzes his Tory pamphlet *Taxation No Tyranny,* one finds that Johnson merely was stating the long-accepted and still valid definition of the word "sovereignty" as a term of politics—not advocating absolutism.

There runs through Johnson's works a strong vein of disillusion and doubt of human powers, a sense of the vanity of human wishes. This is part and parcel of the Christian dogmata that governed Johnson's life. Certainly it shaped his political convictions. Dr. Raymond English speaks of "the rather brutal skeptical streak in Johnson's Toryism. It seems to me that Johnson is rather like Dean Inge in that he combines a profound mystical Christian faith with a fierce pessimism about practical politics. Possibly one should compare both these to St. Augustine, for whom the fall of man had rendered natural law a somewhat inadequate basis for political authority. In a slightly different way, Fitzjames Stephen plays upon a similar theme."

Neither Burke nor Johnson would have been pleased to be styled a "political philosopher." Perhaps Johnson, in his political aspect, is best described as "statist"—which word has a neutral character in Johnson's *Dictionary.* What Ross Hoffman said of Burke is even more true of Johnson: "He took his first principles in politics from the Authorized Version and the Book of Common Prayer." Granville Hicks once wrote of Robert Louis Stevenson, "The

"Dr. Johnson in His Travelling Dress as Described in Boswell's Tour, *Drawn from the Life and Engraved by T. Trotter" (1786).*

Tory has always insisted that, if men would cultivate the individual virtues, social problems would take care of themselves." This is true in essence of Johnson's view of human nature and society; yet Johnson did not ignore the part of institutions in a tolerable social order. Far from being an absolutist, he stood for the rule of law in a polity, the *libido dominandi* checked by custom and Christian doctrine.

"The Whigs will live and die in the heresy that the world is governed by little tracts and pamphlets," Walter Scott wrote once—Scott, who stood directly in the line of Johnson. Into that heresy Samuel Johnson did not slip. His politics did not come from sixteenth- or seventeenth- or eighteenth-century tracts, but from experience of the world, from much reading of the politically wise over many centuries, and from what Eliot calls "the idea of a Christian society," with its concepts of ordination and subordination, charity and justice, divine love, and mortal fallibility.

Whig magnates and demagogic "patriots," Johnson was convinced, meant to break in upon the balance of orders and powers that was eighteenth-century England—an argument later advanced by Disraeli, in the preface to *Sybil.* For Johnson, the Devil was the first Whig because the Whigs stood for insubordination and innovation; Burke was a "bottomless Whig," in Johnson's epithet, because the Whigs clung to no well-defined principles of social order, but lived by expediency and extemporization. Such ejaculations about Whigs, nevertheless, often extracted by Boswell from Johnson in moments whimsical or splenetic, were not Johnson's deeper reflections. At Boswell's request, in 1781, Johnson set down in writing the distinctions between Whig and Tory:

> A wise Tory and a wise Whig, I believe, will agree. Their principles are the same, though their modes of thinking are different. A high Tory makes government unintelligible; it is lost in the clouds. A violent Whig makes it impracticable; he is for allowing so much liberty to every man, that there is not enough power to govern any man. The prejudice of the Tory is for establishment; the prejudice of the Whig is for innovation. A Tory does not wish to give more real power to Government; but that Government should have more reverence. Then they differ as to the Church. The Tory is not for giving more legal power to the Clergy, but wishes they should have a considerable influence, founded on the opinion of mankind; the Whig is for limiting and watching them with a narrow jealousy.

As Leslie Stephen wrote, "The Whigs were invincibly suspicious of parsons." Johnson was not so suspicious.

It may be perceived that the first principles of such a Tory as Johnson and such a Whig as Burke were very nearly identical. To both, the new politics of the dawning era, whether the notions of Rousseau or of Bentham, were abhorrent. Both Johnson and Burke recognized a transcendent moral order, subscribed to the wisdom of the species, were attached to custom and precedent, upheld the idea of the Christian magistrate, and adhered to the venerable concepts of Christian charity and community. The narrow contract-theory of Locke, the skepticism of Hume, the tendency toward individualism in the writings of Smith— these were inimical to both the Toryism of Johnson and the Whiggery of Burke.

When, at the end of his career, Burke refuted Goldsmith's playful reproach by giving to mankind what once he had owed to party, the Old Whig's principles were almost indistinguishable from those of his friend Johnson, who had died before the Deluge of 1789. "I can live very well with Burke," Johnson had said; "I love his knowledge, his diffusion, and affluence of conversation." Or, on another occasion, "Yes, Sir, if a man were to go by chance at the same time with Burke under a shed to shun a shower, he would say—'we have had an extraordinary man here.' "

It was otherwise with Johnson and Smith. Walter Scott, in a letter to John Wilson Croker written in 1829, records someone's account of a meeting between Johnson and Smith at Glasgow—or rather, the account of it said to have been extracted not long later from Adam Smith:

> Smith, obviously much discomposed, came into a party who were playing at cards. The Doctor's appearance suspended the amusement, for as all knew he was to meet Johnson that evening, every one was curious to hear what had passed. Adam Smith, whose temper seemed much ruffled, answered only at first, "He is a brute! he is a brute!" Upon closer examination it appeared that Dr. Johnson no sooner saw Smith than he brought forward a charge against him for something in his famous letter on the death of Hume. Smith said he had vindicated the truth of the statement. "And what did the Doctor say?" was the universal query: "Why, he said—he said—" said Smith, with the deepest impression of resentment, "he said—*You lie*!" "And what did you reply?" "I said, 'You are a son of a bitch!' " On such terms did these two great moralists meet and part, and such was the classic dialogue betwixt them.

Birkbeck Hill doubts the veracity of this incident; however that may be, it represents well enough the degree of esteem in which the two moral philosophers held each other. (pp. 229-31)

[A] gulf was widening even in the last quarter of the eighteenth century between men of intellect who professed Christian dogmata, and men of intellect who had their liberal doubts. Johnson and Burke were of the former party; Smith was Hume's warmest admirer. As Manning said, all differences of opinion are theological at bottom. Smith was no atheist; yet his animadversions on the church, in the first edition of *The Wealth of Nations,* disquieted even his good friend Hugh Blair, the famous liberal preacher of the age, who wrote to Smith in April, 1776: "But in your system about the Church I cannot wholly agree with you. Independency was at no time a possible or practicable system. The little sects you speak of would, for many reasons, have combined together into greater bodies and done much mischief to society." By such remarks, Smith had raised up formidable adversaries, Blair told him. Johnson was one such, no doubt; and Burke, though an energetic friend to religious toleration, was no admirer of the dissidence of dissent.

Finally, there were differences of temperament and social assumptions among these three. Burke was very much an Irishman, Johnson very much an Englishman—and Smith redoubtably a Scot. His mind was the mind of a Scottish Whig, however urbanely professorial Smith might be. William Butler Yeats, in his poem "The Seven Sages," suggests that Burke, though a Whig nominally and occupationally, deep down detested the whole Whig cast of mind and character:

> All hated Whiggery; but what is Whiggery?
> A levelling, rancorous, rational sort of mind
> That never looked out of the eye of a saint
> Or out of drunkard's eye.

Johnson feared Hell and venerated saints; Burke sometimes was facetious in his cups, and read "the fathers of the fourteenth century." Smith appears to have been sober always, and not given to visions of the world beyond the world. It is a great way from Kirkcaldy to Dublin or to Litchfield.

Be that as it may, Burke and Johnson and Smith, in their several ways, described and defended those beliefs and institutions that maintain the beneficent tension of order and freedom. All were pillars of what Burke called "this world of reason, and order, and peace, and virtue, and fruitful penitence"; all knew how men and nations may make choices that cast them "into the antagonist world of madness, discord, vice, confusion, and unavailing sorrow." Such frantic choices are being made two centuries after these three lived and breathed and had their being. So I do not find it at all surprising that some among us, in what we hope will be an era of concentration rather than of eccentricity, are reading afresh Burke and Johnson and Smith. (p. 233)

> *Russell Kirk, "Three Pillars of Order: Edmund Burke, Samuel Johnson, Adam Smith,"* in Modern Age, *Vol. 25, No. 3, Summer, 1981, pp. 226-33.*

Thomas Jemielity　(essay date 1984)

[*Jemielity is an American educator and critic who has contributed essays on the Bible, Restoration and eighteenth-century literature, and satire to several periodicals. In the following excerpt, he argues for the success of Johnson as satirist through detailed exposition of "The Vanity of Human Wishes."*]

A close reading of [**"The Vanity of Human Wishes"**] justifies the . . . view that it succeeds as satire. A variety of reasons present themselves: first, Democritus serves as a fitting guide to the satiric tone of the poem, an appropriateness reinforced by the theatrical imagery appearing in the text; second, the poem maintains a steady, albeit secondary, satiric thrust directed against the retainers, sycophants, and bystanders ever-present and ever-ready in the poem to turn the destruction of others into sources of amusement and gain for themselves; third, Johnson repeatedly and painstakingly fashions a diminished portrait, particularly of his major exampla, and then makes that sketch serve the wider and equally diminishing survey of the poem's specifically explored vain human desires for power, scholarly fame, military glory, long life, and physical attractiveness. This building-block structure, central to the satiric approach of the poem, emerges from and reinforces its opening general survey of human appetite and leads irresistibly to the poem's concluding verse paragraph.

What did Johnson himself expect from satire, and what qualities, in particular, did he seek to invest in his reworking of Juvenal's *Tenth Satire?* The definitions and illustrations he provided in the **Dictionary** for *satire* and its related terms (*satirical, satirick, satirically, satirist,* and *to satirize*) conveniently provide a starting point very close to the time in which Johnson composed and published **"The Vanity of Human Wishes."** Johnson defines satire as "a poem in which wickedness or folly is censured," and proceeds immediately to an important distinction, one that appears in his insistence that Dryden's *MacFlecknoe* is lampoon rather than satire: "proper *satire* is distinguished by the generality of its reflections from a *lampoon* which is aimed against a particular person; but they are too frequently confounded." The related terms and their illustrations characterize satire as censorious and severe in language, employing invective, and written to censure or vilify (for Johnson, the latter term denotes defaming, debasing, and making contemptible). This vein continues: satire is sharp, severe, bold, enterprising, yet it springs from a morally motivated anger, demonstrates a gay wisdom, and directs both hatred and pity at the vice it attacks. Ian Jack has observed, ". . . the declamatory grandeur of Juvenal, with its tone of a dignified public utterance, austere, exacting, sternly censorious, afforded Johnson the precedent and the example he required." Johnson, after all, complained that while earlier translations and imitations had preserved the wit of Juvenal, they neglected "the dignity of the original. The peculiarity of Juvenal is a mixture of gaiety and stateliness, of pointed sentences, and declamatory grandeur." From these sources we can surmise that Johnson sought to bring to his poem a judicial, even prophetic, authority of tone, expressing itself frequently in contempt, indignation, and scorn. Observation wears judicial robes in the poem, to view with the detachment expected of a satirist the panorama of human vanity. Prevailingly scornful and contemptuous of these wishes, Johnson's wit and imagination also demonstrate, T. S. Eliot notwithstanding, "a certain divine levity."

Democritus is summoned to be the guiding spirit of the poem's survey of "the busy scenes of crouded life" (l. 4). Juvenal had offered two philosophical alternatives to this panorama: Heraclitus, to weep over the spectacle, or Democritus, to greet it with derisive laughter. Significantly, Johnson omits the alternatives altogether, calling only upon Democritus to examine the modern trappings of "motly life" (l. 51). What greater opportunities are now afforded his scorn by the antics of "Britain's modish tribe" (l. 61)! The poem expects the philosopher to respond with taunt and gibe at the joys and griefs springing ultimately from the "farce" (l. 67), not of human life, but of vain human machination. The pleasure and woe that come with relentlessly acquisitive human desire are key elements of this farce. Here, as elsewhere throughout the poem, Johnson stresses the farcical quality of human vanity by calling repeatedly on the imagery of the theater, with related figures of fashion and costume, to diminish its pretensions. The two-paragraph introduction of Democritus is studded with such imagery, appearing here in its most frequent and concentrated presence in the poem: "motly life" (l. 51), "unwieldly state" (l. 58), "modish tribe" (l. 61), "solemn toys or empty shew" (l. 65), and, of course, "farce" (l. 67). The actors on this stage come garbed in "the robes of pleasure and the veils of woe" (l. 66). The mob of retainers jamming Preferment's gate find themselves dogged on "ev'ry stage" (l. 77) by those seeking to destroy their peace. Johnson, according to Frederick Hil-

les, "toyed with the idea of having the [young scholar's academic] gown become in the student's imagination the costume of a bishop." The "festal blazes" and "triumphal show" (l. 175) that announce the entry of the poem's military exempla highlight the theatrical vanity of an ambition at odds with Reason's view of war's unequal "game" (l. 185). Xerxes, fittingly, comes in a "gay hostility" (l. 225) that serves as but one instance of the "pompous woes" (l. 223) afforded by war. The listless-eyed dotard insensibly views the entertainment of his "minstrels" (l. 267). The virtuous old man dies a superfluous veteran on "the stage" (l. 308). The death of the elderly, indeed, is a "last scene" replete with amazing "prodigies" (l. 315): Swift dies as a "show" (l. 318), fit entertainment for the midway of human life. The verse paragraph on Beauty, with its reference to "frolick," "dance" (l. 326), and "the latest fashion of the heart" (l. 328), highlights the ephemeral and meretricious quality of achievement by and pride in comeliness. Every state Democritus is asked to survey is ironically and severely reprehended as part of the farce worthy of his piercing glance. Johnson's imagery has made it impossible to view these various human desires with anything other than scorn and contempt.

Democritus is called upon to consider, first, the crowd of "unnumber'd suppliants" at "Preferment's gate" (l. 73). Feverish in their quest for advancement, the poem stresses the evanescent and trivial nature of their ambitions and their success: "They amount, they shine, evaporate, and fall" (l. 76). Dedicators and scribblers are yoked together in a diminishing coupling typical of Johnson's poem and especially of its use of its lists. A semidramatic vignette then develops which brings out not only the emptiness of the success achieved here but even more the venality of those whose self-interest in and instinct for survival leads them to seek "growing names" (l. 81) and "growing wealth" (l. 82) with uncanny instinct. Their old patron is in disgrace, his portrait no longer "the bright Palladium of the place" (l. 84). His "painted face" (l. 83), a fine image of his moral and social whoredom, is indignantly removed from the walls to fodder kitchen fire or at least to salvage the frame. With wit and contempt the poem explores the convenient rationalizations of these sycophants as they justify their change of allegiance, no longer capable now of discerning what once they viewed in awe as "heroic worth, benevolence divine" (l. 88). Like Juvenal before him, Johnson repeatedly uses mob scenes in the poem to direct a second and peripheral satiric blow at these vulturous bystanders seeking the carrion of opportunity in the first signs of weakness or disfavor. No longer like their forebears, the remonstrating sons of Freedom, these retainers have located their patriotism in their pocketbooks and ask now only for "the price of votes" (l. 96).

Like the poem's theatrical imagery, Johnson's scornful attention to the host of self-serving retainers intensifies the satiric thrust of his observations. The roles assumed by these minor figures in the farce are many: hireling ruffians and judges, insidious rivals, gaping heirs, morning worshippers, weekly scribblers and dedicators. As Bate himself has observed, "There are repeated suggestions of thronging jostle" throughout the poem. A "train of state" (l. 109) awaits the moment of Wolsey's fall to become, in turn, scornful suppliants, avoiding Wolsey as they might decaying flesh. Among his lost perquisites Wolsey must number "the menial lord" (l. 116). Academic distinction falls beneath the blow of "meaner minds" (l. 169), and "blockheads" (l. 174) lead Archbishop Laud to his death on the block from which their insensate heads have been fashioned. Military conquerors in disgrace are pushed aside by interrupting court ladies and left to wait on the petty, private squabbles of slaves. Spurred on by the jaundiced motives "of plunder and of praise" (l. 248), allies fly to the aid of oppressed Austria. The defeated conqueror is derided by his foes and upbraided by his subjects, for whom success was clearly the price of allegiance. Like their peers at Preferment's gate, they too have achieved a worldly wisdom, not yet capable, however, of self-examination. The miserly old man is attended by fawning nieces, pampered guests, and those ever-watchful heirs-apparent seeking to manipulate the disposition of his estate. The rival nymph, the enslaved youth, the battering rival, the mining lover, the private friend—discretion surely cautions against public aid—all combine against Beauty in her fall. All of them look on with pleasure as the former objects of their adulation now become hated, because impotent, sources of preferment and grace: "hissing Infamy proclaims the rest" (l. 342). Unlike Juvenal's, the satiric voice of Johnson's poem does not take gleeful, self-satisfied delight in the downfall of the poem's major figures, however scornfully their ambitions are treated. But without exception, the poem relentlessly and ruthlessly exposes, with no extenuation, the unbridled malice, envy, and hatred that motivate the retainers in this poem and provide the dangerous and debilitating framework within which the poem's major figures have chosen to function. What Johnson has so carefully pieced together in **"The Vanity of Human Wishes"** is a mosaic of human pride, dominated by the major exempla of the poem. But the theatrical imagery and the unrelenting exposure of sycophantic ambition effectively highlight the satiric colors in which the major figures appear.

The primary demonstration of the satiric color Johnson maintains throughout **"The Vanity of Human Wishes"** appears in his approach to the major exempla and in the manner in which he uses them as part of the wider survey of vain human desire for power, scholarly renown, military glory, and long life. Like each of his supposedly illustrious peers in the poem, Wolsey, the first gargantuan figure in Johnson's Vanity Fair, enters the stage ironically undercut and already judged. He stands in "full blown dignity" (l. 99), "spread to the utmost extent," in the *Dictionary*'s definition, "as a perfect blossom." But the *Dictionary* includes a second meaning for "full blown"; "stretched by the wind to the fullest extent." This witty, diminishing pun assumes Pauline overtones with its suggestion that power, like knowledge, "puffeth up." A colossal instance of human ego, of the theatrical implications of the "idle shew" which is one of Johnson's definitions of *vanity*, Wolsey's ironic entrance calls up the biblical and satirical overtones of a title drawing on the wisdom of Ecclesiastes. The irony is reinforced by Wolsey's status as a churchman. As the balloon-like ecclesiastic explodes into fragments of canopy, plate, palace, board, army, and lord, the luxury of his material losses receives adjectival stress, while, with deflating anticlimax, he counts among his lost goods, "the menial lord" (l. 116). Does misfortune bring self-awareness? Hardly. Carrying to his death only the sting of "rememb'rd folly" (l. 119), he dies reproaching "the faith of kings" (l. 120), impervious to the demands that faith in another King might have imposed. Wolsey,

however, is only the elaborated instance of the self-indulgent wish to shine in courts, to achieve a power "too great to keep or to resign" (l. 134), that brought ruin not only to him but to Villiers, Harley, Wentworth, and Hyde as well.

Hopes for academic distinction fare no better. Brimful of desire to shake "Bacon's mansion" (l. 140), with "the fever of renown" (l. 137) burning in his veins, a young man enters, undercut at the very outset by the poem's carefully chosen diction. He enters the scene not as "the young scholar," at best a neutral and denotative phrase, but rather as "the young enthusiast" (l. 136), a term Johnson's *Dictionary* defines as "one who vainly imagines a private revelation." The poem, indeed, does not ever address him directly as "scholar." The first images reinforce the private revelation he so vainly imagines. "The strong contagion of the gown" (l. 138), that emisson from one academic body to another, hints at the self-gratifying, self-forwarding impulses of the academic community, especially in its relations among itself. With Bodley's dome and Bacon's mansion under his visionary assault, the poem wryly poses a series of conditions to the "illustrious youth," somewhat mockingly so addressed. A series of parallelisms that form one extensive sentence (ll. 143-60) detail a list of scholarly pitfalls, which do not preclude disappointment even if they are all surmounted. The list is so extensive—ten dangers are specifically enumerated—as to suggest the impossibility of the young enthusiast's successfully avoiding all these obstructions on the road to Science and Truth. The structure of these lines brilliantly conveys the theme, as condition upon condition builds a fabric of visionary absurdity that collapses in the rude, almost totally monosyllabic wisdom about his fate that, ironically, only a pause from letters will provide: "Toil, envy, want, the patron, and the jail" (l. 160). But the young enthusiast, standing in the ruins of this elaborate construction, finds his hopes still undimmed. Delayed recognition, however, may be the product of a slowly acquired wisdom still struggling against meanness of mind. The unshakable dreams of flattery are asked to consider Lydiat and Galileo. Delusion, however, is insuperable, so the young visionary is warned that academic pre-eminence can be fatal. In his last moments on Johnson's stage, the young enthusiast becomes bystander at an execution. Art and Genius weep at their loss, but the executing "blockheads" of Laud sleep undisturbed. The brute, sarcastic force of Johnson's colloquialism brings this delusion to an end. Like Swift before him, in *A Tale of a Tub,* Johnson exposes the enthusiasm that lies at the heart of complex schemes for intellectual renown. But the "Digression on Madness" continues.

Of all the forms of human vanity scrutinized in the poem, however, none receives more extensive treatment than the thirst for military glory. Johnson not only introduces here three fully developed exempla—Charles XII of Sweden, Xerxes, and Charles Albert of Bavaria—but he also provides this section of the poem with the longest of his introductions to one particular human folly. The diminishing note of entrance appears at once as the theatrical imagery of "festal blazes" and "triumphal show" (l. 175) brings on a list of the irresistible forces prevailing over the brave. As ambiguous as these attractions are in themselves, even they are ironically subordinated to the influence of "the senate's thanks" and "the gazette's pompous tale" (l. 177).

"Such bribes" (l. 179), the poem contemptuously comments, set Greek, Roman, and even British armies into motion to "shine" (l. 181) in military exploit in the only way possible to the soldier: by staining "with blood the Danube or the Rhine" (l. 182). Vanity triumphs over virtue in such pursuits, and wasted nations, mortgaged for later generations, enjoy the dearly bought right to regret the wreaths which "rust on medals or on stones decay" (l. 190). The alchemy of warfare, transforming water into blood, has moved through vegetation to its final stage as corrosion and ashes. Such a contemptuous yet witty introduction leaves little reason to assume that the three military exempla who follow will undo the diminished general impression of the soldier's ambition.

The laurels of Charles XII of Sweden display at once a few withered leaves. His "frame of admant" (l. 193)—a stone, in Johnson's **Dictionary**, *"imagined* [my emphasis], by writers, of impenetrable hardness"—and his "soul of fire" (l. 193) are frighted by no danger, fatigued by no labor: he has transcended love and fear. Restless for challenge, he takes no joy in "pacific scepters" (l. 197). "Peace" (l. 201), almost erotically spreading her charms, does so in vain. As nations anxiously watch his eye, an image of his acquisitiveness, Charles begins his march. But "Pultowa's day" (l. 210) transforms him into a "vanquish'd hero" (l. 211) and "a needy supplicant" (l. 213), having to bear in patience and humiliation the interruption of court ladies and the priority of slaves' debates. Was Fate ultimately kind in granting him a hero's death, however? No. Struck by some unknown hand, at "a petty fortress" (l. 220) on "a barren strand" (l. 219), he leaves only a name to point the moral and adorn the tale of military madness.

Xerxes and Charles Albert are both linked in the poem as particular instances of the military showman. Their delight in the "pompous woes" (l. 223) of war underscores their light-hearted, exuberantly cheerful view of bloodshed and carnage as amusement. It is "Persia's tyrant" (l. 224), however, who towers for the moment over the others as the most consummate example in the poem of a military ambition that triumphs over and displaces reason. In what is hardly a compliment, Xerxes marches forth to seize "the certain prey" (l. 227), to starve "exhausted regions in his way" (l. 228). The numbering of his expanding domains only intensifies the desire for conquest. What can be counted is, after all, limited. Flattery impels to a "madness" (l. 231), firing his mind for even more. Now styling himself a god, he adds the winds and the waves to his dominion. The "daring Greeks" (l. 235), not at all overawed by this supposedly divine fury and deriding his pretensions, lop "the spreading god" (l. 234) as they might trim a tree and heap "their vallies with the gaudy foe" (l. 236). Xerxes' "martial show" (l. 235) proves a flop. Defeat, the poem sarcastically comments, impresses Xerxes with "humbler thoughts" (l. 237) as he speeds to the "single skiff" (l. 238) that will carry him in retreat. The carnage that was once his amusement is now the impediment to his escape. Charles Albert pursues his quest in equally ironic terms: "defenseless realms receive his sway" (l. 244). But a "short sway" (l. 245) it is. He falls before the ambiguously motivated resistance of "the fierce Croatian," "the wild Hussar" (l. 249), and "all the sons of ravage" (l. 250). Disgraced and bewildered he suffers the derision of his foes and the blame of his subjects only to steal away finally to a death "from anguish and from shame" (l. 254). In **"The Vanity of Human Wishes,"** war is nothing more than a project, its proponents, ludicrous in their gigantic desires, nothing more than alumni of the Grand Academy of Lagado. The building-block structure of the poem presents "anguish" and "shame" as the fitting conclusion not only for Charles Albert but for all military schemers.

The five verse paragraphs dealing with the suppliant's prayer for "multitude of days" (l. 255) grotesquely reinforce their opening assurance that "life protracted is protracted woe" (l. 258). Another semi-dramatic vignette, thoroughly developed and worthy of Dickens or Waugh, brings on the figure of the listless-eyed "dotard" (l. 263) on his deathbed, puzzled that his meats are tasteless and his wines without joy. He is one of those who has prayed for long life, in health, and, ironically, in sickness. "Dotard" emphasizes the poem's detachment from and severity towards this scene. Perhaps Johnson puns here on the homonym *dottard,* a word he says that "seems to signify a tree that has been kept low by cutting." For it is only the dying trunk of the old man that dominates the grisly scene. In a ludicrous dance of death, the minstrels try vainly to "diffuse the tuneful lenitives of pain" (l. 268). But the dotard remains insensible. As the scene expands from the deathbed, the sneering figures of "the fawning niece and pamper'd guest" (l. 276) emerge: she, fawning to acquire, he, pampered to stay. The watch is tedious: hopes of a legacy can scarcely awe "the gath'ring sneer" (l. 277). A ridiculous yet macabre cacophony swells in the room: as the minstrels play to their insensible audience, the old man adds the cacophonous counterpoint that crowds his tongue: "everlasting dictates . . . / Perversely grave, or positively wrong" (ll. 273-74). Watchful guests, part of that army of malicious and always acquisitive bystanders marching through the poem, appear here too in order to manipulate the dotard against son and daughter with criticism he is only too willing to hear. All the scorn of the scene is condensed into the grim pun that concludes the first verse paragraph of the sketch: they "mould his passions till they make his will" (l. 282). What is left for him except to die? Yet, however lifeless in trunk and branch, Avarice lives "unextinguish'd" (l. 285) in him. With a heart anxious over possible losses, his "cripled hands" (l. 287) defy arthritic pain to review his debtors and mortgages. Suspicious to the end, he "unlocks his gold, and counts it till he dies" (l. 290), a remorselessly presented picture of an old man, defying physical, mental, and emotional debility, to become in death a set of fingers counting coins.

The two verse paragraphs that follow appear to offer a startling yet welcome contrast to this scene. Not everyone, after all, must die a physically and mentally enfeebled miser. What of a virtuous old age, melting away with "unperceiv'd decay" (l. 293), sliding innocently and imperceptibly into death, endearing "peaceful day" (l. 295) with benevolence, and cheering night with "congratulating Conscience" (l. 296)? "Such age there is, and who would wish its end?" (l. 298). Many a reader of the poem perhaps. This first of two verse paragraphs presents what has often been styled a compassionate view of old age. But this first paragraph is a question, and one not devoid of irony: does the possibility of such a sunset justify the wish for a longer day? The answer comes only in the next paragraph. Virtue does not confer an exemption from misfortune. The load of woes flung on the exemplary elderly are manifold and severe. Johnson's diction reinforces this view. Every sunrise dawns on a new sorrow: friendship is "lacerated" (l. 304) by death; year "chases" year, and decay "pursues" decay (l. 305) with relentless speed; and like a vessel near the end of its bountiful contents, joy continuously "drops" from "with'ring life away" (l. 306). Soon "new forms arise, and different view engage" (l. 307). The now superfluous veteran from an earlier stage of human life and activity receives the call to retire in peace. The concessory quality of such a possibility is grim, severe, and unrelenting, yet the next verse paragraph stresses that the concession is limited to "few" (l. 311)! Whatever light and attractive colors flicker in this small bit of Johnson's mosaic, they are dwarfed and overshadowed by the grim colors of the miser's death which precedes and the equally somber hues of the macabre panorama that concludes the poem's sketch of old age. "Life's last scene" (l. 315) is thronged with the carnival-like attractions of surprising monsters, "prodigies" (l. 315). Playing Juvenal's Priam and Hecuba, Marlborough becomes a reservoir of dotage and Swift—the choice of words is key—"expires a driv'ler and a show" (l. 318). Through Johnson's grotesquely effective satiric vision and imagination, Jonathan Swift, in the slaver of senility, is transformed into his own Struldbrugg.

In the overall structure of **"The Vanity of Human Wishes"** the major exempla and the specific vanities they embody reveal with unmistakable clarity the steadily focused object of the poem's attack: vain, merely human, desire. Foolish, insubstantial, and unextenuated appetite takes the already difficult situation of man, described in the opening paragraphs of the poem, and compounds it by chasing "treach'rous phantoms" (l. 9) in so many guises. Man is driven to rest his happiness in something external, something he cannot control. And in this way, Fortune, ironically, does become his goddess. The itch, the fever, the enthusiasm lead to the consequences so pathetically apparent in the poem. Each of the exempla is beaten on his or her own terms; no heavenly judgment chastises them or renders sentence. They are beaten because they have placed their fates out of their own hands by building a fabric of desire that can be laid only on the undermining foundation of the venal and equally acquisitive fools they have supplanted. They are not thrust into these situations; they create them. Hope, desire, fear, and hate, manifesting themselves particularly in boldness, self-indulgence, power, restlessness, and the search for gold—that "wide-wasting pest" (l. 23)—bring them all to the inevitable doom. Johnson's conclusion arises very nicely out of all that has gone before. Ardor and passion, which are inextricably a part of human appetite, cannot receive ludicrous Stoic denial in sedate dispassion, as he "rolls darkling down the torrent of his fate" (l. 346). The intensity of human desire must be recognized and then redirected towards the construction of a fabric man can raise: the internal disciplining of those appetites into patience, obedience, and a love whose demands cannot be exhausted. Where in the exempla has there been the slightest evidence of such internal control? The man willing to set aside their pernicious, ridiculous, and contemptible example in order to embark on this never-ending quest creates his own moral order and equilibrium. Happiness comes of his own making, in his own control, relying on forces within rather than on accidents without. So Fortune is dethroned. Internal moral order results from this muscular, dynamic act. With the effort, "celestial wisdom calms the mind / And

makes the happiness she cannot find" (ll. 366-67) in the externally dependent schemes of men.

Johnson brings us to this point by his skillful use of the major exempla and their wider function in the survey of specific vanities explored in the poem. Each figure and each folly struts from compromised entrance to anticlimactic defeat and departure. Wolsey moves from "full blown dignity" to recriminating death, to but one of several instances of the self-indulgent search for power. The enthusiastic young scholar suffers many setbacks until he too, insuperable in fantasy, must heed the grim warning in the fatal learning that brings Laud to the block. Military ambition of whatever time and place ends in shame and derision, whatever the colossal pretensions that set it into motion. The miserly old man, granted his wish for long life, is but one of many prodigies in the grotesque gallery of the old. And Beauty, heedless, flimsy, and superficial, retires to "hissing infamy" (l. 342). **"The Vanity of Human Wishes,"** Johnson's theater of "idle shew" after "idle shew," does not extenuate this survey with explanatory reply. The exempla march on, already judged, already compromised, through a series of defeats and reversals to be dismissed at the end in pathetic lack of self-awareness. Doom teaches these figures no lessons. The judicial tone that denies extenuation to these fools and follies works together with so much satiric skill in diction, imagery, structure, and tone that sympathetic identification with these victims is rendered impossible. The recurringly unequivocal judgments offer no ground for such loss of detachment. Who wants to be like Wolsey, or even like "the morning worshiper" (l. 80), surrendering self-respect to assume the folly, wickedness, malice, and even insanity unequivocally presented as such in the poem? As Howard Weinbrot observed, the people of the **"Vanity"** do not play for stakes worth having." With satiric contempt, severity, ridicule, and wit, the *dramatis personae* of this farce enter in delusion and exit, not with a bang, but with a whimper: "They mount, they shine, evaporate, and fall." If Samuel Johnson, in **"The Vanity of Human Wishes,"** be not a satirist, where is satire to be found? (pp. 37-45)

Thomas Jemielity, " 'The Vanity of Human Wishes': Satire Foiled or Achieved?," in Essays in Literature, *Vol. XI, No. 1, Spring, 1984, pp. 35-48.*

Geoffrey Hughes   (essay date 1984)

[*In the following excerpt, Hughes discusses Johnson's concerns about the "corruptions" of the English language exerted by "the French, high society, low society, and commerce."*]

In focusing exclusively on Samuel Johnson's role as "a harmless drudge", as he ironically defined the function of the lexicographer, one is, of course, isolating the most famous of his numerous talents. For Johnson, being in addition poet, essayist, novelist, critic, dramatist, conversationalist, pundit and wit, was a literary factotum who might plausibly, if incongruously, be termed a Renaissance Augustan man, or an Augustan Renaissance man.

The titles which were bestowed on him—Ursa Major, implying a constellation of talent, as well as a bearing for literary and critical navigation, and the great Cham of Literature—were not foreseeable when he single-handedly undertook the vast labour of the ***Dictionary*** in 1746. For his writings up to that point had been technically, if not actually, anonymous. (p. 99)

In some nine years he had produced his prodigious *magnum opus,* which the President of the Accademia della Crusca, founded in 1582 for the purification of the Italian language, described as a "very noble work, a perpetual monument of fame to the author [and] an honour to his own country". When Boswell later had the uncharacteristic temerity to suggest that Johnson had not known what he was undertaking, Johnson trenchantly replied:

> I knew very well what I was undertaking, and very well how to do it, and have done it very well.

As usual, few people have seriously disagreed with him. His dictionary may have been overrated in his own time, since a standard was felt to be lacking, and Johnson supplied it with the Augustan virtues of strong-minded intelligence, sanity, clarity and wit. There were then few who could knowledgeably cavil at the deficiencies of his etymology, his bias, his ignorance of "Teutonick", for the great integrating philological discoveries of the nineteenth century lay far ahead. And even when the fine monument of Murray's *Dictionary,* as the *OED* was called by an earlier generation, took shape, Johnson's contribution, particularly the magisterial intelligence and felicitous exactitude of his definitions, was often acknowledged by a simple bracketed capital J.

It would be very easy (and perhaps more profitable) to take up these proceedings with quotations from the ***Dictionary,*** but I shall content myself and, I hope you, with one definition, that of *pedant,* a beast known to us all but quintessentially captured by that most humane of scholars as "A man vain of low knowledge; a man awkwardly ostentatious of his literature". Not surprisingly, Murray recognized this gem (and many others) by simply reproducing it.

Of course, Johnson's was not the first dictionary in English. Ever since the publication of Robert Cawdrey's *Table Alphabeticall of Hard Usuall English Words* in 1604, dictionaries had been growing in size, scope and complexity. Johnson certainly had the benefit of the considerable works of Nathan Bailey, a Stepney schoolmaster, and it has been found that "Johnson's word list and definitions bear a strong resemblance to Bailey's". But it is also true that "under the letter 'L' Johnson included 394 words not found in Bailey, but omitted 909". Though Bailey was in some ways more erudite, Johnson's work became immediately the pre-eminent, authoritative standard.

Like most of the "choice and master spirits of the age", Johnson was highly sensitive and extremely concerned about corruptions in a language which was seen as being in a state of decline. In a memorably pessimistic aphorism, he remarked that "tongues, like governments, have a natural tendency to degeneration". In this view he was broadening the observation of Pope in *An Essay on Criticism:*

> Our sons their fathers' failing language see,
> And such as Chaucer is, shall Dryden be.
>
> (ll. 482-83)

In Johnson's time, of course, prescriptive and proscriptive linguistic attitudes were dominant, in spite of this fatalistic sense of decay and decline which permeated thinking in language matters. His original stance was strongly prescriptive, very much in the manner of a linguistic Newton come to impose order on unruly philology:

> When I took the first survey of my undertaking, I found our speech copious without order, and energetick without rules: wherever I turned my view, there was perplexity to be disentangled, and confusion to be regulated . . .

Swift, whose thinking was often more acutely political than that of his contemporaries, had asserted political causes for linguistic decay. In his *A Proposal for Correcting, Improving and Ascertaining the English Tongue* (1712) he posited this causation:

> The Period wherein the English Tongue received most Improvement, I take to commence with the Beginning of Queen Elizabeth's reign, and to conclude with the Rebellion in Forty-Two. From the Civil War to this present time, I am apt to doubt whether the Corruptions in our Language have not at least equalled the Refinements of it; and these Corruptions very few of the best Authors in our Age have wholly escaped. During the Usurpation [as he damningly referred to the Protectorship], such an Infusion of Enthusiastic Jargon prevailed in every Writing, as was not shaken off in many Years after. To this succeeded the Licentiousness which entered with the Restoration, and from infecting our Religion and Morals fell to corrupt our Language.

Swift's mode of confronting those impurities and "barbarisms" was, typically, by means of ironic parody in letters to the *Tatler.* In one of these in 1710 he urged the editor, Steele, "to make use of your authority as Censor, and by an annual *index expurgatorius* expunge all words and phrases that are offensive to good sense, and condemn all those barbarous mutilations of vowels and syllables".

Johnson was quite specific about the detrimental causes. In his view there were four: the French, high society, low society and commerce.

"The great pest of speech", he asserted, "is frequency of translation." This process surreptitiously imported hundreds of words and, worse, dozens of idioms. Johnson's particular *bête noire* was the French influence which, if it continued unchecked would, in his view, "reduce us to babble a dialect of France".

Of course, the touching vehemence of Johnson's xenophobia or Francophobia only underscores the irony that Englishmen have been babbling a dialect of France ever since 1066. But his hostility was not an individual quirk: it was shared by many of his contemporaries, notably Addison, who in 1711 had written an essay in the *Spectator* deriding the absurd excesses of French influence, and seriously suggesting some form of linguistic control:

> I have often wished that, as in our constitution there are several persons whose business is to watch over our laws, our liberties and commerce, certain men might be set apart as superintendents of our language, to hinder any words of foreign coin from passing among us; and in particular to prohibit any French phrases from becoming current in this king-

dom, when those of our own stamp are altogether as valuable.

This hostility to foreign linguistic infiltration, declared in emotive terms and with the analogy of monetary currency very much in the foreground, had been at the heart of the Inkhorn Controversy 200 years before Johnson's ***Dictionary***. Fine classical scholars like Sir John Cheke, Sir Thomas Chaloner and Thomas Wilson had strongly opposed the wholesale Latin and Greek borrowings of the Renaissance. Cheke, the first Professor of Greek at Cambridge, studiously (and absurdly) resuscitated native terms in his own writings and vehemently declared

> I am of this opinion, that our own tung should be written cleane and pure, unmixt and unmangeled with borrowing of other tunges, wherein if we take not heed by tijm, ever borrowing and never paye-ing, she shall be fain to keep her house as bankrupt.

His sympathizers chimed in with phrases such as "counterfeiting the King's English" and "pouder[ing] their books with ynkehorne termes".

These views, though strongly held, did not carry the day. A policy—or rather an adhocracy—of moderate borrowing became generally accepted. The Inkhorn Controversy simmered down to a good old English compromise. But linguistic xenophobia never dies out entirely.

Johnson clearly saw himself as one of Addison's "superintendents" or as Swift's "censor". "We have long preserved our constitution", he wrote, "let us make some struggles for our language." However, he bridled against the notion of an academy, which had been instituted in France in 1635. Indeed, his ambivalent attitude towards language control is clearly shown in this passage from his **"Preface"**:

> If an academy should be established for the cultivation of our stile, which I, who can never wish to see dependance multiplied, hope the spirit of English liberty will hinder or destroy, let them, instead of compiling grammars and dictionaries, endeavour, with all their influence, to stop the licence of translatours, whose idleness and ignorance, if it be suffered to proceed, will reduce us to babble a dialect of France.

Johnson clearly acted out his hostility to French terms by excluding many from his dictionary, though little or no research has been devoted to this aspect. French words seem to have been more fashionable during the earlier part of the century than when Johnson was compiling his dictionary. An analysis of the *Chronological English Dictionary* reveals an average recorded influx of at least half a dozen words per year during the reign of Queen Anne (1702-14), after which the flow is reduced to a trickle. I am referring here to words which have an obvious French timbre, like *coterie, ennui, connoisseur* and *casserole,* not to terms like *nationalist* and *civilisation,* which—though borrowed from French—have more clearly visible Latin roots.

Words excluded by Johnson (with the earliest *OED* citation) are:

corsage (1481)	champagne (1664)	riposte (1707)
sou (1556)	faux pas (1676)	debris (1708)
bourgeois (1564)	cortege (1679)	clique (1711)
esprit (1591)	contretemps (1684)	beau monde (1714)

unique (1602)	picturesque (1703)	reconnoitre (1714)
spa (1626)	casserole (1706)	bouquet (1716)
hauteur (1628)	cutlet (1706)	roulette (1734)
concierge (1646)	meringue (1706)	vampire (1734)
façade (1656)	envelope (1707)	coterie (1738)

and ennui (1732, though in fact mentioned by Evelyn in 1667)

Johnson, always a pragmatist, did not aim at a wholesale exclusion of French terms. But he did try to prevent the fashionable acceptance of those which, in his linguistic model, represented for him the qualities of "false refinement and declension". Thus *trait* is accepted, but with the hostile comment "scarce English". "*The sublime*", Johnson grudgingly admits, "is a Gallicism, but now naturalized", whereas *cajole* is simply, "a low word". *Voiture* and *role* are, paradoxically, "not in use". His general antipathy to borrowings which he regarded as unnecessary is summed up in this passage:

> The words which our authors have introduced by their knowledge of foreign languages, or ignorance of their own, by vanity or wantonness, by compliance with fashion, or lust of innovation, I have registered as they occurred, though commonly only to censure them, and warn others of the folly of naturalizing useless foreigners to the injury of the natives.

Johnson also employed the condemnatory labels of "a low word" or "cant" to discourage the use of a fair number of words. He often invoked the criterion of etymology, so that a word without respectable roots was regarded as an ill-bred parvenu. Thus *banter* is condemned to outer linguistic darkness as "a barbarous word, without etymology". (It has, of course, survived, despite this handicap, as have *dog, bird, pate* and *smell* whose etymologies are alike uncertain.) Some words regarded as "low" by Johnson still have a colloquial register: they include *bamboozle, budge, coax, flush* (in the sense of temporarily rich), *fuss, glum, job, sham, spick and span, squabble, swop, tiff, touchy, traipse* and—depending on one's attitude to the work ethic—*gambler*. Others, however, seem eminently respectable, such as *belabour, doff, dumbfound, ignoramus, sensible, simpleton* and *volunteer* (verb).

His policy towards the perpetually flourishing but generally unstable language of the underworld or cant was one of straight exclusion. Ironically these were the very words which had occasioned the earliest dictionaries of all, recording and explaining to a curious bourgeois populace the meanings of such terms as *cove, beak* and *fence*. These terms of the underground establishment were at least a century old by Johnson's time and are still heard today, more in some circles than in others.

At the opposing end of the register, he admitted many classically-derived words which Albert C. Baugh regards as having "a very questionable right to be regarded as belonging to the language". Noah Webster even believed that the inclusion of such recherché terms as *assation, ataraxy, conclusible, detention, incompossibility, indigitate* and thousands of others jeopardized the ***Dictionary's*** right to be a "safe standard of writing" and perhaps even constituted a "corruption of the English Language".

Though the adjective *Johnsonian* now denotes alternatively commonsensical wit or polysyllabic elegance in syntax, it would be misleading to see him as solely biased towards classical derivations, for he included without comment several of the four-letter words (though Bailey was the only editor of the time to challenge the taboos of the time by including *all*). In addition he accepted *haggle, hatchet-faced, hen-pecked, huff, jailbird, noodle, numskulled, oaf, pettyfogger, piddle, swig* and *tidbit* without demur. These are liberal inclusions from a man who regarded the "fugitive cant" of the "laborious and mercantile part of the people" as "unworthy of preservation".

Johnson also perceived that affectation in the higher echelons of society contributed to semantic decay. It took the form of exaggerated or melodramatic applications of serious words to trivial contexts. He was diagnosing what is today called *verbicide,* as C. S. Lewis applied the term of Oliver Wendell Holmes, or *weakening.* Johnson's condemning term was the adjective "ludicrous".

It is found in *desperately* as in "she fell despeately in love" from Addison's *Spectator.* Similarly, in *abominable:* "in low and ludicrous language, it is a word of loose and indeterminate censure". *Anthropophaginian* is a "ludicrous word, formed by Shakespeare from *anthropophagi* for the sake of a formidable sound".

Within this area of exaggeration he detected a particular syndrome of feminine affectation. These words he simply condemned as "women's words". *Frightful,* he noted, was "a cant word among women for anything unpleasing"; *flirtation* in the sense of a "quick sprightly motion" is similarly categorized, while *horrid* in women's cant is "shocking; offensive; unpleasing". The echoes can still be heard in fashionable suburbs.

It is very easy to dismiss Johnson's Gallophobia as an academic or nationalist tic and to reject his ostracism of "low" and "ludicrous" usage as the inflexible prescriptivism of an authoritarian age. But even in our times, with their increasingly descriptive ethos, whether eager or grudging in its acceptance of popular usage, one can only admire Johnson's broad, acute and prescient analysis of the insidious effects of commerce:

> Total and sudden transformations of a language seldom happen; conquests and migrations are now very rare: but there are other causes of change, which though slow in their operation, and invisible in their progress, are perhaps as much superiour to human resistance, as the revolution of the sky, or intumescence of the tide. Commerce, however necessary, however lucrative, as it depraves the manners, corrupts the language . . .

Johnson is, of course, describing here a subtle shift in values and in the credibility of many terms, not a clearly isolatable group of key words. One is dealing more with a syndrome than with an influx, with a cynical convention of exaggeration on the part of the advertiser and a cynical connivance on the part of the reader or customer.

As he wrote in the *Idler* of 1759:

> Advertisements are now so numerous that they are very negligently perused, and it is therefore become necessary to gain attention by magnificence of promises, and by eloquence sometimes sublime and sometimes pathetic. Promise, large Promise is the soul of an Advertisement.

Johnson perceived that advertising was even in his time acquiring that convention of incredibility which is now dignified by the legal loophole of "legitimate puffery". Though he might be shocked at the extent of the "hypnotic mendacities of the mass media" and of the institutionalized illiteracy of advertising, he had perceived their root causes.

Even more profound was his perception that there are linguistic forces "superiour to human resistance".

> Those who have been persuaded to think well of my design require that it should fix our language, and put a stop to those alterations which time and chance have hitherto been suffered to make in it without opposition. With this consequence I will confess that I flattered myself for a while; but now begin to fear that I have indulged expectation which neither reason nor experience can justify.

Taking the unanswerable example of human mutability, he continues

> . . . with equal justice may the lexicographer be derided, who being able to produce no example of a nation that has preserved their words and phrases from mutability, shall imagine that *his* dictionary shall embalm *his* language . . .

In similar vein he spoke of the conceit and futility of seeking to "enchain syllables".

Johnson has traditionally been part of a process of 'paternalization', an aspect of the mythology which glorifies individuals of supreme talent who have an intuitive affinity with the *sprachgeist* or spirit of the language. Such a mythology has necessarily declined as the traditional regime of prescriptivism has given way to one of descriptivism, in which language is seen as having its own laws of development which make it impervious to legislation. "Dictionary" Johnson has, perhaps, been lionized as much as a lexicographer as a personality. But his remarkable insights into the complexity of the relationship between language and society and the profound, clairvoyant pessimism of his Preface make him worthy of the accolades of the past, in ways which the past did not fully appreciate:

> As by the cultivation of various sciences, a language is amplified, it will be more furnished with words deflected from their original sense; the geometrician will talk of a courtier's zenith, or the excentrick virtue of a wild hero, and the physician of sanguine expectations and phlegmatick delays. Copiousness of speech will give opportunities to capricious choice, by which some words will be preferred, and others degraded; vicissitudes of fashion will enforce the use of new, or extend the signification of known terms. The tropes of poetry will make hourly encroachments, and the metaphorical will become the current sense: pronunciation will be varied by levity or ignorance, and the pen must at length comply with the tongue; illiterate writers will at one time or other, by public infatuation, rise into renown, who, not knowing the original import of words, will use them with colloquial licentiousness, confound distinction, and forget propriety.

Johnson had, in short, learnt the hard lesson that language is capricious, socially determined and uncontrollable. And yet, paradoxically, his magnificent example inspired the serious, responsible and disciplined attitude to language and the appeal to authority which are still prevalent today. (pp. 99-106)

Geoffrey Hughes, "Johnson's Dictionary and Attempts to 'Fix the Language'," in English Studies in Africa, *Vol. 28, No. 2, 1985, pp. 99-107.*

Malcolm Muggeridge   (lecture date 1984)

[*An English man of letters, Muggeridge has a long reputation as an iconoclast. A socialist and outspoken atheist during the 1930s, he later eschewed socialism and embraced Christianity during the 1960s, which did nothing to mitigate his stinging satire. Organized religion, public education, and egalitarianism were all the objects of his scorn. In the following excerpt from the text of a lecture delivered in 1984, and then published in the* Tablet, *he inspects the religious aspect of Johnson's life, particularly his notion of sin and death.*]

The documentation of Dr Johnson's life is extremely full. There is his assiduous biographer, James Boswell, who travelled with him, listened to him, stirred up his indignation like a matador with his Bull. Also Mrs Thrale, who subsequently became, to Dr Johnson's great indignation, Mrs Piozzi. She knew him intimately, loved him dearly, and recorded her memories of him truthfully and affectionately. There were biographers and numerous reminiscent friends such as Sir John Hawkins, Anna Seward, Arthur Murphy, not to mention the Doctor's own memories, which were liable to pop up, for instance in his *Lives of the Poets* and accounts of his travels.

There is, however, one aspect of Dr Johnson's life, and that a vital one, which is for the most part only superficially conveyed by his friends and biographers—his religion. They knew well enough how seriously he took his religion, if only because of the way he silenced anyone who ventured in his company to introduce an element of facetiousness into a religious discussion. At the time of his death in 1784, he was collecting together prayers he had written down with a view to publishing them, but he died before the task was satisfactorily completed. Even so, the collection of prayers was there, and was subsequently deposited in the library of Pembroke College, Oxford, where Dr Elton Trueblood had access to them sorting them out and arranging them with suitable headings so that they may be read and studied, not just as individual prayers, but as the story of Dr Johnson's inward or spiritual life as distinct from his outward and intellectual life. Blake writes of a Golden String which we must follow:

I give you the end of a Golden String,
Only wind it into a ball,
It will lead you in at Heaven's Gate
Built in Jerusalem's Wall.

The sequence of prayers that Dr Johnson wrote, and that Dr Trueblood has arranged, may be seen as a verbal Golden String, leading, like the others, to Heaven's Gate in Jerusalem's Wall.

I have the good fortune to know Dr Trueblood, a fine scholar and a devout Christian. His handling of the Prayers relates them to one another and to Dr Johnson's own circumstances and aspirations. They are collected into one small volume, with a helpful introduction by Dr Trueblood which sets the scene. Dr Johnson's religious concern began in 1729 when he was twenty, and continued

till his death at seventy-five. The spirit of the age, rather like ours, encouraged scepticism, to the point of assuming that all intelligent people found Christian zeal just amusing. In those days too they had their Don Cupitts. Dr Johnson's piety somehow transcends all this. In his essays he has to take account of the sceptical spirit of the age; in his prayers he is concerned only with his relationship with his Creator and the well-being, spiritual and physical, of those who were dear to him. Thus he prays that he may be delivered from carnal thoughts and impulses, that he may be more regular and assiduous in his work, that however afflicted his body may be God will spare his understanding. Dr Trueblood quotes him as saying in the last paragraph of the last issue of **The Rambler,** a periodical he founded, "The essays professedly serious, if I have been able to execute my own intentions, will be found exactly conformable to the precepts of Christianity and without any accommodation to the licentiousness and levity of the present age."

In a materialist society prayers tend to be a kind of celestial shopping-list; they ask on high for favours, and glory in reminiscences of special responses, sometimes pecuniary, that may have been received. Dr Johnson's prayers are more in the vein of waiting on God; they offer penitence rather than asking for this or that, and earnestly seek help in extricating themselves from any worldly or carnal pursuits in which they may have been involved. In his poem *Prayer* George Herbert assembles a dazzling array of poetic images:

Prayer, the Church's banquet, Angels' age,
God's breath in man returning to his birth,
The soul in paraphrases, heart in pilgrimage,
The Christian plummet, sounding heaven and earth;
Engine against the Almighty, sinner's tower.
Revered thunder, Christ-side-piercing spear,
The six-days' world transposing in an hour.
A kind of tune, which all things hear and fear;
Softness, and peace, and joy, and love, and bliss,
Exalted manna, gladness of the best,
Heaven in ordinary, man well drest,
The milky way, the bird of paradise.
Church-bells beyond the stars heard, the soul's blood,
The land of spices, something understood.

As for waiting on God:

How, then, with fantasy pouring in continuously and variously from every direction, is it possible to find, and to hold on to, reality? I have found, or perhaps I may say been shown, a way which, somewhat diffidently, I herewith describe. First, quite deliberately, make a little clearing in the dark jungle of our ego and will in order to let in light. This involves much cutting down of nettles and brambles, for which I recommend wearing gloves. Then, with patience and true humility, wait on God (note 'on' not 'for'), whose presence, when it comes, as it assuredly will, brings everything into sync. So that out of confused sounds, words with a meaning emerge, and confused happenings sort themselves out and become recognisable. In other words, what seemed to be a Theatre of the Absurd, as Shakespeare puts it, full of sound and fury, signifying nothing, becomes a Theatre of Fearful Symmetry, in which the stage is the universe, and the cast is all mankind, and all the action, be it as minute as a leaf falling, or as far-reaching as a journey to the moon, has its own being and significance as belonging to God's creation, and so being a participant in His purpose for it.

A criticism that is lodged against Dr Johnson is that he is given to melancholy. This, up to a point, is true; he has found life in some respects disappointing, and anyway the cult of cheerfulness is not one that appeals to him. Apart from any other consideration, it conflicts with Christianity, which, as he understands it, is based on a man being crucified, and has taken the Cross as its symbol, in this going right back to the Apostle Paul. His attitude towards the settlers across the Atlantic Ocean in what is now the United States is far from sympathetic. "How is it," he asks, thinking of the role of the slave-traders in the newly developing country, "that we hear the loudest yelps for liberty come from the drivers of slaves?" No answer to his question was forthcoming then, or ever has been. There still lingered about inside him a dream of being offered some distinguished post like an embassy or the governorship of a colonial territory. Boswell, sensing this, took upon himself to remark to Dr Johnson that he wondered how so distinguished a citizen, now provided with a State pension, should be overlooked when it came to filling important posts. All he got in reply was a growl—"You may wonder, Sir." Dr Johnson had provided himself with his own cover-up in the shape of the carefully phrased farewell words of the Sage in *Rasselas.* He had just been told by Imlac that he might at least recreate himself with the recollection of an honourable and useful life, and enjoy the praise which all agree is due to him:

> 'Praise', said the sage, with a sigh, 'is to an old man an empty sound. I have neither mother to be delighted with the reputation of her son, nor wife to partake the honours of her husband. I have outlived my friends and my rivals. Nothing is now of much importance; for I cannot extend my interest beyond myself. Youth is delighted with applause, because it is considered as the earnest of some future good, and because the prospect of life is far extended: but to me, who am now declining to decrepitude, there is little to be feared from the malevolence of men, and yet less to be hoped from their affection or esteem. Something they may yet take away, but they can give me nothing. Riches would now be useless, and high employment would be pain. My retrospect of life recalls to my view many opportunities of good neglected, much time squandered upon trifles, and more lost in idleness and vacancy. I leave many great designs unattempted, and many great attempts unfinished. My mind is burdened with no heavy crime, and therefore I compose myself to tranquillity; endeavour to abstract my thoughts from hopes and cares, which, though reason knows them to be vain, still try to keep their old possession of the heart; expect, with serene humility, that hour which nature cannot long delay; and hope to possess, in a better state, that happiness which here I could not find, and that virtue which here I have not attained.'

These are Dr Johnson's splendid words, and my soul echoes them. Nonetheless, it has to be admitted that he was terrified at the prospect of death, not because it meant the end of earthly living; rather because by his own estimation there was the possibility of finding himself in Hell. It was his sins rather than the termination of his mortal existence that troubled him; in particular three of the Seven Deadly Sins—lust, gluttony and sloth. The last of these has a spe-

cial association with writers. Who among them has not experienced the agony of hours, and sometimes days, with pen and paper ready to hand, an assignment unfulfilled and no words coming?

Also there is the question of Dr Johnson's mental condition. Certain eccentricities of behaviour and speech gave the impression that he was deranged, and perhaps mad. Indeed, with his scrofula and bad eyesight when he was born, in present circumstances there would have been a strong case for doing away with him at birth. Dr Johnson's own tolerance of eccentricity is well exemplified by a conversation he had with Dr Burney about the poet Christopher Smart who was supposed to be mad. "I do not think he ought to be shut up," Dr Johnson said. "His infirmities are not noxious to society. He insists on people praying with him, and I'd as lief pray with Kit Smart as anyone else. Another charge is that he does not love clean linen, and I have no passion for it myself." In the case of Dr Johnson's alleged madness, the suggestion has been made that when he was staying at Streatham as guest of the Thrales, he was subjected to some sort of beating treatment by Mrs Thrale. This strikes me as absurd.

One thing, ladies and gentlemen, seems to me to be certain; in Lichfield Dr Johnson will go on being remembered, not so much for his achievements as a writer as for the mysterious quality of greatness that he exudes. I like to think of him myself, not so much for what he has undoubtedly achieved, his *oeuvre,* some twenty volumes, his travels so well described, his conversation and observations recorded by Boswell and others, but rather in Bolt Court with the strange miscellany of people he assembled there. First, Robert Levet, described as a practiser in physic, on whose death Dr Johnson wrote some beautiful lines:

> Well tried through many a varying year,
> See Levet to the grave descend,
> Officious, innocent, sincere,
> Of every friendless name the friend. . . .
>
> No summons mock'd by chill delay,
> No petty gain disdain'd by pride;
> The modest wants of every day
> The toil of every day supplied.
>
> His virtues walked their narrow round,
> Nor made a pause, nor left a void;
> And sure th' Eternal Master found
> The single talent well employ'd.

Along with him was Mrs Williams, a blind lady, about whom Boswell complained that when dispensing tea she used her finger to find out when the cups were full—a fastidiousness which came ill from Boswell in the light of complaints he had acquired in the course of his debaucheries. Then there were Pol Carmichael, "a Scotch wench", and Mrs Desmoulins, presumably of French descent. Finally, there was Frank, Dr Johnson's black servant, who served him faithfully over a number of years, and to whom the Doctor bequeathed whatever he possessed at the time of his death. There was no apartheid in Bolt Court.

By the deathbed of Catherine Chambers, a servant for many years in his mother's household, Dr Johnson is quite at his best. Alone with her, and kneeling by her, he prays that "the sense of her weakness may add strength to her faith, and seriousness to her repentence." Together, they hope to meet again in a better place; then kiss and part.

As his old friends die off he mourns for them; in the case of Garrick producing a superb requiem: "But what are the hopes of men? I am disappointed by that stroke of death which has eclipsed the gaiety of nations, and impoverished the public stock of harmless pleasure." His **"Life of Savage"** in his ***Lives of the Poets,*** one of his finest achievements, concludes with a masterly sentence: "Those are no proper judges of his (Savage's) conduct who have slumbered away their time on the down of plenty, nor will any wise man presume to say, 'Had I been in Savage's condition, I should have lived or written better than Savage.'" (pp. 47-54)

Malcolm Muggeridge, "Dr. Johnson Looks Heavenward," in his Vintage Muggeridge: Religion and Society, *edited by Geoffrey Barlow, William B. Eerdmans Publishing Company, 1985, pp. 45-55.*

T. F. Wharton   (essay date 1984)

[*In the following excerpt, Wharton treats the principal theme of the "Idler" essays, noting that idleness was of "the utmost personal importance to Johnson."*]

It is generally agreed that **The Idler** is altogether a lighter affair than **The Rambler.** The essays are shorter. There is a quite new sprinkling of topical material. There is an attempt to lighten the style. There is even, in the portrait of 'the ponderous dictator of sentences' (31) or of Sober (36), a parody of Johnson's **Rambler** persona. Even where the **Rambler** tone detectably creeps back, there is a far lower level of moral exhortation than in the earlier periodical.

However, in one sense, **The Idler** is more daring than its predecessor. It handles material of a deep and radical nature; material of which Johnson had a lifelong fear.

The point of entry to such topics is the title-theme of idleness itself. It is a theme of the utmost personal importance to Johnson, obsessed as he was with idleness as sin. Needless to say, the development of this and its related topics is at the expense of others. The first issue of the magazine, establishing the 'Idler' persona, claims that 'scarcely any name can be imagined from which less envy or competition is to be dreaded'. This in itself gives an indication of how completely **The Rambler**'s master-theme of envy now disappears. There are perhaps just two survivals of the powerful theme of neglected merit: the naturalist-author of no. 55, and Gelaleddin the scholar in no. 75. There are only two survivors (nos 29 and 42) of stories of the miseries of dependants. Again, there are just a couple of stories on the subject of marital miseries (nos 28 and 54).

Idleness, on the other hand engrosses the series. There is little of the **Rambler**'s tendency to stress the brevity of life, and the proper use of time as a sacred duty. Rather, the general topic of idleness is used as an invitation to study the seductive distractions of the mind; or the comparative force exerted by mind over sensation. There are eight key essays on such topics in the series. The first is no. 18. In it, the 'correspondent' undertakes to look into a kind of error which, since it is pleasurable in its effects, is rarely examined ('The mind is seldom quickened to very vigorous operations but by pain. . . . We do not . . . willingly decline a pleasing effect to investigate its cause'). This error is, that 'Pleasure is . . . seldom such as it appears

to others, nor often such as we represent it to ourselves.' Johnson proceeds to advance, with utter plausibility, the theory that happiness is a kind of conspiracy of appearances. Starting with the mixed motives of, for instance, concert-goers, among whom more go to be seen, than to hear, Johnson finds his real theme with the idea that each individual's pleasure on such occasions is the result of what might be described as mutual self-deception:

> To every place of entertainment we go with expectation, and desire of being pleased; we meet others who are brought by the same motives; no one will be the first to own the disappointment; one face reflects the smile of another, till each believes the rest delighted, and endeavours to catch and transmit the circulating rapture. In time, all are deceived by the cheat to which all contribute. The fiction of happiness is propagated by every tongue, and confirmed by every look, till at last all profess the joy which they do not feel, consent to yield to the general delusion; and when the voluntary dream is at an end, lament that bliss is of so short a duration.

This exquisite paragraph is unmatched by anything **The Rambler** has to offer. The only trace of a judgement passed is in the splendid comic final clause. The rest is an analysis that strikes the strongest chord of recognition. From the earlier periodicals, the closest Johnson approaches to this kind of analysis is in *The Adventurer* no. 120, some five years earlier; which pronounces that 'The world, in its best state, is nothing more than a larger assembly of beings, combining to counterfeit happiness which they do not feel.' This, however, turns out to be only a matter of keeping up the appearance of wealth. The **Idler** essay is a considerable development. Its only omission is of any explanation of the apparent contradiction, that all are eager to catch the universal rapture, and 'are deceived' by it, yet 'do not feel' the joy they profess. It is an omission which, in due course, Johnson proceeds to correct. No. 50 is the immediate sequel to one of **The Idler's** many portraits. This portrait is of 'Will Marvel' the raconteur, who embellishes the ordinary occurrences of his life into heroic adventures. Its sequel proceeds to excuse Will Marvel, on the grounds that his is merely an extreme manifestation of a universal tendency. Johnson describes how every man enhances what he experiences, either for the benefit of others, or of himself:

> It is certain that without some artificial augmentations, many of the pleasures of life, and almost all its embellishments, would fall to the ground. If no man was to express more delight than he felt, those who felt most would raise little envy. If travellers were to describe the most laboured performances of art with the same coldness as they survey them, all expectations of happiness from change of place would cease. The pictures of Raphael would hang without spectators, and the gardens of Versailles might be inhabited by hermits. All the pleasure that is received ends in an opportunity of splendid falsehood, in the power of gaining notice by the display of beauties which the eye was weary of beholding, and a history of happy moments, of which, in reality, the most happy was the last.

> The ambition of superior sensibility and superior eloquence disposes the lovers of arts to receive rapture at one time, and communicate it at another; and each labours first to impose upon himself, and then to propagate the imposture.

The last paragraph is the significant one, which solves the contradiction between the idea of 'rapture' and 'coldness'. Pleasure is not experienced spontaneously, but is an act of will, albeit an unconscious one. The mind is willed into a receptive and gullible state, so that it may deceive itself as to the quality of the sensory experience transmitted to it. As the reiterated words of 'labour' indicate, much effort is expended, both by the eye itself, and by the struggle to be enraptured. The mind is relieved when it is all over. The 'most happy' moment is 'the last'.

No. 24 is a similar essay. Taking its subject as mental torpor, it somewhat tormentingly fluctuates between direct philosophical discussion, with specific allusions to Locke and Malebranche, and frivolous caricatures of those who live without thought: 'of the sportsman in a rainy month, of the annuitant between the days of quarterly payment, of the politician when the mails are detained by contrary winds'. Its fourth paragraph, however, is entirely serious:

> It is reasonable to believe that thought, like everything else, has its causes and effects; that it must proceed from something known, done or suffered; and must produce some action or event. Yet how great is the number of those in whose minds no source of thought has ever been opened, in whose life no consequence of thought is ever discovered; who have learned nothing upon which they can reflect; who have neither seen nor felt any thing which could leave its traces on the memory; who neither foresee nor desire any change of their condition, and have therefore neither fear, hope, nor design, and yet are supposed to be thinking beings.

At first sight, this seems less depressing in its implications than the essays already discussed. The scathing tone at least implies the *availability* of sensation and reflection. These things are available by acts of will, and the essay concludes by urging that such efforts must be made. Another passage of the essay, however, is less sanguine:

> The waking hours are not denied to have been passed in thought, yet he that shall endeavour to recollect on one day the ideas of the former, will only turn the eye of reflection upon vacancy; he will find, that the greater part is irrevocably vanished, and wonder how the moments could come and go, and leave so little behind them.

The observation is offered as a universal one. The experience was a personal one. It was something he came to record in his *Diaries,* a few years later: 'my time has been unprofitably spent, and seems as a dream that has left nothing behind. My memory grows confused, and I know not how the days pass over me.' Johnson's awareness of the power of fantasy, present since **"London,"** combines, in this *Idler* essay, with one of his most potent metaphors, of a void. The 'eye of reflection', seeking some solid recollection of yesterday's experiences, finds only 'vacancy'. The passage leaves us with the unspoken question, whether the 'thought' of yesterday was not, even at the time, more illusory than real. It is intriguing that the essay's concluding exhortations to arouse the mind from torpor, still uses the language of illusion: 'the passage of life will be tedious and irksome to him who does not *beguile* it by diversified ideas'. The phrase, 'the passage of life', containing once again the metaphor of travel, also contains the ambiguous suggestion, reminiscent of his comments in the *Diaries,* of life passing over the traveller, rather than the other way about.

Three essays later, Johnson grapples with another aspect of 'idleness', and the relationship between mind and matter; the power of habit. He begins by looking at the commonplace moral advice, to know oneself and to reform. He argues that few have the moral energy to do so, preferring an inert 'plunge into the current of life'; but that even those who make the attempt at resolution are defeated by the force of habit. Once again, Johnson is dealing here with a strongly personal theme. No reader of his *Diaries* can miss the frequency with which he forms resolutions of better conduct, at the spiritual climacterics of each year. Each year, too, Johnson records in agony how the last resolutions have been broken. In recognising, in *Idler* 27, the power of habit, Johnson is, moreover, delivering a blow against one of his most cherished spiritual doctrines; of the freedom of the moral will:

> There is nothing which we estimate so fallaciously as the force of our own resolutions, nor any fallacy which we so unwillingly and tardily detect. He that has resolved a thousand times, and a thousand times deserted his own purpose, yet suffers no abatement of his confidence, but still believes himself his own master, and able, by innate vigour of soul, to press forward to his end, through all the obstructions that inconveniences or delights can put in his way.

There is no more telling concession in Johnson than that a man merely *'believes'* himself to be his own master. The breach of resolutions is not, he insists, a matter of hypocrisy. 'There is very little hypocrisy in the world.' 'We resolve to do right, we hope to keep our resolutions, we declare them to confirm our own hope . . . but at last habit prevails.' Not surprisingly, Johnson retreats from this extreme honesty by the end of the essay. Those who are in the power of evil habits 'must' conquer them. Those who are not yet subject to their influence 'may, by timely caution, preserve their freedom'. Yet, these saving clauses, and the use of cautious words such as 'most' and 'commonly' elsewhere, have to fight against at least one downright denial of free-will. Speaking of resolutions, Johnson says that, when forming a good intention, 'the whole soul yields itself to the predominance of truth, and readily determines to do what, when the time of action comes, will be at last omitted'.

This is a very considerable reversal of what Johnson has to say in his *Sermons.* Sermon 5, an important discussion of the problem of evil in the world, and of its compatibility with religious belief, offers the hypothetical prospect of a far happier state of man. If man were simply to improve, he might, 'by the general practice of the duties of religion', 'secure him[self] from misery'. Johnson sternly warns, 'Let no man charge this prospect of things, with being a train of airy phantoms; a visionary scene. . . . To effect all this, no miracle is required; men need only unite their endeavours, and exert those abilities, which God has conferred upon them, in conformity to the laws of religion.' The same Sermon upholds the very concept of free will. Without it, 'Men would be no longer rational, or would be rational to no purpose.' Yet, the ease with which he believes it can be exerted ('men need *only* unite their endeavours') is fundamentally at odds with the conclusions of *Idler* no. 27. In the Sermon, the vision of human improvement is real, not 'airy' or 'visionary'. This ties in with what one normally assumes to be Johnson's strong insistence on the real. One recalls his hatred of Berkeley's philosophy, his common-sense insistence that 'sensation is sensation'. Yet, time and again, the *Idler* essays seem to depict life itself as a kind of dream.

The idea is most fully developed in no. 32. This essay begins on the topic of sleep. Johnson notes with satisfaction the blow to human arrogance that the failure to explain so simple a thing as sleep represents. To sleep, perchance to dream. The rest of the essay turns to the subject of dreams; the dreams both of night and day. In *The Rambler,* Johnson had dealt with dreams in terms of a 'formidable and obstinate disease of the intellect' (no. 89). In *The Idler,* his handling of the subject is both more sensitive and more sympathetic. The relevant passage merits extended quotation:

> There is reason to suspect that the distinctions of mankind have more shew than value, when it is found that all agree to be weary alike of pleasures and of cares, that the powerful and the weak, the celebrated and obscure, join in one common wish, and implore from nature's hand the nectar of oblivion.
>
> Such is our desire of abstraction from ourselves, that very few are satisfied with the quantity of stupefaction which the needs of the body force upon the mind. Alexander himself added intemperance to sleep, and solaced with the fumes of wine the sovereignty of the world. And almost every man has some art, by which he steals his thoughts away from his present state.
>
> It is not much of life that is spent in close attention to any important duty. Many hours of every day are suffered to fly away without any traces left upon the intellects. We suffer phantoms to rise up before us, and amuse ourselves with the dance of airy images, which after a time we dismiss for ever, and know not how we have been busied.
>
> Many know no happier moments than those that they pass in solitude, abandoned to their own imaginations, which sometimes puts sceptres in their hands or mitres on their heads, shifts the scene of pleasure with endless variety, bids all the forms of beauty sparkle before them, and gluts them with every change of visionary luxury.
>
> It is easy in these semi-slumbers to collect all the possibilities of happiness, to alter the course of the sun, to bring back the past, and anticipate the future, to unite all the beauties of all seasons, and all the blessings of all climates, to receive and bestow felicity, and forget that misery is the lot of man. All this is a voluntary dream, a temporary recession from the realities of life to airy fictions; and habitual subjection of reason to fancy.
>
> Others are afraid to be alone, and amuse themselves by a perpetual succession of companions, but the difference is not great, in solitude we have our dreams to ourselves, and in company we agree to dream in concert. The end sought in both is forgetfulness of ourselves.

In this wonderful, mournful essay, Johnson drives deeper and deeper into his theme. Only with the 'sceptres' passage does the impetus slow down for elaboration. The essay is of course less radical than others in the series. It maintains its clear distinction between on the one hand a plain if painful reality and on the other a state of fantasy into which the mind voluntarily retreats. All the same, this is a far stronger acknowledgement of the power of fancy than the more orthodox Johnson would usually permit, being remarkably free from moralising. In fact, when 'misery is the lot of man', and it is acknowledged that 'Many have no happier hours' than their hours of fantasy, the passage conveys no strong sense that Johnson is prepared to condemn the dreamer. Elsewhere, he is far more severe. The fantasy which is here described as 'forgetfulness of ourselves' is represented in the *Sermons*—Sermon 3 is a good example—as forgetfulness of God. Arieh Sachs, working mostly from the *Sermons,* has stressed the side of Johnson which saw the power of fantasy in terms of spiritual danger, to be repressed. Yet here, in an *Idler* essay which is once again unmistakably self-inclusive, particularly in its final paragraph, Johnson extends an uncharacteristic absolution for his own failings and those of other men.

So far, then, Johnson has described a state (no. 24) in which existence almost loses its reality. Even when it seems more real, man may lose his ability to connect with it and influence it, because of the power exercised by mechanical habit (no. 27). He describes (no. 18) the necessity of 'enhancing' experience, so that its impact seems more real. He describes the mind's continual retreat from reality, since reality is painful (no. 32). All this has vital bearing on the topic of idleness, which entirely loses its sinful status when reality and decision are either illusory or unbearable. Johnson's last contribution to the analysis of mind and matter is his treatment of memory in essays 44 and 72.

In no. 44, he describes, in effect, the darkening of life. Acknowledging the existence of a period of life when all is new, and much delightful, he goes on to describe how this openness to experience diminishes with age, and how 'Then it is that the magazines of memory are opened.' Unfortunately, memory is invariably an afflictive power. Its 'agency is incessant'. Without it, 'there could be no other intellectual operation'. These are the opening assumptions of the essay. Yet, when, later in the essay, he comes to handle memory as an aspect of middle age, the 'treasures of remembrance' are seen to be 'blasted'. Memory is not a pure repository of truths, but rather is coloured by the pain of living experienced by each individual:

> The pleasure of recollecting speculative notions would not be much less than that of gaining them, if they could be kept pure and unmingled with the passages of life; but such is the necessary concatenation of our thoughts, that good and evil are linked together, and no pleasure recurs but associated with pain. Every revived idea reminds us of a time when something was enjoyed that is now lost, when some hope was yet not blasted, when some purpose had not yet languished into sluggishness or indifference.

The essay concludes with Themistocles' preference that, rather than learn an art of memory, he could be taught the art of forgetfulness. In a way which is strongly reminiscent of *Idler* 32, and the search for 'forgetfulness of ourselves', this essay decides that 'all shrink from recollection, and all wish for an art of forgetfulness'.

No. 72 pursues the same argument. It begins with the idea of the evanescence of human experience. As in *Idler* 24, Johnson argues how little real impact experience makes on the mind. He puts forward the idea that, if ways could be found of discarding what is useless, the mind would be more free to imprint forcibly what is significant. The rest of the essay, however, records the difficulty of such an idea. The 'memory' which he goes on to describe is one which is abandoned to its own embittered associations, its time being 'uselessly or painfully passed in the revocation of events, which have left neither good nor evil behind them, in grief for misfortunes either repaired or irreparable, in resentment of injuries known only to ourselves, of which death has put the authors beyond our power'. This essay turns out, somewhat unexpectedly, to be the most positive of the key essays of the series. 'Reason will, by a resolute contest, prevail over imagination.' Johnson urges constant employment, since only those 'to whom the present offers nothing will often be looking backward on the past'. He still acknowledges that 'The incursions of troublesome thoughts are often violent and importunate; and it is not easy to a mind accustomed to their inroads to expel them immediately by putting better images into motion.' In the end, the essays on memory take their place alongside the essay on fantasy and daydreams, in describing the mind's retreats from reality. The only difference is that, for Johnson, the memory seems far less pleasurable, handling, as it does, material which has once belonged to reality.

Throughout the key essays, Johnson is directly handling the controversial material of Enlightenment philosophy. He makes continual reference to the philosophers. The whole issue of idleness is jokingly cast in the mode of philosophy in the first essay of the series: 'Some philosophers have called [man] a reasonable animal. . . . Perhaps man may be more properly distinguished as an idle animal.' Johnson touches on the existence of matter, on the nature of mind, on the processes of mind including perception and memory, and on the topics of habit and identity. Finally, in the last and most significant of the key essays, no. 89, he turns to metaphysics. All the other essays have in a sense been preparing for this one. Continually underlying his examinations of daydreams, or memory, or the enhancement of experience is the assumption that 'misery is the lot of man'. The mind's flight from reality is a flight from pain. Even the failure to engage with reality is a failure to engage with pain; though torpor is itself a miserable condition. *Idler* no. 89 proceeds to ask the ultimate question, the question 'why': 'why the only thinking being of this globe is doomed to think merely to be wretched, and to pass his time from youth to age in fearing or in suffering calamities'.

The first explanation offered is of course the orthodox one of the fall of man. 'Misery and sin were produced together.' This is mentioned, however, only to be dismissed. The Garden of Eden is a 'state so remote from all that we have ever seen, that . . . our speculations upon it must be general and confused'. As a 'reason' for pain, therefore, the Fall is set aside. Johnson adopts instead a pragmatic theory that evil at least produces some good: 'Almost all the moral good which is left among us, is the apparent effect of physical evil.' He goes on to explain how none of the three traditional aspects of goodness (soberness, righteousness and godliness) would be practised, but for the enforcements of pain. (pp. 74-83)

The evil of disease enforces on the cautious a sober life. The evils of anarchy enforce a righteous one, since 'the pain of suffering wrong was greater than the pleasure of doing it'; and more positively, 'we are in danger of the same distresses, and may sometime implore the same assistance'. Finally, the evil of discontentment enforces a godly life. This is the most interesting part of the theory:

> Godliness, or piety, is elevation of the mind towards the supreme being, and extension of the thoughts to another life. The other life is future, and the supreme being is invisible. None would have recourse to an invisible power, but that all other subjects had eluded their hopes. None would fix their attention upon the future, but that they are discontented with the present. If the senses were feasted with perpetual pleasure, they would always keep the mind in subjection. Reason has no authority over us, but by its power to warn us against evil.

There are really two alternative explanations here, for the mind's potential resistance to the concept of a god. The one offered at the end of the paragraph is that the mind would, if permitted, be content with present gratifications. Only dissatisfaction in this life encourages the mind to look for gratification elsewhere. The other explanation is only half stated, but can be detected in the sentences, 'The other life is future, and the supreme being is invisible. None would have recourse to an invisible power, but that all other subjects had eluded their hopes.' These sentences seem to say more than that an afterlife is difficult to imagine. They imply that, to the human imagination, an afterlife is an unpalatable concept. But for the misery of the present existence, it would not be believed. (p. 84)

Johnson's philosophical affiliations in this essay are perhaps somewhat unexpected. His theory of 'godliness' finds him citing the idea of a social compact which, he says, 'one of the heathen sages [Plato] has shewn with great acuteness'. But what is not of course acknowledged is that the theory had been pursued far more recently by Hobbes, whom Johnson professed to abominate. As to the invisible power and the supreme being as aspects of human wishes, Johnson's closest companion here is Hume, whose comments on 'belief' include the theory that its 'effect . . . is to raise up a simple idea to an equality with our impressions, and bestow on it a like influence on the passions. This effect it can only have by making an idea approach an impression in force and vivacity.' Hume was another for whom Johnson professed loathing—with a violence which shocked Boswell—but there is a suggestive comment here from Johnson's contemporary, Richard Porson:

> A very old gentleman, who had known Johnson intimately, assured me that the bent of his mind was decidedly towards scepticism: that he was literally afraid to examine his own thoughts on religious matters; and that thence arose his hatred of Hume and other writers.

In fact, even in the *Sermons,* where one might expect to find Johnson at his most orthodox, echoes of Hume are to be found. Sermon 9 is a good example:

> All sin that is committed by Christians, is committed either through an absolute forgetfulness of

God, for the time in which the inordinate passion . . . prevails; or because, if the ideas of God and religion were present to our minds, they were not strong enough to overcome and suppress the desires excited by some object. So that either the love or fear of temporal good or evil, were more powerful than the love or fear of God.

All ideas influence our conduct with more or less force, as they are more or less strongly impressed upon the mind; and they are impressed more strongly, as they are frequently recollected or renewed. For every idea, whether of love, grief, fear, or any other passion, loses its force by time. . . . But by dwelling upon, and indulging any idea, we may increase its efficacy and force . . . and raise it to an ascendant over our passions.

The terminology of Hume is all here, but perversely and confusedly used. 'Idea' seems at one time cognate with 'passions' ('For every idea, whether of love, grief, fear, or any other passion'): at another time it seems to be superior to the passions ('By dwelling upon . . . any idea, we may . . . raise it to an ascendant over our passions'). The answer is of course that Johnson grants to the passions the status of an 'idea' when they are directed towards a worthy end. The 'love or fear of God' amounts to 'the *ideas* of God and religion'. The 'love or fear of temporal good or evil' remains, however, at the level of the 'desires', and should be extirpated. Likewise, *Rambler* no. 203 distinguishes between irrational hopes of mortal happiness, and a rational hope of heaven: 'that hope only is rational, of which we are certain that it cannot deceive us'. In all these examples, Johnson was using some of his own most basic terminology. 'Hope and fear, desire and hate' had been heavily used, from **"The Vanity of Human Wishes"** on. It was a terminology he applied equally to mundane desires and the ideas of religion. There was always the possibility in such a terminology that he might one day leave off the safety-catch of a separation of rational and irrational hopes. When that happened, God would emerge as the emanation of human wishes. This is what happened in *Idler* 89. There is only one other example in Johnson, and that is a private one: the note in his *Annals*, 'Faith in some proportion to Fear'. *Idler* 89 strongly resembles Hume's theory of belief raising up an idea to an equality with our impressions. The only substantial difference is that, rather than the idea influencing the passions, as in Hume, Johnson's passions seem to create the idea. God becomes the ultimate human wish, on which the disappointment of all else 'forces him to fix'. Religion takes its place among the other Johnsonian mechanisms of the mind.

Idler no. 89, and its conclusion that the 'vanity' of life '*forces* him to fix his hopes upon another state', is the culminating point of the personal doubts explored in the key essays of the series. It contains in particularly concentrated form all the major images which Johnson uses in connection with his fears. Chains, rivers, gulphs, mists (familiar from **"The Vanity of Human Wishes"**) and bubbles are all present. Worldly concerns, he concludes, 'chain down the mind . . . to the present scene; nor is it remembered how soon this mist of trifles must be scattered, and the bubbles that float upon the rivulet of life be lost for ever in the gulph of eternity'. Contrary to the impression of Porson's 'very old Gentleman', Johnson could and did confront his fears. It is moving to see the great Christian moralist do so. The only surprise is that his doubts are ex-plored in so comparatively light-weight a context. (pp. 85-7)

> *T. F. Wharton, in his* Samuel Johnson and the Theme of Hope, *Macmillan Press, 1984, 190 p.*

Michael D. Riley　(essay date 1985)

[*Riley is an American poet, critic, and educator who has contributed poetry to numerous periodicals as well as essays on Johnson, T. S. Eliot, and Maurice Merleau-Ponty. In the following excerpt, he posits that "London" is "divided in its deepest instincts between an inclusive philosophical irony capable of embracing the complex world . . . and a more limited normative irony taking on the usual satiric targets."*]

Samuel Johnson was by nature both ironist and satirist. Temperamentally and intellectually, Johnson found both modes powerfully expressive of human experience as he perceived it. Yet, despite that attraction, irony and satire rarely govern any of Johnson's work in a straightforward or uncomplicated way; both modes undergo alterations which tend to deny them finality. Ironic apprehension, in other words, exists for Johnson as a point of view demanding transcendence. In the present essay I would like to pursue the implications of this insight for Johnson's two major poems in English, **"London"** and **"The Vanity of Human Wishes"** (**"VHW"**), in the hope of furthering our appreciation not only of the poems themselves but also of the nature of Johnsonian irony.

"London" and **"VHW"** provide especially attractive vehicles for such analysis because irony is central to both works and because that irony is intensified by poetic context. As "imitations" of Juvenal's *Third* and *Tenth Satires*, respectively, both poems are firmly rooted in the poetic practice of their day, and both poems, owing to their common Juvenalian antecedents, have inevitable similarities. But their differences are even more instructive, and finally more important. The irony of **"London"** is straightforwardly satirical—what I would call *analytical* irony; yet many of **"London"**'s problems (for it has several) can be seen to arise from various displacements of precisely that ironic design; a different perspective impinges frequently but uncertainly, complicating the satiric surface. That complicating philosophical irony provides the essential ingredient of **"VHW"** not only a far greater poem than **"London"** but also a work rightly judged central to Johnson's thought. But the distinction between analytical and philosophical irony, although presented here merely as a helpful rather than a novel concept, perhaps deserves preliminary clarification.

Analytical irony is the type most often associated with satire. It tends toward the rhetorical, toward the status of a device more or less elaborate but always clearly grounded in a controlling normative context. Philosophical irony is exploratory, ultimate in its context but often tentative in practice, frequently mixed or even ambiguous in its final effects. Analytical irony illuminates and exemplifies the norm; philosophical irony questions the reliability or existence of the norm itself. We are reassured by the former, profoundly discomfited by the latter.

Both may be found together, of course, just as both may

be simple or subtle in execution and may be accompanied by many or few incidental ironies along the way. But their effects remain different, and when found together their union is likely to be uneasy. This is the case with **"London."** In the hands of the greatest ironists, however, this union can accomplish the richest artistic possibilities of the ironic mode. This seems to me the case of Pope in the conclusion of *The Dunciad* and of Swift in Book Four of *Gulliver's Travels* and in the "Digression Concerning Madness" in *Tale of a Tub.* It is also the case of Johnson in **"VHW."**

In such works, philosophical irony both complicates and completes the text by confronting the deepest implications of ironic apprehension itself: the threat of disharmony at the heart of existence and/or the failure of harmonizing intellect. The tension peculiar to these texts, however, reflects the finality of the struggle involved. The exploration is coherent, but the reign of order persistently threatens to break away, to reverse or destroy itself. At times the struggle may even surface as a conflict between what an author sees and what he claims to see; a struggle, that is, between a comprehensive imaginative grasp of the subject matter (its images, tonalities, rhetorical patterns as discovered by ironic apprehension), and the author's rational projection of what he claims it all adds up to. In the "Digression Concerning Madness," for example, Swift effectively lacerates traditional satiric targets such as beaus and kings even while he implies, quite powerfully, that madness is in fact the organizing principle of life—an implication which, if granted fully, would render satire itself impossible. Satire would be merely journalism.

But in the greatest works, like the "Digression," this struggle achieves formal coherence, while the evidence of the struggle immeasurably enriches the literary result. This circumstance manifests itself perfectly in **"VHW"** and may throw some light on that poem's complexities; it manifests itself imperfectly in **"London"** and may throw additional light on the nature of that poem's problems.

Juvenal's irony tends toward the philosophical in much the same manner as Swift's in "The Digression," and Juvenal's treatment of the apparently normative contrast between the city and country in the *Third Satire* clearly evidences that complexity of irony. Since that contrast also supplies Johnson's **"London"** with one of its major problems, the topic provides a doubly appropriate starting point.

The relevant passages from Juvenal would include the following:

> Despite the wrench of parting, I applaud my old friend's
> Decision to make his home in lonely Cumae—the poor
> Sibyl will get at least *one* fellow-citizen now!
> It's a charming coastal retreat, and just across the point
> From our smartest watering spot. Myself, I would value
> A barren offshore island more than Rome's urban heart:
> Squalor and isolation are minor evils compared
> To this endless nightmare of fires and collapsing houses,
> The cruel city's myriad perils—and poets reciting
> Their work in *August*!
>
> (*Juvenal,* lines 1-10)

The blend here is typical. Cumae is described as "charming" and right across from Baiae, "our smartest watering spot." Yet translator Peter Green reminds us in a note that "The rise of nearby Puteoli had turned [Cumae] into a backwater." Is Cumae a charming retreat or a backwater? Regardless, the narrator assures us that he himself would find even "squalor and isolation" "minor evils" compared to those found in Rome. The reader might well wonder about such an equation, since the evils supposedly outweighing "squalor and isolation" are in fact fires, faulty housing, and tedious poetry. But the final effect is humorous and subtly balanced: Juvenal daubs the country with the same ironic brush with which he paints everything else.

Similarly, in a lengthy section detailing how hard it is to be poor in Rome (164-186)—not only because of generalized Roman "inflation" but also because "every man jack of us / Is keeping up with his neighbors"—Umbricius compares life in Rome to the modest needs of life in "some rural village." There, "you'd be content enough / And happily wear a cloak of coarse blue broadcloth / Complete with hood," just like everyone else. In most of Italy, no one wears a toga "till the day he dies," not even on public holidays, and not even the magistrates, who "need no better badge of status / Than a plain white tunic." All this seems normative enough, yet even here a slight murmur intrudes. Though "cheerfully staged," those public holidays in their rural manifestation consist of "the same old shows as last year" put up in a "grassgrown theatre." Juvenal's approbation is not complete.

His most undiluted praise of the country occurs in these lines, but the praise goes by quickly:

> What countryman ever bargained, besides, for his house
> Collapsing about his ears? Such things are unheard-of in cool
> Praeneste, or rural Gabii, or Tivoli perched on its hillside,
> Or Volsinii, nestled amid its woodland ridges. But here
> We live in a city shored up, for the most part, with gimcrack
> Stays and props.
>
> (190-95)

All of these, Green notes, "were quiet rural retreats," although Gabii, like Cumae earlier, "was almost deserted."

The last relevant passage appears most frequently in discussions of Juvenal's handling of the country:

> If you can face the prospect of no more public games,
> Purchase a freehold house in the country. What it will cost you
> Is no more than you pay in annual rent for some shabby
> And ill-lit garret here. A garden plot's thrown in
> With the house itself, and a well with a shallow basin—
> No rope-and-bucket work when your seedlings need some water!
> Learn to enjoy hoeing, work and plant your allotment
> Till a hundred vegetarians could feast off its produce.
> It's quite an achievement, even out in the backwoods,
> To have made yourself master of—well, say one lizard, even.
>
> (225-34)

The exquisite balance here deserves the attention it has received, but it does not distinctly differ from Juvenal's treatment of the country as a whole: the country has excellent qualities, and comparison to Rome only enhances their attraction, but the country can hardly be termed either idyllic or convincingly normative. Indeed, no normative element sustains itself for long in any of Juvenal's work. His irony is always extrapolating its effects. And it is this ironic density, I believe, which most drew Johnson into Juvenal's intellectual and artistic orbit.

In **"London,"** however, Johnson does not consistently capture the full ironic potential of his source. He responds to it only fitfully, just enough to set up conflicting levels of irony in the poem. Essentially, in **"London,"** Johnson heightens the specifically normative irony suggested by his source in order to strengthen his own satiric attack; he even draws upon the sanctions of Christianity. (This heightening is most apparent, and most successful, in Johnson's contrast between England's glorious past and its degenerative present.) Yet Johnson cannot entirely resist the larger pull of Juvenal's philosophical irony. Its pessimism and inclusiveness spoke directly to Johnson's own deepest instincts. But neither can he find the means to unite these levels of irony, as he was later to do so brilliantly in **"VHW,"** and **"London"** founders in large part because it attempts to live in two dimensions of irony without building the necessary bridge between them.

These uncertainties of irony emerge most clearly in three areas: the contrast between city and country already mentioned, the integrity of Thales as narrator/satirist, and the moral equation drawn by the poem between the blind operation of "fate" and specifically human culpability. The problem with all of these areas is finally the same: it is the question of Johnson's (and thus the reader's) attitude toward each of them. In this case the contrast between city and country is entirely representative. In most respects Johnson's contrast seems designed to be straightforwardly analytical, a contrast between the iniquitous city and peaceful country. Yet enough goes wrong with this picture

Johnson's wife, Elizabeth Porter, whom he affectionately called "Tetty."

to raise at first the suspicion that Johnson's treatment is ironic. Eventually, another suspicion arises: that Johnson's treatment is simply confused.

The sections of **"London"** corresponding to those of the *Third Satire* are these:

> Tho' grief and fondness in my breast rebel,
> When injur'd Thales bids the town farewell,
> Yet still my calmer thoughts his choice commend,
> I praise the hermit, but regret the friend,
> Resolv'd at length, from vice and London far,
> To breathe in distant fields a purer air,
> And fix'd on Cambria's solitary shore,
> Give to St. David one true Briton more.
>
> For who would leave, unbrib'd, Hibernia's land,
> Or change the rocks of Scotland for the Strand?
> There none are swept by sudden fate away,
> But all whom hunger spares, with age decay:
> Here malice, rapine, accident, conspire,
> And now a rabble rages, now a fire;
>
>   (1-14)
>
> Grant me, kind heaven, to find some happier place,
> Where honesty and sense are no disgrace;
> Some pleasing bank where verdant osiers play,
> Some peaceful vale with nature's paintings gay;
> Where once the harrass'd Briton found repose,
> And safe in poverty defy'd his foes; (43-48)
>
> Has heaven reserv'd, in pity to the poor,
> No pathless waste, or undiscover'd shore;
> No secret island in the boundless main?
> No peaceful desert yet unclaim'd by Spain?
> Quick let us rise, the happy seats explore,
> And bear oppression's insolence no more.
>
>   (170-75)
>
> Could'st thou resign the park and play content,
> For the fair banks of Severn or of Trent;
> There might'st thou find some elegant retreat,
> Some hireling senator's deserted seat;
> And stretch thy prospects o'er the smiling land,
> For less than rent the dungeons of the Strand;
> There prune thy walks, support thy drooping flow'rs,
> Direct thy rivulets, and twine thy bow'rs;
> And, while thy grounds a cheap repast afford,
> Despise the dainties of a venal lord:
> There ev'ry bush with nature's musick rings,
> There ev'ry breeze bears health upon its wings;
> On all thy hours security shall smile,
> And bless thine evening walk and morning toil.
>
>   (210-23)

Perhaps most immediately noticeable in comparing these lines to Juvenal's is not their difference but their similarity. As D. V. Boyd rightly notes regarding the opening lines, "This is a very rugged pastoral indeed, and a rather unlikely ideal of the good life. Ireland is Hibernia, the land of winter, and Scotland is a land of rocks. In both, hunger and age rule human life" (396). Yet Johnson's comparison is no more unlikely than Juvenal's original. The same can be said both for the fact that the Briton only finds repose when he is "safe in poverty" and for Johnson's emphasis on barren isolation in lines 170-175. A similarly unidyllic note of contrast can be found in the availability of the "hireling senator's deserted seat"; the country is not altogether immune from the corruption associated with the city. The basis for all of these non-normative elements, as we have seen, can be found in Juvenal. So the first point to note is that Johnson is quite sensitive to Juvenal's complexities of irony, at least initially.

And the principal reason for that sensitivity is obvious. Philosophically, Johnson is nearly as incapable as Juvenal of constructing a simplistic normative irony and staying with it; Johnson manages it with England's noble past, but that effort seems to strain his resources to the limit. Johnson knew the hardships of the country too well; he knew the pangs of poverty even better. It is significant, in this respect, that in **"London"** poverty and isolation provide the counterpoint to the country's normative satisfactions. For Johnson the pain of poverty and isolation cannot be wished away, even for the sake of satiric exaggeration; they are evils that cannot be idealized, even temporarily. They compel the reader to look *through* as well as *to* the norm, and thus to confront a wider but less secure perspective.

These intrusions, however, do not establish the dominant texture of these lines, and it is in the matter of tonal balance that Johnson fumbles. As Mary Lascelles shrewdly notes, irony itself is ultimately a matter of tone, so that fundamental uncertainties of attitude are bound to be revealed there (40). For example, in lines 170-75 Johnson's indignation at the plight of the city's poor does indeed invest even a "pathless waste" in the country with preferential emotion; at least isolation might be conducive to a ration of self-respect. But other descriptions of the country become, at best, bland cliches: "Some pleasing bank where verdant osiers play, / Some peaceful vale with nature's paintings gay" (45-6). Similarly,

> There ev'ry bush with nature's musick rings,
> There ev'ry breeze bears health upon its wings;
> On all thy hours security shall smile,
> And bless thine evening walk and morning toil.
>
> (220-23)

The conventional rhetoric of such lines by itself renders their effect uncertain, and their union with the more obviously non-normative elements mentioned previously only increases that uncertainty. Poverty and isolation are hardly conducive to peace. In one couplet, Johnson's uncertainty of attitude borders on self-parody: "There prune thy walks, support thy drooping flow'rs, / Direct thy rivulets, and twine thy bow'rs" (216-17).

Yet it is interesting to observe that this couplet, conspicuous in Johnson's context for its self-doubt, contains when read by itself Juvenal's authentic note. The subtle undercutting that Juvenal's readers expect is here, but in Juvenal that recurrent deflation establishes the controlling tone, whereas in Johnson, one cannot be certain deflation is even intended, for throughout the contrast of city and country normative irony has been passionately heightened one moment only to be thrown in doubt the next by placement in a larger field of reference. Johnson's rhetoric too often wages an indecisive war with his sense of the whole truth.

Problems involving Thales as a narrator and the precise nature of **"London"** 's moral universe can be seen as part of the same pattern. Umbricius is a typical Juvenalian spokesman: righteous and self-righteous, courageous and self-pitying, sensitive and callous by turns. He convinces us by the depth of his rage, the accuracy of his vision, and the eloquence of his language, rather than by any consis-

tently sustained moral superiority. It is more as a mouthpiece than a rounded character that we respond to Umbricius: what he sees is more important than what he is. Generally, the same can be said of Johnson's Thales.

But Thales' inconsistencies seem more jarring, and for the same reason as that found in Johnson's handling of city and country. Johnson repeatedly heightens the air of moral superiority surrounding his spokesman, even while he occasionally includes the disturbingly human fallibilities found in Juvenal's spokesman. But unlike Juvenal's portrait, in Johnson's the center will not hold, for the extremes are too far apart. Thales' report of the devastating effects of fire provides a good example of his dubious moral position:

> But hark! th' affrighted crowd's tumultuous cries
> Roll thro' the streets, and thunder to the skies;
> Rais'd from some pleasing dream of wealth and pow'r,
> Some pompous palace, or some blissful bow'r,
> Aghast you start, and scarce with aking sight
> Sustain th' approaching fire's tremendous light;
> Swift from pursuing horrors take your way,
> And leave your little all to flames a prey;
> Then thro' the world a wretched vagrant roam,
> For where can starving merit find a home?
> In vain your mournful narrative disclose,
> While all neglect, and most insult your woes.
>
> (182-93)

This section illustrates in perfect miniature the interpretative problem Thales presents—a problem undiminished by the use of second person, since by the end of the passage it is clear that the subject can only be Thales himself. The early lines effectively destroy any suspicion that we might be hearing the unsullied voice of a holy prophet, despite the fact that much of the poem would nearly support such a description. Like Umbricius, Thales appears merely an Orgilio in embryo—superior only from a lack of opportunity to be anything else. Yet a few lines later we are asked to respond to this complaint: "Then thro' the world a wretched vagrant roam, / For where can starving merit find a home?" Once again, had Johnson caught Juvenal's ironic foundation for his narrator, this plaintive question could have elicited the same smirk of recognition in the reader that such a juxtaposition in Juvenal would create. But here the ironic potential nullifies itself; having been asked to admire Thales so often before, the reader is merely disquieted.

Philosophically, Johnson must have responded to the complex potential of Umbricius as spokesman. Johnson's instinctive pessimism would have approved a satirist embroiled in, rather than above, the battle. Since no one escapes the turpitude of fallen man, such an embattled and imperfect spokesman would also be more morally true to Johnson's views. As a victim of himself as well as the times, such a spokesman would simply be a more complete human being.

But once again Johnson could not consummate rhetorically the marriage of attributes involved in such a complex picture. While he read accurately the ironic opening given him by Juvenal's spokesman, and responded to it in part, he could not endorse the pervasive philosophical skepticism which coherently embeds Juvenal's character in the Roman scene he surveys. When Thales appears strictly as normative satirist, he does so with enriched moral credentials and strident self-righteousness, to the detriment of the ironic potential—and fuller humanity—latent in his characterization. What might have been a complexly human irony remains merely contradictory.

The same problem is especially apparent in the final, and in many ways most important, area of ironic uncertainty in **"London"**: the nature of the moral universe the poem describes. For Edward and Lillian Bloom, the problem is easily resolved: "Like Juvenal, Johnson was pessimistic, but he recoiled from the Stoic premise that evil could be divorced from human agency or volition. The ethic of **"London"** is predicated upon what is for its author a Christian truism: that responsibility for any act must be fixed in the doer" (122). I am not sure what species of Christianity suggests that all the world's evils are traceable to human volition, but I am certain Johnson never subscribed to it. **"London"** is peppered with references to "accident" and "fate" that cannot in fact be disposed of so conveniently. Yet Johnson does Christianize the poem's moral atmosphere so frequently that the problem of evil itself becomes a troubling undercurrent in **"London."** Boyd expresses the actual circumstance admirably: "[Johnson] has no more patience than Voltaire with the complacent distinction between 'the physical evil' and 'the moral evil.' Only the latter, he may know in theory, is a proper subject for satiric indignation; the former, however intolerable, is natural to the human lot. But in practice [in **"London"**] he finds himself unable to separate the two" (393). Johnson's philosophical response to the problem of evil in all its forms, in other words, obtrudes itself uneasily into **"London"**'s normative satiric attack on strictly human immorality.

Once again, Johnson's sensitive reading of Juvenal might well have triggered the problem. For Juvenal, the evils of Rome are both accidental and premeditated, all merely indiscriminate parts of one nasty reality. Admittedly, most of his attacks involve human venality of one sort or another, but he freely includes the dangers of falling roof tiles, deadly pieces of garbage from upper-story windows, huge tree trunks and slabs of marble dangling precariously from wagons, and general economic inflation along with more obvious forms of hypocrisy, fraud, and greed. Since, as we have seen, Juvenal's philosophical stance emphasizes the absurdity of the human condition taken in its entirety, such a confabulation strengthens rather than diminishes the force of his observations. We simply do not look to Juvenal for nice discriminations or *explicit* philosophical explanations.

For Johnson, however, such a confabulation created graver problems. He could readily accept the pessimism inherent in such a view, specifically the fact that evil and suffering are as likely to be random and undeserved as the reverse. But his commitment to more exact philosophical formulation, to a redemptive Christian view of human existence—however distant or limited—and to a rhetorically heightened normative satire, combine to entangle him in weighty difficulties he never quite escapes. Indeed, his failure to suggest solutions is actually aggravated by his Christianizing references. In effect, Johnson's Christian references raise the ante of **"London"**'s philosophical dilemmas without resolving them.

Clear references to chance and "fate" begin Johnson's thematic expansion (all italics are mine):

> Here malice, rapine, *accident*, conspire,
> And now a rabble rages, now a fire; . . .
>
> London! the needy villain's gen'ral home,
> The common shore of Paris and of Rome;
> With eager thirst, by folly *or by fate*,
> Sucks in the dregs of each corrupted state. . . .
>
> *Fate* never wounds more deep the gen'rous heart,
> Than when a blockhead's insult points the dart. . . .

While the second of these examples might be written off as merely fulfilling the need for a rhyme, the other two cannot. In the first the conspiracy between malice and accident is reinforced by the antithesis between distinctly human and merely physical violence in the following line, and in the third example, the same distinction between human volition and chance occurrence is drawn. Although rhetorical slippage occurs often enough in **"London,"** a more persuasive explanation for these instances is Johnson's sensitivity to the problem of evil itself. He cannot neglect the impact of chance on human suffering, even though he does not attend to its implications.

This inattention becomes more acute because of Johnson's Christian reinforcements. In only one instance does Johnson content himself with a strictly pagan reference: "Some secret cell, *ye pow'rs,* indulgent give" (49), Thales begs at one point. In most such situations Johnson uses the term "heaven," which perhaps possesses some ambiguity between the classical and Christian worlds, but not enough. No reader of Johnson's time (or our own) could fail to hear essentially Christian echoes in remarks like these: "Grant me, kind heaven, to find some happier place" (43), "When publick crimes inflame the wrath of heav'n" (66), "Has heaven reserv'd, in pity to the poor" (170), and "Should heaven's just bolts Orgilio's wealth confound" (194). Often the references are even less equivocal, as when Thales and the narrator kiss the "consecrated" earth where Elizabeth was born and recall the past when England's "cross" was "triumphant on the main" (27). We are likewise called upon to survey the "land of heroes and of *saints*" (100) from which "Sense, freedom, *piety*" have been "refined away" (105). London is also the city where a "female atheist talks you dead" (18) and where one of the greatest encroachments of the "fasting Monsieurs" (115) from France is clearly their Catholicism.

One of **"London"**'s finest passages, the effect of the great fire on the wealthy, crystallizes these elements in a particularly revealing way:

> Should heaven's just bolts Orgilio's wealth confound,
> And spread his flaming palace on the ground,
> Swift o'er the land the dismal rumour flies,
> And publick mournings pacify the skies;
> The laureat tribe in servile verse relate,
> How virtue wars with persecuting fate;
> With well-feign'd gratitude the pension'd band
> Refund the plunder of the beggar'd land.
> See! while he builds, the gaudy vassals come,
> And crowd with sudden wealth the rising dome;
> The price of boroughs and of souls restore,
> And raise his treasures higher than before.
> Now bless'd with all the baubles of the great,
> The polish'd marble, and the shining plate,
> Orgilio sees the golden pile aspire,
> And hopes from angry heav'n another fire.
>
> (194-209)

While the overriding emphasis of this passage is on the symbiotic evil existing between the arrogant, omnivorous great and their servile, prostituted dependents, Johnson nevertheless brackets the incident with a wider and more dubious perspective. Providence is called into the affair quite conspicuously, yet its sovereignty is imprecise. It levels Orgilio's ill-gotten gains in a Calvinistic burst of direct retribution, only to find itself embarrassed in the end by prayers for more such remunerative punishment. The force of the problem is increased further by the "laureat tribe's" ironic jeremiad against "persecuting fate," a fate in Orgilio's case which is absolutely just, but only initially. The strictly satiric irony of all this is of course quite effective; the attack on the entire debased system which supports such potentates could hardly be stronger. Yet the hints of final causality remain discordant because unfulfilled. Once again a dimension of philosophical irony is called to witness but is never distinctly heard. (pp. 108-19)

> Michael D. Riley, "Johnson's Proper Irony in 'London' and 'The Vanity of Human Wishes'," in Renascence, Vol. XXXVII, No. 2, Winter, 1985, pp. 108-30.

M. D. Aeschliman   (essay date 1985)

[*An American educator and author, Aeschliman has contributed numerous articles and reviews to periodicals on such diverse topics as biography, philosophy, modern European history, religion, modern satirists, and literature. He is the author of* The Restitution of Man: C. S. Lewis and the Case against Scientism *(1984). In the following excerpt from an essay published in* National Review, *Aeschliman praises the universal appeal of Johnson's writings.*]

Scholars, writers, readers, souls all over the globe, from Cairo to Melbourne, from Johannesburg to Los Angeles—large numbers of them people without any particular background in "Eng Lit"—find something in Johnson that they find in no other voice, save perhaps that of the Lord whom Johnson so faithfully served.

Only the two great dramatic and narrative geniuses of our literature, Shakespeare and Dickens respectively, may be said to exercise so wide an appeal; and Johnson never wrote extensively in their popular fictional and dramatic genres. Dickens was aptly called "the great Christian" by Dostoyevsky; Shakespeare's voice, as Johnson himself noted, is the voice of humanity itself. Johnson's voice, by contrast, is the voice of one person—with a view as wide as the world, to be sure; but the voice of one person nonetheless, unique and extraordinary at the same time that it is general and typical: unique in fact in its very generality and universality. To adapt the words of a modern poet, Johnson is "the impossible possible philosophers' man, / The man who has had time to think enough, / The central man."

Take an instance in which at least part of Johnson's point has been rendered mortal by the passage of time, the famous lines contributed to Goldsmith's "The Traveler":

> How small, of all that human hearts endure,
> That part which laws or kings can cause or cure.
> Still to ourselves in ev'ry place consign'd,
> Our own felicity we make or find.

Clearly Johnson could have had no idea of the political enormities and nightmares that lay in the future, in the much-heralded age of "progress" and rationality foretold by those French *philosophes* whom he so despised for their impiety and wrong-headedness, the age kicked off by Voltaire and Rousseau and initiated in earnest by the French Revolution.

The literature of Dostoyevsky, Kafka, and Solzhenitsyn speaks of a world that Johnson, as unillusioned and unsentimental as he was about human nature, never envisioned. We now know all too well how *large* a part "of all that human hearts endure" laws and kings, equipped with massive technological powers, *can* cause. But, if one may risk saying so, Johnson's insight goes deeper, so deep that Joseph Wood Krutch attributed to him, profoundly Christian as he was, the "tragic sense of life" [see excerpt dated 1944]. Our deepest and most important struggles, Johnson is saying, are usually not with our environments or our fellows, but with ourselves. "I do not know the man so bold," says Emily Dickinson, "who dares in lonely place, / That awful stranger consciousness deliberately face." Johnson unflinchingly faced the stranger, but with none of the masochism, self-dramatization, and self-pity that are characteristic of the Romantic and modern tempers. He wished and worked to be happy, despite crippling disabilities, disadvantages, hardships, and setbacks, and to make others happy; and he saw in loving God and serving his fellows the right way to accomplish these ends: "each laboring for his own happiness, by promoting within his circle, however narrow, the happiness of others." "The business of a wise man," he said to Boswell, "is to be happy."

Johnson's charitable acts are as famous now as they were unostentatious then; his house was often a veritable menagerie and always a resort for the unfortunate, however unattractive. In Joseph Wood Krutch's delightful imaginary dialogue between Johnson and Thoreau, "The Last Boswell Paper," he catches the truth of Johnson's Christian attitude and actions, and even something of his voice: "Several poor wretches live in my house. They do not contribute to its peace. But if they did not live there I do not know where they would live." And however much Krutch also admired Thoreau, the latter can hardly help sounding thin, glib, and eccentric by comparison, both in the imaginary dialogue and in actual life and work. Johnson has precisely that intellectual, moral, social, and religious ballast and balance that so many of our notable American writers—Emerson, Thoreau, Whitman, Melville—so signally lack; a quality that critics from Poe through Santayana to Mark Van Doren and Quentin Anderson have shown to be lacking in them, and which Emerson himself admired in the English at their best. "A strong common sense, which is not easy to unseat or disturb, marks the English mind for a thousand years," he wrote in 1856 in *English Traits,* attributing to the nation and culture the quality that both Newman and Chesterton attributed to Johnson himself in the highest degree. Of our great American writers, in fact, the two most traditional, social, and ethical—Hawthorne and Eliot—venerated Johnson. Hawthorne visited Lichfield, the town of Johnson's birth, as well as Uttoxeter and other sites important in Johnson's life, on "one of the few purely sentimental pilgrimages" of his life; he walked through the house where Johnson was born and touched things in it "because Johnson's hand and foot might have been in those same places."

The adherence of such writers as Eliot, Lewis, and F. R. Leavis to Johnson is less sentimental and more philosophical and ethical; for them his life, standards, and writings represent and transmit the deepest and soundest moral imagination that literature has ever attained, or life reflected. "Johnson is not," Leavis writes, "like the Romantic poet, the enemy of society, but consciously its representative and its voice, and it is his strength—something inseparable from his greatness—to be so." But Johnson's idea of society was moral, and he constantly fought for it. What he said of Addison was still truer of himself: "He was a man in whose presence nothing reprehensible was out of danger; quick in observing whatever was wrong or ridiculous, and not unwilling to expose it." The "laid-back," "tolerant" modern would find him intolerably moralistic, bigoted, sanctimonious, self-righteous, and opinionated, all words that we often employ to hide or justify our own laxity. (As Ogden Nash put it, "what is really mine, / Tolerance, or a rubber spine?")

The truth is that Johnson prepared the way for the great ethical Victorians (e.g., in his hatred of slavery and imperialism and, more generally, of superficiality, amorality, and egotism); for the recovery of the Classical/Christian tradition by writers such as Chesterton, Eliot, and Lewis; and for centrality of belief, thought, and practice anywhere and at any time. He is the least eccentric and provincial of all writers, and therefore he is especially tonic in our time, when, as Joseph Mazzeo has put it, "the idiosyncratic has triumphed over the normative"; and in our place—America—where, as Steven Marcus observed some years ago, "We are still, as Matthew Arnold said of us, . . . a provincial and decentralized society, a society without a center of cultural intelligence and sanity."

No one in life or art provides that intelligence and sanity more dependably than Johnson—a point that Eliot understood, and that a host of recent scholars, including Clifford, Jeffrey Hart, and Donald Greene, have documented. "Without intelligence man is not social, he is only gregarious," Johnson wrote in *A Journey to the Western Islands of Scotland.* This conception of intelligence is insistently, and to many modern ears almost obsessively, moral, for Johnson believed that "he that thinks reasonably must think morally" and insisted, in his lives of Milton and Addison and elsewhere, on the inescapability of moral awareness and obligation as the chief feature of the rational person and of the decent society. ("Prudence and justice are virtues and excellences of all times and all places"; and "we are perpetually moralists.") With great pathos and prescience, Johnson dreaded instances when "society is dissolved into a tumult of individuals, without authority to command, or obligation to obey," where only power and appetite reign. He loved "decent Godly order."

For Johnson, as for his great friend Burke, the heart of society, civilization, and moral order is theism. He would have agreed with the current Wykeham Professor of Logic at Oxford (and would have been delighted that he succeeded an atheist in that Chair) in saying that there is "no satisfactory account of truth or ethics without theism." Johnson was a "mere Christian" who insisted to Boswell that, "For my part, Sir, I think all Christians, whether Papists or Protestants, agree in the essential articles, and that their differences are trivial, and rather political than religious" (June 25, 1763). Yet he knew, as he fought, the

acids of skepticism: "Every thing which Hume has advanced against Christianity had passed through my mind long before he wrote. . . . Truth, Sir, is a cow which will yield such people no more milk, and so they are gone to milk the bull" (July 21, 1763). And he hated smugness and bigotry: "Why, Madam, the greatest part of our knowledge is implicit faith; and as to religion, have we heard all that a disciple of Confucius, all that a Mahometan, can say for himself ?" (April 15, 1778). His rational, orthodox, Christian theism had the same balanced quality and character that he attributed to Addison's: a faith "neither weakly credulous nor wantonly skeptical."

But life is more than mind and spirit, as Johnson knew: "To write, and to live, are very different. Many who praise virtue, do no more than praise it." Or as Auden put it, "Lord, forgive the treason of all clerks, / Whose lives are so much worse than their works." Like Milton, Johnson neither practiced nor could praise a "cloistered virtue"; he lived a life that was in many ways agonizingly painful, unhappy, and, until late in life, very poor, in an enormous metropolis seething with misery, poverty, crime, and temptation; and, as his writings show (especially the prayers and diaries), he struggled doggedly against all of them. But he *did* struggle. In him was none of that "Weariness with the striving to be men" that Leslie Fiedler thinks so typical of our time; none of that "weakened sense of human will" that Lionel Trilling came to think "the most distinctive characteristic of the morality of modern times." Johnson had read the seventh chapter of St. Paul's Epistle to the Romans; he knew what his task was, and whence his help came. Will, not intellect, is the key problem of the moral life: "Most of the crimes and miseries of our lives," he wrote, "arise rather from negligence than from ignorance."

Neurotic, shambling, unkempt, often melancholy, never elegant or "attractive" in his person, Johnson nevertheless valued society and sociability, and exercised his wit and will constantly to maintain, extend, and improve them. He loved beautiful, gracious, and chaste women, marriage, the home, and the family. The birthplace and chief haven of human happiness was for him neither solitude, city, nor state—neither Walden Pond nor Vanity Fair—but the home ("to be happy at home is the end of all human endeavor"); and after the untimely death of his wife, the home of the Thrales and the company of his friends and dependents provided him with the humane settings he so loved and defended.

Outside the Gospels, no other man's recorded utterances, whether written or spoken, have ever sounded so *earned,* and therefore so trustworthy; this authority is apparent even in brief phrases. Johnson is never gratuitously vague or glib or smug; never irreverent or portentous; and he always spoke to be understood. "Some people," he told Boswell, "tell you that they let themselves down to the capacity of their hearers. I never do that. I speak uniformly, in as intelligible a manner as I can" (March 27, 1775). He loved quotation, and he gloried in accrediting and extending the Classical/Christian tradition, which he thought was the living water of the ages. Defending the practice of quotation against a critic, he forthrightly declared: "No, Sir, it is a good thing; there is community of mind in it."

Johnson's talk and writing always contain this "community of mind" as well as "the observations of a strong mind operating upon life"; yet he was not a gloomy moralist, and always valued good cheer and humor: "The size of a man's understanding," he once said, "might always be justly measured by his mirth." And this is the man who secretly wrote law lectures for the Vinerian Professor of Law at Oxford; secretly composed a great series of sermons for John Taylor; wrote some of the greatest poems of the eighteenth century, and one of the greatest of any century; wrote three series of the greatest essays in our language; compiled the first great dictionary of our language, much of which was taken over unchanged by the Oxford English Dictionary; composed *The Lives of the Poets,* the finest short biographies in our language; made some of the finest short translations of classical Greek and Latin poetry in existence; wrote powerfully on politics, and especially against imperialism; produced a classic edition of Shakespeare; wrote a novel of which Hilaire Belloc has said, "Every man ought to read *Rasselas,* and every wise man will read it half a dozen times in his life . . . for never was wisdom better put, or more enduringly."

In the admirable *Dictionary Johnson: The Middle Years of Samuel Johnson,* covering the years 1749 to 1763, James L. Clifford noted that at the Ivy Club Johnson was always "uniformly tenacious" when any question of moral obligation was raised, and went on to show how dogged Johnson's ethical imagination was, not only in novel, poems, essays, prayers, and sermons, but in the *Dictionary* itself, "a great storehouse of philosophy, theology, history, and literature . . . an extensive anthology of English prose and verse." There are 116,000 quotations in the *Dictionary,* helping to make it in itself a great work of literature as well as of lexicography, one on which writers such as Carlyle and Browning cut their teeth. In it, as in everything Johnson touched, he was the man of *sapiens et eloquens pietas*—wise and eloquent piety—as well as Quintilian's *bonus rhetor,* the good man speaking well, vindicating, reaffirming, and transmitting a vast body of humane learning and "the ancient orthodox tradition of ethics." To read Johnson, as C. S. Lewis once said of reading Spenser, is "to grow in mental health." (pp. 49-52)

Sanity has no stronger defender, piety no more eloquent spokesman, genius no greater example. (p. 52)

> *M. D. Aeschliman, "The Good Man Speaking Well," in* National Review, *New York, Vol. XXXVII, January 11, 1985, pp. 49-52.*

Alvin B. Kernan   (essay date 1986)

[*Kernan is an American educator and author of several studies on Renaissance satire and modern theater. He also edited the Yale University Press series on Ben Jonson. In the following excerpt, he relates the linguistic difficulties confronting Johnson while compiling the* Dictionary.]

The first of the great dictionaries in the English language was that of Samuel Johnson, completed in 1755. Johnson's preface describing its composition provides a remarkable insight into the kinds of problems that modern linguists and social thinkers have discovered in language. At the same time, he makes clear in intimately human terms how and why these problems arise and how they are met.

In April 1746, Johnson signed a contract with a conger of booksellers and printers formed to underwrite the considerable costs of a dictionary of the English language that would improve upon earlier ones and rival the great French and Italian dictionaries recently produced in those countries by entire learned academies. Johnson describes his own feelings on the occasion of the launching of the project as pleasure "with a prospect of the hours which I should revel away in feasts of literature; with the obscure recesses of northern learning which I should enter and ransack . . . and the triumph with which I should display my acquisitions to mankind."

The publishers agreed to a total fee of 1,575 pounds, paid at intervals, and Johnson estimated that three years would be sufficient for the project. He proceeded to set up a little dictionary factory in London in the garret of the house at 17 Gough Square (now a Johnson Museum) and settled down to work with six assistants—five of whom were Scots—who were paid 10 shillings a week, half a printer's wage. At the publishers' urgings, Johnson reluctantly addressed a printed plan for the dictionary to Lord Chesterfield, who thus became the nominal patron of the project.

The book was printed in batches, beginning in October 1750. Printing could proceed only when sufficient copy had accumulated and when the printer could conveniently fit the work into his schedule. To provide the necessary steady flow, Johnson developed a production method: he would read a book, underline a word to be used in the *Dictionary,* mark off a passage which defined its meaning, and then note the first letter of the entry in the margin. His assistants would then copy out the marked passages, which were afterwards sorted and pasted up.

The work proceeded much more slowly than planned, partly because of exigencies in the lives of those involved, particularly Johnson's, which he described with his usual felicity: "The English *Dictionary* was written with little assistance of the learned, and without any patronage of the great; not in the soft obscurities of retirement, or under the shelter of academick bowers, but amidst inconvenience and distraction, in sickness and in sorrow." He was referring to the deaths of both his wife and mother, which occurred while he was working on the project, and to his being always pressed for money, forced to beg two-pound advances from the publishers.

A brilliant man, Johnson was often bored by the endless search for words and the attempt to fix their meanings. He worked sitting on a remarkable three-legged chair which he never found time to get fixed. He struggled with and helped his assistants, who were improvident and needy, learned in quirky ways but fond of gambling and drink. He borrowed the books he needed but could not afford to buy, marked them up, and failed to return them, to the annoyance of their owners. Always he was depressed, worried about his health, and uncertain of his place in the world.

In the midst of these disturbances and confusions he had constantly to make a series of precise and absolute linguistic decisions of a kind which W. K. Wimsatt describes very feelingly: "Imagine yourself halfway through Johnson's program of reading for the *Dictionary,* arriving at [a] page of Bacon's *Natural History.* . . . Which of the words and passages on the page would you mark in black lead pencil for your amanuenses to copy? Which would you pass over? By what norms would you make your selection? How many minutes would you need to reach your decisions on one page?"

Johnson described his own feelings in these circumstances in a way that makes clear that his task grew increasingly complex, and as his personal problems and psychic disturbances grew, the language itself began to shimmer and even disappear before his scrutiny:

> Consider that no dictionary of a living tongue ever can be perfect, since, while it is hastening to publication, some words are budding, and some falling away; that a whole life cannot be spent upon syntax and etymology, and that even a whole life would not be sufficient; that he, whose design includes whatever language can express, must often speak of what he does not understand; that a writer will sometimes be hurried by eagerness to the end, and sometimes faint with weariness under a task, which Scaliger compares to the labours of the anvil and the mine; that what is obvious is not always known, and what is known is not always present; that sudden fits of inadvertency will surprise vigilance, slight avocations will seduce attention, and casual eclipses of the mind will darken learning; and that the writer shall often in vain trace his memory, at the moment of need, for that which yesterday he knew with intuitive readiness, and which will come uncalled into his thoughts tomorrow.

Johnson began his work with the belief, which most of us still share, that language existed as an ideal, absolute order underlying the particularities of actual usage and the confusions of life. That assumption appears by implication in a typical remark of his that language had degenerated during the course of history, having been "neglected; suffered to spread, under the direction of chance, into wild exuberance; resigned to the tyranny of time and fashion; and exposed to the corruptions of ignorance, and caprices of innovation." He never entirely gave up this belief that behind historical change and random proliferation there was a "fabrick of the tongue," which the lexicographer could still recover and formalize.

But as Johnson became more deeply involved with the actualities of the language which he had so happily and hopefully undertaken to order—"resolved," he said, "to leave neither words nor things unexamined"—he did not find the Adamic language supposedly spoken in Eden, nor did he find below the *parole* of individual speech acts the *langue* or linguistic structure hypothesized by 20th-century structural linguistics. Instead, he came face to face with what he called "the boundless chaos of a living speech . . . copious without order, and energetick without rules: wherever I turned my view, there was perplexity to be disentangled, and confusion to be regulated; choice was to be made out of boundless variety, without any established principle of selection; adulterations were to be detected, without a settled test of purity."

Not only was there no existing linguistic order, there were, he admitted, not even any certain rules for ascertaining or creating order. Consider the question of fixing the orthography, one of Johnson's first tasks. This might seem relatively straightforward, but he soon discovered that written language rests on speech, and a word which was pronounced differently in various dialects inevitably had dif-

ferent spellings, none authoritative. Furthermore, the vowel sounds of English are so uncertain that no two mouths quite pronounce them in the same way, which also leads to variety in spelling. He complained: "Some combinations of letters, having the same power, are used indifferently without any discoverable reason of choice, as in choak, choke; soap, sope."

Johnson did not like such linguistic uncertainties, which he called "spots of barbarity impressed so deep in the English language, that criticism can never wash them away," but he found them in every area he considered. Pronunciation, where he sought only to mark the primary accent, he found various and arbitrary. Etymologies, an area where he was weak, particularly in the Teutonic languages, were uncertain and "words which are represented as . . . related by descent or cognation, do not always agree in sense." Even the basic question of which words were to be included in the dictionary—i.e., how many *real* English words are there?—brought a plethora of possibilities. Proper names, technical terms, foreign words, compounds, participles, and other derivatives, archaisms, and even a linguistic limbo where he found "words of which I have reason to doubt the existence" combined to open up a great chaos.

It was, however, when he turned to the critical matter of definitions that the full difficulties of the dictionary project became manifest. Meaning began to crumble when he tried to define particles and expletives "of which the sense is too subtle and evanescent to be fixed in a paraphrase," and it disappeared altogether when the great linguist found words "which I cannot explain, because I do not understand them." Even in the case of more apparently solid words, for many "the signification is so loose and general, the use so vague and indeterminate, and the senses detorted so widely from the first idea, that it is hard to trace them through the maze of variation, to catch them on the brink of utter inanity, to circumscribe them by any limitations, or interpret them by any words of distinct and settled meaning; such are bear, break, come, cast, fall, get. . . ." These are the words that make us confront the odd and revealing fact that we can understand words and phrases without being able to define them or consciously focus their meaning.

In the end Johnson inevitably found his way to the critical linguistic fact that the meaning of a word is established not by reference to some objective reality outside language, but by reference to other words. This structuralist view, which modern linguistics describes by saying that language is non-referential, Johnson expressed as a semantic tautology requiring "that *the explanation, and the word explained, should be always reciprocal.*" He considered explanations "unavoidably reciprocal or circular, as hind, the female of the stag; stag, the male of the hind: sometimes easier words are changed into harder, as burial into sepulture or interment, drier into desiccative, dryness into siccity or aridity, fit into paroxysm: for the easiest word, whatever it be, can never be translated into one more easy."

Language, Johnson found in working on the *Dictionary,* is not the product of fact or logic, but of history and human existence. It belongs to a world where "vanity affects peculiar pronunciations and meanings," where the diction of laborers and merchants is "casual and mutable . . . formed for some temporary or local convenience." Advanced societies, he discovered, have the leisure to increase knowledge and to produce new words; fashion and convenience create terms which flourish briefly and die easily; science amplifies language "with words deflected from their original sense." Translation, he remarked, changes grammar itself, altering "not the single stones of the building, but the order of the columns." As he warmed to the subject that engaged his deepest concern, the catalogue of linguistic mutability grows epic:

> The tropes of poetry will make hourly encroachments, and the metaphorical will become the current sense: pronunciation will be varied by levity or ignorance, and the pen must at length comply with the tongue; illiterate writers will, at one time or another, by publick infatuation, rise into renown, who, not knowing the original import of words, will use them with colloquial licentiousness, confound distinction, and forget propriety. As politeness increases, some expressions will be considered as too gross and vulgar for the delicate, others as too formal and ceremonious for the gay and airy; new phrases are, therefore, adopted, which must, for the same reasons, be in time dismissed."

Though traces of a lingering essentialism remain in phrases like "the original import of words," language in the Johnsonian view is finally and inescapably the product of human beings in history and is therefore subject to constant mutation and chance, to mere accident and casual interests. If it can be said to have any overall direction, it is downward, for "tongues, like governments, have a natural tendency to degeneration." He found the radical difficulty grounded in the human thought process itself: "Most men think indistinctly, and, therefore, cannot speak with exactness." But even if language were used more precisely, it would still be flawed, he felt, for experience is larger than language and there are many ideas, feelings, perceptions "which words are insufficient to explain."

Johnson's exploration of language eventually brought him to the very edge of linguistic nothingness, where language is revealed as only a baseless and unsystematic babbling of imperfect people moving through the confusion of life and history. In moments of despair he felt that any attempt to order this Babel was mere folly: "To enchain syllables, and to lash the wind, are equally the undertakings of pride, unwilling to measure its desires by its strength." He understood very well that a dictionary cannot be the record of a pre-existent linguistic order. It can be only a man-made inscription of order on "the boundless chaos of a living speech," admittedly arbitrary, imperfect, temporary.

Johnson was a great conservative of the kind who held "that for the law to be *known,* is of more importance than to be *right,*" especially when there is finally nothing to be absolutely right about. But despite his firm belief in this and other matters that "there is in constancy and stability a general and lasting advantage," the *Dictionary* might never have been completed if the printing business had not moved the project forward in ways that exemplify the way that printed dictionaries have made language real.

The publishers exerted constant pressure on Johnson, urging speed because of the increasing amount of capital absorbed by the venture, which demanded a steady flow of copy and speedy correction of the proof sheets since, as the printer forcefully demonstrated, the press stood idle and the type locked up until author's corrections of proof were made. A few of the proof sheets still exist and reveal that many of the changes Johnson made in proof were not made in type! The publishers cut the number of entries and illustrative quotations in order to save space and money and to keep the final cost of the book down to a reasonable selling price.

Given Johnson's irregular work habits and the enormous unexpected difficulty of the task, the work inevitably dragged. The first folio volume was not completed until 1753, and the second in 1755, at which time the bookseller Andrew Millar, who coordinated the work for the conger, could say on receiving the final sheets of copy, "Thank GOD I have done with *him.*" To which a somewhat deflated Johnson responded: "I am glad . . . that he thanks GOD for anything."

These anecdotes are signs of deeper connections between print and the conception of language objectified in dictionaries. The *Dictionary* was in the first place a practical handbook needed by the printing business to establish authoritative spellings and standardized meanings which print, with its inbuilt tendency toward regularity in all areas—technological, economic, and cultural—required for editing manuscripts and setting type. It was also a book that could not have been conceived without print's characteristic systematization of everything it deals with.

This can be seen in Johnson's perception that the varieties of pronunciation "will always be observed to grow fewer and less different, as books are multiplied," a tendency equally true of spellings and meanings. A dictionary, we might say, is the essential book of print—its secular Bible—at once a supremely useful manual for author, compositor, and proofreader, and a revelation of the essential nature or logic of print's tendency to abstract, order, and idealize language by objectifying it as a theoretical artifact. The extent and the ways in which print shaped the actual assemblage of the dictionary provide a fascinating insight into the detailed ways that technology influences culture.

Johnson laughed at the Borgesian etymologies of Francis Junius (1589-1677) who in his *Etymologicum Anglicanum* derives the word "dream" from "drama," because life is a drama, and a drama is a dream; and who declares, with a tone of defiance, that no man can fail to derive "moan" from "monos" who considers that grief naturally loves to be alone. But Johnson's own method for establishing the meanings of words in the face of the linguistic void is only more familiar, not less arbitrary. Printed books provided his necessary locus of "true" language. He frequently referred to the oral basis of language, but for him a word was real enough for inclusion in the *Dictionary* only when it had appeared in print, and he omitted many familiar terms because, he said, unselfconsciously, "I had never read them."

Print also established the definitions of words. Recognizing that words had at least several meanings and that they changed over time, Johnson recorded a variety of definitions for most words, but he considered a particular meaning legitimate only if it could be reasonably derived from a passage in a printed book. These passages appear in the *Dictionary* in abbreviated form to authenticate definitions that he set down, despite his full awareness that "words are hourly shifting their relations."

But not all books would do as authority for the existence of words and true source of their meanings. Some were excluded because Johnson disapproved of their authors or subjects. Authors whom he considered immoral were not treated as linguistically authoritative. And practical considerations of the amount of reading he could cover forced him to narrow the range still further. In the end he drew his vocabulary from books printed between 1580 and 1660, between Sidney's works and those of the Restoration.

The choice was justified in various ways: the writings of this period were, said Johnson, adapting Spenser's description of Chaucer, "the wells of English undefiled," in which could be found a vocabulary and range of meanings spacious enough that "few ideas would be lost to mankind, for want of English words, in which they might be expressed"; works printed before 1580, it was arbitrarily argued, contained too many obsolescent words and meanings; and works printed after 1660 were too much influenced by the French and were too recent for their language to have been approved by the test of time. In practice Johnson did not stick to his principle and John Locke is quoted more often than any other writer. Roy Harris, the Oxford linguistic philosopher, has aptly called attribution of this kind of linguistic authority to writers, "black-and-white lexicography"—which, he says, "implicitly takes the language of the literate strata of society as having priority, and treats literary, educated usage, preserved for posterity in the published works of major writers, as providing the permanent standard against which to judge any other forms of English."

With all these problems and inconsistencies, the *Dictionary* was at last finished—about 40,000 entries, 114,000 illustrative quotations, over 2,500 double-column pages, a preface, a history of the language and a description of English grammar, all sumptuously printed in 1,000 copies of two folio volumes, and priced at four pounds, ten shillings. Once Johnson's work was accomplished, the "humble Drudge" became "Dictionary Johnson," and his *Dictionary* became the English language objectified in two heavy volumes, ordered word by word alphabetically, and numerically page by page, each entry printed in a regular format—spelling, pronunciation, etymology, historical order of definitions, illustrated, and backed up by quotes from the best English authors. This surely, we still feel, is the language, complete with all the attributes of reality. Yet the famous events gathering around its publication reveal its status as a cultural artifact by revealing its part in the great social struggle going on in the 18th century when middle-class professionals were wrestling cultural and political power from the old aristocracy.

In many ways the noble aristocrat, Philip Stanhope, Fourth Earl of Chesterfield, was a perfect image of the old order. He was a brilliant conversationalist and a notable public speaker—which Johnson, for all his fluency in conversation, was not—famous for his eloquent orations in the House of Lords and for his letters, which he did not deign to print. In all ways he was the ideal of the *ancien regime* of polite letters, an aristocratic amateur who wrote in an elegant fashion for the amusement and instruction of a small circle of friends of similar taste. He was also the arbiter of language, the master of the King's English and of the right, asserted by that term, of the aristocracy to determine polite usage. As such Chesterfield was the appropriate person to serve as the patron of the *Dictionary,* and Johnson was reluctantly persuaded to address the first printed plan advertising it to him.

Chesterfield accepted the homage with a gift of ten pounds, but in the nine years between then and the completion of the work, he expressed no interest and gave no help. In 1754, when the *Dictionary* was about to appear, however, Chesterfield was willing to play the part of the patron again in order to gratify his noted vanity and to assert once again the implicit claim of the patronage system: that letters derived their greatness and language its standards from the manners, tastes, and values of the ruling class. And so he smoothly gave the work his imprimatur with a pretense of democratic spirit, making, he said, "a total surrender of all my rights and privileges in the English language, as a free-born British subject, to the said Mr. Johnson, during the term of his dictatorship."

He went on to offer some advice that by its nature suggests that he and his class were becoming linguistically irrelevant, cautioning Johnson not to fail to trace the origin of the word "flirtation" to "the most beautiful mouth in the world," to define the obscure verb "to fuzz" as "dealing twice together with the same pack of cards, for luck," or to suggest restriction of the overworked word "vastly" as in the description of a snuffbox as "*vastly* pretty, because it was *vastly* little."

Johnson's response, the famous **"Letter to Lord Chesterfield,"** expressed the view of the professional writer for the public marketplace and still stands as the *magna carta* of the modern author—the public announcement that the days of courtly letters are at last ended, that the author is the true source of his work, and that he and it are no longer dependent on the patron or the social system he represents: "Seven years, my Lord, have now past, since I waited in your outward rooms, or was repulsed from your door; during which time I have been pushing on my work through difficulties, of which it is useless to complain, and have brought it, at last, to the verge of publication, without one act of assistance, one word of encouragement, or one smile of favour."

Chesterfield was attempting to preserve the King's English, but Johnson asserted that it was the Author's English, his own and that of his great predecessors: Spenser, Bacon, Shakespeare, Milton, Locke, Pope. He clinched the matter by publishing the *Dictionary* without a dedication and without a reference to the man he now openly declared to be not "a Lord among wits; but . . . only a wit among Lords." The English language, which the *Dictionary* now objectified, was authorized by the writer Samuel Johnson, whose name alone appeared on the title page, and by 114,000 quotations from other authors whose writing established English words and their meaning.

The *Dictionary* was a typical achievement of print, a language book made out of books. It was at the same time an achievement of the professional writer Samuel Johnson, who spoke of his earlier plans to record the language as "the dreams of a poet, doomed at last to wake a lexicographer." Though the book has been supplanted as lexico-graphically authoritative by the *New English Dictionary,* it is still a literary classic. Selections like *"oats—a grain in England generally given to horses, but in Scotland supports the people"* or *"pastern—the knee of a horse—Ignorance, Madam, sheer ignorance"* are frequently collected as instances of the wit and wisdom of Dr. Johnson. The real poetic power of the ***Dictionary*** is in its ordering and fixing the language, abstracting it from the linguistic flux of Babel and giving it boundaries, stability, and permanence.

Linguistic crystallization was achieved by plausibly, but still arbitrarily, using the printed works of famous writers as definitive of what language is and means. In this way Johnson not only solved the practical problem of how to limit and fix speech, but at the same time established the claim of writers, which we now take for granted, that the English language belongs to and is shaped by its great authors and their texts. This authority is so familiar by now that it seems an obvious fact that the literary artist officially rules language, maintains its strength, expands its range of possibilities, creates new words and meanings, reworks the tropes, and in the end is the ultimate authority on wordcraft.

Poetry has always been a high verbal art, but the axiom that the literary text is the source of and the authority for linguistic meaning is not an eternal fact of either culture or nature. It is a print-society concept that has existed in the age between, on the one hand, an older oral poetry where the singers of tales worked with invariable linguistic metrical units fixed by tradition (in which language told the author what he could say), and, on the other hand, increasingly influential modern linguistic views that language is independent of writers, is prior to and generates the text. (pp. 33-8)

> *Alvin B. Kernan, "The Boundless Chaos of Living Speech," in* Princeton Alumni Weekly, *Vol. 87, No. 3, October 15, 1986, pp. 33-8.*

Andrew Varney   (essay date 1989)

[*In the following excerpt, Varney perceives a mental struggle in the narrative voice of Johnson's "London," emphasizing the "motif of the enemy within."*]

Boswell records the enthusiasm with which Oxford greeted the publication of **"London,"** Johnson's imitation of Juvenal's third satire, in 1738: 'Every body was delighted with it; and there being no name to it, the first buz of literary circles was "here is an unknown poet, greater even than Pope." ' Pope himself was impressed by the poem and made efforts to discover, and later to assist, its author; Boswell describes Pope's 'feelings and conduct' on the occasion of **"London"** 's appearance as 'candid and liberal'. Boswell himself calls **"London"** 'this justly celebrated poem', speaks of 'the general blaze of its excellence', and declares that 'it is, undoubtedly, one of the noblest productions in our language, both for sentiment and expression'. (p. 202)

"London" certainly is a political poem. It reflected and contributed to the volatile political atmosphere of 1738 and its popularity was undoubtedly bolstered by its fierce-ly *engagé* content and tone; however, to give a special prominence to its political character may be limiting.

Boswell recognized the political animation of the poem (and felt it unjustified, praising Walpole as 'a wise and benevolent minister'), but the language he uses suggests that **"London"** won warm contemporary approbation for its literary rather than its political qualities. He commends, for instance, in addition to those attributes quoted above, the poem's 'manly force, bold spirit, and masterly versification'. To give very great, or exclusive, weight to the poem's polemical features may be to risk missing the real sources of its distinction and originality. Discussing Johnson's verse in his Warton Lecture (1983), J. D. Fleeman introduces a train of thought very rare in discussion of Johnson's poetry: he quotes T. S. Eliot's remark in *The Use of Poetry and the Use of Criticism* that a finished poem may be very remote from the experience that gave rise to it, and may indeed communicate what 'was not in existence before the poem was completed', and he finds in this a key to Johnson's use of language:

> It is this feature of Johnson's poetry which projects its interest beyond the words which make it. It is projected into a dimension which is not backward from or anterior to those words, but which looks forward to something which is yet to arise from the words. The interest of his words is not so much in where they start but in where they lead [see Further Reading].

To speak of Johnson's writing in this way is a useful admonition: one feels at times that the gravitas of Johnson has oppressed commentary and dissuaded it from giving his writing, whether in verse or prose, the solicitously close attention readily yielded to other writers. In the case of **"London"** interest has centred on 'where the words start'—in Juvenal's third satire and in the political world of 1738—and has not followed 'where they lead'. **"London"** is, I shall argue, a great and profound poem not just because of the accuracy, mordancy, and poetic brilliance with which Johnson has suited Juvenal's satire on the public degeneracy and squalor of Rome to the social and political circumstances of Walpole's London, though these things are real enough, but because Johnson fuses with his public satire a deeply impassioned presentation of the mind in distress that is almost wholly absent from Juvenal and from his other translators and imitators. When, for instance, John H. Johnston describes **"London"** as 'an authoritative indictment of the age' he is evincing that kind of desensitizing that seems to rob Johnson of part of his greatness: it is very easy, because Johnson's manner invites it, to speak of his utterance as 'authoritative', as in a way it is; and it is a very characteristic Augustan voice, but if matters are left there, the strains of querulousness, alarm, unease, fear, and testiness that complicate and enrich the poetic texture of **"London"** may be missed.

Johnson's satire presents us with a society containing in itself the elements of its own destruction, an enemy within which will subvert and betray it. Human minds in this society are fractured, hypocritical, deluded, deceived, or otherwise divorced from their own better interests. Where Juvenal consistently presents an integrated observer, reacting to Rome with a fine *saeva indignatio,* Johnson's Thales is more shaken by the world he decries and may even have taken on something of its fated and self-destructive character. He is more a product of the world he lives in and less independent than Juvenal's Umbricius.

Juvenal's third satire is a vigorous and cutting indictment of specific ills and abuses in Roman life, articulated by one who is about to leave it for a rural retreat. Johnson's Thales, who is on the point of leaving London for Wales, similarly decries his own metropolis, and Johnson exploits and even intensifies the popular emotions of patriotism and xenophobia which form part of Juvenal's rhetorical arsenal. From the very beginning of **"London,"** however, we find something expressed through the antithetical manner of Johnson's verse which is not present in Juvenal's. Juvenal says that while he is disturbed ('confusus', line 1) by his friend's departure he none the less commends his going to take up residence in the deserted town of Cumae:

> Quamvis digressu veteris confusus amici,
> Laudo tamen vacuis quod sedem figere Cumis
> Destinet,
>
> (ll. 1-3)

Juvenal's statement is quite simple, but Johnson carefully examines his divided feelings on his friend's departure:

> Tho' Grief and Fondness in my Breast rebel,
> When injur'd THALES bids the Town farewell,
> Yet still my calmer Thoughts his Choice commend,
> I praise the Hermit, but regret the Friend,
>
> (ll. 1-4)

In one half of this oyster of antithesis we have the pressure of personal emotion, 'Grief and Fondness', and in the other the more ruly and judicious 'calmer Thoughts'. The co-existence of these opposed things in one mind gives rise to the antithesis in line 4 where Johnson's public sense leads him to 'praise the Hermit' while his private feelings make him 'regret the Friend'. The lines are comparatively unimportant to the satirical strategy of **"London"** as a whole, but they are significant in two other ways. First, they mark a new tone and a new theme: neither Juvenal nor any of the major translators and adaptors preceding Johnson (Boileau, Oldham, Dryden) began by stressing any division in the mind. Secondly, Johnson has introduced an image whose implications will give the poem much of its intensity. This is contained in the relationship which Johnson sees subsisting between his emotion and his calmer thought: 'Grief and Fondness in my Breast rebel'. The image of 'rebellion' within is apparently used casually, but not so in fact. The image chosen is rebellion, internecine strife, not international warfare, and it is particularly apt to a poem which will present London as vitiated by its own corruption and by the influence of foreigners (particularly the French) who have come to live in it and on it. The full force of the image as its implications are developed in the poem is to mobilize all those common fears so readily fostered, even in a non-paranoid consciousness, of an enemy within. Even in that first line the rebellious grief and fondness are 'in my Breast'. In its co-operation with the themes of patriotism and xenophobia already mentioned, and with that of the perils daily faced by the individual living in the city, the motif of an enemy within affords one of the strongest emotional threads in the poem.

This enemy within originates with Juvenal, where immigrant Greeks in Rome and imported Greek mores sap Rome's vital strength, and it is used in all other versions

of the satire, but only in Johnson does it gain its full intensity and pervade the whole poem. The subversive enemy within is protean. It may appear in the venality of Members of Parliament:

> Here let those reign, whom Pensions can incite
> To vote a Patriot black, a Courtier white;
> Explain their Country's dear-bought Rights away;
> And plead for Pirates in the Face of Day;
> With slavish Tenets taint our poison'd Youth,
> And lend a Lye the confidence of Truth.
>
> (ll. 51-6)

This is one of the passages frequently adduced in witness to the political nature of **"London."** This is quite right, but attention should also be drawn to the intensity of the language here, to the passion that informs the satire, and to the intimation of a radical disorder from which Johnson has such revulsion: what is the future of a people when its youth is not merely misled but tainted, poisoned, and enslaved, and what is to become of a world where those fundamental perceptions vital to the security of the mind are perverted, where black becomes white and a lie can successfully masquerade as, and take on all the assurance of, truth? Johnson leaves us in no doubt that men such as he describes do hold sway, and in order to indicate their relationship with the sounder element in the commonwealth he again deploys the image of civil discord:

> Behold rebellious Virtue quite o'erthrown,
> Behold our Fame, our Wealth, our Lives your own.
>
> (ll. 63-4)

That it is virtue which is 'rebellious' here is a potent inversion of expected usage as it signifies not merely that the enemy is within the gates but that it has usurped the citadel. As readers of Johnson we would not expect from him any facile optimism about the ultimate invincibility of virtue in this world, but it is worth remembering that the first readers of **"London"** were not as familiar with Johnson as we are. They had never heard this voice before and, as the poem was published anonymously, had no name to put to it. One might add that in crystallizing his vision of what was happening in his world of London in the image of civil war, Johnson was touching a spring that notoriously triggered alarm in the English sensibility through much of the eighteenth century.

The passage which embodies the motif of the enemy within most intensely runs from line 91 to line 157 of **"London."** This important passage, which has attracted comparatively little detailed commentary, possibly as its open xenophobia may have been felt to be a coarse embarrassment, decries the conduct and influence of the French immigrants in London. A glance at it will reveal not only with what passionate disgust Johnson treats the theme but also the peculiar intensifying slant which he gives it.

Describing the sycophantic Greek's excessive willingness to serve his master, Juvenal writes,

> . . . omnia novit
> Graeculus esuriens; in caelum iusseris ibit.
>
> (ll. 77-8)

(Your hungry little Greek knows how to do everything; just tell him to go and he's off to the other world for you.)

Oldham's version dilutes the point of the second half of line 78, but Dryden in his translation remains faithful:

All things the hungry *Greek* exactly knows:
And bid him go to Heav'n, to Heav'n he goes.
            (*The Third Satyr of Juvenal*, ll. 140-1)

Johnson takes the hint from Dryden about how to render 'in caelum iusseris ibit', but he gives it a simple twist:

All Sciences a fasting Monsieur knows,
And bid him go to Hell, to Hell he goes.

            (ll. 115-16)

The substitution of Hell for Heaven does not just make the satire sound more deadly. It also stresses the self-destructive perversion of a mind which will cast itself into damnation merely to ingratiate. Going off to Heaven, in Dryden's rendering, does no violence to the soul.

Comparison with Dryden is always an instructive pointer to the distinctive qualities of **"London."** Dryden's translation is superbly elegant and accomplished (and 191 lines longer than the original) but it does not offer the mordancy of Johnson, or of Juvenal for that matter. The behaviour of the foreign parasites in slavishly following the whims of their masters is described by Dryden in an easy and amusing manner:

Call for a Fire, their Winter Cloaths they take:
Begin but you to shiver, and they shake:
In Frost and Snow, if you complain of Heat,
They rub th'unsweating Brow, and Swear they Sweat.
            (ll. 175-8)

By contrast the compression and verbal energy of Johnson's account of the same phenomenon disturbs, communicating as it does the violent betrayal of nature generated in unhealthy minds. The foreigners are eager to comply with every 'wild Absurdity',

And as their Patron hints the Cold or Heat,
To shake in Dog-days, in *December* sweat.

            (ll. 142-3)

In their pretence of compliance Dryden's Greeks are laughable. Johnson's 'Gauls' shivering in summer and sweating in December wilfully invade the autonomy of their own bodies, which should be governed only by the natural laws of their own physiology: they subjugate what is involuntary and natural to a perverse unnatural will.

It is, however, in the culminating paragraph of this section of the poem that the special qualities of Johnson's rendering are most marked. Juvenal explains how the sycophants get to know their masters' domestic secrets in order to have power over them:

. . . scire volunt secreta domus atque inde timere.
            (l. 113)

Both Oldham and Dryden offer versions of this line, but Johnson dwells on it and expands it. Dryden reads,

They search the Secrets of the House, and so
Are worshipp'd there, and fear'd for what they know.
            (ll. 194-5)

In Johnson the social subversion which Juvenal suggests becomes dramatized through a superbly managed series of couplets as a threat not just to the social structure but to the individual man's spiritual vitals. The movement of rhetorical intensification in his paragraph is accompanied by a movement from the outer social world of 'the Table' to the inner world of the spirit, 'the Heart':

For Arts like these preferr'd, admir'd, carest,
They first invade your Table, then your Breast;
Explore your Secrets with insidious Art,
Watch the weak Hour, and ransack all the Heart;
Then soon your ill-plac'd Confidence repay,
Commence your Lords, and govern or betray.

            (ll. 152-7)

When the heart is ransacked and confidence is repayed with betrayal it is not just society which has fallen victim to the enemy within but individual human personality itself.

"London" goes on to describe other evils of life in the city, not all attributable to pernicious foreign influence, and rises to a climax in the presentation of what we would call the law and order issue. The citizen who goes out at night is exposed to the insults and random violence of the 'fiery Fop' and 'frolick Drunkard', and even when he returns home his house is not secure from the burglar or murderous housebreaker. It is in treating this last threat, to the citizen in his home, that Johnson clinches the theme of the enemy who comes within with an imaginative intensity altogether absent from the original poem and other versions of it.

Once Juvenal has mentioned the danger to the citizen at home he moves quickly on to other matters, and both Oldham and Dryden follow him in this. Only Boileau, whose version of the third satire was distributed between his own first and sixth satires when published, amplifies the point at all. . . . The bourgeois detail here is a nice and quite proper embellishment of Juvenal's four lines, but there is no increase in emotional pressure. Johnson on the other hand gives a terrifying enactment of the scene:

In vain, these Dangers past, your Doors you close,
And hope the balmy Blessings of Repose:
Cruel with Guilt, and daring with Despair,
The midnight Murd'rer bursts the faithless Bar;
Invades the sacred Hour of silent Rest,
And leaves, unseen, a Dagger in your Breast.

            (ll. 236-41)

This nightmare of the imagination is Johnson's culminating vision of the enemy within: it is rendered with great poetical intensity and it brings to a superb climax the passionate presentation of the theme of danger that exists within in **"London."** The paragraph is shaped overall to give maximum emphasis to the terrible irony whereby home, the last retreat and blessed sanctuary of the weary citizen, is the very place where the last, killing blow is struck. (It is interesting that J. P. Hardy, looking at **"London"** as primarily a political poem, finds this passage 'contrived and macabre'.) It is not just in its close focus on the threat that comes into the house that the passage goes beyond Juvenal, however. It is in its detail that it is most telling. The midnight murderer is 'Cruel with Guilt, and daring with Despair'. The psychology is at once apocalyptic and accurate, and it is of a piece with the vision of minds distorted and subverted that has filled the whole of the poem. The very 'Bar' which the murderer breaks, though morally neutral in Juvenal and in any case inanimate, becomes in Johnson another manifestation and instrument of the all-pervading treachery of London: it is 'faithless'. After the violence of the murderer's entrance the scene of the murder itself is presented, by a beautiful and chilling transition, in a sinister dumb-show. The murderer

Invades the sacred Hour of silent Rest,
And leaves, unseen, a Dagger in your Breast.

The word 'unseen', finely poised in the line, gives us the full intensity of Johnson's vision here. The murderer who goes unseen goes also undetected. The enemy within escapes justice. (Johnson worked carefully on the deadly concluding line of this passage. In the existing draft the line reads 'And plants his Dagger in your slumb'ring Breast'. The four revisions in the line as published all intensify its disturbing qualities: 'slumb'ring' was redundant after 'silent Rest', and it could go with the more advantage as it might suggest that the victim would be unconscious of the evil done; the introduction of 'unseen' brings with it the notion of the murderer evading justice; changing 'his Dagger' to 'a Dagger' implies that this was just one of any number of daggers that might be used by now depersonalized assassins; lastly, the substitution of 'leaves' for 'plants' concentrates attention on the helpless corpse of the murdered citizen rather than on the act of violence itself.)

The damage being done to London is registered in Johnson's poem as damage to human integrity. The city has been subverted, and affording no economic or physical security for its native citizens it affords no mental security either. It is very easy to overstate the robustness of the speaker's viewpoint in **"London."** Margaret Doody in her reconsideration of Augustan poetry discusses the standing of Juvenal in the eighteenth century; she notes how he was seen by some as superior to Horace as being more appetitive and vigorous, and goes on to argue that

> Juvenal could seem the more British of the two poets as well as the more sublime. He was praised as the superior moralist, politically independent of corrupt courts whereas Horace the flatterer of Augustus was, as Dryden puts it, 'often afraid of laughing in the right place.' The honest satirist must, it was thought, have something of Juvenal in his composition.

I think it not unlikely that a sense of what Juvenal is like as indicated by Professor Doody has tended to influence our feeling about what **"London"** is like: the crucial thing to bear in mind, however, is that Johnson is not Juvenal, and that Satire III is the starting-point of Johnson's poem and not its destination. (pp. 203-11)

In the poem Johnson's speaker is not a rational observer. He inveighs against the city in a mood of impassioned distress. At one point, particularly inflamed by the way London has become 'The Common Shore [drain or sewer] of *Paris* and of *Rome*' (line 94), he senses that he is getting carried away and pulls himself up with an exclamation of impotent peevishness:

> Forgive my Transports on a Theme like this,
> I cannot bear a *French* metropolis.
>
> (ll. 97-8)

Thales of course is speaking no less than the truth: he *cannot* bear it and is on the very point of departure. In this Thales is in the minority: the majority of London's citizens are staying put. Thales may have started to do what Imlac sees as a manifestation of an unhealthy 'power of fancy over reason', that is to 'fear beyond the limits of sober probability' (*Rasselas,* ch. 44). I do not want to press the implications of this very far, because **"London"** needs to

be understood as an exercise in a number of different modes rather than as an absolute *cri de cœur,* but it certainly adds to the unsettling quality of the piece that it tends to leave us nowhere to turn for an assurance of stability. (The voice of the narrator, which occupies the first 34 lines of the poem, is not sufficiently developed or distinguished to fulfil this role.) It is worth noting that the reference to Thales's 'dissipated Wealth' in line 20 may call into question the motives of his philippic against the city: perhaps he should be scrutinizing his own improvidence. How much of what he says is sour grapes? The reference does not of course necessarily impugn Thales's prudence as it may have been the inevitable expense of city life which has eroded his fortune. In Johnson's **"London"** the worlds inside and outside the head have been undermined. The clarity, security, and confidence of the past (evoked in allusions to a time when England was 'The Land of Heroes and of Saints' (line 100)) have been lost, and before the poet's eyes the social and mental fabric of the city is falling apart. (p. 212)

The poet's despair is made only the more poignant by the fact that he adopts Juvenal's fiction that the indictment of the city comes from the lips of one about to leave it. In this fiction Johnson's friend Thales can solve the problem of London by putting hundreds of miles between himself and the enemy or enemies within. But of course Thales is enacting a fantasy which it is denied to the poet to realize for himself: when Thales glides off on his wherry the poet will remain on the strand at Greenwich, with no choice but to turn back and face the enemy within the squalid metropolis he both inhabits and imagines. (pp. 213-14)

What delighted the literary circles of Oxford and impressed Pope was not just a poem ingeniously adapting Juvenal's scathing satire to the political and social conditions of London in 1738. **"London"** was a great new poem because it brought to Juvenal a new tone and a new theme, and sought to reinforce its presentation of social catastrophe by revealing and exploiting the dangers to the private mind in a world subverted by an insidious enemy from which there was no escape because it (in all its multitude of forms) was entrenched within. (p. 214)

> *Andrew Varney, "Johnson's Juvenalian Satire on London: A Different Emphasis," in* The Review of English Studies, *Vol. XL, No. 158, May, 1989, pp. 202-14.*

Arthur Sherbo   (essay date 1990)

[*Sherbo is an American educator and author of* English Sentimental Drama *(1957) and* Studies in the Eighteenth Century English Novel *(1969). In the following excerpt, he seeks to demonstrate the value of Johnson's Shakespearean commentary for "revealing sidelights into his life."*]

Many eighteenth-century editions of Shakespeare make pleasant reading even when the text is ignored and attention is concentrated solely on the commentary. So often the personality of the editor is clearly discernible from the rambling, digressive notes of these eighteenth-century men of letters, some of them devoted amateurs not too much concerned with the profits to be derived from publication. But editorial practices change with the passage of time, and what was once acceptable is now frowned upon. Modern editors are usually cold, efficient, and above all else economical of words. We learn more about Shakespeare's plays from modern editions, but the editors are for all intents impersonal beings. Anyone who has worked closely with Lewis Theobald, William Warburton, and Samuel Johnson as editors of Shakespeare will be able to spot the notes of the respective editors, and each wrote thousands. One hesitates to predict the same success with the notes of twentieth-century Shakespeareans. Dr. Johnson was not entrusted with an edition of Shakespeare because he was adjudged peculiarly equipped for the task; rather the booksellers thought, quite naturally and shrewdly, that the public would be attracted by his name. The public was expected to ask: What does the Rambler have to say about Shakespeare? not: What advances will this edition of Shakespeare make over its predecessors? And when people bought their copy of the edition they looked as much for the "beauties of Johnson" as they did for the "beauties of Shakespeare." There exists a *Beauties of Johnson;* in it one will find many notes from the edition of Shakespeare, culled exactly because they can be exhibited in isolation as "beauties."

Johnson's personality can be seen in a small group of notes which allow glimpses, or half-glimpses, into his life. The notes are few, and their application must necessarily be accompanied by extreme caution. Although, for example, the extent of Johnson's knowledge of works on the supernatural as revealed in the notes in the edition is important and may even make more understandable his interest in the Cock-Lane Ghost affair, this knowledge is not in the form of a direct statement of personal belief or disbelief; our conclusions are based on the implicit statement. Yet William Kenrick, in his vicious *Review of Dr. Johnson's New Edition of Shakespeare* (1765), seizes upon this very question as the basis for one of his sneers. Johnson had written a long note on *The Tempest* in which he showed some knowledge of spirits and the "System of Enchantment." Kenrick says that he would have passed over the note "But as the world hath been pleased very publickly to impute sentiments to him, which seem incongruous with those he here professes, I cannot pass it over without some little animadversion. The incongruity I mean lies here: the Doctor, I have been frequently informed, very religiously believes in the existence of ghosts and apparitions; although he here strongly insinuates that there *never* was any such thing practised as witchcraft." And he ends his comment, after further "animadversions," with a reference to the Cock-Lane Ghost: "Hence, though I should be brought to believe, that our editor did go from Cock-lane to Clerkenwell, to fulfill an appointment with the ghost of Fanny, I cannot possibly suspect him of ever going there purposely to meet the devil." Kenrick is, of course, distorting Johnson's words to fit his purposes and to give him opportunity for another display of wit.

There are, however, many explicit statements in the notes, not often couched in the first-person singular, it is true, but unmistakably the expression of Johnson's personal views, of his conclusions from first-hand experience, and of his prejudices. When he is prompted to a moral utterance by something in the text it is obviously permissible to assume that the observation is not made solely for the occasion, and hence relatively insignificant, but that it represents the commentator's serious conviction. Again the

wealth of biographical material that we possess is of great value, allowing us to compare bare editorial statements with the facts of Johnson's life. Sometimes the notes make it possible to reconstruct an incident in Johnson's life and, by way of conjecture that borders on certainty, to supplement the still meagre accounts of some events.

Many of the observations on Johnson's character made by Boswell, to start with certainties, are corroborated by Johnson's own works. That is to say, Johnson's moral nature, his melancholy, and his detestation of dishonesty—to choose a few examples at random—might be deduced from *The Rambler, Rasselas,* and the *Letter to the Reverend Mr. Douglas, Occasioned by his Vindication of Milton.* When these same facets of his nature are reflected again and again in other works they are almost as good biographical evidence as Boswell's statements. The presence of notes in the edition of Shakespeare illustrating these and other aspects of Johnson's character make our total picture of him stand out more boldly and clearly.

Johnson's melancholy manifested itself in frequent attacks of hypochondria—the words are actually synonymous in his *Dictionary*—when, for no reason at all, he would fall into a "gloomy, pensive, discontented temper." One suspects, then, that he was impelled, by psychological necessity, to comment on certain passages that touch upon the subject. Thus his note on the Queen's lines in *Richard II* (II, ii, 30-32), "I cannot but be sad; so heavy-sad, / As, though, on thinking, on no thought I think, / Makes me with heavy nothing faint and shrink," comes from personal experience of the very feeling expressed by Shakespeare's character. He writes that "the involuntary and unaccountable depression of the mind, which everyone has sometimes felt, is here very forcibly described," remembering his own state of mind during his attacks of "vile melancholy."

A regard for truth which sometimes was carried so far as to border on the ridiculous is claimed for Johnson by Boswell. For example, Johnson would retire to his garret without telling his servant so that the latter would not be guilty of falsehood when he told visitors his master was not at home. Johnson's objection, critically justifiable or not, to Hamlet's invoking his madness as excuse for wronging Laertes, is prompted by this consideration: "I wish Hamlet had made some other defence; it is unsuitable to the character of a good or a brave man, to shelter himself in falsehood." When Prince John breaks his promise to the rebellious lords (2 *Henry IV*, IV, ii, 112-123), Johnson is shocked into violent objection: "It cannot but raise indignation to find this horrible violation of faith passed over thus slightly by the poet, without any note of censure or detestation." And when the King exclaims to the conspirators in *Henry V:* "Oh, how hast thou with jealousy infected / The sweetness of affiance!" (*Henry V*, II, ii, 126-127), Johnson is moved to compliment Shakespeare's judgment: "one of the worst consequences of breach of trust is the diminution of that confidence which makes the happiness of life, and dissemination of suspicion, which is the poison of society." Equally pertinent are these sentences from a note on the temptation scene in *Othello:* "Deceit and falsehood, whatever conveniences they may for a time promise or produce, are, in the sum of life, obstacles to happiness. Those who profit by the cheat, distrust the deceiver, and the act by which kindness was sought, puts an end to confidence." Twice he deprecates the lightness with which vows are made, and it will be recalled that in his conversation he often inveighed against the practice.

Although these notes, and many more like them, do not afford new insights into Johnson's life they are as revealing as anything in **Rasselas** or **The Rambler.** But the few that follow are even more revealing.

During the period Johnson was working on his **Shakespeare** he was arrested for debt. The publisher Jacob Tonson "extricated" him. This occurred in February 1758; two years earlier (March 1756) he had been arrested for a small debt, and Samuel Richardson, responding to his letter for help, secured his release by lending him the money. If Boswell knew of these two arrests, he chose to be silent about them. It is more likely that Johnson told him nothing. There is no note of poignant distress, no hint of personal shame, in the letters Johnson wrote on these two occasions. Are we then to assume that he was indifferent, that his pride suffered no hurt? A debtor's prison was an extremely unpleasant place; the progress of the prisoner to the "spunging house" was not kept secret; considerations of delicacy seem rarely to have occurred to eighteenth-century London bailiffs. There is no evidence that Johnson was in a debtor's prison or even in a "spunging house" either in 1756 or 1758, but a note in his **Shakespeare** leads to the conjecture that he felt keenly the disgrace of being arrested. He may even have been exposed to public view. The note is a remark on the concluding line of Act II of *2 Henry VI,* Eleanor's words upon her arrest, "Go, lead the way, I long to see my prison." Johnson writes: "This impatience of a high spirit is very natural. It is not so dreadful to be imprisoned, but it is desirable in a state of disgrace to be sheltered from the scorn of gazers." Incidentally, one will find no note on this in the Arden *2 Henry VI* (1957). Is there, perhaps, some connection between these arrests and *Idler* No. 22, **"Imprisonment of Debtors,"** which was substituted for the original, satirical essay upon the republication of the periodical in 1761?

In a sense, what I have done with the note quoted above and what I intend to do with succeeding ones is to interfere between the reader and Johnson's commentary, an ungrateful task which others have perhaps wisely shunned. Walter Raleigh's introduction to *Johnson on Shakespeare* concludes with remarks reminiscent of the closing paragraphs of Johnson's **"Preface."** Johnson had advocated that the reader "yet unacquainted with the powers of *Shakespeare* . . . read every play from the first scene to the last, with utter negligence of all his commentators." Raleigh, speaking of those notes in the edition which record Johnson's "own tastes and habits," rightly considers it "a privilege to be able to hear him talking without the intervention of Boswell; we can in some ways come closer to him when that eager presence is removed." Raleigh comments on a few of these notes in his introduction, but there is no commentary in the book proper. When he cites a note on *Cymbeline* in which Johnson voices an eloquent protest against experiments on live animals he justly observes that we cannot find Johnson's views on this matter in Boswell's *Life.* But he forgets *Idler* No. 17 on vivisection and certain passages in the Soame

Jenyns review. It is very difficult to say something new about Johnson's life and personality.

One fact for which novelty can be claimed is based upon Johnson's changing attitude toward two earlier editors of Shakespeare. When Johnson published his **Miscellaneous Observations on The Tragedy of Macbeth** in April 1745, Lewis Theobald had been dead less than a year (he died Sept. 18, 1744), and in all probability Johnson's work was started while Theobald was still alive. The third note in the **Miscellaneous Observations** concludes with a compliment to Theobald: "For some of his amendments are so excellent, that, even when he has failed, he ought to be treated with indulgence and respect." The note, minus the concluding compliment, is included in the edition of 1765. And there Theobald suffers more than any other critic in Johnson's commentary, on many occasions being patronizingly addressed as "Poor" Theobald. In the 1756 **"Proposals"** Johnson had so far disturbed "the manes of Theobald" (his own words) as if to say of him that "if fame be just to his memory" he "considered learning only as an instrument of gain, and made no further inquiry after his author's meaning, when once he had notes sufficient to embellish his page with the expected decorations." In Johnson's **"Preface"** Theobald is described as "weak and ignorant," "mean and faithless," and "petulant and ostentatious." Theobald had been fair game for others, of course, but Johnson's *volte face* between 1745 and 1756 is hard to explain without impugning his character. And one is not troubled because Johnson failed to realize, as most others had, that Theobald's edition was superior to any up to 1765, but rather because he ill-naturedly berated a man, dead for almost ten years, who deserved better treatment at his hands.

Johnson's reversal of position in regard to Theobald should be compared with his changing attitude to another Shakespearean editor, Sir Thomas Hanmer. After Johnson had finished his notes on *Macbeth* in 1745, Hanmer's edition "fell into" his hands. His opinion of Hanmer's performance, based on his reading of *Macbeth* alone, is low indeed. He concludes the **Miscellaneous Observations** by suggesting that Hanmer would have done better to devote himself to the "arts of policy" in which he excelled rather than to meddle in pursuits of which he knew so little. Hanmer died in 1746, and a highly laudatory *Translation of the Latin Epitaph on Sir Thomas Hanmer Written by Doctor Friend* that appeared in the *Gentleman's Magazine* for May, 1747, has been accepted as Johnson's by the most recent editors of his poetry. Boswell doubts Johnson's authorship of this *Epitaph,* citing the unfavorable remarks in the **Miscellaneous Observations** as evidence. By 1765, when the Preface was written, Johnson, whether he wrote the "Translation" or not, had so far changed his earlier opinion of Hanmer that he praised him highly for his work on Shakespeare. If Johnson was sincere in his praise of Hanmer's editorial performance, he was guilty of incredibly poor judgment, for Hanmer's was, and is, one of the worst editions ever to be published. If this praise was dictated by other considerations, Johnson is again placed in an unfavorable light. He turns on "poor," untitled, unpopular Theobald, after stating that he should be treated with indulgence and respect, and he is suddenly impressed by the abilities of the highly placed and prominent Sir Thomas Hanmer (also recently dead) not too long after refusing to blunt "the weapons of criticism" on him. Possibly these shifts of opinion represent honest reconsideration of the merits of the two men; if so, one is faced with the alternative of an almost inexplicable lapse of critical judgment. What is more, it has been argued that Johnson used the text of the 1757 *Theobald* for much of his own edition. This smacks too much of unpardonable ingratitude. Joseph Ritson, in his *Remarks, Critical and Illustrative . . .* 1783, fastened on this: "It were to be wished that Dr. Johnson had shewn somewhat less partiality to *pride of place;* for, though he professes to have treated his predecessors with candour, Theobald, the best of Shakespeares editors, experiences as much scurrility and injustice at his hands, as Hanmer and Warburton, the worst of them, do deference and respect. For this, however, the learned critic might have his private reasons, which, as they could scarcely have justified his conduct, he did right to conceal." Johnson has been too much praised for his expressed intention to forbear the acrimony, invective, and turbulence displayed by earlier editors and critics. His statement to this effect occurs in the **"Preface,"** but it seems never properly to have been recognized that the **"Preface"** has little to do with the edition, that it was written practically *in vacuo.* The notes in the edition represent what Johnson could do as an editor; the **"Preface"** is merely a comprehensive statement, almost nowhere original, of what an editor should do. Judged by the standards of Johnson's **"Preface,"** Johnson's edition is a failure.

Does Johnson, to pass on to other matters, ever have anything to say about his physical ailments, those conditions which caused him to present such an awkward spectacle as he made his progress along the streets of London? Are there indications that he felt in himself "the pain of deformity?" There are many references in the *Life* to his convulsive starts, his rolling, his shaking his head and body, as well as to his blowing out his breath, his mutterings and inarticulate sounds, and his talking to himself. He suffered from a compulsion to perform certain almost ritualistic acts such as touching posts and entering or leaving a room in a certain way. He cannot have been unaware of the strangeness of his actions and appearance, and on the one occasion when they were remarked on in his presence he endured their mention with "great gentleness." But it must be remembered that the offender was "a very young girl." A man as proud and sensitive as Johnson must, however, have felt some distress as a result of his eccentricities. These eccentricities were, nevertheless, forgotten by those who were close to him, since they were more than amply compensated for by his intellectual powers. Johnson was aware that the "deformed" must divert attention away from their deformity, a fact made evident by two notes in his commentary. The expression "pain of deformity" occurs in one of these as a part of a comment of Falstaff: "Every man who feels in himself the pain of deformity, however, like this merry Knight, he may affect to make sport with it among those whom it is his interest to please, is ready to revenge any hint of contempt upon one whom he can use with freedom." The second note is on the hunchbacked Richard, Duke of Gloucester's, resolution "to o'er-bear such / As are of better person than myself" (*3 Henry VI,* III, ii, 166-167): "Richard here speaks the language of nature. Whoever is stigmatised with deformity has a constant source of envy in his mind, and would counterbalance by some other superiority these advantages which they feel themselves to want. *Bacon* remarks that the deformed are commonly daring, and it is almost

proverbially observed that they are ill-natured. The truth is, that the deformed, like all other men, are displeased with inferiority, and endeavour to gain ground by good or bad means, as they are virtuous or corrupt." And since Richard III, because of his deformity, "cannot prove a lover," he determines "to prove a villain." Johnson comments: "Shakespeare very diligently inculcates, that the wickedness of Richard proceeded from his deformity, from the envy that rose at the comparison of his own person with others, and which incited him to disturb the pleasures that he could not partake." If it be objected that Johnson would not apply the word "deformed" to himself, it must be noted that he thinks of Falstaff's girth as a deformity. Johnson, a virtuous man, endeavoured to gain ground by good means, and if we apply the words of the note to him, we must acquit him of ill-nature. Joseph Wood Krutch remarks, "Perhaps it has never been sufficiently remarked that one reason for his domineering manner, for his insistence upon winning almost every argument by fair means or foul, is to be sought in his realization that he must dominate any group of which he did not expect to become quickly the butt. In many respects he was made to be laughed at."

Johnson was a proud man throughout his life. A strong feeling of independence made him look with suspicion upon unsolicited favors. James Northcote, Sir Joshua Reynolds' biographer, remembers hearing Reynolds observe "that if any drew Johnson into a state of obligation without his own consent, that man was the first he would affront, by way of clearing off the account." A passage in *I Henry IV* which elicits a remark from Johnson is so like this description of Johnson's pride that it merits full quotation. Worcester speaks:

> For, bear ourselves as even as we can,
> The King will always think him in our debt;
> And think, we deem ourselves unsatisfy'd,
> Till he hath found a time to pay us home.
>
> (I, iii, 285-8)

Johnson's note, "This is a natural description of the state of mind between those who have conferred, and those that have received, obligations too great to be satisfied," emerges as a personal confession when compared with Reynolds' comment. Possibly the best-remembered anecdote illustrative of Johnson's pride is that of the boots some well-meaning person left outside his door at Oxford. Johnson, only twenty-one then—and who are more proud than the young?—"threw them away with indignation." Possibly this pride of the young, commented on in his edition, "Shame operates most strongly in the earlier years, and when can disgrace be less welcome than when a man is going to his bride?" offers a clue to an unexplained incident of Johnson's marriage. It is not known why the marriage was performed at Derby rather than at Birmingham. Mr. Aleyn Lyell Reade's explanation is as plausible as any, and is strengthened, I believe, by the note just quoted. Mr. Reade says "Johnson was a young man of twenty-five: Mrs. Porter was a middle-aged woman of forty-six—not the modest forty to which she confessed when the license was applied for. He was practically penniless: she was possessed of a substantial sum of money. We can be extremely tolerant of such events when they have passed into the calms of historic fact, but most of us if alive at the time would have condemned him for cupidity and her for folly. The marriage was probably every whit as distasteful to his relatives as to hers, and both of them would be anxious to have it celebrated on neutral territory." Did the proud young Johnson feel some shame and disgrace when "going to his bride" and therefore resolve that the marriage should take place where he and his bride were not known? In another note in the edition Johnson speaks of the "imprudent generosity of disproportionate marriages." Compare also **Rambler** 167, where Johnson has his recently married correspondents say, "Our fortune was equally suitable, so that we meet without any of those obligations, which always produce reproach or suspicion of reproach, which, though they may be forgotten in the gaieties of the first month, no delicacy will always suppress, or of which the suppression must be considered as a new favour, to be repaid by tameness and submission, till gratitude takes the place of love, and the desire of pleasing degenerates by degrees into the fear of offending."

Admittedly, such conjecture about Johnson's marriage can be regarded only as conjecture; other notes in the edition, however, parallel Johnson's known sentiments so clearly that there can be little doubt as to their pertinence for this supplementary account of him as a man. Who can refrain from a feeling of pity for Johnson when he reads this note on Henry V's soliloquy (IV, i, 247 ff.), "There is something very striking and solemn in this soliloquy into which the king breaks immediately as soon as he is left alone; something like this, on less occasions, every breast has felt. Reflection and seriousness rush upon the mind upon the separation of a gay company, and especially after forced and unwilling merriment"? The reluctance with which Johnson allowed company to take their departure is also too well-known to require documentation. His concern for the feelings of servants or dependents, manifested in many acts of consideration towards the members of his household, is also well known. One remembers Frank Barber, blind Mrs. Williams, and Dr. Levett, among those who were the object of Johnson's regard despite their position of dependency. In **Rambler** 68 he stated that "The highest panegyrick . . . that private virtue can receive, is the praise of servants." And it was precisely this regard for the feelings of his servants that Johnson singled out for praise in the character of Timon. "Nothing contributes more to the exaltation of Timon's character than the zeal and fidelity of his servants. Nothing but real virtue can be honoured by domesticks; nothing but impartial kindness can gain affection from dependants." "Real virtue" and "impartial kindness," these Johnson possessed.

Johnson often remarks that friendship depends on pleasures or interests held in common. The idea finds frequent expression in the **Rambler** (nos. 99 and 160, for example) and is repeated in a note on Falstaff's soliloquy on the virtue of sack (*2 Henry IV*, IV, iii, 86-125). Falstaff says of Prince John, Hal's brother, who has just left him, "Good faith, this same young sober-blooded Boy doth not love me; nor a man cannot make him laugh" (87-89). Johnson reflects that "Men only become friends by *community of pleasures* (my italics). He who cannot be softened into gayety cannot easily be melted into kindness." Here is one of the essential differences, succinctly expressed, between Hal and his brother. Boswell reports Johnson as saying that "Many friendships are formed by a *community of sensual pleasures* (my italics) . . . We form many friendships with bad men, because they have agreeable qualities" and "Most friendships are formed by caprice or by chance,

mere confederacies in vice or leagues in folly." One of the first friends Johnson made in London was Richard Savage. Much has been written about this friendship, and Johnson's biographers have exercised their ingenuity to account for the great moralist's sincere attachment for a man who "was marked," says Boswell, "by profligacy, insolence, and ingratitude." Boswell feared that this association "imperceptibly led Johnson into some indulgencies which occasioned much distress to his virtuous mind." The number of times that Johnson remarks on pleasures shared in common and agreeable qualities in a man as basis for friendship prompts the belief that these, among others, were the reasons for his association with Savage. They lead further to the conjecture that the dark hints of sexual irregularity in Johnson's earliest years in London may have some foundation in fact.

Obviously, there can be no suggestion that Johnson's life is laid bare in the notes to Shakespeare, but, almost as obviously, one cannot dismiss the evidence of his commentary. The temptation to quote more of Johnson's notes is not easy to resist, but too much of a good thing may cloy the appetite. The danger of making capital of notes that seem to illuminate certain shadowy events in his life is so manifest that it should not be necessary to warn against its indiscriminate practice. Documentation of Johnson's opinions, moral utterances, predilections, and the like, has for a long time, however, included quotation of pertinent passages from his work—only sometimes from the commentary to Shakespeare's text. Most scholars, however, have been content to document without reference to the edition of Shakespeare, and it has been my purpose to redirect attention to a fund of information that is, at the very least, highly suggestive. (pp. 53-63)

> *Arthur Sherbo, "Johnson's 'Shakespeare': The Man in the Edition," in* College Literature, *Vol. XVII, No. 1, 1990, pp. 53-65.*

Michael Payne (essay date 1990)

[*Payne is an American educator, essayist, and author. His books include* Irony in Shakespeare *(1974) and* Shakespeare: Contemporary Critical Approaches *(1980). In the following excerpt, he centers on the "imaginative licentiousness" that Johnson displays in his criticism of Shakespeare's works.*]

> Imagination, a licentious and vagrant faculty, unsusceptible of limitations, and impatient of restraint, has always endeavoured to baffle the logician, to perplex the confines of distinction, and burst the inclosures of regularity (**Ram,** 125).

How one writer responds to another is of interest not least because of the ways the predecessor illuminates his critic. This is particularly true of readings of Shakespeare, because of Shakespeare's own repeated insistence that his is a reflective art in which the beholder sees his own face. As Theseus and Hippolyta watch the play of Pyramus and Thisby, Theseus observes that the performance must be amended by imagination, to which Hippolyta adds, "It must be your imagination then, and not theirs" (V.i.212). The Prologue to *Henry V* confesses he lacks "a Muse of fire" and all else that would make him equal to his great subject. Instead, all he and his fellow players can offer is "a crooked figure"; and since they are performing within a "wooden O," they can claim to be only "ciphers" for the epic events of history, unless their performances can work upon the "imaginary forces" of the audience:

> For 'tis your thoughts that now must deck our kings,
> Carry them here and there, jumping o'er times,
> Turning th' accomplishment of many years
> Into an hour-glass; for the which supply. . . .

In the Sonnets the poet argues that his only hope for immortality lies in the participatory imagination of generations of readers. Not only is "perspective . . . best painter's art" and does the eye gild "the object whereupon it gazeth," but also the power of the poet's "eternal lines" to give immortal life to his subject is active only "So long as men can breathe or eyes can see."

Samuel Johnson appears to have had little regard for the Sonnets, and in his annotations in his edition of Shakespeare he passes in silence over the passages just quoted. Johnson does keep returning, however, especially in his **"Preface to Shakespeare,"** to Hamlet's address to the Players, through which Shakespeare seems to insist most strongly that drama has always existed to reflect the moral, temperamental, and historical features of audiences. The purpose of playing, Hamlet says, "both at the first and now, was and is to hold, as 'twere, the mirror up to nature; to show virtue her own feature, scorn her own image, and the very age and body of the time his form and pressure. True Shakespearean that he is, Johnson is not content passively to accept Hamlet's (or Shakespeare's) word. Instead, he so thoroughly engages his imagination with this passage, selecting from it and adding his own emphasis, that he transforms it into nothing less than his own Shakespearean myth. At first Johnson simply turns Hamlet's words back on Shakespeare without explicitly referring to Hamlet or the Players at all: "Shakespeare," Johnson writes, "is above all writers, at least above all modern writers, the poet of nature; the poet that holds up to his readers a faithful mirrour of manners and of life."

There is little reason to doubt that in the original of Johnson's submerged quotation, when Hamlet uses the word *nature,* he means *human nature;* thus, the personifications: "virtue *her* own feature, scorn *her* own image, and the very age and body of the time *his* form and pressure." When we look into the tragic mirror, we see a human face that is in some sense our own with its morality, temperament, and historical situation accentuated. Editors of Johnson have usually assumed that when he calls Shakespeare "the poet of nature" that he also means simply human nature. Johnson's definition of *nature* in his **Dictionary** does not, however, provide much support for this assumption. There he lists twelve definitions, only three of which imply human nature. He concludes his entry for this word by saying that it is a word used so frequently with significations so various and definitions so difficult to determine that Boyle's study of the term is worth "epitomizing." In his *Free Enquiry into the Received Notion of Nature,* Boyle lists eight distinct uses of the word, which Johnson carefully summarizes; all of them refer either directly or indirectly to the material or corporeal world. Similarly, Johnson's illustrative quotations, several taken from *King Lear,* speak unambiguously of the physical world, beginning with Edmund's radical biologism: "Thou, nature, art my goddess." Turning from the **Dictionary** of 1755 to the **"Preface"** of 1765, we should not be surprised to find Johnson praising Shakespeare as "an exact surveyor of the inanimate world." Whereas later poets only partly copy from nature, impressed as they are by the authority of books, Shakespeare (according to Johnson) "shews plainly that he has seen with his own eyes; he gives the image which he receives, not weakened or distorted by the intervention of any other mind."

This sense of Shakespeare as a poet of the inanimate, non-bookish world is fundamental to Johnson's Shakespeare myth. Like all myths, Johnson's is a story embodying a network of images that convey a value system and express desire or longing mixed with dread. Shakespeare, Johnson argues, has become an ancient. Although he may be for that reason dismissed—either by those who are unable to add to truth or by those whose only hope for praise and fame lies in the future—he may also be venerated simply out of a "credulous confidence in the superior wisdom of past ages." It is Shakespeare's antiquity, as well as his careless treatment of his own texts, that justifies producing a modern edition of his works. But Johnson's is a larger claim than that the plays require the benefits of scholarship to enable modern readers to understand them adequately. More than any other writer Shakespeare, in Johnson's view, is in touch with the undisplaced, elemental stuff of life itself. Not only is he a poet *of* nature and his perceptions therefore undistorted by other minds; it would also seem that he is the most ancient of all writers (except, perhaps, Homer):

> Shakespeare's plays are not in the rigorous and critical sense either tragedies or comedies, but compositions of a distinct kind; exhibiting the *real* state of sublunary nature, which partakes of good and evil, joy and sorrow, mingled with endless variety of proportion and innumerable modes of combination; and expressing the course of the world, in which the loss of one is the gain of another; in which, at the same time, the reveller is hasting to his wine, and the mourner burying his friend; in which the malignity of one is sometimes defeated by the frolick of another; and many mischiefs and many benefits are done and hindered without design.

> Out of this chaos of mingled purposes and casualties the ancient poets, according to the laws which custom had prescribed, *selected* some the crimes of men, and some their absurdities. . . . Thus rose the two modes of imitation, known by the names of tragedy and comedy. . . .

Johnson does not, of course, say here that Shakespeare comes chronologically before Sophocles and Aristophanes; rather, he implies Shakespeare's imaginative priority as a kind of pregeneric fecundity. This suggestion that Shakespeare was present before there was literary creation as we now know it enables Johnson to excuse Shakespeare's violation of critical rules. Along with his atavistic naturalism goes his intrinsic freedom. That his practice of mixing tragedy and comedy "is a practice contrary to the rules of criticism will be readily allowed," Johnson admits; "but there is always an appeal open from criticism to nature."

Already in Johnson's myth questions of law and of history arise. As though he were bringing Shakespeare before the bar of criticism, Johnson levels a series of potentially damaging accusations: Shakespeare, he says, "makes no just distribution of good and evil, nor is always careful to shew in the virtuous a disapprobation of the wicked; he carries his persons indifferently through right and wrong"; his plots are as loose as his morality, suggesting that he does not fully "comprehend his own design"; he is careless with endings and resorts to anachronisms "without scruple"; he allows his characters "contests of sarcasm" and gross pleasantries; his tragedies, with their "effusions of passion" are much inferior to his comedies; his narrations and set speeches are wordy and weak; he allows himself to become entangled in "unwieldy" sentiments "which he cannot well express"; his language is not always appropriate to his thought; he mixes emotions too quickly; and he cannot resist the seduction of puns. In a word, Shakespeare is licentious. But like that other keyword, *nature, licentious* has curiously ambivalent meanings and applications. In his **Dictionary,** Johnson associates the word with sexual license and natural power. To illustrate his first definition—"unrestrained by law or morality"—Johnson quotes passages on "licentious lust" from the *Faerie Queene* and from *The Comedy of Errors;* and to illustrate his second definition—"presumptious, unconfined"—he quotes a passage from Roscommon on "licentious waves" flooding a field. In his **"Proposals"** of 1756 and in his **"Preface"** written nine years later, Johnson uses the word to describe Shakespeare's language, but he appears equally concerned with the possibility of his own licentious critical and editorial practice. This anxiety may have arisen from Johnson's reading Upton's *Critical Observations on Shakespeare* (1746), where rules of English grammar are derived from Shakespeare's works. Once these rules are known, Upton claims, readers and editors will be less likely to indulge "the licentious spirit of criticism." After referring explicitly to this passage, Johnson insists that in proposing textual emendations in the notes to his edition, he has not "licentiously indulged" in conjecture but rather has "confined" his "imagination to the margin." On the one hand, there is Shakespeare, poet of nature, spontaneous in perception, in tune with the undifferentiated prima materia of life, free and licentious; on the other hand, there are the laws of criticism, books that dull the senses; the selected abstractions of pure genres, and the rules of grammar and decorum.

Johnson does *not* simply ally himself with the rational laws of criticism against the imaginative powers of poetry. That he does not do so is particularly clear in his exuberant display of his own image-making powers in his final accusation against Shakespeare, which ends up hardly an accusation at all. The accuser is equally guilty of the licentious free-play of linguistic imagination:

> A quibble is to Shakespeare, what luminous vapors are to the traveller; he follows it at all adventures, it is sure to lead him out of his way, and sure to engulf him in the mire. It has some malignant power over his mind, and its fascinations are irresistible. Whatever be the dignity or profundity of his disquisition, whether he be enlarging knowledge or exalting affection, whether he be amusing attention with incidents, or enhancing it in suspense, let but a quibble spring up before him, and he leaves his work unfinished. A quibble is the golden apple for which he will always turn aside from his career, or stoop from his elevation. A quibble, poor and barren as it is, gave him such delight, that he was content to purchase it, by the sacrifice of reason, pro-

priety and truth. A quibble was to him the fatal Cleopatra for which he lost the world, and was content to lose it.

When he turns to writing his notes for *Antony and Cleopatra,* which is one of the plays that seems to have preoccupied him throughout the writing of the **"Preface,"** Johnson continues to associate linguistic excess with Cleopatra; indeed, Johnson's imagination almost becomes licentious, which for him would mean leaving the margin and entering Shakespeare's text. In a note to IV.xii, when Antony calls Cleopatra "Triple-turn'd whore!" Johnson writes:

> Shall I mention what has dropped into my imagination, that our authour might perhaps have written "triple-tongued"? "Double-tongued" is a common term of reproach, which rage might improve to "triple-tongued."

Shakespeare continually emphasizes Cleopatra's identification with the flooding Nile and with all forms of experience that over-flow measure. Her imaginative identification with an audience's point of view is so full that she chooses death in defiance of a boy actor's impersonation of her greatness. She embodies Johnson's two senses of licentiousness: unrestricted lust and unbounded natural power.

If we were to judge only from his notes to the play, we would have ample reason to believe that Johnson had little regard for *Antony and Cleopatra;* for he judges its language obscene, its jests low, its scenes of pathos ridiculous, its conceits far-fetched, and its characters not carefully discriminated. Nevertheless, the play had such a powerful hold on Johnson's imagination that it made him reassess his understanding of the principles of drama. The twenty-seven scene changes of Acts III and IV create the illusion of events occurring simultaneously in different places, as well as occurring in temporal succession. Johnson surprisingly defends Shakespeare against the charge of "violation of those laws which have been instituted and established by the joint authority of poets and of criticks." Based on his own experience as a spectator of plays, Johnson rejects the unities of time and place. He sides with the beauty of variety over the obedience to critical rules. That he cannot resist the Serpent of Old Nile in her "infinite variety" seems almost to surprise Johnson himself. He confesses that he is "frighted at my own temerity" and almost "ready to sink down in reverential silence" before the authorities who support the unities, but he does not. Again, his imagination goes out to Shakespeare in violation of reason, authority, and law. (pp. 66-71)

There is no doubt that Shakespeare, like the Bible, can be quoted to anyone's purpose, but it is rare indeed for critics to follow lines of thought in Shakespeare against their own ideological grain. Johnson does precisely this, putting in jeopardy his own commitments to critical judgment, the accumulated authority of books, and his skepticism about the progress of history. Despite his professed confidence in the progress of Shakespearean textual criticism, Johnson looks back to Dryden for conservative inspiration. Dryden, like the late eighteenth-century painter Fuseli, contemplated the greatness of the past with a sense of despair for the present:

> Our Age was cultivated thus at length,
> But what we gain'd in Skill we lost in Strength.

Our Builders were with Want of Genius curst;
The second Temple was not like the first. ('To My Dear
Friend Mr. Congreve, on his Comedy Call'd The Double
Dealer')

The "burden of the past," as Walter Jackson Bate calls it, fell like a debilitating weight, producing what Dryden says is a "secret shame" in the poet who even thinks of Shakespeare's name. Shakespeare was of the age of Giants before the Flood; Dryden and Johnson think of theirs as an age of lesser men.

At the end of his **"Preface"** Johnson turns to Dryden, who has inspired his Shakespeare myth all along. Dryden, Johnson reminds us, wrote that "the images of nature were still present" to Shakespeare; when he "describes any thing, you more than see it, you feel it too"; he "was naturally learned: he needed not the spectacles of books to read nature." Johnson ends his quotation with the Latin verse from Virgil's First Eclogue concerning "the cypresses among the bending osiers." Much earlier in the **"Preface"** Johnson draws from this Virgilian quotation to complete his myth and to identify his own age. He is comparing Addison's *Cato* to *Othello* when he dismisses poets such as Addison who cultivate "a garden accurately formed." In contrast, Shakespeare "is a forest in which oaks extend their branches, and pines tower in the air." Johnson makes his English substitutions for Virgil's Italian cypresses. There may be weeds and brambles in Shakespeare's woods and meaner minerals among the diamonds in his mines; but the sublime, the delicate, and the beautiful are all there too. The biblical text that supplies first Dryden and then Johnson with their images of literary history locates the Giants, with whom Dryden associates Shakespeare, before the Flood and identifies imagination with the origin of evil that makes the Deluge necessary. Shakespeare is a prehistorical Giant who allows Johnson not only his progressive Whig and conservative Tory historiography, but also his simultaneous celebration and distrust of the imagination. Throughout the **"Preface"** Johnson's visions of history continually cross each other. Shakespeare is the earliest poet in that he is closest to the origins of life, but he is also the product of a barbarous age by which his rudeness and occasional obscenity can be excused. Johnson ends his **"Preface"** by speculating that it was Shakespeare's "superiority of mind" that led him to be so careless of his "own performances" as to give little attention to the preservation of his texts. Here Johnson imagines Shakespeare's comparing his creative "powers" with what he actually produced, suggesting that the texts we have are merely gross displacements of original performances within Shakespeare's mind. After Shakespeare, the smaller men of lesser times compete with each other for fame as they work to restore and explain what Shakespeare has already transcended. When he at last places himself within the mythic vision he has created, Johnson allows the tragic potential in his story to win out. He admits that he is one of those "candidates of inferiour fame" whose belatedness condemns him to wish for powers that he fears he lacks. Johnson thinks of himself, in comparison with Shakespeare, as a belated poet who must confine his imagination to the margin and, in comparison with Dryden, as a belated critic. In his **"Life of Dryden"** (1779) Johnson singles out Dryden's criticism of Shakespeare for special admiration: "In a few lines is exhibited a character, so extensive in its comprehension, and so curious in its limitations, that

nothing can be added, diminished, or reformed; nor can the editors and admirers of Shakespeare, in all their emulation of reverence, boast of much more than of having diffused and paraphrased this epitome of excellence, of having changed Dryden's gold for baser metal, of lower value though of greater bulk."

Little if any of Dryden's influence as an encomiastic critic is manifest, however, in Johnson's *Miscellaneous Observations on the Tragedy of Macbeth,* which appeared twenty years before the **"Preface"** as a specimen of the edition to follow; nor are Johnson's imaginative engagements with Shakespeare's text and his dramatic sense of the effect of stage action on the audience distinguishing features of this early exercise in his Shakespeare criticism. Although Johnson displays his astonishing command of the vast literature on witchcraft and enchantment, he continually resorts to the unfortunate expedient of altering the text when his powers of interpretation fail him. Several of his notes, especially on Macbeth's soliloquies, have never been surpassed. But when Johnson edited his own *Observations* to supply the notes on *Macbeth* for his edition, he suppresses much of his earlier work and argues with a great deal that he lets stand. Indeed, the notes on *Macbeth* display all of the worst features of editorial practice that Johnson enumerates in the **"Preface"**:

> Particular passages are cleared by notes, but the
> general effect of the work is weakened. The mind
> is refrigerated by interruption; the thoughts are diverted
> from the principal subject; the reader is
> weary, he suspects not why; and at last throws
> away the book, which he has too diligently studied.

For the stage direction to the opening scene of *Macbeth,* Johnson supplies a learned history of witchcraft, since a play depending on enchantment would lead to the dismissal of the work and the poet's banishment "to the nursery . . . to write fairy tales instead of tragedies" unless the reader were instructed in placing such a work in the context of the poet's contemporaries. Shakespeare's demonology is a manifestation of "the darkness of ignorance" of his times, the imported effects of "eastern expeditions," and the witchcraft laws enacted during the first year of James I's reign in response to his *Daemonologie.* "This law was repealed in our own time," Johnson remarks proudly. In the notes that follow, Johnson attempts to mediate between Warburton and the editors who preceded him, but in most cases Johnson is too eager to emend the text and to override earlier editor's judgments, allowing his progressive sense of textual history to dominate. For example, in Macbeth's dagger soliloquy in Act II, Johnson rejects Pope's, Theobald's, and Warburton's understanding of Macbeth's descent into homicidal, rapacious bestiality:

> . . . wither'd Murther
> Alarum'd by his sentinel, the wolf,
> Whose howl's his watch, thus with his stealthy pace,
> With Tarquin's ravishing strides, tow'rds his design
> Moves like a ghost.

In refusing to accept the verb "strides"—Johnson would read "sides"—he not only elevates Macbeth but also keeps him from a powerful dramatic enactment of the imagery. It has become traditional for actors to adopt a stealthy pace and ravishing strides, moving first like a wolf and then like a ghost, as they speak these lines. In his notes as they were written for the *Observations* of 1745, Johnson fully identifies with what might be called Macbeth's moral conflicts and provides a superb paraphrase of "If it were done, when 'tis done . . . "; but he is unwilling to think that it is Macbeth's imagination that is tainted with blood, even before he kills the King. Macbeth has carried out murders "yet . . . fantastical" in his imagination apparently long before he takes Duncan's life.

There is a curious but fascinating tradition of Shakespearean criticism within brackets. A. C. Bradley, for example, advances his views of Hamlet's melancholia in two famous lectures in *Shakespearean Tragedy* and then undercuts them in a bold and candid bracketed sentence. Johnson seems to have begun this bracketing tradition in his notes on *Macbeth.* Although he lets stand his arguments from *Observations* for altering the text in Acts II and III, Johnson inserts bracketed arguments against his own earlier views. In 1745 Johnson was ready to deny Macbeth's self-reflexive readiness "to explain his own allusions to himself." This is consistent with Johnson's note on "strides" in that it reduces the multidimensionality of Macbeth's personality. But in response to his own temptation to alter the text when Macbeth speaks of his fears of Banquo—

> There is none but he,
> Whose being I do fear: and, under him,
> My genius is rebuk'd; as, it is said,
> Anthony's was by Caesar.

Johnson produces his own self-reflexive, multi-dimensional critical text. This dialogic character of Johnson's imagination is consistent with Fredric Bogel's perceptive study of Johnson and the role of authority. Bogel claims that "for Johnson the assumption of authority was both necessary and necessarily guilt-ridden, and that he sought ways to assume and disclaim that authority in a single gesture"; he goes on to show that for Johnson authority is "a matter not of personal unity and universal authoritativeness but of energies intrinsically divided by internal conflict and self-questioning." Although Johnson reprints his earlier authoritative judgment against self-division in Macbeth, he adds in brackets the comment beginning,

"Walking up High Street": Johnson and Boswell experience life in Edinburgh by night.

"This note was written before I was fully acquainted with Shakespeare's manner, and I do not now think it is of much weight. . . ." Rather than delete it, as he did with so many of his other early observations on *Macbeth,* Johnson prefers to have us overhear him arguing with himself.

Johnson's notes on *King Lear* are free of earlier published views of that play. In most of his notes Johnson echoes the major themes of the **"Preface"**: Shakespeare's language is "licentious;" and Lear's behavior reflects the vulgarity, "barbarity," and "ignorance of the age." Johnson is, however, silent in his notes concerning those passages on nature that he uses as illustrative quotations in the *Dictionary.* In the **"Preface"** Johnson says that when he studied the emendations of other editors, a caution, like that of a morality play, was "forced" upon him: "I encountered in every page Wit struggling with its own sophistry, and Learning confused by the multiplicity of its views." Johnson enacts this mini-drama himself in his attempts to justify the now notorious Tate version of Cordelia's retiring "with victory and felicity." In Tate's elaborate defense against Shakespearean tragedy, *King Lear* becomes a love story of Edgar and Cordelia. Since they never meet in either the 1608 or 1623 versions of the play, Edgar and Cordelia require much more than Shakespeare provides. Most of Tate's additions lead up to the final rescue of Cordelia and her reunion with Edgar:

> Cord: My *Edgar,* Oh!
>
> Edg: My Dear *Cordelia!* Lucky was the Minute
> Of our Approach, the Gods have weigh'd our
> Suff'rings;
> W' are past the Fire, and now must shine to
> Ages.

Johnson knows that these lines are not Shakespeare's, however shocking and unendurable the genuine ones are for him. Perhaps here more than anywhere else in his edition we might wish that Johnson had not confined his imaginative empathy to the margins. Although Garrick pared down the Tate version, the happy ending of *King Lear* survived until 1823.

When Johnson's *Shakespeare* appeared, it failed to measure up to the expectations Johnson had created with his **"Proposals"** and *Observations.* Although James Barclay, a young Oxford student, came to Johnson's defense, even he was forced to admit that

> Upon the publication of Mr. Johnson's *Shakespeare,* the expectations of the generality . . . were greatly disappointed: They had been induced to expect from his avowed learning and ingenuity, a compleat commentary upon the works of their immortal bard; but through the concurring circumstances of inattention in the Editor, and sanguine expectation in the reader, the performance, I am afraid, has incurred the public censure.

Despite the vicious attacks of William Kenrick, Johnson's edition sold well, earning him an estimated £1,312 10s. Far more damaging than the responses of his contemporaries were the judgments of the Romantics. Schlegel sees in Johnson's criticism merely the continuation of misunderstandings of Shakespeare's "depth of purpose"; Coleridge dismisses Johnson as a "dogmatic Critic and soporific Irenist"; and Hazlitt laments that "Shakespear's bold and happy flights of imagination were equally thrown away upon our author." In these unperceptive attacks can be seen the emergence of the Romantic myth of Dr. Johnson as unimaginative, authoritarian, oppressor of poets. In the flourishing of this unfortunate myth, a clearer perception of Johnson was lost. In 1786 Robert Burrowes read two splendid papers on Johnson's style to the Royal Irish Academy. Burrowes observes that

> Johnson's licentious constructions . . . are not to be conceived as flowing entirely from his passion for substantives. His endeavours to attain magnificence, by removing his stile from the vulgarity, removed it also from the simplicity of common diction, and taught him the abundant use of inversions and licentious constructions of every sort. . . . Metaphorical expression is one of those arts of splendor which Johnson has most frequently employed; and while he has availed himself of all its advantages, he has escaped most of its concomitant faults.

Johnson's imaginative licentiousness is brilliantly manifest in his criticism of Shakespeare. When Johnson sees that aspect of himself reflected back to him when he looks into Shakespearean tragedy, he neither averts his eyes nor hides from his own readers what he has discovered of himself. (pp. 71-7)

> *Michael Payne, "Imaginative Licentiousness: Johnson on Shakespearean Tragedy," in* College Literature, *Vol. XVII, No. 1, 1990, pp. 66-78.*

FURTHER READING

Bate, W. Jackson. *The Achievement of Samuel Johnson.* New York: Oxford University Press, 1955, 248 p.
  Highlights the general themes of Johnson's writings and the character of his thinking.

———. *Samuel Johnson.* New York: Harcourt Brace Jovanovich, 1975, 646 p.
  Biographical synthesis of Johnson's life and works.

Belloc, Hilaire. "On *Rasselas.*" In his *Short Talks with the Dead,* pp. 173-83. 1926. Reprint. Freeport, N.Y.: Books for Libraries Press, 1967.
  Maintains that Johnson's Abyssinian message is "true, important, of good moral effect, and packed." Also relates his impressions of the marginalia in Hester (Thrale) Piozzi's edition of *Rasselas.*

Buono, Carmen Joseph Dello. *Rare Early Essays on Samuel Johnson.* Rare Early Essay Series. Darby, Penn.: Norwood Editions, 1981, 208 p.
  Reproductions of nineteenth-century and early twentieth-century essays on Johnson's life and relationships.

Burke, John J., Jr., and Kay, Donald, eds. *The Unknown Samuel Johnson.* Madison: University of Wisconsin Press, 1983, 182 p.
  Collection of essays which reveals various aspects of Johnson's literary career.

Carlyle, Thomas. "Boswell's Life of Johnson." In *Macaulay's and Carlyle's Essays on Samuel Johnson,* edited by William Strunk, Jr., pp. 65-158. New York: Henry Holt and Co., 1895.
  A reply to Macaulay's essay [see excerpt dated 1856]. Strunk claims Carlyle "goes a little too far in his praise of Johnson."

Chesterton, G. K. "*Rasselas.*" In his *G. K. C. as M. C.: Being a Collection of Thirty-Seven Introductions by G. K. Chesterton,* edited by J. P. de Fonseka, London: Methuen and Co., 1929, pp. 196-201.
  Evaluates *Rasselas* in view of modern readers' tastes.

Courtney, William Prideaux and Smith, David Nichol. *A Bibliography of Samuel Johnson.* Oxford: Clarendon Press, 1968, 185 p.
  Definitive primary bibliography of Johnson's works, including title page facsimiles.

Donaldson, Ian. "Samuel Johnson and the Art of Observation." *ELH* 53, No. 4 (Winter 1986): 779-99.
  Argues that Johnson's powerful reasoning abilities were often hindered by his strong biases.

Edinger, William. *Samuel Johnson and Poetic Style.* Chicago: University of Chicago Press, 1977, 272 p.
  Explicates the logic of Johnson's critical judgments in *The Lives of the Poets.*

Finch, G. J. "Reason, Imagination and Will in *Rasselas* and 'The Vanity of Human Wishes'." *English* XXXVIII, No. 162 (Autumn 1989): 195-209.
  Posits that the operation of reason in Johnson's works is "very equivocal."

Fleeman, J. D. "Johnson's Poetry." *Proceedings of the British Academy* LXIX (1983): 355-69.
  Traces the evolution of Johnson's poetical career.

Greene, Donald J. " 'Pictures to the Mind': Johnson and Imagery." In *Johnson, Boswell and Their Circle,* pp. 137-58. Oxford: Clarendon Press, 1965.
  Focuses on Johnson's critical concern with the effective use of imagery.

Hedrick, Elizabeth. "Locke's Theory of Language and Johnson's *Dictionary.*" *Eighteenth-Century Studies* 20, No. 4 (Summer 1987): 422-44.
  Considers the similarities between Johnson's and Locke's ideas about words, noting evidence of Lockean linguistic notions in Johnson's *Dictionary.*

Henson, Eithne. "Johnson's Romance Imagery." *Prose Studies* 8, No. 1 (May 1985): 5-24.
  Explores the implications of Johnson's Latinate phraseology and its relation to the romance of chivalry.

Hilles, Frederick W., ed. *New Light on Dr. Johnson: Essays on the Occasion of his 250th Birthday.* New Haven: Yale University Press, 1959, 348 p.
  Collection of biographical and critical essays.

Honan, Park. "Dr. Johnson and Biography." *Contemporary Review* 245, No. 1427 (December 1984): 304-10.
  Points out the motivating factors behind Johnson's *Lives of the Poets.*

Hudson, Nicholas. *Samuel Johnson and Eighteenth-century Thought.* Oxford: Clarendon Press, 1988, 272 p.

Considers Johnson's moral and religious thought in the context of eighteenth-century philosophy and religion.

Johnsonian News Letter I— (1940—).
　　Quarterly periodical containing book reviews and articles on many facets of Johnson's life and works.

Kniskern, William F. "Satire and the 'Tragic Quartet' in 'The Vanity of Human Wishes'." *Studies in English Literature 1500-1900* 25, No. 3 (Summer 1985): 633-49.
　　Illustrates how Johnson, through satire, dispels heroic associations connected with the "tragic quartet": Charles XII of Sweden, Charles of Bavaria, Xerxes, and Cardinal Wolsey.

Knoblauch, Cyril H. "Samuel Johnson and the Composing Process." *Eighteenth-Century Studies* 13, No. 3 (Spring 1980): 243-62.
　　Overview of Johnson's opinions of writing and books, noting his preoccupation with the "ironic realization of the insufficiency of the Word."

Korshin, Paul J., ed. *Johnson after Two Hundred Years*. Philadelphia: University of Pennsylvania Press, 1986, 253 p.
　　Collection of essays providing late-twentieth-century perspectives on Johnson's life, intellectual development, and canon.

Korshin, Paul J. and Allen, Robert R. *Greene Centennial Studies*. Charlottesville: University Press of Virginia, 1984, 489 p.
　　Contains several essays on Johnson and his literary career, including "Johnson and Chronology" and "Johnson as Patron."

Leavis, F. R. "Johnson as Critic." *Scrutiny* XII, No. 3 (Summer 1944): 187-204.
　　Praises Johnson's critical writings as "living literature," claiming that they "can be read afresh every year with unaffected pleasure and new stimulus."

————. "Doctor Johnson (Reconsiderations VII)." *The Kenyon Review* VIII, No. 4 (Autumn 1946): 637-57.
　　Examines Joseph Wood Krutch's book, *Samuel Johnson* [see excerpt dated 1944], and provides additional commentary on Johnson's literary achievement.

Lewis, C. S. Letter to W. H. Lewis. In his *Letters of C. S. Lewis,* edited by W. H. Lewis, pp. 128-29. London: Geoffrey Bles, 1966.
　　Reprints a letter dated 2 August 1928, written by Lewis to his brother. Of Johnson, Lewis claims, "I don't know anyone who can settle a thing so well in half a dozen words."

Maner, Martin. *The Philosophic Biographer: Doubt and Dialectic in Johnson's Lives of the Poets*. Athens: University of Georgia Press, 1988, 187 p.
　　Interprets Johnson's biographical techniques, highlighting his skepticism, satire, and critical insights.

McCrea, Brian. "Style or Styles: The Problem of Johnson's Prose." *Style* XIV, No. 3 (Summer 1980): 201-15.
　　Ascertains the extent to which Johnson's prose determines his meaning and his style.

Mencken, H. L. "The Artist." In his *The Vintage Mencken,* edited by Alistair Cooke, pp. 146-47. New York: Vintage Books, 1955.

States that Johnson "left such wounds upon English prose that it was a century recovering from them."

Nath, Prem, ed. *Fresh Reflections on Samuel Johnson: Essays in Criticism*. Troy, N. Y.: Whitston Publishing Company, 1987, 414 p.
　　Collection of essays which consider the impact of Johnson's life and literature on Western thought, including "Sexual Difference and Johnson's Brain" and "Johnson's *Lives* and Augustan Poetry."

Page, Norman. *Dr. Johnson: Interviews and Recollections.* London: Macmillan & Co., 1987, 176 p.
　　Attempts to supplement "the picture given by Boswell" with memoirs of Johnson's acquaintances.

Parker, G. F. *Johnson's Shakespeare*. Oxford: Clarendon Press, 1989, 204 p.
　　Reflects on the intent of Johnson's "Preface to Shakespeare", attempting to recreate the Johnsonian Shakespeare.

Pierce, Charles E. "The Conflict of Faith and Fear in Johnson's Moral Writing." *Eighteenth-Century Studies* 15, No. 3 (Spring 1982): 317-38.
　　Defines the central conflict of Johnson's religion and its place in mid-eighteenth-century morality literature.

Raleigh, Walter. *Six Essays on Johnson*. Oxford: Clarendon Press, 1910, 184 p.
　　Critical and biographical essays written to commemorate the bicentennial of Johnson's birth, such as "Johnson Without Boswell" and "Early *Lives of the Poets*."

Reinert, Thomas. "Johnson and Conjecture." *Studies in English Literature 1500-1900* 28, No. 3 (Summer 1988): 483-96.
　　Seeks to demonstrate that Johnson's proclivity for "figuring out in advance all the ways things can turn out" affected his mode of writing.

Reynolds, Sir Joshua. "Reynolds on Johnson." In his *Portraits,* edited by Frederick W. Hilles, pp. 74-90. New York: McGraw-Hill Book Co., 1952.
　　Eloquent biographical and critical elegy. Discovered only in this century, this essay was probably written in 1786 or 1787, according to Hilles.

Saintsbury, George. "Johnson, Goldsmith, and the Later Essayists." In his *Short History of English Literature,* 613-21. London: Macmillan & Co., 1924.
　　Critical overview of Johnson's life, reputation, writings, and style.

Sherbo, Arthur. "Johnson's Intent in the *Journey to the Western Islands of Scotland.*" *Essays in Criticism* XVI, No. 4 (October 1966): 382-97.
　　Reveals Johnson's intentions in his *Journey,* refuting Jeffrey Hart's critical thesis [see excerpt dated 1960].

Thrale, Hester Lynch. *Dr Johnson by Mrs Thrale,* edited by Richard Ingrams. London: Chatto & Windus, 1984, 137 p.
　　Record of personal observations of Johnson's life and writings.

Van Tassel, Mary M. "Johnson's Elephant: The Reader of the *Rambler.*" *Studies in English Literature 1500-1900* 28, No. 3 (Summer 1988): 461-69.
　　Identifies the intended and actual audience of Johnson's *Rambler.*

Venturo, David F. "The Poetics of Samuel Johnson's Epitaphs and Elegies and "On the Death of Dr. Robert Levet"." *Studies in Philology* LXXXV, No. 1 (Winter 1988): 73-91.

Highlights the influence of Johnson's elegiac and epitaphic principles in his poetry and moral writings.

Vesterman, William. *The Stylistic Life of Samuel Johnson.* New Brunswick, N. J.: Rutgers University Press, 1977, 139 p.

Examines Johnson's prose, narrative, biographical, and poetic styles.

Vulliamy, C. E. *Ursa Major: A Study of Dr. Johnson and His Friends.* London: Michael Joseph, 1946, 340 p.

Biographical and historical perspectives on Johnson's friends. Vulliamy claims, "we cannot really know Johnson unless we make some endeavour to know his friends."

Wahba, Magdi, ed. *Johnsonian Studies.* Cairo: Société orientale de publicité, 1962, 350 p.

Collection of essays by leading Johnsonians, such as Donald Greene and Arthur Sherbo.

Wain, John. *Samuel Johnson.* New York: Viking Press, 1975, 388 p.

Biography focusing on Johnson's literary and social situation.

Watkins, W. B. C. *Perilous Balance: The Tragic Genius of Swift, Johnson, & Sterne.* Princeton: Princeton University Press, 1939, 172 p.

Biographical portraits of Johnson, Jonathan Swift, and Laurence Sterne, underscoring affinities which shaped their literary development.

Watson, George. "Samuel Johnson." In his *The Literary Critics: A Study of English Descriptive Criticism,* pp. 72-101. London: Woburn Press, 1962.

Traces Johnson's "formidable" influence on the historical method in criticism.

Waugh, Arthur. Introduction to *Lives of the English Poets,*

Vol. 1, by Samuel Johnson, pp. v-xv. London: Oxford University Press, 1906.

Describes the circumstances surrounding the composition of Johnson's *Lives* and evaluates its merit.

Wheeler, David, ed. *Domestick Privacies: Samuel Johnson and the Art of Biography.* Lexington: University Press of Kentucky, 1987, 192 p.

Collection of essays analyzing and exploring the uses of Johnson's biographical perspectives in *The Lives of the Poets,* including "Life, Art, and the *Lives of the Poets*" and "Johnson's *Lives* and Modern Students."

Whibley, Charles. "Samuel Johnson: Man of Letters." *Blackwood's Edinburgh Magazine* CCXXI, No. MCCCXXXIX (May 1927): 663-72.

Reviews Johnson's contributions to English letters and examines his literary style.

Whitman, Walt. "Johnson." In *Rivulets of Prose: Critical Essays by Walt Whitman,* edited by Carolyn Wells and Alfred F. Goldsmith, pp. 224-25. New York: Greenberg, Publisher, 1928.

Brief biographical portrait concluding that Johnson "wrote in a latinized style, not simple and with unlearned instincts but pompous and full of polysyllables."

Wimsatt, W. K. *The Prose Style of Samuel Johnson.* New Haven: Yale University Press, 1941, 166 p.

Surveys the rhetoric, theory, and historical implications of Johnson's prose style.

————. "Images of Samuel Johnson." *ELH* 41, No. 3 (Fall 1974): 359-374.

Contrasts variant biographies of Johnson.

Woolf, Virginia. "Saint Samuel of Fleet Street." *The Nation & the Athenaeum* XXXVIII, No. 7 (14 November 1925): 248.

Comments that Johnson's character was endowed with "the peculiar sympathy, the majestic tolerance, the broad humor, which . . . still make the cabmen think of him on a wet night in the Strand."

Giovanni Pico della Mirandola

1463-1494

Italian philosopher.

Recognized as one of the most influential philosophic thinkers of the Italian Renaissance, Pico della Mirandola is perhaps best remembered for his attempt to philosophically reconcile the doctrines of Christianity, Aristotelianism, Platonism, and the Jewish cabala. His thought particularly as expressed in *Oratio de hominus dignitate (On the Dignity of Man)*, marks a significant development in the history of Christian philosophy; Paul J. W. Miller has stated that "Pico found new realms of ideas in his explorations. These new regions remain part of a single world, reflecting God as their cause. The philosophy of Pico della Mirandola expresses the fundamentally religious spirit of the Renaissance."

Born in 1463, Pico was the youngest son of the ruling family of Mirandola, a small domain outside Modena and Ferrara. He was educated by private tutors as a child and displayed an early scholastic inclination. At the age of fourteen he was sent to study canon law at the University of Bologna. Dissatisfied with the law curriculum there, Pico left two years later and went to the University of Ferrara to study philosophy and theology. Leaving for Padua for further instruction in 1480, Pico met several fellow humanist scholars and began writing poetry.

It was at the University of Padua that Pico was introduced to the neoplatonic interpretations of Aristotle. After meeting the renowned Italian philosopher and humanist Marsilio Ficino in 1484, Pico devoted himself to studying the new Platonism. In a quest to uncover further sources for his developing theories, he traveled to the University of Paris, a recognized center of philosophy during the late fifteenth century. Returning to Italy in 1486, Pico settled in Florence, writing his *Commento* on a poem by Benivieni. That year he also published the *Conclusiones*: nine hundred theses based on theology, metaphysics, dialectics, and natural magic. Pico offered to defend his statements in a public debate to be held in Rome, and it was to introduce these debates that Pico composed the *Oration on the Dignity of Man*. However, a papal commission deemed thirteen of the statements heretical, leading Pope Innocent VIII to cancel the proposed disputations. The young philosopher therefore composed his *Apologia,* a defense of his position concerning the thirteen condemned theses, dedicating the work to his friend and benefactor, Lorenzo de'Medici. Pico fled to France to escape Papal wrath and, while there, was imprisoned briefly in Vincennes. Granted permission to return to Florence in 1487, Pico was pardoned by Innocent's successor, Alexander VI, six years later.

During his period of tribulation, Pico relied on the support and protection of such friends as Ficino, de'Medici, and the Dominican reformer Girolamo Savonarola. After his return to Florence, though, he gradually turned from the thinking of Ficino and de'Medici, dedicating himself to Savonarola and composing earnest religious treatises in-

stead. The *Heptaplus* and *De Astrologia* were written during this period. Although Savonarola aspired to convince Pico to join the Dominicans, the latter was never confirmed as a friar. Further, while it seems that Pico did intend to become a traveling missionary, this plan never came to fruition. He died on 17 November 1494, possibly poisoned by one of his servants. Pico was buried in Dominican robes and interred at St. Mark's in Florence.

Although Pico's works mark a significant development in the history of philosophic thought and were highly regarded by his contemporaries for their originality, they have since fallen into relative obscurity. Not all of the philosopher's works are forgotten, however. *On the Dignity of Man* is recognized by many scholars as Pico's most enduring treatise. Composed as the opening speech to the proposed public defense of his nine hundred theses, the *Oration* expands on propositions set forth by Ficino in his *Platonica theologia de immortalitate animorum* (1482). Pico describes a theory of human nature that many scholars deem far more radical than Ficino's. Giovanni Semprini, an early twentieth-century literary critic, theorized that "[while Ficino was] not yet capable of liberating himself from the concept of transcendence, remaining too much an adherent of the negative mysticism of Pseudo-

Dionysius, Pico [succeeded], with a single blow, in delivering man from all dependence on the divine will." Miller has provided support for this statement: "The most remarkable contribution [Pico] makes is his notion that the root of man's excellence and dignity lies in the fact that man is the maker of his own nature. Man may be what he wishes to be; he makes himself what he chooses." This concept has sparked debate over the years as to the extent Pico intended it to be carried. While some scholars have sided with Semprini and claimed that Pico proposed complete freedom from divine will, others take a more tempered approach and maintain that Pico simply suggested self-determination as a way of preparing for the acceptance of religious doctrine. As Russell Kirk has written, "Pico . . . knew that no being can dignify himself: dignity is a quality with which one is *invested;* it must be conferred. For human dignity to exist, there must be a Master who can raise man above the brute creation. If that Master is denied, then dignity for Man is unattainable."

The *Heptaplus* is another of Pico's enduring works. Praised by Ficino, this mystical commentary on the Creation is often regarded as a supplement to the proposals of the *Oration.* As Harriet Waters Preston related: "It was a fixed and characteristic idea of Pico's that God had never suffered the deepest mysteries of any faith to be committed to writing; that the visible text ever conveyed only the lower and more literal meaning, behind which the docile spirit may seek and find the symbolical and the celestial. The [*Heptaplus*] professed to indicate the hidden significance of the Mosaic cosmogony." In addition, Pico developed within this work the idea of the "microcosm": the concept of man as a "little world" that reflects the entire universe, or macrocosm. This concept of a microcosm was neither new nor unique to Pico; it had been a part of philosophy for centuries. As Avery Dulles notes: "Although often described as if it were the appanage of the Renaissance, the microcosm-conception was at least as old as Democritus. It made its appearance in Stoic philosophy, in the Hermetic books, and in the Cabbala. During the Middle Ages it was developed by S. Augustine, S. Thomas and by many others. Nicolas of Cusa stressed the conception heavily; and Ficino expounded it in almost literally the same terms as Pico."

Although Pico never quite succeeded in establishing and defending a firm syncretic theory, his writings influenced philosophical thought for many generations. Hailed by his fellow philosophers, denounced by the religious authorities of his day, and respected by scholars throughout the years, Pico has become, in the words of Nesca Robb, "a living symbol of his age, embodying its diffuse intellectual curiosity, its generous warmth and eagerness of spirit, its belief that nothing on which men have lavished love or interest or endeavour can be wholly without value."

PRINCIPAL WORKS

Commento sopra una canzona d'amore di Girolamo Benivieni (prose) 1486
* [*A Platonick Discourse upon Love,* 1651]
Conclusiones sive theses DCCCC Romae anno 1486 publice disputandae, sed non admissae (prose) 1486
Oratio de hominis dignitate (essay) 1486
Apologia (prose) 1487

Heptaplus (treatise) 1489
De ente et uno (treatise) 1492
   [*Of Being and Unity,* 1943]
† *Disputationes adversus Astrologiam* (treatise) 1494
Opera omnia Ioannis Pici, Mirandulae Concordiaeque Comitis (prose) 1557
De Hominis Dignitate, Heptaplus, De Ente et Uno e Scritti Vari (prose) 1942

*Incomplete translation, published in Thomas Stanley's *Poems.*

† Left in manuscript form at Pico's death.

Walter H. Pater   (essay date 1871)

[*A nineteenth-century essayist, novelist, and critic, Pater is regarded as one of the most famous proponents of aestheticism in English literature. In the excerpt below, he surveys and praises several of Pico's works.*]

The oration which Pico composed for the opening of [his proposed defense of nine hundred paradoxes] still remains; its subject is the dignity of human nature, the greatness of man. In common with nearly all mediæval speculation, much of Pico's writing has this for its drift; and in common also with it, Pico's theory of that dignity is founded on a misconception of the place in nature both of the earth and of man. For Pico the earth is the centre of the universe; and around it, as a fixed and motionless point, the sun and moon and stars revolve like diligent servants or ministers. And in the midst of all is placed man, *nodus et vinculum mundi,* the bond or copula of the world, and the interpreter of nature: that famous expression of Bacon's really belongs to Pico.

> Tritum est in scholis, (he says) esse hominem minorem mundum, in quo mixtum ex elementis corpus et spiritus caelestis et plantarum anima vegetalis et brutorum sensus et ratio et angelica mens et Dei similitudo conspicitur. (*It is a commonplace of the schools that man is a little world, in which we may discern a body mingled of earthy elements and ethereal breath, and the vegetable life of plants, and the senses of the lower animals, and reason, and the intelligence of angels, and a likeness to God.*

A commonplace of the schools; but perhaps it had some new significance and authority when men heard one like Pico reiterate it; and false as its basis was, the theory had its use. For this high dignity of man thus bringing the dust under his feet into sensible communion with the thoughts and affections of the angels was supposed to belong to him not as renewed by a religious system, but by his own natural right; and it was a counterpoise to the increasing tendency of mediæval religion to depreciate man's nature, to sacrifice this or that element in it, to make it ashamed of itself, to keep the degrading or painful accidents of it always in view. It helped man onward to that reassertion of himself, that rehabilitation of human nature, the body, the senses, the heart, the intelligence, which the Renaissance fulfils. And yet to read a page of one of Pico's forgotten books is like a glance into one of those ancient sepulchres, upon which the wanderer in classical lands has sometimes stumbled, with the old disused ornaments and furniture of a world wholly unlike ours still fresh in them. That whole conception of nature is so different from our own. For Pico the world is a limited place, bounded by actual crystal walls and a material firmament; it is like a painted toy, like that map or system of the world, held as a great target or shield in the hands of the grey-headed father of all things, in one of the earlier frescoes of the Campo Santo at Pisa. How different from this childish dream is our own conception of nature, with its unlimited space, its innumerable suns, and the earth but a mote in the beam; how different the strange new awe and superstition with which it fills our minds! "The silence of those infinite spaces," says Pascal, contemplating a starlight night, "the silence of those infinite spaces terrifies me." *Le silence éternel de ces espaces infinis m'effraie.* (pp. 381-82)

It was in another spirit that he composed a Platonic commentary, the only work of his in Italian which has come down to us, on the song of Divine Love, *secondo la mente ed opinione dei Platonici,* according to the mind and opinion of the Platonists, by his friend Hieronymo Beniveni, in which, with an ambitious array of every sort of learning, and a profusion of imagery borrowed indifferently from the astrologers, the Cabbala, and Homer, and Scripture, and Dionysius the Areopagite, he attempts to define the stages by which the soul passes from the earthly to the unseen beauty. A change indeed had passed over him, as if the chilling touch of that abstract, disembodied beauty which the Platonists profess to long for had already touched him; and perhaps it was a sense of this, coupled with that over-brightness of his, which in the popular imagination always betokens an early death, that made Camilla Rucellai, one of those prophetesses whom the preaching of Savonarola had raised up in Florence, prophesy, seeing him for the first time, that he would depart in the time of lilies, prematurely, that is, like the field flowers which are withered by the scorching sun almost as soon as they have sprung up. It was now that he wrote down those thoughts on the religious life which Sir Thomas More turned into English, and which another English translator thought worthy to be added to the books of the *Imitation.* "It is not hard to know God, provided one will not force oneself to define him," has been thought a great saying of Joubert's. "Love God," Pico writes to Angelo Politian, "we rather may, than either know him or by speech utter him. And yet had men liefer by knowledge never find that which they seek, than by love possess that thing, which also without love were in vain found."

Yet he who had this fine touch for spiritual things did not—and in this is the enduring interest of his story—even after his conversion forget the old gods. He is one of the last who seriously and sincerely entertained the claims on men's faith of the pagan religions; he is anxious to ascertain the true significance of the obscurest legend, the lightest tradition concerning them. (pp. 382-83)

It is because the life of Pico . . . is so perfect an analogue to the attempt made in his writings to reconcile Christianity with the ideas of Paganism, that Pico, in spite of the scholastic character of those writings, is really interesting. Thus in the **Heptaplus,** or **Discourse on the seven days of the creation,** he endeavours to reconcile the accounts which pagan philosophy had given of the origin of the world with the account given in the books of Moses—the *Timæus* of Plato with the book of *Genesis.* The **Hetaplus**

is dedicated to Lorenzo the Magnificent, whose interest, the preface tells us, in the secret wisdom of Moses is well known. If Moses seems in his writings simple and even popular, rather than either a philosopher or a theologian, that is because it was an institution with the ancient philosophers either not to speak of divine things at all, or to speak of them dissemblingly; hence their doctrines were called mysteries. Taught by them, Pythagoras became so great a "master of silence," and wrote almost nothing, thus hiding the words of God in his heart, and speaking wisdom only among the perfect. In explaining the harmony between Plato and Moses Pico lays hold on every sort of figure and analogy, on the double meanings of words, the symbols of the Jewish ritual, the secondary meanings of obscure stories in the later Greek mythologists. Everywhere there is an unbroken system of analogies. Every object in the material world is an analogue, a symbol or counterpart of some higher reality in the starry heavens, and this again of some law of the angelic life in the world beyond the stars. There is the element of fire in the material world; the sun is the fire of heaven; and there is in the super-celestial world the fire of the seraphic intelligence. "But behold how they differ! The elementary fire burns, the heavenly fire vivifies, the super-celestial fire loves." In this way every natural object, every combination of natural forces, every accident in the lives of men, is filled with higher meanings. Omens, prophecies, supernatural coincidences, accompany Pico himself all through life. There are oracles in every tree and mountain-top, and a significance in every accidental combination of the events of life.

This constant tendency to symbolism and imagery gives Pico's work a figured style by which it has some real resemblance to Plato's, and he differs from other mystical writers of his time by a real desire to know his authorities at first hand. He reads Plato in Greek, Moses in Hebrew, and by this his work really belongs to the higher culture. Above all, there is a constant sense in reading him, that his thoughts, however little their positive value may be, are connected with springs beneath them of deep and passionate emotion; and when he explains the grades or steps by which the soul passes from the love of a physical object to the love of unseen beauty, and unfolds the analogies between this process and other movements upwards of human thought, there is a glow and vehemence in his words which remind one of the manner in which his own brief existence flamed itself away. (pp. 384-85)

[The] Renaissance of the fifteenth century was in many things great rather by what it designed or aspired to do than by what it actually achieved. It remained for a later age to conceive the true method of effecting a scientific reconciliation of Christian sentiment with the imagery, the legends, the theories about the world, of pagan poetry and philosophy. For that age the only possible reconciliation was an imaginative one, and resulted from the efforts of artists trained in Christian schools to handle pagan subjects; and of this artistic reconciliation work like Pico's was but the feebler counterpart. Whatever philosophers had to say on one side or the other, whether they were successful or not in their attempts to reconcile the old to the new, and to justify the expenditure of so much care and thought on the dreams of a dead religion, the imagery of the Greek religion, the direct charm of its story, were by artists valued and cultivated for their own sake. Hence a new sort of mythology with a tone and qualities of its own.

When the shipload of sacred earth from the soil of Jerusalem was mingled with the common clay in the Campo Santo of Pisa, a new flower grew up from it, unlike any flower men had seen before, the anemone with its concentric rings of strangely blended colour, still to be found by those who search long enough for it in the long grass of the Maremma. Just such a strange flower was that mythology of the Italian Renaissance which grew up from the mixture of two traditions, two sentiments, the sacred and the profane. Classical story was regarded as a mere datum to be received and assimilated. It did not come into men's minds to ask curiously of science concerning its origin, its primary form and import, its meaning for those who projected it. It sank into their minds to issue forth again with all the tangle about it of mediæval sentiments and ideas. In the *Doni Madonna* in the *Tribune* of the *Uffizii,* Michelangelo actually brings the pagan religion, and with it the unveiled human form, the sleepy-looking fauns of a Dionysiac revel, into the presence of the Madonna as simpler painters had introduced other products of the earth, birds or flowers, and he has given that Madonna herself much of the uncouth energy of the older and more primitive mighty Mother.

It is because this picturesque union of contrasts, belonging properly to the art of the close of the fifteenth century, pervades in Pico della Mirandula an actual person, that the figure of Pico is so attractive. He will not let one go; he wins one on in spite of oneself to turn again to the pages of his forgotten books, although we know already that the actual solution proposed in them will satisfy us as little as perhaps it satisfied him. It is said that in his eagerness for mysterious learning he once paid a great sum for a collection of cabbalistic manuscripts which turned out to be forgeries; and the story might well stand as a parable of all he ever seemed to gain in the way of actual knowledge. He had sought knowledge, and passed from system to system, and hazarded much; but less for the sake of positive knowledge than because he believed there was a spirit of order and beauty in knowledge, which would come down and unite what men's ignorance had divided, and renew what time had made dim. And so while his actual work has passed away, yet his own qualities are still active, and he himself remains, as one alive in the grave, *cæsiis et vigilibus oculis,* as his biographer describes him, and with that sanguine clear skin, *decenti rubore interspersa,* as with the light of morning upon it; and he has a true place in that group of great Italians who fill the end of the fifteenth century with their names, he is a true *humanist.* For the essence of humanism is that one belief of which he seems never to have doubted, that nothing which has ever interested living men and women can wholly lose its vitality—no language they have spoken nor oracle by which they have hushed their voices, no dream which has once been entertained by actual human minds, nothing about which they have ever been passionate or expended time and zeal. (pp. 385-86)

Walter H. Pater, "Pico Della Mirandula," in The Fortnightly Review, *Vol. 16, No. LVIII, October 1, 1871, pp. 377-86.*

Henry Osborn Taylor   (essay date 1920)

[*Taylor was an American scholar respected for his studies of the European mind from classical times through the seventeenth century. In the following excerpt from a work originally published in 1920, he theorizes that the sources for Pico's thought include Aristotelian and Platonic theology as well as the Cabala, providing support from the* Conclusiones *and the* Oration on Human Dignity.]

[Pico della Mirandola], who for the sake of philosophy had renounced his princedom, was one of the wonders of the *quattrocento,* and one of its noblest spirits. As a child and as a man, he was prodigious in his intellectual attainments and performances. How many characteristics of his time he represents! Among others, that of being at sea amid the newly flowing currents of Greek philosophy; at sea, as well, with the larger knowledge (craved if not yet won) of nature and the forces moving the universe.

Pico was closely knit in life and sympathy with the Florentine group of Platonists. Like his master Ficino, he was encompassed by his scholastic Aristotelian inheritance, which furnished his habits of thinking. Next, Platonism, in the very widest and loosest sense, may be deemed the source, or rather base, from which sprang his further proclivities, lucubrations, and noble consideration of life. Looking even beyond Platonism, his mind and temper sought appeasement from that fantastic, if soul-satisfying, allegorical interpretation of the Old Testament known as the Jewish Cabbala. With the wise Rabbis and many Christian doctors, Pico believed that its teachings had been secretly revealed by God to Moses, at the time when He delivered to His prophet the tablets of the law. The Cabbala could helpfully be used, he thought, in interpreting the Christian faith; in fact, (as we note) it's elastic symbolism could be compelled to any meaning. In it, moreover, could be discerned the material and intellectual, or prototypal, worlds figured by the Platonists. Holding with them, that a conception is true when it corresponds to the Idea in the Creator's mind, Pico held that our conceptions of the world must accord with the original, immaterial, world existing in the mind of God.

Pico's more direct thoughts of nature seemingly fall within his conception of magic. Let us not be repelled by the word, or conclude at once that Pico's magic did not contain wistful reflections touching nature's processes. "Magia est pars practica scientiae naturalist," says he. But what he meant by *magia,* can be realized only by one who can think in the terms of that Platonism which was fluid enough to run in Cabbalistic moulds, and can also place himself in the fifteenth century and share its lack of a consistent view of nature and physical law. Pico denounces the magic of his time, which relied on demoniac agencies. He wrote a book against Astrology, in which he sought to free men from her deadly web. It is but reasonable to think that he meant something not altogether foolish when he said that *magia* with him is nothing else than "naturalis philosophiae absoluta consummatio"; and again he calls it "nobilissima pars scientiae naturalis." It does no miracles itself, but gathers nature's powers which God scatters through the world, and comes to nature's aid. It investigates and works with the affinities of things, and *marries* terrestrial objects with the forces of the heavenly bodies. There is no virtue existing *seminaliter et separata* in heaven or earth which the true *Magus* cannot *actuare et unire,*—educe, actualize and join together. Such is its value. And so long as *we* think that man can learn of God by reflecting upon His works, we may understand how Pico came to make the following statement which gave umbrage to the Church: "Nulla est scientia quae nos magis certificet de divinitate Christi quam Magia et Cabala":—no other science yields surer proof of the divinity of Christ than Magic and the Cabbala.

Something of Pico's mentality and the nature of his interests may be gathered from the drift of the nine hundred **Conclusiones** or propositions, which he linked together, to make of them perhaps a "golden chain" joining Platonism to Christianity. They were drawn from various sources, or were put forward as his own convictions. One notes the authors upon whom he mainly drew. Twelve propositions he takes from Porphyry, nine from Jamblicus, and from Proclus fifty-five. Then he draws from the supposed mathematics of Pythagoras thirteen, and six from the opinions of Chaldean theologians. Then from the Thrice-great Egyptian Mercury, ten, such as these: "Ubicunque vita, ibi anima; ubicunque anima, ibi mens":—"omne motum corporeum, omne movens incorporeum." Forty-seven *Conclusiones Cabalisticae* follow, pertaining to the secret doctrine of the wise Hebrew Cabbalists, whose memory should be respected. The first one reads: "Sicut homo et sacerdos inferior sacrificat Deo animas animalium irrationalium, ita Michael sacerdos sacrificat animas animalium rationalium." He gives next a variety of *Conclusiones secundum opinionem propriam,* divided into physical, theological, Platonic, mathematical, Chaldaean, Orphic, Magic, Cabbalistical, "Paradoxas dogmatizantes," and "paradoxas conciliantes." His first statement is that Aristotle and Plato are really at one touching all matters natural and theological, although their language seems to conflict. Pico's interpretations were capable of reconciling anything; and so, besides making peace between these two great Greeks, he finds no difficulty in reconciling Aquinas and Duns Scotus. Here we quickly touch the scholastic substratum of his mind shown in his interest in analogies between the nature of an angel and the nature of the soul: "Sicut angelus necessario componitur ex essentia et esse, ita anima necessario componitur ex substantia et accidente."

Pico could be rational, according to our modern notions, and consequently heretical, as when he opposed transsubstantiation, or maintained that Christ did not really descend into Hell, but only *quoad effectum.* Nor can he bring himself to admit the propriety of everlasting punishment for mortal sin. After this he passes to his *Conclusiones* as to Magic, already noticed, and then to the magical significance of the Orphic hymns, and then to the Cabbala.

He publicly supported these nine hundred **Conclusiones** in Rome in the year 1488. Then quickly, as he says in "twenty nights," he wrote his wide-ranging **Apologia,** defending those of his **Conclusiones** which had been dubbed heretical. It was a bristling composition, maintaining, for instance, that the Cross should not be worshipped, that in the Eucharist the substance of the bread remained, and that it does not lie "in the free power of man to believe that an article of faith is true." If he wrote his **Apologia** in "twenty nights," the process, brought against him for these published opinions, lasted intermittently through the remaining years of his short life.

The magnificence of Pico's character, and his lofty consideration of man, appear in his letters, some of which were beautifully translated by Sir Thomas More, and in his oration upon **Human Dignity.** In the first letter, to his nephew, he bids him never wish to please those to whom virtue is displeasing. Then with reference to the Christian faith, he gives his principles and practice: "It is madness not to believe the Gospel, whose truth the blood of the martyrs proclaims, the apostolic voices re-echo, miracles prove, reason confirms, the world attests, the elements utter, the demons confess; but it is far greater madness, when you do not doubt the Gospel's verity, to live as if you did not doubt its falsity."

To Lorenzo de'Medici he writes in courtly praise of his Italian poems, and to Politian in most friendly praise of him and dispraise of himself. As against a narrow classicism, he defends the writings of the great scholastics, showing how their language suited their substance. And in a letter to a man of religion he protests that his first and constant care is to unite piety with philosophy; and says that a sane, firm and robust intellect can be hoped for only from the integrity of life, from goodly conduct and from divine religion.

The **Oration on Human Dignity** nobly expresses Pico's character and the result of his studies. It breathes a new sense of man's God-given freedom. Other creatures are coerced and limited by divine decree; but man's own decision is the arbiter of his nature. He is placed in the midst of the world, so that he may the better discern what it has to offer. God has made him neither heavenly nor earthly, neither mortal nor immortal, in order that he may mould himself to what he will, make himself a brute, or rise to the divine. This liberality from God is man's felicity; through which it is given him to have what he desires and to be that which he wills. Let a sacred ambition invade the mind, that we may strive with all our powers—as we may if we will. Let us despise the earth, and even the heavens, and beyond the courts of the world fly close to God. Thus Pico preaches the great principle—old Greek, human, or Christian—that it is for man to foster his higher nature and suppress the brute. He has taken the world's best to himself, and has brought his truth, the truth of his own nature, from afar:—from Plato, from Aristotle; from the Delphic Apollo's injunctions of temperance and self-knowledge; from the later mysteries—the "Chaldeans," the Cabbala, "Zoroaster," and from Christ.

Toward the close of his Oration, Pico denounces those who use philosophy as a means of gain, and proudly says: "For none other cause have I ever philosophized except in order that I might philosophize. Nor from my studies or my writings have I looked for any pay, or hoped or sought for any other fruit, than cultivation of the mind and the attainment of truth, which always and above all things I desire." In conclusion he advocates wide reading; let one not swear by a single master, be he Thomas or Duns Scotus. Every school has some good of its own. And Pico comments on the merits of the great scholastics, and upon the Greeks; though the names of the latter which he mentions show him to have dwelt with the later and more questionable men, and to have turned more naturally to the commentator and paraphraser, than to the great originals. Yet in spite of much confusing of brass with gold, his scheme of education was a broad one, and his principles of life were of the loftiest.

Pico held a great deal of his time, and also, strangely mixed with it, a great deal of the past, his own genius furnishing the plastic principle, the personal result. He could handle the lucubrations of Scholasticism, and mingle them with Cabbalistic elements to a potent brew, streaked here and there with reason. With demonic energy he sought a short-cut to illumination, an endeavor proper to his time. His short-cut lay through the discovery of secret, hidden, mystery-enfolding writings, which could declare the mystery of life to adepts. He would have the *secret* books of Moses, of Esdras, of Zoroaster, of any dimly adumbrated ancient seer; and from them would draw so quickly the secret of life, suddenly, magically, getting something for nothing, in such mode as Plato and Aristotle knew to be impossible and foolish. The strong character-building and strenuous qualities in Pico knew this too; yet could not keep this Cabbalistic Platonist, this genius of the fifteenth century, from struggling for the short-cut which is folly's cul-de-sac.

Florence was the hearth of the revival of Platonism; and there it became the philosophic fashion. In its origin, it may be taken as part of the strong humanistic revival of letters, which for the fourteenth and fifteenth centuries, had its chief home in Florence. Many of those scholars who were fascinated by "Platonism," were devotees of letters rather than philosophy. So the Platonic revival influenced letters, and diffused itself as an element in art; as one may see in the sonnets of Michael Angelo and the frescoes of Raphael; nor had Leonardo before them been untouched by its suggestiveness.

The revival of any antique system of philosophy could not possibly have any such effect in the fifteenth century as the resurrection of Aristotle had in the thirteenth. Then the systematizing theology and philosophy, called Scholasticism, was reaching the climax of its energy, and was at the same time prepared to adopt the form of a great classic system. The philosophy of Aristotle could supply the desired form and method, and also fill the same with a store of universal knowledge and opinion such as the thirteenth century was very ready to receive. But fifteenth century thought was no longer disposed to bind a novel ancient system on itself; nor did Platonism offer a fresh store of tangible scientific knowledge. The fifteenth century did not expend on it the same unstinted diligence, with the same seriousness of purpose, that the thirteenth had consecrated to Aristotle. And the earlier foundation was not now to be shaken by its rival, which in a measure it had superseded in the late twelfth and thirteenth centuries.

An interest in Platonism passed on from Italy to Spain and France and England. In France, sundry scholars devoted themselves to the elucidation of the immortal Dialogues (poor Dolet did this to his deadly scathe, for the Aristotelianism of the Paris University could be vengeful). And Queen Marguerite of Navarre drew draughts of Platonism from the translations of Ficino. In England, Sir Thomas More took delight in Pico's letters, and incorporated much Platonism in his *Utopia*. But everywhere conservative and anxious orthodoxy, especially at the universities, upheld Aristotle with a grip not to be loosed by anything which Platonism could offer. For indeed, philosophically, intellectually, scientifically, Platonism did not contain and could not offer, what the intellect of the coming time was to demand with a purposeful insistency becoming ever

clearer. The call was for a new view of the universe, for new methods of knowledge, new physical certainties and a larger volume of actually demonstrated fact. (pp. 277-84)

Henry Osborn Taylor, "Aristotle, Platonism, and Nicholas of Cusa," in his Thought and Expression in the Sixteenth Century, Vol. II, *revised edition, Frederick Ungar Publishing Co., 1930, pp. 267-90.*

Avery Dulles (essay date 1940)

[*Dulles is an American educator who has written widely on philosophy and theology. In the following excerpt, he examines the theological beliefs expressed in Pico's writings.*]

It is frequently held that the basis of Pico's religion was not the revealed dogma of Christianity but rather his personal philosophy. This point of view is typically expressed by Kieszkowski:

> Pico's conception of religion does not derive from any particular confessional doctrine, but is related to a philosophic conception of man and the universe.

The exact opposite, however, appears to be the case. Not only Pico's religion, but even his philosophy, is derived primarily from Christian doctrine. He believed, indeed, that the whole function of philosophy was contributory to religion—"If nature is the rudiment of grace," he wrote, "so likewise philosophy is the beginning of religion, nor is that philosophy which removes man from religion." The same evaluation of philosophy is expressed more concisely in a famous epigram from a letter to Aldo Manuzio: "Philosophy seeks; theology finds; religion possesses."

Whether or not one agrees with Pico that philosophy is a department of religion, it is unquestionably true that Pico's own philosophic system revolves about the problem of salvation, or, more generally, the approach to God. The immediate cause of salvation, he held, is divine grace. But man can play a part in his own salvation by making use of the means of grace which God in His mercy has provided. Man should seek his own salvation, not, like Lucifer, by attempting to storm the citadel of heaven, but in humility, by turning to God in prayer.

Prayer, in Pico's religion, was eminently spiritual and interior. "He was not," according to his nephew Gianfrancesco, "very diligent in the observation of external ceremonies." His solicitude to worship God purely in the spirit led him to assert that "neither the Cross of Christ nor any other image is to be adored with latria, even in that manner which Thomas proposes."

This thesis was condemned with the moderate censure of "*de rigore sermonis* scandalous and offensive to pious ears." Pico in the *Apologia* defends his proposition with a wealth of medieval precedent. He cites the statement of Durand of S.-Pourcain that not the Cross, but Christ as remembered through the Cross, is to be adored with latria, and the statement of Robert Holcoth that we ought, strictly speaking, to say that we adore "before" the Cross. More especially, Pico follows the reasoning of Henry of Ghent and John of Guarra, two theologians who had contended that, even *per accidens,* the Cross deserves hyperdulia rather than latria, for it represents primarily the humanity and only secondarily the divinity of Christ.

Garsias, answering Pico, gives a thoroughly interesting disquisition on adoration—its nature, its classes, and its history. He defines adoration as the "interior or exterior cult of anything, shown because of the excellence either formally present in it or attributed to it in any way." He then expounds the degrees of adoration, defining latria as the worship owed to an object of uncreated and infinite excellence, hyperdulia as that owed to an eminent and singular rational creature (for example, the Blessed Virgin or the humanity of Christ), and simple dulia as the worship owed to the excellence of a common rational creature. He explains the difference between formal, material, and accidental adoration, and enumerates the five varieties of the last of these. To images, he concludes, is due imitative accidental worship, and this may be dulia, hyperdulia or latria, according to the excellence of that which is represented. In giving the history of the adoration of images, he tells how the cult of images was altogether abolished under the Old Law because the Judaic peoples were prone to confuse latria with idolatry, and because God, before He assumed flesh, could not yet be properly represented. The worship of images was introduced by the Incarnate Word for various reasons which Garsias repeats from S. Thomas.

Turning to Pico's thesis, the orthodox Spaniard finds that it exposes the faithful to error and lack of devotion, by denying to the Cross on which Christ hung and to most holy images thereof all manner of latria, equally *per se* and *per accidens.* Further, the thesis favors the errors of the Jews and of those who assert that the adoration of images makes the Christians idolaters. To adore the Crucified and not the Cross, according to Garsias, implies a contradiction, since we address ourselves to both in the same act. In other words, it is impossible to dissolve an image into 'that which it represents' and 'that which it is in itself.' Moreover, even if such a dismemberment were possible, it would be absurd to expect the faithful to go through this lengthy rational process before each act of adoration. Garsias concludes that the type of reverence due to images of the Crucified is terminative and imitatively accidental latria.

From Pico's thesis on the adoration of the Cross one might be tempted to infer that he disdained all the forms and instruments of religion. His high reverence for the Sacraments, however, makes it evident that such an inference would be wholly unfounded. "The Sacraments of the New Law," he repeats after S. Thomas, "are a cause of grace—not only *sine qua non,* but also *per quam.*" Pico's interest in the Sacraments is strikingly manifested by his various propositions concerning the Eucharist, two of which were condemned. The first of these [is] that it would be possible for the existence of the bread to remain after the essence had been annihilated. . . .

The second of Pico's condemned propositions concerning the Eucharist asserts that it would be hypothetically possible for Christ to assume the substance of the bread instead of annihilating it or converting it into His body. In other words it could happen, through the absolute power of God, that the three substances—*deitas, humanitas,* and *paneitas*—should be miraculously united. In defending this opinion, Pico argued that he had advanced it simply

as a logical possibility. Moreover, he adds, it had been actually upheld in the ancient confession of Berengar, formerly approved by Pope Nicolas. It had several technical advantages (which had been pointed out by Peter de Palude) over the doctrine of Transubstantiation. For example, this hypothesis removed the necessity of multiplying miracles, since the single miracle of assumption could account for the Eucharist as well as for the Hypostatic Union. Besides, the theory of assumption saved the appearances of the bread and wine.

Garsias, in his refutation of Pico, immediately identifies this thesis as one which had been advanced—and retracted—two centuries earlier by the Thomist, Jean Quidort of Paris. He then breaks down the various articles of Pico's defence. The proposition, he holds, is false, even *de possibile,* since it is incompatible with the form of the consecration and since it contains philosophic absurdities. Specifically, it would be impossible for any material substance to be assumed in such a manner that Christ was totally present in every portion of that substance, as is the case in the Eucharist. In addition, the hypothesis of assumption is not more, but less, economical than that of Transubstantiation. It implies that God assumes a new nature every time the Mass is celebrated, only to drop it a few hours later. Finally, Pico's appeal to the Confession of Berengar is of no avail because he misinterprets the latter and because his opinion patently contradicts the determination of the Church on Transubstantiation.

Still another condemned thesis, while not bearing directly on the Eucharist, deserves mention in this context because of its relation to the Mass. According to this thesis, the words of consecration, in which the priest repeats the utterances of Christ to his Apostles, are spoken not significantively, but materially, or recitatively. Pico here followed the opinion of the Glossator, which had been rejected by most subsequent theologians. (pp. 144-50)

The greatest of the Sacraments, according to Pico, is Baptism. He described it as "the highest gift of the Incarnate Word . . . through which the power of Christ is infused in us and we are regenerated as the sons of God." Specifically, Baptism infuses faith. Unbaptized infants, and likewise all who do not know Christ, can attain their natural felicity; they are "neither deprived of their own nor enriched with divine goods." We who know Christ, however, must fall to either extreme. He who refuses Christ not only makes himself immune to grace, but vitiates nature as well, since it is natural to seek the gifts of the Spirit. By loving Christ we receive Him. The Prophets received Christ under the Old Law, since they believed unquestioningly, hoped eagerly, and ardently desired the future Advent. But since they received Him not as present but as future, therefore they did not experience the fruit of the indwelling Spirit except after He came. These reasonings make it evident that, in Pico's conception, one is saved by believing in Christ and by loving Him.

Pico's conviction that the knowledge and love of Christ were sufficient for salvation is reflected in the assertion that "it is more reasonable to believe that Origen was saved than that he was damned." This proposition was condemned rather mildly as being rash, reprehensible, smacking of heresy, and contrary to the determination of the Universal Church. Pico defends his thesis by seven walls. He argues first that it is not proved that the heretical writings attributed to Origen are genuine. Secondly, granted that they are genuine, it is uncertain whether these heretical views are advanced adhesively or only inquisitively. Thirdly, it cannot be demonstrated that Origen wrote so adhesively as to be guilty of mortal sin. Fourthly, the fact of his impenitence is not established. Fifthly, since we do not know whether or not he repented, it seems reasonable to grant that he was saved, "since his will was in the law of the Lord, and on His law he meditated day and night." In the sixth place the historical evidence that the fifth general council of the Church condemned Origen is dubious; and finally, it does not appear that the determination of the Church on such matters obliges all believers.

Much of the reply of Garsias is devoted to assembling factual evidence for the authenticity of Origen's heretical doctrines and of the decrees of the fifth ecumenical council. More interesting for our purposes is his discussion of the theological issues involved. In answer to Pico's argument that Origen may have advanced his heretical opinions merely inquisitively, Garsias declares with S. Augustine that whatever is written contrary to the substance of the Faith as contained in the Bible is written culpably. Consequently Origen, who was learned in Sacred Letters, is not to be excused for denying the Trinity of the Divine Persons, the resurrection of the dead, and the eternity of rewards and punishments. Origen's persistence in error is sufficiently proved by the fact that he was convicted of pertinacity by an ecclesiastical synod. Moreover, the so-called *Lament of Origen* is manifestly apocryphal.

Turning to the question whether the judgment of the council is binding upon the faithful, Garsias answers at some length. He begins by observing that, as Aristotle proves in his *Ethics,* the type of certitude to be sought on any question is determined by the nature of the matter. Obviously God alone can have certain and evident knowledge of the state of souls before and after death. The Church, however, has certitude, not of evidence but of probability; and according to this type of certainty it proceeds in the canonization of saints and in the condemnation of heretics. Although the particular Church is subject to error in such matters, the universal Church, represented by the community of the faithful, is infallible. It is dangerous to assert, as does Pico, that the Church cannot finally damn anyone after death; for, as we see from experience, it teaches daily that heretics and all who die without Baptism are in hell. Incorrect is Pico's argument that the damnation of heretics is dissimilar to the canonization of saints, insofar as the latter must be confirmed by miracles. It appears from the canonization of martyrs that miracles are not absolutely required. Thus it is evident that the judgment of the Church regarding Origen is binding upon the faithful.

Pico's interest in the salvation of Origen undoubtedly indicates that he was sympathetically disposed toward this third-century Christian Neo-Platonist. The heresies of Origen arose from a sincere effort on his part to create out of the fusion of Neo-Platonism and Christianity a system—Gnostic in character—which should serve both as a philosophy and as a religion. A similar attempt apparently underlay the Florentine Neo-Platonism of the fifteenth century. Pico's work can be described as the continual search for a single system which should be at once *pia philosophia* and *docta religio.* This quest is one of the most important aspects of that great quest for unity which dominated Pico's thought.

In thus identifying philosophy and religion, Pico tended to overlook the distinction between faith and reason, and to ignore the proper spheres of each. He forgot the truth so ably proclaimed by S. Thomas, that while in their objects faith and reason frequently overlap, in their methods and aims theology and philosophy are specifically distinct. Pico carried beyond its true application the Augustinian premise that reason, illuminated by faith, could rise higher than itself.

He proceeded immediately from the principle that "God is a philosopher no less than a priest" to the Gnostic conviction that Revelation pertained to natural philosophy as well as to religion. We have seen that in the *Heptaplus* he undertook to construct an entire cosmology on the basis of Scripture, interpreting the Book of Genesis as though it were a scientific treatise. He believed, as we have remarked, that the Cabbala was a revealed technique for understanding and controlling nature. Moreover, as we have also mentioned, he accepted the theory advanced by Pletho, Manetti and Ficino, that the philosophy of Plato was derived from an inspired tradition. This unitary denomination of wisdom was supposed to have originated with Hermes Trismegistus, and to have been transmitted to historic times by Orpheus, Aglaophemus, Pythagoras, Philolaus, and others.

The inspired sciences, according to Pico, should be treated as mysteries. They should be concealed from the ignorant, and divulged only to the initiate. "Divine matters," he wrote, "either are not written or are written covertly. For this reason they are called mysteries." In the *Oratio* and in the *Heptaplus* he declared that Orpheus, Pythagoras and Plato preferred speech to writing, and, when they did write, expressed themselves in enigmas, so that the vulgar should not understand their meaning. Aristotle, too, according to one of the *Conclusiones,* frequently concealed his meaning by brevity of phrase. Did not even Christ, asks Pico, speak in parables which He interpreted only to His disciples?

Pico, then, believed that divine Revelation pertained to natural knowledge as well as to religion. He likewise held the converse position that human philosophy not only furnished understanding of nature, but also served as the initiation to religion. Such is the sense of his statements that philosophy seeks what religion possesses, and that philosophy is the *inchoatio religionis.* One of the principal arguments, if not the actual theme, of the *Oratio* is precisely that philosophy justifies itself by preparing men for religion.

This conviction is responsible for a definite tendency in Pico's thought to reduce faith to rational knowledge. If he was a fideist in philosophy, he was a rationalist in religion. We have already examined two of Pico's condemned propositions which touch on the relations of faith and reason—his declaration that the manner in which Christ performed miracles is the most certain argument of His divinity, and his thesis that magic and the Cabbala certify the divinity of Christ. In his refutation of each of these conclusions, Garsias observed that Pico was at fault in seeking "certitude of evidence" rather than "firm adhesion of faith."

But Pico's views on the relations between faith and reason

are most clearly expressed in his condemned thesis that "just as no one opines that something is so simply because he wishes to opine thus, so no one believes something to be true simply because he wishes it to be true." As a corollary to this proposition he added: "It is not in the free power of man to believe an article of faith to be true when he pleases, or to believe it to be false when he pleases."

In defending this conclusion Pico declares on the authority of S. Augustine that the mere apprehension of the terms of a proposition does not suffice for belief, but that some probable reason is required in addition. Belief is free in the sense that, once the intellect is determined by the evidence, it is in the free power of man to believe or to refrain from believing; but unfree in the sense that one cannot believe unless the intellect is first persuaded. Pico defends this assertion by the authority of numerous theologians and by five arguments from reason.

First, he declares with Aristotle that opinion does not depend on the will, because, when a doubtful proposition is offered to the mind, one does not incline to either side until new evidence supervenes. Secondly, he argues that what he has proved concerning opinion is applicable to belief, because it is contradictory to believe something which does not appear to the intellect to be true. Thirdly Pico reasons that, since one and the same power cannot be the cause of opposite determinations, the will cannot by itself cause one to assent to some things and to dissent from others. Fourthly, he argues, it is obvious that if we are asked to declare why we believe in Christ, we do not assign as the cause a mere act of will. Finally Pico contends that, as Albertus expressed it, the will acting simply because it wishes to act is like a tyrant, concerning whose actions no reason can be given. In closing his defence Pico explains that his opinion is quite different from that of Robert Holcoth, who had held that the act of belief was wholly unfree inasmuch as both the intellect and the will were determined by the evidence.

Garsias, in his rebuttal of Pico, presents a highly interesting analysis of three positions on the liberty of belief. First he discusses the opinion of Holcoth, Occam and Franciscus de Marchia that the intellect is compelled by miracles, by reasons, and by man's natural credulity. To these nominalist philosophers he replies that the intellect is not compelled to believe anything except self-evident principles and things deduced from self-evident principles. He cites S. Paul's definition of faith as "the substance of things hoped for and the evidence of things unseen" to show that faith is not founded upon experimental knowledge; and he quotes from the Gospel of John to prove that, in spite of the miracles, the Jews were able to disbelieve in Christ.

The second opinion which Garsias analyzes is that of Scotus, Durand of S.-Pourcain and Pico, that the appearance of credibility is one prerequisite, although not the sole cause, of faith. Finally, Garsias expounds the third and, to his mind, correct opinion—that, as Alexander of Hales, S. Thomas and Peter de Palude had maintained, the appearance of credibility is not necessary for Christian belief.

In refuting Pico Garsias considers successively the five arguments of the *Apologia*. Against the first and second arguments he contends that even opinion is contingent upon the will, since the will moves all the powers of the soul to their acts; but granting that opinion is unfree, Christian faith is dissimilar to opinion, in that it does not rest on appearances. To Pico's third argument Garsias replies that not the will *simpliciter*, but the will as specified by infused faith and charity, determines the intellect to assent and dissent. False likewise is Pico's fourth argument in which he maintains that belief not resting upon appearances is irrational. On the contrary, it is most reasonable to wish to believe the First Truth on matters which surpass the faculty of reason. The eight arguments for the Christian faith listed by Scotus are neither sufficient nor necessary for belief. No natural reason is sufficient "unless divine aid be present internally and efficaciously moving the free judgment to belief." Thus the free act of a Christian believer is not, as Pico pretends in his fifth argument, "tyrannical." One accepts the Faith, as S. Thomas declares; because of "an inner instinct of God inviting him."

Pico's proposition *de libertate credendi* is illustrative of a fundamental tendency in his thought. Because he regarded philosophy as a department of religion, he believed that philosophy, as well as revealed truth, played a vital part in the approach of the soul to God. As means of ascending to God, however, both knowledge and faith were inferior to a third method, the method of love. Such is the principal message of the closing chapter of his *De ente et uno:*

> Let us then flee from the world which "lieth in wickedness;" let us depart to the Father Who is the Peace which unifies, Truth itself, the Good itself. But what will give us wings to fly there? The love of things which are on high! What will take them from us? The perverse love of things on earth!

Although *per se* understanding is at least as desirable as love, knowledge alone cannot in this world carry us very close to God. Our understanding reaches its limits at the *lumen ignorantiae* which teaches us to say, "Silence is our praise to Thee." More rewarding is the way of love:

> But behold, Angelo, what madness has seized us! while in the flesh, we can better love God than speak of Him or know Him. In loving we profit more, we labor less, and serve Him better. But we are always inclined to seek through knowledge what we shall never find from seeking, rather than possess through love that which, not being loved, were found in vain.

It is never easy to find labels for a philosophy so complex as that of Pico. In his doctrine of the ascent to God he emphasized so evenly the rôles of thought and love that one cannot call him either a voluntarist or an intellectualist. The same is true of his notion of beatitude. In the *Conclusiones* he declared with S. Thomas that beatitude is essentially an act of the intellect; but he asserted also that the intellect cannot attain felicity without an act of the will, and that the latter is more important than the act of the intellect. Moreover, in felicity itself, he said, allowing that the intellect attains the object of felicity, still the attainment itself would not be felicity without the act of the will. Indeed, Pico conceived of beatitude as an ineffable union transcending both will and intellect. Our last end, he wrote in the *Commento* and in his theses from Plotinus, is union with the first intellect.

In the *Oratio* and in the *De ente et uno* Pico emphasized peace as the chief characteristic of felicity—a peace in which will and intellect, beauty and truth are one. The only true peace, he explained in the latter work, lies in unfailing devotion to God. For if we pursue God today and Baal tomorrow, the law of the spirit one day and that of the flesh the next, our "inner kingdom" will be sundered and devastated. If, on the other hand, unity is bought by the enslavement of reason to the flesh, it will be a false unity, for we will no longer conform to our exemplar in the mind of God. But if we are true to our model, we have only to seek for peace unremittingly and devoutly in this life, and we will receive it through union with God in the next.

In the *Oratio* Pico wrote even more eloquently of peace as the supreme goal:

> When, O Fathers, there is multiplicity in us, then we are torn by discord, which produces conflicts graver than civil wars, and if we wish to escape these, if we aspire to that peace which raises us so high as to place us among the most exalted creatures of the Lord, philosophy alone can repress and compose these discords. . . . Natural reason will pacify the mental strife and dissension which oppress, distract and upset the vexed soul. But it will calm one in such a manner as to force him to recall, as Heraclitus says, that nature was born in war, and for that reason was called by Homer, struggle. It is not in the power of philosophy to give us a true and lasting peace, for this is the gift and privilege of divine theology. Only theology will show us the path to peace and be our guide, and, when we are tired and still far distant, will exclaim: 'Come unto Me, all ye that are heavy laden, and I will give you rest. Come unto Me and I will give you that peace which the world cannot give.' . . . This is that peace which God gives to the blessed in heaven, and which the angels, descending on earth, promised to men of good will, in order that they, ascending into heaven, might become angels.
>
> Let us desire this peace for our friends, this peace for our century and for each home which we enter. Let us wish this peace for our soul, so that it will be made the home of God himself—so that the King of Glory will descend. . . .

In his conception of peace, as in every aspect of his philosophy, Pico remained faithful to the spirit of the Middle Ages. The peace for which he sought was not the mere absence of conflict. His was the Augustinian notion of peace as a positive value—as the tranquility of order. The One, he believed, was in the last analysis identical with the True and the Good. Unity therefore could come only if each man were both True to his exemplar and Good in God's sight. For Pico, as for the scholastics, there could be no unity apart from God, no harmony except that which was founded on the transcendent.

Not only in his view of the method by which peace was to be attained, but in the type of peace which he desired, Pico belonged to the Christian Middle Ages. Peace, for him, was to be found in the spiritual, not in the temporal, kingdom. "Nature," he recognized, "was born in war." Peace neither was nor ever could be a gift of this world. Man, consequently, ought to turn his eyes to God and to pray for "that peace which the world cannot give." The type of tranquility for which Pico longed is an ideal from which succeeding centuries have turned away. Not even in his exaltation of peace does the Prince of Concord speak with the voice of a later age. (pp. 150-64)

Avery Dulles, in his Princeps Concordiae: Pico Della Mirandola and the Scholastic Tradition, *Cambridge, Mass.: Harvard University Press, 1941, 182 p.*

Ernst Cassirer   (essay date 1942)

[*Cassirer was a German-born philosopher and historian who is recognized as one of the foremost interpreters of historical philosophical development. His study of the history of epistemology,* The Problem of Knowledge (1950), *is esteemed for its comprehensive scope and is considered a standard work on the history of human thought. In the following excerpt from the first part of a detailed, two-part study of Pico della Mirandola, Cassirer analyzes the unity of Pico's philosophical thought.*]

In the intellectual panorama of the Italian Renaissance Giovanni Pico della Mirandola is one of the most notable and remarkable figures. For us he is once and for all a part of this panorama and inseparably bound up with it. But the more deeply we study his work, the clearer it becomes that the real significance and substance of his thought can be only very incompletely and inadequately described as belonging to "the Renaissance" in the sense which investigations of the last century in the history of philosophy and of ideas have led us to associate with that term. There is no doubt that Pico belongs among the great representative thinkers of his epoch; but at the same time he falls outside it in many of his characteristics. The intellectual ancestry of his philosophy is to be sought in the ancient world and in the Middle Ages, not in the *Quattrocento*. In many respects he seems to represent and announce a new way of thinking. But on the other hand we find him still completely bound up with and even restricted to a century-old tradition drawn from the most divergent sources. The frame of this tradition Pico never tried to burst asunder. If we understand by "originality" the individual's ability to break through in his thinking and action the limits of what has already been achieved, we cannot in Pico's case look for even the disposition or the will to attain such originality. His intention was to be neither "original" nor "unique"; such originality would have stood in sharpest contradiction to the idea of truth that pervades and inspires his philosophy. For Pico the criterion of philosophic truth consists in its constancy, in its uniformity and sameness. He understands philosophy as *philosophia perennis*— as the revelation of an enduring Truth, in its main features immutable. This Truth is handed down through the ages; but it is generated by no age, by no single epoch, because, as something which eternally is, it is beyond time and beyond becoming.

Such a thinker we can hardly approach immediately with the question of what new trails he has blazed. . . . He is convinced that what is true requires no "discovery," no finding out through any personal inquiry of the individual; rather has it existed from time immemorial. What is characteristic for Pico is hence not the way in which he *increased* the store of philosophic truth, but the way in which he made it *manifest*. His whole thought moves in this direction, and the entire course of his intellectual development is determined by this tendency. If we run over the nine hundred theses which at the age of twenty-three he proposed to defend in Rome, we are astonished not only at their range, but also at the utter disparity of the questions to be treated in them. The first impression we receive from an inspection of these theses can only be one of complete confusion. They touch upon the most incompatible and disparate points; and without any clear or recognizable lines of demarcation the several questions merge into each other. Metaphysics and theological dogmatics, mathematics and astrology, magic and cabbalistic speculation, the history of philosophy, church history, natural history—we encounter them all in motley array. It is as though Pico's ambition was to assemble the positions he desired to treat and defend from every region of the *"globus intellectualis."* This wealth of material seems at first glance bounded or restricted by no intellectual form. But if we look more closely, we find that it is just in this extravagance and excess that a new and distinctive way of thinking comes to light—that the apparent chaos of the nine hundred theses nevertheless takes on the form of an intellectual cosmos.

For the present we shall disregard the question of whether and how far there can be discovered any real internal order in the *contents* of Pico's theses; for this question can find an answer and a clarification only in a later phase of our investigation. For the time being we limit ourselves to the *historical* bearing of the theses, to the way they propose to come to terms with all previous forces and currents in the history of philosophy, the history of religion, and the general history of ideas. What is here characteristic of Pico, and what distinguishes him from all the other thinkers of his time, even from Nicholas Cusanus, is the extent of his intellectual horizon and the breadth of his survey, which tries to exclude or limit no single aspect. It is as though he had made it his goal to render vocal at the same time *all* the intellectual forces which had heretofore cooperated in establishing religious, philosophical, and scientific knowledge. None of them is to be merely attacked or rejected; each of them is granted a definite positive share in the totality of philosophic knowledge and truth. There is no longer for Pico any limitation or dogmatic restriction. He proposes to conjure up the whole great chorus of minds of the past—and to each voice he gives ear impartially and willingly. For he is convinced that only by means of this *polyphony* can that inner harmony be won that is the mark of truth.

Thus we hear from Pico's theses at one and the same time the voices of the great classical tradition, of patristic and medieval theology, of Arabic and Jewish speculation—and each of them he wants to sound forth full and clear and to stand out in its independent significance. Never to such an extent and with such freedom and lack of prejudice had any thinker before Pico examined the fruits of previous intellectual work in the field of philosophy and religion. In Pico's theses we can indeed detect the true spirit of the Renaissance; but in him the Renaissance does not think and feel as something emancipated, as something relying on its own power and will. It sees its real greatness in the complete mastery and intellectual acquisition of whatever the intellectual life of man has worked out in all its different enterprises. It desires to possess and to guard faithfully the heritage of the ages in its entire extent. For Pico this heritage cannot and must not be limited to classical antiquity: the one-sidedness of the humanistic ideal, like every other one-sidedness, he rejected and attacked. His love and his admiration and reverence cannot

be divided; they go out equally to the Middle Ages and to antiquity, to Christianity and to Islam, to the form of the knowledge of God expressed in the writings of the Christian Fathers, of Arabian philosophers or of the Jewish Cabbala. *"Haec est prima et vera Cabala,"* he says in the *Apology* for his nine hundred theses, speaking of his interpretation of the Jewish Cabbalistic sources, *"de qua credo me primum apud Latinos explicitam fecisse mentionem et est illa qua ego utor in meis conclusionibus."*

The same universalistic attitude pervades the whole of Pico's work and gives it its characteristic stamp. In this he differs from his friend and master Ficino. For Ficino wants to further the victory of a definite and particular line of thought, and he feels himself its representative and protagonist. His task is to establish again the main ideas of Platonism, to set forth their agreement with Christianity, and to exhibit them as the foundation of every true philosophic and religious system. But this task which Ficino and the Platonic Academy set themselves was not enough for Pico. He was able to devote himself to it; but he was far from seeing in it the goal of philosophy, of the search for truth in itself. *". . . ego ita me institui,"* he writes in his oration *De hominis dignitate,* *"ut in nullius verba iuratus, me per omnes philosophiae magistros funderem, omnes schaedus excuterem, omnes familias agnoscerem."* Pico does not wish to fight for the rights and the mastery of any particular philosophic school: for him the real meaning and goal of philosophy lies not in fighting, but in peace. The *pax philosophica* is his real ideal, which he sets by the side of the *pax christiana.* *"Cum. . . statutum sit mihi,"* he writes in a letter to Benivieni, *"ut nulla pretereat dies quin aliquid legam ex Evangelica doctrina, incidit in manus. . . illud Christi: Pacem meam do vobis, pacem relinquo vobis. Illico subita quadam animi concitatione de pace quedam ad philosophie laudes facientia tanta celeritate dictavi, ut notarii manum precurrerem."*

But did Pico really manage to complete this great design of his? Did not that idea of a *pax philosophica* that pervades his whole thought remain to the end a mere dream? Indeed, can the goal Pico set himself be formulated and justified from a systematic and philosophic point of view? For Pico the *scholar* it is one of his great and imperishable claims to fame, that in his passionate zeal for learning and in his almost unbounded ability to learn, he left almost no field of knowledge untouched. He came to terms with almost all the great intellectual forces of his time. Not only did he go to school to scholasticism, to Arabian philosophy, to Humanism; in all these movements he himself took part independently and advanced them productively. But it is questionable whether in this advance he made, an advance that historically considered was of great significance and left deep traces, we can see any specifically *philosophical* achievement. If we measure Pico's thought by strictly philosophical standards, we often get the impression that we are here dealing less with a fixed *doctrine* of definite form and clear outline, than with a kind of intellectual alchemy. It is as though Pico never tired of assembling all the positions he encountered, uniting them all with each other, mixing and combining them, in order to see what kind of a product would arise from this treatment. He loves to seek out just the most diverse and curious doctrines, in order to throw them all into the crucible of his thought and to submit them there to a process of purification and clarification. It is as though he thought he could find the philosopher's stone by regarding it as an elixir to be distilled from the most divergent kinds of essences, from an extract of the most incompatible materials. It cannot but give pause when Pico places on the same level propositions from the Platonic and Aristotelian philosophies and ideas which belong to Plotinus, Proclus, or Dionysius the Areopagite, and tries immediately to bring them into harmony. But what result is to be expected when to this he adds propositions and problems from Origen or Augustine, from Thomas Aquinas or Duns Scotus, from Avicenna or Averroes, from the hermetic and cabbalistic literature? Does there not disappear in the end all possibility of distinction, of philosophic criticism—and are we not always in danger of falling into the most obvious contradictions?

This objection has been directed against Pico from the very beginning, and it has determined the traditional estimate of his philosophy. His many-sidedness and comprehensiveness have been admired, but in the same breath his thought has been denied any philosophic value. For men saw in it for the most part nothing but an expression of eclecticism and syncretism. The accounts of the first historians of philosophy who treated Pico in detail, and tried to determine his position in the development of modern philosophy, expressed just such a view. Brucker in his critical history of philosophy sees in Pico's thought nothing but an assembling and confusing of the most incompatible elements: *"inepte miscet omnia et inter se misere confundit."* Later historians have sought to soften this judgment, at least to defend Pico against the charge of being a fool and intellectually incompetent. They too have found the supposed "system" of Pico burdened with the heaviest contradictions; but they have admired the subjective ability and readiness with which Pico succeeded in harmonizing all these contradictions, at least in his own mind, and effecting an apparent reconciliation. Renan speaks of a "wise eclecticism" which Pico sought to preserve in his philosophy. But is there any clear and distinct meaning to be associated with such a phrase? Or is not this oxymoron rather but the expression of the embarrassment into which we fall, when instead of judging Pico's thought by purely historical standards we approach it with genuinely systematic claims? A "wise" eclecticism seems indeed no other and no better than a wooden piece of iron.

Even the most recent Pico literature has brought no final and satisfactory clarification of this point. In recent years two works have appeared, one by Eugenio Garin, the other by Eugenio Anagnine. Garin's work marks an important step in advance: both in systematic interpretation and in the investigation of the sources it has reached new conclusions. But it appears that neither Garin nor Anagnine has fully succeeded in really destroying the force of the charge of "syncretism" brought against Pico's thought. Anagnine indeed refers in the very title of his book to a *"sincretismo religioso-filosofico."* By these words he does not mean that the combination is a wholly uncritical mixture of incompatible elements. In his account Pico appears as by no means a thinker who simply surrendered to the divergent intellectual influences that affected him; he is indeed granted the fullest ability to elaborate all these strains independently. Thus there emerges the picture of a "conscious and tenacious syncretism" (*consapevole e tenace sincretismo*), which is said to be characteristic of Pico's

philosophy. Garin tries still more vigorously to dispel the evil connotations the word "syncretism" bears. One of the main purposes of his account is to show that Pico's work did not remain a *"rudis indigestaque moles,"* an aggregate of ideas thrown together, but possesses a real "inner form" by which it is inspired and pervaded. And in truth it is just at this point that the critical problem lies, from the standpoint of the history of philosophy. Were we forced to deny to Pico's thought any such "inner form," it would then remain but a mere literary curiosity, a document in many respects important and interesting, instructive as to all the manifold and antagonistic interests that motivated the thinking of the Renaissance. But Pico's thought would have to be expunged from the history of genuine *philosophy*. For we can attribute no philosophical significance to an accomplishment that takes no definite *stand* on the great antitheses of metaphysics, epistemology, and ethics; which poses no definite problems and which maintains or rejects no certain solutions. Can we count Pico della Mirandola as belonging to philosophy in *this* sense, and include him in its intellectual development? And what is the distinctive *principle* he set up, and expressed in the whole of his thinking?

To the clarification of *this* question the following study is directed. For it seems to me not to have been exhaustively answered, even by the most recent research on Pico. In detail and in a purely factual respect neither the life of Pico nor the story of the development of his thought seems to confront any insoluble problems. On many difficult and obscure points of his life, as for example his relation to Savonarola, new light has been thrown by modern research. And the genesis and distinctive "filiation" of Pico's ideas are also clear in their main features. His relations to the scholasticism of Paris have been made plain by the valuable investigations of Dorez and Thuasne. His relation to Florentine Humanism and to the Platonic Academy Della Torre has set forth in detail. His relations to Averroe and the Averroistic movement which dominated the Italian universities were traced by Renan. For the understanding of the profound influence Pico received from the medieval Jewish philosophy, Steinschneider's works are fundamental; and the range and significance of these influences, in particular the effect which the Cabbala had on Pico's mind, have once again been placed in a clear light by the most recent works of E. Garin and E. Anagnine. So it seems that for the judgment and the historical understanding of Pico's thought there is nothing essential lacking. We have apparently a firm grasp on the parts: but the intellectual bond that unites them is still absent.

For at this point we come to the most difficult problem, the one that is really critical. Have all the strains that meet in Pico's thought a purely accidental and subjective unity derived merely from himself, from his own individuality? Or does there hold between them a deeper and stricter, a purely objective connection? At first glance we shall hardly be inclined to consider even the possibility of such an objective connection. For what real bond could we conceive capable of bringing together such incompatible materials? Is not Pico effacing all distinction between problems, when in treating the foundations of Christian dogmatics he takes refuge in magic, when he goes so far as to explain that magic is the appropriate and the surest support of the truth of Christianity? *"Nulla est scientia quae nos magis certificet de divinitate Christi quam Magia et Ca-*

bala." And is he not neglecting and destroying every intellectual distinction between particular historical epochs and different cultures, when he jumps immediately from propositions of medieval Christian theology to the rationalism and naturalism of the Arabian philosophy and to hermetic and cabbalistic interpretations? Such doubts are completely justified, and such objections are understandable. But they do not seem to me irrefutable. The following discussion aims to show that the doctrines Pico has collected in his ***Conclusiones*** and expresses in his chief philosophical works, in the ***De Ente et Uno,*** in the ***Heptaplus,*** and in the polemic against astrology, did not just happen to come together accidentally in his mind because of divergent historical influences: they belong together in an internal, objective sense. The principle that unites them is indeed deeply concealed, and can only be brought to light through a careful analysis of the particular strains and ideas. In defending his nine hundred theses Pico himself guarded against the objection that his propositions were only a mere patchwork of completely incompatible ideas. He speaks of an *"occulta concatenatio"* holding between the apparently disparate individual propositions. This "obscure linkage" of his ideas we must make visible. To reveal this unity of arrangement, we must try to reduce Pico's thinking to a few large and general central strains, and to show how these strains are linked together in his mind and united into a distinctive whole.

The One and the Many—God and the World

The ideas of the One and the Many form the two poles about which all philosophic and religious thinking revolves. Metaphysics and theology endeavor, in different ways and by different means, to grasp and clarify the relation between the ultimate First Cause of things, which can be conceived only as absolutely One, and the multiplicity of things, their extension in space and their duration in time. But whenever thought attacks this problem, it is in danger of being caught in an antinomy, in a final and insoluble contradiction. Instead of the intended reconciliation of opposites, on closer analysis one term of the opposition seems to disappear, and thus the whole problem appears to evaporate. If the "First Cause" is really to be conceived as such, i.e., if it is to mean not only the temporal origin of Being, but also its persisting and enduring "Principle," if it is to be that on which all continuance of reality depends and that which it requires at every moment for its existence and character; this means that we cannot effect any real detachment of the Many from the One. The Many must be not only externally dependent on the One. They must remain ever included within it; all the reality we attribute to them they must owe to the One. Hence the Many have scarcely come into being before they must in a sense be taken back once more into the bosom of the One Cause of the World. The latter can suffer nothing besides or outside itself. For any being different from itself, anything that is not itself, would mean a limitation; and this can and must not take place in the absolute and unconditioned Being, which is assumed to be the totality of all perfection, the *ens realissimum et perfectissimum.*

Hence for the "One" to pass beyond itself, and for the Many to proceed out of the One, cannot be conceived in strictly rational terms. Every such proceeding would be either a diminution of the One's own nature, or a multiplying of this nature. And how would a multiplication be possible in what is assumed to be self-contained and perfect? Greek philosophy from the days of Parmenides felt such a multiplication to be contradictory and rejected it. "It is the same, and it rests in the self-same place, abiding in itself. And thus it remaineth constant in its place." Each of the great systems that have followed the Eleatics has brought every resource to bear on freeing Being again from this absolute uniformity and fixity, and on indicating in Being the "possibility" of plurality and change. But this "gigantomachy" of thought, as Plato described it in the *Sophist,* has led to no final solution. None of the attempts at mediation between the opposite poles of unity and plurality, of Being and Becoming, can resolve the contradiction.

Christian speculation rests on the assumptions and the ideas which Greek thought worked out; and at every point it must clothe its own distinctive problem in the *language* of Greek thought, in order to make it accessible and comprehensible to the mind. But its aim is from the outset different from that of Greek dialectic and metaphysics. For it does not inquire, in the same sense as dialectic thinking, into the "Why" of the world and the "Why" of plurality. This "Why" cannot be grasped by pure thought. In the beginning was the *deed*—was the free act of the Divine Will, through which the world came into being. Human reason cannot venture to "conceive" this free act, i.e., to deduce it as necessary from its own concepts and principles. It remains an absolutely unique event, unparalleled, "irrational;" it can be explained or understood through no analogy, through no comparison with anything we encounter in the sphere of our finite, empirical knowledge. But the *certainty* of God's creation and incarnation is not thereby shaken. For it is derived not from rational demonstration but from a fundamentally different source of truth. It is founded on *revelation.*

But *philosophic* thought could not remain with this simple line of division between faith and knowledge, between reason and revelation. All medieval philosophy is filled with attempts to circumvent this division in some way, if only a mediate one, or at least to draw the line of demarcation less sharply than has here been done. The content of revelation is not derived from reason; but on the other hand it can and must not be absolutely inaccessible and impenetrable to reason. Thus there are now repeated on another level all the great typical attempts to solve the problem of the "One" and the "Many." We need not here consider the particular *content* of these attempts at solution. To make clear the general historical context, it is sufficient to have in mind the basic *categories* they rely upon. The specifically Christian and genuinely orthodox solution is determined by the category of *creation.* If this category is accepted, any real *dualism* between the One and the Many, between God and the world, is thereby avoided. For creation is wholly transferred to the interior of the Divine Being; it nowise means that this Being is in any respect dissipated, or lost in anything different from itself.

The real and profound sense of "creation *ex nihilo*" is this: in it the Divine Power is not bound to any *substratum* that could in any way condition or limit it. The world, plurality, has no substratum of that sort. For were such a substratum admitted, it would mean a kind of independence and self-sufficiency, by which the absolute dependence on

God which is here to be displayed would be transformed into its opposite. If God is the content of all reality, there can be no matter "given" to him. This "giveness," this material "subject" for action, holds only for human art, which is thereby once and for all distinguished from genuine and absolute creation.

Quite different from this conception is the relation of unity and plurality, of God and the world, exhibited in all those systems which start from the idea of *emanation* rather than of creation. Here the relation in a certain sense approaches more closely to the rationally comprehensible. For "emanation" stands not in the sign of freedom, but in that of necessity. In it there is expressed no free decree of the will; Being is simply following its own "nature" in passing beyond itself, in allowing something else to arise out of itself. It is not so much a free power that is here expressing itself, as a "must" conditioned and imposed by its essence. Hence there is here a firmly ordered series, based on an intelligible principle: a scale of beings leading down from the One to the Many, in which no step can be passed over. To set up and establish this scale of being is the core of Neoplatonic speculation. This speculation, as it appears above all in the pseudo-Dionysian writings, in the work on the celestial hierarchy and on the hierarchy of the church, puts its stamp on all medieval thinking as well as on the thought of the Renaissance. The work of Pico della Mirandola and his whole intellectual development is completely saturated with the fundamental ideas and presuppositions of the Dionysian writings. The picture of the celestial choirs surrounding the highest Divine Being; the arrangement of the world in accordance with the different celestial spheres and the transmission of effects from above to the "sublunar" earthly sphere: all this forms the basic framework of his metaphysics, his theology and cosmology.

But with this Neoplatonic influence there is joined another, which affected Pico from the very beginning of his intellectual development. In his first academic years in Padua, in 1480-1482, above all through the influence of his teacher Elia del Medigo, Pico fell under the spell of the Averroistic teaching. To it he remained faithful in later years; unlike Ficino, he did not cease to manifest his reverence and admiration for it, even though he did not accept all its consequences. But if we place ourselves on the level of this teaching, at one stroke the problem of unity and plurality, of God and the world, assumes a completely different form. Now it is no longer a matter of solving this problem positively through a basic category of thought, either that of creation or that of emanation. The whole *question* resolves itself into nothing, into a purely dialectical pseudo-problem. On the principles of Averroism there is here nothing that could be significantly asked about—nothing that could raise any problem for the philosophic reason. The problem only arises and can only continue to exist, if reason makes no use of its basic right, the right of independent critical examination, but surrenders itself to dogma. Within the limits prescribed by the medieval picture of the world, Averroism is the attempt at a rational explanation of nature. It seeks to carry through this explanation of nature without the admixture of any dogmatic theological position. What it is looking for is insight into the strict determinism of all occurrences, which follows from the general determinations of matter and motion. What we can know clearly and with certainty is the connection that itself obtains under these determinations, and the way in which they mutually condition each other. But there can be no question of a "cause" of nature in the transcendent sense. For nature as such, the whole of matter and motion, has no beginning in time. To the theological category of creation and to the metaphysical category of emanation there is here opposed the doctrine of the eternality of the world, as it had been established by Aristotle. "Creation *ex nihilo*" becomes an empty word: what we call Becoming is nothing but the continual change of forms and the arising of ever new forms within a matter that is unproduced and without beginning. God is no longer creator, he is only the First Mover. The series of generations is infinite *a parte ante* and *a parte post*. Whatever is possible will at some time arrive at actuality. For in the medium of eternity there is no difference between what can be and what is.

We know the strong influence that Averroism exerted on scholastic thought, and we know how it gradually conquered the entire scientific world. In 1270 Étienne Tempier, Bishop of Paris, summoned the faculty of masters of theology to condemn thirteen Averroistic theses. But not all the prohibitions following each other in quick succession were able to prevent the spread of Averroism in the universities. The humanistic attacks, like those we find with extreme sharpness and violence in Petrarch, likewise rebounded from the iron armor of Averroes almost without effect. Averroism ends by appearing, in the form expressed in the School of Padua, as "science" pure and simple. The reason for this lies less in its empirical content of knowledge than in its conceptual *form* and in the basic theoretical conviction it stood for. For only within the framework of Averroism could there be, under the conditions of medieval culture, anything like an "autonomous" physics, an interpretation of natural phenomena independent of theological presuppositions. It was this function that gave Averroism its meaning, even within the sphere of Christian culture, and secured its exceptional position—despite all the keen criticism directed against it from the side of the real defenders of the Christian faith, like Thomas Aquinas. Within its own field Averroism was invincible, so long as it offered the only possibility and the only assurance of a scientific physics. By John of Jandun Averroes was celebrated as *"perfectus et glorio sissimus physicus,"* as *"veritatis amicus et defensor intrepidus"*; and Michele Savonarola speaks of him, in the book which he composed in praise of the philosophy of the School of Padua, as a thinker who for the acuteness of his mind should be called truly divine.

If we approach Pico's work in the light of these general considerations, we are at once struck by a peculiar and strange trait. All the motives we have just distinguished have entered into Pico's doctrine and put their stamp upon it. He rejected or attacked none of them, and in the different expositions he gave of his fundamental position he impartially made use of them all. In the **Heptaplus** the theme of creation predominates: it is intended as an allegorical interpretation of the Mosaic story of creation. Where Pico follows the Neoplatonic tradition and employs its language, the category of emanation emerges in its systematic significance and moves to the center of his thinking. But he always returned to the support of the Arabian philosophy, and considered it indispensable for the theoretical structure of knowledge. Did Pico possess so little the systematic power of discrimination, that he could simply overlook the difference, and even the complete incompatibility of these fundamental strains, and think he could apply them together and at the same time? Or was the "irenic" drive of his nature so strong, that he was always ready and anxious to blunt the sharpness of contradictions, and to be satisfied with any solution that offered him the show of apparent harmony? Were this true of him, the synthesis he sought to complete in his thought might indeed possess a certain historical and personal interest. But in this case it would lack any general or systematic value.

But such a judgment would by no means do justice to Pico's achievement. For if we examine his work more carefully, we recognize that he was able to employ at the same time the idea of creation, the idea of emanation, and the ideas of Arabian rationalism and naturalism, only because he did not take them simply in their previous meaning, but related them to a definite ideal center, and by thus relating them transformed and enriched their content. No one of these ideas appears with Pico as the complete and exclusive solution to the problem of God and the world. For him they are significant rather as particular moments in the new solution he is seeking. Nor is this solution in any way new, so far as its content alone is concerned: it is not intended to oppose tradition or to break with it in principle. The validity of the principle of authority is still for Pico completely unshaken; and he seeks support for almost every one of his ideas in some one of the great scholastic authorities. But for all that, he is unwilling to subscribe to any particular school unconditionally and without reservation. Even against the Church Pico boldly defends this basic thesis of the *libertas credendi;* he is certain that no one can or ought to be forced to believe. This free attitude toward the Church and toward dogma was possible for Pico because he did not stand for any *doctrine* opposed to theirs, but in opposition to both was trying to assert the validity of his own *principle of knowledge.* He himself hardly formulated this principle clearly and explicitly. But he employed it implicitly in all his writings, to whatever field of inquiry they might belong.

The distinctive category under which he subsumed his doctrine of God, of the world and of man, his theology and his psychology, is the category of *symbolic thought.* Once we ascertain this central point of his thinking, the different parts of his doctrine immediately coalesce into a whole. The basic metaphysical problem of unity and plurality now takes on a specifically different significance. For it is no longer primarily a matter of explaining in what way unity contains plurality in a substantial sense, or by what causal process unity produces plurality out of itself, or passes over into it through a series of intermediaries. All such formulations now appear as merely preliminary, and as more or less inadequate expressions of the problem. Pico is no longer trying to exhibit the Many as the *effect* of the One, or to deduce them as such from their cause, with the aid of rational concepts. He sees the Many rather as *expressions,* as *images,* as *symbols* of the One. And what he is trying to show is that only in this mediate and symbolic way can the absolutely One and absolutely unconditioned Being manifest itself to human knowledge. Metaphysics as well as dialectic or physics can yield no other and no higher truth. They are only different symbols and different interpretations of one and the same meaning, which is the foundation of them all, but which is not capa-

ble of being grasped by us as it is in itself, without any symbolic intermediary.

It is evident that even this fundamental position is not absolutely "new," that it belongs to and takes its place in a great intellectual tradition. At just this point the influence is clear which *mysticism* exerted on Pico and on the whole development of his thought. But what distinguishes Pico from many other forms of mysticism is the circumstance that he is and endeavors to remain primarily a theoretical *thinker.* He was subject to deep mystical experiences and emotions, and in the course of his life, particularly in his contact with Savonarola, these experiences seem to have won greater and greater power over his mind. But he was never willing to give up speculative thinking; nor did he ever believe that such a sacrifice could lead to a genuine and veridical knowledge of God. The true *amor Dei* is for Pico *amor Dei intellectualis:* for only to the intellect is there disclosed the truly Universal, which forms a necessary moment and the real mark of the Divine. Thus Pico also completed the equating of God and the *"intellectus agens": "intellectus agens nihil aliud est quam Deus."* The mystic *"seeing,"* the *"visio intellectualis,"* does not for him therefore coincide with mere mystic *feeling:* it has an independent theoretical meaning and content. Hence Pico is by no means willing to renounce the power of pure thought; he seeks rather to increase it and carry it to the point at which it can be supplemented and enhanced by another purely intuitive kind of knowledge. But at the same time he maintains the position that our thinking and conceiving, in so far as it is directed toward the Divine, can never be an adequate expression, but only an image and a metaphor.

If we can speak of a controlling principle and a controlling method in Pico's thinking, it is to be found in this position. This is the chain that binds together all his theses. And it leads to distinctive and radical consequences: for in the medium of this symbolic form of knowledge the fixed dogmatic content of the Church's teaching begins in some measure to grow fluid. Whatever is substantial and sacramental is dissolved and becomes an intimation, an image of something purely spiritual. Neither word nor picture, neither rite nor any other external action can exhaust the deepest meaning of the religious: *"non in verbis scripturarum esse Evangelium, sed in sensu,"* he says with Jerome, *"non in superficie, sed in medulla, non in sermonum foliis, sed in radice rationis."* Relying on this basic position, Pico arrives at some of his most daring theses, like, for example, the proposition that Christ's visit to Hell is not to be understood in a real and physical sense. Herein lies the great significance he has won for modern religious history. Through the way in which Pico's position sought a pure "spiritualizing" of the doctrines of faith, through the way in which he distinguished the "sacramental" from the "symbolic" he had a marked effect on the transformation and development of doctrine. Especially important is the influence he exerted on Zwingli in these respects.

But we shall not here pursue this religious significance and effect of Pico's thought. We return rather to its purely philosophical content and to its position in the general history of philosophy. And in this respect we find in the central role which symbolic knowledge plays in the structure of Pico's thought further important evidence. For we can recognize from this very trait the close intellectual relationship between Pico and Nicholas Cusanus. In my volume *Individuum und Kosmos in der Philosophie der Renaissance* (1927) I tried to show that the system of Nicholas Cusanus forms one of the most important foci of the whole Renaissance movement, that it offers a center and focus of radiation in every direction. I tried to follow out in detail the influence of Cusanus on the basic ideas of the Platonic Academy in Florence. It has occasionally been objected against this view, that the systematic significance of Cusanus' thought is indeed incontestable, but that I have overestimated the extent of its historical influence, and put it far too prominently in the foreground in the picture of the Renaissance. Even Garin, who in his new account agrees in essentials with my basic conception of Pico's position, has reservations against bringing this position too close to the system of Cusanus. But he himself cites an important piece of evidence I had overlooked. He quotes the assertion in Dorez and Thuasne's book on Pico's stay in Paris, that Pico had planned a trip to Germany, principally in order to visit the library of Cusanus: *"cupiebat proficisci in Germaniam maxime studio visende biblioteca olim Cardinalis de Cusa, et librorum comparandorum causa."* Moreover Garin's own analysis, which is distinguished both by systematic penetration and historical completeness, affords new convincing proof of the connection between Pico and Cusanus. For there here appears as the basic ideas on which Pico's whole work is built the principle of *"docta ignorantia,"* the principle of *"coincidentia oppositorum,"* and the symbolic knowledge of God. To be sure, common prototypes for each of these ideas could be pointed to in the Neoplatonic tradition. But what cannot be explained or derived from that tradition is the characteristic *connection* they possess in both Cusanus and Pico's mind, and the way in which they mutually supplement and support each other. So I think we are in any case entitled to assume a connection between both thinkers.

For the problem that here concerns us, this connection is less significant and important than the *difference* indicated between Pico and Cusanus just because of that connection. If both start with a common interest and a common presupposition, they develop this presupposition in different ways and push it in different directions. In this development, in the new *application* he makes of the principle of "symbolic thinking" and of the principle of *"coincidentia oppositorum,"* there stands revealed the power and the independence of Pico's philosophy. Nicholas Cusanus gives to the traditional ideas of "negative theology" the turn that God in his unity and truth is inaccessible to human knowledge, that he can only be known in the "otherness of assumption" (*in alteritate conjecturali*). But in this "otherness" there are different *degrees* of comprehensibility and of relative accessibility. The true symbol must not be confused with the mere image; the sensible must be strictly distinguished from the intellectual precisely in the symbolic sphere. And genuine precision of intellectual vision belongs to but *one* class of symbols: the symbols of mathematics. If there is any field of human knowledge that gives us an insight, though only by analogy, into the essence of divinity, it is mathematical knowledge. This yields the distinctive, indeed in many respects the unique path that Cusanus follows in his philosophical development. From the mystic vision of God, which is and remains his real goal, and which he sought with the same ardor as the great medieval mystics, he finds himself suddenly transported to the field of mathematics, and he finds himself on the threshold of the problems of modern mathematics, the problems of the analysis of the infinite. And from this position there at times open before him a new vision and insight: for through the medium of mathematics he sees nature also in a new light. The *"praecisio"* he has found in mathematical thinking opens for him the door to the understanding of another new form of *empirical knowledge,* of the nature of physical experimentation, into which he plunges in his book *De staticis experimentis.*

Cusanus remains a strict apriorist: he is convinced that the human mind has the power to construct a closed system of knowledge out of its own basic ideas, out of the ideas of magnitude and measure, of time and number. But at the same time he demands that the intellect should not remain within this system. It must call upon another and opposed power, the power of sense perception, because only by means of sense can it arrive at its own actuality, at its fulfillment and completion. The upward path that leads to God thus includes in itself the downward path that plunges into the intuition of the world in its multiplicity. *"Intellectus. . . in nostra anima eapropter in sensum descendit, ut sensibile ascendat in ipsum. . . . Intellectus qui secundum regionem intellectualem in potentia est, secundum inferiores regiones plus est in actu. Unde in sensibili mundo in actu est."* In a survey and retrospect which Cusanus himself at the end of his life gave of his philosophical development, he characterized this course of his thinking. While I have for many years believed, runs one of the last writings of Cusanus, *De apice theorae,* that the Divine Being must be sought beyond all power of knowledge and before all multiplicity and all contradiction, and that it can be better found in obscurity, it now seems to me that the truth is nearer and more accessible to us in the measure that it is clear. For great is the power of truth—and it speaks to us on the highways and byways, as I have shown in my book *De idiota.*

From this point we can at once clarify the internal *methodological* contradiction between the position of Pico della Mirandola and that of Cusanus, though both start from the idea and the problem of "symbolic knowledge." Pico della Mirandola is neither a mathematical nor an empirical thinker. He is comprehensive enough, and he is seeking too earnestly after genuine philosophic universality to exclude the problems of mathematics and of natural knowledge from his task. But he never escapes the limitations of the scholastic and Neoplatonic tradition. So far as mathematics is concerned, he always tries to employ it for his speculative interpretation of Being; and he thinks the deepest secrets of Being can be treated in the language of numbers and figures. But he never gets beyond the form of the Neopythagorean number mysticism. He never sought mathematics for its own sake, and he never granted it a special or "autonomous" truth-value. For him mathematics possesses neither any independent theoretical content, nor any specific value. And for this reason he concludes that it is harmful to real and genuine knowledge of God: *"Nihil magis nocivum theologo quam frequens et assidua in mathematics Euclidis exercitatio."*

So far as the empirical knowledge of nature is concerned, Pico doubtless has a place in its history; and he must be named amongst its promoters and predecessors. For by his decisive attack on astrology he prepared the path for the modern way of astronomical thinking. But this achievement of Pico's springs, as we shall see, from another source than the empirical observation of nature. It is founded on a purely speculative principle: on his conception of man and of human freedom. From Pico's own basic presuppositions there is thus no path that could lead immediately to a scientific mathematics and to an exact knowledge of nature. From the ideas of Cusanus there extends an influence that leads to Leonardo da Vinci's and Galileo's idea of experience and truth. But the form of mathematics recognized and fostered by Pico's work is essentially *magical* mathematics; it is continued by Reuchlin in his *De arte cabalistica* and *De verbo mirifico.*

For Pico never took the decisive step by which Cusanus introduced the new "orientation" into the knowledge of God. He does not seek God in the bright light of the empirical world and of sensible knowledge; he was convinced that God must be seized in the obscure depths of the human soul. The highest knowledge of which man is capable is and remains a *"scientia abdita."* The human soul, Pico explains in one of his theses, has at its disposal two fundamental forms of comprehending. The one "natural" way of knowing turns to the things of the external world and seeks to represent them in images, by means of perceptions and "phantasms"; these phantasms are then compared by the discursive intellect and reduced to definite classes. But our knowledge of God and of our own soul differs in principle from this natural way. Here there rules a supersensible knowledge, which is alone able to disclose the supersensible nature and the obscure depths of the soul. *"Intelligo de illo intelligere abdito, quod est sine phantasmate, vel adminiculo sensus aut phantasiae et non adhuc de quocumque tali, sed intelligere abdito, directo, et permanente."* Pico does not yet dare to trust empirical knowledge with the same lack of prejudice and the same confidence as Nicholas Cusanus. He is afraid that in looking at the external world the power of genuine "spiritual" knowledge might be weakened. But if this locks for him the real door to natural science in the modern sense of the term, this loss is still not without positive gain. For with all the greater intensity and energy he now turns to the world of the human soul and the human mind alone. In this direction lies his peculiar achievement, which carries him beyond his mystical and Neoplatonic sources: he becomes the herald of a new ideal of human freedom. (pp. 123-44)

> *Ernst Cassirer, "Giovanni Pico Della Mirandola: A Study in the History of Renaissance Ideas," in* Journal of the History of Ideas, *Vol. III, No. 2, April, 1942, pp. 123-44.*

Paul Oskar Kristeller   (essay date 1948)

[*Kristeller is a German-born American educator, editor, and scholar. According to C. B. Schmitt, he has exerted influence "on the philosophico-intellectual side of Renaissance studies . . . greater than that of any of his contemporaries." Among his works are* The Classics and Renaissance Thought *(1955) and* Studies in Renaissance Thought and Letters *(1956). In the following excerpt from his introduction to a translation of the* Oration on the Dignity of Man, *he provides background on*

the influences upon Pico's philosophic thought and its expression in the Oration.]

Giovanni Pico, count of Mirandola, thanks to his social position and to his early death, has always appealed strongly to the popular imagination, while his learning and his thought have earned him the admiration of serious scholars, both in his own time and ever since. The circumstances of his life and death did not permit him to develop his ideas into a mature system of thought. Yet his extant writings display a remarkable wealth of knowledge and erudition and contain brilliant suggestions that were both fruitful and characteristic.

The range of Pico's learning is not only extensive; it assumes additional interest from the fact that he was able to absorb many different ideas and traditions that most of his contemporaries would have considered incompatible. Having enjoyed a thorough classical education, he was familiar with the major works of Latin and Greek literature and philosophy; he cultivated the friendship of some of the leading Humanists of his time; and was able to write letters and treatises in a style which satisfied their meticulous standard of literary elegance. At the universities of Padua and Paris he became acquainted with the logical and philosophical tradition of the Middle Ages and with the writings of the Schoolmen. Pico was not only able to handle their technique of argument and their terminology; he was ready to defend their reputation against the attacks of his Humanist friends. Through his extended stay in Florence and through his friendship with Ficino, he became exposed to the influence of Platonic and Neo-Platonic doctrines emanating from the Florentine Academy. At the same time, because of his different background and ideas, he was able to enrich the thought and influence of that distinguished circle. Adding the study of Hebrew and Arabic to the more common Latin and Greek, he not only gave an impulse to oriental studies but also came into direct contact with the heritage of medieval Arabic and Jewish philosophy. Strongly shaken by his unexpected conflict with the Church authorities over his disputation, in his later years Pico showed an increasing concern for religion and finally became a friend and follower of Savonarola. If we add to this his interest in vernacular Italian poetry and literature, we have the picture of a many-sided if not "universal" intellectual activity that corresponded to the best traditions and ideals of his time.

No less significant are the direct contributions which Pico made to the thought of the Renaissance. His attack on astrology, though prompted by religious and moral rather than by scientific considerations, remains a remarkable episode that made an impression on Kepler himself. Pico's interest in the Cabala led to a broad current of Christian Cabalism which includes, among others, John Reuchlin, and which remained important throughout the sixteenth century.

Even more important are Pico's conception of the dignity of man and his ideal of a universal harmony among philosophers. Both find eloquent expression in the short treatise known as the ***Oration on the Dignity of Man.*** (pp. 215-16)

The first part of the *Oration* attempts a general justification of the study of philosophy. Pico begins with a praise of man. But he rejects as unsatisfactory the traditional views that man owes his distinction to his place in the center of things or to his character as a microcosm. The true distinction of man consists rather in the fact that he has no fixed properties but has the power to share in the properties of all other beings, according to his own free choice. Yet since man has this power of choosing what form and value his life shall acquire, it is his lot and duty to make the best possible choice and to elevate himself to the life of the angels. In this ascent toward the highest form of life he is assisted by philosophy and its various parts. The second part of the **Oration** explains Pico's own interest in philosophy and the plan of his disputation. He is proposing to defend so great a number of theses because he does not follow the teachings of any particular thinker or school but wants to support propositions drawn from many different sources. This leads to a survey of his nine hundred theses, in which he discusses the various thinkers from whom most of them are taken and then emphasizes the original contribution he is trying to make with some of the others. This survey follows on the whole the arrangement of the **Conclusiones** as they appear in the printed editions. The speech ends with an appeal to the supposed audience to begin the disputation.

The general scheme of the **Oration** is obviously adapted to the occasion for which it was written, yet within this setting there stand out two major ideas which give significance to the little work: the dignity of man and the unity of truth.

The idea of the dignity of man has a long and rather complex history. The praise of man as the inventor of the arts and crafts, as a microcosm, as a being distinguished by speech and by reason, is a common theme of ancient thought and literature. The notion that man is closer to God than any other earthly creature appears in Genesis and pervades all the Old Testament. Early Christian emphasis on the salvation of mankind and on the incarnation of Christ also implied a special position of man in the world, and some of the Church Fathers developed this notion and fused it with the conceptions inherited from pagan antiquity. All these ideas were repeated with new emphasis during the Renaissance. Giannozzo Manetti composed a treatise *On the Excellency and Dignity of Man* as a counterpart to Innocent III's work *On the Misery of Man.* Ficino, in his *Theologia Platonica,* gave an additional philosophical importance to the conception by stressing man's universality and his central position in the universe. Pico, who was undoubtedly familiar with most of these previous statements, introduced, however, an important new element. He emphasized not so much man's universality as his liberty. Man is the only creature whose life is determined not by nature but by his own free choice; and thus man no longer occupies a fixed though distinguished place in the hierarchy of being but exists outside this hierarchy as a kind of separate world.

The notion of the unity of truth which dominates the second part of the **Oration** is an attempt to solve a problem that has puzzled many thinkers since ancient times: the variety and contrast between different philosophers and philosophical schools. Ancient skeptics and modern relativists have used the fact to prove that there is no truth or certainty. Another and more satisfying answer to the problem has been the assumption that the opposing schools of philosophy do not merely have a common share in error but that they rather share in a common truth. This

assumption was held in antiquity by the so-called eclectics and by the Neo-Platonists; it was reasserted on different grounds by Hegel; and it still underlies the better part of the studies devoted to the "history of ideas." Pico's notion of a universal truth in which the various thinkers and schools all have a part obviously belongs to this same tradition. It has been suggested that Pico's conception may have had some connection with the Averroistic doctrine of the unity of the intellect. On the other hand, Pico may have tried to give a broader application to Ficino's doctrine of natural religion and to his attempt to reconcile Platonic philosophy and Christian theology. However this may be, Pico's "syncretism" differs from ancient "eclecticism" and modern "perspectivism" on one characteristic point which seems to reflect his Scholastic background: He does not believe with the ancient eclectics that the major philosophers all agree in their doctrines and merely disagree in their words. Nor does he believe with the modern "perspectivists" that every system of thought taken as a whole represents a particular aspect of universal truth. For Pico, truth consists in a number of true statements; and the various philosophers participate in truth in so far as their writings contain, besides numerous errors, a number of specific statements that are true and hence must be accepted. In this sense, his syncretism is exclusive as well as inclusive and further removed from skepticism than its modern counterparts.

The great influence Pico's ideas of the dignity of man and of the unity of truth were destined to exercise in the Renaissance and afterward was due not only to their intrinsic merits but also to their prominent place in the thought of Pico and of his contemporaries. The notion that man owes his distinction to his freedom and that he is emancipated from the hierarchy of being is further developed and emphasized in Pico's **Heptaplus;** the concern for man's freedom is the underlying cause for his attack on astrology, which is the subject of his major extant work. On the other hand, the unity of truth is the underlying conception of Pico's nine hundred theses; and one particular aspect of this unity—the harmony between Plato and Aristotle—was to be the subject of a large work he planned to write, of which the treatise **De ente et uno** is the only extant fragment. It is hence understandable that some scholars consider this syncretism as the central conception of Pico's thought.

Less obvious but equally significant are the links that connect these two conceptions with the Humanistic movement of the early Renaissance. The early Italian Humanists were primarily concerned not with philosophical speculation but rather with the development of a cultural and educational ideal that was based on the study and imitation of classical antiquity. Yet when they were driven to justify that ideal and the significance of their classical studies, they claimed that these studies contribute to the formation of a desirable human being and are hence of particular concern for man as man. This argument is reflected in such expressions as *studia Humanitatis,* the "Humanities," and the "Humanists." This emphasis on man is one of the few ideas—perhaps the only philosophical idea—contained in the program of the early Humanists. When Pico, and Ficino before him, worked out a philosophical theory of the dignity of man in the universe, they were merely giving a more systematic and speculative development to a vague idea that had dominated the thought and aspirations of their Humanist predecessors for several generations. Pico's syncretism is likewise related to the eclecticism of the early Humanists. In their opposition to the exclusive Aristotelianism of the medieval philosophers, the Humanists liked to quote and make use of the teachings of all the different ancient thinkers and schools accessible to them. They did it often in a rather haphazard and superficial manner, but they broadened the horizon and enriched the source material on which profounder thinkers could afterward draw. Pico's syncretism was a philosophical justification of this Humanist procedure and for the first time gave to it something like a positive method and dignity.

Thus the **Oration on the Dignity of Man** is not merely a piece of rhetoric; it contains ideas that are of major importance in the thought of Pico and in the thought of the Renaissance. (pp. 218-22)

> *Paul Oskar Kristeller, "Giovanni Pico Della Mirandola: Introduction," in* The Renaissance Philosophy of Man, *Ernst Cassirer, Paul Oskar Kristeller, John Herman Randall, Jr., eds., The University of Chicago Press, 1948, pp. 215-22.*

Russell Kirk   (essay date 1956)

[*An American historian, political theorist, novelist, journalist, and lecturer, Kirk is one of America's most eminent conservative intellectuals. In the following excerpt from his introduction to a 1956 edition of the* Oration on the Dignity of Man, *Kirk examines the treatise as "the manifesto of humanism."*]

"The enduring value of Pico's work is due, not to his Quixotic quest of an accord between Pagan, Hebrew, and Christian traditions," John Addington Symonds writes, "but to the noble spirit of confidence and humane sympathy with all great movements of the mind, which penetrates it." Out of the bulk of the works of Count Giovanni Pico della Mirandola, who challenged the doctors of the schools to dispute with him on nine hundred grave questions, the only production widely read nowadays is this brief discourse, **The Dignity of Man,** delivered by him in 1486, at Rome, when he was only twenty-four years old. The oration, which was his glove dashed down before authority, lives as the most succinct expression of the mind of the Renaissance. (p. xi)

Now this eccentric genius' **Dignity of Man** is the manifesto of humanism. Man regenerate—"this, visibly," Egon Freidell says, "is the primary meaning of the Renaissance: the rebirth of man in the likeness of God." The man of the Middle Ages was humble, conscious almost always of his fallen and sinful nature, feeling himself a miserable foul creature watched by an angry God. Through Pride fell the angels. But Pico and his brother-humanists declared that man was only a little lower than the angels, a being capable of descending to unclean depths, indeed, but also having it within his power to become godlike. How marvellous and splendid a creature is man! This is the theme of Pico's oration, elaborated with all the pomp and confidence that characterized the rising Humanist teachers. "In this idea," continues Freidell, "there lay a colossal *hy-*

bris unknown to the Middle Ages, but also a tremendous spiritual impulse such as only modern times can show."

The very Cherubim and Seraphim must endure the equality of man, if Man cultivates his intellectual faculty. It is the spirit, the spark of Godhood, which raises Man above all the rest of creation and makes him distinct in kind from all other living things. For all his glorification of Man, however, Pico has no touch of the modern notion that "man makes himself," and that an honest God's the noblest work of man. It is only because Man has been created in the image of God that Man is angelic. God, in his generosity, has said to Man, "We have made thee neither of heaven or of earth, neither mortal nor immortal, so that with freedom of choice and with honor, as though the maker and moulder of thyself, thou mayest fashion thyself in whatever shape thou shalt prefer. Thou shalt have the power to degenerate into the lower forms of life, which are brutish. Thou shalt have the power, out of thy soul's judgment, to be reborn into the higher forms, which are divine."

This, then, is the essence of humanism, which spread out of Italy unto the whole of Europe, reaching its culmination, perhaps, in Erasmus and Sir Thomas More. (More it was who translated the life of Pico by his nephew Giovanni Francisco into English.) God had given Man great powers, and with those powers, free will. Man might rightfully take pride in his higher nature, and turn his faculties to the praise and improvement of noble human nature. A world of wonder and discovery lay before the Renaissance humanist. Yet all this dignity of human nature was the gift of God: the spiritual and rational powers neglected—and through free will Man is all too able to neglect them—Man sinks to the level of the brutes. The humanist does not seek to dethrone God: instead, through the moral disciplines of *humanitas,* he aspires to struggle upward toward the Godhead.

Thus a degree of humility chastened the pride of even the most arrogant humanist of the Renaissance. But the seed of *hubris,* overweening self-confidence, was sown; and a time would come when Man would take himself for the be-all and end-all; and then Nemesis would be felt once more, and—The end, however, is not yet. It has remained for us of the twentieth century to look back upon the course of this *hubris,* diffused over all the world; and to see the oratorical aspirations of the humanists transformed into the technological aspirations of the modern sensual man; and to glimpse the beginning of the Catastrophe, perhaps, in a handful of dust over Hiroshima, or in the leaden domination of the Soviets, or in the pornography and hysteria of the corner news-stand. Robert Jungk, in *Tomorrow Is Already Here,* describes the stage of this progress at which we have arrived: "The stake is the throne of God. To occupy God's place, to repeat His deeds, to recreate and organize a man-made cosmos according to man-made laws of reason, foresight, and efficiency"—this is the ambition of the twentieth-century energumen of progress. And to gratify this ambition, we have moved very near to the dehumanization of Man. In our lust for divine power, we have forgotten human dignity.

By "the dignity of man," Pico della Mirandola meant the high nobility of disciplined reason and imagination, human nature as redeemed by Christ, the uplifting of the truly human person through an exercise of soul and mind. He did not mean a technological or sensate triumph. "The dignity of man" is a phrase on the lips of all sorts of people nowadays, including Communist publicists; and by it, all sorts of people mean merely the gratification of the ego, the egalitarian claim that "one man is as good as another, or maybe a little better." Pico, however, knew that no being can dignify himself: dignity is a quality with which one is *invested;* it must be conferred. For human dignity to exist, there must be a Master who can raise Man above the brute creation. If that Master is denied, then dignity for Man is unattainable.

For despite all the cant concerning the dignity of man in our time, the real tendency of recent intellectual currents has been to sweep true human dignity down to a morass of mechanistic indignity. Joseph Wood Krutch, a generation ago, in his *Modern Temper,* described with a sombre resignation this process of degradation. Without God, Man cannot aspire to rank with Cherubim and Seraphim. Freud convinced the crowd of intellectuals that Man was nothing better than the slave of obscure and arrogant fleshly desires; Alfred Kinsey, unintentionally reducing to absurdity this denial of human dignity, advised his fellow-creatures to emulate, if not the ant, at least the snake—for Man, so the modern dogma goes, lives only to lust. In this fashion phrases linger on in men's mouths long after the object they describe has been forgot.

Pico della Mirandola, Platonist and Christian and sorcerer and rhetorician and mystic, designed his nine hundred questions as an irrefragable proof of Man's uniqueness. Emerson echoed him, five centuries after:

> There are two laws discrete
> Not reconciled,—
> Law for man, and law for thing;
> The last builds town and fleet,
> But it runs wild,
> And doth the man unking.

By a discipline of the reason and the will, to make Man kingly, even angelic—this was Pico's hope, and it has been the hope of all true humanists after him. Thing, nevertheless, has run wild in our time, building town and fleet, bomb and satellite; and the Man has been unkinged; and human dignity is at its lowest ebb, now, when Man's power over nature is at its summit. A real man, in any age, is dignified and nobly human in proportion as he acknowledges the overlordship of One greater than Man. If Things are to be thrust out of the saddle once more, and Man mounted (in Pico's phrase) to "join battle as to the sound of a trumpet of war" on behalf of Man's higher nature, then some of us must go barefoot through the world, like Pico, preaching against the vegetative and sensual errors of the time. (pp. xiii-xx)

> *Russell Kirk, in an introduction to* Oration on the Dignity of Man *by Giovanni Pico Della Mirandola, translated by A. Robert Caponigri, Henry Regnery Company, 1956, pp. xi-xx.*

George Boas (essay date 1957)

[*Boas was an American educator who wrote widely on philosophy. In the excerpt below, he explores Pico's platonic theory.*]

[Pico della Mirandola's] aims and teachings were stated as follows in his famous defense of himself and his thoughts:

> Not satisfied to have added to the common opinions many things about the ancient theology of Hermes Trismegistus, about the disciplines of the Chaldeans, of Pythagoras, and the more secret mysteries of the Hebrews, I have propounded myself as well a great number of ideas discovered and reflected upon by me concerning natural and divine things which required discussion. We proposed first a harmony between Plato and Aristotle which has been accepted by many in former times, but never properly proved. Boethius amongst the Latins promised that he would do this, but never discovered how he could realize his wishes. Simplicius amongst the Greeks attempted the same task, and would that he had succeeded as well as he promised. Even Augustine in his work on the Academics wrote that there were many who had tried to prove the same in their most subtle disputations, that is, to show that the philosophy of Plato and Aristotle were the same. Likewise John the Grammarian, though he said that Plato differs from Aristotle only in the opinion of those who do not understand Plato's language, nevertheless left it to posterity to prove it.

He continues by asserting that he was relying on Duns Scotus and St. Thomas, Averroës and Avicenna, to bring about what he called a *pax philosophica,* a harmony of the philosophers, and to do this by utilizing the numerical methods of the Pythagoreans. He would bring to bear on his problems the doctrine of magic, as understood by the Persian Magi, and the allegorical technique of the Neo-Platonists who interpreted the story of the Odyssey as the search for a single philosophy, and finally the procedures of the cabalists.

Here he clearly assumed that philosophic truth is one and unique, as he believed religious truth to be. Philosophies differed either in the means which they used to expound this unique truth, or in the part of the total truth which they were interested in demonstrating. But it becomes clearer as one reads his writing that the single underlying truth is that of Christianity, as he understood it, and that all philosophies, whether Christian or not, were attempting in his opinion to demonstrate that truth. Whether this program is to be labeled eclecticism or syncretism, both of which terms are in bad odor, is of small importance. Pico apparently saw no difference between Plato and Aristotle, St. Thomas and Scotus, and if one makes a distinction between what a writer says and what he *really* says, if the wanderings of Odysseus can be interpreted as a philosophical myth, then all one can do is expound the unity of thought which lies beneath the diversities of expression. That words do not mean what they say was usually justified at this time by the theory that the common people were not able to understand the truth. The use of parables in the Bible and the legend that the Greeks had secret esoteric doctrines were both called upon as evidence that the popular mind must be protected from a knowledge of philosophic arcana. It is very curious that men who believed in a universal, not a tribal, religion should also have believed in the advisability of keeping its doctrine unexplained in clear and intelligible language. But I suppose that the hierarchical notion of rank and dignity, of the essential unworthiness of the *plebs,* which was certainly current in the Middle Ages, had survived to the detriment of a more charitable idea.

Whatever the reason, Pico firmly discusses man as man and not merely the upper orders of mankind. And man, he maintains, as the Scholastics had as well, God had created to understand rationally the Creation, to love its beauty, and to admire its vastness. But as there was no archetype for such a being, nor any place for him to be located, He made him of an indeterminate nature (*indiscretae imaginis*), that is, *sui generis,* and placed him in the center of the universe. His lack of a larger species to which he might belong, as well as his lack of a peculiar habitat, was a liberation for him. This left him free to contemplate all things both below and above him. He was neither terrestrial nor celestial, so that he could himself make a life for himself. He could either fall to the level of the brutes or rise through regeneration to the level of the divine. There would have been four possibilities open to him: to live the vegetative life like a plant; the sensitive, like an animal; the purely rational, like a "celestial animal"; the intellectual, like "an angel and son of God." But he might too, belonging to no class of beings, withdraw into himself and become a spirit alone with God. The innermost secret of religion is man's mutability—now a vegetable, now an animal, now an angel.

> It is not the bark which makes the plant, but its insensitive nature; not the hide which makes the brute, but its purely sensual soul; not the circular body which makes the heavens, but right reason; not the lack of a body which makes the angel, but his spiritual intelligence. And should you see a man given over to his belly, lying on the ground, he is not a man but a plant; if someone blinded by the empty phantasms of Calypso besmirched with seductive charms, delivered over to the senses, he is a brute, not a man. If a philosopher, discerning all through right reason, you would venerate him; he is a celestial animal, not terrestrial, a more august deity in the dress of human flesh.

Thus man can change himself at will and represent in his ways of living all the beings which are in the universe.

Students of medieval and Renaissance literature will recognize in this an echo of the ancient microcosm-macrocosm leitmotif. If man is to reproduce in miniature all that is in the universe, then clearly his whole life and soul must reproduce all the kinds of life and souls which exist. But he must also not be identified with any particular type. His task as a human being is to emulate the life of all beings and it is in this that he resembles God in Whose image he was made. For God, too, in some mysterious sense is in all things, though Pico also maintains, as his intellectual ancestor had, that He is also above all things. Pico takes over the Aristotelian notion of vegetation being matter in relation to sensitivity, sensation being matter in relation to reason, and adds to it the idea that reason must rise to pure intellection. But his attempt at a fusion of Aristotelian and Platonistic thought leads him to insist that the "parts" of the soul are not literally parts at all, that the soul is a unit, as God is. When man has achieved his destiny, he will be above heaven and earth, like the seraphim, cherubim, and thrones. It goes without saying that he interprets these three choirs of angelic beings as three psychic functions, Love, Intelligence, and Judgment, which functions are precisely the attributes of God. There are few pages in the history of philosophy more eloquent than those in which Pico describes man's life when it is lived in imitation of these powers. The argument behind them is simple. Man must realize his essential nature and his essential nature is found in his kinship with the Creator. Therefore we must live in a manner dictated by that proposition. The thesis is that of the Ancients, though the phraseology is different. Our peculiar status in the universe is that we are not condemned to live according to a fixed and universal rule, as stones must fall, fire must rise, and even the angels must perform their allotted tasks. We are free to move up or down, upward toward God or downward toward matter. Whether we argue like some of the Greeks that we must live "in accordance with Nature," or "in accordance with our nature," the framework of the argument is the same. The Good of each thing is the fulfillment of its essential nature and man's happens to be that of God. He is a peculiar being in that he alone recapitulates the cosmos in all its details. But just as the cosmos manifests different levels of value, as well as different kinds of life, so does man. The fusion of value with the scale of Being complicates the problem, for it entails the belief that since certain levels are inherently better than others, we should make the effort to attain them.

Pico's brave attempt at a syncretism of all philosophies was justified by his consideration of man as man, a being not divided into tribal or sectarian groups. The word "catholic," apparently, he meant to be taken seriously, as meaning *universal.* What more natural than that he should believe all men, whether of his own church or not, to possess a glimpse of the fundamental truths concerning their own being and that of God? How could it have been possible that God would have deprived some of his children of the truth? If that was not possible, then the philosopher must undertake an elucidation of the single truth which was expressed in so many ways. Clearly there must be some ideas which are false, for contradiction exists between various schools of thought. Hence some test of validity must exist and that test is to be found in Christian revelation. Having then decided on what revelation meant, Pico had at his disposal a way of selecting out of all the theories which he studied so zealously those which were true and those which were false. His use of Orphic hymns, of the cabala, of Zoroastrian remnants and Chaldean oracles, of Neo-Platonic interpretations of the Homeric hymns and even the epics was always guided by this principle.

The clash in opinion between the members of the Platonic and those of the scientific tradition lay in what they believed to be the end and purpose of philosophy. For the latter, knowledge was a terminal value; the possession of the truth need not be justified by any further purpose. We are essentially rational beings and we must attain full rationality. To understand suffices. But to the Platonist knowledge had a moral purpose. It must be that peace which passes all understanding, the peace of mind which the Stoics also had sought in their way. "There is indeed," he says, "in us much discord. We are waging within ourselves grave and internal and worse than civil wars. If we do not wish this, if we wish to attain that peace which will bear us aloft until we are placed amongst the Lord's chosen, only moral philosophy can restrain us and seat us there." Dialectics will quiet the strife of philosophies; natural philosophy (i.e., science) will settle the vexing disputes of opinion; and we shall remember, as Heraclitus said, that nature is in a state of war. Remembering this, we shall reach the peace and quiet which theology alone can give. "This is that friendship which the Pythagoreans said was the end of all philosophy, this that peace which God had made in His heavens, which the angels descending to earth announced to men of good will, that through it men themselves ascending to heaven might be made into angels." It was this peace and friendship which he says he was trying to introduce into his age and society.

So much will suffice as a brief outline of Pico's program and of the way in which he thought to realize it. The rest of his work is involved in carrying it out in detail. His hexaemeron, the **Heptaplus,** his **De ente et uno,** and even his attacks on the astrologers were all directed to making clearer the universal basis of those ideas which he believed to be the single Truth revealed in Christianity and expounded in the works of the philosophers and theologians of all places. Since Pico was one of the Italian philosophers who were most read by later writers, it is not difficult to see why a doctrine of a universal religion should have been suggested by his writings. The English Platonists, who had left the Catholic Church, could still take over his main theses and use them to argue to a religion which was naturally implanted in all men regardless of ecclesiastical affiliation. Was it a foresight of that possibility which led his Church to condemn him?

There is but one other work of Pico's which it seems necessary to mention before leaving him. That is his commentary on Benivieni's *Canzona de amore.* Benivieni had written this poem as a short expression of the ideas which Ficino had expounded at greater length in his commentary on Plato's *Symposium.* The work, says Benivieni in his epistle to the reader, was not intended for publication and was in fact published after the death of Pico. It was written as a Christian interpretation of Plato's theory of love. Benivieni is almost ultra-careful to point out that he himself was not attempting in his *Canzone* to state Christian truths, nor was Pico in his commentary doing more than "reciting simply and without any approbation the opinion of another." The *Canzone* consist of nine stanzas, beginning with the usual *apologia* in the form of an invocation to Love, which dwelling within the poet's heart seeks flight to the upper regions of the universe. Love is then presented, as in the last line of the *Paradiso* as that which moves the heavens and rules the world. It is the same force which moves the human heart and urges man to seek God. It is the same love which descends from God to the angels and from them step by step enters into the human mind as rays of light from the sun illuminate the earth and are reflected upward. It is first manifested to us as erotic desires which impel us to unite with the object of our desires, but which are the first evidence of that eternal love which is God's love for His creatures. Out of it is born the Heavenly Venus. Benivieni plays upon the dual relations of love, that which moves us upward and that which moves downward to us. We see the beloved object as beautiful, with the beauty of the body, the spirit, and the mind; and the soul then unites these various beauties into one. In short, the whole poem is an idealization of the force of love in the typical Platonistic manner, containing nothing which had not previously been expressed by a dozen mystics and which was now to be expressed over and over again. To us living in the twentieth century, acquainted with even a portion of the history of poetry and philosophy since the time of the Renaissance, it seems traditional enough to occasion neither surprise nor worry.

Pico's **Commentary** on this poem is really a treatise in itself which can be understood without reference to Benivieni. It begins with making a distinction between three forms of being: causal, formal, and dependent (*participato*). To use his own example, the sun is not hot but is the cause of heat; fire is hot and heat is the form of fire; wood is not hot nor the cause of heat but, by participating in the quality of fire, becomes hot. Of these three forms of being, the causal is the most noble and perfect. God is the purest cause and the cause of all beings, and is therefore above all beings, His transcendence being absolute. There are similarly three kinds of creatures: the corporeal and visible, such as the heavens, the elements, and all things composed of the elements; the invisible and bodiless, which are angelic; and between them, ourselves. Above them all is God, Whose being is the primary source of causality, and from which flow the other natures. But immediately posterior to God in the cosmic hierarchy there is a single incorporeal being which has been produced, not created, *ab aeterno.* This being is as perfect as possible and is called Wisdom (*Sapienzia*), Mind, the Divine Reason, or the Word, according to which philosopher one happens to be reading. It is to be noted that as he develops his argument, he points out that each step is based upon a group of authorities both Christian and Pagan, the Platonists, Hermes Trismegistus, Zoroaster, and "our Theologians." But he is careful to say that Wisdom is not what "our Theologians" call the Son of God.

There follows a section on the two modes of beings, Ideal and Formal, which is important in our context since it establishes clearly the thesis that there exist in the mind certain ideas, which are Platonic essences, in accordance with which individual particulars are created. The Platonic distinction between the essences and the existents is thus retained, and a guarantee of a single and universal and eternal system of truth is established. The importance of this cosmic duality emerges in the writings of the later Platonists who will tend, on the model of Plotinian emanationism, to derive our sensible precepts from our ideas. The difficulty of elaborating a satisfactory theory of truth on the basis of individual perceptions, which presumably must by their very nature be localized and dated, and thus could not form universal and necessary statements, was to loom large in the next century in France and England. But if one could believe that there actually was a complete system of ideas, eternal and universal in their scope, a system called the Ideas in the Mind of God, truth would be established by the adequacy of our particular ideas to these general ideas.

Since man in the **Commento,** as in the **De dignitate,** was in a position midway between the material and the ideal worlds, and "as every mean participates in the extremes, so man is in communication and harmony through his divers parts with all the parts of the world, for which reason we are accustomed to speak of him as a Microcosm, that is a little world." The cosmic hierarchy runs, as throughout the European tradition, from the minerals, through the plants, the animals, the rational animals (men), the angelic minds, above which is God. But similarly in man we find a corresponding hierarchy, running from his body, through his vegetative powers, his sensory and motor powers, his reason, to his intellectual and angelic faculty. It is because of this correspondence that we can participate in the knowledge of the intelligible world. It is not foreign to our nature and the apex of our mind touches it.

With this as an introduction, Pico turns to the theory of Love. Love in its widest sense means our desire for what we consider to be good. Avarice, ambition, piety, friendship, are all forms of love. But in a stricter sense it is the desire for the beautiful, for our other desires differ from love in this sense in that when we are moved by them, the object of our love does not reciprocate our affection. In real love, there must be something reflected back upon us, as, in our love of God, God reflects His love upon us and, in friendship, our friends feel friendly to us as well as we to them. Love is then simply a species of the genus Desire, differentiated from other forms of desire in that it is a desire for the beautiful. Now just as knowledge is a kind of possession—"all things are mine because I know them all"—so there is harmony and similitude between him who desires and that which he desires. Love can exist only between similars, he maintains, and where there is dissimilarity, there is hatred.

But between cognition and desire there is a parallelism. "Appetite follows upon sensation, choice upon reason, volition upon the intellect." In this manner we rise above our animal nature to our angelic nature and arriving there our desire is for the beings of the intelligible world. But as there is a kind of beauty on each level, the beings of the intelligible world have a beauty which is supreme. Our attraction toward ideal beauty is the highest form of love; it is the attraction which the highest part of our soul experiences for that which is closest to its nature. It is our fate to be capable of descending toward the lower realms of the cosmos in our appetites or upward, so that love of intelligible beauty is the fruit of a long education. Such education is always self-education: a man must understand philosophy, must know that there is in the universe a principle of value, must strive to bring into being his better potentialities. For Pico does not maintain that we automatically rise above our bestial natures. Choice, judgment, will are required to discriminate between our goals and decide to seek the highest.

This will suffice as a very brief sketch of the *Commento.* There is no need to dwell upon Pico's elaborate interpretations of Greek and Roman mythology nor to expound in detail his stanza-by-stanza commentary of Benivieni's poem. What we have given here, though necessarily superficial, gives some idea of the metaphysical background of his thought. (pp. 58-66)

> *George Boas, "Italian Platonism," in his* Dominant Themes of Modern Philosophy: A History, *The Ronald Press Company, 1957, pp. 50-69.*

Paul J. W. Miller   (essay date 1965)

[*In the excerpt below, Miller examines various aspects of Pico's philosophy, including "his philosophies of man and of being, which will perhaps disclose the essential character of his thought."*]

Philosophy in fifteenth-century Italy displays characteris-

tics parallel to those of art and letters. Philosophers exhibit a similar enthusiasm for classical antiquity, a zeal for the discovery of hitherto unnoticed ancient source material, a continuing interest in traditional problems formulated in a new manner. Furthermore, Renaissance thinkers could master and associate a great range of ideas in several different fields. All of these traits can be observed in the philosophy of one of the foremost intellects of the time, Giovanni Pico della Mirandola. His thought is not only of the greatest intrinsic interest, but discloses, through one individual, the spirit of the Italian Renaissance. (p. vii)

Pico utilized [a] great mass of philosophical and theological material in accord with certain very curious views about the history of ideas. It is a commonplace of medieval thought that the philosophical conclusions reached by reason, and the content of religious revelation, are in agreement. For Pico, this concord of truth is embodied in the actual history of thought. He considers Greek philosophy and the Judeo-Christian scriptural tradition both as unfoldings of a single pious philosophy. Pico thinks that he is rediscovering the unity of a sacred theology revealed through both Greek reason and Christian revelation.

Greek philosophy, in this view, contains an occult, secret tradition of theological wisdom, running from Hermes Trismegistus, Orpheus, Pythagoras, down to Socrates, Plato, Aristotle, and later thinkers. (Pico even had some misinformation on the "Egyptian" source of Greek thought.) A sacred religious truth was presented by these thinkers in allegorical form, hidden under mythological fables. Even Homer conceals a profound moral and religious doctrine in epic images. The Hermetic tradition had recently been put back into circulation by Pico's older friend Marsilio Ficino, who translated the entire *Corpus Hermeticum* into Latin. These Hermetic and Orphic writings, which are now known to be forgeries dating from late antiquity (mainly the first few centuries of the Christian era), were thought by the Florentine philosophers to be of immense age. They were supposed to contain a continuous occult theology, which Ficino and Pico unveil by symbolic interpretation. Even such presumably clear-thinking rational philosophers as Plato and Aristotle were seen as initiates in a secret tradition of sacred truth.

The Renaissance admiration for the mysterious may seem slightly puerile and affected, yet Ficino and Pico took their work of allegorical exegesis very seriously, for once the inner meaning of Greek religion, thought, and poetry had been grasped, they were seen as a natural revelation of the mysteries of theology. The wisdom of the Egyptians and Greeks was not merely human; it had a religious origin and history which need only be discovered by techniques of exegesis.

Such Renaissance thinkers as Nicholas Cusanus, Ficino, and Pico therefore often exhibited a tolerant eclecticism, an open-minded, receptive attitude toward foreign and ancient philosophies and religions. As previously suggested, this point of view had a perfectly definite metaphysical and historical basis: they believed that the content of these various views was in basic agreement, and that a continuous religious revelation ran through the apparent diversity of human cultures.

The texts of the other set of ideas which Pico made use of, the Judeo-Christian religious tradition, were also interpreted by methods revealing a secret, deeper meaning underneath the crude literal and historical surface. Of course both Jews and Christians had long given the Bible a symbolic interpretation. But Pico believed that he could reveal hitherto unnoticed depths of truth in scripture. For one thing, Pico had a philosophic view of the world, including man, according to which each part of the world is wholly present in every other part. It follows that a truth about any one part immediately reverberates through the whole, and discloses truth about every other part. The very text and literary structure of the Bible is isomorphic with the natural and divine order which it describes. Scripture contains implicit symbolic truths for every branch of science, philosophy, and theology.

Further, Pico's study of Hebrew gave him some access to the *qabbalah,* a Jewish tradition of allegorical commentary on the Bible. He believed that this tradition reached back to Old Testament times. It was an esoteric interpretation of the Law, first revealed by God to Moses alone, then transmitted secretly down to the present. Pico treats the *qabbalah* with more respect than it perhaps deserves. In any case, its influence on his thought has been much exaggerated. Pico merely utilized the *qabbalah* as another tool in his symbolic method of scriptural exegesis. He derived certain new materials from it, but his fundamental method of Biblical commentary is in no way original. Allegorical interpretation had been practiced throughout the Middle Ages, and Pico did not need the *qabbalah* to discover it.

Pico makes independent use of the Hebrew tradition. He rightly points out that he is not subservient to it. Whatever in the Jewish tradition agrees with the Christian Gospel he retains; he refutes whatever in it is foreign to the Gospel. Pico thus makes use of both Greek and Jewish sources of wisdom insofar as he considers them to agree with his own Christian philosophy.

. . . . .

Pico's method of interpreting Scripture can be seen in his **Heptaplus** or **Septiform Narration of the Six Days of Creation.** The principle of his interpretation is the identifying of the truths of science and philosophy with Biblical doctrines. The Greek and Latin Church Fathers, in their commentaries on Genesis, had utilized the cosmology of Plato's *Timaeus.* Pico follows very much in their spirit.

The created world, according to the usual medieval cosmology that Pico uses, is divided into three chief zones, (1) the intelligences or angels, (2) the heavenly bodies, (3) the corruptible earthly bodies. Pico's commentary points out how this hierarchy is present in Genesis, and how Moses already alluded in a hidden way to the facts of natural science as Pico understood them. Biblical concepts also include or signify philosophic concepts. Moses has thus anticipated the findings of Greek philosophers regarding matter, form, etc. Further, the Platonic notion of man as intermediate between the physical and spiritual worlds is held by Pico to be equivalent to the Biblical notion of man as the image of God. Man reunites the multiple orders of creation just as God contains the diverse perfections of creatures in a higher unity.

The natural world, in this sort of interpretation, is a physical embodiment or model of philosophic and religious truth, not a mere symbol or metaphor of a supernatural order: nature actually embodies God's goodness and wis-dom. The parallel between one part of nature and another, between man and nature, or between man and God, is not a poetic fiction but a real isomorphism or identity of structure. Man is the image of God in that he actually reproduces in an imperfect, copied way the perfections of his exemplary cause.

Pico intended this notion of imitation or representation in a realistic, not merely in an aesthetic or metaphorical sense. The permanent interest and value of Pico's view of nature comes from his seeing the physical order as a translation of philosophical and religious truth. In this way, physics, philosophy, and Scripture literally say the same things in different languages.

. . . . .

Since it is impossible to consider all aspects of Pico's philosophy, we shall look at only two major topics, his philosophies of man and of being, which will perhaps disclose the essential character of his thought.

The Italian Renaissance witnessed a renewal of interest in man and his intellectual activities. This study of human culture may be called humanism in a loose sense. In a more correct and strict sense, humanism refers to the ensemble of literary and educational ideals of ancient Greek and Latin culture which were consciously revived and imitated in fifteenth-century Italy. Classical literature had of course continued to be studied and cultivated all through the Middle Ages. Historians are constantly discovering new "renaissances" in medieval culture, which simply indicate the continuous presence of classical letters throughout that period. Still, the Italians felt a new enthusiasm for the classical world, into which they projected all the perfections of an ideal humanity.

This Renaissance humanism was not a philosophy at all, but a cultural and educational program. The humanists were men of letters who employed elegant Latin. They were familiar with certain philosophic concepts, but they were not philosophers. They furnish a plethora of moral platitudes, but not original philosophic ideas. The philosophy of man of such abstract thinkers as Ficino and Pico is altogether distinct and is not derived from the literary movement of humanism.

In fact, fifteenth-century philosophy and literary culture are in many ways opposed. At various times during the Middle Ages there had been analogous conflicts between cultural ideals based on Latin literature and on philosophical speculation. This opposition between literary humanism and philosophic inquiry as ultimate ends of human thought is the subject matter of Pico's celebrated letter of 1485 to the Venetian humanist Ermolao Barbaro. Philosophy need not be written in classical Roman periods, according to Pico, but may employ barbarous medieval Latin, the language of the schools of Paris. For philosophy aims at truth, not at the display of literary virtuosity; it is concerned with reason (*ratio*), not expression (*oratio*). Classical eloquence was wasted on the futilities of myths and fictions, whereas philosophy gives us truth about things human and divine. Pico doubtless derives this contrast between rhetoric and philosophy from Plato, who never tires of opposing the sophist, a virtuoso of persuasive words, to the philosopher, who searches for what is really true. Pico admires the medieval scholastic doctors, Albert, Thomas, Duns Scotus, whose philosophical wisdom written in incorrect Latin is superior to the eloquent but false philosophy of the Roman poet Lucretius. This letter to Barbaro is a particular case of the opposition between a properly philosophic ideal and the cultural program of literary humanism.

The philosophies of man of Marsilio Ficino and Pico are humanistic on a philosophic level. Ficino was the first Renaissance philosopher to formulate a metaphysical view of the nature and place of man in the universe. He was the animating spirit of a loose circle of friends calling themselves the Platonic Academy, and he made the first complete translations of Plato and Plotinus into Latin. His own voluminous writings provide Renaissance thinkers with a view of human nature derived from both Christian and Platonic sources. Man is the metaphysical center of the universe, standing between the physical world of nature and the spiritual world of angels and God. Ficino modifies the hierarchy found in Plotinus in order to obtain a perfect symmetry, with man balanced between the natural and supernatural orders. He considers this placing of man to be in perfect agreement with Christianity, according to which man is the image of God living in the world of physical nature.

Pico's most widely known work, *On the Dignity of Man,* utilizes Ficino's *Platonic Theology.* Yet Pico finds the previous view inadequate, and so unfolds his own philosophy of human nature. The most remarkable contribution he makes is his notion that the root of man's excellence and dignity lies in the fact that man is the maker of his own nature. Man may be what he wishes to be; he makes himself what he chooses.

This celebrated idea is often misunderstood by later critics who interpret Pico in accord with modern philosophies of absolute mind or will. Such interpretations are anachronistic. Pico is not a philosopher of absolute freedom come to torment us before the time. His view of human will is founded on his own perfectly objective philosophy of human nature.

Man has a definite constitution and place in the world, according to Pico. The chief zones of the created universe as mentioned before, are the immaterial angels, the material but incorruptible heavenly bodies, and corruptible earthly bodies. Man unites these three worlds in his own nature. He is not so much another essence as the union of the other three, a lesser model of the whole creation, a microcosmos. This rather trite notion is not a mere symbol or metaphor for Pico; man is made of body and soul, and so literally embodies or reproduces in himself both the angels and physical nature. Thus man has the intermediate place in creation, since he is constituted by the combination of the extremes.

Man also embraces the whole of creation in a further sense, in that he knows it. Any intellectual nature comprehends or includes what it knows. Since the human intellect extends to both spiritual and material objects, man's knowledge is another uniting of extremes.

Not only the created world, but also God is included in man, in that an image embodies and includes its exemplar. Human reason is lord over the senses similar to the way in which God is lord over creatures. One must be careful not to exaggerate the force of Pico's parallel between human reason and God. There is only a similarity of rela-

tion, or analogy, between the way human reason functions and the way God acts. They are both ruling in respect to a lower order of reality. Reason is not a god; it partakes of some of God's functions.

Although man has a definite place in the created world, he is not restricted to some limited form. He gives himself his nature, as a sculptor gives form to a statue. This does not mean that man is an absolute creator of himself, for the making activity of man operates upon potencies which are already given. God has granted to man every kind of seed. They grow as man cultivates them. This notion is as old as Aristotle, who maintained that the virtues are innate in man potentially, but need to be actualized through habituation. The context of Pico's affirmation of man's freedom shows that he is thinking above all of moral freedom, the ability to give oneself the character or set of moral habits that one chooses. Man can make himself into a brute, by choosing the life of the senses, or he can choose supernatural contemplation, which makes man partake of the life of God. Yet Pico is not suggesting that man is outside the definite structure and order of creation; rather, within this order, man selects his own moral nature. The transformation of man into an animal or into the likeness of an angel are symbols derived from Pythagoras and Plato, and represent the ethical choice between good and evil. The citations from Moses and from Plato's *Timaeus* indicate the relation of Pico's view to the Judeo-Christian tradition, in which man is the image of God, and to Platonic philosophy, where man gives himself the sensual life of an animal or the philosophical life of the gods.

If *On the Dignity of Man* emphasizes man's greatness, Pico's later *Heptaplus* remarks his insufficiency. The later work complements the earlier. Both regard philosophy, or natural contemplation, as preparation for higher theological knowledge. The end of man is to return to his first cause, God, where our knowledge is perfected.

Pico formulates this traditional religious notion in Platonic, and particularly Neoplatonic terms. In Plotinus' philosophy, the goal of any being is to return to its first cause. All things partake of a single circular life, descending from and returning to their first principle, the one beyond being. The purpose of all life and thought, in such a philosophy, is to lose all relative being in reunion with absolute unity. The scheme of salvation in Pico's thought is Christian and not Plotinian, but Pico uses Neoplatonic formulas in order to state his own views. For Pico, happiness is a return to God in that man conforms himself to and becomes a perfect image of his exemplary cause. This supernatural elevation of human nature is beyond the natural faculties of reason and will; they are perfected in a higher order by grace.

Pico had a very brief career. It seems most implausible that his writings would present radical changes of viewpoint; a much more likely interpretation is that his philosophy is a consistent whole. In Pico's view, the freedom of man, with its obvious echoes of Plato and Aristotle, is in perfect agreement with the insufficiency of this freedom to attain man's end, based on a religious interpretation of man. The natural order remains perfectly intact while enclosed within a further supernatural order. Pagan Greek philosophies, in Pico, retain their validity even when disclosing their final insufficiency. The concord of philosophies with each other, and with religion, is one of the most fundamental theses of Pico's writings. This agreement is embodied in the collaboration of man's free moral choice with a return to God which we do not make, but receive.

. . . . .

Pico's metaphysics, though less widely known than his ideas on man, is equally significant for the history of philosophy. In his later years Pico was working on a vast *Concord of Plato and Aristotle,* which would have contained his metaphysics. The short *On Being and the One* is a portion of the uncompleted synthesis. It discloses the most fundamental principles of his thought.

Opinions have always been, and still are, divided on the question of the agreement of the chief thinkers of antiquity. Pico adheres to a long tradition of interpretation which maintains that Plato and Aristotle were really expressing the same philosophy in different terms. Neoplatonism, and practically all medieval philosophies, utilize materials from both ancient thinkers, a synthesis made possible by reinterpreting them. The original ideas of Plato and Aristotle are re-used, but in a new sense. This had been going on throughout the Middle Ages, although without benefit of most of Plato's original writings; their content was to some extent accessible through the indirect tradition. Pico was able to utilize all of Plato's works. As will be seen, his manner of interpreting them had much in common with the spirit of medieval philosophy.

The alleged disagreement between Plato and Aristotle centers on one fundamental point. Plato maintained that the one is superior to or beyond being. Aristotle held that the one and being were really the same thing in fact, and differed only in our mental concept or definition. Pico follows the Neoplatonic interpretation of Plato, according to which beings depend on an ineffable one beyond the many, definite formal essences. Being, or the realm of forms, is a second level of reality derived from the one. This region of formal essence is also identified with mind or intellect ($\nu o \hat{\upsilon} \varsigma$). Soul ($\psi \upsilon \chi \acute{\eta}$) is a third level derived from the second; it is mind temporarily present in matter. Finally, the world of physical nature is constituted by soul moving and working in matter.

This interpretation of Plato was widely held until very recent times. There is some evidence that such a philosophy, in which the one rather than being is the first principle, can be found in Plato's own writings. The Neoplatonists constantly quote certain favorite texts in support of their interpretation of Platonic philosophy as a hierarchy of emanations from the one. The good, identified by tradition with the one, is beyond being, but is the source of all being and intelligibility; the one is beyond all definite essence, being, definition, or description; truth about the highest principle is ineffable, beyond the distinctions of reason. The Christian theologian Pseudo-Dionysius the Areopagite identified the Platonic or Neoplatonic one with the monotheist God. Emanation was reinterpreted in terms of creation, not to mention other appropriate improvements. In this Christianized form, Plato's thought exercised an enormous, though indirect, influence throughout the Middle Ages.

Marsilio Ficino, the first Renaissance thinker to know all of the original writings of Plato, continued to interpret Plato within the framework of the Neoplatonic tradition, pagan and Christian, which Platonism had acquired during the previous thousand years; the newly introduced Greek texts were read and understood by all the Florentine thinkers in this perspective. The very title of Ficino's major work, *Platonic Theology,* indicates its content. Although Pico's interpretation of Plato differs in some respects from Ficino's, both Renaissance thinkers follow the long medieval tradition of the fundamental concord of the two Greek philosophers, transformed under the influence of Christianity.

Pico's examination of the problem of being and unity was occasioned by a discussion in which Lorenzo dei Medici had maintained the Platonic view that the one was higher than being. Lorenzo had doubtless been following the traditional ancient and medieval interpretation of Plato's *Parmenides,* adopted also by his friend Marsilio Ficino. Pico's *On Being and the One* was written to show Plato is in merely verbal, not in real disagreement with Aristotle, who maintained that the one is convertible with or equivalent to being.

Modern critics rightly emphasize that the literary form of Plato's dialogues often serves as a key to their philosophic meaning. Pico was one of the first to remark this. He holds that Plato, in the *Parmenides,* did not intend to assert any positive theological or metaphysical doctrines, and that the structure of the eight opposed hypotheses of the dialogue shows that Plato intended only a dialectical exercise. It is a dialogue of method and not of metaphysical content.

Ficino's interpretation had been influenced by the Neoplatonic emphasis on the first hypothesis of the dialogue. This first hypothesis describes the ineffable transcendence of the one, which is above and apart from all being and determination. No being can be affirmed of or connected with the one. This interpretation, which reads the opening hypothesis as a negative description of the one as a pure identity beyond relatedness, had gained added authority and plausibility from the commentary on the *Parmenides* written by the Neoplatonist Proclus. The commentary breaks off at the end of the first hypothesis, with the celebrated texts in which Plato says that the one is beyond any positive being or definition. Any reader who interprets the dialogue more from Proclus' commentary than from the dialectic of all eight hypotheses tends to conclude that these are Plato's last and most profound words on the one. Proclus' commentary had greatly influenced the Christian interpretation of Pseudo-Dionysius, and, in its thirteenth-century Latin translation, had been read by the later medieval and Renaissance thinkers.

Pico's interpretation, that the first hypothesis of the *Parmenides* is no more important than the other seven, and that Plato's intent was not to disclose a profound metaphysical mystery, is based on a new emphasis on the form and method of Plato's dialectic. Pico has attempted to disengage Plato's original meaning from the misleading emphasis of a partial commentary. (Ficino, in his commentary on the *Parmenides,* begun in the same year as Pico's *On Being and the One,* 1492, replies that Pico's interpretation is "against the opinion of all the Platonists." For Ficino, following Plotinus and Proclus, Plato's dialectical form is only an outer covering for a profound metaphysical content.)

Pico's reinterpretation of Plato bears on content as well as form. He shows that Plato's metaphysics is equivalent to

Aristotle's by reinterpreting both, using notions derived from medieval philosophy.

Christians influenced by Plato identify Plato's one with God. The one is a pure identity; it is not another determinate being. What Plato says of the one can be applied to God, since God too is not another determinate essence or nature having certain formal characteristics. God does not have any of the determinations or properties of creatures. Pico attempts to show that, granted the identification of God with the one, it does not follow that God or the one is above being, in any sense which would contradict Aristotle. Aristotle's God, who is the highest or most perfectly actual being, is the same as Plato's. This identity is brought about by Pico's identifying both with the God of Abraham, Isaac, and Jacob.

In a standard medieval distinction, employed by Pico, being may be either (1) all that which is not nothing, or (2) that which does not lack existence (*esse*). In the first sense of being, the things that are, and the things that are one, are exactly the same things. Aristotle rightly said that being and one are merely two ways of describing the same things. Everything that is has both (*a*) being and (*b*) unity. Pico interprets Plato in such a way that Plato is simply assimilated to Aristotle on this point. Plato said that not-being was a principle of relative being, or otherness. Not-being enables beings to be different from other beings. So, in Plato, the many, or the not-one, or the different, are based on not-being. And if the not-one is not-being, then the one must be being. Plato is back in agreement with Aristotle's view that the one and being are the same.

Being in the second sense means that which does not lack existence (*esse*). That which is (*ens*) means whatever participates existence. Pico is here utilizing the metaphysics of St. Thomas Aquinas, who was the first Christian philosopher to base his metaphysics on the real distinction between that which participates existence (*ens*), and the act of existing itself (*ipsum esse*). (There can be no doubt that Pico derived his metaphysic of existence from Thomas. Pico's nephew, Gian Francesco, reports that of ten thousand propositions in St. Thomas, Pico disagreed with only three or four. Of the nine hundred theses Pico proposed for disputation at Rome, forty-five are taken from Thomas, more than from any other philosopher.) The doctrine of existence in Pico turns on the distinction, formulated by Thomas, between God who is his own existence, or is existence itself, and creatures, which are not their own existence, or, which merely participate existence.

The opening verse of Genesis states a religious truth which can be understood by philosophers in different ways. Creatures derive their very being from God. Some Christian theologians, influenced mainly by Platonic metaphysics, consider the distinction between God's being and the being of creatures to be chiefly a difference between eternal being and temporal being. St. Augustine, for example, constantly emphasizes the fact that God is eternally what he is, whereas creatures enjoy their being only transiently and temporally. God is, creatures are always ceasing to be, changing into something else. In a theology of Platonic inspiration, where being is thought of in terms of the self-identity of essence, God possesses eternally and perfectly the identity which creatures possess only imperfectly and for a time. In this sort of philosophy, God's giving tempo-ral being to creatures is taken to mean that God gives them an imperfect possession of essence.

Other theologians, notably St. Thomas, pose the distinction between God and creatures on the level of existence rather than on the level of essence. The difference between God and creatures is that God is existence itself, or is identical with his existence, whereas creatures only participate or share existence. In God, there is no difference between what he is and his act of existing. In creatures, what a thing is, or its essence, is always really different from its act of existing. To say that God created the world is to say that he gave it existence. In this sort of metaphysics, the act of existing is not a mere mode of essence, or way in which essence is (for example, eternal or temporal). *Esse*, real existing, is the final actuality, really different from the actuality of essence, which perfects essence in a different and higher order. Creatures participate existence; that is what they are given in the opening verse of Genesis.

Plato had thought that particular individuals participate in forms or essences. St. Thomas utilizes this Platonic notion of participation in a new way. In his metaphysics, creatures participate not in some essence or manner of being, but in being itself. The difference between God and creatures is the difference between unparticipated and participated existence.

Pico della Mirandola adopts the solution of Thomas, even to the terminology. God is being itself, the act of existing, *ipsum esse*, not another thing which partakes of being. He is being pure and simple, above the things which only have being. Pico takes from St. Thomas his scriptural proof; God tells Moses that his name is "I am who am." Both philosophers take this to mean that God discloses himself as being itself. Other things participate existence (*esse*); God is the plenitude of unparticipated existence.

The apparent disagreement between Plato, who maintained that the one is above being, and Aristotle, who identified the one with being, can now be resolved. The one of Plato, now identified with the Biblical God, is above being in the sense that he is not another thing which has or shares in being. He is not a creature, not something that "is" in the second sense of "having existence" as an attribute. Beings are the things which partake of being; in this sense, God is above beings.

Aristotle held that being was divided into ten categories. God is obviously not a member of any one category; his existence is not a substance, nor a quality, nor a quantity, nor any other category. God is above the ten kinds or categories of being. And so, in Aristotle's view, as interpreted by Pico, God is above being. Plato and Aristotle agree that God is beyond being.

To an observer of the history of philosophy, it is evident that Plato's metaphysics is altogether different from that of Aristotle. Plato's view that being is a relation derived from the pure relation of identity, or the one, is incompatible with Aristotle's view that being means the concrete individual substance. Plato's good beyond being (*ousia*) is not Aristotle's God, who is the first or highest substance or entity (*ousia*). These two Greek philosophies can be made to coincide only when transformed into an altogether different philosophy: the highest principle in Plato turns out to be the same as the highest principle in Aristotle only because they are both identified with a God who is existence itself. God thereby embraces both the one beyond participated being, and the highest substance.

Pico's account of the metaphysical structure of the created world likewise shows a transformation of Greek ideas under Christian influence. The multiple world of creatures contains many natures, many beings, many kinds of good. Yet, while retaining their own being and goodness, creatures at the same time refer to a being and a good beyond themselves. The reality of things is both intrinsic, as in Aristotle's metaphysics, and also referential, as in Plato's. The created world has a double aspect. Creatures have their own being; they exist by virtue of their own act of existing. But this actuality is caused in them; they have it by participation, not by virtue of their own essences. Because creatures have participated existence, they thereby refer to their unparticipated cause.

The same dialectic applies to the notion of the good. Each thing has its own goodness. But it has this good by participation, or, as caused in it by goodness itself. Thus creatures refer to goodness itself, the goodness of God, the way any effect refers to its cause. The good of a creature is in the creature itself, and yet, since it is caused, it leads beyond this instance of good to the good itself.

The most fundamental possible way in which creatures represent or imitate or refer to God is just by existing. What they derive from God is existence, and so they refer to their cause simply by exercising that effect. Of course creatures also derive their formal or essential natures from God, but these are nothing until they exist. Just by virtue of the fact that a thing is, it both has its own being and has it as caused, or by participation, or as referential to absolute being. Plato's relational view of being is equivalent to Aristotle's philosophy of being as substance because Platonic participation has been reinterpreted as a sharing in being itself. Pico's concord of Plato and Aristotle, impossible within their philosophies taken on their own level, has been accomplished by transforming both into a different metaphysics.

This philosophy of participation in being itself has important consequences for the conduct of human life. Pico adopts the traditional Aristotelian view that the good and being are convertible, that is, they differ in thought or in definition but not in fact. Just as the being of man is both intrinsic and yet is a participation from God, even so the good of man has a double dimension. Creatures first attain their own intrinsic good. Aristotle rightly placed this in the proper functioning of a thing's own nature. Pico entirely agrees with Aristotle's view that philosophy, intellectual knowledge on the natural level, guides man to this purely natural or ethical happiness. Yet Pico regards this happiness as imperfect. The true end of each thing is to return to its first beginning, a Platonic notion which Pico doubtless read in Proclus. The supernatural happiness of man, the return to God, who is man's first cause, cannot be brought about merely by philosophical speculation. Aristotle's happiness on the natural level is only a preparation for the supernatural happiness of the return to God. The Neoplatonic notion of return to the one is assimilated by Pico to the Christian idea of divine grace which draws creatures to their Creator. Like Kierkegaard, Pico celebrates the father of faith, Abraham, because he was the first to rise from the level of nature to a supernatural promise.

This scheme of salvation is not a conventional set of pious platitudes but an integral consequence of Pico's metaphysics. In Platonic philosophy, the human soul is divine. It naturally inhabits the super-celestial place, the home of the gods. Plato regards the present life of the soul in the material world as only a temporary misfortune. Pico employs Platonic images to describe the different Christian situation. The human soul is not a god; it is an image of God, according to Pico. When Plotinus in his dying words announced his reunion with the one, he was speaking of the identification of the relative with the absolute, of the loss of human personality in the one beyond being. When Pico speaks of the return of man to God, he uses this language in a different sense. Man in his view becomes a perfect image of God, imitating in a human way the absolute unity of God. Like St. Augustine or St. Thomas, Pico reuses pagan terminology to describe a dialectic which is similar in form to Greek philosophy, but entirely different in content. The divinity of man in this Christian philosophy does not suggest that man is a god. Man participates in the life of God both by his natural being and by his religion, which gives a supernatural life.

. . . . .

Pico della Mirandola called himself an *explorator*. His explorations extended over the whole of philosophy, but were directed by a definite purpose: the discovery of the unity of truth in a harmonious philosophic and religious order, a unity present in a single historical tradition descending through Jewish, Egyptian, and Greek wisdom. Although the unity of truth can hardly be encountered in quite this literal and historical sense, we may still ask whether Pico the explorer found a new world.

The history of medieval philosophy is the story of the assimilation and reinterpretation of ideas derived from Greek philosophy. It is perfectly certain, for example, that the Christian Trinity is not mentioned by Plotinus, nor does Aristotle speak of a God who gives his effects their very existence. St. Augustine found the Trinity and St. Thomas found a God who gives being in Greek philosophy because they transformed it into their own original religious philosophies. These medieval syntheses opened new dimensions of philosophy hardly suggested in Greek speculation.

The Renaissance philosophy of Pico is a new episode in this tradition. The materials of his thought, particularly the works of the Platonic school, are often new. Like his "co-Platonist" Ficino, Pico understood these materials not in a strictly historical way, but in accord with his own constructive purposes. He was convinced of the unity of pagan and Christian thought. This agreement may or may not be encountered as a fact of the history of ideas. Pico created this unity by his own thought; the way in which he assimilated a great variety of doctrines conferred on them their common spirit. He saw the world of physical nature as a stage upon which truths of a spiritual order were embodied and represented. He read pagan literature and philosophy to find in it a prefiguration of religious truth. Scripture was an allegorical unfolding of mysteries. The convergence of all thought and experience, the agreement of philosophies, were, Pico believed, facts of history, but their unity was not merely empirical; Pico understood all aspects of thought and being as disclosing a common truth because they all proceeded from a common source.

Pico encounters in the world, in man, in the good or the one, a system of parts which constitute a unity. The principle of the relations of things is their common descent from God, their exemplary cause. The strongly symbolic, referential character of Pico's world is not based on aesthetic considerations, or on the ideal relations of thought, but arises from the perfectly objective, metaphysical unity which all beings have because they are effects of God, who is being itself. Similarly, in the order of physical and moral action, things come from the goodness of God, and return to it by natural and spiritual inclination. History, the world of nature, the conduct of human life form a whole because they all reflect in different symbolic languages a common providential source.

The materials of Pico's philosophy are characteristic of the Renaissance, and were in many cases unknown in the Middle Ages. His method of understanding these ideas, the form of his thinking, is religious. His thought is a new episode in the history of Christian philosophy.

The art and poetry of the Italian Renaissance have always been admired for the classic perfection of their forms, and the incomparable charm of their symbolism and power of suggestion. Although the secret of beauty remains unknown, much of the attraction of Renaissance works seems to lie in their suggestion of an ideal perfection beyond the particulars present to the senses. Yet this unity reflected by the multiplicity of things is not merely aesthetic. It is religious. Pico found new realms of ideas in his explorations. These new regions remain part of a single world, reflecting God as their cause. The philosophy of Pico della Mirandola expresses the fundamentally religious spirit of the Renaissance. (pp. ix-xxvii)

> *Paul J. W. Miller, in an introduction to* On the Dignity of Man, *translated by Charles Glenn Wallis,* On Being and the One, *translated by Paul J. W. Miller, and* Heptaplus, *translated by Douglas Carmichael, The Bobbs-Merrill Company, Inc., 1965, pp. vii-xxvii.*

Harry Berger, Jr.　(essay date 1969)

[*Berger is an American educator and literary scholar. In the excerpt below, from an essay originally published in 1969, he discusses aspects of neoplatonist idealism found in several of Pico's writings.*]

In the second poem to his *Heptaplus,* Pico divides the universe into three worlds, supramundane, celestial, and terrestrial, bound to one another by the various modalities of logical connection. Man, the fourth world, contains within himself all the aspects of the first three as possibilities, and we may assume that man's very indeterminacy raises him, for Pico, above the determinate universe. Within man all things lose their fixed outlines and are open to whatever new destiny man in his metamorphic freedom may achieve for them. But this achievement takes place *here* in the soul, not *there* in the world, and its validity depends for Pico on an explicit boundary-marking gesture, "Here, not there." For man is somehow in two places at once: *here* he is a frail dweller in the terrestrial world of mortal bodies (*caduca corporum substantia*) sharing with animals a single situation—"unprotected by cover or shade, exposed to rain, snow, sun, heat and cold," and

whether pure or impure, sacred or profane, subject to "the perpetual alternation of life and death." *There,* the all-things-in-all-things of the occult and Neoplatonic literatures are tempered by the fixed hierarchic topography of the essentially Aristotelian world model on which Pico superimposes them.

The two worlds are further distinguished, though not consciously, by a difference of inflection based on what Kant later analyzed as the difference between the external and internal forms of intuition: Pico conceived the *there* in primarily spatial terms, the *here* in temporal terms. *There* is a *where,* but *here* is a *now.* Man must see himself not only in both places but also in two relations: as a fixed object occupying a predetermined *place* in that medieval cosmos where time is a defective image of eternity, and where the eternal is felt primarily in visual or spatial terms; but also as an experiencing subject who occupies a span of time and within whom space and time emerge as modes whereby consciousness conceives its objects. If the language I am using sounds too modern, the distinction can be put this way: a determinate and hierarchic cosmos is one which has been spatially actualized and localized; an indeterminate creature whose central faculties are *ratio* and *voluntas* is a power performing serial operations whose aim is to determine the self by catching the dispersed Many of the cosmos into itself; this process of self-determination involves not only the imaging of the already actualized cosmos but also the acts of exploring and asserting its inner relationships through the dialectical employment of symbol, metaphor and allegory. Though Pico describes man as a fourth world in the *Heptaplus,* in the *Oratio* he treats him as a second creation, a new being and a new mode of existence placed over against the first and distinguished by his *consciousness* (*ratio*) of his situation.

In positing a disjunctive relation between world and man, Pico in effect lays stress on the second world taken by the mind. When God finished the first work of Creation, he "kept wishing that there were someone to ponder the plan of so great a work, to love its beauty, and to wonder at its vastness." Therefore, having made the finite universe perfect in plenitude, order and diversity, he created man "as a creature of indeterminate nature" and placed him at the world's center so that "thou mayest from thence more easily observe whatever is in the world" and so that "with freedom of choice and with honor, as though the maker and molder of thyself, thou mayest fashion thyself in whatever shape thou shalt prefer." The initial assignment of limits is crucial to Pico's position, and consistent in his thought. One finds in Ficino many praises of *homo faber* and these are intended, as André Chastel [in *Marsile Ficin et l'art* (1954)] has observed, "to fix by the analogy of art the manner in which God is present in his creation," and to suggest the comparable dignity of man, *deus in natura:* "His creative activity has its metaphysical justification in the fact that it extends the divine act which makes a perfect masterpiece of the universe." But Pico stresses *homo speculator* rather than *homo faber.* Man is praised for making himself rather than for making things, and he makes himself by his acts of observation, contemplation, and interpretation. Man is like an artist and beholder standing before a perspective picture. The human eye, situated at a proper distance from the object—the universe—sees the whole from a particular subjective viewpoint which is at once ideal and true, a viewpoint which man can vary according to his choice. Placed at a distance which will best allow him *to see,* man's field of activity lies within himself. But this new privilege has as its counterpoise a new distance from God. In his **Commento** on Benivieni's poem, Pico takes issue with Ficino's concept of the beautiful mainly because he wishes to separate God more cleanly from the realm of Ideas than Ficino does. At the same time, he makes this realm a more self-sufficient goal, for in knowing Ideas man somehow truly knows God and possesses the good, and yet, as Cassirer has shown, that is only the truth, knowledge, and possession of symbolic form. Cassirer goes on to draw the consequences:

> Pico is no longer trying to exhibit the Many as the *effect of* the One, or to deduce them as such from their cause, with the aid of rational concepts. He sees the Many rather as *expressions,* as *images,* as *symbols* of the One. And what he is trying to show is that only in this mediate and symbolic way can the absolutely One and the absolutely unconditioned Being manifest itself to human knowledge. . . . There are only different symbols and different interpretations of one and the same meaning, which is the foundation of them all, but which is not capable of being grasped by us as it is in itself, without any symbolic intermediary. . . . he maintains that our thinking and conceiving, in so far as it is directed toward the Divine, can never be an adequate expression, but only an image and a metaphor [see excerpt dated 1942].

And yet in the merely metaphoric, the merely imaginative, lies man's preeminent power of transforming reality as he can. Taking his stand within the relatively limited domain of *poetic* theology, implicitly revising the very significance of the term *ontological,* Pico is able to make and to some extent validate greater claims on man's behalf.

The new position assigned to man is discussed by Pico as that of a *magus* and *interpres.* Distinguishing the good from the bad form of magic, he remarks that the former "is nothing else than the utter perfection of natural philosophy," and he derives the word, on Porphyry's authority, from the Persian *magus,* which "expresses the same idea as 'interpreter' and 'worshiper of the divine' with us." The magus "is the servant of nature and not a contriver," one who

> does not so much work wonders as diligently serve a wonder-working nature . . . having clearly perceived the reciprocal affinity of natures, and applying to each single thing the suitable and peculiar inducements . . . [he] brings forth into the open the miracles concealed in the recesses of the world, in the depths of nature, and in the storehouses and mysteries of God, just as if she herself were their maker . . . and [he] weds lower things to the endowments and powers of higher things.

Sorcery or witchcraft is a presumptuous assertion of power which betrays itself as weakness: the attempt to be a contriver or wonder-worker "makes man the bound slave of wicked powers" and subjects him to the "enemies of God." Its motivation seems connected with the uncontrolled desire of the lower faculties, the urge of the pleasure principle to do away with all difficulty and obstacles to ease. The sorcerer is a false god trying to create a false nature, bypassing the discursive questing of natural philosophy to attain the false image of that peace which can be granted only by theology. . . . If we consider Pico's at-

A terra cotta bust of Lorenzo de' Medici, a great patron of Pico.

titude toward astrology, we may infer that interpretation, or natural magic, is the normative mean between two forms of surrender: astrological determinism which would do away with the responsibility of the thinking creature *now* (*here*), and utopian magic which would wish away the natural limits of the human animal *there* in the terrestrial world.

This process of interpretation may be concretely illustrated on a small scale by a passage from the **Oration** in which Pico considers how man may return to the divine source; the passage begins with an exhortation:

> Let us disdain earthly things, despise heavenly things, and finally, esteeming less whatever is of the world, hasten to that court which is beyond the world and nearest to the Godhead. There, as the sacred mysteries relate, Seraphim, Cherubim, and Thrones hold the first places; let us, incapable of yielding to them, and intolerant of a lower place, emulate their dignity and their glory. If we have willed it, we shall be second to them in nothing.

> But how shall we go about it, and what in the end shall we do? Let us consider what they do, what sort of life they lead. If we also come to lead that life (for we have the power), we shall then equal their good fortune.

The key word here is *emulate—aemulemur.* Emulation is aggressive imitation, an agon between the emulating self and its exemplar. The method of emulation about which Pico asks is most fully demonstrated at the level of style, by the grammatical and rhetorical strategies of his answer. The angels are first treated as exemplars at a distance from the self, superior and independently real. . . . Their reality is grammatically affirmed in the true Aristotelian manner: the angelic substance is the subject, the predicate includes its *energeia* in the mode of essential attribute. By imitating the activity, man may come to share in the attribute. . . . The situation calls for metaphor only in its Aristotelian sense of the transfer of quality. But in the next two sentences the relation between angel and man becomes more fluid, more symmetrical:

> Above the Throne, that is, above the just judge, God sits as Judge of the ages. Above the Cherub, that is, above him who contemplates, God flies, and cherishes him, as it were, in watching over him.

Here the attribute is focused as a genus of which angels and men may be species—the class of just judges, or of contemplative creatures—while the angelic title seems to be transferred from its proper reference to this genus. In effect Pico has replaced the substance with the power as the subject of thought. This leads to the following statement, whose syntax may allow us to see the Seraph reduced to a vehicle or symbol of man as lover:

> Whoso is a Seraph, that is, a lover, is in God and God in him, nay, rather, God and himself are one. Great is the power of Thrones, which we attain in using judgment, and most high the exaltation of Seraphs, which we attain in loving.

Thus Pico has converted the Seraph from reality to metaphor, from angelic substance to human operation, from remote exemplar to indwelling attribute.

In the next passage, the Cherub as contemplation seems at first to have the status of a mere emblem:

> Moses loved a God whom he saw and, as judge, administered among the people what he had first beheld in contemplation upon the mountain. Therefore, the Cherub as intermediary by his own light makes us ready for the Seraphic fire and equally lights the way to the judgment of the Thrones. This is the bond of the first minds, the Palladian order, the chief of contemplative philosophy.

Pico will later convert Moses in the same way, but here the historical figure provides an exemplar: man as complex embodiment of the simple qualities abstractly signified by "angels." Yet from this point on, Pico stylistically suggests a return of the Cherub to his original reality. At first this is merely implicit in the Cherub's reoccupation of the grammatical subject; he is still treated as an artificial model. . . . (pp. 190-96)

In the process of emulation embodied in this passage, boundaries are marked, dissolved, reasserted between the mind and the reality which is its model and object. The *ascensus* of the mind is thus unequivocally internal, poetic, metaphoric—the movement "upward" is diagrammatically conceived as a movement inward. The Piconian metamorphoses through which "man becomes all things" and so creates his own nature are processes of imagination. They are neither magical nor merely fictional: not magical, because the word "becomes" really means, for Pico, "plays the roles of "; not fictional, because the transformational activity of mind which his language mirrors is part of the growth of a real self and adumbrates a reality *an*

sich: the very passage, as an *aemulatio,* is a historic moment in the development of Pico della Mirandola. The process whereby angels are converted to abstractions or hypothetical figures thus has ontological significance. But the reference of *ontological* is in transit here, for the domain of objective spirit is less congruent with *cosmos* and more with *homo* than it is even in Ficino. Where Ficino usually speaks of *anima,* Pico usually addresses or speaks of *homo.* This is significant, since there is a World Soul but not a World Man. The individual soul may easily be envisaged as in or part of the universe, a portion of the World Soul, its epistemological counterpart, etc. But *man* is a self-contained unit whose body and soul may be set over against the world as well as envisaged within it. *Spiritual* tends in its connotations to move toward "psychological," "mental," "imaginative"; therefore the play of metaphor becomes a more substantial activity so long as it is circumscribed as such. . . . But an image becomes an image-of, a noumenon, only through that final self-limitation whereby the mind bounds the area in which it has given play to its constitutive power and distinguishes that area from the transcendent realm where Cherubs are ineffable. Pico's seems a casual or conventional rather than a felt gesture of limitation. The dominant vector of his thought is from world to self, from reality/history/nature to mind, from mystery to metaphor. (pp. 196-97)

In all this, the functions of self, mind and metaphor were exercised in place—place being defined by two coordinates, the earthly center of the cosmos and the human middle of the hierarchy of creatures. The point of invoking angelic exemplars lay in the presupposition of their greater perfection and higher reality. (p. 198)

In moving from description to critique, we have to keep in mind the difference between Pico's stated intentions and those "motives" which a later interpreter elicits from his work. The present essay is concerned primarily with the life, thought, personality, motives, and in general the "activity of spirit" which the work itself renders. With Pico, as with Ficino, Bruno, and many others loosely called Renaissance Neoplatonists, we are confronted with a body of work which is second-rate from a literary or philosophical point of view, but of great significance to the history of culture and ideas. Nesca Robb, whose judgments are always shrewd and perceptive, has summed it up this way [in *Neoplatonism of the Italian Renaissance* (1935)]:

> There are writers who live though their works die, and Pico is one of them. . . . it is Pico himself rather than his work that is still vital. He was the raw material of a poet, lacking in literary gift yet possessed of an inherent poetry of mind and character that illumines his life and breaks in veiled flashes through the inchoate clouds of his learning.

In exploring a gap of this sort between the man *behind* the work and the man *in* the work, our attention may most profitably be directed toward the formal, structural and stylistic exigencies which are entailed but not realized by Pico's "philosophy."

The assumptions and motives of Pico the man are familiar and may be set forth briefly: he believes that God's language is the language of symbol—"hieroglyph"—and that divine symbols display their transcendent origin by being hermetically obscure; they hide their meanings and thus spur the mind of man to interpretation. The cosmos is the greatest symbol, and the Mosaic scripture—especially Genesis—is its preeminent verbal representation. Moses is a model for all writers because he was inspired to set down in a single synoptic text a vision of the cosmos which infolded all possible interpretations. Pico treats the inspired account of Creation as the product of intuitive or noetic thought—having received the Word from the same Spirit who presided over Creation, Moses is called *aemulator naturae*. Less fortunate interpreters who are not thus inspired must fall back upon discursive modes of apprehension normal to fallen man. Pico resorts to *ratio*, to philosophy and discursive interpretation, to get beyond them and attain to a simultaneous intuitive vision of God. Though his often labored pursuit of correspondences appears nothing if not rational, the context of pursuit is an emotive and mystical quest. His interpretive exercises may seem little more than a game, yet they have a serious psychological function: through them he hopes to work himself up to a state in which the vision will (seem to) flood his mind with its light. He is of course aware that man is not and cannot become God, that human dignity entails the tragic limitation, that if man could literally become a god he would lose the essential mark of his greatness, that is, the impulse to transcend a condition of mortality which in one sense cannot ever be transcended.

The distinction between discursive and noetic knowledge, between the human and angelic forms of apprehension, is very old, but Pico's concern with it derives immediately from Ficino. In *Theologica Platonica* III. 1 Ficino cites the field seen and painted by Apelles:

> It is the field which gives Apelles' soul at one and the same moment the perception of the view and the desire to paint it, but if Apelles sees and paints one blade of grass, then another, in successive moments, this is no longer an effect of the field but of Apelles' soul, which by nature is capable of seeing and performing things not simultaneously but successively.

As André Chastel remarks, the example is intended to distinguish "the normal modes of our inner activity from the operations aroused by the intervention of God and the angelic world, where intuitions are given as simultaneous wholes; and it is precisely toward the splendors of the superior vision and its symbols that Ficino's curiosity tends." Ficino's conception derives from Plotinus' famous misinterpretation of the hieroglyph:

> The sages of Egypt . . . in order to reveal to us their wisdom . . . symbolized objects by hieroglyphs, and in their mysteries symbolically designated each of them by a particular emblem. Thus each hieroglyphic sign constitutes a kind of science or wisdom; and without discursive conception or analysis places the thing under the eyes in a synthetic manner.

But Ficino passed on to Pico an interest not so much in the mystical character of the symbol as in the discursive content and the process leading up to the intuition embodied in the image: "Unless one knows what a hieroglyph means, one cannot see what it says. But once one has acquired the relevant knowledge, 'unfolded' by more or less exoteric instruction, one can take pleasure in finding it 'infolded' in an esoteric image or sign." To see the whole universe as a radiant hieroglyph, or rather to strip away the veil and see it all at once in angelic vision, was the goal of Ficino's philosophic quest. His spiritualization of the humanist praise of man was ambiguous to the extent that this goal made him sensible of the life in time as fragmentary and unsatisfactory, an exile from man's true home. Time, itself like a hieroglyph, existed to be transcended. The particular symbol Ficino uses in his gloss on Plotinus is curiously emblematic of his central concern:

> Your thought of time . . . is manifold and mobile, maintaining that time is speedy and by a sort of revolution joins the beginning to the end. It teaches prudence, produces much, and destroys it again. The Egyptians comprehend this whole discourse in one stable image, painting a winged serpent, holding its tail in its mouth.

The emblem *visualizes* the prior acts of thought whereby the mind came to the intuition the image represents. It is not *time*, but *the thought of time* which the symbol infolds. The interest in the discursive process thus leads the mind, whether consciously or not, to symbolize its own interpretation rather than the object giving rise to the interpretive impulse.

This tendency is more assertive in Pico. He strives to establish in the object of his attention some *otherness* which is to be overcome—or more precisely, to establish it *in order to overcome it*. This otherness may be something exemplary, or neutral, or recalcitrant, or partial, or defective, but whatever it is, its function is to stimulate him to confront it, transform it, assimilate it—in short, to dissolve the world into the self as a first phase in the process of self-transcendence, a first step on the ladder to God. When we turn our attention from the man and his motives to the work and its character, we may locate one important cause of failure in this tendency, for it produces an unbalanced interest in the subject, the self, and tends to dissipate the very sense of otherness which makes self-transcendence possible. In his polemic against astrology, for example, he distinguishes natural (physical and spiritual or intelligible) causes from occult causes in the cosmos: the former influence nature but not man, the latter are not astral or demonic forces but human fictions, symbols, projections. But Pico's aim, as Cassirer has shown, is the liberation of man, not the objective revaluation of nature. Unlike the cosmologists and scientific philosophers of the later Renaissance, his attempt to improve human power does not proceed by freeing nature from human idols, striving to make it more independent and real so that it may be confronted as it is in itself. His attempt proceeds rather by freeing man from nature and restricting all nonhuman influences. The result, as Cassirer says in *Individual and Cosmos*, simply extends the thesis introduced in the **Oration:** " . . . not a new way of conceiving nature, but a new way of conceiving man's worth. Now, against the power of 'Fortuna' is opposed the power of 'Virtus'; against destiny, the will conscious of itself and trusting in itself."

Cassirer remarks that Pico sees in man's sinfulness "nothing but the correlate and counterpart to something other and higher":

> Man must be capable of sin, that he may be capable of good. For this is just Pico's underlying idea, that in good as in evil man is never a completed being, that he neither rests ever securely in good, nor is ever a hopeless prey to sin. The way to both lies

ever open before him—and the decision is placed within his own power. . . . Hence however high he may rise, man must always expect a Fall: but at the same time no Fall, however deep, excludes the possibility of his rising and standing erect once more.

Pico's main interest is in the rising vector: sin and evil are less real to him than human power; they are dialectically necessary rather than existentially present in his writing. That is, they function as alien obstacles to be overcome so that man may fulfill the main tendency of his nature, which is to keep moving. Thus, if natural philosophy reminds us that it is not in her power, "to give us in nature a true quiet and unshaken peace," this is not because of human limits but simply because of the limits of natural philosophy, which passes the baton to "holiest theology."

Even when God is the object of inquiry, the same tendency to establish then dissipate the otherness of the object makes itself felt. In the longest and most important chapter of the *De ente et uno* (chapter 5), Pico leans heavily on Pseudo-Dionysius' negative theology to characterize God as "the being who infinitely transcends all that can be imagined." The purpose of the chapter is "to show that not only with the Platonists and Peripatetics, who disagree with one another, but often in the same single writer, there can be, with respect to the divine attributes, many affirmations and many negations equally just." The argument exemplifies Pico's attitude as described by Cassirer: "Our thinking and conceiving, insofar as it is directed toward the Divine, can never be an adequate expression, but only an image and a metaphor." Pico arranges the quest for knowledge of God in four degrees, in the third of which God is conceived as superior to whatever is signified by the transcendental terms (the one, the true, the good and being). "In the fourth degree, finally, we know Him as superior not only to these four transcendentals, but also to every idea which we could form, to every essence which we could conceive Him to be." After two short chapters disposing of Platonist difficulties in regard to prime matter and multiplicity, Pico devotes the eighth chapter to showing how "being, unity, truth, and goodness, are present in all that exists beneath God." This leads to a curious reversal in Chapter 9, "In which it is indicated how these four attributes pertain to God," for they can be referred to Him not only—as we might expect—"as He is the cause of other beings," but also "as He is taken absolutely in Himself." The tone of the discourse at this point makes it difficult for us to believe that Pico has taken seriously his own strictures on the limits of attribution, for he seems to have shifted in an unqualified manner from negative to positive theology:

> We conceive God, then, first of all as the perfect totality of act, the plenitude of being itself. It follows from this concept that He is one, that a term opposite to Him cannot be imagined. See then how much they err who fashion many first principles, many gods! At once it is clear that God is truth itself. For, what can He have which appears to be and is not, He who is being itself? It follows with certainty that He is truth itself.

We cannot tell whether Pico has lowered God or whether he has simply given up God-as-He-is and retracted his discussion to the symbolic form of God, God-as-He-is-conceived. In the tenth and final chapter, at any rate, he draws a moral from the treatise by using the transcendentals as the ground of an *aemulatio Dei*. . . . It is not God's love for us but our love of higher things, not the grace of God but the grace of truth, which will urge us upwards.

The treatise in this fashion ultimately reduces God to a terminus for man, and even the remoteness of the God of mystical theology may serve chiefly to indicate how high man can soar by the proper use of his own powers. There is little feeling in Pico of human action as *a response* to divine pressure, as part of a dialogue with a God who is both present in the soul and wholly other. The God who cannot be determined as an object exists indeed as a noumenon for Pico, but as such is of little functional or methodological importance.

It may of course be argued that the *De ente et uno* is not meant as mystical theology, but this is the point: Pico uses the strategy of the *via negativa* merely to respond "to the arguments which the Platonists invoke to sustain against Aristotle . . . the superiority of the one over being." The chapter is an episode in his unfinished attempt to reconcile Aristotle and Plato, and at its conclusion the brief essay into theology is abruptly terminated:

> From all this we conclude that God is . . . the being who infinitely transcends all that can be imagined, as David the prophet put it in the Hebrew: "Silence alone is Thy praise."

> So much for the solution of the . . . difficulty. The window is now wide open for a true understanding of the books composed by Denys the Areopagite on *Mystical Theology* and *The Divine Names*. Here we must avoid two mistakes: either to make too little of works whose value is great, or, seeing that we understand them so ill, to fashion for ourselves idle fancies and inextricable commentaries.

Since Pico does not avail himself of the newly opened window, his Q.E.D. would be a non sequitur except that it underlines his main theme, which has less to do with God and Denys than with trying to solve old problems in new ways. Here, as in the *envoi* of the final chapter with its somewhat inconsistent and irrelevant though characteristically Piconian attention to the rising vector, we cannot be sure whether Pico is more serious about the body of the argument or about the reflective envelope in which he has placed it.

It is something of a jolt to see the transcendental terms used in the tenth chapter in a purely figurative manner, after they had been treated with scholastic seriousness in previous sections. The tenth chapter has ostensibly the structural function of a return—from God to man, from contemplation to action, from intellectual withdrawal to moral application. But in fact it seems to display itself chiefly as a rhetorical triumph: the topics previously referred to God have now been neatly transferred to man; the subject of the *De ente et uno* has been verbally assimilated to the familiar assertions about the dignity of man. There is a "return" in name only, since the areas of mystical, metaphysical and ethical discourse are but nominally distinct. And the "return" is itself an exhortation to renewed withdrawal: "Let us fly from the world and soar to the Father, imitating Him by becoming unified, true, and good; since these three attributes are united to being, we do not exist if we do not possess them, and are in a state of continuous death." The notions of nonexistence and death aroused here are no less imprecise, no less hyperbolic, than the image of soaring, which means—reduced to literal terms—retiring within oneself and meditating *on* the Neoplatonic ascent. (pp. 201-07)

> *Harry Berger, Jr., "Pico and Neoplatonist Idealism: Philosophy as Escape," in his* Second World and Green World: Studies in Renaissance Fiction-Making, *University of California Press, 1988, pp. 189-228.*

Raymond B. Waddington   (essay date 1973)

[*Waddington is an American educator and essayist. In the following excerpt he examines the structure of, and the inherent meaning of that structure to, the* Heptaplus.]

Thirty years ago Ernst Cassirer braved the labyrinth of Pico della Mirandola's bewildering intellectual syncretism. Following the thread *symbolic thought* which he had used so effectively with Nicolaus Cusanus, Cassirer emerged triumphant to proclaim that the concept of human freedom from the oration **On the Dignity of Man** solves the riddle of consistency in Pico's *opera:* "To our surprise we then become aware that the whole of that work and its internal structure is determined by the same underlying idea that Pico has made central in his oration. Pico's metaphysics, his psychology and theology, his ethics and natural philosophy—these all now appear as a continuous unfolding of the underlying theme here announced." Since that time it has become conventional to read the oration as the ideational key to this most complex and important figure.

Recently Cassirer's thesis concerning the idea of freedom has been extended and refined significantly by Frances A. Yates, who depicts Pico as a Christian magus, wedding Hermetic and Cabalistic modes of magic to give the natural magic of his friend and mentor, Marsilio Ficino, a more directly religious thrust. Miss Yates, like Cassirer, admits that the content of the oration is nothing new, but finds the particular interest in the emphasis:

> [The] orthodox notions are in the oration on the Dignity of Man, but the Dignity of Man as Magus, as operator, having within him the divine creative power, and the magical power of marrying earth to heaven rests on the gnostic heresy that man was once, and can become again through his intellect, the reflection of the divine *mens,* a divine being. The final revaluation of the magician in the Renaissance is that he becomes a divine man.

Somewhat more implicitly than Cassirer, Miss Yates, too, sees the oration as the thematic key to Pico's thought: "Pico's oration on the Dignity of Man echoes throughout with the words Magia and Cabala; these are the basic themes of his whole song." Whereas Cassirer was concerned to identify the particular philosophic originality of Pico della Mirandola and its impact upon subsequent Renaissance thought, the task to which Miss Yates has addressed herself is the proper discrimination and assessment of the influences upon Pico which made that originality possible. Nonetheless, there is, I think, an essential

consonance in the contours of the intellectual *terra incognita* that they have mapped.

Miss Yates's vision of the magician Pico has not, however, met with the almost unanimous approval accorded to her Hermetic Bruno. The most thoughtful dissenter has been Charles Trinkaus, who, apparently conceding Yates's argument for the oration in itself, chooses the **Heptaplus** for his central text and makes this demur:

> This vision of man, fulsome as it is, should be noticed to be a metaphysical and a religious vision of man as demi-god, and not a vision of man as an active earthly creature making himself a ruler and knower of all. I do not think the appellation of *Magus,* which Miss Yates wishes to apply to this conception of man, is fitting, because it is surprisingly non-operative, extraordinarily passive, almost statuesque, with man almost literally seen as the emblem of God in the middle of the world with all its parts and creatures doing him service.

For Trinkaus "Pico's image of man is basically a religious image, and also a poetic one," and in the **Heptaplus** Pico reveals an "extraordinarily anthropocentric" (i.e., human without the divinity of the magus) vision of the universe, which vision "is cognate also to his **Oratio de dignitate hominis.**" Moreover, pursuing his emphasis upon the anthropocentrism of the **Heptaplus,** Trinkaus attempts to relate this theme to the symbolic structure of the treatise. As Pico explains in the "Second Proem to the Whole Work,"

> I have divided the whole exposition into seven books or treatises, rather to imitate Basil and Augustine than because the integrative attention of the reader may be refreshed by frequent breaks. Moreover, since the seven expositions are arranged in seven books and each book is divided into seven chapters, the whole corresponds to the seven days of creation.

Trinkaus interprets the structure figuratively, and remarks upon its apparent collapse:

> His fourth book deals with the fourth world of man. One must recognise a certain lack of clarity in his organisational schema. The fourth is the middle book of seven, and man is in his view, as in Ficino's, the node or centre of the cosmos. But man was created, according to *Genesis,* on the sixth day. Each book follows through the seven days of creation and rest in its seven chapters, so that the fourth chapter of the fourth book is the exact centre of the work, if it is conceived of like an acrostic, as Pico conceived of it. But he is unable to make his exegesis of *Genesis* come out thus neatly.

Caught in the intricacies of his own symbolic numerology, according to Trinkaus, Pico attempts to place his major thematic revelation at the mathematical center of the treatise; but, baffled by the unavoidable chronology of the Mosaic creation, he is forced to comment, instead, upon the fourth day's creation of the sun and moon at the midpoint of **Heptaplus,** thereby flawing the structural scheme which is the basic organization.

Trinkaus is the only one of these intellectual historians to give any considerable attention to the **Heptaplus.** Independently, however, literary historians have discovered the **Heptaplus** as a seminal document in formulating the Renaissance conception of poetry as creating a "world" that is directly analogous to the world of God's own creation. As Maren-Sofie Røstvig explains, Pico links Augustine's conception of the world as God's poem with a Neoplatonic (or Hermetic) interpretation of the Mosaic creation. The poet creates with the word, just as the Word of God, in the Gospel of St. John, was responsible for the entire creation. Genesis, therefore, necessarily provides the archetype for any subsequent literary creation, and, being the first and most direct inspiration from God, contains within it all the secrets, the entire order of creation, presenting the model for all poems, as Moses presents the model for all poets. . . . Combining, as Miss Røstvig suggests, Solomon's dictum that God created everything in number, weight, and measure (Wisdom 11.21) with his Platonic/Pythagorean predilection for conceiving the world order in terms of mathematical harmony, Pico would have a natural disposition to recreate the Genesis model by means of a numerological structure.

Perceiving the significance of the *Heptaplus* for literary theory, however, has the concomitant effect of making Trinkaus' charge of structural failure all the more damning. If the *Heptaplus* is to be seen not primarily as exegetical commentary but itself as a literary construct which reveals the pattern of the original creation, the fault cannot be trivial. Pico says "truly the scripture of Moses is the exact image of the world;" and "since a writer copies nature," the failure to imitate correctly the literary archetype of all nature strikes at the heart of Pico's audacious enterprise.

From the critical dialogue I have traced here, several issues emerge: first, is Trinkaus correct in his assessment of the structural deficiency of the *Heptaplus*? Since his response to the structure is predicated upon his prior conclusion about the meaning of the work, one must ask, further, if the treatise is indeed radically anthropocentric. How should the nature of man in the vision of the treatise be perceived—as passive and limited, as Trinkaus describes it, or as boldly free, divine, magical, as Cassirer and Yates would have it? This last question has the consequence of taking us from the narrow boundaries of execution and meaning in a specific work to the more general matter of thematic consistency between the *Heptaplus* and the oration, and, thereby, philosophic coherence in Pico's *opera*. The purpose of this essay is to arrive at some provisional answers by focusing upon the interrelationship of structure and meaning in the *Heptaplus.*

If to a philosopher the "controlling principle and [the] controlling method in Pico's thinking" is symbolic thought, it is suggestive that to a literary historian the striking thing about Pico is his interest in symbolic form. The seven-times-seven numerological structure of the *Heptaplus* implies, on Pico's own justification, a concept with both spatial and temporal dimensions. The division into seven books of exposition "to imitate Basil and St. Augustine" makes a spatial separation of levels of meaning, which are, as Pico carefully acknowledges, actually simultaneously present, thus creating a symbolic exfoliation similar to Augustine's division of *The City of God* into twenty-two books. But just as Pico's interpretation itself is a creation ("producing a work completely new from the beginning," so it follows the pattern of creation in dividing each book into seven chapters, corresponding to the seven days of creation, each chapter explicating the Mosaic account of that day's labors in accord with the governing level of exposition. The first four levels of exposition constitute the four "worlds" of nature—elemental, celestial, angelic, and human—followed by a fifth book on the "successive order" of these worlds and the "discordant concord" between them; a sixth book on the unity of all things; and the seventh on the felicity which is eternal life, and so the reunion of all creation with God.

Although the first six books of expositions do not exploit the potential analogy of the stages of creation, Pico shifts his perspective with the last, permitting a conflation of dimensions:

> Finally, just as the six days of creation were followed by the Sabbath, that is, by a rest, it is fitting that after treating the orders of things proceeding from God and explaining their union and diversity and their bonds and habits, we should in a seventh, and, as it were, sabbatical exposition, touch lightly on the felicity of creatures and their return to God, which through Mosaic and Christian law was granted to man, though we were long separated from it through the sin of our first parent.

The implications of Pico's decision to write, not a conventional *Hexameron,* but a *Heptaplus* should not be ignored. As a Cabalist he is committed to the proposition that the book of Moses contains all wisdom, the secrets of all nature; as a Christian he believes that nature to be spiritual as well as physical, the creation to include the invisible world of the soul as well as the visible one of matter. The deficiency of the common expositor is his shortsightedness in stopping with the end of the material creation on the sixth day, instead of going on to the spiritual state symbolized by that Sabbath of everlasting rest and now attained only through the agency of Christ. Therefore, just as the seventh day of Moses is the Sabbath of rest, so the seventh chapter of each exposition shall always be devoted to Christ, "who is the end of the law and is our Sabbath, our rest, and our felicity."

Both organizational principles arrive at a common end, the week of chapters (repeated sevenfold) in the Sabbath that is Christ and the seven books in a veritable academic sabbatical, which is devoted to an exposition of history in the Christian perspective. Pico knows, uses, and explicitly refers to the tradition, stemming from the thousand-year "day of the Lord" (Psalms 90.4), that the six days of creation correspond to the anticipated six-thousand-year life of the world. The Proem to Book VII, which is by far the longest of proems to individual books, establishes the overreaching Christian view of history: "whoever does not put his faith in Christ after recognizing Him is rightly deprived not only of the first felicity, but also of the second, the natural, since it is only a corrupt and fallen nature that does not desire grace." Chapters 1 and 2 do not mention Christ; Chapter 3 refers to him only toward the end, as if in preparation for the revelation of 4; Chapter 4, the millennium into which the Savior was born, is devoted to his nature; thereafter Pico considers the correspondence between the remaining days and what occurred after the coming of Christ. Thus temporal order ultimately dominates Pico's exposition of Genesis, and, as is customary in Christian exegesis of a temporal nature, the vision unmistakably is a prophetic one: "Here we shall disclose what in the present scripture Moses clearly hid about these, so that this explicit prophecy of the advent of Christ, of the increase of the Church, and of the calling of the gentiles, may be read plainly."

In support of his contention that the **Heptaplus** is Pico's essay on man, Trinkaus points out that the principal discussion of man occurs in Book IV; but because man was created on the sixth day, the sixth chapter of each book is devoted to man, as the seventh chapters are devoted to Christ, "the exemplar of man." Stressing Pico's use of *primum in aliquo genere* in I.7, "If, as the philosophers say, all perfection in each class is derived by the other members from the most perfect one as from a fountain, no one may doubt that the perfection of all good men is derived from Christ as a man," Trinkaus seemingly concludes that this exemplary function establishes the role that Christ fulfills throughout the treatise. But to so read is to level out distinctions by missing the implications of Pico's conceptual scheme. In fact the presentation of Christ varies from book to book in accordance with the dominant level of exposition. Thus I.7 emphasizes class and genus in a quasi-scientific way appropriate to the elemental world. II.7, in the celestial world, urges us not to forge astral talismans in metal, but to shape the image of Christ, the word of God, in our souls. Similarly, III.7 (angelic world) argues Christ's power to elevate and perfect the angels; IV.7 (human world) presents the typological conception of Christ as the second Adam; V.7 (order of the worlds) envisions Christ as the unifying link, who is, himself, all in all; VI.7 (affinity of the worlds) describes Christ as the mediator, the only door from earthly to heavenly life. In VII.7 (eternal life) Pico explains that heavenly man (i.e., Christ), not earthly man, was made in God's image, ending the **Heptaplus** with the promise that those who are reborn through baptism will attain the image of both Son and Father.

Granted that Pico consistently emphasizes the mystery of the incarnation—Christ's dual nature as man-God—even so, it seems a distortion to see Christ only as the uppermost range of the nature of man, which constitutes the major theme. Perhaps this is simply a matter of emphasis. For me, however, **Heptaplus** predominantly is a celebration of the nature of Christ; rather than anthropocentric, it is profoundly Christocentric. It should be remarked that Pico breaks, or expands, his expositional pattern to dedicate his sabbath, the entire seventh book, to Christ; he does not do this with man in Book VI.

If one can make a considerable case, then, for the treatise as focusing upon Christ and not man, what corroboration does that symbolic center, the mathematical mid-chapter provide? Certainly it relieves the strain of arguing that the creation of man in IV.6 should somehow have been wrenched out and placed two chapters earlier; but is IV.4 any more demonstrably about Christ than about man? "This according to his acrostical scheme is the very centre of the work, but not fitting the six labours, it also deals with man's physical beauties and faults symbolised by the fourth day's work of creating night and day, darkness and light, moon and sun.

Although he has spoken of the rational nature in IV.1-2, Pico tells us he must now speak of its "adornments" and its "royal furnishings"; this is what Moses meant by placing sun, moon, and stars in the firmament. While recent philosophers would call the sun the active intellect, "we shall so expound it in the meantime that wherever the soul turns toward the waters above, toward the Spirit of the Lord, it shall be called sun, because it becomes bright all over," according with the Platonic concept of *dianoia*. Although Pico ostensibly wishes to allegorize the creation of the celestial bodies in terms of the rational nature and thereby couches his discussion in a philosophic context, the language and thrust of his chapter serve to suggest another, more specifically religious, intention:

> When the day of future life has dawned, we shall be parted from our senses and turned toward more divine things, understanding them by means of another, nobler part. Therefore, it is rightly said that this sun of ours presides over the day and the moon over the night. Likewise, because after having cast off this mortal garment we shall contemplate solely by the light of the sun that which in this wretched night of the body we try to see with all our strength and power rather than do see, the day on that account is bright with the sun alone.

The interpretive clue to this intention and to the undermeaning of the entire chapter is provided, I believe, by turning to VII.4, the directly corresponding chapter of the book celebrating Him whose nature fulfills and perfects that of natural man. Book VII, as I noted earlier, consists of a review of the "week" of sacred history in accordance with the stages and demarcation of the week of Genesis, interpreting, in effect, the Genesis creation as a prophetic type of the subsequent spiritual progress of the world. In Chapter 4 Pico reaches the events of the fourth millennium of history:

> Then came the fourth day, on which the sun, the lord of the firmament, that is, Christ, the lord of the law, and the moon-like Church, the bride and consort of Christ, and the apostolic doctors who would educate many to justice, like stars in the firmament, began to shine forth for eternity, calling the world to eternal life. The sun did not destroy the firmament, but perfected it, and Christ came not to destroy the law, but to perfect it.

Pico urges his reader to consider "how true and sound the scheme of my interpretation is," and seeks to establish his case by concentrating upon three issues: proving from "The testimony of the Jews" that the works of the fourth day foreshadow the coming of Christ; "that nothing represents the Messiah to us more fittingly than the sun"; and that Jesus of Nazareth was truly the Messiah promised to the Hebrews. He uses biblical chronology to establish that Christ came in the very middle of the fourth millenium, or thousand-year day of the Lord; within the same day "the light of the moon, the Church, shone upon the whole world," and within five hundred years of Christ's death the apostles and martyrs "illuminated the shadows of our night and the darkness of the firmament, that is, of the law." Pico then cites rabbinical authorities to argue that the period of the law was to extend into the fourth day, but that the Messiah would come before the fourth had elapsed, concluding from this that, unquestionably, Christ is the Messiah. Finally he sets out to prove by the "similarity of metaphor" that the sun is the image of Christ:

> He placed his tabernacle in the sun, and he sprang from the tribe of Judah, whose emblem is the lion, the animal of the sun, and when Plato in the *Republic* calls the sun the visible son of God, why may we not understand it as the image of the Invisible Son?

> If he is the true light illuminating all minds, does
> he not have as his most exact likeness the sun,
> which is the light of the senses illuminating all bo-
> dies? But why do we look for anything else? Let us
> ask the sun itself, which, eclipsed behind the moon
> during Christ's passion, clearly showed us the ac-
> cordance of its nature.

In effect, Pico has quite literally patterned his treatise
upon the form of Genesis—as he understands it. Just as
Moses' creation hides at its midpoint the prophecy of
Christ's advent, so Pico's interpretation of the Mosaic account does exactly the same thing. And yet, true to his
principle that the interpretation must be "self-consistent
and coherent" from beginning to end, not "an arbitrary
and violent sort of exposition," he takes care to include
within the treatise itself the information necessary to apprehend that mystery hidden at the center: the emergence
of the sun on that fourth day is a prophetic revelation of
the *solem iustitiae,* the god incarnate who called himself
the light of the world.

The hidden Son at the mathematical center of the treatise
implies a symbolic spatial pattern, which probably can be
fully apprehended only with a grasp of the whole (including, necessarily of course, that outermost sabbath book).
Biblical typology, upon which Pico conceives his scheme,
always is an art of hindsight prophecy; to recognize the
type one has to know the antitype. But there is an implicit
temporal pattern as well. Miss Røstvig comments, "The
number 4 applies with equal justice to the gospels, the sun,
and Christ; the sun is fourth in the sequence of the planets
and it was created on the fourth day, so that it holds the
middle both temporally and spatially." The temporal
movement in the **Heptaplus** is linear, as the reader proceeds through the books of the treatise in sequential order.

As Trinkaus correctly perceives, the ordering of the four
worlds—elemental, celestial, angelic, human—intimates a
value hierarchy, an ascending sequence. Moreover, the arrangement cannot be other than a deliberate one, since it
is different from the preliminary explanation in the second
proem to the whole: "Highest of all is . . . the
angelic. . . . Next to this comes the celestial world, and
last of all, this sublunary one which we inhabit. . . .
There is, moreover . . . a fourth world in which are found
all those things that are in the rest." The introduction of
the human world leaves its placement indefinite—it could
be either first or last, or simply outside the sequence. Otherwise, the ordering is highest to lowest, the opposite of
the lowest to highest succession actually followed in the
treatise. Pico reinforces the ascending sequence by imagery of vertical movement: "Let us rise from the elements
to the heavens" (Proem to II); "Who will now give me the
wings of a dove . . . ? I shall fly above the heavenly region" (Proem to III); III.7 explains how Christ "so elevates" human nature as to set man "over" the angles.
Having reached this peak of speculation, the movement
inverts, causing the reader to undergo a descent. Book V,
"Of All the Worlds, in Successive Order of Division," reverses the order of the worlds presented in the first four
books: V.1 discusses the angelic, V.2 the heavenly, V.3 the
elemental, V.4-5 heavenly bodies and animals, and V.6
man. The introductions to the final two books avoid language suggesting vertical movement, effectively committing the reader to horizontal progression, keeping him on
the same level to which he had descended in Book V. If

the temporal movement of the reader were to be dia-
gramed, the shape of **Heptaplus** would be that of a pyramid.

Or, to accept the image which Pico provides for us at the
start, the shape of a mountain. The circumstances of
Moses' prophetic transfiguration plainly signify for Pico
the state of spiritual elevation and the unparalleled favor
which Moses received; citing Exodus 25.40, Pico stresses
the manner in which Moses learned exactly to imitate the
form of the world: "just as we also read that on the mountain where he learned these things, he was commanded to
make everything according to the pattern that he had seen
on the mountain." More than this, however, the process
of ascending the mountain seems to become for Pico an
archetype of the arduous spiritual discipline necessary to
attain that summit of revelation, something achieved only
by the chosen few:

> If the few disciples of the Lord, chosen from so
> many thousands, could not bear so many things,
> could the whole people of Israel—tailors, cooks,
> butchers, shepherds, slaves, and maidservants, to
> all of whom the law was given to be read—have
> borne the weight of the whole of Mosaic, or rather
> divine, wisdom? On the summit of the mountain,
> that very mountain on which the Lord also often
> addressed his disciples, the face of Moses used to
> become wonderously bright, illuminated by the
> light of the divine sun; but since the people with
> their owl-like and unseeing eyes could not endure
> the light, he used to speak to them with his face
> veiled.

Pico, in other words, makes his reader figuratively emulate the role of Moses in ascending to the summit of the
mountain; but, as himself a Mosaic word-artificer, he veils
his light so that those who are blind cannot see the sun.

Why does Pico feel obliged to conceal this perfectly orthodox and thoroughly familiar Christian back-reading of the
Pentateuch? To understand this requires the willing suspension of disbelief in several areas. First, one must appreciate the consequences of the intellectual milieu of Platonic mystagogue and Hermetic magus, which Edgar Wind
and Miss Yates have reconstructed for us. The Moses posited by Pico is a magus, "deeply learned in all the lore of
the Egyptians," from whom Pythagoras learned the art of
silence and Plato the technique of concealing doctrine beneath the language of mysteries:

> Therefore if in his books Moses seems an unpol-
> ished popularizer rather than a philosopher or
> theologian or master of great wisdom, let us call to
> mind that it was a well-known practice of the sages
> of old either simply not to write on religious sub-
> jects or to write of them under some other guise.
> For this reason these subjects are called mysteries.

Pico's knowledge of the Cabala served to convince him
that he had mastered the "secrets of the book of Moses,"
penetrating almost the very source of wisdom, which experience caused him to venerate Moses more than the gen-
tile *Prisca Theologia,* whose genealogies of wisdom so en-
grossed the Hebrew-less Ficino.

Holding this esoteric conception of Moses and believing
that Moses is "the pattern for perfection in a writer," Pico
can only present himself in the role of Moses. Harry Berger, Jr., for whom Pico's idealism is a selfish and trivializ-

ing escapism, remarks that the figure of Moses in the *Oration on the Dignity of Man* is "Pico playing the role of Moses." The perception is acute, though it refuses to take seriously enough the image of Moses or the importance of role playing as the means of effecting that self-creation which is the theme of the oration. Moses in the oration, however, is only one actor in a cast almost as numerous as the conclusions Pico proposed to defend; in the *Heptaplus* he is on stage throughout.

If it seems improbable that Pico would so elaborately and intricately construct an expository treatise only to conceal a part of the meaning, it may be argued that he follows scrupulously the model of the Mosaic artist (albeit a model created by himself). Speaking of mysteries in the riddling language of mysteries, he reveals part but not all: "I remembered the provision of the Mosaic law that one should not harvest his field completely but should leave a portion of it untouched so that the poor and needy might get sheaves and handsful to satisfy their hunger." Pico emphasizes the commandment to create according to the *pattern* seen on the mountain, and the incarnation of this pattern preserved in the scriptures written by Moses. Correspondingly, the *Heptaplus* must be read as a work of literary art; as in a poem, here form and structure should be considered to convey meaning as significantly as discursive statement. Both Moses and Pico would require an act of creative understanding by the reader.

This theory of symbolic form derives from, and is governed by, Pico's essential allegorical principle—everything is in everything:

> Bound by the chains of concord, all these worlds exchange nature as well as names with mutual liberality. From this principle (in case anyone has not yet understood it) flows the science of all allegorical interpretation. The early Fathers could not properly represent some things by the images of others unless trained, as I have said, in the hidden alliances and affinities of all nature.

A knowledge of the hidden affinities makes possible, too, the self-consistency and internal coherence which Pico requires of himself. An example of this internal coherence, Pico probably would think, can be seen in the almost punning fashion in which he cues the reader's attention to the presence of allegory in IV.4: "Now we must speak of its adornments and what I may call its royal furnishings" (Nunc de ornatu et, ut ita dixerim, regia eius suppellectile dicendum).

In his study of allegory Angus Fletcher reminds us that "the Greek term *kosmos* has a double meaning, since it denotes both a *large-scale order* (macrocosmos) and the small-scale *sign of that order* (microcosmos)." *Kosmos* signifies both a universe and a symbol implying a hierarchical rank. This duality (which survives precisely in English with *cosmos* and *cosmetic*) obtained as well in Latin through the relationship between *ornare* (furnish, embellish) and *ordinare* (order, arrange). In this sentence Pico calls attention to the fact that he is reducing the macrocosm to a microcosm, the universe to the order within man, but by employing language associated with cosmic allegory, he manages to leave the reader conscious of allegorical manipulation, and thus responsive to the shift when celestial macrocosm becomes microcosm to the greater spiritual universe. The play upon *regia* involves the

same sliding scale of correspondences in terms of rank; man, sun, and Christ all hold analogous positions in their respective worlds.

The meaning is there for those who know how to find it. Once again the burden is upon the reader. Pico, emulating what he saw in Moses, conceals while providing a model for arriving at revelation. The process is discovery, coming, as Pico exults in VII.4, in "the fullness of time." "Et ecce temporis plenitudo." (pp. 69-84)

> *Raymond B. Waddington, "The Sun at the Center: Structure as Meaning in Pico della Mirandola's 'Heptaplus'," in* The Journal of Medieval and Renaissance Studies, *Vol. 3, No. 1, Spring, 1973, pp. 69-86.*

William G. Craven   (essay date 1981)

[*In the following excerpt, Craven surveys several critical interpretations of Pico's theory of man as a microcosm, as revealed in the* Heptaplus *and the* Oration.]

Several authors have insisted that Pico rejected the idea of man as a microcosm. This is a curious position, because the evidence to the contrary is so clear. In the *Oratio* Pico states that he "was not satisfied by the many assertions made by many men concerning the outstandingness of human nature". Included among these is the idea that man is the bond tying the world together, which could reasonably be taken as equivalent to the microcosm. However, it is not accurate to say that he rejects the ideas he lists. He says of them "these reasons are great but not the chief ones". The same idea of man as the bond of the world is invoked later in the *Oratio* to justify the rather eccentric interpretation of "Know thyself" as an exhortation to investigate nature. It is valid, but is not the image best suited to his purposes in the *Oratio.*

In the *Heptaplus,* on the other hand, the microcosm is integral to his scheme. The entire work is built on correspondences, on the principle that all is in each. The phrase quoted by Garin and Cassirer, "Tritum in scholis . . . ", "It is a commonplace in the schools that man is a lesser world", is not an attack on the microcosm. It is clear from the context that the opposite is intended. "Tritum" means that the idea is so generally accepted that its use will need no justification. There is an interesting parallel usage in the *Disputationes* when Pico refers to the doctrine of the heavens being the universal cause as "tritum apud philosophos". He certainly did not wish to impugn a doctrine which, as something generally accepted even by astrologers, was to be the foundation of his argument. The idea of the microcosm has a similar function in the argument of the *Heptaplus,* and it should have been clear from the work as a whole that "tritum" could not imply disparagement. Pico is quite explicit about his purpose. He intends to vindicate Moses, by showing that beneath the surface of what appears to be a simple, even primitive story, there are hidden the treasures of all true philosophy, as well as prophesies concerning Christ. This is possible because of the precise and complete correspondences between the four "worlds" of creation, the angelic, celestial, elemental and human. In writing about one, Moses could convey truths simultaneously about each of the others. This is the justification for Pico's sevenfold exegesis. For his elaborate scheme, it is essential for man to be a microcosm, containing whatever is in the other worlds.

Pico insists, moreover, that man must contain everything in reality. Garin was mistaken in his view that Pico proposed a convergence in human knowledge, not human nature. On the contrary, he explicitly dismisses such a convergence as inadequate. In the fifth exposition he explains the meaning and significance of man as microcosm. He repeats with emphasis "Dico autem re ipsa", "I say in reality", because the angels and all intelligent creatures contain all things in some way in knowing them. What makes man unique is that he contains them in reality. Pico sees this not as reducing man to an aggregate, but as his peculiar privilege. This is the meaning of Moses' words, that man was made in God's image. Whereas God "assembles and unites the total perfection of the true substance of things" in himself as their origin, man "collects and joins to the completeness of his substance all the natures of the world" as their centre. Thus, man's microcosmic nature and his central position in the universe are both clearly affirmed.

Kristeller has argued in several of his lectures that the *Heptaplus* echoes the doctrine of man in the *Oratio* because in it Pico places man outside the hierarchy of being, making him a fourth world apart from the others. Yet man in the *Heptaplus* is certainly part of the system, firmly tied to it by correspondences. As the fourth world, he corresponds part by part to the rest of creation, and it is all in him. In fact, Pico says that he is "not so much a fourth world, like some new creature, as he is the bond and union of the three already described". His position in the universe is quite explicit. He is at the centre, placed there as the image of God, like a founder's statue in the centre of a city. Moreover, as Kristeller himself had noted, man contains all natures precisely as "medium", things below him in a higher form, things above him in a lower form. His position on the cosmic ladder is clearly defined; man has his proper place in the hierarchy of being.

While it is not true to say that the idea of the microcosm is rejected in the *Oratio,* the image of man displayed in the *Heptaplus* is certainly in marked contrast to the conventional picture of man free to choose his own nature. In the one case, man can become all; in the other, he is all. This is, or should be, a challenge to historians who wish to find in Pico a consistent doctrine of man. Garin's statement, that man was everything because he could be everything, merely evades the issue by juggling words. Charles Trinkaus, on the other hand, explicitly recognised the difficulty when he observed that the picture of man in the *Heptaplus* was "surprisingly non-operative, extraordinarily passive, almost statuesque". It was surprising and extraordinary in contrast to the conventional view of the *Oratio.* De Lubac also noted the contrast, pointing out the microcosmic elements in the *Oratio* and insisting that any interpretation must accommodate both themes. He was convinced that Pico had achieved a synthesis of the two. The emphasis differed, but neither element was emphasised to the detriment of the other. Just how the union between the two was effected, however, de Lubac did not succeed in making clear. The contrast remains between a dynamic view of man who is potentially all, and a static view of man who is actually all.

One can understand, therefore, the reaction of those who have tried to avoid the difficulty by ignoring the *Heptaplus,* or else by seeking to discredit it as a retreat from the boldness of the *Oratio,* a loss of nerve after Pico's condemnation. At the time of writing the *Heptaplus,* however, Pico showed no sign of retreating, and was insisting that the pope should rehabilitate him on his own terms. Besides, there was no reason why he should have felt it necessary or even diplomatic to change his ideas about man. They were not touched by the condemnation, and in any case they remained unpublished. Other historians have taken a less cavalier approach, and have tried to accommodate the *Heptaplus* to the *Oratio.* One such endeavour was Kristeller's insistence that man in the *Heptaplus* was outside the hierarchy of being, in spite of his firm location as *medium.* Trinkaus approached the problem from another angle. Admitting that man in the *Heptaplus* was involved with the cosmos, he argued that the opposite was not only true but more true. Pico subjectivised or personalised the cosmic elements, thus undermining the metaphysical order. Man was not being tied to a rigid system. The universe, like man, was alive and quivering with soul. It was an extraordinarily anthropocentric vision of the universe. In his search for distinctive doctrines, however, Trinkaus lost sight of Pico's reason for emphasising the mutual correspondences in creation. It is essential for his elaborate exegetical scheme that each world should correspond to the others, so that whatever Moses says about one can be true of all. To single out one of the worlds and make it the dominant pattern would destroy the symmetry. The balance must be preserved, so that the allegory works both ways. What is said of man must be true of the other worlds, but the contrary must also be the case. The intention of the work as a whole must be kept in mind.

A more elaborate attempt to accommodate man in the *Heptaplus* to the fable in the *Oratio* was made by Raymond Waddington [see excerpt dated 1973]. Arguing with great ingenuity from the structure of the *Heptaplus,* he concluded that its subject was Christ. He interpreted it as an invitation to the reader to emulate Moses, who, like Christ, was a Promethean figure. Moreover, such emulation would be role-playing, akin to self-creation. In this way he made man in the *Heptaplus* look more like the allegedly Protean-Promethean man of the *Oratio.* The image of man ceased to be passive and statuesque; instead, "the stage is dominated by a concatenation of Promethean figures, Pico, Moses, and—at the center—the first and last of creators, Christ. The human world may be a microcosm of the creation, but this active operator and controller of nature is a microcosm of the creator. A magus." Regrettably, Waddington's interpretation piles supposition upon supposition: that the mid-point of the work must be laden with significance, that Moses is a magus, that Pico represents himself as Moses. He saw his account as enjoying "a closer affinity to Pico's expressed intentions", yet it was precisely these it had to disregard. Pico states repeatedly that the *Heptaplus* is an exegetical commentary. There is no real textual justification for seeing it as a work of creation, in Waddington's numinous sense, making Pico a Moses and a creator. Waddington took the words "producing a work completely new from the beginning", and invested them with a grander significance than they have in context, where they are explicated by the phrase "without reference to earlier works". All Pico claims is that he is writing a commentary more complex than anything hitherto, which will not use earlier, similar works. It will be new in its complexity, but in its content and approach it will be similar enough to earlier commentaries for him to deny that he is using them. A further point which must be noted is that Waddington was not discussing the image of man in the *Heptaplus.* He pushed that inconvenient phenomenon into the background by asserting that the treatise was Christocentric, not anthropocentric. What he discussed was the supposedly Promethean role exercised by Pico, and expected by him of the reader. Finally, Waddington's whole exercise is an attempt to find in the *Heptaplus* ideas resembling the conventional view of the *Oratio*: self-creating man, man the magus. This view, I will now argue, it itself a misunderstanding of Pico's words and intentions.

In Pico's fable, the unique privilege bestowed by God on man was the power to determine his own nature, to be his own maker. Could he have intended this literally, as a philosophical statement? An essential step is to examine the way Pico uses the word "natura" in his other works. It will become apparent that he always uses it in its scholastic sense, meaning something prior to all choice, something which is a precondition for any choice, because it establishes the proper finality of the subject who chooses. All activity is directed towards an end, which is the good corresponding to the agent's nature. When a choice is made by a rational agent, the particular good is referred to the end which corresponds to the nature. Without reference to that end, no choice would be possible. The idea of man literally choosing his own nature, in a metaphysical sense, would have been nonsensical to Pico. Several examples can be quoted to show how he used and took for granted this framework of ideas.

In the *Commento,* written in the same year as the *Oratio,* there is a chapter on natural desire. Defining this concept, Pico says that since every creature has some perfection proper to itself, by participation in the divine goodness, it is necessary that it should have a definite end. He takes for granted the metaphysical framework in which each nature has its proper perfection, defined by its end, for which it has a "natural desire". It might be objected that the *Commento* is a work of exegesis rather than a statement of Pico's own position. The same ideas are presupposed, however, in both the *Heptaplus* and *De ente et uno.*

The fourth book of the *Heptaplus* is concerned with the human world and the nature of man. The first chapter proposes to "say some things about human nature in advance". Pico is content to state the commonplace that "man consists of a body and rational soul". His nature is clearly something given. Later, Pico assumes the scholastic concept of nature when he writes: "Man resembles man and animal, animal, because they share the same sort of essence, whether of species or of genus". Again, in an extended discussion of the two kinds of beatitude, natural and supernatural, he notes that each nature has its limits:

> In regard to man, although different philosophers hold different opinions, nevertheless all have kept within the narrow bounds of human capacity . . . I neither reject nor despise their arguments and opinions, if they are taken as speaking only of natural felicity. [For] it is certain that through this, neither men nor angels can be exalted any more highly than they say. This is strongly confirmed by the fact that since nothing can rise above itself by relying on its own strength (otherwise it would be stronger than itself), so nothing relying on itself can attain a felicity any greater or more perfect than its own nature.

Corresponding to human nature there is its natural fulfillment, and man cannot exceed this by his own efforts. The nature and its proper fulfillment are definite and circumscribed. Certainly, man can be elevated beyond these limits by grace, but this is not a matter of his own choice or endeavours.

Most clearly of all, the scholastic notion of nature is assumed in *De ente.* There the priority of nature to any choice is made explicit:

> In the first place, there is a natural being of things, as for a man to be man, for a lion to be lion, for a stone to be stone. Natural goodness undividedly follows this being . . . Consequently, just as all things desire the good, even so all things desire being, and first of all they desire that goodness that follows upon natural being, since this goodness is the foundation of subsequent goodnesses, which are added to it in such a way that without this goodness the others cannot be.

In other words, just as the natural being is the foundation for all accidental forms of being, so the natural good is the foundation for all desire, and therefore choice.

The references to "nature" in Pico's other writings make it clear that he thought of human nature as something given, something with its own proper finality and fulfillment, and with its definite limits which man could not alter or exceed by his own efforts. All choice is made with reference to the nature and its corresponding good. This framework of ideas Pico took for granted, and nature determined by choice would have been inconceivable. The only reasonable conclusion is that the words of God to Adam must have been intended as something other than strictly philosophical discourse. In fact, their character is clear enough from their place in the *Oratio.* The fable is simply a story with a moral. When Pico has elaborated his answer to the question of why man is worthy of wonder, he asks rhetorically why it should be given so much emphasis. His purpose in acclaiming man's privilege, he answers, is so that we may recognise it and make the best use of it. "Let a certain holy ambition invade the mind, so that we may not be content with mean things but may aspire to the highest things and strive with all our forces to attain them: for if we will to, we can". The opening part of the *Oratio* is an exhortation, and the celebration of man's possibilities is directed precisely towards this end. It is meant to generate ambition, to inspire effort. It is a moral exhortation not to vegetate, not to act like animals, when it is within our power to be angelic and even godly. From its immediate context, one would expect the creation fable to refer to the moral order. Its meaning would be simply that man is free to choose, for better or for worse, his level of moral existence.

Pico's interest in human freedom is quite specific and limited. He is not concerned with the philosophical explanation or defence of freedom. He does not try to explain, for example, how freedom is metaphysically possible, how man can choose the lower in preference to the higher. The question is by no means a focus for his thinking or an abiding theme. Neither of the examples usually quoted, his thesis "de libertate credendi" and his attack on astrology, lends support to the idea of a "passionate concern for freedom". As will appear later, the former sets limits to the freedom of the act of faith, while the latter is remarkable for neglecting to use the argument from human liberty. Pico's precise concern at the beginning of the *Oratio* is with the use men make of their freedom. The reason for his concern is that the possible consequences of this use range so dramatically from the heights to the depths.

A careful reading of what Pico wrote underlines the extravagance of the conclusions historians have drawn from the fable: like Cassirer's idea that man is never a completed being, and that mutability has become the basis of human dignity; Garin's assertion that man is nothing but makes himself all; Edgar Wind's rhapsodies on Protean man. Wind wrote of the *Oratio:*

> The fact that [man's] orbit of action is not fixed like that of angels or of animals, gives him the power to transform himself into whatever he chooses, and become a mirror of the universe. . . . In his adventurous pursuit of self-transformation, man explores the universe as if he were exploring himself. And the further he carries these metamorphoses, the more he discovers that all the varied phases of his experience are translatable into each other: for they all reflect the ultimate One, of which they unfold particular aspects.

This ignores Pico's explicit statement of his purpose in emphasising man's mutability, which is to warn of the degradation which is possible for him, and to exhort him to the highest of his possibilities. The celebration of man's possibilities is not a mere eulogy of human versatility. It is anything but an invitation to protean adventuring, to promiscuous metamorphosis. Equally fanciful was Garin's vision of man as lord of the world of forms, with power to hurl everything into the darkness of chaos or to transfigure, transform and remake it. In the *Oratio,* man makes and transforms only himself. He has no mandate over the world of forms, no active cosmic function. Man's sphere of operation is within himself, his own moral and religious life.

It is difficult to see why historians have been so consistently unwilling to admit that Pico was speaking metaphorically, of the moral order. The reason, perhaps, is that if man's choosing his nature is a metaphor, then there is nothing very remarkable about it. The idea of man rising or sinking according to the way he acts was, as de Lubac has amply shown, a favourite one among the Fathers and twelfth-century spiritual writers, and there is a particularly close parallel to Pico's version of it in Nicholas of Cusa. A traditional metaphor would be neither new nor daring; it would not liberate man from a constricting cosmos or from creaturely dependence.

Another consequence of admitting the moral and metaphorical character of Pico's fable is that it cannot be represented as a serious philosophical statement about man. By using the word "natura" so loosely, Pico precluded philosophical investigation. His elaboration of the idea of mutability is rhetorical, adding authorities and parallels, but not subjecting it to scrutiny. This is why there was no problem for him in using two different images of man. There was no question of working out a consistent doctrine of man. Pico uses whichever image suits the particular purpose of the work. In the *Heptaplus,* it was necessary

to show man as a microcosm, so that what Moses said about man could be applied to the universe, and vice versa. To have stressed man's mutability would have ruined the elaborate symmetry of the work. The idea of the microcosm is not subjected to scrutiny, however; it is simply accepted as commonplace, "tritum in scholis". In the *Oratio,* on the other hand, Pico the moralist wishes to stress the contrasting possibilities open to man, depending on his own effort or lack of it. For this purpose, the static image of the microcosm is not particularly helpful, so he turns to the mutability of man and the transformation myths. What the two works have in common is that they both take traditional ideas about man and use them as subordinate elements in the working out of a larger theme. Neither theme required a philosophical investigation of man, and in neither case did Pico undertake such an investigation. The nature of man was not one of his concerns as a philosopher. (pp. 29-36)

> *William G. Craven, in his* Giovanni Pico Della Mirandola, Symbol of His Age: Modern Interpretations of a Renaissance Philosopher, *Librairie Droz, 1981, 173 p.*

Peter Carravetta　(lecture date 1986)

[*In the following excerpt from the text of a lecture originally delivered in 1986, Carravetta provides a concise, insightful analysis of the* Commento.]

Let's look at the *Commentary* on Benivieni's canzone. In Book I, Pico starts out by inscribing the horizon of his interpretation with the three modes of being, which are A) Causal, "the noblest," B) Formal, and C) Participated. The critical text says: "Che ogni cosa creata ha lo essere in tre modi," but a variant reading reported by Garin states, "Che ogni cosa si può intendere in tre modi." The difference between "having to be"—i.e.: being "must" have three modes of givenness—and "it can be understood (as)" is not slight, for the accepted critical text postulates these three modes of being as categorical, whereas the variant reveals a less dogmatic and more hypostatic situation, a proleptic tendency where becoming is more crucial than being, where interpreting is more fundamental than ontology. In the course of his exposition, Pico will exhibit the tendency to problematize the dynamics among the modes of being, rather than the question of its foundation. Proceeding with (neo)Platonic referents, he subsequently lists three Grades of being, according to which entities can be a) Invisible and Incorporeal, or angelic and intellectual by nature; b) Visible and Corporeal, in other words, manifest themselves as the Elements; and c) Formal and Agent, or emanations of the Rational Soul, which is incorporeal, invisible and immortal. In short, we have God, the Angelic Mind or Intellect, and the Rational Soul. We will not delve into the symbolic correspondences with the figures of Uranus, Jupiter, Saturn and others for reasons that will be discussed in a moment. There are, however, two important assertions worth taking notice of: first, that we have already "enough which is necessary for understanding [*cognizione*] the treatment of love," and secondly, concerning the philosophical tradition, Pico will not follow—at least for now—the Alexandrian neo-platonists (Proclus, Hermias, Syrianus, in short Dionysus the Aeropagite), preferring rather to develop the line of Plotinus, Porphyry and "most of the more *perfetti* Platonists [who] place between God and the World-Soul only one creature, which they call the Son of God, because it was directly produced by God." Thus whereas the first tradition is "alone . . . true in itself," he will continue along the lines of the second because "it is more philosophical, truer to Plato and Aristotle and followed by all the Peripatetics and better [*migliori*] Platonists." Thus we have, on the one hand, a positing of ontological presuppositions which will legitimate the cognitive and methodological moves required by the act of interpretation; moreover, an awareness of the existential temporalness of the interpreting itself *in re* is expressed by his stating that "for the time being," he has enough materials, a valid and strong enough interpretive platform, to get on with the task he set for himself. On the other hand, Pico cannot totally divorce himself from the historical and hermeneutic legacy of these pro-blematics, and his pointing to a specific set of precedents means that he is well aware of what today is variously known as the historicity of understanding, the conflation of horizons (Gadamer) or even reader expectations. Moreover, we must recall that this very situation entails as well that the interpreter allow for the twisted and contorted relation to the canon, a situation which during every interpretive effort calls for a recovery, a *Verwindung,* and thus a necessary distortion, of given predecessors and phenomena. It is within these parameters that Pico takes leave of Avicenna as well as, and more importantly, of Ficino's ontology, which granted only the precategorical God and Souls. Pico's approach, his very method, gave him no option but to "expand" the system by adding Mind between God and Souls. This notion of Mind could be profitably developed at the figural level because for Pico "son of God" does not mean Christ, but rather Wisdom, Divine Reason, the Word, and, in a way, it harks backward to Hermes and points forward toward Blake's and Nietzsche's allegories. The radical alteration brought to both method and theory means that his notion of symbol and allegory was being altered also. For, as we read in Chapters Eight through Eleven, and then again in Book Two, Chapter Twenty-two et infra, the symbolism and figural impact of ideas as embedded in myths such as those of Uranus, Jupiter and so on, can and in fact do serve as a double hermeneutic principle, because

> Jupiter and Saturn and all the other gods can mean both the idea of Saturn and Jupiter and all the other gods and the natural, not the ideal, Saturn and Jupiter.

In short, for Pico *Idea* is an Archetype, Intelligible Being, *Form* is Matter, Sensible Being, and *Participated Being* is Rational Being. The ontological triad partakes of the ontic givenness of being when it is realized as figure, when it turns up as Matter, ergo as a concrete tangible "thing," artwork or whatever. But this figure, this myth incarnate being no longer, or at least exclusively, Pure idea, must be something else, and so it will be given currency by man's participated being, his real being-with-others. The fact that this being-with-others has no ontological provisions for universal, precategorical being *for* others, in other words, that it does not respond to the tuning forks of nineteenth and early twentieth century theory, should not blind us to the net "rupture" it represents with respect to the approaches on the scene during his time. Above all, we should mention his ending the slavery of method to

substantia, which means that ontology was now ready to embark upon a linguistic search of its own statute. Unless one insists in wallowing still in the dichotomies and the syllogistic common (despite obvious differences) to both Scholasticism and Structuralism, Pico's epistemic triangle is actually a precursor of more recent multiperspectival methods of inquiry. It might be interesting to try a comparison of this interpretive model with Peirce's phenomenology. At any rate, the fact that one of the angles of the triangle is still identified with a Universal Constant or God implies that Pico was still on the ridge that separates semiotics from hermeneutics, though he will subsequently open up the former to the latter.

In Book Two of the **Commentary** Pico expounds the Principles of this parahermeneutic. Every word is ambiguous, says the philosopher, so the first task is to explain what something is. In the case of the word Love, its deepest sense seems to be that it is an "inclination," a tending towards a "what" which in turn gives it its specific meaning. More broadly, Love is a desire for beauty, and so the determination of what beauty is will have a direct bearing upon one's conception of Love. We must leave aside the question of whether Pico introduced anything radically new in the Ficino originated tradition of *Trattati d'amore:* it appears he did not, and his comments on Cavalcanti's poetry tell us more about Pico than about the *stilnovista.* What is of more pressing interest here is this phenomenology of the interpretive mind which is careful to point out a hidden ontological agreement between Christianity and Plato concerning love as Eros, as Vision, while insisting on the unbridgeable duality of beauty at times physical at times intellectual. According to Pico, insofar as it is material cause, love can only be engendered by beauty, but beauty is ever displaying manifold masks, it being at any given time one of several possible Venuses. Now if this is the case, it follows that the Rational Soul will place a premium value on the proper identification of which Venus we are confronted with. Pico observed earlier that to know is to possess and that different cognitive natures entail different appetites. The question of having to decide among the manifold of experience, when the principles are solidly pinned to the sky and man's nature cannot be relied upon as it is at heart characterized by a dynamic vision, by an imaginary projecting, means that interpretation here coincides with judgment and with an ever shifting or unstable coincidence of being and method. Beauty equals harmony, complexity, but beauty also arises there where is contrariety, discord, difference:

> Below Him begins beauty, because contrariety begins, without which there can be no created things, but there would be only God. This contrariety and discord [contrarietà e discordia] of diverse natures is not enough to constitute a creature unless through proper proportion the contrariety becomes unified and the discord concordant, which can be assigned as a true definition of beauty, that it is nothing other than a *friendly enmity* [amica inimicizia] and a concordant discord [concorde discordia]. Heraclitus therefore called war and strife the father and progenitor of all things, and in Homer whoever speaks ill of strife is said to have blasphemed against nature.

Can we conjecture a notion of beauty as fundamental difference, as a dynamic ontological condition that discloses things as they are and/or have been, in contrast, for example, to a notion of beauty grounded upon the identity principle and things as they ought to be? Indeed: we have here the possibility of an idea of love and beauty that reveals evil, strife, suffering and other ills, for instance, the inevitability of contradiction, which in turn demands a principle of action, a will to representation and repetition. There are moreover underground connections with certain Romantics, even with the younger Nietzsche up to *Beyond Good and Evil*. But also much like the *later* Nietzsche and the post-symbolists of our day, this primary compulsion to image-building and to posit values entails a confrontation with the rhetoric of otherness, and this can only lead to the terrain of allegory, as we shall see. But to return to love and beauty, once understood as being the negative of a value ultimately invented by man the believer and maker of his universe, it is inconceivable to think of beauty without having an idea of what is not beautiful, to desire strength without at the same time qualifying weakness, to attempt a doctrine or system of analysis without knowing what chaos or disorder are. Acknowledging this "negativity" means that the only hierarchy possible is a generic "distinction"—and not a "difference"—between what love is and what it is not, who can love and who cannot, what is good and what is evil, and perhaps what is of the few—the aristocratic strain in Pico—and what is accessible to the many—the vulgus as herd.—Beauty and Love may be equal to the One and Perfect Being in their profounding within God, but love and beauty among humans is actually perceived and lived within the dynamics of the Intellect and the Rational Soul. Therefore, they partake in the interpretive game, and turns into a question of rhetorics. The philosopher shows here uncanny critical flexibility and matches the model to the text in such a way that one may even say the text actually speaks its own intention, compelling the reader to recreate a logical equivalent of its rhetorical structure. For instance, of Benivieni's lines,

> Because the lovely Cyprian's fair breast
> Sustained that god when first he saw the light,
> It roused his appetite
> To track her living beauty's blazing sun.

> [Questi perché nell'amorose braccia
> Della bella Ciprigna in prima nacque
> Sempre seguir li piacque
> L'ardente sol di sua bellezza viva]

Pico writes:

> The perfect knowledge of anything consists in the understanding both of its particular nature and of all the properties which follow that nature. Sometimes through the properties known to us we investigate the nature of the thing, and sometimes, by an opposite process, from a knowledge of the nature itself one arrives at an understanding of the properties, and this method [e questo modo], which is a great deal better, our Poet has followed here, having stated the nature of love in the third stanza, deriving from that in the present one of its principal property and then assigning the reason for the noblest effects which love works in us. *Questi perché*... This assigns the first property with its reason, and since this is the first and true love, on which every other love depends, born of ideal beauty, which is called the Cyprian, or Venus, for the above reason every love and beauty must direct itself towards these, and on that account no desire

for anything deformed or shameful can claim for itself the most sacred name of love.

A perfect system of correspondences has been established between Christian theology and Pico's version of Neoplatonism, and once again we can point out the epistemological-methodological assumptions at work. Yet there are two indications toward an overcoming of the strictures of method: one is that the casual interpretation of the figures, still somewhat mechanical, couches an emblematic remark—". . . of ideal beauty, which is called the Cyprian, or Venus . . ."—which activates two substitutions that open the text vertically, so to speak; the other is the identification, and commentary along the lines, of a logical pattern underlying the poem: rhetorics as the other, the "ghost" of method. Once again, rhetorics and method are the *recto* and *verso* of the same coin. (pp. 145-50)

> *Peter Carravetta, "In Pursuit of the Chameleon: The Interpretations of Pico," in* Italiana, *Albert N. Mancini, Paolo Giordano, Pier Raimondo Baldini, eds., Rosary College, 1988, pp. 141-52.*

Pauline Moffitt Watts   (essay date 1987)

[*In the following excerpt, Watts provides a concise outline of the* Heptaplus, *examining the significance of natural magic as a thematic element of this work.*]

In the **Heptaplus,** Pico discussed four worlds, the angelic, the celestial, the sublunary or elemental, and the world of man. For his exposition of the angelic and celestial worlds, he relied heavily, though certainly not exclusively, upon the works of the pseudo-Dionysius. In the Proem to the second book of the **Heptaplus,** his exposition of the heavenly world, Pico refers to the pseudo-Dionysius as the "glory of our theology" (along with Thomas Aquinas) and in the Proem to the third book, his exposition of the angelic world, he says that he treads in the footsteps of the Areopagite.

In a general description of the three worlds given in the Second Proem, Pico manifests his debt to the pseudo-Dionysius:

> In the first world, God, the primal unity, presides over the nine orders of angels as if over many spheres and, without moving, moves all toward himself. In the middle world, that is, the celestial, the empyrean heaven likewise presides like the commander of an army over nine heavenly spheres, each of which revolves with an unceasing motion; yet in imitation of God, it is itself unmoving. There are also in the elemental world, after the prime matter which is its foundation, nine spheres of corruptible forms.

In addition to accepting the monadic-triadic structure of the pseudo-Dionysian cosmos, Pico also accepts the pseudo-Dionysian idea of the cosmos as an emanative *sympatheia*. Again in the Second Proem, Pico says,

> It should above all be observed, a fact on which our purpose almost wholly depends, that these three worlds are one world, not only because they are all related by one beginning and to the same end, or because regulated by appropriate numbers they are bound together both by a certain harmonious kin-

ship of nature and by a regular series of ranks, but because whatever is in any of the worlds is at the same time contained in each, and there is no one of them in which is not to be found whatever is in each of the others.

Pico's belief that the universe is a monadic-triadic *sympatheia* leads him to conceive of language and symbolic thought in a way that is distinct from that of Cusanus. According to Pico, words and images are part of a theophanic cosmic code:

> The early Fathers could not properly represent some things by the images of others unless trained, as I have said, in the hidden alliances and affinities of all nature. Otherwise there would be no reason why they should have represented this thing by this image, and another by another, rather than each by its opposite. But versed in all things and inspired by that Spirit which not only knows all these things but made them, they aptly symbolized the natures of one world by those which they knew corresponded to them in the other worlds. Therefore those who wish to interpret their figures of speech and allegorical meanings correctly need the same knowledge. . . .

For Pico, therefore, words had a "natural" as distinct from a conventional" signification, and by extension, affirmative theology and its goal of *gnosis* assumed for him a centrality in the "science of God" which it did not have for Cusanus. Moreover, it was Pico's conviction that there was a cosmic code to be cracked that was the basis of his attraction to "natural" magic.

In the famous **Oration** prefacing the nine hundred *conclusiones* which he proposed to debate publicly in Rome, Pico discussed "natural" magic in some detail, always carefully distinguishing it from demonic magic. Of "natural" magic, Pico says:

> Having carefully investigated the harmony of the universe, which the Greeks very expressively call $\sigma\upsilon\mu\pi\alpha\theta\epsilon\iota\alpha\nu$, and having looked closely into the knowledge that natures have of each other, this second magic, applying to each thing its innate charms, which are called by magicians $\iota\upsilon\gamma\gamma\epsilon\zeta$, as if it were itself the maker, discloses in public the wonders lying in the recesses of the world, in the bosom of nature, in the storerooms and secrets of God. And as the farmer marries elm to vine so the magician marries earth to heaven, that is, lower things to the qualities and virtues of higher things.

Pico devoted twenty-six *conclusiones* to the subject of "natural" magic. The nineteenth through twenty-fourth *conclusiones* reveal that for Pico, it is particular words and calls which have magical power in that they derive ultimately from the voice of God. In the twentieth conclusion he succinctly expressed this belief, saying that "whatever magical power a word has, it has to the extent that it is fashioned by the voice of God." (*Quelibet vox virtutem habet in Magia, inquantum Dei voce formatur.*)

It was Pico's belief in the magical power of words that led him into the arcane world of Cabalism, in which transpositions, anagrams, and invocations deriving from the ten names of God that composed the Sephiroth and the twenty-two letters of the Hebrew alphabet would lead to a comprehension of the secrets of God and the cosmos. At the conclusion of the **Heptaplus,** Pico claimed that all *gnosis*

lay concealed in the Pentateuch, and that this "Mosaic profundity" could be made accessible through the Cabalistic art. Taking the first four verses of Genesis as his example, Pico began by explaining what he proposed to do:

> This whole passage is composed of 103 letters, which, arranged, as they are, make up the words which we read, displaying nothing but the common and trivial. But this arrangement of letters, this text, composes the shell of a secret kernel of hidden mysteries. If we open up the words and take the same letters separately and, according to the rules which the Hebrews hand down, join them together properly into the sayings that can be made up of them, they say that there will appear to us, if we are fit for hidden wisdom, many wise and wonderful doctrines. If this is done with the whole law, there will finally be brought to light by the proper placing and connecting of its elements all learning and the secrets of all the liberal disciplines.

Pico went on to show how through the rearrangement of the letters of the first four verses of Genesis, the following passage would emerge: "the father, in the Son and through the Son, the beginning and end or rest created the head, the fire, and the foundation of the great man with a good pact." And for Pico this decoding represented the "holy pact" of creation in which the "little world" that is man is bound together with the "great man" that is the world in a microcosmic-macrocosmic symbiosis. (pp. 289-93)

> *Pauline Moffitt Watts, "Psuedo-Dionysius the Areopagite and Three Renaissance Neoplatonists: Cusanus, Ficino, and Pico on Mind and Cosmos," in* Supplementum Festivum: Studies in Honor of Paul Oskar Kristeller, *James Hankins, John Monfasani, Frederick Purnell, Jr., eds., Medieval & Renaissance Texts & Studies, 1987, pp. 279-98.*

FURTHER READING

Review of *Giovanni Pico della Mirandola: His Life, by His Nephew Giovanni Francesco Pico; also Three of His Letters; His Interpretation of Psalm XVI; His Twelve Rules of a Christian Life; His Twelve Points of a Perfect Lover; and His Deprecatory Hymn to God. The Athenaeum,* No. 3284 (4 October 1890): 441-43.
> Concise biographical overview of Pico's life.

Cassirer, Ernst. "Giovanni Pico della Mirandola: A Study in the History of Renaissance Ideas (Part II)." *Journal of the History of Ideas* 3 (1942): 319-46.
> Second part of the critically acclaimed study of Pico by the eminent Renaissance Italian literature scholar. (See excerpt dated 1942 for the first part of this article.)

Craven, William G. "Pico and His Modern Interpreters." In his *Giovanni Pico della Mirandola: Symbol of His Age,* pp. 1-20. Geneva: Librairie Droz, 1981.
> Surveys the critical reception of Pico's ideas and works by twentieth-century literary scholars, historians, and critics. This essay includes discussion of studies by Paul

Oskar Kristeller, Avery Dulles, and Ernst Cassirer, among others.

Dulles, Avery. "Pico's Principal Works"; "Cosmology: The Visible Hierarchy"; "Anthropology: The Dignity of Man." In his *Princeps Concordiae: Pico della Mirandola and the Scholastic Tradition,* pp. 11-24, 76-104, 105-28. Cambridge: Harvard University Press, 1941.
Surveys and examines the history of philosophical ideas dominant during the Renaissance which permeate Pico's works.

Kristeller, Paul Oskar. "Renaissance Platonism." In his *Renaissance Thought: The Classic, Scholastic, and Humanistic Strains,* pp. 48-69. New York: Harper Torchbooks, 1961.
Traces the history of the Platonic tradition during the Renaissance.

Kristeller, Paul Oskar, and Randall, John Herman, Jr. Introduction to *Renaissance Philosophy of Man: Petrarca, Valla, Ficino, Pico, Pomponazzi, Vives,* edited by Ernst Cassirer, Paul Oskar Kristeller, and John Herman Randall, Jr., pp. 1-20. Chicago: University of Chicago Press, 1948.
Explores the concept of humanism as it pertains to the works of Francesco Petrarca, Lorenzo Valla, Marsilio Ficino, Pico, Pietro Pomponazzi, and Juan Luis Vives.

Michener, Richard L. "The Great Chain of Being: Three Approaches." *Ball State University Forum* XI, No. 2 (Spring 1970): 60-71.
Examines the concept of the Great Chain of Being as exemplified in the works of Pico, John Donne, and Alexander Pope.

Preston, Harriet Waters. "An Early Humanist." *The Atlantic Monthly* LI, No. CCCVI (April 1883): 494-506.
Chatty, anecdotal essay concentrating on Pico's life.

Rigg, J. M. Introduction to *Giovanni Pico della Mirandola: His Life, by His Nephew Giovanni Francesco Pico; also Three of His Letters; His Interpretation of Psalm XVI; His Twelve Rules of a Christian Life; His Twelve Points of a Perfect Lover; and His Deprecatory Hymn to God,* translated by Sir Thomas More and edited by J. M. Rigg, pp. v-xl. London: David Nutt, 1890.
Biographical survey of Pico's life, with critical discussion of his theological doctrines and works.

Symonds, John Addington. "Third Period of Humanism." In his *Renaissance in Italy: The Revival of Learning,* pp. 309-91. New York: Henry Holt and Co., 1888.
Biographical and critical profile which hails Pico as the embodiment of Renaissance ideals. *On the Dignity of Man* is highly praised, as is Pico's spirited attacks on the validity of astrology as a source of knowledge; Symonds laments, however, Pico's falling "victim to the hybrid mysticism and magical nonsense of the Cabbala."

Wirszubski, Chaim. *Pico della Mirandola's Encounter with Jewish Mysticism.* Cambridge: Harvard University Press, 1989, 292 p.
In-depth study of the history of the Cabala and its doctrines, the significance of Christian Cabalism, and Pico's uses of the Cabala in his works.

Sir Joshua Reynolds

1723-1792

English artist, essayist, sketch writer, and dialogist.

Reynolds is widely revered as the greatest portrait-painter in English history, having produced striking portraits of Samuel Johnson, David Garrick, and members of the late-eighteenth-century English monarchy, nobility, and upper classes. He articulated his artistic principles in a series of fifteen discourses delivered during his long tenure as foundation president of the Royal Academy of Arts. The collected *Discourses* reflect Reynolds's ideals, which, though not closely followed in his own work, were long considered essential to any student of art or art criticism. Reynolds also founded and served as president of the Literary Club: a gathering of writers, statesmen, and others who met regularly for the purpose (according to Reynolds) of listening to Johnson express his opinions at length in after-dinner conversation. Reynolds's achievement in diverse disciplines prompted James Boswell to write, in the dedicatory preface to his *Life of Samuel Johnson, LL.D.* (1791): "Your excellence not only in the Art over which you have long presided with unrivalled fame, but also in Philosophy and elegant Literature, is well known to the present, and will continue to be the admiration of future generations."

Reynolds was born in Plympton, Devonshire in 1723. His father, Rev. Samuel Reynolds, was a schoolmaster in Plympton and a former fellow of Balliol College, Oxford. He attempted to steer Joshua into a career as a physician, but upon being convinced of the latter's artistic leanings, supported him in his training. Reynolds was deeply impressed by Jonathan Richardson's *Essay on the Art of Painting* (1715), with its call for the founding of an English national school of art similar to the academies already established on the Continent. As a young man Reynolds was apprenticed to Richardson's son-in-law, Thomas Hudson, who was at the time considered the foremost portrait painter in London. Within two years' time Reynolds rivaled Hudson in skill, earning the master's jealousy and his own dismissal from the apprenticeship. After a few years of painting portraits on his own, he traveled to the Mediterranean as a guest aboard a warship commanded by his friend, Captain Augustus Keppel. Reynolds disembarked in Italy, where he resided for nearly three years studying paintings by the Italian Renaissance masters, notably Michelangelo, Raphael, and Correggio. While examining Raphael's frescoes in the Vatican, he caught a severe cold that resulted in lifelong deafness. The ear-trumpet Reynolds used for the rest of his life came to be regarded as one of his most distinguishing characteristics. (Once, he even painted a portrait of himself holding the trumpet to his ear.)

Reynolds returned to London in 1753 and began in earnest his career as a portrait painter. He moved into a house with his youngest sister, apprenticed young painters, and grew quite wealthy as a result of his labors. An important portrait he painted of Commodore Keppel marked the true beginning of his career. For nearly forty years he

painted British royalty, military men, members of the peerage, numerous other celebrities, and their children. Commenting on Reynolds's great productivity, Frederick Keppel stated that the artist considered a hundred and fifty finished portraits "a fair year's work." This industry was reflected in Reynolds's own words: "Those who are determined to excel in art must go to their work whether willing or unwilling; morning, noon, and night." In 1760 Reynolds moved into a spacious house on Leicester Square, where he lived with his sister for the rest of his life. This house became the scene of many dinner parties, which were often attended by members of the Literary Club, founded at Reynolds's suggestion in 1764. The Club, which met regularly at the Turk's Head tavern, eventually included such personages as Richard Brinsley Sheridan, Thomas Warton, Edmund Burke, Garrick, Boswell, and Reynolds's best friend, Oliver Goldsmith, among several others. But it centered around and was dominated by Johnson. "The Great Cham of Literature" had engaged Reynolds to write three essays for the "Idler" on artistic theory in 1759, and the two remained friends until Johnson's death in 1784. Johnson, commenting upon Reynolds's agreeable personality, said that he considered his friend "the most invulnerable man I know; whom, if I should quarrel with him, I should find the most difficulty how to abuse him." The near-sighted Johnson was irritated, though, by Reynolds's painting a portrait of him holding a book close to his one good eye, and muttered to Boswell, "Sir, he may paint himself as deaf as he chooses, but I *will not* go down to posterity as 'Blinking Sam.' "

In 1768 Reynolds was elected president of the new Royal Academy of Arts, in which capacity he served for over two decades except for a brief hiatus. His election was confirmed by George III, who knighted him. As president Reynolds skillfully guided the Academy, attempting—as had been urged by Richardson over sixty years earlier—to form a school of national painters who would choose not only Biblical and classical themes but scenes from England's historic past, as well. Also, Reynolds presided at the Academy's annual awards dinner, delivering a discourse at that event every year or two until 1790. These discourses promote his artistic ideals—and, after Reynolds's death, sparked two centuries of spirited debate as to their worth to the practicing artist. During the course of his presidency Reynolds was opposed in policy by his chief rival in portraiture, the outspoken Thomas Gainsborough, who refused to send his own paintings to the Academy's exhibition for two years. Yet Reynolds's "Fourteenth Discourse," delivered after Gainsborough's death, paid elegant tribute to the latter's accomplishment. Reynolds briefly resigned the presidency in 1790 after Academy members rudely refused to approve one of his own nominations for membership. (Asked to reconsider his action by the shaken members—and by the king—he resumed the presidency.)

In 1790, in the midst of painting a portrait, Reynolds realized he had gone completely blind in one eye. Unwilling to risk damaging his still-healthy eye, he quit painting and spent his last two years in quiet retirement, attending the theater and being visited by former students and the surviving members of the Club. Poor health necessitated Reynolds's resigning all obligations to the Academy late in 1791. Burke was at his bedside when he died, on 23 February 1792. The distinguished statesman wrote a widely praised obituary of Reynolds that reads, in part, "His talents of every kind, powerful from nature, and not meanly cultivated by letters, his social virtues in all the relations and all the habitudes of life, rendered him the centre of a very great and unparalleled variety of agreeable societies, which will be dissipated by his death. He had too much merit not to excite some jealousy, too much innocence to provoke any enmity. The loss of no man of his time can be felt with more sincere, general, and unmixed sorrow."

The *Discourses* are Reynolds's major contribution to aesthetic theory, though he left his notebooks, and a few character sketches, as well. In addition there are the "Idler" essays, which, as critics have noted, contain the germ of the ideas treated at length in the *Discourses.* The latter, long considered an essential text to artists, art critics, and art students, have remained in print since their first publication over two centuries ago, with notable editions published by Edmond Malone, Edmund Gosse, Austin Dobson, Roger Fry, and Robert R. Wark.

The individual discourses each treat discrete themes and issues. The first and second discourses (both delivered in 1769) state the importance of studying the artistic principles of established masters and emphasize rendering accurate portraits from life. "The Second Discourse," further,

urges the novice to examine carefully the "grand style"—but also to develop his own talents and to experiment in derivations from established practices. In the third (1770) and fourth (1771) discourses, Reynolds propounds and develops a theory of beauty and artistic intent similar to that stated by Imlac in Johnson's prose romance *Rasselas, Prince of Abyssinia* (1759), holding that the artist must pursue the beautiful by concentrating upon general matters, not detailed or particular ones. (As Johnson's Imlac says, "The business of the poet . . . is to examine, not the individual, but the species; to remark upon general properties and large appearances: he does not number the streaks of the tulip, or describe the different shades in the verdure of the forest.") In "The Fourth Discourse" Reynolds also demarcates the "grand" and "ornamental" styles of painting. "The Fifth Discourse" (1772) returns to the theme of the first two, addressing the nature and extent of the student's variations upon recognized techniques and styles.

In "The Sixth Discourse" (1774), Reynolds attempted to define genius and to fix its relation to artistic industry. "The Seventh Discourse" (1776) further extends the concept of beauty (described in the third and fourth discourses) to include everything that brings lasting satisfaction to the soul and posits the immutable nature of right and wrong in both morals and taste. Reynolds demonstrated the practical application of his general principles to specific cases in "The Eighth Discourse" (1778) while warning against the danger of overly strict obedience to rules. The short "Ninth Discourse" (1780) salutes the Academy upon its moving into a new building and reiterates Reynolds's belief that true art must address the mind through appealing to the senses. "The Tenth Discourse," delivered late in 1780, is generally considered the weakest of the fifteen, addressing a subject with which Reynolds was not truly conversant, the art of sculpture.

"The Eleventh Discourse" (1782) returns to the issue of genius, specifically examining the relationship between design and accomplishment. In "The Twelfth Discourse" (1784), Reynolds addressed the advantages to be gained by art students who travel abroad. "The Thirteenth Discourse" (1786) develops the topic of the sixth: the definitions and proper functions of imitation and imaginative derivation. "The Fourteenth Discourse" (1788) contains a touching account of Reynolds's complete reconciliation with Gainsborough at his old rival's deathbed and an eloquent assessment of the man Reynolds called "one of the greatest ornaments of the Academy." In his fifteenth and final discourse Reynolds summarized his pedagogical intents and purposes, concluding his oration with a salute to his master, "Michael Angelo."

From the beginning, whether liking or disliking the intent of the individual discourses, critics have considered them eloquent statements of artistic belief—so eloquent, in fact, that for a time during the eighteenth century there was some speculation that Johnson and Burke had written some of them. Reynolds himself, though, denied that they were the work of anyone but himself, and critics have concurred with this judgment since the early nineteenth century. Reynolds did credit Johnson with having shaped his views, going so far as to state that Johnson had, to a large extent, taught him how to think. Reynolds's general theory of art fell out of favor during the Romantic period, with

William Hazlitt and William Blake, among others, publicly abusing Reynolds's theories on several occasions. (They abused the memory of Reynolds himself as well, with Dante Gabriel Rossetti dubbing him "Sir Sloshua.") In particular, they held that it is indeed the artist's role to "number the streaks of the tulip": to concentrate upon the particulars of their subjects. They also argued that Reynolds's emphasis upon imitation and recognition of past masters was ill-suited to the true man or woman of rootless genius, whom the Romantics held as their ideal. Finally, Hazlitt noted what he considered inconsistencies within the discourses themselves and inconsistencies between the artist's theories and practices. The latter issue has remained a subject of commentary to the present day. Critics today acknowledge this difference, but hold that Reynolds's view of painting from the general subject was somewhat different from that recognized by his contemporaries and the Romantics; according to W. R. M. Lamb, Reynolds's close study of the Italian Renaissance masters "seems to have educed in him a peculiar force of magnifying and ennobling vision, which enabled him to perceive and portray, not merely the general or typical qualities, but something greater and finer than others could observe, something divine, in the persons who sat to him in London," leaving to posterity "that marvelous series of pictures to show what portraiture can do to dignify society and elevate a nation's character in its own eyes." Scholars have further noted that in the *Discourses* Reynolds attempted to inculcate artistic ideals into the thinking of students rather than provide fellow masters a finished catalogue of theory based on a lifetime of work.

During his day, as John Ruskin was moved to write, Reynolds was "the prince of portrait-painters." He was acknowledged as such even by his rivals, influencing artistic practice in his country through the age of J. M. W. Turner. (Viewing the wide range of poses and techniques in Reynolds's paintings, Gainsborough was moved to exclaim, "Damn him, how various he is!") As founder of the Literary Club, he made possible the close association of the minds who produced the outstanding English art and literature of the second half of the eighteenth century. He thus provided the setting for Johnson to hold forth in the inimitable manner recorded by Boswell. And in the *Discourses,* Reynolds left a record of artistic ideals that were long considered essential to understanding the artist's intent and role—documents that remain of critical interest today.

PRINCIPAL WORKS

Seven Discourses Delivered in the Royal Academy by the President (essays) 1778
*Works (essays and criticism) 2 vols. 1797
Johnson & Garrick (dialogues) 1816
The Literary Works of Sir Joshua Reynolds. 3 vols. (essays, journals, sketches, and criticism) 1835
Letters of Sir Joshua Reynolds (letters) 1929
Portraits (sketches) 1952

*This collection contains all fifteen discourses delivered by Reynolds to the Royal Academy. The *Discourses* have appeared in many editions in the years since 1797, with the most authoritative being *Discourses on Art,* edited by Robert R. Wark, published in 1959.

Oliver Goldsmith   (essay date 1774)

[*Goldsmith is recognized as one of the most important writers of the English Augustan Age. Although he distinguished himself during his lifetime as a narrative poet, he has since been acclaimed for two nonpoetic works:* The Vicar of Wakefield *(1766), a novel that helped pioneer the use of a protagonist as narrator, and* She Stoops to Conquer *(1773), a drama written as a reaction against the English tradition of sentimental and moral comedy. In the following excerpt from* Retaliation *(1774), a poem filled with mock epitaphs of his still-living friends, Goldsmith expresses his high regard for Reynolds's accomplishment and character. (The following lines were the last ever written by Goldsmith, who died several days after setting them to paper.)*]

Here Reynolds is laid, and, to tell you my mind,
He has not left a wiser or better behind;
His pencil was striking, resistless, and grand,
His manners were gentle, complying, and bland:
Still born to improve us in every part,
His pencil our faces, his manners our heart.
To coxcombs averse, yet most civilly steering,
When they judged without skill, he was still hard of hearing:
When they talked of their Raphaels, Corregios, and stuff,
He shifted his trumpet, and only took snuff.

(p. 121)

Oliver Goldsmith, "Retaliation," in his Poems, Plays and Essays, *Thomas Y. Crowell & Co., 1890?, pp. 115-21.*

Joseph Warton   (essay date 1782)

[*Warton was an accomplished literary critic who is best remembered for* An Essay on the Genius and Writings of Pope, *the first volume of which was published in 1756. In the following excerpt from the fourth (1782) edition of that work, he extols the artistic theories and influence of Reynolds's* Discourses.]

One cannot forbear reflecting on the great progress the art of painting has made in this country . . . : a progress, that, we trust, will daily encrease, if due attention be paid to the incomparable discourses that have been delivered at the Royal Academy: which discourses contain more solid instruction on that subject than, I verily think, can be found in any language. The precepts are philosophically founded on truth and nature, and illustrated with the most proper and pertinent examples. The characters are drawn with a *precision* and *distinctness,* that we look for in vain in *Felibien, De Piles,* and even *Vasari,* or *Pliny* himself. Nothing, for example, can be more just and elegant, as well as profound and scientific, than the comparison betwixt *Michael Angelo* and *Raffaële,* page 169 of these **Discourses.** *Michael Angelo* is plainly the hero of Sir *Joshua Reynolds,* for the same reasons that *Homer,* by every great mind, is preferred to *Virgil.* (pp. 394-95)

Joseph Warton, in a chapter in his An Essay on the Genius and Writings of Pope, Vol. II, *1782. Reprint by Gregg International Publishers, 1969, pp. 385-411.*

Horace Walpole   (letter date 1783)

[An English author, politician, and publisher, Walpole is best known for his memoirs and voluminous correspondence. Both provide revealing glimpses of life in England during the second half of the eighteenth century. In the following excerpt from a letter written to William Mason on 10 February 1783, he appraises the just-published "Fourth Discourse."]

Sir Joshua has lately given me too his last *Discourse* to the Academy, which I will tell you *entre nous,* is rather an apology for or an avowal of the object of his own style, that is, effect or impression on all sorts of spectators. This lesson will rather do hurt than good on his disciples, and make them neglect all kind of finishing. Nor is he judicious in quoting Vandyck, who at least specified silks, satins, velvets. Sir Joshua's draperies represent clothes, never their materials. Yet more, Vandyck and Sir Godfrey Kneller excelled all painters in hands, Sir Joshua's are seldom even tolerably drawn. I saw t'other day one of, if not the best of his works, the portrait of Lord Richard Cavendish; little is distinguished but the head and hand; yet the latter, though nearest to the spectator, is abominably bad; so are those of my three nieces, and though the effect of the whole is charming, the details are slovenly, the faces only red and white; and his journeyman, as if to distinguish himself, has finished the lock and key of the table like a Dutch flower-painter. (pp. 284-85)

> *Horace Walpole, in a letter to William Mason on February 10, 1783, in his* Horace Walpole's Correspondance with William Mason, Vol. II, *W. S. Lewis, Grover Cronin, Jr., Charles H. Bennett, eds., Yale University Press, 1955 pp. 284-86.*

Edmund Burke   (essay date 1792)

[Considered a founder of Anglo-American conservatism, Burke was an Irish-born English statesman, philosopher, and critic. Throughout his career in Parliament he aligned himself with such causes as the abolition of the slave trade, taxation reform for the American colonies, and removal of political restrictions on Roman Catholics in Ireland. A champion of custom, convention, and prescription, Burke at no point sanctioned radicalism; among his most renowned works is a condemnation of the French Revolution, Reflections on the Revolution in France *(1790). Burke also wrote a pioneering work in the field of aesthetics,* A Philosophical Inquiry into the Origin of Our Ideas of the Sublime and the Beautiful *(1756), and in 1759 founded the* Annual Register, *a yearly review of important events. The following excerpt is from the obituary notice Burke wrote a few hours after Reynolds's death and published in the* Gentleman's Magazine *shortly afterward.]*

Sir Joshua Reynolds was, on very many accounts, one of the most memorable men of his time. He was the first Englishman who added the praise of the elegant arts to the other glories of his country. In taste, in grace, in facility, in happy invention, and in the richness and harmony of colouring, he was equal to the great masters of the renowned ages. In portrait he went beyond them; for he communicated to that description of the art, in which En-

glish artists are the most engaged, a variety, a fancy, and a dignity derived from the higher branches, which even those who professed them in a superior manner did not always preserve when they delineated individual nature. His portraits remind the spectator of the invention of history, and the amenity of landscape. In painting portraits he appeared not to be raised upon that platform, but to descend to it from a higher sphere. His paintings illustrate his lessons, and his lessons seem to be derived from his paintings.

He possessed the theory as perfectly as the practice of his art. To be such a painter, he was a profound and penetrating philosopher. (pp. 629-30)

His talents of every kind, powerful from nature, and not meanly cultivated by letters, his social virtues in all the relations and all the habitudes of life, rendered him the centre of a very great and unparalleled variety of agreeable societies, which will be dissipated by his death. He had too much merit not to excite some jealousy, too much innocence to provoke any enmity. The loss of no man of his time can be felt with more sincere, general, and unmixed sorrow. (p. 630)

> *Edmund Burke, in an extract in* Life and Times of Sir Joshua Reynolds, Vol. II *by Charles Robert Leslie and Tom Taylor, John Murray, 1865, pp. 629-30.*

Edmond Malone   (essay date 1797)

[Malone was an Irish literary critic and Shakespearean scholar. A friend of Reynolds, Samuel Johnson, and Horace Walpole, and a member of The Club, Malone was an unusually perceptive editor. He was among the first to chronologize the works of Shakespeare and to question the authenticity of both William Ireland's Shakespeare forgeries and Thomas Chatterton's "Rowley" poems. In addition, he assisted his close acquaintance James Boswell in revising both Journal of a Tour to the Hebrides *(1785) and* The Life of Samuel Johnson, LL.D. *(1791). In the following excerpt from the prefatory "Life" (1798) in his edition of Reynolds's collected works, Malone highly praises the value of the* Discourses.]*

It was no part of the prescribed duty of his office to read lectures to the Academy; but [Mr. Reynolds] voluntarily imposed this task upon himself, for the reasons which he has assigned in his **"Fifteenth Discourse"**:

> If prizes were to be given, it appeared not only proper, but almost indispensably necessary, that something should be said by the President on the delivery of those prizes; and the President for his own credit would wish to say something more than mere words of compliment; which, by being frequently repeated, would soon become flat and uninteresting, and by being uttered to many, would at last become a distinction to none: I thought, therefore, if I were to preface this compliment with some instructive observations on the art, when we crowned merit in the artists whom we rewarded, I might do something to animate and guide them in their future attempts.

Such was the laudable motive which produced the fifteen **DISCOURSES,** pronounced by our author between the 2d of Jan. 1769, and the 10th of Dec. 1790: a work which contains such a body of just criticism on an extremely difficult subject, clothed in such perspicuous, elegant, and nervous language, that it is no exaggerated panegyrick to assert, that it will last as long as the English tongue, and contribute no less than the productions of his pencil to render his name immortal. (pp. xl-xlv)

> *Edmund Malone, "Some Account of The Life and Writings of Sir Joshua Reynolds," in* The Works of Sir Joshua Reynolds, Knight, Vol. 1, *third edition, T. Cadell, Jun. and W. Davies, 1801, pp. iii-cxxiv.*

Francis Horner   (essay date 1801)

[*Horner was a Scottish authority on political economy and finance and a member of Parliament. His death at age 38 was deeply mourned in Westminster, where he was admired as much for his upright character as for his accomplishments as a political economist. In the following excerpt from his journal entry of 1 April 1801, he praises Reynolds as a man of genius and as a public benefactor.*]

[Next] to the writings of Bacon, there is no book which has more powerfully impelled me to revolve [sentiments concerning the improvement of one's character] than the **Discourses** of Sir Joshua Reynolds. He is one of the first men of genius who have condescended to inform the world of the steps by which greatness is attained: the unaffected good sense and clearness with which he describes the terrestrial and human attributes of that which is usually called inspiration, and the confidence with which he asserts the omnipotence of human labour, have the effect of familiarising his reader with the idea that genius is an acquisition rather than a gift; while with all this there is blended so naturally and so eloquently the most elevated and passionate admiration of excellence, and of all the productions of true genius, that upon the whole there is no book of a more *inflammatory* effect. (p. 153)

> *Francis Horner, in a journal entry on April 12, 1801, in his* Memoirs and Correspondence of Francis Horner, M.P., Vol. I, *edited by Leonard Horner, Little, Brown and Company, 1853, pp. 151-53.*

William Blake   (essay date 1820?)

[*Critics view Blake, an English poet and artist, as one of the most important literary figures of the nineteenth century. His works are esteemed for their dense thematic texture, compressive and allusive style, the original system of mythology they present, and their impassioned, prophetic tone. Virtually unknown in literary circles and often dismissed as a lunatic in his own time, Blake is still considered the most extreme of the English Romantic writers, but critics today acknowledge his stature as one of the greatest poets of his age. Not at all an admirer of Reynolds's thought, Blake covered the pages of his copy of Reynolds's* Works *with derisive marginalia. One scholar dates Blake's notations to about 1820. In the following sample from this marginalia, Blake expresses his*]

scorn for the theories of Reynolds, Edmund Burke, John Locke, and Sir Francis Bacon.]

Burke's *Treatise on the Sublime and Beautiful* is founded on the opinions of Newton and Locke. On this treatise Reynolds has grounded many of his assertions in all his **Discourses.** I read Burke's treatise when very young, at the same time I read Locke on *Human Understanding,* and Bacon's *Advantages of Learning.* On every one of these books I wrote my opinions, and on looking them over found that my notes on Reynolds in this book were exactly similar. I felt the same contempt and abhorrence then that I do now. They mock inspiration and vision. Inspiration and vision was then and now is and I hope will always remain my element, my eternal dwelling-place. How then can I hear it contemned without returning scorn for scorn? (p. 296)

> *William Blake, in an extract in* The Discourses of Sir Joshua Reynolds *by Sir Joshua Reynolds, edited by Edmund Gosse, Kegan Paul, Trench & Co., 1884, p. 296.*

William Hazlitt   (essay date 1821)

[*An English essayist, Hazlitt was one of the most important critics of the Romantic age. He was a deft stylist, a master of the prose essay, and a leader of what was later termed "impressionist criticism"—a form of personal analysis directly opposed to the universal standards of critical judgment accepted by many eighteenth-century critics. Like Charles Lamb, Hazlitt utilized the critical techniques of evocation, metaphor, and personal reference—three innovations that greatly altered the development of literary criticism in the nineteenth and twentieth centuries. Many of Reynolds's artistic theories ran counter to Romantic sensibility, and Hazlitt took strong exception to them in several essays. In the following excerpt from the second of two essays on the* Discourses, *published in the first volume of his* Table Talk; or, Original Essays (1821-22), *Hazlitt seeks to demonstrate the presence of inconsistencies and other critical flaws in Reynolds's theories.*]

The first inquiry which runs through Sir Joshua Reynolds's **Discourses** is, whether the student ought to look at nature with his own eyes or with the eyes of others, and on the whole, he apparently inclines to the latter. The second question is, what is to be understood by nature; whether it is a general and abstract idea, or an aggregate of particulars; and he strenuously maintains the former of these positions. Yet it is not easy always to determine how far or with what precise limitations he does so.

The first germ of his speculations on this subject is to be found in two papers in the Idler. In the last paragraph of the second of these, he says,

> If it has been proved that the Painter, by attending to the invariable and general ideas of nature, produces beauty, he must, by regarding minute particularities and accidental discriminations, deviate from the universal rule, and pollute his canvas with deformity.

In answer to this, I would say that deformity is not the being varied in the particulars, in which all things differ (for on this principle all nature, which is made up of individuals, would be a heap of deformity) but in violating general rules, in which they all or almost all agree. Thus there are no two noses in the world exactly alike, or without a great variety of subordinate parts, which may still be handsome, but a face without any nose at all, or a nose (like that of a mask) without any particularity in the details, would be a great deformity in art or nature. Sir Joshua seems to have been led into his notions on this subject either by an ambiguity of terms, or by taking only one view of nature. He supposes grandeur, or the general effect of the whole, to consist in leaving out the particular details, because these details are sometimes found without any grandeur of effect, and he therefore conceives the two things to be irreconcileable and the alternatives of each other. This is very imperfect reasoning. If the mere leaving out the details constituted grandeur, any one could do this: the greatest dauber would at that rate be the greatest artist. A house or sign-painter might instantly enter the lists with Michael Angelo, and might look down on the little, dry, hard manner of Raphael. But grandeur depends on a distinct principle of its own, not on a negation of the parts; and as it does not arise from their omission, so neither is it incompatible with their insertion or the highest finishing. In fact, an artist may give the minute particulars of any object one by one, and with the utmost care, and totally neglect the proportions, arrangement and general masses, on which the effect of the whole more immediately depends; or he may give the latter, *viz.* the proportions and arrangement of the larger parts and the general masses of light and shade, and leave all the minuter parts of which those parts are composed a mere blotch, one general smear, like the first crude and hasty getting in of the ground-work of a picture: he may do either of these, or he may combine both, that is, finish the parts, but put them in their right places, and keep them in due subordination to the general effect and massing of the whole. If the exclusion of the parts were necessary to the grandeur of the whole composition, if the more entire this exclusion, if the more like a *tabula rasa,* a vague, undefined, shadowy and abstracted representation the picture was, the greater the grandeur, there could be no danger of pushing this principle too far, and going the full length of Sir Joshua's theory without any restrictions or mental reservations. But neither of these suppositions is true. The greatest grandeur may co-exist with the most perfect, nay with a microscopic accuracy of detail, as we see it does often in nature: the greatest looseness and slovenliness of execution may be displayed without any grandeur at all either in the outline or distribution of the masses of colour. To explain more particularly what I mean. I have seen and copied portraits by Titian, in which the eyebrows were marked with a number of small strokes, like hair-lines (indeed, the hairs of which they were composed were in a great measure given)—but did this destroy the grandeur of expression, the truth of outline, arising from the arrangement of these hair-lines in a given form? The grandeur, the character, the expression remained, for the general form or arched and expanded outline remained, just as much as if it had been daubed in with a blacking-brush: the introduction of the internal parts and texture only added delicacy and truth to the general and striking effect of the whole. Surely a number of small dots or lines may be arranged into the form of a square or a circle indiscriminately; the square or circle, that is, the larger figure, remains the same,

whether the line of which it consists is broken or continuous; as we may see in prints where the outlines, features, and masses remain the same in all the varieties of mezzotinto, dotted and line engraving. If Titian in marking the appearance of the hairs had deranged the general shape and contour of the eyebrows, he would have destroyed the look of nature; but as he did not, but kept both in view, he proportionately improved his copy of it. So in what regards the masses of light and shade, the variety, the delicate transparency and broken transitions of the tints is not inconsistent with the greatest breadth or boldest contrasts. If the light, for instance, is thrown strongly on one side of a face, and the other is cast into deep shade, let the individual and various parts of the surface be finished with the most scrupulous exactness both in the drawing and in the colours: provided nature is not exceeded, this will not nor cannot destroy the force and harmony of the composition. One side of the face will still have that great and leading distinction of being seen in shadow, and the other of being seen in the light, let the subordinate differences be as many and as precise as they will. Suppose a panther is painted in the sun: will it be necessary to leave out the spots to produce breadth and the great style, or will not this be done more effectually by painting the spots of one side of his shaggy coat as they are seen in the light, and those of the other as they really appear in natural shadow? The two masses are thus preserved completely, and no offence is done to truth and nature. Otherwise we resolve the distribution of light and shade into *local colouring.* The masses, the grandeur exist equally in external nature with the local differences of different colours. Yet Sir Joshua seems to argue that the grandeur, the effect of the whole object, is confined to the general idea in the mind, and that all the littleness and individuality is in nature. This is an essentially false view of the subject. This grandeur, this general effect, is indeed always combined with the details, or what our theoretical reasoner would designate as *littleness* in nature: and so it ought to be in art, as far as art can follow nature with prudence and profit. What is the fault of Denner's style? It is, that he does *not* give this combination of properties: that he gives only one view of nature, that he abstracts the details, the finishing, the curiosities of natural appearances from the general result, truth and character of the whole, and in finishing every part with elaborate care totally loses sight of the more important and striking appearance of the object as it presents itself to us in nature. He gives every part of a face; but the shape, the expression, the light and shade of the whole is wrong, and as far as can be from what is natural. He gives an infinite variety of tints, but they are not the tints of the human face, nor are they subjected to any principle of light and shade. He is different from Rembrandt or Titian. The English school, formed on Sir Joshua's theory, give neither the finishing of the parts nor the effect of the whole, but an inexplicable dumb mass without distinction or meaning. They do not do as Denner did, and think that not to do as he did is to do as Titian and Rembrandt did; I do not know whether they would take it as a compliment to be supposed to imitate nature. Some few artists, it must be said, have 'of late reformed this indifferently among us! Oh! let them reform it altogether!' I have no doubt they would if they could; but I have some doubts whether they can or not.—Before I proceed to consider the question of beauty and grandeur as it relates to the selection of form, I will quote a few passages from Sir Joshua with reference to what has been said on the imitation of particular objects. In the **"Third Discourse"** he observes,

> I will now add that nature herself is not to be too closely copied. . . . A mere copier of nature *can never produce any thing great; can never raise and enlarge the conceptions, or warm the heart of the spectator.* The wish of the genuine painter must be more extensive: instead of endeavouring to amuse mankind with the minute neatness of his imitations, he must endeavour to improve them by the grandeur of his ideas; instead of seeking praise by deceiving the superficial sense of the spectator, he must strive for fame by captivating the imagination.

From this passage it would surely seem that there was nothing in nature but minute neatness and superficial effect: nothing great in *her* style, for an imitator of it can produce nothing great; nothing 'to enlarge the conceptions or warm the heart of the spectator.'

> What word hath passed thy lips, Adam severe?

All that is truly grand or excellent is a figment of the imagination, a vapid creation out of nothing, a pure effect of overlooking and scorning the minute neatness of natural objects. This will not do. Again, Sir Joshua lays it down without any qualification that

> The whole beauty and grandeur of the art consists in being able to get above all singular forms, local customs, peculiarities, and *details* of every kind.

Yet [later] we find him acknowledging a different opinion.

> 'I am very ready to allow' (he says, in speaking of history-painting) 'that *some* circumstances of minuteness and particularity *frequently* tend to give an air of truth to a piece, and *to interest the spectator in an extraordinary manner.* Such circumstances therefore cannot wholly be rejected: but if there be any thing in the Art which requires peculiar nicety of discernment, it is the disposition of these minute circumstantial parts; which, according to the judgment employed in the choice, become so useful to truth or so injurious to grandeur.

That's true; but the sweeping clause against 'all particularities and details of every kind' is clearly got rid of. The undecided state of Sir Joshua's feelings on this subject of the incompatibility between the whole and the details is strikingly manifested in two short passages which follow each other in the space of two pages. Speaking of some pictures of Paul Veronese and Rubens as distinguished by the dexterity and the unity of style displayed in them, he adds—

> It is by this and this alone, that the mechanical power is ennobled, and raised much above its natural rank. And it appears to me, that with propriety it acquires this character, as an instance of that superiority with which mind predominates over matter, by contracting into one whole what nature has made multifarious.

This would imply that the principle of unity and integrity is only in the mind, and that nature is a heap of disjointed, disconnected particulars, a chaos of points and atoms. In the very next page, the following sentence occurs—

> As painting is an art, they (the ignorant) think they ought to be pleased in proportion as they see that art ostentatiously displayed; they will from this

supposition prefer neatness, high finishing, and gaudy colouring, to the truth, simplicity and *unity* of nature.

Before, neatness and high finishing were supposed to belong exclusively to the littleness of nature, but here truth, simplicity and unity are her characteristics. Soon after, Sir Joshua says, 'I should be sorry if what has been said should be understood to have any tendency to encourage that carelessness which leaves work in an unfinished state. I commend nothing for the want of exactness; I mean to point out that kind of exactness which is the best, and which is alone truly to be so esteemed.' This Sir Joshua has already told us consists in getting above 'all particularities and details of every kind.' Once more we find it is stated that

> It is in vain to attend to the variation of tints, if in that attention the general hue of flesh is lost; or to finish every so minutely the parts, if the masses are not observed, or the whole not well put together.

Nothing can be truer: but why always suppose the two things at variance with each other?

> Titian's manner was then new to the world, but that unshaken truth on which it is founded, has fixed it as a model to all succeeding painters; and those who will examine into the artifice, will find it to consist in the power of generalising, and in the shortness and simplicity of the means employed.

Titian's real excellence consisted in the power of generalising and of *individualising* at the same time: if it were merely the former, it would be difficult to account for the error immediately after pointed out by Sir Joshua. He says in the very next paragraph:

> Many artists, as Vasari likewise observes, have ignorantly imagined they are imitating the manner of Titian, when they leave their colours rough, and neglect the detail: but not possessing the principles on which he wrought, they have produced what he calls *goffe pitture*, absurd, foolish pictures.

Many artists have also imagined they were following the directions of Sir Joshua when they did the same thing, that is, neglected the detail, and produced the same results, vapid generalities, absurd, foolish pictures.

I will only give two short passages more, and have done with this part of the subject. I am anxious to confront Sir Joshua with his own authority.

> The advantage of this method of considering objects (*as a whole*) is what I wish now more particularly to enforce. At the same time I do not forget, that a painter must have the power of contracting as well as dilating his sight; because he that does not at all express particulars, expresses nothing; yet it is certain that a nice discrimination of minute circumstances, and a punctilious delineation of them, whatever excellence it may have (and I do not mean to detract from it), never did confer on the artist the character of Genius.

At page 53, we find the following words:

> Whether it is the human figure, and animal, or even inanimate objects, there is nothing, however unpromising in appearance, but may be raised into dignity, convey sentiment, and produce emotion, in

the hands of a Painter of genius. What was said of Virgil, that he threw even the dung about the ground with an air of dignity, may be applied to Titian; whatever he touched, however naturally mean, and habitually familiar, by a kind of magic he invested with grandeur and importance.

No, not by magic, but by seeking and finding in individual nature, and combined with details of every kind, that grace and grandeur and unity of effect which Sir Joshua supposes to be a mere creation of the artist's brain! Titian's practice was, I conceive, to give general appearances with individual forms and circumstances: Sir Joshua's theory goes too often, and, in its prevailing bias, to separate the two things as inconsistent with each other, and thereby to destroy or bring into question that union of striking effect with accuracy of resemblance in which the essence of sound art (as far as relates to imitation) consists.

Farther, as Sir Joshua is inclined to merge the details of individual objects in general effect, so he is resolved to reduce all beauty or grandeur in natural objects to a central form or abstract idea of a certain class, so as to exclude all peculiarities or deviations from this ideal standard as unfit subjects for the artist's pencil, and as polluting his canvas with deformity. As the former principle went to destroy all exactness and solidity in particular things, this goes to confound all variety, distinctness, and characteristic force in the broader scale of nature. There is a principle of conformity in nature or of something in common between a number of individuals of the same class, but there is also a principle of contrast, of discrimination and identity, which is equally essential in the system of the universe and in the structure of our ideas both of art and nature. Sir Joshua would hardly neutralise the tints of the rainbow to produce a dingy grey, as a medium or central colour: why then should he neutralise all features, forms, &c. to produce an insipid monotony? He does not indeed consider his theory of beauty as applicable to colour, which he well understood, but insists upon, and literally enforces it as to form and ideal conceptions, of which he knew comparatively little, and where his authority is more questionable. I will not in this place undertake to shew that his theory of a middle form (as the standard of taste and beauty) is not true of the outline of the human face and figure or other organic bodies, though I think that even there it is only one principle or condition of beauty; but I do say that it has little or nothing to do with those other capital parts of painting, colour, character, expression, and grandeur of conception. Sir Joshua himself contends that 'beauty in creatures of the same species is the medium or centre of all its various forms;' and he maintains that grandeur is the same abstraction of the species in the individual. Therefore beauty and grandeur must be the same thing, which they are not; so that this definition must be faulty. Grandeur I should suppose to imply something that elevates and expands the mind, which is chiefly power or magnitude. Beauty is that which soothes and melts it, and its source I apprehend is a certain harmony, softness, and gradation of form, within the limits of our customary associations, no doubt, or of what we expect of certain species, but not independent of every other consideration. Our critic himself confesses of Michael Angelo, whom he regards as the pattern of the great and sublime style, that 'his people are a superior order of beings; there is nothing about them, nothing in the air of their actions or their attitudes, or the style or cast of their limbs or features, that reminds us of their belonging to our own species. Rafaelle's imagination is not so elevated: his figures are not so much disjoined from our own diminutive race of beings, though his ideas are chaste, noble, and of great conformity to their subjects. Michael Angelo's works have a strong, peculiar, and marked character: they seem to proceed from his own mind entirely, and that mind so rich and abundant, that he never needed or seemed to disdain to look abroad for foreign help. Rafaelle's materials are generally borrowed, though the noble structure is his own.' How does all this accord with the same writer's favourite theory that all beauty, all grandeur, and all excellence, consist in an approximation to that central form or habitual idea of mediocrity, from which every deviation is so much deformity and littleness? Michael Angelo's figures are raised above our diminutive race of beings, yet they are confessedly the standard of sublimity in what regards the human form. Grandeur then admits of an exaggeration of our habitual impressions; and 'the strong, marked, and peculiar character which Michael Angelo has at the same time given to his works,' does not take away from it. This is fact against argument. I would take Sir Joshua's word for the goodness of a picture, and for its distinguishing properties, sooner than I would for an abstract metaphysical theory. Our artist also speaks continually of high and low subjects. There can be no distinction of this kind upon his principle, that the standard of taste is the adhering to the central form of each species, and that every species is in itself equally beautiful. The painter of flowers, of shells, or of any thing else, is equally elevated with Raphael or Michael, if he adheres to the generic or established form of what he paints: the rest, according to this definition, is a matter of indifference. There must therefore be something besides the central or customary form to account for the difference of dignity, for the high and low style in nature or in art. Michael Angelo's figures, we are told, are more than ordinarily grand: why, by the same rule, may not Raphael's be more than ordinarily beautiful, have more than ordinary softness, symmetry, and grace?— Character and expression are still less included in the present theory. All character is a departure from the commonplace form; and Sir Joshua makes no scruple to declare that expression destroys beauty. (pp. 131-38)

Sir Joshua's theory seems to rest on an inclined plane, and is always glad of an excuse to slide, from the severity of truth and nature, into the milder and more equable regions of insipidity and inanity! I am sorry to say so, but so it appears to me.

I confess, it strikes me as a self-evident truth that variety or contrast is as essential a principle in art and nature as uniformity, and as necessary to make up the harmony of the universe and the contentment of the mind. Who would destroy the shifting effects of light and shade, the sharp, lively opposition of colours in the same or in different objects, the streaks in a flower, the stains in a piece of marble, to reduce all to the same neutral, dead colouring, the same middle tint? Yet it is on this principle that Sir Joshua would get rid of all variety, character, expression, and picturesque effect in forms, or at least measure the worth or the spuriousness of all these according to their reference to or departure from a given or average standard. Surely, nature is more liberal, art is wider than Sir Joshua's theory. Allow (for the sake of argument) that all forms are in themselves indifferent, and that beauty or the sense of pleasure in forms can therefore only arise from customary association, or from that middle impression to which they all tend: yet this cannot by the same rule apply to other things. Suppose there is no capacity in form to affect the mind except from its corresponding to previous expectation, the same thing cannot be said of the idea of power or grandeur. No one can say that the idea of power does not affect the mind with the sense of awe and sublimity. That is, power and weakness, grandeur and littleness, are not indifferent things, the perfection of which consists in a medium between both. Again, expression is not a thing indifferent in itself, which derives its value or its interest solely from its conformity to a neutral standard. Who would neutralise the expression of pleasure and pain? Or say that the passions of the human mind, pity, love, joy, sorrow, &c. are only interesting to the imagination and worth the attention of the artist, as he can reduce them to an equivocal state which is neither pleasant nor painful, neither one thing nor the other? Or who would stop short of the utmost refinement, precision, and force in the delineation of each? Ideal expression is not neutral expression, but extreme expression. Again, character is a thing of peculiarity, of striking contrast, of distinction, and not of uniformity. It is necessarily opposed to Sir Joshua's exclusive theory, and yet it is surely a curious and interesting field of speculation for the human mind. Lively, spirited discrimination of character is one source of gratification to the lover of nature and art, which it could not be, if all truth and excellence consisted in rejecting individual traits. Ideal character is not common-place, but consistent character marked throughout, which may take place in history or portrait. Historical truth in a picture is the putting the different features of the face or muscles of the body into consistent action. The *picturesque* altogether depends on particular points or qualities of an object, projecting as it were beyond the middle line of beauty, and catching the eye of the spectator. It was less, however, my intention to hazard any speculations of my own, than to confirm the common-sense feelings on the subject by Sir Joshua's own admissions in different places. In the Tenth Discourse, speaking of some objections to the Apollo, he has these remarkable words—

> In regard to the last objection (*viz.* that the lower half of the figure is longer than just proportion allows) it must be remembered, that Apollo is here in the exertion of *one of his peculiar powers,* which is swiftness; he has therefore that proportion which is best adapted to that character. This is no more incorrectness, than when there is given to an Hercules an extraordinary swelling and strength of muscles.

Strength and activity then do not depend on the middle form; and the middle form is to be sacrificed to the representation of these positive qualities. Character is thus allowed not only to be an integrant part of the antique and classical style of art, but even to take precedence of and set aside the abstract idea of beauty. Little more would be required to justify Hogarth in his Gothic resolution, that if he were to make a figure of Charon, he would give him bandy legs, because watermen are generally bandy-legged. It is very well to talk of the abstract idea of a man or of a God, but if you come to any thing like an intelligible proposition, you must either individualise and define, or destroy the very idea you contemplate. Sir Joshua goes

into this question at considerable length in the Third Discourse.

> To the principle I have laid down, that the idea of beauty in each species of beings is an invariable one, it may be objected . . . that in every particular species there are various central forms, which are separate and distinct from each other, and yet are undeniably beautiful; that in the human figure, for instance, the beauty of Hercules is one, of the Gladiator another, of the Apollo another, which makes so many different ideas of beauty. It is true, indeed, that these figures are each perfect in their kind, though of different characters and proportions; but still none of them is the representation of an individual, but of a class. And as there is one general form, which, as I have said, belongs to the human kind at large, so in each of these classes there is one common idea which is the abstract of the various individual forms belonging to that class. Thus, though the forms of childhood and age differ exceedingly, there is a common form in childhood, and a common form in age, which is the more perfect as it is remote from all peculiarities. But I must add further, that though the most perfect forms of each of the general divisions of the human figure are ideal, and superior to any individual form of that class; yet the highest perfection of the human figure is not to be found in any of them. It is not in the Hercules, nor in the Gladiator, nor in the Apollo; but in that form which is taken from all, and which partakes equally of the activity of the Gladiator, of the delicacy of the Apollo, and of the muscular strength of the Hercules. For perfect beauty in any species must combine all the characters which are beautiful in that species. It cannot consist in any one to the exclusion of the rest: no one, therefore, must be predominant, that no one may be deficient.

Sir Joshua here supposes the distinctions of classes and character to be necessarily combined with the general leading idea of a middle form. This middle form is not to confound age, sex, circumstance, under one sweeping abstraction: but we must limit the general idea by certain specific differences and characteristic marks, belonging to the several subordinate divisions and ramifications of each class. This is enough to shew that there is a principle of individuality as well as of abstraction inseparable from works of art as well as nature. We are to keep the human form distinct from that of other living beings, that of men from that of women; we are to distinguish between age and infancy, between thoughtfulness and gaiety, between strength and softness. Where is this to stop? But Sir Joshua turns round upon himself in this very passage, and says, 'No: we are to unite the strength of the Hercules with the delicacy of the Apollo; for perfect beauty in any species must combine all the characters which are beautiful in that species.' Now if these different characters are beautiful in themselves, why not give them for their own sakes and in their most striking appearances, instead of qualifying and softening them down in a neutral form; which must produce a compromise, not a union of different excellencies. If all excess of beauty, if all character is deformity, then we must try to lose it as fast as possible in other qualities. But if strength is an excellence, if activity is an excellence, if delicacy is an excellence, then the perfection, *i.e.* the highest degree of each of these qualities cannot be attained but by remaining satisfied with a less degree of the rest. But let us hear what Sir Joshua himself advances on this subject in another part of the ***Discourses.***

> Some excellencies bear to be united, and are improved by union: others are of a discordant nature: and the attempt to unite them only produces a harsh jarring of incongruent principles. The attempt to unite contrary excellencies (of form, for instance) in a single figure, *can never escape degenerating into the monstrous but by sinking into the insipid; by taking away its marked character, and weakening its expression.*
>
> Obvious as these remarks appear, there are many writers on our art, who not being of the profession, and consequently not knowing what can or cannot be done, have been very liberal of absurd praises in their description of favourite works. They always find in them what they are resolved to find. They praise excellencies that can hardly exist together; and above all things are fond of describing with great exactness the expression of a mixed passion, which more particularly appears to me out of the reach of our art.
>
> Such are many disquisitions which I have read on some of the Cartoons and other pictures of Raffaelle, where the critics have described their own imaginations; or indeed where the excellent master himself may have attempted this expression of passions above the powers of the art; and has, therefore, by an indistinct and imperfect marking, left room for every imagination with equal probability to find a passion of his own. What has been, and what can be done in the art, is sufficiently difficult: we need not be mortified or discouraged at not being able to execute the conceptions of a romantic imagination. Art has its boundaries, though imagination has none. We can easily, like the ancients, suppose a Jupiter to be possessed of all those powers and perfections which the subordinate Deities were endowed with separately. Yet when they employed their art to represent him, they confined his character to majesty alone. Pliny, therefore, though we are under great obligations to him for the information he has given us in relation to the works of the ancient artists, is very frequently wrong when he speaks of them, which he does very often, in the style of many of our modern connoisseurs. He observes that in a statue of Paris, by Euphranor, you might discover at the same time three different characters; the dignity of a Judge of the Goddesses, the Lover of Helen, and the Conqueror of Achilles. A statue in which you endeavour to unite stately dignity, youthful elegance, and stern valour, must surely possess none of these to any eminent degree.
>
> From hence it appears, that there is much difficulty as well as danger in an endeavour to concentrate in a single subject those various powers, which, rising from various points, naturally move in different directions.

What real clue to the art or sound principles of judging the student can derive from these contradictory statements, or in what manner it is possible to reconcile them one to the other, I confess I am at a loss to discover. As it appears to me, all the varieties of nature in the infinite number of its qualities, combinations, characters, expressions, incidents, etc. rise from distinct points or centres and must move in distinct directions, as the forms of different species are to be referred to a separate standard. It is the object of art to bring them out in all their force, clearness, and precision, and not to blend them into a vague, vapid, nondescript *ideal* conception, which pretends to unite, but in reality destroys. Sir Joshua's theory limits nature and paralyses art. According to him, the middle form or the average of our various impressions is the source from which all beauty, pleasure, interest, imagination springs. I contend, on the contrary, that this very variety is good in itself, nor do I agree with him that the whole of nature as it exists in fact is stark naught, and that there is nothing worthy of the contemplation of a wise man but that *ideal perfection* which never existed in the world nor even on canvas. There is something fastidious and sickly in Sir Joshua's system. His code of taste consists too much of negations, and not enough of positive, prominent qualities. It accounts for nothing but the beauty of the common Antique, and hardly for that. The merit of Hogarth, I grant, is different from that of the Greek statues; but I deny that Hogarth is to be measured by this standard, or by Sir Joshua's middle forms: he has powers of instruction and amusement that 'rising from a different point, naturally move in a different direction,' and completely attain their end. It would be just as reasonable to condemn a comedy for not having the pathos of a tragedy or the stateliness of an epic poem. If Sir Joshua Reynolds's theory were true, Dr. Johnson's *Irene* would be a better tragedy than any of Shakespear's.

The reasoning of the ***Discourses*** is, I think then, deficient in the following particulars:

1. It seems to imply that general effect in a picture is produced by leaving out the details, whereas the largest masses and the grandest outline are consistent with the utmost delicacy of finishing in the parts.

2. It makes no distinction between beauty and grandeur, but refers both to an *ideal* or middle form, as the centre of the various forms of the species, and yet inconsistently attributes the grandeur of Michael Angelo's style to the superhuman appearance of his prophets and apostles.

3. It does not at any time make mention of power or magnitude in an object as a distinct source of the sublime (though this is acknowledged unintentionally in the case of Michael Angelo, etc.), nor of softness or symmetry of form as a distinct source of beauty, independently of, though still in connection with another source arising from what we are accustomed to expect from each individual species.

4. Sir Joshua's theory does not leave room for character, but rejects it as an anomaly.

5. It does not point out the source of expression, but considers it as hostile to beauty; and yet, lastly, he allows that the middle form, carried to the utmost theoretical extent, neither defined by character, nor impregnated by passion, would produce nothing but vague, insipid, unmeaning generality.

In a word, I cannot think that the theory here laid down is clear and satisfactory, that it is consistent with itself, that it accounts for the various excellences of art from a few simple principles, or that the method which Sir Joshua has pursued in treating the subject is, as he himself expresses it, '*a plain and honest method.*' It is, I fear, more calculated to baffle and perplex the student in his progress, than to give him clear lights as to the object he should have in view, or to furnish him with strong motives of emulation to attain it. (pp. 140-45)

William Hazlitt, "The Same Subject Continued," in his Table Talk; or, Original Essays, J. M. Dent & Sons Ltd., 1908, pp. 131-45.

Henry William Beechey   (essay date 1835)

[*Beechey was an English painter and explorer. With his brother, G. D. Beechey, he explored the Nile and surveyed the northern African coastline from Tripoli to Derna from 1821 to 1822. As an author, Beechey published and illustrated a report on the North-African expedition in 1828 and contributed a lengthy biographical preface to the 1835 edition of* The Literary Works of Sir Joshua Reynolds. *In the following excerpt from the latter work, he highly recommends the* Discourses *to students of painting.*]

We are firmly convinced that by pursuing the line of study pointed out in Sir Joshua's incomparable **Discourses,** the student in painting will do more for himself, on the basis of his well-grounded academic education, than any other mode of instruction can secure to him; and that the method of study which he has recommended—the study of the works of the best ancient masters—will be found, in the present advanced state of the arts, when so great a portion of mechanical dexterity and so good a view of nature have already been acquired, to afford the best means, if not indeed the only ones, of directing the painter to those important excellences which nothing but theory can teach, and which are at present nearly all that remain to be acquired.

Sir Joshua has availed himself in his **Discourses** of much valuable matter on the general principles of art, brought together with great labour, and selected with much discrimination by the author of an excellent little treatise on painting written nearly two centuries ago; and which would probably have never been practically useful if Reynolds had not forced its contents into notice, and given them the form which they assume in his lectures. The admirable manner in which he has illustrated the principles contained in that interesting volume, which are chiefly derived from Greek and Roman authorities, has given them a value which they would never have possessed in the form in which they were arranged, and a much more extensive circulation than the author of the work could have ever anticipated. (pp. 291-92)

So far from detracting from the merit of the **Discourses,** we think the use which Sir Joshua has made of the contents of the volume alluded to is at once highly creditable to his judgment in distinguishing their merit, to his ability in their selection, illustration, and arrangement, and to the unassuming spirit with which he has adopted the principles which others suggested to him. (p. 292)

Henry William Beechey, "Memoir of Sir Joshua Reynolds," in The Literary Works of Sir Joshua Reynolds, First President of the Royal Academy, Vol. I by Sir Joshua Reynolds, T. Cadell, 1835, pp. 31-300.

John Ruskin   (essay date 1843)

[*Ruskin was an English critic, essayist, historian, poet, novella writer, autobiographer, and diarist. Endowed with a passion for reforming what he considered his "blind and wandering fellow-men" and convinced that he had "perfect judgment" in aesthetic matters, Ruskin wrote over forty books and several hundred essays and lectures that expounded his theories of aesthetics, morality, history, economics, and social reform. Although his views were often controversial and critical reception of his works was frequently hostile, Ruskin became one of the Victorian era's most prominent and influential critics of art and society. Perhaps as well known today for the eloquence of his prose as for the content of his works, he is also considered one of the greatest prose stylists in the English language. In the following excerpt from his* Modern Painters (1843), *Ruskin examines and attacks Reynolds's theories of High Art as outlined in the second of Reynolds's three* Idler *essays.*]

We speak of great truths, of great beauties, great thoughts. What is it which makes one truth greater than another, one thought greater than another? This question is . . . of peculiar importance at the present time; for, during a period now of some hundred and fifty years, all writers on Art who have pretended to eminence, have insisted much on a supposed distinction between what they call the Great and the Low Schools; using the terms "High Art," "Great or Ideal Style," and other such, as descriptive of a certain noble manner of painting, which it was desirable that all students of Art should be early led to reverence and adopt; and characterising as "vulgar," or "low," or "realist," another manner of painting and conceiving, which it was equally necessary that all students should be taught to avoid.

But lately this established teaching, never very intelligible, has been gravely called in question. The advocates and self-supposed practisers of "High Art" are beginning to be looked upon with doubt, and their peculiar phraseology to be treated with even a certain degree of ridicule. And other forms of Art are partly developed among us, which do not pretend to be high, but rather to be strong, healthy, and humble. This matter of "highness" in Art, therefore deserves our most careful consideration. Has it been, or is it, a true highness, a true princeliness, or only a show of it, consisting in courtly manners and robes of state? Is it rocky height or cloudy height, adamant or vapor, on which the sun of praise so long has risen and set? It will be well at once to consider this.

And first, let us get, as quickly as may be, at the exact meaning with which the advocates of "High Art" use that somewhat obscure and figurative term.

I do not know that the principles in question are anywhere more distinctly expressed than in two papers in the *Idler,* written by Sir Joshua Reynolds, of course under the immediate sanction of Johnson; and which may thus be considered as the utterance of the views then held upon the subject by the artists of chief skill, and critics of most sense, arranged in a form so brief and clear, as to admit of their being brought before the public for a morning's entertainment. I cannot, therefore, it seems to me, do better than quote these two letters, or at least the important parts of them, examining the exact meaning of each passage as it occurs. There are, in all, in the Idler three letters on painting, Nos. 76, 79, and 82; of these, the first is directed only against the impertinences of pretended connoisseurs, and is as notable for its faithfulness, as for its wit, in the description of the several modes of criticism in an artificial and ignorant state of society; it is only, therefore, in the two last papers that we find the expression of the doctrines which it is our business to examine.

No. 79 (Saturday, Oct. 20th, 1759) begins, after a short preamble, with the following passage:

> Amongst the painters, and the writers on painting, there is one maxim universally admitted and continually inculcated. Imitate nature is the invariable rule; but I know none who have explained in what manner this rule is to be understood; the sequence of which is, that every one takes it in the most obvious sense, that objects are represented naturally when they have such relief that they seem real. It may appear strange, perhaps, to hear this sense of the rule disputed; but it must be considered, that, if the excellency of a painter consisted only in this kind of imitation, Painting must lose its rank, and be no longer considered as a liberal art, and sister to Poetry, this imitation being nearly mechanical, in which the slowest intellect is always sure to succeed best; for the painter of genius cannot stoop to drudgery, in which the understanding has no part; and what pretence has the art to claim kindred with poetry but by its power over the imagination? To this power the painter of genius directs him; in this sense he studies nature, and often arrives at his end, even by being unnatural in the confined sense of the word.
>
> The grand style of painting requires this minute attention to be carefully avoided, and must be kept as separate from it as the style of poetry from that of history. (Poetical ornaments destroy that air of truth and plainness which ought to characterise history; but the very being of poetry consists in departing from this plain narrative, and adopting every ornament that will warm the imagination.) [In a footnote Ruskin adds: "I have put this sentence in parentheses, because it is inconsistent with the rest of the statement, and with the general teaching of the paper; since that which 'attends only to the invariable' cannot certainly adopt 'every ornament that will warm the imagination.'"] To desire to see the excellencies of each style united—to mingle the Dutch with the Italian school, is to join contrarieties, which cannot subsist together, and which destroy the efficacy of each other.

We find, first, from this interesting passage, that the writer considers the Dutch and Italian masters as severally representative of the low and high schools; next, that he considers the Dutch painters as excelling in a mechanical imitation, "in which the slowest intellect is always sure to succeed best;" and, thirdly, that he considers the Italian painters as excelling in a style which corresponds to that of imaginative poetry in literature, and which has an exclusive right to be called the grand style.

I wish that it were in my power entirely to concur with the writer, and to enforce this opinion thus distinctly stated. I have never been a zealous partisan of the Dutch school, and should rejoice in claiming Reynolds's authority for the assertion, that their manner was one "in which the slowest intellect was always sure to succeed best." But

before his authority can be so claimed, we must observe exactly the meaning of the assertion itself, and separate it from the company of some others not perhaps so admissible. First, I say, we must observe Reynolds's exact meaning, for (though the assertion may at first appear singular) a man who uses accurate language is always more liable to misinterpretation than one who is careless in his expressions. We may assume that the latter means very nearly what we at first suppose him to mean, for words which have been uttered without thought may be received without examination. But when a writer or speaker may be fairly supposed to have considered his expressions carefully, and, after having revolved a number of terms in his mind, to have chosen the one which *exactly* means the thing he intends to say, we may be assured that what costs him time to select, will require from us time to understand, and that we shall do him wrong, unless we pause to reflect how the word which he has actually employed differs from other words which it seems he *might* have employed. It thus constantly happens that persons themselves unaccustomed to think clearly, or speak correctly, misunderstand a logical and careful writer, and are actually in more danger of being misled by language which is measured and precise, than by that which is loose and inaccurate.

Now, in the instance before us, a person not accustomed to good writing might very rashly conclude, that when Reynolds spoke of the Dutch School as one "in which the slowest intellect was sure to succeed best," he meant to say that every successful Dutch painter was a fool. We have no right to take his assertion in that sense. He says, the *slowest* intellect. We have no right to assume that he meant the *weakest.* For it is true, that in order to succeed in the Dutch style, a man has need of qualities of mind eminently deliberate and sustained. He must be possessed of patience rather than of power; and must feel no weariness in contemplating the expression of a single thought for several months together. As opposed to the changeful energies of the imagination, these mental characters may be properly spoken of as under the general term—slowness of intellect. But it by no means follows that they are necessarily those of weak or foolish men.

We observe however, farther, that the imitation which Reynolds supposes to be characteristic of the Dutch School is that which gives to objects such relief that they seem real, and that he then speaks of this art of realistic imitation as corresponding to *history* in literature.

Reynolds, therefore, seems to class these dull works of the Dutch School under a general head, to which they are not commonly referred—that of *Historical* painting; while he speaks of the works of the Italian School not as historical, but as *poetical* painting. His next sentence will farther manifest his meaning.

> The Italian attends only to the invariable, the great and general ideas which are fixed and inherent in universal nature; the Dutch, on the contrary, to literal truth and minute exactness in the detail, as I may say, of nature modified by accident. The attention to these petty peculiarities is the very cause of this naturalness so much admired in the Dutch pictures, which, if we suppose it to be a beauty, is certainly of a lower order, which ought to give place to a beauty of a superior kind, since one cannot be obtained but by departing from the other.

If my opinion was asked concerning the works of Michael Angelo, whether they would receive any advantage from possessing this mechanical merit, I should not scruple to say, they would not only receive no advantage, but would lose, in a great measure, the effect which they now have on every mind susceptible of great and noble ideas. His works may be said to be all genius and soul; and why should they be loaded with heavy matter, which can only counteract his purpose by retarding the progress of the imagination?

Examining carefully this and the preceding passage, we find the author's unmistakable meaning to be, that Dutch painting is *history;* attending to literal truth and "minute exactness in the details of nature modified by accident." That Italian painting is *poetry,* attending only to the invariable; and that works which attend only to the invariable are full of genius and soul; but that literal truth and exact detail are "heavy matter which retards the progress of the imagination."

This being then indisputably what Reynolds means to tell us, let us think a little whether he is in all respects right. And first, as he compares his two kinds of painting to history and poetry, let us see how poetry and history themselves differ, in their use of *variable* and *invariable* details. I am writing at a window which commands a view of the head of the Lake of Geneva; and as I look up from my paper, to consider this point, I see, beyond it, a blue breadth of softly moving water, and the outline of the mountains above Chillon, bathed in morning mist. The first verses which naturally come into my mind are—

> A thousand feet in depth below
> The massy waters meet and flow;
> So far the fathom line was sent
> From Chillon's snow-white battlement.

Let us see in what manner this poetical statement is distinguished from a historical one.

It is distinguished from a truly historical statement, first, in being simply false. The water under the castle of Chillon is not a thousand feet deep, nor anything like it. Herein, certainly, these lines fulfil Reynolds's first requirement in poetry, "that it should be inattentive to literal truth and minute exactness in detail." In order, however, to make our comparison more closely in other points, let us assume that what is stated is indeed a fact, and that it was to be recorded, first historically, and then poetically.

Historically stating it, then, we should say: "The lake was sounded from the walls of the castle of Chillon, and found to be a thousand feet deep."

Now, if Reynolds be right in his idea of the difference between history and poetry, we shall find that Byron leaves out of this statement certain *un*necessary details, and retains only the invariable,—that is to say, the points which the Lake of Geneva and castle of Chillon have in common with all other lakes and castles.

Let us hear, therefore.

> A thousand feet in depth below.

"Below?" Here is, at all events, a word added (instead of anything being taken away); invariable, certainly in the case of lakes, but not absolutely necessary.

> The massy waters meet and flow.

"Massy!" why massy? Because deep water is heavy. The word is a good word, but it is assuredly an added detail, and expresses a character, not which the Lake of Geneva has in common with all other lakes, but which it has in distinction from those which are narrow or shallow.

"Meet and flow." Why meet and flow? Partly to make up a rhyme; partly to tell us that the waters are forceful as well as massy, and changeful as well as deep. Observe, a farther addition of details, and of details more or less peculiar to the spot, or, according to Reynolds's definition, of "heavy matter, retarding the progress of the imagination."

> So far the fathom line was sent.

Why fathom line? All lines for sounding are not fathom lines. If the lake was ever sounded from Chillon, it was probably sounded in metres, not fathoms. This is an addition of another particular detail, in which the only compliance with Reynolds's requirement is, that there is some chance of its being an inaccurate one.

> From Chillon's snow-white battlement.

Why snow-white? Because castle battlements are not usually snow-white. This is another added detail, and a detail quite peculiar to Chillon, and therefore exactly the most striking word in the whole passage.

"Battlement!" why battlement? Because all walls have not battlements, and the addition of the term marks the castle to be not merely a prison, but a fortress.

This is a curious result. Instead of finding, as we expected, the poetry distinguished from the history by the omission of details, we find it consist entirely in the *addition* of details; and instead of being characterized by regard only of the invariable, we find its whole power to consist in the clear expression of what is singular and particular!

The reader may pursue the investigation for himself in other instances. He will find in every case that a poetical is distinguished from a merely historical statement, not by being more vague, but more specific, and it might, therefore, at first appear that our author's comparison should be simply reversed, and that the Dutch School should be called poetical, and the Italian historical. But the term poetical does not appear very applicable to the generality of Dutch painting; and a little reflection will show us, that if the Italians represent only the invariable, they cannot be properly compared even to historians. For that which is incapable of change has no history, and records which state only the invariable need not be written, and could not be read.

It is evident, therefore, that our author has entangled himself in some grave fallacy, by introducing this idea of invariableness as forming a distinction between poetical and historical art. What the fallacy is, we shall discover as we proceed; but as an invading army should not leave an untaken fortress in its rear, we must not go on with our inquiry into the views of Reynolds until we have settled satisfactorily the question already suggested to us, in what the essence of poetical treatment really consists. For though, as we have seen, it certainly involves the addition of specific details, it cannot be simply that addition which turns the history into poetry. For it is perfectly possible to add any number of details to a historical statement, and to make it more prosaic with every added word. As, for instance, "The lake was sounded out of a flat-bottomed boat, near the crab-tree at the corner of the kitchen-garden, and was found to be a thousand feet nine inches deep, with a muddy bottom." It thus appears that it is not the multiplication of details which constitutes poetry; nor their subtraction which constitutes history; but that there must be something either in the nature of the details themselves, or the method of using them, which invests them with poetical power or historical propriety.

It seems to me, and may seem to the reader, strange that we should need to ask the question, "What is poetry?" Here is a word we have been using all our lives, and, I suppose, with a very distinct idea attached to it; and when I am now called upon to give a definition of this idea, I find myself at a pause. (pp. 19-26)

I come, after some embarrassment, to the conclusion, that poetry "is the suggestion, by the imagination, of noble grounds for the noble emotions." I mean, by the noble emotions, those four principal sacred passions—Love, Veneration, Admiration, and Joy (this latter especially, if unselfish); and their opposites—Hatred, Indignation (or Scorn), Horror, and Grief,—this last, when unselfish, becoming Compassion. These passions in their various combinations constitute what is called "poetical feeling," when they are felt on noble grounds, that is, on great and true grounds. (p. 27)

Farther, it is necessary to the existence of poetry that the grounds of these feelings should be *furnished by the imagination.* Poetical feeling, that is to say, mere noble emotion, is not poetry. It is happily inherent in all human nature deserving the name, and is found often to be purest in the least sophisticated. But the power of assembling, by *the help of the imagination,* such images as will excite these feelings, is the power of the poet or literally of the "Maker."

Now this power of exciting the emotions depends of course on the richness of the imagination, and on its choice of those images which, in combination, will be most effective, or, for the particular work to be done, most fit. And it is altogether impossible for a writer not endowed with invention to conceive what tools a true poet will make use of, or in what way he will apply them, or what unexpected results he will bring out by them; so that it is vain to say that the details of poetry ought to possess, or ever do possess, any *definite* character. (pp. 27-8)

In like manner, in painting, it is altogether impossible to say beforehand what details a great painter may make poetical by his use of them to excite noble emotions: and we shall, therefore, find presently that a painting is to be classed in the great or inferior schools, not according to the kind of details which it represents, but according to the uses for which it employs them.

It is only farther to be noticed, that infinite confusion has been introduced into this subject by the careless and illogical custom of opposing painting to poetry, instead of regarding poetry as consisting in a noble use, whether of colors or words. Painting is properly to be opposed to *speaking* or *writing,* but not to *poetry.* Both painting and speaking are methods of expression. Poetry is the employment of either for the noblest purposes.

This question being thus far determined, we may proceed with our paper in the Idler.

> It is very difficult to determine the exact degree of enthusiasm that the arts of painting and poetry may admit. There may, perhaps, be too great indulgence as well as too great a restraint of imagination; if the one produces incoherent monsters, the other produces what is full as bad, lifeless insipidity. An intimate knowledge of the passions, and good sense, but not common sense, must at last determine its limits. It has been thought, and I believe with reason, that Michael Angelo sometimes transgressed those limits; and, I think, I have seen figures of him of which it was very difficult to determine whether they were in the highest degree sublime or extremely ridiculous. Such faults may be said to be the ebullitions of genius; but at least he had this merit, that he never was insipid, and whatever passion his works may excite, they will always escape contempt.
>
> What I have had under consideration is the sublimest style, particularly that of Michael Angelo, the Homer of painting. Other kinds may admit of this naturalness, which of the lowest kind is the chief merit; but in painting, as in poetry, the highest style has the least of common nature.

From this passage we gather three important indications of the supposed nature of the Great Style. That it is the work of men in a state of enthusiasm. That it is like the writing of Homer; and that it has as little as possible of "common nature" in it.

First, it is produced by men in a state of enthusiasm. That is, by men who feel *strongly* and *nobly;* for we do not call a strong feeling of envy, jealousy, or ambition, enthusiasm. That is, therefore, by men who feel poetically. This much we may admit, I think, with perfect safety. Great art is produced by men who feel acutely and nobly; and it is in some sort an expression of this personal feeling. We can easily conceive that there may be a sufficiently marked distinction between such art, and that which is produced by men who do not feel at all, but who reproduce, though ever so accurately, yet coldly, like human mirrors, the scenes which pass before their eyes.

Secondly, Great Art is like the writing of Homer, and this chiefly because it has little of "common nature" in it. We are not clearly informed what is meant by common nature in this passage. Homer seems to describe a great deal of what is common;—cookery, for instance, very carefully in all its processes. I suppose the passage in the Iliad which, on the whole, has excited most admiration, is that which describes a wife's sorrow at parting from her husband, and a child's fright at its father's helmet; and I hope, at least, the former feeling may be considered "common nature." But the true greatness of Homer's style is, doubtless, held by our author to consist in his imaginations of things not only uncommon but impossible (such as spirits in brazen armor, or monsters with heads of men and bodies of beasts), and in his occasional delineations of the human character and form in their utmost, or heroic, strength and beauty. We gather then, on the whole, that a painter in the Great Style must be enthusiastic, or full of emotion, and must paint the human form in its utmost strength and beauty, and perhaps certain impossible forms besides, liable by persons not in an equally enthusiastic state of mind

Dutch, I mean not the moderns, but the heads of the old Roman and Bolognian schools; nor did I mean to include, in my idea of an Italian painter, the Venetian school, *which may be said to be the Dutch part of the Italian genius.* I have only to add a word of advice to the painters, that, however excellent they may be in painting naturally, they would not flatter themselves very much upon it; and to the connoisseurs, that when they see a cat or a fiddle painted so finely, that, as the phrase is, it looks as if you could take it up, they would not for that reason immediately compare the painter to Raffaelle and Michael Angelo.

In this passage there are four points chiefly to be remarked. The first, that in the year 1759, the Italian painters were, in our author's opinion, sunk in the very bathos of insipidity. The second, that the Venetian painters, i.e. Titian, Tintoret, and Veronese, are, in our author's opinion, to be classed with the Dutch; that is to say, are painters in a style "in which the slowest intellect is always sure to succeed best." Thirdly, that painting naturally is not a difficult thing, nor one on which a painter should pride himself. And, finally, that connoisseurs, seeing a cat or a fiddle successfully painted, ought not therefore immediately to compare the painter to Raphael or Michael Angelo.

Yet Raphael painted fiddles very carefully in the foreground of his St. Cecilia,—so carefully, that they quite look as if they might be taken up. So carefully, that I never yet looked at the picture without wishing that somebody *would* take them up, and out of the way. And I am under a very strong persuasion that Raphael did not think painting "naturally" an easy thing. (pp. 29-32)

> John Ruskin, "Of the Received Opinions Touching the 'Grand Style'," in his *Modern Painters*, Vol. III, *John Wanamaker, 1843, pp. 17-32.*

Actress Sarah Siddons as the Tragic Muse, one of Reynolds's most renowned portraits.

to be looked upon as in some degree absurd. This I presume to be Reynolds's meaning, and to be all that he intends us to gather from his comparison of the Great Style with the writings of Homer. But if that comparison be a just one in all respects, surely two other corollaries ought to be drawn from it, namely,—first, that these Heroic or Impossible images are to be mingled with others very unheroic and very possible; and, secondly, that in the representation of the Heroic or Impossible forms, the greatest care must be taken in *finishing the details,* so that a painter must not be satisfied with painting well the countenance and the body of his hero, but ought to spend the greatest part of his time (as Homer the greatest number of verses) in elaborating the sculptured pattern on his shield.

Let us, however, proceed with our paper.

> One may very safely recommend a little more enthusiasm to the modern painters; too much is certainly not the vice of the present age. The Italians seem to have been continually declining in this respect, from the time of Michael Angelo to that of Carlo Maratti, and from thence to the very bathos of insipidity to which they are now sunk, so that there is no need of remarking, that where I mentioned the Italian painters in opposition to the

Charles Robert Leslie and Tom Taylor (essay date 1865)

[*Leslie was an English painter, editor, essayist, and biographer. He edited the* Memoirs of John Constable, R. A. *(1843) and wrote* A Hand-book for Young Painters *(1855), the latter a collection of his lectures to students of the Royal Academy written when he was Professor of Painting (1847-51). He began what he intended to be the most complete critical biography of Reynolds to date, but he died before completing it. This work was completed by the biographer and dramatist Tom Taylor in 1865. In the following excerpt from this biography, Leslie and Taylor survey and discuss what they consider the most noteworthy discourses in Reynolds's collection.*]

The *Discourses* should be considered quite as much pleas for the intellectual claims of Art, urged before audiences which included many of the most distinguished men of the time, as lectures for the instruction of students. Such pleading was eminently required at a time when the tone and habits of painters, and the shallow affectations and coxcombries of connoisseurs, were little calculated to prepossess intelligent or refined minds in favour of the Arts. Whatever we may think of the road into which the President's *Discourses* directed the student, there can be no doubt it led upwards.

"The First Discourse" was introductory. It enumerates the advantages to be hoped from the institution of a Royal Academy, which, besides furnishing able men to direct the student, would be a repository for great examples of the art. To the objection that Raffaelle never studied in an academy, it is answered that all Rome was an academy. One advantage the lecturer claims for an Academy in this country—that our artists had nothing to unlearn. Then he recommends (as certain principles,—the first of them, the enforcing of implicit obedience on the part of the *young* students to the rules of Art as established by the practice of the great masters. Rules, he remarks, are not the fetters of genius; they are fetters only to men of no genius. When the pupil becomes a master he may consider what liberties he will take with the rules which he has heard inculcated. The stage when the student is passing into the painter is the one, in the President's view, most carefully to be watched. Then, more than ever, the importance of "scrupulous labour" above "fallacious mastery" is to be impressed upon the aspirant. He is to be told again and again that labour is the only price of solid fame. But his industry must be rightly directed. He must be taught to strive for purity of outline rather than readiness of hand—to think more of the disposition of drapery than of the imitation of its texture: above all, absolute exactness in drawing the model must be insisted on. The lecture closes with the expression of a wish and hope that the present age may vie in Arts with that of Leo X., and that the dignity of the dying art (quoting from Pliny) may be revived under the reign of George III. (pp. 318-19)

On the 11th of December [1769] came the first distribution of prizes at the Royal Academy—silver medals for academic studies from the living model and architectural drawings; gold medals for the best picture, basrelief, and architectural design from given subjects. . . . The President's **"Second Discourse"** was delivered at this ceremony, and is as appropriate to its occasion as the first. In it he proposes to direct the student in his course of study, with a just and modest deprecation of the charge of vanity, on the score of his long experience and constant assiduity. Much of that experience had been purchased, he says, by a series of mistakes; but "the history of error, properly managed, often shortens the road to truth." The chief object of his precepts is "to prevent the misapplication of industry." He divides the student's career into three epochs. In the first he has to acquire "the language of his art"—the power of drawing, modelling, and using colours with some degree of correctness. In the second, he is to endeavour "to collect subjects for expression—to amass a stock of ideas." The whole of preceding art is now to be his master; but he must still be afraid of trusting his own judgment, and of deviating into any track in which he cannot find the footsteps of some former master.

In the third epoch he is to trust his own judgment, to consider and separate the principles of different modes of beauty. As, in the preceding stage, he ought to know and combine all excellences; in this he is "to learn to discriminate incompatible perfections." From this stage onwards he is a master. Instead of comparing works of art with each other, he is to test art itself by nature, and may now first try the power of his imagination.

Here I may pause to ask the question, how the combination of excellences can be prior to the discrimination of incompatible perfections? It seems to me that the second process involves the third: nor can I see how the student is to understand excellences and defects in art at all, except by use of that test of nature which he is only to employ, according to Sir Joshua, after passing his third stage.

We now return to the second stage—to show the readiest path that leads to distant excellence.

"A great part of every man's life," Sir Joshua insists, "must be spent in collecting materials for the exercise of genius. Invention is little but new combination. Nothing can come of nothing. Hence the necessity for acquaintance with the works of your predecessors." But of these, who are to be models—the guides? The answer is, "Those great masters who have travelled with success the same road."

Here again I would pause to point out that this course implies the need of a long study of previous masters, before nature is ventured upon. But no account is taken of those varieties of character and temperament, which must make the masters, whose study is invaluable to one man, comparatively valueless to another. How is the nature, attuned to Teniers and Ostade, to profit by Raphael and Michael Angelo? Perhaps Reynolds would have answered such an objection by giving permission to the student to choose his masters and models according to his bent—on condition that he chose those of long established excellence in the particular line. But I do not think any sufficient recognition of this right will be found in the *Discourses.*

The President goes on, in his considerations of modes of study, very wisely to condemn the practice of general and finished copying. Even colouring, he points out, may be better learned by close observation than by attempts at imitating. To acquire the art of colouring he sends the student to nature, but only "after he has clearly and distinctly learned (from pictures) in what good colouring consists."

Then follow suggestions as to the really useful way of copying; to select the best parts and characteristic excellences of the picture copies; instead of copying touches, to copy conceptions (he means modes of conception); instead of treading in other men's footsteps, to labour only to keep in the same road. "Try to imagine how a Michael Angelo or a Raffaele would have conducted themselves, and work yourself into a belief that your picture is to be seen and observed by them. Even enter into a kind of competition with these great masters; paint a subject like theirs; a companion to any work you think a model. Test your own work with the model."

I cannot but think that there reigns through all these recommendations a characteristic fear of leaving the student enough to himself; an exaggerated respect for the old ways of conception and treatment; a failure to recognise the truth that art is multiform, but that the Muse, while ever renascent, never reappears in the body she has once worn and outgrown.

Sir Joshua goes on to recommend a master in style, which he considers the same in painting as in writing; and his choice settles on Ludovico Caracci. He thinks the choice justified by his breadth of light and shadow, his simplicity of colouring, and the solemn effect of his diffused twilight, which he considers better adapted to grave and dignified subjects than "the more artificial" brilliancy of sunshine which enlightens the pictures of Titian.

Here I must say I am stopped short by my inability to understand how "sunshine" can be more artificial than "twilight"—how a habitual dimness is less a trick than a habitual brilliancy—and, trick for trick, why the gloomier and sadder should be supposed better suited to dignified subjects than the brighter and more cheering. Is Titian's *Cornaro Family* less dignified than L. Caracci's *St. Jerome*—the *Assumption* of Venice than the *Transfiguration* of Bologna?

At the risk of the gravest charges of presumption, had I been a hearer of Sir Joshua's I must have protested alike against his choice of a model of style, and his reasons for it. I see in this excessive glorification of the Caracci style the influence of the taste of the time upon the speaker, rather than the conclusion of his *genuine* judgment; and I appeal from the Pall-mall Discourse to the Venetian Notes. I *am sure* that, whatever Sir Joshua's pen might maintain, his whole artistic heart leapt to Titian and Tintoret and Veronese, and flung to the winds, in its enjoyment of their splendour, all the "gravity" and "dignity" of Caraccesque twilight.

To return to the Discourse. No exception can be taken to all that Sir Joshua says of the need of labour to the student. It holds true of the greatest genius, as of the humblest plodder, that "excellence is granted to no man but as the reward of labour." Continual application is the thing. "Let your portcrayon be never out of your hands. Draw till you draw as mechanically as you write. But, on every opportunity, *paint* your studies instead of *drawing* them. Painting comprises both drawing and colouring. The Venetians knew this, and have left few sketches on paper."

Even the crowning lesson of the lecture,—often excepted against, and not altogether true,—if considered *quoad hoc,* as advice given to students, is sound: "Have no dependence on your own genius: if you have great talents, industry will improve them; if you have but moderate abilities, industry will supply their deficiency. Nothing is denied to well-directed labour—nothing is to be obtained without it." This is wholesome doctrine for hearers, whose real powers are still latent or in the germ.

The peroration is admirable.

> I cannot help imagining that I see a promising young painter equally vigilant whether at home or abroad, in the streets or in the fields. Every object that presents itself is to him a lesson. He regards all nature with a view to his profession, and combines her beauties, or corrects her defects. He examines the countenances of men under the influence of passion, and often catches the most pleasing hints from subjects of turbulence or deformity. Even bad pictures themselves supply him with useful documents, and, as Leonardo da Vinci has observed, he improves upon the fanciful images that are sometimes seen in the fire, or are accidentally sketched upon a coloured wall.

A most true and exhilarating description; enough to kindle the young listeners on the benches before the speaker into a glow of wholesome determination and passionate eagerness for work. But it shows us the student in constant perusal of the book of nature. Could the lecturer have pro-

duced any such effect by describing the student poring over pictures? Did Reynolds himself get his marvellous facility, his grace, his life, his happiness of attitude, his truth of character, from study of pictures, or from constantly applied natural powers of keenest observation? Did he not bring to the profitable study of pictures—even at twenty-nine—long and trained habits of observing faces and forms? Was not his study of pictures, in point of fact, only the completion and accompaniment of his study of life, instead of a distinct and preliminary stage of his labour, such as he would make it for all these young men? I fear we must answer, in the affirmative, with Reynolds the painter against Reynolds the discourser on painting. (pp. 336-42)

On the 11th of December [1770] the Gold and Silver Medals adjudged in 1769 by the Council of the Royal Academy were distributed. (p. 370)

The President's **"Third Discourse"** was delivered on occasion of this distribution. This lecture is an expansion of one of his early papers in the *Idler,* on the grand style and the right imitation of nature. In it he warns the student that the mere copying of nature will never produce anything great; that there is something higher than mere imitation; that the great style must be the aim of the painter who would raise and enlarge the conception and warm the heart. Then he attempts to define in what this great style consists, and his conclusion is that "the whole beauty and grandeur of the art consists in being able to get above all singular forms, local customs, particularities, and details of every kind."

So far as this definition means that the painter is to correct nature by herself; to distinguish and reject accidental deficiencies, excrescences, and blemishes from the perfect and normal forms of objects, no exception can fairly be taken to it.

But the President goes further. He maintains that there is a general perfection of beauty which combines all the special perfections of particular types. "The perfection of form is not to be found in the Hercules, the Gladiator, or the Apollo, but in a figure that partakes equally of the activity of the Gladiator, the delicacy of the Apollo, and the strength of the Hercules." But where, the critic is compelled to ask, is such a figure to be found? If found, must it not of necessity be something characterless, insipid, and essentially devoid of vitality?

I venture to think that this notion of a central type of form, to combine all the various graces and perfections of the most opposite characters, is an imagination of the President's generalizing brain, and cannot be practically sought after by the student without risk of falling into that vice which is called "academicism," for want of a better word.

The President goes on to insist upon the necessity of separating the accidental from the essential, "of disregarding all local and temporary ornaments, and looking only on those general habits which are everywhere and always the same." The thoughtful reader again must ask, What habits are these? where are they to be found?

Sir Joshua illustrates his theory of "the neglect of separating modern fashions from the habits of nature," by referring to the absurd effect of pictures which give to Grecian heroes the airs and graces practised in the Court of Louis XIV.

But this is not enough. His argument requires for its support that we should find some means of representing Grecian heroes without the attributes and accidents of Grecian heroic life; that we should paint Achilles, not as Homer describes him, complete in accoutrements and dress, in habits, accomplishments, and ways of life, but in some "general" dress and with some "general" accompaniments and belongings which belong to no time in particular and to all times alike. I confess that such an abstract Achilles is to me just as difficult of comprehension as Martinus Scriblerus's abstract Lord Mayor.

I think it must be admitted by all unprejudiced minds that Mr. Ruskin's criticism on this theory of Sir Joshua's,—which makes the essential characteristic of the grand style to be the avoidance of temporary and local circumstances and precise details—is sound and searching [see excerpt dated 1843], and that his own definition of the grand style is as much superior to that of Sir Joshua in comprehensiveness and sound philosophy as it is in the eloquence of its expression.

Mr. Ruskin defines the grand style by four characteristics:—

1st. Choice of noble subject.

2nd. Introduction into the conception of the subject of as much beauty as is consistent with truth.

3rd. Inclusion of the largest possible quantity of truth in the most perfect possible harmony.

4th. Inventiveness: that is, the work must be produced by the imagination.

The direction of the President's reasoning may however be at once explained, and in some degree justified, by the fact that he was speaking at a time when very low and unworthy ideas on art prevailed, and when there was a tendency to prize works of minute and puerile imitation far beyond their true value.

Sir Joshua's **"Third Discourse,"** if read as a protest against the undue exaltation of the petty and trivial in detail, is full of useful warning and guidance to the student.

He expressly guards himself against the charge of depreciating good works in styles below the highest.

> None of them . . . are without their merit, though none enter into competition with this universal presiding idea of the art. The painters who have applied themselves more particularly to low and vulgar characters, and who express with precision the various shades of passion as they are exhibited by vulgar minds (such as we see in the works of Hogarth), deserve great praise; but as their genius has been employed on low and confined subjects, the praise which we give must be as confined as its object. The merrymakings or quarrellings of the boors of Teniers, the same sort of productions of Brouwer or Ostade, are excellent in their kind, and the excellence and its praise will be in proportion as in their limited subjects and peculiar forms they introduce more or less of the expression of those passions as they appear in *general* and more *enlarged* nature. This principle may be applied to the battle-pieces of Bourgognone, the French gallantries of Watteau, and, even beyond the exhibition of animal life, to the landscapes of Claude Lorraine and the sea-

views of Vandevelde. All these painters have, in general, the same right, in different degrees, to the name of a painter which a satirist, an epigrammatist, a sonnetteer, a writer of pastorals or descriptive poetry, has to that of a poet.

We may surely ask, on this, what would be the worth of any definition of poetry which should exclude from the rank of poet Horace, Juvenal, Dryden, Theocritus, Thomson, and Wordsworth? Sir Joshua, in fact, throughout his Discourse, confines the name of painter to the painter of one class of subjects only—the high historical and religious: or what he calls "the great mode of painting." To hold this up as an object of pursuit to all students alike, whatever their bent or calibre, may be in a certain sense the best mode of dignifying the art; but I must be excused for doubting if it be the most profitable and soundest teaching. (pp. 370-75)

"The Fourth Discourse" was delivered, as usual, at the distribution of premiums, on the 10th of December [1771].

Its main purpose is to show that generality ennobles art; particularity debases it. The concluding paragraph sums up the argument.

> On the whole . . . it seems to me that there is but one presiding principle which regulates and gives stability to every art. The works, whether of poets, painters, moralists, or historians, which are built upon general nature, live for ever; while those which depend for their existence on particular customs and habits, a partial view of nature, or the fluctuations of fashion, can only be coeval with that which first raised them from obscurity. Present time and future may be considered as rivals, and he who solicits the one must expect to be discountenanced by the other.

A consolatory reflection this for unsuccessful men,—a sentence which has given comfort to many a baffled and hungry votary of High Art. It seems to me, however, that this doctrine of the President's, like many of the doctrines in his *Discourses,* is inexactly stated. The truth of the matter is that the greatness of Art does not depend on expressing general ideas and neglecting personal, local, and minute ones,—for by this road we only get to Martinus Scriblerus's abstract Lord Mayor—but on expressing the largest possible amount of enduring truth and beauty in the particular form or subject chosen.

Thus limited, Sir Joshua's doctrine is sound; taken as he expresses it, it is utterly inconsistent with the facts of the case. Is not Homer minute, local, and personal? Does he "generalize" the armour, the dress, the meals, the battles of his heroes,—he who paints every figure on the shield of Achilles; who shows us his warriors arming, and dressing, garment by garment, piece by piece, from the triple cone of horsehair to the burnished greaves, not sparing us a fold, a thong, or a buckle; who gives us the very dishes of Achilles's bill of fare; the ingredients in Machaon's medicine for flesh wounds; the name of every ship in the fleet; the force of every contingent in the hosts; the order and names of the fruit-trees and beds of Alcinous's garden; the particulars of Nausicaa's family-wash, and the game at romps that followed it; every detail of the foot-bath of Odysseus? Why, Homer is full of the most trivial details. . . . What makes it a great work is not its generalization, but the penetration, precision, and insight with which the minutest facts of the particular history have been looked into, the force with which they have been grasped, the vigour and life with which they have been reproduced. The lessons of the history may be useful and applicable to the end of time, but this in no way affects the fact that they are involved in deductions from a special set of occurrences transacted on a narrow theatre, and most minutely recorded.

The certain effect of this holding up of "general ideas" as the test and *"differentia,"* or special characteristic, of High Art, was to make "High Art" empty, academic, and lifeless; to kill it, far more certainly than it could be killed by any amount of Dutch literalness or Venetian ornament.

So far as the tendency of this part of his teaching goes, or has gone, I cannot but think Sir Joshua's **Discourses** among the unsafest of all guides to the student. I should like to see an appendix of limitations and cautions bound up with every copy of the book given away by the Academy to the winners of its medals. The best thing to be said for it is that the President's teaching, however misdirected, tends, as I have said already, undeniably upwards. (pp. 419-22)

In short, I find myself protesting, with the most thorough heartiness of conviction, against almost every deduction of this **"Fourth Discourse."** I am satisfied, and I believe every intelligent person conversant with the facts of art will be satisfied, by a careful and unbiassed reading of it, that Sir Joshua was led away by his adhesion to the untenable theory that *the Grand* style of art is to be attained by seeking the "general," and sinking the "individual;" the truth—which had served as the germ of this theory—being, that "the Grand style" in art depends on the degree in which its productions embody dignity, truth, beauty, and invention, consistently with their subjects. (pp. 425-26)

His **"Fifth Discourse"** was delivered, as usual, at the Distribution of Premiums on the 10th of December [1772]. Inasmuch as it involves less sweeping theory than the fourth, it is sounder and safer. He begins by insisting on the great circumspection necessary in any attempt to unite excellences, lest they should prove mutually destructive. And here he refutes one of the unsound deductions of his own **"Third Discourse."** There he told the student that the perfection of human form was "not to be found in the Hercules, nor in the Gladiator, nor in the Apollo; but in that form which is taken from all, and which partakes equally of the activity of the Gladiator, of the delicacy of the Apollo, and of the muscular strength of the Hercules." In this **"Fifth Discourse"** he warns the student that "the attempt to unite contrary excellences—of form for instance—in a single figure, can never escape degenerating into the monstrous but by sinking into the insipid, by taking away its marked character, and weakening its expression."

So, instead of now telling the students to aim only at the highest, to set themselves to trial measurements of their conceptions against Raphael and Michael Angelo, they are recommended "to try themselves, whenever they are capable of that trial, what they can, what they cannot do; and instead of dissipating their natural faculties over the immense field of possible excellence, to choose each some particular walk in which he may exercise all his powers, so as to become each the first in his way." Now, too, it

seems to have occurred to Sir Joshua on reflection that in his last year's Discourse he had too harshly severed the ornamental from the grand style. He admits that "the principles of the ornamental style may be cautiously employed in softening the harshness and mitigating the rigour of the grand style as it was employed by Ludovico Caracci." Sir Joshua then proceeds to point out that the greater excellency of the great masters will be found in their frescoes. His teaching on this point only needs the fuller illustration it would have derived from a closer acquaintance with the frescoes of the century before Raphael, and a recognition, which is not to be found in the **Discourses,** of the double function, decorative and instructional, of those noble works which clothed the churches, and chapels, the cloisters, and cemeteries of Northern and Central Italy with the purest splendours of colour and the most vivid representations of God's dealing with mankind.

Then follows an elaborate and often-quoted comparison of Raphael and Michael Angelo; and then, from the grand style, of which they are the highest exemplars, the lecturer passes to what he calls the "original" or characteristical style, *i.e.* the style impressed less with elevated character than with the special spirit of the master; exemplified by opposites in Salvator Rosa and Carlo Maratti, in Rubens and Poussin. Lastly, the student is warned to be as select in those whom he endeavours to please as in those whom he endeavours to imitate. (pp. 462-64)

On the 10th of December [1774] the medals were awarded as usual, when Mr. James Jeffreys carried off the gold medal for painting (subject, 'Seleucus and Stratonice'); and Charles Banks for sculpture (subject, 'Pygmalion'). (p. 91)

On the same day Sir Joshua delivered his **"Sixth Discourse."** The subject was "Pictorial imitation—the following of other masters, and the advantage to be drawn from the study of their works." Sir Joshua insists, characteristically and soundly, that a painter must of necessity be an imitator of the works of other painters, just as much as an imitator of the works of nature. (pp. 91-2)

But in recommending imitation and study of other men's works, it is not meant that such works are to be copied; nor is nature to be neglected. "Nature is, and must be, the fountain which alone is inexhaustible, and from which all excellences must originally flow." (p. 93)

The following passage is quoted, as exactly describing Sir Joshua's own method of studying and using the works of his predecessors:—

> The sagacious imitator does not content himself with merely remarking what distinguishes the different manner or genius of each master; he enters into the contrivance in the composition, how the masses of lights are disposed, the means by which the effect is produced, how artfully some parts are lost in the ground, others boldly relieved, and how all these are mutually altered and interchanged, according to the reason and scheme of the work. He admires not the harmony of colouring alone, but examines by what artifice one colour is a foil to its neighbour. He looks close into the tints, examines of what colours they are composed, till he has formed clear and distinct ideas, and has learned to see in what harmony and good colouring consists. What is learned in this manner from the works of

others becomes really our own, sinks deep, and is never forgotten; nay, it is by our seizing on this clue, that we proceed forward, and get further and further in enlarging the principles, and improving the practice of our art.

There cannot be sounder advice than this, for here Sir Joshua was speaking from his own experience, not generalizing in the development of a thesis.

Excellent remarks follow on "manner," as being generally the result of defects, and not to be imitated: on the danger of falling into a worship even of mannerism by studying only one school, or one master: with a well-chosen list of servile and one of more liberal imitators.

When the student has collected materials by diligent study of the arts, from these sources, the fire of his own genius, working on these materials, is to produce new combinations—illustrated by the well-known image of the Corinthian brass.

The President then addresses himself to another and more special kind of imitation,—"the borrowing a particular thought, an action, attitude, or figure, and transplanting it into your own work. This will either come under the charge of plagiarism, or be warrantable and deserve commendation, according to the address with which it is performed." All this part of the Discourse must be read as Sir Joshua's plea for his own practice, which was vehemently assailed by his brother painters and the critics. He has certainly the best of the argument, and his own adaptations of the ideas of other painters were exact illustrations of what he here says: "Such imitation is so far from having anything in it of the servility of plagiarism, that it is a perpetual exercise of the mind, a continual invention."

Sir Joshua then points out how wide the field of such imitation is—how bad as well as good work may be fruitful of suggestions—how the student may "pick up from dunghills what, by a true chemistry, passing through his own mind, shall be converted into gold; and how under the rudeness of Gothic essays he will find original, rational, and even sublime inventions."

From this point of view he reviews the different schools, and shows what each will furnish of peculiar merit for the student's use. All this part of the Discourse shows the soundness of his taste and the essential catholicity of his judgment, when not warped or fettered by theory. This is especially shown by his remarks on Watteau and Jan Steen, in which he does justice to the grace of the one, and the strength, sagacity, and penetration of the other.

He sums up his plea for catholicity of study, and the universal right of appropriation, in a noble passage:—

> To find excellences, however dispersed; to discover beauties, however concealed by the multitude of defects with which they are surrounded; can be the work only of him who, having a mind always alive to his art, has extended his views to all ages and to all schools, and has acquired from that comprehensive mass which he has thus gathered to himself a well-digested and perfect idea of his art, to which everything is referred. Like a sovereign judge and arbiter of art, he is possessed of that presiding power which separates and attracts every excellence from every school; selects both from what is great and what is little; brings home knowledge

from the east and from the west; making the universe tributary towards furnishing his mind, and enriching his works with originality and variety of inventions.

> Thus I have ventured to give my opinion of what appears to me the true and only method by which an artist makes himself master of his profession; which, I hold, ought to be one continued course of imitation that is but to cease with his life.

There has never been bolder or better pleading for eclecticism. But it is impossible not to feel in every part of this Discourse, that, however true as a description of the formation of an accomplished artist, it is *not* a description of the working of creative genius. (pp. 93-6)

At the distribution of the prizes for the year, on the 10th of December [1776], the President delivered his **"Seventh Discourse."** Its argument is directed to prove the reality of a standard of taste, as well as of corporal beauty; taste being the power of distinguishing right from wrong applied to works of art, and taste, united with the power of execution, constituting genius. What can we say of a definition of genius which excludes the imaginative power altogether? Led away, as usual, by his generalizing tendency, Sir Joshua in this part of his argument entirely confounds things so fundamentally distinct as science and fine art, when he ventures on the assertion that "it is the very same taste which relishes a demonstration in geometry that is pleased with the resemblance of a picture to an original, and touched with the harmony of music." "Truth," he says, "is the object of the mind's natural appetite; and truth may be found in the agreement or equality of original ideas among themselves (geometric), from the agreement of the representation of any object with the thing represented (pictorial), or from the correspondence of the several parts of any arrangement with each other (musical)."

It follows, if this be so, that wherever truth of representation is found taste will be gratified. The proposition only needs to be thus stated to be rejected. But "besides real truth," says the President, "there is apparent truth, opinion, or prejudice. In proportion as this is generally diffused and long received, the taste which conforms to it approaches nearer the taste which conforms to truth. Thus opinions are a kind of truth upon sufferance. In proportion as they are local and transitory, they recede from truth." In trying to grasp the exact connexion of Sir Joshua's argument—not an easy matter always—I find that he infers the fixity of rules of taste from the fixity of what he calls "the general idea of nature." I confess I cannot succeed in grasping the meaning of this phrase. "Beauty and nature," I am told, a few sentences farther on, "are different modes of expressing the same thing." "Deformity is not nature, but an accidental deviation from her accustomed practice." We are told that it is a sad misapplication of terms to praise Rembrandt and the Dutch painters for nature. "How can particularities, such as they paint, be nature, when no two individuals are the same in them?" The conclusion is deduced that "a work is in good or bad taste according as it is produced under the influence of general or partial ideas."

When I ask myself as to the practical effect of this teaching, I must confess I can get no satisfactory answer. Admitting—which is much—that there is such a thing as "general nature" in form, how am I to look for it in individual character, in dress, or in manners? Is art to be debarred the use of these? It seems to me that this is the conclusion to which Sir Joshua's doctrine forces us; and that art which records contemporary events, or strives to call up the past as it was, has no place within the limits of the theory which underlies this lecture, and, indeed, the whole of the *Discourses.* The President seems to have felt this, if somewhat dimly, as he follows out his chain of reasoning, and he is forced to admit that there is a taste which hits on what is right in what he calls "ornament" in art, *i.e.* such secondary matters as dress in men and women, and colouring, in the requisites of a picture. I may pause to direct attention to this undervaluing of colour in comparison with form, which is not more strenuously insisted on by Sir Joshua's theory than it is contradicted by his practice. In these matters the President maintains the duty of respecting long-established associations. They may even acquire, he says, such a stability and spread as to approximate to laws of general nature. As examples, the President insists on the propriety of putting the statues of great men into the classical dress, ignoring altogether the commemorative or historical value of all records of dress or equipment. His theory on the subject of dress-portraiture is in accordance with his frequent, though—happily, as I think—not his constant practice.

> He, therefore, who in his practice of portrait-painting wishes to dignify his subject—which we will suppose to be a lady—will not paint her in the modern dress, the familiarity of which alone is sufficient to destroy all dignity. He takes care that his work shall correspond to those ideas and that imagination which he knows will regulate the judgment of others, and therefore dresses his figure something with the general air of the antique, for the sake of dignity, and preserves something of the modern, for the sake of likeness.

I imagine that most lovers of Reynolds's pictures will agree with me in thinking that his most beautiful, as well as most interesting, portraits are precisely those in which he has admitted least of the general air of the antique, and adhered most closely to the fashions of his time.

The following passage is characteristic in its cautious good sense: "Whoever would reform a nation, supposing a bad taste to prevail in it, will not accomplish his purpose by going directly against the stream of their prejudices."

With a good deal of sound and well-expressed incidental remark, this Discourse seems to me one of the vaguest and least satisfactory of the series. (pp. 169-72)

At the meeting for the distribution of prizes, on the 10th of December [1778], Sir Joshua delivered his **"Eighth Discourse."** Its argument is directed to prove that the Principles of Art, whether poetry or painting, have their root in the mind: in our love of novelty, variety, and contrast, which, however, in their excess become defects. A moderation is to be observed between variety and unity, between profusion of ornament and nakedness, between simplicity and exuberance. Throughout this is an excellent lecture. It contains hardly any of that dangerously broad generalization which was Reynolds's rock ahead, and is eminently practical in character. It puts with great clearness the distinction between principles and rules. In what is said of portraiture, nothing can be better than the contrast between the turgid flutter of Rigaud and the grand simplicity of Titian. There is an admission that in the earlier Discourses the President had undervalued the ornamental part of the art, but he explains: "I said then what I thought it was right at that time to say. I supposed the disposition of young men more inclinable to splendid negligence than perseverance in laborious application to acquire correctness; and therefore did as we do in making what is crooked straight; by bending it the contrary way, in order that it may remain straight at last." "The painter must add grace to strength, if he desire to secure the first impression in his favour." "There are some rules whose absolute authority, like that of our nurses, continues no longer than while we are in a state of childhood." "The various modes of composition are infinite. . . . Whatever mode of composition is adopted, every variety and licence is allowable. This only is indisputably necessary, that to prevent the eye from being distracted and confused by a multiplicity of objects of equal magnitude, these objects, whether they consist of lights, shadows, or figures, must be disposed in large masses, and groups properly varied and contrasted; that to a certain quantity of action a proportioned space of plain ground is required; that light is to be supported by sufficient shadow; and, we may add, that a certain quantity of cold colour is necessary to give value and lustre to the warm colours." In this lecture occurs the dictum which Gainsborough is always said to have defied in his 'Blue Boy' painted the year after this. "It ought, in my opinion, to be indispensably observed that the masses of light in a picture be always of a warm mellow colour, yellow, red, or a yellowish white; and that the blue, the grey, or the green colours be kept almost entirely out of these masses, and be used only to support and set off these warm colours; and for this purpose a small proportion of cold colours will be sufficient." It is worth noting that this remark (certainly too sweepingly expressed) occurs in a lecture intended to guard students against attaching too much weight to rules. Gainsborough may have thought it well to show by an example that Sir Joshua's doctrine might be pushed further. The concluding remarks of the lecturer, questioning the right of Timanthes to the praise that has been generally given him for concealing the face of Agamemnon in his picture of the 'Sacrifice of Iphigenia,' derive additional significance from the fact that this was the subject of the year's competition in painting. Probably all the students had followed the practice of the Rhodian painter. To them was addressed the last sentence of the lecture: "If difficulties overcome make a great part of the merit of art, difficulties evaded can deserve but little commendation." (pp. 225-27)

On the 10th of December [1780] at the distribution of prizes, Sir Joshua delivered his **"Tenth Discourse"**—on Sculpture. It must, I think, be rated low among his Discourses, and shows a very inadequate conception of the subject. It opens with the assumption that sculpture has but one style, an assertion which will astonish students of the Gothic and Renaissance, from the works of the Pisans, and the French cathedral sculptors, down to the workers in terra-cotta and marble, who have flung their wealth of invention so lavishly into the chapels and cloisters of the Certosa. The lecture has its value, however, as showing, by its elaborate exposure of the faults of Bernini and the Flamboyant school, how much Reynolds feared the influence of Roubiliac, the cleverest representative of that style, on our few students of sculpture. The Discourse is not unsound in its criticism of this most vicious school. It insists, well and wisely, on correctness and perfection of form as the essential points of the sculptor's art; and pronounces the perfection of that art to be reached when to these are added grace, dignity, and appropriate expression. But between the Antique and Bernini there might, for all that appears in this Discourse, have been no sculpture whatever. Even the sight of casts from the Gates of Ghiberti, on the walls of the lecture-room, only suggests to Sir Joshua a remark on the deficiency of their light and shadow. Of the works of the Pisan school; of the profuse invention of those nameless men who in the thirteenth and fourteenth centuries filled the porches and niches of the cathedrals of England, France, Germany, and Italy with their fair, or quaint, or sublime creations; of the abounding fancy and luxurious wantonings of Renaissance imagination; even of the power of Michael Angelo, there is not a word in this Discourse. It is scarcely necessary to add that the whole historical side of sculpture is ignored. The decisive condemnation of modern dress for statues is not to be wondered at. It was not many years since West's Death of Wolfe had been considered a daring innovation, if not quite below the dignity of history-painting; history-sculpture was even more dignified. Sir Joshua had probably in his mind the statue of the Duke of Cumberland in Berkeley Square when he solemnly says, "In this town may be seen an equestrian statue in a modern dress, which may be sufficient to deter future artists from any such attempt." It is odd that Charles I. at Charing-Cross did not occur to him, on the other side. Had he not seen, too, Verocchio's mighty Colleoni at Venice, on his great horse, "in his armour as he lived"? Time has decided dead against the President. No sculptor now would ever think of clothing a monumental statue in any but the dress of the wearer's time, country, and calling. (pp. 310-12)

On the 10th of December [1782] the **"Eleventh Discourse"** was delivered on the distribution of the prizes. It is an attempt, certainly not successful, to define pictorial genius; and the general upshot of the argument is, that this consists "in the power of expressing what employs the pencil, as a whole." "A nice discrimination of minute circumstances and a punctilious delineation of them, whatever excellences it may have"—and Sir Joshua does not detract from them—"can never confer upon the artist the character of genius." This is, in effect, the presentation from another point of view of the theory more fully elaborated in the **"Third"** and **"Fourth Discourses,"** that "the grand style" consists in the avoidance of detail; and I must refer my readers to the reasons given in my analysis of those Discourses against the lecturer's conclusions. Walpole (writing to Mason) mentions this Discourse

> as, *entre nous*, rather an apology for, or an avowal of, the object of his own style, that is, effect or impression on all sorts of spectators. This lesson will rather do hurt than good to his disciples, and make them neglect all kind of finishing. Nor is he judicious in quoting Vandyke, who at least specified silks, satins, velvets. Sir Joshua's draperies represent clothes, never their materials. Yet more: Vandyke and Sir Godfrey Kneller excelled all painters in hands; Sir Joshua's are seldom even tolerably drawn [see excerpt dated 1783].

He further exemplifies his objections by reference to the pictures of Lord Richard Cavendish and the three Ladies Waldegrave.

There is good ground for this criticism. But it is unfair, I think, to charge Sir Joshua with accommodating his theory to his practice. He rather squared his practice to his theory. The slightness of his work in his portraits might plausibly be attributed to haste and eagerness to get money; but when we find the same exaggerated breadth degenerating into emptiness in the works on which he wished to found his reputation as a historical painter, as, for example, the Ugolino, it must be admitted that he was working on a principle in this respect. It seems to me that the practical result in his pictures is as damaging to the theory as the arguments in its support are unsound. We ought, however, carefully to distinguish the masterly facility often seen in Sir Joshua's pictures from the calculated emptiness visible in so much of the Ugolino. (pp. 386-87)

On December the 10th [1784], at the distribution of the prizes, the **"Twelfth Discourse"** was delivered. The theme is the education of the artist. I have little doubt that the motive which determined Sir Joshua's choice of subject was Barry's fierce attack on him as a feeble plagiarist in his pamphlet on the Adelphi pictures. The Discourse might be called a defence of invention at secondhand. It begins with a sensible estimate of the value of prescribed methods of study, and points out the obvious truth, that the minds of men are so differently constituted that it is impossible to prescribe one method for all. This thesis is worked after Sir Joshua's generalising fashion, till the argument resolves itself into this (something like Omar's for the burning of the Alexandrian Library)—"It is of no use to prescribe to those who have no talents; and those who have talents will find methods for themselves." "The most skilful master can do little more than put the clue into the hands of his scholar by which he must conduct himself." He cautions the indolently disposed not to allow their natural supineness to master them, under the guise of fastidious love of method; those of ready invention against too easy contentment with first thoughts. Rapid sketching is very well; but the artist must not rest there. He must correct from nature, and *"look about him for whatever assistance the works of others will afford him."* This opens the way to what I conceive the main purpose of the Discourse, a defence of the practice of borrowing, and a distinction between the "theft" that is felonious in art, and the "appropriation" that is not only excusable, but praiseworthy. The description of pictorial practice is no doubt founded on Sir Joshua's own way of working. When the painter sits down to his work (he says), he starts with the knowledge of the figure, the general principles of composition, and a view in his mind's eye of the effect of his masses and light and shadow. All this belongs to his conception of his design as a whole.

> It is a subsequent consideration to determine the attitude and expression of individual figures. It is in this period of his work that I would recommend to every artist to look over his portfolio or pocketbook, in which he has treasured up all the happy inventions, all the extraordinary and expressive attitudes, that he has met in the course of his studies; not only for the sake of borrowing from those studies whatever may be applicable to his own work, but likewise on account of the great advantage he will derive by bringing the ideas of great art-

ists more distinctly before his mind, which will teach him to invent other figures in a similar style.

(pp. 462-64)

All that follows in the Discourse is a defence of the practice of borrowing. Raffaele borrowed from Masaccio. *He did not consider the practice disgraceful, for the source of his two St. Pauls and his 'Thoughtful Listener' was in the Brancacci Chapel at Florence, open to all. Raffaele did not steal from poverty, but from the value he set on the thing stolen,* "enriching the general store with materials of equal or of greater value than that which he had taken." "Such men," he concludes, with direct reference doubtless to the tone of Barry's strictures, "surely need not be ashamed of that friendly intercourse which ought to exist among artists, of receiving from the dead and giving to the living, and perhaps to those who are yet unborn." (pp. 464-65)

Sir Joshua everywhere inculcates reverence for Nature and constant resort to her.

> I have heard painters acknowledge—though in that acknowledgment no degradation of themselves was intended—that they could do better without Nature than with her; or, as they expressed themselves, *that it only put them out.* A painter with such ideas and such habits is, indeed, in a most hopeless state. The art of seeing nature, or, in other words, the art of using models, is in reality the great object, the point to which all our studies are directed. He who recurs to nature at every recurrence renews his strength. The rules of art he is never likely to forget; they are few and simple; but nature is refined, subtle, and infinitely various, beyond the power and retention of memory; it is necessary, therefore, to have continual recourse to her. In this intercourse there is no end of his improvement; the longer he lives the nearer he approaches to the true and perfect idea of art.

So ends the Discourse; and its conclusion may be dwelt on as proving that pre-eminent respect for nature, which in Sir Joshua struggled with what the feeling of the present day is likely to condemn as an overweening respect for earlier art, and undue licence in appropriation from it. Had Sir Joshua been less of a portrait-painter, I doubt not he would have been still more of a plagiarist. Happily his enforced resort to actualities—due to that which Barry so scorned and grieved over, the predominance of portraiture in English painting of that day—preserved him from the Correggiosity of Correggio, and the Raffaelism of Raffaele, into which he has fallen in his few sacred compositions, and would have fallen more and more, had he not been preserved by contact with the living men and women whose portraits he painted. (pp. 466-67)

> *Charles Robert Leslie and Tom Taylor, in their* Life and Times of Sir Joshua Reynolds, *Vols. I & II,* John Murray, 1865, 532 p., 646 p.

F. S. Pulling (essay date 1880)

[*An English historian, Pulling wrote biographies of Reynolds and the Marquis of Salisbury. In the following excerpt from his life of Reynolds, originally published in 1880, he favorably describes the style and tone of the Discourses.*]

A word as to [Reynolds's] style. There is a clearness and perspicuity about it which enables us at once to perceive the drift of his remarks; he does not conceal himself in a dense mass of verbiage, nor does he write ambiguously, hinting at this and suggesting that, but arrow-like goes straight to his point. Withal, there is no baldness; every sentence is carefully constructed, and there are everywhere marks of the *labor limæ;* perhaps here and there it savours somewhat too much of elaboration. Still, it is a very graceful style; just what we should expect from a cultured, well-tempered mind,—scholarly without pedantry, easy without vulgarity. He is of course tainted somewhat with the classical heresy, and often uses a trisyllable where we should prefer a monosyllable, or a word of Latin origin in preference to one of native English growth. But for a man who had lived so much in Johnson's society, he is no great sinner in this respect; and all is so natural and so unaffected, that we are certain it was done, not out of a desire to parade his learning, but simply because it was the ordinary style of the time.

His matter is as pleasant as his manner. No trace of that lofty superiority, that assumption of infallibility, which the critic generally thinks it necessary to put on, is to be found in Reynolds. His own views he puts forward as being in his opinion the right ones, not as the *only* ones it is possible to hold. He is severe on pretenders, on sham connoisseurs, but the severity is always tempered with a playful banter or a half-excuse. And his opinions are those of a sensible, unprejudiced man: he has his favourites among the old masters, but he respects every great name. Fault-finding is not his *forte,* and often we find him touching lightly on errors and defects, only to pause over the excellences of the artist he is criticising. His advice to students is, I should conceive, most valuable and practical; but of this I have really no means of judging. It seems, however, to me, that having rescued English Art from the degradation in which he found it, his great object in his *Discourses* was to prevent its ever sinking to that state again. (pp. 100-01)

> *F. S. Pulling, in his* Sir Joshua Reynolds, *1880. Reprint by Sampson Low, Marston, Searle, & Rivington, 1886, 116 p.*

Edmund Gosse (essay date 1884)

[*A distinguished English literary historian, critic, and biographer, Gosse wrote extensively on seventeenth- and eighteenth-century English literature. His commentary in* Seventeenth-Century Studies *(1883),* A History of Eighteenth Century Literature *(1889),* Questions at Issue *(1893), and other works is generally regarded as sound and suggestive. Gosse is also credited with introducing the works of Norwegian dramatist Henrik Ibsen and other Scandinavian writers to English readers. In the following excerpt from the preface to his 1884 edition of the* Discourses, *Gosse defends the essays' importance, placing them in the historic context of English art criticism.*]

The perspicuous and graceful *Discourses* of Sir Joshua Reynolds have long ago ceased to be held as oracles by the student anxious merely to listen and be taught. Neither the lecturer's facts nor his opinions are authoritative enough to pass unscathed under a modern scrutiny. Comparatively little was known about the history of art in his time, and that little was concealed from him by his ignorance of the German language. His earliest discourse might have gained much from Lessing and from Winckelmann; his latest is just as innocent of the erudition of those writers. He knew nothing about Greek sculpture, nothing about Venetian painting. He passed close by the hiding-places of the great monuments of art, and never suspected their presence. If we allow ourselves to be vexed at this, and to wish he would talk about Giotto when he is speaking to us about Le Sueur, we shall miss what he has to give us. But, on the other hand, we shall fall into an error just as grave if we fail to perceive his limitations and shortcomings.

It is commonly an idle thing to wish that events which lay in one direction had lain in another. Yet we cannot help desiring that Reynolds had read the *Laokoon*. All that was brightest and most sensible in the Englishman would have leaped up to greet the freshness of Lessing's intuition of the principles of art. As it was, the best we can say of Reynolds, merely as a critic, is that he was the most gifted, and the most entertaining of the old dogmatic school. He lived in an age when his great friend Burke, and Spence, the author of *Polymetis,* and that barbarous creature Batty Langley, were the acknowledged authorities on art in England, when criticism of plastic things was nothing more than a sort of empirical æsthetic philosophy. It must be remembered that there was a very great excuse for this. The camel had to be evolved from the traveller's internal consciousness. There was nothing to be seen, no typical collections, no public galleries, no catalogued libraries, no selected museums. (pp. v-vi)

The prestige of a phalanx of allied French critics was still unshaken in the west of Europe. The quaint shades at which Lessing had tiled in the *Laokoon,* Dufresnoy and Caylus, Félibien and De Piles, were still listened to with entire deference. Reynolds, though he girds at them, still regards them with a certain awe. He quotes them with a respect which may mystify our generation, which has entirely forgotten them all. The iniquity of oblivion hath blindly scattered his poppy over the pompous hexameters of the *De Arte Graphica,* and Longinus himself, who was the remote but direct ancestor of all these wordy critics, is no longer looked upon as a practical guide. But there was a reason why Reynolds should regard the French writers on art with more deference than he spared for Spence or for Harris. Like himself, these men had been painters. They were not evolving the laws of æsthetics without having ever seen or painted a picture. Dufresnoy, at least, whom they all followed, had been an industrious, though a singularly unfortunate professional painter; Caylus was not merely a dilettante scribbler of romances and regulations, he was an active and indefatigable etcher, and such men could take refuge from the fallacies of their theories in the practice of their work.

It is to a similar circumstance that the *Discourses* owe their vitality and charm. If Félibien and Dufresnoy had painted better, their notes and their verses on the theory of art might have possessed greater value. In Reynolds the qualities were united which were wanting to those narrow and pedantic Frenchmen. The President of the Royal Academy did not come forward to instruct the students until he had secured a broad reputation as one of the most

superb of modern painters. He spoke, it is true, in the old pedantic accents, or, rather he took for granted the correctness of the old pedantic formulas; but he translated them into the language of a man who had moved among men, and learned the secret of the world. That shrewd analyst of character, Dr. Samuel Johnson, knew what he was saying when he remarked that of all the men he had met Joshua Reynolds was the one who had passed through life with most observation of it. His *Discourses,* like his pictures, show that he did not always comprehend his own limitations. Perceiving his sympathies to be broad, he fancied that they were boundless, and he stumbled over a *Death of Cardinal Beaufort,* or an examination of the laws of bas-relief. When he soared too high, when he put forth his hand and touched the ark of the highest imagination, the fate of Uzzah overtook his work. And this uncertainty about his own limitations, combined with his great and necessary ignorance of the facts of art, is what makes certain pages of this volume powerless to instruct or fire us.

But how few works of the class have borne the attacks of time with so signal a success! The full and eloquent periods have not a little of the suavity which the incomparable pencil of the master possessed, yet we are never conscious of any striving after effect in style. As a lecturer we find Reynolds earnest, courteous, convincing; his images are discreetly chosen, and are almost always apt; his final appeal is ever to that technical experience which no one of his hearers could gainsay. In comparison with the work of his immediate contemporaries, of Burke, of Goldsmith, of Gibbon, his prose is perhaps a little formal, a little wanting in animation. His thought is sometimes veiled by a slight obscurity, and this was, no doubt, what his enemies caught at when they called him Sir Obadiah Twylight, and dubbed his careful style "sub-fusk." But, on the other hand, when he can quite forget his Dufresnoy and his De Piles, and is thinking solely of the eager faces before him, and of the budding Aaron's rod of English art, his dignified sentences attain a clear and almost an impassioned accent. He is thoroughly engaged in brain and hand; his whole heart is bound up in what he is saying, and we listen not merely to a splendid painter or a deep and trained thinker, but to a spirited enthusiast. (pp. vi-ix)

There are many ways in which it would be possible to annotate the *Discourses* of Reynolds. . . . I have also amused myself by transcribing from the British Museum copy of Malone's *Life and Works of Reynolds,* which belonged to William Blake, a few hitherto inedited notes and verses which the famous visionary has scribbled on the margin. In his *Life of Blake* Gilchrist described this curious relic, which he supposed to date from about 1820. I have printed nothing which had already seen the light in the chapter which Gilchrist dedicates to these notes of Blake's. They occur only in the first volume of the work, but they are extremely numerous, disfiguring almost every page. The title contains this quatrain, which I may print, as it has been incorrectly given in both the editions of Gilchrist:—

> Degrade first the Arts if you'd mankind degrade;
> Hire idiots to paint with cold light and hot shade;
> Give high price for the worst, leave the best in disgrace,
> And with Labours of Ignorance fill every place.

That is Blake's final judgment on the *Discourses* of Reynolds, a book with which it was impossible that his transcendental and ill-trained enthusiasm could be in sympathy. To have printed many of his entertaining diatribes would have been to edit Blake under the guise of editing Reynolds, but I hope that the specimens given may amuse, and yet suffice. (pp. x-xi)

> *Edmund Gosse, in a preface to* The Discourses of Sir Joshua Reynolds *by Sir Joshua Reynolds, edited by Edmund Gosse, Kegan Paul, Trench & Co., 1884, pp. v-xi.*

Claude Phillips   (essay date 1894)

[*In the following excerpt, Phillips writes glowingly of Reynolds's literary ability, then describes the key works of Reynolds's career.*]

Nothing is more remarkable in the great career of our master [Reynolds] than the genuine literary ability which he developed by degrees, side by side with, yet quite independently of, his artistic capacity. And we must wonder the more when we remember that he received not more than the education of the average school-boy of his time, and in the course of his well-filled and practically uninterrupted career was unable to supplement early deficiencies by any sustained course of reading or study. We have before us the instance of a mind developed and a talent matured as it were from without, by constant contact with the noblest intellects of the time; with all that was most brilliant and most weighty in the world of literature; most able and most aspiring in the world of statesmanship and politics; most sprightly and most distinguished in the worlds of aristocratic and literary fashion; most fascinating in that world within a world—the stage. (pp. 389-90)

The kernel of his theories may, no doubt, be found in those three short letters to the *Idler,* written in 1759, at the instance of Dr Johnson; but here the writer is at once more absolute and less felicitous in his generalisations, more inclined to paradox in his enunciations, both of theory and of fact, than he becomes later on in the *Discourses.* Moreover, as we pass from the earlier to the later of these, we perceive a marked increase in their literary and didactic value. There becomes evident a very notable desire to correct the occasional excess and exaggeration of statement into which the President of the Royal Academy, addressing its students *ex cathedrâ,* and seeking to underline as strongly as he can the theories and precepts which he inculcates, has been betrayed.

Sir Joshua, as the man of letters, as the theorist and preceptor in the art of which he is, in his own peculiar way, so brilliant a practician, need not be looked for far beyond the *Fifteen Discourses.*

The notes to William Mason's translation of Alphonse Du Fresnoy's *Art of Painting* constitute, however, an excellent supplement to these, with here and there a practical piece of advice to the artist, or a pithy condensation of artistic experience strikingly put; but in general they are at one with the principles more elaborately and with more of oratorical dignity enunciated in the *Discourses.*

So masterly a passage as the following piece of satire, veiled in precept—contained in the painter's note on the line,

'Twas not by words Apelles charm'd mankind,

cannot be passed over in silence:—

> As Fresnoy has condescended to give advice of a prudential kind, let me be permitted here to recommend to the artist to talk as little as possible of his own works, much less to praise them; and this not so much for the sake of avoiding the character of vanity, as for keeping clear of a real detriment; of a real productive cause which prevents his progress in his art, and dulls the edge of enterprise.

> He who has the habit of insinuating his own excellence to the little circle of his friends, with whom he comes into contact, will grow languid in his exertions to fill a larger space of reputation. He will fall into the habit of acquiescing in the partial opinions of a few; he will grow restive in his own; by admiring himself he will come to repeat himself, and then there is an end of improvement. In a painter it is particularly dangerous to be too good a speaker; it lessens the necessary endeavours to make himself master of the language which properly belongs to his art—that of his pencil. This circle of self-applause and reflected admiration is to him the world, which he vainly imagines he has engaged in his party, and therefore supposes that further enterprise becomes less necessary.

This state of things obtains to a far greater extent in our own day than it could possibly have done in Sir Joshua's. His words of wisdom conjure up for us, as vividly as may be, the many little pontiffs, each of a separate artistic religion, complacently snuffing up the fumes of the incense offered them by disciple and imitator, and letting genius pale and wither by too carefully shrouding it from the keen blast of public opinion.

The *Journey to Flanders and Holland in the year 1781* is chiefly remarkable as containing much valuable appreciation and criticism, by an artist of eminence, of his great predecessors among the Flemish masters, and chiefly of Rubens and Van Dyck. It is in the form, not of a sustained work, but of notes on the individual pictures, very many of them still to be found in the same places in which Reynolds inspected them. A word has already been said [in an unexcerpted portion of this book] about the remarkable "Character of Rubens," with which the notes conclude. It is an excellent summing up of the merits and defects of the mighty Antwerper, whom he had avowedly learnt to love and to understand better since he had studied him at his proper home in the churches of Flanders, and in the Dusseldorf Gallery, then enriched with the famous series of pictures by the Flemish master which are now one of the chief glories of the *Alte Pinakothek* of Munich.

There is much here that serves as a corrective to the too extreme pronouncements of the Sir Joshua of the *Discourses* on the "grand style," on the sublimities of Michelangelo, and the rare perfections of the "Bolognian" school, the praises of which he therein so often finds occasion to sing, with an eloquence and an enthusiasm that cannot be other than genuine. Much earlier—at the close of his Italian tour—we find him, with an intuitive sympathy, analysing and commenting on the masterpieces of sixteenth-century Venetian art, with an attention to the relative proportions of light and shade, and to technique generally, such as he had hardly paid, even to the much-worshipped productions of Buonarroti and Sanzio in the

Vatican. Now, again, notwithstanding the strictures and criticisms with which he deems it necessary to qualify his admiration, we see how spontaneous, how ardent is his sympathy with the great Venetian of Flanders.

He loves, and almost fears to love too well, the painter of whom he says, "the effect of his pictures may be not improperly compared to clusters of flowers;" whom, in those final words of his, he appears to be defending, not only against the strictures of others, but against his own in another place:—

> Those who cannot see the extraordinary merit of this great painter, either have a narrow conception of the variety of art, or are led away by the affectation of approving nothing but what comes from the Italian school.

How strangely contrasts with this enthusiasm the curt, dry paragraph devoted by the master to the description of one of the world's noblest works—the "Adoration of the Lamb" of Hubert and Jan van Eyck at Ghent; then seen there in its entirety, and not, as now, despoiled of the wings, which we have to seek out at Berlin and Brussels:—

> In a chapel is a work of the brothers Van Eyck, representing the Adoration of the Lamb, a story from the Apocalypse. It contains a great number of figures in a hard manner, but there is a great character of truth and nature in the heads, and the landskip is well coloured.

This is the "hard, Flemish manner," of which Sir Joshua, even in praise, speaks *disprezzando,* and which Horace Walpole—let it always be remembered to his credit—could appreciate at a moment when in England he was almost alone in so doing.

But it is, after all, to the *Discourses* that we must look for the authoritative statement of Sir Joshua's views on the theory and practice of his art; and none was more keenly aware than himself how little his life-work, supremely succesful as it was, conformed to, or illustrated, those views. At the same time it must be borne in mind that the lectures in question were all—with the exception of the **First** and the **Ninth**—prepared for and delivered to the students of the Royal Academy; that the lecturer accordingly felt bound to enunciate for their benefit, as strongly and definitely as possible, those principles which he judged best calculated to guide and strengthen the pupil in the beginnings of an artistic career. (pp. 390-95)

> *Claude Phillips, in his* Sir Joshua Reynolds, *Charles Scribner's Sons, 1894, 415 p.*

Sir Walter Armstrong   (essay date 1900)

[*Armstrong was a highly respected nineteenth-century Scottish translator, journalist, and art historian. In the following excerpt from a critical biography originally published in 1900, he offers generally dismissive opinions of Reynolds's style and theories. Armstrong also compares Reynolds's style to that of Samuel Johnson and Edmund Burke.*]

The fame of Sir Joshua's *Discourses* is at first sight a little difficult to understand. For a hundred years it has been the fashion to treat them as models of literature and monuments of critical profundity. Their style has been thought

so much too good for their putative author, that the great shades of Burke and Johnson have been descried at Sir Joshua's elbow, controlling his expression and even suggesting his ideas. Again, their reasoning on the foundations of art has been so far accepted by those who ought to know, that they have been put, as a text-book, into the hands of some twenty generations of students. And yet Sir Joshua's style is good only through its sincerity; and his teaching sound only if meant to be superficial. (p. 213)

To us who have the advantage of a distant perspective, it seems extraordinary that any one should ascribe the eminently human, but somewhat invertebrate periods of Sir Joshua first to Johnson and afterwards to Burke. As a writer Reynolds was, of course, an amateur. He had never been drilled in the use of language, or compelled to notice how the practised writer avoids those involutions and cacophonies which spring from the unguarded expression of complex ideas. He piles relative on relative and participle on participle, until his sentences become so long drawn out that we have to read them twice to grasp their meaning. As interpreted by a good speaker, they would, no doubt, be clear enough. Vocal modulations would bring out the sense. But Reynolds, we are told, had a very bad delivery, and so it is not surprising that his colleagues paid him the compliment of a request to print his sermons! . . . Beside Burke and Johnson, Reynolds was a bungling writer, taking a long time to say what he had to say, and showing almost complete ignorance of those contrivances by which the cunning scribe prevents the reader from knowing he is bored. And yet, a century and a quarter old as it is, his prose is strangely fresh. Its easiness is by no means inherent in the subject of which it treats, for even the art critic does not cling, voraciously, to a page of art criticism! To put it frankly, Reynolds is neither profound in induction, nor logical in deduction, nor clear in expression, and yet his *Discourses* have vitality, and successive generations of students have read them with interest, and with a pleasant sense that a real personality strove for expression in their unconvincing periods. As a rule an Englishman of good education takes more interest in poetry, and vastly more interest in politics, than he does in art. And yet I feel pretty sure that more readers work their way through the *Discourses* than through the best works of either Johnson or Burke. Why is this? I believe it to depend on exactly the same instinct as that which makes us prefer the fifteenth century to the sixteenth in Italian painting.

In reading Sir Joshua, we feel that he is inside his subject, groping his way out. His guesses are often unhappy, and lead him to conclusions which are little else than absurd. But there he is, nevertheless, inside, and doing his best to understand his *milieu,* and to get a right conception of the whole matter. His methods of expression are imperfect, and leave us with the idea that his conceptions are too complicated to be rendered in such words as he can command. He who has more imagination than expressive power is more interesting to his fellow creatures than one in whom the proportions are reversed. His striving is a guarantee that he has done his best, and leaves us with a sense of something to be filled in by ourselves. With writers like Burke and Johnson it is different. Their methods are apt to be more complete, as methods, than their ideas are, as ideas. So that instead of being inside their subjects, they are outside, or even detached and a little contemptuous. The kernel of human interest seems to have shrunk away and to be rattling, dry and sapless, within the fine externals of their style. Perfect art, no doubt, demands that imagination and expression shall each rise to the same level, and that style and thought shall be so nearly one that we shall find it difficult to determine where the one leaves off and the other begins. This, however, is a consummation not often reached, and our choice lies, as a rule, between extreme sincerity with more or less halting expression, on the one hand, and less sincerity with greater fluency, on the other. Sir Joshua's *Discourses* belong to the former class.

Before going on to speak of Sir Joshua's æsthetic theories, I must say something about those other writings in which more literary skill is to be found than in the *Discourses.* I mean the two famous *Dialogues.* The short one, especially, in which Sir Joshua attempts to uphold his own and Garrick's importance against the Doctor, is a little masterpiece—dramatic, full of character, and light in touch. The second is nearly as well done, and more pregnant. The two endings show that Reynolds had not been so faithful to Covent Garden and Drury Lane for nothing. The first dialogue is cut off sharply, and yet exactly in the right place, by the angry Johnson; to the second he provided a peroration so vigorous that it makes an excellent "curtain" for both.

The rest of Sir Joshua's writings, whether published or not, are greatly inferior. The character of Johnson is only a rough draft; the three "Idlers" are happy neither in form nor substance; while the *Journal of his Tour in the Netherlands* is only a journal and his notes to Du Fresnoy only notes. As a writer his reputation depends on the fifteen *Discourses* and the two *Dialogues.* The superiority of the latter suggests that he might, had he tried, have made a reputation as a playwright.

Turning to his ideas about art, the first thing to strike us is the remarkable contradiction between his expressed opinions and his own practice. The whole drift of his *Discourses* is towards the promotion of those forms of art which spring from and appeal directly and solely to the reason, over those which excite emotion by the expression of more or less sensuous ideas. I do not think it is putting the matter unfairly to say that Reynolds, the theorist, did all he could to promote the belief that fine art is a question of teaching and a good memory, like spelling; while Reynolds, the painter, spent his energies in showing that all risks may be run for the sake of clothing a pictorial idea in a gorgeous envelope. (pp. 215-20)

In spite of his independence, Reynolds was not an original thinker. He accepted the ideas of his time as the foundation for his own reasoning, and seems to have felt no impulse to go behind, and test their value for himself. It is impossible to believe that the painter of the "Nelly O'Brien," and the "Lord Heathfield" could have felt any sincere emotion before the dry melodrama of Salvator Rosa or the cold futility of Le Sueur. But instead of confessing his indifference, he wasted his mental energies in searching after "rules" by which their hold on fashion and pretence to set a standard might be confirmed. If he had begun by telling the students that the essential part of art was neither to be learnt nor taught, and that all the academy could do was to enable young men to become such masters of their tools that those born to art could step into

visible possession of their birthright, he would have done something to put his theories in their proper place.

The truth is that Sir Joshua, with all his study and introspection, never hit upon a real theory of art at all. His mind took too narrow a sweep. The notion of collating one art with another occurred to him but once, and then he made a most unhappy use of it. It never struck him that a theory of art which might fit a picture but would be absurd if applied to a teapot could not be a universal theory. He never suspected that beneath the whole body of artistic things which man had created lay a deep, solid, and universal foundation on which the beauty of them all was built. He examined phenomena, and when he had collected a certain number of these from famous works of art, he concluded they were the causes of excellence. Raffaelle was great, Raffaelle painted draperies in the abstract, not silks and velvets, *ergo,* abstract draperies are the cause of greatness. In all seriousness that is too often the fashion of Sir Joshua's reasoning. His objective was false and so, of course, was his way of stepping towards it. His aim was not to help the young men who hung upon his words in making the most of any artistic faculties with which nature had endowed them, but to teach them how to produce imitations of the Carracci, at least, if they could not manage Raffaelle and Michelangelo. So far does he sometimes go in this direction that one is almost tempted to believe his teaching insincere, to suspect that he was speaking against his convictions, under the belief that it was better for students to believe that hard work could do everything, than to know the artist is not school-made, but conceived in his mother's womb.

I alluded just now to the one attempt made by Sir Joshua to carry his theories beyond the art of painting. This was in that **"Tenth Discourse,"** in which he spoke of sculpture. A more convincing proof of his inability to step outside the area of his own experience, could scarcely be given. He makes no real attempt to determine the natural æsthetic boundaries which control the modeller. He takes them as already decided by the practice of the ancients and of such moderns as he chooses to admit into their company. "Sculpture has but one style," he declares, and therefore "can only to one style of Painting have any relation." So far as this was true, and even a century ago it was but a partial truth, it was due to the survival of so many masterpieces of ancient art. With these to imitate, men were slow to explore new paths for themselves. Since the days of Reynolds they have done so, with splendid results; and it is not, perhaps, unreasonable to think that an artist of his distinction ought to have foreseen the feasibility of such a new departure. He was blinded, however, by his system. He tested art, not by its own immutable conditions, but by the forms into which accident had led it. All his theorising rests on the assumption that man had nothing more to discover, no new thoughts to express, no changed forms of civilisation to illustrate, no new beliefs to insist upon. He takes one form of the world's art wealth as it existed in his own day, and, instead of attempting to discover the vitalising principle which ran through it all and brought it into line with sister forms, marshals its mere external phenomena into rules to control the new generation, and prevent any future repetition of such free developments as those which make the glory of Greece and Italy. (pp. 221-24)

Sir Walter Armstrong, in his Sir Joshua Reynolds, First President of the Royal Academy, *William Heinemann, 1905, 236 p.*

Lord Ronald Sutherland Gower   (essay date 1902)

[*Gower was a member of Parliament, an art historian, and a trustee of the National Portrait Gallery. In the following excerpt, he emphasizes contradictions he perceives between Reynold's theories and practices as well as contradictions within the individual discourses themselves.*]

Sir Joshua Reynolds' **Discourses** to the Students of the Royal Academy were considered at the time at which they were given as most valuable aids to the study of art. His opinions of certain schools and painters, notably of Correggio and the Carracci brothers, are wholly at variance with the trend of art opinion to-day; and it is surprising that a painter in whose pictures a vivid naturalness constitutes their first charm, should have seen the masterpieces of the early Italian painters with so cold an eye. (p. 128)

Apart from opinions that no longer concern an age in which the general knowledge of art is infinitely wider, and in which opinion is not overshadowed by the pseudoclassicalism of the eighteenth century, these **Discourses** tend in their advice to the perpetuation of mediocrity amongst painters. First comes the advocating of the idea that imagination is superior to Nature as a source of the artist's inspiration, followed by the pronouncement that industry and continual study make the great artist rather than genius: "You must have no dependence on your own genius," says Sir Joshua in his **"Second Discourse"**—that "On the Methods of Study." "If you have great talents, industry will improve them; if you have but moderate abilities, industry will supply their deficiency. Nothing is denied to well-directed labour; nothing is to be obtained without it. Not to enter into metaphysical discussions on the nature or essence of genius, I will venture to assert that assiduity unabated by difficulty, and a disposition eagerly directed to the object of pursuit, will produce effects similar to those which some call the result of natural powers." Such a statement is tantamount to saying that industry alone will produce the works of genius, and, as Hazlitt very justly observes, "Industry alone can only produce mediocrity; but mediocrity in art is not worth the trouble of industry. Genius, great natural powers, will give industry and ardour in the pursuit of their proper object, but not if you direct them from that object into the trammels of common-place mechanical labour. By this method you neutralise all distinction of character—make a pedant of a blockhead, and a drudge of a man of genius."

Sir Joshua himself was a living example of the heights to which genius may attain when aided by unceasing industry; and so unbalanced an opinion as he expresses in this Discourse can surely only have arisen from a belief that his own powers were the outcome of "assiduity," rather than "highly cultivated natural gifts." Throughout the **Discourses** Sir Joshua seems to insist that every great artist has formed himself by the study of the works of his predecessors, and that "the daily food and nourishment of the mind of the Artist must be found in the works of his predecessors;" and "that by imitation only, variety and even originality is produced;" adding, "I will go further: even

genius, at least, what is so-called, is the child of imitation." Yet in speaking of Carlo Maratti, after detailing all the masters of painting at whose feet he sat in whole-souled imitation, Sir Joshua says, "Carlo by diligence made the most of what he had; but there was undoubtedly a heaviness about him, which extended itself uniformly to his invention, expression, his drawing, colouring, and the general effect of his pictures. The truth is, he never equalled any of his patterns in any one thing, and he added little of his own." This description scarcely supports Sir Joshua's assertion that "assiduity will produce effects similar to those which some call the result of natural powers." The President's inconsistency of theory is further shown by his advice to the students to study Nature, after he propounded the idea that "all beauty, grace, and grandeur, are to be found, not in actual Nature, but in an idea existing in the mind." "He who recurs to Nature," he says at the conclusion of the **"Twelfth Discourse,"** "at every recurrence renews his strength. The rules of art he is never likely to forget, they are few and simple; but Nature is refined, subtle, and infinitely various, beyond the power and retention of memory. It is necessary, therefore, to have continual recourse to her. In this intercourse there is no end to his improvement: the longer he lives the nearer he approaches to the true and perfect idea of art."

Happily Sir Joshua's inconsistencies and opposed opinions on art were confined to these **Discourses.** (pp. 128-30)

Lord Ronald Sutherland Gower, in his Sir Joshua Reynolds: His Life and Art, *George Bell and Sons, 1902, 144 p.*

Roger Fry   (essay date 1905)

[*Fry was an English artist, art critic, art historian, and translator who gained fame as an influential theorist and as an advocate of modern art. He was a member of the Bloomsbury Group, which included such artists and authors as Virginia Woolf, Clive Bell, and Lytton Strachey. Inspired by the work of such artists as Paul Cézanne, Vincent van Gogh, and Paul Gaugin, whom he named "postimpressionists," Fry stressed the paramount importance of color and form in art, defining art itself as "meaningless form." He was a versatile scholar whose expertise also included Renaissance art. Fry's edition of the* Discourses, *with critical prefaces to each discourse, was long considered the most important edition of Reynolds's best-known work. In the following excerpt, Fry appraises Reynolds's accomplishment in the* Discourses, *assesses the value of that work for succeeding generations, and then explicates and comments upon each discourse individually, but for the first.*]

The notion that Reynolds as a critic ought to have bound himself within the limits of his own talent as an artist, that he was to recommend others to do no more than he had done himself, is palpably absurd. It is just because he had the gift, an unusual one among artists, of rising to a general view of art as a whole, and of regarding his own performance with objective impartiality, that he is so remarkable as a critic. He was, moreover, intensely optimistic about the future of art in England, and he, therefore, looked forward to a generation which should surpass himself as much, or more, than he had surpassed Hudson and Richardson. That he put before the rising generation ideals higher than he himself could compass is a sign only of his generosity and detachment from personal feelings.

In considering Reynolds as a critic we come to the crucial question of the value of Reynold's *Discourses* for the artist and amateur of to-day. The present edition has been undertaken from a belief that their value still persists, that the *Discourses* are not merely a curious and entertaining example of eighteenth-century literature, but that they contain principles, and exhibit a mental attitude, which are of the highest value to the artist. The artist can make as little use of the pure æsthetics of professed philosophers as the practical engineer can of the higher mathematics; what he requires is an applied æsthetics, and it is rarely indeed that a writer has at once the practical knowledge and the power of generalisation requisite to produce any valuable work in this difficult and uncertain science. Reynolds was one of the first, and he remains one of the best, who have attempted it. He keeps, as a rule, close to the point at which the artist must attack the problems of æsthetics, and he succeeds in proportion as he does so. When he endeavours to find support in abstract philosophical principles he is less happy, though he never fails to be ingenious and suggestive. It results from this—from his approaching the subject with the artist rather than with the philosopher—that his methods will often be found of real value even when the greater knowledge and greater critical insight which our generation may justly claim, invalidate his conclusions.

Reynolds' limitations are obvious enough to us; for him classical sculpture was summed up in the Apollo Belvedere and the Portland Vase, and Italian painting began with Michelangelo and Raphael. To suppose that this argues a lack of critical power on Reynolds' part is unfair; he was the child of his time, and his caution prevented him from venturing on what would have appeared impossible paradoxes to his contemporaries. Rather, one may well be surprised at the many small indications of his appreciation of primitive art. It is not improbable that in his *Discourses* he may have minimised this admiration out of deference to contemporary opinion, for the strongest expressions of it are found in his more intimate notes on a *Journey to Flanders and Holland.* There we find a genuine admiration of Hubert van Eyck's altarpiece at Ghent; and a comparison between Jan van Eyck's altarpiece at Bruges with two heads by Rubens to the disadvantage of the latter. Elsewhere he admires pictures by Pieter Breughel and Quentin Matsys. (pp. ix-xi)

As it is, however, the difference between his survey of art and that which we now command is great enough to make it a question for us how far it destroys the value of his teaching.

The two great discoveries made since Reynolds wrote are the discovery of Greek as opposed to Græco-Roman art, and the discovery of the art of the Middle Ages and early Renaissance. These discoveries both make in the same direction—the discovery of Greek art has dissipated for our eyes the over-blown beauties of that art which kindled the enthusiasm of Winkelmann and Goethe. The discovery of Botticelli and Van Eyck, though it has not lessened our love for Michelangelo, and has hardly interfered with Raphael's fame, has made us unfairly indifferent to the beauties of seventeenth-century Italian art. Moreover, we now recognise the essential kinship between Greek and Gothic sculpture. Classic and Gothic have ceased to be opposites, and the frontier has become one of time rather than place. The degree of development of an art, not the race or the religion that produced it, has become the essential point. Our warmest affections have turned from a later to an earlier stage of that development; we love sincerity and intensity of feeling more than the artifices of a careful rhetoric.

And hence arises a question which must be faced. It is impossible for us to doubt that the beauties we find in Mantegna and Van Eyck are real artistic beauties, and yet most of Reynolds' precepts are directed towards a kind of beauty which is at least very different from theirs, possibly incompatible with it. There runs throughout the *Discourses* a constant appeal to the student to aim, above all, at unity. He is to look with the "dilated eye," to seize the general effect, to avoid all detail which will interfere with this; to subordinate and sacrifice parts, however excellent and expressive in themselves, to this general agreement and coherence of the parts in the whole. Reynolds does not deny that other methods are possible to the artist, as his unstinted praise of Jan Steen declares, but he appears to deny that any other method is compatible with the lofty key of great imaginative art. And in so far as he does this we are bound, I think, to differ from him, and to admit the possibility of another kind of unity, even in the grand style.

There are, in fact, two contending principles in art—one of which makes for richness of content, the other for unity of expression. Some kind of balance between these seems to be necessary for a great work, since, on the one hand, a chaos of unrelated forms, however beautiful in themselves, would distress us by the impossibility of bringing them together; and, on the other hand, a skilfully arranged composition of vapid and meaningless forms could only arouse a languid interest in the artist's dexterity. (pp. xii-xiv)

If, then, Reynolds' value as a critic is not altogether impaired for us by his ignorance of certain aspects of art with which we are now familiar, we shall certainly be ready to admit his value as a teacher. Nor has there ever been a time since their first publication when the main tendencies of his teaching were likely to be better understood than the present. Reynolds' contention was that art was not a mechanical trick of imitation, but a mode of expression of human experience, and one that no civilised human society could afford to neglect; that this expression required for its perfection serious intellectual effort, and that, however diverse the forms it might take, it depended on principles which were more or less discoverable in the great traditions of past masters. He regarded this tradition as embodying, approximately, these fundamental principles somewhat as the actual laws of a country embody the ideals of jurisprudence. Finally, he maintained a belief in the possibility of an organised cooperative advance in the knowledge of these principles of artistic expression comparable in some degree with the advance in scientific knowledge.

That his hopes in these respects have not been fulfilled is no proof that they are altogether vain. There have been times when tradition did secure this community of knowledge, this gradual building up, step by step and generation after generation, of positive acquisitions in the knowledge of how to find artistic expression for feelings and ideas, and there is nothing chimerical in hoping for their recurrence. (pp. xix-xx)

We are tired of a too self-assertive individualism; the cult of genius has passed its climax with the death of Whistler; and we are ready to listen with profit to the sage counsels and constructive policy of Reynolds.

Whether we accept his indications of the laws of artistic expression or not—and he himself would have welcomed investigation and correction—we may at least admit that he remains one of the few writers who have approached the subject from the artist's point of view, and that he more than any other has suggested the lines along which profitable generalisations may be deduced from past experience. The mere belief in the existence of law in an activity which is assigned, by romantic enthusiasts on the one hand, and by contemptuous sceptics on the other, to caprice, is already much, and in that belief Reynolds never faltered. His creed may be defined in Goethe's words: "The genuine law-giving artist strives for artistic truth; the artist who knows no law, but follows a blind inner instinct, strives for natural verisimilitude." (p. xxi)

The **"Second Discourse"** is devoted to giving the student his proper orientation in the domain of art. Reynolds shows alike his knowledge of art and his genial understanding of human nature. Recognising as he does that the language of art is difficult, not only to speak, but even to understand aright, he feels bound to impress on the student a feeling of reverence for accepted standards of worth. To "accept the world's verdict rather than his own" is the only way to build a sure foundation of critical understanding. To be prepared to find the experience of the past valid is the right attitude for one who would hope to be able ultimately to modify and improve its judgments. And for the young artist, liable as he is to be captivated by minor excellences which answer to some personal predisposition, it is no less important to enlarge and correct his sympathies by a willing docility. Reynolds, perhaps, hardly allows enough for the necessity to the artist of specialising in his appreciations. Few artists can be as eclectic as Reynolds without suffering shipwreck; and the method he had found good for himself is not for everyone. Appreciation and admiration of a general kind for all that has been canonised by the consensus of past criticism an artist may well cultivate, but his personal devotion and passionate study must be given to a few whose work can help him towards the making of his own style.

But Reynolds sees too the dangers of the docility he inculcates and he endeavours to mitigate them. Since the destruction of the guild and apprentice system of the Middle Ages, when a man learned painting almost as one now might learn engineering, there has been no real education in art. All that the schools and academies can do is to provide the possibilities of a man's teaching himself; and it is towards this self-education that the *Discourses* are directed. Reynolds' calm and observant temperament led him to a just and detached view of human nature, and in his advice to students he never assumes impossible virtues or even inculcates heroic ones. He tells the student to take his own nature with all its proneness to vanity and indolence as it is, and to try only to get the best possible out of it. He enforces humility, but would not have the student press this too far, or crush his self-confidence by an immoderate rigour; he is even to indulge that "affection

which we bear to the teacher" when we learn from ourselves. It is indeed remarkable, considering the addiction of his age to moral precepts, how free Reynolds is from that particular kind of untruthfulness which is supposed to make for edification. (pp. 17-18)

In the **"Third Discourse"** Reynolds endeavours to lay the foundations of his principles of æsthetics, principles which he constantly appeals to in the remainder of the *Discourses* and which merit close inquiry. His main thesis is that in works which aim at an exalted imaginative effect, particular and individual forms are out of place; that the forms in such work must be general and representative; that, for instance, in a great dramatic composition the introduction of literal portraiture would lower the imaginative key, and deprive the work of its exalting and ennobling effect. In this main contention Reynolds' verdict is, to put it on purely empirical grounds, borne out by the practice of the greatest masters: Giotto, Masaccio, Leonardo, Raphael, and Michelangelo stand as witnesses to this truth.

It is not, however, so easy for us to follow Reynolds in his proofs as in his conclusions, nor is it possible to acquit him altogether of confusion of thought and inconsistency in the use of words. Above all, that difficult and dangerous word *"Nature"* is used by him with a wilfulness which reminds one of the control over the meanings of words which Humpty Dumpty vaunted to Alice. He uses it (1) in the ordinary sense in which artists use the word—as the sum of visible phenomena not made by artifice. "There are excellences in the art of painting beyond what is commonly called the imitation of Nature." (2) It is used in an Aristotelian sense as an immanent force working in the refractory medium of matter towards the highest perfection of form. "The terms beauty, or nature, which are general ideas, are but different modes of expressing the same thing." (3) Finally, Nature is not only what Nature actually produces, or what Nature strives to produce, but whatever is agreeable to the affections and predispositions of the mind. "In short, whatever pleases has in it what is analogous to the mind, and is, therefore, in the highest and best sense of the word, natural."

Of these senses the second Aristotelian sense is that with which the present Discourse is most concerned. For Reynolds here endeavours to show that the beautiful in every species is the "common form" of the species, the specific type-form from which every individual departs in some particular. Beauty is the lowest common denominator of the forms of the individual members of the species. It is the average, and might almost be arrived at by taking a compound photograph of all the individuals that compose that species. In the third letter to *The Idler* this theory of beauty as the mean of all the possible individual variations is more fully developed. Reynolds says: "Every species of the animal as well as the vegetable creation may be said to have a fixed or determinate form, towards which Nature is continually inclining, like various lines terminating in the centre; or it may be compared to pendulums vibrating in different directions over one central point; and as they all cross the centre, though only one passes through any other point, so it will be found that perfect beauty is oftener produced by Nature than deformity." He then goes on, in anticipation of Herbert Spencer, to explain that our acceptance of this common form as beauty is due to nothing other than use. "As we are, then, more accustomed to beauty than deformity, we may conclude that to be the reason why we approve and admire it, as we approve and admire customs and fashions of dress for no other reason than that we are used to them; so that though habit or custom cannot be said to be the cause of beauty, it is certainly the cause of our liking it."

In this passage Reynolds denies any fundamental predilections of the human sense organs for one kind of stimulus rather than another. He denies, rashly we think, for the sense of sight that preference for certain rhythmic stimuli which are undeniable when we consider the sense of sound. He eliminates the musical element in art, and makes of beauty merely an affair of use and wont. Fortunately, he is not consistent with such a sceptical and empiric view, as his use of Nature in the third sense indicates.

But we must return to a closer examination of the idea of the common specific form. This is clearly derived, though probably indirectly, from Aristotle. In Aristotle Nature is herself an artist working always for perfection of form, but obstructed by the refractory nature of matter, by "accident." The artist frees the form of its accidental obscurities, and reveals it as "Nature" intended. In Reynolds a similar idea of the artist's function is given: he is to find Nature by eliminating the particular and the accidental. But a difference comes in. With Aristotle the higher reality, $\tau o \; \beta \epsilon \lambda \tau \iota o \nu$, which the artist discovers, is an ideal form more perfect and more harmonious than any that Nature produces. It is that form towards which it is the nature of every individual to strive; it is the end proposed by Nature but never reached. Reynolds, already anticipating the attitude of the nineteenth century, finds the ideal in a mere average. But he still keeps the Aristotelian distinction of Nature and Accident. His average specific form is what Nature aims at but is always diverted from by accident.

Let us inquire what meaning this idea has for us in the light of subsequent scientific thought. In the first place, the word Accident might give rise to a difficulty, since for us all results, deformity as well as regularity, are equally the result of immutable laws. However, the idea of Accident still holds good when we consider any particular order of events. Thus we do recognise that, as regards any particular organism, the conditions in which it has been placed are either adverse or favourable to its development, so that we talk of a well-grown or a stunted specimen of a flower or tree. But, as a matter of fact, the well-favoured specimen is not the average specimen, but the one which has had exceptionally favourable circumstances of soil, of light and temperature, and so forth. Similarly, in human beings we recognise that some are well formed and others ill; and we notice that it is among the aristocracy of any race, those members who have succeeded in getting the best conditions of nourishment, the widest range of sexual selection, that the finer specimens are to be found. From the Darwinian point of view, therefore—which regards species as nothing but the form corresponding to a particular set of conditions—the ideal specific form would be one which had every organ as perfectly developed for its functions as was compatible with the full development of every other organ. So that in a man it would have the utmost muscular strength compatible with the utmost swiftness, the utmost brain power compatible with physical de-

velopment, and so on. But in this idea of harmonious development, which would certainly have an æsthetic value as well as a scientific, we are probably unconsciously importing those æsthetic elements which we then proceed to find. If we choose as our specific type one in which there is what we call a harmonious development of the parts, what wonder that we find harmony and proportion in it. But Nature is indifferent to this: if conditions arise which demand the abnormal development of an organ, no compunctions about harmony or proportion stand in her way. She will drag out the proboscis of an insect to five times the length of its body, or make an ape's arms half as long again as its legs, and at the same time dock it of a tail, which might have balanced their monstrous overgrowth. In the case of the human species this is becoming evident. The type which tends to predominate is no longer that of the Greek athlete but that of the city magnate, as highly specialised for certain functions as is the giraffe or the elephant. We take the Greek athlete as the central type of humanity because it is beautiful, not because it is, or ever was, really central. There is beauty and ugliness in Nature, but it is we, not Nature, who decide which is which. (pp. 39-43)

But for us the unsatisfactory nature of Reynolds' theory of specific type-forms as the basis of beauty becomes still more evident when we consider that modern science hesitates to define species. The purely empirical definition of species as a group of organisms capable of interbreeding with fertile results has given place to the Darwinian view of species as the response of organic nature to particular sets of conditions. But biologists are becoming increasingly uneasy as to whether after all this explanation will cover the whole range of facts.

It does not, of course, follow that because we cannot define species it may not contain the clue to ideal beauty, but it becomes increasingly difficult to look to it for any basis of æsthetic theory. In Reynolds' time the absolute nature of species was not questioned. God had created all species definitely, and it was, therefore, not impossible to suppose that there existed for each species a kind of divine archetype, such as Plato conceived, the form of which might be arrived at by comparison and induction, and that if it could be discovered, this divine archetype would have perfect beauty. This seems, indeed, to have been the inspiring idea of all those attempts at canons of proportion for the human figure which have occupied thoughtful and ingenious artists, like Leonardo and Dürer.

To sum up, then, we must abandon Reynolds' theory of beauty as the "common form" of the species, while we accept the conclusion to support which he constructed it. Still more decisively must we dismiss the theory of use and habit as the ultimate cause of our recognition of beauty which he derived from it.

Reynolds' theory is, in point of fact, a development of classical notions of æsthetics derived, as we have seen, primarily from Aristotle, repeated by Latin writers, and taken up by the French and Italian æsthetic writers of the seventeenth century. It was probably from a passage in Bellori, quoted by Dryden in his preface to Du Fresnoy's "Parallel between Poetry and Painting," that Reynolds actually derived his main ideas, though he has developed them with an ingenuity and resource that are all his own. The theory of common form was evidently developed as an afterthought. His practice as an artist, and his fine critical sense, had convinced him already of the need of generalisation, and from Bellori's passage he thought he could draw a philosophical support for his convictions. For us his convictions have naturally more value than his philosophy. Nor was Reynolds himself quite at ease about his theory. In this very Discourse he finds himself bound to modify it seriously. He has throughout had in his mind the idea that this common specific form was expressed in Greek, or rather in Græco-Roman, sculpture, but he bethinks him that among these sculptures there is far too great a variety to refer them all to this specific type-form—"the beauty of the Hercules is one, of the Gladiator another, of the Apollo another." He consoles himself, however, by saying: "Still, none of them is the representation of an individual, but of a class." This, of course, destroys the value of the specific type-form as a basis, since each of these figures is the "common form" of a group, arbitrarily selected by the artist from the whole species, and has, therefore, no authority from Nature for its beauty such as the specific type-form lays claim to. Reynolds too perceived this, for he adds as a corrective: "Yet the highest perfection of the human figure is not to be found in them, but in that form which is taken from all."

But further reflection—a reminiscence, perhaps, of Raphael's cartoon of the Healing of the Cripple—suggests to Reynolds' mind an even more serious difficulty, and one which, had he pursued it, might have greatly changed his æsthetics.

What about deformity? This too enters into art and into the works of the grand style. And he adds: "There is likewise a kind of symmetry, or proportion, which may properly be said to belong to deformity." And yet the whole effort of the artist in his search for the "common form" was precisely to distinguish between beauty and deformity, and reject the latter. With this, and one other sentence to the same purpose, Reynolds dismisses the whole subject of the ugly in art, apparently unconscious of its immense importance. Had he gone in where he thus lightly skates over he would have been the originator of a new world of æsthetic speculation.

Being thus, unfortunately, compelled to reject Reynolds' explanation of the necessity for generalisation in works of the grand or imaginative style, we may, perhaps, since we agree with his conclusion, desire to find other and surer grounds for a result so important to the artist.

We must look for them not in Nature, regarded objectively, but in the reaction of the human mind to Nature, being satisfied if we can find in that a sufficiently wide basis to give our conclusions validity for the ordinarily constituted human being without seeking for a divine sanction. There is in all probability some scientific and objective validity for the classification of species of animals. But with regard to species with which we are closely familiar, we are forced, in order to deal with the infinite number of individuals which we encounter, to adopt a further classification which is practical and imaginative rather than scientific. In the case of our own species in particular, this classification is very extensive, and of such importance, that the mere names of the classes often awake reverberations in the recesses of our imagination. The mere names king, knight, beggar have such power because of the rich significance for life of the types they represent. And for each of these classes we carry in our mind a vaguely outlined typical form, a kind of mental compound photograph of the various individuals who compose the class, so that we can say at once, by applying these type-forms of the mind, that a man has, for example, a lawyer's or a coachman's face. It is the part of poetry to draw on these organs of our imaginative existence by the vague evocation of words. It is the part of such poetical design as Reynolds is here concerned with, at once to call up the mental type-form, and to give it greater precision and content than it had before. (pp. 43-6)

The principle of generalised form laid down in the last Discourse is here [in The **"Fourth Discourse"**] applied, and the necessity for it shown in each of the stages of the execution of a work—Invention, Composition, Expression, Colouring. In carrying out this investigation Reynolds comes upon a class of work which, as an artist, he cannot but admire, and yet which does not conform strictly to the canons laid down for the highest kind of imaginative design.

For this class he discovers, therefore, another and lower aim, that of being ornamental, of giving us pleasing and delightful combinations of form and colour, the disposition of which is not controlled by any great imaginative idea. The pleasure from this class of work is, he urges, of a lower kind, inasmuch as it is more sensual and less intellectual. These two styles, the grand and the ornamental, Reynolds considers as entirely distinct, and governed by opposite principles, inasmuch as particular and local features may properly be introduced into the latter, while they must be rigidly excluded from the former. The exponents of the grand style are found chiefly in the Roman, Florentine, and eclectic Bolognese schools, and in the French school of the seventeenth century. Somewhat strangely, Reynolds classifies the Venetian and Dutch schools together, as belonging to the ornamental. In the England of the eighteenth century, when even the lesser Venetians were eagerly bought by our country gentlemen, such an apparent slight upon the Venetians could not pass without comment, and Reynolds is conscious of the need to defend his attitude. In the first place, he excludes Titian, and gives him almost to a nicety the position which most critics of to-day would adopt. Then he admits that the Venetians attained to perfection in their lower line of effort; elsewhere he enlarges this by admitting that success in the lower is more admirable than ambitious failure in the higher style, so that he would have had nothing to object to our preferring a Paolo Veronese to the great mass of Bolognese or French art; indeed, his own judgment would have confirmed such a view. True, he quotes Vasari's hard sayings upon Tintoretto; but, much as these go against the general current of the taste of to-day, a really impartial study of the mass of Tintoretto's work will show that they contain a profound truth: that Tintoretto is frequently capricious, superficial, and essentially frivolous. While, when we come to the lesser Venetians, to Pordenone, Bordone, and Bonifazio, we may fairly admit that the splendour of decorative and non-significant colour is almost the only claim they have to our reverence.

In this attack upon the Venetians, which is certainly excessive in some phrases, Reynolds seems to have been striving at a judicial impartiality in the face of his own instinctive feelings. He was himself so entirely at home in Venetian art; he felt its appeal so intensely, even basing upon it his own most magnificent designs, and learning from it the secret of his rich and transparent colouring, that in the endeavour not to rate beyond its worth a style of which he himself was a master, he actually decried it more than justice required. Indeed it is curious to find that Tintoretto appealed to him so strongly that in his Italian sketch-book there are more notes made of his dispositions of chiaroscuro than of any other artist's.

But this effort at judicial impartiality, which leads Reynolds to incline the balance against his feelings, is one proof of the genuine critical poise of his mind. Indeed, whether we accept this application in detail or not, the whole Discourse contains principles of criticism of the widest scope and profoundest significance—ideas that can be applied to the education of taste with the most fruitful results. For there is nothing which stimulates more a true critical appreciation of art than the attempt to go beyond the mere judgment that a work is excellent, to inquire of what kind its excellence is, and how it stands in regard to other excellences. In one point alone it seems that it might be possible to alter Reynolds' classification so as to agree better with the judgment of recent times. The sharp line between the grand and ornamental styles seems rather arbitrary; and a classification which separates Tintoretto entirely from Titian, and places him alongside of Teniers, is something of a shock to our feelings. It might be fairer to say that there are infinite gradations in the degree of imaginative intensity of a conception, and that what is required of a work of art is the exact correspondence of the expression to the imaginative key. Then we shall find that Reynolds' principle holds true, that a greater particularisation is possible in the lyrical key of a Correggio than could be allowed in the epical of a Michelangelo or the dramatic of a Leonardo, and that as we descend through Watteau's pastorals to the prose of Metsu and Terborgh the particular and local are increasingly appropriate. It is the want of this proper adjustment that shocks us so much in the inflated ambitions of some Italianising Northerners. (pp. 67-9)

It follows of necessity from the principles laid down in the last Discourse—namely, that every degree of imaginative elevation in the theme must have its corresponding degree of generalisation and abstraction from the particular in the forms which give it expression—it follows from this, that a mixture of the qualities of different degrees—or styles, as Reynolds calls them—and any attempt to unite their various excellences, must produce a discord. It is this application which Reynolds, eclectic though he was, here [in The **"Fifth Discourse"**] enforces. His advice to the student is to keep his attention fixed on the higher excellences: "If you compass them, and compass nothing more, you are still in the first class." Somewhat dangerous advice, and hardly borne out by his own practice, since it omits the case, which is certain to be a frequent one, of an artist who might have succeeded on the lower plane, failing entirely on the higher.

Reynolds goes on to point out the dangers of a too theoretical eclecticism to which the student might have been inclined by following incorrectly his remarks on the grand style—the danger, namely, of insipidity. That is the danger which we now feel, more clearly even than Reynolds did, to have beset the art of the seventeenth century of Bo-

logna and France when it attempted the grand style. The generalised and ideal type-form can only satisfy the imagination when it contains as full and definite a content, when it is as *real*, as the particular form. In so far as it fails of this, though it may answer generally to the vague compound image of the type which we carry in our minds, it will not heighten or enrich it, and we have a sense of disappointment: we miss the expected stimulus, and find the work insipid, however admirable our intellect tells us it should be. It is our growing sense of the importance of this content of the type-forms which has forced us to transfer our affections increasingly from the art of the seventeenth century to that of the fifteenth. We have seen already that Reynolds himself was not without a suspicion of the justice of this view.

As against this danger of insipidity, Reynolds proposes to the student the study of yet a third style, the "characteristic," of which he takes Salvator Rosa and Rubens as types. The merit of this style consists not so much in the propriety of the forms chosen as in their perfect consistency. Reynolds' use of the word "characteristic" is here somewhat different from the modern sense. We should be inclined to call a style characteristic in which the characters of natural objects were strongly accentuated. We should, for instance, apply the word to such a style as Pollajuolo's, Signorelli's, or Dürer's. But Reynolds appears rather to mean a style in which the character of the artist is strongly impressed on everything that he does; or, as we might now say, a temperamental style. (pp. 107-08)

The **"Sixth Discourse"** is devoted to Reynolds' famous exposure of the theory of genius, and it contains, in spite of the dry and sceptical attitude that the author discovers, some of the most eloquent and persuasive passages in the whole series of the *Discourses,* and this because in disposing of a false and romantic superstition about the nature of the creative imagination the author appeals to principles of order and reason as against caprice and accident. It is only to thoughtless and uncultured minds that this attempt to replace chance by law, in the realm of the imagination will appear a lessening of its dignity and charm.

"It must of necessity be that even works of genius, like every other effect, as they must have their cause, must likewise have their rules." That is the charter by which alone the student has a right to expect any reward for his labour. Against this the theory of genius, as it is ordinarily held, sets up the notion of a capricious and incalculable fate, which may reward the careless and condemn the assiduous devotee. The theory of genius as thus held by the public has reacted disastrously on the modern artist. Its destructive effects are, however, due to the half-truth it contains. All men have not equal gifts, as Reynolds would, in his anxiety for the student's welfare, seem to suggest; and though the effects of genius have their causes, these are so hidden or complex that the results, like those of meteorology, always surprise us, and defy alike analysis and prediction.

Reynolds quite rightly insists on the exercise of his conscious intelligence by the artist; but modern scientific speculation shows that, however important this is, the synthetic power, the act of putting things together in a new order, and, with a new significance which we call creation, is a function of a part of our mind over which we have no direct and immediate control. And though the fruits which the artist may reap from his "subliminal self" will be richer in proportion to the kind and quality of the seed implanted by his conscious intelligence, the nature of the soil, over which he has no control, will still be the largest factor in the result. Reynolds, therefore, is right in inducing his hearers to do all that a determined will and active intelligence can, to improve their science and taste, but assuredly wrong in holding out to them the hopes of a more certain and calculable reward than the diversity of human nature allows. It is only right to add, seeing how much misunderstanding and criticism Reynolds' words have aroused, that he elsewhere [in this Discourse] shows (in the passage about Maratti . . .) that he was conscious of the inequality of natural gifts, and that he only wished to emphasize here, even at the cost of some exaggeration and some inconsistency, the more hopeful aspect of the situation, which the value of conscious intelligent effort supplies.

The artist, indeed, does well to work as though the special gift which we call genius did not exist, even though he possesses it—the critic can hardly be blind to its overwhelming importance. But even the critic may in justice admit what a superstitious public will hardly allow—namely, that a poor and uncultured genius may be of less importance in the influence his art exerts than an artist who has only general capacity, which he has cultivated to its utmost by thoughtful and well-reasoned methods; that, for example, Reynolds himself, whose genius is not his most conspicuous trait, was, on the whole, a more important figure in the history of British art than Gainsborough, who had genius of the most striking kind.

Incidentally, Reynolds here gives what is, perhaps, the truest account of the functions of art criticism that has ever been framed. He declares that, though he must believe in the existence of underlying laws, even in the most surprising effects of genius, "these refined principles cannot be always made palpable like the more gross rules of art; *yet it does not follow, but that the mind may be put in such a train, that it shall perceive, by a kind of scientific sense, that propriety which words can but very feebly suggest.*" It is on the basis of a belief in this logic of the sensations and emotions, however difficult or even impossible it may be to define, that all criticism and discussion of works of art must rest.

The rest of the Discourse is devoted to the discussion of how the artist can best cultivate his gifts by the imitation of what is great in the art of the past. The wisdom and caution of Reynolds' advice on this head, the care with which he discriminates between the investigation into the principles of a great work, and the thoughtless imitation of its accidents of manner, leave nothing to be desired. (pp. 137-39)

To substitute in matters of taste "rational firmness" for "vain presumption" is the object of [the **"Seventh Discourse"**]. Its aim, and the general attitude it inculcates, are invaluable at all times, since the denial of the existence of a standard of right and wrong, of better and worse, is as disastrous in art as a similar denial would be in morals. It is, moreover, a denial that is almost universally made by those who lack the sensibility or the cultivation to enable them to make right judgments, and who, therefore, have an interest in bringing the whole matter into a chaos of conflicting individual opinion. "De gustibus non dispu-

tandum," and "One man's opinion is as good as another," are the war-cries of aggressive Philistinism. Unfortunately, that general consensus of trained experience, which is all that can be demonstrated to such sceptics, is neither exact, nor detailed enough, to impress them very profoundly; and though those who have the sensibility and training to pronounce upon a work of art, believe, not, as is supposed, implicitly in their own infallibility, so much as in an objective rightness of judgment towards which they continually strive to approximate, it is hardly possible for them to justify their faith to those who are "so continually in the agitation of gross and merely sensual pleasures, or so occupied in the low drudgery of avarice, or so heated in the chase of honour and distinction, that their minds, which had been used continually to the storms of these violent and tempestuous passions, can hardly be put into motion by the delicate and refined play of the imagination."

But however this may be, Reynolds hardly succeeds in what he sets out to demonstrate, and the whole teaching suffers from a certain discursiveness and want of construction that are unusual with him: it contains, nevertheless, some very important passages. Reynolds endeavours to distinguish between artistic truth which is absolute, and as far as human things go eternal, and that which has its basis upon conventions, fashions, and habits which are local and temporary, but which, if they are long continued and widely spread, may almost take on the air of absolute truth. The absolute truth would correspond to those specific type-forms which were discussed in the third Discourse, while an example of a relative, but still widely-extended, artistic truth is given in the eighteenth-century practice of wrapping a modern senator in a toga when he stood for a statue.

As we have, in the introduction to [the **"Third] Discourse,"** tried to show the impossibility of any such absolute external standard of beauty as Reynolds conceived, we are thrown back upon one principle, that of the conformity, within certain limits of variation, of human nature. In every great work of art, of whatever time or country, there are expressed certain ideas which are of universal acceptance, while there are many others which can only be appreciated by the artist's countrymen and contemporaries. It is thus that a good judge of Western art is able at once to recognise the beauty of an Egyptian statue or a Chinese painting. There is sufficient of what is universally applicable to human nature to allow of this, but in neither case will he understand the work of art completely. Many beauties will depend on a recognition of local imaginative or religious ideas to which the critic may have no clue; much will depend on associated ideas which could only be present in their full force to the artist's countrymen and contemporaries. This view, however, only reinforces, though from a different standpoint, Reynolds' main conclusion, that the more the appeal is made to what is common and universal in human nature the wider in space and the longer in time will be the acceptance of the work.

As part of the systematic education of taste, Reynolds again discusses the artist's attitude to Nature, the necessity for him to do more than copy the forms of Nature as they are presented to him; but he gives us yet another meaning for Nature than that employed in the third Discourse, and one that carries with it consequences which he scarcely foresaw. In [the **"Third] Discourse"** Nature is the mean of all the particulars of a species, the end towards which existence constantly aims. We come here to that third sense of the word Nature to which allusion was made, in anticipation, in the Introduction to [the **"Third] Discourse."** According to this, Nature "comprehends not only the forms which Nature produces, but also the nature and internal fabric and organisation, as I may call it, of the human mind and imagination"; and, farther on, "whatever pleases has in it what is analogous to the mind, and is, therefore, in the best and highest sense of the word, *natural."* Reynolds, it is true, puts alongside of this, as though no difference existed, his former idea of Nature and beauty as the common specific form.

But, really, we have got hold here of an entirely new principle; for when Nature is defined by Reynolds as what is agreeable to our mental desires and aspirations, and when he adds that the artist should follow Nature in this sense, he allows much more than before. Man's mental appetites and affections have demanded that there should be beings of human form with wings, and a similar but rather perverted appetite, to which Reynolds was himself subject, demanded that there should be babies' heads with wings and no bodies; but Nature, taken even in Reynolds' second or Aristotelian sense, shows no indication of striving in this direction.

We have, therefore, got in this definition a new principle, which cuts away the foundations, as it obviates the necessity of the idea of beauty as the common form of each species. We are now allowed to make beauty independent of the forms of external nature, and to base it on what is found to satisfy most completely and permanently the demands of our common human nature. If we like to call this "Nature," as Reynolds does, the artist still follows Nature; but the term is now so wide that there is little good gained in using it. But, at least, we have here a principle of æsthetics which will allow us to include in the beautiful the strangest dreams of human fancy; to discuss on common terms the complete realisations of human form in Greek sculpture, and the impossible but intensely significant contours of Simone Martini's Madonnas or Utamaro's ladies. As we showed in discussing the third Discourse, it is perfectly possible to substitute this view for Reynolds' own view of beauty as the common form, without invalidating his main conclusions; and here at last we have Reynolds himself, though apparently unconscious of what might result from it, really acknowledging this larger and more fundamental principle. (pp. 177-80)

Reynolds begins [the **"Eighth] Discourse"** with what looks like a reminiscence of Burke's *Treatise on the Sublime and Beautiful.* That it is unconscious we gather from a note towards the end in which he refers to that work. But though he begins by applying abstract ideas, such as novelty, variety, and contrast, these are not systematically carried through, and he soon takes up particular instances and applications of general rules, discussing them with a clear idea of the painter's needs in practice. We may differ from particular interpretations that he gives to the rules, but the spirit in which he reasons about them, his cautions against a rigid and unintelligent application of them, are of the utmost value to artists. There are few pieces of art criticism which come so close to the questions at issue for the artist. (p. 223)

To Reynolds the establishment of the Royal Academy, and its installation in a great public building, was primarily of importance as an outward and visible sign—a public confession by a nation which has always inclined to utilitarianism—of the real value of art as a form of disinterested intellectual activity. Once more [in the **"Ninth Discourse"**] he declares that its proper function is the appeal to the imagination through the senses, not the mere gratification of the senses without further issue. (p. 259)

The **"Tenth Discourse"** is in many ways one of the least satisfactory; the subject is too large for such a slight treatment; and Reynolds, speaking no longer from actual experience, loses himself in confusing and contradictory qualifications. For all that, the main thesis that sculpture should aim, more exclusively than painting needs to do, at the essential generalities of form is sufficiently borne out by an examination of what has actually been done. If we rule out, as of a different category, miniature sculpture and bas-relief we shall find but few instances where the lower imaginative keys, genre, the pastoral, the lyric, or even prosaic portraiture—have been successfully treated in the round. A few Roman portrait heads, some of the more lyrical and fantastic of French fourteenth-century sculptures, the portraits of Desiderio, Rosellino, Mino da Fiesole, and Leone Leoni, and for pure genre, certain figures by Guido Mazzoni of Modena, and finally a considerable mass of eighteenth-century French and German sculpture, are, perhaps, the chief examples that one may bring forward. There is nothing—that is to say in sculpture—that can at all correspond with the painting of artists like Palma, Veronese, and Rubens. Sculpture in miniature is altogether different; there we are by no means so immediately conscious of the imitation of nature; the language is nearly as conventional as that of painting, and almost anything is allowable that may charm or amuse. We need not complain of the topical genre of a Tanagra figure; and a Meissen porcelain has as good a right to its extravagant drapery and capricious conceits as the painting of a Lancret or Pater. Even humorous grotesque and caricature, which would shock us intolerably on a large scale, may be used in minute sculpture with perfect propriety. Had Reynolds made this distinction his denunciation of the unfortunate attempts of the sculptors of his own day to introduce the rococo into sculpture would have been entirely justified.

It is not by any means so easy to follow Reynolds in two other principles which he here lays down as regards sculpture: first, that correctness is of its essence; and secondly, that formal beauty should be its only aim to the exclusion of expressive beauty. To both of these limitations of the art we may oppose one word that Reynolds himself could scarce have gainsaid—Michelangelo. There is hardly a figure in the Medici Chapel which does not depart from the correct proportions of the human figure in some way or another; and who would base their admiration of either the Pietà in the Duomo at Florence, or that still more wonderful sketch in the Rondanini Palace, upon their formal beauty? Sculpture, indeed, aims at the expression of the profoundest imaginative truth by the simplest and most effective method of appeal that the senses admit, that of the hollow and the boss; but it is by the disposition of these in their most expressive, and not merely in their most correct or elegant relations, that its highest achievements are attained. (pp. 265-66)

In the **"Eleventh Discourse"** Reynolds returns once more to the question of genius, but he uses the word in a more particular sense to describe what we may call the specific talent of the painter. Genius in the sense of creative power may exist apart from any one particular aptitude for expression. The higher parts of genius, the intellectual power which "enables the artist to conceive his subject with dignity," lie outside of any special aptitude. But Reynolds is here concerned with that special aptitude for pictorial expression which, one has sadly to admit, is sometimes given to those who lack the higher power of noble conception. One can, perhaps, best understand these two aspects of genius by an example. Rossetti was pre-eminently a man of genius in the general sense, endowed with the profoundest and most original notions; but he had very little specific talent, and this may account for his forcing parallel roads for his ideas through language and design. Millais was, on the other hand, richly gifted with the specific talent for artistic expression, with genius, as Reynolds here uses the word, but without any corresponding distinction of thought or feeling.

What then, Reynolds inquires, are the marks of this specific talent? He finds it in the power of seizing the general characters of objects. From this he slips inadvertently into talking of this power as though it were the same as that power of comparing and choosing out the central form of a class which he has proclaimed as the method of the grand style. In truth, there is a distinction, since this specific talent occurs in connection with the lower as well as the higher branches of art, and we must try to recognise and isolate it whether it is occupied upon pots and pans or upon gods and angels. It consists then, according to Reynolds, in the power of seizing the general characteristics of whatever is represented, but this is quite consistent with a particularising and individualising which are altogether rejected from the grand style. In portraiture, for instance, as Reynolds says, it consists in placing the features correctly before or even without, drawing them minutely; but the doing of this may be used to give mere likeness of the most prosaic kind. It is, in fact, more than anything else, the secret of literal likeness. Reynolds is right, then, in fixing upon this power of seizing at once upon the general relations of the parts as *par excellence* the artist's gift, but we have no right in this particular connection to go further and prescribe the end to which this power may be used. It may be used merely to arouse the sense of likeness, or it may be used to express the noblest conceptions. In whichever class of painters it occurs, whether in the rhiparographer or the divine, we must acknowledge genius in this sense of the word.

One further amplification of Reynolds' thesis must be made in order that it may fit with our more catholic appreciations of art. Reynolds seems to imply that the use of detail is in itself a sign of the want of this power. Here he shows himself the child of his century, the period of all others when artists were most easily satisfied with a casual and superficial vision. We may be contented if the artist seizes and holds the general characteristic relations of the parts, and need not inquire whether he goes on to elaborate them or not. He may merely place the features with

unerring certainty on the mask, as Mr Sargent does, without saying very much what they are; or he may go on to describe every wrinkle, and count every eyelash, as Dürer did. Providing he holds those main characteristic relations firmly all the time, does not cease to see the wood, and make it visible to the spectator, because of the trees, he will have given equal if not superior proof of the specific talent of the artist. (pp. 287-89)

Reynolds here [in the **"Twelfth Discourse"**] touches once more on the ground of his **"Second Discourse."** He displays the same humorous good sense, the same indulgent and playful recognition of human weakness and folly, and gives us once more the measure of his own kindly and genial nature. His attitude to education in art is, as always, mildly sceptical—and one can understand that he was not a good teacher in practice. His view is that the pupil first of all learns what he calls the grammar of art—namely, to draw correctly whatever object is placed before him. He is then to receive a set of general principles—principles of choice and selection, which it must be left to him to apply in practice. He is to deduce his art from these general ideas, and he is continually to refer to the great works of art in which those ideas and principles are embodied, while he is always to go to Nature for filling out the content of these schematic designs derived from the study of art. The scheme is, perhaps, as good a one as can be devised for training an artist born at a time when there is no great and vital tradition of design—and that has been the fate of artists ever since the Academy replaced the Guild. But it is well to remember that this programme is very different from that which the great masters whom Reynolds exhibits for imitation passed through.

The artist of the Renaissance never learned the grammar that Reynolds presupposes. For by this correct drawing of any object is meant an indifferent exactitude, a passionless and disinterested *précis* of facts—in short, an unartistic drawing. Now, the artist of the Renaissance learned first an artistic formula, the formula of his time as understood by his master, and this became so much of a second nature to him that when he looked at Nature he saw it in terms of this formula. If he was an inferior artist he repeated this more or less exactly to the end; if he had original power he gradually modified this formula until it expressed his own temperament. But he never passed through a stage of indifferent and coldly exact representation. He passed from one biassed and interested vision to another equally biassed and interested, but one which suited him more exactly. (pp. 319-20)

In this connection it may be well to recapitulate the distinction already suggested by Reynolds [in the **"Sixth Discourse"**] between different kinds of borrowing from works of art. There is the taking over of the actual mode of vision and manner of an artist, as Raphael took over that of his master Perugino; and there is the borrowing of particular inventions of another artist, and the accommodation of them to the artist's own personal style, as Raphael later on borrowed from Filippino and Masaccio. The former more intimate imitation of a master is what all great artists began with, but what few artists can safely do after their apprenticeship. The taking over of another man's formula in youth is a proper confession of inexperience, and a way towards self-perfection; the adoption of such a formula in maturity is the confession of want of independence, and almost invariably a sign of incapacity. Of the second kind of borrowing no artist need ever feel ashamed at any time if, as Reynolds says, he conceals his theft—that is, if the incident or motive is so thoroughly transmuted into the borrower's own mode of conception that it becomes an integral part of his creation. (p. 320)

The **"Thirteenth Discourse"** is perhaps the most masterly as it is the most subtly reasoned of all Reynolds' works. We may notice that as he proceeds Reynolds relies more and more on the conformity of a work of art to the demands of the cultivated intelligence, and less on any principles derived from external nature. He bases beauty, that is, on the uniformity of human nature, and judges that whatever is most universal in its appeal approaches most to absolute artistic truth; while he finds for temporary and partial predilections of the human mind a proportionate degree of relative artistic truth. In effect, the **"Thirteenth Discourse"** is an eloquent and noble protest against the demands made on art by the untrained appetites of the public. It is also more applicable to-day than when Reynolds delivered it. With the social and intellectual emancipation of the lower middle classes the demand for crude sensational effects, for vivid appeals to a lazy curiosity, and love of novelty, has become imperious. It would no longer be possible to-day, as it was in 1786, to appeal from art to the practice of the stage, as showing how by deviation from mere imitation the higher ranges of emotion may be conveyed to the imagination and feelings, because the stage too has suffered from precisely those evils which Reynolds deplores in art; and the power to die with a perfect imitation of every physiological circumstance has become the test of greatness in an actress, while the introduction of a real hansom cab, a real waterfall, or what not, is the proof of scenic completeness.

The end of art—Reynolds is never weary of pressing the point—the end of art is to appeal to the cultivated imagination; and as the cultivation of the imagination is not only rare, but is looked upon as something extravagant and subversive of the comfortable routine of existence, serious art is likely always to remain, as indeed it always has been in this country, a sporadic and isolated phenomenon. It must be practised almost in secret like a proscribed religion, while a safe and palatable substitute is solemnly paraded for the acclamations of the populace. For this Discourse alone Reynolds deserves to be held in reverence by all those who think that art is more than a relaxation from the serious cares of the money market. (pp. 347-48)

[The **"Fourteenth Discourse"**] is described by one of Reynolds' coldest admirers as "perhaps the most interesting passage in the Discourses." It is interesting for the light it throws on Reynolds' character as a man and as a critic, and it is highly favourable to both. Gainsborough had quarrelled with the Academy in 1783, and since then had refused to exhibit. In this quarrel he was possibly in the right, but his conduct was not likely to please the Academy's President. Nor had Gainsborough accepted Reynolds' advances very cordially. They were too much opposed in character both as men and as artists ever to be intimate. Such are the circumstances that generally produce the bitterest professional jealousy. But Reynolds' love of art was too sincere to allow of any such personal feelings, even if he had not dispelled them entirely in that touching final reconciliation which is here so delicately de-

scribed. But it is not only Reynolds' superiority as a man that is shown by this Discourse, but his admirable critical sense. It may seem to us now to be cold praise to say that Gainsborough is greater than Raphael Mengs, or Pompeo Battoni, but that is only because Reynolds' prophecy has come so entirely true. It always requires some courage, some power of conviction, and some force of imagination to see a contemporary as a really great man. Reynolds had known him all his life as Mr Gainsborough, and it required a firm effort of the imagination to divine what a rich sound the word Gainsborough would one day have to our ears. Everything was against his forming so just and so exalted an opinion of his rival, and yet he did not hesitate to place him, where he still stands, at the very head of the English school. (p. 371)

It is characteristic of the rounded completeness, the deliberation, and method of all Reynolds' works, that [with the **"Fifteenth Discourse"**] he was able to bring his Discourses to so fitting and apt a close. He seems almost to have set about dying with the same calm deliberation that had characterised the actions of his life. A little more than a year before the delivery of this Discourse, "while finishing a portrait of the Marchioness of Hertford, he felt a sudden decay of sight in his left eye. He laid down the pencil, sat a little while in mute consideration, and never lifted it more." The apparent ease with which he resigned himself to the inevitable loss of his one supreme interest in life, the tranquillity and cheerfulness with which he endeavoured to amuse himself in these last darkened days, embittered as they were by quarrels and jealousies within the Academy itself, give one the idea that beneath the "complying" blandness of his manners there was something of stoical fortitude. He, at least, knew when to resign, when to disappear gracefully from public life; and the last Discourse is ennobled by the dignity of this attitude. In it he touches on nothing that was not worthy of the occasion, and touches the greatest things worthily. In this apologia for his work as an educator of taste he shows neither false humility nor undue pride, and his opinion of his own work is as just as his judgment of others'. He had no illusions about his own genius, he knew himself incapable of the highest ranges of imaginative creation, but no tinge of envy mars his celebration of the triumphs he could not share. If one realises all the circumstances under which it was delivered, the concluding paragraph of this Discourse must count as itself attaining to that grandeur of style which he so consistently and so disinterestedly admired. (pp. 399-400)

Roger Fry, in introductions to Discourses Delivered to the Students of the Royal Academy *by Sir Joshua Reynolds, Seeley & Co. Limited, 1905, 445 p.*

Laurence Binyon   (essay date 1906)

[Binyon was an English art historian, critic, translator, dramatist, and poet. He wrote numerous books on art, including Painting in the Far East *(1908), and lectured throughout the world on art and literature. A prolific and respected poet, he succeeded T. S. Eliot as Norton Professor of Poetry at Harvard University. In the following excerpt from a review of Fry's edition of the* Discourses, *Binyon praises Reynolds as a worthy instructor*

of art students and as an authoritative guide to distinctly English portraiture.]

We must remember that [Reynolds, in the ***Discourses,***] was not interpreting works of art to the world; he was teaching students the principles that should govern practice. He avows the difficulty of a subject in which so much must elude verbal explanation; he did not try to teach what could not be taught, and wisely chose for illustration paintings in which the main principle of unity was obvious and explicit. If, like most eighteenth-century minds, he relies too much on conscious rule and theory, constructing too much from the outside, the value of his teaching is scarcely impaired. Individual moderns may take some recreating element from early art, Rossetti adding a new richness of content, Puvis de Chavannes a new sense of the value of space; but a practical teacher is bound to take up art at the point where he finds it. What Reynolds omitted to enforce is of little account compared with what he does enforce. The insistence by Ruskin on the importance of copying plumage, plants, and rocks, illustrates the disastrous effect of elevating "richness of content" to a positive governing principle. The anarchy and helplessness of the present day illustrate the danger of 'following Nature,' and of concession to caprice. For the value of academic teaching is that it provides a norm or standard, and its fruitful effect comes, as often as not, from the personal reaction it stimulates. Hence its supposed futility. But, since our Academy left off being academic, there has been nothing even to provoke such wholesome reaction.

Reynolds, with masculine concentration of purpose, kept the essential things always in view. Knowledge of our national mental character, its tendency to laziness and impatience of discipline, may have accentuated his emphasis on the paramount value of thought and purpose in painting, his eloquent appeals to learn from the great men of the past. Yet he nourished a splendid faith in the imaginative capacity of his race; his generous ideal was of a national art surpassing his own in creative scope and grandeur; he conceived of tradition not merely as a code of rules, but as initiation into the company and ennobling emulation of the masters who are not dead but immortal. (pp. 106-07)

> *Laurence Binyon, "The Teaching of Reynolds," in* The Independent Review, *Vol. VIII, No. 28, January, 1906, pp. 103-07.*

R. Brimley Johnson (essay date 1927)

[*Johnson was an English editor of collected editions of works by major figures in English literary history. In the following excerpt, he praises* Johnson & Garrick: Two Dialogues *as a work in which Reynolds successfully recreates Dr. Johnson's conversational style.*]

[*Johnson & Garrick: Two Dialogues was originally*] printed in "Red Lion Passage" in 1816, but "not published"; being ingeniously "imitated" by Sir Joshua Reynolds from the conversation of Dr. Johnson; the most skilful parody, I think, ever produced of the great man's dictatorial methods of maintaining his opinions against all comers, without the least hesitation in contradicting himself.

Sir Joshua knew very well that Johnson loved talking for talking's sake; that he was perfectly ready to champion a cause or run down a friend for the pleasure of contradic-

tion; and would strongly resent being called to account for anything he may have said on "T'other side," last Wednesday at Thrale's:—no doubt, an irritating habit.

But he was wise enough, also, to see that it was the dictator's abuse of his friends one should therefore discount, not his generous praise. He has given us the real Johnson by producing three pages "against," and ten "for," David Garrick: a very proper proportion to represent the real nature of the man.

No careful reader of Boswell and Johnson's letters can fail to realise his simple and warm-hearted affection for his fellow-men, despite the verbal intolerance with which at times, it delighted him to assert his own superiority. There is scarcely a name of any importance among the great and little ones of that vigorous generation of whom he has not somewhere spoken a kind word with discriminating generosity. And when he speaks to praise, it is usually with greater care and at greater length, that is, more seriously and sincerely; than when he snaps out scorn or drowns the voice of justice with his growling thunder.

The ***Dialogues*** most truly reflect this truth of Johnson, with a subtlety of understanding far more skilful than mere verbal imitation. Though here, too, Sir Joshua has happily combined his friend's decided partiality for big words and ponderous sentences, with that gift for incisive brevity in vigorous Anglo-saxon; which is the more significant part of his contribution to the building of English prose.

Wm. Cotton describes the ***Dialogues*** as being "compiled from collected scraps of Johnson's conversation"; as Croker had dismissed "so tame an imitation composed from recollected scraps"; but this is only to repeat the old, foolish, contempt for the "stretch of mind and prompt assiduity" with which Boswell "preserved, collected, *and arranged*" the materials of his immortal Life. Both men, in fact, were artists in composition, not shorthand reporters of the spoken word; and Sir Joshua's ready adaptation of colloquial wit reveals an aspect of his personality, in pleasant contrast to the more polished periods of his ***Discourses*** on Art.

It is true that actual opinions expressed by Johnson are embodied here. Boswell gives us, in other words, the characteristic mockery of 'little' great men—mimics, painters, tobacconists or what you please; and the insolent suggestion that many desired "the credit of having it said, that they held an argument with Sam Johnson" on questions beyond their powers to comprehend. No doubt he actually called Garrick a "great repeater. . . . but a faint approach towards being a great man." Boswell, again, reports what is here invented: the loyal defence of "little" David, against the charge of parsimony, with loud assertions of his generous nature and conduct; including the curious anecdote of Peg Woffington and her "blood-red" cup of tea. We know that Johnson often declared, with his usual commonsense, that we all love money; that he despised the cant, "fit for kitchen-wenches and chambermaids," that an actor himself felt the emotions he displayed; that he more than once contrasted the gentleman-buffoonery of Garrick with Foote's vulgar wit; though, on this point, the player himself once charged Johnson with so much ignorance of good manners as to praise the

Facsimile of Reynolds's handwriting.

"courtly vivacity of the most vulgar ruffian that ever trod the boards."

Everything here, indeed, may be found in Boswell; but it is so retold and reframed as to make it Sir Joshua's own: a genuine parody of a master of conversation. (pp. 5-8)

> *R. Brimley Johnson, in an introduction to* Johnson & Garrick: Two Dialogues *by Sir Joshua Reynolds, The Cayme Press, 1927, pp. 5-8.*

Frederick Whiley Hilles (essay date 1929)

[*Hilles was an American educator who specialized in the works of Samuel Johnson and his contemporaries, notably Reynolds. He wrote prolifically on Reynolds's life and work, editing* Letters of Sir Joshua Reynolds *(1929) and the character sketches published as* Portraits *(1952). In addition, his* Literary Career of Sir Joshua Reynolds *(1936) is widely considered an essential biographical and bibliographical study of Reynolds's influences and literary career. In the following excerpt from his preface to* Letters of Sir Joshua Reynolds, *Hilles describes the style and tone of Reynolds's letters, conclud-*

ing his assessment by reprinting a short poem by Reynolds's contemporary, Hester Thrale.]

To many this collection [*Letters of Sir Joshua Reynolds*] will seem surprisingly small, since it is to be expected that the letters of a man who rose to such eminence would have been carefully preserved. But like Goldsmith, who "never wrote a letter in his life", Sir Joshua wrote sparingly. He used to say that his friend Astley, the painter, would rather run three miles to deliver his message by word of mouth than venture to write a note; the same remark applied to himself. "Familiar letters by Sir Joshua", wrote his pupil, James Northcote, "are . . . very scarce: he was too busy and too wise to spend his time in an occupation which is more congenial to the idle and the vain, who are commonly very voluminous in their production of this article". From the same source we learn that in early life he "was too much occupied in his studies to dedicate much time to epistolary correspondence", and in his closing years, when threatened with blindness, he naturally refrained as much as possible from writing. Throughout his correspondence we note phrases which admirably illustrate this. "I write with continual interruption, having so little to say, and so little time to say that little, that I believe I should not have ventured to have wrote, if I had not had an opportunity of inclosing my letter in a cover to Mr. Frazer". "I intended writing to you from London, and have still a frank for that purpose; but you know what a bad correspondent I am." "I am forced to write in a great hurry, and have little time for polishing my style."

Such passages as these serve to explain the careless and hasty manner in which many of the letters are written, a manner that is in marked contrast to that of his published writings. Marks of punctuation are sparingly used, as might be expected in informal correspondence, but that the author of the *Discourses* should be guilty of glaring inaccuracies in construction and spelling may surprise some readers. In his letter to Bishop Lowth, for example, he uses the word *parallelism* three times, writing it *Parellelisms, parelelisms, paralelism,* and he frequently misspells the names of his most intimate friends (*e.g. Burk, Keppell, Whitford, Wilks*). Indeed, so careless is he in such matters that John Williams, when publishing the letters to Miss Weston, stated that they would "totally remove the long received idea, that he was the author of the Discourses delivered at the *Royal Academy,* or a man of that learning which it has been generally supposed". To refute this, it is only necessary to compare his letters with those of the two contemporaries most conspicuous in literature, Goldsmith and Johnson. If the author of *The Vicar of Wakefield* can be guilty of such grammatical mistakes, if the first great English lexicographer can show such inconsistencies in spelling, it is absurd to consider Reynolds illiterate. "Orthography and punctuation, it should be remembered, were laxly regarded in those days, even by men of culture."

Not only did he write carelessly, but with great difficulty. Surely Sir Robert Edgcumbe is mistaken in stating that "he had a ready pen, and wrote with but few corrections". I have seen and studied with care the MS. of the lengthy *Apologia* written after his quarrel with the Academy, the original of the character-sketch of Dr Johnson, and many loose folios which were apparently fragments of his *Discourses,* and in every case the pages are covered with additions and corrections. His method of composition was the reverse of Gibbon's; the polish seen in his published writings was the result of constant revision. Even when composing mere letters, he seems to have made it his practice to write first a rough draft, which he later copied. "I have no doubt", he wrote to Dr Parr, "but that you are surprised to receive a letter in this form. The truth is, this was intended only as a rough draft, but the weakness of my eyes must prove my excuse in not writing it over fair".

It was Boswell's hero Paoli who once declared that he could decide on the character and disposition of a man whose letter he had seen. Certainly the character and disposition of the "dear Knight of Plympton" stand revealed in the letters which follow. No one can say of him what Cowper did of Pope, "the most disagreeable maker of epistles I ever met with" because he "seems to have thought that unless a sentence was well-turned, and every period pointed with some conceit, it was not worth the carriage". For in Sir Joshua's letters the conscious element is lacking, and what is thus lost in correctness and elegance is gained in sincerity. His letters ring true. They are not witty ("I never was a wit in my life"); they are not spiced with scandalous anecdotes; but they do reveal that mildness, that genuineness, that devotion to his calling, for which he was praised by all who knew him.

> When Johnson by strength overpowers our mind,
> When Montague dazzles, and Burke strikes us blind,
> To Reynolds well pleased for relief we must run,
> Rejoice in his shadow and shrink from the sun.

(pp. xi-xvi)

Frederick Whiley Hilles, in a preface to Letters of Sir Joshua Reynolds, *edited by Frederick Whiley Hilles, Cambridge at the University Press, 1929, pp. xi-xviii.*

John Steegmann   (essay date 1933)

[*In the following excerpt, Steegmann justifies Reynold's intent and accomplishment in the* Discourses.]

Five years after Sir Joshua's death his executor, Malone, published the authoritative edition of the fifteen *Discourses,* which immediately became matter for controversy: who was their real author? At first they were fathered on Johnson, but after his downright remark: "Sir Joshua would as soon have asked me to paint for him as to write for him," another begetter had to be found; so Burke was, inevitably, selected. Comparison with the styles of Burke and Johnson makes it at once clear that neither of them could possibly have been the author; subject-matter apart, the *Discourses* are not the work of a practised writer, for in many passages the style is involved and the meaning obscured through lack of skill in exposition. . . . Reynolds himself had supervised the publication of the first ten *Discourses* in 1778, and had prepared and polished for the press the remainder as they were delivered.

As to their content, it has often been observed that the precepts laid down by Reynolds therein are not in accordance with his own practice; that they contain but little instruction and a great deal of generalisation; that, while he may help his listeners to learn how to look at pictures, he does not give them the least hint of how to make pictures themselves; and that, while there is much wisdom in all of them, there is little inspiration in any. It must, however, be remembered that he never regarded it as part of his duties to instruct either the pupils in his studio or those in the Academy School; that was the function of the teaching staff, of the Professor of Painting, the Professor of Perspective, and the others; his business was to impart a knowledge of the principles of the art; but since he was a student and a scholar rather than an original thinker, he did not concern himself to evolve a final theory, a philosophy of æsthetic. He did not believe in the finality of any one form of criticism as opposed to any other, and he was fully aware that new conditions would produce new critical standpoints; yet in the *Discourses,* despite this knowledge, he accepted without question the axiom that antique sculpture and Renaissance painting represent the two final perfections of what, again without question, he took to be sister arts. His audience, he remembered, was composed of young men, no more and no less intelligent than any other young men embarking on any other profession; experience of art students had convinced him that the number of potential Masters was exceedingly small, and, rightly or wrongly, he preferred to devote himself to the many who would never become Gainsboroughs or Holbeins or Reynoldses rather than to the very few who possibly might. The instruction that he imparted was, therefore, strictly orthodox, and in accordance with the rules laid down by the Augustans early in the century, the rules of Good Taste.

The *Discourses* may be described as the official guide to the study of painting for Academy students; they prescribe a course of study by adopting which the student will at least be able to produce pictures reminiscent of the most approved Masters; a method of training which, if not calculated to encourage much originality can hardly be said to differ very greatly from the methods of most art schools to-day. (pp. 120-23)

John Steegmann, in his Sir Joshua Reynolds: Great Lives, *Duckworth, 1933, 136 p.*

Ellis K. Waterhouse   (essay date 1941)

[*Waterhouse was an English art historian, educator, and editor. Considered one of the most prominent art historians of his generation, he made many contributions to the study of art. Among his many books on art history are* Reynolds *(1941) and* Gainsborough *(1958), both highly regarded, and* Painting in Britain, 1530-1790, *first published in 1953 and still considered a standard. In the following excerpt, he outlines each of the fifteen* Discourses.]

It is neither unfair nor unflattering to say that Sir Joshua's literary gifts were as considerable as his virtues as a painter of portraits. The *Discourses* are the most vital contribution of the eighteenth century to the literature of criticism, and they are also the monument of Reynolds' ability as a writer, just as the successful establishment of the Royal Academy is the monument of his practical sagacity. They are almost wholly concerned with the training needed by a "history" painter, and they remain valid and instructive for any artist to-day, even though Sir Joshua himself showed no very great aptitude to profit by the lessons which he has shown himself competent to formulate. Their teaching, however, remains the most illuminating approach to his own work. Since they are the single aspect of his activity which has been treated with the scholarship and thoroughness which it deserves, a brief outline of their teaching is all that need be given. (p. 21)

The fundamental postulate of the *Discourses,* which is no-where explicitly stated but impregnates every theory and every practical suggestion included in their teaching, is that the purpose of an Academy is to train a young artist not merely to be a competent practitioner in his own field and in his own country. If his work is worth anything at all, its value must be assessed by standards by which all Western art may equally be measured. Reynolds would have considered such standards as absolute, but our subsequent knowledge of non-European arts makes this qualification necessary to-day. The foundation of the Academy meant for Reynolds that British art need no longer be parochial, something despised (as it was) by the cultivated patron who was familiar with the art of Italy and Flanders: it was to become part of the European tradition.

This is the point he stresses in the **"First Discourse"**: "The principal advantage of an Academy is, that . . . it will be a repository for the great examples of the Art. These are the materials on which Genius is to work, and without which the strongest intellect may be fruitlessly or deviously employed." The idea of a National Gallery had not then been formulated, but it is clearly implied in this conception of an Academy, which "will bring us nearer to that ideal excellence which it is the lot of genius always to contemplate, and never to attain". In reading this we should remember how foreign to the ideas of Lely, Kneller, or Hudson, was any ideal excellence beyond their own attainments: there was no place in the planning of their busy careers for any such hypothesis. In this Discourse he names only Raphael, Michelangelo and Annibale Carracci, and he makes only one practical suggestion, based on what he has been able to deduce of the method by which these great examples attained perfection. The *young* student must copy all the accidents of the model before him with naturalistic fidelity: style must come later, it must not be taught at the beginning.

The **"Second Discourse"** is addressed to the more advanced student "whose business is to learn all that has been known or done before his own time": such is the ideal obligation Reynolds proclaims for the young artist. But he gets down at once to practical suggestions on the method by which this is to be achieved, which he explains with astonishingly sound psychological insight and freedom from cant. His scepticism about the value of most direct copying, and his recommendation to make frequent studies directly in colour from the model, are almost heretical, as he admits.

Here Reynolds is entirely explicit about his conception of Genius and how it must be trained. "You must have no dependence on your own Genius. . . . Nothing is denied to well-directed labour, nothing is to be obtained without it." Instruction can help to direct this labour well by hints on method; perhaps it can do very little else, for "Few have been taught to any purpose who have not been their own teachers". Since "Invention, strictly speaking, is little more than a new combination of those images which have been previously gathered and deposited in the memory" most of an artist's time must be spent in gathering these images. The models from which we learn these best are the

great masters of the past, and "with respect to the pictures you are to choose for your models, I could wish that you would take the world's opinion rather than your own". For, by studying pictures admired by the world, you will come at length to see what it is that the world (rightly or wrongly) admires in them, and such knowledge is always valuable. It was thus, against his own first opinion, that Reynolds took to studying Raphael, and came at length to appreciate his enormous virtues.

"Discourse Three" is dangerous stuff for the advanced student and is perhaps the central hub of the *Discourses,* containing, as it does, a more or less reasoned account of what Reynolds held to be the nature of Beauty, and indications of how the artist was to attain it.

Beauty, for Reynolds, rests in an average, deduced from particulars and with the imperfections which exist in all particular examples pared off. It is more or less parallel to the Platonic theory of ideas, and, accordingly, "Nature herself is not to be too closely copied". The "wish of the genuine painter is . . . to improve mankind by the grandeur of his ideas (i.e., these generalizations from nature): . . . he must strive for fame by captivating the imagination". "This great ideal perfection and beauty are not to be sought in the heavens, but upon the earth", and the representation of them is the "great style". He admits, however, that it is difficult to "describe by words the proper means of acquiring it, if the mind of the student should be at all capable of such an acquisition". Experience of innumerable examples and comparison are the methods to be employed and the only way of shortening the road is the imitation of ancient statuary. He goes on to emphasize that the painter must learn to make the difficult distinction between what is Natural and what is Fashionable and that he must divest himself of all prejudice in favour of his own (or any other) age or country: although in fact he recommends a strong prejudice in favour of classical antiquity.

On top of this training for the Great Style a wide general education is also necessary: for, having mastered Beauty and Simplicity, he must learn to animate his figures with the proper qualities and this can only be done "by him who enlarges the sphere of his understanding by a variety of knowledge, and warms his imagination with the best productions of ancient and modern poetry".

The **"Fourth Discourse"** applies the defining principles of the Great Style, already given in the Third, to the various elements which make up a work of art—Invention, Composition, Expression and Colouring. In doing this Reynolds finds it necessary to discuss the Venetian, Flemish and Dutch schools, which cannot be subsumed under the Great Style, and for which—as his own practice showed—he had an especial predilection. These he calls examples of the "Ornamental Style" and he concedes them great virtues of their own on a lower level. By over-emphasizing the defects of his own favourites he shows most clearly the critical poise of his mind.

The practitioner of the Great Style must avoid the seductions of the Ornamental, since "the great style is always more or less contaminated by any meaner mixture": but the Ornamental Style has its own peculiar excellences, and under it come portraits, landscapes, still life paintings and so on. This type of painting is raised in character by borrowing some of the simplicity of the grand manner, and, in this way, Reynolds rationalizes his own practice in portrait painting, and shows how necessary, even for an artist who has no higher ambition than to excel in one of the humbler branches of the art, is some comprehension of the principles of the Great Style.

The **"Fifth Discourse"** begins with an attempt to clear up certain misunderstandings which Reynolds fears may have followed from what he has said about the Grand Style, and he does this by defining the characteristics of its two greatest exemplars, Raphael and Michelangelo. There are limits to what the Great Style can achieve. "Some excellences can bear to be united . . . others are of a discordant nature"—and he shows, from the example of Guido Reni, how the attempt to illustrate strong passions and retain at the same time a serene beauty of countenance, leads the painter into insipidity.

The discussion of insipidity leads to an alternative dichotomy of styles, which will include certain qualities worthy of admiration which the contrast of the Great and the Ornamental Styles did not cover. Now we have the Great Style and "the original or characteristic style", and the examples given of the latter are Salvator Rosa, Rubens, and Nicholas Poussin. These last three painters, differing from one another in everything else, have in common that they produce illustrations each of a perfectly self-consistent world, and one which bears always the strong impress of their own personality. Even their defects are essential to this consistency, and Reynolds uses them as examples to provide a warning against the insipidity arising from too great eclecticism, of which he gives Maratta as an example. The whole discourse seems to have been planned as an antidote to a too one-sided application of the rules he had laid down in the two previous ones.

In the **"Sixth Discourse"** Reynolds gives an account, based on his own practice, of the development of an artist's mind throughout the whole of his life. He scouts altogether the popular conceptions of "genius" and inspiration, although he admits some painters have more natural capacity for improvement than others. The only way in which an artist can become a master of his profession he holds to be by "one continued course of imitation, that is not to cease but with his life". "A painter must not only be of necessity an imitator of the works of nature . . . but . . . as necessarily an imitator of the works of other painters. . . . No man can be an artist, whatever he may suppose, upon any other terms." He describes the nature of this imitation and also the method of "borrowing" or "transplanting" figures or ideas from the works of other artists, and he defends the proper exercise of these practices from being identified with plagiarism. It is a remarkably rational and conscious description of the workings of an artist's mind, especially of those workings which are often held to be subconscious. It has proved too wounding to professional vanity to be generally accepted, but is perhaps the most valid account which has ever been put in words. As a touchstone of Sir Joshua's critical objectivity it has no rival among his writings.

The **"Seventh Discourse"** is an attempt at tracing the fixed principles of criticism. In the **"Sixth"** he had demolished the popular conception of "Genius", in this he does the same for the popular conception of "Taste". "The real substance . . . of what goes under the name of taste, is fixed and established in the nature of things." To form this just taste is undoubtedly within the power of the artist and is a help to his work. It is a power which is acquired "by the same slow progress as wisdom or knowledge of every kind", a power of distinguishing right and wrong, and it is attained by becoming sufficiently conversant with poetry and the other arts, by a certain study of what we would now call psychology, and also from the "conversation of learned and ingenious men". This is an account of Reynolds' own method of acquiring his judgment in the arts. In defining further he becomes diffuse and unexpectedly confused, mixing such statements as that the general end of all the arts is to please, with a system of qualitative grading, in which the highest arts are those which unfold truths that are useful to mankind and which make us better and wiser.

In the **"Eighth Discourse"** Reynolds urges moderation in all things—in the amount of variety and contrast, in the degree of novelty, in ornament, even in simplicity and the observance of rules. This leads to an enquiry into the "true meaning and cause of rules" and into the question of their correlation with fundamental dispositions of the passions. He gives practical notes, illustrated by examples, about colouring, relief, etc., and gives a side-line on his own style in the statement that the practice of leaving any detail or incident (unless too horrible) in a picture to the imagination is opposed to the principles of the art of painting. The **"Ninth Discourse"** is merely a stately utterance on the value to society of cultivating intellectual pleasures, made when the Academy moved to Somerset House.

The **"Tenth Discourse"** is a discussion of Sculpture and what Reynolds conceived to be its limitations in comparison with Painting. It is the least happy of the Discourses and based on the least knowledge. In it he makes no statement which bears upon his practice as an artist.

In the **"Eleventh"** he returns to his favourite subject, the question of "Genius", being afraid, perhaps, that he had left the impression that mere industry was sufficient to acquire it. He aims at giving a right direction to this industry and emphasizes that the "great business of study is to form a *mind*". Mere industry often leads to a pre-occupation with high finish and Reynolds was interested in the problem—which was particularly apparent to him as a portrait painter—that the most perfectly and highly finished imitation of anything often conveys a less appearance of likeness than something more sketchy. He concludes that the peculiar "genius of mechanical performance" in the art of painting consists in "the power of expressing your subject *as a whole*". Using Raphael's frescoes and Titian as his examples, he examines the nature of this power of generalizing and makes suggestions for arriving at a proper economy of statement. But he says: "I commend nothing for want of exactness: I mean to point out that kind of exactness which is best, and which is alone truly to be so esteemed." By what he has overlooked in some of the examples he quotes (e.g. the minuteness of much of Titian's finish, as Mr. Fry points out), he supplies his authority for his own, often too summary, treatment of accessories.

The **"Twelfth Discourse"** starts out with the suggestion that he is going to answer a question which he was often asked, and which many still ask to-day—what course of study is the young painter to pursue when he gets to Italy. His answer is that all pre-arranged plans of study are useless. Method "has certainly many advantages in dispatch of business" but he has "little confidence of its efficacy in acquiring excellence in any art whatever". His profoundly practical mind was aware that accident and opportunity had an overwhelming part in shaping the course of his own studies and he merely recommends the continual experience of the greatest masters as enthusiasm or occasion directs. For what is to be got from them he reverts again to his thesis of the nature of artistic borrowing, and its being both proper and necessary. This he illustrated by examples of Raphael's borrowing from Masaccio and he gives in parenthesis an interesting encomium on Masaccio, which marks almost the beginnings of the appreciation of Quattrocento art. He even adumbrates, in his description of how gestures may be borrowed and adapted, the ideas which are at the back of the work being done today by the Warburg Institute. The most valuable clue to his own practice lies in the recommendation that, when you borrow a pose from an earlier artist, you must paint it from nature. The "great object to which our studies are directed" is "the art of seeing nature, or, in other words, the art of using models".

The **"Thirteenth"** is the most eloquent and most crucial of the **Discourses.** Reynolds is no longer addressing students of a greater or less degree of proficiency, but is making an impassioned appeal for all the arts, as possessing something of divinity, and a vigorous protest against the ever-recurring criticism that the aim of art, and the standard by which it should be judged, is its degree of imitative success. The test for a work of art is not whether it successfully imitates nature, but whether it genuinely affects the cultivated imagination.

The necessity of education for a proper appreciation of the arts is a point he stresses. Only the lowest and purely imitative forms of art are naturally pleasing, the higher require education for them to move the imagination and sensibility. He draws parallels from the other arts, especially the eighteenth century stage and opera and poetry, where the acceptance of a highly artificial convention is more clearly of the essence than it is in painting, and he examines the different ways in which these arts deviate from nature. Each art has its own special manner of deviation, and by studying their mutual correspondence and relation to nature we may arrive at a true critical faculty. A full knowledge of critical theory along these lines he thinks is perhaps not the proper study for a practising artist, but he must remember that, in judging works of art, experience gives him a sort of sagacity, whose operations appear akin to intuition, which is much more reliable than cold reason. This will probably enable him to judge correctly, without being able to formulate in words the principles of his criticism.

The occasion of the **"Fourteenth Discourse"** was the recent death of Gainsborough, and it contains a remarkably fair appraisal of a man with whom Reynolds had nothing in common except an intense love of his art. Gainsborough never attempted the higher style of painting, he perhaps would not even have admitted that it was "higher" than the style of the landscapes, subject-pieces and portraits in which he excelled. Even while warning the students against imitation of Gainsborough's impressionism, Reynolds recognizes its aptness to secure the effect Gainsborough intended, and it is probable that no more just and

generous tribute to an unsympathetic rival has been written. Otherwise the Discourse is not important.

The same cannot be said of the **"Fifteenth"** and last Discourse, which is much more than a speech of farewell. It is the profession of faith of a nearly blind old man, who had had many months' leisure, since he was last able to paint, to think over and appraise what he had said before, and to think how best he could reinforce whatever in his teaching seemed to him most precious. He acknowledges, not without decent pride, everything he has taught in the twenty years over which the writing of the **Discourses** was spread, and he emphasizes the serious and deliberate character of their teaching, saying that he has "succeeded in establishing the rules and principles of our art on a more firm and lasting foundation than that on which they had formerly been placed". But the bulk of the Discourse is reasoned praise of Michelangelo, whose grand style is what he would aspire to, if he had his life over again. If one has high aspirations it is Michelangelo that one must study; his great style "presupposes in the spectator a cultivated and prepared artificial state of mind", and it may not be appreciated at first, but it is the highest to which painting has ever attained, it is "the language of the Gods". (pp. 21-9)

Ellis K. Waterhouse, in his Reynolds, *Kegan Paul, Trench Trubner & Co. Ltd., 1941, 300 p.*

Frederick W. Hilles   (essay date 1949)

[*In the following excerpt, Hilles examines the characteristics of Reynolds's writing style, comparing it to the styles of Joseph Addison and Samuel Johnson.*]

On a May afternoon in 1776 Sir William Forbes was host to a distinguished company at his villa near London. One of his guests, Sir Joshua Reynolds, remarked that beauty could not be discriminated. George Colman, disagreeing, suggested that there was a difference between languishing beauty and lively beauty, and when Boswell pointed out that " 'twas of stile Sir Joshua had talked," Colman stuck to his guns, saying that styles too could be distinguished by their excellence. "Tell me then," challenged Reynolds, "the distinctive quality of Addison's style."

On a July afternoon in 1807 Sir Harry Englefield entertained a similar group at his home in London. The conversation turned on English prose, "and after much had been said, it was allowed by all present that Sir Joshua Reynolds, in His Lectures, wrote with more purity & simplicity than any other modern writer, & might for the excellence of His style in that respect be compared with Addison;—having clearness, ease, and no affectation."

Much has been written of the **Discourses,** but to the best of my knowledge the question of style has been passed over, or dismissed with a few vague adjectives. And yet that question calls forth others more specific. Is Sir Joshua's prose Addisonian, as Sir Harry's friends imply? Reynolds himself said he was of Johnson's "school." Is his prose Johnsonian? Herbert Read classifies him as a traditionalist. What are the characteristics of the traditional style as revealed in his writings?

As a stylist Sir Joshua must be judged by his **Discourses** and the three letters to *The Idler* which antedate them. With a few negligible exceptions he allowed nothing else of his to be published in his lifetime. We have no way of knowing what alterations he would have made before printing his journals, his jeux d'esprit, and his admirable biographical sketches. Nor can our study include his personal letters, if we are to understand the comments which critics have made of his prose style. (pp. 49-50)

Fortunately, to limit ourselves to the ***Discourses*** and *Idlers* is not a serious restriction. The letters to *The Idler* were printed in 1759, when the author was thirty-six years old, a successful painter but still relatively unknown. The final discourse was printed in 1791, a year before Sir Joshua's death, at a time when he was generally regarded as the greatest living painter. There is a gap of thirty-two years between his first and last publication. If his style changed as he matured, an examination of the *Idlers* and ***Discourses*** should reveal the fact.

But examination reveals little difference between the early and the late writings. . . . I for one should find it very difficult to distinguish from internal evidence between what Reynolds wrote in 1759 and what he wrote in 1769 or 1779.

In general we may apply to his style what Johnson said of the man; it is the same all the year round. Here and there a purple passage is to be found, such as the one Northcote heard Reynolds read to Burke. And the concluding paragraphs of the final discourse reveal an emotion in the speaker which is not characteristic. Here and there, too, we meet with clumsy writing, like the phrase which a contemporary reviewer extracted from the **"Eighth Discourse"**: "by recommending the attention of the artist to an acquaintance with the passions." But I consider unjustified such sweeping statements as that by Horace Walpole, ordinarily an acute critic in such matters. He reported that the **"Twelfth Discourse"** "was observed to be much more incorrect in the style than any of his former." To me the twelfth seems no more "incorrect" than those which were written earlier or later. I should characterize it as a polished piece of writing, typical of what is to be found in the other discourses.

Without further ado, then, I shall present two extracts as characteristic of their author. One is from the first discourse, the other from the last, although I am not concerned with the time when either was written. I have selected them almost, as the phrase goes, at random. They are long enough for the development of a thought, short enough to be used in an essay of this length. A careful scrutiny of these selections should make clear to us how Reynolds put words and sentences together. The blind man judging the shape of an elephant by feeling its trunk? I reply with the Latin tag popular in the eighteenth century: *ex pede Herculem*. From the **"First Discourse"**:

> I would chiefly recommend, that an implicit obedience to the *Rules of Art,* as established by the practice of the great MASTERS, should be exacted from the *young* Students. That those models, which have passed through the approbation of ages, should be considered by them as perfect and infallible guides; as subjects for their imitation, not their criticism.

> I am confident, that this is the only efficacious method of making a progress in the Arts; and that

he who sets out with doubting, will find life finished before he becomes master of the rudiments. For it may be laid down as a maxim, that he who begins by presuming on his own sense, has ended his studies as soon as he has commenced them. Every opportunity, therefore, should be taken to discountenance that false and vulgar opinion, that rules are the fetters of genius; they are fetters only to men of no genius; as that armour, which upon the strong is an ornament and a defence, upon the weak and mis-shapen becomes a load, and cripples the body which it was made to protect.

How much liberty may be taken to break through those rules, and, as the Poet expresses it,

To snatch a grace beyond the reach of art,

may be a subsequent consideration, when the pupils become masters themselves. It is then, when their genius has received its utmost improvement, that rules may possibly be dispensed with. But let us not destroy the scaffold, until we have raised the building.

From the **"Fifteenth Discourse"**:

> In reviewing my Discourses, it is no small satisfaction to be assured that I have, in no part of them, lent my assistance to foster *newly-hatched unfledged* opinions, or endeavoured to support paradoxes, however tempting may have been their novelty; or however ingenious I might, for the minute, fancy them to be; nor shall I, I hope, any where be found to have imposed on the minds of young Students declamation for argument, a smooth period for a sound precept. I have pursued a plain and *honest method;* I have taken up the art simply as I found it exemplified in the practice of the most approved Painters. That approbation which the world has uniformly given, I have endeavoured to justify by such proofs as questions of this kind will admit; by the analogy which Painting holds with the sister Arts, and consequently by the common congeniality which they all bear to our nature. And though in what has been done no new discovery is pretended, I may still flatter myself, that from the discoveries which others have made by their own intuitive good sense and native rectitude of judgement, I have succeeded in establishing the rules and principles of our Art on a more firm and lasting foundation than that on which they had formerly been placed.

I assume everyone will agree that these passages are highly characteristic of Sir Joshua's thinking. The reverence for the past, the abhorrence of ingenious and novel opinions, the emphasis on good sense and judgment, ideas which Sir Joshua held in common with Burke and Goldsmith and Johnson, underlie all that he wrote. But our concern is with manner rather than matter, and here too the passages seem to me highly characteristic of the author.

The first thing to be noticed is that although twenty-two years elapsed between the writing of the two passages, the tone and rhythms are the same. The author has plenty of time. The sentences are long, and there is a marked tendency to wordiness. And yet, owing to careful balance, the sentences do not get out of hand. It is not a diffuse style. A certain crispness and control are secured through antithesis, and the varied rhythms of the individual sentence form part of a more sustained rhythm.

In a belated obituary we are told that "there was a polish in the exterior of Sir Joshua, illustrative of the Gentleman and the Scholar." The extracts reveal this polish. In the one he quotes Pope; in the other he has italicized the two phrases from *Hamlet*. The earlier selection contains the elaborate armor simile and concludes with a metaphor. These "decorations," as Sir Joshua would have termed them, are functional. Together with other elements, they retard the tempo and support the prevailing tone, which is dignified, deliberate, urbane.

There is a smooth, easy-flowing quality to the phrasing, partly due to initial connectives, partly to syntax. To show how each sentence or each paragraph moves into the next would be tedious. Two examples from the second selection should suffice. The "nor shall I . . . be found to have imposed" is a dominant seventh which is resolved in "I have pursued," and this sentence in turn, ending with "the most *approved* Painters," is followed by the most obvious inversion in either selection: "That *approbation* which the world has uniformly given, I have endeavoured to justify. . . ." Here the object of the sentence, placed out of its normal position, binds the sentence more closely to what precedes it. Throughout these selections there is a high degree of coherence.

The style is smooth; it is also emphatic. And the emphasis is achieved in various ways. Never going to the extremes of Johnsonese, Sir Joshua gains emphasis through parallelism. When Old Masters are called "perfect" and "infallible" guides, the second adjective is redundant. "False" and "vulgar" differ in meaning but, when yoked together as here, result in nothing more than an added weight to the thought. The same is true, as Polonius might have admitted, of *"new-hatch'd unfledg'd."* Significantly Reynolds has amplified the other Shakespearean phrase, writing "plain and *honest*" instead of *"honest."*

More conspicuous is parallelism when coupled with anaphora, "however tempting . . . however ingenious," or when there are three elements in each member, "intuitive good sense . . . native rectitude of judgement." It is possible to distinguish between "intuitive" and "native" or between "good sense" and "rectitude of judgement," but in this passage each phrase seems to mean no more than "innate right thinking." Repetition of the idea deepens the impression.

Needless to say, when a parallel structure is used to bring out opposites, emphasis is increased. Early in the second selection Reynolds contrasts "a smooth period" with "a sound precept." Here three elements in each member are linked by alliteration and the two members contrasted in meaning. But the phrase is the more noticeable because it in turn is in apposition to what precedes it. The result is a double antithesis, two parallelisms forming a third: "declamation" rather than "argument," "a smooth period" rather than "a sound precept."

There is no doubt that diction also plays its part in making the style emphatic. Sir Joshua, like all educated writers of his time, preferred words of Latin rather than Anglo-Saxon ancestry, the long word rather than the short. It is because of this and because of his tendency to write impressive-sounding phrases, that his style has been dubbed "presidential." For example, "those models, which have been passed through the approbation of ages," might be

in simpler language "models tested by time." Again "helped to promote" would be less pompous than "lent my assistance to foster," and we have already noticed "rectitude of judgement," a phrase which sounds Johnsonian and which had been used by Burke.

Frequently it is not the long word itself but the way in which it is used that colors the passage. Like Johnson, Reynolds naturally thinks in abstractions. Hence he speaks of "that *approbation* which *the world* has *uniformly* given." And often an abstract quality is made subject of a sentence. "Their genius has received its utmost improvement," he writes. "Novelty" is "tempting," "discovery" is "pretended," "art" is "exemplified." In this connection a study of a sentence near the end of the first selection is rewarding. The subject, a compound clause of twenty-six words, can for our purpose be reduced to "How much liberty may be taken." The simple predicate is "may be a subsequent consideration." Colloquially we might say, "you may think about breaking the rules later."

The passive voice seems to dominate throughout. Rules are "established" by masters, obedience "should be exacted" by teachers, models "should be considered" by students, opportunity "should be taken" by all, armour "was made" by unspecified artisans, liberty "may be taken" and rules "dispensed with" by artists. Reynolds is "assured" by [we suppose] his friends and will not "be found [by anyone] to have imposed" on the minds of novices. We learn further that "in what has been done [by me] no new discovery is pretended" [by me]. Among other effects such writing re-enforces generalization.

Related to this, I believe, is the normal unemphatic use of the expletive "it" or "there." Almost any page written by Reynolds will provide an example. Midway in the first selection we read, "it may be laid down as a maxim, that . . ." Remove these words, and the sentence is a somewhat Johnsonian aphorism, "He who begins by presuming . . ." The aphorism itself is general: the reference is to anyone who behaves in this way. But when the words which we have removed are restored, the generality is heightened. It may be laid down by whom? The subject is impersonal.

In the text, immediately before the example just cited, we read: "He who sets out with doubting, will find life finished before he becomes master of the rudiments." Where Johnson and Reynolds begin a phrase with "he who," Addison and Steele commonly write "a man who." Now "man" in this context is not particularized, but an added abstraction creeps in when the indefinite "he" is substituted for the generalized noun.

So much for analysis. Only by descending to particularities can we give meaning to those adjectives which have been applied to Sir Joshua's style: clear, easy, unaffected, perspicuous, elegant, nervous. Doubtless if other passages were subjected to the same sort of treatment, some alteration of the lights and shadows would occur, but the general impression would remain the same. Sir Joshua was an artist. The dignity which he advocated in painting he achieved in writing.

Many of the characteristics noted in our analysis are to be found in Johnson's prose. It would be surprising if this were not so. The two men were contemporaries, they were close friends, they were both generalizers. In his penetrating study of Johnson W. K. Wimsatt writes:

> What he said about the dignity of generality has its most obvious reflection in the fact that his own writing may, as we have said, be characterized as exceptionally general and abstract. Johnson, the last great neoclassicist, the reactionary, was the one who most seriously attempted to put into artistic practice the neoclassic uniformitarian ideal. . . . In his elaborate system of parallelism and antithesis, in the "philosophic" pomp of his diction, he devised a way of lending to the abstract an emphasis, a particularity and thickness. . . . By limiting himself faithfully to the abstract, he achieved more with it than did any other neoclassicist.

Here the key word is in the first sentence. Johnson's writing is *exceptionally* general. We have seen that Sir Joshua, a later neoclassicist, a less positive reactionary, adopted the Johnsonian devices, and that his writing is emphatically abstract. The difference between the two styles is one of degree. (pp. 50-7)

Throughout his ***Discourses*** we come across Johnsonian echoes. We find phrases like "that slow progression of things, which naturally makes elegance and refinement the last effect of opulence and power"; sentences like "At that age it is natural for them to be more captivated with what is brilliant, than what is solid, and to prefer splendid negligence to painful and humiliating exactness"; paragraphs like "These instructions I have ventured to offer from my own experience; but as they deviate widely from received opinions, I offer them with diffidence; and when better are suggested, shall retract them without regret." And we have already noticed Sir Joshua's fondness for the Johnsonian aphorism. Here are a few culled from the ***Discourses:*** "Nothing can come of nothing: he who has laid up no materials, can produce no combinations." "But let no man be seduced to idleness by specious promises. Excellence is never granted to man, but as the reward of labour." "What has pleased, and continues to please, is likely to please again." (p. 57)

Reynolds was profoundly influenced by Johnson and acknowledged his indebtedness. Nevertheless, no one has accused him of writing Johnsonese. His style is what Saintsbury called characteristic. Herbert Read, as was said earlier, terms it traditional. And it is not difficult to account for this.

Buffon's famous dictum is to the point. How did Sir Joshua's friends characterize him? Johnson: "The most invulnerable man I know; the man with whom if you should quarrel, you should find the most difficulty how to abuse." Burke: "his native humility, modesty, and candour, never forsook him, even on surprise or provocation; nor was the least degree of arrogance or assumption visible to the most scrutinizing eye, in any part of his conduct or discourse." His temper, according to Malone, was modest and equable, according to Boswell equal and placid, according to Barnard mild, according to Mrs. Thrale peaceful. His manners, according to Goldsmith, were gentle, complying, and bland.

Such a man would instinctively shy away from the overemphatic, would avoid all extremes, would strive to appear normal. "Peculiar marks," he wrote, "I hold to be, generally, if not always, defects; however difficult it may

be wholly to escape them." Hence he expresses himself in a style which admits of no eccentricities, no mannerisms. I have tried without success to discover the distinctive quality of his style. It is that of the cultured gentleman of his day.

A few months before Reynolds became author, Horace Walpole in an unpublished letter to Dalrymple remarked: "a good style (in writing) has grown almost as common as a good print." This good style, everyone knows, derived from Addison, and there are passages in the *Spectator*, particularly when the pleasures of the imagination are discussed, which Reynolds might have written. I should say that Sir Joshua's style is basically Addisonian with Johnsonian overtones. It is the middle style, "exact without apparent elaboration . . . elegant but not ostentatious." (pp. 58-9)

> *Frederick W. Hilles, "Sir Joshua's Prose," in* The Age of Johnson: Essays Presented to Chauncey Brewster Tinker, *edited by Frederick W. Hilles, Yale University Press, 1949, pp. 49-60.*

Joseph Wood Krutch   (essay date 1952)

[*Krutch is widely regarded as one of America's most respected literary critics. A conservative and idealistic thinker, he was a consistent proponent of human dignity and the preeminence of literary art. His criticism is characterized by such concerns; in* The Modern Temper *(1929), for example, he argued that because scientific thought has denied human worth, tragedy has become obsolete, and in* The Measure of Man *(1954) he attacked modern culture for depriving humanity of the sense of individual responsibility necessary for making important decisions in an increasingly complex age. In the following excerpt, Krutch reviews* Portraits, *focusing upon Reynolds's acidic portrait of Garrick and the general unevenness of the entire collection.*]

Samuel Johnson once explained why great men are often disappointing to meet. "Uncommon parts," he said, "require uncommon opportunities for their exertion." Yet The Club to which he himself belonged was great just because its most distinguished members were exceptions to the rule and needed no special opportunities. Burke without a rostrum, Garrick without a stage, and Reynolds without a canvas were still obviously remarkable men and they set one another off as though they had been imagined by a novelist for the purpose.

James Boswell was not a man to overlook this fact and it is not surprising that he once toyed briefly with the possibility of following his life of Johnson with a life of Reynolds. This probably explains why several fragmentary compositions by Reynolds turned up among his papers and made possible this third volume [***Portraits***] in the popular Yale edition of his vast literary remains. That Reynolds could write as well as paint was no secret to his contemporaries, but two of the brief fragments here made public for the first time are truly brilliant. One is an hilarious skit intended to demonstrate how hopelessly Oliver Goldsmith could bungle an anecdote; the other is a quietly acid portrait of Garrick in the role of a man who "made himself a slave to his reputation."

What Reynolds says is by no means irreconcilable with what other contemporaries are known to have said. Garrick appears to have been a man who was essentially a performer, who acted off stage as well as on, and from whose conversation no "good things" are remembered despite the fact that he lived in an age pre-eminent for witty talk. But Reynolds' portrait does nevertheless constitute the most vivid and quietly damning picture drawn by any reliable contemporary. Garrick, he says, prepared his social appearances as carefully as he prepared for a public performance. "The habit of seeking fame in this manner left his mind unfit for the cultivation of private friendship. Garrick died without a real friend, though no man had a greater number of what the world calls friends."

That Reynolds was by nature neither malicious nor censorious makes the picture seem all the more damning and if it is accurate one can only conclude that the vivacity and superficial charm of the man must have been, as Reynolds himself admits, almost as extraordinary as his professional talent. After all Johnson, Burke, Goldsmith and Reynolds himself seem to have been glad to have him in their company.

If there were in this volume a few other things as good as the short bits about Goldsmith and Garrick it would be rewarding indeed and almost as good as Boswell's own "London Journal." Unfortunately, however, the total of the new Reynolds material is contained within a few pages and to allow it a whole volume suggests that those responsible for this edition of the Boswell papers may be spreading things a bit thin.

> *Joseph Wood Krutch, "As Sir Joshua Reynolds Saw His Friends," in* The New York Times Book Review, *November 16, 1952, p. 6.*

Walter John Hipple, Jr. (essay date 1957)

[*Hipple is an American educator who has written extensively on aesthetic theory. In the following excerpt from an essay originally published in a different form in the* Journal of Aesthetics and Art Criticism, *he considers the appropriateness of the theory of the central form to Reynolds's system as a whole.*]

[The] chief subject of the discourses is "that grand style of painting, which improves partial representation by the general and invariable ideas of nature." This general nature is, consistently with Reynolds' philosophical principles, a conception in the mind of the artist; for although the conception is formed by abstraction from external reality, the ideal itself has only a potential existence prior to its comprehension. Accordingly, the same distinction between copying (on one hand) and invention, recombination, and improvement (on the other) obtains in the imitation of nature as in the imitation of artists: "Upon the whole, it seems to me, that the object and intention of all the Arts is to supply the natural imperfection of things, and often to gratify the mind by realizing and embodying what never existed but in the imagination."

It is noteworthy that in the *Discourses* Reynolds does not advance the peculiarly literal conception of general nature which he expounded in the third of his *Idler* papers. Beauty was there arbitrarily confined to form alone, and was found to be the medium or center of the various forms of a species or kind (that form which is more frequent than any one deviation from it—not necessarily an average); this definition carried as corollaries, that the beauty of an individual could not be judged prior to the collection of statistics on its species, and that there could be no comparison in point of beauty between species. Refutations of Reynolds' theory from the eighteenth century to the present day have more often than not directed their battery against this paper, either directly or by reading the *Discourses* as an expansion of it and criticizing them accordingly. Thus, Sir Uvedale Price, who attempts to account for beauty by a mechanism partly nervous, partly associational, criticizes the *Idler* theory sharply, for beauty to Price does not depend on comparison within a species; Richard Payne Knight, who employs an elaborate faculty psychology in accounting for the several "beauties" of the various faculties, sees Reynolds as confining his notions to the intellectual qualities of things exclusively; and Dugald Stewart, attempting to subsume previous theories with the aid of a theory of philosophical language, finds the Reynolds view narrow and inadequate. The moderns, diverting attention from the systematic interrelations of Reynolds' ideas to their sources, or the sources of the terminology in which they are couched, rarely see Reynolds' thought as more than a *pasticcio;* but Roger Fry at least has deemed the theory of the central form worthy of refutation.

I shall not enter upon the question of the validity of this doctrine; rather, I should like to consider briefly the formal or constitutive question of its appropriateness to Reynolds' system as a whole. I think that, viewed in this light, it is a misstep. The peculiar virtue and merit of a Platonic system of criticism consists in the flexibility or "ambiguity" of its terms, a flexibility which permits their analogical application to a range of subjects and the consequent isolation in those subjects of the universal traits or "ideas" to which the terms refer. If it be asked, how can undefined terms isolate anything? the reply must be, that each such term receives definition in each context by comparison with and opposition to other terms of the system; in each application the meaning of the term emerges from its use in the argument, the "dialectic." If this indeterminacy of terms is a prerequisite for a Platonic system that is not to be dogmatic, it is apparent that Reynolds erred in attempting to tie down so literally the meaning of "beauty" in the *Idler* papers. Ideality is not to be defined or given statistical delimitation.

In the *Discourses,* the first of which was delivered ten years after the *Idler* papers were written, the freedom of the dialectic is unimpaired by dogmatic definition. Yet Reynolds never abandoned outright his early theory. In a letter to Beattie in 1782, commenting on the manuscript of the essay on beauty which Beattie had submitted to him, he observes: "About twenty years since I thought much on this subject, and am now glad to find many of those ideas which then passed in my mind put in such good order by so excellent a metaphysician. My view of the question did not extend beyond my own profession; it regarded only the beauty of form which I attributed entirely to custom or habit. You have taken a larger compass, including, indeed, everything that gives delight, every mental and corporeal excellence. . . . ." . . . In the discourses, too, Reynolds speaks of "presenting to the eye the same effect as that which it has been *accustomed* to feel, which in this case, as in every other, will always produce beauty. . . . " But habit is not advanced as the single cause of all beauty, and in the discourses the earlier theory is quietly modified by sloughing off all the literal limitations on the concept of beauty. By so doing, Reynolds made his system one of the permanent alternatives of aesthetic theory.

It is apparent that beauty, treated in the manner of Reynolds, has the energy and grandeur customarily associated with the sublime; and, indeed, it is difficult to see how there could be more than one ideal type of general nature—Reynolds' mode of reasoning automatically obviates the distinction between sublime and beautiful. Yet a distinction so pervasive in the literature of the century is certain to leave its mark; and Reynolds occasionally bifurcates his concept of the beautiful, setting the sublime against the "elegant." These two characters are not coordinate; the dichotomy is between a higher beauty, the sublime, and a lower, the elegant. The elegant may be paired with taste and fancy, while the sublime is connected with genius and imagination; alternatively, the elegant may be judged sensual. But the sublime, in any event, sweeps all before it:

> The sublime in Painting, as in Poetry, so overpowers, and takes such a possession of the whole mind, that no room is left for attention to minute criticism. The little elegancies of art in the presence of these great ideas thus greatly expressed, lose all their value, and are, for the instant at least, felt to be unworthy of our notice. The correct judgment, the purity of taste, which characterize Raffaelle, the exquisite grace [elegance] of Correggio and Parmegiano, all disappear before them.

When Reynolds is treating of art, Raffaelle stands for him "foremost of the first painters," but when attention is directed towards genius and sublimity, then Michael Angelo, though he cannot match Raffaelle in balance and completeness of artistic equipment, is supreme.

There are passages in which Reynolds' sublime and elegant correspond pretty closely in application with Burke's sublime and beautiful. Reynolds draws, for instance, the inescapable contrast between the sublime landscapes of Salvator and the elegant scenes of Claude, between bold projections and gentle slopes, abruptly angular and gradually inclined branches, clouds rolling in volumes and gilded with the setting sun, and so forth. It is significant, however, that this coincidence of doctrine occurs in discussion of landscape, precisely where the difference of the two systems is minimum. In landscape, the sublime is not of higher order than the elegant; both Claude and Salvator are painters of the first rank, and the distinction between their styles is literal and descriptive. But in human subjects, the sublime springs from and appeals to higher faculties. The tastes of Burke and Reynolds, to be sure, are less different than their fashions of accounting for their tastes; but the difference in their accounts is radical. Burke's literal distinction of beauty and sublimity is often dissolved by Reynolds, and when not abandoned it is so transformed in content and established on so different a foundation that only in isolated contexts does any considerable resemblance appear. Burke's famous distinction had become a verbal commonplace for succeeding aestheticians, to no two of whom did it convey the same meaning.

Although Reynolds refers to Burke as a truly philosophical aesthetician, and although Burke is the only writer so praised, his influence on Reynolds' thought was slight. Even the essay on taste prefixed to the second edition of the *Sublime and Beautiful* (to which Thompson and Bryant assign some weight in determining Reynolds' opinions) has no clear relation to the theory of Reynolds. For Burke, taste is "that faculty or those faculties of the mind which are affected with, or which form a judgment of, the works of imagination and the elegant arts," whereas for Reynolds taste is "that faculty of the mind by which we like or dislike, whatever be the subject," a faculty which judges in the productive, practical, and theoretical sciences alike. In the system of Burke, the aesthetic excellences rest upon very different foundations from the moral virtues, but throughout the system of Reynolds there runs a recurrent analogy between beauty and virtue, and another between beauty and truth. Burke, in short, operates within a scheme of separate sciences and is in search of closely literal definitions of the aesthetic qualities he treats (even though those qualities pervade both nature and art), while Reynolds tends always to analogize the sciences and to "define" analogically and dialectically. The occasional verbal and doctrinal resemblances, then, are only isolated points of community in systems which are radically and fundamentally distinct.

The criterion of taste for Reynolds is of course generality. Not only should the audience whose taste is appealed to *be* universal (always and everywhere), but it should appeal to general principles in judging works and their producers. Nature (true art) is distinguished from fashion (false art) by the test of enduring and universal fame. Great works, therefore, "speak to the general sense of the whole species; in which common . . . tongue, every thing grand and comprehensive must be uttered." Yet at the same time, the artist may envisage an elect few—his great predecessors—as his audience; and this is not a contradiction, for *these* are the few who have sloughed off fashion and rejected particularity—they are not men, but Man. Indeed, the appeal is never to the untutored taste of the multitude (which will always exhibit local and temporary particularity) but always to the taste the natural potentialities of which have been cultivated by art. For criticism both *is* an art and is developed through art, requiring for its cultivation the enthusiasm inspired by works of genius: "It must be remembered," says Reynolds, "that this great style itself is artificial in the highest degree, it presupposes in the spectator a cultivated and prepared artificial state of mind. It is an absurdity, therefore, to suppose that we are born with this taste, though we are with the seeds of it, which, by the heat and kindly influence of . . . genius, may be ripened in us." There is a hierarchy of criticisms as there is a hierarchy of imitations, each stage more inclusive than the preceding: comparison of works and masters within an art (which first test "must have two capital defects; it must be narrow, and it must be uncertain"); comparison of arts and their principles with one another; and comparison of all such principles "with those of human nature, from whence arts derive the materials upon which they are to produce their effects," which style is at once the highest and the soundest, "for it refers to the eternal and immutable nature of things."

Taste so conceived is no different from genius, save that to genius there supervenes a power of execution. Indeed, all the elements of the system—artist, audience, style, and subject—are merged when in their perfected state: "The *gusto grande* of the Italians, the *beau ideal* of the French, and the *great style, genius,* and *taste* among the English, are but different appellations of the same thing." Genius, then, is only the imaginative power of apprehending general nature; but it is related to the universal in another sense as well, since it involves a collective effort, each artist being inspired by his own predecessors. Many of the Longinian passages in the discourses center about this last theme: "Whoever has so far formed his taste, as to be able to relish and feel the beauties of the great masters, has gone a great way in his study," Reynolds declares, "for, merely from a consciousness of this relish of the right, the mind swells with an inward pride, and is almost as powerfully affected, as if it had itself produced what it admires"; I need not quote the eulogy of Michael Angelo with which the discourses conclude. Even the "genius of mechanical performance," the painter's genius *qua* painter, participates in generality: it consists in "the power of expressing that which employs your pencil . . . *as a whole*," contracting into one whole what nature has made multifarious by working up all parts of the picture together instead of finishing part by part.

The paradox that genius is the product of art is the chief purport of the discourses: "The purport of this discourse, and, indeed, of most of my other discourses, is, to caution you against that false opinion . . . of the imaginary powers of native genius, and its sufficiency in great works." Because of the identifications already remarked upon, the purpose of the discourses can also, of course, be stated in terms of taste ("My purpose in the discourses . . . has been to lay down certain general positions, which seem to me proper for the formation of sound taste") or in terms of the art itself (it became necessary, in order to reconcile conflicting precepts, "to distinguish the greater truth . . . from the lesser truth; the larger and more liberal idea of nature from the more narrow and confined; that which addresses itself to the imagination, from that which is solely addressed to the eye. . . . [The] different rules and regulations which presided over each department of art, followed of course . . . "). Keeping, however, to the aspect of the discourses which centers upon genius—it was certainly not Reynolds' view that natural powers have no efficacy, or that an Academy can make a Michael Angelo of any daubing student; a "man can bring home wares only in proportion to the capital with which he goes to market." But natural powers are only a potentiality, and as a professor addressing students, or (more widely) as an aesthetician addressing artists and critics with the view of forming taste and directing practice, Reynolds deals with what is within human powers to alter, not with what is given by nature; the question is, how to realize natural endowment and how to direct its efforts. Thus the relation of genius to rules can be stated variously: the opposition of genius to the narrow rules of any rigid intellectual system is a conventional topic; nonetheless, Reynolds urges, "what we now call Genius, begins, not where rules, abstractedly taken, end; but where known vulgar and trite rules have no longer any place. It must of necessity be, that even works of Genius, like every other effect, as they must have their cause, must likewise have their rules. . . ." These rules depend on the imagination and passions. The active principle of the mind demands variety, novelty, contrast; the passive, uniformity, custom, repose; and per-

fection lies in a mean. This is all obvious; noticeable is the slightness of the *axiomata media* under the guidance of which the universal qualities are found or embodied in particular works. But it is generally true of Platonic systems of criticism that instead of "rules" governing the relations of parts in a whole directed towards a specific end, "touchstones" are supplied which facilitate the recognition of the universal virtues in their concrete manifestations. So while Reynolds occasionally vouchsafes a rule (as that the masses of light in a picture be always of a warm, mellow color), these rules are few and slender, and the emphasis is on a complicated balancing of artists who embody the various aesthetic virtues and defects.

All the problems of genius, of taste, and of art, then, are given their peculiar form in Reynolds' aesthetics by the dialectical method and psychological orientation of the system. Since the root is not a supernal nature but a terrestrial, the ideal universe being a product of imagination, the faculties of the mind play a crucial role. But Reynolds' view of the faculties is neither original nor complex; sense perceives, fancy combines, reason distinguishes. Appropriately, since imagination is the combining and generalizing power, the arts depend upon it for their higher qualities, and upon sense only by a condescension to the necessities of human nature. Such condescension is inevitable, however, and art strives to give each faculty gratification: "Our taste has a kind of sensuality about it, as well as a love of the sublime; both these qualities of the mind are to have their proper consequence, as far as they do not counteract each other; for that is the grand error which much care ought to be taken to avoid." In the same way, opinion as well as truth must be regarded by the artist, and its authority is proportioned to the universality of the prejudice; "whilst these opinions and prejudices . . . continue, they operate as truth; and the art, whose office it is to please the mind, as well as instruct it, must direct itself according to opinion, or it will not attain its end." Such concessions, however guarded, mark the difference of this system from that of Plato, for whom the highest art of Reynolds would be second-best; for Plato, true art is dialectic, whereas for Reynolds, such an identification is prevented by the laws of the mind. Reason (as discriminating faculty) plays its role not in dictating the subjects of art but in assisting the artist to "consider and separate those different principles to which different modes of beauty owe their original . . . to discriminate perfections that are incompatible with each other." Reason and taste may be identified with one another in some contexts, but when reason is "grounded on a partial view of things," in contrast with the habitual sagacity of imagination, it must give way—in art, imagination is "the residence of truth."

The distinction of levels of argument is often accompanied by the bifurcation of concepts and the identification of the concepts on the higher level. This tendency is in Reynolds sometimes imperfectly realized or difficult to trace. Imagination and fancy, for instance, are not consistently or radically distinguished by him; in only one passage are they explicitly contrasted: "Raffaelle had more Taste and Fancy; Michael Angelo more Genius and Imagination. The one excelled in beauty, the other in energy. . . . Michael Angelo's works . . . seem to proceed from his own mind entirely. . . . Raffaelle's materials are generally borrowed, though the noble structure is his own." The couplings here suggest a difference of degree, imagination rearranging more freely and powerfully. Fancy is sometimes "capricious" and connected with the picturesque. But although the distinction made familiar by Coleridge is here sought in vain, there is an obvious differentiation of artistic powers paralleling the contrast of the arbitrary, fashionable, and ornamental with the natural, simple, and beautiful. The distinction of sublime from elegant, and the identification of taste, genius, and style on the higher level, have been enough insisted upon.

Reynolds' elaborate hierarchy of styles and species is made possible by the differentiation of mental powers and aesthetic characters which has been outlined. One set of distinctions depends upon dignity of subject: history, genre, landscape, portraiture, animal painting, still-life, and so on—many of which classes are themselves susceptible of subdivision. Cutting across this hierarchy of genres is the contrast of a higher and a lower manner. In history, for instance, the grand style of Rome and Florence is set against the ornamental style of Venice and Flanders; and in the lower genres of the art, there is "the same distinction of a higher and a lower style; and they take their rank and degree in proportion as the artist departs more, or less, from common nature, and makes it an object of his attention to strike the imagination of the spectator by ways belonging specially to art. . . . " Arts employing different means from painting are handled similarly in terms of object and manner, although some media may render the lower manner intolerable: sculpture (which Reynolds instances at length) must design in simplicity proportioned to the simplicity of its materials. Even the "non-imitative" arts of architecture and music exhibit parallel distinctions, with the higher quality related to the imagination by association rather than imitation, and the lower connected with utility and sense. The argument is always flexible, however; excellence in a lower style is preferred to mediocrity in a higher (a principle which Reynolds illustrates in the critique of Gainsborough), and it is erroneous to introduce the grand manner into a lower rank to which a different mode of achieving a qualified generality is appropriate. In portraiture, for instance, universality is achieved not by idealizing beyond recognition but by catching the likeness "as a whole." Still another dimension is introduced in discussion of the "characteristical" style, peculiar to the cast of mind of an individual painter; while such peculiarity is not referable to a true archetype in nature, and is not a proper object of imitation, it has its proper excellence in consistency and unity, "as if the whole proceeded from one mind."

But Reynolds' attention returns always to the grand style, the keystone of the arch. The grand style is universal in cause and in effect, in subject and in style; it is beautiful by abstracting from the particular forms of nature, simple by rejecting the influence of fashion. Although grandeur requires simplicity—which is truth—it is still contrary to truth, when truth is particular and historical. The grand style concerns itself rather with "that ideal excellence which it is the lot of genius always to contemplate, and never to attain." (pp. 140-48)

Walter John Hipple, Jr., "Sir Joshua Reynolds," in his The Beautiful, The Sublime, & the Picturesque in Eighteenth-Century British Aesthetic Theory, *The Southern Illinois University Press, 1957, pp. 133-48.*

Robert R. Wark   (essay date 1959)

[A Canadian-born American art scholar and educator, Wark has edited numerous collections of art commentary and catalogues of artwork. His edition of Reynolds's Discourses on Art *(1959) is considered definitive. In the following excerpt, he examines and defines the perceptible tension between the rational and the imaginative in Reynolds's artistic theory.]*

The works of Sir Joshua Reynolds form one of the most instructive documents in the history of European art during the second half of the eighteenth century. Nowhere else do the distinctive features of the period find more comprehensive and eloquent presentation.

To many it may appear parochial to push Reynolds' claims for attention among the major European artists of the middle and late eighteenth century; for within the span of Reynolds' productive years (1750-1790) there was much going on elsewhere that appears, superficially at least, more beguiling and exciting than the work of this English portraitist. In Italy, during the early part of Reynolds' career, Tiepolo and Canaletto were still painting; France was enjoying the magic of Fragonard and Chardin. Before Reynolds died, the French were startled by the propaganda paintings of David, the Spanish encountered the first works of Goya, and the Italians saw the monuments of ancient Rome reflected through the eyes of Piranesi.

The mere mention of such names immediately indicates in some measure the changes that were taking place in European art between the time Reynolds started to paint in the middle of the eighteenth century and the day in July 1789 when his failing sight obliged him to lay aside his brush. The shift was from a decorative and predominantly gay type of art to one generally more emotional, from an art of striking uniformity in style and intention to one of great individuality and variety. The extent to which Reynolds reflected this change in his work has not been generally recognized. His painting and writing have usually been considered apart from their European context. Yet there were few more clearly aware than he of the shifting temper of the time. And one doubts whether there was any artist who strove more conscientiously to reconcile the developing attitudes with what he considered best in the tradition he inherited.

In Reynolds' writings, and particularly in the ***Discourses,*** one senses clearly the dilemma confronting the artists of the late eighteenth century. The ***Discourses,*** or lectures on art delivered to the Royal Academy, are the most important and imposing part of Reynolds' literary output. (p. xv)

Reynolds states his controlling ideas concerning art in a fine sweeping passage at the close of the **"Ninth Discourse"**:

> The Art which we profess has beauty for its object; this it is our business to discover and to express; but the beauty of which we are in quest is general and intellectual; it is an idea that subsists only in the mind; the sight never be held it, nor has the hand expressed it: it is an idea residing in the breast of the artist, which he is always labouring to impart, and which he dies at last without imparting; but which he is yet so far able to communicate, as to raise the thoughts, and extend the views of the spec-

tator; and which, by a succession of art, may be so far diffused, that its effects may extend themselves imperceptibly into publick benefits, and be among the means of bestowing on whole nations refinement of taste: which, if it does not lead directly to purity of manners, obviates at least their greatest depravation, by disentangling the mind from appetite, and conducting the thoughts through successive stages of excellence, till that contemplation of universal rectitude and harmony which began by Taste, may, as it is exalted and refined, conclude in Virtue.

This is the essence of Reynolds' claim for art; most of the basic ideas of the *Discourses* are at least implicit in the passage. But clearly there is much here that calls for elucidation. The crux of the matter lies in understanding what Reynolds means by "beauty."

To the twentieth-century mind, nurtured on nonrepresentational values in art, it may be a little disconcerting to be told that Reynolds' criteria of beauty are phrased almost entirely in terms of the image (the physical object the artist has chosen to represent) and the ethical and moral properties of that image. Reynolds is perfectly able to consider such elements as line, shape, light, and color apart from any image they may form. For him, however, the primary importance of these elements lies in the extent to which they may be controlled by the artist in giving embodiment to his perception and understanding of the world around him. The thought that painting might exist without a direct and immediately perceivable point of contact with the world about us is quite alien to Reynolds, although some of his contemporaries were beginning to explore that possibility.

The artist, then, must derive his ideal of beauty from the physical world. Just how this is to be done is a problem that occupies a great deal of Reynolds' time throughout the *Discourses.* In the passage already quoted from the **"Ninth Discourse"** it is evident that Reynolds believes this ideal of beauty is not directly seeable. It is rather a sublimation in the mind of the artist of what he has already observed in the world about him. To abstract from these direct observations the ideal, which for Reynolds is true nature, is a problem involving much study and understanding.

In attempting to lead his students toward the perception of this ideal, Reynolds propounds the theory of what he calls *general* as opposed to *particular* nature. "All the objects," he says in the **"Third Discourse,"**

> which are exhibited to our view by nature [i.e., *particular* nature], upon close examination will be found to have their blemishes and defects. The most beautiful forms have something about them like weakness, minuteness, or imperfection. But it is not every eye that perceives these blemishes. It must be an eye long used to the contemplation and comparison of these forms; and which, by a long habit of observing what any set of objects of the same kind have in common, has acquired the power of discerning what each wants in particular. This long laborious comparison should be the first study of the painter, who aims at the greatest style. By this means, he acquires a just idea of beautiful forms; he corrects nature by herself, her imperfect state by her more perfect. His eye being enabled to distinguish the accidental deficiencies, excres-

cences, and deformities of things, from their general figures, he makes out an abstract idea of their forms more perfect than any one original; and what may seem a paradox, he learns to design naturally by drawing his figures unlike to any one object. This idea of the perfect state of nature [i.e., *general* nature], which the Artist calls the Ideal Beauty, is the great leading principle, by which works of genius are conducted. . . . Thus it is from a reiterated experience, and a close comparison of the objects in nature, that an artist becomes possessed of the idea of that central form, if I may so express it, from which every deviation is deformity.

The line of reasoning that Reynolds here follows had a long and venerable tradition going back to Plato and Aristotle. The assumption was that by generalizing from the particular, by eliminating what is specific and individual, we proceed to a "higher" more universal truth and we approach the abstract idea embodied in a family of forms. Truth and beauty were thus identified with the general. It is a concept at the core of most Renaissance theories of art, although the writers do not always agree about the precise way in which this general idea is to be obtained. Reynolds is more empirical than many of his predecessors; that is, he relies more on direct observation and a sort of averaging process rather than on what might be called inspiration. The question of whether or not beauty and truth should be identified with the general is a philosophical problem that has been much debated during the nineteenth and twentieth centuries. But Reynolds certainly accepted the proposition as true, and his aesthetic system cannot be understood without that assumption.

Although the physical world is the source from which all knowledge of beauty must ultimately be derived, the artist should avail himself of the achievements of his predecessors in their approaches to that general idea of nature abstracted from the particular. In this way, Reynolds felt, the road to excellence could be shortened a little and needless repetition of effort avoided. But a moot problem arises in the selection of those predecessors who may most suitably be taken as models. Making and justifying this selection is one of the major tasks Reynolds assumes in the *Discourses.* His voice is given for the sculpture of Greek and Roman antiquity and for the painting of the High Renaissance in Italy, especially that of Raphael and Michelangelo and their seventeenth-century Bolognese and French followers. In their use of materials derived from the physical world, these artists achieved something that approached Reynolds' ideal general nature, and they were accordingly the most valuable models for students to study.

There can be no doubt, from what has already been said about his concept of beauty and how it is to be discovered, that Reynolds considered hard work and disciplined thinking essential for any artistic achievement. He makes the point in the **"First Discourse"** and returns to it again in nearly all the later ones: "The impetuosity of youth is disgusted at the slow approaches of a regular siege, and desires, from mere impatience of labour, to take the citadel by storm. They wish to find some shorter path to excellence, and hope to obtain the reward of eminence by other means, than those which the indispensible rules of art have prescribed. They must therefore be told again and again, that labour is the only price of solid fame, and that whatever their force of genius may be, there is no easy method of becoming a good Painter."

Although the theme of disciplined work and industry as prerequisites of achievement is a leitmotiv that runs through all the discourses, in the later ones, when Reynolds is addressing more advanced students, he elaborates the idea, introducing qualifications. In the initial phases of learning an art, Reynolds concedes, the labor is to a great extent mechanical, directed simply toward acquiring a command over the tools. Thereafter, however, the labor is mental; the knowledge and intelligence of the student then become the factors of importance. Likewise, as the student's own understanding matures, dependence on imposed rules and dogma relaxes. Reynolds emphasizes that "an implicit obedience to the *Rules of Art* . . . should be exacted from the *young* Students." But he later admits that "There are some rules, whose absolute authority, like that of our nurses, continues no longer than while we are in a state of childhood."

And yet for Reynolds the creative act, even in the fully developed artist, is always clearly deliberate and conscious, operating according to a rational and discoverable pattern.

> It must of necessity be, that even works of Genius, like every other effect, as they must have their cause, must likewise have their rules; it cannot be by chance, that excellencies are produced with any constancy or any certainty, for this is not the nature of chance; but the rules by which men of extraordinary parts, and such as are called men of Genius work, are either such as they discover by their own peculiar observations, or of such a nice texture as not easily to admit being expressed in words; especially as artists are not very frequently skilful in that mode of communicating ideas. Unsubstantial, however, as these rules may seem, and difficult as it may be to convey them in writing, they are still seen and felt in the mind of the artist; and he works from them with as much certainty, as if they were embodied, as I may say, upon paper.

Having given voice on many occasions to his conviction that intellectual effort is essential for achievement in the arts, Reynolds feels obliged to discuss how far constant application will in itself, apart from innate talent, be effective in producing great art. It is a question he returns to many times, and, one must admit, he does not always seem to give the same answer. Reynolds may well have found himself here in something of a dilemma. The whole existence of the institution of which he was president rested on the assumption that disciplined training is necessary in order to create anything of value in the arts. He naturally wished to encourage the students to pursue that training with as much ardor as possible. On one occasion he permits himself to say: "Nothing is denied to well directed labour: nothing is to be obtained without it. Not to enter into metaphysical discussions on the nature or essence of genius, I will venture to assert, that assiduity unabated by difficulty, and a disposition eagerly directed to the object of its pursuit, will produce effects similar to those which some call the result of *natural powers.*" Yet at another time Reynolds says equally emphatically: "It is of no use to prescribe to those who have no talents; and those who have talents will find methods for themselves, methods

dictated to them by their own particular dispositions, and by the experience of their own particular necessities."

It is not easy to reconcile the implications of these two statements, even when one admits the qualification, which Reynolds himself immediately applies to the second, that this doctrine is not to be extended to the younger students. They, like other schoolboys, must necessarily live a life of restraint. However, if it is not entirely clear what Reynolds feels may be achieved by mere industry in the absence of talent, it is evident that he is never shaken in his belief that talent without disciplined training, directed from without or within, will achieve nothing.

The broad line of Reynolds' thought as outlined thus far is this: the ultimate function or the end of art is moral and ethical; art seeks to achieve this end through the pursuit of beauty; beauty is an ideal distillation from the objects in the physical world and can be approached only through intense study both of those objects and of the work of previous artists who have striven toward the same goal. In this train of reasoning there is nothing that would in any way surprise Reynolds' contemporaries and predecessors, nothing that they would regard as bizarre or deviating from a sane, well-tempered version of most current opinion on such matters. Reynolds himself would be the first to disclaim originality for his ideas. If one were to seek grounds for praise, he would much rather it would be for the Augustan virtue of expressing clearly and well what others had thought in a nebulous or partial fashion. In his last discourse he states his claim directly:

> I have pursued a plain and *honest method;* I have taken up the art simply as I found it exemplified in the practice of the most approved Painters. That approbation which the world has uniformly given, I have endeavoured to justify by such proofs as questions of this kind will admit; by the analogy which Painting holds with the sister Arts, and consequently by the common congeniality which they all bear to our nature. And though in what has been done, no new discovery is pretended, I may still flatter myself, that from the discoveries which others have made by their own intuitive good sense and native rectitude of judgment, I have succeeded in establishing the rules and principles of our Art on a more firm and lasting foundation than that on which they had formerly been placed.

The judgment of posterity has generally substantiated Reynolds' claim. The ***Discourses*** are considered one of the most eloquent, as well as one of the last, presentations of the ideas that dominated European art criticism and theory from the mid-fifteenth to the mid-eighteenth century; they are regarded as a sort of coda in which the principal themes of the movement are given a final statement before another, or perhaps a variant, subject is developed. (pp. xviii-xxiii)

From what has already been said of the substance of the ***Discourses*** Reynolds appears as a rationalist, with a clear, coherent conception of the nature of art and the creative process, the lectures themselves as "what oft was thought, but ne'er so well express'd." This is the way the ***Discourses*** are generally assessed, and it is, by and large, a valid assessment. But the picture, viewed in detail, is in fact more complicated. The ideas with which Reynolds is dealing are so broad that within the main stream there is ample opportunity for many eddies and even crosscurrents. During the three hundred years when these ideas dominated European art criticism, refinements and qualifications are constantly occurring in the thought patterns that reflect the changing temperament of individual theorists and the phases into which European thought falls from the fifteenth to the eighteenth century. Reynolds is no exception in giving expression to the particular idiosyncrasies of his period, and there is much in the *Discourses* that stamps them clearly as late eighteenth-century documents. They reveal their time of origin not so much in particular statements as in the emphasis and relative importance given to variations on the principal theme. For the historian of art and art criticism these deviations from the general pattern are of great interest. They are most evident in the emphasis Reynolds places on association as a factor in aesthetic response, in his insistence that art must appeal to the imagination, and in his willingness to accept considerable individualism in the matter of style. None of these ideas is intrinsically new. All of them can be located within the writings of Reynolds' predecessors. But they are ideas fundamentally at variance with the main current of thought he inherited and were ultimately to displace it. The emphasis Reynolds gives to these ideas and, in particular, his efforts to strike a compromise between them and the major traditional tenets, are characteristic of the man and his generation.

The increasing stress on association of ideas as a consideration that may enter into and even govern our response to a work of art is one of the primary factors enforcing a transformation of the outlook that dominated European art criticism from 1450 to 1750. The thought certainly did not originate with Reynolds. It was so widespread by the time he wrote (at least in English criticism) as to be an earmark of the period.

Reynolds indicates clearly what he means by the concept when he talks about architecture:

> as we have naturally a veneration for antiquity, whatever building brings to our remembrance ancient customs and manners, such as the Castles of the Barons of ancient Chivalry, is sure to give this delight. Hence it is that *towers and battlements* are so often selected by the Painter and the Poet, to make a part of the composition of their ideal Landskip; and it is from hence in a great degree, that in the buildings of Vanbrugh, who was a Poet as well as an Architect, there is a greater display of imagination, than we shall find perhaps in any other; and this is the ground of the effect which we feel in many of his works, notwithstanding the faults with which many of them are justly charged. For this purpose, Vanbrugh appears to have had recourse to some principles of the Gothick Architecture; which, though not so ancient as the Grecian, is more so to our imagination, with which the Artist is more concerned than with absolute truth.

Reynolds even goes so far as to imply that our whole idea of beauty is strongly influenced by association and custom. When speaking of the architectural orders inherited from Greek and Roman antiquity, he states that "if any one . . . should . . . invent new orders of equal beauty, which we will suppose to be possible, they would not please; nor ought he to complain, since the old has that great advantage of having custom and prejudice on its side." This type of preference Reynolds considers to be based on *apparent* rather than *real* truth. "However,

whilst these opinions and prejudices, on which it [apparent truth] is founded, continue, they operate as truth; and the art, whose office it is to please the mind, as well as instruct it, must direct itself according to *opinion,* or it will not attain its end."

The admission that the response to a work of art may be influenced by custom and the associations the object can arouse is of great importance. One sees its effect particularly clearly in the attitude of artists toward the work of their predecessors. We have already discovered Reynolds advocating the study of the masters as a means of acquiring the wisdom that has accumulated concerning an art, thus leading one's own work toward perfection. Now he suggests that in addition it is possible to borrow directly from earlier works or allude to them in such a way that a train of thought will be aroused through association that will enhance the appeal of the later work. This idea opens possibilities not entirely compatible with the first attitude. They are, to be sure, rather equivocal possibilities, and they led eventually to some of the features of mid-nineteenth-century art most distressing to modern critics. In the writings of Reynolds and his contemporaries, however, the concept is just beginning to unfold and is held firmly in place by other considerations.

One of the principal factors contributing to the emphasis Reynolds and his contemporaries placed on the doctrine of association of ideas was a renewed wave of subjectivism and emotionalism in art, after the rationalism dominant for the previous hundred years. Reynolds himself fought a rear-guard action against this development all his life; yet its positive influence is felt in many ways throughout his work. Another manifestation, in addition to the emphasis on association, is his constant insistence that the aim of art is to be accomplished through an appeal to the spectator's imagination. And it is clear that what Reynolds means is an appeal going beyond what can be immediately rationalized in the mind of the spectator. Reynolds is much taxed to explain just how this conception is to be reconciled with his convictions about the cerebral and intellectual side of artistic activity. He concludes that although the appeal may transcend anything reason can explain at once, yet there are factors determining this appeal that may with patience be unearthed and understood. One should not, therefore, distrust imagination and feeling, for they are to be regarded as a type of suprareason. "Reason," Reynolds insists, "without doubt, must ultimately determine every thing; at this minute it is required to inform us when that very reason is to give way to feeling."

The line of thought is becoming rather tenuous. Here, as in the suggestion that our ideal of beauty may be influenced if not determined by association, there is a tug against the main current of rationalistic thought concerning art and beauty that is the foundation of Reynolds' aesthetic. Art is a rational and intellectual pursuit, yet it is to appeal to the spectator in a way that is emotional rather than intellectual. . . . The compromise Reynolds seems to strike between the two attitudes, reliance on simple reason, on the one hand, and on emotion and instinct, on the other, is a solution characteristic of a late eighteenth-century mind.

A third manifestation of the same broad shift in emphasis appears in the way in which Reynolds treats the problem of style and the different schools or species of painting, sculpture, and architecture, which are defined in terms of differences in style. From the sixteenth century on, the various regional schools of painting in Europe had been recognized, and fairly accurate, though not always sympathetic, investigations of the differences in style among them had been made. A hierarchic scale of values had been established that comprehended both the manner, or style, in which the work was executed and also the theme or subject matter. Where painting was concerned, the High Renaissance in Rome, particularly as exemplified in the work of Raphael, was placed at the top of the ladder. The evident order and clarity of the style, the adherence to the precepts of general or ideal nature, the lofty subject matter, all gave to this painting the most likely opportunity to fulfill the high ethical aim Reynolds and his predecessors set for art. The more sensuous character of Venetian and Flemish paintings placed them below the Roman in the scale of values, while the lack of discrimination in approaching the problem of general nature placed Dutch painting, with its very direct empirical approach to the world around it, even lower. Painting that dealt with portraiture, landscape, genre, and still life was also low in the scale of values, for the subject matter lacked the intellectual dimension considered necessary for the greatest art.

Reynolds generally subscribed to this system of hierarchic scaling established by his predecessors. Yet he gives a distinctive twist to the problem. Whereas for most of the earlier theorists the final outcome of academic training was supposed to be an ability to combine the most desirable features of many masters and schools into one composite style, for Reynolds the third and last period in the development of an artist takes on a different complexion: "In the former period he sought only to know and combine excellence, wherever it was to be found, into one idea of perfection: in this [the last period], he learns, what requires the most attentive survey and the most subtle disquisition, to discriminate perfections that are incompatible with each other."

Time and again in the **Discourses** one senses in Reynolds the recognition of the validity of a type of individualism in art that would have puzzled many of his predecessors. Although he agrees with the traditional judgment that the Roman school, for instance, is "greater" than the Venetian, he insists much more strongly than had been customary that the two groups are not attempting to do comparable things and suggests, at least by implication, that comparisons of their relative merits are not always possible or relevant. In dealing with the problem Reynolds establishes his own categories of style and artistic intention. His principal divisions are the "grand" or the "great" style and the "ornamental," typified by the Roman and Venetian schools, respectively. He also admits a third category, the "characteristic," which runs across the first two. In this third bracket he includes all artists, however different their intentions, who have strongly marked individual characteristics or manners. Thus Poussin, Rubens, and Salvator Rosa come together in this group. That Reynolds was able to recognize and accept the artistic integrity of three such completely different artists suggests a catholicity of taste that is rare in his predecessors.

Reynolds' inclination toward this type of individualism and the acceptance of various styles and artistic intentions as legitimate is kept firmly in check by his general adherence to the old hierarchic system. On many occasions, however, one senses an impatience with the established dogma, especially when it interferes with the enjoyment of fine paintings in other than the grand style. "Indeed perfection in an inferior style may be reasonably preferred to mediocrity in the highest walks of art." Reynolds also asks more than once that the performance be judged according to the intention and not according to some rule applied indiscriminately to all art.

Once again, in weaving his way between intense individualism and academic insistence upon conformity to a clearly established pattern of values, Reynolds attempts a compromise that is evidence of a late eighteenth-century, and particularly a late eighteenth-century English, outlook.

It is probably not particularly important what labels are attached to the two attitudes between which Reynolds constructed a compromise. That which concerns individualism, imagination, and the value of association is usually called "romanticism"; the other, involved with uniformity, reason, and ideal form is usually called (at least by historians, philosophers, and students of literature) "classicism." The difference between the two (as between most such outlooks) is, in the last analysis, one of degree; and it would be difficult to find a man whose work is a pure example of one untouched by any suggestion of the other. Romanticism and classicism as states of mind may, and do, occur at any time and in endless combinations. It is artificial and inaccurate to attempt to confine them within chronological limits. Nevertheless it is true that classicism was the prevalent and dominant outlook during the late seventeenth and early eighteenth centuries, just as romanticism predominated at the end of the eighteenth and the beginning of the nineteenth centuries. This preponderance of opinion justifies, to some extent, calling the earlier period the Enlightenment, or Age of Reason, and the later one the Romantic period. In the main framework of his thought about art there can be little doubt that Reynolds appears strongly imbued with the ideas of the earlier outlook, the Age of Reason; and this is the estimate of the man that has generally prevailed. But the latter part of this essay has emphasized that there is also a generous component of what may be called romanticism in his thought. (pp. xxiv-xxx)

In his practice of painting as in his theory of art Reynolds maintained a balance between the classical ideals that had dominated the thought of his predecessors and the romantic ones that were to assume such importance in the production of early nineteenth-century artists. Although he felt free to manipulate his style in accordance with changing aims, his variations were nearly always in terms of the precursors he admired, and the variety he sought never degenerated into that carnival of styles of which Pugin complained in English architecture some fifty years after Reynolds' death. Likewise in his exploitation of the associative values of an image he never forgot the formal values of painting on which his predecessors placed such stress.

Thus the positions Reynolds takes up in the theory and practice of art are closely related and completely consistent one with the other. He stands in both as a figure particularly probable in the late eighteenth century, a man deeply sensitive to the value of a tradition that was waning in popular estimation, but sympathetically aware of the shifts in opinion and outlook taking place around him. (p. xxxv)

> *Robert R. Wark, in an introduction to* Discourses on Art *by Sir Joshua Reynolds, edited by Robert R. Wark, Huntington Library, 1959, pp. xv-xxxv.*

Eugene Clinton Elliott   (essay date 1962)

[*Elliott is an American educator and essayist who has written widely on art and aesthetics. In the following excerpt, he compares the artistic theories of Reynolds with those of his critical antagonist William Hazlitt, illuminating the key difference in viewpoint articulated in the latter's criticism.*]

A dominant impression, after a reading of Hazlitt's insistence upon his differences with Reynolds, is how much the positions of the two men are alike. Both believed that art serves a moral purpose in expressing an ideal, and so recognized a hierarchy of kinds of art. Both maintained that only a good man can be a good painter, though both recognized various kinds of excellence. Both held that art is imitation—Hazlitt insisted upon it—and they agreed that the basis of all art is the first effect of objects upon the imagination. With so much agreement on the ultimate purpose and nature of art, where do their differences lie?

The first difference of real significance is in the nature of the ideal. Sir Joshua explained his thought in the **"Ninth Discourse."**

> As the senses, in the lowest state of nature, are necessary to direct us to our support, when that support is once secure there is danger in following them further; . . . it is therefore necessary to the happiness of individuals, and still more necessary to the security of society, that the mind should be elevated to the idea of general beauty, and the contemplation of general truth . . . [The artist] deserves just so much encouragement in the state as he makes himself a member of it virtuously useful, and contributes in his sphere to the general purpose and perfection of society. The Art which we profess has beauty for its object; this it is our business to discover and express; but the beauty of which we are in quest is general and intellectual; it is an idea that subsists only in the mind; . . . which, if it does not lead directly to purity of manners, obviates at least their greatest depravation . . .

Hazlitt equated Reynolds' general beauty and general truth with ideal beauty, the neo-classic *beau idéal,* and opposed to it another notion of the ideal. "The ideal is only the selecting a particular form which expresses most completely the idea of a given character or quality." "The concrete, and not the abstract, is the object of painting, and of all the works of imagination." For Hazlitt, it was absolutely necessary that the highest works of art in painting should depict concrete individuality, for the notion of character, which was of the essence of the ideal, to his way of thinking implied individuality.

Reynolds' ideal was social; Hazlitt's ideal was individualistic. On the basis of this opposition, Hazlitt selected six major points on which he took issue with Reynolds. (pp. 73-4)

These he stated in different ways in different essays. Others have made sufficiently clear the fact that Hazlitt did not always bother to understand Reynolds. He fixed his mind on their fundamental disagreement and adhered firmly to that as he belabored his six points.

First, he objected to Reynolds' idea that the imitation of nature is an inferior object in art, and that all beauty, grace, and grandeur are to be found, not in actual nature, but in an idea existing in the mind. Hazlitt insisted that art is first and last the imitation of nature, and that the highest art is merely the imitation of the finest nature.

Second, he protested the idea that the great style in painting depends on leaving out the details of particular objects. Using observation of the natural world as an example, he insisted that representation of detail is not inconsistent with perception of the larger masses and proportions that Reynolds called general nature. Reynolds, in his **"Eleventh Discourse,"** had admitted that no general idea can be represented other than in a particular form, but he distinguished "those minute differences in things which are frequently not observed at all" from the "great characteristick distinctions, which press strongly on the senses, and therefore fix the imagination." The issues lose their sharpness with Hazlitt's statement that "abstract truth or ideal perfection does not consist in rejecting the peculiarities of form, but rejecting all those which are not consistent with the character intended to be given . . . "

The third and fourth points must be considered together. Hazlitt denied that beauty or ideal perfection was to be sought in a central form or norm; rather he insisted that ideal form was the expression of a strong, unique character and therefore appeared in extreme, highly individualistic traits; and he stated that Reynolds rejected character as an anomaly. This difference is important in understanding the two men, and it had its origins in complicated changes in the notion of character during the eighteenth century. Certainly, the idea of a norm as the standard of beauty would preclude the notion of character as Hazlitt understood it, which might be defined as a quality of individual nature sufficiently intense to manifest itself throughout the object in which it resided. Reynolds, however, held no such idea of character. To him, character was typical. An object had character insofar as it was expressive of a type.

In putting his ***Discourses*** together, Reynolds drew heavily upon earlier works, particularly those which originated in the French *Académie royale.* The discussions of character there were based upon a seventeenth-century psychology rapidly becoming obsolete, but which persisted, especially in technical works on painting, because of the great utility of the doctrine of the passions in so-called history painting. To state this psychology briefly, the *complexion* of a person, which made him ruddy or sallow, was the peculiar mixture of *humours* that determined his *temperament.* Temperament, plus the effects of age, sex, nation, class, and occupation, gave him also a certain *character,* a unique appearance from which an observer might deduce the forces that had worked to make him what he was. Considered in these terms, character was essentially external. (pp. 74-5)

Due largely to the seventeenth-century vogue for that form of literature known as *character-writing,* the word *character,* from designating the external forms of appearance and behavior which were signs of forces acting on the individual, came to designate the forces themselves, and more specifically the internal nature. In literary criticism around 1750, the word was used ambiguously to mean now one and now the other. In books on painting, the older usage persisted longer. Reynolds' conception of character as typical is entirely consistent with this notion of character as external signs of a number of forces, and, so far from eliminating all detail, it was originally a theory for determining detail. This fact is clear in Fuseli where he speaks [in his Fifth Lecture] of the discriminations of the characterizing forces; it is less clear in the *Discourses,* for Reynolds intended to deal only with general principles and left the details of practise to the professors of painting at the Academy.

For Reynolds, character was basically external and typical. When Hazlitt used the word *character* he meant exclusively internal nature, and as it was this core of individual integrity that was the foundation of his stand against an evil society, he was not disposed to recognize any other meaning.

The last two points of difference again must be discussed together, and they relate also to the changing concept of character of which I have just spoken. Hazlitt stated that Reynolds did not understand expression but considered it hostile to beauty; and he denied that genius or invention consisted chiefly in borrowing the ideas of others, or in using other men's minds.

Reynolds, when he spoke of expression, referred almost exclusively to the representation of the passions, though there are indications that he would have extended the meaning of the term to include attitude and decorum. Hazlitt also most often dealt specifically with facial expression but the term expression had a much larger significance for him. *Gusto* or expression was "the conveying to the eye the impressions of the soul, or the other senses connected with the sense of sight, such as the different passions visible in the countenance, the romantic interest connected with scenes of nature, the character and feelings associated with different objects." Expression gave interest and signification to forms and was the basis of judging their imitation—the greater the sympathy of the artist, the closer will be the affinity between the imitation and the thing imitated. Finally, therefore, expression is the test and measure of genius.

Once again to understand what is involved here we must go back to earlier theory. The doctrine of expression evolved against a background of interest in the possibility of conveying abstract ideas through images. In art and literature this interest created a vogue for emblem books, and in psychology it was represented by statements such as Bacon's, that "emblem . . . reduces intellectual conceptions to sensible images."

As made explicit in *conférences* at the *Académie royale* near the end of the seventeenth century, the most general sense of the word *expression* was the principle that "all parts of the composition of a picture should contribute to the depicting of the subject to be represented—all parts should bear the characteristic marks of that subject—in order that the idea of the subject might be transferred from the picture to the mind of the beholder, leading him to respond with appropriate feelings." (pp. 75-6)

Hazlitt reshaped the concept to his own purposes. Expression was no longer the characteristic mark of the subject distributed throughout the picture. It had become the effect of a powerful sympathy enabling the artist to enter into his object, to penetrate to its nature. Great art, then, was not the exact imitation of visual appearance. A true portrait demanded a comprehension of the whole, that is, of a varied mass of physical appearances through which the subject might pass, which could only be known through the activity of a moral sense—sympathy; and the picture finally responded to a preconceived judgment—an ideal image of the object in the mind of the artist.

Here Hazlitt seems in full contradiction to his denouncing of Reynolds for holding that grace and beauty are an ideal in the mind rather than in nature. One thing saved him. The character that was portrayed was, to him, nature, the internal determinant, the essential individual nature of the thing pictured, manifesting itself in every particular feature of the representation. He related expression not so much to the whole picture, as to each object. Hazlitt had located the universal in the individual. In society and politics, truth lay in common sense, the feeling-judgments all men had within them. In morals, human sympathy was inherently good if man would but be guided by it. And in art, beauty and grandeur stemmed from character, the ideal that was nature in motion, harmonizing and unifying the various forms.

Not the least surprising fact to come out of a comparison of these two men is that Hazlitt, the romantic, insisted upon an almost literal imitation of nature as the end of art, whereas Reynolds, the neo-classicist, was equally emphatic that imitation was the means of art but not the end. The end of art which he sought, securing the happiness of individuals and the well-being of society by the revelation of general truth and general beauty, might well be served by using depicted objects as signs to convey an idea subsisting only in the mind. Reynolds borrowed attitudes and compositional patterns from other painters and played upon the associations and connotations they brought with them in an intellectual game not unrelated to that played by Jacob Cats when he created the emblems Reynolds copied in learning to draw.

In art as in life, Hazlitt could trust abstract ideas only if their truth was vouched for by direct testimony of experience. In spite of the fact that in his own prose style he wove innumerable quotations into the very texture of his sentences, with no other acknowledgement than the use of quotation marks, he insisted that such borrowing as Reynolds' was plagiary. For Hazlitt, originality, the essence of genius, required direct sensual experience, especially that intensity of sympathy (the moral sense) which, directed by congeniality to temperament, led great men to discover some property or quality in nature which had never been seen before.

The difference between Reynolds and Hazlitt depended upon Hazlitt's radical individualism. Certainly a heightened individualism is part of the romantic movement, as is also the kind of enthusiastic sympathy Hazlitt identified with expression. But Hazlitt's individualism and enthusiasm did not lead to a subjective individualistic art. The principle of analogy by which he explained the spectator's understanding of the meaning and truth of the details of a picture was not romantic suggestion but part of the association of ideas by which he believed all understanding was accomplished; and far from being obscure, because it was physiognomic in principle, it required an almost literal imitation. As for the actual practice of painting, Hazlitt's differences with Reynolds seem to be differences of interpretation rather than of kind, and become significant only in relation to underlying differences of social outlook. The point of absolute disagreement between these two men lies in their definitions of genius: Hazlitt required a degree of originality that Reynolds would have found excessive. But even Hazlitt's pure novelty, looked at in terms of the usual romantic criteria, was limited to the discovery of qualities in nature and was susceptible of being judged by common sense.

There seems to be, in Reynolds' conception of the ideal, an assumption that the artist should put himself at the service of the state. At least, he should contribute to the general purpose and perfection of society, and Reynolds seems not to question the role of the state in the society of his time. The painter deserved encouragement from the state to the extent that he made himself virtuously useful. Hazlitt's ideal was more in line with the assumptions of Adam Smith's economic liberalism, that every individual's pursuing his own ends would providentially assure the well-being of the whole. This ideal led him to distrust the allegorical morality of neo-classic history painting and to define history as nature in action. In the end, Hazlitt's comments on painting supported the detailed realism of the pre-Raphaelites and some of the later Victorians, which is not to say that he would have approved of their pictures. (pp. 77-8)

> *Eugene Clinton Elliot, "Reynolds and Hazlitt," in* The Journal of Aesthetics and Art Criticism, *Vol. XXI, No. 1, Fall, 1962, pp. 73-9.*

Catherine Neal Parke (essay date 1978)

[*Parke is an American educator and essayist. In the following excerpt, she argues that in the* Discourses *Reynolds "offers ideals expressive of his listeners' best selves" and that in his lectures he aimed "to develop a 'mind adapted and adequate to all occasions.'"*]

In the **Discourses** Reynolds holds his listeners up to ideals expressive of their best selves. He offers the rules of art as formal embodiment, as a kind of translation of the lectures' aim to develop a "mind adapted and adequate to all occasions." For Reynolds this central Neoclassical tenet is not only the foundation for the creation of lasting excellence in the arts, but also an immediate practical necessity for everyday living. And, since the power of any conceptual system (its capacity for answering the needs of the mind and desires of the heart) depends on how well the system can encompass large issues and accommodate small, Reynolds' variation on this Neoclassical theme offers, both emotionally and philosophically, a nearly irresistible combination. (p. 152)

The "art of true orientation," the subject of the **Discourses,** is a martial and meditative discipline. Its aims are survival and excellence, adaptation and adequacy to every situation and to all times. Since these activities require the mind's eye to see, at an instant, the laws governing the facts at hand, to cultivate "an intuitive flair for the essentials of a situation," we learn, by way of them, a man's style. *Style,* according to Reynolds, is a man's characteristic power over the materials he chooses or within the circumstances in which he finds himself. Now, style comprehends excellence and survival. With a good eye to the laws governing the facts at hand, a man can respond to these facts not merely as a *collection of facts,* but rather as a *subject.* And by responding to the facts as subject, a man aligns himself to a rhythm of meaning: the form of the thing seen. To see form always involves "casting what [is] seen into manageable models," thereby finding an equilibrium "between the demands of the object and the tendencies in the observer." When this equilibrium is accurately found, which is to say also when the use of models is adequately understood, explanation becomes a plan for action. The observer then understands what he is to do with what he has seen. He knows how to act. He knows, in other words, what he wants to do with what he knows. As it becomes clear in the course of the lectures, Reynolds intends the rules of art to serve the attractive purpose of helping the observer, whether artist or audience to find this significant equilibrium between truth and desire. (p. 153)

In "Discourse II" Reynolds gives an historical example of true orientation, an example for his students to imitate. Philopoemen, "one of the ablest Greek generals," lived a life of "perpetual meditation." His biography offers "a striking picture of a mind always intent on its profession," always "prepar[ing] itself by laying in proper materials at all times and in all places." In other words, Philopoemen's life offers an image of a mind in the process of adapting and making itself adequate to all times and occasions. Here for the first time Reynolds brings the Neoclassical criterion for artistic excellence into the present moment, into the world of change and process, and into biography. This pattern characteristic of the **Discourses** accounts for their trustworthy tone and their continuing usefulness. . . . After Reynolds tells Philopoemen's story, he makes the connection. He instructs every "promising young painter" to be "equally vigilant, whether at home, or abroad, in the streets, or in the fields" and to "regard all Nature with a view to his profession." As a way of encouraging young artists to begin a long, often tedious course of study, Reynolds' way is canny. Who among us would not want to be associated in our labors with the glamors of a general? But the Philopoemen example is both encouraging and true—a fairly unusual combination—because the glamor does not betray the simple, working center of the comparison. Having the reputation for being one of the ablest Greek generals is glamorous indeed, but the way Philopoemen earned that reputation was not so in the least: the man worked all the time. And of course, Reynolds intends this as a major lesson of the story.

But if Philopoemen worked all the time, he worked, so to speak, at his leisure, and he was always his own teacher, a practice Reynolds recommends throughout the lectures. By comparison with the immediate purpose to which this general aimed all his work (saving his life in a real ambush), all this self-instruction *was* easy, leisurely, relaxed;

leisurely in its rhythm of habitual repetition, a rhythm with which Philopoemen came, no doubt, to identify himself. And relaxed in that especially attractive, highly charged way which comes only when a man knows he is using his imagination to the full in practicing, beforehand, for something very important, like saving his life. Such a study is unquestionably worth the work. It is, perhaps, the one aim surely calculated to keep most men honest and, as they turn a clear eye on their mistakes, to become, for their own good, their own best enemies. Philopoemen takes his time exactly by working all the time. The man will not be rushed or pressed. He works slowly, imaginatively to save his life. His attempt takes energy from the deep, simple seriousness of its purpose. But to achieve this simpler purpose of survival, the man invents a system which itself makes a counterstatement to pressing need. Philopoemen makes space for himself within the seemingly confined topic of survival, and in so doing he embodies that virtue of excellence: when the most serious accuracy finds a way to take its own time to invent its shape and discover its form. (pp. 154-55)

While Philopoemen perpetually meditates on every imaginable ambush in every new territory he visits, he is, of course, travelling over the territory of his own mind. He imagines himself as attacker and defender, a practice Reynolds calls "doubling" in his book *The Portraits.* Based on the way he understands the mind to work best and also to like best to work, Reynolds recommends thinking about two things at once:

> The mind appears to me of that nature and construction that it requires being employed on two things in order that it may do one thing well. . . .
> If I was to judge from my own experience, the mind always desires to double, to entertain two objects at a time.

In order to make an imaginary history of the ideas of battle, Philopoemen thinks of himself *as himself* and *as his enemy.* He passes through a geography both real and ideal. The territory really does exist. But turned so consistently to imaginative use, projected into the future as a place where the general must be currently both himself and his antagonist, this geography becomes ideal too—the location for an exercise in "doubling," a preparation for the right use of models.

Now, if this meditative landscape is to serve the purpose Philopoemen intends (preparing the mind for a real ambush), it must be seen really, accurately: the imagination's task is to imagine the real. But exactly because the general's purpose is to prepare his mind for an ambush, he must maintain, absolutely, an equivalence of the ideal and the real. It would be hard to invent a better example than this one to dramatize the central hypothesis of the *Discourses,* the belief which provides both their structure and subject: the world, being the world of man, is necessarily a world of ideas. Being a world of ideas, our environment requires us, whether artists or audience, always to see in the facts a potential for two simultaneously satisfying truths: a truth appropriate to those facts and a truth appropriate to us who are looking at the facts. The second truth often appears different from the first, but, according to Reynolds, rarely is; because the two truths are reciprocal parts of nature, linked by the mind's sense of a "principle of congruity, coherence, and consistency, which is a real existing

principle in man." The second truth involves our desires toward the facts of the first truth and our relation to them. In the case of Philopoemen, the *desire* is survival and victory within the facts of war. The *relation* is the general's amphibious role as both himself and his enemy. The relation is the structure which empowers the specific desire to function, to attain its end. And the desire—to anticipate things to come in this essay—makes sense out of and tests the relation. Desire is the *telos* of the *Discourses.* Within the rather leisurely pace and tone of the lectures, taken as a whole, the teleology of desire forms a center of urgency.

Reynolds explicates this center of urgency in ["**Discourse XII**"] where he clearly establishes the identity between "the art of seeing nature" and "the art of using models": "*The art of seeing Nature,* or in other words, the art of using Models, is in reality the great object, the point to which all our studies are directed." By establishing this identity, Reynolds applies his definition of Nature (the form of things and the structure of the mind) to the practical matter of learning to paint. To learn to paint and to continue to improve, the artist must learn to imitate, to use models. Using models rightly involves mastering, once again like Philopoemen, the art of doubling, the art based on the mind's natural instinct to think about and to think best about two things at once. The mind's desire to imitate, to imagine, to experience or to know something through an act of embodiment always leads the mind back to greater self-knowledge. Because, as Vico has taught us, we know ourselves best by what we make.

When the art of seeing nature or the art of using models becomes practically the point to which an artist directs all his studies, then and only then is "the service of nature . . . *perfect freedom.*" Reynolds grounds this identity of service and freedom (with its Christian resonance) in a radical epistemology of faith, a faith which in turn originates in the mind's desire to see things fit together, make sense, come out right, discover form. Tone for this epistemology is set when in **"Discourse II,"** Reynolds describes the severe consequences which result whenever the student pursues inadequate methods of study and later in **"Discourse XII"** when he questions any use of method. "Few men," he writes, "have been taught to any purpose who have not been their own teachers." The artist who fails to live a life of personal, aggressive comprehension (the perfectly free service of nature) will never achieve excellence. Worse, he will live his life, fearful and jealous, like the juggler who guards his meager skill. Here Reynolds describes the good artist:

> Conscious of the difficulty of obtaining what he possesses, [the well-grounded painter] makes no pretensions to secrets of closer application. Without conceiving the smallest jealousy against others, he is contented that all shall be as great as himself, who have undergone the same fatigue; and as his preeminence depends not upon a trick, he is free from the painful suspicions of a juggler, who lives in perpetual fear lest his trick should be discovered.

The juggler (and the juggler-artist) learns his skill quickly. His mechanical trick is thin, a gimmick, and in proportion to this thinness, his fear of loss. The true artist, like Philopoemen, on the other hand, knows from experience the fatigue of skill. Reynolds suggests that the very fatigue of this long labor accounts for the true artist's contentment with other artists' success; a contentment grounded partly in the knowledge of how few men are willing to work as hard as he did. The "perfect freedom" of nature's service means then, in part, a freedom from the self-destructive passion, jealousy. The good artist is the good man. He wishes other artists well. He embodies the two meanings of *virtue:* goodness and strength. He gains strength for his profession through the fatigue of study. (To prepare the student for being very tired, Reynolds makes this positive case for weariness.) And his strength is like weight, ballast steadying him against destructive emotions tossing other artists who do not take into their bodies the heaviness of hard work.

With this negative example of the juggler to focus the ideal and make it memorable, Reynolds concludes the example of Philopoemen's "life of perpetual meditation." The juggler offers a dark warning. His image reverses the practical ideal of "perfect freedom" which Reynolds evokes in the telling of Philopoemen's story and by his tone throughout the succeeding thirteen lectures. The fears and jealousies which naturally accompany trick-learning fall outside the area of substantial learning and perpetual meditation. Substantial learning makes a man feel safe because he knows the simple truth about how he learned what he knows: he worked hard. And in turn, feeling safe helps any of us to be good. A course of study offering to help a man *feel* safe and thereby *be* better is attractive.

Philopoemen's life is thus a metaphor for the whole of the positive process of study Reynolds maps over the twenty-one years of the *Discourses.* The general studied, literally and figuratively, in the open. He studied *Nature:* the forms of things and the structure of the mind. As the occasion came, he studied either alone or with others—nothing hidden, no secret to guard. And in double contrast with the juggler whose very skill becomes a source of fear and jealousy, Philopoemen's learning not only spares him those mean fears, but also substantially prepares his mind against the fear of sudden attack. The matters here are serious and the stakes are high. But the tone of this epistemology of survival, part of the larger epistemology of faith directing the *Discourses,* is really quite cheerful and bracing. Both epistemologies are grounded in the belief that the nature of things welcomes inquiry, that answers can be found, and that, as Reynolds puts it, "one truth teaches another." These assumptions lead to a wholesome belief in the value and pleasure of repetition. And this pair of beliefs is possible only when the attempt to learn something is understood to be, essentially, a hopeful process of self-correction, continued for the simplest and most energetic of reasons: because one wants to. The energy, good sense, and high ideals of the *Discourses* come from their grounding in the unarguable premise of desire.

For as powerfully as Reynolds depends on the traditional connection between rhetorical theory and the principles of art, insisting on this isomorphism, and for as heavily as he borrows rhetorical terms, encouraging young artists to "collect," "invent," and "compose," still he does leave a major part of the artist's education to a different kind of activity, an activity which is a form of self-instruction based on intuition and love. In contrast to that earlier example of the juggler (an example of what not to do), Reynolds advises the young artist travelling abroad on a study tour to employ himself first off "upon whatever he has been incited to by any immediate impulse." He continues:

"It is impossible that any thing should be well understood or well done, that is taken into a reluctant understanding, and executed with a servile hand." Any talented art student "will find methods for [him]self, methods dictated to [him] by his own particular dispositions . . .". Better than any other methods he could learn from another man, his own will teach him best. The truly talented artist will always find the right ways to teach himself. Like his paintings, his methods will be "congenial and natural to the mind . . . giv[ing] him by reflection his own mode of conceiving." In counterpoint to his insistence upon formal training, with its unquestioning subordination of the imagination to reason, and upon systematic practice, Reynolds offers this image of the young student's education:

> Every seminary of learning may be said to be surrounded with an atmosphere of floating knowledge, where every mind may imbibe somewhat congenial to its own original conceptions.

By inventing his own methods, which is to say also by eventually finding his own style, the young artist will make a good beginning on his long study to locate himself in relation to his predecessors. He will see himself separate enough from them to feel his work worth something. These complementary orientations are necessary in a course of study, like Reynolds', based on imitation, and, from what we know of Reynolds' methods of composition, grounded in autobiography. (pp. 156-60)

When for the first time Reynolds discusses the place and importance of copying masterpieces, he takes time to discuss this stage of the artist's education carefully. If he begins copying wrong, the student will never arrive at that perfect freedom of nature's service; he will never be sufficiently himself to use models (to imitate nature) with confidence and accuracy. The young student should paint what Reynolds calls "a companion" to the original. And this companion, another application of the art of doubling, should imitate only the concept of its original. Paint, Reynolds advises, as if the master artist himself were coming to see your version:

> . . . enter into a kind of competition, by painting a similar subject, and making a companion to any picture that you consider as a model. You will not only see, but feel your own deficiencies more sensibly than by precepts, or any other means of instruction.

The passage offers an attractive harmony of near-opposites for the artist's round of self-instruction: entering into *competition* by making a *companion.* Reynolds understands the struggle each new generation of artists wages with those who came before. His method of competition and companionship recognizes the ambivalence any student will feel toward what "is indeed a severe and mortifying task, to which none will submit, but such as have great views, with great fortitude sufficient to forego the gratifications of present vanity for future honour." Yet the tone of the full passage on the importance of copying is a tone of affirmation, affirmation not simply of the end results, but even of the process of getting there. The student's long course of imitation will always involve severity and mortification and will always call for fortitude. But into the balance Reynolds throws the heavier weight of trusting the student to be able to see his own mistakes. If left alone to the active contemplation of sound examples, the student will recognize his weaknesses. And in seeing these weaknesses for himself, he finds substantial proof that he is already beginning to move beyond his current mistakes. Like Philopoemen, the student who can learn to detach himself from himself enough to play his own enemy, will find in this very activity the confidence and energy he needs to get on with his learning.

Clearly for Reynolds the consequences of error are not overpowering. His measured, even cheerful attitude toward the positive uses of error would make the ***Discourses,*** if one read them for nothing else, a document of continuing interest: and especially of interest to us in the twentieth century, as writers like Michael Polanyi turn our epistemological focus to an understanding of learning as the paradigm of knowledge. As Reynolds sees the matter, error is considerably less frightening than some of the alternatives, particularly the "danger of slow proficiency." The young student should not fear mistakes that come from "bold and arduous attempts" and from his "passion for his art," because by learning on his own, the student discovers his own deficiencies. When he conceives the attempt himself, when he does not simply follow another man's course, the student will more likely see where he went wrong. Only at the very beginnings of a new study can one man learn from another. After that, the teacher "can do little more than put the end of the clue into the hands of his Scholar, by which he must conduct himself."

When he attempts more than he can do, the student learns from his own mistakes. More importantly, however, he protects himself from that possibility more dangerous than failure: "the danger of slow proficiency" from "too easy tasks." I should say here, parenthetically, that Reynolds quickly acknowledges the real pain of failure and admits that repeated failures often do real damage. As a teacher, he is not naive. Neither is he one who from his secure position as a successful artist easily recommends to beginners the usefulness, while underestimating the pain, of failure. Although Reynolds does not specifically call "the slow proficiency of too easy tasks" an evil until **"Discourse XI,"** his unspoken warning has guided us all along. The moral psychology expressed in this warning (that easy tasks almost surely lead to no good and usually damage us) returns the reader to that pair of opposites from the second lecture: the general and the juggler. And this return elaborates the significance of that emblematic pair.

To put it simply, the general must look at the whole territory, watching for the particular attack. This training steadies him in the art of an intense equilibrium, an orientation like that of the Samurai who was always the first to see an attack coming where his comrades still saw only the vacant horizon. By our normal standards of inattention, such feats appear a kind of supersensory perception. But they are, as Reynolds goes on to argue, as necessary for the decent and shapely conduct of our lives as they are necessary for good art. The general, like the young artists who should copy him, learns to study equally well on his own or with others, at any time and any place. He is perfectly flexible. He has nothing to hide or protect. And he shares his knowledge. The juggler performs a balancing act, too, but he focuses literally, narrowly on the balls he throws into the air. For his context he takes only his body and that slight extension of the body's perimeter: the arcs described by the juggling balls. This narrow focus is both

a metaphor and condition for the fearful, jealous way he protects his simple, mechanical skill. The student who educates himself by "too easy tasks" is like the juggler. The student who always tries the hard lesson is the general. And the consequences for a man's moral education, based on the course he chooses, are a major interest of the ***Discourses.*** (pp. 160-62)

In his book, *The Dying Self,* Charles M. Fair writes that we recognize the truly good people we meet in our lives by this characteristic: ". . . their powers are available to them. . . ." Their bodies are quick; their minds, agile. They move with a speed and grace (or sit quite still, like Reynolds, when the accident of the moment dictates that choreography), we know can come only from a long apprenticeship during which "one truth teaches another . . . till that contemplation of universal rectitude and harmony which begun by Taste, may, as it is exalted and refined, conclude in Virtue."

With the word *virtue,* we are back to the beginning of this essay. Etymologically *virtue* comprehends goodness and power. We call an artist's "power over his materials," Reynolds says, his *style.* An artist develops his style by imitation, that exercise in applied taste: the power of distinguishing right from wrong. As an audience, we recognize this power manifest not only in excellent art, but also in virtuous life; in those acts performed where, like a successful painting, "all the parts are compact, and fitted to each other, everything being of one piece." Whether in life or in art, these acts are the most memorable, because the most natural. They stand the test of time because they are uncluttered, economical. They express a man's skill in leaving out as well as putting in. And they reflect to the observer "his own mode of conceiving." The mind works this way: even familiar objects seldom leave more than an impression of their general effect, "beyond which we do not go in recognising them." We are all naturally abstractionists. The man who successfully incorporates into his art these daily, survival workings of the human mind directs art, at one and the same time, toward its highest excellence.

Appropriate to his own theory of art, Reynolds ends the ***Discourses*** with a memorable image: the figure of Michelangelo. Withdrawing himself, Reynolds pairs every young art student with Michelangelo for his teacher. As Reynolds presents him, Michelangelo is the artist who took the pictorial arts to the border of those non-imitative arts, music and architecture. And while maintaining this crucial distinction between the imitative and non-imitative, he borrowed from the power of these allied arts to speak directly to the imagination. By studying the master's works, the student locates himself individually, but more than personally, in a line of inheritance and tradition of memory. Beginning his career by copying the art of Michelangelo, the young artist takes into his body the practical knowledge of this man's genius, until "what is learned in this manner from the works of others becomes really our own, sinks deep, and is never forgotten . . . " (pp. 172-73)

Catherine Neal Parke, "The Image of the Good Man in Sir Joshua Reynolds' Discourses," in THOUGHT, *Vol. LIII, No. 209, June, 1978, pp. 151-73.*

Nicholas Penny   (essay date 1986)

[*Penny is an English educator, essayist on art, and curator at the Ashmolean Museum in Oxford. In the following excerpt, he considers several of the key points made in the* Discourses.]

It is easy to demonstrate that the leading ideas in the **Discourses** were not new. But on some subjects Reynolds provided a novel outlook: in particular, his severe account of the proper boundaries of the art of sculpture anticipated and helped to shape the neo-classicism of the end of the century, and his painter's view of architecture did much to encourage the 'picturesque' aesthetic. Reynolds impresses us as having accepted nothing on trust: he is frequently critical of earlier academic authorities and questions, very much in the spirit of Johnson, many of the 'rules' they propounded. He may at times have sounded like a voice from the past: such, indeed, was his intention. But it was a voice from the distant, not the recent, past, and it had an urgent and uncompromising message for the present.

In his **"Third Discourse,"** delivered at the prize-giving on 14 December 1770, he warned that 'a mere copier of nature can never produce any thing great; can never raise and enlarge the conceptions, or warm the heart of the spectator'. The 'genuine painter', he continued to an audience of young painters who no doubt considered themselves genuine enough, would have higher aspirations: 'instead of endeavouring to amuse mankind with the minute neatness of his imitations, he must endeavour to improve them by the grandeur of his ideas; instead of seeking praise, by deceiving the superficial sense of the spectator, he must strive for fame, by capturing the imagination.'

Reynolds could be far less positive and far more reflective, more of a philosopher and less of a pedagogue, as, for example, in the conclusion to his Discourse delivered a decade later on the opening of the Academy's new building, where he alludes to platonic conceptions of beauty and to art as an indirect agent of enlightenment:

> The Art which we profess has beauty for its object; this it is our business to discover and to express; but the beauty of which we are in quest is general and intellectual; it is an idea that subsists only in the mind; the sight never beheld it, nor has the hand expressed it: it is an idea residing in the breast of the artist, which he is always labouring to impart, and which he dies at last without imparting; but which he is yet so far able to communicate, as to raise the thoughts, and extend the views of the spectator; and which, by a succession of art, may be so far diffused, that its effects may extend themselves imperceptibly into publick benefits, and be among the means of bestowing on whole nations refinement of taste: which, if it does not lead directly to purity of manners, obviates at least their greatest depravation, by disentangling the mind from appetite, and conducting the thoughts through successive stages of excellence, till that contemplation of universal rectitude and harmony which began by Taste, may, as it is exalted and refined, conclude in Virtue.

The confession of the artist's inevitable deficiency, the repeated conditional 'may', and the qualification ('if it does not lead directly') fail to impede the optimistic moral progress of this long sentence. We are left, however, with a pious hope rather than a firm conviction. (pp. 30-1)

> *Nicholas Penny, "An Ambitious Man: The Career and the Achievements of Sir Joshua Reynolds," in* Reynolds, *edited by Nicholas Penny, Harry N. Abrams, Inc., Publishers, 1986, pp. 17-42.*

FURTHER READING

Banner, D. H. "Joshua Reynolds, 1723-1923: The Cultivation of Taste." *The Nineteenth Century* XCIV, No. DLVIII (August 1923): 200-09.
> Discursive survey of Reynolds's artistic principles.

Bate, Walter Jackson. "Johnson and Reynolds: The Premise of General Nature." In his *From Classic To Romantic: Premises of Taste in Eighteenth-Century England,* pp. 59-92. 1946. Reprint. New York: Harper & Row, 1961.
> Studies Reynolds and Samuel Johnson as stewards of the moral imagination, concluding that "the premises of English neoclassicism found in Reynolds their most broadly representative expression and in Johnson their most triumphantly humane application."

Bosker, A. "Sir Joshua Reynolds." In *Literary Criticism in the Age of Johnson,* pp. 178-84. 2d ed., rev. New York: Hafner Publishing Company, 1953.
> Short discussion of several aspects of Reynolds's aesthetic theory.

Clough, Wilson O. "Reason and Genius—An Eighteenth Century Dilemma (Hogarth, Hume, Burke, Reynolds)." *Philological Quarterly* XXII, No. 1 (January 1944): 33-54.
> Examines efforts by William Hogarth, David Hume, Edmund Burke, and Reynolds to define the relative roles of genius and reasoned industry in determining artistic achievement.

Farington, Joseph. *Memoirs of the Life of Sir Joshua Reynolds, with Some Observations on His Talents and Character.* London: Cadell & Davies, 1819, 786 p.
> Sympathetic critical biography by a contemporary. Farington defends Reynolds as the sole author of the *Discourses.*

Goldstein, Harvey D. "Ut Poesis Pictura: Reynolds on Imitation and Imagination." *Eighteenth-Century Studies* I, No. 3 (March 1968): 213-35.
> Closely examines the *Discourses,* maintaining that there is great unity in Reynolds's critical thought, not "inconsistencies" as claimed by William Hazlitt and others.

Hazlitt, William. Review of *Memoirs of the Life of Sir Joshua Reynolds,* by Joseph Farington. *The Edinburgh Review* XXXIV, No. LXVII (August 1820): 79-108.
> Negative review of Farington's life of Reynolds, with dismissive criticisms of Reynolds's artistic theories.

——. "On Certain Inconsistencies in Sir Joshua Reynolds's *Discourses.*" In his *Table Talk; or, Original Essays,* pp. 122-30. 1821-22. Reprint. London and Toronto: J. M. Dent & Sons; New York: E. P. Dutton & Co., 1908.

> Examines the *Discourses,* bringing together numerous passages that "from their contradictory import seem to imply some radical defect in Sir Joshua's theory, and a doubt as to the possibility of placing an implicit reliance on his authority."

Hilles, Frederick Whiley. *The Literary Career of Sir Joshua Reynolds.* 1936. Reprint. New York: Archon Books, 1967, 318 p.

> Heavily footnoted biographical and bibliographical history of Reynolds's literary career. Robert R. Wark described this study as "a mine of information about the *Discourses* and an indispensable tool for every serious student of Reynolds."

———. "Reynolds among the Romantics." In *Literary Theory and Structure: Essays in Honor of William K. Wimsatt,* edited by Frank Brady, John Palmer, and Martin Price, pp. 267-83. New Haven and London: Yale University Press, 1973.

> Compares critical estimations of Reynolds made by Romantics William Blake, Benjamin Robert Haydon, and William Hazlitt, who all agreed "in opposing the Johnsonian concept of the Concrete Universal. To them it was right and proper to number the streaks of the tulip; to them great thoughts were specific."

Hudson, Derek. *Sir Joshua Reynolds: A Personal Study.* London: Geoffrey Bles, 1958, 276 p.

> Full-length biography that incorporates material from Frederick Whiley Hilles's works and other recent sources. Reynolds's *Journey from London to Brentford* is printed in the back of this volume, appearing in print for the first time.

Johnson, Edward Gilpin. Introduction to *Sir Joshua Reynolds's "Discourses,"* pp. 13-51. Chicago: A. C. McClurg and Co., 1891.

> Biographical and historical overview of Reynolds's life and times, with a short, approving critical summary of Sir Joshua's importance.

Keppel, Frederick. "Sir Joshua Reynolds." *Scribner's Magazine* XV, No. 1 (January 1894): 93-108.

> Biographical essay, touching upon Reynolds's friendships with Oliver Goldsmith, Samuel Johnson, and other members of the Literary Club.

Lamb, W. R. M. Introduction to *The Discourses of Sir Joshua Reynolds, P.R.A.,* pp. vii-xxv. Glasgow: Robert Maclehose and Co.; London: Macmillan and Co., 1924.

> Short biographical and critical essay, surveying all fifteen discourses and attempting to trace "a real connection between [Reynolds's] theory and his practice."

Lynd, Robert. "Reynolds, Goldsmith, Burke, and the Years of the Dictatorship." In his *Essays on Life and Literature,* pp. 113-31. London: J. M. Dent & Sons; New York: E. P. Dutton & Co., 1951.

> Biographical sketch of Reynolds, primarily as a friend of Samuel Johnson.

Mahoney, John L. "Reynolds's *Discourses on Art:* The Delicate Balance of Neoclassic Aesthetics." *The British Journal of Aesthetics* 18, No. 2 (Spring 1978): 126-36.

> Close reading of the *Discourses,* arguing that these lec-

tures are "part of that liberal tradition of Neoclassic theory extending as far back as Dryden and as far forward as Samuel Johnson."

Northcote, James. *The Life of Sir Joshua Reynolds.* 2 vols. London: n.p., 1818.

> Revealing portrait of Reynolds's life, contemporaries, and works, written by a pupil and apprentice of Reynolds. This work is a revised edition of Northcote's earlier *Memoirs of Sir Joshua Reynolds* (1813).

Simon, Irène. "Reynolds on Custom and Prejudice." *English Studies* 65, No. 3 (June 1984): 226-36.

> Attempts to show that "Reynolds's defence of prejudice applies only to a very small area of art—drapery," and that while Reynolds admittedly fought a "rear-guard action against 'newly-hatched unfledged opinions'" he was nevertheless "hardly the hide-bound conservative that [Robert W.] Uphaus makes him out to have been" (see Further Reading entry below).

Smith, James Harry, and Parks, Edd Winfield. "Sir Joshua Reynolds (1723-1792)." In *The Great Critics: An Anthology of Literary Criticism,* edited by James Harry Smith and Edd Winfield Parks, pp. 479-82. 3rd ed., rev. New York: W. W. Norton & Co., 1951.

> Short biographical and critical study written to introduce and explicate the principles of Reynolds's "Thirteenth Discourse." This, according to the editors, "reveals a line of thought which, if not contradictory to the doctrines previously laid down, is a least outside them."

Thompson, Elbert N. S. "The *Discourses* of Sir Joshua Reynolds." *PMLA* XXXII, No. 3 (1917): 339-66.

> General essay on the *Discourses,* addressing Reynolds's theories within the context of eighteenth-century European critical thought and examining the extent of Samuel Johnson's influence.

Trowbridge, Hoyt. "Platonism and Sir Joshua Reynolds." *English Studies* XXI, No. 1 (February 1939): 1-7.

> Seeks to demonstrate that Reynolds, a man often taken as a representative proponent of eighteenth-century Neoplatonism, actually shows "a tendency away from Platonism much more prominently than any attraction towards it." Further, Trowbridge argues that "the true philosophical affinity of Reynolds' classicism is not Plato but John Locke."

Uphaus, Robert W. "The Ideology of Reynolds' *Discourses on Art.*" *Eighteenth-Century Studies* 12, No. 1 (Fall 1978): 59-73.

> Posits an essentially conservative philosophical basis, both implied and explicit, underlying the *Discourses.* Uphaus's conclusion is opposed by Irène Simon (see Further Reading entry above).

Wilson, John. "April MDCCCXXIX." In his *The Works of Professor Wilson of the University of Edinburgh,* Vol. II: *Noctes Ambrosianæ,* edited by James Frederick Ferrier, pp. 213-49. Edinburgh and London: William Blackwood and Sons, 1855.

> Reprints commentary from an 1829 issue of *Blackwood's Edinburgh Magazine.* Wilson praises Reynolds's artistic and literary accomplishment, writing that "as to Sir Joshua's writings, their spirit is all in delightful keeping with his pictures. One of the few painters . . . who could express by the pen the principles which guide the pencil.

'Tis the only work on art which, to men not artists, is
entirely intelligible."

Thomas Warton

1728-1790

English literary historian, critic, and poet.

The writings of Warton mark a milestone in English literary history. His *History of English Poetry from the Close of the Eleventh Century to the Commencement of the Eighteenth Century* is widely considered the most significant literary history to be published in the eighteenth century. Along with his critical works on John Milton and Edmund Spenser, this work helped revive interest in medieval and Elizabethan literature and promote the study of literature as an art. In addition, his early poetry reflects a love of Gothic elements and nature, placing him as a predecessor of the Romantic poets of the nineteenth century.

Thomas Warton was born on 9 January 1728 in Basingstoke, Hampshire, the son of Thomas and Elizabeth Warton and the younger brother of literary scholar and poet Joseph Warton. Under the tutelage of his father, young Thomas exhibited an early love of reading and writing. In a 1737 letter to his sister, Jane, the nine-year old Thomas enclosed a translation from Martial, "On Leander's Swimming over the Hellespont to Hero." This precocity was encouraged by Warton's father in a variety of ways, and included taking his son to visit such places of historical interest as Stonehenge and Windsor Castle. A well-known account of Warton's intellectual curiosity and sensitivity is related by Clarissa Rinaker: "[While] the father and older brother were examining every detail [of Windsor Castle] with eager and voluble attention, the younger observed what he saw with so quiet a regard that his father misconstrued his silence as lack of interest and remarked to Joseph, 'Thomas goes on, and takes no notice of any thing he has seen.' Joseph, however, came later to realize how deeply impressed with everything he saw the younger boy had been, and remarked, 'I believe my brother was more struck with what he saw, and took more notice of every object, than either of us'." Antiquarian studies remained a strong interest of Warton's his entire life.

In 1744, Thomas enrolled at Trinity College, Oxford. He was elected one of Trinity's scholars in 1745, greatly relieving the family's financial burden of educating two sons. Following the death of Thomas Warton the elder that same year, the scholarship made possible the continuation of Thomas's education. Warton received his B.A. in 1747, was ordained, and became a tutor at Trinity. There are many anecdotes in regard to Warton's ineffectiveness as a tutor. Lord Eldon relates: "Poor Tom Warton! He was a tutor at Trinity; at the beginning of every term he used to send to his pupils to know whether they would *wish* to attend lecture that term." While the intellectual life of Oxford during the eighteenth century had declined considerably from earlier times, impressive facilities for study were still available to dedicated scholars such as Warton. In addition, he found the atmosphere created by Oxford's Gothic architecture especially favorable for writing poetry. The opportunity to do so arose in 1748, after William Mason's "Isis: An Elegy" was published, attacking alleged Jacobite activity at Oxford. The president of Trinity re-

quested that Warton compose a rebuttal. The result was the 1749 publication of "The Triumph of Isis," a heroic poem in defense of Oxford, glorifying the men of note who had studied there while occasionally suggesting that the scholarly environment of the university, enhanced by its distinguished architecture dating from the Middle Ages, had inspired these students to achieve academic eminence. Although he focused his energies in later life on literary history and criticism, Warton never completely gave up writing poetry. Warton received his M.A. in 1750 and secured a fellowship at Trinity in 1751. Warton continued his studies and in 1754 published *Observations on the Faerie Queene of Spenser,* an acclaimed critical work which showed Warton to be a literary critic of merit.

His scholarly reputation greatly enhanced by the warm reception of *Observations on the Faerie Queene,* Warton was elected professor of poetry at Oxford in 1757 and served in the post for ten years. It was during this time that he wrote *A Companion to the Guide and Guide to the Companion* (1760), a humorous satire of popular guidebooks. In this work Warton gently ridiculed other antiquarians of the time by claiming to have "discovered" several unknown halls and libraries at Oxford. Warton's most enduring comic work, however, is *The Oxford Sausage; or*

Select Poetical Pieces Written by the most Celebrated Wits of the University of Oxford, which he edited anonymously and published in 1764. Some of Warton's contributions to this work include "A Panegyric on Oxford Ale" and "Ode to a Grizzle Wig," which reveal the playful side of his personality.

Warton's studies culminated in his earning a bachelor of divinity degree in 1767. He was appointed to the parish of Kiddington in Oxfordshire, but chose to continue living at the university. Warton had begun to collect the materials that would eventually be compiled into his famous *History of English Poetry from the Close of the Eleventh Century to the Commencement of the Eighteenth Century,* published in three separate volumes from 1774 to 1781. Warton's well-received works earned him the respect of London literary society. The renowned lexicographer Samuel Johnson, a friend and admirer of Warton since the publication of *Observations on the Faerie Queene,* helped him gain admittance to the Literary Club in 1782. Warton proved very popular with the chief members of the Club, which included Sir Joshua Reynolds, James Boswell, and Edmund Burke, among others. His friendship with Johnson had been occasionally strained to the limit over the years, but as of a visit by Johnson and Boswell to Oxford in 1776 relations were smoothed over and their friendship reaffirmed.

Warton was elected Camden professor of history at Oxford in 1785 and was also named poet laureate in April of the same year, succeeding William Whitehead. He held these posts until his death. Warton suffered an attack of gout in early 1790 and traveled to Bath to recover. Returning to his responsibilities at Oxford, Warton suffered a massive stroke on 20 May in the common room of Trinity. He died the following day and was buried in the antechapel of Trinity College.

Poetry occupied a great deal of Warton's attention throughout his life. His verse was somewhat popular during the eighteenth century, with one collection reaching four editions in Warton's lifetime alone. He was a versatile poet, writing on many subjects and in several different veins, ranging from the humorous to the scholarly. Critics recognize Warton's importance in reviving the sonnet, a verse form neglected since Milton's death. In addition, his poetry reveals an interest in antiquarian studies and a reverence for nature, with some scholars identifying Warton as a precursor of the nineteenth-century Romantic poets. One critic has written that "the versification was often uncouth, but Warton's sincere admiration for nature and antiquity alike, though not expressed in his sonnets or elsewhere with much subtlety, arrested attention in his own time by its novelty, and lent distinction to his poetic achievements."

While Warton wrote a fairly substantial amount of poetry, it is as a scholar, critic, and literary historian that he gained the greatest amount of lasting recognition. Of his first notable critical work, Rinaker wrote: "The result of Warton's combined poetical enthusiasm and scholarly study of Spenser was that he produced in the *Observations on the Faerie Queene* the first important piece of modern historical criticism in the field of English literature. By the variety of its new tenets and the definitiveness of its revolt against the pseudo-classical criticism by rule, it marks the beginning of a new school." Essentially a well-received

and respected scholarly work, *Observations on the Faerie Queene* was vehemently denounced in a 1756 pamphlet by William Huggins, *The Observer Observ'd, or Remarks on a Certain Curious Tract, Intitl'd, Observations on the Faerie Queen of Spencer, by Thomas Warton, A.M.* Over the years, however, the majority of literary historians and critics have tended to lend support to Rinaker's observation.

Warton's continued efforts in literary studies resulted in his greatest contribution to English literary history, *The History of English Poetry.* Warton intended for this work to trace English literary history from the late eleventh to the early eighteenth centuries, but his death terminated the project. At that time, three volumes had been published and a fourth started, but the study had progressed only to the end of the sixteenth century. Although incomplete, it is still considered by many critics to be a seminal work in English literary history. There has been some debate over the originality of Warton's plan for this historical overview. Both Alexander Pope and Thomas Gray had composed plans for a history of English literature, but neither acted upon these intentions. Gray stated in 1768 that he had decided against completing the project, and Warton's first volume of the *History* went to press the next year. In 1770 Gray sent Warton the outline of his intended history upon the suggestion of Richard Hurd. This outline revealed that Gray had intended to group authors according to their critical affiliations. In the first volume of *The History of English Poetry,* just published, Warton had arranged his authors in chronological order. This approach was maintained in the second and third volumes, indicating to most critics that Warton did not steal Gray's plan in either concept or content, but detractors continued to espouse the opposite argument.

Of Warton's works, *The History of English Poetry* has received the most critical attention due to both its groundbreaking nature and intended scope. Both Edward Gibbon and "Christopher North" (John Wilson) praised the work for its innovativeness and completeness, especially in terms of the attention given to minor authors. Many twentieth-century critics claim that while some of the information contained in *The History of English Poetry* is faulty, it should nevertheless be recognized as an important piece of English literary history. The work indeed contains some errors in dates and fact, and the arrangement of authors and works is often incorrect. In addition, translations of foreign languages were occasionally imperfect. Joseph Ritson, Horace Walpole, and Sir Walter Scott all denounced the work on these and other counts. But modern-day scholars also acknowledge the influence this work had in piquing interest in medieval and Elizabethan literature and in drawing attention away from the neoclassical prose style popularized by such authors as Pope.

Literary critics from the eighteenth century to the present day have recognized the groundbreaking nature of much of Warton's works in a variety of genres. The interest expressed in antiquarian elements and nature in his poetry classifies him in some respects as a forerunner of the English Romantic movement. The significance of both *Observations on the Faerie Queene of Spenser* and *The History of English Poetry from the Close of the Eleventh Century to the Commencement of the Eighteenth Century* as seminal pieces of literary history has long been recognized by literary scholars. In words of praise for the latter work which may summarize the modern perspective of Warton's canon, Rinaker has stated that "although Warton was unable to free himself from many of the faults of his age, which he inherited together with its virtues, he added to them many of the conspicuous merits of the next century, which he was able in a remarkable way to anticipate."

PRINCIPAL WORKS

Five Pastoral Eclogues: The Scenes of Which are Suppos'd to Lie Among the Shepherds, Oppress'd by the War in Germany (poetry) 1745
The Pleasures of Melancholy (poetry) 1747
The Triumph of Isis (poetry) 1749
Newmarket, a Satire (poetry) 1751
The Union: or, Select Scots and English Poems [editor] (poetry) 1753
Observations on the Faerie Queene of Spenser (criticism) 1754
A Companion to the Guide and Guide to the Companion (prose) 1760
The Oxford Sausage; or Select Poetical Pieces Written by the Most Celebrated Wits of the University of Oxford [editor] (poetry) 1764
†*The History of English Poetry from the Close of the Eleventh Century to the Commencement of the Eighteenth Century.* 3 vols. (history and criticism) 1774-81
Poems. A New Edition, with Additions (poetry) 1777
‡*Specimen of a Parochial History of Oxfordshire* (prose) 1782; also revised as *Specimen of a History of Oxfordshire,* 1783
Verses on Sir Joshua Reynold's Painted Window at New College, Oxford (poetry) 1782
Milton's Poems upon Several Occasions, English, Italian and Latin, with Translations by John Milton [editor] (poetry) 1785

*Several critics do not attribute these poems to Warton.

†Eighty-eight pages of a fourth volume were published in 1789.

‡The revised edition is the most widely recognized work; the original edition consisted of twenty privately distributed copies.

––––––––––––

Samuel Johnson   (letter date 1754)

[*Samuel Johnson was a preeminent figure in English literature. He was a prolific lexicographer, essayist, poet, and critic, best known for his* Dictionary of the English Language *(1755). In the following excerpt from a 1754 letter to Warton, first published in James Boswell's* The Life of Samuel Johnson *(1791), Johnson praises* Observations on the Faerie Queene of Spenser, *predicting that it will help "the advancement of the literature of our native country."*]

SIR,

It is but an ill return for the book [*Observations on the Faerie Queene of Spenser*] with which you were pleased to favour me, to have delayed my thanks for it till now. I am too apt to be negligent; but I can never deliberately shew

my disrespect to a man of your character: and I now pay you a very honest acknowledgement, for the advancement of the literature of our native country. You have shewn to all, who shall hereafter attempt the study of our ancient authours, the way to success; by directing them to the perusal of the books which those authours had read. Of this method, Hughes, and men much greater than Hughes, seem never to have thought. The reason why the authours, which are yet read, of the sixteenth century, are so little understood, is, that they are read alone; and no help is borrowed from those who lived with them, or before them. Some part of this ignorance I hope to remove by my book, which now draws towards its end; but which I cannot finish to my mind, without visiting the libraries of Oxford, which I therefore hope to see in a fortnight. I know not how long I shall stay, or where I shall lodge; but shall be sure to look for you at my arrival, and we shall easily settle the rest. I am, dear Sir,

　　　　Your most obedient, &c.
　　　　SAM. JOHNSON.
[London] July 16, 1754. (p. 160-61)

> *Samuel Johnson, in a letter to Thomas Warton on July 16, 1754, in* The Life of Samuel Johnson, LL.D., *by James Boswell, 1791. Reprint by Dutton, 1978, pp. 160-61.*

Thomas Warton   (essay date 1774)

[*In the following excerpt from his preface to the first volume (1774) of* The History of English Poetry, *Warton explains his intent and organization of the work.*]

In an age advanced to the highest degree of refinement, that species of curiosity commences, which is busied in contemplating the progress of social life, in displaying the gradations of science, and in tracing the transitions from barbarism to civility.

That these speculations should become the favourite pursuits and the fashionable topics of such a period is extremely natural. We look back on the savage condition of our ancestors with the triumph of superiority; we are pleased to mark the steps by which we have been raised from rudeness to elegance: and our reflections on this subject are accompanied with a conscious pride, arising in great measure from a tacit comparison of the infinite disproportion between the feeble efforts of remote ages, and our present improvements in knowledge.

In the mean time, the manners, monuments, customs, practices, and opinions of antiquity, by forming so strong a contrast with those of our own times, and by exhibiting human nature and human inventions in new lights, in unexpected appearances, and in various forms, are objects which forcibly strike a feeling imagination.

Nor does this spectacle afford nothing more than a fruitless gratification to the fancy. It teaches us to set a just estimation on our own acquisitions, and encourages us to cherish that cultivation, which is so closely connected with the existence and the exercise of every social virtue.

On these principles, to develop the dawnings of genius, and to pursue the progress of our national poetry, from a rude origin and obscure beginnings, to its perfection in a polished age, must prove an interesting and instructive investigation. But a history of poetry, for another reason, yet on the same principles, must be more especially productive of entertainment and utility. I mean, as it is an art, whose object is human society: as it has the peculiar merit, in its operations on that object, of faithfully recording the features of the times, and of preserving the most picturesque and expressive representations of manners: and because the first monuments of composition in every nation are those of the poet, as it possesses the additional advantage of transmitting to posterity genuine delineations of life in its simplest stages. Let me add, that anecdotes of the rudiments of a favourite art will always be particularly pleasing. The more early specimens of poetry must ever amuse, in proportion to the pleasure which we receive from its finished productions. (pp. 3-4)

I have chosen to exhibit the history of our poetry in a chronological series: not distributing my matter into detached articles, of periodical divisions, or of general heads. (p. 4)

A few years ago, Mr. Mason, with that liberality which ever accompanies true genius, gave me an authentic copy of Mr. Pope's scheme of a *History of English Poetry,* in which our poets were classed under their supposed respective schools. The late lamented Mr. Gray had also projected a work of this kind, and translated some Runic odes for its illustration, now published; but soon relinquishing the prosecution of a design which would have detained him from his own noble inventions, he most obligingly condescended to favour me with the substance of his plan, which I found to be that of Mr. Pope, considerably enlarged, extended, and improved.

It is vanity in me to have mentioned these communications. But I am apprehensive my vanity will justly be thought much greater, when it shall appear, that in giving the history of English poetry, I have rejected the ideas of men who are its most distinguished ornaments. To confess the real truth, upon examination and experiment, I soon discovered their mode of treating my subject, plausible as it is, and brilliant in theory, to be attended with difficulties and inconveniencies, and productive of embarrassment both to the reader and the writer. Like other ingenious systems, it sacrificed much useful intelligence to the observance of arrangement; and in the place of that satisfaction which results from a clearness and a fulness of information, seemed only to substitute the merit of disposition and the praise of contrivance. The constraint imposed by a mechanical attention to this distribution appeared to me to destroy that free exertion of research with which such a history ought to be executed, and not easily reconcileable with that complication, variety, and extent of materials which it ought to comprehend.

The method I have pursued, on one account at least, seems preferable to all others. My performance, in its present form, exhibits without transposition the gradual improvements of our poetry, at the same time that it uniformly represents the progression of our language.

Some, perhaps, will be of opinion, that these annals ought to have commenced with a view of the Saxon poetry. But besides that a legitimate illustration of that jejune and intricate subject would have almost doubled my labour, that the Saxon language is familiar only to a few learned antiquaries, that our Saxon poems are for the most part little more than religious rhapsodies, and that scarce any compositions remain marked with the native images of that people in their pagan state, every reader that reflects but for a moment on our political establishment must perceive, that the Saxon poetry has no connection with the nature and purpose of my present undertaking. Before the Norman accession, which succeeded to the Saxon government, we were an unformed and unsettled race. That mighty revolution obliterated almost all relation to the former inhabitants of this island; and produced that signal change in our policy, constitution, and public manners, the effects of which have reached modern times. The beginning of these annals seems therefore to be most properly dated from that era, when our national character began to dawn.

It was recommended to me by a person eminent in the republic of letters, totally to exclude from these volumes any mention of the English drama. I am very sensible that a just history of our stage is alone sufficient to form an entire and extensive work; and this argument, which is by no means precluded by the attempt here offered to the public, still remains separately to be discussed at large and in form. But as it was professedly my intention to comprise every species of English poetry, this, among the rest, of course claimed a place in these annals, and necessarily fell into my general design. At the same time, as in this situation it could only become a subordinate object, it was impossible I should examine it with that critical precision and particularity which so large, so curious, and so important an article of our poetical literature demands and deserves. To have considered it in its full extent, would have produced the unwieldy excrescence of a disproportionate episode: not to have considered it at all had been an omission, which must detract from the integrity of my intended plan. I flatter myself, however, that from evidences hitherto unexplored I have recovered hints which may facilitate the labours of those who shall hereafter be inclined to investigate the ancient state of dramatic exhibition in this country with due comprehension and accuracy.

It will probably be remarked, that the citations in the first volume are numerous, and sometimes very prolix. But it should be remembered, that most of these are extracted from ancient manuscript poems never before printed, and hitherto but little known. Nor was it easy to illustrate the darker and more distant periods of our poetry, without producing ample specimens. In the meantime, I hope to merit the thanks of the antiquarian, for enriching the stock of our early literature by these new accessions: and I trust I shall gratify the reader of taste, in having so frequently rescued from oblivion the rude inventions and irregular beauties of the heroic tale or the romantic legend. (pp. 4-6)

Thomas Warton, in a preface to his History of English Poetry from the Twelfth to the Close of the Sixteenth Century, Vol. I, *edited by W. Carew Hazlitt, revised edition, 1871. Reprint by Georg Olms Verlagsbuchhandlung, 1968, pp. 3-6.*

Horace Walpole   (letter date 1774)

[*Walpole was an English author, politician, and publisher. He is best known for his memoirs and voluminous correspondence. In the excerpt below from a 1774 letter to William Mason, Walpole criticizes Warton's literary*

style, claiming that it lessens the value of The History
of English Poetry.]

Well, I have read Mr Warton's book [**The History of English Poetry**]; and shall I tell you what I think of it? I
never saw so many entertaining particulars crowded together with so little entertainment and vivacity. The facts
are overwhelmed by one another, as Johnstone's sense is
by words; they are all equally strong. Mr Warton has
amassed all the parts and learning of four centuries, and
all the impression that remains is, that those four ages had
no parts or learning at all. There is not a gleam of poetry
in their compositions between the scalds and Chaucer: nay
I question whether they took their metres for anything
more than rules for writing prose. In short, it may be the
genealogy of versification with all its intermarriages and
anecdotes of the family—but Gray's and your plan might
still be executed. I am sorry Mr Warton has contracted
such an affection for his materials, that he seems almost
to think that not only Pope, but Dryden himself have
added few beauties to Chaucer. (pp. 143-44)

> *Horace Walpole, in a letter to William Mason
> on April 7, 1774, in* Horace Walpole's Corre-
> spondence with William Mason, Vol. I, *edited
> by W. S. Lewis, Yale University Press, 1955,
> pp. 143-47.*

Thomas Thomson   (essay date 1803)

[*The following excerpt is from an unsigned review of
Richard Mant's edition of* The Poetical Works of the
Late Thomas Warton *in* The Edinburgh Review *which
is attributed to Thomas Thomson. In the excerpt, he ex-
amines Warton's poetry and critiques* The History of
English Poetry.]

At an early age, Mr Warton began to be distinguished as
a poet; and, in his first and rudest efforts, he discovered
the same cast of genius and manner which characterise all
his serious compositions. His most prominent feature is a
fancy splendid and vigorous, which delights to form its objects in picturesque and fantastic groupes, but which appears to draw his materials less from an extensive and
original observation of nature, than from a memory richly
stored with images rifled from the poetical treasures of a
former period. Without being insensible to the charms of
classical learning, he appears to have been still more powerfully attracted to the literature of what may be called the
heroic ages of modern Europe. His mind seems to have ri-
oted in the gaudy fictions of the Gothic chivalry and romance. In quest of 'Gothic manners,' and 'Gothic arts,' he
did not shrink from the fatigue of exploring the more remote and neglected sources of this fairy lore: but, above
all, the writers from whom he probably first caught this
enthusiasm, who had themselves been under its powerful
influence, and whose works were fitted to afford it the
most full and exquisite gratification, were unquestionably
Spenser and Milton. Indeed, we might perhaps be war-
ranted in saying, that his fond admiration of the peculiar
beauties of these two poets, had, in a great degree, subdued
his own originality of genius. The obvious character, and
most obvious defect of the poetry of Warton, is a too servile imitation, or rather an adoption of their imagery and
language. It gives to many of his larger and most successful compositions, too much of the air of a parody or a

cento: and, even when his ideas may have been derived
from other sources, or may be regarded as his own, they
seem, involuntarily, to have embodied themselves in the
borrowed language, and set phrases of his great masters.

As it is not our intention to enter into a particular criticism on the poems of Warton, which have been long in the
possession of the public, it would be of little utility or interest here to follow his biographer through the detail of
their respective dates, which he has very properly, and we
presume very accurately given. Of his poetry so much has
now been said, only as it serves to indicate the general
character of his mind, and the particular direction which
it gave to his literary pursuits. A still more decided proof
of the indulgence he had given to his favourite propensities, was afforded by his **Observations on the Fairy Queen
of Spenser,** first published in the year 1754; and of which
an enlarged edition was given in 1762. Of the merits of this
work a very fair estimate, we believe, has long been formed
by the public. The chief praise, unquestionably, is due to
the discovery which it made of a new track of research in
the literature of early English poetry and romance, which
is certainly by no means incurious or uninteresting in itself, and which on all hands must be admitted to possess
very great attractions, as conducting almost exclusively to
the full illustration of the great writers of a later period.
This track of research, Warton himself continued to pursue with great ardour; and even in the earliest specimen
of his critical talents, we may discern the commencement
of those investigations which ultimately led him to the accomplishment of his greatest and most important work,
The History of English Poetry.

Although the compilation of this elaborate work must
have occupied much time, and exacted no common share
of diligence and industry, yet we find the intermediate period, preceding the appearance of the first volume in 1774,
filled up with many other literary pursuits. Of these, Mr
Mant has given a particular chronicle. They sufficiently
serve to indicate the ardour and versatility of Warton's
mind; but are not, in general, of such a kind as essentially
and permanently to affect his fame. The most considerable
among them is his splendid edition of Theocritus; a work
which we believe was received by critical scholars with
disappointment, and from which, certainly, his reputation
has not derived much increase. The undertaking is said to
have been pressed on him by the exhortations of some of
his literary friends; but we suspect that he had, by this
time, become too much a 'truant to the classic page,' to
perform, with adequate diligence and zeal, the toilsome
duties of an editor. (pp. 254-55)

We will confine our remarks [on the **History of English
Poetry**] to a single point. When taken as a whole, it is impossible to deny that there is a certain lifeless massiveness
in [this work] which, in the perusal, becomes extremely
oppressive, and which, with various excellencies in other
respects, has already, we suspect, condemned it to be in
the number of those books which are oftener praised than
read. This, we apprehend, is not to be ascribed to the bulk
of the work, to the minuteness of its details, or to the pro-
fuseness of its quotations from obscure and antiquated
writers. To those who are not mere loungers in reading,
there is in all this a richness and fullness which would not
be without powerful attractions. To us it appears, that the
fault is intimately connected with the general frame and

construction of the work. In adopting a simply chronological arrangement of his materials, instead of a systematic method founded on some leading principle, Mr Warton is known to have deviated from the projected plans of Pope, and of Gray; and, in doing so, he has been at pains to vindicate his choice, by assuring us, that it proceeded from an experimental conviction of the utter impracticability of the latter. How far such an experiment had been ever fairly made, might perhaps be questioned, from the rapid and slovenly manner in which the composition of the work appears to have proceeded. But the real difficulty of the attempt we are inclined to ascribe, not so much to its own impracticable nature, as to the absence of those scientific powers and habits which were requisite to its successful execution. No ordinary shares of genius and of taste may be allowed to Warton; and we sincerely believe, that in point of mere literary accomplishment, few men could have been found so well qualified for the execution of the particular parts of such a work. But, unquestionably, to powers of that higher order which, by a sort of magical influence, could have given the unity, and simplicity, and strength of a whole, to an infinite number of scattered and various parts, the pretensions of Mr Warton were extremely moderate. We would not be understood to insinuate, that the plans suggested by Pope, and by Gray, were very happily conceived, or very judiciously digested, or that the simple adoption of them by Warton would have cured the radical defect of his book. Neither do we mean to state, that an arrangement of a chronological nature was in itself utterly incompatible with that higher species of excellence which he has failed of attaining. The excellence of which we speak, is by no means essentially dependent on mere mechanical arrangement; and, by the infusion of an informing spirit into the whole mass, we should even conceive it possible to vanquish the disadvantages of an awkward and unnatural method. The successful execution of the plan might probably be attended with the sacrifice of some of those collateral details which Warton has not scrupled to collect in his long and desultory course; yet it may be safely presumed, that, with a tolerable share of address, almost every thing might be retained and incorporated which is not an offensive excrescence even on the miscellaneous pages of his curious and amusing work.

During the publication of the successive volumes of the *History of English Poetry,* and after the appearance of the last of them, Mr Warton continued to amuse and instruct the public by various inferior literary productions. Among these, was his short, but satisfactory detection of the forgeries of Chatterton; which appeared at a period when it was regarded as some merit, to have been among the foremost to expose the shallow impostures of that wonderful boy. But the most important of his later works was his edition of the Juvenilia of Milton, with very copious annotations, in which he gave full scope to that species of critical discussion in which he was best fitted to excel. His early and intimate acquaintance with the poetry of Milton, and his liberal use of Miltonic imagery and language, we have formerly noticed. In return, he here employs himself in tracing the obligations of Milton to his poetical predecessors, but in his detections there is nothing invidious, or that will not tend to heighten, rather than to lower the admiration of that mighty genius. (pp. 256-57)

Thomas Thomson, in an originally unsigned essay entitled "Mant's 'Warton's Poetical Works'," in The Edinburgh Review, *Vol. II, No. III, April, 1803, pp. 250-61.*

Sir Walter Scott   (essay date 1804)

[*Scott was a Scottish novelist, poet, historian, biographer, and critic. In the excerpt below, from a review originally published in the* Edinburgh Review *in 1804, he praises the subject matter and comprehensiveness of* The History of English Poetry, *but criticizes the lack of "plan and system."*]

The late Mr. Warton, with a poetical enthusiasm which converted toil into pleasure, and gilded, to himself and his readers, the dreary subjects of antiquarian lore, and with a capacity of labour apparently inconsistent with his more brilliant powers, has produced a work of great size [*The History of English Poetry*], and, partially speaking, of great interest, from the perusal of which we rise, our fancy delighted with beautiful imagery, and with the happy analysis of ancient tale and song, but certainly with very vague ideas of the history of English poetry. The error seems to lie in a total neglect of plan and system; for, delighted with every interesting topic which occurred, the historical poet pursued it to its utmost verge, without considering that these digressions, however beautiful and interesting in themselves, abstracted alike his own attention, and that of the reader, from the professed purpose of his book. Accordingly, Warton's *History of English Poetry* has remained, and will always remain, an immense commonplace book of *memoirs to serve for such an history.* No antiquary can open it, without drawing information from a mine which, though dark, is inexhaustible in its treasures; nor will he who reads merely for amusement ever shut it for lack of attaining his end; while both may probably regret the desultory excursions of an author, who wanted only system, and a more rigid attention to minute accuracy, to have perfected the great task he has left incomplete. (p. 11)

Sir Walter Scott, "On Ellis's 'Specimens of the Early English Poets'," in his Critical and Miscellaneous Essays of Sir Walter Scott, Vol. I, *Carey and Hart, 1841, pp. 9-19.*

Nathan Drake   (essay date 1810)

[*Drake was an English physician and literary essayist. In the following excerpt, he discusses Warton's writing style in the early poetry.*]

The bias of Mr. Warton's mind towards poetry and elegant literature was early shewn; in his ninth year, in a letter addressed to his sister, he sends her a translation from Martial; and it has been affirmed, that in 1745, when only in his eighteenth year, he published **"Five Pastoral Eclogues,"** the scenes of which are laid among the shepherds of Germany, ruined by the war of 1744. The authenticity of this production has, however, been much doubted by Mr. Mant, who says, "I do not learn that they ever had the name of Warton affixed to them, and can assert, on the authority of his sister, that he absolutely disclaimed them." Yet it cannot be denied, that a vein of description runs through these Eclogues of a kind very similar to that which Mr. Warton was afterward accustomed to indulge:

the . . . allusion, for instance, to the chivalric combat, in Eclogue the 3d, and the subsequent picture of the convent, in Eclogue the 4th, are of this cast. (p. 167)

The close imitation of Milton, too, in Eclogue the 2d, the description of the Hermit's Cell in Eclogue the 5th, and various other passages, of considerable merit for the age at which they are supposed to have been written, might, not without reason, lead to the attribution of these pieces to our author.

It must, indeed, be admitted, that the first acknowledged production of Mr. Warton, **"The Pleasures of Melancholy,"** published in 1747, but composed in 1745, is in a strain superior to the Eclogues. This beautifully romantic poem, though executed at a period so early in life, betrays almost immediately the tract of reading, and the school of poetry, to which its author had, even then, sedulously addicted himself. Every page suggests to us the disciple of Spenser and Milton, yet without servile imitation; for, though the language and style of imagery whisper whence they were drawn, many of the pictures in this poem are so bold and highly coloured, as justly to claim no small share of originality.

The year succeeding this effusion he wrote, on the recommendation of Dr. Huddesford, President of his college, **"The Triumph of Isis,"** in reply to Mr. Mason, who had published an Elegy, under the title of "Isis," reflecting, rather harshly, on some circumstances which had lately occurred, of a political nature, in the university of Oxford. **"The Triumph of Isis"** was printed in 1749, and received with a burst of applause, as a noble and spirited vindication of the honour and reputation of his Alma Mater. It has, moreover, the merit, though written upon a temporary subject, of containing imagery and sentiment which must always please and interest. That it is superior to the poem which gave rise to it, has been, not only the opinion of the public, but of Mr. Mason himself, who, writing to Mr. Warton in 1777, for the purpose of thanking him for a present of his poems, which he had then just published, but in which, out of delicacy to his former opponent, he had omitted the **"Triumph of Isis,"** says with much candour,

> I am, however, sorry to find that the **"Triumph of Isis"** has not found a place near the delicate **"Complaint of Cherwell,"** to which it was a proper companion; and I fear that a punctilio of politeness to me was the occasion of its exclusion. Had I known of your intention of making this collection, most certainly I should have pleaded for the insertion of that poem, which I assure you I think greatly excels the Elegy which occasioned it, both in its poetical imagery, and the correct flow of its versification.
>
> (pp. 169-71)

On the genius of Warton, as a Poet, an adequate value has not yet been placed; for in consequence of a sedulous imitation of the diction of our elder bards, especially of Spenser and Milton, originality of conception has been very unjustly denied him. To his brother Joseph, with whom he has been commonly ranked, he is greatly superior, both in vigour and fertility of imagination, though, perhaps, less sweet and polished in his versification.

In the rhymed pentameter, indeed, and in blank verse, he is inferior, in point of versification, to Dryden, Pope, and

Milton; but in the eight-syllable metre, to which he was particularly partial, he has exhibited, almost uniformly, great harmony and sweetness. The mixture of *trochaics* of seven syllables, and *iambics* of eight, which has been objected to him as a fault, in this species of verse, I am so far from considering as a defect, that, as in Milton and Gray, I esteem it productive of much beauty and much interesting variety.

Against the antique cast of expression which he has so frequently adopted in his poems, the disciples of Dryden and Pope have brought many complaints. That an *indiscriminate* use of the phraseology of our elder bards must be admitted as a blemish will not be denied; but when, as in Warton, the theme is drawn from the bosom of legendary lore, and abounding in pictures of Anglo-Norman arts and manners, a judicious admixture of old words throws a richness and mellowness over the composition that admirably blends with the nature of the subject, and which no other expedient can supply.

The imagery, indeed, throughout the greater part of the poetry of Warton is altogether antiquated; it is founded on the costume of the chivalric ages, and is every where thickly strewn with feudal pictures and embellishments. The language is accordant, and has given to these glowing sketches a tint which, as removing all rawness and glare of colouring, appears the work of time. In fact, more than any other poet since the era of Spenser, our author may be termed *The Bard of Gothic Painting.* In lyric poetry he approaches nearer the genius of *Collins* than of *Gray;* for, like the former, he was strongly addicted to the *wild,* the *wonderful,* and the *romantic.* In *these departments,* after enumerating our three great poets, *Spenser, Shakspeare,* and *Milton,* may we not add, as forming the closest approximation, the names of *Collins* and of *Warton?* (pp. 174-76)

> *Nathan Drake, "Sketches, Biographical and Critical of the Occasional Contributors to the Rambler, Adventurer, and Idler," in his* Essays: Biographical, Critical, and Historical, *Vol. II, W. Suttaby, 1810, pp. 35-236.*

William Hazlitt   (essay date 1818)

[*Hazlitt was one of the most important literary critics of the Romantic age. He was a deft stylist, a master of the prose essay, and a leader of what was later termed "impressionist criticism"—a form of personal analysis directly opposed to the universal standards of critical judgment accepted by many eighteenth-century critics. Like Charles Lamb, Hazlitt utilized the critical techniques of evocation, metaphor, and personal reference—three innovations that greatly altered the development of literary criticism in the nineteenth and twentieth centuries. In the following excerpt, Hazlitt commends Warton's talent as a sonneteer.*]

Warton was a poet and a scholar, studious with ease, learned without affectation. He had a happiness which some have been prouder of than he, who deserved it less— he was poet laureate.

> And that green wreath which decks the bard when dead,
> That laurel garland crown'd his living head.

But he bore his honours meekly, and performed his half-yearly task regularly. I should not have mentioned him for this distinction alone (the highest which a poet can receive from the state), but for another circumstance; I mean his being the author of some of the finest sonnets in the language—at least so they appear to me; and as this species of composition has the necessary advantage of being short, (though it is also sometimes both 'tedious and brief',) I will here repeat [one] of them. . . .

Sonnet. Written at Stonehenge.

Thou noblest monument of Albion's isle,
Whether, by Merlin's aid, from Scythia's shore
To Amber's fatal plain Pendragon bore,
Huge frame of giant hands, the mighty pile,
T' entomb his Britons slain by Hengist's guile:
Or Druid priests, sprinkled with human gore,
Taught mid thy massy maze their mystic lore:
Or Danish chiefs, enrich'd with savage spoil,
To victory's idol vast, an unhewn shrine,
Rear'd the rude heap, or in thy hallow'd ground
Repose the kings of Brutus' genuine line;
Or here those kings in solemn state were crown'd;
Studious to trace thy wondrous origin,
We muse on many an ancient tale renown'd.

Nothing can be more admirable than the learning here displayed, or the inference from it, that it is of no use but as it leads to interesting thought and reflection.

That written after seeing Wilton House is in the same style, but I prefer concluding with that to the river Lodon, which has a personal as well as poetical interest about it.

Ah! what a weary race my feet have run,
Since first I trod thy banks with alders crown'd,
And thought my way was all through fairy ground,
Beneath the azure sky and golden sun:
When first my Muse to lisp her notes begun!
While pensive memory traces back the round
Which fills the varied interval between;
Much pleasure, more of sorrow, marks the scene.—
Sweet native stream! those skies and suns so pure
No more return, to cheer my evening road!
Yet still one joy remains, that not obscure
Nor useless, all my vacant days have flow'd
From youth's gay dawn to manhood's prime mature,
Nor with the Muse's laurel unbestow'd.

(pp. 186-87)

> *William Hazlitt, "On Swift, Young, Gray, Collins, etc.," in his* Lectures on the English Poets, *1818. Reprint by Oxford University Press 1924, pp. 160-89.*

Thomas Campbell   (essay date 1819)

[*Campbell was a Scottish poet, biographer, and historian. In the excerpt below from a work first published in 1819, he offers a mixed valuation of Warton's poetic skill.*]

Every Englishman who values the literature of his country, must feel himself obliged to Warton as a poetical antiquary. As a poet, he is ranked by his brother Joseph in the school of Spenser and Milton; but this classification can only be admitted with a full understanding of the immense distance between him and his great masters. He had, indeed, "spelt the fabled rhyme;" he abounds in allusions to

the romantic subjects of Spenser, and he is a sedulous imitator of the rich lyrical manner of Milton: but of the tenderness and peculiar harmony of Spenser he has caught nothing; and in his resemblance to Milton, he is the heir of his phraseology more than of his spirit. His imitation of manner, however, is not confined to Milton. His style often exhibits a composite order of poetical architecture. In his verses to Sir Joshua Reynolds, for instance, he blends the point and succinctness of Pope, with the richness of the elder and more fanciful school. It is one of his happiest compositions; and, in this case, the intermixture of styles has no unpleasing effect. In others, he often tastelessly and elaborately unites his affectation of antiquity, with the case-hardened graces of modern polish.

If we judge of him by the character of the majority of his pieces, I believe that fifty out of sixty of them are such, that we should not be anxious to give them a second perusal. From that proportion of his works, I conceive that an unprejudiced reader would pronounce him a florid, unaffecting describer, whose images are plentifully scattered, but without selection or relief. To confine our view, however, to some seven or eight of his happier pieces, we shall find, in these, a considerable degree of graphic power, of fancy, and animation. His **"Verses to Sir Joshua Reynolds"** are splendid and spirited. There is also a softness and sweetness in his ode entitled **"The Hamlet,"** which is the more welcome, for being rare in his productions; and his **"Crusade,"** and **"Grave of Arthur,"** have a genuine air of martial and minstrel enthusiasm. Those pieces exhibit, to the best advantage, the most striking feature of his poetical character, which was a fondness for the recollections of chivalry, and a minute intimacy of imagination with its gorgeous residences, and imposing spectacles. The spirit of chivalry, he may indeed be said, to have revived in the poetry of modern times. His memory was richly stored with all the materials for description that can be got from books: and he seems not to have been without an original enthusiasm for those objects which excite strong associations of regard and wonder. Whether he would have ever looked with interest on a shepherd's cottage, if he had not found it described by Virgil or Theocritus, may be fairly doubted; but objects of terror, splendour and magnificence, are evidently congenial to his fancy. He is very impressive in sketching the appearance of an ancient Gothic castle, in the following lines:

High o'er the trackless heath, at midnight seen,
No more the windows, ranged in long array,
(Where the tall shaft and fretted nook between
Thick ivy twines) the taper'd rites betray.

His memory was stored with an uncommon portion of that knowledge which supplies materials for picturesque description; and his universal acquaintance with our poets supplied him with expression, so as to answer the full demand of his original ideas. Of his poetic invention, in the fair sense of the word, of his depth of sensibility, or of his powers of reflection, it is not so easy to say any thing favourable. (p. 657)

> *Thomas Campbell, "Thomas Warton," in his* Specimens of the British Poets, *revised edition, Henry Carey Baird, 1853, pp. 655-57.*

John Wilson (essay date 1838)

[*In the following excerpt, Wilson surveys the background, content, and literary style of several of Warton's poems.*]

In the **"Pleasures of Melancholy,"** composed in his seventeenth year, there are some passages of no mean power—and that will bear comparison with any thing written at so early an age by the best of our poets. Indeed, we agree with Thomas Campbell in thinking that "it gives promise of a sensibility which his subsequent poetry did not fulfil;" and, though it cannot be truly said that in after life he did not follow the bidding of his own genius, yet, by following it, he seems to have allowed to languish in disuse many feelings and emotions with which his thoughtful heart had in early boyhood been familiar, and almost to have forgotten them in his devotion to the lore of Chivalry and Romance. (p. 554)

In [the passages of the **"Pleasures of Melancholy"**], equally as in the productions of his maturer genius, Warton discovers "that fondness for the beauties of Architecture which was an absolute passion in his breast." But there is in them, if we mistake not, a depth of feeling hardly to be found in the best descriptions of the same objects and places in his later poems. They are always brought by him before our eye with wonderful distinctness—but rather by a vivid conceptive than imaginative power; and his pictures, beautiful or solemn though they be, want, we fear, what Wordsworth could have given them,

> The Consecration and the Poet's Dream.

Yet we may be doing them injustice—and you may prefer the celebrated passages—for once they were celebrated—in his **"Triumph of Isis,"** written in his 21st year—and in his **"Verses on Sir Joshua's Painted Window at New College,"** written in advanced life—and justly called by Campbell "spirited and splendid—blending the point and succinctness of Pope with the richness of the older and more fanciful school" [see excerpt dated 1819]. (p. 555)

But by far the noblest of Warton's inspirations are his two odes—**"The Crusade"**—and **"The Grave of King Arthur."** "They have," quoth the author of Hohenlinden and Lochiel, "a genuine air of martial and minstrel enthusiasm." And again, "the spirit of Chivalry he may indeed be said to have revived in the poetry of modern times." Scott took a motto for the Minstrelsy of the Border from Warton—a most appropriate one—

> The songs, to savage virtue dear,
> That won of yore the public ear;
> Ere polity, sedate and sage,
> Had quenched the fires of feudal rage.

But Scott was indebted to Warton for far more than a motto—and has somewhere acknowledged the obligation—his genius was kindled by **"The Crusade,"** and **"The Grave of Arthur"**—nor has he surpassed, if indeed he has equalled them in any of his most heroic strains. The *composition* is more perfect than that of any thing Scott ever wrote—the style more sustained—and the spirit more accordant with the olden time.

"The Crusade" is supposed to have been the Song composed by Richard and Blondel, and sung by that minstrel under the window of the Castle in which the King was imprisoned by Leopold of Austria. (p. 559)

"The Grave of King Arthur" is even a still nobler strain. King Henry the Second having undertaken an expedition into Ireland to suppress a rebellion raised by Roderic, King of Connaught, commonly called O'Connor Dunn, or the brown Monarch of Ireland, was entertained in his passage through Wales with the songs of the Welsh Bards. The subject of their poetry was King Arthur, whose history had been so disguised by fabulous inventions that the place of his burial was in general scarcely known or remembered. But in one of those Welsh poems sung before Henry, it was recited that King Arthur, after the Battle of Camlan in Cornwall, was interred at Glastonbury Abbey, before the high altar, yet without any external mark or memorial. Afterwards, Henry visited the Abbey, and commanded the spot, described by the bard, to be opened; when, digging near twenty feet deep, they found the body deposited under a large stone, inscribed with Arthur's name. This is the groundwork of the ode; but it is told with some slight variations from the Chronicle of Glastonbury. The Castle of Cilgarran, where this discovery is supposed to have been made, now a ruin, stands on a rock descending to the river Teivi in Pembrokeshire, and was built by Roger Montgomery, who led the van of the warriors at Hastings. (p. 560)

These two Odes work on our imagination more powerfully than "The Bard" of Gray. To us they appear to be more poetical, and you may laugh at us for saying so, as sardonically as your face will permit. "Was ne'er prophetic sound so full of woe," cannot with any truth be said of the rhetorical style of that Ode—and we should not have suspected from the stately composure of his speech, occasionally corrugated with affected vehemence, that with haggard eyes the Prophet stood on a rock. Yet it was on same occasion during the current year that we heard some simple soul like ourself called over the coals for the heresy we now have been guilty of, by some truculent critic who seemed to think his own character involved, heaven knows how, in the lyrical genius of Gray.

By the way, Thomas Warton has, in our opinion, described Abbeys and Cathedrals, within and without, much better than Walter Scott.

> If thou wouldst view fair Melrose aright,
> Go visit it by the pale moonlight;
> For the gay beams of lightsome day
> Gild, but to flout, the ruins grey.
> When the broken arches are black in night,
> And each shafted oriel glimmers white;
> When the cold light's uncertain shower
> Streams on the ruin'd central tower;
> When buttress and buttress, alternately,
> Seem framed of ebon and ivory;
> When silver edges the imagery,
> And the scrolls that teach thee to live and die;
> When distant Tweed is heard to rave,
> And the owlet to hoot o'er the dead man's grave,
> Then go—but go alone the while—
> Then view St David's ruined pile;
> And, home returning, soothly swear,
> Was never scene so sad and fair.

The second couplet has no business there—and forcibly brings before us an image which should have been totally excluded from the picture. Omit these two lines and you will at once feel how the effect is deepened of the night vision. Besides, they are in themselves bad—for daylight did never yet "*gild* ruins grey"—much less "*flout*" them—and these are, moreover, ugly words. The next four lines are excellent; though to our ear and eye, in so short a passage, so many monosyllabic epithets sound and look oddly— "fair," "pale," "gay," "grey," "black," "cold." The buttresses are alternately in light and in shadow—and the Last Minstrel says "alternately they seem of ebon and ivory." That is pure nonsense. They seemed to be of stone. The change of substance is the reverse of a process of imagination—for it destroys the shadowy beauty given to the edifice by moonlight, substituting in its place something to the last degree fantastic—say at once ridiculous. We doubt the truth of "silver edges the imagery and the scrolls," but you may like because you understand it. The silver as well as the ebon and the ivory had been far better away. But the fatal fault—and it is to us an astounding one—is, "And the owlet hoots o'er the dead man's grave." That line not only disturbs but destroys the spirit pervading—or intended to pervade—the description—that of stillness—sadness—beauty—peace—"Was never scene so sad and fair!"—"Then view St David's ruined pile" is a needless repetition—and comes in very awkwardly after "ruined central tower,"—nor is that an inconsiderable blemish in such a picture. "Soothly swear" seems to us rather silly—but if you admire it we shall try to do so too—and 'tis but a trifle. . . . (p. 562)

Sir Walter says in a note, that it is impossible to conceive a more beautiful specimen of the lightness and elegance of Gothic architecture, when in its purity, than the eastern window of Melrose Abbey, and alludes to Sir James Hall's ingenious idea, that the Gothic order, through its various forms and cunningly eccentric ornaments, may be traced to an architectural imitation of wicker-work, of which, as we learn from some of the legends, the earliest Christian churches were constructed. Possibly. But that affords no justification of such a description as this, natural or not in itself—poetical or prosaic; for it is utterly destructive of the solemn—the awful feelings which it was the aim of the Minstrel to awaken and to sustain. He had just said,

> O fading honours of the dead!
> O high ambition lowly laid!

And this fanciful or rather fantastic affair of the Fairies must, at such a juncture, be offensive to every reader who accompanies Doleraine and his guide in a state of any emotion. 'Tis a prettiness worthy but of a lady's Album.

With the exception of Cibber, the Poets Laureate of England have all been respectable—some have been—one is now—illustrious. Warton wore the laurel gracefully; and some of his odes—classical in conception and execution—are delightful reading to this day. Dr Mant says well, "Sure I am that he has executed the office with surprising ability; that he has given variety to a hackneyed argument by the happiest selection and adaptation of collateral topics; and has shown how a poet may celebrate his sovereign, not with the fulsome adulation of an Augustan courtier, or the base prostration of an Oriental slave, but with the genuine spirit and erect front of an Englishman." "The Probationary odes," witty as they were, are now forgotten; and Warton's are not remembered. We believe the rogues printed the Laureate's first ode, which was rather a rum concern, among the Probationary; and sent him a copy

with an editorial letter expressing their gratitude to him, for having set "the example of a Joke"—"an inimitable effort of luxuriant humour." Dr Joseph says, that his brother "of all men felt the least, and least deserved to feel, the force of the Probationary odes, written on his appointment to the office; and that he always heartily joined in the laugh, and applauded the exquisite wit and humour that appeared in many of those original satires." Laureates do not like to be laughed at, more than other office-bearing men—but Warton had more humour and as much wit as the Set—and, on this occasion, rubbing his elbow, merely chuckled, "black-letter dogs, Sir." (p. 563)

Warton had a fine eye and a feeling heart for nature—as indeed he had for every thing good—and perhaps some of his unambitious descriptive verses may please you more than his statelier Odes. It has been said that they are rather deficient in sentiment—too purely descriptive; some of them are so—others not—and we think that objection will by none be felt to lie against his delightful lines entitled **"The Hamlet."** Headley calls it "a most exquisite little piece," and says "it contains such a selection of beautiful rural images as perhaps no other poem of equal length in our language presents us with." Headley, we think, was a Trinity man, and as such must have loved Warton, and his praise may need pruning; but he was a good judge because a fine genius. **"The Hamlet"** is "written on Whichwood Forest" which lies towards the western side of Oxfordshire, and near the Poet's parish of Cuddington. (p. 565)

Headley remarks, too, that the leading idea of these lines was suggested by an account of the life of a peasant in Phineas Fletcher's "Purple Island." Dr Mant agrees with him; but we see small reason or none for thinking so, and believe that the "leading idea," which is obvious to all mankind, was suggested to Warton many hundred times during his walks in the Forest of Whichwood. (p. 566)

Verily there is poetry in [the verses of **"On the Approach of Summer"**]—nor are they, to our mind at least, the worse but the better of being besprinkled with colourings from Milton. We do not call that plagiarism—nor is it borrowing; Warton lays no claim to a diction peculiarly his own; and having studied Milton all his life, he had become imbued with the language of his minor poems, which he rejoiced to use in love and reverence of his mighty master. The flow of thought, and sentiment, and imagery proceeds from his own genius thus enriched; and had he not been a true poet (nobody calls him a great one), his familiarity with Milton would have been shown but in Centos.

His **"Humourous Pieces"** are very pleasant—and **"The Progress of Discontent"** (written in his eighteenth year) has been pronounced by Dr Joseph to be "the best imitation of Swift that has yet appeared." (p. 569)

> *John Wilson, in an originally unsigned essay entitled "A Glance Over the Poetry of Thomas Warton," in* Blackwood's Edinburgh Magazine, *Vol. XLIV, No. CCLXXVI, October, 1838, pp. 533-72.*

W. Carew Hazlitt (essay date 1871)

[*Grandson of the famous essayist, W. Carew Hazlitt was an English bibliographer, essayist, and literary critic. In*

the following excerpt from his preface to his edition of
The History of English Poetry, *he admits that Warton
possessed some literary talent, but contends that the success of the work was due to there being "absolutely no
competitor in sight."*]

The time seems to have arrived, when the truth should be
spoken freely. Warton was an amiable man, a scholar, and
a person of sound literary tastes. His reading had been
considerable, and his views in many points were unusually
enlarged. He possessed, in no mean degree, that faculty so
deficient in some who have followed him in the same line
of investigation—the faculty of *selection*. He enjoyed the
advantages of a pleasing and easy style, and of the friendly
co-operation of some of the most eminent antiquaries and
poetical students of the age. He entered on his task, moreover, under exceptionally favourable circumstances, when
criticism upon old English literature was in a very unformed and immature state, and when, therefore, it was
tolerably certain that an indulgent estimate would be
taken of any work on the subject, which should be of respectable merit. But Warton was excessively indolent,
equally careless, and, it must be candidly owned, not particularly well-informed on several branches of the inquiry
which he had proposed to himself. It was his rare good fortune to be enabled to take possession of the field at a period
when there was absolutely no competitor in sight; and,
added to that, but of course in a certain degree consequently upon it, the very uncommon distinction has since
fallen to his lot of being glossed by the foremost scholars
(in this particular way) of each succeeding generation.
These gentlemen, instead of aspiring to produce a new
History of English Poetry, worthy of the subject and of
the country, have uniformly condescended to become the
exponents and scholiasts of Warton, a man, with all his
virtues and abilities, certainly in many essential respects
incompetent for his self-appointed task. (pp. vii-viii)

> *W. Carew Hazlitt, in a preface to* History of
> English Poetry from the Twelfth to the Close
> of the Sixteenth Century Vol. I *by Thomas
> Warton, edited by W. Carew Hazlitt, revised
> edition, 1871. Reprint by Georg Olms Verlags-
> buchhandlung, 1968, pp. v-xvi.*

Charles D. Deshler   (essay date 1879)

[*In the excerpt below, Deshler praises the subject matter
of and imagery in Warton's sonnets.*]

Warton's numerous sonnets cover a wide range; but are
particularly noteworthy for the increased attention they
give to natural objects, and for the transition in the application of the sonnet to poetical subjects of a descriptive
kind which this increase denotes. Instead of being confined, as the sonnet had been very generally, to amatory,
elegiac, or complimentary subjects, or to the sublimation
of some abstract sentiment or idea, his sonnets largely celebrate historical or familiar scenes and places, chosen by
him for the picturesqueness of their environments, or for
the interesting associations that were clustered around
them. Many of the local descriptions in these brief poems
are very attractive; and, indeed, there is scarcely one of his
sonnets, whatever their theme, but will reward us by the
gracefulness and delicacy of its sentiments, and the correctness of its diction and structure. It is true they make

no great pretensions, but the level plain on which they
travel reveals so many inviting bits of retired loveliness,
and affords so many charming glimpses of quiet beauty,
that we wonder his poems are so little known and prized.
Probably, however, the neglect into which they have fallen
is due to an excess of correctness of finish and an over-
refinement of taste, which impart to them an air of stiffness and effeminacy that a closer inspection would mea-
surably dissipate. To my mind, the transcripts of English
sights and scenes in Warton's sonnets are extremely pleasing, and will bear close scrutiny. (pp. 178-79)

> *Charles D. Deshler, "Fifth Afternoon," in his*
> Afternoons with the Poets, *Harper & Broth-
> ers, Publishers, 1879, pp. 155-212.*

Thomas Humphry Ward   (essay date 1880)

[*In the excerpt below, Ward provides a brief discussion
of Miltonic and pseudoclassical influences on Warton's
poetry.*]

Thomas Warton is in his poetry chiefly imitative, as was
natural in so laborious a student of our early poetical literature. The edition of his poems which was published by
his admirer and his brother's devoted pupil, Richard
Mant, offers a curious example of a poet 'killed with kindness'; for the apparatus of parallel passages from Spenser,
Shakespeare, Milton, and others, is enough to ruin any little claim to originality which might have been put forward
for him. The **"Pleasures of Melancholy"** is a cento of *Il
Penseroso, Comus,* and *The Faerie Queene;* the **"Ode on
the Approach of Summer"** is a mere echo of *L'Allegro.*
Again, the influence of Gray makes itself far too strongly
felt in Warton's elegiac poems and odes. But there are reasons why his genial figure should not be altogether excluded from a representative English anthology. It has often
been said that his **History of English Poetry,** with Percy's
Reliques, turned the course of our letters into a fresh channel; but what is more noticeable here is that his own poetry—or much of it, for he is not always free from the taint
of pseudo-classicalism—instinctively deals with materials
like those on which the older writers had drawn. In reaction against the didactic and critical temper of the earlier
half of his century, he is a student of nature; he is even an
'enthusiast,' in Whitehead's sense. He has two passions,
well expressed in the two sonnets [**"Sonnet Written in a
Blank Leaf of Dugdales 'Monasticon'"** and **"To the River
Lodon"**]—the passion for 'antiquity' and the passion for
nature; for the Bodleian Library and for

> The field, the forest, green and gay,
> The dappled slope, the tedded hay;

and, we may add, for Oxford, his home for forty-seven
years, at whose service he was always ready to place his
invention, his humour, and his gift of satire. The real Warton is to be looked for in the writings in which these passions find their vent; in the **History,** in the **Sonnets** (a form
of composition which he revived among us), and in the
Humorous Pieces; not in the 'quit-rent odes' which were
wrung from him by the unhappy necessities of his laure-
ateship. (pp. 382-83)

> *Thomas Humphry Ward, "Thomas Warton,"
> in* The English Poets: Addison to Blake, *Vol.
> III, edited by Thomas Humphry Ward, 1880.*

Reprint by The Macmillan Company, 1921, pp. 382-88.

Thomas R. Lounsbury   (essay date 1892)

[*Lounsbury was an American educator and literary historian and critic. In the following excerpt, he praises* The History of English Poetry *for the advances in literary criticism it reveals, while attacking the self-absorbed "spirit that pervades the work."*]

It is the observations contained in Thomas Warton's *History of English Poetry* that denote the high-water mark of the eighteenth-century judgment of Chaucer. To the oldest writers of English literature Warton was attracted both by the bent of his mind and the nature of his studies. In the first critical work he produced—the *Observations on the Faerie Queene of Spenser,* which came out in 1754—he took occasion to deplore the then prevalent indifference to the writings of the earliest of our great poets. His words still have a good deal of interest for the light they throw upon contemporary opinion.

> I cannot dismiss this section . . . without a wish that this neglected author, whom Spenser proposed as the pattern of his style, and to whom he is indebted for many noble inventions, should be more universally studied. This is at least what one might expect in an age of research and curiosity. Chaucer is regarded rather as an old than as a good poet. We look upon his poems as venerable relics, not as beautiful compositions; as pieces better calculated to gratify the antiquarian than the critic. He abounds not only in strokes of humor, which is commonly supposed to be his sole talent, but of pathos and sublimity not unworthy a more refined age. His old manners, his romantic arguments, his wildness of painting, his simplicity and antiquity of expression, transport us into some fairy region, and are all highly pleasing to the imagination. It is true that his uncouth and unfamiliar language disgusts and deters many readers; but the principal reason of his being so little known, and so seldom taken into hand, is the convenient opportunity of reading him with pleasure and facility in modern imitations.

Both the progress of appreciation and the lack of full appreciation are clearly discernible in this passage. The feelings that inspired the view pervading it are displayed still more fully in the chapters of Warton's *History* that are devoted to Chaucer. It was twenty years later—that is, in 1774—that the volume containing these appeared. After that time a new order of things set in, and new ways of looking at the early poet began to prevail. But these chapters will always be of interest and value for the information they give us of the sentiments of the transition period through which Chaucer's reputation was now passing. Warton's criticisms, though in the main following the old lines, showed plainly the greatness of the advance in knowledge that had been made. It is the work of a man who had read the writings of which he spoke, and not merely read about them. His selection of passages for commendation, and of passages characteristic of the poet's style, were usually taken from the genuine productions, and not, as had often been the case, from those which are now recognized as spurious. The praise, moreover, which he bestowed was so hearty that it excited comment, and

in some instances dissent. . . . Walpole's feelings were outraged by the preference apparently exhibited—for nothing of that nature is openly expressed—for the originals of Chaucer to the modernizations of Pope, and even of Dryden. Warton also added much matter illustrative of the poet's compositions, to which all succeeding writers have been under obligation. His work, indeed, is one which it will perhaps be always necessary to consult for its facts, its references, and its inferences; and though in many points it needs to be corrected, a long time will certainly elapse before it will be superseded.

All this can be said, and be said truly. But while the substantial merits of the chapters on Chaucer need not be denied, they are very far from being perfectly satisfactory. They were marked in particular by the defects which invariably characterized the writings of both the Wartons. In certain ways these two scholars were the most irritating of commentators and literary critics. Their object was never so much to illustrate their author as to illustrate themselves. Instances of this disposition occur constantly in those sections of the *History of English Poetry* which treat of Chaucer. Warton is constantly wandering away from his legitimate subject to furnish information about matters that concerned very remotely, if at all, the business in hand. Much of the material he collected is introduced not to throw light upon the question under consideration, but to parade his knowledge. Still, it is the spirit that pervades the work which is especially objectionable. About it lingered the apologetic air of the eighteenth century, which talked as if it had something of a contempt for itself for taking interest in an age when neither language nor poetry had reached the supreme elegance by which both were then distinguished. Warton's words make upon the mind the impression that he admired Chaucer greatly, and was ashamed of himself for having been caught in the act. Whenever he abandons conventionally accepted ground, we recognize at once the timid utterance of the man who feels called upon to put in a plea in extenuation of the appreciation he has manifested. At the very outset we are treated to a specimen of that sort of critical comment which is never able to stand alone, but must always bolster itself upon the crutches of other people's opinions. Warton probably knew more about the early writers of our speech than any man then living. His authority on the subject was certainly at that time reckoned supreme. Yet he felt it necessary to summon to his support men whose views in this matter were of scarcely any authority at all. He began his account of Chaucer with the remark that this early writer had been "pronounced by a critic of unquestionable taste and discernment"—by whom he meant Dr. Johnson—"to be the first English versifier who wrote poetically." (pp. 244-48)

Thomas R. Lounsbury, in his Studies in Chaucer: His Life and Writings, Vol. III, *1892. Reprint by Russell & Russell, Inc., 1962, 512 p.*

George Saintsbury   (essay date 1904)

[*Saintsbury was an eminent English literary historian and critic. In the excerpt below, he provides a critical discussion of* Observations on the Faerie Queene of Spenser *and* The History of English Poetry, *praising*

Warton for bringing the historical study of poetry to the fore.]

For a combination of earliness, extension, and character no book . . . exceeds in interest Thomas Warton's ***Observations on Spenser.*** To an ordinary reader, who has heard that Warton was one of the great ushers of Romanticism in England, and that Spenser was one of the greatest influences which these ushers applied, the opening of the piece, and not a very few passages later, may seem curiously half-hearted and unsympathetic. Such a reader, from another though closely connected point of view, may be disappointed by the fragmentary and *annotatory* character of the book, its deficiency in *vues d'ensemble,* its apologies, and compromises, and hesitations. But those who have taken a little trouble to inform themselves on the matter, either by their own inquiries or by following the course which has been indicated in this book, will be much better satisfied. They will see that he says what he ought to have said in the concatenation accordingly.

It is impossible to decide how much of yet not discarded orthodoxy, and how much of characteristic eighteenth-century compromise, there is in the opening about "depths of Gothic ignorance and barbarity," "ridiculous and incoherent excursions," "old *Provençal* vein," and the like. Probably there is a good deal of both; there is certainly a good deal which requires both to excuse it. Yet before long Warton fastens a sudden petard on the main gate of the Neo-Classic stronghold by saying: "But it is absurd to think of judging either Ariosto or Spenser by precepts which they did not attend to." Absurd, indeed! But what becomes of those antecedent laws of poetry, those rules of the kind and so forth, which for more than two hundred years had been accumulating authority? It is no good for him to go on: "We who live in the days of writing by rule. . . . Critical taste is universally diffused . . . " and so on. The petard goes on fizzing and sparkling at the gate, and will blow it in before long.

In the scattered annotations, which follow for a long time, the attitude of compromise is fairly kept; and even Neo-Classics, as we have seen, need not necessarily have objected to Warton's demonstration *pièces en main,* that Scaliger "had no notion of simple and genuine beauty"; while the whole of his section on Spenser's stanza, &c., is full of *lèse-poésie,* and that on Spenser's inaccuracies is not much better. But the very next section is an important attack on the plagiarism-and-parallel-passage mania which almost invariably develops itself in bad critics; and the defence of his author's Allegory, nay, the plump avowal of him as a Romantic poet, more than atones for some backslidings even here. Above all, the whole book is distinguished by a genuine if not always understanding *love* of the subject; secondly, by an obvious refusal—sometimes vocal, always latent—to accept *a priori* rules of criticism; thirdly, and most valuably of all, by recurrence to contemporary and preceding models as criteria instead of to the ancients alone. Much of the last part of the book is occupied with a sort of first draft in little of the author's subsequent ***History;*** he is obviously full of knowledge (if sometimes flawed) and of study (if sometimes misdirected) of early English literature. And this is what was wanted. "Nullum numen abest si sit *conscientia*" (putting the verse aside) might almost be the critic's sole motto if it were not that he certainly cannot do without *prudentia* itself. But Pru-

dentia without her sister is almost useless: she can at best give inklings, and murmur, "If you are not conscious of what has actually been done in literature you can never decide what ought and ought not to have been done."

This is what gives the immense, the almost unequalled importance which Warton's ***History of English Poetry*** should possess in the eyes of persons who can judge just judgment. It has errors: there is no division of literature in which it is so unreasonable to expect accuracy as in history, and no division of history to which that good-natured Aristotelian dictum applies so strongly as to literary history. Its method is most certainly defective, and one of its greatest defects is the disproportion in the treatment of authors and subjects. When the author expatiates into Dissertation, he may often be justly accused of first getting out of his depth as regards the subject, and then recovering himself by making the treatment shallow. And I do not know that his individual criticisms betray any very frequent or very extraordinary acuteness of appreciation. To say of the lovely

Lenten is come with love to town,

that it "displays glimmerings of imagination, and exhibits some faint ideas of poetical expression," is surely to be, as Dryden said of Smith and Johnson in *The Rehearsal,* a "cool and insignificant gentleman"; and though it is quite accurate to recognise "much humour and spirit" in *Piers Plowman,* it is a little inadequate and banal.

But this is mere hole-picking at worst, at best the necessary or desirable ballast or set-off to a generous appreciation of Warton's achievement. If his erudition is not unflawed, its bulk and mass are astonishing in a man of his time; if his method and proportion are defective, this is almost inevitable in the work of a pioneer; and we have seen enough since of critics and historians who make all their geese swans, not to be too hard on one who sometimes talked of peacocks or humming-birds as if they were barndoor fowls or sparrows. The good which the book, with its wealth of quotation as well as of summary, must have done, is something difficult to realise but almost impossible to exaggerate. Now at least, for England and for English, the missing links were supplied, the hidden origins revealed, the Forbidden Country thrown open to exploration. It is worth while (though in no unkind spirit) once more to recall Addison's *péché de jeunesse* in his *Account of the English Poets,* in order to contrast it with the picture presented by Warton. Instead of a millennium of illiteracy and barbarism, with nothing in it worth noticing at all but Chaucer and Spenser—presented, the one as a vulgar and obsolete merryandrew, and the other as half old-wives'-fabulist and half droning preacher—century after century, from at least the thirteenth onward (Warton does not profess to handle Anglo-Saxon) was presented in regular literary development, with abundant examples of complicated literary kinds, and a crowded bead-roll of poets, with specimens of their works. Men had before them—for the first time, except in cases of quite extraordinary leisure, opportunities, taste, and energy—the *actual* progress of English prosody and English poetic diction, to set against the orthodox doctrine that one fine day not so very early in the seventeenth century Mr Waller achieved a sort of minor miracle of creation in respect of both. And all these works and persons were accorded serious literary and critical treatment, such as had been hitherto reserved for the classics of old, for the masterpieces of what Cal-lières calls *les trois nations polies* abroad, and for English writers *since* Mr Waller. That Warton did not gush about them was no fault; it was exactly what could have been desired. What was wanted was the entrance of mediæval and Renaissance poetry into full recognition; the making of it *hoffähig;* the reconstitution of literary history so as to place the work of the Middle Period on a level basis, and in a continuous series, with work ancient and modern. And this Warton, to the immortal glory of himself, his University, and his Chair, effected. (pp. 68-72)

George Saintsbury, "The English Precursors," in his A History of Criticism and Literary Taste in Europe from the Earliest Texts to the Present Day, Vol. III, *1904. Reprint by William Blackwood & Sons Ltd., 1935, pp. 52-88.*

W. P. Ker (essay date 1910)

[*Ker was a noted Scottish scholar of medieval literature and an authority on comparative European literature and the history of literary forms. In the following excerpt, he commends Warton's efforts as a literary historian, while admitting some weak points in his methodology.*]

The Renaissance worked itself out in one direction to a sort of thin culture or polite literature which found substantial erudition much too laborious and expensive. Bentley was scoffed at by people with very scanty furniture of their own. Some of the most famous men of that time are light in material knowledge, at least so far as is shown in their writings—Berkeley, for example, as compared with Hobbes before him or Hume after him. The great difference between Berkeley and Hume is that Hume wrote the *History of England.* Even Dr. Johnson, who has so much of the old-fashioned regardless love of reading, makes little use of it in his works, apart from the *Dictionary;* his depreciation of history and historians is well known. But it was from history that fresh supplies had to be drawn, to save polite literature from dying of inanition; and supplies of this sort were given by Thomas Warton in his **Observations on Spenser,** in his **Milton,** and above all in his **History of Poetry.** He was not afraid to plunge, and he was not too careful about form. The **History of English Poetry** was censured for its want of method. But method may be bought too dear, when there is a want of material; and method may be applied, when sufficient material is found. Warton had to work hard to make his way among the manuscripts of the Bodleian and Lambeth, the British Museum, and the Colleges of Oxford and Cambridge. No doubt he took all the help he could get, and owed much to his advisers and coadjutors; but with all allowances he had still more than enough to do. The main thing wanted was a report on the extant works, and that was what he gave. Method, after all, is far less required in literary than in political history. The political historian has to extract the essence from masses of documents that in themselves are unmeaning. The historian of literature deals with documents which in themselves are intelligible, which have, or which at any rate were by the authors of them thought to have, an immediate, present, independent value, quite apart from their bearings on other things or the inferences that might be drawn from them. Literary history is more

like a guide-book than a geography. It may be amusing in itself at a distance from the realities of which it speaks, but it is not properly effective until it brings the traveller on his way, so that he sees for himself the temples and towers and mountain passes with his bodily eyes. Some historians of literature go wrong and spoil their work by writing as if their matter were all past, like the events of history; treating plays and poems like battles or sieges or constitutional reforms, to be described indirectly by a reconstructive gentleman in his study, doing his best to explain what he cannot see. Some part of literary history no doubt is busied conjecturally with epic poems and others which (as Paulin Paris said) have the misfortune not to exist. But the main part of it deals with extant things, which live for the present day when the seeing eye falls on them; they are unjustly treated when they are kept by the historian at a distance from the eye, as unrealized though permanent possibilities of sensation. That was not Thomas Warton's policy. As well as he could, he put forward the results of his explorations in large samples, and he was right. Those who read his history see and know a good deal of old poetry at first hand; and those who find what they want will not be troubled at the careless profusion of the show. There are many mistakes, no doubt, which Ritson the accuser was ready to fix upon. But they do not really damage the general character of the book. There are omissions and failures. It is a pity that Warton should have slighted the ironical grace of the dispute between the Owl and the Nightingale, that wonderful anticipation of Chaucer in a rustic thirteenth-century dialect. It is strange that he never found the Cottonian MS. *Nero* A. x, with the *Pearl* and *Sir Gawayne.* But these are accidents.

It seems that Warton deliberately refused to be methodical or philosophical. A scheme of the history of poetry had been drawn by Pope, divided like the history of painting into schools. Gray, who took up the subject after Pope, and who resigned it to Warton, would have put into it more order and construction than his rambling successor. (pp. 353-55)

The history of poetry, even when, like Warton's, it is random and informal, is part of history at large. It has its inconveniences and limitations; it can never be a harmonious work of art, like Gibbon's history, just for the reason already given, that works of art are what it deals with, and that art and literature are living things which assert themselves against the historian and cannot be made into mere matter for a narrative. Nevertheless the history of literature, like political history, is part of the memory of the world; it is philosophical, like the history of philosophy itself, a record of fashions of thought, of ideas. Thomas Warton, who took up the history of Gothic architecture as well as poetry, had a knowledge of the past life of England most ample, fresh, and variegated. He took an honourable share in that business of historical investigation which was itself the most important new fashion of thought in the eighteenth century. Partly through the store of new matter that it provided for the 'reading public', partly through the zest and enthusiasm of its students—the spirit of adventure, which is the same in Warton as in Scott—it did more than any theory to correct the narrow culture, the starved elegance, of the preceding age. It is not to be forgotten that Johnson, who was disrespectful to history in general, and, occasionally, unkind to Warton, became himself an historian of literature in his *Lives of the Poets.*

Warton's historical work began in admiration, particularly of Spenser and of Milton's early poems. This, like Joseph Warton's critical work also, was due to their father. Thomas Warton the elder had discovered the early poems of Milton, in the volume of 1645, when as yet there were few to praise them. (As late as 1782, Joseph Warton in his essay on Pope speaks of Milton's 'smaller and neglected poems'.) The neglect and the recovery of them is described by Thomas the son in the preface to his edition of 'Poems upon several occasions, by John Milton'. This is one passage:—

> My father used to relate that when he once at Magdalene College Oxford mentioned in high terms this volume to Mr. Digby the intimate friend of Pope, Mr. Digby expressed much surprise that he had never heard Pope speak of them, went home and immediately gave them an attentive reading, and asked Pope if he knew anything of this hidden treasure. Pope availed himself of the question: and accordingly we find him soon afterwards sprinkling his *Eloisa to Abelard* with epithets and phrases of a new form and sound, pilfered from *Comus* and the *Penseroso.*

The work of Thomas Warton as a commentator was very largely the tracing of resemblances and possible borrowings—an estimate, in detail, of the reading and booklearning of Spenser and Milton. But it is more than an essay on what is called in so many German professional treatises the *Belesenheit* of authors. Nor is it like the work of those 'parallelists' (the word is Warton's own) who 'mistake resemblances for thefts'. It is a liberal interpretation of the minds of the poets, through their reading. Warton justifies himself, modestly and sensibly, at the end of his chapter 'of Spenser's imitations from old romances'.

> Many other examples might be alledged, from which it would be more abundantly manifested that our author's imagination was entirely possessed with that species of reading, which was the fashion and the delight of his age. The lovers of Spenser, I hope, will not think that I have been too tedious in a disquisition which has contributed not only to illustrate many particular passages in their favorite poet, but to display the general cast and colour of his poem. Some there are, who will censure what I have collected on this subject as both trifling and uninteresting; but such readers can have no taste for Spenser.

Without admiration, Warton's work would not have been done; and the same may be said of Joseph Warton's exhilarating criticism. This is even more remarkable, inasmuch as he praises the work of Pope with no mean or ungenerous exceptions or cavillings, while at the same time he refuses to take 'acute understanding' as a substitute for 'creative and glowing imagination'. (pp. 355-57)

> *W. P. Ker, "Warton Lecture on English Poetry," in* Proceedings of the British Academy, *Vol. 4, 1909-10, pp. 349-59.*

Clarissa Rinaker   (essay date 1915)

[*Rinaker wrote widely on the works of the Warton fami-*

ly. In the excerpt below from her critical study of Thomas Warton, she explores the development of his poetic talent. (The chapter excerpted below originally appeared in the Sewanee Review *in 1915.)*]

Naturally enough Warton first attempted to express his genius in poetry, and the bulk though not the best of his poems were written while he was yet a young man. Then, because the age in which he lived was unfavorable to poetry, especially the new kind that he was writing, and because, as Christopher North said, 'the gods had made him poetical, but not a poet,' he turned later to criticism and history where he won more immediate as well as more enduring fame. He did not, however, so completely abandon poetry as not to produce some pieces which, when compared with the work of his contemporaries, have real intrinsic value and take an important place in the development of poetry in his century. Moreover, his early verse, though largely imitative, imitates new models, the poet's favourites, Spenser and Milton, more than the pseudo-classical models, and shows a real originality in its introduction of the Gothic or mediæval subjects in which the poet was always deeply interested, in its genuine interest in nature, and in its attempts of the sonnet form. Besides this, his verse illustrates more completely than that of any one of his contemporaries the whole change that was taking place in English poetry; it includes practically every tendency of the new movement: the repudiation of the pseudo-classical models, the Spenserian and Miltonic revivals, the return to nature, the cult of solitude, the melancholy of the 'grave-yard school,' the interest in the supernatural, and the Gothic revival. Although Warton lacked the lyrical sweetness and poetic insight of his friend Collins—whose qualities he could at least appreciate—and the poetic fire and inspiration of Gray—to whom he paid the tribute of a sonnet—these are the poets with whom one feels bound to compare him. If he had less poetical genius than either of them, he had at least a greater variety of interests, and he made distinguished contributions in the direction of his principal interests.

Warton's first published poem, printed without his name in his brother's thin quarto of *Odes on Various Subjects* in 1746, was, like his earlier school-boy exercise, a classical imitation. The year before it appeared, when the poet was but seventeen, he had written his first long poem, **"The Pleasures of Melancholy,"** and he published it anonymously in a quarto pamphlet in 1747. The poem shows how devoted a student of Milton the young poet was, the tone and diction being decidedly Miltonic although the title and the form were obviously directly suggested by Akenside's much less romantic "Pleasures of Imagination." The poem follows the general plan of *Il Penseroso,* being a description of the various pleasures which the man devoted to melancholy contemplation may enjoy, and it is full of personifications of abstractions and Miltonic epithets and diction. A few typical passages will illustrate both Warton's command of blank verse and the influence of Milton:—the invocation,—

> Mother of musings, Contemplation sage,
> Whose grotto stands upon the topmost rock
> Of Teneriff;

and such direct allusions as,—

> . . . . . the dazzling spells

> Of wily Comus cheat th' unweeting eye
> With blear illusion, and persuade to drink
> That charmed cup, which Reason's mintage fair
> Unmoulds, and stamps the monster on the man;

and,—

> The taper'd choir, at the late hour of pray'r,
> Oft let me tread, while to th' according voice
> The many-sounding organ peals on high,
> The clear slow-dittied chaunt, or varied hymn,
> Till all my soul is bath'd in ecstasies,
> And lapp'd in Paradise.

The whole poem is saturated too with the melancholy of the graveyard school of poets, and passages can be selected which seem to have been directly inspired by various of their poems. The young poet gives every evidence of having tried his hand in the style of each of them; but he combined the results into a whole with some characteristic additions of his own. (pp. 24-6)

This choice of models was not accidental even from the first; it was part of a consistent and deliberate reaction against the prevailing models and a rejection of them. His preference for Spenser rather than Pope Warton stated expressly in this first long poem and defended on the very "romantic' ground that livelier imagination and warmer passion are aroused by the artless magic of the *Faerie Queene* than by the artificial brilliance of the *Rape of the Lock*,—

> Thro' POPE's soft song tho' all the Graces breathe,
> And happiest art adorn his Attic page;
> Yet does my mind with sweeter transport glow,
> As at the root of mossy trunk reclin'd,
> In magic SPENSER's wildly warbled song
> I see deserted Una wander wide
> Thro' wasteful solitudes, and lurid heaths,
> Weary, forlorn; than when the fated fair
> Upon the bosom bright of silver Thames
> Launches in all the lustre of brocade,
> Amid the splendors of the laughing Sun.
> The gay description palls upon the sense,
> And coldly strikes the mind with feeble bliss.

Warton's relation to the melancholy group of poets who drew their inspiration largely from *Il Penseroso* is, moreover, not that of a mere imitator. He made positive contributions to that style of poetry by contriving to preserve a more objective tone in his own melancholy and by introducing the Gothic note that later frequently became dominant in his own verse and constituted his distinctive contribution to poetry. Of even greater importance is the fact that he may fairly be credited with having influenced pretty directly the greatest poem of the elegiac school, Gray's "Elegy in a Country Church-yard." (p. 27)

Warton's devotion to his Alma Mater inspired the **"Triumph of Isis,"** in 1749, the first poem to attract the attention of the academic world. The year before, William Mason, in "Isis: an Elegy," had glanced at the Jacobite leanings of Oxford as they had given rise to a foolish drunken out-break which had been carried to the King's bench and had reflected dishonour upon the heads of some of the colleges. Warton, encouraged by Dr. Huddesford, the president of Trinity, hastened to the defense of his university in a poem that at least surpassed Mason's. The youthful poet received a substantial compliment from Dr. King, whom he had especially commended, and who left

five guineas with Daniel Prince, the bookseller, to be given to the author. The **"Triumph of Isis"** is not one of Warton's best poems. It is largely pseudo-classical in its use of the heroic couplet, its artificial diction,—such as 'vernal bloom,' 'oliv'd portal,' 'pearly grot,' 'floating pile,' 'dalliance with the tuneful Nine,'—and in its stereotyped classical allusions. It is full of Miltonic personifications of abstractions and places mingled with the deities and heroes of classical myth and history; we meet with Freedom and Gratulation, Cam and Isis, Muse and Naiad, Tully, Cato and Eurus. But there is quite as much mediæval colouring. Warton's characteristic love of the past appears in one of the finest passages in the poem in which his admiration for Gothic architecture is only second to his love of Oxford.

Following the appearance of these poems Warton was asked to contribute to the *Student, or, the Oxford, and Cambridge Monthly Miscellany,* and brought out four poems of earlier composition which were printed over various signatures. One, **"Morning. The Author confined to College,"** in six line stanzas, shows some influence of Milton and a personal enjoyment of natural scenes, and one is a paraphrase of Job XXXIX in heavy couplets, unlike any other of Warton's verse. Two of the poems were humorous academic verse, experiments in satire and burlesque in the taste of the Augustans. The earliest of them, the **"Progress of Discontent,"** written in 1746, was considered by the poet's brother, who may not have been an impartial critic, the best imitation of Swift that had ever appeared. It is a mild satire upon the career of many a young man who, with discontented indolence rather than ambition, sought advancement through the university and church, and the story is told in vigorous Hudibrastic measure with considerable relish and spirit. The **"Panegyric on Oxford Ale"** is probably the best of his humorous academic pieces. It is a burlesque of Milton's epic style after the manner of Phillips's "Splendid Shilling." The blank verse is well managed, and the mock dignified humour well kept up throughout the poem. The models are unmistakable; there are direct allusions to both, and the poem concludes with comparing the unhappiness of the poet whose supply of ale is cut off with that of Adam shut out from Paradise,—a grief he professed to share in common with his master, the author of the "Splendid Shilling,"—

> Thus ADAM, exil'd from the beauteous scenes
> Of Eden, griev'd, no more in fragrant bow'r
> On fruits divine to feast, fresh shade and vale
> No more to visit, or vine-mantled grot;
>
> . . . . .
>
> Thus too the matchless bard, whose lay resounds
> The SPLENDID SHILLING'S praise, in nightly gloom
> Of lonesome garret, pin'd for cheerful ALE;
> Whose steps in verse Miltonic I pursue,
> Mean follower: like him with honest love
> Of ALE divine inspir'd, and love of song.
> But long may bounteous Heav'n with watchful care
> Avert his hapless lot! Enough for me
> That burning with congenial flame I dar'd
> His guiding steps at distance to pursue,
> And sing his favorite theme in kindred strains

In the same year Warton made two other modest offerings, both of slight importance. **"Newmarket, a Satire,"** published anonymously, was a somewhat heavy Popeian satire in closed couplets with balance, antithesis, and not infrequent epigrammatic turns of thought. Another pamphlet contained an academic poem, and **"Ode for Music,"** written for the anniversary in commemoration of the benefactors to the university, and performed at the Sheldonian Theatre, July 2, 1751.

In all these attempts the poet was evidently trying to find both himself and his public. That he felt the need of winning an audience for poetry which was deliberately different from the prevailing fashion is shown by the fact that much of it was published anonymously and that in his next publication, to which he did not affix his name,—*The Union: or Select Scots and English Poems,* containing some of his brother's odes, Collins's "Ode to Evening," and Gray's "Elegy," a few ancient Scottish poems, and minor poems by some of his contemporaries,—he asked for the verdict of the public upon two new poems of his own which he included without owning them. (pp. 28-30)

Of the two poems thus modestly proffered, the **"Pastoral in the Manner of Spenser"** was patently inspired by the poet whose work Warton was then studying carefully both as poet and critic, and the **"Ode on the Approach of Summer"** was obviously Miltonic. The former is a double imitation, a paraphrase of the 20th *Idyllium* of Theocritus in the manner of Spenser's *Shepherd's Calendar* with pseudo-Spenserian diction. But like other eighteenth century imitators of Spenser—of whom, it will be remembered, his father was perhaps the first—Warton had not enough knowledge of Spenser's language to escape such solecisms as 'did deemen', nor could his admiration save him. (p. 30)

That Warton was not simply an imitative poet was steadily proved by each new poem, and by none more strikingly than by two sonnets published in 1755 in Dodsley's *Collection.* He was a constant experimenter with forms as well as subjects of poetry. It may have been—pretty certainly was—his admiration for Milton again that interested him in the sonnet, but the subjects of his sonnets are not only so unMiltonic but so original in their use of the form to express personal emotion in the presence of natural scenes as to show him a real and important innovator. Warton was not, however, the first eighteenth century poet to write sonnets; Mason, Stillingfleet, and Edwards had each written a few, so that the whole credit for its revival cannot be claimed for any one of them. But certainly Warton's greater importance as a man of letters and the superior merit and originality of theme of his sonnets make his influence greater in the revival of the sonnet than that of any of his predecessors.

The **"Sonnet Written at Winslade in Hampshire"** 'about 1750' is the better of the two. It is not free from the influence of Miltonic diction—though not the diction of the sonnets; it is distinctly personal and reflective in tone, and further it indicates Warton's feeling that in their poetical inspiration the native charms of the village were peculiarly adapted to his genius. It shows that his interest in natural scenes as the source of poetic emotion was as conscious and deliberate in his early verse as his interest in the past for the same purpose,—

> Her fairest landskips whence my Muse has drawn,
> Too free with servile courtly phrase to fawn,
> Too weak to try the buskin's stately strain.

The **"Sonnet on Bathing"** is likewise Miltonic in diction, but it wholly lacks the personal note that distinguishes the other. Both are written in the Miltonic form, with better rhymes than some of his later sonnets. (pp. 32-3)

In 1764 he was the unconfessed editor of a miscellany of humorous verse called *The Oxford Sausage; or, Select Poetical Pieces: Written by the Most Celebrated Wits of the University of Oxford.* His own earlier academic verse with several new pieces of inferior merit were included in this miscellany with a great many similar poems by his contemporaries. The preface, in mock-serious style, explained the purpose and praised the novelty of such a collection and poked slyly at the growing fondness for poring over manuscript collections: 'That nothing might escape us, we have even examined the indefatigable Dr. Rawlinson's voluminous collection of manuscripts presented to the Bodleian Library, but, we must acknowledge, without success; as not one poignant ingredient was to be found in all that immense heap of rare and invaluable *originals.*' Of the two poems little need be said. The not very amusing dialogue between the **"Phaeton and the One-Horse Chair"** is, apparently, as a reviewer in the *Monthly Review* observed, an imitation of Smart's fable of the *Bag-Wig and Tobacco-Pipe.* More clever is the little **"Ode to a Grizzle Wig"** in which Warton, while comparing the relative merits of 'bob' and 'grizzle', frequently burlesqued with relish the manner of Milton's shorter poems. These poems and the *Oxford Newsman's Verses* were evidently dashed off with more enjoyment of the fun than poetry, and their chief interest lies in the fact that they show the poet in his most robust and genial mood. (pp. 33-4)

Warton's apparent abandonment of poetry at the very moment when he seems to have been passing from poetry largely imitative to poetry with considerable originality and intrinsic value demands some explanation. The reasons for Warton's partial desertion of poetry and turn to critical and historical studies are in part the same. It is generally recognized that the eighteenth century was conspicuously an age of prose, of reason, of skepticism, of didacticism; its characteristic poetry was either prosaic or merely brilliant and correct; and its attitude toward imagination, enthusiasm, romance, decidedly hostile. It was not the age to encourage such a poet as Thomas Warton with his enthusiastic love of the older neglected poets and his fondness for romance, nor to be moved by descriptions of the glories of the past. The standards and ideals of the school of Pope were not yet overthrown,—Warton himself did not immediately escape from their influence in his own poetry,—and there probably were few who read his verse with sympathetic appreciation. And Warton's poetical genius was not sufficiently robust to weather the storms of unfavourable criticism. Later in his life his sensitiveness to ridicule of his poetry—he could endure with composure the most virulent abuse of his other work—cost him the friendship of Dr. Johnson; at this period criticism simply repressed his poetic fervor. It is characteristic of his natural modesty as well as of his appreciation of the general lack of sympathy with his Gothic muse that, except in very early letters to his brother, although he wrote freely of his plans, his progress with all his other work of all sorts, there is no mention of his poetry, even in his letters to Price, to whom he wrote intimately.

As far as we can judge from the poetry which Warton wrote, excellent as some of it is, his was not a great poetical genius. Poetical taste, feeling and enthusiasm he had in abundance, but there seems to have been a lack of the creative spark. (pp. 34-5)

The poems that belong to Warton's later period, that is, those that appeared for the first time in the collected edition of 1777 and were presumably written after the publication of the ***Oxford Sausage,*** the laureate odes, and other occasional later poetry, show, as would be expected, a considerable advance over his earlier work in the direction of the new movement. They are far less imitative; not only are Pope and Swift largely ignored, but even Milton and the early romanticists, Thomson, Parnell, Young, exert less influence. They begin to show, too, some influence of contemporary romanticists, especially of Gray. They are also more markedly characterized by those peculiar qualities which had appeared in Warton's early work, the love of the past and the love of nature.

Four poems in the volume are significant of Warton's poetical taste; three show that his allegiance to the older English poets was unchanged, and one helps to account for Gray's influence. The **"Ode sent to Mr. Upton, on his Edition of the Faerie Queene"** expresses his early fondness for 'romantic Spenser's moral page' and his joy in reviving his ancient pageantry, and the sonnet **"On King Arthur's Round Table, at Winchester"** rejoices that

> Spenser's page, that chants in verse sublime
> Those Chiefs, shall live, unconscious of decay.

In the **"Monody, written near Stratford upon Avon"** the thought of the 'bard divine' who made here his 'infant offering' of 'daisies pied' transforms, 'as at the waving of some magic wand', a vision of natural loveliness to a fanciful vision of tragedy. The sonnet **"To Mr. Gray"** expresses the poet's gratitude

> For many a care beguil'd
> By the sweet magic of thy soothing lay,
> For many a raptur'd thought, and vision wild.

The influence of Gray is strong in one of the most interesting and significant of Warton's later poems, the **"Ode Written at Vale-Royal Abbey in Cheshire."** It is apparent throughout the poem, from the form, the elegiac quatrain, to the atmosphere of pensive melancholy which pervades it. The poem begins

> As evening slowly spreads his mantle hoar,
> No ruder sounds the bounded valley fill,
> Than the faint din, from yonder sedgy shore,
> Of rushing waters, and the murmuring mill,

and continues with a scene not unlike that with which the elegy opens. But there is an important difference between Gray's poem and Warton's. The former is classical and universal in its application and appeal; the scene might be any village church-yard; the conventional moralizing is exactly the sort which dignified the eighteenth century, and which makes an almost constant appeal both because of its truth and because of the perfect form which Gray gave to it. Warton, however, was describing a particular ruined abbey, and it called up in his mind visions of the past in which he was deeply interested. He delighted to reconstruct the ruined abbey, to recall its departed glories, to dwell on the themes dear to him, its architecture, its learning, its minstrelsy, and its romance.

> Here ancient Art her dædal fancies play'd

> In the quaint mazes of the crisped roof;
> In mellow glooms the speaking pane array'd,
> And rang'd the cluster'd column, massy proof.
>
> Here Learning, guarded from a barbarous age,
> Hover'd awhile, nor dar'd attempt the day;
> But patient trac'd upon the pictured page
> The holy legend, or heroic lay.
>
> Hither the solitary minstrel came
> An honour'd guest, while the grim evening sky
> Hung lowering, and around the social flame
> Tun'd his bold harp to tales of chivalry.

Both poets portray the transitoriness of human life; Gray advances from the description of an evening scene to contemplation of the dignity and worth of rustic life; Warton to the celebration of vanished glories prized even in an ampler age.

This love of the past, this revival of mediæval glories especially, which occasionally showed in the earlier poems and appeared more strongly in many of his later ones, connects Warton most closely with the romantic movement and constitutes his most original contribution to it. His mediæval poems have also a close relation to his other literary work; they give expression to the same master passion that urged him, as critic and historian, to exploit the beauties of Spenser and the forgotten poets of early English literature. In two of Warton's best and most characteristic odes, he concerned himself wholly with the past. These very romantic poems are **"The Crusade"** and the **"Grave of King Arthur."** The first purports to be the song that Richard Cœur de Leon and Blondel de Nesle composed together, by which the minstrel was able to discover his master in prison. The poem has a fine swing, from the beginning of the song

> Syrian virgins, wail and weep,
> English Richard ploughs the deep!

to the defiant close,—

> We bid those spectre-shapes avaunt,
> Ashtaroth, and Termagaunt!
> With many a demon, pale of hue,
> Doom'd to drink the bitter dew
> That drops from Macon's sooty tree,
> Mid the dread grove of ebony.
> Nor magic charms, nor fiends of hell,
> The christian's holy courage quell.
> Salem, in ancient majesty
> Arise, and lift thee to the sky!
> Soon on thy battlements divine
> Shall wave the badge of Constantine.
> Ye Barons, to the sun unfold
> Our Cross with crimson wove and gold!

The favourite ode, however, will always be **"The Grave of King Arthur,"** in which a story of the national British hero of romance is skilfully set into a brilliant framework of mediæval splendour. Warton explained in a short preface that the story was adapted from the Chronicle of Glastonbury and dealt with a Welsh tradition that Arthur was not carried away to Avalon after the battle of Camlan but was received by monks and buried before the high altar in Glastonbury Abbey. This story, told to Henry II by Welsh bards at Cilgarran Castle, induced him to go to the abbey, find the grave, and, as the ode has it, establish a chantry at its shrine. The description of the feast with which the poem opens is gorgeously romantic, and splendidly sug-

gests the great mediæval of the next century, Sir Walter
Scott. Warton's richness and harmony of diction, his stirring and vigorous appeal to the imagination were continued, but scarcely eclipsed, in the poems of his great successor. (pp. 129-32)

Warton's love of the past was the inspiration also of three
of his sonnets. Two were suggested by relics of the early
history of England: one by King Arthur's Round Table,
hanging in the old Norman castle at Winchester, and the
other by the mysterious monument of 'wondrous origine'
unknown at Stonehenge on Salisbury Plain.

The third of the mediæval group, the most interesting of
Warton's sonnets, if not the most interesting of all his
poems because it affords a characteristic glimpse of the
poet-scholar, is the one **"Written in a Blank Leaf of Dugdale's Monasticon."** It has for its subject the delightful,
the æsthetic, side of antiquarian study. That aspect made
to Warton an appeal quite as strong as the scholarly one;
it was to him an influence as potent in poetry and art as
the other was in history and scholarship. The antiquary
has never had a better defense and justification than the
following lines:—

> Deem not, devoid of elegance, the Sage,
> By Fancy's genuine feelings unbeguil'd,
> Of painful pedantry the poring child;
> Who turns, of these proud domes, th' historic page,
> Now sunk by Time, and Henry's fiercer rage.
> Think'st thou the warbling Muses never smil'd
> On his lone hours? Ingenuous views engage
> His thoughts, on themes, unclassic falsely stil'd,
> Intent. While cloister'd Piety displays
> Her mouldering roll, the piercing eye explores
> New manners, and the pomp of elder days,
> Whence culls the pensive bard his pictur'd stores.
> Nor rough, nor barren, are the winding ways
> Of hoar Antiquity, but strown with flowers.

The same note of interest in the past is struck rather frequently, but never so forcibly, in his last poems, the laureate odes. Aside from this element, the odes have very little
merit indeed. They are dignified, conventional, and often
perfunctory. Warton was not interested in contemporary
events, and George III made no great imaginative appeal;
therefore Warton, like many another laureate, took refuge
in singing the glories of English heroes of the past, of Alfred and the British legacy of liberty; of William Conquer-
or and the barons who obtained Magna Charta; of Edward
and the victories in France; and in lauding his great predecessors, the laureates of England.

These celebrations of ancient days, together with Warton's neglect of the ostensible subjects of his odes, were
cleverly ridiculed by 'Peter Pindar', a poet whose coarse
but frequently humorous satires were more successful
than his serious verse. In "Ode upon Ode" he parodied
Warton's celebration of the past; in "An Expostulary
Epistle from Brother Peter to Brother Tom," derided his
neglect of the present, and in his "Advice to the Future
Laureat," written after the death of Warton, he pointed
with some cleverness to his learning as the cause of his ill
success as a laureate.

> Tom prov'd unequal to the Laureat's place;
> Luckless, he warbled with an Attic Grace:
> The language was not understood at Court,
> Where bow and curt'sy, grin and shrug, resort;

> Sorrow for sickness, joy for health, so civil;
> And love, that wish'd each other to the devil!

> Tom was a scholar—luckless wight!
> Lodg'd with old manners in a musty college;
> He knew not that a Palace hated knowledge,
> And deem'd it pedantry to spell and write.
> Tom heard of royal libraries, indeed,
> And, weakly, fancied that the books were *read*.

The second important characteristic of Warton's poetry,
the interest in natural scenes as the subject of poetry,
which had been in his early period largely coloured by the
influence of Milton and Spenser, was equally conspicuous
in his later work. In the later poems, however, although
he justified his selection of such subjects from the practice
of these favourite poets, it is pretty evident that he was
painting directly from nature. The following short passage
from the ode on **"The First of April"** illustrates the closeness of Warton's observation of simple details which the
pseudo-classicist would have thought beneath the notice
of a poet,—

> Scant along the ridgy land
> The beans their new-born ranks expand:
> The fresh-turn'd soil with tender blades
> Thinly the sprouting barley shades:
> Fringing the forest's devious edge,
> Half rob'd appears the hawthorn hedge;
> Or to the distant eye displays
> Weakly green its budding sprays.

The modernity of Warton's poetry in which the rustic delights of simple life are celebrated was attested by the fact
that his **"Hamlet, an Ode written in Whichwood Forest,"**
was republished in 1859 with fourteen etchings by Birket
Foster, a popular engraver, who made illustrations for editions of Milton, Goldsmith, Scott and Wordsworth, and
that a second edition was called for in 1876. Yet for all its
'softness' and 'sweetness', the poem is not one of Warton's
best efforts.

In two sonnets Warton shows an ability to use the sonnet
for that combination of observation of nature and personal
reflection which prevailed in the poetry of the next century; they are as reactionary in the direction of the return
to nature as the mediæval sonnets were in that of the return to the past. One of these is a study of nature and
mood, in the furtherance of which the poet assumed the
contrast between the hopeful and the disappointed lover.
It is apparent that at least the changeful Surrey landscape
was real, whatever the state of feelings in which it was
viewed.

> While summer-suns o'er the gay prospect play'd,
> Through Surry's verdant scenes, where Epsom spreads
> Mid intermingling elms her flowery meads,
> And Hascombe's hill, in towering groves array'd,
> Rear'd its romantic steep, with mind serene,
> I journey'd blithe. Full pensive I return'd;
> For now my breast with hopeless passion burn'd,
> Wet with hoar mists appear'd the gaudy scene,
> Which late in careless indolence I pass'd;
> And Autumn all around those hues had cast
> Where past delight my recent grief might trace.
> Sad change, that Nature a congenial gloom
> Should wear, when most, my cheerless mood to chase,
> I wish'd her green attire, and wonted bloom!

The second nature sonnet, **"To the River London,"** is even
more interesting intrinsically as well as historically. Al-

though one is seldom justified in interpreting poetry biographically, and though Warton was extremely reticent, I cannot but find in this sonnet something of that personal note which was characteristic of the new poetry. It is in the mood of melancholy reflection upon a natural scene that was so congenial a vein to Warton's pupil, William Lisle Bowles.

> Ah! what a weary race my feet have run,
> Since first I trod thy banks with alders crown'd,
> And thought my way was all thro' fairy ground,
> Beneath thy azure sky, and golden sun:
> Where first my Muse to lisp her notes begun!
> While pensive Memory traces back the round,
> Which fills the varied interval between;
> Much pleasure, more of sorrow, marks the scene.
> Sweet native stream! those skies and suns so pure
> No more return, to cheer my evening road!
> Yet still one joy remains, that not obscure,
> Nor useless, all my vacant days have flow'd,
> From youth's gay dawn to manhood's prime mature;
> Nor with the Muse's laurel unbestow'd.

Closely akin to these nature poems are those that celebrate the joys of rustic life, poems that, still echoing Milton, stand between "The Deserted Village" and "The Task." Of these the **"Inscription in a Hermitage"** is the most Miltonic in its praise of studious solitude, but the poet's joy in the blackbird's 'artless trill', the wren's 'mossy nest', his concern to count 'every opening primrose', to guide 'fantastic ivy's gadding spray' show the close observer and real lover of nature. In the **"Ode to Solitude, at an Inn,"** the genial poet shows a keen enjoyment of a solitude shared with nature,—

> Then was loneliness to me
> Best and true society,—

but an equal impatience with the unrelieved solitude of an inn,—

> Here all inelegant and rude
> Thy presence is, sweet Solitude.

The **"Sonnet Written after seeing Wilton-House"** perhaps belongs in this group; it affords an imaginative variation of Johnson's and Goldsmith's theme that

> Our own felicity we make or find.

Warton celebrates the 'pleasure of imagination,' the power of Fancy' to

> Bid the green landskip's vernal beauty bloom
> And in bright trophies clothe the twilight wall,

a sentiment as characteristic of the author as it is remote from the moralizing of those sturdy classicists.

Reflection and sentiment have got the better of nature in two odes that, although popular with Warton's contemporaries, fail to move the modern reader. The ode **"To Sleep"** is reminiscent of Young; it invokes sleep to assuage grief, to 'calm this tempest of my boiling blood.' **"The Suicide,"** the favourite ode of many contemporary readers, has fallen into obscurity in spite of, or perhaps because of, its representation of austere virtue triumphing over weak sentimentality. The most interesting feature of the poem now, at least, is the vivid portrayal of nature in a forbidding mood as the background for the sombre theme. (pp. 133-38)

Classical characteristics are not so obvious in Warton's poetry as love of the past and of nature. Although it is difficult to point out particular instances of classical influence in his poetry, the careful reader gains from the whole a definite impression that the writer was thoroughly familiar with the best classical poetry and alive to its characteristic beauties. Mant, the editor of Warton's poems, painstakingly pointed out a number of parallels to passages from such classical poets as Theocritus and Pindar, Virgil, Horace, Ovid and Lucretius. Some few of the poems were, indeed, frank imitations from Horace and Theocritus. But Warton's classicism is not so clearly manifested in imitations from classical poetry or allusions to it as in his recognition of the fact that there is no inevitable antipathy between the classical spirit and 'Gothic' poetry; that they have in common that imaginative quality which is a distinguishing characteristic of the mediæval romances and which the poets of a pseudo-classical age lost by too close an adherence to the form instead of an independent recognition of the spirit of classical poetry. Much of Warton's own poetry, therefore, dealt with mediæval subjects with the deliberate purpose of restoring by that means this essential quality of great poetry which had disappeared in an age of reason.

Because he recognized the close relation between the mediæval and the classical spirit, Warton distinctly resented, in the sonnet on Dugdale's *Monasticon,* the designation of antiquarian studies as 'unclassic'. And in the **"Verses on Sir Joshua Reynolds's Painted Window"** he pointed out the possibility of a relation between the spirit of the middle ages and that of classical antiquity, as illustrated, in this instance, by their application to ecclesiastical architecture. Reynolds, as a typical representative of the eighteenth century school of art, saw an incompatibility between the 'softer touch', the 'chaste design', the 'just proportion', and the 'faultless forms of elegance and grace' of classical art; and the 'vaulted dome' and 'fretted shrines', the 'hues romantic' that 'ting'd the gorgeous pane',—the 'Gothic art' of ancient magnificence; the acceptance of one meant for him the denial of the other. Not so with Warton, whose feeling was all for their essential unity.

The common suggestion that Warton's profession of conversion to the classical school of art, his profession that he had been

> For long, enamour'd of a barbarous age,
> A faithless truant to the classic page,

was probably not quite whole-hearted and did not even deceive the friend to whom it was addressed, does not reveal the full significance of the poem. Its importance in this connection is neither its generous recognition of the beauties of Attic art, nor even the more extended and sympathetic description of the magic of Gothic art, but the suggestion of the possibility of combining classical and mediæval ideals to the advantage of both. With a just sense of their characteristic beauties, the greater naturalness and universality of one, the stronger appeal to the imagination of the other, Warton realized that in art, as in poetry, perfection lay in their union, and therefore he proposed that the great classical artist should

> . . add new lustre to religious light:
> Not of its pomp to strip this ancient shrine,

But bid that pomp with purer radiance shine:
With arts unknown before, to reconcile
The willing Graces to the Gothic pile.

The immediate and later reception of Warton's poetry indicates that it belongs much more to the new than to the old school. Johnson and Hazlitt may fairly be taken as typical critics of the two schools: the former could see no merit in the performance of his friend; the latter could not praise it too highly. Dr. Johnson was repelled by Warton's enthusiasm for the past; he could appreciate the benefits to be derived from the study of antiquities in illuminating the history and progress of mankind, but he had no sympathy with Warton's enthusiasm for the intrinsic beauties of old literature and art, nor with his attempt to reëmbody something of their spirit and charm in modern poetry; he saw in his poetry only strangeness of language and form, or at best, revival of what was not worth reviving. Although he protested that he still loved the fellow dearly for all he laughed at him, he wrecked his friendship with Warton by ridiculing his verse thus,—

Wheresoe'er I turn my view,
All is strange, yet nothing new;
Endless labour all along,
Endless labour to be wrong;
Phrase that time has flung away;
Uncouth words in disarray,
Trick'd in antique ruff and bonnet,
Ode, and elegy, and sonnet.

Hazlitt, on the other hand, although disposed to blame Warton for the defects of his age in scholarly method, repeatedly acclaimed him a 'man of taste and genius', 'a poet and a scholar, studious with ease, learned without affectation', and 'the author of some of the finest sonnets in the language',—praise which accords well with Warton's vogue among the poets who were Hazlitt's contemporaries.

Interesting as Warton's poetry is in showing his own development from nearly pseudo-classical to pretty romantic ideals, and valuable as much of it is intrinsically, its greatest importance is to the student of literary history as a factor in the development of the new movement. The influence of the romantic poetry of this laureate poet can scarcely be, and certainly has not been, overestimated, though it has not been altogether overlooked. 'If any man may be called the father of the present race', wrote Southey in the *Quarterly* in 1824, 'it is Thomas Warton, a scholar by profession, an antiquary and a poet by choice'. (pp. 138-40)

> *Clarissa Rinaker, in her* Thomas Warton: A Biographical and Critical Study, *1916. Reprint by Johnson Reprint Corporation, 1967, 241 p.*

Raymond D. Havens   (essay date 1928)

[*In the excerpt below, Havens challenges the claim that Warton was "one who lifted high the banner of literary revolt."*]

Thomas Warton is usually thought of as one who lifted high the banner of literary revolt "with gems and golden lustre rich imblazed." We picture him, both in critical theory and in poetic practice, a conscious rebel against the school of Pope. Such a misconception is natural enough, since we usually read both his prose and his poetry in anthologies that aim to give not his most typical, but his most significant writings, and his significance is thought to lie in revolt. Even if we turn to his complete works, we commonly read them with an eye for indications of romanticism; and, in any case, it is heterodoxy rather than conformity that makes the strongest first impression. As a result, we pass over the hundreds of satirical heroic couplets, the translations from Horace, the paraphrase of a chapter of Job, as well as the dozen humorous pieces and fasten upon **"The Pleasures of Melancholy," "The Grave of King Arthur,"** and **"The Crusade."** In emphasizing these last two we do right, for they represent the real man, but **"The Pleasures of Melancholy"** does not. Though supposed to be typical of the Wartons and of their period, it is really typical of adolescence and tells us little about its sixteen-year-old author except that he was young, poetic, and a lover of Spenser and Milton. To be sure, it says a good deal about midnight, tombs, Gothic vaults, and solitude; but it is no more gloomy than is a ghost story. Its title describes it accurately, **"The Pleasures of Melancholy."** "Is there," the young bard asks, "a pleasure like the pensive mood,"

To bend
Th' uncertain step along the midnight mead,
And pour your sorrows to the pitying moon?

Far from being plunged in despair, he is having an excellent time and is very well satisfied with himself:

Few know that elegance of soul refin'd,
Whose soft sensation feels a quicker joy
From Melancholy's scenes, than the dull pride
Of tasteless splendour and magnificence
Can e'er afford.

And a hundred lines later he repeats, "These are delights . . . which alone the pensive soul can taste." He piles up macabre and gloomy details, not because he really enjoys tombs and fogs, nor because he is discouraged and wishes his surroundings to accord with his mood; quite the contrary, out of the fullness of youth he seeks the thrill of a complete antithesis to the comfort, health, and high spirits that he enjoys. Partly it is bravado and partly roughing it from an easy chair. We do not judge Goethe by *Werther,* yet *Werther* describes a real phase of Goethe's development, whereas there is no reason to believe that Warton ever

Genuine transport found, as on some tomb
Reclin'd . . . [he] watch'd the tapers of the dead.

Nor did he actually prefer a rainy, foggy, scowling morning to all the sweetness of a May dawn; but in his ignorance of the emotions he attempted to describe he fell into exaggeration. Such pseudo-romanticism might well be significant if it were the affectation of one who had reached "years of discretion," but in the work of a boy not yet seventeen it has the same meaning as down on the lip and unpredictable breakings in the voice. At this particular time, indeed, it meant even less, for grave-yard poetry was just coming into vogue. Dyer's "Ruins of Rome" appeared in 1740, Young's *Night Thoughts* at intervals between 1742 and 1745 (the year in which **"The Pleasures of Melancholy"** was written), Blair's "Grave" in 1743, Hervey's *Meditations among the Tombs* in 1745-46, and in 1742

Gray began his "Elegy." The first three of these works, which (like his own effusion) were in blank verse, almost certainly influenced Warton, who also very naturally adopted the gloomy themes, congenial to an adolescent boy, that such productions were bringing into fashion.

Yet it is not because of his poetry alone that Thomas Warton has been pictured as one of the powers that led the enbattled seraphim to war against the neo-classic despotism. For in his *Observations on the Fairy Queen* (1754) he is said to have "produced a revolution in criticism." No doubt there is the possibility of a revolution in his remark, "It is absurd to think of judging either Ariosto or Spenser by precepts which they did not attend to," but unfortunately this utterance is not original and by no means represents his critical position. I have said "position," but the plural should be used, since in the very section which contains this comment he twice shifts his ground and employs no fewer than three conflicting critical standards. If the shifting were deliberately done in order to present contrasting points of view, it would indicate unusual keenness of discrimination and catholicity of taste; but it is unconscious and is due to the confusion in his mind, a confusion shared by many of his contemporaries. (pp. 36-8)

By beginning his *Observations* with the consideration "Of the plan and conduct of the *Fairy Queen*" Warton seems to lay great stress upon the architectonic element, and by finding the poem seriously deficient in this particular he seems to be condemning it as a whole. In so doing he was merely accepting the neo-classic assumptions and canons and repeating what Dryden, Hughes, and others had said before him. But he was not satisfied; he felt that something was wrong, though he did not know just what, and, accordingly, in the last two paragraphs of this first chapter, he attempts a defence of his beloved poem: "But it is absurd," he tells us, "to think of judging either Ariosto or Spenser by precepts which they did not attend to. We who live in the days of writing by rule, are apt to try every composition by *those* laws which we have been taught to think the *sole* criterion of excellence. Critical taste is universally diffused, and we require the *same* order and design which every modern performance is expected to have, in poems where they never were regarded or intended." It is here implied that a great poem must have order and design, must be tried by some laws, but that the neo-classic rules are not "the sole criterion of excellence." We are led to infer that a study of poetry which was free from preconceptions and not limited to the ancient classics and to the French and English works patterned after them would give us other laws, other concepts of order and design, and that with these the *Faerie Queene* might be found to accord.

This is a most illuminating suggestion and might, had it been followed up, have led to great things. But it is merely an afterthought which was added in the second edition. Warton does nothing more with it and that, as is clear from his immediately passing to another idea (which he treats as the same), because he has never thought it through but has merely appropriated it from John Hughes. In the preface to his edition of Spenser (1715), Hughes had said of the *Faerie Queene:* "The whole Frame of it wou'd appear monstrous, if it were to be examin'd by the Rules of Epick Poetry, as they have been drawn from the Practice of *Homer* and *Virgil*. But as it is plain the Au-

thor never design'd it by those Rules, I think it ought rather to be consider'd as a Poem of a particular kind, describing in a Series of Allegorical Adventures or Episodes the most noted Virtues and Vices: to compare it therefore with the Models of Antiquity, wou'd be like drawing a Parallel between the *Roman* and the *Gothick* Architecture." It is to Hughes, therefore, a much more liberal, original, and penetrating critic than Warton, that all the credit for the often-quoted passage from the *Observations* is due.

Warton continues as follows:

> Spenser . . . did not live in an age of planning. His poetry is the careless exuberance of a warm imagination and a strong sensibility. It was his business to engage the fancy, and to interest the attention by bold and striking images, in the formation, and the disposition of which, little labor or art was applied. . . . Exactness in his poem, would have been like the cornice which a painter introduced in the grotto of Calypso. . . . we scarcely regret the loss of ["arrangement and oeconomy"] . . . while their place is so amply supplied, by something which more powerfully attracts us: something, which engages the affections the feelings of the heart, rather than the cold approbation of the head. If there be any poem, whose graces please, because they are situated beyond the reach of art, and where the force and faculties of creative imagination delight, because they are unassisted and unrestrained by those of deliberate judgment, it is this.

Such criticism is sheer lawlessness. It belittles labor, judgment, selection, revision, and the entire architectonic, intellectual element to exalt spontaneity and emotional appeal as the only important things in poetry. According to it, the elaborate, monumental creation of "our sage and serious Spenser" is a piece of careless exuberance possessing little plan or art and owing its greatness largely to its faults, to the absence of "exactness" and "deliberate judgment." Furthermore, it seems to imply what Warton unconsciously have believed that subject matter is the main thing in literature, that Spenser's work is great not because of its beauty, its art, but mainly because it furnishes the mind with a pleasant land in which to wander.

It should be observed that all three appraisals of the *Faerie Queene* stand: first, that it lacks plan; second, that it has plan but not that of the classic epic; third, that it is without plan and is better so. They are regarded not as optional but as supplementary one to another; Warton believed them all. To be sure, he writes, "It is absurd to think of judging either Ariosto or Spenser by precepts which they did not attend to;" yet he does so judge them. He lets his condemnation of Spenser's irregularity remain and even places it at the beginning of his book. Furthermore, in his penultimate paragraph he repeats the neo-classic condemnation though with suggestion of the other two positions. "In analysing the Plan and Conduct of this poem, I have so far tried it by epic rules, as to demonstrate the inconveniencies and incongruities, which the poet might have avoided, had he been more studious of design and uniformity. It is true, that his romantic materials claim great liberties; but no materials exclude order and perspicuity . . . I have so far conformed to the reigning maxims of modern criticism, as . . . to recommend classical propriety." In saying "his romantic materials claim great liberties," Warton seems to touch on his own earlier suggestion that the *Faerie Queene* should be judged by more liberal rules than those of neo-classicism; yet he concludes that, after all allowances have been made, it cannot be brought into conformity with any just standards. Does he, then, fall back upon the romantic justification? By no means. "Nothing is more absurd or useless," he asserted in the Postscript, "than the panegyrical comments of those, who criticise from the imagination rather than from the judgment, who exert their admiration instead of their reason, and discover more of enthusiasm than discernment." Yet, useless and absurd as it was, he had done it, just as he had vaguely held, and probably continued to hold, three conflicting standards of esthetic judgment. In so doing, he showed himself to be much like the rest of us and thoroughly typical of the unsettled, transitional age to which he belonged.

He was an antiquary and a poet with little interest in the problems of literary criticism. The critical theories of his own and the immediately preceding age, he accepted, since they seemed to be in harmony with all the criticism he knew from Aristotle down, but probably gave them little real thought, just as he gave little space in his ***Observations*** to the subjects with which neo-classic criticism had been chiefly concerned. He seems not to have been analytical or to have cared much for the structural element in art—his own writings are notably lacking in it—but, since something had to be said about the plan and the unity of the *Faerie Queene,* he said it. So slight was his interest in such things that he merely repeated the condemnation of his predecessors, together with the suggestion of one of them that Spenser should not be judged by rules which he did not attend to. In his own words, "I have so far conformed to the reigning maxims of modern criticism, as . . . to recommend classical propriety." Yet his real taste and feelings are to be found in the earlier comment: "We scarcely regret the loss of these [proprieties] while their place is so amply supplied, by something which more powerfully attracts us; something, which engages the affections the feelings of the heart, rather than the cold approbation of the head."

This critical dualism, this sharp separation of judgment from enjoyment vitiates Warton's criticism. A writer who condemns what he really likes and approves of what he is actually indifferent to is a dubious guide in matters of taste. If Warton could have faced the issue squarely with a respect for his true likings and instincts, if he had asked himself, for example: "What are the things that I really like in Spenser? Are these things the bases of great poetry? Should the *Faerie Queene* be judged as a classic epic? How serious are the defects that have been pointed out in its plan? What effect did Spenser try to secure? Did he choose the best means to secure it? Are the effects and the means worthy of great poetry? if he had asked himself such questions and had possessed the ability to discuss them, he would have given us a really important book. But this is demanding too much. The hand of tradition lay heavy upon criticism and could not lightly be shaken off. None of the writers who felt the charm of medieval literature and architecture possessed at once the courage, the inclination, and the ability to furnish a reasoned justification for their novel taste. Certainly the easy-going Thomas Warton was unequal to so difficult a task; he had too much respect for tradition (natural enough in a lover of the past) and too little power of keen, analytical discrimination. Furthermore, it did not trouble him to condemn as a critic

what he enjoyed as a reader; he showed no desire to prove that the beggar with whom he had fallen in love was really a princess in disguise. (pp. 39-44)

In Warton's case, this inconsistency, this divided allegiance between wife and mistress, appears in the poetry as well as the criticism. **"The Suicide,"** for example, pictures with notable understanding and sympathy the sufferings of an unfortunate, melancholy man who finally makes way with himself. But the poem does not end on the note of sympathy for the sinner. In the last four stanzas a "cherub-voice" speaks reproof and brings the poem into accord with orthodoxy and propriety:

> Forbear, fond bard, thy partial praise;
> Nor thus for guilt in specious lays
> The wreath of glory twine:
> In vain with hues of gorgeous glow
> Gay Fancy gives her vest to flow,
> Unless Truth's matron-hand the floating folds confine.

Here again Warton straddles. A little conventional morality patched on at the close will, he feels, do no harm and will prevent any possible misunderstanding. He has not thought the matter through and so does not see that his concluding stanzas seriously impair the unity and effectiveness of the poem which owes its original inception and all its vitality to that very sympathy for the sinner which its apparent purpose is to condemn.

A similar attempt to serve both God and Mammon disfigures the ode **"Written at Vale-Royal Abbey."** The first twenty stanzas of this poem are devoted to a pensive description of the ruins and to wistful imaginings of the days long since departed—harmless enough, it would seem, but the piece is not allowed to end so. Instead, "severer Reason" is brought in to remind us of the "more useful institutes . . . and new civilities" of modern life and of how

> Science, on ampler plume, a bolder flight
> Essays, escap'd from Superstition's shrine;
> While freed Religion, like primeval light
> Bursting from chaos, spreads her warmth divine.

It is safe to say that the poet-professor who rarely went to London but devoted his leisure to ancient manuscripts and medieval ruins had little real concern about "useful institutes" or "new civilities" and that he was more interested in Gothic superstitions than in the science which displaced them; yet, unlike later medievalists, he never asserted and probably would have denied the superiority of the middle ages to the modern. The enlightened eighteenth century was of course better—only he preferred to devote himself to a less civilized period.

Of all the vanished pomps of yesterday, that which seems to have appealed most strongly to Warton was Gothic architecture. Many of his vacations were given over to visiting old churches and castles and to making notes on them in preparation for an extensive work on medieval buildings. Like almost everything else he wrote, his poems give abundant evidence of this enthusiasm; yet they also leave no doubt that he regarded the Gothic as inferior to the classic. In the **"Ode for Music,"** written in 1751, when he was only twenty-three, he says of the Oxford buildings:

> Nor wants there Graecia's better part,
> 'Mid the proud piles of ancient art,

Whose fretted spires, with ruder hand,
Wainflet and Wickham bravely plann'd.

and thirty-one years later, in one of his last pieces, he not
only condemns but ridicules the noble art which had been
his study and his diversion in countless happy hours. So
great an apostasy could not have sprung simply from seeing the pretty windows which Sir Joshua Reynolds painted for New College, Oxford. These were only the occasion
which brought out once more the fundamental antagonism between what Warton liked and what his reason approved of, and again the palm was given to reason. "Ah,
stay," he cries,

Ah, stay thy treacherous hand, forbear to trace
Those faultless forms of elegance and grace!

After a most sympathetic picture of the pleasure he has
found in Gothic buildings, he again addresses the painter:

Ah, spare the weakness of a lover's heart!
Chase not the phantoms of my fairy dream,
Phantoms that shrink at Reason's painful gleam!

Yet "of ravish'd pleasures why complain?" He acknowledges the "chaste design"

The just proportion, and the genuine line;
Those native portraitures of Attic art

of Reynolds's work and exclaims

Thy powerful hand has broke the Gothic chain,
And brought my bosom back to truth again;
To truth, by no peculiar taste confin'd,
Whose universal pattern strikes mankind . . .
To truth, whose charms deception's magic quell,
And bind coy Fancy in a stronger spell.

He now finds humor in the "brawny prophets," the proud
saints, the fiercely-frowning virgins, and the mundane angles of Medieval stained glass and bids them

No more the sacred window's round disgrace,
But yield to Grecian groupes the shining space.

The point should be stressed; Warton ridiculed medieval
stained glass, its colors as well as its drawing, and wished
it banished from churches! Surely the force of reason could
no further go! The explanation is obvious: by no conceivable distortion of the canons of classic art as they were
then understood could highly-colored windows filled with
naïve, confusing, badly-drawn details be justified. They
could not be brought into the fold as Addison had brought
"Chevy Chase" and the "Children in the Wood;" they
must be justified in accordance with another aesthetic or
abandoned. Warton abandoned them. Their beauty, the
pleasure he had for years found in them, the importance
of their contribution to Gothic interiors—all these were
as nothing in the face of their non-conformity.

Reynolds's "Grecian groups" did not seem to the laureate
out of place in a Gothic church. On the contrary, their
presence suggested that a happy union might be made of
antique and medieval art. It was Reynolds's achievement

Not of its pomp to strip this ancient shrine,
But bid that pomp with purer radiance shine:
With arts unknown before, to reconcile
The willing Graces to the Gothic pile.

Warton does not stress the point, which may be little more

than a graceful compliment; and there is no reason to believe that he had thought much about it or dreamed of a
higher synthesis of the two styles. He loved the Gothic but
realized that it did not conform to the classic principles.
Could it not be made to conform by the use of such expedi-
ents as "Greek" windows? What he had in mind was
merely a superficial tinkering or patching up which should
not interfere with the charm or the essential character of
the medieval church but which should satisfy the rules.
Such an attitude is typical of the man. To the last he remained true to the orthodox, neo-classic principles and at
the same time a devoted admirer of medieval art which
those principles condemned. The condemnation apparently troubled him little; it seems not to have interfered with
his enjoyment and certainly did not drive him to any thorough-going examination of the bases of his taste. Criticism
he seems to have regarded as a kind of intellectual golf,
a game in excellent repute, played according to somewhat
arbitrary rules of its own, but quite apart from the realities
of life. If he had really grasped the principle underlying
his oft-quoted assertion of the folly of "judging either Ariosto or Spenser by precepts which they did not attend to"
he would not have condemned Gothic architecture as a
"fond illusion" but would have come to see that it has its
own laws, its own "reason," "truth," and "just proportion" quite as much as does the Greek.

"It may be," some one will perhaps reply, "but what of
it? Do Warton's opinions matter much any way?" To
which we may answer with a paradox "which comforts
while it mocks" that the truth of Warton's opinions does
not matter but their inconsistences and other limitations
do. We read the ***Observations*** and the **"Verses on Reynolds's Window,"** not for light on the *Faerie Queene* or on
Gothic architecture, but on a subject about which we
know much less,—the mid eighteenth-century. If we are
ever to understand this period, it will be through a careful
study of such typical figures as Thomas Warton, a study,
not only of their successes, but of their failures, a study
which does not overlook their conventionality and conservatism in its search for originality and liberalism. Such a
study will convince us of the impossibility of tagging the
writers of the time as "romantic" or "classic." We have
seen that the **"Pleasures of Melancholy"** is in the main
pseudo-romantic, that its author's critical position is usually neo-classic, and had we discussed his best poems, we
should have found in them romantic strains predominate. Even true classicism might be discovered in his Latin
poetry and his editions of the Greek anthology and of Theocritus. Yet in everything he wrote, characteristics may be
discovered that are usually termed neo-classic, together
with other characteristics commonly called romantic. Frequently the two are to be found on the same page, often
in the same sentence. But, although evidence of both these
qualities, is abundant, there is no warrant for attaching to
Thomas Warton the epithet which is often associated with
his name,—that of rebel. (pp. 45-50)

*Raymond D. Havens, "Thomas Warton and
the Eighteenth-Century Dilemma," in* Studies
in Philology, *Vol. XXV, No. 1, January, 1928,
pp. 36-50.*

Sir Edmund Gosse (essay date 1928)

[*Gosse was a distinguished English literary historian, critic, and biographer who wrote extensively on seventeenth- and eighteenth-century English literature. In the following excerpt, he gives the history of* The Oxford Sausage, *commenting on its accuracy as a portrayal of eighteenth-century Oxford life.*]

Picked up on a suburban bookstall, a little volume, annoying me at first by what seemed its impenetrable reserve, ended by exciting my curiosity to the last degree. *The Oxford Sausage* bears no editor's name, its anonymous preface is designed to mislead, and its contents show no evidence of design. It is a collection of facetious copies of verse, illustrating university life, and its title-page claims that all of them are witty, *tota, merum sal. Tota* is going too far, but many of the poems are funny, and all are unfamiliar. But they cannot have been highly familiar even to readers of this reprint of 1815, since the Oxford they illustrate was the Oxford of more than half a century earlier than that.

The Oxford Sausage, as I will presently explain, emanated from Trinity; in the following year, 1816, a graceful youth named John Henry Newman matriculated at that college. The contrast between old and new could not be made more emphatic. The first discovery about the *Sausage* is that it was, in 1815, a reprint; the original having appeared, with a like furtiveness, in 1764. Half a century had made a great difference in social manners, yet there is no change, or very little, in the verses. . . . (p. 169)

The carefully concealed editor of *The Oxford Sausage* was a man famous in his day and by no means forgotten now, Dr. Thomas Warton. He was the author of the earliest and long the best *History of English Poetry,* he was a poet himself and in his day a metrical innovator, but he was above all an Oxford man. His whole life was spent in the odour which breathes around *The Oxford Sausage,* an atmosphere of strong tobacco and foaming ale, Latin quotations, and endless conversation. By 1764 Warton was already a Fellow of Trinity College and Professor of Poetry, as well as the author of many serious works; so that he might well not be anxious to appear as the compiler of a book of local songs, all frivolous, and some not decent. So he wrote a preface, warning readers not to try to discover who the editor was, and especially not to suppose him to be the author of the anonymous *Companion to the Guide to Oxford* and of *Terræ Filius,* because "most unluckily the author of those pieces will never be known."

This was very sly, because these were not the same person, *Terræ Filius* being the work of a rapscallion called Nicholas Amhurst, long dead by 1764; and the *Companion*—oh! what a deceitful professor—being written by Warton himself! He slipped into the *Sausage* several poems of his own, of course without his name. Dr. Hunt has identified some of them for me, but there is one, the satire called **"Newmarket,"** which there could be no mystery about, since Warton had openly published it thirteen years earlier. . . . (pp. 170-71)

The exposure of university life which Gibbon makes in his *Autobiography* has often been quoted, and has been charged with exaggeration. "The Fellows or monks of my time were decent, easy men who supinely enjoyed the gifts of the founder. . . . From the toil of reading, writing, or thinking they had absolved their consciences." The verses in *The Oxford Sausage,* whether satirical, Bachanalian, or merely frivolous, confirm the judgement of Gibbon. Here is part of a picture of "the peaceful Fellows," probably from the pen of Warton himself:

> No chattering females crowd their social fire,
> No dread have they of discord and of strife,
> Unknown the names of Husband and of Sire,
> Unfelt the plagues of matrimonial life.
>
> Oft have they basked along the sunny walls;
> Oft have the benches bowed beneath their weight;
> How jocund are their looks when dinner calls!
> How smoke their cutlets on the crowded plate!
>
> O, let not Temperance too disdainful hear
> How long our Feasts, how long our Dinners last;
> Nor let the Fair with a contemptuous sneer
> On these unmarried men reflections cast!

Historians, such as Mr. Christopher Wordsworth, confirm the impression which these verses give. In the generation previous to *The Oxford Sausage,* the University, strongly Jacobite and disloyal to the House of Hanover, had been kept from stagnation by its political anxieties. But after 1745 slumber fell on Oxford. Professors were silent, college tutors grew inefficient, discipline was relaxed. The first Lord Malmesbury, writing of the very year when the *Sausage* appeared, describes the utter looseness of rule. Undergraduates could absent themselves when they pleased, and go off to town. His own tutor, "a worthy man," did not "concern himself with his pupils." This is the tone revealed throughout the verses of *The Oxford Sausage.*

But Thomas Warton himself was far removed from the lazy type of the college don, who

> to thoughtless ignorance a prey,
> Neglects to hold short dalliance with a book.

He was full of intellectual curiosity and creative energy. . . . (pp. 171-72)

Good-natured in the extreme, Warton shows his easy temper by printing in *The Oxford Sausage* a skit upon himself; or, perhaps, was that a blind—who knows? Michael Wodhull, of Brasenose, was the author of the "Ode to Criticism," which ridicules **"The Triumph of Isis,"** a serious poem which Warton had published in 1749. But Wodhull was a famous book-collector, whose library contained black-letter treasures which Warton may have been anxious to consult. He is not so kind to all contemporary antiquaries, since a parody of the ballad of "Chevy Chase" pokes fun at Browne Willis, whose books about the English cathedrals are still of value. . . . (pp. 173-74)

Light is thrown by various poems in the *Sausage* on the relaxations of University life. The gentlemen commoners, being men of fashion, affected riding, horse-racing, and driving. On Sundays they rode

> With hat new-cock'd, and newly laced,
> O'er mutton-chops and scanty wine
> At humble Dorchester to dine.

Cock-fighting in the pit in Holywell had been forbidden by the Vice-Chancellor, but was winked at elsewhere. There was some tennis for the richer and some billiards for the poorer men, but very little. Undergraduates, scarcely more than boys in those days, amused themselves with walks, skittles, and quoits. There is here a mention of rowing for pleasure:

> No more the wherry feels my stroke so true;
> At skittles in a grizzle can I play?
> Woodstock, farewell! and Wallingford adieu!
> Where many a scheme relieved the lingering day,

sighs the scholar promoted to the immobility of a Fellowship. . . . (p. 175)

The editor of *The Oxford Sausage* was but thirty-six years of age, but his ways were already settled, and it is notable that he consistently looks backward and not forward. He would not have sympathised with Lord Haldane's call to the heights, nor is there the slightest hint that he saw around him any revival of enthusiasm or earnestness. Warton had plenty of humanism, but it was not in the least idealistic, and in this respect he was abreast of his time and not a step in front of it. But he looked back with veneration on the isolated scholars who had preserved Oxford from reproach in the previous generation, and particularly on the wonderful and isolated figure of Thomas Hearne, the *architypographus* to the University, whom Warton can scarcely have known in person, since Hearne died, in his rooms in college, in 1735, when Warton was a child. The **"Epistle"** from Hearne is doubtless a mystification; in it the spirit of the great persecuted antiquary sarcastically congratulates Warton on the disfavour now shown by the Oxford fellows to every kind of research. I fail to grasp the allusion in the lines:

> Cruel as the mandate
> Of mitred priests, who Baskett late enjoined
> To throw aside the reverend letters black,
> And print Fast Prayers in modern type.

But it is part of a lamentation appropriately put in the mouth of Hearne, who, though no house in Oxford "had so rich a furniture" in his eyes as the Bodleian, was not merely dismissed from his post there as a punishment for his non-juring convictions, but was positively forbidden in the midst of his unrivalled investigations, to enter the Library. This was a shameful piece of tyranny. I find little reference in *The Oxford Sausage* to discord between Whigs and Jacobites, doubtless because after 1760 the Jacobite question ceased to be a burning one. . . . (pp. 176-77)

From a **"Panegyric on Oxford Ale,"** which I am disposed to attribute to the pen of Thomas Warton himself, I take a passage characteristic of English versification in 1764, modified as it had become by the influence of Thomas and Young, and equally descriptive of the duller side of college life:

> All powerful ALE! Thy sorrow-soothing sweets
> Oft I repeat in vacant afternoon,
> When tatter'd stockings crave my mending hand
> Not unexperienced; while the tedious toil
> Slides unregarded. Let the tender swain
> Each morn regale on nerve-relaxing Tea,
> Companion meet of languor-loving nymph:
> Be mine each morn, with eager appetite
> And hunger undissembled, to repair
> To friendly Buttery; there on smoking crust
> And foaming Ale to banquet unrestrained,
> Material breakfast!

Tea, at about a shilling an ounce, was still a luxury, not to be wasted on a serious meal like breakfast, but to be reserved for some special occasion when, as *Terræ Filius* tells us, the scholar had the privilege of sipping it, "after Prayers, with some celebrated toast." (pp. 177-78)

> *Sir Edmund Gosse, "The Oxford Sausage," in his* Selected Essays, *first series,* William Heinemann Ltd., *1928, pp. 169-78.*

Frances Schouler Miller (essay date 1938)

[*In the following excerpt, Miller discusses the influence of Warton's antiquarian studies on his poetry.*]

Thomas Warton was a poet-antiquary—perhaps the foremost of the eighteenth century—whose observations and editions, literary history and verse were dominated by the historic sense. . . . (p. 71)

What briefly is the historic sense? It is, perhaps, most significantly the realization that men of the past were unlike those of the present in manners and customs, in dress and in dwellings, in religious feeling and modes of thought, a realization usually accompanied by a sympathetic rather than a superior attitude toward the past. It is not simply the interest in the past that is almost as old as history itself, but the interest in the "differentness" of the past; not merely the critical sense of the historian that enables him to evaluate documents and to weigh evidence, but the ability of artist, play-producer or layman that enables him to judge an early work of art as a product of the times in which and of the taste for which it was created. (p. 71)

It is significant that no chronological division can be made between Warton's creative and critical activities. He was writing and publishing poetry simultaneously with his observations, histories, and editions. And all his writing was influenced by his historical sense. His criticism, for example, was less of the judicial type and more that of the literary historian. Rambling and digressive antiquary that he was, Thomas Warton had little interest in the fundamental problems of criticism. He had no theories to propound of the nature of tragedy, of the connection of life with literature, of the relation of art to morality, to utility, to truth. In discussing those "isms" to-day termed romanticism, classicism, realism, primitivism, and humanism, Warton made statements that are either contradictory or too general and indefinite to be attacked. He pointed out beauties rather than faults, he admired rather than analyzed. Interested in particulars, his forte was explaining individual passages and tracing parallels. His important use of the comparative method is more to his credit as literary historian than as critic.

It is, however, precisely because of his essentially historical approach to criticism that Warton's literary history is so interesting as an exhibition of the historic sense. Indeed, his writing a history of poetry at all is significant. Before the eighteenth century there had not even been an attempt. Two poets before Warton—Pope and Gray—had each drawn up a sketch of English poetry by the "schools" method, but neither went farther than the outline. That Warton wrote his as an historical development of poetry shows him in line with the growing eighteenth-century interest in the writing of histories; that he abandoned the "schools" method in favor of the freer "exertion of research" exhibits his open-mindedness as a scholar.

Similarly striking is the national, almost nationalistic, aspect of the *History of English Poetry.* Warton tried to begin his history with the birth of the English national character. That he began with the wrong period, the eleventh century, as more scholarly scholars from Ritson on have made clear, is immaterial for this discussion. What is significant is that Warton as an Englishman wrote a *History of English Poetry* and not a history of the poetry written in English. One doubts if Gray could have written his history of poetry with so much national feeling.

In a second way Warton's literary history exhibits the historic sense; it is essentially antiquarian. Like an antiquary, he usually ignores aesthetic values. Specifically, he shows great interest in literature as a picture of early manners and customs. . . . Such antiquarian interest has definite results. It means enlarging the definition of literature to include any document which, regardless of its aesthetic merits, tells us of the life and habits of our ancestors. In his Preface to the *History of English Poetry* Warton wrote:

> But a history of poetry . . . [besides showing the dawn of the national genius] . . . must be more especially productive of entertainment and utility. I mean, as it is an art, whose object is human society: as it has the peculiar merit, in its operations on that object, of faithfully recording the features of the times, and of preserving the most picturesque and expressive representations of manners: and, because the first monuments of composition in every nation are those of the poet, as it possesses the additional advantage of transmitting to posterity genuine delineations of life in its simplest stages. Let me add, that anecdotes of the rudiments of a favourite art will always be particularly pleasing.

This constitutes an oblique thrust at absolute criticism, which judges literature solely by its aesthetic merits and not by its historical values. At all events, such a statement is not congruent with the narrower neo-classical conception of literature. Not that Warton was particularly conscious of the implications. If we take his Preface literally, he, too, was more interested in "finished productions" of poetry, by which he undoubtedly meant the polished literature of the eighteenth century, than in the rudimentary verse picturing a more primitive society.

Warton's historic sense enabled him to be tolerant of anachronisms. That is, his knowledge of the past helped him to detect flaws in the historical coloring of a piece of literature, while his historic sense at the same time made him realize that the naïve handling of the classical past constituted part of the charm and flavor of medieval literature. . . . (pp. 72-5)

But Warton's historic sense had a more vital effect on his methods: his knowledge of past times enabled him to use non-literary material in treating the history of literature. In the *Observations* he learned to show the relationship of what the poet sees to what he feels and writes, in other words, the effect of environment. The "source material" of history (contemporary chronicles, travel literature, and letters) he used to explain everything from Spenser's gardens and interior decorations to his choice of allegorical personages and the reality of chivalric conventions in the

Faerie Queen. Again, as a proof of the popularity of certain motifs in romance, Warton uses what might be called the "archeological" evidence of tapestries. The novelty of Warton's method here should not be underestimated; this is not the more common comparison of poetry and of painting or the realization of "the necessary connection between literary composition and the arts of design." (p. 76)

The most important critical result of Warton's historic sense is his historical point of view. The contention of Miss Rinaker, that Thomas Warton was the first to use the historical point of view, Dr. Sheppard and Dr. Havens have refuted. Dr. Sheppard has shown that the historical viewpoint was a recognized method of criticism long before Thomas Warton busied himself with the *Fairie Queen* or made hit-or-miss translations of Middle English manuscripts; Dr. Havens has demonstrated that Warton in applying the historical point of view to his criticism of the plan and structure of the *Fairie Queen* was not at all consistent [see excerpt dated 1928]. With all Warton's limitations as a historical critic adequately discussed by these two scholars, it remains to point out that Warton practically stumbled on the historical point of view. As a comparison of the two editions of the *Observations* will show, Warton read more widely in Spenser's predecessors and contemporaries between the first edition of 1754 and the second of 1762. In the latter Warton constantly explains Spenser's choice of incidents as indebtedness to the general romance tradition rather than to specific authors. Especially impressed by the persistent popularity of Arthurian romance in Elizabethan England, he explained that it had influenced Spenser's subject matter far more than the eighteenth century realized. His "track of reading" had broadened in another direction too—that of Spenser's Italian models. By 1762 Warton could recognize a reference to the "pearls" and "corals" of a lady's teeth and lips as common to the "italian poets" rather than a direct borrowing from Ariosto. Although he could by no means approve whole-heartedly the plan and conduct of the *Faerie Queen* and perhaps even wished Spenser's bosom brought "back to truth again," he realized—and made his readers realize—that the example of Tasso and Ariosto had influenced Spenser's method tremendously.

Having widened his "track of reading," Warton began to formulate certain doctrines of literary history. It is necessary, he insisted, to study a poet's predecessors and contemporaries in order to understand the poet himself.

> And here it may be observ'd, that in criticising upon Milton, Johnson, Spenser, and some other of our elder poets, not only a competent knowledge of all antient classical learning is requisite, but also an acquaintance with those books, which, though now forgotten and lost, were yet in repute about the time in which each author respectively wrote, and which it is most likely he had red.

Warton practised what he preached with especial thoroughness in his edition of Milton's *Minor Poems,* the footnotes to which are chiefly citations of parallel passages from Milton's less-known predecessors and contemporaries. By the application of this doctrine, too, he showed the relationship between the pastoral portions of the *Fairie Queen* and Sidney's *Arcadia,*—in fact, the whole Elizabethan pastoral fashion. Now it was the application of this idea that so impressed Warton's contemporaries. Dr. Johnson wrote a well-known letter praising the method; an unknown correspondent commended it in a letter to the *Gentleman's Magazine* published earlier than Johnson's; Hurd also praised the method. These letters, incidentally, throw light on Miss Rinaker's contention that Thomas Warton was one of the original exponents of the historical point of view. It is not the viewpoint itself that Warton's contemporaries praise as new but the application of the historical point of view to the methods of literary scholarship. Not the critical theorists but the practical editors and scholars applauded.

There is, indeed, little doubt that Warton enjoyed finding out parallels or that he became increasingly absorbed in the "manners and customs" aspect of history and of literature. Soon he discovered for himself the theory of milieu. This theory, closely allied to his application of the historical point of view to scholarship, postulates that a poet should be studied in relation to his environment and his era, not in a critical vacuum. For example, Warton explained the "platonic cast" of Spenser's "Hymns of Heavenly Love and Beauty" by the interest of Spenser's friend Sidney and others in the system of Plato. More concretely, the "emblematical personages" of Elizabethan shows and spectacles tempted Spenser, said he, as much as the example of Ariosto to write an allegorical poem. . . . His most general statement of the theory of milieu follows:

> In reading the works of a poet who lived in a remote age, it is necessary that we should look back upon the customs and manners which prevailed in that age. We should endeavour to place ourselves in the writer's situation and circumstances. Hence we shall become better enabled to discover, how his turn of thinking, and manner of composing, were influenced by familiar appearances and established objects, which are utterly different from those with which we are at present surrounded. For want of this caution, too many readers view the knights and damsels, the tournaments and enchantments, of Spenser, with modern eyes; never considering that the encounters of chivalry subsisted in our author's age; that romances were then most eagerly and universally studied; and that consequently Spenser, from the fashion of the times, was induced to undertake a recital of chivalrous achievements, and to become, in short, a ROMANTIC POET.

This passage also shows that the historical point of view as exemplified in Warton was not cold theory but practice. His was a reconstruction of the past requiring two faculties: accurate historical knowledge and sympathetic imagination. This theory is also the converse of his recognition that any writing is literature that gives us a picture of old manners. Old literature helps one to a knowledge of "ancient manners" and a knowledge of "ancient manners" is necessary to the understanding of the elder poets. Perhaps then it was his original antiquary's interest in medieval poetry as a reflection of medieval life that enabled Warton to state his theory of milieu.

For the historical point of view and its corollary, the theory of milieu, Warton had still another use. By these valuable critical principles he could justify what he liked but felt contemporary taste would not approve, for example, Spenser's imaginative but unorthodox use of ancient fable and mythology. Warton was not entirely satisfied with the plan of the *Faerie Queen*, yet his understanding of Spen-

ser's contemporaries and era prevented a wholesale condemnation. Finally in the *History of English Poetry* he used the historical point of view to explain what he thoroughly disapproved, apparent irreverence and obscenity.

> It is in an enlightened age only that subjects of scripture history would be supported with proper dignity. But then an enlightened age would not have chosen such subjects for theatrical exhibition. It is certain that our ancestors intended no sort of impiety by these monstrous and unnatural mixtures. . . . They had no just idea of decorum, consequently but little sense of the ridiculous: what appears to us to be the highest burlesque, on them would have made no sort of impression.

Or again:

> Not that I mean to palliate the levity of the story ["The Miller's Tale"], which was most probably chosen by Chaucer in compliance with the prevailing manners of an unpolished age, and agreeable to ideas of festivity not always the most delicate and refined. Chaucer abounds in liberties of this kind, and this must be his apology.

Warton, in short, used the historical point of view not only to explain what he did like, but to explain away what he did not like.

In spite of his occasional cavalier references to antiquaries, Thomas Warton was very much of an antiquarian. What is more, he defended antiquarianism—again by the historical point of view. This valuable critical principle served not only to justify the ways of Spenser by the analogy of ancient literature but to justify the by-ways of Thomas Warton's interest in old manners and customs. At the end of the second edition of the *Observations* he wrote:

> Mechanical critics will perhaps be disgusted at the liberties I have taken in introducing so many anecdotes of ancient chivalry. But my subject required frequent proofs of this sort. Nor could I be persuaded that such enquiries were, in other respects, either useless or ridiculous; as they tended at least, to illustrate an institution of no frivolous or indifferent nature. . . .
>
> I am still further to hope, that, together with other specimens of obsolete literature in general, hinted at before, the many references I have made, in particular to Romances, the necessary appendage of ancient Chivalry, will also plead their pardon. For however monstrous and unnatural these compositions may appear to this age of reason and refinement, they merit more attention than the world is willing to bestow. They preserve many curious historical facts, and throw considerable light on the nature of the feudal system. *They are the pictures of antient usages and customs; and represent the manners, genius, and character of our ancestors.*

Finally, Warton uses the assumption that it is necessary to study contemporary authors and customs to illustrate an old English classic (in short, the historical point of view) in defense of scholarship. In a vigorous passage added in the second edition of the *Observations* he declared:

> Pope laughs at Theobald for giving us, in his edition of Shakespeare, a sample of
>
> "———All such READING *as was never read.*"

But these strange and ridiculous books which Theobald quoted, were unluckily the very books which Shakespeare himself had studied; the knowledge of which enabled that useful editor to explain so many difficult allusions and obsolete customs in his poet, which otherwise could never have been understood. For want of this sort of literature, Pope tells us that the DREADFUL SAGITTARY in *Troilus and Cressida,* signifies Teucer, so celebrated for his skill in archery. Had he deigned to consult an old history, called the DESTRUCTION OF TROY, a book which was the delight of Shakespeare and of his age, he would have found that this formidable archer, was no other than an imaginary beast, which the grecian army brought against Troy. *If Shakespeare is worth reading, he is worth explaining; and the researches used for so valuable and elegant a purpose, merit the thanks of genius and candour, not the satire of prejudice and ignorance.* That labour, which so essentially contributes to the service of true taste, deserves a more honourable repository than The TEMPLE of DULNESS.

In sum, Warton's use of the historical point of view was pragmatic and "occasional." That is, he used it when he wanted to defend the plan of the *Faerie Queen,* to account for the seeming irreverence of his ancestors, or to justify the antiquarian nature of his own *Observations.* Since its use resulted less from theoretical conviction than from practical need, there is small wonder that at times he was inconsistent.

Self-evident as is Warton's love for antiquity, his conception of the past needs further discussion. For historical facts are more or less constant, but the selection of facts or generalizations on the basis of facts are variables, and the variations are wide from person to person and generation to generation. Warton, like most men of his time, believed in the progressive development of poetry; more questionable is the thoroughness with which he thought out his beliefs. Indubitably he found popery a more poetical religion than the reformed. . . . He nearly berates Milton for his bitterness towards Catholicism, a bitterness that Warton disliked almost as much as the poet's republicanism. "No man was ever so disqualified to turn puritan," he wrote, because Puritanism meant turning even farther away from the more poetic Catholicism. (This, a personal reaction of Warton, was not typical of the age; indeed, his brother Joseph thought him rather hard on Milton.) However condescendingly he might speak of its crudeness and irrationality, Warton undoubtedly found the whole medieval period more poetical than enlightened "modern" times.

Nevertheless his common sense enabled him to avoid some of the pitfalls into which an indiscreet apologist for the past is likely to slip. Much as he hated to relinquish belief in the authenticity of Rowley's poems, Warton realized the dangers in valuing the old simply because it is old. Accordingly doubting Thomas declared of dubious Thomas:

> It is with regret that I find myself obliged to pronounce Rowlie's poems to be spurious. Antient remains of English poetry, unexpectedly discovered, and fortunately rescued from a long oblivion, are contemplated with a degree of fond enthusiasm: exclusive of any real or intrinsic excellence, they afford those pleasures, arising from the idea of antiquity, which deeply interest the imagination. With

these pleasures we are unwilling to part. But there is a more solid satisfaction, resulting from the detection of artifice and imposture.

By insisting that Spenser painted "real manners" and that the moving castles of romance were founded on the instruments of war used in sieges during the Crusades, Warton avoided the fairy-tale approach to the past made by many. On the other hand, he did show decided preference for the more "romantic" aspects of early English literature and life. Knightly legend, chivalry, and the gorgeous rather than the grim aspects of feudalism fascinated him; he paid little attention to realistic fabliau and satire, to bourgeois commerce and city life. One would never gather, for example, from the emphasis in Warton's criticism of Chaucer, especially in the *Observations,* that Chaucer was a poet of realism who depicted the manners not only of the court but of all classes. Such, then, was Warton's attitude towards the past: now poetic, now prosiac, now regretful of its "pastness," now superior to its crudities.

His poetry also was influenced by his early historical interests; apparently an early visit to Windsor Castle was particularly influential on the future poet. . . . (pp. 77-84)

A second influence, apparently, was home training. Whatever else was included in the diet and catechism of the Warton family, the two boys were early given an appreciation of Gothic architecture and the poetry of Spenser and Milton. From the younger Thomas Warton's approach to the poetry of Milton and his master Spenser, one might judge that these two loves may very well have reinforced his love for old poets, romances, and architecture. Perhaps long residence at Oxford helped to develop Warton's historic sense. There he lived with Gothic buildings; there he saw the survival of medieval customs; possibly the patrons and "famous alumni," especially Alfred and the Black Prince, influenced the subject matter of his poetry. His visits to his brother Joseph while the latter was headmaster of the school at Winchester, Alfred's capital and home of the Table Round, produced the sonnet on Arthur's Round Table and gave Warton access to old records utilized in the *History of English Poetry.* (pp. 84-5)

How did Warton handle the historical subject matter he had chosen? One remembers Ker's statement that "the Middle Ages have influenced modern literature more strongly through their architecture than through their poems." Certainly in Warton's poetry there is much—and very good—exact description of architecture. He had his eye on the object when he wrote of the "thousand torches" illuminating "the vaulted roof " and "the lofty-window'd hall" hung with "storied tapestry" of Cilgarran Castle or "the fretted nook," "the clustur'd column," and "windows, rang'd in long array" of Vale Royal Abbey. Moreover, architectural, or at least archaeological, remains are frequent starting points for Warton's reconstruction of the past. Of the former type are the ode on Vale Royal Abbey and the verses on the birth of the Prince of Wales (which begin with Windsor Castle); of the latter, the sonnets on Stonehenge and King Arthur's Round Table. It is just as evident, however, that Warton is capable of giving the manners and customs, interiors and costumes belonging to the life lived in such abbeys or castles; he wrote as confidently of Windsor Castle's "proud Tilts, unmatch'd for hardy deeds" as of the Castle itself, or of the Vale Royal Abbey, where

the solitary minstrel came
An honour'd guest, while the grim evening sky
Hung lowering, and around the social flame
Tun'd his bold harp to tales of chivalry.

This ability to describe the life in the castle, though stimulated originally by first-hand experience of architectural "reliques," was probably derived in part from Warton's reading of romance. For example, a note of Mant à propos of

The golden fans, that o'er the turrets strown,
Quick-glancing to the sun, wild music made

shows that Warton in *The History of English Poetry* comments several times on such fans. In **"The Crusade"** Warton uses the "moving castles" which in *The History of English Poetry* he insisted were not originally fictions of romantic poets but actual engines of war. Thus it is entirely possible that Warton's reading of old literature colored the architectural details derived from first-hand observation. In other words, Thomas Warton's historical poetry results not merely from his interest in Gothic architecture but from his literary studies as well.

Whatever the source of his inspiration and background, Warton's portrayal of medieval people while not exact, is not so completely unconvincing as is that of some eighteenth-century plays dealing with the Middle Ages. King Richard on a Crusade, the bard who sings of Arthur's grave, and the hermit are all sufficiently medieval not to be mistaken for moderns. Warton, however, never quite caught the fanaticism that lay behind two such different phases of religious feeling as the Crusades and extreme asceticism or the equal fervor of the Arthurian belief. But Warton, after all, whether dealing with nature or the past, with himself or others, was hardly a psychological poet.

In the third place, Warton demonstrates real ability to show in the same poem two "levels" of antiquity, the period of Henry II and that of King Arthur, an ability all the more surprising in view of the difficulty many of his contemporaries experienced in portraying accurately even one level of antiquity. To put it differently, Warton could show both past perfect and pluperfect when others could scarcely show the simple past tense. In **"The Grave of King Arthur"** Warton suggests the interval of time by references to the "ruthless Dane" and Henry's "Norman pike-men" as well as by direct mention of time and oblivion; he contrasts the time-setting of Henry's stately feast and meditated conquest of Ireland with Arthur bleeding beneath a Saxon spear and encountering a "paynim foe" admidst wild scenery reminiscent of "The Bard"—a far more difficult task than simple "progress pieces" such as **"Ode XIX"** on poetry or the **"Ode for Music."**

To the past, or occasionally "pasts," Warton makes several approaches. The first, the retrospective, he uses in the **"Ode on Vale Royal Abbey,"** where, by repeopling a ruined monastery, Warton creates a picture of monastic life in by-gone days. The second approach, the comparison of past with present or of present to past, appears in his laureate odes and, somewhat less obviously, in the complimentary poems on the marriage of the king and the birth of the prince. Finally, Warton exhibits the "historic-dramatic imagination." In his **"Inscription on a Hermitage"** the poet speaks directly in the person of the hermit; in **"The Crusade"** and **"The Grave of King Arthur"** the

poem, without any preliminaries, assumes the time and place of action as silently as a play.

Warton's poetical handling of historical material continues to be notable throughout his work. Historical subject matter is found in his earliest known poem, the adolescent **"Pleasures of Melancholy,"** and continues through his laureate odes. It appears in a nature poem, the **"Ode on the Approach of Summer."** Indeed, much as others use nature for their figures of speech, Warton uses historical tropes. Great imaginative power may not lie in such passages as:

Again the lords of Albion's cultur'd plains
March the firm leaders of their faithful swains;
As erst stout archers, from the farm or fold,
Flam'd in the van of many a baron bold.

or

Firm as the castle's feudal roof,
Stands the Briton's social home.

but they are certainly historical. Clio, in short, was the Muse who dictated, if not inspired, much of Warton's poetry.

In poetry as in criticism, Warton's attitude toward the past is not that of an extremist or fanatic. Although he loves ancient architecture and old manners, his common sense tells him he is better off in the world of to-day. Warton, indeed, suffered from a conflict similar to the eighteenth-century dilemma diagnosed by Dr. Havens. Not only did Warton waver between absolute and historical criticism, between Grecian and Gothic architecture; he also could not make up his mind about the medieval past. Sometimes, as he thinks of the *Faerie Queen,* he grieves "that envious Time so soon o'er the lov'd strain had cast his dim disguise"; sometimes he sees through his own illusion "of fair images of ancient things" that "the captive bard's obsequious mind beguiles," and dispels this illusion by the use of "severer Reason." . . . (pp. 86-9)

Warton's historical poetry, then, is frequent, plentiful, though not always consistent. Is it original? Mant states flatly:

In one department he is not only unequalled, but original and unprecedented: I mean in applying to modern poetry the embellishment of Gothic manners and Gothic arts; the tournaments and festivals, the poetry, music, painting, and architecture of "elder days."

Warton's originality is relative but real. In the first place, Elizabethan topographical poetry, such as Drayton's *Polyolbion,* was definitely historical. So was Daniel's *Civil Wars.* Yet these minor Renaissance epics had died out, never to be revived. Besides, Mant refers to modern poetry, by which he meant no more than the eighteenth century, perhaps only the latter half. But even within this century Pope had used historical material. In "Windsor Forest" he wrote:

Oh wouldst thou sing what heroes Windsor bore,
What Kings first breathed upon her winding shore,
Or raise old warriors, whose ador'd remains,
In weeping vaults her hallow'd earth contains!
With Edward's acts adorn the shining page,
Stretch his long triumphs down thro' every age,
Draw monarch's chain'd, and Cressi's glorious field,

The lilies blazing on the regal shield. . . .
Let softer strains ill-fated Henry mourn,
And palms eternal flourish round his urn.
Here o'er the martyr-king the marble weeps,
And, fast beside him, once-fear'd Edward sleeps.

Now in his poem **"On the Marriage of the King"** Warton catalogued for Queen Charlotte's benefit the historical attractions of England:

Lo! this the land, where Freedom's sacred rage
Has glow'd untam'd through many a martial age.
Here patriot Alfred, stain'd with Danish blood,
Rear'd on one base the king's the people's good:
Here Henry's archers fram'd the stubborn bow,
That laid Alanzon's haughty helmet low . . .
Here Chivalry, stern school of valour old,
Her noblest feats of knightly fame enroll'd;
Heroic champions caught the clarion's call,
And throng'd the feast in Edward's banner'd hall.

In the earlier and greater poet, one notices the absence of localizing details; in Warton, their presence. He writes of the bows of Agincourt, chivalric training, and, subsequently, Druid songs, "cunning Bards at ancient banquets" who "sung of paynim foes defied, and trophies hung," Spenser who "tun'd his mystic minstrelsy, and dress'd in fairy robes a Queen like Thee." Undoubtedly Charlotte would have learned more specific history from Warton's poem than from Pope's. The chief difference here between Warton's work and Pope's is not in subject matter but in the "ancient manners" that Warton was the first to use so freely. Nor could his contemporaries really contest his claim to originality. Gray did not exploit the same field of history, but confined himself to the more primitive Celtic and Norse fields, barely touching the Elizabethan in his humorous "Long Story." Besides, what in Gray could be described as "Gothic manners?" Moreover, his friends and Warton himself were conscious of the originality of his historical poetry. In 1762 Percy wrote Warton a letter with this important postscript:

That pleasing cast of antiquity, which distinguished those beautiful poems of yours, in ye late Collection of Oxford Verses, & which gave them so great an advantage over all others, would be finely adapted to such an undertaking; And, let me add, nothing would fix your fame upon a more solid basis, or be more likely to captivate the attention of the public, which seems to loathe all the common forms of poetry; & requires some new species to quicken its pall'd appetite.

To this Warton replied:

I thank you for thinking me qualified to complete Chaucer's *Squiers Tale.* . . . You are certainly right in thinking that the Public ought to have their Attention called to Poetry in new forms; To Poetry endued with new Manners and new Images.

This, one of Warton's few symptoms of revolt, comes early and precedes the writing of most of his historical verse. Much later, indeed, Warton wrote, in his rather ambiguous fashion, of one of Milton's Latin poems:

And here, more particularly in displaying the glories of heaven . . . his fancy, to say nothing of the apocalypse, was aided and enriched with descriptions in romance. By the way, this sort of imagery,

so much admired in Milton, is much more practicable than many readers seem to suppose.

Is this to be interpreted that Warton was campaigning for the introduction of the imagery of romance, such as he himself used? Unmentioned by Mant, another aspect of Warton's originality as an antiquarian poet is his defence in the already-quoted **"Sonnet written in a blank Leaf of Dugdale's Monasticon"** of antiquarianism.

In summation, Warton's literary history is closely connected with his creative work. Both poetry and prose show the same enthusiasm for the past, treat the same periods, reveal the same interests: courtly legend, the Crusades, king rather than peasant and high life rather than low, the poetical and picturesque side of popery, and especially "ancient manners" and architectural remains. His poetry as well as his prose deals with the literary life of the past: the minstrels and Chaucer, Spenser and Shakespeare.

Moreover, Warton's approach to the past is fairly realistic. His insistence on the reality of Spenser's "manners" or of the moving castles of romance is paralleled by his relatively realistic treatment of the past in poetry. Although he did choose to describe the more picturesque, gorgeous, and "romantic" aspect of the past, he wrote of what actually did or could take place in by-gone times. In his verse there are no supernatural transactions as in "Christabel" or eerie transitions as in "The Admiral's Ghost," where Noyes suggests that Nelson was Drake come back to save England. In **"The Grave of King Arthur"** the supernatural disappearance of Arthur is refuted; a story of normal death and burial is substituted. Fairies, indeed, would have been no anachronism in medieval verse, but Warton keeps his feet on the earth and off fairy ground. Nor does he invent any medieval stories; his "real events" all take place in historic castles. In short, Warton shows very little imaginary, though plenty of imaginative, reconstruction of an actual past.

Finally, Warton's verse and prose both reveal a "medieval conflict." In both he shows that the present is more enlightened and reasonable, less superstitious and primitive than the past, yet he loves withal the religion, manners and literature of by-gone times. It is not for us to psychoanalyse Thomas Warton and decide how or whether he resolved this conflict, or whether he should have done so, but only to record this conflict of enlightened reasonableness with a love of the past as another product of his very acute historic sense. (pp. 89-92)

> *Frances Schouler Miller, "The Historic Sense of Thomas Warton, Junior," in ELH, Vol. 5, No. 1, March, 1938, pp. 71-92.*

Hoxie Neale Fairchild　(essay date 1942)

[*Fairchild was an American educator and literary historian. In the excerpt below, he discusses the influence of medieval Catholicism and superstition on Warton's poetic works.*]

Thomas Warton the younger (1728-1790) shared many of his brother's tastes, but the two men are easily distinguishable. Compared with Joseph, Thomas is more of a scholar and less of a critic; less "poetical" but a better poet; less religious but a stronger Churchman; more concerned with the Middle Ages and less with "simple" nature; and despite his cultivation of preromantic fashions, more in harmony with the nonsentimental trends surviving in the Johnson circle. He was partly a wit and completely a don; very convivial and not averse to low company. Perhaps his rough exterior concealed a heart of gold, or perhaps he was hard to the core—the point is disputed. (p. 345)

This Troy professor was no Dr. Dryasdust. His researches were carried on with real emotional enthusiasm and were closely related to his poetry. Being a scholar, he was a specialist even in his sentimentalism. He lived by his feelings, but his feelings drew him toward the glamorous past. When he writes a retirement piece in his brother's favorite vein he imagines himself as a learned hermit:

> At eve, within yon studious nook,
> I ope my brass-embossed book,
> Pourtray'd with many a holy deed
> Of martyrs, crown'd with heavenly meed:
> Then, as my taper waxes dim,
> Chant, ere I sleep, my measur'd hymn;
> And at the close, the gleams behold
> Of parting wings bedropt with gold.

In those half-lyrical, half narrative poems which so clearly foretoken the verse of Scott, Warton responds, at least dramatically, to the spirit of Christian chivalry:

> O'er the sepulchre profound,
> E'en now with arching sculptures crown'd,
> He plans the chantry's choral shrine,
> The daily dirge, and rites divine.

Blondel and his royal master join in singing:

> Fearless we climb this hostile shore!
> And thou, the sepulchre of God!
> By mocking pagans rudely trod,
> Bereft of every awful rite,
> And quench'd thy lamps that beam'd so bright;
> For thee, from Britain's distant coast,
> Lo, Richard leads his faithful host!

The bearing of such passages on Warton's personal religion is not easy to determine. Burrowing through his folios, this bookworm of sensibility came face to face with medieval Catholicism. He never quite knew what to make of it. Nothing in his type of High Churchmanship would give him any real sympathy with it, but something in its flavor appealed to his imagination. It was inseparable from those qualities in poetry and architecture that stirred him most deeply. Repugnant to reason, it was delightful to fancy. And so, paying no heed whatever to the doctrines of Catholicism, he obtained a quasi-religious thrill from its superficial trappings. One of the choicest **"Pleasures of Melancholy"** is to walk at night through the aisles of a ruined abbey,

> where mused of old
> The cloyster'd brothers: thro' the gloomy void
> That far extends beyond their ample arch
> As on I pace, religious horrour wraps
> My soul in dread repose.

Apparently he sees no difference between this pleasantly superstitious fear and the feelings of the monks themselves. He does not allow such moods to interfere with his devotion to truth and liberty, for the dedication of the Radcliffe Camera in 1749 inspires these lines in praise of Oxford dons of the preceding century:

> And see yon sapient train! with liberal aim,
> 'Twas theirs new plans of liberty to frame;
> And on the Gothic gloom of slavish sway
> To shed the dawn of intellectual day.

But Gothic gloom is very effective aesthetically, and Warton has no religion which can firmly be separated from "fancy." The conflict emerges clearly in the **"Verses on Sir Joshua Reynolds' Painted Window"**:

> But chief, enraptur'd have I lov'd to roam,
> A lingering votary, the vaulted dome,
> Where the tall shafts, that mount in massy pride,
> Their mingling branches shoot from side to side;
>
> . . . . .
>
> Where Superstition with capricious hand
> In many a maze the wreathed window plann'd,
> With hues romantic ting'd the gorgeous pane,
> To fill with holy light the wondrous fane.

Gothic architecture is indubitably romantic; but is it holy or superstitious? And what is the difference? On such questions it is unprofitable to press Warton very hard.

In this extremely polite epistle he recants his Gothic tastes, for Sir Joshua's window has won him over to the bright, explicit reasonableness of classicism:

> Sudden, the sombrous imagery is fled,
> Which late my visionary rapture fed:
> Thy powerful hand has broke the Gothic chain,
> And brought my bosom home to truth again;
> To truth, by no peculiar taste confin'd,
> Whose universal pattern strikes mankind;
> To truth, whose bold and unresisted claim
> Checks frail caprice, and fashion's fickle claim;
> To truth, whose charms deception's magic quell,
> And bind coy Fancy in a stronger spell.

This conversion, however, is not permanent. The old conflict between head and heart reappears when Warton sees the remains of Vale-Royal Abbey. He cannot help loving the place:

> For though the sorceress, Superstition blind,
> Amid the pomp of dreadful sacrifice,
> O'er the dim roofs, to cheat the tranced mind,
> Oft bade her visionary gleams arise,

the abbey was the abode of hospitality, pious contemplation, and, above all, art and learning:

> Here ancient Art her daedal fancies play'd
> In the quaint mazes of the crisped roof;
> In mellow glooms the speaking pane array'd,
> And rang'd the cluster'd column, massy proof.
>
> Here Learning, guarded from a barbarous age,
> Hover'd awhile, nor dar'd attempt the day;
> But patient trac'd upon the pictur'd page
> The holy legend, or heroic lay.

Here too the minstrel came and "Tun'd his bold harp to tales of chivalry." But although "th'ingenuous Muse" must be forgiven for these picturesque recollections,

> Severer Reason forms far other views,
> And scans the scene with philosophic ken.
>
> From these deserted domes new glories rise;
> More useful institutes, adorning man,
> Manners enlarg'd, and new civilities,

On fresh foundations build the social plan.

Science, on ampler plume, a bolder flight
Essays, escap'd from Superstition's shrine;
While freed Religion, like primeval light
Bursting from chaos, spreads her warmth divine.

The poems of Thomas Warton, then, in no way controvert the thesis that eighteenth-century sentimentalism is the child of Protestantism. One may legitimately argue that such affection for the Middle Ages, despite its waverings and inconsistencies, ultimately helped to break down anti-Catholic prejudices and thus paved the way for the Oxford Movement. But to imagine an interview between Warton and a group of nineteenth-century Tractarians is to be convinced that there is nothing essentially Catholic in his medievalism. He would repudiate any attempt to trace a connection between his antienthusiastic High Churchmanship and his fondness for stained glass. The former belongs to reason, he would say; the latter to fancy. His Protestantism has reached so nearly complete a state of liquefaction that he can, though not without uneasiness, sentimentalize the externals of a religion in which he has no serious belief. (p. 345-49)

> *Hoxie Neale Fairchild, "Aesthetic Sentimentalists," in his* Religious Trends in English Poetry, 1740-1780: Religious Sentimentalism in the Age of Johnson, Vol. II, *Columbia University Press, 1942, pp. 338-64.*

A. M. Kinghorn   (essay date 1963)

[*Kinghorn is an English educator and literary historian. In the following excerpt, he examines the content of* The History of English Poetry, *commenting on Warton's critical perception.*]

The first historian of English poetry, properly speaking, was Thomas Warton, who combined an immense erudition with a classical unity of theme and a singleness of purpose, and brought these qualities to bear on the task of writing literary history.

Warton had prepared the ground for twenty years and his *Observations on the Faerie Queene of Spenser* may be taken as a preliminary work revealing his methods. His object was to write the *History of English Poetry* in such a way that the early poets would gain critical respectability and would thereby be considered worthy of further research into their works and times. Warton did not follow the plan of Pope and Gray which, by insisting upon classification into literary types, neglected historical development; instead, he approached his subject chronologically, and tried to show how one age gradually and imperceptibly melted into another. Occasionally he drew attention to the relationships between English and Continental European literature. It is a pity that his *History* was not continued as far as the eighteenth century, for then Warton's readers might have been encouraged to consider the links between contemporary literature and the literary traditions up to that time. This, in turn, might have compelled them to set a truer value on the works of their own age. As it was, the periodical reviewers, though friendly, interpreted Warton's work as a tracing of the emergence of English poetry from barbarism to their own refined times and concluded that this demonstrated the superiority of con-

temporary writings. Warton himself rarely forgot that he was an Augustan despite his love for the romantic past and he invariably respected the tastes of his century by curbing his antiquarian enthusiasms in accordance with the peculiar smug resistance characteristic of the 'literati'. In the Preface to the first volume of the *History,* for example, we encounter a remark which we would not normally expect from a professed literary historian.

> We look back on the savage condition of our ancestors with the triumph of superiority; we are pleased to mark the steps by which we have been raised from rudeness to elegance: and our reflections on this subject are accompanied with a conscious pride, arising in great measure from a tacit comparison of the infinite disproportion between the feeble efforts of remote ages, and our present improvements in knowledge.

It is hardly likely that Warton subscribed to the full and boundless conceit of this statement, but his mission was to some extent that of a populariser and so he probably deemed it politic to make his own deferential concession to the complacency of an age of 'bon ton'. Few English scholars, let alone popular readers, would have admitted at that time that their own early literature was part of a rich heritage or that it possessed any merit as literature.

Warton's task was a formidable one of monumental pioneering, for he had to tap original sources in what Thomas Tyrwhitt, whose editing of the *Canterbury Tales* proceeded side by side with Warton's historical researches, referred to as 'those sepulchres of MSS, which, by courtesy, are called libraries'. His method was to select one or more poems from each writer whom he introduced and to give generous quotations from them. When appropriate he would provide a summary or paraphrase of one or two major works with the addition of his own commentary. There is as much quotation as text in the *History* and the latter is frequently irrelevant. Warton could not help digressing, particularly in the direction of the old romances, but his digressions were useful in that they showed the eighteenth century that the Middle English period was not an unlearned chaos, and that hitherto isolated and apparently unconnected facts were really closely connected and formed units of a coherent pattern. His work has been severely castigated by modern historiographers on the ground that it is formless and more of a reference work than a history but, since much of the material presented was unavailable elsewhere at the time, the fullness of his quotations is defensible. Many of the works from which he took extracts were only accessible in the form of original MSS or scarce prints.

The first volume was dominated not by Old English literature but by Chaucer. Warton, who was hostile to the Germanic alliterative tradition, omitted the Anglo-Saxon period entirely and began at the twelfth century because, as he claimed, Anglo-Saxon literature was not an integral part of English literature and nothing of poetical value remained from that time. As a substitute for this omission, he inserted two *Dissertations,* in the first of which, called **'Of the Origin of Romantic Fiction in Europe'**, he accepted Warburton's theory tracing the romances to an Arabian origin. The old romances were Warton's delight, and his discussion of them, though often ill-informed and generally oversimplified, was lingering and full. The metrical romances, along with the popular ballads, represented two kinds of early literature which had an appeal for an audience outside the more scholarly circles at which the *History* as a whole was aimed, so that it is likely that Warton was indulging both himself and the popular reader by including an essay on this subject. The second dissertation, **'On the Introduction of Learning into England'** serves to reveal Warton's belief that there was little or no learning in England until after the Conquest had dispelled the mists of ignorance which characterised the 'Dark Ages'. It is a brief sketch, but nothing more, of the standard eighteenth-century view of the period.

Most Chaucer criticism before Warton, Dryden's excepted, was patronising, and Warton did not really advance much on this attitude, declaring himself surprised when he had to praise Chaucer, a true poet whose faults were attributable to 'an age which compelled him to struggle with a barbarous language and a national want of taste'. He obviously regarded Chaucer as fortunate in having French and Italian models to work from and imitate, though he does admit the existence of a national genius for characterisation, a literary quality which eighteenth-century critics never tired of discussing. In general, Warton's account of Chaucer's poetry betrays its author as a man nurtured on Renaissance humanism who had no understanding of literary forms other than the Classical ones. The result of this prejudice was a denial that mediaeval literature had any kind of pattern imposed on it; the 'prolixity' and 'want of art and method' which Warton found in Dante were, as far as he was concerned, the inevitable outcome of a neglect of Classical forms and a reliance on a 'Gothic' or extravagant imagination. Chaucer's 'good sense and judgment' is, in Warton's view, continually engaged in disciplining his 'strong imagination, unacquainted with selection and arrangement of images'. What Warton has to say about Chaucer's adaptations from Boccaccio is therefore not particularly enlightening even on the critical standards of the eighteenth century. His discussion of the *Canterbury Tales* assumes that, since 'the figures are all British', Chaucer has at last been emancipated from the bad effects of his models, and is now writing in his own poetical personality, of which the chief talent is that of humour, 'unassisted and unalloyed'. The *Canterbury Tales* reveal for Warton surprisingly modern 'talents for satire and for observation on life; qualities which usually exert themselves at more civilised periods'. Yet he refers to the *Tales* as 'these curious and valuable remains' before going on to outline the characterisation of a dozen of Chaucer's pilgrims; it is clear that he regards the *Tales* more as an important document of social history than as a subject for the literary critic to study, and Chaucer's poetic quality as an inexplicable paradox in a gross age. However, when we compare Warton's treatment of Chaucer with that of most of his contemporaries, who preferred to read the poet in modernised versions, it is plain that Warton is more receptive to the rhythms and cadences of Chaucer's verse than critics who believed that 'Spenser's elegance and Dryden's fire' provided a substitute for Chaucer which far surpassed the original. A year after the first volume of Warton's *History* appeared, the publication of Thomas Tyrwhitt's scholarly edition of the *Tales*, with his long essay on Chaucer's language and versification, inaugurated modern Chaucer study.

When he comes to deal with Chaucer's contemporaries and successors, however, Warton's judgment is more in accord with that of later critics who enjoyed a greater perceptive of knowledge and had better texts from which to work. He did not magnify the worth of the late mediaeval poets, as Gray did of Lydgate or Ritson of Minot, nor did he try to compare them invidiously with eighteenth-century poets, as Tytler did when trying to extol the works of James I of Scotland. Gower he found dull and open to attack on account of his anachronisms and misrepresentations, which Warton thought strange in a scholar. Gower, he considered, was one who sacrificed poetry to the affectation of appearing learned, and Warton reveals his own powers of discrimination when he transcribes four of the *Cinquante Balades* written when Gower was a young man. He says that these 'place our old poet Gower in a more advantageous point of view than that in which he has hitherto been usually seen'. This is another way of saying that the poems are free of the heavy pedantry and weighty allusiveness of the *Confessio Amantis;* they are in fact very much in accord with late eighteenth-century ideals of sentimental lyricism.

Lydgate's academic versatility he admired but his long-windedness he describes as 'tedious and languid'; he held that his chief excellence lay in the flowery diction admitted by certain kinds of descriptive writing. He quoted *The Life of our Lady* by way of illustration and gave a full account of *The Temple of Glass* which he found completely derivative, either from Chaucer or the classics. He praised Hawes' *Pastime of Pleasure* as being 'almost the only effort of imagination and invention which had yet appeared in our poetry since Chaucer' but consigns Barclay's *Ship of Fools* to limbo on account of its prosaic lack of inspiration. He is wrong about Skelton, about whom he talks disparagingly and at length, but it is expecting too much of Warton to think that he could possibly stand so aloof from the poetical traditions of Spenser and Milton as to find even the slightest virtue in Skelton's ragged rhyming and apparently coarse buffoonery. After all, only the most recent studies take any other view.

Warton planned to touch only the high points of Scots poetry, as suggested in Gray's design, but in the end gave quite a full account of the 'makars', starting with Dunbar, whom he admired as an allegorist, 'the first poet who has appeared with any degree of spirit in this way of writing since [Langland]'. Much of what he says is taken from Lord Hailes' *Ancient Scottish Poems* of 1770. The most interesting feature of this portion of Warton's *History* is his quotation of most of the description of May in the *Prologue* to the XIIth book of Douglas's *Aeneid* and his rendering of it into modern English prose in order to show that its poetic power was not dependent upon either its form or its vocabulary. Such critical paraphrasing was an original experiment for its time and it well catches the temper of the highly-coloured description, which Warton declared to be the distinguishing mark of an original mind 'not overlaid by the descriptions of other poets'. He found similar qualities in Lyndsay, from whom he quotes extensively, and in Blind Harry's *Wallace*. More recent critics have been unwilling or unable to find poetical qualities in either of these and it is edifying to read Warton's critique, arbitrary though it is. His account of *The Kingis Quair*, given in a note, preceded Tytler's by several years. He quotes the twentieth and twenty-first stanzas from the poem and identifies the MS, but though he reveals his familiarity with Major's reference to James I's *libellus artifi-*

ciosus, called by Bale *Super Uxore futura,* Warton did not associate either with what he himself referred to as 'The King's Complaint'. Nevertheless it is Warton, not Tytler, who deserves the credit of having discovered *The Kingis Quair* for the eighteenth century.

Warton leaves his beloved Middle Ages with a great deal of reluctance and enters into an account of the effects of the Classical Renaissance on English poetry of the sixteenth century. He is obliged to point out, as a 'civilised' man, that 'soon after the reign of Elizabeth, men attained that state of general improvement and filled those situations with respect to literature and life, in which they have ever since persevered', but it is clear from the tone and atmosphere of the remainder of his *History* that Warton feels the loss of the romantic spirit. 'Ignorance and superstition, so opposite to the real interests of human society, are the parents of imagination', he declares, and goes on to regret the operations of 'the tacit compact of fashion, which promotes civility by diffusing habits of uniformity'. Faced with the choice between the supposed barbarities of feudal society and the good taste imposed on literature as a result of the wider dissemination of classical learning Warton is forced to an expression of the intellectual dilemma of his own age and concludes: 'We have parted with extravagancies that are above propriety, with incredibilities that are more acceptable than truth, and with fictions that are more valuable than reality'. It was left to Scott to find a suitable means of expressing in popular terms the yearnings of a sophisticated public for a painless escape into the realms of chivalry. (pp. 198-203)

A. M. Kinghorn, *"Warton's History and Early English Poetry,"* in English Studies, *Netherlands, Vol. 44, No. 4, June, 1963, pp. 197-204.*

John A. Vance (essay date 1983)

[*Vance is an American educator and literary critic. In the excerpt below, he examines Warton's various poetic styles.*]

Encouraged and stimulated by his father, his brother Joseph, and his own desire to express what was running through his fertile mind, Thomas Warton, at age seventeen, entered the ranks of English poets with the anonymous *Five Pastoral Eclogues: The Scenes of Which are Supposed to Lie Among the Shepherds, Oppressed by the War in Germany,* published by Dodsley in March 1745. (p. 27)

In the first eclogue, Alphon attempts to convince a saddened Lycas that they should retire with their flocks to a sanctuary farther back in the woods. But Lycas' grief over the loss of his favorite lamb, trampled by the soldiers' horses, renders him immobile. We are angered that Lycas' simple life has been spoiled: "Thou know'st my little flock; three tender ewes / Were all my mean ambition wish'd or sought." The "monsters" have also looted Alphon's cave, scattering and ruining his meager belongings—even the "hoard of choicest chestnuts" he had collected for his love. The first eclogue ends emotionally with a pathetic Lycas pointing to the places where his favorite lamb had played:

see there the spring
Where oft he wont to slake his eager thirst!

And there the beech, beneath whose breezy shade
He lov'd to lie, close covert from the Sun!
See yet the bark smooth-worn and bare remains,
Where oft the youngling rubb'd his tender side!

In Eclogue 2 Warton takes us deeper into nature, where we find Acis and Alcyon enjoying their refuge from the turbulence of war. Here the poet depicts nature as inspirational to the soul. All is quiet and slow; the eye observes and appreciates the simple and the delicate; there is no vice within this idyllic setting. But the "din of clashing arms" soon "disturbs the softer scene." Alcyon speaks of a weary reaper:

Whistling he home returns to kiss his babes,
With joyful heart, his labour's sweet reward!
But ah! what sudden fears amaze his soul
When, near approaching, all before he sees
His lowly cottage and the village 'round
Swept into ruin by the hand of war,
Dispers'd his children, and his much-lov'd wife.

Here the emotional impact is more controlled, though no less effective, than Lycas' reminiscences of his favorite lamb. Most poignant is Alcyon's interruption of Acis' delightful song on the sounds, sights, and scents of morning: "methinks I hear the deathful sounds / Of war approaching, and its thunders roar."

The third eclogue tells of Alcon, who was walking with his dear Lucilla when a soldier rode up and tore the maid "With brutal hand from his contending arms, / Weeping in vain, and shrieking for his aid." The distraught Alcon wanders deeper into the "dark and pathless" woods thinking of the "helpless virgin, subject to the will / Of each rude ravisher" and envisioning her eventually cast off, wandering the friendless earth, calling his name, and begging bread on which to survive. Upon the acceptance of his loss, Alcon seeks death by the wolves who roam the "savage forest."

In Eclogue 4, a dialogue between Mycon and Philanthes, we learn that the soldier's ax has leveled the venerable forest, marring the beauty of nature. Philanthes describes his climb to the top of a hill and the view of the fighting on the other side:

Sudden a burst of brightness smote my sight,
From arms, and all th' imblazonry of war
Reflected far, while steeds, and men, and arms
Seem'd floating wide, and stretch'd in vast array
O'er the broad bosom of the big-swoln flood,
That dashing roll'd its beamy waves between.

Mycon adds to this panoramic scene his account of the ravaging soldiers who plundered a convent: "the shrieking sisters fled / Dispers'd and naked thro' the fields and woods." The following morning Mycon examines the ruins and considers how future generations might view the remains: "Unknowing how it fell, with pious awe." Warton's implication is interesting: antiquarians and sightseers too frequently romanticize the remains of abbeys and castles without associating the violence and chaos which prompted such desecration and destruction.

In the fifth eclogue, Corin and Calistan describe their world as moribund due to the effects of war. Although the soldiers have now moved on to another battle, nature will never regain her tranquillity. . . . The mood at the end of the eclogue depresses the spirit: Calistan, mentioning that the youngling lamb "hangs his sickly head," points to the darkened west and to an approaching storm.

Warton's *Five Pastoral Eclogues* certainly suggests a new poet at work: several of the pastoral allusions are trite; there is too much repetition of expletives like "But Ah"; and at times the depictions of grief and suffering are too saturated with emotion. But there is much in the *Eclogues* to praise: Warton is effective in providing a visual and panoramic backdrop, in contrasting the sights and sounds of peaceful nature to those of chaotic strife, and in involving the reader emotionally with those affected by the war. We come away from the *Eclogues* convinced, not that we have read a superlative poem, but that we have experienced a powerful expression of the poet's antiwar sentiments. (pp. 27-30)

Melancholy as subject matter for poetry was well established by the time Warton published **"The Pleasures of Melancholy"** in 1747. (An initial version seems to have been completed by 1745). Robert Burton's *Anatomy of Melancholy* influenced not only Milton's *Il Penseroso* but several early eighteenth-century poets who wrote of the gloom of night and the decay of buildings. Young, Parnell, and Dyer are the better-known poets of melancholy and retirement before Warton, but to this list we may add lesser poets like William Broome, whose "Melancholy: An Ode" in the 1720s leaves no doubt that Warton's poem culminated rather than ushered in an era. Regardless, **"The Pleasures of Melancholy"** remains the most representative eighteenth-century poem on the subject.

The opening stanza invokes Contemplation:

> Raptur'd thou sitt'st, while murmurs indistinct
> Of distant billows sooth thy pensive ear
> With hoarse and hollow sounds; secure, self-blest,
> There oft thou listen'st to the wild uproar
> Of fleets encount'ring, that in whispers low
> Ascends the rocky summit, where thou dwell'st
> Remote from man, conversing with the spheres!

The poet shows no fear of the imposing goddess; he falls on his knees and implores her to lead him to "solemn glooms" congenial with his soul: "to cheerless shades, / To ruin'd seats, to twilight cells and bow'rs, / Where thoughtful Melancholy loves to muse." The "laughing scenes" of spring no longer charm the poet.

The first stanza shows a poet wishing to escape from the follies of society, but unlike the author of *The Enthusiast* he desires to dwell apart from any community of fellowmen. Instead of sharing daily experiences with primitive but noble Indians, the poet asks only to sit alone beneath "yon ruin'd abbey's moss-grown piles." The ruins, however, are only one component of the overall mood: Warton includes in the same stanza the "lone screech-owl's note," "mouldering caverns dark and damp," "Midnight's raven," a "hollow charnel," a "ghostly shape," and "far-winding vaults" to convey the sense of melancholy. His pleasure in contemplating these sights and sounds would increase, he admits, if he could stand among the bones of the dead, watching a taper shed "a livid glare / O'er the wan heaps." As he rises from his couch at the "solemn noon" of night, he notices that all is silent:

> Roars not the rushing wind; the sons of men
> And every beast in mute oblivion lie;
> All nature's hush'd in silence and in sleep.

> O then how fearful is it to reflect,
> That thro' the still globe's awful solitude,
> No being wakes but me! . . .

His choice of images in this powerful and frightening portrait of the night triggers the imagination, and we add our own details of horror to his scene.

Warton believes that the gloom of night is as or more conducive to creativity than a lovely spring morning in nature:

> But let the sacred Genius of the night
> Such mystic visions send, as Spenser saw,
> When thro' bewild'ring Fancy's magic maze,
> To the fell house of Busyrane, he led
> Th' unshaken Britomart; or Milton knew,
> When in abstracted thought he first conceiv'd
> All heav'n in tumult, and Seraphim
> Come tow'ring, arm'd in adamant and gold.

Remote from "Mirth's mad shouts" may the poet best contemplate this "fleeting state of things":

> This sober hour of silence will unmask
> False Folly's smile, that like the dazzling spells
> Of wily Comus cheat th' unweeting eye
> With blear illusion, and persuade to drink
> That charmed cup, which Reason's mintage fair
> Unmoulds, and stamps the monster on the man.
> Eager we taste, but in the luscious draught
> Forget the poisonous dregs that lurk beneath.

Warton thus advocates pensive melancholy not as a destructive exercise in self-pity, but rather as a healthy intellectual endeavor.

Warton also indicates his position on imaginative versus "correct" poetry:

> Thro' POPE's soft song tho' all the Graces breathe,
> And happiest art adorn his Attic page;
> Yet does my mind with sweeter transport glow,
> As at the root of mossy trunk reclin'd,
> In magic SPENSER's wildly-warbled song.

Warton conceives the poetry of Pope's school as the morning light, clarifying an otherwise vague and darkened landscape, but such verse pales by comparison with the vivid but mysterious images in imaginative poetry. Finally, in the passage on the ruins of Persepolis, we find that the bat and adder have usurped the obelisk where once ruled "elegance and art": "Far as the sight can pierce, appear the spoils / Of such magnificence!" Other than an obvious comment on mutability, the ruins are to Warton a palace of pleasure, where the pensive man can retire undisturbed with his thoughts and cultivate an independent and imaginative artistic expression. In contrast to the formal columns of the classical structure, the ruins are symbolic of the mysterious and unrefined—two marks of the creative imagination. (pp. 34-7)

In 1748 William Mason, of Cambridge University, composed *Isis: An Elegy,* a poem which cast a frowning glance at the supposed Jacobitism of Oxford. Compelled to answer the charge, George Huddesford, president of Trinity College, called upon Thomas Warton to reply, and the young tutor responded with **"The Triumph of Isis"** in 1749. His initial retaliatory strike at Cambridge hits with force: "Still sing, O Cam, your fav'rite Freedom's cause; / Still boast of Freedom, while you break her laws." Proud of the "massy piles of old munificence" which symbolize the endurance and permanence of Oxford, Warton reflects on the "gifted sons" of her storied past:

> Tuning to knightly tale his British reeds,
> Thy genuine bards immortal Chaucer leads:
> His hoary head o'erlooks the gazing quire,
> And beams on all around celestial fire.
> With graceful step see Addison advance,
> The sweetest child of Attic elegance.

Warton also recalls the likes of Walter Raleigh and John Locke and then looks further back in time to the "sable-suited" Black Prince and the "patriot king" Alfred the Great, who by tradition founded Oxford: " 'Twas Alfred first, with letters and with laws, / Adorn'd, as he advanc'd, his country's cause." Alfred's spirit is well-pleased that at Oxford freedom "rests her weary feet": "That here at last she takes her destin'd stand, / Here deigns to linger, ere she leave the land." An acknowledged success (even Mason allowed its superiority to his own *Isis*), **"The Triumph of Isis"** was followed by another poem extolling both university and country, **"Ode for Music"** (performed at Oxford on 2 July 1751), in which Warton notes that learning and liberty have always been the hallmark of Oxford. Isis flowed during England's earliest days and heard in the golden dawn the promise of greatness: "Nor was the pious promise vain; / Soon illustrious Alfred came, / And pitch'd fair Wisdom's tent on Isis' plenteous plain." It is doubtful Oxford could have selected a more enthusiastic spokesman (or propagandist) than Thomas Warton.

Four important events at court prompted verses from Warton in the period 1751-62. His **"Elegy"** on the death of the Prince of Wales in 1751, published along with other Oxford offerings, is both traditional and predictable in its tribute to the prince, but the second poem, **"On the Death of George the Second,"** which concludes a 1761 collection of Oxford verses on the occasion, is more of a request to the then Secretary of State William Pitt than a lament over the death of George. After many lines of blatant flattery Warton states his business:

> O Pitt, while honour points thy liberal plan,
> And o'er the Minister exalts the Man,
> Isis congenial greets thy faithful sway,
> Nor scorns to bid a statesman grace her lay.

And there is precedent, Warton continues, for endowing the university: "From kings she claim'd, yet scorn'd to seek, the prize, / From kings, like George, benignant, just, and wise."

Warton's **"On the Marriage of the King"** (1761) is addressed to George III's new bride, Charlotte of Mecklenburg-Strelitz. Portraying England as the land of military heroes (Alfred, Edward III, and Henry V) and literary genius (Spenser, Shakespeare, and Milton), Warton invites the queen to explore the delights of and near Oxford. Hopefully, Charlotte will be predisposed to favor the university with her presence and, more importantly, with her and her husband's patronage. In 1762 Warton again honored the royal family with **"On the Birth of The Prince of Wales"** (the future George IV). Not only did he contribute this poem but he also oversaw all 114 contributions in the Oxford volume dedicated to the event. Warton directs his overture to George III through the king's infant son: "Him the bold pattern of his patriot sire / Shall fill

with early fame's immortal fire." Warton then invokes the memory of the infant's most magnificent ancestor, Edward the Black Prince. The new prince will soon view the medieval treasures at Windsor Castle, and there Edward's "sable mail shall strike his eye" and "fire the youth, to crown his riper years / With rival Cressys, and a new Poitiers." Lest one forget his ulterior motive, Warton reminds George III that the Black Prince was an Oxford man. But, while he lauded the military prowess of the Black Prince, Warton could not suppress his aversion to war in general:

> Full oft, too rashly glows with fond delight
> The youthful breast, and asks the future fight;
> Nor knows that Horror's form, a spectre wan,
> Stalks, yet unseen, along the gleamy van.

At the end of the poem we note again Warton's realization that the romantic aspects of the past (the "Gothic trophies"), though enjoyable and inspirational to contemplate, should not be lamented:

> Those elfin charms, that held in magic night
> Its elder fame, and dimm'd its genuine light,
> At length dissolve in Truth's meridian ray,
> And the bright Order bursts to perfect day.

To repeat, Warton arrived at such a conclusion long before he wrote the verses on Reynolds's window. Finally, although he is not above overt flattery in these occasional poems, he uses them as vehicles to improve Oxford's relationship with the court, to praise his university and nation by unfurling the colorful banners of the past, and to warn the present and future king that war must not be romanticized but rather viewed in its horrifying light. For these reasons, the occasional poems have more than a passing interest.

That Warton seemed especially well-suited for occasional poetry was likely a factor in his selection as Poet Laureate in 1785—his duties being to write two odes per year: one for the New Year, the other for the king's birthday. But when Warton was named to succeed William Whitehead on 26 April he had little time in which to contemplate and write his first ode—the king's birthday falling on 4 June. The results were disappointing; the ode little suggests the work of an experienced and talented poet:

> To kings like these, her genuine theme,
> The Muse a blameless homage pays;
> To George of kings like these supreme
> She wishes honour'd length of days,
> Nor prostitutes the tribute of her lays.

One misses Warton's taste for historical analogue and his praise of British liberty in this frankly dull and seemingly hurried exercise. He writes like a man unsure of what is expected of him. . . . (pp. 40-3)

In most of his laureate odes Warton emphasizes the beauties of peace, freedom, and domestic achievement. In the New Year's Ode for 1786 (Ode 16) he praises not only Britain's successes at sea and in warfare, but also her accomplishments in agriculture and commerce. He points out in the New Year's Ode for 1787 (Ode 18) that although songs of war were fitting in the age of chivalry, now "the Bard in alter'd tones / A theme of worthier triumph owns," and that is of kings who diffuse "commerce, peace, and art." And in the Birthday Ode for 1787 (Ode 19) Warton establishes, as he does in his Birthday tribute for 1786 (Ode 17), firm precedents for flattering his king by mentioning the efforts of Chaucer, Spenser, and Dryden during the reigns of Edward III, Elizabeth, and Charles II. Admittedly, one hardly envisions George within such a charmed circle, but Warton's intent is to elevate to noble stature the "peaceful prowess" reflective of the current reign.

In the New Year's Ode for 1788 (Ode 20) Warton traces the history of medieval Windsor Castle during times when the sounds of war were heard over the land. Although stressing that George is committed to peace, Warton adds that if war is inevitable Britain must "arise" and "wake the slumbering fire." But he cannot bring himself to endorse completely the hurling of the "Vindictive dart": "Or, arm'd to strike, in mercy spare the foe; / And lift thy thundering hand, and then withhold the blow!" The Birthday Ode for 1788 (Ode 21) exalts liberty as reflected in Britain's heritage. Warton's praise for George is not overdone or strained: he only says that the king adds "new lustre . . . to native laws." This ode, one of his best laureate productions and a far cry from the first in 1785, suggests how comfortable Warton could feel writing in the historic vein.

Warton did not compose New Year's Odes for 1789 or 1790. Due to his attack of madness in October 1788, George was in no condition to hear the 1789 tribute, and there was no court at Windsor or St. James in 1790. Even so, George's condition, temporarily improved, is the subject of the Birthday Ode for 1789 (Ode 22). In what amounts to a get-well card to George, the ode states that he is a "father, friend, and lord" to his subjects. Misconceptions about George III's popularity suggest that Warton's remark was highly exaggerated, but in fact the king's illness had much to do with his being the first of the Hanoverians to elicit warmth and sympathy from his subjects—especially due to the deplorable behavior of his sons during his sickness. And George's condition is the subject matter of Warton's final Birthday Ode, completed shortly before his death in May 1790: here the Goddess Health beckons the king to share her cup "of precious cure." In summary, Warton's Odes, except for the first, are marked by rich imagery, vivid allusions, and a celebration of peace. Although Warton flatters George awkwardly in a few places, we do not sense that the laureate has compromised his integrity as a poet by commending his king.

Warton was able to enjoy a work like the *Probationary Odes* because he possessed a delightful sense of humor himself. One may not envision a pensive antiquary, literary historian, and poet laureate having much to laugh about, but some of his verse reveals him in a lighthearted moment, attempting nothing serious, perhaps only escaping temporarily from his scholarly work: for example, poems like **"Ode to a Grizzle Wig,"** Warton's version of "the wig makes the man," **"The Castle Barber's Soliloquy,"** *The Oxford Newsman's Verses,* and **"The Phaeton and the One-Horse Chair,"** an elementary attempt at moralizing ("The pace that's slow is often sure"). Swiftean in spirit, the **"Prologue on the Old Winchester Playhouse"** depicts the activity in a butcher shop right below the playhouse: "The Monarch swaggers, and the Butcher swears! / Quick the transition when the curtain drops, / From meek Monimia's moans to mutton chops!"

In 1751 Warton composed *Newmarket, A Satire*—210 lines of rhyming couplets—which portrays the frivolous and irresponsible life of young well-to-do's. In a mock-heroic tone, Warton assails racing, a summer delight in Oxford:

> See, like a routed host, with headlong pace,
> Thy members pour amid the mingling race!
> All ask, what crouds the tumult could produce—
> Is Bedlam or the Commons all broke loose?

Warton's vision of the future is rather bleak:

> Go on, brave youths, till in some future age
> Whips shall become the senatorial badge;
> Till England see her thronging senators
> Meet all at Westminster, in boots and spurs;
> See the whole House, with mutual frenzy mad,
> Her patriots all in leathern breeches clad:
> Of bets, not taxes, learnedly debate,
> And guide with equal reins a steed or state.

Glancing at Swift, Warton wonders how a "virtuous Houhnhym" would disdain seeing that "meanest spawn of man's half-monkey race; / In whom pride, avarice, ignorance, conspire, / That hated animal, a Yahoo 'Squire."

No other poem by Warton exhibits such frenzied activity, successful word play, and spirited satire of human foibles, but at the end of *Newmarket* he appears to lapse into an awkward equation between the current situation and the fall of ancient Greece. Knowing Warton, however, the last forty lines, filled with inflated rhetoric, are surely a tongue-in-cheek parody of similar comparisons with the past in other poems of the day. While he was at times guilty of employing conventional images, Warton was too good a poet to damage seriously a humorous poem with such an ending. It is difficult to imagine his being so distressed at England's interest in gambling and popular amusement; instead he is adding yet another level of humor and satire to his poem by trivializing, not the amusements, but rather the excessive moral seriousness with which they were viewed.

We cannot know how often Warton attended the races, but we may be certain that **"A Panegyric on Oxford Ale"** (1750) reflects frequent experience. One senses much sincerity in Warton's opening statement: "Balm of my cares, sweet solace of my toils, / Hail, JUICE benignant!" Wine, that "riot-stirring" beverage and "unwholesome draught," cannot begin to compare to the delights of ale:

> My sober evening let the tankard bless,
> With toast enbrown'd, and fragrant nutmeg fraught,
> While the rich draught with oft-repeated whiffs
> Tobacco mild improves. Divine repast!

The poet informs us that his tutorial duties and studies are not neglected, but when friends call, "To Pot-house I repair, the sacred haunt, / Where, ALE, thy votaries in full resort / Hold rites nocturnal." Warton finds important precedent for indulging in his favorite brew:

> Be mine each morn with eager appetite
> And hunger undissembled, to repair
> To friendly buttery; there on smoaking crust
> And foaming ALE to banquet unrestrain'd,
> Material breakfast! Thus in ancient days
> Our ancestors robust with liberal cups

Usher'd the morn, unlike the squeamish sons
Of modern times: nor ever had the might
Of Britons brave decay'd, had thus they fed,
With British ALE improving British worth.

But into his Eden slides the dreaded serpent: "Sudden (dire fate of all things excellent!) / Th' unpitying Bursar's cross-affixing hand / Blasts all my joys, and stops my glad career." Paradise was lost.

Although the **"Panegyric"** is bold and comical, one should also note the poet's recurring conclusion regarding the joys of escape, which must end eventually. The same theme is evident in **"The Progress of Discontent"**—published initially in 1750 although first written in 1746. Here we find a talented lad who cannot adjust to the "heavy chains" of college regulations: "In garret dark he smokes and puns, / A prey to discipline and duns." The young man struggles to a fellowship after nine long years, but is yet unsatisfied with his life: "who can bear to waste his whole age / Amid the dulness of a college, / Debarr'd the common joys of life." The man's departure from academic life brings him some luck at first: he secures a living in his fortieth year and weds a cousin of the country squire. He performs his "duties" as country parson so well that he reaps profit enough to support for a time his carousing lifestyle. But the weight of everyday domestic and financial annoyances moves him to lament his ever leaving the college: "Return, ye days, when endless pleasure / I found in reading, or in leisure!"

Although the poet's satire and moral are obvious, **"Progress"** has autobiographical and thematic implications worthy of note. During the 1746-50 period, Warton must have seriously contemplated his future at Trinity College, and as we can gather from **"Morning: The Author confined to College"** (Ode 8), written perhaps as early as 1745, he might have considered a life in the country free from academic demands and restraints. Warton may therefore have composed **"Progress"** as a reminder to himself that all is not idyllic on the other side of the Isis or Cherwell. And the poem argues once more that there is no permanent escape: the parson realizes this and pines for the sanctuary of an academic life. (pp. 44-9)

Thomas Warton's poetry encompassed several modes, topics, and themes during his forty-five years as a publishing poet, and his interests remained consistent over that long period. At times stumbling badly over his own diction and penchant for alliteration, he nevertheless filled his verses with rich and at times powerful natural and historical imagery and allusion. Although he dipped freely into Spenser and Milton for allusions or inspiration, there is both originality and delight in his treatment of the past, his depiction of nature, his love of freedom and distaste for war, his defense of the contemplative man and antiquarian scholar, his ability to chuckle at his own life-style, and his reflections on the loss of innocence and the dilemma of escape versus security. . . . A good deal of Warton's poetry approaches the best of the age; at worst, he is one of the better poets of the period 1745-90. (pp. 52-3)

> *John A. Vance, "The Poetry," in his* Joseph and Thomas Warton, *Twayne Publishers, 1983, pp. 14-53.*

FURTHER READING

Austin, Wiltshire Stanton and Ralph, John. "Reverend Thomas Warton." In their *The Lives of the Poets-Laureate,* pp. 316-32. London: Richard Bentley, Publisher, 1853.
Biographical sketch with a brief discussion of Warton's impact on English literary criticism.

Beers, Henry A. "The School of Warton." In his *A History of English Romanticism in the Eighteenth Century,* pp. 186-220. New York: Henry Holt and Co., 1916.
Brief examination of the romantic aspects of Warton's poetry.

Dennis, John. "The Wartons." In his *Studies in English Literature,* pp. 192-225. London: Edward Stanford, 1876.
Biographical piece with occasional unfavorable critical commentary.

Fairbanks, A. Harris. " 'Dear Native Brook': Coleridge, Bowles, and Thomas Warton, the Younger." *The Wordsworth Circle* VI, No. 4 (Autumn 1975): 313-15.
Supports the premise that both Warton's "To the River Lodon" and William Lisle Bowles's "To the River Itchin" greatly influenced Samuel Taylor Coleridge's "To the River Otter."

Ferguson, Oliver W. "Warton and Keats: Two Views of Melancholy." *Keats-Shelley Journal* XVIII (1969): 12-15.
Explores Warton's influence on John Keats, with supporting references to parallel passages in "The Pleasures of Melancholy" and "Ode to a Nightingale."

Harvey, A. D. *English Poetry in a Changing Society: 1780-1825.* London: Allison and Busby, 1980, 195 p.
Provides general background information on poetical movements through the eighteenth century, with special attention given to lyrical ballads and lyric poetry.

Hopkins, Kenneth. "Thomas Warton." In his *The Poets Laureate,* pp. 92-108. Rev. ed. New York: Barnes and Noble, 1973.
Biographical information, with some discussion of Warton's reception at the beginning of his tenure as poet laureate.

[Lee, Henry Boyle.] "Thomas Warton." In *The Cornhill Magazine* (June 1865): 733-42.
Biographical material with some discussion of Warton's interest in Gothic architecture.

Pittock, Joan H. "The Taste for the Gothic: Thomas Warton and the History of English Poetry." In her *The Ascendancy of Taste: The Achievement of Joseph and Thomas Warton,* pp. 167-214. London: Routledge and Kegan Paul, 1973.
Traces Gothic elements in literature prior to Warton and analyzes his use of such elements in his critical and historical works.

————. "Thomas Warton and the Oxford Chair of Poetry." *English Studies: A Journal of English Language and Literature* 62, No. 1 (January 1981): 14-33.
Discusses the history of the Oxford Chair of Poetry and Warton's tenure in the position. In addition, some treatment of the content of Warton's lectures is given.

Sambrook, A. J. "Thomas Warton's 'German Eclogues'." *The Review of English Studies* XX (February 1969): 61-2.
Brief argument in favor of Warton's authorship of the

German Eclogues, providing supporting evidence from a letter from Warton's publisher.

Vance, John A. "Samuel Johnson and Thomas Warton." *Biography* 9, No. 2 (Spring 1986): 95-111.
      Focuses on the friendship between Warton and Samuel Johnson, suggesting that Johnson felt more attached to the relationship than Warton.

Literature
Criticism from
1400 to 1800
Cumulative Indexes

This Index Includes References to Entries in These Gale Series

Contemporary Literary Criticism Presents excerpts of criticism on the works of novelists, poets, dramatists, short story writers, scriptwriters, and other creative writers who are now living or who have died since 1960.

Twentieth-Century Literary Criticism Contains critical excerpts by the most significant commentators on poets, novelists, short story writers, dramatists, and philosophers who died between 1900 and 1960.

Nineteenth-Century Literature Criticism Offers significant passages from criticism on authors who died between 1800 and 1899.

Literature Criticism from 1400 to 1800 Compiles significant passages from the most noteworthy criticism on authors of the fifteenth through eighteenth centuries.

Classical and Medieval Literature Criticism Offers excerpts of criticism on the works of world authors from classical antiquity through the fourteenth century.

Short Story Criticism Compiles excerpts of criticism on short fiction by writers of all eras and nationalities.

Poetry Criticism Presents excerpts of criticism on the works of poets from all eras, movements, and nationalities.

Children's Literature Review Includes excerpts from reviews, criticism, and commentary on works of authors and illustrators who create books for children.

Contemporary Authors Series Encompasses five related series. *Contemporary Authors* provides biographical and bibliographical information on more than 97,000 writers of fiction, nonfiction, poetry, journalism, drama, motion pictures, and other fields. Each new volume contains sketches on authors not previously covered in the series. *Contemporary Authors New Revision Series* provides completely updated information on active authors covered in previously published volumes of *CA*. Only entries requiring significant change are revised for *CA New Revision Series*. *Contemporary Authors Permanent Series* consists of updated listings for deceased and inactive authors removed from the original volumes 9-36 when these volumes were revised. *Contemporary Authors Autobiography Series* presents specially commissioned autobiographies by leading contemporary writers. *Contemporary Authors Bibliographical Series* contains primary and secondary bibliographies as well as analytical bibliographical essays by authorities on major modern authors.

Dictionary of Literary Biography Encompasses three related series. *Dictionary of Literary Biography* furnishes illustrated overviews of authors' lives and works and places them in the larger perspective of literary history. *Dictionary of Literary Biography Documentary Series* illuminates the careers of major figures through a selection of literary documents, including letters, notebook and diary entries, interviews, book reviews, and photographs. *Dictionary of Literary Biography Yearbook* summarizes the past year's literary activity with articles on genres, major prizes, conferences, and other timely subjects and includes updated and new entries on individual authors.

Concise Dictionary of American Literary Biography A six-volume series that collects revised and updated sketches on major American authors that were originally presented in *Dictionary of Literary Biography*.

Something about the Author Series Encompasses three related series. *Something about the Author* contains well-illustrated biographical sketches on juvenile and young adult authors and illustrators from all eras. *Something about the Author Autobiography Series* presents specially commissioned autobiographies by prominent authors and illustrators of books for children and young adults.

Yesterday's Authors of Books for Children Contains heavily illustrated entries on children's writers who died before 1961. Complete in two volumes.

Literary Criticism Series
Cumulative Author Index

This index lists all author entries in the Gale Literary Criticism Series and includes cross-references to other Gale sources. References in the index are identified as follows:

- **AAYA:** *Authors & Artists for Young Adults,* Volumes 1-3
- **CAAS:** *Contemporary Authors Autobiography Series,* Volumes 1-11
- **CA:** *Contemporary Authors* (original series), Volumes 1-131
- **CABS:** *Contemporary Authors Bibliographical Series,* Volumes 1-3
- **CANR:** *Contemporary Authors New Revision Series,* Volumes 1-29
- **CAP:** *Contemporary Authors Permanent Series,* Volumes 1-2
- **CA-R:** *Contemporary Authors* (revised editions), Volumes 1-44
- **CDALB:** *Concise Dictionary of American Literary Biography,* Volumes 1-6
- **CLC:** *Contemporary Literary Criticism,* Volumes 1-63
- **CLR:** *Children's Literature Review,* Volumes 1-23
- **CMLC:** *Classical and Medieval Literature Criticism,* Volumes 1-6
- **DC:** *Drama Criticism,* Volume 1
- **DLB:** *Dictionary of Literary Biography,* Volumes 1-101
- **DLB-DS:** *Dictionary of Literary Biography Documentary Series,* Volumes 1-7
- **DLB-Y:** *Dictionary of Literary Biography Yearbook,* Volumes 1980-1988
- **LC:** *Literature Criticism from 1400 to 1800,* Volumes 1-15
- **NCLC:** *Nineteenth-Century Literature Criticism,* Volumes 1-29
- **PC:** *Poetry Criticism,* Volume 1
- **SAAS:** *Something about the Author Autobiography Series,* Volumes 1-11
- **SATA:** *Something about the Author,* Volumes 1-62
- **SSC:** *Short Story Criticism,* Volumes 1-6
- **TCLC:** *Twentieth-Century Literary Criticism,* Volumes 1-39
- **YABC:** *Yesterday's Authors of Books for Children,* Volumes 1-2

Author Index

Emecheta, (Florence Onye) Buchi
1944- . . . . **CLC 14, 48**
See also CA 81-84

Emerson, Ralph Waldo
1803-1882 . . . . **NCLC 1**
See also DLB 1, 59, 73; CDALB 1640-1865

Empson, William
1906-1984 . . . . **CLC 3, 8, 19, 33, 34**
See also CA 17-20R; obituary CA 112;
DLB 20

Enchi, Fumiko (Veda) 1905-1986 . . . **CLC 31**
See also obituary CA 121

Ende, Michael 1930-. . . . . **CLC 31**
See also CLR 14; CA 118, 124; SATA 42;
DLB 75

Endo, Shusaku 1923- . . . . . **CLC 7, 14, 19, 54**
See also CANR 21; CA 29-32R

Engel, Marian 1933-1985. . . . . **CLC 36**
See also CANR 12; CA 25-28R; DLB 53

Engelhardt, Frederick 1911-1986
See Hubbard, L(afayette) Ron(ald)

Enright, D(ennis) J(oseph)
1920- . . . . **CLC 4, 8, 31**
See also CANR 1; CA 1-4R; SATA 25;
DLB 27

Enzensberger, Hans Magnus
1929- . . . . **CLC 43**
See also CA 116, 119

Ephron, Nora 1941- . . . . **CLC 17, 31**
See also CANR 12; CA 65-68

Epstein, Daniel Mark 1948- . . . . **CLC 7**
See also CANR 2; CA 49-52

Epstein, Jacob 1956- . . . . **CLC 19**
See also CA 114

Epstein, Joseph 1937-. . . . . **CLC 39**
See also CA 112, 119

Epstein, Leslie 1938- . . . . **CLC 27**
See also CANR 23; CA 73-76

Erdman, Paul E(mil) 1932- . . . . **CLC 25**
See also CANR 13; CA 61-64

Erdrich, Louise 1954-. . . . . **CLC 39, 54**
See also CA 114

Erenburg, Ilya (Grigoryevich) 1891-1967
See Ehrenburg, Ilya (Grigoryevich)

Eseki, Bruno 1919-
See Mphahlele, Ezekiel

Esenin, Sergei (Aleksandrovich)
1895-1925 . . . . **TCLC 4**
See also CA 104

Eshleman, Clayton 1935-. . . . . **CLC 7**
See also CAAS 6; CA 33-36R; DLB 5

Espriu, Salvador 1913-1985. . . . . **CLC 9**
See also obituary CA 115

Estleman, Loren D. 1952- . . . . **CLC 48**
See also CA 85-88

Evans, Marian 1819-1880
See Eliot, George

Evans, Mary Ann 1819-1880
See Eliot, George

Evarts, Esther 1900-1972
See Benson, Sally

Everett, Percival L. 1957?- . . . . **CLC 57**
See also CA 129

Everson, Ronald G(ilmour) 1903- . . . **CLC 27**
See also CA 17-20R

Everson, William (Oliver)
1912- . . . . **CLC 1, 5, 14**
See also CANR 20; CA 9-12R; DLB 5, 16

Evtushenko, Evgenii (Aleksandrovich) 1933-
See Yevtushenko, Yevgeny

Ewart, Gavin (Buchanan)
1916- . . . . **CLC 13, 46**
See also CANR 17; CA 89-92; DLB 40

Ewers, Hanns Heinz 1871-1943 . . . **TCLC 12**
See also CA 109

Ewing, Frederick R. 1918-
See Sturgeon, Theodore (Hamilton)

Exley, Frederick (Earl) 1929- . . . . **CLC 6, 11**
See also CA 81-84; DLB-Y 81

Ezekiel, Nissim 1924-. . . . . **CLC 61**
See also CA 61-64

Ezekiel, Tish O'Dowd 1943- . . . . **CLC 34**

Fagen, Donald 1948-. . . . . **CLC 26**

Fair, Ronald L. 1932-. . . . . **CLC 18**
See also CANR 25; CA 69-72; DLB 33

Fairbairns, Zoe (Ann) 1948- . . . . **CLC 32**
See also CANR 21; CA 103

Fairfield, Cicily Isabel 1892-1983
See West, Rebecca

Fallaci, Oriana 1930-. . . . . **CLC 11**
See also CANR 15; CA 77-80

Faludy, George 1913-. . . . . **CLC 42**
See also CA 21-24R

Fante, John 1909-1983. . . . . **CLC 60**
See also CANR 23; CA 69-72;
obituary CA 109; DLB-Y 83

Farah, Nuruddin 1945-. . . . . **CLC 53**
See also CA 106

Fargue, Leon-Paul 1876-1947 . . . . . **TCLC 11**
See also CA 109

Farigoule, Louis 1885-1972
See Romains, Jules

Farina, Richard 1937?-1966. . . . . **CLC 9**
See also CA 81-84; obituary CA 25-28R

Farley, Walter 1920- . . . . **CLC 17**
See also CANR 8; CA 17-20R; SATA 2, 43;
DLB 22

Farmer, Philip Jose 1918-. . . . . . . **CLC 1, 19**
See also CANR 4; CA 1-4R; DLB 8

Farrell, J(ames) G(ordon)
1935-1979 . . . . **CLC 6**
See also CA 73-76; obituary CA 89-92;
DLB 14

Farrell, James T(homas)
1904-1979 . . . . **CLC 1, 4, 8, 11**
See also CANR 9; CA 5-8R;
obituary CA 89-92; DLB 4, 9; DLB-DS 2

Farrell, M. J. 1904-
See Keane, Molly

Fassbinder, Rainer Werner
1946-1982 . . . . **CLC 20**
See also CA 93-96; obituary CA 106

Fast, Howard (Melvin) 1914- . . . . . . **CLC 23**
See also CANR 1; CA 1-4R; SATA 7;
DLB 9

Faulkner, William (Cuthbert)
1897-1962 . . . . **CLC 1, 3, 6, 8, 9, 11, 14,**
18, 28, 52; SSC 1
See also CA 81-84; DLB 9, 11, 44;
DLB-Y 86; DLB-DS 2

Fauset, Jessie Redmon
1884?-1961. . . . . **CLC 19, 54**
See also CA 109; DLB 51

Faust, Irvin 1924-. . . . . **CLC 8**
See also CA 33-36R; DLB 2, 28; DLB-Y 80

Fearing, Kenneth (Flexner)
1902-1961 . . . . **CLC 51**
See also CA 93-96; DLB 9

Federman, Raymond 1928- . . . . . . **CLC 6, 47**
See also CANR 10; CA 17-20R; DLB-Y 80

Federspiel, J(urg) F. 1931-. . . . . **CLC 42**

Feiffer, Jules 1929-. . . . . **CLC 2, 8**
See also CA 17-20R; SATA 8; DLB 7, 44

Feinberg, David B. 1956-. . . . . **CLC 59**

Feinstein, Elaine 1930-. . . . . **CLC 36**
See also CAAS 1; CA 69-72; DLB 14, 40

Feldman, Irving (Mordecai) 1928-. . . . **CLC 7**
See also CANR 1; CA 1-4R

Fellini, Federico 1920-. . . . . **CLC 16**
See also CA 65-68

Felsen, Gregor 1916-
See Felsen, Henry Gregor

Felsen, Henry Gregor 1916- . . . . **CLC 17**
See also CANR 1; CA 1-4R; SAAS 2;
SATA 1

Fenton, James (Martin) 1949-. . . . . . **CLC 32**
See also CA 102; DLB 40

Ferber, Edna 1887-1968. . . . . **CLC 18**
See also CA 5-8R; obituary CA 25-28R;
SATA 7; DLB 9, 28

Ferlinghetti, Lawrence (Monsanto)
1919?- . . . . **CLC 2, 6, 10, 27; PC 1**
See also CANR 3; CA 5-8R; DLB 5, 16;
CDALB 1941-1968

Ferrier, Susan (Edmonstone)
1782-1854 . . . . **NCLC 8**

Feuchtwanger, Lion 1884-1958 . . . . . **TCLC 3**
See also CA 104; DLB 66

Feydeau, Georges 1862-1921. . . . . . **TCLC 22**
See also CA 113

Ficino, Marsilio 1433-1499 . . . . **LC 12**

Fiedler, Leslie A(aron)
1917- . . . . **CLC 4, 13, 24**
See also CANR 7; CA 9-12R; DLB 28, 67

Field, Andrew 1938-. . . . . **CLC 44**
See also CANR 25; CA 97-100

Field, Eugene 1850-1895 . . . . **NCLC 3**
See also SATA 16; DLB 21, 23, 42

Fielding, Henry 1707-1754 . . . . **LC 1**
See also DLB 39

Fielding, Sarah 1710-1768. . . . . **LC 1**
See also DLB 39

Fierstein, Harvey 1954-. . . . . **CLC 33**
See also CA 123

Figes, Eva 1932-. . . . . **CLC 31**
See also CANR 4; CA 53-56; DLB 14

Gifford, Barry (Colby) 1946-....... CLC 34
See also CANR 9; CA 65-68

Gilbert, (Sir) W(illiam) S(chwenck)
1836-1911 .... TCLC 3
See also CA 104; SATA 36

Gilbreth, Ernestine 1908-
See Carey, Ernestine Gilbreth

Gilbreth, Frank B(unker), Jr.
1911- .... CLC 17
See also CA 9-12R; SATA 2

Gilchrist, Ellen 1935-.......... CLC 34, 48
See also CA 113, 116

Giles, Molly 1942-.............. CLC 39
See also CA 126

Gilliam, Terry (Vance) 1940-
See Monty Python
See also CA 108, 113

Gilliatt, Penelope (Ann Douglass)
1932- ....CLC 2, 10, 13, 53
See also CA 13-16R; DLB 14

Gilman, Charlotte (Anna) Perkins (Stetson)
1860-1935 ....TCLC 9, 37
See also CA 106

Gilmour, David 1944-
See Pink Floyd

Gilroy, Frank D(aniel) 1925-........ CLC 2
See also CA 81-84; DLB 7

Ginsberg, Allen
1926- .... CLC 1, 2, 3, 4, 6, 13, 36
See also CANR 2; CA 1-4R; DLB 5, 16;
CDALB 1941-1968

Ginzburg, Natalia 1916-...... CLC 5, 11, 54
See also CA 85-88

Giono, Jean 1895-1970.......... CLC 4, 11
See also CANR 2; CA 45-48;
obituary CA 29-32R; DLB 72

Giovanni, Nikki 1943-........ CLC 2, 4, 19
See also CLR 6; CAAS 6; CANR 18;
CA 29-32R; SATA 24; DLB 5, 41

Giovene, Andrea 1904-............. CLC 7
See also CA 85-88

Gippius, Zinaida (Nikolayevna) 1869-1945
See Hippius, Zinaida
See also CA 106

Giraudoux, (Hippolyte) Jean
1882-1944 .... TCLC 2, 7
See also CA 104; DLB 65

Gironella, Jose Maria 1917-....... CLC 11
See also CA 101

Gissing, George (Robert)
1857-1903 .... TCLC 3, 24
See also CA 105; DLB 18

Gladkov, Fyodor (Vasilyevich)
1883-1958 .... TCLC 27

Glanville, Brian (Lester) 1931-...... CLC 6
See also CANR 3; CA 5-8R; SATA 42;
DLB 15

Glasgow, Ellen (Anderson Gholson)
1873?-1945 .... TCLC 2, 7
See also CA 104; DLB 9, 12

Glassco, John 1909-1981 .... CLC 9
See also CANR 15; CA 13-16R;
obituary CA 102; DLB 68

Glasser, Ronald J. 1940?- .... CLC 37

Glendinning, Victoria 1937-........ CLC 50
See also CA 120

Glissant, Edouard 1928-.......... CLC 10

Gloag, Julian 1930- .... CLC 40
See also CANR 10; CA 65-68

Gluck, Louise (Elisabeth)
1943- .... CLC 7, 22, 44
See also CA 33-36R; DLB 5

Gobineau, Joseph Arthur (Comte) de
1816-1882 .... NCLC 17

Godard, Jean-Luc 1930-.......... CLC 20
See also CA 93-96

Godden, (Margaret) Rumer 1907-... CLC 53
See also CLR 20; CANR 4, 27; CA 7-8R;
SATA 3, 36

Godwin, Gail 1937-........ CLC 5, 8, 22, 31
See also CANR 15; CA 29-32R; DLB 6

Godwin, William 1756-1836...... NCLC 14
See also DLB 39

Goethe, Johann Wolfgang von
1749-1832 .... NCLC 4, 22

Gogarty, Oliver St. John
1878-1957 .... TCLC 15
See also CA 109; DLB 15, 19

Gogol, Nikolai (Vasilyevich)
1809-1852 .... NCLC 5, 15; SSC 4
See also CAAS 1, 4

Gokceli, Yasar Kemal 1923-
See Kemal, Yashar

Gold, Herbert 1924-....... CLC 4, 7, 14, 42
See also CANR 17; CA 9-12R; DLB 2;
DLB-Y 81

Goldbarth, Albert 1948-........ CLC 5, 38
See also CANR 6; CA 53-56

Goldberg, Anatol 1910-1982 .... CLC 34
See also obituary CA 117

Goldemberg, Isaac 1945-.......... CLC 52
See also CANR 11; CA 69-72

Golding, William (Gerald)
1911- ..... CLC 1, 2, 3, 8, 10, 17, 27, 58
See also CANR 13; CA 5-8R; DLB 15

Goldman, Emma 1869-1940....... TCLC 13
See also CA 110

Goldman, William (W.) 1931-.... CLC 1, 48
See also CA 9-12R; DLB 44

Goldmann, Lucien 1913-1970 ...... CLC 24
See also CAP 2; CA 25-28

Goldoni, Carlo 1707-1793 .... LC 4

Goldsberry, Steven 1949-......... CLC 34

Goldsmith, Oliver 1728?-1774....... LC 2
See also SATA 26; DLB 39

Gombrowicz, Witold
1904-1969 .... CLC 4, 7, 11, 49
See also CAP 2; CA 19-20;
obituary CA 25-28R

Gomez de la Serna, Ramon
1888-1963 .... CLC 9
See also obituary CA 116

Goncharov, Ivan Alexandrovich
1812-1891 .... NCLC 1

Goncourt, Edmond (Louis Antoine Huot) de
1822-1896 .... NCLC 7

Goncourt, Jules (Alfred Huot) de
1830-1870 .... NCLC 7

Gontier, Fernande 19??-.......... CLC 50

Goodman, Paul 1911-1972.... CLC 1, 2, 4, 7
See also CAP 2; CA 19-20;
obituary CA 37-40R

Gordimer, Nadine
1923- .... CLC 3, 5, 7, 10, 18, 33, 51
See also CANR 3; CA 5-8R

Gordon, Adam Lindsay
1833-1870 .... NCLC 21

Gordon, Caroline
1895-1981 ....CLC 6, 13, 29
See also CAP 1; CA 11-12;
obituary CA 103; DLB 4, 9; DLB-Y 81

Gordon, Charles William 1860-1937
See Conner, Ralph
See also CA 109

Gordon, Mary (Catherine)
1949- .... CLC 13, 22
See also CA 102; DLB 6; DLB-Y 81

Gordon, Sol 1923-................ CLC 26
See also CANR 4; CA 53-56; SATA 11

Gordone, Charles 1925-.......... CLC 1, 4
See also CA 93-96; DLB 7

Gorenko, Anna Andreyevna 1889?-1966
See Akhmatova, Anna

Gorky, Maxim 1868-1936 .... TCLC 8
See also Peshkov, Alexei Maximovich

Goryan, Sirak 1908-1981
See Saroyan, William

Gosse, Edmund (William)
1849-1928 .... TCLC 28
See also CA 117; DLB 57

Gotlieb, Phyllis (Fay Bloom)
1926- .... CLC 18
See also CANR 7; CA 13-16R

Gould, Lois 1938?-............. CLC 4, 10
See also CA 77-80

Gourmont, Remy de 1858-1915.... TCLC 17
See also CA 109

Govier, Katherine 1948-.......... CLC 51
See also CANR 18; CA 101

Goyen, (Charles) William
1915-1983 ....CLC 5, 8, 14, 40
See also CANR 6; CA 5-8R;
obituary CA 110; DLB 2; DLB-Y 83

Goytisolo, Juan 1931- .... CLC 5, 10, 23
See also CA 85-88

Gozzi, (Conte) Carlo 1720-1806 .. NCLC 23

Grabbe, Christian Dietrich
1801-1836 .... NCLC 2

Grace, Patricia 1937-............. CLC 56

Gracian y Morales, Baltasar
1601-1658 .... LC 15

Gracq, Julien 1910- .... CLC 11, 48
See also Poirier, Louis

Grade, Chaim 1910-1982 .... CLC 10
See also CA 93-96; obituary CA 107

Graham, Jorie 1951-............. CLC 48
See also CA 111

Graham, R(obert) B(ontine) Cunninghame
1852-1936 .... TCLC 19

Heat Moon, William Least   1939-... CLC 29

Hebert, Anne   1916- .... CLC 4, 13, 29
See also CA 85-88; DLB 68

Hecht, Anthony (Evan)
1923- .... CLC 8, 13, 19
See also CANR 6; CA 9-12R; DLB 5

Hecht, Ben   1894-1964 .... CLC 8
See also CA 85-88; DLB 7, 9, 25, 26, 28

Hedayat, Sadeq   1903-1951 .... TCLC 21
See also CA 120

Heidegger, Martin   1889-1976 ...... CLC 24
See also CA 81-84; obituary CA 65-68

Heidenstam, (Karl Gustaf) Verner von
1859-1940 .... TCLC 5
See also CA 104

Heifner, Jack   1946- .... CLC 11
See also CA 105

Heijermans, Herman   1864-1924 ... TCLC 24
See also CA 123

Heilbrun, Carolyn G(old)   1926- ..... CLC 25
See also CANR 1; CA 45-48

Heine, Harry   1797-1856
See Heine, Heinrich

Heine, Heinrich   1797-1856 .... NCLC 4

Heinemann, Larry C(urtiss)   1944- .. CLC 50
See also CA 110

Heiney, Donald (William)   1921-
See Harris, MacDonald
See also CANR 3; CA 1-4R

Heinlein, Robert A(nson)
1907-1988 ...... CLC 1, 3, 8, 14, 26, 55
See also CANR 1, 20; CA 1-4R;
obituary CA 125; SATA 9; DLB 8

Heller, Joseph
1923- .... CLC 1, 3, 5, 8, 11, 36, 63
See also CANR 8; CA 5-8R; CABS 1;
DLB 2, 28; DLB-Y 80

Hellman, Lillian (Florence)
1905?-1984 ..... CLC 2, 4, 8, 14, 18, 34,
44, 52
See also CA 13-16R; obituary CA 112;
DLB 7; DLB-Y 84

Helprin, Mark   1947- ..... CLC 7, 10, 22, 32
See also CA 81-84; DLB-Y 85

Hemans, Felicia   1793-1835 ...... NCLC 29

Hemingway, Ernest (Miller)
1899-1961 ... CLC 1, 3, 6, 8, 10, 13, 19,
30, 34, 39, 41, 44, 50, 61; SSC 1
See also CA 77-80; DLB 4, 9; DLB-Y 81,
87; DLB-DS 1

Hempel, Amy   1951- .... CLC 39
See also CA 118

Henley, Beth   1952- .... CLC 23
See also Henley, Elizabeth Becker
See also DLB-Y 86

Henley, Elizabeth Becker   1952-
See Henley, Beth
See also CA 107

Henley, William Ernest
1849-1903 .... TCLC 8
See also CA 105; DLB 19

Hennissart, Martha
See Lathen, Emma
See also CA 85-88

Henry, O.   1862-1910 ... TCLC 1, 19; SSC 5
See also Porter, William Sydney
See also YABC 2; CA 104; DLB 12, 78, 79;
CDALB 1865-1917

Henry VIII   1491-1547 .... LC 10

Hentoff, Nat(han Irving)   1925- ..... CLC 26
See also CLR 1; CAAS 6; CANR 5;
CA 1-4R; SATA 27, 42

Heppenstall, (John) Rayner
1911-1981 .... CLC 10
See also CA 1-4R; obituary CA 103

Herbert, Frank (Patrick)
1920-1986 .... CLC 12, 23, 35, 44
See also CANR 5; CA 53-56;
obituary CA 118; SATA 9, 37, 47; DLB 8

Herbert, Zbigniew   1924- .... CLC 9, 43
See also CA 89-92

Herbst, Josephine   1897-1969 ...... CLC 34
See also CA 5-8R; obituary CA 25-28R;
DLB 9

Herder, Johann Gottfried von
1744-1803 .... NCLC 8

Hergesheimer, Joseph
1880-1954 .... TCLC 11
See also CA 109; DLB 9

Herlagnez, Pablo de   1844-1896
See Verlaine, Paul (Marie)

Herlihy, James Leo   1927- .... CLC 6
See also CANR 2; CA 1-4R

Hermogenes   fl.c. 175- .... CMLC 6

Hernandez, Jose   1834-1886 ...... NCLC 17

Herrick, Robert   1591-1674 .... LC 13

Herriot, James   1916- .... CLC 12
See also Wight, James Alfred

Herrmann, Dorothy   1941- .... CLC 44
See also CA 107

Hersey, John (Richard)
1914- .... CLC 1, 2, 7, 9, 40
See also CA 17-20R; SATA 25; DLB 6

Herzen, Aleksandr Ivanovich
1812-1870 .... NCLC 10

Herzl, Theodor   1860-1904 .... TCLC 36

Herzog, Werner   1942- .... CLC 16
See also CA 89-92

Hesiod   c. 8th Century B.C.- ...... CMLC 5

Hesse, Hermann
1877-1962 .... CLC 1, 2, 3, 6, 11, 17, 25
See also CAP 2; CA 17-18; SATA 50;
DLB 66

Heyen, William   1940- .... CLC 13, 18
See also CA 33-36R; DLB 5

Heyerdahl, Thor   1914- .... CLC 26
See also CANR 5, 22; CA 5-8R; SATA 2,
52

Heym, Georg (Theodor Franz Arthur)
1887-1912 .... TCLC 9
See also CA 106

Heym, Stefan   1913- .... CLC 41
See also CANR 4; CA 9-12R; DLB 69

Heyse, Paul (Johann Ludwig von)
1830-1914 .... TCLC 8
See also CA 104

Hibbert, Eleanor (Burford)   1906- .... CLC 7
See also CANR 9; CA 17-20R; SATA 2

Higgins, George V(incent)
1939- .... CLC 4, 7, 10, 18
See also CAAS 5; CANR 17; CA 77-80;
DLB 2; DLB-Y 81

Higginson, Thomas Wentworth
1823-1911 .... TCLC 36
See also DLB 1, 64

Highsmith, (Mary) Patricia
1921- .... CLC 2, 4, 14, 42
See also CANR 1, 20; CA 1-4R

Highwater, Jamake   1942- .... CLC 12
See also CAAS 7; CANR 10; CA 65-68;
SATA 30, 32; DLB 52; DLB-Y 85

Hikmet (Ran), Nazim   1902-1963 .... CLC 40
See also obituary CA 93-96

Hildesheimer, Wolfgang   1916- ..... CLC 49
See also CA 101; DLB 69

Hill, Geoffrey (William)
1932- .... CLC 5, 8, 18, 45
See also CANR 21; CA 81-84; DLB 40

Hill, George Roy   1922- .... CLC 26
See also CA 110

Hill, Susan B.   1942- .... CLC 4
See also CA 33-36R; DLB 14

Hillerman, Tony   1925- .... CLC 62
See also CANR 21; CA 29-32R; SATA 6

Hilliard, Noel (Harvey)   1929- ...... CLC 15
See also CANR 7; CA 9-12R

Hilton, James   1900-1954 .... TCLC 21
See also CA 108; SATA 34; DLB 34

Himes, Chester (Bomar)
1909-1984 .... CLC 2, 4, 7, 18, 58
See also CANR 22; CA 25-28R;
obituary CA 114; DLB 2, 76

Hinde, Thomas   1926- .... CLC 6, 11
See also Chitty, (Sir) Thomas Willes

Hine, (William) Daryl   1936- .... CLC 15
See also CANR 1, 20; CA 1-4R; DLB 60

Hinton, S(usan) E(loise)   1950- ..... CLC 30
See also CLR 3, 23; CA 81-84; SATA 19

Hippius (Merezhkovsky), Zinaida
(Nikolayevna)   1869-1945 ...... TCLC 9
See also Gippius, Zinaida (Nikolayevna)

Hiraoka, Kimitake   1925-1970
See Mishima, Yukio
See also CA 97-100; obituary CA 29-32R

Hirsch, Edward (Mark)   1950-... CLC 31, 50
See also CANR 20; CA 104

Hitchcock, (Sir) Alfred (Joseph)
1899-1980 .... CLC 16
See also obituary CA 97-100; SATA 27;
obituary SATA 24

Hoagland, Edward   1932- .... CLC 28
See also CANR 2; CA 1-4R; SATA 51;
DLB 6

Hoban, Russell C(onwell)   1925- .. CLC 7, 25
See also CLR 3; CANR 23; CA 5-8R;
SATA 1, 40; DLB 52

Hobson, Laura Z(ametkin)
1900-1986 .... CLC 7, 25
See also CA 17-20R; obituary CA 118;
SATA 52; DLB 28

Laughlin, James 1914-............ **CLC 49**
See also CANR 9; CA 21-24R; DLB 48

Laurence, (Jean) Margaret (Wemyss)
1926-1987 .... **CLC 3, 6, 13, 50, 62**
See also CA 5-8R; obituary CA 121;
SATA 50; DLB 53

Laurent, Antoine 1952- .... **CLC 50**

Lautreamont, Comte de
1846-1870 .... **NCLC 12**

Lavin, Mary 1912-...... **CLC 4, 18; SSC 4**
See also CA 9-12R; DLB 15

Lawler, Raymond (Evenor) 1922- ... **CLC 58**
See also CA 103

Lawrence, D(avid) H(erbert)
1885-1930 .... **TCLC 2, 9, 16, 33; SSC 4**
See also CA 104, 121; DLB 10, 19, 36

Lawrence, T(homas) E(dward)
1888-1935 .... **TCLC 18**
See also CA 115

Lawson, Henry (Archibald Hertzberg)
1867-1922 .... **TCLC 27**
See also CA 120

Laxness, Halldor (Kiljan) 1902- .... **CLC 25**
See also Gudjonsson, Halldor Kiljan

Laye, Camara 1928-1980 .... **CLC 4, 38**
See also CA 85-88; obituary CA 97-100

Layton, Irving (Peter) 1912- ..... **CLC 2, 15**
See also CANR 2; CA 1-4R

Lazarus, Emma 1849-1887........ **NCLC 8**

Leacock, Stephen (Butler)
1869-1944 .... **TCLC 2**
See also CA 104

Lear, Edward 1812-1888 .... **NCLC 3**
See also CLR 1; SATA 18; DLB 32

Lear, Norman (Milton) 1922- ...... **CLC 12**
See also CA 73-76

Leavis, F(rank) R(aymond)
1895-1978 .... **CLC 24**
See also CA 21-24R; obituary CA 77-80

Leavitt, David 1961?-............. **CLC 34**
See also CA 116, 122

Lebowitz, Fran(ces Ann)
1951?- .... **CLC 11, 36**
See also CANR 14; CA 81-84

Le Carre, John 1931-... **CLC 3, 5, 9, 15, 28**
See also Cornwell, David (John Moore)

Le Clezio, J(ean) M(arie) G(ustave)
1940- .... **CLC 31**
See also CA 116

Leconte de Lisle, Charles-Marie-Rene
1818-1894 .... **NCLC 29**

Leduc, Violette 1907-1972........ **CLC 22**
See also CAP 1; CA 13-14;
obituary CA 33-36R

Ledwidge, Francis 1887-1917...... **TCLC 23**
See also CA 123; DLB 20

Lee, Andrea 1953- .... **CLC 36**
See also CA 125

Lee, Andrew 1917-
See Auchincloss, Louis (Stanton)

Lee, Don L. 1942-................. **CLC 2**
See also Madhubuti, Haki R.
See also CA 73-76

Lee, George Washington
1894-1976 .... **CLC 52**
See also CA 125; DLB 51

Lee, (Nelle) Harper 1926- ...... **CLC 12, 60**
See also CA 13-16R; SATA 11; DLB 6;
CDALB 1941-1968

Lee, Lawrence 1903- .... **CLC 34**
See also CA 25-28R

Lee, Manfred B(ennington) 1905-1971
See Queen, Ellery
See also CANR 2; CA 1-4R, 11;
obituary CA 29-32R

Lee, Stan 1922-.................. **CLC 17**
See also CA 108, 111

Lee, Tanith 1947-................ **CLC 46**
See also CA 37-40R; SATA 8

Lee, Vernon 1856-1935 .... **TCLC 5**
See also Paget, Violet
See also DLB 57

Lee-Hamilton, Eugene (Jacob)
1845-1907 .... **TCLC 22**

Leet, Judith 1935- .... **CLC 11**

Le Fanu, Joseph Sheridan
1814-1873 .... **NCLC 9**
See also DLB 21, 70

Leffland, Ella 1931- .... **CLC 19**
See also CA 29-32R; DLB-Y 84

Leger, (Marie-Rene) Alexis Saint-Leger
1887-1975
See Perse, St.-John
See also CA 13-16R; obituary CA 61-64

Le Guin, Ursula K(roeber)
1929- .... **CLC 8, 13, 22, 45**
See also CLR 3; CANR 9; CA 21-24R;
SATA 4, 52; DLB 8, 52

Lehmann, Rosamond (Nina) 1901- ... **CLC 5**
See also CANR 8; CA 77-80; DLB 15

Leiber, Fritz (Reuter, Jr.) 1910-.... **CLC 25**
See also CANR 2; CA 45-48; SATA 45;
DLB 8

Leino, Eino 1878-1926........... **TCLC 24**

Leiris, Michel 1901-.............. **CLC 61**
See also CA 119, 128

Leithauser, Brad 1953-........... **CLC 27**
See also CA 107

Lelchuk, Alan 1938-.............. **CLC 5**
See also CANR 1; CA 45-48

Lem, Stanislaw 1921-........ **CLC 8, 15, 40**
See also CAAS 1; CA 105

Lemann, Nancy 1956-............ **CLC 39**
See also CA 118

Lemonnier, (Antoine Louis) Camille
1844-1913 .... **TCLC 22**

Lenau, Nikolaus 1802-1850 ...... **NCLC 16**

L'Engle, Madeleine 1918- .... **CLC 12**
See also CLR 1, 14; CANR 3, 21; CA 1-4R;
SATA 1, 27; DLB 52

Lengyel, Jozsef 1896-1975.......... **CLC 7**
See also CA 85-88; obituary CA 57-60

Lennon, John (Ono)
1940-1980 .... **CLC 12, 35**
See also CA 102

Lennon, John Winston 1940-1980
See Lennon, John (Ono)

Lennox, Charlotte Ramsay 1729 or
1730-1804 .... **NCLC 23**
See also DLB 39, 39

Lennox, Charlotte Ramsay
1729?-1804.................. **NCLC 23**
See also DLB 39

Lentricchia, Frank (Jr.) 1940-...... **CLC 34**
See also CANR 19; CA 25-28R

Lenz, Siegfried 1926-............. **CLC 27**
See also CA 89-92; DLB 75

Leonard, Elmore 1925-....... **CLC 28, 34**
See also CANR 12; CA 81-84

Leonard, Hugh 1926- .... **CLC 19**
See also Byrne, John Keyes
See also DLB 13

Leopardi, (Conte) Giacomo (Talegardo
Francesco di Sales Saverio Pietro)
1798-1837 .... **NCLC 22**

Lerman, Eleanor 1952-............ **CLC 9**
See also CA 85-88

Lerman, Rhoda 1936-............. **CLC 56**
See also CA 49-52

Lermontov, Mikhail Yuryevich
1814-1841 .... **NCLC 5**

Leroux, Gaston 1868-1927........ **TCLC 25**
See also CA 108

Lesage, Alain-Rene 1668-1747....... **LC 2**

Leskov, Nikolai (Semyonovich)
1831-1895 .... **NCLC 25**

Lessing, Doris (May)
1919- .... **CLC 1, 2, 3, 6, 10, 15, 22, 40;**
SSC 6
See also CA 9-12R; DLB 15; DLB-Y 85

Lessing, Gotthold Ephraim
1729-1781 .... **LC 8**

Lester, Richard 1932-............. **CLC 20**

Lever, Charles (James)
1806-1872 .... **NCLC 23**
See also DLB 21

Leverson, Ada 1865-1936........ **TCLC 18**
See also CA 117

Levertov, Denise
1923- .... **CLC 1, 2, 3, 5, 8, 15, 28**
See also CANR 3; CA 1-4R; DLB 5

Levi, Peter (Chad Tiger) 1931-..... **CLC 41**
See also CA 5-8R; DLB 40

Levi, Primo 1919-1987........ **CLC 37, 50**
See also CANR 12; CA 13-16R;
obituary CA 122

Levin, Ira 1929- .... **CLC 3, 6**
See also CANR 17; CA 21-24R

Levin, Meyer 1905-1981 .... **CLC 7**
See also CANR 15; CA 9-12R;
obituary CA 104; SATA 21;
obituary SATA 27; DLB 9, 28; DLB-Y 81

Levine, Norman 1924- .... **CLC 54**
See also CANR 14; CA 73-76

Levine, Philip 1928-.. **CLC 2, 4, 5, 9, 14, 33**
See also CANR 9; CA 9-12R; DLB 5

Levinson, Deirdre 1931-........... **CLC 49**
See also CA 73-76

Levi-Strauss, Claude 1908- .... **CLC 38**
See also CANR 6; CA 1-4R

McEwan, Ian (Russell)　1948-　......　CLC 13
　　See also CANR 14; CA 61-64; DLB 14

McFadden, David　1940-..........　CLC 48
　　See also CA 104; DLB 60

McGahern, John　1934-.......　CLC 5, 9, 48
　　See also CA 17-20R; DLB 14

McGinley, Patrick　1937-.........　CLC 41
　　See also CA 120

McGinley, Phyllis　1905-1978　......　CLC 14
　　See also CANR 19; CA 9-12R;
　　obituary CA 77-80; SATA 2, 44;
　　obituary SATA 24; DLB 11, 48

McGinniss, Joe　1942-............　CLC 32
　　See also CA 25-28R

McGivern, Maureen Daly　1921-
　　See Daly, Maureen
　　See also CA 9-12R

McGrath, Patrick　1950-..........　CLC 55

McGrath, Thomas　1916-　......　CLC 28, 59
　　See also CANR 6; CA 9-12R, 130;
　　SATA 41

McGuane, Thomas (Francis III)
　　1939-　..............　CLC 3, 7, 18
　　See also CANR 5; CA 49-52; DLB 2;
　　DLB-Y 80

McGuckian, Medbh　1950-.........　CLC 48
　　See also DLB 40

McHale, Tom　1941-1982.........　CLC 3, 5
　　See also CA 77-80; obituary CA 106

McIlvanney, William　1936-........　CLC 42
　　See also CA 25-28R; DLB 14

McIlwraith, Maureen Mollie Hunter　1922-
　　See Hunter, Mollie
　　See also CA 29-32R; SATA 2

McInerney, Jay　1955-............　CLC 34
　　See also CA 116, 123

McIntyre, Vonda N(eel)　1948-　.....　CLC 18
　　See also CANR 17; CA 81-84

McKay, Claude　1890-1948........　TCLC 7
　　See also CA 104; DLB 4, 45

McKuen, Rod　1933-.............　CLC 1, 3
　　See also CA 41-44R

McLuhan, (Herbert) Marshall
　　1911-1980　..................　CLC 37
　　See also CANR 12; CA 9-12R;
　　obituary CA 102

McManus, Declan Patrick　1955-
　　See Costello, Elvis

McMillan, Terry　1951-　........　CLC 50, 61

McMurtry, Larry (Jeff)
　　1936-　.........　CLC 2, 3, 7, 11, 27, 44
　　See also CANR 19; CA 5-8R; DLB 2;
　　DLB-Y 80, 87

McNally, Terrence　1939-......　CLC 4, 7, 41
　　See also CANR 2; CA 45-48; DLB 7

McPhee, John　1931-.............　CLC 36
　　See also CANR 20; CA 65-68

McPherson, James Alan　1943-　.....　CLC 19
　　See also CANR 24; CA 25-28R; DLB 38

McPherson, William　1939-　........　CLC 34
　　See also CA 57-60

McSweeney, Kerry　19??-..........　CLC 34

Mead, Margaret　1901-1978........　CLC 37
　　See also CANR 4; CA 1-4R;
　　obituary CA 81-84; SATA 20

Meaker, M. J.　1927-
　　See Kerr, M. E.; Meaker, Marijane

Meaker, Marijane　1927-
　　See Kerr, M. E.
　　See also CA 107; SATA 20

Medoff, Mark (Howard)　1940-　...　CLC 6, 23
　　See also CANR 5; CA 53-56; DLB 7

Megged, Aharon　1920-.............　CLC 9
　　See also CANR 1; CA 49-52

Mehta, Ved (Parkash)　1934-.......　CLC 37
　　See also CANR 2, 23; CA 1-4R

Mellor, John　1953?-
　　See The Clash

Meltzer, Milton　1915-.........　CLC 26 13
　　See also CA 13-16R; SAAS 1; SATA 1, 50;
　　DLB 61

Melville, Herman
　　1819-1891　......　NCLC 3, 12, 29; SSC 1
　　See also SATA 59; DLB 3, 74;
　　CDALB 1640-1865

Membreno, Alejandro　1972-　.......　CLC 59

Mencken, H(enry) L(ouis)
　　1880-1956　.................　TCLC 13
　　See also CA 105; DLB 11, 29, 63

Mercer, David　1928-1980.........　CLC 5
　　See also CA 9-12R; obituary CA 102;
　　DLB 13

Meredith, George　1828-1909......　TCLC 17
　　See also CA 117; DLB 18, 35, 57

Meredith, William (Morris)
　　1919-　..............　CLC 4, 13, 22, 55
　　See also CANR 6; CA 9-12R; DLB 5

Merezhkovsky, Dmitri
　　1865-1941　..................　TCLC 29

Merimee, Prosper　1803-1870......　NCLC 6

Merkin, Daphne　1954-.............　CLC 44
　　See also CANR 123

Merrill, James (Ingram)
　　1926-　......　CLC 2, 3, 6, 8, 13, 18, 34
　　See also CANR 10; CA 13-16R; DLB 5;
　　DLB-Y 85

Merton, Thomas (James)
　　1915-1968　.............　CLC 1, 3, 11, 34
　　See also CANR 22; CA 5-8R;
　　obituary CA 25-28R; DLB 48; DLB-Y 81

Merwin, W(illiam) S(tanley)
　　1927-　......　CLC 1, 2, 3, 5, 8, 13, 18, 45
　　See also CANR 15; CA 13-16R; DLB 5

Metcalf, John　1938-.............　CLC 37
　　See also CA 113; DLB 60

Mew, Charlotte (Mary)
　　1870-1928　.................　TCLC 8
　　See also CA 105; DLB 19

Mewshaw, Michael　1943-...........　CLC 9
　　See also CANR 7; CA 53-56; DLB-Y 80

Meyer-Meyrink, Gustav　1868-1932
　　See Meyrink, Gustav
　　See also CA 117

Meyers, Jeffrey　1939-............　CLC 39
　　See also CA 73-76

Meynell, Alice (Christiana Gertrude
　　Thompson)　1847-1922　........　TCLC 6
　　See also CA 104; DLB 19

Meyrink, Gustav　1868-1932......　TCLC 21
　　See also Meyer-Meyrink, Gustav

Michaels, Leonard　1933-........　CLC 6, 25
　　See also CANR 21; CA 61-64

Michaux, Henri　1899-1984　......　CLC 8, 19
　　See also CA 85-88; obituary CA 114

Michelangelo　1475-1564...........　LC 12

Michener, James A(lbert)
　　1907-　.............　CLC 1, 5, 11, 29, 60
　　See also CANR 21; CA 5-8R; DLB 6

Mickiewicz, Adam　1798-1855　.....　NCLC 3

Middleton, Christopher　1926-......　CLC 13
　　See also CA 13-16R; DLB 40

Middleton, Stanley　1919-......　CLC 7, 38
　　See also CANR 21; CA 25-28R; DLB 14

Migueis, Jose Rodrigues　1901-　.....　CLC 10

Mikszath, Kalman　1847-1910　.....　TCLC 31

Miles, Josephine (Louise)
　　1911-1985　........　CLC 1, 2, 14, 34, 39
　　See also CANR 2; CA 1-4R;
　　obituary CA 116; DLB 48

Mill, John Stuart　1806-1873　.....　NCLC 11

Millar, Kenneth　1915-1983　........　CLC 14
　　See also Macdonald, Ross
　　See also CANR 16; CA 9-12R;
　　obituary CA 110; DLB 2; DLB-Y 83

Millay, Edna St. Vincent
　　1892-1950　.................　TCLC 4
　　See also CA 104; DLB 45

Miller, Arthur
　　1915-　......　CLC 1, 2, 6, 10, 15, 26, 47
　　See also CANR 2; CA 1-4R; DLB 7;
　　CDALB 1941-1968

Miller, Henry (Valentine)
　　1891-1980　.......　CLC 1, 2, 4, 9, 14, 43
　　See also CA 9-12R; obituary CA 97-100;
　　DLB 4, 9; DLB-Y 80

Miller, Jason　1939?-..............　CLC 2
　　See also CA 73-76; DLB 7

Miller, Sue　19??-................　CLC 44

Miller, Walter M(ichael), Jr.
　　1923-　.....................　CLC 4, 30
　　See also CA 85-88; DLB 8

Millhauser, Steven　1943-.......　CLC 21, 54
　　See also CA 108, 110, 111; DLB 2

Millin, Sarah Gertrude　1889-1968　..　CLC 49
　　See also CA 102; obituary CA 93-96

Milne, A(lan) A(lexander)
　　1882-1956　..................　TCLC 6
　　See also CLR 1; YABC 1; CA 104; DLB 10

Milner, Ron(ald)　1938-...........　CLC 56
　　See also CANR 24; CA 73-76; DLB 38

Milosz Czeslaw
　　1911-　........　CLC 5, 11, 22, 31, 56
　　See also CANR 23; CA 81-84

Milton, John　1608-1674.............　LC 9

Miner, Valerie (Jane)　1947-........　CLC 40
　　See also CA 97-100

Minot, Susan　1956-　.............　CLC 44

Minus, Ed　1938-................　CLC 39

Miro (Ferrer), Gabriel (Francisco Victor)
    1879-1930 .... TCLC 5
    See also CA 104

Mishima, Yukio
    1925-1970 .... CLC 2, 4, 6, 9, 27; SSC 4
    See also Hiraoka, Kimitake

Mistral, Gabriela   1889-1957 .... TCLC 2
    See also CA 104

Mitchell, James Leslie   1901-1935
    See Gibbon, Lewis Grassic
    See also CA 104; DLB 15

Mitchell, Joni   1943-.............. CLC 12
    See also CA 112

Mitchell (Marsh), Margaret (Munnerlyn)
    1900-1949 .... TCLC 11
    See also CA 109; DLB 9

Mitchell, S. Weir   1829-1914 ...... TCLC 36

Mitchell, W(illiam) O(rmond)
    1914- .... CLC 25
    See also CANR 15; CA 77-80

Mitford, Mary Russell   1787-1855.. NCLC 4

Mitford, Nancy   1904-1973......... CLC 44
    See also CA 9-12R

Miyamoto Yuriko   1899-1951...... TCLC 37

Mo, Timothy   1950-................ CLC 46
    See also CA 117

Modarressi, Taghi   1931- .... CLC 44
    See also CA 121

Modiano, Patrick (Jean)   1945-..... CLC 18
    See also CANR 17; CA 85-88

Mofolo, Thomas (Mokopu)
    1876-1948 .... TCLC 22
    See also CA 121

Mohr, Nicholasa   1935-............ CLC 12
    See also CLR 22; CANR 1; CA 49-52;
    SATA 8

Mojtabai, A(nn) G(race)
    1938- .... CLC 5, 9, 15, 29
    See also CA 85-88

Moliere   1622-1673 .... LC 10

Molnar, Ferenc   1878-1952........ TCLC 20
    See also CA 109

Momaday, N(avarre) Scott
    1934- .... CLC 2, 19
    See also CANR 14; CA 25-28R; SATA 30,
    48

Monroe, Harriet   1860-1936....... TCLC 12
    See also CA 109; DLB 54

Montagu, Elizabeth   1720-1800 .... NCLC 7

Montagu, Lady Mary (Pierrepont) Wortley
    1689-1762 .... LC 9

Montague, John (Patrick)
    1929- .... CLC 13, 46
    See also CANR 9; CA 9-12R; DLB 40

Montaigne, Michel (Eyquem) de
    1533-1592 .... LC 8

Montale, Eugenio   1896-1981... CLC 7, 9, 18
    See also CA 17-20R; obituary CA 104

Montgomery, Marion (H., Jr.)
    1925- .... CLC 7
    See also CANR 3; CA 1-4R; DLB 6

Montgomery, Robert Bruce   1921-1978
    See Crispin, Edmund
    See also CA 104

Montherlant, Henri (Milon) de
    1896-1972 .... CLC 8, 19
    See also CA 85-88; obituary CA 37-40R;
    DLB 72

Montisquieu, Charles-Louis de Secondat
    1689-1755 .... LC 7

Monty Python .... CLC 21

Moodie, Susanna (Strickland)
    1803-1885 .... NCLC 14

Mooney, Ted   1951-............... CLC 25

Moorcock, Michael (John)
    1939- .... CLC 5, 27, 58
    See also CAAS 5; CANR 2, 17; CA 45-48;
    DLB 14

Moore, Brian
    1921- .... CLC 1, 3, 5, 7, 8, 19, 32
    See also CANR 1; CA 1-4R

Moore, George (Augustus)
    1852-1933 .... TCLC 7
    See also CA 104; DLB 10, 18, 57

Moore, Lorrie   1957-........... CLC 39, 45
    See also Moore, Marie Lorena

Moore, Marianne (Craig)
    1887-1972 ... CLC 1, 2, 4, 8, 10, 13, 19,
                                        47
    See also CANR 3; CA 1-4R;
    obituary CA 33-36R; SATA 20; DLB 45

Moore, Marie Lorena   1957-
    See Moore, Lorrie
    See also CA 116

Moore, Thomas   1779-1852........ NCLC 6

Morand, Paul   1888-1976 .... CLC 41
    See also obituary CA 69-72; DLB 65

Morante, Elsa   1918-1985....... CLC 8, 47
    See also CA 85-88; obituary CA 117

Moravia, Alberto
    1907- .... CLC 2, 7, 11, 18, 27, 46
    See also Pincherle, Alberto

More, Hannah   1745-1833 .... NCLC 27

More, Henry   1614-1687............. LC 9

More, (Sir) Thomas   1478-1535 ...... LC 10

Moreas, Jean   1856-1910 .... TCLC 18

Morgan, Berry   1919-.............. CLC 6
    See also CA 49-52; DLB 6

Morgan, Edwin (George)   1920-..... CLC 31
    See also CANR 3; CA 7-8R; DLB 27

Morgan, (George) Frederick
    1922- .... CLC 23
    See also CANR 21; CA 17-20R

Morgan, Janet   1945- .... CLC 39
    See also CA 65-68

Morgan, Lady   1776?-1859....... NCLC 29

Morgan, Robin   1941-.............. CLC 2
    See also CA 69-72

Morgenstern, Christian (Otto Josef Wolfgang)
    1871-1914 .... TCLC 8
    See also CA 105

Moricz, Zsigmond   1879-1942 ..... TCLC 33

Morike, Eduard (Friedrich)
    1804-1875 .... NCLC 10

Mori Ogai   1862-1922........... TCLC 14
    See also Mori Rintaro

Mori Rintaro   1862-1922
    See Mori Ogai
    See also CA 110

Moritz, Karl Philipp   1756-1793 ...... LC 2

Morris, Julian   1916-
    See West, Morris L.

Morris, Steveland Judkins   1950-
    See Wonder, Stevie
    See also CA 111

Morris, William   1834-1896 .... NCLC 4
    See also DLB 18, 35, 57

Morris, Wright (Marion)
    1910- .... CLC 1, 3, 7, 18, 37
    See also CA 9-12R; DLB 2; DLB-Y 81

Morrison, James Douglas   1943-1971
    See Morrison, Jim
    See also CA 73-76

Morrison, Jim   1943-1971......... CLC 17
    See also Morrison, James Douglas

Morrison, Toni   1931-..... CLC 4, 10, 22, 55
    See also CA 29-32R; DLB 6, 33; DLB-Y 81;
    AAYA 1

Morrison, Van   1945- .... CLC 21
    See also CA 116

Mortimer, John (Clifford)
    1923- .... CLC 28, 43
    See also CANR 21; CA 13-16R; DLB 13

Mortimer, Penelope (Ruth)   1918-.... CLC 5
    See also CA 57-60

Mosher, Howard Frank   19??-...... CLC 62

Mosley, Nicholas   1923- .... CLC 43
    See also CA 69-72; DLB 14

Moss, Howard
    1922-1987 .... CLC 7, 14, 45, 50
    See also CANR 1; CA 1-4R; DLB 5

Motion, Andrew (Peter)   1952-...... CLC 47
    See also DLB 40

Motley, Willard (Francis)
    1912-1965 .... CLC 18
    See also CA 117; obituary CA 106

Mott, Michael (Charles Alston)
    1930- .... CLC 15, 34
    See also CAAS 7; CANR 7; CA 5-8R

Mowat, Farley (McGill)   1921- .... CLC 26
    See also CLR 20; CANR 4; CA 1-4R;
    SATA 3; DLB 68

Mphahlele, Es'kia   1919-
    See Mphahlele, Ezekiel

Mphahlele, Ezekiel   1919-......... CLC 25
    See also CA 81-84

Mqhayi, S(amuel) E(dward) K(rune Loliwe)
    1875-1945 .... TCLC 25

Mrozek, Slawomir   1930-........ CLC 3, 13
    See also CA 13-16R

Mtwa, Percy   19??-.............. CLC 47

Mueller, Lisel   1924-........... CLC 13, 51
    See also CA 93-96

Muir, Edwin   1887-1959.......... TCLC 2
    See also CA 104; DLB 20

Muir, John   1838-1914 .... TCLC 28

Literary Criticism Series
Cumulative Topic Index

This index lists all topic entries in the Gale Literary Criticism Series *Contemporary Literary Criticism, Literature Criticism from 1400 to 1800, Nineteenth-Century Literature Criticism,* and *Twentieth-Century Literary Criticism.*

Topic Index

LC Cumulative Nationality Index

AMERICAN
Bradstreet, Anne **4**
Edwards, Jonathan **7**
Eliot, John **5**
Knight, Sarah Kemble **7**
Munford, Robert **5**
Taylor, Edward **11**
Wheatley, Phillis **3**

CANADIAN
Marie de l'Incarnation **10**

CHINESE
Lo Kuan-chung **12**
P'u Sung-ling **3**
Ts'ao Hsueh-ch'in **1**
Wu Ch'eng-En **7**
Wu-Ching-tzu **2**

DANO-NORWEGIAN
Holberg, Ludvig **6**
Wessel, Johan Herman **7**

DUTCH
Spinoza, Benedictus de **9**

ENGLISH
Andrewes, Lancelot **5**
Arbuthnot, John **1**
Aubin, Penelope **9**
Behn, Aphra **1**
Brooke, Frances **6**
Bunyan, John **4**
Burke, Edmund **7**
Carew, Thomas **13**
Charles I **13**
Chatterton, Thomas **3**
Churchill, Charles **3**
Cleland, John **2**

Collier, Jeremy **6**
Collins, William **4**
Congreve, William **5**
Davenant, William **13**
Davys, Mary **1**
Day, Thomas **1**
Defoe, Daniel **1**
Delany, Mary **12**
Dennis, John **11**
Donne, John **10**
Drayton, Michael **8**
Dryden, John **3**
Elyot, Thomas **11**
Fanshawe, Anne, Lady **11**
Fielding, Henry **1**
Fielding, Sarah **1**
Foxe, John **14**
Garrick, David **15**
Goldsmith, Oliver **2**
Gray, Thomas **4**
Haywood, Eliza **1**
Henry VIII **10**
Herrick, Robert **13**
Howell, James **13**
Hunter, Robert **7**
Johnson, Samuel **15**
Jonson, Ben **6**
Julian of Norwich **6**
Kempe, Margery **6**
Killegrew, Anne **4**
Lanyer, Aemilia **10**
Locke, John **7**
Lyttelton, George **10**
Malory, Thomas **11**
Manley, Mary Delariviere **1**
Marvell, Andrew **4**
Milton, John **9**
Montagu, Mary Wortley, Lady **9**
More, Henry **9**

More, Thomas **10**
Parnell, Thomas **3**
Pepys, Samuel **11**
Pix, Mary **8**
Pope, Alexander **3**
Prior, Matthew **4**
Reynolds, Joshua **15**
Richardson, Samuel **1**
Roper, William **10**
Rowe, Nicholas **8**
Sheridan, Frances **7**
Smart, Christopher **3**
Smith, John **9**
Spenser, Edmund **5**
Sterne, Laurence **2**
Swift, Jonathan **1**
Trotter, Catharine **8**
Walpole, Horace **2**
Warton, Thomas **15**
Winchilsea, Anne Finch, Lady **3**
Wollstonecraft, Mary **5**
Wycherley, William **8**
Young, Edward **3**

FRENCH
Boileau-Despréaux, Nicolas **3**
Christine de Pizan **9**
Crébillon, Claude Prosper Jolyot de, (fils) **1**
Duclos, Charles Pinot **1**
Holbach, Paul Henri Thiry, Baron d' **14**
La Fayette, Marie-Madelaine, Comtesse de **2**
Lesage, Alain-René **2**
Malherbe, François de **5**
Marat, Jean Paul **10**
Marie de l'Incarnation **10**
Marivaux, Pierre Carlet de Chamblain de **4**
Marmontel, Jean-François **2**
Molière **10**

Cumulative Index to Titles

Title Index

Title Index

Title Index

Title Index

Title Index

Title Index